FOR
DISTINGUISHED CONDUCT
IN THE FIELD

FOR
DISTINGUISHED
CONDUCT
IN THE
FIELD

The Register of the
Distinguished Conduct Medal
1939–1992

George A. Brown

'For Distinguished Conduct in the Field'

hardly describes the examples of extreme courage and undaunted feats achieved by the recipients of this honour.

From the Crimea in 1855 to the Gulf War in 1992, these men have performed acts of bravery. This book records those achievements from 1939 to 1992.

The list of the recipients contained herein is in alphabetical order for easier reference. The rank, serial number and regiment or corps of the recipient are given and the full citation from the original document (where these are not available, the London Gazette entry is given, if published).

I had originally intended to provide the terms of reference of the Distinguished Conduct Medal, but after consideration, I would suggest that the reader consult the excellent book on British Gallantry Awards by P. E. Abbott and J. M. A. Tamplin.

Their book is the Bible on British Gallantry Awards.

I sincerely hope that this small tribute to all Military Forces will prove not only interesting to the general reader, but also as a reference source for fellow collectors and historians.

George A. Brown

Dedicated to Lori-Ann, John, Cheryl, Margot & Greg

Acknowledgements

The production of this book has been exciting and rewarding.

I have wanted, for some time, to tell the stories of these brave men and their unbelievable feats of arms, for they are examples of extreme courage, often in the face of great dangers and overwhelming odds.

The citations for the awards are from the official was records and for his considerable assistance in researching these I wish to record my sincere appreciation to Mr. David A. E. Morris.

I sincerely hope that this small tribute to the Military Forces will prove not only interesting to the general reader but also as a reference source for fellow collectors and historians.

EDITORIAL NOTE

This book has been compiled from the original recommendations typed or handwritten in the field at the time of the action and subsequently passed up the chain of command for approval. Some must have been almost illegible from the start; others have lost their edges or their continuation sheets, or have had filing holes punched through key words. Such illegible or missing words are indicated by square brackets.

On balance, we are more than fortunate that so much has survived.

The text faithfully follows the original citations, except that, in order not to tire the reader, minor spelling mistakes have been corrected, some abbreviations have been given in full and the military use of capitals for proper nouns has been suppressed.

A

Abbey, Albert Henry Royce, Sergeant
VX 113314, 14/32 Australian Infantry Bn. (Immediate)
For great gallantry and inspiring leadership at Waitavalo, New Britain.

On 17 Mar 45 Sjt. Abbey took over 17 Platoon after his platoon commander was wounded. In the afternoon he was ordered to launch an attack on Mt Sugi a most strongly defended enemy position, which the Jap was holding with all his remaining strength, the platoon objectives being the most vital of those allotted to the company.

Shortly after the attack commenced the platoon came under intense fire from 3 HMGs and many LMGs. The axis of the advance was up a precipitous slope, slippery from rain and through dense bush. At this stage the resistance was so strong that the platoon was halted. Sjt. Abbey completely ignoring the enemy's fire, went forward alone to find positions from which each of his Bren guns could best neutralise the enemy pillboxes. Having found good positions he called his men forward, section by section, directing their fire.

Later on, when other enemy LMGs to both flanks again halted the advance, Sjt. Abbey moved to each section in turn and so inspired and encouraged them with his complete disregard of danger that they again followed him forward, broke the enemy resistance, and finally consolidated their objectives. Sjt. Abbey personally accounted for at least two of the enemy during this action. The foothold so gained was the pivot of a later attack which finally shattered the last enemy resistance.

On the previous day as platoon serjeant, Sjt. Abbey had shown great coolness in steadying his men under fire from enemy 105 mm mortars. On the subsequent day he continued his task as platoon commander with the same high standard of devotion to duty.

Through the whole action Sjt. Abbey proved himself to be one of the most outstanding NCOs I have ever seen. His appreciation of vital ground, his cheerfulness and complete absence of fear, were of tremendous value to his platoon and an inspiration to the whole battalion.
(L.G. 3.7.45)

Abbott, William Henry, Private
NX 2233, 2/2 Australian Infantry Bn.
On the morning of 3 Jan 41 at Bardia one post in particular, covered by four Field guns and at least two Breda A/Tk Guns, was offering considerable resistance to the advance up the wadi.

Pte. Abbott seeing this, at once volunteered to attack the post single-handed under covering fire from Carrier Section. This he did and assisted by a Carrier Crew succeeded in driving out and capturing at least 120 men and two L.M.G.s.

Meanwhile the supporting Field Guns laid down a heavy barrage making this area particularly dangerous. Pte. Abbott however, completely ignored this and by his action greatly inspired all men near him and enabled them to move forward.
M.I.D. 15.12.42   *(L.G. 9.5.41)*

Abols, David, Corporal
24355246, Parachute Regt.
During the early hours of 28th May 1982 the 2nd Battalion The Parachute Regiment were ordered to attack enemy positions in the area of Port Darwin on the island of East Falkland. The enemy were well entrenched in strength and fierce fighting ensued all day.

In the heat of the battle Corporal Abols dashed through enemy fire to drag a wounded comrade to safety. When another Corporal was wounded he again crossed an exposed forward slope to rescue him.

Later, well to the fore, he destroyed an enemy position which resulted in effective enemy resistance being ended in that area. His actions throughout showed extreme courage. *[From L.G.]*   *(L.G. 19.9.78)*

Abraham, Albert Joseph, Private
SX 10515, 2/10 Australian Infantry Bn. (Broadview, South Australia) (Immediate)
K.B. Mission Action, Milne Bay, New Guinea, night 27/28 Aug 42.

For conspicuous gallantry and devotion to duty on the night 27/28 Aug 42.

This soldier was in charge of a Bren L.M.G. when he was wounded by five bullets through his feet and legs at about 0030 hrs. His Company withdrew shortly afterwards, but in the darkness he was not missed and continued to serve his gun against enemy tanks and infantry at point blank range.

Six hours later at dawn, a patrol under Lieut. K. R. Erskine-Wilson found Pte. Abraham still gamely fighting off a Japanese Patrol of 10 men. Of these he had accounted for 6, and the remainder were dealt with by Lieut Erskine-Wilson's Patrol.

In a subsequent march of 5 days' duration through dense jungle, during which period Pte Abraham was carried on the shoulders of his comrades, he bore severe pain gaily and unflinchingly, and was a inspiration to his comrades.   *(L.G. 4.2.43)*

Abukr, Mohamed, Ombashi
40602, No. 2 M.I.Coy W.A.C.
This Ombashi, after the surrender of Socota Fort on the 26th April 1941, accompanied O.C. of the Force and was of the greatest assistance in extricating Italians from the Patriots. After dark O.C. withdrew with six Italian

wounded; the Ombashi, without orders, returned to the Fort and, although the Patriots were shooting and bombing indiscriminately, he brought out six more Italians and by using an Italian car returned with them to camp at midnight. All the Italians were naked and four wounded which indicated that they were actually removed from the Patriots. To return alone and without orders into the chaos of Socota Fort in the dark to rescue Italian wounded, shows in my opinion a very high degree of courage and resource.

[D.C.M.—but to await decision of the Colonial Office]

Acaster, Leonard, Trooper
7888516, 4 Royal Tank Regt. (Leeds) (Immediate)
On the night of the 30th Nov 1941, Tpr. Acaster was driver of an 'I' Tank which went into action when the Sqdn counter-attacked on El Duda. A shell penetrated his Tank, killing the Gunner and wounding Tpr. Acaster in the face. The Tank halted and being close to the enemy was quickly invested by them in the darkness. Tpr. Acaster with great presence of mind feigned death, and the remainder of the crew were taken prisoner. As soon as the enemy moved off Tpr. Acaster started up his Tank again, and drove it back in the direction of our lines where he met other soldiers who helped him out and led him to a R.A.P.

Tpr. Acaster was badly wounded in the face and his eyes were filled with blood, rendering him half blind, while the pain was intense. His courage and presence of mind was most conspicuous and his devotion to duty in thus saving his Tank from Capture under the most trying conditions sets an example which has rarely been equalled in the Service.   *(L.G. 24.2.42)*

Adams, Albert Henry, Warrant Officer Cl. I (R.S.M.)
6134495, 1st Bn. East Surrey Regt.
R.S.M. Adams' conduct during an attack on this Battalion was most gallant and praiseworthy and was an example to all ranks. The facts are that at about 1000 hrs on 27th November 1942, BHQ, which was in a strip of wood in the railway station at Tebourna was attacked by tanks and infantry. The tanks halted short of the wood and fired into it with guns and M.G. Infantry had succeeded in establishing themselves in houses and trees over the railway line which overlooked BHQ and were firing down into the wood at very short range. There was a great deal of fire which at first caused some confusion by its suddenness. RSM Adams completely ignored all enemy fire and gave orders to various BHQ parties to man positions to deal with the situation and very quickly restored confidence among the men under his command. A lorry of wounded dashed across the railway line into the HQ area. RSM Adams at once organised stretcher parties under very heavy fire and succeeded in getting all the wounded out safely.
M.I.D. 20.12.40   *(L.G. 11.2.43)*

Adams, Claude William, Warrant Officer Cl. II (actg.)
4040919, 4th Bn. King's Shropshire Light Infantry (Dixey) (Periodic)
This W.O. came out with the battalion to France and has fought throughout the campaign with this battalion. He came to France as a Platoon Sjt, but his Platoon Commander was wounded in the Caen break-out battle, and CSM Adams commanded the Platoon with outstanding success from that day onwards until he was promoted W.O.II in April, 1945. His platoon had a run of unbroken success, and this W.O. was to a very large extent responsible for this success. By his aggressive leadership, cheerfulness and coolness under fire, he so inspired his men, that they never knew failure in battle.

In the battle for Antwerp this W.O. with his platoon was responsible for the capture of some 100 enemy, who had to be driven out from concrete emplacements in the centre of the town. Whenever a Section was temporarily held up in this battle, CSM Adams would go up to it, encourage it, and so lead it that the opposition was overcome.

Again, in the battle for Asten this W.O.'s platoon did remarkably well and again the success was due in the main to the example set by this W.O.

No praise can be too high for the magnificent example set by this W.O. over a long period of almost continuous fighting.   *(L.G. 24.1.46)*

Adams, Harry, Corporal
4464727, Military Police (Bradford) (since killed in action)
No citation.   *(L.G. 14.2.46)*

Adams, John Henry, Private
14716652, 6 Green Howards (Bucknell) (Immediate)
Pte. Adams was a member of a platoon in a defensive position near Bemmel which was subject to a strong enemy attack on 1 Oct. 44.

Two platoons of an adjoining battalion were overrun and enemy infantry reached a point sixty yards away, when they were stopped by small arms fire. After a brief interval two Panther tanks came forward, leading on the enemy infantry again. Pte. Adams seized the platoon Piat, crawled along a ditch, calmly placed a bomb in the gun and fired. This caused the leading tank to run into a ditch, from which its crew kept up a heavy fire, as did the second tank in support. With a complete contempt of danger, Pte. Adams moved about the tank and hit it three times more. The crew baled out and abandoned it. The second tank came up firing HE and MG, but Adams again changed position, firing a further bomb which hit the second tank which quickly halted, turned and made rapidly off.

This soldier had been in action for only three days. His exemplary coolness under heavy fire, his disregard for his own safety, and his determined and outstanding gallantry not only destroyed one and damaged a second tank but completely halted and broke up the enemy attack.   (*L.G. 1.3.45*)

Adams, Joseph, Corporal
2/London Irish Rifles (Belfast)
Ref. Map Italy 1/25,000 Sheet 160II NW Pignataro Intesamna.

On 16 May 44 during the Battalion attack on Colla Monache Cpl. Adams was commanding a section in 14 Platoon which was the right forward Platoon of 'G' Company (the right forward Company). The Company was being subjected to heavy shelling and small arms fire and after advancing about 500 yds 14 Platoon had had all its NCOs and its Platoon Commander made casualties with the sole exception of Cpl. Adams. Cpl. Adams immediately assumed command of the Platoon, re-organised his sections and pressed on with great personal courage which heartened his men and enabled him to lead them on to the capture of the final objective.
Recommended for M.M.   (*L.G. 7.12.44*)

Adamson, John Izatt, Sergeant
2754237, Black Watch (Hill of Beath, Fife)
At Heracklion on 21.5.41 Sjt. Adamson showed conspicuous courage and leadership when ordered to take his platoon forward to destroy an enemy strong point. In spite of the strength of the enemy being greater than was previously supposed he pressed home the attack until held up by heavy fire at close range. He then showed great courage by standing up so as to persuade the enemy to surrender. This he successfully accomplished with the result that twenty five men, one M.G. and several submachine guns were captured and further casualties amongst our troops prevented.

Throughout the battle Sjt. Adamson showed coolness, courage and initiative of the highest order setting a fine example to the men under his command.
                                         (*L.G. 4.11.41*)

Adamson, Robert James, Guardsman
2718310, 1st Bn. Irish Guards (Morpeth, Northumberland) (Immediate)
In the Anzio Beach head.

This Guardsman was member of a platoon of No. 3 Company which on the night 21/22nd Feb took over positions from the II/6th U.S. Regiment. Gdsm Adamson and a Gdsm Montgomery were allotted to a forward outpost position. On the way up they picked up an abandoned American Browning M.G. and ammunition. With this M.G. and a box of grenades these two men established themselves well forward of the company position and spent the night harrying German posts and breaking up German patrols. Just before dawn, Gdsm Adamson went back to the former American positions where he found another Browning and more ammunition. These he brought forward, and then for the rest of the day these two Gdsm, Gdsm Adamson and his companion, conducted a private war against the enemy. They

operated on the ridges forward of the company positions and could be quite clearly seen as they moved from place to place, covering each other with great skill, till they came to the final phase of each little [...]eration, when under covering fire from his companion, Gdsm Adamson closed in on the sniper or spandau posts, and, not having the means or inclination to take prisoners, shot the Germans with a Tommy Gun, which was his original equipment. Gdsm Montgomery was eventually wounded and had to withdraw, so Gdsm Adamson continued operations alone and for the three last hours of daylight gave the enemy no rest and no chance to form up for an organized attack. At dusk, Gdsm Adamson came in to Company H.Q. and asked a stretcher bearer to dress what he called a slight wound on the side of his face. While this was being done he fainted, and it was seen that he had a severe wound which must have been causing him intense pain. It is impossible to find out when exactly Gdsm Adamson was wounded, but it is certain that for some time he must have been fighting while handicapped by excruciating pain, which would have incapacitated a man of lesser physical and mental determination and complete devotion to duty. Guardsman Adamson's remarkable and persistent gallantry, his initiative and skill and his complete disregard of danger and suffering, on top of a long and excellent record as a fighting man in Tunisia and Italy, deserve in my opinion the immediate award of the D.C.M.   (*L.G. 15.6.44*)

Adcock, Sidney Steytley, T/Sergeant
60445, 1/2 S.A. F.F. Bn., South African Forces
For conspicuous and distinguished services in action, and outstanding devotion to duty continuously over a period of the past twelve months to the end of July 42.

When the outpost at Temrad was attacked and forced to withdraw on the 6th April, Sjt. Adcock through his initiative and quickness in bringing his section of machine-guns into action enabled the troop of Field guns which he covered to withdraw unscathed. Several enemy detachments had advanced to within a few hundred yards of the guns and were in the process of erecting mortars, when with great presence of mind he swung his section of machine-guns into position and effectively engaged the enemy, inflicting heavy casualties and causing them to abandon their mortars.

On the 13th April, he was in command of a section of armoured Cars acting as a screen to a column of all arms operating against the enemy defences at Temrad. In spite of intense artillery and machine-gun fire he led his section to within a few hundred yds of the enemy positions, and effectively engaged enemy OPs which were putting down heavy artillery fire on the column, causing them to withdraw. He only withdrew under orders when the column was being threatened by an enemy tank attack.

He was in command of numerous foot patrols which successfully penetrated the enemy defences forward of the Gazala line, gaining valuable information. He was badly wounded when our position South of the El Alamein box was being consolidated, but in spite of his wounds he insisted on returning to duty within a few days. He has consistently borne himself with the utmost efficiency and fearlessness in the execution of his duties in action.   *(L.G. 18.2.43)*

Aitken, James, Warrant Officer Cl. II (C.S.M.)
2818488, 5th Bn. Seaforth Highlanders (London, N.4)
(Immediate)
This W.O.'s Company took part in the attack on Corradini on 21 January 1943. The Company was subjected to very heavy mortar and M.G. fire and the Company Commander was wounded. Throughout the whole operation C.S.M. Aitken moved freely amongst the men of his company, encouraging and steadying them when there was risk of them becoming disorganised as a result of the difficult country and the weight of enemy fire. He showed powers of leadership above those expected of his rank, and a complete disregard for his own safety.

The success of his company must be largely attributable to the very great example he set to his men.
M.I.D. 20.12.40   *(L.G. 22.4.43)*

Albrecht, Kingsley George, Corporal
SX 7830, 2/48 Australian Infantry Bn. (Immediate)
For personal gallantry, grim determination and leadership in destroying an enemy tank crew holding up the advance of his Platoon in the night attack.

On the night 25/26 Oct 42 in the attack on Trig 29 (Miteiriya Ridge) Cpl Albrecht was leading his Section when his Platoon was held up by heavy Machine Gun and Anti Tank Gun fire, apparently coming from an enemy strong post.

Without thought of personal danger Cpl Albrecht charged the post with rifle and bayonet only to find the post was a dug in German Mark II Tank. Cpl Albrecht then attacked the tank, in the face of heavy fire, with a 73 Grenade rendering the crew unconscious—they were then killed by grenades.

This gallant and speedy action allowed Albrecht's Platoon to continue its advance to its objective.

Although wounded by shrapnel in the head and covered with blood Cpl Albrecht continued to lead and control his Section during the reorganisation phase and refused to be evacuated until his Section had completed digging in and was ready for any enemy counterattack.

Cpl Albrecht's personal bravery, grim determination and leadership was responsible for the success of his Platoon's final capture of the objective. *(L.G. 11.2.43)*

Alcock, William Mernie, C.Q.M.S.
3311243, 2 Highland Light Infantry (Fraserburgh)
(Periodic)
This NCO has served with distinction throughout his service in the Battalion since 1935. As one of the original Carrier Platoon NCOs, on the formation of the Platoon

in Palestine in 1938 he took part in the many raids and searches of villages during the Palestinian troubles.

Throughout the Eritrean campaign owing to there being no officer available, he commanded the Carrier Platoon with distinction, and in the advance which led up to the capture of Barentu, and Maasawa, his work in patrolling materially assisted in the gaining of information vital to the plan for these battles. After the capture of Cheren as a result of his knowledge and efficiency he commanded the Brigade Carriers in the advance from Cheren to Asmara and from Asmara to Ghinda. At the battle of Barentu C/Sjt. Alcock led the Brigade Carriers, and largely due to his courage, determination, and disregard of personal safety, together with his abililty to size up the situation, and render accurate reports, the Battalion was able to effect its capture.

In Libya, during the action at Bir El Tamar on 5th June 1942, this NCO was conspicuous in his coolness under fire and in the calm and efficient manner in which he led his detachment of carriers. Throughout the action he continuously led his section to and from the front line over open shell swept ground evacuating wounded. By his untiring efforts and fine leadership a large number of wounded men were brought to safety.

His work during the last four years has always been of the highest standard and his abililty, courage, determination, and untiring efforts in every duty performed are an example to all his subordinates.*(L.G. 14.10.43)*

Alexander, Robert [James], Warrant Officer Cl. I
(R.S.M.)
3440088, 2nd Bn. Lancashire Fusiliers (Birkdale)
(Immediate)
During operations in the mountains on 14th April, 1943, when the 2nd Battalion The Lancashire Fusiliers, was holding the Dj Bettiour feature. A platoon of D Company, was pinned down by heavy shell fire whilst advancing to the attack.

No 3440088 RSM Alexander with amazing coolness and complete disregard for his own safety walked out from cover into the shell swept area and stood encouraging the platoon to go forward out of the danger area, thereby saving the platoon from heavy casualties. He then organised the collecting of wounded, being exposed the whole time to enemy fire. On the 15th April when Battalion HQ was attacked by the enemy under cover of a mist RSM Alexander was wounded in the face and chest by a bursting grenade but insisted on carrying on with his duties after his wounds had been dressed until he was ordered to the rear 24 hrs later.

Throughout the Battalion's three day engagement with the enemy RSM Alexander's personal bravery and leadership was of an exceptionally high standard and had an inspiring effect on all ranks.

I consider his conduct of such a high standard that I recommend him for an immediate award.

(L.G. 15.6.43)

Allan, Donald Stewart, C.Q.M.S.
L.12550, South Saskatchewan Regiment (Periodic)
Since the 3rd of September 1944 Company Sergeant-Major Allan has been with 'A' Company of the South Saskatchewan Regiment. During his tenure in this capacity he has taken part in every action his Company has been engaged in. His personal courage, devotion to duty and outstanding leadership has many times been responsible for the success of his Company in attacks which they have successfully accomplished.

During the night of the 14th of October 1944 at the northwest end of Groote Meer Lake in square 6617, when the enemy had infiltrated and surrounded 'A' Company, thus cutting off the Company Commander who had gone to liase with the tank Commander some 400 yards distance, Company Sergeant-Major Allan so organized and inspired his men that they were eager to hold and fight. He knew full well that the Company was surrounded and that immediate help was unlikely, and by his example of calmness and determination so inspired his men that they repulsed the counter attack of enemy tanks and infantry, even though the position was under heavy machine gun and cannon fire by the enemy. Without his determination the Company could well have become disorganized very easily. He kept the battalion Commander in the picture at all times by 18 set despite the fact that the signaller with him had become a casualty.

His willingness to overcome severe handicaps does not only apply to the case above but is in evidence in all work that Company Sergeant-Major Allan undertakes. He is one of the finest types of soldier in the Canadian Army.

(L.G. 17.3.45)

Allan, Harold Charles, Sergeant (A/W.O.II (S.S.M.))
7892792, 4th City of London Yeo., Royal Armoured Corps (Paignton) (Immediate)
This Warrant Officer has been conspicuous for his outstanding bravery and love of battle throughout the operations, he was fearless and untiring and a great help to his Squadron Leader. On 28th Dec. he was in the thick of the fighting all day. He engaged the enemy at very short range accounting for at least six enemy tanks himself.

During the withdrawal he took part in the rear guard action and was one of the last to come out of action.

No man could have done more with the material and ammunition at his disposal. On 30th Dec. he was again in the thick of the fighting all day and again accounted for several enemy tanks.

On at least three occasions during these battles he towed broken down tanks out of the firing line, personally supervising the task himself outside his tank.

(L.G. 19.3.42)

Allan, James Snodgrass, Lance Corporal
2693403, 5 L. of C., Military Police
Green, S., Lance Corporal
4915273, 2 Div. R.A.S.C.
Clark, G.H., Gunner
877372, 209/53 A./Tk. Bty., Royal Artillery
(1) L/Cpl. Allan
I received a head wound near Lille on 18 May 40 and was taken to the hospital at Camiers, which on 20 May, was taken over by the Germans.

On 1 July, with other wounded, I was moved, in a lorry through Hesdin, Lille (2 July) and Renaix (4 July) to Loekeren (6 July), where we were packed like sardines in barges and, after 3 days, reached Emmerich. We were then taken on to Dortmund. While I was there 7 Irishmen and 4 Welshmen were interviewed by a German official in the presence of an individual who bore, on the lapel of his coat, a badge with the letters I.R.A. None of the men interviewed subscribed to these efforts to win him over and all of them rejoined us.

By this time I was convalescent and on about 16 July was taken by rail, a 4 days' journey, to Thorn (Poland), Stalag XX A.

After a fortnight I was transferred to a working camp (No. 354) at Pischnitz (Popolaska) also known as Hoch Stublau. This camp was about 50 kms. S.E. of Danzig and P/W were employed on roadwork on a new road which is to run from Berlin to Danzig. Although an N.C.O. I was compelled to work, but P/W who were unfit, at the instigation of a British M.O. Major Tucker, R.A.M.C. were excused from this levy. This officer did magnificent work in attending to sick P/W, although he had little equipment and constant hindrance.

By contrast at Thorn, R.S.M. Davidson (the camp leader) and a Pte. Puttinger (who wore the crown of a S.M.) curried favour with the Germans and were very harsh with P/W. Similarily, C.S.M. Dean, at the working camp, insisted on our working, to the limit of our capacity, in order to placate and win personal favour from the Camp Commandant.

The guards at both camps could be divided into two categories, those who were over 25, who treated us fairly and those who were younger and brutal. As far as I know no guard would accept a bribe.

While I was a P/W at Pischnitz (4 Aug—17 Sept 40) we received one parcel on 28 Aug, which was divided between 41 men; my portion being 12 cigarettes and half a tin of kippers. Camp rations were poor; we had two meals a day. All money and valuables were confiscated. Each man was given one blanket and all overcoats and spare clothes were taken from us. There was no issue of soap and towels, so that we were generally lousy and filthy.

The first requisite for escaping is a large scale map of the vicinity of the camp. I was able to make a copy of a map, which had been brought into the camp by some white Russians who were awaiting repatriation. Poles came into the camp and worked alongside us on the road.

They did not give us any escape material but were, practically to a man, willing to help escapers.

(2) L/Cpl. Green

My unit was formed into a rearguard to fight, a delaying action on the canal at La Bassée. By 26 May 40 we were reduced to ten men, four of whom were wounded, when we were overwhelmed and taken prisoners.

I was marched away in a long column through Lille, Arras, Cambrai and Malmedy, where we were entrained for Dortmund. Dortmund was then used as a collecting and transit camp for P/W and, after 14 days, we went on to Thorn (31 July).

Conditions in this camp were as described by L/Cpl. Allan. No copy of the Hague Convention was available for P/W.

I got away from the camp on 5 Aug 40, while on a working party, but was recaptured 6 days later, as, having no map, I lost my way and was soon exhausted.

Having been escorted back to the camp, I was taken down to the punishment cells, stripped and beaten with a rubber truncheon into insensibility. I was kept there for 26 days with one meal a day of bread and water. For the first twelve days I lost my memory and was later transferred to the working camp at Pischnitz.

Escape by L/Cpls. Allan & Green and Gnr. Clark

On 17 Sep 41, 20 of us were out working under one guard. We were digging up bombs, made of iron and concrete. The guard left us and we remained under the charge of a German-Pole. We seized our opportunity and slipped away and, once out of sight, made off in an easterly direction. (Allan was wearing a Polish uniform, Green had a Polish tunic and British army slacks and Clark was in Battle dress.)

Our course was Gostynin, Borazanov and Kenpa. (There Allan stayed behind, while Clark and Green went on.)

Journey from Kenpa to Moscow (Clark and Green)

We were directed and helped by the Poles (chiefly poor Jews) from Kenpa through Sochachev, Lasky and Modlin to Warsaw. Here we were sent to an important secret organization; they were well equipped with wireless, a printing press and a large clerical staff. We were later guided to the Russian frontier through Ostroleka and were given 50 Roubles each and a letter addressed to Mon Molotoff but, on entering Russia, (24 Sept) were arrested, and spent 4 months in the Luvianko prison. At the end of Jan 41 we were removed to the concentration camp at Smoklensk, where we remained until our release. (Clark was retained subsequently by the Embassy for duty as an orderly).

Journey from Kenpa to Russia (Allan)

At Kenpa I was parted from the other two as the Poles thought it better to split us up.

On about 1 Oct 41 I was guided by way of Sochechiev to Warsaw, where I was sheltered and looked after by the official Polish organization. Later I was taken by train to the Russian frontier, passing through Siedlice and Nemmoijki. I crossed the river Bug in a boat, while Polish scouts kept a watch for any German patrol. I climbed over the barbed wire fence into Russia and handed myself over to the authorities within five minutes of crossing the frontier. I was searched very thoroughly and everything was taken away from me. I was put in a small cell for one night. I was then taken on to another place (I do not know the name) and stayed there for 10 days in company with Polish prisoners. Then I was sent to Bialystock prison where I stayed for about a month together with several Polish soldiers. The food was terrible and the conditions were extremely bad. There was no room to lie down in the cell at night. I then went to Minsk where conditions were just as bad. On the 6th January I was sent to Moscow where the conditions were better. I was in a room with 25 English and French. The food was good and cigarettes were provided.

While I was a Minsk I had learnt two Russian sentences—'I must speak to the Prison Governor'; 'When can I speak to the Prison Governor'—which I used in the Moscow prison but with no result. With me at this time were: Lovegrove, Briggs, Bateman, Boughton.

We were given paper to write to England, but I did not avail myself of this opportunity as I thought the letters would not be sent. In order to force the Russians to allow us to see the Govenor we went on a hunger strike for five days. On the third of this strike I was taken away and put in a cell by myself as I was considered to be the ring-leader. At the end of the five days my friends were moved to another room where I joined them. This was about the 6th February. Three or four days later my friends were taken away and from then on I did not know anything about them. The following day I was taken from my cell and put in another with three Frenchmen. I stayed there until about the 25th February when I was taken out and put in a cell alone. I was there for five weeks and, at the end of the time, was beaten up by the prison guards. During this period I was perpetually interrogated and asked why I had come to Russia and also questioned concerning the Secret Police organization in England. I told them the story of my escape and asked to see the British consul. I stayed another nine weeks alone in the cell, during which time I was again beaten up. The Russian—German war then broke out and we were taken to Capatob to a very bad prison; 10 men were packed into one small cell and there was scarcely room to stand. I stayed there until the 7th September, when the deputy govenor came to my cell and brought me out. I was then placed in the first class part of the prison and given cigarettes and all the food I could eat. My clothes were washed and they made a great fuss of me. The following morning I was taken to Moscow under escort of two Lieutenants. I stayed in the Lubianka prison for one night where I was extremely badly treated. The following morning I was taken back to my old prison, but put in the third class part where I stayed alone in a cell for three weeks. They then came and gave me a bath, hair-cut, etc., but refused to give me any food. They then took me before two civilians who questioned me as to my name, etc., and then told me I was free. I asked for some food and this was brought immediately. They told me the address of the British Embassy but as I did not know my way about Moscow they had to take me there in a car. They pointed out the Embassy to me and then stopped the car 300 yards away from it. I rushed straight in.

During the period I was in prison I was forced to sign certain documents in Russian which, naturally, I could not understand. A revolver was used in order to persuade me to do this.

On board H.M.S. London a full account of my experience was taken down in shorthand under instructions from either Lord Beaverbrook or Lt. Gen Ismay, in Lord Beaverbrook's cabin. It took about two hours. I told them the story of my escape with particular empahsis on my experiences in Russia. I mentioned the name of a Pole who had helped me but was immediately warned by Brig. Ismay that I must, on no account, mention names. *(L.G. 2.12.41)*

Allan, Ronald David, Sergeant
15229, Royal Australian Infantry Corps
For Vietnam *(L.G. 10.12.68)*

Allan, William, Lance Sergeant
3132466, 4/5th Bn. Royal Scots Fusiliers (Crieff)
(Immediate)
On the morning of the 26th Oct, after the landing South of Hoedekenskerke in South Beveland 'A' Company were ordered inland in the LVTs. Owing to three of these breaking down the Company Commander was obliged to order all the Company into three LVTs. The Company arrived at the railway station W of Baarland, which was its objective, when a German anti tank gun opened up on the first amphibian at a range of twelve yds. Two shots were fired and both missed. The first amphibian was crowded out with personnel and stores. The crew were unable to open the doors and release the personnel. Cpl Allan jumped out of the tank, dashed forward to the gun position, and dominated the site with sten gun fire, until the personnel were able to disembark.

He was fired at from different angles, one shot becoming lodged in his pack and another going through his clothes. In all he tackled five pits, killing three Germans and, but for his prompt action, many more casualties would have been sustained. During the course of the whole action Cpl Allan displayed great leadership and courage. *(L.G. 22.3.45)*

Allen, Mark Haselock, Corporal
2875307, 2nd Bn. Gordon Highlanders (Sheffield 9)
During the action at 41 Milestone on the Ayer Hitam—Johore Rd in Jan 42, this non-commissioned officer displayed gallantry under intense machine gun fire. He organised and led carrying parties for ammunition which he successfully delivered to the forward troops at a very critical juncture. Subsequently he brought back several casualties at a time when machine gun fire and shelling were continuous in the area. Throughout the fighting in Johore and Singapore Cpl Allen set a most inspiring example to his men by his cheerful demeanour, determination and courage. *(L.G. 13.12.45)*

Allen, Richard Wesley, Private
SX 18234, 2/10 Australian Infantry Bn. (Immediate)
For conspicuous gallantry and bravery during the Sanananda Action.

At 0930 hrs 21 Jan 43 two Platoons of C Company attacked a strongly defended Japanese position on the beach between Sananada Point and Wye Point. After capturing two pill boxes both Platoons were held down by heavy MG fire and sniping from both flanks. 14 Platoon who had turned right were in a particularly dangerous position as the enemy had the advantage in ground and cover. Pte Allen who had moved left with 13 Platoon happened to notice their plight and immediately moved with his Bren gun to a position on the open beach from which he engaged the enemy post with fire. Another enemy post observed his move and opened fire on him with a LMG. In spite of this fire which tore his haversack and equipment to shreds, Pte. Allen continued to engage the post on 14 Pl's front and killed at least 3 of the enemy who were endeavouring to get an LMG into position. In addition he called warnings to 14 Platoon when he saw movement of snipers, enabling that Platoon to deal with them. He remained in his exposed position for more than one hour, the rising tide finally forcing him to withdraw. In the meatime both Platoons although still unable to move forward had dug in and established fire superiority over the enemy posts.

But for Pte Allen's tenacity, initiative and utter disregard for personal safety, 14 Platoon would have suffered heavy casualties and probably both Platoons would have had to be withdrawn. As it was the position was held and troops of 2/9 Battalion were able to advance without casualties under our covering fire and mop up the resistance between C company and 2/9 Battalion. Pte Allen's conduct was of the highest order and an inspiration to all who witnessed it. *L.G. 22.4.43)*

Allenberg, William Harry, T/Sergeant (A/W.O.II)
53046, 4/6 S.A. Armoured Car Regt., S.A.T.C., South African Forces (Immediate)
On 5 Nov 42 Allenberg's Squadron was operating behind enemy lines South of Daba—one of his Squadron cars attacking 14 German trucks had been hit and captured with its crew—at last light. Allenberg—observing the approximate Leager area—set forth after dark in a 15 Cwt bug accompanied by 6 O/Ranks. At approx 02.00 hrs on 6 Nov the leager was discovered and the party approached to within 50 yards and opened up with their automatic rifles. Allenberg, showing splendid leadership and outstanding bravery—led his party in and finally recaptured the men taken prisoner in the early evening together with the 14 Enemy trucks and 25 prisoners.

One of Allenberg's party was killed and one seriously wounded.

I recommend WOII Allenberg for the immediate award of the M.M.

Recommended for M.M. M.I.D. 15.12.42

(L.G. 25.2.43)

Allison, Millard Jasper, Corporal
K38586, Royal Canadian Armoured Corps
No citation   (L.G. 24.1.46)

Almond, James, Corporal
4451276, Durham Light Infantry (Cheadle)
No citation   (L.G. 18.10.45)

Amon, Private
77, 1st Northern Rhodesia Regt.
Somaliland. For conspicuous gallantry on August 12th at Tug Argon when as a Battalion H.Q. runner Pte. Amon twice carried important messages to an isolated company over some 500 yards of ground which was swept by M.G. and S.A. fire. On numerous other occasions from Aug 11th to Aug 15th Pte Amon carried messages through shell and S.A. fire and was so reliable that he did more than his fair share of this dangerous work. His example to his comrades was consistently a high one and his devotion to duty at all times, great.
To be dated 11.2.41 and substituted for the award of the African D.C.M. announced in the L.G. of that date.

(L.G. 21.7.42)

Anderson, George Knight, Corporal (A/Sgt.)
2983211, 2 Cameron (Bonnybridge) (Immediate)
During the Cassino operations, this NCO was attached to an Advanced Dressing Station of 17 Field Ambulance as NCO in charge of a party of stretcher bearers.

On the night 17/18 February 1944, 1/2 G.R. were involved in an attack on the Monastery of Montecassino. During this action the Battalion suffered very heavy casualties and the advance was halted in very close proximity to most strongly held enemy positions.

At approximately 0430 hrs in the morning of 18th February information was received at the ADS to the effect that casualties had been incurred in the RAP of 4/6th Raj Rif. Corporal Anderson at once organised a party of stretcher bearers and proceeded up the treacherous and exposed hill path to the unit. Although the track was under shell and mortar fire he went direct to the RAP and successfully evacuated the casualties. Soon after his return assistance was asked for by 1/2 G.R. Immediately Corporal Anderson volunteered for duty and set out with a party without delay.

Owing to the attack the enemy was employing all his available fire power both on the Battalion positions and on the approaches. On the route that had to be taken by Corporal Anderson's party snipers were very active and the whole journey was undertaken through an inferno of shelling and mortar and small arms fire.

On arrival at the RAP he found that the Commanding Officer was badly wounded and would undoubtedly die if speedy surgical attention were not available. At once he preceeded with his squad to carry this officer back a distance of one mile over the route on which—such was the intensity of enemy fire—there seemed no chance of survival. Throughout the ensuing nightmare journey Corporal Anderson's only thoughts were for his patient and he refused to endanger him or cause him discomfort by undue hurry or jolting.

Happily this task was successfully accomplished and the officer received the necessary attention in time to save his life.

Corporal Anderson then sent his squad back to rest and then without a thought for himself proceeded to organise further parties of bearers, each of which he led personally with cheerful encouragement back to the RAP.

Altogether he made four more such journeys to the RAP and back.

Corporal Anderson's self-sacrifice, indomitable courage and cheerful determination were the direct means of saving at least one life and of bringing twenty more stretcher cases to safety. His conduct throughout was beyond all praise.   (L.G. 24.8.44)

Anderson, James Harold, Corporal
VX 34703, 2/24 Australian Infantry Bn.
For outstanding gallantry and devotion to duty at El Alamein 25-31 Oct 42.

During the attack of night 25/26 Oct Cpl Anderson's Platoon when about 400 yds from its objective was subjected to intense fire from a very well sited enemy MG post at about 50 yds range and suffered heavy casualties.

Cpl Anderson, seeing his Platoon held up rushed forward calling out to his Platoon Commander 'I'll get them', firing the TSMG continually from the hip and, though subjected in the bright moonlight to the concentrated fire of two Spandaus at point blank range, stormed, singlehanded, the enemy post, killed the four German gunners in the post and silenced the guns.

By this great action of bravery, Cpl Anderson saved further casualties in his Platoon and enabled it to gain its objective.

Again on the night 30/31 Oct in the attack astride the railway line A and D coys were held up by extremely heavy fire from a MG Post and again Cpl Anderson leapt up and charged the post with his TSMG blazing and, rushing through intense fire, again silenced, singlehanded, this post killing the occupants with his TSMG.

Though very severely wounded in the leg in this action, Cpl Anderson crawled back to his Acting Company Commander to report the silencing of the post. This NCOs conduct throughout these attacks was such as to defy description. His bravery and utter fearlessness inspired all who were in contact with him and his two singlehanded acts referred above were such as to turn difficult situations into successful actions and very materially assisted in the main action of the unit.

(L.G. 11.2.43)

Anderson, Vincent, Corporal
QX 8109, 2/15 Australian Infantry Bn.

Throughout the operations near Alamein from the night 23/24 Oct 42 until 5 Nov 42, Cpl Anderson showed outstanding courage, leadership and initiative.

During the initial attack on west Pt 23 on the night 23/24 Oct, when he commanded a forward section on the left flank of the battalion, he led his section with courage and dash, overcoming the resistance of an enemy post whose fire was enfilading the battalion advance, and quickly continuing the advance after passing back his prisoners and reorganising his section.

During a further battalion attack north of Pt 29 on night 28/29 Oct 42, Cpl Anderson again led the left forward section of the battalion with coolness and resolution. On the following morning he was directly responsible for the capture of two 50mm guns and their crews. As the half-tracked vehicles towing these guns approached his position Cpl Anderson held the fire of his section until they were within 200 yards of him. The section then opened fire, setting one vehicle alight. He then immediately went forward with his section and captured the two crews, the two guns, and the remaining vehicle.

M.I.D. 24.6.43   *(L.G. 11.2.43)*

Anderson, William, Sergeant
3244515, 46th Reconnaissance Regt. (Motherwell)
(Immediate)

On 19 Jan 44 'C' Sqn's two dismounted troops, under command 2/5 Queens, were ordered to occupy the small wooded feature lying East of P.216(9000). Sjt. Anderson's Troop were first pushed out along P.216 to observe and supply information of the enemy to assist the Squadron Commander in making his plan.

They detected the presence of enemy on the objective, and also three Spandau positions covering the re-entrant, lying N.W. of P.216, which would have to be crossed to reach the objective.

Sjt. Anderson proved especially able in this observation, and put his section on to one of these positions, killing one of the crew.

In the attack on the objective, the Assault Troop were pushed through Sjt. Anderson's Troop, but despite the smoke screen laid to cover the passage of the re-entrant, came under very heavy fire.

Sjt. Anderson pushed his section further forward to assist the Assault Tp by keeping the Spandau crews' heads down, without regard to the fact that he thus exposed himself to the fire of the enemy on the objective.

Two of his men were hit, and in addition to encouraging them, he crawled forward to bandage the wounds of Tpr. Cranney, risking the Spandau fire to do so.

Meanwhile the remainder of the sqn had pushed forward, and by fire and movement silenced the enemy on the objective, but still could not reach it owing to the continued presence of the Spandaus and the fact that ammunition had run out.

Sjt. Anderson then re-disposed his section so as to cover the left flank and rear, in the event of a counter-attack, and by skilful control of fire managed to check any attempt of the Spandau crews to make any movement, despite the fact that he was reduced himself to a magazine and a half of Bren Ammunition.

At the end of the day Sjt. Anderson was the only survivor of the five Sjts who were in the force, and his Tp Commander also had been killed.

In the re-organisation of sections, checking of arms and re-issue of ammunition, when everyone was very tired, Sjt. Anderson was a tower of strength, working indefatigably for both Troops, being the only Sjt.

The example he showed during the action, and after it, was excellent.   *(L.G. 29.6.44)*

Anderson, William, Sergeant
3313030, 5 Highland Light Infantry

On 14 Jun 40 at Ferriere et Clocher this N.C.O. carried the message, by motor cycle, from Battalion H.Q. to Company H.Q. ordering the withdrawl of the Company. He had to approach through a hail of L.M.G. fire which might well have caused him to give up the attempt. His very outstanding courage and coolness undoubtedly saved the lives of every person at Company H.Q. and by getting the message through he saved the whole Company which was rapidly being surrounded by overwhelming numbers, from being completely cut off. It is impossible to praise too highly his courage.

(L.G. 20.12.40)

Andrew, Richard Ivor, Sergeant
5439010, 1/7 Battalion Queen's Royal Regt.
(Ponsanooth, Cornwall) (Immediate)

On 6th March 1943, 5439010 Sjt. Andrews was in command of an Infantry 6 pdr anti-tank gun crew covering the southern approaches to the Bde position. This position was heavily attacked at an early hour when seventeen enemy tanks approached moving fast. They deployed for the attack, and passed across the front of Sjt. Andrew's gun. With remarkable fire discipline, and with the intention of obtaining the full destructive effect of the anti-tank layout, Sjt. Andrews held his fire and remained concealed until four enemy tanks had passed across his sights.

The tanks were about at 1,000 yards range and passed his position, when Sjt. Andrews opened fire knocking out the first tank with a succession of shots, and also the tank following. This onslaught stopped the initial attack.

A Mark IV Special then went into a hull-down position, and systematically shelled the gun pit, to which Sjt. Andrews replied repeatedly hitting the enemy tank, but causing no vital damage owing to the shots glancing off the heavily armoured turret. Another tank then took up a similar hull-down position and acted as an armoured O.P. to an 88 mm in position behind a ridge, which came into action against the gun.

The shelling became so severe that Sjt. Andrews ordered his crew into cover, but himself lay quietly beside the gun awaiting an opportunity for further action. It was clear that the enemy thought the gun silenced, as some time later the Mark IV that he had been watching came slowly forward. Sjt. Andrews seized his opportunity, loaded and fired the gun himself, and scored a hit. The tank withdrew and was found the next day abandoned.

For the next hour Sjt. Andrews continued to fire his gun single handed while continually being shelled and machine gunned. The parapet of his position was completely shot away, and the gun shield pierced by bullets, and an A.P. shot, while a 75 mm H.E. shell had exploded actually in the gun pit.

When the fire had sufficiently lost its intensity, Sjt. Andrews recalled his crew, and for the remainder of the day maintained his gun in action under continuous enemy fire of all natures. In all 64 rounds were fired by the gun. The gun and crew were in full view of a large portion of the main position, and the magnificent example set by Sjt. Andrews undoubtedly had an effect that was probably decisive in encouraging others to stand firm under circumstances which at times became nearly desperate. When it is understood that Sjt. Andrews had never before been in a determined enemy tank attack, nor had he ever fired his gun in action before, the exceptional gallantry of his behaviour throughout the day can be realised.

Recommended for V.C.   *(L.G. 4.5.43)*

Andrews, Alfred Albert Percy, Sergeant
781600, Royal Artillery
No citation
M.I.D. 20.12.40   *(L.G. 27.8.40)*

Andrews, George Ramsay, Warrant Officer Cl. I
2640, 18 Bn., New Zealand Military Forces
For outstanding gallantry and coolness under fire.

During the action at Galatos on 25 May 41 this Warrant Officer was wounded in the arm. While waiting to have his wound attended to he reported to the 10 Brigade H.Q. and asked for employment. The Germans were advancing fast, there were many stragglers and some confusion. He was instructed to rally parties and take them into position, which he did in fine fashion, having a large share in preventing panic.

He then organised and led a party to rescue some wounded who were being abandoned and then asked permission to leave as he had received three additional wounds. He was under fire the whole time and his outstanding gallantry and coolness had an invaluable steadying effect.

M.C. 21.6.45, M.I.D. 11.1.45 *(L.G. 30.12.41)*

Anstee, Reginald Arthur, Sergeant
2031345, 7th Bn. Royal Welch Fusiliers (Kidwelly)
During 5 Jan 44 Sjt Anstee was commanding a Platoon of the right forward company engaged in the advance through the thick forest area South of Sur Waha 368491. The difficult country made control extremely difficult, and our advance was opposed with determination by enemy MG posts concealed in the thick woods. Throughout the advance Sjt Anstee led his Platoon with great dash and showed considerable skill in outflanking enemy MG posts, and it was largely owing to the action of his Platoon that his Company reached their objective by about midday. During the reorganisation on the objective the company was subjected to heavy shelling, and Sjt Anstee continued to provide a most inspiring example of complete indifference to danger.

At about 1600 hrs a heavy counter attack with considerable artillery support developed on the left flank of the battalion position. Sjt Anstee's Company Commander was severely wounded, and all the company officers and the CSM having already become casualties, he assumed command of the Company. By his admirable personal example, and complete calmness he kept the company quite steady, and the company position intact. After the position had been stabilised, the Company locality on the left having been largely over-run by the enemy it was necessary to readjust the dispositions of Sjt Anstee's Company in order to prevent any further penetration. With the enemy still in close contact, his own troops tired, and in the face of enemy shell fire, this, in the gathering darkness was a most delicate operation. Sjt. Anstee, however, continued to keep complete control of his men, and the readjustment had been successfully carried out before an officer arrived to take over command of the Company.

Throughout a day of hard fighting under the most unpleasant conditions Sjt Anstee showed leadership of the highest order. The magnificent example and tremendous energy of the NCO undoubtedly had a very marked effect on his company and contributed materially to the successful outcome of the entire operation.

          (L.G. 12.4.45)

Anton, William, Driver
1869824, 58th C.W. Coy & 232nd Coy (T.A.), Royal Engineers
Prior to Capture
About the end of May in the general retreat my party, in a lorry, were separated from the main column, got lost and made for Lille, hoping to get instructions there.

Capture
On approaching Lille we ran into an ambush and were taken prisoners. We were told to abandon our arms and the eight of us were shepherded down a road by two Germans who, when they saw another party of Germans further on, left us.

First Escape

We ran down a side street and were directed by a woman to the village of Fives. Here, in a café, we were given assistance and a suit of clothes was found for one man. I wandered off into the village, was able to find some civilian clothes for myself and then returned to the café. By this time the Germans were pouring through the village and those of us, who had not been able to get civilian clothes, remained hidden in the café. The other man, now in civilian clothes (Spr. Hurschal of 232 Coy. T.A.) and I left Fives. It was then evening and we marched all night across country and at dawn, found ourselves in Belgium on the Tournai road.

Recapture

Here a German car pulled up and an officer, who asked us the way to Tournai, recognised us as being English and handed us over to some German motor cyclists. We were taken to the Race Course at Lille where P/W were being collected. Here Hurschal and I, being in civilian clothes, were placed with other civilian prisoners. I lost sight of Hurschal at this time and was later interrogated by a German officer who, as he did not understand a word of English did not believe my statement that I was not a spy and actually ordered a firing party; fortunately, a moment later, another officer appeared and called for an Interpreter, who proceeded to interrogate me. I gave him false dates as to my landing in France and made out that I was a Pioneer. He then ordered me to rejoin the other civilian prisoners, but, on the following day, I was placed with military P/W, of whom there were about twenty altogether. The next morning we marched off towards Belgium by way of Tournai and Ath, and, after eight days, reached Nivelles. Here we were put in the town jail for two days and were then placed on a train for Germany.

Second Escape

Our journey by train took us through Wavre and Gennapes to Waterloo where, when the train slowed down, I managed to jump off. The train did not halt nor did the guards fire at me, so it is possible that the latter did not see me. I made off at once in the opposite direction and reached La Louviere, east of Mons. In La Louviere, looking for a way South, I asked directions from a woman who gave me food and, with the help of others directed me to an Englishman, who lived in the town. They had already warned me not to attempt to go through France, but to make for the coast, in the hopes of finding a boat. The Englishman repeated this advice, gave me provisions and 20 frs. and I made off on foot for the coast, striking it near Middelkerke. From there I wandered up the coast towards Holland and got as far as Heyst, Knocke and so just into Holland; but all the time I saw not the slightest trace of a boat. During the next three weeks I wandered round in this district and, towards the end of this period, got down to Thourout.

Recapture

In the village of Eeson, somewhere near Alost, I was betrayed by a woman, who owned a farm, to the Belgian Gendarmerie who locked me up and, next morning, handed me over to two Gendarmes who took me to Bruges in a car, where I was put in the town jail. I was taken to the German Kommandantur and interrogated. Here I again gave false information and later, on the same day, was interrogated a second time when I confirmed the information I had given earlier in the day. The next day I was taken by lorry to Termonde, which was a sort of Transit Camp, where I had to await the arrival of a column of prisoners who arrived the same day, fifty-six of whom were English soldiers.

Third Escape

The following day we started to march towards Ghent. On the way we stopped, after about three hours, for a ten minutes' break. Here local inhabitants brought food for the prisoners and, in the scramble for it, when the guards were fully occupied in trying to control the men, I slipped away into a field of standing crops. I crawled into a ditch and waited until all was quiet. Two men passed me and later brought me food and asked if I wanted clothes. One of these men later led me across the fields and put me on my way. Walking in a southerly direction, I came to a farmhouse where I was allowed to listen to the radio and heard the English news, from which I learnt for the first time that France's Armistice Terms had been agreed upon, and that certain zones were to be demilitarised within the next three weeks (about 25th June). I made for the frontier but did not hurry as I thought it might be better to wait until the three weeks for demilitarisation were up. I reached La Louviere again, via Mons, where I learnt that the Germans were sending families from Cologne to Beaudore (?). I reached the frontier and crossed it through cornfields, eventually arriving at Avesgnes where I received food and accommodation at a farm for one night, but had to hide when a German agent (a Frenchman) came to the house to check up the numbers of cattle to be commandeered. The next big town through which I passed was Vervisn (?) where I decided to make for Rheims. I reached Neufchâtel and found that I could not cross the river as the bridge had been blown up. A German pioneer company were building a trestle bridge. I made my way to Guignicourt where there were two such bridges.

Recapture

I crossed the first bridge over the river at Guignicourt, but was stopped on the second bridge, over the canal, and taken to the Kommandantur. After interrogation, I was taken to a château in the village which served as a P/W camp for Frenchmen, of whom there were about 130 other ranks and 2 officers. I was given the work of cooking for them. Most of the men were suffering from colic brought about by the supply of water and the monotonous diet of lentils, twice a day, with a little black bread.

Final Escape

On the night of the 4th day there I managed to get away, in spite of the fact that my French companions watched me constantly as the Germans had told them that in the event of my escaping the senior French officer and ten men would be shot. I got out of the sleeping quarters, which I shared with the cooks, by pretending to have the prevalent colic, made my way through the back garden, over a wall, down the street and out of the village. As it was raining very hard and pitch dark I lost my way and found myself back again in Guignicourt, where I entered a deserted house, found a bed and went to sleep. On the following day the owner of this house, who had been evacuated, returned to find me in residence, but he was very helpful, gave me food and, the day after, brought the Maire who gave me 20 frs. and counselled me to leave, which I did.

On leaving Guignicourt an old woman gave me a hoe and basket, as camouflage, and advised me to leave behind my overcoat, as it was rather a good one and therefore conspicuous. I tried to cross the river at Neufchâtel, but the current was too strong, so I followed the road on the northern bank as far as Soissons. I crossed the river here by the stone bridge (the other two were destroyed) and went on to Meaux. From Meaux I made for Melun, Fontainebleau, Montargis, Gien, Aubigny, Neuvy and so to the line of demarcation at Quincy, which I reached in the late evening. The village itself in in Unoccupied France, but I was able to cross the river in the morning, as it was only waist deep and, by doing so, avoided the German guards who were stationed on the iron bridge there.

From here I headed south again by way of Issoudun, Chateauroux, Limoges, Brive, Cahors and so to Toulouse. From Toulouse I went on through Parmiers, Foix, Ax Les Thermes and so to L'Hospitalet. Beyond the village of L'Hospitalet I got as far as Porte where I was stopped and interrogated by French Mobile Police who took me to St. Cyprien, where I was interned. From there I was sent to Agde where I met Dvrs. McAngus and Tull with whom I continued the rest of my journey. (See S/P.G.(F)99/100)

Military and Air Intelligence

At Bruges there was every sign of a big dump of ammunication *(sic)* and a great many Army vehicles, about 300 yards from the Canal.

At Bouizon, near Vierzon, on the line of demarcation there was a wireless installation—4 masts and a large three storey building in the centre, completely isolated from all houses.

Information supplied by inhabitants was that German planes when taking off for a raid came from different aerodromes and formed up in the air itself before setting out. The purpose of this was to avoid congregating a lot of planes on the ground in one place.

There were aerodromes outside each large town, notably those at Nivelles and Ath.   *(L.G. 7.3.41)*

Applebee, Frederick, Sergeant
6010746, 1st Essex Regt. (Bradford)
Was commanding a Platoon of 'D' Coy. On 26 Nov this Company was the leading Company in the attack and

for some time, held an objective [...]00 to [...]00 yds South of the road, unsupported on either flank, having previously suffered heavy casualties. During this time, the Company was counter attacked by some enemy tanks and infantry. Sjt. Applebee kept moving from section to section under close range fire from both tanks and infantry, encouraging and directing his sections with complete disregard to personal danger, and thereby maintaining the position. On 29 Nov when attacked by tanks from the West and infantry from the South, Sjt. Applebee again at great personal risk kept visiting and directing his sections. His platoon was thus able to drive off an enemy infantry attack from the South which reached to the wire, at a time when tanks had penetrated to within 100 yds of his right flank and the Company on his right flank had been completely wiped out or taken prisoner. There is no doubt that the courageous actions of this N.C.O. was largely responsible for his platoon and Company holding on to their positions and thus enabling El Duda to be re-established. *(L.G. 24.2.42)*

Appleby, Allan, Sergeant
5498305, Bn. Royal Tank Regt. (Bournemouth)
(Immediate)
Sjt. Appleby was commanding a troop of three 'I' Tanks and was the left troop of the leading Squadron in the attack on 'Tiger' on 21.11.41. Two of his tanks blew up on a minefield, sustaining broken tracks and other local damage. The rest of the Squadron went on. This was at 0700 hrs. Throughout the day, the enemy made intermittent attacks with Infantry supported by artillery fire from the West. Small arms, mortar, and Molotov cocktails were used against him. He repulsed these attacks with the utmost energy and initiative, directing the fire of the immobile tanks, and manœuvring the fit tank with considerable skill. During lulls, although continuously subjected to Artillery and M.G. fire, he commenced the repair of the tanks, and by nightfall had completed them. He then took in tow another tank which he found damaged by a mine and led them all back within the Tobruk perimeter to the night leaguer and the unit. Sjt. Appleby's initiative, drive and skill in fighting his troop although two tanks were immobile, and his devotion to duty in carrying out the repairs while most of the time the troop was under fire set an example of determination and courage which must rank highly in the service. He was acting as troop commander in place of an Officer, whose normal command it would be.
(L.G. 24.2.42)

Arbuthnot, Edward, Private (A/Cpl.)
2978024, 1st Bn.Green Howards (Edinburgh)
(Immediate)
On the occasion of the break-out from the Anzio Bridgehead on 23rd May 1944, 1 Green Howards launched an attack onto the left coastal sector of the enemy positions. Cpl. Arbuthnot was a member of a Platoon of 1 Green Howards who were given the task of

escorting a R.E. Gapping Party, and carrying ladders to the point on the river Moletta at which assaulting Companies were to cross the River.

During the move of this party from our forward positions to the Moletta river, a newly laid minefield was encountered and casualties were caused by the explosion of several mines. These casualties included the Platoon Commander of the Green Howards' Platoon, the Officer i/c the R.E. detachment and 40% of the entire party.

In spite of the very difficult situation caused by this initial reverse and the fact that the enemy were now opening fire on the survivors, Cpl Arbuthnot took command of the party and led them, with as many ladders as could be carried, through the remaining mines to the banks of the Moletta.

It was entirely due to the determination and leadership of this N.C.O. that ladders were placed in position in time to enable the assaulting companies to cross zero hour. Cpl Arbuthnot was wounded twice during this exploit but later in the action volunteered to go forward and take over a section position at a critical stage in the action. *(L.G. 21.9.44)*

Archibald, John Murray, Sergeant (A/W.O.II (C.S.M.))
2986699, 7th Bn.Argyll & Sutherland Highlanders (Carron, Falkirk) (Immediate)
On 6th Mar 43, when the Germans attacked the battalion position on the Segdel ridge the main weight of the attack fell on C.S.M. Archibald's company which was continuously engaged with machine gun, mortar and artillery fire from 0800 hrs till sunset. As the day passed, the enemy worked his machine guns and mortars up closer and in greater numbers, and the company was subjected to constant shelling and machine gunning until a counter-attack at last light finally drove the enemy off. In these difficult circumstances C.S.M. Archibald gave an outstanding display of devotion to duty. All through the day he moved about the Company area with complete disregard of the enemy fire, visiting platoons and passing orders. When an observation post was driven in by fire, he personally led a party back to it and then went by himself to a position in the flank where he remained sniping the advancing infantry and observing and reporting their movements, and the effect of our own fire. Throughout the action, C.S.M. Archibald's coolness and disregard of danger were an inspiration to the men of his company and of invaluable assistance to his Company Commander.
Recommended for M.M. M.M. 22.7.43   (L.G. 4.5.43)

Armitage, Brian Lindsay, Sergeant (temp.)
35856, 1/2 F. F. Bn. South African Forces (Immediate)
For most conspicuous gallantry, personal initiative, and resourcefulness.

On the night of 31 Aug/1 Sep when Patrol HQ and the Infantry Platoon protecting the HQ were surprised by approx. 150 Germans, and a few minutes later surrounded and attacked by this numerically superior enemy force, it was Sjt. Armitage who observed the enemy, warned his HQ, and immediately brought his V.M.G. into action, thus initiating an attack by our own troops.

In spite of a wound received during the first stages, he kept on firing until the V.M.G. was knocked out by enemy fire. With great presence of mind, Sjt. Armitage then returned to HQ, fetched the Armoured Car there, and himself manning the V.M.G., pushed right in amongst the enemy in the face of heavy and concentrated L.M.G. fire at very short range. His action in moving up and down amongst the enemy in the Armoured Car and keeping up sustained V.M.G. fire not only caused many enemy casualties, but so completely demoralised the Germans, and drove them into such disorder, as to allow the supporting Infantry Platoon to reorganise and re-establish themselves, completely restoring the position.

Through his unfailing courage, and without thought of self, Sjt. Armitage was instrumental in capturing 14 German prisoners, inflicting numerous casualties, and compelling the enemy to withdraw, thus saving a desperate situation which might easily have developed into one embracing the loss of many of our own troops.
Recommended for M.M.   *(L.G. 5.11.42)*

Armstrong, Denis Wemyss, Sergeant
4224, Royal Natal Carbineers (Immediate)
For Conspicuous Gallantry in Action at Combolcia Pass on 22 Apr 41. Sjt. Armstrong stalked two M.G. posts and shot the crews. After failing to dislodge two more M.G.'s by bombs he again stalked the position and shot the crews. This action saved his Company many casualties. *(L.G. 21.10.41)*

Armstrong, George Thomas, Warrant Officer Cl. II (C.S.M.) (Drill Sergeant)
2022288, 5th Bn. Grenadier Guards (S. Elkington, Lincs.)
During the fighting on the Anzio Bridgehead the 5th Battalion Grenadier Guards was almost continuously in action from the 25 Jan—9 Feb 1944 and this Warrant Officer was acting as RSM. Throughout the period D/Sjt Armstrong was suffering severe pain from rheumatism, but refused to go sick.

On the night 7/8 Feb the enemy broke through the front and heavily attacked Battalion HQ, which was practically surrounded. This Warrant Officer led the defence with Tommy gun and hand grenades and by his extreme gallantry and powers of leadership succeeded in holding his position. He was twice blown over by enemy hand grenades, but this made no difference to his continuous disregard for his own safety and his ability to fight the enemy with the means at his disposal.

Throughout the period that the Battalion was in close contact with the enemy D/Sjt Armstrong's cheerfulness and devotion to duty were an inspiration to all with whom he came in contact, and his conduct is deserving of the highest commendation.

M.I.D. 23.9.43   (*L.G. 15.6.44*)

Armstrong, James, Warrant Officer Cl. II
3851803, 2nd Bn. King's Regt. (Preston) (Immediate)
Ref Map Italy, 1/25,000. Sheet 100, IV. NW.

At 0600 hrs on 14th Nov, 1944, 'C' Company, 2nd Battalion the Kings Regiment, had captured the area around Road Junc 433209, and were consolidating under a new Company Commander, the previous one having been wounded a short time before.

Company HQ and one Platoon were established in a house and the whole position was subjected to extremely heavy shellfire, when the house received three direct hits from an enemy 88mm gun. The house was demolished, the new Company Commander was seriously wounded, the Company 2nd-in-Comd completely stunned, and one Platoon Commander and some men wounded. No. 3851803 CSM J. Armstrong although himself very shaken immediately took control extricating and evacuating wounded to places of safety under continual heavy shell fire. His untiring efforts without help from any senior officer, his encouragement to the wounded and control of the other platoons nearby quickly established order out of a situation which might have got out of hand.

He supervised the complete evacuation of the wounded and reorganized the company for the 2nd-in-Comd to take forward into battle about one hour later.

Such was CSM Armstrong's conduct in adversity that the Company continued the advance without hesitation and such was his initiative that no time was lost in reorganisation or in the momentum of the advance.

'C' Company had no Officers other than the acting Company Commander, during the ensuing advance to San Martino (408229), and in consequence CSM Armstrong moved from one platoon to another quite regardless of his own safety during very heavy shelling and spandau fire, urging the men to get on and giving words of encouragement and advice throughout the action.

That the action was successful must in a very large way be credited to CSM Armstrong. He showed an example to his Officer and men of the highest traditions of the British Army and never at any time did he sow any concern for himself. He had only one object in view, the fulfilment of the Company task and loyalty to the cause under the most extenuating circumstances.

(*L.G. 26.4.45*)

Armstrong, John, Private
4393111, 6th Bn. Green Howards (Langley-on-Tyne) (Immediate)
On the night of the 25/26 Oct 42 during the attack on Pt. 94 in the Munassib Depression, Pte. Armstrong was advancing with his Platoon Commander when they were fired on by a machine gun post. The Platoon Commander was wounded and unable to carry on. With complete disregard for his own safety, Pte. Armstrong went forward and destroyed this post and enabled his Platoon to move forward. Again the Platoon was held up by another machine gun post and flash bombs. Pte. Armstrong again went forward with Pte. Charlish and put this post out of action, killing and wounding 7 Italians.

The following day under intense mortar fire on our consolidated positions, Pte. Armstrong kept up a continual fire on an enemy sniper post, subsequently killing at least one sniper and forcing them to evacuate the position.

Recommended for M.M.   (*L.G. 28.1.43*)

Arndt, Robert Julius, Corporal
M.167678, The Perth Regiment, Canadian Infantry Corps (Immediate)
On 29 April 1945 Corporal Arndt was commanding a section in 'A' Company the Perth Regiment. The Company was engaged in a night attack on a very strong enemy position, in the area immediately south of the village of Nansum.

When the leading troops of the Company reached a point approximately 100 yards from the southern edge of the village a strong belt of wire was encountered and the enemy in a house 100 yards distant opened fire.

Corporal Arndt's section was ordered to breach the wire and assault the house from which the enemy was firing. Under the brilliant leadership of this Non-Commisioned Officer the section succeeded in getting through the wire and across a deep water-filled ditch. The enemy fire became more intense and machine guns were now firing at the section from both flanks as well as from the house, Corporal Arndt silenced some of the enemy by throwing a grenade through a window after which he dashed into the house alone firing his weapon. The enemy gave way before this determined assault and the section took 70 prisoners in addition to wounding six and killing several of the enemy. Six enemy machine guns were captured.

Several hours after the capture of the house a force of approximately 30 enemy, armed with machine guns and bazookas, counter attacked and attempted to recapture the house. During this counter attack Corporal Arndt, himself occupied a slit trench covering the left flank of the position. With great coolness and determination, he withheld his fire until the enemy were approximately ten yards from him. When he opened fire he killed five of the enemy, including two officers, and completely disorganized and routed the enemy.

(*L.G. 22.9.45*)

Arnold, George Henry Charles, Lance Corporal
7885476, 3 Bn. Royal Tank Regt.
In April 1941 Arnold was captured in Greece, and later taken to a Prisoner of War Camp at Woltzburg in Austria. Here he was put in charge of small working camps, which

enabled him to gain information and learn the language while travelling from camp to camp.

On September 15 at a small camp near Vienna, Arnold and a friend arranged to escape. At 9 p.m. they attacked the two guards at the gate with bars unscrewed from some windows and struck out in a S.E. direction.

As a result of previous unsuccessful attempts to escape it was decided not to travel by night, but masquerade as German officers on leave in civilian clothes travelling openly by day. Whenever it looked as though they were to be spoken to, they said 'Heil Hitler' thus creating an impression of Gestapo in plain clothes.

As no help was forthcoming from the civil population of Austria they had to exist on what they could steal from the land such as turnips and grapes.

On crossing the Border into Yugo-slavia they stopped at a house to ask for food and on finding the Ustache in occupation, Arnold and his friend used great presence of mind in following up their story of German officers on leave and convinced their hosts that their papers had been stolen. They spent the night in this house and left on their travels the following morning furnished with a considerable amount of information about location of units etc.

They were finally picked up by the Partisans and returned to the British after a very difficult spell trying to convince the Partisans that they were escaped British Prisoners of War and not German spies.

Apart from making an outstanding escape and showing great initiative, Arnold was able to pass on valuable information which will help future escapees. He has also volunteered to go back into enemy occupied territory and help his companions escape in the same way. This is an excellent example of courage and initiative and I thoroughly recommend that this soldier be awarded the D.C.M. for his great achievement.

(L.G. 24.8.44)

Arnold, George Luke Sidney, Warrant Officer Cl. II
(S.S.M.)
7871727, 7th Bn. Royal Tank Regt. (Scarborough)
Tobruch 21st—30th November, 41.

Over a period of ten days during which The Squadron has taken part in six separate actions, S.S.M. Arnold has been responsible for maintaining supplies of ammunition and fuel under the most trying circumstances. In particular on 22nd November, he led his lorry out of the perimeter on the heels of the tanks and through intense artillery fire. On various occasions he has supplied the squadron under artillery and mortar fire and in the face of snipers. As a result of his disregard for his own safety, no tank in the squadron was ever short of supplies. He has been a magnificent example to all ranks.

(L.G. 24.2.42)

Arrowsmith, James, Warrant Officer Cl. I (actg.)
3520954, 11th Bn. Lancashire Fusiliers (Bury)
(Periodic)
RSM Arrowsmith carried out valuable work as CSM during early operations in the Gothic Line. In October 1944 he was appointed RSM in the field. When the Battalion took over positions from U.S. Troops in Monte Grande area, he was responsible for all forward administration, the defence of Battalion HQ area, and for the reception of reinforcements.

This work was carried out by RSM Arrowsmith in the most difficult conditions. Supply and maintenance was carried out by night and often under heavy enemy fire, but by calm leadership and example, often doing work himself under shellfire and in exposed positions which he might well have left to others, he ensured that at no time was the enemy allowed seriously to interfere with the operation.

Owing to shortage of man power, there were periods when Battalion HQ was itself responsible for the defence of a locality. On these occasions RSM Arrowsmith displayed a high sense of leadership and personal courage. When enemy fire was heaviest, he was constantly in evidence, ensuring that the position was securely held and by his example of complete indifference to personal safety giving inspiration to his men.

This Warrant Officer's high sense of duty and discipline, in action and at rest and his constant exemplary example with which he allowed no condition of discomfort, danger or fatigue to interfere, has always been a fine example to all ranks and has contributed enormously to the discipline, training and morale of the battalion as a whole.

Recommended for M.B.E.   *(L.G. 13.12.45)*

Arsenau, Paul, Lance Sergeant
D62214, Canadian Infantry Corps
No citation   *(L.G. 9.2.46)*

Ashby, Herbert Hector, Private
SX.10570, 2/48 Australian Infantry Bn.
For courage, leadership and determination to fight on against great odds for a period of 15 hrs although his section was isolated from the remainder of the Company.

At Tell el Eisa on 22 Jul 42, Pte Ashby was in command of his Section, in an attack on strong German positions.

The attack was commenced at 0615 hrs and early in the advance the Company received heavy casualties from artillery and MG fire. All the offrs were killed or wounded and Pte Ashby's Sec became isolated from the remainder of the Company. After assaulting and subduing several enemy MG posts the Sec was held up by intense fire from the front and flanks.

Although at times his position appeared to be impossible he flatly refused to consider withdrawal and insisted on fighting on. By his alertness and fire control he was able to release from capture a crew of three from a Valentine tank and two members of his Sec, killing or wounding all the enemy who had seized them.

With great personal courage he sniped continuously at enemy nearby and by his leadership and dogged determination inspired his men who inflicted heavy casualties on the enemy during an engagement lasting all day.   *(L.G. 24.9.42)*

Ashton, Anthony, Lance Sergeant
2721511, 1st Bn. Irish Guards (Burnley) (Immediate)
This L/Sjt. took part in the attack on Pt 212 on 27th April '43 and was a leading figure in the defence of Pt. 214 throughout the whole period till the position was relieved. 0300 1st May. As the Senior Sergeant left in No 3 Coy. he took over command when Lt. Kennard was wounded on the morning of 30th April, and proved a worthy successor. But before this also he displayed the highest courage and devotion to duty and was an example of all that an excellent soldier should be.

He was with Lt. Kennard in the attack on the M/Gs it was he who turned one gun on the retreating Germans, and then brought it back to our positions, having destroyed the other. After the Armoured Car, which had got up on to the Ring contour north of pt. 214 had been halted, it was he who prevented the crew from dismounting their guard by his skilful and accurate LMG fire, and having got them pinned, handed over the gun, crawled forward with a small party and eliminated the crew, who had either gone to ground or were hiding inside the car. In this way, he removed a serious threat to the Bn's position, and no other armoured car attempted to come up that way again. During the attacks and counterattacks he was always to the forefront, and probably has the largest total individual score of Germans to his credit. I strongly recommend this N.C.O. for his numerous acts of bravery and initiative, of which only two have been mentioned.   *(L.G. 8.7.43)*

Ashton, Hartley Edward, Sergeant
930746, 124 Field Regt. (N) T.A., Royal Artillery
    (Wallasey) (Immediate)
At Lentini on the 14th July 1943 Sgt Ashton was in action with the rest of 48 Field Battery. His task was to cover the approaches into the position. Hearing that there were enemy approaching the area he went to investigate and met an enemy motor cyclist armed with a machine gun. He shot the motor cyclist and returned to command his gun. At this stage in the action the volume of fire was considerable and exitement was running high so that there was some danger that troops in rear would fire into the back of Sjt. Ashton's Troop which was in a forward position. Sjt. Ashton took adequate steps to prevent this happening. When the tanks came up the road towards him, firing as they came, Sjt. Ashton took control and engaged them. As a result the leading tank was brought to a standstill after charging the wall at the side of the road. A number of other tanks then piled up behind the leading one and the volume of fire became even greater.

Appreciating the fact that the tank crews might surrender if firmly attacked at close quarters Sjt. Ashton by personal leadership and example carried the men of his troop with him up to the wall lining the lane along which the tanks were trying to move. Covered by the fire of the remainder he himself with several men leapt into the road and climbing on top of the tanks forced many of the crews to surrender. Later he accompanied the patrol into the forward areas. Throughout the action Sjt. Ashton showed exceptional initiative and power of command. His bearing under heavy and sustained small arms fire, to which Gunners are not normally subject, was an example not only to his troop but to the whole regiment.
Recommended for M.M.   *(L.G. 21.10.43)*

Ashton, Peter John, Corporal
4720051, Royal Australian Infantry Corps
For Vietnam   *(L.G. 12.2.71)*

Askew, William Henry, Platoon Sergeant Major
4388271, 1st Bn. The Green Howards
For conspicuous gallantry and devotion to duty at Otta on 28th April, 1940.

This W.O. was actg as Company Sjt. Mjr of 'Y' Company. His Company was astride the river with one platoon detached on the Eastern bank. Early in the day his Company Commander had gone to the detached platoon and was unable to get back. PSM Askew was left in command of the remainder of the Company. He fought his Company throughout the whole day with skill and determination and great courage, inflicting considerable losses on the enemy, and showing complete disregard for his own personal danger. On being ordered to withdraw he effected the withdrawal of his Company from close contact with the enemy in perfect order and without any losses. Throughout the action he showed a splendid example to all ranks.

Assan, Lance Corporal
11321, Somaliland Camel Corps
For continuous gallantry at Mill Hill in the Tug Argan position from the 11th to 13th August, 1940. By his bravery and disregard for danger he set an example to his men and at one time when under heavy fire stripped down and cleaned a Bren Gun which had stopped firing.
To be dated 11.2.41 and substituted for the award of the African D.C.M. announced in the L.G. of that date
                                               (L.G. 21.7.42)

Asseltine, Walter, Corporal
B.78719, Irish Regt. of Canada (Immediate)
During the night 16/17 April 1945 a strong enemy force consisting of approximately one thousand men supported by self-propelled guns attacked the town of Otterloo, Holland. The Irish Regiment of Canada was responsible for defending this town which was a key point in the main axis of advance of 5 Canadian Armoured Division and the location of Divisional Headquarters. The enemy

succeeded in infiltrating into the town and bitter fighting continued throughout the entire night.

By 0600 hours approximately 300 of the enemy had succeeded in infiltrating into a vital sector and were securely dug-in along the verges of the narrow road. Corporal Asseltine, commanding a section of three flame-throwing carriers (Wasps) was ordered to clear this vital sector. When the section, with Corporal Asseltine in the leading carrier, moved onto the road, it immediately came under intense small arms fire from three sides at point blank range, in many instances as close as four or five yards. Disregarding the enemy fire this gallant Non-Commissioned officer, with great coolness, directed the work of his section and opened fire with his flame-thrower, spraying ditches and slit trenches on both sides of the road. A concealed Bazooka position opened up at approximately 30 yards range and the second carrier was put out of action. Corporal Asseltine immediately rushed the position and with one burst from his Bren Gun killed the crew. Visibility was limited by fog to fifty yards but this Non-Commissioned Officer advanced up the road a distance of three hundred yards until his fuel was exhausted and then continued his advance firing small arms until this vital sector was cleared of the enemy. He then turned around, picked up the crew of the carrier which had been put out of action, and returned to his headquarters to re-fuel.

As a result of this Non-Commissioned Officer's magnificent leadership and courage seventy of the enemy were killed, many wounded and the remainder so demoralised that the tactical picture was completely changed and the town was quickly cleared of the enemy.
(L.G. 22.9.45)

Aston, Nash William, Lance Corporal
553237, 3 Hussars, Royal Armoured Corps
On 11th December 1940, the tank in which this N.C.O. was travelling became bogged and was knocked out by enemy gunfire from a range of approximately 400 yards. After managing to escape from his tank this N.C.O., in spite of being under very heavy enemy fire, assisted his wounded comrades from the disabled tank. He then assisted the Medical Officer in carrying wounded back to a more covered position. He continued assisting the Medical Officer in dressing and attending wounded men, being the whole time under heavy fire from artillery and machine guns.

His gallantry is worthy of the highest praise and was the means of saving many lives.   *(L.G. 25.4.41)*

Atkins, Herbert John, Warrant Officer Cl. II
(C.S.M.)
6346229, 5th Bn. Queen's Own Royal West Kent Regt.
(Sanderstead) (since died of wounds) (Immediate)
On 16th Dec. 43 the Coy. took part in a night attack on point 269 on the Orsogna—Ortona road. On reaching the objective two German tanks were discovered. CSM. Atkins, under considerable small arms fire, succeeded

in contacting the reserve Platoon which had got isolated owing to the heavy cordite fumes from the damage and the darkness. He led these men in, attacked the tanks, both of which were captured intact. Some 20 minutes later a third German tank, a flame thrower, started firing from about 100 yds. away on the left flank. CSM Atkins went forward across the road, contacted both forward Platoons. and under heavy fire, successfully assisted in the re-organisation necessary to deal with the new threat. A Platoon of 'C' Coy., sent to deal with this, was met and shown the situation by him. Subsequently during heavy enemy shelling, CSM Atkins, by showing complete disregard for his own safety was a great inspiration to all ranks and played an important part in the successful re-organisation of the position.
Recommended for M.M.   *(L.G. 4.5.44)*

Atkinson, Clarence Cecil, Private
NX 4314, 2/3 Australian Infantry Bn.
For conspicuous gallantry and devotion to duty on 27 Jun 41 whilst holding a defensive position on Jebel Mazar feature, 10 platoon were 'pinned' down by the fire of an enemy Hotchkiss gun for a period of three hours. One section of 12 Platoon endeavoured to outflank the enemy gun despite the number of snipers. Eventually the section was held up, one man being killed.

Pte. Atkinson then with a haversack of grenades dashed forward amongst the rocks hurling grenades, clearing the area of enemy and capturing the Hotchkiss gun. On moving forward, Pte. Atkinson became the target of intensive fire, from the area, but he continued on, displaying amazing courage.
Recommended for M.M.   *(L.G. 12.2.42)*

Atkinson, Ernest, Corporal (A/Sgt.)
4128852, 6th Bn. Cheshire Regt. (Knutsford)
(Immediate)
On 17 Sep 43, Sjt. Atkinson was in command of a machine gun section in a very forward position at S. Lucia (South of Battipaglia). Enemy infantry attacked the positions at dawn in very superior numbers. For [...] hours he directed the fire of his section under intense mortar and machine gun fire. Eventually the enemy infiltrated into the rear of the position from cover on the left flank. Sjt. Atkinson swung his gun round and engaged the enemy at a range of only a few yards. At this critical moment the gun developed a stoppage which could not be rectified. Sjt. Atkinson seized a Bren gun which had been dropped near his gun pit and continued to fire until the few magazines with the gun were exhausted. He then took the pistol from his No. 1 who was lying mortally wounded besides the gun and whilst firing the pistol with one hand, rectified the machine gun stoppage with the other. During this time he was hard pressed from all quarters and had ignored a demand for surrender made by the enemy. He later successfully reorganised his section without loss to guns or equipment. The enemy mortar and machine gun fire was intense throughout the

action. His courage and leadership inspired the men of his section to continue fighting in the face of desperate odds.   *(L.G. 13.1.44)*

Attewell, William George, Sergeant (A/W.O.II (C.S.M.))
6137322, 1st Bn. East Surrey Regt. (Colchester)
On 17th June 1944 'C' Company, 1st Battalion The East Surrey Regt was engaged in a battalion attack in the Citta del Pieve A.3684 area. During the morning the Company Commander was killed and the only other officer severely wounded. At this time a German counter attack was launched, which recaptured a house and temporarily disorganised the Company. CSM Attewell, the Company Sergeant Major of the Company, reformed the Company, led a counter attack on to the house in the face of heavy machine gun and mortar fire, recaptured the house, and consolidated the company position. He then personally sited every Bren gun and Piat in the Company and held his position until relieved that night. By his personal courage, initiative and leadership this Warrant Officer not only reorganised the Company after its officers had been made casualties, but, under constant fire, so imbued the men with the offensive spirit that the whole position was regained and the Germans driven out of their stronghold.   *(L.G. 7.12.44)*

Austin, Gerald Alexander, Sergeant (actg.)
14531142, 1 Queen's Own Royal West Kent Regt. (Llandudno Junc.) (Immediate)
Ref Map: Italy, Sheet 109, 1/25,000
On 18 Sep, 1944 Sjt. Austin was in command of 9 Platoon. At approx 0230 hrs the leading platoon of the Company, No 7 Platoon, had just crossed the S.L. for an attack on to La Ventura (822903) when it came under severe mortar and MG fire from all flanks and rear. As a result both the platoon commander and platoon sjt, as well as many others, became casualties, and the platoon was temporarily pinned down. Realising the situation, Sjt. Austin at once crawled forward under fire and took control of the remnants of the platoon. In very open country, where visibility was quite good, Sjt. Austin organised both pls for an attack forward to a house from which considerable fire was being directed. Sjt. Austin himself led the charge down hill and the position was over-run.

Still more enemy MG posts now opened up and again Sjt. Austin organised and led an attack. This, however, was not so successful and the platoon was in addition caught in the enemy Defensive Fire. Oblivious of any personal danger Sjt. Austin now crawled from sec to sec and, on orders just received, withdrew his platoon slightly to better cover and proceeded to engage the enemy afresh.

Sjt. Austin's leadership and complete command of the situation did much to press home the initial attack and his personal example did much to inspire his men under difficult circumstances.
Recommended for M.M.   *(L.G. 8.3.45)*

Averill, Maurice, Sergeant (A/W.O.II (S.S.M.))
7880509, Royal Tank Regt., Attd. G.H.Q., Reconn. Unit. (Periodic)
S.S.M. Averill was captured by German parachutists near Corinth on 26.4.41 and after two days they were taken to Corinth P/W camp, where he met Sjt. Britton who subsequently escaped with him and has also been recommended for recognition.

Conditions in the camp were very bad. The food was poor and there was much brutality. A colonel was struck down for obeying an order too slowly, and a sergeant stripped and beaten for singing.

On 8.6.41 S.S.M. Averill entrained at Kalamaki with those detailed to be taken to Germany. They changed trains at Athens and on the following day were detrained at Gravia and marched towards Lamia. When they reached a rocky track the Austrian guard, who had been talking to S.S.M. Averill, went ahead to show off how quickly he could go over the loose rocks. S.S.M. Averill then slipped away with Sjt. Britton and hid.

No search was made, so they spent that night in the hills and the following day reached the monastery at Damasta. Here one of the brothers looked after them, warned them if enemy patrols were in the district and afterwards, when the head of the monastery returned and threatened to hand them over to the enemy if they came within a mile of its walls, continued to feed and help them.

They then lived for a time in the hills, dressed as shepherds and supported by two Greeks.

At the end of October they went to Dernitza but returned to their friends in the hills in November.

They were consistently on the look out for a chance to get away and were now becoming desperate—especially as they had been joined by other escapers: their Greek friend said he would find transport and come with them, but was clearly rather frightened; a rich Greek woman had promised help but could do nothing; and a caique owner they had contacted dared not risk a journey as he had just been imprisoned for helping escapers.

On 2.1.42 they at last found a caique and S.S.M. Averill, Sjt. Britton and the party of five Palestinians and their Greek friend which they had collected, made their way to the water's edge, where they embarked. They had to avoid Italians manning search lights and A.A. guns in the district.

There was no wind so they took turns in rowing. They put in for water to a village on the north coast of the bay next day, opposite the coast of Eubœa.

The afternoon of the 6.1.42 they reached Skiathos, sailing close to the coast on the S.E. corner of the island. Here they were joined by three Australian privates who had been on the island ten days.

On 8.1.42 they left for Skopelos and landed in a bay opposite Strongyli Island. They lived at a monastery while they were on the island, trying vainly to find a caique for Turkey. Meanwhile the wife of the caique captain, who had taken them to Skiathos, had betrayed them and the Australian who returned to Skiathos to find a caique had been shot by Italians defending himself. Two days later the Italian patrol had already reached Glossa. Their only chance of escape was a caique from Halonnesus. This they found fortunately, and after being well looked after by the Mayor of Halonnesus and a shepherd on Skantzoura Island, where they were forced to land because of bad weather, they reached Chesme on 5.2.42.

S.S.M. Averill and Sjt. Britton, in spite of a protracted time in enemy territory under the most trying conditions, never once gave up persevering in their attempts to escape—nor did they forget their responsibilities to other escapers they met and ably led their small party back to Turkey. It was a highly meritorious performance often calling for much courage and quick thinking in the face of unexpected danger.
Recommended for M.B.E. *(L.G. 9.9.42)*

Avery, Frederick, Private
4689158, 1/King's Own Yorkshire Light Infantry
(Gateshead)
On the 13th July at Casa Belluza this soldier showed great courage and determination. He was one of a small party that reached the objective under intense enemy fire. On entering the position a M.G. was seen to be firing down a strong point. Pte. Avery at once advanced towards it and put it out of action by throwing grenades into the position. 3 further M.Gs still continued to harass the advance of our troops. Again Pte. Avery went forward, and with his small party was responsible for destroying all of them. He later located a sniper firing from the cover of a tree. He at once proceeded to work his way behind him and took him prisoner. Again on the 22nd July Pte. Avery acted with great coolness and bravery when his platoon was suffering heavy casualties from a M.G. firing from an enemy pillbox. He immediately dashed forward and hurled grenades into the post destroying the M.G. crew. He set a splendid example to all ranks.
M.M. 29.6.44 *(L.G. 18.11.43)*

Ayre, John, Warrant Officer Cl. II
3244343, 7th Bn. Cameronians (Fromdon Grange)
(Immediate)
At Selston, during the night 21 Jan 45, a strong counter-attack supported by enemy armoured vehs developed against the battalion front. Sjt. Ayre's Company Commander was mortally wounded almost immediately. There were no Officers left in the company and this NCO took over command. Sjt. Ayre immediately went round all his company positions through heavy spandau fire and shelling at great personal risk and it was largely due to his personal example and initiative that the company was able to deal with the counter-attack so successfully. In addition, he organised the evacuation of casualties and supply of amn with great coolness. *(L.G. 12.4.45)*

B

Babe, George Kenneth, Sergeant
410329, 21 N.Z. Bn. (Immediate)

This NCO was in charge of a platoon during the fighting in Cassino from 20-25 Mar 44. On the morning of 21 Mar his platoon was ordered to capture and clean out a building in which an enemy tank had just been destroyed. Despite the extremely heavy shelling and MG fire brought down by the enemy to secure the building and despite the fact that he and his platoon had been engaged in heavy and strenuous fighting involving many casualties, he boldly led his men forward across the open approaches. His personal example, dash and determination were mainly responsible in securing the building and cleaning out the major portion with grenades and small arms fire. He continued to hold his gain until, with the building gradually collapsing on account of direct fire, he was ordered to withdraw.

Sjt. Babe displayed a courage, initiative and cheerfulness under continued fire which quite inspired his men and proved an invaluable aid to his Company.

(L.G. 3.8.44)

Bach, Conrad William, Driver
T/128199, R.A.S.C. (Twickenham)

About 9 Jun 40 my unit 116 Coy, R.A.S.C. was in the neighbourhood of St. Valery. I was left with a few other men manning an anti-tank gun position. We discovered after a time that the rest of our Coy had left after scuttling their lorries, so we drove our own lorry down to St. Valery. An acting Q.M.S. there formed up about 15 of us and told us to try and hold our position in a wood, but we were forced to withdraw. We reached the beach to find that several thousand men were under fire of the German light artillery and M.G's on the surrounding cliff. Finally the white flag was hoisted and the men marched up to surrender. I got permission from the German guards to go back and row out to a burning gun boat, on which my C.O., Major Mackintosh, had been seen. There were a number of bodies in the boat, but I saw no sign of the Major.

We were marched all across Belgium and Holland to the Dutch German frontier. Conditions on this march, which took three weeks, were bad. After a train journey of a few hours, we went by boat up the Rhine to Camp Heimrich, where a few days were spent cleaning up. A two and a half days journey across Germany, without any food and in very bad conditions, finally brought us to Stalag XX A, at Thorn. Conditions in the old forts in which we were quartered were very bad indeed, and in Dec 40 I was moved to Camp 13(a), situated in some barracks nearby, where conditions were, if anything, even worse. Red Cross parcels started coming in very slowly, but later improved to about one parcel per man every

two or three weeks. The camp food was very meagre indeed, but men who went to work outside the camp got much better food, and men were always keen, therefore, to get outside work. As I had a very good knowledge of German, having been educated in Switzerland, I was employed throughout as interpreter and translator. In Thorn there was a very lively Black Market trade going on, mainly run by Poles. I concentrated on cornering the coffee market, as coffee was the most highly prized barter merchandise, and could be sold for as much as 80 marks per kilo. Thanks to this trade I scraped together between 500 and 600 R.M. and 8 Swiss frs. As I consider it difficult to escape successfully from this camp, I did all I could to get transferred.

After trying for five months, in May 41 I succeeded in getting a Sonderführer (Kommandant of Prison Labour parties), for whom I was working, to have me moved to Berlin Stalag III D, where I was to be interpreter at a factory which was being built by British, Polish and French P/W. After about a month here, I was sent to Stalag III D(a) Schoenenberg. This was situated about 150 yds away from a brewery which had been completely demolished by an R.A.F. raid and was being rebuilt by the P/W at III D(a). Here I soon got friendly with the guards, and my duties as interpreter made it possible for me to go to and fro between the camp and the brewery without escort. I now set about procuring civilian clothes, and with great difficulty I was finally able to get a civilian suit and overcoat, for which I had to give a gold ring, gold cigarette case and 200 R.M. These clothes I obtained from a civilian worker.

On Friday 31 Oct at about 0620 hrs, that is just after roll call, I left the camp by the main gate as though to go to the officers barracks adjoining the brewery, where I had been working daily as translator and interpreter for about 6 weeks. Strictly speaking I should have had to show my camp pass, but I had purposely got out of the habit of doing this during the many journeys to and fro which I had to make each day in the course of my duties. I had with me the small suit case in which I carried my papers, and which the sentry had lost the habit of examining. On this particular day I had my civilian suit tucked away in it amongst some papers. I changed quickly in a tool shed nearby and slipped away to a tram stop. After changing several times I reached the Anhalter Bahnhof at about 0700 hrs. As I saw no signs of any special formalities required at the ticket office I booked a ticket to Stuttgart. The train, which left Berlin at 0730 hrs, went straight through and there was no control apart from that by the ticket collector for civilians, whereas soldiers' papers were examined. I arrived at Stuttgart at about 2000 hrs, walked about the town, had a coffee and then caught a train about 0200 hrs to Lorrach. I changed trains at Geisingen and reached Lorrach about noon 1 Nov.

I decided not to make for Schaffhausen as according to rumours the frontier was very closely watched in that neighbourhood. I knew the Swiss side of the Basle frontier well, having spent holidays there and I had picked up all the information I could, especially from a Belgian P/W, who knew the German side accurately. (I also had a map with me which a Belgian civilian, who was involved in our Black Market in the camp, had bought for me in Berlin). The advice given to me was to avoid the northern part of the Riehen Salient, between Lorrach and Basle, which was reputed to be wired, and to make for Grenzach. A high rock cliff in the hill on the right of the road about 1 km West of Grenzach, would enable me to be absolutely sure of recognising my position. I was told to look out for a level crossing just below this and cross over it, follow the road for a short distance— about 50 yds—and go through a big iron farm gate (on the right of the road) which cannot be missed, as it is the only one thereabouts. I was to go carefully between a farmhouse and a barn until a ditch was reached, which runs N.W. along the left hand side of the railway track. My route lay along this ditch for about 200 yds, great care being taken to avoid a sentry patrolling the line, until I saw a wooden hut or sentry box ahead of me. I must then make for a light about 100 yds away half right, by turning sharp right (N.E.) and across the railway line into Switzerland.

I followed these instructions accurately. As soon as my train arrived at Lorrach I left the village by a road running due East, and then went up on to the hillside above it, keeping the road in view. As it turned South I carried on southward across country and saw a sign post pointing to Grenzach. At one point on my route I saw a sign board which said 'Grenze 700 m.' and I saw barbed wire between trees and posts at a point which I cannot place accurately on the map. Before descending to the Syhlen—Grenzach road I had a rest, wash and shave by a stream. In the dusk I walked along this road through Grenzach. I recognized the Grenzacher Horn rockface and I knew that I had to be extremely careful from now on. I proceeded very cautiously through fields on the north side of the road. I was very tired by now and decided not to cross that night so I climbed up into the woods above the vineyards north of Grenzach, and found an old disused dugout, which afforded some protection from the cold, and where I lay low for the night. When I got there in the early evening I could see the glare from the lights of Basle clearly. I could hear dogs during the night but did not actually see any. There were several disused bits of fortifications nearby and I had seen wire along the frontier above my dugout.

At dawn on 2 Nov I ventured out very slowly through the thick undergrowth and suddenly got a full view of the Rhine. Below I could see the railway line and the level crossing just east of Horn, and in the distance the cemetery opposite which I was to get across the frontier.

I waited until evening and then dropped down to the level crossing, found the farm gates which I had to pass, crept abut ten yards under cover of a wall and then dropped into a ditch, partly covered with bushes and long grass, which runs along the west side of the railway line, north of the hamlet of Horn. I had to crawl along this ditch for about 300 yds, taking care to move only when the single sentry, who patrols the railway line from the level crossing to the frontier—walking on the north side of the track on a slight embankment—was moving away from me. when I saw the wooden hut ahead of me I stopped and waited for some time, unable to make up my mind to make a dash for it. Finally, as the guards footsteps faded into the distance, I sprang across the railway line, having first assured myself of the cross-roads light, of which I could only see the glow from my ditch below the railway line. There was no wire here and no Swiss sentries to be seen. Once across the line I had to go through some long grass, cross a small track and go straight ahead till I reached a road, where I was in Switzerland. Under cover of a high wall on the right of the road (the cemetery wall) I made for the cross-roads light and then kept straight on under a railway bridge until I came to a cross-road with tram lines. I caught a tram into Basle, whence I took the next train to Zurich. There I got a connection to Winterthur and thence to Islikon, where I walked up to my uncle's house, arriving there just after midnight 2/3 Nov. I telephoned to the Embassy at Zurich and went there next morning. After a very friendly interview with the Swiss Police I was sent back to my uncle's house, where I remained until I was repatriated. *(L.G. 10.11.42)*

Baddeley, Ronald Mountford, Sergeant
2763122, 1st Bn. Black Watch (Bolton) (Immediate)
For exceptional courage and powers of leadership at the crossing of the Ouadi Akarit on 6 Apl 43.

Our forward troops having been heavily counter-attacked, it became necessary to get forward reinforcements to help them. The only means of doing this was by way of a narrow gap through a minefield and then along the anti-tank ditch. The enemy had this gap, which was some 250 yards across, accurately registered, and as soon as the reinforcements started to arrive, he brought down an intense artillery concentration on it and on the anti-tank ditch; whilst at the same time his M.Gs were firing along the wadi from a flank. During the crossing, all the Officers and the C.S.M. of Sjt. Baddeley's Coy were either killed or wounded. Although not the senior NCO in the Coy, he immediately took charge, and with a complete disregard for his own safety placed himself on the bank above the anti-tank ditch and from this exposed position controlled the passage of his Coy into the ditch.

He then led the Coy down the ditch and out into the open to the unreconnoitred positions it was intended to occupy, although those were only some 500 yards from the enemy. Here he reorganised the Coy and held off the enemy's counter-attack till nightfall. Sjt. Baddeley's great courage, and his ready and able assumption of command were largely responsible for our being able to maintain our bridgehead on the far bank of the wadi.

(*L.G. 22.7.43*)

Bagley, William Henry, Sergeant
22244111, Rifle Brigade
For skill, endurance and courage during three years of operations in the jungles of Malaya. On more than one occasion his first class leadership and determination in the face of hostile fire resulted in the successful accomplishment of his tasks. *[From L.G.]*

(*L.G. 23.5.58*)

Bailey, Edward Bell, Sergeant
967465, 32 L.A.A. Regt., Royal Artillery (Eston,
   Middlesborough) (Immediate)
This NCO is detachment commander of a Bofors gun on Ta Kali aerodrome. On 12 Mar 42, during a raid on Ta Kali, a number of bombs fell in this position, demolishing the billet and destroying ammunition. He kept his gun firing against enemy bombers and displayed great coolness. On 20 Mar 42, during a very heavy raid in the morning, his gun position was again bombed while he was engaging planes coming in from another direction. Heavy bombs again fell within 20 yds of his gun but by his example, the detachment remained steady and continued engaging until a further stick of bombs fell very close to the gun putting it out of action by bomb splinters. One man was wounded and several of the detachment received slight injuries from blast.

Another gun was put in early the following morning and in the first engagement with Me. 109 bombers Sjt. Bailey's detachment successfully engaged. 3 hits were obtained and the plane was claimed to have been destroyed. Subsequent reports prove that a plane fell into the sea during this engagement.

Sjt. Bailey's inspiring leadership and devotion to duty always and especially on the above occasions during these very heavy attacks has been most marked and has contributed largely to the detachments excellent fighting spirit.   (*L.G. 13.8.42*)

Bailey, Ernest, C.Q.M.S.
1917194, Royal Engineers
No citation.   (*L.G. 20.12.40*)

Bain, William Tennant, Warrant Officer Cl. II
(C.S.M.)
2873412, 1st Bn. The Royal Scots (Dover) (Immediate)
At Indin, Burma on 4/6th April 1943.
   CSM W. Bain was in command of a platoon holding an isolated position at point 544013 to prevent the enemy from reoccupying the feature which had previously been captured. The pl took over this position at about 2000 hrs 4th Apr and owing to heavy sniping and enemy fire it was not possible to furnish rations to this party until

after nightfall. The ration party which set out the following night was surprised by an enemy patrol and was unable to get through. During the night of 5/6 Apr a force of approx 40 enemy passed through his area with whom he dealt effectively. A similar number appeared at about 0630 hrs 6 Apr and were similarly dealt with. CSM Bain had over-heard on his wireless that the other two pls in his area had been already withdrawn and that he was in an isolated position. In spite of lack of rations and water, he remained in his position until ordered to withdraw on the morning of the 6th and during the whole action maintained the highest morale amongst the men under his command, this in spite of the obviously precarious position of the platoon and the fact that they had had no sleep for 3 nights. CSM Bain displayed courage and leadership of outstanding order.

(*L.G. 22.7.43*)

Bainbridge, Robert, Corporal
843466, 8th Durham Light Infantry
See Pte. Joseph Waller   (*L.G. 4.11.41*)

Baird, Graham Weir, Corporal (A/Sgt.)
2761852, 2/5th Bn. Queen's Royal Regt. (Methil,
   Fifeshire) (Immediate)
Anzio Bridgehead, 26 and 27 February, 1944
   Sjt. Baird was Platoon Sjt. of No. 7 Platoon, 'A' Company, 2/5 Queen's, engaged in an attack to capture Rap House (Italy 1/50,000 sheet 158 IV Ardea 843302) on the evening of 26 Feb 1944 in order to open up communications with the forward company of 10th Bn Royal Berkshire Regt. His Platoon was directed on the left of the enemy positions by the house, one section being sent in to clear the house itself. During the dark, touch was lost with this section and Sjt. Baird decided himself to go to the house and investigate the position.

   Within a few yards of the house he was shot through the throat by a Schmeiser but continued until he found the section commander, also wounded, by the house. He put a dressing on his wounds and got him away, rejoining the remainder of the Platoon, which had now connected with a Berks Platoon in a wadi just north of the house.

   During the night Sjt. Baird lost a considerable amount of blood from his throat wound and it was clear that he must soon be evacuated. He would not go, however, until light, volunteering to get back for the Berkshires to their Bn H.Q. with information about the attack, possibility of communications and the best routes past the enemy positions. To get back he had to pass an enemy position, which he did in daylight and under fire, having to crawl nearly 500 yds. By the time he reached the forward company of the Queen's he was very weak and was sent to the RAP. He however passed two RAPs and an ADS and continued back to the Royal Berkshires' HQ, where he gave a long and detailed account of the position of their own troops, enemy locations, action to be taken against the enemy and a possible route for the following night. It was not until he had given similar detailed and valuable information to his own Bn HQ that he would allow himself to be taken away.

Throughout the night of the attack and during the following morning, Sjt. Baird set a most splendid example. His great endurance, courage and determination could not have been surpassed. While his strength lasted he gave throughout a most conspicuous demonstration of devotion to duty.   *(L.G. 15.6.44)*

Baker, Albert, Lance Corporal
2614133, Grenadier Guards (attd. to S.S.T. No. 1
   Commando) (Stanningley, Yorks)
         First recommendation (for M.M.)
On 23rd February 1943 in the area of Cemetery Hill the Germans carried out an assault in force on the left flank troop of No. 1 Commando.

The attack was put in with great determination from the rear left. L/Cpl Baker was the No. 1 of a MMG supporting B Sub-Section of Morgan's Troop on the left.

When the attack opened up this NCO immediately brought fire to bear on the enemy. However, as the Germans were advancing from behind they were outside the arc of fire of the MMG. Seeing this L/Cpl Baker with complete disregard for his own safety and with the help of his No. 2 moved the gun into a position from which he could bring fire to bear on the enemy. In order to do this L/Cpl Baker had to change his position in the gun pit and by doing so left himself exposed to the enemy. As a result of the fire, however, he was instrumental in beating off the attack. The gun position was under heavy fire throughout the engagement and the attack was so determined that some enemy were found dead within 20 yds of the gun. The great courage, coolness, and devotion to duty of L/Cpl Baker was instrumental in preventing the position from being over run.
         Second recommendation (for D.C.M.)
Throughout the period 26th February 1943 to 4th March 1943 during which time his troop were constantly engaged with the enemy, the above NCO has at all times shown the highest powers of leadership, courage and devotion to duty.

During the attack on Hill Point 231 on 2nd March 1943 he was acting as No. 2 on the bren gun. Altogether, with his No. 1 (Pte Williams 83) he was instrumental in destroying a large number of the enemy and enemy machine-gun positions. When his troop position was being over-run by the enemy his bren gun was responsible for covering the withdrawal of his sub-section. This he carried out to such effect that the section withdrew without loss. After the section had withdrawn successfully this NCO together with his No. 1 advanced under heavy fire and captured two enemy machine-gun positions killing their crews. During this action L/Cpl Baker sustained an injury but he carried on and with his troop succeeded in getting back to the Mine near Sedjenane.

Before the battle of Sedjenane started L/Cpl Baker was sent down to the advance dressing station. He found the battle of Sedjenane had started. He thereupon refused treatment and joined with the 6th Lincolns and was put in charge of a MMG. During the battle of Sedjenane he directed the fire of his team to such good effect that a great many casualties were inflicted on the enemy. Throughout the whole period of operations L/Cpl Baker has at all times shown the highest standard of leadership, courage and devotion to duty.   *(L.G. 22.4.43)*

Baker, Charles Thomas, Private
14661145, 7th Bn. Duke of Wellington's Regt. (York)
   (Immediate)
At Haalderen 7566 at 0315 hours 4th Dec 1944 the enemy launched a full scale attack on the positions of 7 D.W.R. in an attempt to secure the Nijmegen bridge. The enemy companies were first sighted and engaged by a Bren gun team of three men. Their fire drew the fire of at least four Spandaus and one man was killed immediately. The enemy then attacked the post with grenades and cup dischargers and isolated it from the rest of the platoon. Pte. Baker was one of the two remaining soldiers. Incensed by the death of his comrades, Pte. Baker took charge, held his fire so his exact location would not be pin pointed in the darkness. When the enemy section was within 5 to 10 yards of the position, he opened fire and completely wiped out the enemy force, killing 6 Germans. He then engaged the remainder of the enemy battalion which had overrun other posts and was advancing along the road and caused further considerable casualties, only ceasing fire when his ammunition was completely exhausted. The enemy then attempted to search for the post but the men went to ground in the ruins of a house until a counter attack cut off the enemy who had penetrated deeply into the battalion position. From then onwards they blocked the road and by noises and shouts prevented the enemy withdrawing. When the enemy force was finally rounded up, Pte. Baker crawled from his weapon pit still carrying his gun and an armful of empty magazines. Pte. Baker's great heroism and initiative when cut off and great determination to deny his post until the last, not only resulted in the death of many Germans, but was one of the outstanding factors in the destruction of the enemy attempt on the Nijmegen bridge. The fact that Pte. Baker is only 19 years old makes his feat more remarkable.
                              (L.G. 5.4.45)

Baker, Frank, Sergeant
6086968, Queen's Royal Regt.
No citation.   *(L.G. 11.7.40)*

Baker, Jack, Sergeant
780231, Royal Artillery
No citation.   *(L.G. 20.12.40)*

Baldwin, Alfred, Warrant Officer Cl. II (C.S.M.)
2208942, 508 Fd. Park Coy., Royal Engineers
On 20-21 May, at a bridge near Bethune, was in charge of demolitions and road-blocking, although subject to continual bombing and air-machine-gun attacks, carried the work through with exceptional coolness and personal courage, setting a splendid example to his men. At all times from 10 May until evacuated from Dunkirk he showed great efficiency and courage in all his duties, which were carried out with cheerfulness and promptitude.   *(L.G. 11.7.40)*

Ball, Harry James, Corporal
VX 29458, Australian Military Forces
No citation.   *(L.G. 14.10.43)*

Ball, Herbert, Lance Corporal
3663228, 2nd Bn., King's Own Scottish Borderers (Manchester 11)
11th March 1944. 162 Feature—East Mayu Range
On the 11th March 1944 L/Cpl. Ball led a patrol of 2 men to feature 162 near Buthidaung. He himself approached to within a few yards of an enemy strong point. With a burst of tommy-gun he killed a sentry before returning with valuable information.

Three days later with an officer and a private soldier he again went on a daylight patrol to the same feature. While swimming the Letwedet Chaung the Officer and private got into difficulties. L/Cpl. Ball first helped the officer across and then returned for the private who had in the meantime sunk. Although under observation from the enemy post he had previously located he searched the river for half an hour for his comrade. He then returned to the officer who was unconscious and applied artificial respiration until he regained consciousness. Having carried the officer under cover he returned to his company to obtain aid in bringing back the officer. With this party he again swam the river and brought the officer back to safety.

Between October 1943 and April 1944 L/Cpl. Ball has consistently led successful patrols and brought back valuable information without regard to his own safety.
                                               (L.G. 8.2.45)

Bambling, Reginald Harvey, Private
QX6943, 2/15 Aust. Inf. Bn.
Private Bambling displayed outstanding qualities of leadership, courage and determination during an attack made by 2/15 Aust. Inf. Bn. at West Point 23 near Tel el Elsa on 1 September 1942.

Bambling's section was the rear section of the platoon and had been given the task of 'mopping up' behind the two forward sections. As the section crossed the outer wire of the enemy position the section commander was killed. Bambling at once took command of the three men left in the section and led them through the inner wire. Inside this he could see an enemy post, which had been passed by our forward troops and was firing on them.

Bambling charged this post at the head of his section, firing his Bren from the hip, killing 5 of the enemy and taking 1 officer and 10 other ranks prisoner.

Detailing one man to take the prisoners to the rear, Bambling led his remaining two men in an attack on another post 50 yards away, again firing his Bren from the hip, but was himself shot in the back and left shoulder, and while he lay in the open had his legs badly lacerated by mortar fire.

Subsequently one of our tanks appeared and although wounded Bambling pointed out to the tank commander that the enemy post was still resisting and asked him to bring fire on it. This was done, five enemy being killed and 14 more being taken prisoner by the two men with Bambling. Ten more enemy frightened by the appearance of the tank whose fire Bambling had directed, emerged from another post with their hands up and were taken to the rear by the same two men, who later carried Bambling out of the battle.

By his resolution, disregard of personal danger, and coolness Bambling was thus responsible for causing the deaths of 10 enemy and the capture of an officer and 34 other ranks, as well as silencing the fire of the two Spandaus and two 81mm mortars, which were found in the first post, and two Spandaus and five machine pistols found in the second.   *(L.G. 5.11.42)*

Bamess, Benjamin Alder, Private
WX 10180, 2/43 Aust. Inf. Bn. (Chinocup, W.A.) (Immediate)
On 29 Nov 43, Pte. Bamess was a member of 7 Pl. 2/43 Aust. Inf. Bn. during a coy attack on enemy positions 60757185 on the Bonga Wareo track (Fortification Pt 1/25000).

Pte. Bamess was the Bren Gunner of the leading section, and during the advance under heavy enemy mortar and machine gun fire, the section commander was killed. Pte. Bamess immediately took command and led the section into the attack until held up by concentrated fire from two LMG's sited in depth. Pte. Bamess moved forward and silenced the first gun with his Bren, killing the crew. He then penetrated into the enemy position and silenced the second gun. Still under fire from the flanks, he reorganised the section and led them through the position killing the remainder of the enemy.

His personal courage and disregard for his own safety was an inspiration to his whole coy, and his action was largely responsible for the success of the operation.
                                               (L.G. 23.3.44)

Banks, Joseph John, Lance Corporal
5187360, 1st Bn. Royal Welch Fusiliers (Ladywood, Birmingham) (Immediate)
Donbaik, Burma. 18th March 1943.
During the attack of 'A' Coy of this battalion on to an enemy strong point, Lance Corporal Banks displayed the utmost tenacity and outstanding leadership. One platoon which had already suffered heavy casualties was

still trying to gain an entrance into the enemy stronghold, when Lance Corporal Banks' section was ordered to go to their assistance. This NCO led his section into the attack and, failing to make headway on the left, reformed his men and attacked again from the right. Again they met a hail of bullets, mortar bombs and grenades and began to fall back. Lance Corporal Banks, however, stood his ground and urged his men forward once more, shouting 'Come on boys, let's get them.' Again the section moved forward, met the same heavy fire and stumbled. The dust and smoke obscured the scene for some moments but when it temporarily cleared Lance Corporal Banks was seen standing about ten yards from the post waving and shouting his men forward. They rallied and charged with the bayonet but three men fell, one being Lance Corporal Banks. Although wounded he still gave orders to his section until, finally, realising that the opposition was far too strong, he ordered the remnants of his section back. His great bravery and inspiring leadership set a wonderful example to all around him. *(L.G. 1.6.43)*

Barber, Harold Richard, Corporal
7910964, 2nd Bn. Royal Tank Regt. (London, S.W. 8)
(Immediate)
At Thadodan on 14 April 42, a number of lorries and guns were stuck in the river crossing. The bridge had been bombed and accurate and observed shell fire was coming down on the bridge and the diversion. Cpl. Richard Barber towed a number of vehicles out with his tank, himself getting out under shell fire and attaching the tow rope. Although wounded early on in the shoulder by a splinter, he carried on, and even helped to salvage medical kit from an ambulance which could not be towed out.

Again at Yenanyaung on 17th, 18th and 19th Apr. 42, this NCO showed great bravery and coolness under fire. On the 18th he accompanied another tank on a valuable recce through an enemy occupied village and himself brought back a quantity of information.

On the 19th when attacking an enemy gun, his tank received three direct hits and had to be abandoned. He stood by his tank seeing that the whole crew were safely out although the tank received another direct hit at this time. Although suffering from shock and deafness, he later took over command of another tank, in which he brought up the rear of the break through in the afternoon, and in which he returned as a guide for the Div. Commander, thus making three journeys through the danger area in which he came under heavy and accurate mortar fire.

By his courage and devotion to duty, this NCO has proved an inspiration to his comrade and has carried out invaluable work. *(L.G. 30.6.42)*

Barham, Jack Arthur, Sergeant
2734613, 3 Bn. Welsh Guards on attachment to 1 Cdn
Light Anti-Aircraft Bn. (London, N.16) (Immediate)
On 3 September 1944, the 1 Canadian Light Anti-Aircraft Battalion was advancing towards an objective near Misano. Enemy sniper and mortar fire was very heavy and about six hundred yards short of the objective the Company Commander and the only remaining Platoon Commander were both seriously wounded. At the same time two Panther tanks appeared and started to overrun the Company, which by this time was in imminent danger of becoming disorganised.

Sjt. Barhan, who was acting as Company Sergeant-Major, immediately took over the Company, rallied the men, and, showing great initiative, so disposed the anti-tank weapons that the enemy armoured attack was beaten off.

The mortar and machine-gun fire was still intense but Sergeant Barhan crawled over open ground from one Platoon position to another, encouraging and directing his men. He then continued to lead the Company forward until the objective was reached and consolidated.

On the following morning the Company, under a new Company Commander, continued its advance, again through heavy mortar and shellfire. On reaching the objective the new Company Comander was killed by shellfire and once again Sjt. Barhan took over the Company. Under increasingly heavy fire he organised a strong defensive position and commanded the Company until he was relieved that evening. His courage was indomitable and his coolness under fire an example and an inspiration to the rest of the Company.

This Non-Commissioned Officer was directly responsible on both occasions for his Company being able to hold the ground it had gained. His courage, devotion to duty, initiative and leadership upheld the very highest traditions of the Service. *(L.G. 8.3.45)*

Barlow, Jack, Tpr.
554969, 7th Q.O. Hussars
During the action at Mechili on January 24th 1941 against an enemy column; protected by medium tanks, the bullet proof glass block in the driver's visor in front of his eyes was shattered by an enemy projectile and he received severe wounds in the face including both eyes, totally blinding him, at any rate for the time being. (He may recover the sight of one eye and be able to see something with the other.)

In spite of these wounds he continued to drive his tank in accordance with the directions of its Commander, and succeeded in extricating it in reverse away from an extremely exposed position, until it had reached cover. It was then discovered that he had been severely wounded and totally blinded.

Had it not been for his most gallant behaviour, it is certain that the tank with its crew would have been lost as the enemy cruisers were following up knocking out any light tanks they could get close to.

Trooper Barlow has been commended by his Squadron Leader in several other actions and for his efficiency, courage, and endurance throughout the campaign.
Recommended for V.C.

Barnard, John William, Sergeant
VX 28837, 2223 Bn. Australian Military Forces
In a raid against enemy positions of unknown strength west of Tobruk on 22 April 1941, this NCO took command of the raiding party when his two officers became casualties 3,500 yards from our foremost defended localities. He saw to the destruction of two enemy anti-aircraft guns with Mills bombs and then coolly commanded the party on its fight back to the perimeter under the most withering artillery, mortar, machine gun, and anti-tank gun fire. As instance of his courage, he did all this despite a wound in the shoulder from an explosive bullet. During the withdrawal considerable mopping up was necessary, and further casualties were inflicted on the enemy, a total of 47 prisoners being brought in.

Fine leadership of this description is a magnificent example to the remainder of the battalion.

(L.G. 18.7.41)

Barnes, Laurence, Private
V 180274, 24 Aust. Inf. Bn.Australian Military Forces
(Immediate)
South Bougainville. For outstanding courage and devotion to duty in holding a machine gun position against sustained enemy attacks.

Private Barnes, at Hiru Hiru on 6 May 45, displayed outstanding courage in holding a forward position for two and a half hours and causing heavy casualties to the enemy during their sustained attacks on his Company.

As a bren gunner in 7 section 18 Platoon D Company 24 Australian Infantry Battalion (Australian Imperial Force) Private Barnes manned a forward pit in his platoon's defensive position astride the main Buin road on the East side of the company area. At 0830 hrs a strong enemy force launched a traditional fanatical bayonet charge against the company with the obvious intention of cutting the road and preventing the movement of another company to the Hongorai River. With great coolness Private Barnes held his fire in the initial attack until the enemy were ten yards from his pit and then, with deadly accuracy, mowed down the screaming Japanese. Each time the enemy reformed and charged again, Barnes repeated his tactics with similar success. Throughout the morning he also engaged tree snipers with deadly effect. Although he exhausted his ammunition on one occasion Private Barnes refused to leave his gun, carrying it back to the dump he obtained fresh supplies and returned to his position to continue the fight. After the enemy had been finally defeated, with very heavy casualties, thirteen dead were counted outside

Barnes' pit, the nearest being only eleven feet from his gun.

Private Barnes' coolness, courage and skilful handling of his weapon was an inspiration to his comrades and assisted materially in the crushing defeat which was inflicted on the enemy, thus allowing our forces to rapidly advance and seize the important Hongorai river crossing.

(L.G. 24.8.45)

Barnes, Raymond Alexander, Warrant Officer Cl. II (temp.)
1410972, Royal Australian Infantry
For Vietnam   *(L.G. 23.7.71)*

Barnett, James Henry, Sergeant
3521772, 1/8 Bn. Lancashire Fusiliers (Colchester)
(Immediate)
At Kyaukse on 4 Feb 1945, Sjt. Barnett was pl sjt. of 15 pl C Coy 1/8th Bn. The Lancashire Fusiliers. The task allotted to the Bn was to capture and hold the village of Kyaukse (sq 3264 map Ngazun sheet 4) and at the same time destroy the enemy. The enemy strength was estimated to be approx 120, well dug in, in bunker posns. C Coy was the right hand Coy in the attack which started at 1100 hrs, with the object of clearing the Southern part of the village. At approx 1415 hr the Coy objective had been reached by 15 pl, when Sjt. Barnett pointed out to his pl Comd that there was enemy activity in the Pagoda 332644, to the South, and suggested that the posn should be dealt with immediately. The pl Comd agreed and the pl continued to adv. Shortly after the adv had continued the pl Comd and a Fusilier were killed by a direct shot from a 37 mm A/Tk gun sited in the Pagoda. This incident held up the advancing pl, but Sjt. Barnett immediately took command of the pl and recovered the bodies of his pl Comd and the fusilier. He then told the pl to remain in their present posn and himself went across to the tks who were working with the pl at the time and explained the situation. After arranging with the tks and without orders from his Coy Comd, Sjt. Barnett re-organised the attack on the enemy posn. He then lead the attack himself with two secs, coming under heavy fire from an L.M.G. and a 37 mm gun. Sjt. Barnett however pressed home the attack and over ran the posn, he himself killing many Japs out of the 32 accounted for, and also capturing a 70 mm gun and a 37 mm gun.

Sjt. Barnett then re-organised the pl in a def posn on the objective while the guns were being dug out and a search made. During this period they were continually being sniped. After the guns had been dug out and the posn searched, he returned with his pl to his Coy, on orders from the Coy Comd.

It was only as a result of the outstanding leadership displayed by Sjt. Barnett, the fine example shown to the men under his Comd, and his grim determination, that the enemy posn, (which if it had been allowed to remain in enemy hands would undoubtedly have severely handicapped the consolidation of the village) was successfully taken, the enemy killed and the guns captured.

(L.G. 19.4.45)

Barnhouse, Kenneth Arthur, Sergeant
*M.51216, 28 Cdn. Armd. Regt. Canadian Armoured
Corps (Immediate)*
On 23 Oct 44 D Coy Alg R with two tps of tks of 28 Cdn
Armd Regt under comd was ordred to secure a br head
over the Roosendallsche Canal at MR 743187 (sheet 24
NW 1/25000 Brecht). The tks were to lead the adv. Sjt.
Barnhouse was crew comd of the pt tk. As Sjt.
Barnhouse's tk reached the cross rds at MR 743185
which was held by German inf with three Bazookas and
a 75 mm SP gun, he observed the enemy in the ditches
aiming their Bazookas at the tks. The tks could not
depress their guns sufficiently to bear on the enemy. Sjt.
Barnhouse, quickly appreciating the situation turned his
tk into cover behind a building. Then, armed only with a
pistol and three #36 grenades, he jumped from the turret
of his tk and with complete disregard for his personal
safety ran at the enemy posn firing his pistol. Upon
reaching the first weapon pit he threw a grenade into it
and raced on to the second one. His daring and
determined attack forced the enemy to surrender and the
inf took over the posn. Sjt. Barnhouse's coolness and
quick wittedness under fire were of the highest order on
this occasion. By his prompt and daring action he
disposed of the immediate threat to the tks, captured
twelve prisoners and cleared the crossing of the canal
for the force.

(L.G. 13.1.45)

Barratt, Charles Henry, Lance Sergeant
*6029742, Royal Armoured Corps, attd. No. 1 Special
Force, H.Q. S.O.(M) C.M.F. (Ilford) (Immediate)*
Sjt. Barratt first parachuted into the Appenine area of
enemy occupied Italy on 29 Jul 44. He completed 7
months behind the enemy lines maintaining WT contact
with the utmost regularity and passing vital information
to the Allies. During this time Sjt. Barratt and his mission
were on many occasions hunted by the enemy and were
forced to be constantly on the move. They suffered
severely from shortage of food and the rigourous winter
conditions of the Appenines. On 10 Feb 45, although
still prepared to remain on at his post, Sjt. Barratt was
ordered to make his way through the enemy lines for a
rest.

After several weeks at Base Sjt. Barratt volunteered
for an extremely hazardous operation. He was dropped
blind into enemy territory in March, 1945, together with
a British officer and two Italians. The party had
volunteered to contact partisan forces known to be
operating in the Po Valley which were vital to 15th Army
Group's spring offensive. Sjt. Barratt again acted as
operator to the party, which landed safely in spite of the
many enemy garrisons in the area. He soon made wireless
contact with Base and maintained excellent contact
throughout many weeks. At times his party was in
extreme danger and on more than one occasion he got

his contacts with Base despite the fact that the enemy
were living in the same house in which he was hiding.
Through his diligence and bravery vital information
relative to the move of the 92nd Panzer Grenadier
Division was passed to 15th Army Group immediately
prior to the offensive.

On one occasion Sjt. Barratt with his officer was
surprised whilst resting in a house. They were unarmed
and held up at the point of an automatic by a Fascist
Officer. Regardless of the risk they leapt on to the Fascist,
disarmed him, and killed him by kicking and strangling
him. Finding the house surrounded by Fascist troops they
shot their way out with the assistance of local partisan
forces who had been attracted by the shooting.

Throughout his service behind the enemy lines this
NCO has shown outstanding bravery and a high sense
of duty and he is strongly recommended for the award
of the Immediate DCM.

(L.G. 4.10.45)

Barrett, Francis Alfred, Warrant Officer Cl. II
NX.18434, Australian Military Forces
No citation.

(L.G. 9.9.42)

Barrett, Henry Kokoro, Corporal
25813, 29 N.Z. (Maori) Bn. (Immediate)
During the attack at Pascuccio Ridge on 7 Dec 43 Cpl.
Barrett's Pl was held up by heavy LMG fire from the
top of a steep escarpment 400 yards from the objective.
Leading his section Cpl. Barrett climbed hand over hand
to the top and personally dealt with the first LMG post.
Calling up his men his section under his leadership
cleared two more LMG posts and then with fixed
bayonets charged the remaining enemy and gained their
objective astride the Orsogna-Ortona Rd.

While reorganising his Pl came under fire from a
house some 400 yards away. Cpl. Barrett with six men
rushed the house and destroyed that post also.

During subsequent counter attacks Cpl. Barrett
showed the same vigorous aggressiveness which was an
inspiration to his whole Platoon and an example of high
courage and devotion to duty.

(L.G. 6.4.44)

Barter, Jack, M.M., Sergeant
*6096731, 2/7 Queen's Royal Regt. (London, N.9)
(Immediate)*
On 16 Apr 45 near Menate Sjt. Barter commanded a Pl
of 'D' Coy 2/7th Bn The Queen's Royal Regiment
advancing along an open road on the Western shores of
Lake Commachio. At about 0700 hrs Sjt. Barter's Pl
came under extremely heavy fire from two collections
of houses and casualties were caused including key
personnel. With complete disregard for the enemy MG
fire Sjt. Barter moved amongst his Pl and reorganised
them. Despite enormous difficulties including an Anti-
personnel minefield and absence of any covered
approaches, Sjt. Barter prepared a brilliant plan for the
assaulting of the positions. He personally led the final
charge shouting wild cries which inspired his men to

greater efforts and helped enormously to weaken the enemy's determination. By the time the first collection of houses was reached Sjt. Barter was a long way ahead of the remainder of his Platoon and without hesitation kicked open the door of the main building and single handed cleared the house. He alone accounted for at least 6 Germans and took a further 10 prisoners.

Immediately Sjt. Barter continued to lead his men to the second objective and such was his determination and complete contempt for enemy fire that his inspired Platoon assaulted this last position with an unbelievable gusto.

This NCO has commanded a Pl during the fighting on the River Senio and throughout the recent battles. At all times he has shown a similar extremely high standard of courage and leadership; on the above occasion, however, his conduct was outstanding and deserving of immediate recognition.   *(L.G. 18.10.45)*

Bartholomew, George Bernard, Sergeant
33950, 8 N.Z. Field Coy., N.Z.E. Bde.
As leader of an engineer party attached to a Battalion of the 6 (NZ) Bde from 17/7/42 to 31/7/42 Sjt. Bartholomew displayed outstanding devotion to duty and untiring effort in performing valuable patrol work, in demolishing enemy equipment; and in locating and lifting enemy minefields. For three successive nights prior to the 6 NZ Bde attack on the night 21/22 Jul 42 Sjt. Bartholomew went out with fighting patrols and successfully demolished enemy machine-guns and other equipment, and then on the two night immediately previous to the main attack he patrolled the Brigade front, sometimes under sharp machinegun fire, and located and brought in full and accurate information of enemy minefields. During the Brigade attack on the night 21/22 Jul 42 he led his party of Sappers and despite the occurrence of casualties from enemy mortars and machinegun fire which continued throughout the mineclearing operation he led and encouraged his men in the dangerous task of detecting and lifting enemy booby traps and mines through a 300-yd field. As a result of his daring and inspiring leadership mines were rapidly cleared to allow carriers and other supporting transport to move forward. It was due almost entirely to the personal effort and courageous example of Sjt. Bartholomew that enemy minefields on the battle front did not hold up the attack.
                (L.G. 31.12.42)

Bartholomew, Maurice Jachon Boar, Lance Corporal
7886054, Royal Tank Regt. (Blandford)
No citation.   *(L.G. 13.9.45)*

Barton, Richard Stephen, Trooper
5569985, 5th Bn. Royal Tank Regt. (Trowbridge)
(Immediate)
In the area approx. 3 miles South of Eleut el Tamar

On the evening of June 2nd 1942, Tpr. Barton was driver on a tank which was left in front of the guns awaiting recovery. The crew were taken off the tank with the exception of Tpr. Cunliffe 75 gunner and Tpr. Barton driver. The remainder of the Sqn moved off and were later engaged by 80 enemy tanks. 20 of these tanks came round the flank to attack the guns. On seeing this Tprs. Barton and Cunliffe mounted the Tank and manned the 75mm. They engaged the 20 enemy tanks and claimed one hit.

Their own tank was hit by a shell from an enemy tank and Tpr. Cunliffe was badly wounded and the tank set on fire. Tpr. Barton dragged Cunliffe from the tank and although under heavy machine gun fire from the app-roaching tanks he pulled Cunliffe into a slit trench. The enemy tanks then passed over his position and overran the guns. Barton stayed with Cunliffe that night during which time Tpr. Cunliffe died. Later the enemy tanks withdrew again and Tpr. Barton succeeded in making good his escape and rejoined his Regiment.

I recommend therefore that he be given an immediate award of the D.C.M.   *(L.G. 15.10.42)*

Barton, Samuel, Sergeant
3190057, 4 King's Own Borderers (Hawick)
(Immediate)
During the adv on to Koningsbosch on 19 Jan 45 Sjt. Barton was comd the leading pl of the Bn, and was travelling in the leading armd carrier. At a pt only 200 yds from the town Sjt. Barton's carrier came under 88 mm and very hy small arms fire. Notwithstanding this, Sjt. Barton debussed his pl, org his pl, and led the attack on the enemy posn. This attack was so speedily and effectively org that enemy resistance was soon overcome and the posn captured. 60 PW were taken and two 88 mm guns captured by this pl. Cas had already been suffered by armd vehs during this adv from these two guns and I consider that by Sjt. Barton's quick and resolute action further such cas were undoubtedly saved.
                (L.G. 12.4.45)

Barton, Stanley John, Warrant Officer Cl. II (A.Q.M.S.)
1071767, 52nd L.A.A. Workshops, R.A.O.C. (Havant, Hants)
Crete. 22 May, 1941.
For conspicuous gallantry and devotion to duty in the Sternes Area on about 22nd May, this W.O. and 2 NCO's proceeded to a Bofors Gun site to carry out urgent repairs. En route the party, which was proceeding in a Bren Carrier, run into an ambush when the driver was killed and one NCO wounded, the party got through, warned the gun crew and assisted in the dispersal of the parachute troops and then completed the repairs.

On the following night the same three with a small party of fitters, proceeded to Korares. They were again attacked en route but made their way through and under continuous sniping succeeded in changing the barrels of three 3.7″ A.A. Guns, a very remarkable feat, and by this act enabled the battery half section to come into action by the next morning. These are only two of many similar occasions where Q.M.S. Barton, by his work, maintained guns in action.   *(L.G. 4.11.41)*

Basset, Denis Morton, Private
12518, 23rd Tng. Bn., 2 N.Z.E.F. (att. L.R.D.G.)
On 30/12/41 near El Agheila; a party of LRDG trucks was shot up and destroyed by enemy aircraft. Pte. Basset with great foresight collected his prismatic compass and a tin of water from his burning vehicle, although still under heavy fire from the attackers. The crews of the trucks, numbering 10 O.R.s, were then faced with the alternative of a short walk to the nearest enemy post, and surrender, or of a long march of 200 miles over waterless desert to safety at Gialo. They chose the latter alternative and covered the distance in 9 days led and navigated by Pte. Basset to whom the main credit of the successful march is due.   *(L.G. 19.3.42)*

Bassett, Albert Donald, Corporal
VX141784, 57/60 Aust. Inf. Bn. (Immediate)
South Bougainville—Hongorai River—Pororei River area.

For outstanding leadership, devotion to duty and conspicuous gallantry in fierce fighting during the operations of the Commando Road which forced the enemy from his defensive positions on the Hongorai River and eventually led to the capture of the important Oso Track Junction.

Cpl. Bassett was a section leader in 10 platoon B company when on commencing to move from its defensive position on the west bank of the Pororei River at approximately 0700 hours 18 May, the company was attacked from the south by a strong enemy force using light machine guns, rifles, and knee mortars.

10 Platoon was caught on an open bombed out piece of ground and was pinned down by heavy enemy automatic fire. After a fierce fight which lasted for two hours, the enemy commenced an encirclement with fire.

Cpl. Bassett was ordered to take his section to the left flank and oppose the enemy encirclement. Showing great leadership and determination he led his section across open ground through heavy enemy fire to a position in which he disposed his section to meet the encircling enemy.

The section engaged the enemy with accurate fire and after inflicting casualties forced the enemy to withdraw to their original positions. Cpl. Bassett and his section remained in position until half an hour later when the enemy commenced an encirclement from the right. He was then ordered to take his section back over the open ground and oppose the enemy from the right flank.

Again, with untiring energy and forceful leadership, he led his men across the open ground through heavy fire. His Bren gunner was wounded before the section reached its new position but Cpl. Bassett quickly reorganised his section under fire and dragged the wounded man to safety. His section continued, and under the inspiring leadership of Cpl. Bassett reached its position in time to oppose the enemy attack, once again inflicting casualties on the enemy and repulsing the attack.

During this engagement two enemy light machine guns opened fire on the section wounding another man. Appreciating that further casualties would be caused unless bold action was taken, Cpl. Bassett gallantly moved out to an exposed position from which he could observe these light machine guns, and by directing the fire of his own light machine gun succeeded in silencing the enemy guns.

Throughout the four hour engagement with the enemy, Cpl. Bassett displayed leadership of the highest order, and by his own personal courage and devotion to duty so inspired the men in his section that they were able to repulse the enemy attacks on each flank with heavy losses and permitted the company to continue its advance to complete its task.   *(L.G. 20.9.45)*

Bassett, Lewis James, Sergeant
A37403, Canadian Infantry Corps
No citation.   *(L.G. 24.1.46)*

Baston, Frederick William, Sergeant
5335070, Royal Berkshire Regt.
Sjt. Baston was in comd of a locality which was subjected to continual shelling and small arms fire for 36 hrs. The loss of this post would have been vital. By his determination, zeal and devotion to duty he held the post until only himself and 2 other NCOs were left in a fit state to carry on. He kept the locality intact until relieved.
     (L.G. 22.10.40)

Batchelor, Eric, Sergeant (actg.)
16827, 23 N.Z. Bn. (Immediate)
On the 21st Jul 1944 at San Donato Sjt. Batchelor was in command of the forward Platoon of his Coy and with a small covering patrol on his own initiative cleared all the houses of the enemy on the feature taking a total of nine prisoners; five of which he took single handed, thus allowing the advance of the Coy to continue.

A short time later strong opposition was encountered from an enemy strong point which dominated Strada ridge, and which held up the advance. Again Sjt. Batchelor by outstanding leadership, lead his Pl in a successful attack on the position against heavy enemy machine gun and artillery fire.

Again at S. Andrea Sjt. Batchelor took out a small patrol to investigate a suspected enemy occupied house. Leaving his party outside with total disregard for personal safety he single handed entered the house and captured two enemy snipers. Throughout the whole of the action Sjt. Batchelor showed extraordinary powers of leadership and initiative and set a magnificent example by his personal courage and supreme devotion to duty under severe conditions.   *(L.G. 10.5.45)*

Batchelor, Eric, D.C.M., Sergeant   **Bar**
16827, 23 N.Z. Bn. (Immediate)
On the night 14/15 December Sjt. Batchelor was platoon
serjeant in one of the forward companies in the attack
on Celle. His platoon commander wounded on the start
line this NCO immediately took command and led his
men spiritedly into the attack. In a long advance over
broken country and without contact on either flank he
showed great skill and personal bravery in the liquidation
of three enemy strongpoints, killing eight, wounding
eleven and capturing twenty prisoners. On the following
night when ordered to proceed across country to his
Company HQ Sjt. Batchelor mistakenly passed deep into
enemy territory and on entering Casa Salde was
confronted not by his Coy Commander but some thirty
Germans. Although he had but three men with him, with
initiative of the highest order he made a rapid
appreciation of the surprise his entry had caused the
enemy and immediately engaged them, deploying his
small force to great effect.

From the resultant fierce and confused fracas in which
Sjt. Batchelor became involved in a shot for shot duel
between himself and the German NCO the party emerged
with 19 prisoners, leaving behind them 5 killed and 4
wounded. The capture of this strongpoint undoubtedly
assisted the next day's advance very greatly. Throughout
a long and difficult operation against a seasoned enemy,
Sjt. Batchelor has by his great personal courage, initiative
and outstanding leadership been an inspiring example
to all ranks. The work of his platoon under his inspiration
was largely responsible for the firm hold that the
Battalion had on its objective.   *(L.G. 21.6.45)*

Bateman, Kenneth William, Bandsman
4188640, 1/Royal Welch Fusiliers
Boughton, E., Pte.
5570076, 2/Wiltshire Regiment.
(1) Bndsmn. Bateman
My unit was in the line at Robecq, ten kms. from
Béthune and I was attached for duty to the R.A.P. caring
for 17 wounded, when on 25 May 40 we were taken P/
W by a detachment of German 'Death Head' Hussars
(converted into a Tank Bn). We were taken to their H.Q.
at Cambrai and later, by train, through Tournai straight
across Germany to Thorn (Torun) to the Stalag XXA,
where we arrived on 6 June 40.
(2) Pte. Boughton
When captured at the R.A.P., on 23 May 41, I was a
casualty with a wound in my left foot. Although in some
pain I was compelled to march with other walking
wounded, through Cambrai, from where we were taken
by train across Germany to Stalag XXA at Thorn (Torun)
in German occupied Poland.
Account by Bndsmn. Bateman and Pte. Boughton
From the central depot for O.R. P/W at Thorn, we
were immediately relegated to Fort 13 (Boughton spent
a short while at the Camp hospital in Fort 14, two miles
distant from Fort 13, and where there were then 2 British

M.Os and some 3,000 O.R.s. Fort 14 held at least 5,000
O.Rs). On arrival at Fort 13 we were searched and all
property confiscated with the exception of our paybooks.
We were not interrogated, apart from our registration.
We were issued, a week after arrival, with a shirt and a
pair of underpants apiece. We were housed in wooden
huts, 25 men to a room, and slept in straw with one
blanket. Rations were poor and short; discipline was very
severe.

In early July we were both transferred to a working
camp at Kulm (Chermno) about 25 miles North of the
main camp at Thorn, and where we remained for 32
months. Conditions and treatment were similar to those
in our previous camp. During this time we were twice
issued with Red Cross parcels, the first lot ran to one
parcel between 20 P/W and the second batch was enough
to allow 2 men to share a parcel. All our letters were
censored.

We were told by other P/W who had been in Fort 17
(near Thorn railway station), that their Senior Officer in
that Fort, a Lt-Col. of the Leicesters, encouraged all to
escape. As a contrast in Fort 11, CSM MacDonald
warned all ranks against revealing escape schemes to
two NCOs, RSM Davidson, 6/D.L.I. and RSM Letts,
RASC, who were strongly pro-German and had already
betrayed men.

P/W in general kept cheerful, but there was a lot of
dysentery, of which 38 men died (July/Oct) and both
scabies and diphtheria were prevalent. Some of our
guards who were on leave in Stettin on 6 Oct 40 and
experienced air raids there, returned very disheartened
and reported a shortage of fats and scarcity of clothes.
To our certain knowledge there were cases of Germans
deserting to Russia.

We decided to make a break from Kulm although we
could get little provision of food and had no map or
compass. (Boughton had got together a map, compass
and some clothes, while he was in Fort 13, but as the
move to Kulm was made without warning, he was obliged
to leave this collection with Gnr. Abrahams, R.A. who,
as a Jew, was not allowed to go to a working camp, where
rations were more ample.

On 18 Oct at 0100 hours we climbed the lavatory
wall, crawled through the barbed wire and got away into
some woods, of which we had previously made a note.
Our direction during the next four weeks lay through
Rypin, Mlawa, and Makow. At the last place on about 3
Nov we were nearly picked up by a German patrol and
lost our Polish helpers, who had directed our journey to
this point.

On 19 Nov we succeeded in crossing into Russian
Occupied Poland, but soon afterwards were arrested and
had some weeks in prison at Celestor and Minsk. In Feb
41 we were moved to an internment camp at Smolensk,
where we remained until our release on 8 July, after a
week in a hotel in Moscow.   *(L.G. 4.11.41)*

Bates, Richard Russell, Lance Corporal
2696584, 1st Bn. Scots Guards (Liverpool 8)
(Immediate)
Anzio Beachhead.

This Guardsman, a member of an A.Tk gun crew, showed the greatest courage and cheerfulness throughout the battle, knocking out altogether three enemy tanks and capturing a Recce car in the following circumstances:—

(1) On January 26th, when there was a very heavy concentration of shells on the area, six enemy tanks appeared and started shelling and machine-gunning our positions. This Gdsn immediately leapt from his slit weapon pit and engaged the tanks. One of our guns was knocked out, but this Gdsn, regardless of his own safety, continued to fire at the tanks, completely destroying one, damaging another, and causing the remainder to withdraw.

(2) During the same afternoon a few enemy tanks approached the position again. On this occassion Gdsn Bates loaded, laid and fired the gun singlehanded, knocking out another tank.

(3) On February 7th, during very heavy enemy artillery fire and also under snipers' fire from short range, this Gdsn with two others, crept up to his gun and knocked out a third tank, causing other enemy tanks to withdraw.

(4) On February 6th, a German Recce car got through our minefield and stopped fifty yards from the coy position. Gdsn Bates, with one other Bdsn, advanced on the car and took prisoner its three occupants, and also captured the car, which contained among other equipment, a map with enemy mortar and gun positions marked on it. *(L.G. 15.6.44)*

Batten, Arthur John, Sergeant (A/W.O.II (B.S.M.)
835455, Royal Horse Artillery, Western Desert Force
Corps, A.I.F. (Southbourne, Hants)
I wish to bring to your notice and to recommend for the highest award No. 835455 Battery Sergeant Major Arthur John Batten, R.H.A., A.I.F.

Early on the morning of the 14th April a number of German heavy tanks broke through the forward defences of Tobruch, and in the half light attacked his Battery, Royal Horse Artillery. B.S.M. Batten immediately left the command post, and went to No. 1 gun of the troop. This was the flank gun which was being most heavily engaged at close range by the enemy. His coolness and courage was a splendid example to the gun detachments, who fought magnificently. Finally the gun was hit by enemy fire, and the detachment was killed. Although himself wounded, he refused to leave the position, and assisted in dressing other wounded, and encouraging the other detachments until the fight was over.

During this action his Bty accounted for 5 heavy tanks at close range, and caused the remainder of the enemy tanks to turn tail and withdraw. *(L.G. 18.7.41)*

Batten, Christopher, Private
NX126254, 2/3 Aust. Inf. Bn. (Periodic)
For distinguished conduct in the field.

During the Aitape—Wewak campaign British New Guinea from 1 Apr 45 to 15 Aug 45 Pte. Batten was a company stretcher bearer. His devotion to duty and the rare unflinching courage he displayed in carrying out tasks allotted are beyond praise. Heedless of his own personal danger he never hesitated to attend and evacuate wounded men, even in the most dangerous and difficult situations.

On the 6 May 45 Pte. Batten was attached as stretcher bearer to a platoon on patrol in the vicinity of Koanumbo Village when contact was made with the enemy. The section commander of the forward section was wounded and fell in an exposed position which was swept by enemy fire. Regardless of his own personal safety Pte. Batten rushed forward to the aid of the wounded man, coolly dressed his wound and carried him to safety. It appeared impossible to move forward without being at least wounded, but Pte. Batten never hesitated a moment to perform what he knew to be his duty despite the great risk involved.

Again on 1 Jun 45, during a company advance south of Boram Plantation in the Wewak area Pte. Batten was a stretcher bearer attached to the leading platoon when it encountered intense machine gun fire from enemy in bunker positions guarding the approach to Feature 910. The forward section commander and three of his men were wounded. Although it was extremely dangerous, and despite the fact that he himself was grazed by enemy bullets, he immediately went to their aid, dressed their wounds and supervised their evacuation to the rear. Then during a two and a half hour carry to the RAP his constant care and nursing ability, far beyond the normal capacity of a company stretcher bearer, undoubtedly helped to save the lives of these men.

Throughout the entire campaign Pte. Batten has displayed initiative, gallantry and devotion to duty of the highest order. Several men in his company owe their lives to his prompt and expert care delivered under conditions that demanded from him the utmost in self control and disregard of danger. His outstanding ability and conscientiousness so imbued the men with confidence as to materially contribute to the success of his platoon on every occasion it engaged the enemy. *(L.G. 6.3.47)*

Batty, Leonard William Charles, Sergeant
SX 7605, Western Desert Forces Corps, Australian
Military Forces
His great bravery and dash when he took his bren gun Carrier directly up to an enemy battery under heavy fire from anti-tank and machine guns and engaged it at a distance of 50 yards and his valour and determination in leading a section of carriers during a raid by C coy on an enemy position on a ridge known locally as Carrier Hill at Tobruk on 22 April 41. The raid which was made at

daylight had as its object the clearing of the enemy position and the destruction of a battery of artillery which had been established there. The operation resulted in the capture of the battery by the killing or capture of the gun crews, the destruction of some if not all the guns, the capture of 368 prisoners the infliction of heavy casualties on the enemy and the destruction of a quantity of enemy war material. Sjt. Batty took his carrier towards the enemy position with great dash. As it came over the ridge it was fired on by enemy machine guns and anti-tank guns which were in position near a battery of field guns. Without hesitation he ordered the driver to drive up to the enemy guns and circle round them. The carrier got to within 50 yards of the battery and drove round them several times. As the carrier circled the battery it engaged the gun crews with a bren gun and anti-tank rifle. The other carriers followed after an interval followed by our infantry and the battery was taken. Sjt. Batty then took his carrier to another centre of enemy resistance where it again engaged the enemy. Sjt. Batty and one of the other members of the crew were wounded. Batty's audacious determination and bravery in the face of the fire from the enemy's machine guns and anti-tank guns impressed and encouraged the other troops engaged. It was a big factor in maintaining the vigour of the attack and in the success of the operation.   *(L.G. 18.7.41)*

Batty, Walter, Sergeant
22909, 6 N.Z. Rd. Regt.
On the morning of 1st December 1941 at Bel Hamed the 6 Regt NZA were withdrawing in the face of very heavy opposition in the shape of tanks and infantry. A troop had succeeded in extricating itself from the main position and were forming up to be led to a new position some distance away. Sjt. Batty was with his gun and tractor and had nearly reached the troop forming-up place when the troop was subjected to a hail of tank shells and small arms fire. One tank was actually in the process of charging the troop. With firm determination Sjt. Batty ordered 'Halt, action rear,' brought his gun into action and with his first shot disposed of the charging tank and proceeded single-handed to engage another eight tanks at long range. By now the remainder of the troop had deployed for action and the tanks not relishing the fate of their leader made off. The prompt and determined action of Sjt. Batty in accepting battle single-handed undoubtedly saved the remainder of the troop who were at the time reforming and not able to accept a tank attack from this particular quarter.   *(L.G. 19.3.42)*

Baty, Eric Lawrence, Private
7793, 4 Fd. Amb., N.Z.M.C.
Baty was captured by German paratroops on the Corinth Canal, Greece on 26 Apr 41 and was sent via Wolsberg, Spital-am-Semmering, Oberwart and Landeck to Spital an der Drau (Stalag XVIII Z).

In June 41, with the help of four other P/W, a tunnel was started in his room, but this was abandoned on the instructions of the Senior British Officer. A year later he took advantage of a failure of the camp lighting to climb over the double wire fence at Wolsberg. After two days he was arrested by the Gestapo while asleep in a bush. Only a few weeks elapsed before he crawled through a drain passing under the wire, but he was recaptured after 14 hours' liberty.

In May 43 with a companion he walked out of the camp area at Spital-am-Semmering where P/W were allowed to walk freely over the 1200 acres belonging to the farm. After walking for three days in uniform they were apprehended. His fifth attempt was made on 17 Sep 43. Whilst the gates were unguarded during a distribution of Red X parcels, Baty and two others drew their parcels and walked out of camp. They were recaptured five days later.

Although he received 21 days' cells after each escape attempt, he did not hesitate to join two other P/W in their escape from a working camp near Graz. In Apr 44 they found no great difficulty in unlocking the doors of their farmhouse billet and escaping whilst the guards were in their own sleeping quarters. As they had been unable to secure civilian clothes, they travelled by night only. The River Drau was crossed on an improvised raft, and after eight days of severe weather, they reached Yugoslavia. On 20 Apr 44 they met Partisan soldiers and were guided to the British Mission at Radnagora. A month later they were evacuated by air to Italy, reaching Bari on 9 Jun 44.   *(L.G. 14.9.44)*

Bauer, Marcus, Sergeant
1488893, 72 Anti Tank Regt. Royal Artillery
(Stornoway, Isle of Lewis)
Pont du Fahs—Robaa (0.6881) (sheet 8) 31 Jan 43.

On 31 Jan 43, this NCO was in command of a 6 pr gun covering the Pont du Fahs—Robaa road at 0.6881 (sheet 8). When the enemy tanks moved down the road in front of his position, Sjt. Bauer was the first to open fire at the leading Mk VI, which he stopped at a range of about 650 yds. This brought considerable fire from 88mm, 75mm, and small arms from the following tanks, which wounded the layer. Sjt. Bauer promptly took over and laid and fired the gun himself. His gun became exposed to the following tank, but he continued to fire and after firing another 15 rounds the four following Mk III's were all disabled. On the Comd's instruction (Lt. Edwards) Sjt. Bauer continued to fire at the leading Mk VI, in an attempt to set it on fire, but every round was replied to by the rear Mk VI which was hull down on his right flank. That night the infantry covering the position withdrew, leaving Sjt. Bauer unprotected from covering infiltration. Although the enemy surrounded him, and at one point came within 15 feet of the gun, Sjt. Bauer remained in action until the situation was restored by the arrival of more infantry. The platoon Comd (A Coy, 5 Buffs) states that every round fired from Sjt. Bauer's gun scored a hit on an enemy tank.   *(L.G. 23.9.43)*

Bauer, Rupert Edward, Private
F800160, 2 Bn. Royal Canadian Regt.
For Korea   *(L.G. 18.4.52)*

Bauleni, Wisiki, Corporal
DN 9327, King's African Rifles
No citation.   *(L.G. 22.3.45)*

Bay, Joseph Albert, Pte.
C52868, 48th Highlanders of Canada (Immediate)
Ref Map Italy 1/25,000 Sheet 89 III SW Russi—
Bagnacavallo

On the morning of 16 December 1944 'C' Company
of the 48th Highlanders of Canada attacked a group of
buildings known as Casa Baschi at MR 394345. C-52868
Private Joseph Albert Bray was a Bren gunner of 14
Platoon in 'C' Company.

The position was strongly held, and the enemy
machine gun and rifle fire from the position was intense.
In spite of this fire, Private Bray's section advanced
steadily towards a brick shed, from which the final assault
on the objective was to be made. Before the shed was
reached, however, the section came under small arms
fire from the right flank. The section leader was wounded
in the neck and Private Bray himself was seriously
wounded in the stomach by fire from a Scmeisser.
Despite his wounds however Private Bray immediately
took charge, rallied and organized the section in a fire
position, and himself attacked the enemy firing on him.
He engaged and killed with his Bren gun two enemy
armed with Schmeissers. Having dispersed this post, he
returned to the section near the shed.

He had hardly reached this spot when an enemy party,
about 12 in number, made an immediate counter attack.
Without hesitation Private Bray moved back into the
open and killed two of the advancing Germans and
dispersed the remainder. The enemy, having reorganized,
again counter attacked and again Private Bray, although
wounded a second time by a bullet that broke his leg,
continued his fire until the enemy had once more been
dirven off.

This soldier's actions are worthy of the highest praise.
At great risk to his own life and despite serious wounds
and weakness from loss of blood, Private Bray showed
supreme courage in the face of great odds. Almost
entirely due to his resolution and fortitude, an enemy
counter attack in vastly superior strength was broken,
and the platoon position saved.

Bays, Walter Patrick, Lance Bombardier
*H35279, 5 Cdn. Fd. Regt., Royal Canadian Artillery
(Immediate)*
On the evening of 20 February, 45, L/Bdr. Bays was
acting as assistant to the Artillery Forward Observation
Officer with 'C' Company, Régiment de Maisonneuve.
At the time, our infantry was moving into position on
the high ground south west of Moyland preparatory to
an assault on Moyland Castle the following day. This
castle had been converted into an enemy strong point
and dominated the Cleve—Calcar highway, control of
which was vital to the enemy's defence of the sector.
Shortly after arriving in the area, the artillery officer
became a casualty and was no longer able to carry on at
the observation post he had established. L/Bdr. Bays
immediately took over command and for the next twenty
four hours provided artillery support for the infantry.

Notwithstanding the fact that any movement in the
area brought down heavy enemy mortar and small arms
fire, L/Bdr. Bays continued to occupy his exposed
position and engage enemy strong points with effective
fire. With complete disregard for his own safety, he
maintained contact with the infantry commander by
crossing and re-crossing the open ground between his
observation post and company headquarters.

At approximately 1400 hours on 21 February, the
Régiment de Maisonneuve attacked and captured
Moyland Castle thus clearing the main highway and
paving the way for further advances towards Calcar. Prior
to and during this critical action, L/Bdr. Bays continued
to man his observation post and by his effective control
of artillery made a direct contribution to the success of
the attack.

Throughout the entire engagement, this Non-
Commissioned Officer displayed courage and determination of the highest order and beyond the call of duty.
His coolness and resource, whilst in a dangerously
exposed position and whilst fulfilling the duties of a
Foward Observation Officer, were an inspiration to all
ranks.   *(L.G. 12.5.45)*

Bazabarimi, Hassan, Sergeant
*GC13275, Gold Coast Regt., Royal West African
   Frontier Forces*
No citation.   *(L.G. 19.4.45)*

Beal, Alick Frederick, Corporal (A/Sgt.)
*320224, 1st King's Dragoon Guards (Hanley)
   (Immediate)*
On 21 July 44 at 403346, Sjt. Beal who was leading a
patrol of armd cs recceing a route to Anghiari (427410)
when he ran into a strongly held position of four coys
strength on the slopes just south of Veriano. The enemy
opened up with heavy shell, mortar and small arms fire
from all sides. He quickly organised his party into two
parts and attacked the enemy positions with his guns
and 6 men on their feet, which was far exceeding his
task. The result of his attack was that 17 posns were
silenced, 50 men known to have been killed and that
night the enemy retired from that posn. He himself was
wounded and clambered out of his car to enable his
second sergeant to take over the command car and lost
consciousness in getting to the ground, where he was
dragged under cover by his leading dingo comd before
coming round. Whereupon he staggered into his car again
took over control and continued to shoot up the enemy
inflicting many more casualties silencing most of the

posns before withdrawing. Before withdrawing he personally went to the rescue of a crew of an M.10 which had been set on fire, and which was still under heavy fire of all kinds and brought back three of the crew who were wounded. Upon getting back under cover he lost consciousness and was evacuated.

Through his cool and skilful handling of the patrol no one was injured, but himself and the crew of the M.10 and left many dead enemy, destroyed four bazookas and captured 14 prisoners, including two officers.

(*L.G. 7.12.44*)

Beale, Leslie Edward, Lance Corporal
VX 63991, 2/24 Aust. Inf. Bn. (Immediate)
For outstanding qualities of leadership, initiative and personal gallantry in the battalion attack on a strongly defended feature on Tarakan.

At 1200 hrs 3 Jun 45 an attack was launched by 8 Pl A Coy 2/24 Aust. Inf. Bn. on the feature Poker 3. This feature was dominating ground and the right flank strongpost on a vital ridge. The only approach was a razor-back spur on which the enemy defences, consisting of tunnels and foxholes, were sited in depth for 100 yards and the advance could not be made on more than a two man front.

When 4 (the leading) section came under fire after moving only 4 yards the section commander and three other were wounded. L/Cpl. Beale commanded 5 section and passing it through the leading section was checked immediately by fire from MGs, rifles, and grenades. Showing complete fearlessness for the heavy enemy fire, L/Cpl. Beale personally carried out a reconnaissance forward and to the flank, locating the enemy positions and engaging a MG post with grenades.

He returned, and collecting the Bren gunners of both his and 4 section, sited them to bring effective fire on the enemy. At this juncture the platoon commander and 6 section commander became casualties and L/Cpl. Beale immediately assumed command of the platoon.

He sited the Bren gun of 6 section and reorganising both 5 and 6 sections he threw phosphorus grenades and personally led the assault on the enemy position under cover of the planned supporting fire of the three well sited Bren Guns, and smoke from the grenades. The attack was successful, the feature captured and 13 enemy killed. L/Cpl. Beale immediately disposed his force to hold the captured ground, and 7 platoon passed through to exploit.

Undaunted, L/Cpl. Beale armed with a Bren gun firing from the hip, led 7 platoon's leading section after the retreating Japanese to capture a further 200 yards of the vital ridge.

Throughout the action, L/Cpl. Beale displayed leadership of the highest order, outstanding courage and complete disregard for his own safety. By his gallantry and leadership, although twice wounded early in the action, L/Cpl. Beale held the whole platoon as a fighting

force after it had suffered 12 casualties and his example fired his comrades to success.   (*L.G. 24.8.45*)

Bear, Lindsay Alfred, M.M., Sergeant
VX 17821, 2/14 Aust. Inf. Bn. (Immediate)
Action at Kumbarum 11 Oct 43.

On the night 10/11 Oct 43 a Jap Force of one Company approximately 60 strong established themselves in strongly dug-in positions on a dominating feature overlooking Kumbarum and connected to Kings Hill by a razor edge ridge approximately 700 yards long. The enemy completely cut the supply line to the 2/27 Aust. Inf. Bn. and overlooked positions occupied by the 2/14 Aust. Inf. Bn. They also caused panic and casualties amongst the native carrier trains which attempted to get through to the 2/27 Aust. Inf. Bn.

It was only possible to use one platoon in the attack owing to the extremely difficult and narrow approach. This led a distance of 700 yards from Kings Hill along a razor edge which fell sharply away into a precipice on each side. The attacking platoon advanced in single file under cover of heavy supporting fire to within 40 yards of the objective before making the final assault. This was made with two sections in charge of VX 17821 Sjt. Bear L. A. (MM) who led the assault throughout. One section moved on the left of the ridge and the other on the right supported by fire from the third section. Sjt. Bear and the section on the right fought their way up an almost sheer cliff face through heavy fire and a barrage of grenades rolled down from above. The first to reach the top was Sjt. Bear who, although wounded three times, emptied his rifle amongst the enemy and then fought his way along the top of the ridge bayonetting two and causing the death of at least ten more by driving them over a sheer precipice. The objective was gained resulting in over thirty (30) of the enemy being killed and the L of C being cleared. The success of this most difficult attack was largely due to the magnificent part played by Sjt. Bear. He showed complete disregard for his own safety and displayed outstanding personal gallantry throughout the attack. The example he set was an inspiration to his men.   (*L.G. 20.1.44*)

Bearman, Frederick James, Lance Sergeant
6348301, 2/7 Queen's Royal Regt. (Aylesford, Kent)
(since died of wounds) (Immediate)
At 0600 hrs on 13 Sep 44 'A' Coy 2/7 Queen's was ordered forward to attack objectives about 1000 yds in front of their positions on the Croce—San Savino ridge. Immediately the attack started the Coy Comd was wounded and command of the Coy was handed over to 9 Pl Comd. This left L/S. Bearman in charge of 9 Pl. Shortly afterwards the remaining officers in the Coy were wounded.

L/S. Bearman who started the attack as a Section Leader now found himself commanding a Pl in a Coy with no Officers and notwithstanding the fact that the Coy had at this time come under very heavy enemy shell and spandau fire gallantly led his Pl forward, walking about under heavy fire and urging the men on with complete disregard for his own safety.

Under his command the Pl was responsible for destroying at least 2 Spandau positions which had caused heavy casualties in the Coy and not long afterwards L/S. Bearman himself was wounded by the explosion of an enemy mortar bomb.

This NCO displayed very high qualities of initiative, leadership and resourcefulness and was an inspiration to the men under him. *(L.G. 8.2.45)*

Beaulieu, Jean Marie, Corporal
D.157871, Le Regt. de Maisonneuve (Immediate)
On the 14 April 1945 Le Régiment de Maisonneuve was ordered to attack the southwestern outskirts of Groningen, Holland. The last phase of the battalion attack was the capture by B company of Le Régiment de Maisonneuve, of a bridge over a canal which was a dominating position that dominated the line of advance of the Calgary Highlanders into the built up area of the town. Cpl. Beaulieu the leading section commander of 'B' company skilfully worked his section to within seventy five yards of the bridge and found it to be intact but covered with fire from two 20mm guns on the far side of the canal and also by very heavy machine gun fire which by this time had pinned his platoon to the ground, preventing any further advance.

Realizing that the objective could not be taken unless these guns were dealt with Cpl. Beaulieu with complete disregard for his own safety got up and rushed across the bridge. In spite of the steady and intense enemy fire he succeeded in reaching the bank on the far side and after crawling to a position on the flank he engaged the first gun with his sten. The enemy gun crew now outflanked surrendered and Cpl. Beaulieu turned on the second gun and engaged it while his section crossed the bridge and secured a bridgehead on the far side.

All through the action Cpl. Beaulieu showed outstanding leadership and devotion to duty. His alertness in appreciating the situation and his coolness and bravery under fire were directly responsible for the capture of the company objective. *(L.G. 21.7.45)*

Beaumont, Walter, Private
4802944, Lincolnshire Regt. (Scunthorpe)
No citation. *(L.G. 4.1.45)*

Bebbington, William Yarwood, Sergeant
3525822, 1/9 Bn. Manchester Regt.
Sjt. Bebbington as acting platoon Commander was ordered to carry out a reconnaissance prior to the occupation of a position. As soon as he set out to perform this duty he was wounded which considerably handicapped his work. He completed his reconnaissance and insisted in personally issuing his orders to his section commander although this meant travelling a considerable

distance in great pain, and delaying attention to his wound. *(L.G. 27.8.40)*

Beck, Arthur John, Lance Corporal
14424561, 6 King's Own Scottish Borderers (Croydon)
On 2 Nov 44 L/Cpl. Beck was a Sec Comd in 'D' Coy, 6 KOSB. On that day 'D' Coy led an adv against considerable opposition from enemy shell and mortar fire and finally occupied a posn near Neerkant. The firm tenure of this posn was essential to the def plan of the Bn and as a base for future ops.

During the adv the Pl Comd, Pl Sjt. and all senior NCOs of the Pl in which L/Cpl. Beck was serving became cas. The confidence of the men became badly shaken and it appered as if the adv would be held up.

L/Cpl. Beck quickly appreciated the gravity of the situation and without hesitation assumed comd of the pl. Without regard to personal risk he put himself at the head of the adv and, by personal example and inspiring leadership instilled such confidence and encouragement in his men that the adv continued without delay and the posn was reached.

Shortly after the occupation of the posn the enemy became aware of the presence of the Coy and proceeded to bring down a furious bombardment of shell and mortar bombs, accurately aimed and obviously corrected by observation. Throughout this whole bombardment, L/Cpl. Beck's conduct was of an exemplary nature. He firmly refused to take any cover and devoted himself to visiting and encouraging the men in the most exposed outposts of his pl posns. Even when wounded slightly he refused to allow this to interfere with his important and valuable example. As a result the posn was held and reinforced, thus enabling subsequent ops to take place as planned. There is no doubt that this important success was only achieved through the determined spirit and indomitable personal valour of this junior NCO.

(L.G. 22.3.45)

Beckett, Harold, Warrant Officer Cl. II (actg.)
3658104, 2 Bn. West Yorkshire Regt. (from the S. Lancashire Regt.) (Longsight, Lancs.) (Periodic)
Throughout this period in the Imphal area Sjt. Beckett has been in command of a platoon and has distinguished himself in every action which his Coy has fought.

His dogged courage and skilful leadership have been most noticeable on all occasions.

As an example, during an attack on a Japanese position on the Kohima Road his platoon was assigned the task of going ahead of the tanks and covering the party searching the road for anti-tank mines. The platoon immediately came under effective small arms fire but with great determination pursued their task and drove a deep wedge into the enemy's position, inflicting a number of casualties. This enabled the mine lifters to complete their task and thus allow the tanks to get up onto the feature and complete the destruction of the enemy. The operation was one which called for grit and skilful leadership, both qualities which Sjt. Beckett never fails to display in the highest degree.   *(L.G. 28.6.45)*

Beckham, Harold Frederick, Lance Corporal
634020, 24 N.Z. Bn. (Immediate)
At 1700 hrs on 20 Apl 45 L/Cpl. Beckham's pl was across the Idice River defending a large building close to the river bank. An attempt was made to put another coy across. A forward pl of this coy came under close and accurate fire of two enemy MGs which had previously remained concealed, suffered casualties and were pinned down. The position was quickly appreciated by the pl across the river and L/Cpl. Beckham volunteered to deal with the enemy MG posts. Supported by covering fire and followed by two men this NCO tackled the first post on his own, killing the three occupants. From then on he could not be supported by covering fire, but he cleverly worked his way up a communication trench, killing two more parachutists on his way and finally reaching the second gun and killing its two man crew. He then searched a nearby house found it empty and returned to his pl. L/Cpl. Beckham's action freed the pl which was pinned down and enabled it to cross the river and take up its position without further casualties. Other troops followed and the bridgehead was made secure. This NCO has always displayed a fearless courage and a complete disregard for his own personal safety and had been a splendid example to all those privileged to serve with him.*(L.G. 18.10.45)*

Bedworth, W. E., Lance Sergeant (A/Sgt.)
5102817, Royal Artillery
No citation.   *(L.G. 27.9.40)*

Beeston, Eric, Sergeant
4128900, 6th Bn. Cheshire Regt. (Stockport)
(Immediate)
Sjt. Beeston was Pl Sjt of a M.G. Pl supporting 2/6 Queens during the attack on Montecorvino airfield on 9 Sep 43. Early in the action, his Pl Comd was seriously wounded. Sjt. Beeston took over the Pl, which destroyed two enemy aircraft and inflicted heavy casualties on enemy personnel. During the action one section of the Platoon was almost completely surrounded by a much larger enemy force, who assaulted the section position, causing the men to withdraw. Sjt. Beeston and one other man went forward under intense M.G. fire, regaining the section position. During the subsequent enemy counter attack by mortars, M.Gs and tanks, this NCO displayed courage and leadership of the highest order, and his indifference to his personal safety was a constant and fine example to the whole platoon. *(L.G. 13.1.44)*

Bell, Bertram Riley, Colour Sergeant (A/W.O.II (C.S.M.)
5825326, Hampshire Regt. (Littleport, Cambs.)
No citation.   *(L.G. 26.10.44)*

Bell, Harry James, Cpl.
VX 29458, 2/32 Aust. Inf. Bn.
For distinguished service and personal bravery during the period 23 Oct 42 to 23 Jan 43 and in particular during the operations in the vicinity of El Alamein in Oct/Nov 42.

During the attack by 2/32 Aust. Inf. Bn. on German positions at the railway line in the vicinity of Point B 11 South East of Sidi Abd El Rahman, and subsequent fighting from 30 Oct to 5 Nov 1942, Cpl. Bell commanded number Eight Section in C Company. During the attack the company was held up by shell fire short of its final objective. An enemy machine gun and an anti-tank gun were firing on the company from the left flank and causing a number of casualties. Cpl. Bell's platoon attacked these positions with his section in front led by himself. He attacked the machine gun post killing one gunner and probably two others with his Tommy Gun and a grenade while two of his section drove the crew from the anti-tank gun. On one occasion his platoon commander seemed certain to be hit at close range by an enemy rifleman but was saved by the quick action of Cpl. Bell. On the following day he fought his section with inspiring bravery and determination when that portion of the front was attacked by 26 tanks.

On the night 2/3 Nov his section took part in a raid and destroyed an enemy machine gun post. His platoon commander was wounded and despite bright lighting from Pyretechnics and very heavy fire he dressed his wound and brought him out. Owing to the danger the officer ordered them to leave him but Cpl. Bell remarked '15 Platoon had never left one of its men and they will not start now.'

Cpl. Bell has shown great initiative, bravery and devotion to duty throughout the period and has been a fine example to all in his Platoon.

Bell, Harry Langford, M.M., Corporal
3607113, 2nd Bn. Royal Inniskilling Fusiliers (Liverpool 7) (Immediate)
Ref Map: Italy-1/25,000—Argenta—Sheet 88-I NE.

On the 17th April, 1945 Cpl. Bell was commanding a section in No. 17 Platoon 'D' Company, 2nd Bn The Royal Inniskilling Fusiliers. The task of 'D' Company was to break out of a small bridgehead already formed over the Fossa Marina (292618) the first part of the Battalion's task of cutting Route 16, to seal off the enemy tanks, S.P. guns and infantry in Argenta. Speed in this operation was essential.

When forming up on the perimeter of the bridgehead the company came under very heavy mortar and shell fire. Cpl. Bell was imperturbed by this, although the rest of his section were lying down, he walked about giving his final orders, calmly smoking a cigarette. On two occasions he was blown off his feet. His bearing gave the greatest encouragement to his section and platoon.

Shortly afterwards the advance commenced, and Cpl. Bell led his section in an attack on two Spandau posts in a group of houses across 300 yards of bullet swept ground. The houses were successfully stormed, both gun-posts were silenced by Cpl. Bell who personally killed the 2 gunners.

Cpl. Bell was wounded in the arm during this attack, but he did not hesitate, without further orders, he continued in an assault on another house 100 yards ahead. In spite of heavy small arms fire, this house was taken, the automatic weapons silenced and 6 prisoners captured. Cpl. Bell refused to be evacuated.

The platoon then reformed and prepared to attack a house 400 yards away, which had been converted into an enemy strong-point, containing several light automatics and an S.P. gun or Mark IV Tank.

Undeterred by this heavy concentration of fire, Cpl. Bell led his section, now reduced to himself and 3 men, across 400 yards of very open country, under heavy and continuous automatic fire. He charged straight for the strong-point. Cpl. Bell personally destroyed one enemy machine gun before a heavy mortar barrage finally stopped the section. All of the section except one being either killed or wounded.

During this attack Cpl. Bell received a serious wound in his buttock and his right arm all but severed at the elbow.

The platoon commander ordered the section to be evacuated but Cpl. Bell, although still capable of evacuating himself, continually refused to move until all his section had been taken to safety. He lay under the spasmodic fire of snipers for 2 hours.

This NCO throughout the day, more than fulfilled the task demanded of him. He continued to lead his section though wounded, he led an advance of nerly 800 yards and it is doubtful, but for his speed and determination, if the Battalion could have carried out their important task of cutting Route 16.

Cpl. Bell's self-sacrificing actions and inspiring courage was the talk of all who saw him and his name is now a byword in the Battalion.

Statement by 100240 T/Capt. J. M. Campbell—'D' Company.

On the 17th April, 1945 I was commanding No. 17 Platoon, 'D' Company 2nd Bn The Royal Inniskilling Fusiliers. The Battalion was to put in an attack. 'D' Company was the leading company and 17 Platoon the leading platoon of 'D' Company. Our task was to break out of a small bridge-head already formed over the Fossa Marina (292618) and to reach the Argenta—Ferrara road, thus cutting off the enemy forces fighting in Argenta. Cpl. H. Bell, M.M., was a section leader in my platoon.

The platoon formed up for the attack on the perimeter of the bridge-head and while so doing, it was subjected to an intense concentration of enemy shell and mortar fire. While this was on Cpl. Bell, quite imperturbed walked about his section, which, like the remainder of the platoon was lying flat on the ground, giving out his final orders for the attack.

When the concentration lifted the attack went forward. The first objective was a group of houses some 300 yards from the perimeter. These houses Cpl. Bell stormed at the head of his section, silencing two Spandau-posts and killing two of the enemy himself. During this action he was wounded in the right arm. He bound a handkerchief round the wound and refused to be evacuated. He was then fired on from a house some 100 yards further on. Without hesitation and in spite of his wounds he led his section into this house, silencing another Spandau-post and taking six prisoners.

The platoon reformed for an assault on another strong-point, which consisted of a house containing several light automatics and an S.P. gun or Mark IV tank. The house was also covered by fire from enemy positions to each flank. During the assault Cpl. Bell led his section, now reduced to four, straight across about 400 yards of open ground.

Cpl. Bell personally destroyed an enemy machine gun; continuing towards the strong point a heavy mortar barrage finally stopped this section wounding all except one man. Cpl. Bell himself receiving very bad wounds.

I made arrangements for the evacuation of the section, an operation which took some two hours to complete, as my communication by wireless to Company HQ was not working and the stretcher bearers had other casualties to deal with. All this time Cpl. Bell, although badly wounded in the right arm and having an enormous wound in his right buttock, lay out there with his other two wounded men and refused to be evacuated until all his section had been carried to safety. The men as they lay there were subjected to intermittent fire from enemy snipers and light automatic fire from the house some 40 yards away.

Never before have I seen displayed on any battlefield such magnificent courage and devotion beyond the call of duty. His actions were an inspiration to the whole platoon, which accomplished its task that day, taking some 30 prisoners and killing several of the enemy on the way.

Statement by 85301 T/Major P. J. Blake, M.C., Commanding 'D' Company.

On 17th April, 1945 Cpl. H. Bell, M.M. was commanding a section in No. 17 Platoon, 'D' Company 2nd Bn The Royal Inniskilling Fusiliers. The task of the company was to break out of the bridgehead, already formed over the Fossa Marina 292618 (Sheet I N.E. 1/25,000 Argenta) and cut off the retreat of the enemy from Argenta.

On the perimeter of the bridgehead some 400 yards from the crossing place, 17 platoon came under a devastating enemy barrage when forming up to attack a group of houses some 300 yards west, but Cpl. Bell quite unperturbed by this, wandered about among his section issuing his final orders. His bearing was a great example to his section and the rest of the platoon. On two occasions he was blown off his feet.

Shortly afterwards the attack commenced and Cpl. Bell well at the head of his section charged two enemy machine gun posts, killing two of the occupants and silencing both guns. While doing this he was wounded in the arm. Not content with taking his objective he sighted another enemy post some hundred yards away, but in spite of considerable enemy fire he again charged the post, completely overcoming the enemy, capturing six prisoners. Though badly wounded he refused to be treated or evacuated. Cpl. Bell's section was now four in strength. The attack continued and a house converted into a strong point was encountered but Cpl. Bell not waiting for any orders led his section in a charge straight for the post, he himself destroying one enemy machine gun. A heavy enemy mortar concentration was put down right on Cpl. Bell's position and all the section were wounded or killed but for one man. Cpl. Bell's platoon Commander ordered all those capable of withdrawing to come back but Cpl. Bell refused point blank to leave until all others were evacuated though he was wounded in three places, his right arm all but severed at the elbow. For two hours he lay there in that condition and for a great deal of the time was being shot at by enemy snipers. Throughout this day his deeds were the talk of all who saw him and but for his dash and complete disregard for his own personal safety it is doubtful if the task required of the company could have been completed. His name is a byword with his whole company and Battalion.

Statement by No. 6975565, Sjt. Gilligan, F., 'D' Company.

On the 17th April, 1945, Cpl. H. Bell, MM was commanding a section of 17 platoon of which I was platoon sjt. The platoon crossed the river and reached a house on the perimeter of the bridge-head, where we were forming up for the attack, when the enemy brought down a very heavy 'stonk' from artillery and mortars on the area. Everyone lay down except Cpl. Bell, whom I saw walking about amongst his section, wearing a soft hat and smoking a cigarette and issuing orders to his section in the most imperturbable manner. The attack soon started and Cpl. Bell led his section in an attack on a group of houses 300 yards away, under heavy automatic fire.

He and his section stormed the houses, silenced two Spandau-posts, killed two of the enemy, and went straight on to take another house about 100 yards further on. Here he captured 6 prisoners. During the attack on the first house he received a wound in the right arm but refused to be evacuated.

The platoon then reformed for a further attack on a strong-point, consisting of a fortified house, inside which was a tank or an S.P. gun. During this attack I was working with a section on the right flank. Cpl. Bell's section was on the left flank. I did not see his section in action for some time until I rejoined Platoon Headquarters. I then discovered that all Cpl. Bell's section except for one man had been wounded. It took a long time to evacuate the wounded men who were all lying out in the open, some 40 yards from the final objective, and were being fired at by enemy snipers. I noticed that Cpl. Bell was the last man to be brought back and that he had very bad wounds in his right arm and his buttocks.

Cpl. Bell by his superb gallantry and coolness under very difficult conditions was an inspiration and a shining example to the remainder of the platoon.

(*L.G. 18.10.45*)

Bell, Victor Frederick, Sergeant
5887631, 2nd Bn. Northamptonshire Regt.
(Northampton)
At 0900 hrs 18 Jan 44 Sjt. Bell, in command of 9 Pl 'A' Coy 2nd Bn The Northamptonshire Regt., was ordered to mop up an enemy strong point established on the banks of the R. Garigliano and which had been by-passed during the previous night's advance across the river.

The bank was thickly laid with A/P mines.

When the leading section was about 250 yds from the strongpoint it was met with very heavy Spandau fire. Sjt. Bell lost no time in making a plan to deal with this strongpoint, and it was very largely due to his masterly appreciation of the situation that the enemy O.P. was over-run.

He ordered two assault sections under the Pl Sjt. to move forward to within 40–50 yds from the house. As the sections moved to this point the enemy opened fire with five machine guns and rifle grenades. Under Sjt. Bell's inspiring leadership they moved to the assault covered by a smoke screen he had ordered to be fired by the 2≤ mortar, as the assaulting sections moved forward.

He ordered the fire section to move to a point to the left of the buildings in order to cut off the enemy.

Whilst completing the 'mopping up' of the enemy his T.S.M.G. jammed. He picked up an enemy machine gun and used it against the 2 remaining enemy machine guns still in position.

Seven prisoners, all wounded, were captured. 4 Br prisoners were released, 4 enemy machine guns a large quantity of ammunition, and other war material was captured and the enemy was killed while trying to escape.

It was undoubtedly due to Sjt. Bell's inspiring and magnificent leadership and complete disregard for his own personal safety that this enemy strong-point was so successfully and completely routed. His ruthless determination, and his carefully laid and well executed plans which were carried through in spite of a hail of machine-gun and light automatic fire from very close range were an inspiration to the men under his command.

(*L.G. 29.6.44*)

Belo, Semisi, Sergeant
356, Fiji Military Forces
No information available.   (*L.G. 6.6.44*)

Bennet, Ronald Arthur, Sergeant-Artificer
1420914, Royal Artillery
No citation.   (*L.G. 27.8.40*)

Bennett, Austin, Sergeant
F76599, Canadian Infantry Corps
No citation. *(L.G. 24.1.46)*

Bennett, Frederick Clifford, Sergeant
2694917, 1st Bn. Scots Guards (Grasshoughton,
Yorks.) (Immediate)
Anzio Bridgehead.

On the night 29/30 January 1944, Sjt. Bennett was commanding the leading platoon of his company in an attack against strong enemy positions.

As these positions were very much stronger than had been anticipated, Sjt. Bennett was ordered to lead the way down a ditch and infiltrate to the objective regardless of any enemy holding out on the flanks. In the course of the advance four enemy positions were encountered along the ditch, but in each case Sjt. Bennett led the leading section in a surprise rush and overcame the positions. In the fourth and final attack before the objective was reached he was wounded in the shoulder, arm and side but he immediately rallied his platoon and led them to the objective. He then returned and led back down the ditch the 35-40 prisoners which he had captured in the course of the advance and with one other wounded Guardsman he managed to escort them back to Bn H.Q. in spite of the fact that the enemy was still firmly established on either side of the ditch down which he had to go.

This NCO's gallant bearing and initiative were an inspiration to his company. *(L.G. 15.6.44)*

Bennett, Joseph William, Warrant Officer Cl. III
(Pl.S.M.)
5105015, Royal Warwickshire Regt.
No citation. *(L.G. 20.8.40)*

Bennett, Sydney Leonard, Corporal (A/Sgt.)
6349878, 4th Bn. Queen's Own Royal West Kent Regt.
(Walthamstow) (Immediate)
At Kohima in the D.C.'s bungalow area on the night 10/11 April 1944 the platoon to which Sjt. Bennett was platoon Sjt. was heavily mortared and shelled, the left forward section received a direct hit and was knocked out. Sjt. Bennett realising the importance of this position, without hesitation got together such men of Pl HQ who were near him and led them forward under heavy fire, occupied the position and held it in spite of frequent attacks until he was relieved later by a section from the reserve platoon.

Throughout the period 5–20 April Sjt. Bennett was an inspiration to his platoon showing leadership and courage of a high order and a complete disregard for his personal safety under heavy enemy fire.

Recommended for an immediate award of the Distinguished Conduct Medal. *(L.G. 27.7.44)*

Bentham, Eric, Lance Corporal
4694246, 2/4 King's Own Yorkshire Light Infantry
(Bradford)
During the action at pt 290 on 21 Apr L/Cpl. Bentham assisted his Platoon Commander in evacuating a wounded man from a burning farm. This they did under fire from M.G.s and Mortars. As soon as he reached Coy HQ about 15 enemy were seen coming over the hill. He immediately organised 8 R.A. men who were there into a Section, got them into a fire position and opened fire, preventing the enemy from penetrating any further in to the battalion positions. He had been slightly wounded when returning from the farm but refused to be evacuated.

During the attack on Argoub Hamra on 22 Apr 43, on his own initiative he led his section to re-inforce the left forward platoon under heavy M.G. and Mortar fire. He then led his section up the right of the hill to silence a M.G. post which he did by throwing grenades.

During the actions on both days the initiative, leadership and courage shown by L/Cpl. Bentham were of the highest order. *(L.G. 15.6.43)*

Bentley, Allen Richard, Sergeant
NX 21473, 2/13 Aust. Inf. Bn.
Sjt. Bentley was platoon Sjt of the A Tk gun platoon of 2/13 Aust Inf bn during the operations near Alamein commencing on 23 Oct 42. Throughout these operations until he was evacuated wounded on the afternoon of 25 Oct 42 he showed conspicuous bravery and devotion to duty. During the night 23/24 Oct 42 and morning of 24 Oct the platoon had suffered considerable casualties, including its officer. Sjt. Bentley assumed command and visited each gun at intervals—often under heavy shell fire. During the afternoon of 25 Oct the enemy made a counter attack with tks and lorried infantry on the ground which 2/13 Aust. Inf. Bn. had gained. During this attack, owing to the reduction in the numbers of his men Sjt. Bentley himself helped to man a gun. He held his fire until the leading tk was within 200 yds, then firing, knocked it out with the first shot. Under heavy machine gun fire from enemy tks Sjt. Bentley with great courage and resolution, kept his gun in action and accounted for five other tks before he and two other members of the gun crew were badly wounded. Before being evacuated, and although in a very weak condition, he continued (until he collapsed and became unconscious) to give orders for the re-organisation of the platoon, checked reports of the casualties to his men and guns and gave directions for the next senior NCO to take over command. His example and devotion to duty were an inspiration to his platoon who maintained their guns in action under heavy fire and were responsible for knocking out a number of the enemy tanks. *(L.G. 11.2.43)*

Bentley, Thomas Cyril, Sergeant
6400234, 10 Bn. Parachute Regt., Army Air Corps
(Caversham)
At Oosterbeek on 20 Sep 44 Sjt. Bentley who had already
shown conspicuous bravery in much hard fighting since
he dropped on 13 Sep, was in charge of a detachment of
mortars, using the top floor of a house as O.P. in the
hard pressed north eastern corner of the Div. perimeter.
The position was held by the remnants of the bn, about
50 strong, constantly under fire and frequently heavily
attacked. From his O.P. he not only directed telling fire
on the enemy, but secured informtion vital to the defence,
which he was obliged to take in person to his CO
under fire from close range on each occasion. When the
side of his house was blown in by a S.P. gun at point
blank range he fell from top floor to basement but crawled
out and carried on from another. He was located and
shot out again more than once that day but set a
magnificent example of determination to carry on and
during the operation was responsible for the discovery
and repulse of a dangerous infiltrating movement from
an unexpected quarter [...] the Bn H.Q. house: the CO
was wounded and the few men there captured. The
mortars were lost. That night Sjt. Bentley led a patrol
into the enemy occupied area and brought the mortars
out, operating them from then on under heavy fire, under
the personal direction of the Brigadier, for whom they
were the last two mortars in the Bde.

It is difficult to praise too highly this NCO's courage,
coolness, endurance and competance or to overestimate
his contribution, both material and moral, in a difficult
operation.   *(L.G. 20.9.45)*

Bernard, Joseph Edmund, Warrant Officer Cl. II
(actg.)
G.23269, North Shore (N.B.) Regt., Canadian Infantry
Corps (Immediate)
Company Sergeant Major Bernard on 26 February 1945
during the assault on the village of Keppeln when 'B'
Company were pinned down in the open, Map Ref
972452, under intense machine gun, mortar and artillery
fire evacuated several of the wounded and gave
encouragement to the remaining men.

The advance was resumed after some artillery fire
had partially neutralized the enemy fire. A machine gun
position again pinned down the company. Company
Sergeant Major Bernard with utter disregard for his own
personal safety rushed forward and wiped out this enemy
position single handed, killing three and taking the
remainder prisoners, thus allowing the Company to
proceed.

In the further advance of the company the Company
Commander was killed and all three platoon commanders
became casualties. Company Sergeant Major Bernard
immediately took command and led the company into
the village clearing the company's objective. Company
Sergeant Major Bernard then assumed command of the
complete company and reorganised it. The company

made firm the bridge-head obtained in the village,
allowing the remainder of the battalion to pass through.
The bridgehead enabled the battalion to complete its task
and seize the battalion objective, the village of Keppeln.
                                    (L.G. 16.6.45)

Berresford, Lawrence, Sergeant
2613330, 4 Tk. Grenadier Guards (Tydfil, Glam.)
(Immediate)
On 5 Nov 44 at Meijel, Sjt. Berresford commanded a
Troop of No. 2 Sqn. The Sqn had been ordered to attempt
a dash round the enemy right flank. Having penetrated
behind the German lines some 400 yards, the Sqn became
bogged in soft ground and in a minefield as well. Several
tanks were knocked out by A/Tk gun fire. Throughout
the day from 0745 hrs until dark Sjt. Berresford continued
to fire the weapons of his Tp at any target which presented
itself. He continued engaging the local farm buildings
from which the Germans were attempting to Bazooka
him, and also he continued firing at any opposition which
might be giving trouble to the Inf in Schans. Although
his Tp was mined, bogged, immobile and also marooned
several hundred yards behind the enemy postions he
continued to inspire in his Tp a most offensive spirit and
succeeded in killing a large number of Germans.
Throughout the day the Tp was under continual hostile
fire which at times became intense. The fire consisted of
observed A/Tk fire, arty and mortars. Just before dark
an attempt was made by the Recce Tp to come to the aid
of the remainder of the Sqn. It did not succeed in reaching
Sjt. Berresford's Tp. He therefore remained with his tks
until after dark by which time his ammunition became
exhausted. Having received permission to evacuate his
tks he collected his Tp and formed them into a patrol.
Leading this patrol he set forth to approach the German
lines from the rear. He encountered two enemy patrols
on the way which he successfully dealt with. His party
was continually shot at whilst it was passing through the
German lines from rear and front. Furthermore, his party
was heavily mortared. During this operation four of his
men were wounded. He succeeded in bringing back all
his wounded as well as the remainder of his patrol. His
personal example and leadership was of a standard
altogether out of proportion to the command he held.
His determined spirit inspired in his Tp the will to
continue fighting an offensive action throughout the day
some hundreds of yards behind the enemy lines, during
the whole of which time the Tp was under continued
observed hostile fire.

Finally, his grim determination to fight his way back
through the enemy lines inspired his Tp with tremendous
confidence and the will to win through. *(L.G. 1.3.45)*

Berrison, Chinyama, Sergeant
11958, King's African Rifles (Immediate)
For outstanding courage and [...] leadership under fire

On the night 29/30 October 1944 Sjt. Berrison, an
African Pl Sjt. had a section of his platoon forward close

under a strongly held Japanese position on a feature known as Point 500 near Chinmag[...] Burma. Sjt. Berrison worked his men forward in spite of showers of grenades thrown by enemy down precipitous stone; eventually Sjt. Berrison found he was right under the lip of the Japanese position with a small tree only seperating him from the enemy grenader in the trench four feet above him. Sjt. Berrison then sent his men to the left to carry out an encircling movement while he himself remained immediately in front of the Japanese grenadier whose who attention was thus drawn to Sjt. Berrison. While the section worked round to the left a grenade battle at a few yards range developed between Sjt. Berrison and the enemy who had the overwhelming advantage of a dug in position on higher ground. Sjt. Berrison continued the engagement until he had exhausted his supply of grenades. Moving in the darkness he rejoined his section, took a fresh supply of grenades, and encouraged his men and directed them further on their line of advance and then returned to his original position under the lip of the Japanese position. The grenade engagement started once more and an enemy grenade was tossed so that it would have landed on Sjt. Berrison had it not by good fortune caught in the roots of the small tree and burst just above his head. Sjt. Berrison was undeterred by this occurence and continued to throw his grenades at the two enemy positions he had by this time located. He managed to lob one of his grenades into the Japanese position immediately above his head. The occupant was seriously injured and rendered unconscious, being taken prisoner next morning. Sjt. Berrison also managed to get a direct hit with a grenade in the second enemy position and the Japanese grenadier was silenced, his mutilated body being found when the feature was eventually captured. Meanwhile the enemy had opened heavy fire and were sending [...] showers of grenades from other position. His company Commander then sent a runner to Sjt. Berrison and ordered him to withdraw. The NCO moved from his isolated position, collected his men, and displaying fine judgement and control withdrew them with only minor casualties.

Sjt. Berrison's [...] courage [...] and personal disregard for safety were [...] casualties [...]   (*L.G. 22.3.45*)

Berry, George Thomas, Sergeant
VX 31716, 2/24 Aust. Inf. Bn.
For conspicuous gallantry and devotion to duty at El Alamein 25/26 Oct 42.

During the attack of night 25/26 Oct Sjt. Berry was acting OC 11 Pl. Throughout this attack his fearless leadership under heavy fire of all natures inspired his men with confidence and enabled them unhesitatingly to follow him through intense fire. With utter disregard for his own safety he rushed and silenced two enemy posts on his own in this action.

Upon the Coy objective for this action there was a strong enemy post cunningly sited which the Coy Comd decided to use all three Pls to assault. Sjt. Berry's Pl was the left hand Pl for this assault and when this assault was made Sjt. Berry was the first man of the whole Coy into the post and carried out terrible execution with the bayonet until he received a wound which broke his arm. This NCO's dashing leadership and fearless courage set a brilliant example not only to his own Pl but to all who saw him and set the tempo for the whole Coy attack, contributing very largely to the success of the unit's operation for the night.   (*L.G. 11.2.43*)

Berry, Myron, Private
M 106615, Loyal Edmonton Regiment (Immediate)
Reference Map Italy 1/25,0000 Sheet 100–11 Cesena.

On the night 22/23 October 1944, 'D' Company of the Loyal Edmonton Regiment was given the task of enlarging a bridgehead over the Savio River which had already been established by the Battalion. Number 18 Platoon under command of the Platoon Sergeant, was to capture a house at MR 582097.

During the attack the Platoon Sergeant was seriously wounded, and, as there was no other NCO left within the platoon, M-106615 Private Myron Berry immediately took charge. Owing to casualties and the rough and muddy going the platoon had become somewhat disorganised but Private Berry by his personal example and coolness soon rallied them. With great calmness he selected a suitable spot, formed the platoon up for attack and with loud shouts to his comrades and with absolute disregard for his own personal safety he led them in a charge across 25 yards of open ground which was swept by machine gun fire, into the house where under the inspiration of his leadership they quickly disposed of the enemy, killing two and wounding three.

After consolidation, the house and surrounding trenches were subjected to considerable enemy pressure, and heavy shell and mortar fire. Private Berry continually made the rounds of his men, visiting each position, encouraging and cheering the others and ensuring that all was well. During the most of this time he was in the open himself, exposed to the enemy small arms and shell fire. He remained in command for 18 hours, until he was wounded on 23 October 1944.

This soldier's demonstration of courage and coolness at all times throughout this action was highly commendable. His gallant acceptance of great responsibility at a very critical moment was an inspiration and an example to all within his company, and his actual leadership of the charge which cleared the house, without doubt was responsible for the platoon's success and the ultimate success of his company.   (*L.G. 17.2.45*)

Berry, Richard, Private
5437631, 1 Bn. Duke of Cornwall's Light Infantry
On the night of 31 May 40 my Section was placed in a position on the left flank of D Company between Nieuport and Dunkirk. Next morning we found that the rest of the Company had disappeared, presumably

towards Dunkirk. On the instructions of our Section Commander we also reached the beach at Dunkirk, but were unable to embark and were captured on the outskirts of the town on 1 Jun 40.

I was sent via Belgium and Holland to Stalag VIIIB (Lamsdorf, Upper Silesia), where I was kept for five weeks. In August I was sent to work in a coal mine at Hindenburg, near Beuthen, as one of a party of about 60 British P/W. Conditions were good and we were paid a Mark a day.

On 22 Sep I escaped with Gunner Brindley, John, R.A., and (?) Pte. Haig, Robert, Gordon Highlanders. We knew that an Eastbound coal train stopped just outside the camp about midnight each night. We were working on the night-shift, and, after climbing through the barbed wire, boarded the train, which took us to Cracow. There we tried to get off and hide, but, as we were in British battle dress, we were stopped by the civilian police. We said we had escaped from Lamsdorf and were sent back there. Our punishment was 10 days' solitary confinement.

In Oct 40 I was one of a party who were sent to work on the roads in the Sudetenland near Neisse. On 9 Nov I escaped with Brindley, Dvr. Ferris, R.A.S.C., and Pte. McLean, Ronald, R.A.O.C. Our idea was to walk to Hungary, which was then neutral, but we got lost in the hills and, as we had no food, we had to let ourselves be caught after four days. We were again returned to Lamsdorf and received 10 days' imprisonment.

In Feb 41 I was sent back to Hindenburg. Ten of us planned to escape, and waited till the Red Cross Parcels had begun to come through. In the early morning of 10 Mar Pte. Bloom, Alfred John, East Kents, and myself left as the second party. I got out first, followed by Bloom. Another man was to have accompanied us, but did not turn up. All those taking part in the escape were working on the morning shift, which meant that we were up at 0400 hrs. The guards were very lax, as there had been no attempt for about nine months, and the man on duty near our hut on that particular day was not very intelligent. We eluded him ad crossed the barbed wire at the back of our billet. We walked for about 6 or 7 miles and hid all day. After dark we made for the railway station and boarded an Eastbound train.

We left the train near Cracow and went to a house. We told the Pole there that we were English, and he sheltered us all day and at night directed us to the next town, where we jumped another train and got to another small town. There we got food again from Poles, walked another night, and boarded another goods train which took us to Tarnow. Here we met a Pole who spoke English. He supplied us with civilian coats and hats (so far we had been wearing battle dress) and put us into a timber wagon on a goods train bound for Nisko. There a gang of Poles working on the railway under a German foreman, provided us with food and put us on another train, the engine driver of which they instructed to let us off near the frontier which then existed between German-

occupied and Russian-occupied Poland. The driver put of off near the River San, advising us to seek shelter. One man hid us for a night and took us next day to a neighbouring village where an English-speaking Pole sheltered us for one day.

On the night of 20 Mar 41, we swam the River San. I went across first, and failed to find Bloom on the other side, though I waited for him. I then went to the nearest house and asked for the Russian authorities. Two armed soldiers took me to a barracks where I was questioned. All my documents were taken from me. They included Part II of my A.B.64, private letters and photographs, and the German Stalag identity disc. I said I was a British soldier, and was asked if I spoke German. I said I spoke a little German, and was then questioned for five hours by a Russian Corporal, whose knowledge of German was also very small. The end of the interrogation. I was thrown into a little room without food, matress, or heating. There was no glass in the window, just bars. My clothes, which had got wet when I crossed the river, were frozen on me. I was kept alone in this cell for 24 hours.

I was then taken by car to Przemysl, where I was again questioned for about two hours, being asked where I was born, what school I had attended, the names of my parents, my profession, regimental number, where I was captured, and where I had escaped from. I kept asking to get in touch with the British Embassy or Consulate. I was told I would be free in two or three weeks, and after my fingerprints and photograph had been taken, I was put in a cell besides some Poles. A little later I was put into another cell, again with Poles. One Pole, a new arrival to this cell, told me that Bloom was in the cell next door, but I did not see Bloom either there or anywhere else in Russia. I was again questioned by the Russians and asked the name of my companion. I told them I had been with Bloom.

After 11 or 12 days in this prison, I was transferred to another one, also in Przemyl. I was detained there until 22 Jun, the day of the outbreak of the war between Germany and Russia. In this second prison I was questioned several times, always at night or in the early morning and chiefly in German. Generally there were three or four Russians sitting round the table, and they frequently fired questions at me in different languages. I was made to sit under a bright light. On 22 Jun the Germans attacked the town, and the Russians made us march Eastwards. At one stage we were actually in the middle of an engagement between about 100 Germans and 1000 Russians. After two days' walking we reached Sambor (24 June), where we stayed two or three days. I was told by Poles that Bloom and Cpl. Jowell, Stanley, were also in Sambor, but I did not see either of them.

From Sambor we were transported by rail to Ziatoust in the Urals. The journey lasted 21 days. Most of the prisoners were Russians, Poles, Jews, and Ukrainians. There were 62 in each wagon, and our only food was bread and water. On arrival in Ziatoust on 17 July, I was put into prison where I remained until 4 Mar 42. During the whole of that time the prisoners had no blankets or mattresses and were sleeping on the stone floor. We had a bath and delouse once in six weeks. The food consisted of 450 grammes of black bread and a litre of soup a day. Exercise each day lasted 20 minutes. The rest of the time was spent in the cell. I was moved from cell to cell, but most of the time I was in solitary confinement. In Feb 42, about a month before I left, I was interrogated once by a Russian NCO in German. I was asked the same questions as before. Though the interrogator did not accuse me directly of being a German spy, he asked if I had heard of the Gestapo or the German Secret Service, and gave me the impression that he thought I was other than I said I was. The interrogation lasted about half an hour.

On 4 Mar 42 I was sent by train with three Russians and a Jew to Chelyabinsk, a journey of a day. On arrival I was put in a cell with 300 men. As the cell was too small to accommodate that number, platforms had been erected round the walls for prisoners to live on. Every day when new arrivals were put in, there were fights for accommodation among the prisoners, and I saw several of them killed. I was three weeks in this cell. At one time I was sick, but got no medical attention; the other prisoners stole my food when I was ill. The food again consisted of black bread and soup, and again there was 20 minutes' exercise a day; but no one went for fear of losing his clothes and place. About the middle of Jun I was questioned by a Russian who spoke English. I asked for the British Embassy and was told it 'cut no ice' there. I lost my temper and called the Russian a few names. I was taken back to my cell. There I was beaten up by two soldiers. One hit me under the chin. I went down. When I recovered consciousness, I had bruises and lumps on my body and head. I remained in the big cell till 20 Jul when I was questioned by a Russian who could speak good English. He seemed very sympathetic and asked me the same questions as before. A prison official wrote down all the answers in Russian, and when he had finished I was asked to sign this statement.

I carried on in the same way till 10 or 11 Aug when I was taken to Kuibyshev by train. I was kept in prison there until 23 Aug, when I was put into a motor car and driven for about five minutes. The Russians then put me out of the car and, after pointing out the British Embassy, drove off. At the third attempt I found the right place and went inside. I was told that the Embassy had been expecting me all day. I gathered that they had first heard of me when a Pole, freed by the Russians in Mar 42, had gone to the Embassy with the information that there was a British soldier imprisoned in Zlatoust.

The food in the last prison in Kuibyshev was worse than at any time during my captivity, but the prison itself was cleaner and better organised. The day before I left they gave me a shirt, underpants, and socks, all of which I had been without all the time I was in Russia. I was interrogated again in English and asked the same old questions. When the interrogator had finished he said, 'The Committee sat yesterday and set you free.'

(L.G. 7.1.43)

Berry, Theodore Waldemar, Lance Corporal
1883728, 1 Field Squadron, Royal Engineers (Ryde, I. of W.) (Periodic)
At Alamein on the evening of the 1st Nov 42, this NCO with a party of 3 sappers went out from the head of Double Bar Track to destroy four 88 mm guns. As they proceeded towards the guns, the party came under intense small arms and machine gun fire. L/Cpl. Berry with great coolness ordered the 3 sappers of his party to open fire at the nearest enemy position, whilst he went forward on foot and fixed the demolition charge to the first of the 88 mm's. He succeeded in doing this and returned to his party. The enemy by this time were determined to recover the remaining 3 guns, and L/Cpl. Berry was unable to destroy the other 3 guns owing to mortar fire being opened on the guns. He moved the party to a position where their fire would have greater effect, and again went forward, and despite mortar and machine gun fire intensifying, he succeeded in destroying the other 3 guns. The hazardous nature of this NCO's deed was increased owing to the fact that he had to carry on his back, explosive charges required for the demolition.

On the 7th Nov 42, this NCO during the approach march to Bir Khalda, was despatched on reconnaissance with one vehicle and one driver. During his reconnaissance he came under fire from two 3-tonners. Dismounting from his vehicle he went forward on foot and fired his Bren gun at the two lorries. After exchanging fire, 20 Italians who were with the 3-tonners surrendered, and this NCO returned with them to Squadron Headquarters. *(L.G. 14.10.43)*

Berthelot, Guy Bernard, Lance Corporal
L.13504, South Saskatchewan Regt.
During the operation at Dieppe 19 Aug 42, when his Platoon Sjt. was wounded and the platoon temporarily disorganised by heavy enemy fire from the top of a hill, Berethelot with the assistance of Pte. Haggard, took charge of the platoon and decided on a plan of attack. The enemy was strongly situated in weapon pits. Berthelot firing from the corner of a house with a Bren gun was to cover the advance of a section. But, as this mode of attack proved unsuccessful, Berthelot, alone advanced up the open hill into the pit area, firing from the hip straight down into the enemy pits. His section followed up this daring and inspired assault with grenades and rifle fire. Twenty-seven dead and thirty prisoners were accounted for. *(L.G. 2.10.42)*

Bevan, Charles William, Sergeant
7881318, 5th Royal Inniskilling Dragoon Guards
On 27th May, 1940, Sjt. Bevan was ordered with his tank to cover the withdrawal of the rear elements of infantry in his sector near Neuve Chapelle. He remained

in position in the face of heavy fire anti tank fire until the infantry had passed to safety and his ammunition was exhausted. Then when he and the remainder of his crew were wounded and their vehicle was in flames he withdrew.   *(L.G. 20.12.40)*

Bevan, Morgan, Lance Sergeant
1068689, 2nd Regt., Royal Horse Artillery
  (Pontypridd)
On 14.6.42 'I' Battery were in action South of Acroma. L/Sjt. Bevan was No. 1 of a 25 pr gun. At about 0830 hrs enemy tanks advanced from the south and when about 1000 yards from the Tp position they came under direct observation from L/Sjt. Bevan's gun.

L/Sjt. Bevan was ordered to engage the enemy tanks gun control. His was the only gun firing in the Tp and in consequence the enemy concentrated their fire on his gun. For about one hour L/Sjt. Bevan continued to engage the enemy tanks over open sights. Every time the enemy tried to come on they were forced back to a hull down position. Several direct hits were scored.

Two of L/Sjt. Bevan's detachment were killed and two wounded during this action. L/Sjt. Bevan showed a fine disregard for danger and was an inspiration to the remainder of his detachment.   *(L.G. 15.10.42)*

Beya, Asana, Sergeant
SLA 26943, Sierra Leone Regt., Royal West African
  Frontier Forces
No citation.   *(L.G. 22.3.45)*

Bhimbahadurpun, Warrant Officer Cl. II
21132012, 1/2nd King Edward VII's Own Gurkha
  Rifles
For Malaya   *(L.G. 4.4.50)*

Billingham, Eric, M.M., Lance Sergeant
947984, 288/124th Field Regt., Royal Artillery
  (Barnsley)
On May 26th and 27th when his troop was heavily engaged at Fachri (Gazala Line), L/Sjt. Billingham was in charge of his Troop wagon lines and amn supply. Any movement between Troop and Wagon lines brought down heavy gun fire. Already one Quad had been temporarily put out of action. Rather than risk a succession of Quads running to the Troop with amn, L/Sjt. Billingham took it upon himself to run the gauntlet driving his Quad alone with a long trail of amn trailers behind. This he did twice under heavy shell fire. By this courageous and gallant act he enabled the Troop to carry on firing at a critical moment in the action when amn was running low.

Later on June 14th and 15th in the Gazala breakthrough a column of vehicles in which he was driving became involved with mine-fields. After the Officer in charge of the column had found a safe passage L/Sjt. Billingham 'policed' the whole column through to safety, although the area was being harrassed by shell fire. Later

between Jun 28th and July 1st he was largely instrumental in extracting the Troop vehicle unde his charge from positions around Deir el Shein which were under hostile fire from Guns, Tanks, and M.G.s.

L/Sjt. Billingham has always shown the greatest initiative and his infectious cheerfulness and courage are an example to all the men who were with him.
                                            (L.G. 18.2.43)

Bilsborrow, Albert Edward, Warrant Officer Cl. II
  (C.S.M.)
3758960, 8th (Irish) Bn., King's Regt. (Maghull,
  Lancs.)
During the landing on the Normandy Coast on 6 June 44, this WO landed at H hour with the recce party of his company under his Company Commander. The beach was under enemy mortar fire and shortly after landing, CSM Bilsborrow's Coy Commander was wounded. The Company 2 i/c was also hit by an enemy mortar bomb, and CSM Bilsborrow immediately took over the Company, and completed the reconnaissance although under constant enemy fire. He remained in command of the company until H plus 2 hours when another officer arrived, and during this time he did invauable work in helping to clear the beaches. I consider that the high example and devotion to duty displayed by this Warrant Officer is outstanding and that he should be given some recognition for his services.
Recommended for M.M.   *(L.G. 31.8.44)*

Bingham, G. J. W., Signalman
N.X.51770, Australian Military Forces
No citation.   *(L.G. 5.3.42)*

Bingham, Joseph, Corporal
C58593, 21 Cdn. Armd. Regt. (G.G.F.G.) (Immediate)
The 21 Cdn Armd Regt (GGFG) on 26 Feb 45, was ordered to assault, capture and hold the high ground NE of Udem area MR 0043:1/25,000 sheet 4303 Udem. This ground was a dominating feature, commanding Udem, and the surrounding terrain was comparatively flat. No. 3 Sqn undertook to assault this feature when No. 2 Sqn who had been originally ordered to carry out the task became bogged down and came under very heavy A Tk fire. Cpl. Joseph Bingham was a crew comd in one of the tps in No. 3 Sqn. On the approach to the start line minor defects appeared in his tank which at any moment might have rendered it useless for fighting. Although fully aware of this Bingham pressed fwd to the attack crossing the start line with a section of infantry riding on the tank. Almost immediately the tp came under heavy A Tk fire and the tp leader's tk was hit and brewed. Ordering the inf to ground cover this NCO manœuvered his tank into a hull down posn and searched for the enemy guns by speculative shooting. One enemy A Tk gun located at approx 990452 fired, obtaining a glancing strike on Cpl. Bingham's tk temporarily sealing the drivers hatch. By calm and speedy action this NCO

rallied his shaken crew and brought fire to bear on the enemy gun, forcing it to withdraw. This enabled the remainder of the tp to press fwd up the slope and Bingham maintained a heavy fire from all his weapons until they had passed out of sight. He then moved fwd towards the objective in an effort to rejoin his tp. On the way an inf offr was seen waving frantically from a slit trench slightly to his right and without hesitation Bingham halted, dismounted and crossed the bullet swept ground on foot. The offr and men were members of the Lake Sup R (M) and were being pinned down by SA fire coming from the house at 995445. Returning to his tk Cpl. Bingham engaged the house with 75 mm HE and within a few seconds the enemy, five in number, came out with hands upraised and the inf were able to continue on the fwd objective. By this time Cpl. Bingham was far to the rear and complete darkness had descended. Fully realizing that every tank gun and man would be required to hold the objective he ordered his tank fwd to the high ground. On arrival he became bogged down at such an angle that it was impossible to traverse the turret and thus to fight the tanks. Cpl. Bingham ordered his crew to ground and dismounting two Browning MGs he dug in in a def role. Two enemy counter attacks developed against No. 3 Sqn's posn during the night but Cpl. Bingham and his crew kept up a withering fire from their ground posns and greatly aided in inflicting cas and driving enemy from the feature. Throughout this op the courage, coolness under fire and initiative of this NCO was of the highest calibre. His crew, encouraged by his superb example and leadership were able to fight their tk in a most outstanding manner, assisting the inf fwd, accounting for numerous enemy cas, and adding in no small measure in the capture of this vital high ground.
(*L.G. 12.5.45*)

Birch, William John, Corporal
3445776, 2 Lancashire Fusiliers (Bury, Lancs.)
At Bdj Kochok on 11th Dec 42 showed conspicuous gallantry in the face of the enemy whilst in command of a section. After an unsuccessful attempt had been made to dislodge an enemy post, Birch called for volunteers to go forward with him to recover a wounded Sjt. and to recce the enemy position. Leaving one man with his Sjt., Birch took Fusilier Ryan forward with him, and rushed the enemy position, using Hand Grenades and Sub-Machine Guns. The enemy surrendered and nine prisoners, including two Officers were captured.
(*L.G. 23.9.43*)

Bishop, Dennis Alfred, Warrant Officer Cl. II (B.S.M.)
*818430, 11th Field Battery, 1st Field Regt., Royal
    Artillery (Larkhill, Wilts.)*
On Jan 25 near Msus when the battery which formed part of a small column was attacked on three sides by Tanks and some Artillery BSM Bishop under very difficult conditions collected and controlled the Wagon Lines close to the guns. He showed great initiative and

coolness in leading them to successive areas where they were best placed as successive attacks were made and by his alertness enabled the Battery to move rapidly out of action, when further withdrawal was ordered. Previous to this and on many subsequent occasions between Nov and February he has brought ammunition up to the guns under the most adverse conditions, under heavy fire, never failing to be there when it was wanted in a hurry and anticipating orders when things happened too quickly for him to be given them. The steadiness and command shown by this W.O. have invariably been at their best under shell fire and his work throughout has been exemplary.
(*L.G. 9.9.42*)

Black, Gavin, Corporal
7884495, 7 Royal Tank Regt. (since killed in action)
This NCO was tank commander during the action on 9 Dec 40 at Nibeiwa and Tummar West, fighting his tank with gallantry and coolness engaging enemy guns at close range in spite of many direct hits one of which damaged his radiator and put one engine out of action. In spite of this he brought his tank back to the rallying point.
His coolness and devotion to duty were remarkable.
(*L.G. 25.4.41*)

Blackham, Leslie, Sergeant
*4387223, 6th Green Howards (Middlesborough)
    (Immediate)*
On the night of the 16/17th March 1943, when the Battalion was attacking the outposts of the Mareth line, Sjt. Blackham was Platoon Sergeant of the leading platoon. He led his platoon right up into the Anti personnel minefield behind the R.E. party helping the Sappers to clear a gap in this very deep minefield. As soon as he was through the minefield he organised the platoon quickly and with supreme coolness despite intense enemy Machine Gun fire and shell fire. At this stage he was wounded and lost one finger, but continued to organise Platoon Headquarters. When a mortar bomb wounded all the personnel in the Headquarters he picked up an anti tank rifle, charged and took a Machine gun post, flung grenades at another causing it to surrender. His dash and leadership, his disregard for his personnel safety and encouragement, was a great inspiration to his men.
(*L.G. 17.6.43*)

Blackman, Herbert Ernest, Private
*14756962, 1 Gordon Higlanders (Twickenham)
    (Immediate)*
Whilst engaged on the very difficult operation of clearing the town of Rees of fanatical German paratroopers Pte. Blackman showed such outstanding bravery and complete disregard for the enemy's fire and his own safety, that the men around him willingly accepted him as their leader after the Sec Comd had been killed. They followed him with great cheerfulness under the most difficult circumstances.

On 24 Mar 45 in Rees, Pte. Blackman's section was ordered to attack and clear a large factory strongly held by the enemy: half-way to their objective through the intensity of the fire, the section became temporarily held up, but his initiative, great leadership and courage in going round encouraging the others, so rallied them that with him in the lead they rushed and stormed the factory and cleared it against great odds. Immediately the section had finished the task of clearing it, the enemy started to bazooka the factory from close range and attempted a counter-attack. Once again this soldier's personality, supreme bravery and example was the cause of the post remaining firm and the splendid reactions of this section caused the enemy further casualties.

Later on the same day, during a further attack by the platoon, the Pl Comd was severely wounded and lay out in the open under intense fire, it being impossible for anyone to reach him—several attempts having failed. Pte. Blackman, however, seeing his section were well organised in their position, quietly slipped out on his own and after about an hour's crawl in daylight and under full enemy observation, managed to reach his Pl Comd and dressed his wounds and remained with him till darkness came, when he organised his evacuation.

The superb example and devotion to duty the soldier showed was beyond praise and his actions were largely responsible for keeping up the morale of his Company, who had had a very bitter and difficult previous 36 hrs fighting. His cheerfulness, energy and personal courage under conditions, which had to be seen to be believed, were exceptional even for an experienced NCO.

(L.G. 7.6.45)

Blackmore, George Edward, Warrant Officer Cl. II (B.S.M.)
952598, 70th Field Regt., Royal Artillery (Ealing)
For conspicuous gallantry and leadership during the period 3rd–17th March 1943.

BSM Blackmore's troop was subjected to observed counter-battery fire almost continuously throughout this period and was dive-bombed on eleven occasions. The troop was often called on to produce fire whilst being shelled and/or bombed itself. BSM Blackmore, who, on account of officer casualties, was acting as troop leader as well as troop sergeant major, set a sterling example ensuring that fire orders reached the guns and checking the lay of the guns in the midst of the enemy shelling and with complete disregard for personal safety. Whenever gun teams were hit, BSM Blackmore went immediately to the gun in question, attended to the wounded and arranged for them to be evacuated immediately and the gun to be got firing again with the minimum of delay.

On one occasion on March 8th when the troop received particularly heavy casualties, and one gun team was reduced to two men, he, himself, acted as No. 1 to that gun and kept the troop firing as a four gun unit. His example throughout the whole period was an inspiration

to all on the gun position and never once did he lose his grip of the situation.   *(L.G. 15.6.43)*

Blackwell, Alun Trevor, Lance Corporal
3655742, South Lancashire Regt., No. 1 S.S. Bn. & S.O.E.
L/Cpl Blackwell belonged to the Malta Independent Company under the direct orders of Capt Simpson RN commanding 10th Submarine Flotilla. He was a picked man and had been specially trained in the handling of folbots and their use in night operations. In November 1941 he took part in a special operation for landing two agents and their equipment on the coast of Tunisia from an MTB, but the folbot in which Blackwell landed the party was wrecked and they were all arrested by local police and interned. When the Germans entered Tunisia in November 1942 Blackwell escaped from prison and in company with the same two agents proceeded to form a secret organisation for passing information to the Allied Forces as to German movements and intentions. Blackwell took over the Information side of the group and a total of 585 reports were passed to Allied HQ in the space of four months. The quality of the information was frequently described by the Military Intelligence Branch at AFHQ as most useful.

The group was continually harassed by German counter espionage activities and eventually in March 1943 after six prominent members had been arrested, Blackwell took over leadership and the output of information continued steadily.

Finally Blackwell was himself arrested in April 1943, despite a last desperate attempt to escape by jumping from a second story window, but unfortunately he broke his leg and was eventually deported to Germany. He has recently been repatriated suffering from tuberculosis.

A stout hearted North countryman who displayed courage and resource of a very high order.

(L.G. 2.8.45)

Blackwell, James Ernest, Lance Sergeant
5502956, 1st Bn. Hampshire Regt. (Greenwich)
(Immediate)
During the advance on Pachino on 10 July 43, an enemy position, which was still in action, was harassing two Bns by fire from their rear. With two other men, L/Sjt. Blackwell attacked the enemy. With great dash and daring he got to close quarters using hand grenades and tommy-gun. His small party killed several enemy and captured 2 Officers and 55 men with a quantity of weapons. In this engagement L/Sjt. Blackwell behaved with great coolness and enterprise under fire and showed complete disregard for danger. His conduct on subsequent occasions was of the same high standard.
(L.G. 21.10.43)

Blagg, Daniel Kenneth, Private
4975304, Sherwood Foresters (attd. 2 West Yorkshire Regt.) (Worksop) (Immediate)
On 14 Jan 44, Pte. Blagg was with his section on a standing patrol about 1000 yards in front of his coy at Bagona, Arakan. During the night, the coy was attacked and this patrol in accordance with its orders, tried to rejoin its coy. They were unable to do so, one man being wounded in the attempt. The Sec Comd decided then to work round the flank and try to reach Bn HQ, but they got badly lost amongst the maze of chaungs in that area. For two day and nights they wandered, losing one man by drowning but still carrying the wounded man. Pte. Blagg, being the only strong swimmer of the party, was indefatigable in his efforts, and had to ferry the wounded man across all the chaungs. In addition he made two attempts to rescue the drowning man. The party got split up, but eventually Pte. Blagg reached Bn HQ with the wounded man and gave a very accurate report of the happenings. Again on the night of 22 Jan, Pte. Blagg's platoon was ordered to attack an enemy strong post at Nyunggyaung, which had been holding up two coys of another unit. During the advance, the platoon came under very heavy fire, killing the pl comd, and holding up the advance. Pte. Blagg worked his way forward and silenced an MG post by throwing grenades, thus enabling his section to gain their objective. During the operations he has shewn remarkable coolness and has set a high example to his comrade by his courage and determination
(L.G. 20.4.44)

Blain, Robert [Strachan], Warrant Officer Cl. II (C.S.M.)
2978067, King's Regt. [The Dorsetshire Regt. on AFW 3121] (Glasgow, E.2) (Immediate)
Operations in Burma—March 1943.
This Warrant Officer belonged to the Sabotage Squad of his Column, and took a leading part in the destruction of the railway to Myitkyina. On 6th March, 1943, working with great speed he destroyed a bridge south of Nankan, cutting a box girder with a span of 120 feet, and blowing the abutments of another span. He also cut the railway in many other places, laid a number of booby traps using 3″ mortar shells for bursting charge, and then withdrew his men safely to the rendezvous some miles distant.
On 23th March 1943 at Pago, he and his party of ten men helped to ambush a Japanese company, inflicting a number of casualties. Later, near Nyaung Bintha on the Shweli River, his section ambushed an enemy party of twice his strength, destroying about half of them. On all occasions and at all times he upheld the finest traditions of a British Warrant Officer. *(L.G. 5.8.43)*

Blair, Clive, Corporal
QX38364, 49 Aust. Inf. Bn. (Immediate)
During a Bn attack on the morning of Monday 7th Dec '42, after the Coy Comd of B Coy had been killed, for awhile the attack became disorgaised. Cpl. Blair immediately summed up the situation and under fire collected the men in the viciity and enabled the attack to push on. Later, when the Pl was pinned down by MG fire he outflanked the enemy posn, silenced it and returned to lead his men on. It was then whilst endeavouring to silence a further MG that he was wounded. Blair however continued to lead his men and only withdrew when his injury would not allow him to carry on. Cpl. Blair was an outstanding example to the men he led and right throughout the action showed outstanding courage, determination and leadership under fire. *(L.G. 30.3.43)*

Bland, Tom, Sergeant
856956, 257 Bty 65 A. Tk. Regt., Royal Artillery (Grimsby) (Immediate)
At Wetteren on 6 Sep 44 this NCO was in charge of a Tp of 17 pr A Tk guns defending Wetteren Br. When the position was attacked by enemy inf supported by Mortars and A Tk guns, Sjt. Bland organised a party of his men to fight as inf in sp of the RE who had become desperately engaged. Armd with one Bren gun and rifles they played a very distinguished part in the subsequent battle and when 40 Germans had been pinned down in the cellar of a house, Sjt. Bland volunteered to attack them with his detachment.
Leading his men across completely open ground he reached the house, entered it and ejected the whole of the enemy force, which was mown down by Besa fire from the Tks as they fled across open ground.
There is no doubt that Sjt. Bland, by his initiative, leadership and courage contributed greatly to the success of the defence.
This action is an outstanding example and deserving of an immediate award of the DCM. Sjt. Bland set an example at a very critical period and shewed complete disregard of his own personal safety. *(L.G. 21.12.44)*

Blandford, Arthur, Warrant Officer Cl. I (Staff Sgt.-Maj.)
726541, 9th Lancers, Royal Armoured Corps
On 5th June, 1940, S.S.M. Blandford was ordered to carry out a patrol at Toeufles, S.W. of Abbeville, to protect the right flank of the 153rd Infantry Bde. At Toeufles he established contact with a patrol of the Black Watch who reported the enemy in large numbers N.E. of the village. S.S.M. Blandford with his patrol of two light tanks immediately went towards the position where those enemy were reported. He there surprised and engaged a large number of German infantry at close range. He inflicted heavy casualties on the enemy in position, and followed up those who ran away. While engaging these infantry an enemy anti-tank gun opened fire from a flank, hit one of his light tanks and set it on fire. S.S.M. Blandford was instrumental in having the fire put out, the tank driven out of action, and subsequently towed to safety. *(L.G. 27.9.40)*

Bloomfield, Alexander, Corporal (A/Sgt.)
2976964, Argyll & Sutherland Highlanders
(Greenock, Renfrew)
On the 23rd May 1941 during the Battle for Crete Sjt. Bloomfield was Platoon Sergeant of a Platoon of 'A' Company. This platoon was given the task of clearing a wood held by the enemy. This task it successfully accomplished, but in doing so the Platoon Commander was wounded. Sjt. Bloomfield took command of the Platoon and led it forward to exploit its success. The Platoon soon came under heavy Machine Gun and Mortar fire and suffered several more casualties. Sjt. Bloomfield successfully extricated his Platoon. He then returned to the scene of the action to try and retrieve the dead and wounded. He observed one wounded man attempting to move and in full view of the enemy and under intense Machine Gun fire Sjt. Bloomfield went forward alone and carried the wounded man back to safety.

On the following day, 24th May, Sjt. Bloomfield with his Platoon were again in action. At the end of the action Sjt. Bloomfield went forward himself and under intense Machine Gun fire succeeded in carrying back to safety another wounded man.

On the 26th May Sjt. Bloomfield was in command of his Platoon near Heraklion. At 6.15 a.m. his Platoon was heavily attacked by a large body of enemy. His personal example and leadership inspired his Platoon which successfully repelled the attack.

During all these operations Sjt. Bloomfield set a fine example, displayed courage of a high order and at all times carried on with entire disregard to his own personal safety.   *(L.G. 4.11.41)*

Boardman, Christopher, Lance Sergeant
3522635, 1 East Lancashire Regt. (Blackburn)
(Immediate)
On 22 Sep 44, during the attack on Bladel, after wireless communication between the forward platoons and Company Headquarters had broken down, L/Cpl. Boardman volunteered to go forward and contact the forward platoon commanders. To do this, L/Cpl. Boardman had to advance over flat open ground swept by Machine Gun fire. Not only did L/Cpl. Boardman contact both Platoon Commanders, but he successfully guided the right hand platoon forward a distance of 300 yds up into line with the left platoon in the face of heavy enemy fire. For some time he took command of this platoon as the Pl Comd and Pl Sjt had become casualties.

During one of his many journeys between Coy H.Q. and the Platoons he gave first aid to two wounded men, and single-handed shot three Germans and put a fourth to flight, who attempted to interfere with him when he was bandaging up the wounded men.

Throughout the whole action which lasted from first light to 0900 hrs on the following day, he displayed great courage and initiative and an entire disregard for his own personal safety. His cheerfulness throughout the night,

despite hunger and all the dangers of street fighting was inspiring to those around him.   *(L.G. 1.3.45)*

Bober, Walter Lorne, Sergeant (A/W.O.II (C.S.M.))
M16370, The Loyal Edmonton Regt. (since killed in action) (Immediate)
At first light on 23 October, 1943, the Loyal Edmonton Regiment was attacking the town of Colle d'Anchise and 'B' Company, in which Sergeant Bober was acting as platoon commander of the leading platoon, was attacking on the left flank. When his platoon first came under fire, Sergeant Bober observed a fortified enemy strong point dug in behind the stone walls and manned by at least 30 of the enemy. This strong point was forward of the other rifle companies of the Regiment, and was engaging them with machine gun fire from four machine guns and a number of other automatic weapons. It was essential, therefore, that this enemy locality be destroyed. With the authority of his Company Commander, Sergeant Bober turned over the command of his platoon and then worked forward alone across open ground and up an exposed slope carrying with him a Piat. Throughout his advance of approximately 150 yards he was under concentrated enemy fire from this locality, but he persisted and by skilful fieldcraft reached a position 20 yards from the strong point. He immediately fired five Piat bombs into the position, completely destroying it, inflicting nine casualties (killed) on the enemy. This gallant action allowed another rifle company on the right flank to continue its advance without loss, and although Sergeant Bober was wounded during the action, he returned to his platoon, resumed command, and continued to fight it throughout the battle.
                                    (L.G. 16.3.44)

Bohlen, William Henry, Sergeant
2057831, 246 Fd. Coy., Royal Engineers
This NCO, although wounded in the head, remained at his post in command of his section for three hours after his section officer had been killed (Lieut. Evans). During the whole of this time the portion of the canal bank held by the section was heavily bombarded both by artillery and mortars, and was finally attacked by German infantry who were repulsed. The successful defence of the sector was largely due to Sjt. Bohlen's presence of mind, personal gallantry, and devotion to duty. These events took place on the afternoon of 30 May. *(L.G. 11.7.40)*

Boland, Edgar Frank, Lance Corporal
NX 8670, 2/2 Aust. Inf. Bn.
On the morning of 3 Jan at Bardia after his Pl Commander had been killed and the Pl Sjt. had become detached from the Pl. L/Cpl. Boland assumed command, reorganised the pl and successfully led it throughout the remainder of the day, capturing some 16 gun positions and setting his pl a wonderful example of courage, determination and devotion to duty.   *(L.G. 9.5.41)*

Bollam, Reginald James, M.B.E., Warrant Officer Cl. II (C.S.M.)
5614925, 2nd Bn. Devonshire Regt. (Basingstoke)
(Immediate)
On 1st August 1943 on Regalbuto Ridge the Battalion was heavily counter attacked and temporarily lost the forward end of the ridge. As soon as the enemy advance had been checked 'D' Company was ordered to attack round the right flank. The Company Commander became a casualty almost immediately and the one remaining officer was some distance away on the flank. CSM Bollam at once took command of the Company and drove the enemy off the ridge, personally shooting [...] German machine gunners in doing so. The remaining officer had now become a casualty and CSM Bollam reorganised the Company on the objective under heavy fire from mortars and M.G.s, and held the position until relieved. He showed great bravery under heavy fire throughout the action. *(L.G. 4.11.43)*

Bollands, D., Sergeant
6397264, Royal Sussex Regt.
No citation. *(L.G. 11.7.40)*

Bolton, George, Sergeant
3854511, 1st Bn. Loyal Regt.
On June 1st at Bencous during heavy enemy shelling this NCO displayed complete disregard for his own safety and rendered air to the wounded. Later in the day during a counter-attack on the enemy he showed dash and determination. After rallying a few men he worked his way forward under severe enemy M.G. fire, and inflicted loss on the enemy. Later during the withdrawal of his company he covered his platoon with fire and did not withdraw himself until all were safe. His conduct was of a very high order without. *(L.G. 22.10.40)*

Bolton, William, Sergeant
3709974, 2nd Bn. King's Own Royal Regt. (Bolton)
(Immediate)
On 8th May 1944 No. 2 Platoon 46 Coln was occupying an important hill feature in 'Blackpool' Block. The Comd and two sections were absent on duty leaving Sjt. Bolton and two sections with one section M.M.Gs on the position.

At approx 0100 hrs the position was attacked by enemy estimated at one platoon. In the ensuing battle which lasted 3 hours Sjt. Bolton organised the defence so that the attack was beaten off with estimated enemy losses of 20. At first light he took a party of men forward and recovered the bodies of a Jap Officer and man from whom valuable identifications and information were obtained.

On 11th May 1944, No. 2 Platoon 46 Coln were outside the perimeter wire of Blackpool Block as a fighting patrol and the enemy in dug-in positions were encountered. The Comd. and several men were wounded in the first exchange of shots. Sjt. Bolton with utter disregard for his own personal safety rushed forward to within ten yards of an enemy L.M.G. firing his carbine killing one Jap for certain and quietening the L.M.G. thereby enabling the wounded to escape. He brought back a wounded NCO and then coolly withdrew the remainder of the platoon. On the subsequent roll call it was discovered that two wounded men had left behind 1 L.M.G. and 1 carbine on the enemy post. Sjt. Bolton immediately organised a section and personally led it under enemy fire and recovered the weapons.
(L.G. 31.8.44)

Bond, Bernard John, Corporal
23880355, Special Air Service Regt.
For Oman *(L.G. 25.5.76)*

Boniface, Duncan Joseph, Private
83223, 4 N.Z. Armd. Bde. Wksps., N.Z.E.M.E. Corps
(Periodic)
As driver of a D-8 tractor of the 4 NZ Armd Bd Rec Section, Pte. Boniface has displayed cool courage of a particularly high standard over a long period.

During the advance over the Morro river he proceeded across the river ahead of the tanks to assist them to cross and for the three following nights under heavy mortar and Spandau fire he worked continuously keeping the roads clear and assisting tanks forward.

For a period of weeks he worked under enemy fire every night recovering vehicles and tanks and on more than one occasion he recovered tanks within 300 yards of the enemy under such heavy fire that the crews of the tanks had been withdrawn by the Regt.

At Cassino the cool calculated courage previously displayed was even exceeded. Day after day he recovered tanks in full view of the enemy and under continuous fire and on six different nights he worked on the lateral road between Route 6 and the Railway within earshot of the enemy. Such heavy fire was brought down by the noise of his tractor that the 21 NZ Bn finally refused to allow him to work there any longer owing to the casualties being suffered by the Infantry.

Another job taken in his stride was the recovery of a T-2 P[...] tank belonging to the Americans. Everytime recovery was attempted very heavy fire had been brought to bear on this valuable vehicle and the Americans only abandoned further attempts after suffering casualties.

At the conclusion of the Cassino battle a certain number of tanks were stranded on the steep road north of the Monastry. After the Poles had lost several over a 400 ft cliff in attempting to recover them Eighth Army considered the rest impossible of recovery and instructed that they be blown up. However, Pte. Boniface did not concur in this decision and was largely instrumental in the eventual recovery of these tanks. His courage, skill, endurance and extremely high sense of duty was once again evidenced in the battle of Florence where his work inspired his comrades to such extent that despite heavy tank casualties every tank was recovered within one day of the cessation of heavy fighting.

Throughout the whole of the operations of this Division in Italy Pte. Boniface has displayed energy, endurance and cool courage of an extremely high order and he has so inspired his unit that the tank recovery of 2 NZ Division is unexcelled in Italy.   *(L.G. 21.6.45)*

Booker, Richard John, Warrant Officer Cl. II
*NX 191699, Aust. New Guinea Administrative Unit,
Australian Military Forces (Immediate)*
WOII Booker was a member of Angau party which landed with 2 Sqn (5 Cav 1 US Cav Bde) at Momote, Los Negros Is, Admiralty Group on 29 Feb 44.

After the enemy had attacked our beach head perimeter on the night of 29 Feb—1 Mar, Brig-Gen Chase, comdg General of the landing force, urgently required that a patrol should penetrate the enemy's line to the south of Los Negros in order to ascertain enemy strength, dispositions, artillery locations and ammunition dumps. WO Booker volunteered to lead a patrol and with one member of the RPC he led 10 US troops through the enemy lines to a distance of approx 12 miles. The patrol discovered large dumps of ammunition, located trench and pill box positions and many anti-aircraft and HMG emplacements. The guns were rendered useless by the patrol. WO Booker discovered many enemy documents which proved most valuable, as the comdr of the Task Force was able to gauge the enemy's capabilities and direction of his attack. This enabled the Task Force Comdr to meet the threat on our flank. During the same night the enemy attacked but was repulsed with heavy losses. The knowledge gained by the patrol and the fact that the enemy's guns were rendered useless by the patrol undoubtedly saved the landing force from being wiped out.

On 2 Mar WO Booker accompanied by a single native member of RPC carried out a recce to the 'Skidway'—a tactical point on the right flank of our perimeter. WO Booker succeeded in getting through the enemy's lines and on the roadway which connected the enemy's spearhead to his base at Salami on Seeadler Harbour foreshore. WO Booker located MG emplacements already occupied by the enemy and large ammunition dumps. Position of land mines were noted. WO Booker had to take to the jungle to evade a party of 30 Japanese which was approaching him. He followed a trail and came upon a tent—the occupants of which were temporarily absent. WO Booker crept into the tent which proved to be a unit HQ. He seized as many important looking papers and maps as possible and successfully got through the enemy lines to return to our perimeter. Interpretation discovered that some of the documents gave plans for attack that was to occur that night. That night the enemy made his strongest counter attack on our right flank. The attacking force was wiped out to the last man. Brig-Gen Chase personally commended

Booker and was high in his praise of the work of the 'two-man patrol.'

On the 3, 4 and 5 of Mar, Booker conducted many patrols and brought back much information of enemy strength and locations. A large number of enemy documents were turned in by him. On 5th, he was attached to Col. Kirk of the 5 US Cav Regt which fought their way to Salami and established a beach head on Seeadler Harbour. His knowledge of the local country was of utmost value, when the leading patrol was fired on by the enemy, Booker and one member of the RPC went ahead and caused a diversion. The enemy strong point was overcome by the rest of the patrol.

On 10 Mar, Booker accompanied Capt. Hoggard of Angau to Lemondrol Creek, Los Negros Is. WO Booker became separated from Capt Hoggard but located large ammunition and food dumps with enemy troops present. His prompt and accurate signal back to our lines resulted in our artillery completely destroying the dumps. Later in the day Booker was forced to retreat by a strong enemy patrol. He returned to HQ that night with information of many enemy strong points. The following day Booker took three native scouts and again got through the enemy lines to locate the Japanese HQ in Papitalai Hills. On 18 Mar he landed at Bear Point and crossed the island to reach Laniu village. En route he found a strong force of Japanese securely entrenched in the limestone caves. This was the first indication that was received of the enemy using and enlarging the caves to make a network of tunnels. WO Booker then contacted 300 natives. Despite the presence of the enemy which guarded the Loniu passage from the limestone caves, he contrived to get the entire village population to an evacuation point at the harbour side of the passage. The removal of the civil population from the operations area undoutedly saved many native lives.

On 24 Mar, Prisoners of war were urgently needed by 1 Cav Div. WO Booker proceeded to Tong Is with 12 US Troops and two natives, members of RPC. Booker considered that the presence of white troops would jeopardise his chances of taking prisoners, he therefore sent the 12 soldiers back to Los Negros and with the two natives located 4 armd Japs. WO Booker enlisted the aid of several Tong Is natives and with great skill surrounded the Japanese and captured them after a brief struggle. There were no casualties. After two days the party and prisoners were picked up by a PT boat.

On 4 Apr, WO Booker accompanied a squadron of the 12 Cav Regt to Rembutyo Is. as guide. During the landing, the greater part of the enemy force escaped into difficult hill country. On 6 Apr Booker set out with two natives to track the Japanese force. The small party was ambushed by the enemy who opened fire on them with machine guns and automatic weapons. Booker left the two natives to watch the enemy movements and raced back alone to lead a US patrol back to the spot. Booker led the patrol back but on entering a gorge was again fired on by the enemy. Capt. Crass, US Army was severely wounded in the chest and two others were wounded. Booker volunteered to make his way back to the Sqn HQ so as to have an aircraft or PT boat ready to evacuate the wounded. This he succeeded in doing and again led a party to pick up the wounded. As a result of his action, the badly wounded officer was evacuated in time to save his life. At the request of Brig-Gen Chase, WO Booker again visited Rambutyo Is to plan the final mopping up of the Japanese troops there. On a final patrol Booker killed three Jap soldiers who tried to ambush him. For the second time Brig-Gen Chase commended the WO.

During the campaign, WO Booker displayed a courage and resourcefulness that made his name a byword throughout the American Division. He constantly volunteered for patrol duties without regard for his own safety and his intelligence reports were of great value to our forces. *(L.G. 23.8.44)*

Booth, John Hamilton, Corporal
2824715, Seaforth Highlanders, No. 1 S.B.S.
(Glasgow, S.1.)
For particularly meritorious service in action against an armed German Naval Auxiliary vessel off Suda Bay on the 21st April, 1942, when his courage and skilful shooting with the bren gun were worthy of the highest praise. The words of the official report were as follows:—
'Some really splendid shooting with the bren gun by Corporal J. Booth of the Seaforth Highlanders had been successful in preventing the enemy from manning their foremost gun and he had just (literally) flattened the crew of the midship gun when our first direct hit completely destroyed this gun, which appeared to be blown over the side. Fire from her machine-gun, which had been ineffective, had now ceased and an attempt to man the after gun was frustrated by Corporal Booth, the gun's crew preferring to jump over the stern rather than face the fire of his bren gun.'
On 13th April as lookout this NCO sighted the masts of an enemy ship at great range in the Ionian Sea and on two patrols his keenness to take his share in all the work of the submarine has been most marked and appreciated. His previous service in the flotilla has included the patrol in HMS *Osiris* in January when a complete failure of the shaft lubrication system occurred and Booth worked in two watches to lubricate the bearings by hand for the entire return passage, and a patrol in HMS Thunderbolt in October 1941, when he successfully accomplished his special task and, with Sergeant Sherwood, landed eight agents on the enemy coast. Before this he saw service in the Tenth Submarine Flotilla at Malta, and there is no doubt that Corporal Booth is the best type of NCO to achieve co-operation and good results in combined operations between the services. *(L.G. 5.11.42)*

Bosse, Maurice, Sergeant (actg.)
D.57848, Le Régiment de Maisonneuve (Immediate)
On the ninth of March, during the advance from Zanten, Germany, toward Wesel, Sergeant Bosse was in command of a section of flame-throwing carriers attached to 'C' Company of Le Régiment de Maisonneuve.

'C' and 'D' Companies were to capture a group of houses and a wood to the rear. Before reaching their objectives both companies came under intense enemy machine gun fire and shelling. The fire seemed to be coming mostly from the houses and the edge of the wood and flame throwing tanks which were supporting the attack exhausted their fuel in an unsuccessful attempt to neutralize it.

Appreciating that the entire attack might well fail unless this fire could be stopped, Sergeant Bosse immediately ordered two of his carriers to set fire to the houses while he would take care of the wood alone. As they sped forward Sergeant Bosse, standing, in the front of his carrier, covered their approach with sweeping fire from a Browning machine gun. While doing so he was hit in the left arm by a burst of enemy machine gun fire and his Browning gun ran out of ammunition.

Disregarding his injury Sergeant Bosse ordered his driver to go forward and grabbed his Bren gun with which he continued to fire on the enemy machine gun posts. Although hit again, in the right hand, he did not falter but continued firing.

As they reached the edge of the wood Sergeant Bosse was hit in the stomach, his third wound. He fell in the carrier but in spite of his injuries gathered sufficient strength to fire two shots of flame into the enemy machine gun positions silencing them. His driver then turned the carrier and took him to the Regimental Aid Post.

Meanwhile the other crews, inspired by his leadership and gallant example had managed to neutralize the fire from the houses, and the two forward companies rushed thir objectives successfully overcoming all resistance.

The outstanding bravery and devotion to duty shown by this Non-commissioned Officer throughout this action in which his battalion successfully smashed a German counter-attacking force and over two hundred prisoners were taken, were undoubtedly a decisive factor in the conclusion of the battle. *(L.G. 16.6.45)*

Boughton, Edward, Private
5570076, 2/Wiltshire Regt.
See Bateman, Kenneth William   *(L.G. 4.11.41)*

Bounsall, Denis Arthur Harrison, Bandsman
5725602, 1 Dorsetshire Regt. (Parkstone, Dorset)
(Immediate)
(1) On 19 Jul 43 during the advance towards Agira two rifle Coys came under very heavy mortar fire and machine gun fire from some high ground to the front and flank of their positions. They were pinned to the ground and any further movement became impossible. Under this heavy fire Pte. Boundsall, one of the Bn

Stretcher Bearers, with absolute disregard to his own personal safety, walked about amongst the Coys, dressing and collecting casualties, and brought them back a short distance to the rear, where he placed them under cover of a small bank. He then called in the assistance of more stretcher bearers and personally took control of this small party of stretcher bearers which he had by then collected. Several times he came forward collecting casualties and each time he was subjected to heavy fire. Having seen the last of these casualties evacuated to the R.A.P. he finally returned to his Coy.

(2) *Second Occasion.*

On 21 Jul 43 Pte. Boundsall accompanied a platoon who were sent out on patrol. During the course of this patrol the platoon came under heavy mortar and automatic fire from positions to the flank, and were fored to withdraw. Pte. Boundsall with the assistance of a volunteer went forward across the bullet swept ground and brought back at least four casualties. There was then only one casualty remaining out and unaccounted for. Pte. Boundsall went out by himself for this man whom he did not find until late that evening. He stayed out with him until late that night, dressing his wounds, and eventually carried him back two miles before dawn the following morning where he handed him over to the R.A.P.   *(L.G. 4.11.43)*

Bowditch, James, Sergeant
QX13703, Z Special Unit, Australian Military Forces (Periodic)

From 14 Apr 44 to the cessation of hostilities this NCO has performed outstanding services, calling for the highest degree of courage, leadership and initiative. From 24 Apr to 3 May 45, Sjt. Bowditch was a sub party commander of the Special Operational Party inserted into Tarakan Is. for the purpose of collecting pre-invasion intelligence. With great daring and initiative, Sjt. Bowditch carried out a special patrol to Tg Djorata and located enemy dispositions and coastal artillery.

Between 24 May to 2 Jun 45 Sjt. Bowditch took part in an enemy deception plan in support of 9 Aust Div operation Oboe VI in British North Borneo. Again by his utter disregard for his personal safety, Sjt. Bowditch was of great assistance to the Party Leader and his example was an inspiration to the other members of the party.

On 6 Jul 45, Sjt. Bowditch was a member of a party inserted by parachute in the Manakam River Lakes area of Dutch Borneo to take part in Special Operations. The party remained in the field until 12 Aug '45 during the whole period Sjt. Bowditch was in charge of a sub party of 2 white soldiers and 30 native guerillas. The sub party under the leadership of Sjt. Bowditch carried out many successful patrols to contact native chiefs and destroy enemy food dumps. On 10 Aug '45 Sjt. Bowditch was sent to reinforce a small S.R.D. patrol at the mouth of the Kahala River, which was being heavily engaged by a Japanese patrol sent out from Noketax[?] to liquidate

the party. By his personal courage and leadership, Sjt. Bowditch was mainly instrumental in killing 30 of the Japanese and pinning down the remainder at the mouth of the river where they were later destroyed.

Throughout all the above operations, Sjt. Bowditch has displayed great devotion to duty and courage of the highest order.   *(L.G. 6.3.47)*

Bowen, John, Sergeant
8304764, 52nd Fd. Regt., Royal Artillery

As Battery NCO i/c Signals, he kept the line communications of his battery open throughout operations. Whenever bombing and shelling destroyed the telephone lines, he restored communication, and showed complete disregard of danger by working on his lines under very heavy fire, especially on the perimeter of Dunkirk between May 28th and June 1st.   *(L.G. 11.7.40)*

Boyce, Charles Bernard, Sergeant
4080833, 53rd Reconnaissance Corps (Birmingham 1) (Immediate)

On 27 April 1945 A Troop of 'C' Squadron had received orders to seize the bridge at Kluversborstel 0005 (Germany). This Troop was supported by a section of anti-tank guns commanded by Sjt. Boyce. On arriving at a bend in the road about 800 yards from the bridge, at a point where the road turned to run parallel with the river, the leading car came under observed mortar and spandau fire from a position on a rise on the far side of the river. The armoured cars deployed to their right and returned the enemy fire. Sjt. Boyce also deployed the leading gun and, still under fire from the opposite bank of the river, gave the crew orders for action. When this gun was engaging the enemy position with H.E., Sjt. Boyce returned to his second gun and found that the Number One and the Loader had both been badly wounded in the legs and were unable to get their gun into action. He hastily made a reconnaissance for a suitable position and, replacing the wounded men with others from his headquarter detachment, got the gun into action. The flat and open ground to the right of the road was the only place where the guns could be got into action quickly. This meant that the operation would have to be carried out for some distance in full view of the enemy. This whole area was consequently subjected to continual mortar and machine gun fire from the enemy position on the opposite bank. When satisfied that his guns were effectively engaging the enemy, Sjt. Boyce in full view of the enemy ran to the wounded men and after applying field dressings placed one of the men, whom he realised had a broken leg, on a gate which he found nearby and dragged him back for a distance of 300 yards. He then returned to the second man and as he also had a fractured leg placed him on the gate and dragged him back to safety.

Sjt. Boyce's actions undoubtedly saved the lives of his two men, while he effectively maintained his section of guns in action against the enemy. This contributed largely towards the success of the Troop operation in which the bridge was captured and held. *(L.G. 2.8.45)*

Boyde, Robert Thomas, Warrant Officer Cl. II
2979240, 7th Bn. Argyll & Sutherland Highlanders (Bishopton) (Immediate)
On the night of 24th March 'D' Coy was ordered to attack and capture a large farm south of Bienen which was known to be strongly held. The leading Pl having dealt with the opposition to their front was held up by M.M.G.'s firing from the embankment to the left and the Coy. Comd ordered CSM Boyde to bring up the reserve pl., their Officer having been wounded, and deal with the situation with the assistance of two wasp flamethrowers. CSM Boyde got his pl into a fire posn behind a large bank and under their covering fire ordered the flame throwers to work their way to a ruined building where they could get a good posn to shoot their flame along the embankment. As soon as they fired he led the Pl in a bayonet charge and killed or captured the enemy, who had been manning the spandaus. He then led his Pl on to the objective but they were held up by some snipers firing from a small out-house. CSM Boyde organised covering fire on the windows and himself ran forward and threw two grenades into the building which killed one German and caused the remainder to surrender.

This W.O. handled the Pl and the flame throwers most skilfully under difficult and trying conditions against a very resolute enemy and showed personal courage and initiative far above the average. As a result of his actions the farm was finally captured and a large number of enemy either killed or made prisoner.   *(L.G. 21.6.45)*

Boyle, Gilbert Magnuss, Sergeant
4802362, 1st Bn. Lincolnshire Regt. (Doncaster)
Sjt. Boyle came into the Field as a Platoon Serjeant. After a short period he took over the command of a Platoon and led his platoon in action at Donbaik, Burma, on 18th March, displaying coolness and skill.

He later led his platoon into action at Taungmaw Burma on 28th March. His initiative and skill resulted in his platoon reaching its objective. Later in the day he was surrounded by the enemy and once again his coolness and exceptional control over his men enabled the platoon to remain in position for 7 hours without suffering any casualties. When ordered to rejoin his Company, his brilliant leadership enabled his platoon to get back from a most dangerous position again without the loss of a single man.

Throughout the campaign, Sjt. Boyle's inexhaustible energy, his steadiness under fire, personal courage and really brilliant leadership, have been of inestimable value to his superior commanders and a fine example and encouragement to his men.   *(L.G. 16.12.43)*

Boyle, Gilbert Magnuss, D.C.M., Sergeant (A/Colour Sergeant)   **Bar**
4802362, 1st Bn. Lincolnshire Regt. (Doncaster) (Immediate)
On 7th April, 1944, at Kohima, Burma, C/Sjt. Boyle was ordered to command a pl in an attack on a Jap position, owing to a shortage of pl. commanders. The first objective was taken, and the second objective, about 150 feet higher was still to be tackled. The leading pl suffered heavy casualties in attempting the assault. C/Sjt. Boyle on his own initiative brought up his reserve pl, and on being ordered to assault, led his men up a jungle clad precipice which was covered by enemy fire. He led the way cutting the jungle and making a path, encouraging his men with Battle Cries. At the top, the hill was bare and the enemy brought accurate fire to bear on it. C/Sjt. Boyle found he had only ten men available owing to casualties, and knew that there might be further enemy along the ridge. At once he continued in face of cross fire and ran alaong the open ridge to the end. He took 30 Japs by surprise, who were running out. For 10 minutes he organised accurate fire and killed at least 10 of the enemy himself firing 50 rounds from his rifle. Having turned the enemy off the ridge, he and a L/Cpl. continued down the North slope. This was bare, and a Jap MG opened up on him; he had no cover. He remained in that position, returning the fire for 5 minutes and then withdrew. He organised his men and reported the last objective clear.

During the next 24 hrs, C/Sjt. Boyle's behaviour was outstanding. He repeatedly visited his forward men to give them food and amn every time drawing enemy fire. He assisted in rescuing a wounded man who had been hit by an enemy MG and whilst doing so was under fire. When heavily shelled he remained with his Coy Comd, and went round giving encouragement to his men.

C/Sjt. Boyle's leadership was of the very highest order. He led his men with great gallantry, he held them together by his cheerfulness and amazing example, and when finally ordered to withdraw, he withdrew them in an orderly and efficient manner.

His conduct was an inspiration to his whole Coy. For his rank he showed outstanding skill, a sense of duty and powers of leadership of the very highest order.
    (L.G. 22.6.44)

Bracegirdle, Kenneth Barry, Sergeant
WX.4251, Australian Military Forces
No citation.   *(L.G. 9.9.42)*

Bracewell, Reginald Charles, Corporal (A/Sgt.)
6851044, 2nd Bn. King's Royal Rifle Corps (Tolworth, Surbiton) (Immediate)
For outstanding courage and leadership.

On June 4th at Bir el Hacheim Sjt. Bracewell was in command of a section of 2 Pdr. A/T. gun which was acting as escort to the forward O.P. As they went forward they suddenly came under heavy enemy fire which forced the O.P. to withdraw. Sjt. Bracewell and his section covered this withdrawal, returning the enemy's fire with energy and skill. While this action was in progress one enemy A.P. shell killed the No. 3 and removed Sjt. Bracewell's arm. In spite of this severe injury Sjt. Bracewell continued to engage the enemy, and eventually after the O.P. had withdrawn, successfully brought his section out of action. He has proved himself to be an N.C.O. of the highest courage and exceptional ability.

(L.G. 15.10.42)

Bradfield, Ronald Pierce, Corporal
WX 981, 2/11 Bn., Australian Military Forces
This young NCO was ill with dysentery in the hospital at Malleme, Crete on 19 May 41 when it was captured by German parachutist, and with others was made to walk in front of them. The party was fired on by [...] and in the confusion Cpl. Bradfield escaped, secured a rifle, joined the first Australian unit he saw and fought with them for four days clad only in pyjamas. Cpl. Bradfield escaped with others from Aphakia in a boat [...] which took 10 days to reach Sidi Barrani. The party had nothing to eat at all during the last six days, and on arrival more than half the men had to be carried ashore and taken to hospital. Cpl. Bradfield however returned immediately to his Bn looking cheerful and well. A good example.

(L.G. 4.11.41)

Bradford, Thomas Morton, Corporal
7921285, 1st Lothians & Border Yeomanry (Berwick)
Near Dieteren on 17 Jan 45, Cpl. Bradford was commanding a tank in a troop which had been ordered to flail a path up to a water obstacle and from there to sp by fire the inf attack on Dieteren. When the inf had gone through, the Troop was to cross a scissors bridge and clear a path for a bulldozer up to a second water obstacle. The first part of the operation was successful, but the scissors bridge collapsed as Cpl. Bradford's tank was crossing, leaving only the Bulldozer and his tank on the far side. He duly flailed a path up to the next obstacle and then returned to the first obstacle. A bridge was now being built which brought down heavy enemy artillery and mortar fire, and at 2000 hrs the bulldozer was hit and went on fire. As it was blocking the exit from the bridge, Cpl. Bradford got out of his tank, fixed on the tow-rope and towed the blazing bulldozer clear.

During the night the enemy made three separate attempts to reach the bridge but on each occasion were spotted by Cpl. Bradford, fired on and forced to withdraw.

There was an intermittent ground fog which made firing from a tank at night even more difficult, but he was so accurate, that he was able to shoot H.E. at some flashes he saw with the result that there was a big explosion and cessation of fire from that quarter.

He was, at all times during the night, of the greatest assistance to the R.Es. who were building the bridge, conveying verbal reports and messages, usually under fire, and relaying them through his own wireless back to his Squadron H.Q.

At 1000 hrs next morning armd colns crossed the bridge and carried on with the advance on Echt. It is now known from PW that the enemy made determined efforts to reach and destroy the bridge but were held up by fire from the tank.

The bridge was the only one over this obstacle. It was vital for the success of the whole operation that it should be held, and for a considerable part of the night Cpl. Bradford was its sole defender. Although it was a constant target for the enemy artillery and mortars, Cpl. Bradford remained in close proximity in order to make quite certain that no enemy could approach. In this he was eminently successful and materially contributed to the success of the whole operation. He displayed throughout a sense of responsibility, alertness and determination far above average.   *(L.G. 12.4.45)*

Bradley, David, Sergeant (A/Staff Sergeant)
23910792, Light Infantry
For Northen Ireland   *(L.G. 19.3.74)*

Brahatis, Stanislaus, Sergeant (actg.)
NX101098, 2/8 Aust. Commando Sqn. (Immediate)
On the morning of 26 Feb 45, enemy in strength were found by recce to be occupying a strongly dug in position on the southern bank of Maxwell's Crossing (Ref Rumiki sheet Bougainville 1:25000 Series 917523). The position dominated a main Japanese escape route leading south from Mosigetta area.

Lieut. Maxwell's section was detailed to attack the position. Evidence showed that the Jap defences were new and manned by fresh troops with at least 3 LMGs and 1 Juki. The attacking force was organised in two groups, viz *(a)* Support Group with EY rifles *(b)* Assault Group.

Sjt. Brahatis was in command of the Assault Group.

At 1645 hrs 26 Feb the attack was launched with the assault group advancing under cover of the support group fire. They were faced with an almost sheer 40 ft bank on the crest of which was the enemy. Led by Sjt. Brahatis only 4 men managed to reach the crest, where Brahatis personally cleared the first two enemy positions with hand grenades and Owen gun, exhausting the ammunition. His Bren gunner was wounded and rolled off the bank leaving his gun. Unhesitatingly and under heavy fire, Brahatis raced along the crest, picked up the gun, and using it from the hip, charged two LMG positions and silenced them. Then directing the fire of his two remaining men, he advanced, engaging the Juki in the open at 40 yards range, killing the No. 1 and temporarily silencing the gun. At this stage the barrel of his Bren flew off. Brahatis promptly charged and with his pistol shot a Jap at 6 ft range, recovering the barrel, and again temporarily silencing the Juki. His ammunition ran out and so, covering with his pistol his two remaining men of whom one was wounded, he withdrew his entire force in perfect order with their wounded.

By his action, Sjt. Brahatis practically over ran the position single handed, eliminating 2 LMGs and their crews and twice silencing the Juki. To do this he consecutively used Owen, Bren, grenade and pistol. He personally killed 4 enemy and wounded an unknown number. With the ammunition exhausted he crowned his performance by directing the completely successful evacuation and withdrawal of his force.

His inspired action was far beyond the call of duty. He showed utter disregard for his personal safety, being continuously under heavy fire without cover and twice slightly wounded.

He still remains on duty, and his courage determination and leadership are shining example to his men.
(L.G. 21.6.45)

Brammer, John McAlister, Corporal (A/Sgt.)
NX 152731, 2/6 Aust. Cav. (Commando) Sqn.
(Immediate)
For most conspicuous courage, resourceful leadership and devotion to duty in action at Uria River in the Dumpu area.

On 8 Oct 43 Cpl. Brammer was 2 i/c of a patrol up the Uria River, led by Lieut J. H. Graham. At 1650 hours the patrol was ambushed by a party of enemy securely positioned about 30 feet above our troops firing 3 LMGs, rifles and grenades at less than 70 yards range. The patrol leader and one man were killed and another wounded almost immediately. When Cpl. Brammer who had been sent to a flank got back to the patrol, he found it in a desperate situation. By quick resource he got the patrol under cover while he himself with three others kept the enemy under fire. Seeing the main party clear he courageously exposed himself to heavy fire on open ground, while he ascertained that the officer and man were dead, and secured their personal effects which may have been of value to the enemy. He then withdrew the remainder of the patrol. The withdrawal was so successfully carried out over open ground, commanded by enemy fire that only one additional casualty was incurred. This man who was unable to move himself was moved under fire to safety by Cpl. Brammer and Pte. Little, and part carried, part floated, down the river for about 400 yards, when Cpl. Brammer so splinted and dressed a compound fractured leg as to win high praise from Sqn M.O. when the patrol and casualties got safely back to the Sqn base. The patrol killed or severely wounded at least four enemy in action. *(L.G. 20.1.44)*

Bramwell, Harold Joseph, Sergeant
62490, 21 N.Z. Bn. (Immediate)
On the night 23/24 Oct 42 at Miteiriya Ridge, Sjt. Bramwell rallied his men when they were badly shaken by heavy Mortar fire and led them to their objective. While moving forward the platoon ran into an enemy MG nest. Sjt. Bramwell, using two sections to engage

the enemy, worked round to a flank and rushed the post with the third, killing several of the enemy and capturing one heavy and two light MGs.

On the night 24/25 Oct he took out a fighting patrol and captured an enemy post which had been machine gunning their position during the day, capturing 2 MGs and ten prisoners. Sjt. Bramwell's conduct in this and earlier engagements has always been an inspiration to his men. *(L.G. 28.1.43)*

Branch, Alfred John, Sergeant (actg.)
5961370, 1st Bn. Hertfordshire Regt. (Hoddesdon)
(since died of wounds) (Immediate)
For conspicuous gallantry and devotion to duty at Banzuolo Ridge on 11 Oct 44.

On the night 10/11 Oct 1 Coy was ordered to capture and hold a prominent feature known as Banzuolo Ridge. The enemy were believed to be in some farm buildings at Pt 528 at the Eastern end of the feature and in another farm at Pt 412 at Western end.

At approximately 0230 hrs on the 11 Oct the leading platoon came under heavy MG fire from the area of the buildings at Pt 528. They replied, and the enemy brought down defensive fire which pinned the leading platoon to the ground.

Sjt. Branch who commanded the Reserve Platoon of 1 Coy was ordered to do a flanking attack on Pt 528. Time was short, and Sjt. Branch quickly assembled his platoon in the bright light of a waning moon, and despite heavy mortar and artillery fire, led them safely to the forming up positions.

Sjt. Branch personally led the assault, which was supported by fire from the remaining platoon. As he approached within twenty five yards of the objective a Spandau opened up on his advancing men (by this time his covering fire had ceased). Quickly locating the post, Sjt. Branch doubled forward and silenced it with a grenade, then shouting to his section commanders to follow his example he threw his remaining 77 and 36 grenades into the farm buildings which caught fire.

By his prompt action he succeeded in completely demoralising the enemy who hurriedly withdrew. The advance of the Coy continued and by daylight the Eastern end of the objective had been gained. There can be no doubt that the ultimate success of the attack was primarily due to this NCO's inspiring leadership and complete disregard for his own personal safety. *(L.G. 10.5.45)*

Brand, James Edward, Lance Sergeant
2364346, Royal Signals (Darlington, Yorks)
No citation. *(L.G. 23.3.44)*

Brann, Curtis, Warrant Officer Cl. III (Pl.S.M.)
23759, Wiltshire Regt.
No citation. *(L.G. 27.8.40)*

Brant, Bert, Sergeant
6092085, 2/7 Queen's Royal Regt. (Bilston, Staffs.)
(Immediate)
On 27 Oct 43 'B' Coy 2/7 Queen's was ordered to clear
the West side of the River [...]one near Montanaro. By
the morning of 28 Oct 43 a bluff overlooking the sunken
lane which formed the Western approach to the crossing
had been gained.

On 28 Oct 43 Sjt. Brant's Platoon crossed the river
by Reconnaissance Boats under artillery support and
despite confusion caused by shellfire in the area of the
crossing, gained his first objective—a bluff overlooking
the sunken lane. He proceeded to his next objective in
the face of heavy automatic fire and, despite several
casualties, used his automatic weapons with great effect
to work his way forward by bounds. The Platoon on his
right was held up, but he continued to advance steadily
against increasing opposition, until forced to withdraw
owing to his exposed position.

This skilful infiltration deep into the enemy defences
had a great part in forcing the enemy to withdraw soon
afterwards and contributed greatly to the establishment
of Montanaro bridgehead. Sjt. Brant's cool leadership
and very fine handling of his platoon gave great
confidence to his men, who openly expressed their
admiration of his bearing and devotion to duty throughout
the action.   *(L.G. 10.2.44)*

Bray, Joseph Albert, Private
C52868, Canadian Infantry Corps
No citation.   *(L.G. 7.4.45)*

Bray, Wallace, M.M., Lance Sergeant
5445070, 2 Duke of Cornwall's Light Infantry
(Cheltenham) (Immediate)
On the night 20/21 Nov, 1944, an attempt was made to
establish a bridgehead (386209) across the River Cosina.
Civilians had reported that the near bank of the river
was protected by a belt of mines, to a depth of some 50
yards, running the entire length of our front. On the far
bank were a number of known enemy positions and there
was every indication that there were tanks in support of
his forward infantry. The river, in itself, presented a
difficult infantry obstacle and the approaches to it were
covered by very heavy arty and M.G. defensive fire.

L/Sjt. Bray, MM, was acting as Pl Sjt. of one of the
leading Pls of 'A' Coy., 2 D.C.L.I. The Pl comd became
a casualty in the minefield, and very heavy enemy fire
came down in the immediate area causing the men to go
to ground. L/Sjt. Bray, who was at the rear, dashed to
the head of the Pl and took charge. He got the men going,
led them through the minefield under heavy M.G. fire,
across the river and attacked the first objective. The
enemy put in a counter-attack supported by two tanks.
L/Sjt. Bray seized the Pl P.I.A.T. and scored a hit with
his first shot, causing both tanks to withdraw. The
counterattack was repulsed, and thereafter neither tank
made any attempt to leave its hide and molest our troops.

It was entirely due to L/Sjt. Bray's courage, initiative
and leadership that the Pl was able to gain and to hold its
objective.   *(L.G. 26.4.45)*

Breakey, Frank Keam, Warrant Officer Cl. II
(C.S.M.)
H100061, Canadian Infantry Corps
No citation.   *(L.G. 24.1.46)*

Brennan, Thomas, Gunner
900926, 288 Fd Bty., 124th Fd Regt. (N) T.A., Royal
Artillery (Newcastle-on-Tyne) (Immediate)
On the night of the 'Gazala' 'Break-out' on June 14/
15th Dvr Brennan was driving an Armd O.P. After dark
further effective Arty support was impossible and Dvr
Brennan's Carrier found itself with our own forward
troops still attacking. Our Infantry were held up by a
number of very active hostile weapon posts. As Bren
Carriers were scarce at that time and were employed
elsewhere, Dvr Brennan took it upon himself to use his
Armd O.P. as a light tank, and at once charged a firing
A/Tk gun, and crushed it. Wheeling about he charged
and overran another weapon post of Light Automatics.
Through this cool and daring action (although his role
as O.P. driver did not require him to do so) he enabled
the infantry to get ahead in this part of the advance. Later
that night he extracted two ditched Bren Carriers under
a hail of automatic and M.G. fire and enabled them to go
into action again. Later he found a Staff car which had
broken down just outside an enemy tank leager. He took
the Staff car in tow and brought it through the leager.
After towing it for 30 miles he repaired it and got it on
the road again.   *(L.G. 5.11.42)*

Bridgeman, Alfred George, Colour Sergeant (actg.)
5338566, 2/6th Bn. Queen's Royal Regt. (Hornsey
Rise) (Immediate)
On the 14 Apr 45, this NCO's Company were ordered
to capture two houses as a preliminary to our advance
on the village of Bindella. To reach these houses the
Company had to cross a bottle neck formed by two canals
with very open country on both sides. This bottle neck
was covered by an enemy SP gun and a spandau. Sjt.
Bridgman with his platoon Piat group was in position to
cover the advance of another platoon, under smoke, onto
the first house. Having accomplished this he had to catch
up with his own platoon who were advancing onto the
second house. To do this he had to advance across 300
yards of open country at a time when the smoke screen
had lifted and the ground was covered by a spandau.
When crossing the road with his Piat group and the
reserve section to join the other two sections of his
platoon, who were already across, the enemy SP gun
fired HE into the 77 grenade smoke screen he was using
to cover his crossing, killing three men and wounding
another and also damaging his last Piat bombs.

During the whole time that his platoon were in
position on their objective Sjt. Bridgman recrossed this

open stretch of ground under fire six times to get support from the other platoon, fetch ammunition and more Piats. As all the 77 grenades had been expended, he had no smoke to cover him and the journey was almost suicidal, especially as he could not move fast when laden with ammunition. At his first attempt he took one man with him to help carry the amn but this man was immediately killed and Sjt. Bridgman from then on made all the crossings by himself, in spite of the spandau and SP gun which were repeatedly causing casualties in his platoon. There is no doubt that his personal example and the fact that he arrived with amn at a time when nearly all grenades had gone and the remaining brens had only two magazines left, was very largely responsible for keeping his platoon in a very unpleasant position after a long march and a severe knock taken during the attack.
(L.G. 23.8.45)

Briggs, Charles Thomas, Warrant Officer Cl. II (C.S.M.) (A/W.O.I (R.S.M.))
5378508, 7 Oxfordshire & Buckinghamshire Light Infantry (Lowestoft) (Immediate)
This W.O. acted as RSM during the period 15-21 Feb 44 when the Bn was surrounded and over-run by superior enemy forces. On the night 19/20 Feb 44 only small elements of the Bn remained in a perimeter formed round Bn HQ. Attacks on the perimeter were incessant and from all directions, and mortar and artillery fire heavy. After one of the many attacks the enemy established himself in a strong position behind a disabled tank, from where he could bring to bear accurate and heavy fire on the remaining positions at close range. CSM Briggs, realising the urgency of the situation quickly and under heavy fire organised a small party for a counter-attack. Regardless of his personal safety he encouraged his small party and led them to the assault. Enemy fire increased in intensity in a desperate effort to annihilate this gallant party, but the example and courage displayed by this W.O. fired his part with such determination to close with the enemy, that they charged and the enemy fled in disorder. The example set by this W.O. was of the very highest order and an inspiration to all. The successful holding of the last vital position at Regtl HQ against such great odds was due in no small degree to his outstanding conduct. *(L.G. 15.6.44)*

Briggs, George Stanley, Warrant Officer Cl. III (T.S.M.)
543103, 15/19 Hussars, Royal Armoured Corps
My Squadron was surrounded by German infantry at Brusselghem, between Brussels and Louvain, on 18 May 40 and, when our ammunition was exhausted, we had no alternative but to surrender. With other P/W I was marched to Louvain, where we entrained for Bocholt. Here I remained for twelve days in Stalag VI F. Our equipment, including steel helmets, were taken from us on capture. At Bocholt we were searched and all our money and personal property confiscated, including spare

clothing such as scarves and cardigans. Our Army pay books were inspected and returned to us.

On 1 June 40 British P/W were taken across Germany by train in closed cattle trucks. No provision of food or blankets was made for this three days' journey, apart from a stop outside Berlin, when soup was given out.

On 3 June we arrived at Thorn and were placed in Stalag XXA (3) the reception and main Camp. From here I was taken to Fort 13, a mile from the railway station (the hospital is in this fort), later to Fort 12, another mile further on, and finally to Fort 17, which is close to Fort 13.

On arrival at the last Camp I was searched but allowed to retain my pay book and personal property. We were not interrogated. No issue of clothing was made during my stay.

Conditions were very bad. P/W, who slept on mattresses on the floor, were so closely packed that everyone soon became plagued with lice. Food was insufficient, the daily ration of mouldy bread being 400 grams per man. There was also a lack of fresh drinking water and many P/W were in hospital with stomach troubles. Discipline at first slack was later tightened up as British P/W were not easy to handle. All letters were censored. Rooms were rarely searched. During my stay of seven weeks no parcels arrived or were distributed. P/W were sent out to work, but as an NCO, I did not do so. Roll call was taken at 0700 and 1900 hours. The camp was invariably floodlit at night. P/W of Irish extraction were removed after identification.

On 21 July 40 I was taken, with 149 others, to a working camp at Winduga (Stalag SS Z) (?), where as senior NCO I was made Camp Leader. Six days later, having acquired a sailor's pull-over and a suit of overalls from a Polish carpenter, who came into the Camp, I escaped at dusk with 5302 Petty Officer Maurice Barnes of H.M. Submarine Seal. Working camps, at that period, only had a single wired fence and it was comparatively easy to get through. Men were continually getting out but were usually rounded up after a few hours liberty. We headed S.E. with the intention of making for Roumania and, the first two days lived on raw potatoes. A search for water obliged us to approach houses. We carefully avoided houses carrying wireless aerials, as we knew that the Poles were not allowed to have receiving sets and argued that evidence of wireless indicated German occupants.

The Polish inhabitants, on learning that we were British, made us very welcome and advised us to make for Russia. We were passed on, from farm to farm, until we came to Warsaw (by way of Plonsk). Here we met an organisation, composed of Polish ex-officers and headed by a former General, who looked after us and guided us, through Melkinica, to the Polish—Russian frontier, which we reached on 9 Sep 40. Our escort to this point (sent by the Organisation) was armed, but we did not see any German patrols. We left our helpers once we got into the stretch of no-man's land between German and Russian occupied Poland. On approaching the Russian sentries we were fired on, and both of us fell flat. I heard Barnes groaning but was immediately seized by the Russians and marched off and did not see Barnes again. I heard later that he had been hit in the leg and was taken to a Russian hospital. I believe the N.A. Moscow is investigating his case. I spent a short while in prison at Belostok and then was taken to the Luvianko prison in Moscow, where I remained until Jan 41. Conditions were indescribable as the prison was overcrowded with Poles, food was scarce and bad, and there was inadequate provision for heating and washing. In the early part of Feb I was taken to an internment camp at Micrurin near Smolensk, where I met the other 13 O.Rs who had escaped and where conditions were slightly better.

Here we were kept until 22 June when the Germans invaded Russia and we were put on a train said to be going to Siberia. On about 26 June the train was halted and all of us (British) were taken off, embraced by the guards and then sent back to Moscow, where we were given quarters in a small hotel and given good rations. On 8 July we were released and handed over to our Embassy.   (*L.G. 4.11.41*)

Bright, Frederick Gordon, Private
WX 4186, 2/16 Aust. Inf. Bn.

This soldier revealed outstanding courage and resourcefulness during the attack on Damour River on 6 Jul 41. This sig in company with sigs Cpl. Bremner & Pte. Hickey set out at 0130 hrs with fd telephones, cable, & a 108 pack wireless set to provide comn between HQ & coys at earliest time possible. They were pinned down at various times & were subjected to very heavy enemy fire under which on one occasion the wire was cut by shrapnel & was repaired by this party in full view of the enemy. During this period comn was maintained by this party with HQ & valuable infm was transmitted in respect to what could be seen of the enemy's activities. This party carried on with their hazardous duties from 0130 to 2200 hrs & during most of this period were subjected to vigorous MG fire by enemy snipers as well as arty barrages.

On the morning of 9 Jul 41 at 1000 hrs Pte. F. G. Bright, together with Pte. J. A. Woods, was ordered to lay telephone cable from Adv HQ 2/16 Aust. Inf. Bn. to the Mosque, on the south side of the Litani river. Pte. Bright immediately came under shell fire from enemy destroyers, but he continued with his task until he reached the Mosque. From this point, accompanied by Pte. Woods he decided to cross the Litani river. He was under fire continuously from MGs and snipers. On crossing the river he commenced laying cable, still under fire, until he reached a point in vicinity of the fwd coys. Capt. D. J. Horley and an arty FOO took over this telephone the location of which, made it possible to direct effective fire on many MG and mortar nests. The outstanding courage of Pte. Bright, his coolness under fire and his

conception of his duty were a material factor in the successful crossing of the Litani River by our forces.

Pte. Bright is recommended for the immediate award of the Military Medal.
Recommended for M.M.   (*L.G. 12.2.42*)

Brisson, Maurice, Private
G21012, Carlt. & York Regt., Canadian Infantry
   Corps

During the course of an attack on 18 Jul 43 on Spot Height (762) South East of Enna in Sicily it became imperative that an M.G. post be assaulted. As the Platoon was being otherwise engaged, the Platoon Comdr & his batman & Pte. Brisson advanced on this post and in the course of the Advance the Platoon Comdr was killed & the batman critically injured. Pte. Brisson showing great bravery, complete disregard for his own life, and devotion to duty carried on with the assault and got to the rear of the post and shot two of the enemy there & killed the third with the butt of his rifle. The wiping out of this post permitted the two other sections to advance and achieve their objective.   (*L.G. 23.9.43*)

Brittlebank, John, Bombardier
930882, Royal Artillery, No. 3 & 8 Commando & 1
   S.B.S.

On the night of the 5th of September 1942, Bombardier Brittlebank accompanied Captain Wilson in a folbot to make an attack with experimental torpedoes on an enemy ship in Crotone harbour.

The craft was so skilfully manœuvred into position by Bombardier Brittlebank that it remained undetected in spite of the dangerously calm water within the harbour.

After the attack had been delivered, the folbot party succeeded in withdrawing from the harbour, although by this time the enemy were actively hunting for them. This enemy activity prevented HM Submarine P.42 from keeping the agreed rendezvous, and so Bombardier Brittlebank and Captain Wilson were forced to spend the night at sea in their craft which gradually became damaged by the sea as the weather deteriorated. This fact obliged them to beach the folbot in order to carry out some necessary repairs before setting a course for Malta, some 250 miles distant. In doing so, both Captain Wilson and Bombardier Brittlebank were detected and captured. Captain Wilson reports that throughout the operation Bombardier Brittlebank's conduct and reactions to the varying circumstances left nothing to be desired, and that during the interrogations subsequent to his capture, he set a fine example of reticence. When told that he was to be shot at dawn, his only request was that he might be granted permission to write to his next-of-kin.

This non-commissioned officer previously had taken an active part in the raid on Field Marshal Rommel's Headquarters and had succeeded in finding his way back to his unit after being 40 days in the desert behind the enemy lines. His selection for this further difficult and dangerous task in Crotone harbour appears to have been thoroughly justified. I consider that his determination and devotion to duty on this occasion were well worth the award for which I now recommend him.

(L.G. 20.12.45)

Broad, Thomas Harold, Sergeant
408913, 5th Royal Inniskilling Dragoon Guards (Hereford) (Immediate)

On 17 Apr 45 4 DG and 7/9 RS were given the task of clearing the 7 Armd Div Cl between Walstrode and Soltau. Owing to the close nature of the country, with thick woods in which gps of inf with spandaus, bazookas and some a.tk guns were operating progress during the early part of the day was slow.

In the early afternoon the adv was held up by a.tk guns and inf dug in north of Mittelstendorf 3885, the leading veh of the recce tp having been knocked out by a.tk gun fire. 3 Tp Recce Sqn was ordered to recce and alternative route further to the East through Messhausen 4086. PW reports indicated that the village of Tetendorf 4188 was an enemy strong pt incl at least one a.tk gun and that the woods SW of the village were occupied by inf with pzfaust. Sjt. Broad was comd of the ldg veh of the patrol.

Although fully aware of the danger to his lt veh this NCO worked fwd with the greatest boldness and confirmed the presence of parties of enemy to the east of the rd. He by-passed these gps and reached the SW edge of the Tetendorf woods. While halted in observation he heard veh mov and then spotted a small party of Germans mov East towards Tetendorf. With great promptness he changed posn, engaged and destroyed the leading veh and killed one German offr and two other ranks. He then continued his adv in spite of the danger from pzfaust and reached the crossroads west of Tetendorf, thus outflanking the enemy posn on the main Cl. Here he est himself, maintained observation on the approaches to Soltau in spite of incessant sniping and continually engaged and dominated the enemy in the woods to his rear and east of the road until B Sqn and a coy of 7/9 RS passed through the route he had opened and entered Soltau.

Although mounted in a lt tk working in close country and under constant threat from pzfaust teams Sjt. Broad showed the greatest courage, coolness and contempt for danger throughout the op. By his energy, initiative and resource in opening and keeping open this new route, turning the flank of the enemy's main posn, he was personally responsible for enabling a sqn of tks and coy of inf to penetrate the town of Soltau from an unexpected quarter, in consequence of which the remaining perimeter defs were quickly overcome.

Recommended for M.M. *(L.G. 2.8.45)*

Broadbent, Albert Glen, Trooper
M.104610, 29 Cdn. Armd. Recce Regt. (S. Alta. R.) (Immediate)

On 29 Jan 45 two tks of A Sqn 29 Cdn Armd Recce Regt with under comd one Stuart tk from RHQ were supporting the inf in an attack on a strong enemy posn in the dyke at Kapelsche Veer, MR 098497 Holland Sheets 10 NW & SW, series GSGS 4427. Tpr. Broadbent was gnr in the tp leader's tk. At approx 0400 hrs 30 Jan 45 the tks and inf were working fwd to an intermediate objective along the south side of the dyke when the inf came under hy mortar and MG fire and were forced to withdraw. During this action the tp leader, Lt. Kennedy, was wounded by an enemy sniper and Tpr. Broadbent, acting on his own initiative, took over comd of the tp.

He successfully laid down covering fire for the withdrawal of the inf, covered the other tks out and finally withdrew his own tk to evac Lt. Kennedy to the inf RAP. His orders to his tp were clear and concise, and he had complete control of the situation at all times, despite the fact that he was constantly being sniped at from very close range. At 0700 hrs Lt. Hill came fwd to take over comd of the tp and at 0800 hrs the inf made another attack, sp by the tks. Tpr. Broadbent's tk came up over the dyke and he spotted enemy mov. Without hesitation he ordered the tk to halt, indicated the enemy to Lt. Hill, and proceeded to engage them. Five prisoners were taken by the inf at this pt. Later interrogation of one PW, a S/Sjt., whose statement is att, proved that the alertness and initiative demonstrated by this OR resulted in the complete destruction of one enemy pl. Again hy mortar fire forced the inf to dig in two hundred yds short of the objective from which pt a further attack with inf, tks and flame throwers was planned to take place at 1430 hrs. Owing to a misunderstanding of orders, the flame-thrower and one tk started the attack too soon. Lt. Hill was out of his tk at inf HQ and Tpr. Broadbent was again in comd of the tp. He immediately contacted his Sqn Comd, explained the situation and was ordered to move fwd to give sp and keep the enemy down until the inf could be sent in. He took control of the tp and moved them fwd so effectively that the inf were able to follow along and firm up on the objective before last light. After dark the enemy put in a hy counter-attack and the pl on the objective was forced to withdraw. Tpr. Broadbent, who had remained in comd of the tp when Lt. Hill became a cas, maint his tks in posn, keeping up a covering fire in front of the posn, until the inf were clear. He then withdrew to a posn behind the dyke and continued to harrass the enemy posns. The following morning, when a new tp came fwd to take over the tks, Tpr. Broadbent sent his men out, but remained behind to take the new offr around on foot and indicate all the known enemy posns. Throughout this entire action Tpr. Broadbent showed the greatest initiative and leadership. On three separate occasions he took over the tp and comd it with such skill that severe losses were inflicted upon the enemy forces. The courage and complete disregard for personal safety shown by this OR was far beyond the call of normal duty. His leadership and the skilful manner in which he emp his forces was undoubtedly a major factor leading to the final success of this op.

PW Statement

Herewith is a complete description of the commendation mentioned in the sidelined passage of the enclosed Isum. PW is Stab Feldwebel Heinrich Fischer comd 3 pl 9 coy of 17 Para Regt in the brhead. He is an old soldier describing himself as militarily a fox and his praise for the tk comd in question is prompted by 'a soldier's admiration of a good job well done,' even though in this case it accounted for most of his pl. This particular tk appeared on the 30 Jan approx at 109494 several hundred yards from his own slit trench. It manœuvred into posn in a small bend in the dyke from where it could depress its guns sufficiently to rake the north slope of the dyke with MG fire. PW states that the other tks, which he believes were two in number, made no attempt to get into a favourable posn and consequently were prevented from using their armament effectively. The first tk, however, was painfully alert for mov. PW caught only a fleeting glimpse of the tk comd searching the ground with binoculars but the slightest attempt to leave the slit trench brought down an immediate burst of MG fire. Most of his pl being young and inexperienced were betrayed by their own carelessness and were picked off one by one with what PW describes as sniper accuracy. PW believes this tk responsible for the total of 17 killed and 5 wounded in his pl.   *(L.G. 21.4.45)*

Brockbank, James, Private
4546440, 2nd East Yorkshire Regt. (Preston)
(Immediate)
During the assault on the beaches at La Brèche, France, on 6 Jun 44, this soldier landed with an assault coy of his Battalion. The beach was under heavy mortar, MG, and artillery fire and the coy suffered many casualties, making it difficult to deal with the fixed defences. This soldier took command of a number of men whose leaders were casualties and led them against the fixed defences. He showed great initiative and was fearless under fire, leading his party from one objective to another, until finally the beach objective was cleared. At the last pillbox this soldier went forward alone, broke open the door, and single-handed killed the three enemy occupying it. It was largely due to his action that the beach objective was captured.   *(L.G. 31.8.44)*

Brooke, Harry, Warrant Officer Cl. II (C.S.M.)
2319013, Force 133 M.E.F., Royal Signals
In Crete before the occupation he was taken prisoner during the campaign and later escaped. He remained in the Island and joined our mission, rendering very valuable service through his knowledge of the terrain and language which he had acquired.

Withdrawn from Crete in the Summer of 1942, he returned to the field in June 1943. During the whole time he has been in enemy-occupied territory he has shown unfailing devotion to duty under difficult and often dangerous conditions. When under enemy fire in circumstances of extreme danger his cool courage and resourcefulness had been an example to all present.

He distinguished himself especially on the 3rd Oct. 43 when his station was surrounded and all were in imminent danger of capture. By his personal example under heavy fire he rallied the party, organised their escape through the enemy lines. Thereafter, regardless of danger he returned and succeeded in saving his W/T set and all station stores including explosives and records before the place was overrun by the Germans.

He is recommended for an award of the DCM.
                    (L.G. 4.1.45)

Brooks, John William, Warrant Officer Cl. II (C.S.M.)
4263339, 2nd Bn. Royal Northumberland Fusiliers
For conspicuous gallantry and devotion to duty at all times during the action of the B.E.F. in retiring from Belgium. This Warrant Officer commanded his platoon with great initiative, courage and cool headedness during the whole action. His conduct was an example to his men, which kept them going, although tired and hungry. His cool thinking saved what might have been a serious situation on the Canal near Wolveringham, when he organised a successful counter attack with three men from his platoon and the remains of an infantry platoon.
                    (L.G. 20.12.40)

Brooks, Richard Leonard Lancelot, Warrant Officer Cl. II
2010, 4 N.Z. Fd. Regt. (Periodic)
In Jan 1944 'D' Tp was short of officers and the Tp was detailed to a sniping section about 1000 yards from the FDLs at Orsogna. WOII Brooks acted as GPO to this forward section and displayed courage and skill in this difficult duty.

In Feb 1944 at Cassino he was again called on to perform officers duty. On one occasion while the Tp position was being heavily shelled by 170 mm's two gunners were wounded. Disregarding his own safety, he carried the wounded men to the stretcher Jeep and drove them himself to the RAP.

In Jun 1944 on the advance up the Atina—Balsorano valley, WOII Brooks was acting as BSM. Ammunition supply was difficult owing to continued movement and the road from Sora forward was under shellfire for long periods. Due to his untiring work day and night, he maintained the service to the guns, many times bringing his amn up the road under fire.

During the advance from San Donata to Florence WOII Brooks again acted as BSM. His untiring efforts in maintaining and servicing the guns resulting in the smooth running of his Battery. At times he worked for two to three days and nights without rest in order to accomplish this.

At all times during his long service, WOII Brooks has displayed skill at his job. He was an excellent No. 1 and by his energy earned accelerated promotion. His cheerfulness, personality and outstanding courage under difficult conditions have been an inspiration to his men. His exceptional devotion to duty has been a wonderful contribution to the smooth running of his Battery.

(L.G. 21.6.45)

Broome, William Wilfred, Sapper
A.19124, 7 Cdn. Fd. Coy., Corps of Royal Canadian Engineers
On 26 April 1945 7 Canadian Field Company, Royal Canadian Engineers was supporting the advance of 5 Canadian Infantry Brigade from Delmenhorst towards Oldenburg. Number 3 Platoon of 7 Field Company was ordered to support the Calgary Highlanders whose objectives were the villages of Gruppenbuhren and Bulterei. The infantry had attained their objectives, but the main road between the two towns had not been completely cleared of mines and road blocks. This road had to be completed as quickly as possible in order to permit supporting tanks and carriers to move up to the forward positions. Number 3 Platoon was still on the job. Mines had been encountered on the roads and verges and around two road blocks. Sapper Broome was detector man with number 9 section working up the road when, at approximately 2015 hours enemy shellfire came down very close to the sapper party. The five men in Broome's party naturally stepped towards the ditch for cover and in doing so, Sapper Broome stepped on a mine. 'S' mines had been found previously and by the fact that only the 'jumping' charge was detonated, the nature of this mine was made known to the sapper.

Instead of throwing himself into the ditch for protection before the final charge exploded, Sapper Broome remained exactly where he was, in a crouching position, and allowed the mine to explode under his leg.

The remaining four men of his party were all within 10 yards of Broome; yet none were in any way injured by the explosion of this 'S' mine. By his unselfish action Sapper Broome undoubtedly saved his companions from serious injury or possible death while the cost to him was the loss of his lower left leg.

Statement by L/Cpl Bewlay, R. S.
I, L51530, L/Cpl. Bewlay R.S., was with the section on the evening of 26 Apr 45 in support of the Calgary Highlanders 5 Cdn Inf Bde. Spr Broome was a member of my section, and while moving up the road we came under enemy shellfire. We took to the ditch for protection and Sapper Broome landed on an 'S' mine. With great presence of mind he held his foot on the mine holding it in the ground. This action in all possibility saved the lives of myself and three more of our section.
Statement by A19151 L/Sjt. Bentley S. H.
On the evening of Thursday, 26 Apr 45, the section of which I was in charge was clearing roads and verges in support of the Calgary Highlanders. We were finding

many mines of various types. Sapper Broome was a member of the detector party.

The enemy commenced to shell the area, and it became necessary for the party to take cover. On doing so Sapper Broome rolled onto an 'S' mine, but with great presence of mind remained lying on it thus stopping the mine from functioning properly and leaving the rest of the party uninjured at the expense of his leg.

I was a few yards ahead of Sapper Broome's party and observed the incident and have no doubt that Sapper Broome's action saved the rest of the party from injury and possible death.
Statement by C90056 Spr. McDonald G. T.
I, C90056, Spr. McDonald G. T., was a member of the party engaged in sweeping verges for mines in support of the Calgary Highlanders on the night of 26 Apr 45 when A19124 Spr. Broome W. W. stepped on an 'S' mine. Realizing the danger to those around him, Sapper Broome threw himself on the mine which exploded under him. The explosion threw me to the ground, but Sapper Broome remaining on the mine saved me certain serious injury.
Recommended for B.E.M., then G.C. *(L.G. 22.9.45)*

Brown, Frank Maurice, Private
4801400, Army Catering Corps [1st Bn The Lincolnshire Regt. on AFW 3121] (Lincoln)
At Taungmaw, Burma, on the 28th March, 1943, Pte. Brown, the Company Cook, volunteered to accompany his Coy which was under strength, into action, when it put in an attack on the enemy occupying a ridge. His platoon having gained its objective, remained in position, while Pte. Brown accompanied his officer forward for 100 yards to ascertain if the enemy were still in position further forward. The enemy were surprised and Pte. Brown was responsible for killing at least three of them personally. Heavy fire was directed at this party and it withdrew. Pte. Brown regardless of his own safety, remained in position until he had covered his Officer back to the platoon. Later, Pte. Brown was ordered to take over command of his section owing to his platoon comd. becoming a casualty. Whilst in command, his section was counter-attacked, but Pte. Brown, himself standing up in the face of heavy small arms fire and throwing many grenades, so directed the fire of his section that the attack was repulsed and his section was responsible for killing at least six of the enemy.

The same afternoon, having been ordered to withdraw, Pte. Brown's section was the last to leave the ridge, which was then under heavy L.M.G. fire. Having ensured that all his men had gone back, Pte. Brown himself remained on the ridge to cover his Officer back. Having withdrawn, Pte. Brown learned that the Coy wireless set had been left on the ridge. He went back and recovered it under heavy fire.

His coolness, personal gallantry and determination to close with the enemy, set an example to the other men of his platoon, the value of which could not be too highly estimated. *(L.G. 30.9.43)*

Brown, George Henry, Lance Corporal
6913435, 2nd Bn. Rifle Brigade
This NCO accompanied Lt. C. H. Liddell on two reconnaissane patrols on the nights 2/3 December 1940 and 7/8th December. He and one other NCO crawled right up to the enemy defences, which had sentries posted about 50 yards apart. He got through these and scaled the wall of the defences and got inside the camp. He then crept back again and was thus able to bring very valuable information about the size and strength of the defences and location of A/Tk mines. Again on the night 7/8th he managed to crawl up to another side of the camp and get up very close. He was able to report a gap in the defences closed by night by enemy tanks, which was of the greatest value. These two patrols took a very long time and required endless patience, skill and courage in eluding the watchfulness of the sentries.
Recommended for M.M.   *(L.G. 25.4.41)*

Brown, George Meldrum, Sergeant
2754751, 2 Black Watch (Kirkcaldy) (Immediate)
On 21 Nov 41 in the bn attack on Tiger from the Tobruch perimeter, Sjt. Brown as pl Sjt. and finally Pl Comd of the left fwd coy, showed the most conspicuous and continuus gallantry and tenacious devotion to duty. When all his Coy officers were casualties nearing the final objective, and his CSM was killed, this NCO with coolness and determination led on his Pl, now depleted by over 50% and fought his way to the far side of the German Bn posn commanding Tiger. There assisted by two tanks, he was largely instrumental in completing the rout of the enemy and the capture of a large quantity of LMGs, A.Tk guns and mortars. He then remained with a few other fwd tps covering the flank movement of the bn towards the consolidation of Tiger, thereafter withdrawing when signalled, in perfect order, on the bn posn, under heavy fire. *(L.G. 24.2.42)*

Brown, Horace Reginald, Trooper
7912813, 2nd Bn. Royal Tank Regt. (West Croydon)
(Immediate)
On the 3rd March, 1942, No. 7 Troop, 'B' Squadron, 2nd R. Tanks, commanded by 2/Lt. Yates was advancing across open country to cover a canal junction near Waw, when at about 400 yards range they came under heavy fire from guns of 75 mm calibre. These were concealed in a wood on the far side of the canal. The shelling was intense and at very short range, all the tanks being hit a number of times, one shell exploding in the cupola killing the tank commander & gunner outright while the operator, Tpr. J[...] was severely wounded. Although Tpr. Brown's tank was so badly damaged that it could only turn in one direction, he managed to manœuvre it back to help the other tanks. While still under heavy fire at short range, he gained touch with the surviving members of the crews of the other tanks and ascertained that they could get back to the road along a bank. Further he made sure that the remaining occupants of the tanks were dead. Then despite the difficulty of steering his tank he returned to his Squadron Commander two miles away, having to make a detour through territory of which he had no map. After giving a clear and concise report of the action he immediately volunteered to drive another tank.

Throughout this man showed the greatest disregard of danger in the face of heavy fire which at much close range was devasting. The conduct, coolness and initiative of Tpr. Brown when left with the wounded and two dead members of his crew, were an example to all.
(L.G. 23.4.42)

Brown, John Henry Owen, B.Q.M.S.
1445560, 226/57th Anti-Tank Regt., Royal Artillery
This NCO was serving with the BEF in France when he was captured on 29 May 1940 at Caestre. After a few weeks at Stalag VIIIB (Lamsdorf) he was sent to Blechammer, E.3 Kommando, where he devoted his energies to the welfare of the men and to general escape work until he was returned to the main camp in January 1942. Shortly afterwards he was transferred to a working camp in Berlin (N. 806, attached to Stalag IIID). Five months later he was again sent to Blechammer, and in June 1943 he was appointed Camp Leader at Genshagen holiday camp.

Realising that the German intended to use this camp subversively for their own ends he determined to thwart them. Despite the very real danger involved, he pretended to be working for the Germans, whilst at the same time he was really using the comparative freedom accorded to him to further the cause of the Allies; even when the Gestapo became suspicious BQMS Brown did not hesitate to continue his work.

Acting as he did entirely on his own initiative, he fully realised that in all probability he might be suspected of betraying his own country. This did in fact happen, but it has now been established without question that BQMS Brown did acquire and transmit to this country valuable information.

Through his continuous efforts the British Free Corps, which the Germans hoped to expand from the men sent to Genshagen, gained few recruits, and eventually the project became a complete failure. In addition BQMS Brown used the frequent change of personnel at the camp to establish inter-camp communication, passing on information and escape aids.

It is remarkable that whilst busy with all these activities, he did not neglect his duties as Senior NCO, Genshagen was excellently run, and men who have been there have shown marked respect and esteem for Brown.

When the camp closed in December 1944 BQMS Brown was again sent to Lamsdorf, and with the other personnel he was later evacuated to Hehenfels (Stalag 383). On 22 April 1945 this camp was liberated by an American unit. *(L.G. 27.9.45)*

Brown, John, Sergeant
*40557, 6 N.Z. Field Coy., N.Z.E. New Zealand
Military Forces (Immediate)*
During the attack on Miteiriya Ridge on 23/24 Oct 42.
Sjt. Brown was Section Sjt. with the Field Coy. party
clearing the Northern gap through the enemy minefields.
Very early in the attack the section came under heavy
shelling and machine-gun fire, and the Section Officer
was wounded and had to be evacuated. Sjt. Brown
promptly took charge and continually reorganised the
clearing party as the numerous casualties occurred. With
total disregard for personal safety he led and directed
his men. Before reaching the first minefield the vehicles
in rear carrying the mine clearing and gap marking stores
became boxed in with the supporting carriers and other
transport and completely lost direction thus increasing
Sjt. Brown's difficulties. During all this time the section
was under heavy fire and casualties continued to occur,
but Sjt. Brown calmly set about collecting and extricating
his transport and stores and then carried on with the
direction of his men in the clearing of a lane through the
enemy minefields. He, himself, repeatedly investigated
'booby' traps and lifted mines. As a result of his initiative
and courage he overcame a most difficult situation and
by his inspiring leadership and personal example he
encouraged his men to complete their hazardous task
with expedition and efficiency. *(L.G. 28.1.43)*

Brown, Percy James, Warrant Officer Cl. II (T/Sgt.-
Maj.)
532671, 1st Fife & Forfar Yeomanry, T.A.
During the period May 19th-29th this W.O. showed a
very high standard of leadership and courage and was
an excellent example to those in his Squadron. His troop
were under fire and bombing on numerous occasions and
each time he showed initiative and disregard for personal
danger, employing his troop to the best advantage and
gaining valuable information. On May 29th, at Vyfweg
(3 miles S.E. of Bergues) during the withdrawal, although
his tank was damaged, he remained behind to cover the
withdrawal of infantry, causing numerous casualties to
the enemy. *(L.G. 20.8.40)*

Brown, Percy Reginald, Warrant Officer Cl. II
5173452, Gloucestershire Regt. (Stonehouse, Glos.)
No citation. *(L.G. 25.10.45)*

Brown, Reginald Albert Sidney, Warrant Officer Cl.
III (Pl.S.M.) (A/W.O.II C.S.M.)
5718503, 2 Dorsetshire Regt.
On 27 May P.S.M. Brown was comdg. the right fwd pl
of the bn. At 5 am. that morning the enemy broke through
on his right flank and for ten hrs P.S.M. Brown by his
example, coolness and leadership maintained his original
posn. despite very heavy shell fire and three strong attacks
by the enemy during which period his pl suffered very
heavy casualties. On the eventual orders to withdraw
P.S.M. Brown extricated his pl under heavy fire. His

conduct throughout the operations was an inspiration to
all ranks. *(L.G. 22.10.40)*

Brown, Ronald Andrew, Sergeant
3769644, 2 Queen's Own Cameron Highlanders
During the 'mopping up' of enemy centres of resistance
in Nibeiwa Camp on 9/12/40, this NCO attacked an
enemy M.G. post single handed, and destroyed it by
successful use of hand grenades. Later, on 10/12/40,
during the attack on Sidi Barrani and in the course of
'mopping up' operations, this NCO led his pl with great
gallantry and complete disregard to personal safety. His
conduct on both days set a fine example to all ranks.
(L.G. 25.4.41)

Brown, Sidney, Warrant Officer Cl. III (Pl.S.M.)
5720440, 2 Dorsetshire Regt.
On 27 May P.S.M. Brown was in comd. of a fwd pl
guarding an important crossing of the La Bassée canal.
This pl held its original posn throughout the day despite
being in full view of the enemy and being under constant
heavy shell and M.G. fire. P.S.M. Brown by his coolness
and leadership kept his pl together drove off two major
attempts by the enemy to cross the canal and finally when
ordered to withdraw extricated his pl under heavy fire.
(L.G. 22.10.40)

Brown, Thomas Wright, Warrant Officer Cl. II
(C.S.M.)
*2753247, Scots Guards att. 2 Coldstream Gds.
(Caerphilly, Glam.) (since killed in action)
(Immediate)*
On 28 May, the bn were ordered to capture and hold the
Piccolo feature (6530). The Scots Gds Coy (att to the
bn) were directed on to the Western high point of the
feature and gained their objective shortly before first
light. Throughout the day the Coy was subjected to heavy
arty and mortar fire, to sniping and attempted infiltration
and early in the day all the officers in the Coy were either
killed or wounded and evacuated. CSM Brown then took
command of the Coy and handled it with such
outstanding skill that the feature was held in spite of
determined and prolonged assault on it by the enemy
and in consequence the bn was able to carry out its task
of holding its objective. An officer finally took over from
CSM Brown at nightfall.

CSM Brown's personal bravery in walking about
under constant fire, his coolness in action and his
capability of making quick decisions at critical moments
of the day were an inspiration to all ranks.
(L.G. 7.12.44)

Brown, William Cary, Private
K.2190, Calgary Highlanders (Immediate)
On 23 October 1944 'D' Company of the Calgary
Highlanders CA(O) was ordered to attack a strongly held
German position on a Holland dyke near Osendrecht.

At approximately 1600 hours, 16 platoon which was the lead Platoon of the Company came under very heavy enemy machine gun and rifle fire and were pinned down. Private Brown, the Company Runner, went forward on his own to ascertain the difficulty and found that the Platoon Commander and all the NCOs were out of action, so he took over the Platoon and by crawling up to the top of a ditch he directed the fire of 16 Platoon's Bren Guns onto the enemy. At this time the Company Commander and 18 Platoon Commander were both wounded and the Company Sergeant Major took over and sent Private Brown back for more ammunition. He had to go back under heavy fire. On his return with the ammunition he saw our tank support moving into position and regardless of personal danger he went over to them and personally directed their fire on the enemy positions which he had located previously. He then returned to the forward Platoon with the ammunition.

Brown's coolness and quick thinking in taking control of the forward platoon and later assisting them by directing the tank fire on the enemy undoubtedly saved the Company from very heavy casualties and made it possible for them to carry on and take their objective. At all times throughout the action Private Brown's extreme courage, coolness and complete disregard for his personal safety were an inspiration to all those with him.

(L.G. 13.1.45)

Brown, William Frederick James, M.M., Sergeant (A/ W.O.II (C.S.M.))
5501356, 2/4 Hampshire Regt. (Fleet) (Immediate)
This NCO was assisting the Officer Commanding 'Y' Crossing of the R. Gari on the night of 11/12 May 1944. By his personal example and great courage he was instrumental in maintaining the constant flow of boats across the ferry under heavy MMG and mortar fire. His total disregard for personal danger was in itself an inspiration and an encouragement to his gallant ferrymen and a very large contributary factor to the success of the ferry service.

Early on, two of the four boats were put out of commission by enemy action. Sjt. Brown, under heavy enemy fire launched two more and finally ended up with three when the operation was cancelled.

His unceasing and untiring efforts, his magnificent example and his personal courage was an inspiring sight and his coolness under fire something to remember and hope to emulate.

On the evening of 14 May 1944, during the attack by the Bn on the Massa Vertechi feature, the leading tanks had failed to cross the SL (a stream) and were hopelessly bogged. The leading coys had come under heavy enemy DF and suffered many casualties, especially amongst Coy Comds and Pl Comds. Sjt. Brown's Coy, which had the gruelling experience of the river crossing ferrying where they lost their Coy Commander and suffered many casualties—had done an attack on to objective Brown

on 13 May and were depleted—lost all officers on the SL.

Sjt. Brown, by his great courage and example and great powers of leadership, rallied what men he could and led them on to the objective. The Bn only reached the objective 150 strong and but for his action it is doubtful whether the objective could either have been reached or held.

(L.G. 26.10.44)

Browne, Laurence Hamilton, Corporal
4444, Long Range Desert Group, N.Z. Army Service Corps, New Zealand Military Forces
This NCO displayed exceptional gallantry and resource during the raid on Murzuk on Jan. 11th, 1941. He commanded his vehicle most efficiently and maintained his lewis gun in action with coolness and telling effect on the enemy. His example did much to keep the patrol steady at a critical time when enemy fire was causing casualties. Although wounded in the foot he remained at his post.

In the action at Gebel Sherif, South-West of Kufra on Jan. 31st his coolness was instrumental in saving his vehicle and crew when subjected to a determined low-flying bombing and M.G. attack by an enemy aircraft.

Throughout all the L.R.D.G. operations in Libya this NCO has held the responsible post of patrol navigator, and has shown the utmost devotion to duty.

(L.G. 8.7.41)

Browning, Sydney, Corporal
410507, 7th Queen's Own Hussars, Royal Armoured Corps (New Inn, Farsley, Yorks.)
South of Sidi Rezheg on 23.11.41, whilst acting as wireless operator and loader in the Officer Commanding 7th Hussars' tank this NCO was wounded in the head. When opportunity occurred to relieve him with another operator he absolutely refused to leave his duties and though in pain he continued to carry on during the action on 24.11.41, and maintained wireless communication until the tank was evacuated on 25.11.41. On 24.11.41, when under fire he got out of the turret and cleared a round stuck in the barrel. Twice he repaired the damaged trigger mechanism and generally set a magnificent example of coolness and determination to continue his duties of maintaining the damaged gun in action and his wireless working.

(L.G. 20.1.42)

Bruce, John James, Sergeant
3379660, 4th Bn. East Lancashire Regt.
On various dates between 10.5.40 and 31.5.40 this NCO who was Battalion Signal Sergeant rendered invaluable service to the Battalion by maintaining intercommunications under very difficult and dangerous circumstances. During most of the time he also carried on his shoulders the responsibilities of the Bn. Signalling officer who was evacuated to hospital. After being captured by the enemy at Cost Cappel on 29.5.40 and marched back about a

mile into their lines he made his escape down a sewer and adjoined the unit.   *(L.G. 11.7.40)*

Brunton, William Lancelot, Sergeant
1032936, 12th A.A. Bty., Royal Artillery
Although wounded himself and in considerable pain Sjt. Brunton carried on the work of attending the wounded on the beach at Bray Dunes on the 1st June 1940. He continued this work under shell fire until all the wounded had been dressed. At all times he has shown conspicuous coolness and devotion to duty.   *(L.G. 20.12.40)*

Bruton, Albert [Henry] George, Sergeant
407204, Queen's Bays (2nd Dragoon Guards), R.A.C.
(Cirencester) (Immediate)
Ref Map Italy 1/50,000 88 II (Imola) 88 I (Argenta)
From the time his Regiment went into action on April 11th until he was severely wounded when his tank was knocked out on April 17th when breaking through the Argenta Gap, Sjt. Bruton displayed outstanding courage, powers of leadership and resource.

One particular incident was on 13th April. Sjt. Bruton was Tp Sjt of 4 Tp 'B' Sqn which was in support of D Coy Royal Inniskilling Fusiliers, who were advancing North from the bridgehead over the Santerno River to the River Reno. This Company, after an advance of three thousand yards, was out by itself, as flanking formations had been held up. The enemy launched a heavy counter-attack from the left. Sjt. Bruton was ordered to go alone and counter this threat. Although several deep ditches had to be negotiated he showed great resource in getting his tank into action. He drove right in amongst the attacking enemy causing many casualties, though all the time under accurate fire from a supporting SP gun and bazookas. As a result of his vigorous action not only was the counter-attack broken up, but our own advance quickened all along the front and over 100 prisoners were taken in the particular area in which Sjt. Bruton was operating.

Sjt. Bruton's courageous and energetic action not only caused great enemy loss but also gave fresh momentum to the advance towards Bastia, which could not have taken place except for Sjt. Bruton's decisive and determined action.   *(L.G. 23.8.45)*

Bryant, Roy Chevallier Bisson, Corporal (A/Sgt.)
7890130, 3rd County of London Yeomanry, Royal
Armoured Corps (Immediate)
On 30 Nov 43 Sjt. Bryant was commanding a tank in the Rocca Giovanni area where the Squadron was heavily engaged in fighting infantry supported by S.P. guns. Owing to the nature of the ground two tanks of his troop were stuck in the mud, and were being attacked by snipers and rifle-grenades. Sjt. Bryant realising the urgency of getting these tanks mobile, under heavy fire he dismounted from his tank and attached a tow rope, thereby freeing one tank which was ordered away.

The country was very close and by this time the Troop Leader's tank was surrounded by enemy, this tank had both its guns out of action, Sjt. Bryant beat off four attempts of the enemy to destroy this tank with his tommy gun and hand grenades. Eventually the enemy withdrew leaving twelve dead, eight prisoners and much equipment including tank destroying bombs, twenty pack horses, four L.M.G.'s, one mortar and one valuable range finder.

There is no doubt that Sjt. Bryant saved two tanks from destruction and through initiative and bravery captured much valuable equipment.   *(L.G. 6.4.44)*

Bryant, William James, Sergeant
6465352, 6 Queen's Own Royal West Kent Regt.
(London, S.E.14)
On 13 Apr 43 D Coy was one of the two fwd Coys in the attack on Dj Bou Diss. The Coy's objective was the summit itself—pt 617. After one of the forward platoons had met stiff opposition when nearing the summit and were beginning to fall back, Sjt. Bryant led his platoon through with great dash and reached the top. The platoon suffered severe casualties but owing to this NCO's inspiring example the remainder of the pl remained on the objective despite heavy fire. Sjt. Bryant was also instrumental in wiping out the chief enemy M.G. nest that had, up to this time, held up the Coy on the left.

Sjt. Bryant's cool courage and fine leadership on this and many other occasions in this campaign has been an inspiration to all around him.   *(L.G. 15.6.43)*

Brygider, Adam, Corporal
H.19715, Queen's Own Cameron Highlanders of
Canada
This NCO's cool efficiency and courageous conduct throughout the Dieppe operation 19 Aug 42, contributed greatly to his Coy's success. In the house-to-house fighting in Pourville he was in the forefront of the action. At one stage he dragged a wounded comrade through heavy fire for 400 yards to shelter, and then returned under fire to attack and clear further houses. On the withdrawal to the beach, he with Cpl. Kellar organized in a most efficient manner the withdrawal and protection of wounded personnel. With complete disregard for their own safety, these two NCO's repeatedly returned through the wire, advanced to exposed positions and brought back wounded men, through heavy fire. This NCO directed the successful evacuation of the casualties to the L.C.As. His gallant conduct throughout resulted in the lives of many soldiers being saved.   *(L.G. 2.10.42)*

Bryson, John Huntingdon, Guardsman
2694706, Scots Guards (Immediate)
As No. 1 of a Bren gun section of a platoon on the left flank, Gdsmn Bryson not only played a major part in stemming the enemy advance for six hours, but also, during this action, handed over his gun to his No. 2, and single handed rescued wounded comrades from no man's land on two occasions under heavy fire. Most of this

action took part in a wood, the enemy using mortars, machine guns and tommy guns to assist their flanking attack. This called for something more than ordinary qualities as the defending troops had to change their positions time and again to meet the attack as it developed from all sides.

Guardsman Bryson displayed these qualities in full measure. With complete disregard for his own safety he moved his gun from one position to another, sometimes firing from behind rocks, and sometimes resting his gun in the fork of a tree, as the situation demanded. He was an inspiration not only to those in contact with him, but also to the whole Bn. He inflicted very heavy casalties on the enemy. *(L.G. 6.8.40)*

Buckley, Cornelius Timothy, Warrant Officer Cl. II (S.S.M.)
401150, Kings Dragoon Guards, Royal Armoured Corps
5th and 6th February, 1941 at Sidi Saleh.

During the Battle at Sidi Saley, on February 5th and 6th, SSM Buckley set a magnificent example of resource, boldness and courage. On several occasions, by his fearlessness and deterination he captured with his own Armoured Car, unsupported by other vehicles, large numbers of prisoners amounting to 2 or 3 hundred. Two instances of his behaviour are outstanding.

On the evening of 5th February, SSM Buckley who had taken some prisoners back, was ordered to escort, with his Armoured Car, the echelon up to his Squadron, who had been ordered to hold a position off the main road leading South from the Battlefield. It was just dark and the situation was complicated by the number of small enemy parties who were moving across country in an effort to break through to the South. SSM Buckley missed the Squadron, went on in the dark for a further 10 miles South towards the enemy, thinking that the Squadron might have moved. In doing so, he encountered an enemy party. Although he was followed by four unarmed lorries, SSM Buckley attacked with such speed and determination that after a number had been killed the enemy surrendered. SSM Buckley then turned his convoy around and brought it, and his 100 prisoners back. All this was done in the dark without lights.

The following morning, February 6th, SSM Buckley was sent back down the road to bring in a few of the prisoners that he had not been able to the night before. On his way he attacked the Fort of Sidi Farag with his A/T Rifle and caused the garrison of fifty to surrender. These, with several others, he put in a derelict lorry and towed them back to the Regiment behind his Armoured Car.

In both these instances Sergeant Major Buckley was acting alone, without wireless, in a country where there were armed mechanised parties. But the knowledge of this did not affect his determination to capture every Italian he could find and he set a magnificent example to his Squadron. *(L.G. 16.5.41)*

Bugg, Leonard Frederick, Private
TX 1394, 2/12 Aut Inf Bn. (Immediate)
Period 22 Jan—6 Feb 44

Pte. Bugg was a member of 16 Pl D Coy 2/12 Aust. Inf. Bn. and was given command of a Section immediately prior to going into action. During the advance on Prothero II (ref map Paipa 1:25,000 642659) on 22 Jan 44 the leading platoon of Pte. Bugg's coy was held up by MMG fire and snipers hidden in trees to a flank. Pte. Bugg with his Bren gun rushed forward and engaged the enemy from a distance of 30 yards. The Bren mag pouches he was wearing were hit and set on fire, but Pte. Bugg threw them off and continued firing. He ordered his section to move round a flank under his covering fire during which time he killed the enemy machine gunner, allowing his sec to gain its objective. By his action the advance of the Coy was greatly facilitated. In this and subsequent actions Pte. Bugg was continually in the forefront of the fighting and his courage and aggression were an inspiration to the remainder of his sec and helped materially in the success his Coy achieved in the operation. *(L.G. 30.3.44)*

Bull, William Thomas St. Clair, Sergeant
5253132, 7th Bn. Worcestershire Regt. (Dudley)
16th May to 16 August 1945.

Sjt. Bull, 7th Bn The Worcestershire Regt, was employed as platoon Sjt of 11 Platoon, 'B' Coy, 7th Bn The Worcestershire Regt, during the operations at Kohima and subsequently from the Chindwin to the crossing of the Irrawady, leading up to the capture of Mandalay and until the Bn was flown out of Central Burma in May 1945. On many occasions Sjt. Bull by his leadership and personal bravery in acting on his own initiative enabled his Pl Comd to reorganise and hold ground under heavy fire. His flair for organising supporting 2″ mortar and Bren fire on his own initiative led to his platoon carrying out many successful attacks. At Myingatha near Shwebo, during the Bn attack when 'B' company was a leading company, one section of 11 platoon became cut off from the remainder by heavy enemy L.M.G. and spring grenade fire. Sjt. Bull on his own, and with complete disregard for his safety crossed the open ground, reorganised the section and led it back again over open ground to rejoin the remainder of his platoon. It was by his initiative and courage that 11 platoon were able to continue the attack successfully capturing its objective. Again, after the capture of Shwabo and during the advance southwards, 11 Platoon were holding a forward position across the main road. A platoon from 'D' Company passed through to reconnoitre ahead. This patrol was seriously ambushed and became pinned to the ground by heavy enemy cross fire. In the absence of his platoon commander Sjt. Bull collected the isolated remnants of the patrol, took his 2″ mortar, went forward under extremely heavy fire and put down H.E. and smoke onto the enemy position which enabled the remainder of the patrol to bring out their wounded and withdraw without further casualties. Although both his own mortar men were wounded, he sustained the mortar fire and eventually withdrew recovering both the mortar and his wounded man. At Tedaing on the banks of the Irrawady when 11 Platoon was detached and holding the village on its own, Sjt. Bull was visitng his sentries by night when a enemy raiding force penetrated his perimeter. Sjt. Bull and his orderly lay down and waited until the Japs were a few yards from them, when he threw his two grenades which killed five and caused panic and the withdrawal of the enemy. Sjt. Bull then visited each post and the perimeter personally and inspired confidence into his men who eventually beat off a heavy enemy attack. Throughout the whole campaign Sjt. Bulls devotion to duty, cheerfulness willingness and bravery were an inspiration to all ranks of his platoon. His personal disregard for his own personal safety was at all times worthy of the highest praise. *(L.G. 6.6.46)*

Bullock, Donald Charles, T/Corporal (A/T/Sergeant)
Ch./X.3346, Royal Marines (Bexley, Kent)
No citation   *(L.G. 27.6.44)*

Bullock, Norton, Lance Sergeant
2615150, Grenadier Guards
No citation   *(L.G. 27.8.40)*

Burdett, Julian, Corporal
PO36660J, Royal Marines
On the night of 11th/12th June 1982, on the Island of East Falkland, 45 Commando Royal Marines launched a silent night attack against strongly held enemy positions on the craggy hill feature of Two Sisters, ten kilometres to the west of Port Stanley. As Section Commander, Corporal Burdett was leading his Section when they came under heavy fire from enemy Mortars. Two of his men were killed instantly and he himself severely wounded. Despite these setbacks, he continued to encourage and steady his section as they moved forward.

Ignoring his wounds Corporal Burdett also continued to pass further important reports of enemy positions. Simultaneously he organised the evacuation of his wounded colleagues until he himself was carried from the scene of the fighting. Despite serious losses, Corporal Burdett's selfless and distinguished leadership inspired his men to continue their advance. *[From L.G.]*
                                   (L.G. 19.9.78)

Burfield, Edward Victor, Private
6089331, 1/6 Bn. Queen's Royal Regt.
1. Capture
I was captured at Oudenarde (Belgium) on 21 May 40 while the remnants of my company were attempting to withdraw from a position which was surrounded by the enemy. After being marched to Brussels I was sent to Stalag XX A (Thorn), arriving on 5 or 6 Jun 40.

2. Camps in Poland
See Section 2 S/P.G.(P) 1976 (L/Cpl. Lloyd).
3 Attempted Escapes
I made altogether 11 attempts to escape, all of which are described in L/Cpl. Lloyd's report, except my first attempt. This was made in Sep 40 when I escaped from Biscrofsberg, a working camp in Danzig. I got out of the camp by cutting the wire, and was captured in Poland. This was seven days later. I had walked part of the way, and had stolen a bicycle the day before I was caught. I intended making for Russia. I was arrested for not having an identity card.
4. Escape
See Section 4 S/P.G.(P) 1976.   *(L.G. 3.8.44)*

Burgess, Horace, M.M., Sergeant
2034237, 501 Field Coy., Royal Engineers (London, S.W.1) (Immediate)
On 25th Feb 1944 at approx 0600 hrs Sjt. Burgess who was by himself in a wadi, was surprised and set upon by a patrol of five of the enemy. As a result he was captured and taken to where four other men had also been taken prisoner. Sjt. Burgess, although now unarmed, refused to except the position, and, while keeping his captors employed, issued orders in English for all the prisoners to attack. At a given signal these prisoners led by Sjt. Burgess rushed the German patrol. A stand up fight ensued in which 2 Sappers were killed. Undaunted the remainder continued at close grips with their armed opponents and eventually the German patrol fled in disorder. Three of them were subsequently captured. Sjt. Burgess showed exceptional coolness and courage in organising this unarmed attack, and carried out his own part of it with great dash and skill. *(L.G. 15.6.44)*

Burke, Frank, Sergeant
1473858, 3 Nigeria Lt . Bty. W.A.A., Royal Artillery (Beeston, Leeds) (Periodic)
At the Kyingri Loop (Map sheet 84 16 map reference 939608) Sjt. Burke was employed as Observation Post Assistant to [...] his Troop Commander. At 0630 [...] on the 19th March 1944 'D' Coy 4th Nigeria Regt with which the O.P. was situated was heavily attacked by the Japanese. In the first assault Capt Barnaby was killed; Sjt. Burke who had been sent by Capt. Barnaby to the bottom of the hill the O.P. was on returned onto the hill, took charge himself and fired the guns. 'D' coy was driven off the hill but Sjt. Burke remained to the very end engaging the enemy with his Sten Gun and was then wounded himself. He then withdrew to the bottom of the hill, teed in his telephone on the line and again controlled the fire of the guns; the Japanese were then about 20 yards away and Sjt. Burke rang up the G.P.O. and told the guns to fire onto the O.P. knowing that he himself would be in the danger area. I then ordered him over the telephone to withdraw, he then collected what was left of the O.P. party and got them back when an Infantry Officer ordered him to the A.D.S. to which he

then went. This B.N.C.O. showed a very high devotion to duty.

Recommended for M.M.   *(L.G. 16.11.44)*

Burke, Ronald Leslie, Lance Sergeant
23315, New Zealand Military Forces
No citation.   *(L.G. 20.1.42)*

Burke, Thomas, Sergeant
7811235, 42nd Divisional Signals, Royal Signals, T.A
16 May 40 to 29 May 40

Sjt. Burke T. was the section Sergeant of 'B' Cable Section. By untiring energy and inspiring leadership he encouraged his men to lay and maintain lines throughout the whole period of the operations under shell fire, bombs, and machine gun fire.   *(L.G. 22.10.40)*

Burley, Donald, Sergeant
6202602, Queen's Bays (2nd D.G.), (Edgware)
(Periodic)

On 20 Sep 44, NW of M dell Arboreta, the left flank of leading elements of 2 Armd Bde were heavily engaged from high ground of the Corinao Spur (780914). This vital position had been held by infantry of the division operating on the flank of the 2 Armd Bde, but they had been forced to withdraw, leaving wounded on the ground, by an enemy counter-attack.

One Troop of the The Queen's Bays, of which Sjt. Burley was Tp Sjt was ordered to go and assist in driving the enemy from this area. During this move both his Tp Ldr's tk and the Cpl's tk were knocked out leaving Sjt. Burley to carry on the operation by himself.

Realising that the ground over which he would have to attack was almost entirely covered by enemy A/T guns, he dismounted and set off to find out a covered way of approach up the hill to the enemy position.

This he did and managed to return, though he was constantly under close and accurate fire of all descriptions. He found an Infantry Company Commander and told him what he had found out on his reconaissance and suggested a suitable plan of attack.

The plan was agreed to and Sjt. Burley led the infantry into the enemy position, using his guns so effectively that they arrived there with few casualties. The enemy were temporarily routed, and under cover of the tank fire were able to evacuate the casualties who had been left there in the first instance and consolidate.

Later the enemy counter-attacked again. Sjt. Burley inflicted severe casualties on them, but whilst he was on foot, reconnoitring an alternative fire position for his tank, he was badly injured. He was able to walk back to his tank and, though in great pain, and suffering from loss of blood, he continued to fight his tank until the enemy had again been dispersed.

This NCO, throughout, showed resource, initiative, powers of planning, and skill in execution, which would be considered outstanding in a commander of much higher rank. In addition, he showed great personal courage in continuing to command his tank when so severely wounded. The fighting spirit of Sjt. Burley undoubtedly inspired all who co-operated with him in this action.

Sjt. Burley was back again in time to take part in the advance from the River Montone to beyond the River Lamone. At the passage of the Marzino he commanded his tank with marked ability and in the hard fighting west of Faenza and across the Lamone he commanded his troop in the absence of his Troop Leader. His was one of the first Troops over the Lamone and throughout he led his tanks with great courage and resource causing many casualties amongst the enemy and materially assisting the infantry in holding their bridgehead against severe enemy counter-attacks.   *(L.G. 28.6.45)*

Burnett, James, Lance Corporal
1/400092, Royal Australian Regt.
For Korea   *(L.G. 15.7.52)*

Burnett, Richard, Fusilier
4268489, 2nd Bn. Royal Northumberland Fusiliers
(Immediate)

For conspicuous gallantry and devotion to duty near Bulcamp [...] the Bruges—Gurnes Canal on 31st May, 1940.

His Company Commander called for volunteers to take the Machine Gun position across the canal. He at once volunteered and advanced with his gun and tripod under heavy shell fire. Having established his gun in a very exposed position this soldier inflicted great losses on the enemy, though under fire, until his ammunition was expended. The bridge was destroyed before he returned by swimming across with the gun, having had to abandon the tripod.   *(L.G. 20.12.40)*

Burns, James Swetenham, M.M., Sergeant
557104, 2nd Lothians & Border Yeomanry
(Immediate)

On 14 May 44, in the area south of Cassino, Sjt. Burns was Troop Sergeant of one of the leading Troops of the Squadron of tanks in support of the Black Watch (RHR) in the widening of the Bridgehead over the River Rapido. Visibility was reduced to practically nil with the result that some of the tanks lost contact with the infantry. Sjt. Burns tank was one of the four which reached the objective with the infantry. When the mist lifted it became obvious that the enemy had brought up S.Ps between these tanks and the remainder of the squadron and that a counter attack was imminent. Sjt. Burns commanded his tank with such skill that he was able to inflict considerable casualties on the enemy, thus breaking up the threatened counter attack. Although given the chance to withdraw, he refused to do so until the position was fully consolidated. In the afternoon his tank was hit for the third time, but he did not cease firing until it was actually ablaze. He then organised the surviving crews and fought dismounted with the infantry for twenty four hours. He then returned to his Squadron where he got a new tank which was knocked out in action on the following day. Having seen his crew to safety he returned to his Squadron Leader's tank and calmly pointed out the direction from which the fire was coming. Throughout this prolonged action Sjt. Burns showed remarkable coolness and courage and a complete disregard for his own safety. His determination to engage the enemy was a fine example to all who saw him, undoubtedly contributed largely to the ultimate success of the operation.   *(L.G. 26.10.44)*

Burrage, Stanley, Corporal (A/Sgt.)
7885179, 6th Royal Tank Regt. (Driffield, E. Yorks.)
   (Immediate)
At Sidi Rezegh on the 23rd November, 1941 he showed the greatest coolness and courage during most difficult circumstances. As a tank commander he held his fire until the last moment and knocked out two enemy tanks. When his tank was finally put out of action and his crew killed, he acted magnificently under heavy fire, evacuating wounded men and forming a small first aid post himself. Throughout this action he caused many casualties to the enemy and was instrumental in saving the lives of many wounded, and his personal example of outstanding calmness and bravery under fire was an inspiration to all.   *(L.G. 19.3.42)*

Burton, John Henry, Sergeant
7907475, 15/19th King's Royal Hussars (Wilberfoss)
   (Immediate)
On 14th April 1945 Sjt. Burton was commanding 2nd Tp 'A' Sqn which was the leading Tp of the Sqn advancing down the road towards Winsen 4755 in support of 'D' Coy 1 Chesh. The country was thickly wooded on both sides of the road which made visibility very difficult and movement off the road practically impossible. The leading tank of the Tp was hit by an 88mm gun firing straight down the road. As soon as this happened Sjt. Burton with great speed and skill manœuvred his Tp into position on the side of the road and brought down fire with such speed and accuracy on the area where the gun was, although he could not see it, that it was abandoned by its crew. In the meantime Sjt. Burton set off himself on a recce on foot, to try to find a way through the woods round this gun, in spite of the presence of a considerable number of enemy infantry and much S.A. fire which was holding up our own infantry. With great initiative and complete disregard for his own safety Sjt. Burton by going forward on foot found a possible way round to the right through the woods which was not apparent from the map and could not have been found without spending some time on foot out by himself in most dangerous and unpleasant conditions. Meantime however another foot recce discovered that the enemy A/Tk gun had been abandoned and so Sjt. Burton moved his Tp on down the road. Shortly afterwards the Besa of the leading tank got a

jammed round and in trying to clear this the commander of the tank was killed and the gunner wounded by S.A. fire from enemy inf in the woods close by. Shortly afterwards Sjt. Burton's own gun became jammed and while dismounted in order to clear this and also to look after the wounded on his other tank, he was himself shot in the head by S.A. fire. In spite of this he reported the situation calmly and clearly and when another Tp was brought up, withdrew his Tp to get their guns in order and rendered first aid to other wounded men in his Tp and bandaged up his own head. Throughout the whole operation Sjt. Burton had handled his Tp with great skill and shown the greatest courage and initiative. His personal courage and conduct had been an example and inspiration to everybody present.   *(L.G. 21.6.45)*

Busanga, Zakare, Lance Corporal
12572, Gold Coast Regt.
To be dated 30.9.41   *(L.G. 21.7.42)*

Buxton, Richard George, Sergeant
SX 3460, Royal Canadian Infantry Corps
For Korea   *(L.G. 18.7.52)*

Byce, Charles Henry, M.M., Sergeant (actg.)
H.45944, Lake Superior Regt. (Motor) (Immediate)
On the morning of 2 Mar 45, 'C' Coy Lake Sup R (Mot) was ordered to pass through posns held by 'A' and 'B' Coys in the gap south of the Hochwald Forest. Their objective was a group of buildings at MR 055408. The attack was launched at 0430 hrs and by 0600 hrs 'C' Coy was on its objective. At first light their posn became apparent to the enemy and they were immediately subjected to hy shelling and mortaring. Their three supporting tks were knocked out and the Coy Comd and all the other offrs became cas. A/Sjt. Byce immediately assumed comd of his pl, whose task it was to consolidate the left flank. The enemy were entrenched not more than seventy-five yards away and subjected his pl to continuous MG fire. Sjt. Byce realized that his posn was untenable as long as the enemy retained possession of their dugouts. He at once organized and personally led an assault on the posn and the enemy were driven out after suffering some twenty cas. By this time the SA and mortar fire had become most intense. Nevertheless Sjt. Byce continued to move about from post to post directing the fire of his men and maintaining contact with the other pls. At this time enemy tks were seen to be manœuvring into posn for an attack. Sjt. Byce appreciated that a counter-attack was imminent and, taking the only remaining Piat, he proceeded to stalk the tks. His first and second shots at the leading tk missed, thus giving away his posn, and the tks directed their MG fire onto him. However, Sjt. Byce calmly took aim again and knocked out the tk. As the crew evacuated they were killed to a man by MG fire from Sjt. Byce's pl. An enemy tk then appeared at a railway under-pass at MR 055406 and Sjt. Byce realized that if he could destroy it in the

under-pass it would block the others from attacking his posn. He then went fwd to a house which was a pt of vantage but found it occupied by the enemy. Sjt. Byce and his single companion cleared the building with hand grenades, but by this time the tk was through and moving onto his posn. He issued orders to his pl to let the tks, 4 in number, go through them and then to open up on the inf which was following behind. This they did and the attack was broken up, the enemy inf withdrawing. The tks, however, remained commanding the posn and, with no further anti-tank weapons available, Sjt. Byce realized that his pl was no longer effective. He then proceeded to extricate what remained of 'C' Coy. At this phase the enemy called upon Sjt. Byce to surrender but he refused and ordered his men back across the bullet swept ground, returning to 'A' Coy lines at 1500 hrs. Despite the fact that he had accomplished so much and had fought steadily under the most trying circumstances, Sjt. Byce refused to cease fighting. He took up a sniper's posn and for the remainder of the afternoon fired at enemy inf on the railway embankment. He was seen to kill seven and wound eleven. By this action he prevented the infiltration of the enemy into the Coy area dead ground which was visible only to him in his commanding posn. The magnificent courage and fighting spirit displayed by this NCO when faced with almost insuperable odds are beyond all praise. His gallant stand, without adequate weapons and with a bare handful of men against hopeless odds will remain, for all time, an outstanding example to all ranks of the Regt.   (L.G. 2.6.45)

Byrne, John, Lance Corporal
2616748, 3rd Bn. Grenadier Guards (Birkenhead)
On Thursday, 4th Feb 43, at about 1500 hrs, the Coy of the a/n L/Cpl. attacked Alliliga Hill nr Bou Arada. For the next 24 hrs L/Cpl. Byrne and his three Company Stretcher Bearers, worked without a break; the conditions under which they laboured were appalling; the ground was of a rocky, precipitious nature, with almost vertical slopes, and interspersed with thick scrub and bushes; throughout the 24 hrs L/Cpl. Byrne and his bearers were subjected to heavy mortar fire, machine gun fire, and, whilst tending the wounded, deliberate sniping; in no way did this deter L/Cpl. Byrne from organising and encouraging his bearers in a calm continuance of the many and great tasks which faced them that afternoon and night. As one example only of what he did during the action, I would cite the case of a L/Sjt. whom he and another bearer carried for 2 miles over this difficult country, from 1600 hrs to 0100 hrs, in order to bring him eventually to an advanced RAP, dressing, and attending six wounded men en route. Having done this he at once returned to his company, made an improvised stretcher with rifles, and helped carry his C.S.M., who ultimately died, for a mile, over what could practically be called impossible going. According to all reports the powers of stamina as displayed by L/Cpl. Byrne during the action were amazing, his example of devotion to duty,

a very fine one, and the encouragement and leadership he gave to those working under him, quite outstanding. One of his stretcher bearers, incidentally, became a casualty during the night; as a result of L/Cpl. Byrne's work during the engagement, some thirty casualties were tended under fire and successfully evacuated. I recommend L/Cpl. Byrne for the immediate award of the D.C.M.   (L.G. 8.4.43)

Byrne, John Patrick, Lance Sergeant
3855811, 10 Lancashire Fusiliers (Ashton-under-Lyne) (Immediate)
Before Rathe Drung.
On Jan 9th 1943 during an attack on West Hill Sjt. Byrne was acting as Pl Commander. Throughout the action he showed courage and coolness and fine leadership. His pl was badly caught in the open by heavy cross-fire. He reorganized them and held on to the ground he had captured. When ordered to withdraw some four hours later, he withdrew from a difficult position skilfully, and although severely wounded continued to command his pl until ordered to the rear to be attended to.   (L.G. 8.4.43)

Byrne, John Vincent, Corporal
2060658, Gordon Highlanders, 1st Special Air Service Bde., attd. H.Q. 8th Army
1. Capture
In Mar 42, while serving with 1st Special Air Service Brigade, I was engaged on a sabotage mission near Benghazi. While returning alone from this mission on 27 Mar, and after walking for about 8 days I saw a Chevrolet truck South of Mekili. I thought that I was by now in the British lines, and walked towards the truck. While I was thus engaged a German car drew up beside me and a German officer stuck a revolver in my ribs.
2. Captivity
On 28 Mar 42 I was taken to a German Infantry camp at Barce. Near here I was searched and interrogated in English. My interrogators noticed that I was wearing the special tunic of the Special Air Service Brigade. They asked me my unit, but I gave them only my name, rank and number. They then told me the name of my unit and of my Commanding Officer (Lt.-Col. David Stirling, Scots Guards). They were most anxious to ascertain the nature of the operation on which I hd been engaged. I gave them no details of this.
After interrogation I was sent back to Barce, and shortly afterwards handed over to Italian custody in Benghazi. Here I was lodged in a Police station. An Italian officer, purporting to be an Italian parachutist, and speaking good English, took me to his house, gave me a good meal and some cigarettes, and asked me to tell him about the operation upon which I had been engaged prior to my capture. I refused all information. On 30 Mar 42, I was taken to a small camp at Miserata. Here I was again asked the name of my unit. I gave my interrogator my name, rank, and number only. I was then

taken to a small reception camp nearby, given some food, and put into a room containing four beds. I went to sleep, but early the next morning, 31 Mar, a man speaking good English, and wearing the uniform of an officer in the British Fleet Air Arm, entered the room. He had a bandage round his head, and said that he had been wounded. With him was a British Sergeant in an Anti-Tank Battery, R.A. The Fleet Air Arm officer happened to leave the room for a moment, and during his absence the Sergeant warned me that the officer was a stool-pigeon.

When the 'officer' returned he talked about incidents in the campaign in North Africa, praising the work of the K.D.G's, and criticizing that of the 1st Armoured Division. He stated that he had operated from Malta, and talked a good deal about conditions there. While he was talking, I happened to put on my Special Air Service Brigade tunic. He then began to ask me questions about my unit and Commanding Officer. I told him that I was a parachutist, but nothing else. He then told me that if I had any information which I wished sent back to England, I could safely give it to him, since all British Officer P/W had special facilities for transmitting such information. I then introduced into my conversation with him the fact that I was aware that the Italians sometimes employed stool-pigeons. I produced from my pocket a hacksaw blade, which my searchers had not noticed, and remarked that if ever I met a stool-pigeon I would like nothing better than to use it upon his throat. The officer agreed with me, but soon afterwards called the guard, and left the room. I did not see him again. About an hour afterwards some Italians entered the room and took away my tunic, giving me an Italian tunic in place of it. A little time afterwards, whilst still in North Africa, I happened to meet a genuine British officer of the Fleet Air Arm. I cannot remember his name, but he told me that his uniform had been taken from him for examination, and had not been returned.

On 1 Apr 42, I was removed to another camp at Miserata, where I was kept in solitary confinement, and deprived of all food for two days. On 5 Apr with some other British P/W, I was taken to the main transit camp at Tripoli where I was allowed to mix with other P/W. On 6 Apr I was taken by car back to Miserata, and on 8 Apr was removed to Derna and handed over to German custody.

Here I was given a good meal, and a German officer produced a Red Cross form. It contained a space for the name of my unit, and also a paragraph inviting complaints. I refused to complete this form, and it was left lying on the table. I was quite well treated for the remainder of my time here, and managed to exchange my Italian tunic for a Greek uniform.

On 12 Apr I was taken to an airport and flown to Crete, and thence immediately to Athens. On 13 Apr I left Athens by train with an escort. Travelling in the same compartment with me was an R.A.F. Sergeant named Salmon. We travelled via Salonika, Belgrade and Vienna.

While in Greece, at every stop the train was besieged by starving Greeks trying to exchange cigarettes for bread. The Germans on the train sometimes gave them the ends of bread wrapped up to resemble a whole loaf. We arrived at Dulag Luft (Oberursel), near Frankfurt, about 18 Apr 42.

At Dulag Luft, Salmon and I were immediately taken to the hospital. I was lodged in a private ward and all my clothes were removed. After a time my clothes were brought back. I saw four R.A.F. sergeants here but they were in separate cells. A German soldier who spoke English with an American accent, and was known as 'The Sheriff,' produced a Red Cross Form, having a space for the name of my unit and a paragraph at the bottom for complaints. I filled in the complaint paragraphs only.

Next day I was brought some food, but was otherwise undisturbed for two days. Then a German officer who spoke English came into my room, gave me a cigarette, and took me to another room where he asked me some general questions about my civil life. He then said that though he did not want any real military information from me, he would like to know the name of my unit, and the nature of the operation upon which I had been engaged prior to capture. In the course of his subsequent conversation he asked me whether I knew of an attempt to make a sea landing at Tripoli, what 'Squadron' had invaded Rommel's H.Q., whether there were any glider planes in the M.E., whether I was a Regular soldier, where I had performed my training, and what I and my friends thought about the course of the war. I refused to answer these questions. My interrogator then told me that he thought that my attitude, as an NCO, should have been 'more intelligent.' I was taken back to my cell, and was allowed to wash and change my clothes.

Next morning another officer of quite a different type took me into the same room in which I had had my previous interview. He was very friendly and confidential, and insisted that he did not really want me to give him any military information, but that he required some information about my next-of-kin. He said that in order to help him he needed to know the name of my unit. I told him that I would not answer his questions unless I was allowed first to consult with a British officer. I was then taken back to my cell. Half an hour afterwards a guard took me to a photographer's and told me that I was to be photographed and to have my finger prints taken. I refused to submit to this treatment. My guards told me that everyone had to submit to it, and that my attitude was unreasonable. They did not attempt to coerce me by physical force. In the passage outside the photographers' I met four R.A.F. sergeants and some other P/Ws who had been photographed and finger-printed. When I had seen them I decided to allow myself to be treated in a similar way.

With these R.A.F. sergeants I was then taken to a part of Dulag Luft known as the Reception Camp.

Later a British sergeant took me to see the S.B.O., S/Ldr. Elliott. S/Ldr. Elliott warned me against talking carelessly.

I was not interrogated further at Dulag Luft. On 23 Apr 42, with a number of other P/W, I was sent to Stalag Luft III (Sagan).

On arrival here I was taken to an outer compound and searched. Next day, 24 Apr, I met a F/Sjt. Ross who said that he was in charge of Security in the camp. He warned me against possible stool-pigeons. He then told me that a Lt. Bonnington of my unit, was in the Officers' camp, and wished to talk to me. At a pre-arranged time I walked down to the fence separating the Officers' camp from the NCO's and spoke through it to Bonnington. He told me that Capt. Thompson, my former Adjutant, was with him.

3. Conditions in Stalag Luft III, 23 Apr 42-Sep 42.

Between Apr—Sep 42, the S.B.O. of the Officers was W/Cdr. Day and that of the NCO's was Sjt. Deans.

As a matter of routine the Germans searched one block every day, and there were occasional other searches. There were many individual tunnel schemes.

Between Apr and Jul 43, there were a number of U.S.A.A.F. personnel here, as well as British and Dominion personnel, and a new compound was being constructed to house them. The camp was divided into two compounds, East and West. The East compound contained British NCO's, and their S.B.O. was Grp/Capt. Kellett. The West compound contained British and American Officers. The S.B.O. of the joint party in the West compound was W/Cdr. Day. The number of American officers was about 600.

In Jun 43 nearly all the British personnel were moved to a new camp, Stalag Luft 6 at Heidebrug, near Memel. About 100 NCO's were left behind as a rear party.

After some time I volunteered to work as an officer's servant, in the hopes of being transferred to another camp from which escape would be easier. A number of other NCO's including Sjt. Wareing (S/P.G.(P)1018) did the same. In Sep 42, with about 100 officers, 15 NCO's were transferred to Oflag XXI B. (Schubin).

4. Oflag XXI B. (Schubin).
First attempted escape

Each day one British P/W orderly was allowed to go down to the camp pigsties with swill, accompanied by a German guard. I used to work in the cook-house and I decided, with the approval of Lt. Comdr. Buckley, a member of the Escape committee, to attempt to escape while acting as swill orderly. I collected a quantity of chocolate, raisins, cheese and cigarettes from Red Cross parcels. I still possessed my Greek uniform from which I removed the pockets and buttons. I made a civilian cap from blanket material, and also procured some maps and a compass. As I cannot speak German I did not provide myself with any form of identity card or Ausweis.

I went out with the swill on two occasions, but could not find an opportunity to get away from the guard.

Eventually, in Oct 42, with Cpl. Sampson (an Australian), and the usual German guard, I wheeled some swill on a handcart to a garage opposite the pigsties. We contrived to manœuvre the cart so that it partially blocked the entrance to the sties.

I noticed a bicycle lying nearby. We emptied the swill into the feeding troughs, and while Sampson was washing the swill tubs, and the guard was engaged in locking the door of the sties, I ran round a corner, put on my cap, mounted the bicycle, and rode off.

I saw a signpost pointing to Bromberg. Unfortunately, when I had gone a little way through the town of Schubin, a German civilian and a soldier shouted at me. The civilian then grabbed the front wheel of my bicycle, and I fell off and was caught. I was then taken to the local police station and searched. My maps were hidden in my belt, and my compass inside my wrist watch, and neither were found by my captors. I was sent back to the camp and confined in a cell for 13 days. Apparently the camp authorities never discovered that I had escaped on account of the slackness of one of the guards, and as someone in the camp had obligingly taken my place at roll calls they were not even certain as to the precise time and day when I had got out of the camp. After this escapade I was not allowed to proceed outside the camp. The only NCO who was allowed to do so was Sjt. Wareing, who profited by this privilege to make a successful escape two months later.

Second Attempted Escape

In consequence of an attempted mass escape on 9 Mar 43, the vigilence of the camp guards became intense. It was now only possible for P/W to leave the camp to perform coal fatigues which involved a journey of about 10 yards beyond the main gate. I contrived to go on one of these fatigues, and as I entered the coal yard I noticed a garage nearby which seemed to me to offer a temporary hiding place for an intending escaper. I then asked W/Cdr. Kyle for permission to make a second attempt to escape, and obtained his approval readily. He gave me some synthetic food, and maps of the route from Schubin to Danzi, and from Schubin to Warsaw. He also offered me money but as I cannot speak German, I declined it. For the same reason I did not attempt to provide myself with any form of identity card.

A Sjt. Carter who worked in the tailor's shop in the camp, procured for me a pair of blue pin-striped trousers, a black morning coat, and a civilian cap. I put on these garments underneath my battledress, and wore an army overcoat over that. I carried a compass, and stowed my food, some chocolate, a razor, and soap, in bags under my arms.

On two occasions thus attired, I went out with coal parties, but had no opportunity to get away.

On the third occasion, on 15 Mar 43, I went out with a coal party, and managed to slip into the garage and behind a fire-engine there. I then quickly removed my army clothes. The other members of the party and their guard shut the door of the garage, leaving me inside.

When they had gone, I immediately got through a window in the garage, made my way to the pigsties, and by luck again found a bicycle there.

I mounted this and rode through the town of Schubin, and about 4 kms. towards Bromberg. I then turned down a side road and hid my bicycle among some trees. After walking along a foot-path for about an hour I hid in a wood until dark. My plan was to make for Warsaw if possible.

On 16 Mar I reached the Grn Kan Notecki (G.S.G.S. 3982. Europe 1:250,000, Sheet N.33/9.) There were some barges and boats in this canal, but they had no oars. In walking about I fell into a pond and got soaked. I therefore took off my clothes in a wood and tried to dry them. At dawn on 17 Mar I cleaned myself up, shaved, and walked through Labiszyn and then towards Hohensalza (Inowraclow, Sheet N.33/12). I was much handicapped by the fact that the names of my map were Polish, but the names of all signposts were in German. By now my feet had begun to swell, and in order to wear my boots I had to take off my socks. I therefore thought I had better try to board a train travelling South into Austria.

I lay in a ditch near a railway and saw a number of coal trains passing and stopping. Eventually I climbed into the guards wagon of an empty train and was shunted into a marshalling yard. I then climbed into the guards' cabin of another train laden with hay. I stayed here for about two hours, and then climbed through the window of an empty wagon in a third train. Shortly afterwards the train moved off. Next morning, 18 Mar, I found I was at a station called Barcin (Sheet N.33/12.) Later my wagon was shunted into a factory yard. I saw that a number of workmen were beginning to open and sweep out other wagons, so I jumped out of the window. I thought that I saw the station to be names Wapnau (?). Then I noticed some wagons labelled Elsenau, and a little later a signpost pointing south and bearing the same name. Following the signpost I walked to the railway station at Elsenau (Damastawek, Sheet N.33/12), and hid in a lavatory. While here I shaved with water from the W.C. pan. I then lay down for a time in an old railway wagon. My feet were now in a very bad state and I could not run.

On getting out of the wagon on 20 Mar I was accosted by a German railwayman. As I could speak no German, I was handed over to the police. I then told them who I was and they identified me from a police gazette. They took from me my maps and my food, but I managed to retain my compass. I was then sent under guard to Stalag Luft III (Sagan), where I received 24 days solitary confinement.

5. Escape

Towards the end of Jun nearly all the British personnel were moved to a new camp, Stalag Luft VI, at Heidekrug, near Memel. Since I am a soldier, I had repeatedly applied to be sent to an Army camp but the German camp authorities had refused my application. In Jul 43, I remained behind at Stalag Luft III, with the rear party of about 100 NCO's.

On 15 Jul 43, with F/Sjt. Callander, D. V. M., and four other R.A.F. P/W, I was taken under guard to Berlin, and thence to Koenigsberg by train en route for Stalag Luft VI. I was wearing British Army battledress, having no pockets or badges. I wore no head-dress.

We arrived at Koenigsberg on the evening of 16 Jul, and were placed in a transit camp for the night.

I noticed that this camp had only a thin wire fence round it. The six of us, with three guards, were lodged in half a hut, the other half being occupied by some French medical orderlies.

Callander had served with the French Foreign Legion, and spoke fluent French. When we saw that the orderlies were allowed to bring us hot water and to talk to us, Callander and I together decided to escape if at all possible. Callander therefore asked a Frenchman to help him. This man gave him 10 Reichmarks and 100 French francs in exchange for 'Lagergeld.' The Frenchmen wore either French or British uniforms, with the words 'Zivil' in a diamond on their left arms. The man to whom Callander spoke said that they were free to walk about Koenigsberg, and that any Frenchman there would help us, or, at least not betray us to the Germans.

When it got dark our German guards noticed Callander removing from his tunic his badges and medal ribbon. They therefore posted an extra guard at the door of our hut, and our own three guards took it in turns to sit up with us inside. Despite this we tried to cut through the wall of the hut with knives which we had, but were stopped by the NCO of the guard.

About 0800 hrs next morning 17 Jul, we were let out of the hut into the compound, and allowed to visit the latrines. These were out of sight of the guard at the door of the hut. Callander and I agreed that if either of us saw an opportunity of escape, we would take it independently. He gave me 5 Reichsmarks.

I then went to the latrine. Near here, on the other side of a wire fence, I noticed a number of Russian P/W. Some of these motioned me that they wanted cigarettes, and I threw two packets over to them. I then noticed that from their compound I could reach a road, under cover and out of sight of any guards. The drain from the latrine ran underneath the wire into the Russians compound. At this moment a Frenchman came to the latrine, and I told him to tell Callander to join me at once. As I told him this a party of French P/W entered my compound, and temporarily distracted the attention of the guards posted there. Unfortunately I dared not wait for Callander to join me.

I lowered myself into the latrine drain which was about 2 feet deep, and slid under the wire into the Russians' compound. I then scrambled into some thick grass near the wire fence separating this compound from the road. This wire was old and rotten. I broke it with my hands, crawled out on to the road, and walked away. The whole of this procedure took about 5 minutes.

The road on which I now stood ran parallel to a railway line, and between the road and the railway there was a large number of rusty metal bins. I lifted one up and got underneath it. Here I remained until dark.

After dark I walked along the railway line into a railway station in Koenigsberg. Leaving the station, I noticed many people walking about in the dark. I walked towards the docks and eventually could see the water.

Near the road on which I was walking there were about a dozen railway lines and a number of empty goods wagons. I entered one of these and spent the night in it. Next morning, 18 Jul 43, I noticed a number of gangs of Russians and Frenchmen, walking about near by. The Russians were guarded, but the Frenchmen were not. I lay in the wagon all day, and about 1800 hrs saw a gang of Frenchmen leaving the docks and apparently going home. There was no guard with them, and they all wore British battledress trousers. A few of them also wore British battledress blouses, and all had on their left arms the 'Zivil' badge. I got out of the train and mingled with them, shaking hands with those nearest to me. While I was walking along I explained to one of them who could understand English that I was an 'English airman.' He said 'Come.'

After walking for some time this man took me into the hut where he lodged. He then brought an Englishman who had served in the French Army, and I was able to explain that I wished for help to escape. This man took me to his billet and told his French companions not to talk about me. I asked him to procure for me a 'Zivil' badge. He gave me his own and made another for himself. From him I learned that there was no shipping in Koenigsberg other than a few small coal boats going to Finland. He told me that it would be hopeless for me to escape from Koenigsberg by sea. He gave me 50 Reichsmarks, and one of his friends gave me 150 francs.

I learned that my companions were going to be issued with some form of passport next day. They said that I could remain with them for as long as I wished, and that they would try to procure me civilian clothes, one of their passports, and a permit to go on leave as if I were one of their number. One of my helpers worked on the railway, and told me that the railway wagons were sealed by the French workers themselves. He added that he could arrange to provide me with plenty of food and to conceal me in a wagon which would take my 'anywhere I liked,' into Germany, Austria, France, or even Turkey. The only difficulty was that I was bound to be shunted about for weeks during the journey, and that he could not arrange to supply me with sufficient water for so long a time.

By now a number of Frenchmen were aware of my presence, and one of my helpers told me that he thought I should leave Koenigsberg as soon as possible. I told him that a friend of mine (Sjt. Wareing) had escaped from Danzig to Sweden—a fact which I had learned in Stalag Luft 3 from R.A.F. personnel who had been lectured by Wareing upon his escape, after his arrival in England. I then said that if my helpers could get me some civilian clothes, I would try to steal a bicycle and get to Danzig.

They gave me a suit of blue overalls to cover my uniform, a beret, and a haversack of food, and also offered me more money, which I refused. What money I had, I stitched into my trousers. Before I left they said that they would be glad to help any future escaping P/W's who might come their way.

Next morning, 19 Jul 43, after my helpers had gone to work, I walked into the town. Finding a bicycle inside a gateway, I stole it and rode off.

My map showed the Danzig area up to the town of Elbing. I noticed a number of signposts marked 'Elbing' leading from the town, and I followed these along the coast road.

About 12 kms from Elbing, I noticed a road block ahead, where travellers were having their passes examined. I managed to turn down a side path into a wood where I hid until dark. I then walked across country, carrying my bicycle most of the way, until I had by-passed the road block. I hid my bicycle under a hedge, climbed into a tree, and spent the rest of the night among the branches.

At dawn on 20 Jul 43, I descended, washed myself and resumed my journey. I had my shaving kit with me, but found it was not necessary to shave at this time.

I passed through Elbing without incident, but about 15 kms. west of it, my front tyre punctured while I was going through a village. I walked through the village, took my bicycle into a wood, and stuffed the punctured tyre with grass. I then proceeded until I came to a pontoon bridge over the River Vistula. This bridge was guarded, but there was much traffic upon it, and the guard took no notice of me. I crossed the bridge, and then rode and walked alternately until I reached the outskirts of Danzig just before dark. I then hid my bicycle, walked along a path beside a railway line and hid in an old signal box.

Early next morning, 21 Jul 43, I saw a man wearing French uniform, I told him that I was an English 'airman' and said that I wished to go somewhere where I could wash and change. He took me to a small station and gave me coffee and hot water. I washed and shaved here.

I told the Frenchman that I wished to get down to the docks at Danzig and board a Swedish boat. He remarked that my tunic was bulging underneath my overalls, so I took it off. He also told me that my 'Zivil' badge was no use in Danzig, and the French P/W here wore two crosses and the letter of their prison camp on their left arms. He likewise offered me money, which I declined. I left my haversack and battledress blouse with him, and he told me that if I was unsuccessful in finding a ship at the docks I could return to him.

I then walked towards the docks, mingling with people going to work. I noticed some piles of coal alongside some ships painted with the Swedish colours. There was a German guard nearby engaged in examining travellers' papers. I approached him, rolling a cigarette, and as I passed him I turned my head away from him and spat. He allowed me to pass without incident. There were a number of workmen walking in the same direction, and he probably did not notice me.

I now found myself on a cinder track parrellel to the wharf where the Swedish ships were berthed. Between the track and the ships there was a wire fence with gaps in it opposite each ship. At each gap a German guard was posted.

On the opposite side of the track to the wharf there was a latrine. I entered this and watched closely. I noticed a number of Russian workmen wearing overalls and old civilian clothes, walking through a gap near me on to one of the Swedish boats. Other workmen were leaving this ship and passing through the gap outwards.

About 1000 hrs it began to rain, which may have temporarily distracted the attention of the guard at this gap. Choosing a suitable moment I mingled with other workmen, walked past the guard, and up a companion way on board the Swedish ship. Almost immediately I found a place where I could see the boiler room, which was empty.

I climbed down a ladder into the boiler, opened a door between two of the boilers, and entered a narrow passage on each side of the boilers, whence I wa able to look into the boiler room. I stayed here until the evening. I then came out, and finding no one about, dropped into the coal bunker, and hid amongst the coal. Here I remained for two days. The only food I had was a pound of chocolate and I had no water. From time to time I was able to peer out of my hiding place.

On the morning of 23 Jul a man came down into the bunker and flashed a torch about. Shortly afterwards a bell rang, and the ship began to move.

I remained in my hiding place until about 1500 hrs on 24 Jul, when I clambered up to my spy-hole and looked out. I then approached one of the Swedish sailors, told him that I was an Englishman, and that I wished to see the Captain. When the Captain saw me, he asked me to prove to him that I was English. I then handed to him my two British Army identity discs, which I had managed to retain on my person since my capture in Africa. The Captain congratulated me, and said 'You ought to be in England in a week.'

He then sent me to the crew's quarters where I was scrubbed down, given some clothes, and fed. My old clothes were thrown overboard, and with them my 50 Reichsmarks and 150 francs. I retained my maps.

The ship arrived in Goteborg at 1100 hrs on 25 Jul. Here I was handed over to the Swedish police. After taking my particulars, they conducted me to a hospital where I was disinfected. That evening I was taken to the Police Station, but I refused to give any information until I saw the British Vice-Consul. Eventually he arrived and took me to his office. That night I was sent to Stockholm by train, alone.

I arrived at Stockholm next morning, 26 Jul, and took a taxi to the British Legation, where the Military Attaché met me. I remained in Stockholm until 14 Aug 43, when I left by air for the U.K.   (*L.G. 7.10.43*)

Byrne, Patrick, Warrant Officer Cl. I (R.S.M.)
6340124, 6 Queen's Own Royal West Kent Regt.
(Ashford) (Immediate)
From March 20th—27th 1944 the Bn occupied the area of Cassino Castle and Pt 175. Circumstances dictated that supplies were off-loaded at the base of the hill in a quarry which was under direct enemy observation and which was shelled continuously throughout the battle for Cassino and in the following days. RSM Byrne was in charge of this area and of the organisation of the nightly carrying parties. These invariably took place in the dark under shellfire, and every day took its toll of casualties. Throughout the period RSM Byrne showed such outstanding coolness and disregard for his own safety that the men kept perfectly steady and the difficult operation was carried out in good order. Time and again during the most intense periods of shelling he would be seen calmly walking about encouraging the men and organising the evacuation of the wounded. On the last night a dump of 900 mortar bombs was set alight, and for two hours the small quarry was filled with explosions and flying shrapnel. RSM Byrne's superb example in these trying circumstances was again instrumental in maintaining order and saving many casualties.
(*L.G. 20.7.44*)

C

Cabot, Cyril Charles, Lance Sergeant
5058217, 1st Bn. North Staffordshire Regt. (Calcutta)
On the evening 6 May 43 in the area of milestone three on the Maungdaw—Buthidaung road L/Sjt. Cabot was a platoon Sjt in a composite force under Lt Wise. This force was ordered to attack and occupy a hill feature to the N of the road. At about 1830 hrs the platoon in which L/Sjt. Cabot was Sjt was ordered to move round the right flank and secure a limited objective. Under cover of darkness they moved through particularly thick and difficult country and at first light found that they had over run their objectives and were within the enemy lines. On proceeding towards their original objectives they came under very heavy enemy MG and rifle fire, when three men were killed and three men wounded. The platoon withdrew under cover to a temporary defence position. L/Sjt. Cabot repeatedly went back to the wounded dressing their wounds and took water. On each trip he was exposed to very heavy fire, but despite this he rescued the wounded and brought them back to cover; and succeeded in burying two of the dead. Finally he made a reconnaissance again subjected to very heavy enemy fire and eventually discovered a route by which the platoon returned with the wounded and subsequently rejoined Lt. Wise's force.

Throughout the entire action L/Sjt. Cabot showed a complete disregard of personal danger and courage of the highest order. The acting platoon commander and the personnel of the platoon cannot speak too highly of this NCO. It was undoubtably due to his personal courage and example that the platoon commander and the personnel of the platoon was able to evacuate the wounded and rejoin a weak force, who needed the extra weapons to carry out their task.

For his proven courage and staunchness in battle on previous occasions L/Sjt. Cabot was selected for a particularly audacious patrol, consisting of one B.O. and two B.O.Rs which set out for the Maungdaw area on 17 June 43 with the object of capturing a Japanese prisoner. After 36 hours in the enemy lines watching the enemy movements an opportunity arose at Zantelarara near Maungdaw. At about noon on 19th June 43 a Jap patrol of six men and a traitor Muslim entered the village and three (including the Muslim) entered a house. By a clever ruse the patrol succeeded in capturing one Jap, killing the others and possibly killing the Muslim. L/Sjt. Cabot assisted in the capture of the prisoner and throughout the entire operation displayed those qualities of personal courage and staunchness worthy of the highest traditions of the British NCO without which the patrol could not have been a success. At all times in action L/Sjt. Cabot has set a fine example and has displayed courage of the highest order. I consider that his individual acts and …
[completion missing] (L.G. 16.12.43)

Cairns, Alexander, M.M., Sergeant
3191131, 8th Bn. Durham Light Infantry (Glasgow)
On the morning of 6 June 42 enemy posns were located to the south of 8 DLI Outpost. It was decided to attack these posns with 4 Carriers and a Sec of Inf. Sjt. Cairns led the Carrier attack with such dash and determination that the enemy posns were overrun and 10 Officers, 200 men and a number of A/Tk Guns, heavy and light M.Gs captured.
M.M. 20.12.40 (L.G. 24.9.42)

Calder, Harry Watt, Private
14421247, R.A.M.C. (attd. No. 40 RM Commando & HOC) (Peterhead) (Immediate)
Operation 'Impact' 11th–12th April 1945.

At daybreak, two troops of the Commando, plus Tactical HQ, to which Pte Calder was attached in the capacity of medical orderly, found themselves on the tip of a narrow dyke with impassable mud and water on either side. From one flank they were subjected to intense and accurate artillery and mortar fire; and from the other they were under close and accurate small arms and snipers' fire. Within a few minutes eight officers and men were killed or seriously wounded, and one of the troop medical orderlies who had tried to reach them was forced to take cover in some swampy grass.

At this stage Pte Calder crawled forward, and when all cover gave out he tied some white bandage round one arm in lieu of his Geneva Cross which he had lost and advanced in the open. He was followed by Sgt Bostock RAMC, who witnessed the next incident. Calder was now so close to the enemy position that a German NCO, thinking he wished to surrender, came out and signaled to him to come in; Calder somehow managed to make him understand that he intended to look after the casualties; the German politely agreed and returned to his strongpoint.

Calder and Sgt Bostock evacuated the only surviving casualty successfully. Throughout the next three hours Calder left his slit-trench repeatedly to deal with other casualties as they occurred: during which time he had repeated narrow escapes. As soon as the enemy strongpoint in the pumping-station was captured Pte Calder advanced entirely on his own initiative to help with the casualties there. It now became known that the troop that had advanced to the canal bridge (our main objective) had been attacked from both sides by the enemy, supported by two self-propelled guns, and had been wiped out.

Without a word to anyone Pte Calder set off alone down another dyke which was completely devoid of cover and subjected to heavy fire of all kinds. He swam a gap through which flood water was pouring, which had been deemed impassable to troops, and near the bridge found the bodies of the medical orderly and other members of the missing troop.

Although he was now half a mile in advance of the Commando's most forward position he pushed on beyond the bridge. Here he found two seriously wounded men of the Commando, one of them lying in the water. He did what he could for them and then pushed on half a mile further through still uncaptured territory until he found a stretcher party of the 2/5 Queens in Menate village. He led these back to rescue the two wounded men, and then returned alone to our positions. Throughout the whole day he continued to display a complete indifference to danger and a cheerful stoicism that was most remarkable.

His behaviour was an outstanding display of the most exceptional initiative and courage with which he is endowed, and which he has shown on several previous operations. *(L.G. 18.10.45)*

Calistan, Charles Vivian, M.M., Lance Sergeant
6915040, 2nd Bn. Rifle Brigade (Stratford, E. 15)
Sjt. Calistan was Section Commander of a section of 6 pdr anti-tank guns sited on the west flank of the snipe position 866295 on 26 & 27 Oct 42. Sjt. Calistan's troop was engaged by enemy tanks both during the night and the following morning; by midday 27 Oct all the other guns in his troop had been knocked out, and all the other numbers of his own gun crew but himself wounded and incapaitated. The troop was almost out of ammunition.

At about 1300 hrs 15 German tanks attacked his sector. The Commanding Officer arrived at his position and acted as loader while he laid the gun and acted as No. 1. With the greatest courage and coolness he waited until the tanks were 200–300 yds away, and hit and set nine of them on fire. He then had no more ammunition left. Unperturbed he waited while his troop commander fetched more ammunition, and when it had arrived, hit three more enemy tanks in as many shots, and so broke and repelled the enemy attack. He continued to operate his gun for the rest of the day. After dark he received orders to close on to Coy HQ, and withdrew with the rest of his company. He set off to walk the 400 yds to Coy HQ under heavy MG fire from 3 German tanks, carrying one of the wounded members of his crew. The wounded man was hit and killed in his arms. He immediately returned to his troop position to fetch the last remaining wounded man, whom he brought safely back, still under intense & accurate fire.

Throughout the action, the quality of his determination was such that, when the last point of human endurance & ability to continue to fight had been reached, Sjt. Calistan took a new lease of courage. This he communicated to all around him, and with their help he

saved the day, so enabling his Battalion to withdraw safely from a critical position, after inflicting losses of 57 tanks burnt on the enemy.

During this action, his superb gallantry was outstanding among many courageous acts performed. *M.M. 13.8.42* *(L.G. 14.1.43)*

Callaghan, Thomas, Guardsman
2716776, 1st Bn. Irish Guards (Immediate)
On the 15th May 1940, H.M.T. 'Chrobry' was bombed, set on fire and subsequently abandoned. The bomb, or bombs, dropped in the cabins occupied by the senior officers of the 1st Bn Irish Guards. Gdsmn Callaghan saved the lives of a number of men who were trapped below by lowering a rope to a porthole and hauling them up to the top deck.
(M.M., L.G. 27.9.40, amended to D.C.M. L.G. 7.3.41)

Calvert, Arthur, Warrant Officer Cl. III (Pl.S.M.)
2654108, 2nd Bn. Coldstream Guards
On the 1st June on the Yser Canal north of Hondschoote, P.S.M. Calvert handled his platoon with sound common sense, thereby saving casualties to his own men and inflicting heavy loss on the enemy. After the officers of his company had been killed or wounded he was ordered to withdraw his platoon from the canal bank. He executed the withdrawal in face of the enemy without further loss. He showed a fine example of initiative. His calmness and courage under M.G. and shell fire were an example to all ranks. *(L.G. 27.8.40)*

Calvert, George Edward, Warrant Officer Cl. II (C.S.M.)
4389328, 6 Bn. Green Howards (Sunderland)
(Immediate)
On 11 June 1944 near Oristot CSM Calvert was CSM of 'A' Coy during the attack on an enemy position in close country. When the coy were ordered to reorganise on the ground they had won, one pl was cut off from the rest and despite assistance by three tanks was under heavy Spandau fire causing casualties. The C.O. ordered the Coy Comd to extricate them and take up another position. The Coy Comd went forward and was killed instantly. CSM Calvert organised a support group of three bren guns and set about reorganising the pl. Only when two bren gunners had been wounded and the other had run out of ammunition did this W.O. move back to the rest of the coy carrying with him a wounded man and himself bringing up the rear. His courage, leadership and example inspired all about him during three hours of continuous fighting.
M.I.D. 20.12.40, Belgian Decoration Militaire, 14.5.48 *(L.G. 31.8.44)*

Cameron, Desmond Robert, Warrant Officer Cl. II (temp.)
214866, Royal Australian Infantry Regt.
For Vietnam *(L.G. 2.4.70)*

Cameron, Donald George, M.M., Warrant Officer Cl.
II (temp.)
5410081, Royal Australian Infantry Corps
No citation. *(L.G. 28.3.69)*

Cameron, Duncan Iain, Corporal
T/92464, R.A.S.C. (Pitlochry, Perthshire)
M.I.D. 25.1.45 *(L.G. 23.3.44)*

Campbell, Alexander George, Staff Sergeant
*7597284, R.E.M.E., LAD attd. 142 Regt., R.A.C.
(Glasgow)*
At Sbiba on 21st Feb 43 after the Meftah Ridge action
the F.O.O., reported his Cruiser tank had broken down
in No Man's Land during the withdrawal. I ordered S/
Sjt. Campbell to go out with a covering party provided
by the Coldstream Guards and recover the tank. As soon
as the A.R.V. was heard advancing the Germans lit up
the area in which it was working with parachute flares
and then shelled and machine-gunned the area. S/Sjt.
Campbell was quite imperturbed and made it plain to
his crew that all the German shot, shell & lights ever
manufactured would not prevent them recovering the
tank. The tank was recovered.

On 21st Apr 43, his Sqn Comd's tank was badly
disabled in a minefield. Quite regardless of personal
safety and under shell and mortar fire, S/Sjt. Campbell
made repeated journeys, through the minefield which
had not been swept, to the tank to evacuate every single
item of equipment possible.

After the Meftah Ridge and all the other actions he
has always been the first person to inspect and evacuate
derelict tanks whether in minefields or not and arrange
for their recovery, and given valuable assistance to the
R.D., R.E.M.E., R.A.M.C. and Padre.

His endless energy and cheerful attitude even after
working non-stop day and night for days on end have
been a model of outstanding leadership under the most
trying and dangerous battle conditions. His work and
conduct throughout the campaign have equalled the
highest traditions of the R.E.M.E.

His courage, loyalty, command of men, and radiation
of energy and determination, and his confident cheerful
outlook combined with an enlivening sense of humour
have turned tired men into veritable lions working for
him in battle.
M.I.D. 23.5.46 *(L.G. 8.7.43)*

Campbell, Robert Millar, Sergeant
*53072, 2 S.A. Armd. C. Recce Bn., S.A.T.C., South
African Forces*
On 13 Apl 42 T/Sjt. Campbell, R. M. was in comd of a
sec of Armd C's with a coln which was attacked by at
least 15 Tanks at U8588 (ref map Ain-el-Gazala). When
withdrawing with the coln he noticed some infantry
running in front of the advancing tanks and immediately
turned his Armd C round and moved forward about 500
yards under intense tank, arty and M.G. fire to endeavour

to rescue some of these men. He approached to within
about 200 yards of the tanks and picked up three men. In
spite of the fact that his car stopped on this journey owing
to engine failure he returned twice more under similar
circumstances and rescued a further two men on each
trip, one of them being wounded.

This NCO's coolness, courage, devotion to duty and
utter disregard of his own safety in the face of the enemy
fire was instrumental in the rescue of seven of his
comrades and was an inspiration to everyone.
(L.G. 9.7.42)

Canning, Oliver, Warrant Officer Cl. I (Staff Sgt.-Maj.)
546720, 10th Hussars, Royal Armoured Corps
On 27th May, 1940, at Huppy S.S.M. Canning was
attacking enemy machine gun nests in position. S.S.M.
Canning's tank was having great difficulty manœuvring
on heavy plough, and was unable to engage machine
gun nests which were very well sited on reverse slope
positions. Without hesitation S.S.M. Canning dismounted from his tank and destroyed an enemy machine
gun team with his revolver. S.S.M. Canning's action was
responsible in destroying an important enemy machine
gun position and was a splendid example to his men.
M.B.E. 1.1.52 *(L.G. 27.9.40)*

Cardy, Kenneth Francis, Sergeant
*6025124, R.E.M.E. attd. 2nd (Armd. Recce Bn. Welsh
Gds.) (Orsett, Essex) (Immediate)*
On 9 Apr 45 near Menslage, he was driving behind a
tank which was hit by 2 H.E. shells and burst into flames.
All the crew were wounded.

Sjt. Cardy, completely disregarding his own personal
safety since he was under heavy shellfire from heavy
calibre German Guns, rushed to the tank and, single-
handed, fought the flames and put them out, thereby
saving the vehicle which could, therefore, be repaired
and was actually put back into service the next day. Later
in the same evening this NCO recovered a tank under
observation of the enemy who were putting down fire
upon the area where he was working. Sjt. Cardy
deliberately drove his ARV between two blazing houses
to recover this tank although he was under intense
shellfire at the same time.

By this cool and gallant action, and by showing such
a very great devotion to duty, he had saved two tanks for
the Battalion at a time when it was extremely short of
vehicles. *(L.G. 12.7.45)*

Carey, Keith, Sergeant
NX 4546, 2/3 Aust. Inf. Bn.
New Guinea. For outstanding gallantry and devotion to
duty.

During an attack by 'C' Coy near [...] New Guinea
on 6 Nov 42, Sjt. Carey was in command of the left
platoon. The enemy held a narrow uphill spur well
covered by M.G. fire. As casualties were suffered Sjt.
Carey rallied his men and pressed forward with great

determination. The commander of the right platoon was wounded and Sjt. Carey immediately assumed command of both platoons and pressed forward until the objective was reached. The Coy then came under severe infilade fire and in a very short time only 12 men remained unwounded. Sjt. Carey pressed home the attack and an enemy heavy machine gun was captured. Pressing further forward he held the high ground under very heavy enemy pressure until the arrival of reinforcements put the enemy to flight. Throughout the action Sjt. Carey's coolness and courage were outstanding and an example to his men. The success of the attack was largely due to his skill and leadership, and to his determination especially when casualties were heavy. *(L.G. 30.3.43)*

Cargill, William, Warrant Officer Cl. II
2754158, 2nd Bn. Black Watch (Arbroath)
This Warrant Officer has been Coln Sjt Major throughout the period of training, and operations in Burma.

During the action north of Nathkokyin on 8 May 1944, Warrant Officer Cargill displayed outstanding qualities of courage and resourcefulness in assisting to direct the immediate defence of the Command Post. As casualties occurred, he attended to them under frequently heavy fire in addition to his other duties.

Finally with complete disregard for his personal safety and by coolness in the handling of his weapons he was largely responsible for beating off the first enemy counter-attack.

Eventually, after the engagement lasting some 5 hours had been broken off Warrant Officer Cargill was a member of a party of approx 90 men including eleven casualties which was faced with an exceptionally arduous march through mountainous country. Throughout the 24 hour march, with complete indifference to personal fatigue, he maintained a very high standard of discipline amongst exhausted troops, largely as a result of which the party rejoined safely the main force as a formed body with no stragglers, and every man with his arms, ammunition and equipment as he left the battle-field.

Throughout operations this Warrant Officer has shown the highest possible sense of duty, and his courage, determination and cheerfulness have been an inspiration to all.

Warrant Officer Cargill has previously served with distinction, first as a Corporal and then as a Sjt in Crete, Syria and Tobruk. *(L.G. 26.4.45)*

Carpenter, Frank Herbert, Lance Sergeant
46696, 7th Field Sqn., Royal Engineers (Ipswich)
(Immediate)
During the night 23/24 Oct, 1942, about M.R. 87552957, this NCO continuously shewed the greatest courage and devotion to duty. While his Troop were held up by enemy fire on the first field L/Sjt. Carpenter with the greatest coolness went into the field and neutralised booby traps. Later in the night he again carried out this dangerous work under fire on the third enemy field and together

with his Troop Leader charged an enemy post which was firing on the troop making the gap, taking the occupants prisoner.

Throughout the whole of the night, no matter how heavy the fire L/Sjt. Carpenter carried on his hazardous task of lifting booby traps. His coolness, courage, and tenacity was outstanding and remarked by all who saw him. *(L.G. 14.1.43)*

Carpenter, Herbert Charles, Sergeant (actg.)
6465807, 2nd Bn. Royal Fusiliers (Virginia Water)
(Immediate)
On the afternoon of 11 Nov 1944, 'Z' Coy were ordered to move from X roads to capture some houses. On approaching some factory buildings, the Company came under intense fire at close range from MGs and bazooka stationed in these buildings. The right hand platoon was completely pinned down and the left hand one No. 16 platoon, commanded by Sjt. Carpenter went to ground. Sjt. Carpenter quickly rallied his platoon and leading them in a skilful left flanking movement succeeded in by-passing the factory and infiltrating his platoon to a FUP for an attack on his final objective taking 5 prisoners on the way. These houses were strongly held and the enemy opened heavy small arms fire on No. 16 platoon. In spite of this Sjt. Carpenter led his platoon in an attack on the houses which he succeeded in capturing, killing three Germans and taking a further 8 prisoners. The platoon was now almost surrounded, with enemy at very close quarters, but Sjt. Carpenter consolidated his objective and later made his way back alone to guide 'X' Company forward to reinforce his position. He then, under orders, withdrew his platoon into 'Z' Company reserve, and thereafter throughout the night organised and led carrying parties with food for the forward troops of both 'X' and 'Z' Companies who were in very close contact with the enemy. His unbounded cheerfulness throughout was a wonderful inspiration to all ranks. His daring and initiative in getting his platoon through the enemy positions to capture his objective, and finally his personal courage and dash in the final assault and clearance of the houses turned the immediate stalemate into a very favourable position, forced the enemy to withdraw from the factory buildings before daylight, and proved to be the deciding factor in the success of the whoe battalion operation. *(L.G. 26.4.45)*

Carr, Edwin Frank, Corporal
188487, 24 NZ Bn. (Immediate)
On the night of 7 Dec 43, during the earlier stages of the bitter fighting in the attack on Orsogna, Cpl. Carr's section was forced to retire a hundred yards. This NCO then discovered that one of his section was lying wounded in the lost ground. With no regard to his personal safety, Cpl. Carr went forward under intense small arms fire and brought the wounded man back to safety. He then rejoined his section. One hour later, at about 2000 hrs, Cpl. Carr's section, which then consisted

of himself and three men, were left forward section of a leading platoon. Shortly after they advanced again to attack and the whole platoon came under intense spandau fire from a ridge to the left. With complete disregard to danger and with great coolness, Cpl. Carr and one of his section moved straight up the ridge and wiped out the first machine gun post. This NCO then carried on and with outstanding bravery successfully accounted for two more machine gun posts single handed. He then lead his section to wipe out a fourth post. After a further hundred yards advance of very bitter fighting the company was ordered to withdraw and whilst doing so, Cpl. Carr was wounded in the arm. Before leaving he handed over his section to one of his men and walked back to the RAP unassisted. Throughout the whole five hours fighting Cpl. Carr showed outstanding leadership and bravery and set a fine example to the other members of his section and company.

M.I.D. 23.5.46   *(L.G. 6.4.44)*

Carr, Francis Arthur, Sergeant
1867740, Royal Engineers, No. 5 Commando
(London, S.E.14)
On 28th March 1942, during the Commando Raid at St. Nazaire, France.

Sgt Carr was NCO i/c the demolition party commanded by Lieut Robert Burtenshaw.

Before reaching the demolition site, Lieut Burtenshaw was killed and immediately Sgt Carr took command and led the party, against heavy enemy opposition, to the dry dock gate.

Sgt Carr then reported to Lieut Brett who commanded another demolition party also detailed to assist in destroying this gate. Lieut Brett had been wounded in the legs and could only move with difficulty. Sgt Carr assisted Lieut Brett in supervising the two parties in their laying of the explosive charges on the dry dock gate. The charges were about to be fired when fighting broke out in the area, forcing the demolition party to take cover. Sgt Carr then went forward alone and fired the charges which completely destroyed this gate.

Sgt Carr then continued to assist Lieut Brett in organising the withdrawal of both parties to the point of re-embarkation. Sgt Carr throughout the entire action showed outstanding courage and devotion to duty. His leadership was magnificent.

M.I.D. 20.12.40   *(L.G. 5.7.45)*

Carr, Jack Theobald, Sergeant
1052363, 2 Svy. Regt., Royal Artillery
This NCO was in H.M.S. 'Grafton' on May 29th 1940 when the ship was struck by a torpedo in Dunkirk harbour. He was among a party of troops of various units between decks. When the torpedo struck there was a rush for the nearest exit. Sjt. Carr immediately took charge and by his cool behaviour stopped the panic and kept the men quiet between decks until the order was given to embark on the rescue ship. Sjt. Carr then assisted

wounded men and did all in his power to help the evacuation of the ship. His final act before leaving the 'Grafton' was to go back below decks and rescue a wounded man who had been forgotten. *(L.G. 27.8.40)*

Carr, Peter, Sergeant
3128552, 2nd Bn. Royal Scots Fusiliers
No. 3128552 Sjt. P. Carr, 2nd Bn. The Royal Scots Fusiliers is recommended for the award of the Distinguished Conduct Medal.

On the night 26/27th May, 1940 the platoon officer was missing and Sjt. Carr took charge of the Platoon. He showed great courage and was very cool under enemy fire from sniper, machine guns and mortars. He continually visited section posts and kept the men very cheery.

On the night of 26th May, 1940 it was reported that No. 3127993 Fusilier Strain was wounded and that no one could get to him. This NCO crawled under heavy fire and brought back Fus. Strain, who was very badly wounded, he then went forward and brought back the gun which had been used by Fus. Strain.

On the morning of the 27th May, 1940 when the order was given to withdraw Sjt. Carr again went forward and brought back more wounded. He reorganised his platoon and took up another position on the railway in rear of Hill 60.
Silver Star L.G. 14.5.48   *(L.G. 27.8.40)*

Carr, Raymond, Sergeant
408479, 5th Royal Inniskilling Dragoon Guards
(Moulton, Northants.) (Immediate)
On 24 Oct 44 Sjt. Carr was leading a Tp of 'A' Sqn. During the night 23/24 Oct two bns of 158 Inf Bde had advanced from Rosmalen along the railway to the Eastern outskirts of s'Hertogenbosch under cover of darkness.

On the morning of 24 Oct 'A' Sqn was ordered to move up to support 1 E Lancs in that area. Preliminary recce revealed that the route taken by the infantry below the embankment was too boggy to be practicable for tanks. The only possible route for the tanks was along the railway which was raised on an embankment 15 ft above the surrounding country and in full view of enemy positions on both flanks.

Anti-Tank guns had already been reported in action in the area Hintham 3447 some 400 yards south of the rly and though being engaged by another sqn were not known to have been neutralized, others were reported along the dyke between Herven 3248—Heinis 3448 500–1,000 yards north of and dominating the rly. Sjt. Carr with complete disregard for his personal safety, led his troop with the greatest determination and dash along the rly line itself for 1000 yards and was then able to find a passable route north of the embankment. This route though defiladed from the south by the embankment was still in full view of the enemy positions to the north. Sjt. Carr continued his advance reporting the state of the going to his Sqn Leader as he did so and succeeded in reaching s'Hertogenbosch and making contact with 1 E Lancs in the town.

As a result of Sjt. Carr's gallant and hazardous advance the remainder of the sqn were able to move up to support 1 E Lancs and complete the operation of mopping up the Eastern outskirts of the town.

(*L.G. 1.3.45*)

Carroll, Michael Rupert, Sergeant
212555, Royal Australian Infantry Corps
For Vietnam   (*L.G. 18.2.69*)

Carruthers, John, Sergeant
4456094, 8 Durham Light Infantry, T.A
Sjt. Carruthers showed great courage and coolness under hy fire when employed with the Br Carrier Pl on a standing patrol, to watch for enemy tanks. He engaged enemy L.M.G. posns, thus drawing their fire away from British tanks, which were retiring nearby. He continued at his gun under heavy fire until all his amn was expended. This occurred on 21 May 40. (*L.G. 11.7.40*)

Carruthers, William Ernest, Corporal (A/Sgt.)
Ch.x.3[.], Royal Marines
For Malaya   (*L.G. 19.10.51*)

Carter, Charles William, Sergeant
20462, 21 NZ Bn. (Immediate)
On the night 9/10 Jul, 42, Sjt. Carter led a fighting patrol into Elmreir depression. He attacked with grenades a large enemy gun and tractor, killing the crew. He then led his patrol against an Italian strong point doing great execution with both LMG and grenades. Sjt. Carter showed good judgment and splendid fighting qualities in this action and also 15/16 Jul, 42, at Ruweisit Ridge he led his platoon and displayed good leadership and showed a splendid fighting example to his men.

(*L.G. 26.11.42*)

Carter, Eric Reginald, Sergeant
5628590, 2nd Bn. Hampshire Regt. (Reading)
(Immediate)
On the 25th October, 1943, 'Y' Company had been ordered to seize the bridge at 931751. There were known to be at least four M.Gs covering this bridge, and night fighting patrols had failed to deal with these. Sjt. Carter was placed in command of an assault party of six men and ordered to attempt a crossing of the bridge in daylight. Sjt. Carter led his party to the bridge and directed intensive fire on to all known enemy posts. With great dash he then led the way across the bridge and himself knocked out the nearest M.G. post with grenades. The enemy outnumbered his party by at least two to one but, under Sjt. Carter's direction they were taken prisoner or driven out. At least six dead Germans were found later. An unlocated M.G. post from the right then opened up and prevented re-inforements crossing the bridge. Sjt. Carter organised the four remaining men already across

into a defensive bridgehead and held on until further reinforcements were brought across. He then led the party with great determination and completed the capture of the bridgehead. The success of this operation was undoubtedly due to Sjt. Carter's courage, leadership and personal example which led the enemy to think that his assault detachment was far larger than it in fact was.

(*L.G. 24.2.44*)

Carter, John Alexander, Trooper (T/Corporal)
38317, Royal Australian Armoured Corps
At approximately 1800 hours 18th August 1966 Corporal John Carter was the Crew Commander of an armoured personnel carrier of 3 Troop First Armoured Personnel Carrier Squadron. This troop had been given the task of carrying a relieving force of Infantry to assist D company 6 Battalion Royal Australian Regiment which was in heavy contact with a Brigade sized enemy force. Orders were for the carrier troop to advance with two sections forward. Weather conditions at the time were extremely difficult due to a severe rain storm.

When contact was made with the enemy, Corporal Carter's vehicle was engaged by fire from a 57 millimetre recoilless rifle, machine gun and small arms fire. The projectile from the 57 recoilless rifle missed his vehicle and exploded against a rubber tree. Corporal Carter returned the fire using his 50 calibre machine gun. The gun jammed. He then grasped the driver's Owen Machine Carbine and without hesitation leapt on to the top of his vehicle and returned fire killing the 57 millimetre recoilless rifle team a fraction after another 57 millimetre recoilless rifle round had been fired. This round exploded and dazed the crew and passengers. Corporal Carter still undeterred continued to fire killing five other enemy.

By his actions Corporal Carter also drew additional fire on to himself enabling the other vehicles of the troop to advance.

Through the action which was fought at very close range, Corporal Carter showed outstanding courage, initiative and determination. His actions were an inspiration to all his comrades and contributed greatly to the success of the assault by the relief force, the heavy casualties inflicted on the enemy, and, immediately afterwards, the relief of D Company 6 Batalion, The Royal Australian Regiment. [*From L.G.*]   (*L.G. 1.8.67*)

Carter, Kenneth, Private
5445267, 2nd Bn. Duke of Cornwall's Light Infantry
(Hayle, Cornwall) (Immediate)
On 8 August, 1944, during the attack by 2nd Bn D.C.L.I. on the Incontro Monastery 889659, B Coy reached the S.E. corner of the outside wall and 15 pl were ordered to advance to the N.E. corner. The platoon came under very heavy M.G. fire from an enemy locality on the Eastern slope of the feature. The Platoon Commander decided to attack the position round the right flank, supported by a fire group from the left. Pte. Carter was the No. 1 of the bren gun in this fire group, and it soon became

obvious that his was the only position from which the target could be effectively engaged. Opening fire, Pte. Carter immediately became the target for the enemy fire, and he was very severely wounded; one bullet entering his neck and another passing through one cheek and out of the other, smashing his jaw bone.

Although in great pain and almost unconscious, Pte. Carter continued to give effective covering fire until the flanking force reached its objective. He then collapsed. Had he failed, the attacking sections could not have reached their objective without heavy casualties.

(L.G. 7.12.44)

Carter, Thomas John, Sergeant
2041039, 1st Bn. East Surrey Regt. (Bromley)
(Periodic)
On 2 Jun 44 a recce patrol of tanks and carriers with a mine-sweeping detachment from the Pioneer Platoon under Sjt. Carter was sent out to find out whether Fulmone (Map ref Ferentino Sheet 151–2–SW 409473) 3 miles in front of our own lines was held by the enemy. The tanks and carriers were stopped by a demolition 2 miles from Fulmone. An Italian arrived shortly after and said that 8 Germans were in his house and had killed his wife. Sjt. Carter asked for volunteers and left to capture them with a L/Cpl and Pte of the Carrier Platoon and his 2 Ptes of the mine-sweeping detachment. They took two LMGs and three TSMGs. After a walk of a mile over the hills they found the house empty, but saw below them, 1000 yards away at the foot of the Fulmone Hill an 88 mm gun and crew. Sjt. Carter ordered the Bren guners to open fire. One man at least was wounded. Immediately after, they heard and saw a large explosion at the gun position. Sjt. Carter and the L/Cpl, covered by the Bren guns, walked down to the gun which they found in the middle of the road. It was demolished and there was blood round it. After calling down the Bren gunners Sjt. Carter ordered the house [...] parties of Germans were seen; one was engaged by TSMG fire [...]away by Bren gun fire. At least one man in each group was wounded. As [...] was now getting dusk Sjt. Carter led his patrol home three [...]. By his extremely resourceful leading of the patrol wh[...], once the carriers were stopped, might well have turned back, and by his personal courage, this NCO was responsible for the wounding of at least three Germans and for causing them to destroy their 88mm gun. This action was most commendable since Sjt. Carter knew that he could not be supported by tanks or carriers if he got into trouble, and that he was three miles in front of our lines.

This NCO has commanded the Bn Pioneer Pln since 31 Jul 43 with great distinction. He has invariably undertaken the most dangerous work himself and his personal example on many occasions under fire has proved an inspiration to his pln. During the period the Bn was in the line on the R Rapido (Map ref Italy 1/100,000 Cassino 8815) Sjt. Carter supervised mine-lifting operations by his pln on a number of consecutive nights. These operations entailed dealing with new types of booby traps and the new wooden box mine. In addition a number of German and uncharted American minefields were located and marked by this NCO. All these operations were invariably carried out under enemy shell and mortar fire and it was largely due to Sjt. Carter's outstanding leadership that casualties in his pln were low.

(L.G. 7.12.44)

Carter, Thomas Robert, Corporal
1866710, 23 Fd. Coy. Royal Engineers
At Tressin on the night 24–25 May the demolition charges on two bridges only 30 yds apart were to be fired simultaneously by lighting two fuses. Actually only one fuse was lit, the other failed to light. Cpl. Carter who was R.E. representative on the spot, although he knew that one fuse was already lit & burning went forward and succeeded in lighting the fuse of the second bridge. He had only just gained cover when the first bridge blew up.   *(L.G. 22.10.40)*

Cartwright, H. F., Warrant Officer Cl. II (C.S.M.)
6190073, 47 Company, Auxiliary Military Pioneer
Corps
During the period of evacuation of the B.E.F to Boulogne, May 18/24, this Warrant Officer worked unceasingly, and it was largely due to him that the Company arrived intact at Boulogne. He organized and commanded a detachment of armed men in the fighting in Boulogne, and his personal example inspired his men, who were largely untrained for fighting, to put up a successful defence.
M.I.D. 26.7.40   *(L.G. 3.9.40)*

Carudel, Andrew George, Warrant Officer Cl. II
4461574, Durham Light Infantry
After successfully accomplishing a most dangerous mission in France in 1943 lasting nearly a year, for which he has been recommended for the M.M., this W.O. with great gallantry, volunteered for a second mission, although by then well known to and actively pursued by the enemy.

This work entailed extensive travelling under dangerous conditions in enemy occupied territory; Carudel was obliged to pass enemy Check Posts and came under scrutiny of enemy train guards. The risks which he ran were greatly increased owing to the fact that he was not a Frenchman, also by the fact that he was a well known figure on the French race courses as a jockey. If it had not been for his exceptional coolness and courage, especially on occasions when his travel papers which were invariably forged were not entirely 'in order,' it would not have been possible for him to continue this dangerous work. Apart from this, the dangers which he ran when reorganizing the compromised sector of his reseau during his first tour of duty in enemy occupied territory were extreme and increased the risks incurred on his return to France; in fact he had become well known to the Gestapo figuring on their counter espionage lists as British Lieutenant.

Some time after his arrival he was arrested with the head of the intelligence reseau to which he was attached. He endeavoured to save his chief but, finding this impossible, made his escape under enemy fire and succeeded in warning all concerned. Shewing great personal courage, he organized another attempt to effect the escape of his chief and, having failed, took over control of the organisation. With complete disregard for his own safety he succeeded in regrouping it and maintaining contact with London under the most difficult conditions until the liberation of France. Command of his reseau ranked in the eyes of the French Resistance Movement as a Lieutenant Colonel's appointment and he was in fact deemed to hold, whilst in the field, the honorary grade of Commandant.

Captured documents show that during the whole of the period his organisation was considered by the enemy counter-intelligence services as one of the most dangerous in France, and that all the means at their disposal were employed in the effort to achieve its destruction.

Throughout his mission, although in constant danger, C.S.M. Carudel exhibited the greatest qualities of courage, determination and leadership, inspiring all members of his organisation by his example of unsparing effort and unfailing cheerfulness.

M.M. 20.12.45   *(L.G. 20.12.45)*

Casey, Raymond Samuel, Sergeant
L18011, 5 Bdn. A.Tk. Regt., Royal Canadian Artillery
(Immediate)
The A & S H of C and the Linc & Welld Regt secured and for two days held a small brhead on the east side of the canal at Moembruggm 8794 (1/50000 Sheet 21 and 31) during which time a br was built. The brhead was limited in depth to about 300 yds due to hy mortar and MG fire. Sjt. Casey was Tp Sjt of 'A' Tp 96 Cdn A Tk Bty IC of two 17 pr M10s which with three tks of 29 Cdn Armd Recce Regt crossed into the brhead at 0700 hrs 10 Sep. With one tk of 29 Cdn Armd Recce Regt and one M10 Sjt. Casey proceeded to MR876945 where the two AFVs came under MG and rifle fire which could not be located due to the fog. Mov and what appeared to be an enemy AFV was seen but no accurate recce could be made from the vehs. Sjt. Casey went fwd on foot under fire to investigate and located 9 Germans in the backyard of the house all of whom he took prisoners. He took them back to the tk and returned to the house, re-entered and brought out 2 more Germans. One member of the tk crew who could speak German ascertained from the prisoners that they were members of the mortar pl and that the remainder of the pl with 3 mortars were in another house to the west. Sjt. Casey, with another member of his crew approached this house under fire and captured the remaining 14 members of the enemy pl who were found to be in trenches there. By his gallantry under fire and total disregard of his own safety, Sjt. Casey

liquidated an enemy mortar pl which had pinned down our tps in this area thereby enabling us to extend our brhead and permit our adv to continue. *(L.G. 9.12.44)*

Cassettari, Bruno, Private
14399391, 2/6th Bn. Queen's Royal Regt. (London,
E.6) (Immediate)
On 8 Sep 1944 'B' Company, 2/6th Bn The Queen's Royal Regiment carried out an attack on Gemanno which was strongly held by the enemy. During their advance to the objective, the Section Commander and all the members of Pte. Cassettari's section were either killed or wounded, by close range fire from an enemy machine post.

Pte. Cassettari armed himself with the bren gun and advanced single handed on the enemy post, killing all three of the enemy manning the machine gun. Pte. Cassettari then continued to advance to his objective, which he held alone until relieved by a section from the reserve platoon. Throughout this action, Pte. Cassettari showed complete disregard for his own personal safety and his individual action was of great assistance in enabling the Company to gain their objective.

            (L.G. 8.3.45)

Cassford, Arthur James, Warrant Officer Cl. III
(Pl.S.M.)
2613030, 3rd Bn. Grenadier Gds
On May 21, 40, this W.O. in spite of being wounded remained at his post and organised repeated counter attacks to stop enemy infiltration. His personal disregard for danger was an inspiration to all. *(L.G. 11.7.40)*

Catchpole, Austin Edward, Sergeant
7886150, 48th Bn. Royal Tank Regt. (M[..]on)
(Immediate)
Ref Maps: Italy 1/50,000 Sheet 88 I (Argenta) & 76 II (Portomaggiore).

On 18 April, 1945 'C' Sqn 48th Bn. Royal Tank Regiment was placed under comd 5 Buffs and was ordered to move north from Conselice 2749 and clear Route 16. No. 2 Tp comprising two tks under Sjt. Catchpole was in sp of B Coy. At 0500 hrs the Coy and tp were ordered to occupy a group of large buildings just north of Benvignante 2068. It was just starting to get light, the infantry were clearing the buildings. Sjt. Catchpole had dismounted and was guiding the leading tk into a posn in some nearby trees, when a S.P. from the area of the trees opened fire, penetrating the turret and badly wounding two of the crew. Sjt. Catchpole totally disregarding his own safety remained in the open and guided the tk around the corner of the building before it could be hit again. Here he attended to the wounded and then taking the second tk commenced manœuvering it into a posn where it could cover the S.P. While he was doing this a second S.P. opening up at almost point blank range hit the tk, later withdrawing slightly under cover of H.E. Two of the crew of this tk were also badly wounded and as before Sjt. Catchpole attended to them himself and carried them into one of the buildings.

At this juncture the posn was that the buildings were occupied by about half a Coy of Inf, the two damaged tks were useless and the two S.P.s covered the line of withdrawal. The whole party was in a rather disorganised state and Sjt. Catchpole, realising the seriousness of the posn immediately assumed command and organised the place for defence. Communication with the rest of the Bn and Sqn was severed so he ordered the infantry to cover him while he went to his tank, with the object of seeing if he could get his 19 Set working. As he was entering the tk by the side door it was bazookaed.

Later at 1100 hrs the situation in this area became apparent and a smoke screen was put down in the hope that it would enable the party to withdraw. This was duly successful, Sjt. Catchpole again playing a prominent part. He himself did not withdraw until he had stripped the 'Tabby' equipment and removed the breech block and firing mechanism from the tks.

This NCOs personal bravery, devotion to duty and leadership were beyond praise. He was entirely responsible for saving the situation and turning what might well have been a disaster into an orderly withdrawal. I can not speak too highly of his conduct.
(L.G. 23.8.45)

Catchpole, Reginald Arthur, Warrant Officer Cl. II (C.S.M.)
6342338, 4 Queen's Own Royal West Kent Regt.
For conspicuous gallantry and devotion to duty at the Foret de Nieppe between 25th and 28th May 1940.

When acting R.S.M. of his Bn. on 26th May, C.S.M. Catchpole did very valuable work in collecting stragglers of other units and escorting them under heavy fire to rifle companies which were in urgent need of reinforcements. This Warrant Officer by his example of bravery and disregard of personal safety was an inspiration to the men and the greatest value to his Commanding Offr during the period given above.   *(L.G. 11.7.40)*

Caveney, John, Warrant Officer Cl. III (Pl.S.M.)
3592593, 4th Bn. East Lancashire Regt.
At Cherens, on the night 24th/25th May, 1940, this P.S.M. led a fighting patrol of fifteen men which fought and probably destroyed the bulk of an enemy patrol of twenty five men and a reinforcement of twelve men. He brought back his own party without casualty displaying exceptional skill and courage. This was the first patrol the Bn. had carried out in face of the enemy and the moral effect throughout the Bn. was considerable.
(L.G. 22.10.40)

Chadwick, Walter Lees, Guardsman
2696194, 2nd Bn. Scots Guards (Widnes) (Immediate)
In the night attack on the Tobacco Factory Area Battipaglia on Sept 11th, this Guardsman showed outstanding bravery and dash. He personally accounted

for several German machine-gunners with his own bayonet. On one occasion a Spandau opened up at him at short range, one bullet grazed his lip, one went through his steel helmet and three through his haversack—he at once charged the post and killed the occupants. He was last seen in company with a Sjt. and another guardsman attacking a more distant Spandau post and was later reported 'Missing.' On Nov. 2nd he walked into our lines in civilian clothes.   *(L.G. 24.2.44)*

Challice, Clifford Lloyd, Private
C. 33169, Lincoln & Welland Regt., Canadian Infantry Corps
On the night 3/4 Apr 45, Linc & Welld R was ordered to attack and seize a bridgehead on the north side of the Twente Canal near Deldern, Holland. C Coy was on the right with No 12 Platoon detailed to seize the initial foothold and establish a firm base for the balance of the coy to pass through. During the crossing, the platoon sjt, who was in command, was severely wounded and the depleted platoon eventually found themselves on the far side of the canal, without leadership and under intense small arms and machine gun fire. Acting on his own initiative, Pte. Challice assumed command and organized his small group to defend a house which was the key point of the platoon position. The enemy immediately launched a vigorous counter-attack and in the early stages Pte. Challice suffered a broken right arm from enemy small arms fire. Despite the intense pain this soldier resited the remainder of his men, slung a Bren gun over his left shoulder and, with other wounded changing and loading magazines for him took up a fire position on the left of the house. In this manner he fought off the counter-attack almost single-handed, killing five of the enemy 50 feet from the window and wounding many more, thereby disorganizing the enemy and holding the bridgehead for the remainder of his coy to pass through. The immediate attack over, he assisted in the bandaging and evacuation of the wounded as best he could until he finally collapsed from exhaustion and shock and was himself removed to the RAP. By his initiative in assuming responsiility far beyond the call of duty, his disregard of great personal pain, and his refusal to attend to his own safety, Pte. Challice accounted for five of the enemy and inspired his men to successfully withstand every attempt by the enemy to cut off his coy. His courage was a magnificent example to all who saw him, and had a profound effect on the success of the action.
(L.G. 11.8.45)

Challington, William Albert, Lance Sergeant
3515161, Queen's Own Cameron Highlanders, No. 2 Commando (Birmingham)
On 28th March, 1942, during the Commando raid at St. Nazaire, France.

Sgt Challington was in an assault group covering the dry dock area. Disembarking from the burning bows of HMS Campbeltown on to the dock gates, Sgt Challington immediately engaged the enemy gun-crews who were on the roof of the pumping station and whose plunging fire was intense in the immediate area. Under his devastating covering fire, the assault onto the roof of the pumping station and the consequent destruction of the crews and guns was successfully completed. Later, when his assault group formed a covering force in the area in which the demolitions were taking place, this NCO, showing total disregard for his own safety, engaged and knocked out an enemy machine gun position which was bringing heavy fire to bear on the Operational HQ. Continuing to display great courage and initiative, his group later became engaged in the street fighting in the town of St. Nazaire and during the fighting he alone engaged an enemy motor cycle combination which approached at high speed firing an automatic gun from the sidecar.

During this street fighting, this NCO's dash and initiative was outstanding and with a small party he managed to regain the open country through the town in an attempt to escape to Spain. He was captured only after organising other members of his party to set off in pairs to freedom.   *(L.G. 5.7.45)*

Chalmers, Hugh, Rifleman
5836648, London Irish Rifles (Stonferry Hill, Yorks.)
Map Ref Italy 1/25,000 Sheet 160–II

Rfn. Chalmers is the Bren Gunner of a section of 17 Pl 'H' Coy. During the attack through The Gustav Line at Colla Monache Rfn. Chalmers' Section Comd was wounded. The Bren Group at this stage was apart from the rest of the section who were pinned down by close range small arms fire from Germans in buildings close by. There was also a determined group of Germans firing at the rest of the platoon from trenches on the Right Flank and the whole advance was temporarily held. Rfn. Chalmers then, without any orders to do so, decided to destroy the latter position. This necessitated crawling 100 yds up a ditch and then an assault across another 60 yards. This he did although under heavy fire all the time from a variety of directions. He then charged across the open himself firing his Bren Gun from the hip. The German post contained eight men and two M.G.s. Rfn. Chalmers killed one and the rest surrendered. This acted of gallantry was carried out not because he was ordered to do it, but purely because he conceived it his duty to do it. Rfn. Chalmers was alone responsible for dislodging this post and enabling the platoon to advance and force an entry into the village. His conduct throughout the whole of this battle was exemplary and his merry attitude and a determination to close with the enemy had an inspiring effect not only on his section, after the loss of their leader, but throughout his whole platoon.
                        (L.G. 7.12.44)

Chalmers, John James, Trooper
125837, 4 S.A. Armd. Car Regt., South African Forces
On 1 June 42 this soldier was commanding a car on the Trig Enver Bey. He was sent to assist No. 3 Troop which was attacking 50 met coming from Meteifel. Seeing the direction of their attack he maneouvred to cut off the head of the enemy column and in spite of very heavy Breda fire he put 18 shots from his 37 mm into the column while closing with it. His fire set three enemy troop carriers on fire and killed the driver of the leading lorry. This resulted in the breaking up of the convoy and freeing 48 POW's of 50 Div. He showed courage, initiative and daring and I recommend him for the Immediate award of the Military Medal.
Recommended for M.M.   *(L.G. 13.8.42)*

Chalmers, Ralph William, Sergeant
409323, 5th Royal Inniskilling Dragoon Guards
(Belfast) (Immediate)
On 9 Apr C Sqn was leading the adv from Twistringen NW to secure Wildeshausen and cut one of the main escape routes of the para army retreating in front of 30 Corps. By late afternoon the sqn had reached the main rd Harpstedt—Wildeshausen and turned west to clear the last mile to the town. At this pt the main rd was enclosed on both sides by thick woods in which there were found to be inf with Spandaus and panzerfaust. There was also sniping. It was therefore necessary to clear the woods with inf so that the sqn could pass through and seize the Northern outskirts of the town. Sjt. Chalmers who was comdg 1st Tp was given the task of sp the inf who were to clear the wood with one pl on each side of the rd. Tks were unable to move off the rd. This NCO himself led his tp in the asslt and had succeeded in working through to within two hundred yds of the further edge of the wood when a determined counter attack was made on the right hand pl from the rear. In order to reorganise and renew the attack on a different axis it became necessary to withdraw the inf to the Eastern edge of the wood. In spite of the fact that he was surrounded by enemy inf incl snipers and bazooka teams Sjt. Chalmers maintained his posn and covered the withdrawal both of the inf and of the remaining tks in his tp. His steady and accurate fire broke the counter attack and enabled the inf to disengage successfully. His tk was four times hit by bazookas and he eventually returned himself on foot. This NCO showed exceptional coolness and gallantry under heavy fire and in a most dangerous and exposed posn. He was mainly responsible for the successful disengagement of the inf as a formed body capable of continuing the operation and for killing a large number of the enemy who made the counter attack.
Croix de Guerre (French) App—3.4.45 (L.G. 21.6.45)

Chambers, James Henry, Warrant Officer Cl. I
3304958, 6th Bn. Highland Light Infantry
(Musselburgh) (Periodic)
At Achim, Germany, on 22 Apr. 45, the area of the Bn. P.O.W. Cage was shelled at a time when RSM Chambers was temporarily in sole charge of approx. 30 POW. Regardless of the danger to which he was exposed, RSM

Chambers remained in the open, marshalling and organising the prisoners until they were safely evacuated.

On 24th Apr. 45, at Mahndorf, Germany, Bn HQ was subjected to continuous and heavy enemy artillery fire for a period of 22 hours, during the initial stages of which two vehs, containing explosives, 75 grenades and ammunition, were set on fire. Despite the danger from recurrent explosions, RSM Chambers organised the removal of several vehs in the vicinity, personally driving away a carrier full of ammunition which was in great danger of catching fire. Shortly after this act, the flames caused the tins of petrol in a trailer to explode setting the HQ on fire. RSM Chambers worked incessantly throughout under enemy shellfire at great personal risk, and it was largely due to his enterprise and complete disregard for his own safety that most of Bn HQ transport was moved to comparative safety.

These are but two instances of the qualities of coolness and resource under fire which have been characteristic of RSM Chambers during many of the actions in which this Unit was involved in the N.W.E. Theatre of operations, during the period Sep. 44 to May 45.

(L.G. 24.1.46)

Chambers, Robert, M.M., Sergeant
*4270293, No. 3 Indep. M.G. Coy., Royal
Northumberland Fusiliers (Newcastle) (Immediate)*
At Briquessars on 17 June 44, Sjt. Chambers was in command of a MG section during the attack by the enemy on positions held by 1/6 Bn Queen's R.R. During the whole attack which lasted from 1200 hrs until dark, the example set by this Sjt. was magnificent. He personally directed the fire of his guns with complete disregard for his own safety, and inflicted heavy casualties on the enemy, although his position was under continuous mortar and artillery fire.

On one occasion enemy snipers in trees were giving considerable trouble, and Sjt. Chambers walked forward in front of his section position with a bren gun, utterly regardless of very heavy fire, and standing up in full view firing from the hip, he shot down several of the snipers.

Later he took one MMG to flank by himself, and waited until the advancing enemy were within 80 yards. He then opened fire and forced what was left of them to retire in complete disorder.

His utter fearlessness and courage in directing his guns resulted in heavy casualties to the enemy.

(L.G. 31.8.44)

Chandler, Joseph Thomas, Sergeant
*4861085, 2 Leicestershire Regt. (Leicester)
(Immediate)*
On 27 March 44, 71 Coln was heavily attacked by the Japanese. In our counter-attack one offr and 4 ORs were killed. Sergeant Chandler, Platoon Sjt, [...] Platoon, took a section to recover the five bodies. Despite very heavy enemy automatic fire and grenades Sjt. Chandler by cool and skilful handling of his section, succeeded in

recovering all the bodies. Five Japanese were killed, Sjt. Chandler personally accounting for two. His excellent example and leadership were an encouragement to his whole column.

On 12 Apr 44, an ambush party from 17 and 71 colns were blocking the rly Naba—Mawlu, [...] 602. Sjt. Chandler, now commanding 15 Platoon, was heavily attacked by Japanese, first by automatic fire and grenades, then by assault. Sjt. Chandler's personal leadership in the hand to hand fighting enabled the platoon to withstand the assault. At least 15 Japanese were killed. During this action Sjt. Chandler was wounded, first by a bullet through his shoulder, but continued to lead his platoon until again shot, this time through his side. He was then evacuated by [...] when the ambush withdrew. Despite his painful journey of ten miles, he remained cheerful throughout. His leadership and courage throughout the action were magnificent and his cheerful determintion, once wounded, a fine and effective example to all.

(L.G. 27.7.44)

Chapman, Arthur Edward, Warrant Officer Cl. III (Pl.S.M.)
2207990, 4 Queen's Own Royal West Kent Regt.
For conspicuous gallantry at Audenarde on 22nd May 1940.

Carried out invaluable work by taking command when his Coy Comd was killed. He personally attacked two German machine gunners with his pistol, wounding one and driving off the other. Personally loaded wounded on to trucks after the flank guard had retired—withdrew his men and those of other units with skill. Showed a total disregard of personal danger and outstanding qualities of leadership.

Initials are A. W. not A. E. *(L.G. 11.7.40)*

Chapman, Edwin Kerwyne, Sergeant
6014477, 1/4th Bn. Essex Regt. (Romford)
Sjt. Chapman was NCO i/c of a Sec. of Carriers forming part of a mobile column which left Mersah Matruh on the afternoon of June 26th. During the hours of darkness many columns were encountered, and the only means of identifying them as friend or enemy was by sending the Sec. of Carriers forward to investigate. On every occasion, Sjt. Chapman carried out this role with great dash and enthusiasm, although often encountering considerable enemy opposition. On one particular occasion, he identified a column as hostile, but continued his investigation so close to the enemy that he was able to procure an Officer prisoner, in spite of heavy fire. On a later occasion he identified two German aircraft on the ground, and wrecked them both by small arms fire and grenades, again under enemy fire. Throughout the entire operation of the column he displayed a magnificent offensive spirit, which, coupled with a complete disregard for his own personal safety, was a great inspiration to the whole column. Furthermore, his quick and accurate identification of enemy columns enabled

considerable damage to be inflicted on them, and at a later stage was of great assistance in enabling the column to get back when completely surrounded.

(L.G. 24.9.42)

Chapman, Gilbert Allen, Lance Corporal
6344856, 44 Reconnaissance Regt., Reconnaissance Corps (London, S.E.13) (Immediate)
On the night 6/7 February, L/Cpl. Chapman was 2IC of a section post in a house at 321330, close to the Senio River near San Severo. At about 0230 hours the house was raided by a strong enemy party of about 20 men. It was a very dark night and the enemy crawling up subjected the house to Bazooka and intense light automatic fire on two sides. The Section Sergeant and two men were killed instantly and another man wounded, leaving one side of the house undefended. Communications also failed. L/Cpl. Chapman immediately took charge of the situation and with his own accurate Tommy Gun fire dispersed and confused the approaching enemy thus giving himself time to replace the casualties in the exposed sector and get the wounded man into the house. After a brief lull, during which time considerable fire was directed against the house, the enemy attacked again and a German officer approached under cover of a shower of grenades and demanded surrender. He was immediately shot dead. Several more attempts were made to rush the house but in each case they were beaten off and the enemy finally withdrew.

Shortly after this a heavy shell and mortar concentration was directed against the house which caused the roof to collapse on three men inside. L/Cpl. Chapman, with only one unwounded man besides himself and the house still under small arms and mortar fire, immediately set about digging out the buried men until help arrived shortly afterwards. Four Germans were found dead on the ground and later a deserter reported that seven others had been wounded in the raid. There is no doubt that the quite exceptional coolness, courage and devotion to duty shown by L/Cpl. Chapman against very superior odds and in very difficult circumstances saved the lives of several of his comrades and caused the enemy raid to be a complete failure with serious casualties. The action of this NCO, only promoted the day previously, was a stirring and inspiring example to his Squadron.

(L.G. 21.6.45)

Chapman, John, Warrant Officer Cl. II (actg.)
4199944, 4th Bn. Royal Welch Fusiliers (Chathill) (Periodic)
A/CSM Chapman as a platoon Sjt. in Normandy, Holland and Germany has shown outstanding courage and leadership under most difficult circumstances. He has led many patrols, taken command of the platoon when his officer has become a casualty and has always been a great source of inspiration to the men of his platoon and latterly as CSM to his Company during some very hard battles. To quote one particular action at Bocholt when

his Company was putting in an attack with a squadron of tanks on the night of 28 Mar 45. Sjt. Chapman was commanding the leading platoon. Thick fog, apart from the darkness made this attack doubly difficult. As Sjt. Chapman's leading section approached the objective it was held up by Spandau fire from two houses. Placing himself at the head of his remaining two secs, Sjt. Chapman led them forward under heavy enemy arty and MG fire, captured the two houses and took 20 [...]. When dawn broke he found himself under fire from some further houses on his flank. Thereupon he organised a raid, after some fierce fighting occupied the houses and took further PWs all of a Para Div. At this point the CSM of the Coy was wounded and Sjt. Chapman took over his duties—a task which he performed most creditably for another two attacks.

Throughout this period his keenness to close with the enemy, his courage and his example were all above praise.

(L.G. 24.1.46)

Chapman, Joseph Douglas, Gunner
1491336, 259 A/Tank Bty., Royal Artillery (Newcastle) (Immediate)
On 1 Dec 41 when his gun was in position on portee in defence of 6th N.Z. Infy Bde H.Q., 3000 yards North of Sidi Rezegh (430406), he showed exceptional calm and accuracy in laying in the face of an attack by between 20 and 30 tanks and dismounted infantry. When his No. 1 was for the second time wounded, Gunner Chapman took charge of the gun. Shortly after this a direct hit through the shield killed and remaining two of his detachment. He continued firing with the driver of the portee, until this man, too, was wounded and the gun put out of action. Gunner Chapman then brought in the wounded driver and regardless of personal risk, searched for and found the A.D.S. to which he assisted him. During this action, it is believed that at least five tanks were totally destroyed by this gun.

(L.G. 24.2.42)

Chard, Dennis Albert, Rifleman
6920612, 2nd Bn. Rifle Brigade (Hayes, Middlesex) (Immediate)
During an action on Oct 26/27 on the Snipe position 866295 Rfn. Chard was No. 3 on a 6 pdr A/Tk Gun. In the first attack at night his No. 1 was wounded but he still continued to engage the enemy. At night he allowed two enemy tanks to approach to 200 yards firing their machine guns at his gun before he opened fire. He hit one which caught fire and so damaged the other that its guns were silenced and it was immobile. During the whole of this action his gun was under heavy machine gun fire from the rear. At first light he attended to the wounded whilst he was himself still under fire. When the position was attacked by infantry he manned a bren gun and caused casualties to the enemy. In the last tank attack in the evening at about 1700 hrs he turned his gun completely round from S.E. to N.W. and then held his fire till three enemy tanks had approached to 200 yds.

Two of them caught fire and the third was damaged. Owing to shortage of ammunition he was unable to set the third tank on fire. During this action his crew was killed by the fire from these tanks but he still continued to fire his gun. During the action he was responsible for the destruction of ten enemy tanks, and by coolness and courage was an inspiration to his platoon in very critical circumstances. *(L.G. 14.1.43)*

Charnick, George Joseph, Warrant Officer Cl. II
7015055, 2/London Irish Rifles, Royal Ulster Rifles
  (Dagenham)
During Apr 45 CSM Charnick was CSM of a Rifle Coy. On three occasions, in the attack on the bridge over the Conselice Canal south of Lavenzola (Italy sheet 88 317535), in the over-running of an enemy battery of 150 mm guns near Coltra (Italy 76 256677) and the attack on the bridge at Quartesena (Italy 76 211821) he showed great courage, resourcefulness and leadership under fire. His cheerfulness and willingness to carry out any task was a constant source of encouragement to the men of his coy.

In Oct 1944 in the attack on Casa Spinello (Italy 99 031253) he took charge of a difficult situation when all three officers in a rifle Coy had been killed, and despite darkness, rain and mud, enemy minefields and heavy fire, he consolidated the position, supplying the position with ammunition and personally evacuating one casualty from the interior of an uncharted minefield. In Nov 43 in the attack on Fossecessia on the Sangro CSM Charnick showed great gallantry in engaging and destroying singlehanded an enemy post which had been holding up his Company's advance and causing casualties.

CSM Charnick has been CSM of a rifle Company since Mar 1943 has been twice wounded, has fought in every important battle in which the Battalion has been involved since the beginning of the North African campaign and has been once previously unsuccessfully recommended for a decoration.

He has shown himself to be the type of Warrant Officer who is a credit to the highest traditions of his Regiment and the Infantry.
M.I.D. 29.11.45, Silver Star (USA) 25.3.49
  (L.G. 13.12.45)

Chartrand, Roger, Sergeant
E5634, Canadian Infantry Corps
No citation. *(L.G. 24.1.46)*

Chatterley, Charles Alfred Attwood, C.Q.M.S.
2585253, Royal Signals
No citation. *(L.G. 9.8.45)*

Cheevers, Richard Murdock, Warrant Officer Cl. II (C.S.M.)
7011848, 13th Bn. King's Regt. (Northfleet, Kent)
  (Immediate)
Operations in Burma—March 1943.

On 30th April 1943, No. 8 Column and HQ No. 2 Group, 77 Ind. Inf. Bde, had completed their crossing of the Kaukkwe Chaung by raft, and were forming up within their bridgehead to move off, when fire was opened by a strong force of Japanese from the landward direction on the side of the river on which the British force was. Serjeant Major Cheevers directed Column HQ, which was under his immediate command, to make its way along the river bank with the main body, and immediately proceeded to the edge of the perimeter to prevent the enemy interfering with the withdrawal. Almost at once he saw a Japanese machine gun which was being manœuvred into a position from which the withdrawing column would be caught by a devastating fire. Serjeant Major Cheevers opened fire with his sub-machine gun and killed the enemy gun crew. He was immediately fired on himself from a few yards to his left by another machine gun; he turned his fire on this and again wiped out the crew. No further enemy being visible in his immediate neighbourhood, he reported back to his Column Commander and asked to be given another task. By now the withdrawal was well under way, and thanks to the respite gained by Cheever's prompt and resolute action the Column was in a position to acquit itself well and without suffering casualties during the attempt by the enemy to bring on a running fight. Cheever's conduct on this day was typical of the resolution and determination which he displayed throughout the whole campaign. *(L.G. 5.8.43)*

Cheney, Cyril Arthur, Bombardier (A/Sgt.)
897730, A/Tk. Bty., Royal Horse Artillery
  (Hornchurch) (Immediate)
At about mid-day on 30/5/42 near Bir Harmat a section of 6 prs led by Capt R. R. Oakey, RHA went to the flank and ahead of the fire line of a Sqn of Grant tanks to engage what they thought to be 1 or 2 enemy 50mm guns which had come into action amongst some derelicts to the flank of our tks. The mirage was very bad at the time and this section had to advance a long way before they could locate the enemy guns. When they did so they found that there were 6 enemy 50mm guns. These were engaged at once; one of the portees was hit almost immediately and caught fire, and the other gun was under intense MG and shell fire from three sides. Sjt. Cheyney however continued to fight his gun to cover the withdrawal of the other detachment, of whom several were wounded. During this time he knocked out one 50mm gun with a direct hit and while engaging the others a Mk III tk appeared amongst the derelicts. This he quickly engaged and put up in flames.

He then worked his way towards the burning portee and picked up Capt. Oakey. The fire from his gun was so accurate that the 50mm guns ceased firing and later pulled out. Sjt. Cheyney showed conspicuous courage in continuing to engage a superior force and by his fine leadership set a very high example to the rest of the section and as result of his action a truck was enabled to come up and collect the wounded and the threat to the tks was dispelled. *(L.G. 13.8.42)*

Cheshire, Allan Gee, Corporal (A/Sgt.)
M17017, Edmonton Regt. (Immediate)
On the evening prior to the dawn attack by the Edmonton Regt. on Agira from the West, 29 Jul 43, a Fighting patrol of one section under Cpl. Cheshire was sent out North West, across rugged and difficult country, to attack and destroy at daybreak, an enemy machine gun and mortar post, which dominated a road leading from Agira to the East.

Just before daybreak as the patrol approached the enemy position, its presence was discovered, fire was opened at short range from a ledge half way up a rugged feature some 300 feet high, and two soldiers became casualties. Cpl. Cheshire quickly appreciated the situation, disposed his section in a position from which it could give him covering fire, and heedless of his own safety, went o [...] one.

By skilful use of cover he got behind the feature, then scaled [...] the semi darkness an almost vertical cliff 50 feet in height, stalked his quarry, and with grenades, rifle and bayonet charged the post, killed six and captured six German prisoners. *(L.G. 23.12.43)*

Chikena, Yaya, Staff Sergeant
NA/29660, 1st Bn. Nigeria Regt., Royal West African Frontier Forces
NA/29660 Sjt. Yaya Chikena is the African Pl Sjt. of the Pl which led his Coy's attack on 5 Mar 45 on a feature occupied by the Japanese. Sjt. Yaya Chikena was with the rear section of the leading Pl which had come under heavy LMG fire when it debouched into a stretch of one hundred yards of open paddy field.

Sjt. Yaya Chikena worked his section towards the enemy LMG position, rushed the position and himself killed the crew of the LMG with a grenade. Later in the engagement, Sjt. Yaya Chikena saw that the Pl Comd of the second Pl had become a casualty. He immediately took over comd of this Pl in addition to his own and completed the task of consolidating them on their objective.

This African Sjt. showed great personal courage and initiative throughout this engagement and his actions were those of a brave and determined man who kept a clear head under fire and dealt most successfully with all situations as they occurred. *(L.G. 21.6.45)*

Chikoya, Warrant Officer Cl. II (C.S.M.)
7124, Somaliland Camel Corps
For continuous gallantry in the face of the enemy from the 11th to 13th August, 1940, during the attack on Mill Hill and the subsequent withdrawal. By his bravery he set an example to the NCOs and men of his company and regardless of danger assisted the British Officers and NCOs in distributing ammunition under heavy fire.

To be dated 11.2.41 and substituted for the award of the African D.C.M. announced in the L.G. of that date
(L.G. 21.7.42)

Childs, Leonard Herbert, Lance Corporal
3512009, 5 Northamptonshire Regt. (Guildford)
(Immediate)
Italy, 1:100,000 Sheet 76 Farrara at MR 214898
During the morning of 24 Apr, C Coy encountered an enemy strongpoint protected by outposts, and sited on the far bank of a deep and wide canal. This NCO was sent on patrol to gain information about the width and banks of the canal, to find likely crossing places and locate enemy Spandau positions.

Although under continuous small arms fire, this NCO waded the canal and moved along the bank until he found a Spandau post, which opened murderous fire at close range. Regardless of personal safety, L/C Childs attacked the post single handed, inflicted casualties, and then returned with his invaluable information. Soon after, as the tanks had not arrived to assist the Coy forward, he took a Piat and alone engaged a Spandau post in a house, which greatly assisted the Coy to cross the canal. This action was carried out under most heavy and accurate fire from small arms and mortars.

L/C Childs was an inspiration to all in his Coy, and acted with complete disregard for his personal safety. The success of his Coy was due almost entirely to his unselfish & courageous action. *(L.G. 18.10.45)*

Chinn, George Ernest, Warrant Officer Cl. I
3975, Royal Australian Infantry
WO Cl I George Ernest Chinn served with both the Australian Military Forces and the Royal Australian Air Force during World War II. At the conclusion of the war he continued his service as an infantry soldier in the 22nd Battalion and the Royal Australian Regiment. He was an instructor at the Royal Military College, Duntroon, from 1952 to 1960 when he was appointed Regimental Sergeant Major of the 1st Special Air Service Company, Royal Australian Infantry. In April 1964 WO Chinn joined the Australian Army Training Team in Vietnam and was posted as an advisor at the Dong Da National Training Centre in Thua Thien Province.

While temporarily detached from the Training Centre he accompanied the 32nd Vietnamese Ranger Battalion during operation LAM SON 115 near Lavang from the 18th to 28th April 1964.

During the helicopter assault landing, WO Chinn landed in the first wave under Viet Cong ground fire which caused several casualties. Realising the effect this fire would have on the second wave of troop loaded helicopters, he assisted in the deployment of sub units and the clearing of the Viet Cong out of range of the landing zone with complete disregard for his own safety and in the face of Viet Cong fire. The second wave were able to land without casualties.

Immediately after the Ranger Force had cleared the Viet Cong training camp they were again attacked by the Viet Cong. WO Chinn personally drew Viet Cong fire, allowing the organisation of a successful reaction force. *[From L.G.]*   *(L.G. 29.10.65)*

Chivers, George, Sergeant
6457700, 1st Bn. Royal Fusiliers (Hornchurch, Essex)
   (Immediate)
For conspicuous gallantry and devotion to duty at Agordat on 31st January 1941.

Sergeant Chivers commanded his platoon during the attack on the enemy's position, and throughout the day he led his platoon with marked skill and determination. During the initial advance he realised the ground to his front was open and that he was coming under machine gun fire from a strong position to his left. He skilfully extricated the platoon and led them under cover to another position to be in touch with the Company on his right. Later in the day he took over a portion of the enemy's trenches for the Company on his right and during this operation the enemy counter-attacked. He himself personally fired a Bren gun and repulsed the attack, killing fifteen of the enemy. During the whole day his platoon were under machine gun fire or being constantly sniped. Sergeant Chivers showed great skill, determination and power of leadership during the action.
                                       (L.G. 18.7.41)

Christian, John Herbert, Corporal (actg.)
3776385, 2nd Bn. The Monmouthshire Regt., South
   Wales Borderers (Dalby, I.O.M.) (Immediate)
On the morning of 24 Feb 45, the Bn had been ordered to capture an objective approximately half way between Goch and Weeze. L/Cpl. Christian was commanding a Sec in the Coy on the right flank of the attack. The enemy brought down extremely heavy defensive fire of all natures, and his platoon, in its advance across completely open country, suffered heavy casualties, including the Platoon Officer and all senior NCO.

L/Cpl. Christian immediately assumed comd of the platoon and led them forward through extremely heavy fire. The platoon's intermediate objective was a fortified farmhouse on which L/Cpl. Christian led a spirited attack which resulted in the killing or capture of 18 Germans in it. The platoon was then directed on to its final objective. At this time, the platoon consisted of only 15 private soldiers, the majority of whom were in action for the first time. Heavy enemy fire was being brought down on the objective, which was a wood, but he led the platoon forward with great skill and dash, clearing the wood and establishing a position on the forward edge.

For the next two days and nights, the whole area was subjected to the most intense shelling and mortaring and owing to casualties, it was impossible to provide a more senior platoon commander. L/Cpl. Christian was, therefore, left in command and set a magnificent example of leadership, bravery and endurance, maintaining his platoon position under very heavy fire and the constant threat of counter-attack by enemy infantry and S.P. guns in the immediate vicinity of the position. His superb example undoubtedly contributed greatly to the success of the whole operation.   *(L.G. 10.5.45)*

Christie, Victor Julius, Corporal
27391, 2 T.S., South African Forces
For conspicuous bravery and good leadership at Salum on 11 and 12 Jan 42. His platoon came under very effective enfilade fire from an enemy position on left flank. Quickly and with great resolution he crossed a wide open space and was then able to get near enough to shoot a machine gunner with his pistol. Closing in he threw a hand grenade into an occupied and well protected house, resulting in the surrender of 1 Officer and 17 men. This cleared the way for a further advance. The whole occurrence took place under heavy enemy fire.
                                       (L.G. 19.3.42)

Christmass, Keith Charles, Private
WX22774, 2/24 Aust. Inf. Bn., (since died)
   (Immediate)
For conspicuous bravery and devotion to duty in the attack on the important feature south of Droop—Tarakan 422711, May 45.

During the advance south from Djoeata along the Dutch track, whilst C Coy 2/24 Aust Inf Bn were exploiting forward after the air strike on feature Droop with the object of gaining as much ground as possible before darkness, they were held up south of feature Droop at 422711 by rifle and LMG fire and grenades form a strongly defended enemy post at Approx 19090 hrs 27 May 45.

3 Sec 13 Pl, in which Pte. Christmass was an Owen gunner, was ordered to a flank to encircle the enemy and cut the track in rear of the enemy position.

The section succeeded in cutting the track and with Pte. Christmass leading, attacked the strongly defended position along the razor back track. Pte. Christmass came under rifle fire about 15 to 20 yards from the enemy position and was wounded by a bullet in the chest, causing him to fall. With complete disregard of his own safety, and in spite of being wounded he rose, and firing his Owen gun killed one enemy and proceeded to advance killing another enemy before he himself was again wounded in the right arm, prveenting his further use of the Owen gun. With great courage and resource, he immediately contacted his section commander and pointed out enemy positions before allowing himself to be evacuated.

By his conspicuous bravery when wounded, and great devotion to duty, he was an example to his section and was instrumental in his section continuing the attack, inflicting further casualties on the enemy and capturing the position, enabling the Coy to advance a further 300 yards and gain vital ground before last light.
To be dated May, 1945   *(L.G. 18.7.45)*

Christoff, George Joseph, Sergeant
NX 54034, 2/30 Bn., A.I.F.

Sjt. Christoff was in charge of an armoured car and on 21st to 23rd January 1942, whilst the Battalion was in a position at Yong Peng was detailed to proceed along the Young Peng—Muar Road beyond the forward line and endeavour to ascertain the position regarding the 2/19 and 2/29 Bns which had been cut off by enemy at Bakri. With great daring and dash he took his car through the enemy lines to a point several miles in the enemy's rear where he interrogated natives. He subsequently drove further and was only stopped when an enemy road block was encountered. He had several encounters with the enemy but returned without having contacted troops of the 2/29 and 2/29 Bns. The next morning as a result of information that some men of the two isolated Bns were trying to return he again went on the same journey, this time locating one officer and 19 men of the two bns which he ferried to our position. Sjt. Christoff made four trips with his armoured car on that day, each time encountering the enemy. *(L.G. 10.1.46)*

Christsen, James William, Sergeant
QX 6940, 2/15 Aust. Inf. Bn.
Tobruch—Period April/October 1941.

During operations at Tobruk over the period March–October 1941, Sjt. Christsen has exhibited valuable qualities as a leader; his personal bravery under fire and his aggressiveness and determination have created an example which has produced a strong fighting spirit in the members of his platoon. On April 14 he commanded a carrier which was utilised in cooperation with a platoon of infantry for the purpose of driving a large number of German machine gunners from a position which they had hastily occupied in the Anti Tank ditch surrounding portion of the inner line of defences of Tobruk. His action played a large part in the success of the operation which resulted in breaking up of the enemy position and the capture of ninety four German prisoners, with machine guns and equipment.

On 2 May 41 when in command of three Carriers, Sjt. Christsen went forward towards the newly formed Salient to ascertain enemy dispositions. After proceeding 500 yds the Carriers were engaged by heavy MG and A Tk fire. He ordered his carriers about and after returning 200 yds noticed that a carrier had stopped. He immediately turned about and under continued heavy fire proceeded to the disabled carrier, jumped out and hooked a tow rope from his own to the damaged carrier and towed it to safety. In the damaged carrier one man was killed and another badly wounded from A Tk fire.

During subsequent operations Sjt. Christsen has frequently led his carriers outside the perimeter on recce patrols and obtained valuable information concerning enemy dispositions.
M.I.D. 30.12.41   *(L.G. 16.4.42)*

Cini, Gilbert, Lance Corporal
1637423, Intelligence Corps, I.S.L.D., G.H.Q., M.E.F., R.A. (London, S.W.6)

This wireless operator worked behind the enemy lines for 22 months in 1942 and through his all round ability and enterprise in this and other spheres was mainly responsible for the success of the mission. He volunteered for a second mission and remained for two months until its work was completed. His party was on one occasion subjected to heavy bombing, resulting in casualties and loss of much equipment but nevertheless he maintained unbroken communication and continued to discharge his duties faithfully and well. *(L.G. 14.10.43)*

Clare, Walter Howard, Warrant Officer Cl. II (C.S.M.)
H.16361, Princess Patricia's Canadian Light Infantry (Immediate)
Reference Map Italy 1/25,000 Sheet 101 III SW Rimini.

During the heavy fighting which followed the break through of the Gothic Line, 'C' Company Princess Patricia's Canadian Light Infantry on 22 September advanced across the River Meccia to San Martino (MR 808992). On reaching the objective the position was consolidated under heavy enemy fire. In the early morning of 22 September 1944 the Company Commander was killed; he was the third 'C' Company Commander killed in three successive days. Command of the company fell to Company Serjeant Major Walter Howard Clare.

At this time the whole company position was being subjected to extremely heavy and continuous fire from enemy 88mm guns, 10cm mortars and SP guns firing AP and HE shells. This fire lasted throughout the day. Company Headquarters, which was established in a house, received several direct hits. The roof and two sides of the house collapsed and Company Serjeant Major Clare ordered the personnel to Company Headquarters to take refuge away from the house. The wireless set, which was the Company's only means of communication with Battalion Headquarters, was lost in the dust and falling debris. Company Serjeant Major Clare remained behind in the house, dug the set out, and carried it 150 yards to another building where he reorganised company Headquarters. The signallers, however, could not be found, so Company Serjeant Major Clare re-assembled the set and operating it himself, thereby regained communication with Battalion Headquarters. During the day under continuous enemy shell fire he visited the three platoons, encouraging the men and keeping them deployed and in position. Under his command the company defeated a local counter attack, killed two of the enemy, took five prisoners and evacuated all company casualties.

Company Serjeant Major Clare's coolness and courage were an inspiration to the whole company at a time when control was most difficult. The company had been in action for five days and all ranks suffered from fatigue as a result of almost continuous shelling. His

quick action in assuming command of the company, his disregard for his own personal safety, and his determined leadership were of the highest order and merit award.
(L.G. 20.1.45)

Clark, Benjamin, Lance Bombardier
*L.55515, 15 Cdn. Fd. Regt., Royal Canadian Artillery
(Immediate)*
On 10 Oct 44, during the op to clear Breskens and the pocket north of the Leopold Canal, L/Bdr Clark acted as OPA for Capt Campbell, E.E., FOO with the SD & G Highrs. The bn was ordered to capture and hold Hoofdplaat. During the assault on the objective, although the FOO and crew were repeatedly under enemy fire, they directed arty fire effectively throughout. L/Bdr Clark was particularly noticeable by his coolness and efficiency. On gaining the objective, an OP was est in the attic of a house. Shortly after first light the next morning the enemy commenced counter-attacking the OP came under mortar fire and the FOO was wounded. L/Bdr Clark helped to bring the offr to safety, then returned, re-organised the OP and continued to direct arty fire himself, although the building was still under enemy fire. The FOO returned and a new OP was est to sp the leading coy which was moving to the outskirts of the town to meet other counter attacks. This OP also came under hy fire, and the FOO was again wounded. L/Bdr Clark assisted him to safety and again returned and carried on with direction of arty fire, although the enemy fire continued. Two of the remaining three members of the OP party were wounded but L/Bdr Clark continued to keep the OP under control and to direct fire, inspiring all who saw him by his coolness and efficiency. He continued to carry out the sp of the inf in this way until he was finally relieved at the end of the day. As a result of his bravery and efficiency the inf were able to obtain the continuous arty sp, which was largely responsible for keeping them on their objective in the face of repeated enemy counter attacks. *(L.G. 13.1.45)*

Clark, Charles Albert, Staff Sergeant
C.97586, Canadian Postal Corps
No citation.   *(L.G. 15.6.46)*

Clark, Frank, Sergeant
*5566242, 7 Fd. Coy., Royal Engineers (Chippenham)
(Immediate)*
Sjt. Clark's example has been magnificent throughout the action especially during the last few days. Although H.Q.Sjt., he volunteered for every possible dangerous job. During the initial river reconnaissances in spite of his age (37), he swam R. Cari and measured the gap. On the first attempt at building 'Congo' assault Bailey Bridge he returned to the river after the Company had left time and again assisting in the collection of wounded and removing vehicles under fire. During the 'Amazon' assault Bailey Bridge operation he worked from the start to the finish of the operation continually under fire and

greatly assisted in completing the task. Early on 17 May 1944 he was acting as Platoon Sjt. of a platoon which was constructing a forward track under fire. Two Bulldozer operators were killed and he, with a Cpl, operated the Bulldozer under fire until 80 yds of track were completed. On the same morning his platoon officer was found to be missing and he went back twice under fire in his efforts to find him. He has inspired all ranks by his great courage and example. *(L.G. 26.10.44)*

Clark, George Edward, Warrant Officer Cl. II (C.S.M.)
5821003, Suffolk Regt.
No citation.   *(L.G. 11.7.40)*

Clark, George Henry, Gunner
877372, 209/53 A./Tk. Bty., Royal Artillery
See Allan, James Snodgrass   *(L.G. 2.12.41)*

Clark, George Stanley, Private
*G22945, N. Shore Regt., Canadian Infantry Corps
(Immediate)*
During the initial assault on 6 Jun 44, on the beaches at St. Aubin-sur-Mer, Pte. Clark, G. S., was a member of a section of 'A' Coy which landed at H plus 5 mins. Both the section leader and 2 IC Sec became casualties and Pte. Clark, on his own initiative, took over comd of the section.

In the afternoon, in the vicinity of Tailleville, his was the forward section of the leading pl which came under heavy MG and mortar fire. There was no cover for his men near at hand and recognizing this fact, he unhesitatingly lead his men across 800 yds of open country under fire to attack the enemy posn in the wood and neutralize the fire. By this action he made it possible for the remainder of 'A' Coy and the whole of 'D' Coy to cross the same ground to close with the enemy and carry on with the attack. During the whole of the operations on D Day, Pte. Clark showed himelf ready to assume unexpected responsibilities, quick at appreciating difficult situations and decisive in his action to overcome them. His display of personal courage enabled him to maintain firm control of his men and was at all times an inspiration to all ranks.

There is no doubt that his qualities of leadership and resolution made possible this local success of 'A' and 'D' Coys and thereby contributed greatly to the success of the bn.   *(L.G. 19.8.44)*

Clark, Roland Arthur, Sergeant
5379128, 1 Oxfordshire & Buckinghamshire Light Infantry (Winkfield)
On 16 Jul 44 near Cahier 9062, Sjt. Clarke took part in his Coy in Operation 'Villa' in an artificially illuminated night attack on a small copse full of dense undergrowth. When just short of the objective a German MG 42 opened on the Coy and pinned it to the ground. Sjt. Clarke, without hesitation, went fwd alone and without orders over a distance of fifty yards and disappeared into the

wood which was the Coy's objective. He re-appeared a few moments later carrying the German MG 42 on his shoulder and driving a German prisoner before him. Sjt. Clarke had killed the remaining members of the team. By this remarkable action his Company was able to reach its objective. Thereafter in spite of a GSW in the leg which he persisted in describing as a 'twisted knee' Sjt. Clarke showed a coolness and courage beyond all praise during some three hours of hand to hand fighting. The intensity of the fighting was such that one offr, eight effective NCOs and eighteen privates were killed and eighteen wounded in his Company. *(L.G. 19.10.44)*

Clark, William David, Sergeant
VX6215, 2/8 Aust. Inf. Bn.
Act of gallantry and devotion to duty in the face of the enemy on 21 May 1941 in Crete.

On 21 May 41 Sergeant Clark, in charge of a fighting patrol consisting of one platoon, went forward to contact an enemy force which, from information obtained from the Greeks, consisted of approximtely 20 men armed with sub machine guns situated on high ground in front. A Greek Company which was to support the patrol did not arrive at the rendezvous and with only about six Greeks, acting independently, Sergeant Clark decided to carry on and engage the enemy. Almost immediately the position became precarious as intense machine gun and 5≤ mortar fire was brought to bear on the patrol, whose position was fairly exposed. The opposing force was then estimated to have at least three machine guns and a 5≤ mortar in support. Under these circumstances Sergeant Clark did an extremely good job to hold the platoon together and by skilful placing of his sections he was able to return some fire and engage the enemy with success with the loss of one man wounded only, until he was eventually forced to withdraw. His platoon had been pinned down for almost three hours. Later it was decided that the task was too big even for a Company, as the force was far larger than anticipated. Sergeant Clark's leadership and personal bravery was a real inspiration to the men under his command in these extremely trying conditions.

He showed conspicuous courage and devotion to duty throughout the whole campaign in Crete in the capacity of acting platoon commander. *(L.G. 4.11.41)*

Clarke, Arthur Leonard, M.B.E., Warrant Officer Cl. I (R.S.M.)
1060781, 1st Regt., Royal Horse Artillery (Rhyl, Flintshire) (Periodic)
For extremely valuable and gallant services throughout both the defence of Tobruk, and in subsequent operations.

His remarkably fine understanding of the critical position last May enthused him to get sundry derelict enemy guns into action. He gradually developed such an extremely efficient organisation over several miles of the perimeter that 'Mr. Clarke's Guns' became recognised as an extremely important factor in Tobruk's defences, as well as their constant use for harassing and counter battery. He directed a very large amount of enemy ammunition most effectively at the enemy.

Casualties in the recent operations necessitated his taking on as Gun Position Officer to the Rocket Troop, RHA. Although outside his normal role as an RSM, no one could have carried out this important technical duty more efficiently or been a finer example in the severe fighting, than he proved himself to be. *(L.G. 9.9.42)*

Clarke, Sydney, Sergeant
3650449, 1st Bn. Border Regt., 1st Air Landing Bde.
At Arnhem on the 25th Sept 1944, Sjt. Clark was in command of a platoon detailed to clear the enemy from some woods where they were becoming a threat to our main position. On entering the wood the platoon was pinned down by enemy fire from inside the wood. Sjt. Clark, however, regardless of any personal danger, carried on the advance himself, throwing grenades amongst the enemy. At the far end of the woods there was an enemy tank, hull down, engaging the position on the left. Sjt. Clark immediately collected some grenades, rushed to the tank, opened the top of the turret and dropped the grenades inside, setting the tank on fire. During the whole of this period he was under heavy fire. His gallantry, leadership and devotion to duty were beyond all praise. *(L.G. 9.11.44)*

Clay, William Frederick, Lance Sergeant
5344864, 10th Bn. Royal Berkshire Regt. (Chichester) (Immediate)
On 22 Jan 44 on the Damiano Ridge, 'B' Coy had seized the 411 height and was being counter-attacked in strength. Sjt. Clay was in command of a 3″ mortar detachment with 'B' Coy on the Ridge. In the first phase of the fighting all the amn was expended, having been used with great effect on the enemy in his forming up places and approach lines, which were defiladed from arty fire. At this time the Ridge and the Bn position below were being subjected to the most intense artillery and mortar bombardment. In the height of this Sjt. Clay led his men back to Pl H.Q. to bring up Amn. Encouraging them by word and by his bearing of cheerful indifference to enemy shelling, he successfully brought up a load of amn, although all other amn parties had been immobilised by casualties in the attempt. The enemy was now close in and Sjt. Clay without thought of personal safety completely exposed himself at his O.P. to enable him to bring fire close in on the enemy. Though continuusly fired at he continued standing at his O.P. controlling his fire until his amn was again expended. The Coy was now hard pressed and Sjt. Clay led his men forward to fight with their rifles. In the ensuing fighting Sjt. Clay displayed the most aggressive initiative, on two occasions he went forward himself to attack the enemy who had infiltrated, killing three and wounding two. The cheerful courage and fearless spirit displayed by Sjt. Clay was an

heartening to the men of the Coy, as his deadly mortar fire had been before.   *(L.G. 15.6.44)*

Cleere, Patrick, Sergeant
553943, 7th Queen's Own Husssrs, Royal Armoured Corps

On January 22nd, 1941, this NCO Troop Sjt. when his troop advanced under heavy fire towards the wire at Tobruch. He shewed great courage, coolness and initiative, when his Troop leader's Tank was blown up on a mine. He took his tank up to the damaged tank and after directing his gunner to give covering fire, he got out under heavy and point blank anti-Tank Rifle and small arms fire and helped his Troop Leader to put on a tow rope. He then towed the tank abut a thousand yards, when the soft ground caused the damaged tank to swivel round, pulling his own tank broadside to the enemy fire. This NCO again got out under heavy fire in an effort to find some other way to tow the tank. Both tanks were then hit by A/T Rifle fire and his operator wounded. Sjt. Cleere then tried to get out the driver of the damaged tank, but he was dead and it was decided to abandon the tank. Sjt. Cleere then picked up the crew of the damaged tank and got them out of Action.

Throughout the whole campaign this NCO has done consistently well, shewing initiative, coolness and courage.

M.B.E. 13.6.59   *(L.G. 9.5.41)*

Clements, Percy Priestly, Sergeant
2564415, Leicestershire Regt. [Army Air Corps on AFW 3121]

Sergeant Clements was a member of a party of parachutists dropped in Calabria in February, 1941, to blow up an aqueduct, who were subsequently captured by the Italians. Shortly after capture they were taken to Camp 78, Sulmona, where Officers and Other Ranks were placed in separate compounds, no communication between them being allowed. Despite this regulation, Sergeant Clements, who took charge of the most secret communications in the Other Ranks compound, managed to maintain clandestine communication with the Officers, and exchanged with them particulars of all secret messages received from the War Office. He also arranged the despatch of similar messages to the War Office in selected Other Ranks' letters and later, when the Officers were moved to another camp, was responsible for maintaining all communication between the Camp and the War Office.

On the 12th September, 1943, following the Italian armistice, when all attempts to escape were strictly forbidden, Sergeant Clements escaped to the hills. From there, on the 14th September, 1943, he watched the Germans enter the camp, and he then, with another NCO, started walking south, continuing as far as Morrone, their journey lasting twenty-two days.

At Morrone they hid up for a week until they were able to join the British Force at Casacalenda, on the 13th

October, 1943. Throughout their escape Sergeant Clements was in charge.

M.C. 12.4.45, M.M. 20.6.46   *(L.G. 2.3.44)*

Clift, Kenneth Rochester, Signalman
NX 3698, 'J' Sec. Sigs., Australian Military Forces

On 21 Jan 41 during the Battle of Tobruch at approx. 1000 hrs. Sigmn. Clift, McKeague and Bruce proceeded in the direction of 2/3 Bn to lay cable back to Bde. H.Q. They had been informed that 2/3 Bn. was in front. They proceeded as directed, but after going about two miles, realized that they were too far ahead and swung left. Shortly afterwards they saw an Italian Bty.

Sigmn. Clift, in charge of the line party, immediately decided to attack the battery. They headed for the battery firing with their only weapons, two pistols. When about 50 yds away, the Bty. Comdr. ordered the guns to stop firing and held up a white flag. The line party then disarmed the officers and men and marched them in the direction of a column of prisoners. Then the party found 2/3 Bn. H.Q. and laid cable back to Bde. H.Q.

It was only by the quick decision, initiative and daring of Sigmn. Clift that this party was able to eliminate this battery, which was still firing at our troops in rear.

(L.G. 9.5.41)

Clout, Albert, Corporal
6399689, 1st Bn. Lincolnshire Regt. (Brighton)
(Immediate)

On 7th April, 1944, at Dongyaung, Burma, Pte. Clout was Coy runner, when his Coy assaulted and held an enemy position. In the initial assault, Pte. Clout was with his Coy Comd. When the enemy first opened fire, the Coy Comd was hit, and Pte. Clout at once found the enemy and killed him with his rifle. During the assault, he remained with his Coy Comd, supplying him with verey lights; at the same time, 2 bunkers were met and fire came from them. Without hesitation, and in the lead, Pte. Clout ran to the first bunker threw in a grenade, fired his rifle and silenced the enemy single-handed.

In the second assault, Pte. Clout once again was at his Comd's side. The final objective was captured, the forward troops slightly beyond were separated from the main body by heavy fire, and an open ridge. Pte. Clout went forward through the fire, obtained a report, and came back to HQ. HQ. then came under fire. Pte. Clout returned the fire, supplied his Comd once again with grenades and verey lights, and then went back to the rear pl. for information. Whilst doing so, he again met fire, but went on.

On the afternoon of 7 April, 1944, a man was wounded in a trench. Pte. Clout went to rescue him. Pte. Clout crawled along the ridge and was hit in the buttock. He crawled on and got to the man. The man was then hit again by a burst of fire. Pte. Clout pulled him out slowly, enemy fire still continuing, and brought him single-handed to safety.

On the morning of 8th April, 1944, the enemy shelled Coy HQ continuously for ten minutes. Pte. Clout was in a trench, but knowing his Coy Comd was out in the open, went to look for him. He saw his commander, but was then hit by a splinter in the back and neck; he tried to go on but fell. He was brought to safety.

Throughout a period of 36 hours, Pte. Clout performed many hazardous missions, and 3 individual gallant actions. His coolness and bravery and his disregard for his personal safety were beyond all praise. His great gallantry in knocking out a bunker, and rescuing a wounded comrade under heavy fire inspired and amazed all around him. His was a magnificent effort which showed a sense of devotion to duty which would be hard to equal. *(L.G. 22.6.44)*

Coad, Albert Victor, Sergeant
6913317, 10th Rifle Brigade (London, N.W.5)
'B' Coy 10 R.B. were under command of the 2nd Lothians & Border Horse during the operations from 6 May 43 to [...] May 43.

At 0530 hours on 9 May 43, when Sjt. Coad's Platoon was ordered to advance into Hammam Lif, his Platoon Officer and two other ranks were seriously wounded by enemy M.G. fire. In spite of heavy mortar and small arms fire and continual sniping, this Sergeant, with the aid of Cpl. Steggles, succeeded in taking the two wounded men, in consecutive journeys, to a place of safety. He went back a third time and brought back the officer to a safe place where he could receive medical attention. Sjt. Coad then returned into the battle and assumed command of the Platoon, and remained in position until ordered to withdraw.

Later in the same morning at 0830 hours the Company went forward to attack the same town. Sjt. Coad was commanding the Platoon when the Company was pinned down by artillery, mortar and heavy M.G. fire. His platoon suffered more casualties and the platoon on his left had their officer killed and the Sergeant wounded. On seeing this Sjt. Coad immediately assumed command of both platoons and succeeded in getting all the wounded back to a place of safety. He rallied and encouraged the men who remained and carried out an organised and successful withdrawal of both Platoons, stage by stage, when ordered.

In these actions Sjt. Coad displayed the highest qualities of leadership, and by his coolness and courage and complete disregard of his own personal safety undoubtedly saved the lives of many men in a critical situation. *(L.G. 22.7.43)*

Coe, Laurence Arthur, Private
7516742, Army Dental Corps
This soldier was captured near Dunkirk in May, 1940, and after being placed in various prison camps was eventually sent to a camp in German occupied Poland. One morning in October, by a clever ruse of insinuating himself into a working party of 20 men who had already

been counted, he managed to slip away from the sentry, knowing that he would not be missed when the party returned to the camp in the evening. After remaining hidden for some time he made his way to the Docks at Danzig, and dodging the sentries, stowed himself away on a steamer which was about to sail.

After four days at sea he was forced by hunger to give himself up to the Captain of the ship, which turned out to be a Swedish ship bound for Gothenburg. He was imprisoned at Gothenburg for ten days before being released by the offices of the British Consul.

Private Coe was repatriated from Stockholm in February, 1941. *(L.G. 21.3.41)*

Coehn, Gunther Rene, Corporal
546662, South African Forces
No citation.
Published as Koen, amdt to Coehn 11.9.44
M.I.D. 3.8.44 *(L.G. 18.10.45)*

Coffin, Wilfred Rubin, Sergeant
829605, Royal Artillery, 6 Armd. Div. (Deptford)
(Immediate)
For conspicuous gallantry and devotion to duty at Thala on 22 Feb.

Sjt. Coffin's gun was defending the forward 25 pdrs which by that time were in a very exposed position. Sjt. Coffin and four of his detachment were wounded by enemy shell fire. Sjt. Coffin kept his gun in action, directed the evacuation of his wounded, and refused to leave his post himself. Although wounded he remained with his gun throughout the day and later succeeded in shooting down a Ju.88 which fell about two miles north of Thala. His conduct was an outstanding example to all ranks. *(L.G. 8.4.43)*

Coitino, Michael, Lance Corporal
24161744, Parachute Regt.
For Northen Ireland *(L.G. 19.9.78)*

Colbert, Kenneth Bede Thomas, Corporal
NX 126259, 2/3 Aust. Inf. Bn. (Immediate)
For distinguished conduct in action.

During a company advance south of Boram in the Wewak area British New Guinea, on 1 June 45, Cpl. Colbert was in command of the section which led the advance. The section encountered intense machine gun fire from enemy in bunker positions covering the approach to Feature 910. In a sharp engagement Cpl. Colbert and three of his men were wounded. Despite his wound, he engaged the enemy position with his Sub-machine gun covering the evacuation of his wounded. Then, on his own initiative, he went forward alone and made a thorough reconnaissance of the enemy position, drawing fire from several different points. Shortly afterwards he repeated the reconnaissance with his Company Commander.

On the information gained on this reconnaissance a plan was evolved for a company attack on the following day which was entirely successful.

During this attack, Cpl. Colbert led his section in an assault on a heavily defended bunker position. Heavy Machine gun fire at point-blank range held up the section but Cpl. Colbert, displaying magnificent courage and with complete disregard for his own safety, dashed forward up a steep slope firing his Owen Gun from the hip. He killed the enemy machine gun crew and captured the gun. Immediately he rallied his section moved forward and engaged another machine gun which was enfilading the company endangering the advance of the left forward platoon. He directed the fire of the section on to this machine gun with such effect that it was quickly silenced.

During the whole action which lasted an hour, Cpl. Colbert's gallantry under fire, inspiring leadership, determination and devotion to duty were of an unusually high order. His aggressive and decisive action undoubtedly contributed towards the complete success of the operation. *(L.G. 24.8.45)*

Cole, William, Sergeant
6137453, 1 East Surrey Regt.
This NCO took out a fighting patrol across the river. He successfully reached the buildings on the far side and killed a civilian sniper who had been doing a lot of damage. He withdrew in the face of superior opposition although his communications consisted only of a very delapidated boat. He had previously commanded his pl and held his post to the end on the R. Escaut when his pl comd was hit, and successfully stopped all enemy attempts to adv.
Recommended for M.M. *(L.G. 20.8.40)*

Coleman, Cyril Charles, Bombardier (A/Sgt.)
896272, 211/64th Med. Regt., Royal Artillery (Partick, Glasgow)
16th April 1941, Servia Pass Greece
The Troop was ordered to withdraw in the evening 16/4/41 from the Troop Position near Servia. The only approach to the Gun position was across the skyline. A hostile battery which had been shelling the Troop consistently and accurately opened fire immediately the vehicles drove on to the position.

The Guns were deep in mud and owing to the difficult nature of the ground and approach every gun had to be winched out. For the last hour and a half of daylight and under continual shellfire Lt. A. C. Darnborough and Sjt. Coleman worked on the saving of the guns. On one occasion Sjt. Coleman was knocked down by the blast of a shell which landed in the gun pit and he was bruised and covered in debris but he carried on the work.

After dark the stone bridge over a waddy on the gun position collapsed and two A.E.C. tractors and one gun fell into the waddy and again Sjt. Coleman's unceasing work helped to extricate the vehicles and gun.

All the guns of the troop were saved and the last gun finally left the position at 0400 hrs 17th April. Throughout the night Sjt. Coleman worked ceaselessly and showed exceptional bravery and calmness under fire and was a fine example to the men under him.
(L.G. 30.12.41)

Coles, Edward Francis, Lance Sergeant
B66765, Canadian Infantry Corps
No citation. *(L.G. 9.2.46)*

Coles, Ronald Falcon Charles, Lance Corporal
5345780, 10th Bn. Royal Berkshire Regt. (Reading)
(Immediate)
On the night 10/11 Nov 43, 10th Bn. The Royal Berkshire Regt. had just relieved another Bn in the Calabritto position when intense shelling, mortar and MG fire was opened which proved to be the prelude to a determined enemy attack.

At about 1900 hrs when the enemy fire was at its height an Offr was seriously wounded. L/Cpl. Coles, one of the stretcher bearers attached to a reserve Coy near the Bn HQ area, immediately left the cover of his slit trench and ran forward some 200 yds to where the Offr lay. Completely ignoring the enemy shelling he dressed the Offr's wounds and then carried him single handed to a Bantam, during part of which journey he had to pass through heavy enemy MG fire. Placing the Offr in the Bantam he drove it himself to the RAP, along a road which was also at the time under accurate shell fire. He then immediately returned to his coy, and on six other and separate occasions during the night went out and attended to wounded men despite the fact that shells and mortar bombs were still falling and that MGs were sweeping the area.

At first light on 11 Nov, he took out stretcher bearers and searched for wounded to ensure that none had been left unattended. During his search he discovered a wounded man, and despite the fact that he was in full view of the enemy who was still firing, he attended the man's wounds and carried him to safety.

On the night 11/12th when the Bn HQ area was once again subjected to very heavy fire which caused several casualties, L/Cpl. Coles again went out under this fire to attend to the wounded men, moving from one to another, dressing their wounds and heartening them by his own personal cheerfulness and imperturbable manner. He continued to search throughout the night until he was satisfied that all wounded had been collected and cared for.

On the evening of 12 Nov the Coy to which L/Cpl. Coles was attached was sent to regain touch with one of the leading Coys, round which considerable numbers of enemy had infiltrated. Information was received that a Sjt had been wounded, that it had not been possible to bring him in, and that he was probably in an area occupied by the enemy. On hearing this, L/Cpl. Coles immediately set off on his own initiative to look for this Sjt; with the utmost calm he advanced under heavy and close MG fire, and began to search the area. It was not until he was ordered by an Offr to desist that he gave up his efforts to find the wounded man.

Throughout the whole period of some 40 hours, L/Cpl. Coles refused to rest. Oblivious to his own persnal danger, he displayed courage of the very highest order and set a standard of selflessness and devotion to duty which was an inspiration to all who were privileged to witness it. By his gallant conduct he undoubtedly saved many lives.
Recommended for V.C. (*L.G. 23.3.44*)

Collett, Alfred Alexander, Corporal of Horse
316329, Life Guards (Immediate)
On 30 Apr 45 CofH Collett was in comd of a sec of No 7 tp that was sp an armd C tp which had orders to seize and hold a br near Dienste. This br was important for the adv of the Gds Armd Div. This br was found to be held by a party of about 30 enemy, armd with Spandaus and bazookas with which the enemy were putting up a tenacious resistance. A bazooka, missing an armd car, struck a tree and CofH Collett was wounded. The centre of resistance was a trench manned by 6 men from which a considerable weight of fire was coming. CofH Collett adv 30 yds in full view and firing shot for shot with the enemy sec, rushed their post, killing 3 and taking the remainder PW. He then led his sec with great skill and dash in clearing some nearby houses from enemy who were still resisting strongly and continued for an hr driving the enemy from a wood, thus making the br secure.

The example of this NCO was an inspiration to all who witnessed this action, and contributed substantially to the success of the action. (*L.G. 23.8.45*)

Collins, Franklin Zeal, Sapper
B44464, 5 Cdn. Machanical Equipment Section, Corps of Royal Canadian Engineers (Immediate)
B–44464, 5 Cdn Armd Div, 1 Cdn Corps, On the 20th December 1944, Spr. Collins was operating an Armoured Bulldozer with 'B' Squadron, 1 Assault Regiment who had been given the task of preparing an assault crossing over the Fosso Munio in support of 11th Canadian Infantry Brigade. A first attempt during the night had failed and an Armoured Dozer had been knocked out and the operator killed. At 0745 hours, Spr. Collins, who was in reserve, was called forward to the site. Mortar and shellfire was constant and heavy. Acting on instructions from the Officer i/c Assault Group, he dozed an approach to the water so that an AVRE could place a fascine. The site was under full enemy observation and for 15 minutes, while completing his task, the shelling and mortaring became intense. A fascine was successfully placed by an AVRE and Spr. Collins was next instructed to go out and push spoil across the fascine to the far side, making a rough tank crossing. Mortar and shellfire again became very intense while he was

working. He succeeded in pushing spoil across the fascine, but his D–7 would not mount the 'step' on the far side. He returned and reported that while, still an obstacle to his D–7, a few tanks could cross and he could then complete the task. Tanks were ordered forward to attempt the crossing but the first three were knocked out by an Anti-tank gun which covered the approach. This caused a long delay, but at 1500 hours, under cover of smoke, three tanks got forward. The first two crossed successfully, but the third blinded by smoke, drove off the side of the fascine and blocked the crossing. It was decided that the only solution was to remove the ditched tank and put an Ark over the fascine. Spr. Collins backed his dozer up to the tank and aided by a REME officer and two of his men, winched the derelict clear of the site. Movement forward was, to a large extent, concealed by the ditched tank, but as soon as it started to move, a most intense concentration of fire, mostly 88 mm HE fell on the crossing. Spr. Collins then waited while an Ark was put in place and the crossing was proven suitable for all vehicles. For a period of nine hours, Spr. Collins remained near the site and was never out of mortar or shellfire. Each time he moved onto the task, he was in full observation and brought down a tremendous weight of fire on himself. His outstanding courage and cool judgement under fire were largely responsible for the success of the operation which, at that time, could not proceed without armoured support. (*L.G. 3.3.45*)

Collins, John Francis, Sergeant (A/C.Q.M.S.)
5384577, 1st Bn. Dorsetshire Regt. (Ayr) (Immediate)
On 4 Oct 44, Sjt. Collins was commanding his platoon in one of the fwd Coys during the Bn attack north of Bemmel. The first part of the advance was over very open ground, and was made in the face of intense small arms fire from S.S. elements and very heavy enemy arty D.F. In spite of heavy casualties Sjt. Collins led his platoon to the elimination of three spandau posts. The objective was reached when there were only six men left in the platoon, three of whom were wounded. Sjt. Collins never faltered and himself, with sten and grenade, routed the last of the enemy, of whom several were killed. Throughout the action Sjt. Collins showed complete disregard for his own safety, and it was entirely due to his leadership that the enemy were driven out. His behaviour was an inspiration to all. (*L.G. 1.3.45*)

Collins, Norman, Lance Sergeant
4393999, 6th Green Howards (Halifax) (Immediate)
On the night 16/17th March 1943, L/Sjt. Collins was a member of a fighting patrol which captured an outpost on the Mareth line. Despite intense enemy fire from the flank, this NCO led his part of the patrol round a flank with supreme courage and calmness, later he charged a 37 mm gun which was firing at him with his Thompson Sub Machine Gun, killing or capturing the crew and the gun. He again charged another post single handed, which had suddenly opened fire at the patrol at close range and

throwing 69 grenades he captured the post. The action of this NCO, his devotion to duty and supreme courage inspired those about him and were largely responsible for the capture of the position. *(L.G. 17.6.43)*

Colman, Alwyn Charles, Gunner
SX 561, 2/3 Fd. Regt., Australian Military Forces
On April 27th, 1941, in Greece, near Raft Bay, B Troop Guns were subjected to a vicious M.G. attack from the air and three Quads were set on fire. Gnr. Colman was told that Gnr. Dignum was missing and may still be in the burning Quad. The shells in the Quad were by this time exploding and Colman went back to find out. Dignum was not in the Quad but just as Colman was leaving a shell exploded and the nose cap hit him on the shoulder. Despite this injury he assisted Bdr. Sage to [...] the wounded subsection. *(L.G. 4.11.41)*

Comm, Philip Anthony, Corporal (actg.)
14334514, 7 Somerset Light Infantry (Bath)
(Immediate)
On 27 Mar 45 Cpl. Comm commanded the leading sec of a fwd pl in an encadre attack on the Autobahn at Vehlingen. The adv was stopped short of the objective by hy MG fire from several well-dug-in and mutually sp posts and Cpl. Comm's sec suffered cas. He at once brought accurate fire to bear on the enemy: himself got the wounded back, continued to neutralize the opposition and indicated the posns to the sp tks.

Under the tks' fire this NCO then led his sec fwd under a hail of crisscrossing enemy bullets. He then by bold and clever use of ground crawled right up to the enemy defences and got to close quarters. Thirty Boche gave themselves up; several dead were counted.

This brave and skilful adv under exceptionally hy fire at once enabled flanking pls to adv and close with the enemy. Cpl. Comm's gallantry, initiative and leadership without a doubt turned the whole enemy defence line, consisting of an ideal posn and trenches full of amn.
(L.G. 7.6.45)

Conaghan, James, Sergeant
2989967, 75th Anti-Tank Regt., Royal Artillery
(Falkirk) (Periodic)
During the period from 23 Jun 44 until the conclusion of the op between the Rivers Maas and Rhine in Mar 45 Sjt. Conaghan has commanded a towed 17-pr gun det. His gun has been in action in the fwd area supporting the Inf Bde throughout the whole period. At all times Sjt. Conaghan showed sustained gallantry; he was frequently under heavy shell and mortar fire but he remained cheerful and his fine disregard for his own personal safety encouraged his men to endure the heaviest shelling without flinching.

Before the crossing of the R Rhine his Regiment was converted into a composite force of two SP Btys A Tk and two Coys of Inf formed from the towed 17-pr Btys. Sjt. Conaghan trained his gun det as an Inf Sec and

throughout the op after the crossing of R Rhine led it with great dash and skill until he was wounded 7 May 45. His action on that occasion was typical of many he has carried out. His sec was acting as adv gd between Lebenau and Lemke when it came under heavy fire from a house strongly held by SS tps inside.

At all times this NCO has shown the greatest devotion to duty and his bravery and cheerful and determined leadership have been the inspiration of his men.
(L.G. 24.1.46)

Condie, William Thomson, A/Captain
493077, Special Air Service Regt.
For Oman *(L.G. 5.2.74)*

Conlon, Pat Joseph, Corporal
6913641, 2nd Bn. Rifle Brigade
For conspicuous gallantry and devotion to duty.
At Sidi Saleh on 6th Feb., this NCO was platoon Sergeant of a platoon whose area had been penetrated by an enemy medium tank and was being surrounded by the enemy infantry. Although one other section was forced to withdraw by heavy enemy fire, he protected the A/tk. guns on the right of the position by engaging the advancing infantry with L.M.G. fire. He subsequently went forward under fire, rescued two wounded men and brought them and the section truck back to safety, the remainder of the section having been killed or wounded.
(L.G. 9.5.41)

Conn, George, Lance Sergeant
6468001, 9th Bn. Royal Fusiliers (Steeple Morden,
Herts.) (Immediate)
During the attack made by this Bn on 9 May near Enfidaville L/Sjt. Conn was with the left forward Coy. This Coy was held up by intense M.G. fire just short of the enemy's positions. At this point this NCO was detailed to carry a message to the reserve Coy asking for support. To do this it was necessary to cross a hundred and fifty yards of ground swept by fire on two sides and also intense heavy shell fire. This NCO was seriously wounded about a hundred yards from this Coy, he crawled on and although in a state of collapse insisted on delivering the message to the reserve Coy Commander in person. This NCO's complete disregard for his own wounds and outstanding devotion to duty were an inspiration to all who witnessed the incident.
(L.G. 9.8.43)

Connell, John, Lance Sergeant
4034147, 6th Bn. Durham Light Infantry
(Birmingham) (Immediate)
On the 13th July this NCO's Company took part [...] attack on some strongly held positions outside [...]no. The country was rough and difficult and there were many small enemy posts and snipers. During the advance the Company came under heavy small arms fire but Sjt. Connell's Platoon was first to get into the enemy's

defensive area. Sjt. Connell immediately located a Breda Gun which he started to rush, but the crew withdrew down a track to a new position. Waiting until a Bren Section came up, he immediately seized the Gun himself and advancing down the track opened fire on the crew, who were completely wiped out. In addition he took one officer and many other ranks prisoner. On continuing the advance to an enemy R.A.P., still with the Bren, he and the section were sniped from a tree. Seeing the sniper, Sjt. Connell immediately killed him. This NCO has been an example to his Company, for his [...] and bravery have been outstanding. His leadership has been magnificent.   *(L.G. 18.11.43)*

Connell, William, Warrant Officer Cl. II (C.S.M.)
5669089, 4 Royal Sussex Regt.
The above named W.O. was C.S.M. of 'A' Coy. On May 21st, 1940, the Bn was awaiting orders at Anseghem, when it came under heavy shell fire. In 'A' Coy there were several casualties, including two stretcher bearers attached to the Coy whose stretchers were at the time on the Coy truck.

C.S.M. Connell on his own initiative, having helped to steady the Coy whose first experience of shell fire this was, went in search of the truck and stretchers. After a time, he returned, dragging two stretchers behind him. He then organised the evacuation of the wounded to a cellar, himself helping to carry them. The whole area was being heavily shelled throughout.

C.S.M. Connells' calmness and steadiness under fire, of which it was his first experience, his initiative and complete disregard of personal danger were an inspiration to all around him, and were of the greatest value in steadying the Coy as well as the means of getting the wounded to safety.

In subsequent action at Caestre this W.O.'s behaviour was of equally high standard. During the march to Dunkirk with only one officer with the Coy his leadership and cheerfulness contributed to the eventual safe arrival of the Coy.   *(L.G. 11.7.40)*

Constable, Anthony Laurence George, Corporal
    (actg.)
3443234, 2nd Bn. King's Regt. (Carshalton)
Ref maps Italy, 1/100,000, Sheets 160, 122.

Cpl. Constable has served as a stretcher bearer in all the actions that the bn has fought in Italy. At all times he has shown the highest courage and devotion to duty. His leadership of the other coy stretcher bearers has always been exemplary, and his conduct throughout has been far in excess of his duty. When casualties have occurred this NCO has gone out immediately without hesitation and brought them into safety. He has always shown complete disregard for his own personal safety and there is no doubt that the high state of morale and willingness in which the men of his coy have gone forward into the attack has been due to a large extent to the men's confidence in the Coy S.Bs.

On May 9th, 44, when the bn was in a concentration area behind Mount Trocchio, (894186) a report was received by his Coy that a young Officer of another unit was lying on the side of the mountain with his foot blown off by a 'S' mine. Although the mountain side was strewn with mines, Cpl. Constable without hesitation moved straight up to where the Officer was, alone, and then organized the evacuation of the Officer from the Mine Field.

During the crossing of the R. Gari, (866173), on the night of 11/12th May, 44, Cpl. Constable worked for 36 hours without rest and food rescuing the many wounded from both banks of the river. The area was constantly under extremely heavy and concentrated shell fire. Cpl. Constable walked about between the wounded quite oblivious to any danger. His example on this occasion was an example to all ranks of the bn.

On the 26th June, 1944, the bn attacked Gigiella, (W.348915), the Company was in reserve and while concentrated behind Lopi, (3590), was subjected to heavy concentrations of artillery fire. The CSM was killed and many of the company wounded. Again Cpl. Constable's conduct in evacuating the wounded under this shell fire was exemplary.

This NCO's magnificent example and steadfast devotion to duty have been a source of encouragement and inspiration to confidence for all ranks of the bn.
                                              (L.G. 19.4.45)

Constable, Leslie Peter Harold John, Sergeant
319120, 8th King's Royal Irish Hussars (Sidcup)
    (Immediate)
On 30 Mar Sjt. Constable was tp sjt of the leading tp adv north towards Oding. On reaching the woods two thousand yds south of the village the tp was heavily engaged by small arms fire and Panzer Fausts. The tp ldr riding in the second tk was killed and his tk knocked out. Another tk was also knocked out. Sjt. Constable took charge of the remaining two tks and continued to advance to the outskirts of the village where he encountered a rd block and considerable resistance. He was wounded in the jaw by shrapnel, but continued to engage the enemy at close range for a period of more than an hour whilst attempts were being made to clear the route behind him to bring up inf and reinforcements. Sjt. Constable was again wounded in the head, this time seriously. He refused to allow his crew to evacuate him: they were ordered to do so by the Sqn Ldr. At this time the only remaining tk was knocked out.

By his striking example of courage and leadership, Sjt. Constable did all in his power, even when twice wounded, to retain the initiative and close with the enemy.   *(L.G. 21.6.45)*

Convery, John James, Marine (A/T/Sergeant)
Ply/X.1394, Royal Marines, No. 40 RM Commando
    (Gateshead) (Immediate)
Termoli 3rd October 1943

Sgt Convery in Q Troop became the only SNCO in the troop remaining unwounded after all three officers had become casualties. He took command of the troop and carried on holding the left flank where severe fighting was taking place. Later when ordered over to the right flank he himself killed 15 Germans with a bren gun. Throughout the action Sgt Convery displayed courage and leadership of the very highest order and he was responsible for organising the troop in its defensive position during two counter-attacks.   *(L.G. 8.2.44)*

Conway, Franklin Gordon, Sergeant-Major
1038, Divisional Cavalry Regt., New Zealand Military Forces
For conspicuous gallantry.
During the occupation of Galatos by the Div. Cav. detachment over a period of approximately six days Sjt.-Major Conway on at least three occasions led patrols deep into enemy country gaining valuable information as to enemy positions and capturing several enemy Maxim machine guns, spare parts, and large supplies of ammunition. These guns and supplies were used to great advantage during the remainder of the campaign. In addition Sjt.-Major Conway during the whole of the campaign showed exceptional devotion to duty. The initiative and courage he displayed was an inspiration to others.   *(L.G. 30.12.41)*

Conway, James Sheppard, Sergeant
876831, 2 Fd. Regt., Royal Artillery (Glencraig, Fifeshire)
On 30 Jan 44, Sjt. Conway was performing the duties of OPA to Capt. Dunn, who was acting as an FOO with the 1st Bn KSLI, during their attack on Campoleone Railway line. During the advance the OP vehicle became bogged. Capt. Dunn and Sjt. Conway continued to do their work on foot, using a telephone to their vehicle. They became separated. Sjt. Conway returned to the truck after dark and arranged to move it to Bn HQ, where Capt. Dunn eventually rejoined it. An OP was established by first light. Capt. Dunn was wounded and became unfit for duty at 0730 hrs 31 Jan 44. An officer sent to replace him was also wounded before his arrival at the OP. From 0700 hrs until midnight on 31 Jan, Sjt. Conway carried out shoots, controlling the fire of his whole battery, passed back much valuable information and carried out the task of an OP officer with great success in spite of being subjected to heavy shelling, mortar and MG fire. Sjt. Conway's action contributed much to what the CO of the 1st KSLI has termed the 'magnificent support' afforded to them by the artillery.   *(L.G. 15.6.44)*

Cook, James Walter, Corporal
5347151, 10th Bn. Royal Berkshire Regt. (Henley-on-Thames) (Immediate)
At the Anzio Beach-head on the night 6/7 Mar 44 Cpl. Cook was ordered to occupy with a standing patrol of 10 men, a house known as Law's Folly in order to protect the left flank and comns to A Coy locality. At 2045 hrs an enemy patrol of 10 men approached the house. Cpl. Cook ordered his patrol to hold their fire until the enemy were within 20 yds of the house, and then, with the first burst of fire killed 2 of the enemy. The remainder of the patrol at once began to withdraw down a ditch under cover of a Spandau. Cpl. Cook crawled forward alone to within 10 yds of the enemy automatic and then charged it firing his TSMG. He killed both the enemy gunners and silenced the MG; as a result the rest of the enemy patrol was put to flight. Cpl. Cook at once switched his fire down the ditch and succeeded in wounding two more. He then returned to his patrol to await events. At 2345 hrs an enemy fighting patrol of 30 men with 4 Spandaus attacked, but were pinned in some outhouses by the accurate S.A. fire of Cpl. Cook's party. Shortly after, one of the Bren guns was damaged and put out of action. During the next 45 mins the enemy tried to rush the house three times but at each attempt they were beaten back by the accurate SA fire and also by a grenade throwing party which Cpl. Cook had organised in the top rooms of the house. Eventually the enemy withdrew leaving behind 6 dead and carrying several wounded with them. The patrol withdrew at first light intact. Throughout this small action Cpl. Cook displayed the highest qualities of leadership and courage; he had with him 5 men who were new to battle, and there is no doubt that his own personal example and utter disregard for his own safety so inspired the men that they were able utterly to defeat three determined attacks although heavily outnumbered, and to inflict considerable casualties without loss to themselves.   *(L.G. 20.7.44)*

Cook, Thomas, Warrant Officer Cl. II (C.S.M.)
2927262, 1st Bn Qeen's Own Cameron Highlanders (Leith, Edinburgh) (Immediate)
During an attack on a Japanese strong point at Sachema, Assam, on 14 Apr 44, this warrant officer displayed conspicuous gallantry and leadership especially after his Coy Comd had been wounded. He personally led his coy HQ in attack on Japanese positions with complete disregard for his personal safety. He charged and bayonetted the Japanese officer in command of the position and relieved him of his sword. His personal example throughout was an inspiration to all.
                               (L.G. 22.6.44)

Cook, William, Sergeant (A/C.Q.M.S.)
4543011, 1st Bn Parachute Regt., Army Air Corps
McAuley, Vincent Cronkite, A/S/Ldr.
J.4761, 7 Sqn, Bomber Command, RAF
Nightingale, Frederick Kitchener, F/Sjt.
618551, 7 Sqn, Bomber Command, RAF
1. Capture
S/Ldr. McAuley and F/Sjt. Nightingale
We were members of the crew of a Stirling aircraft (Pathfinder Force), which left Oakington (Cambs) at approximately 1700 hrs on 11 Dec 42 to bomb Turin.

The other members of the crew were:—F/Lt. Christie, W., D.F.M. (pilot) (killed while baling out and believed buried in Cuneo, Italy)

Sjt. Jagger, R.N.Z.A.F. (navigator)
F/Sjt. McDonald (bombardier)
F/Sjt. Jerries, (flight engineer)
F/Sjt. Falkingham (wireless operator)
and Sjt. McGraw, R.C.A.F. (rear gunner)

With the exception of F/Lt. Christie, all the above are known to be P/W in Italy.

We reached our target, but the weather was very hazy, and we had to descend to 7,000 feet to carry out our task properly. We were then hit by flak, about 2100 hrs, and the aircraft was set on fire. We jettisoned our flares and bombs over Turin, and set a course for home. We were losing height, and the pilot thought it inadvisable to try to cross the Alps, so he turned South West, towards the French frontier. About 2145 hrs, as we were still losing height, the pilot gave the order to bale out. We were then somewhere in the neighbourhood of Cuneo, in Piedmont (Italy).

S/Ldr. McAuley

I destroyed my secret equipment before leaving the aircraft.

My parachute did not open properly, and I must have been unconscious when I landed. At 2335 hrs I regained consciousness, and found myself, with a dislocated right shoulder, lying in a ditch in an orchard. I had great difficulty in freeing myself from my parachute harness, and had not sufficient strength to conceal either my parachute or mae west. I heard troops moving about close by. I opened my escape box, took a Horlick's tablet and got out my compass. With its aid I began walking West. I could not get my tunic off or remove my badges, but I managed to pull my trousers over my flying boots.

In a short time I reached a canal about 15 ft wide, with steep sides. I realised that in my condition I could not cross it. I threw my pistol into it, and sat down in a field close by. In about an hour some Italian soldiers came. They shouted at me and fired their rifles in the air over my head. I then gave myself up. They spoke some kind of French dialect of which I could understand a few words. I think I must then have fainted.

The soldiers took all my belongings from me except my watch. They then fetched a stretcher, and carried me to a house where an old woman gave me a drink of sherry. Later I was taken to the 'Headquarters of No. 7 Commando.' which I think must have been near Cuneo. Here my boots were taken off, and I was laid on a table. A doctor came and gave me some kind of anaesthetic.

When I came to, there was an officer with a note book, and a Blackshirt in civilian clothes, standing beside me. The offier asked me a number of questions in English, such as the type of my aircraft, my squadron number, route, target, bomb-load, the number of men in the crew, and their names. I told him the type of aircraft, the number of men in the crew, and a few of their names including McGraw's. He told me that they had already captured

Falkingham, and that my shoulder would be attended the next day.

I was put in a cell with two guards, and Falkingham was put in a similar cell next to me. I was given some food, but could get no sleep. There was a man in my cell writing at a desk. One of my guards who could speak French, (which I can speak a little) asked me several further questions.

About 0800 hrs on 12 Dec an officer brought Falkingham into my room, but we were not allowed to converse. I was then interrogated by an English-speaking Intelligence Officer who had come from Turin. He asked me if I had had a pistol, and I told him that I had thrown this away. He also asked me my address in Canada, which I gave him. He told me that he liked English people, but that his own house in Genoa had been destroyed by R.A.F. raids. He added that the Italians had found our aircraft and that Nightingale and McDonald had been captured.

About 1100 hrs Falkingham was taken out of my room, and I was taken by car by a senior officer to a Military Hospital of Fossano. I arrived here about 1130 hrs, and was put in a single room. Three guards, however, also slept in it, and there were generally three people there throughout the day.

About 1600 hrs I was taken to have my shoulder x-rayed. While this was being done several of the Italian patients came and jeered at me. That night a doctor set my dislocated shoulder. He did this in a manner which I thought deliberately brutal, and he and several other onlookers jeered at me during the process. The Sisters in the hospital, on the other hand, were extremely kind to me.

Next day (13 Dec), an Intelligence Officer came to see me, and produced a Red Cross Form which contained a space for my squadron number, (which he knew), and my Station (which he did not). He told me that Christie had been killed, and the aircraft destroyed, and that they had captured all the crew except McGraw.

He then asked me a number of questions about the armament, petrol load, and speed of my aircraft, how long my flight from England had taken, what methods of navigation were used in bad weather, and, most insistently, what was my Station. I did not answer these questions. This officer saw me twice later during my stay in the hospital. He did not ask me further questions, but on the last occasion he told me that McGraw had been captured. On 14 Dec my right arm was put in a plaster cast. Later I was told that Nightingale was in the same hospital, but I was not allowed to see him.

On the evening of 22 Dec I was given back my clothes, and with Nightingale was taken by car to Fossano station, and thence by train to Turin. At Turin we had to wait for about an hour and a half. During this time some Italian soldiers came and shook their fists at us, and made various offensive remarks.

F/Sjt. Nightingale

I baled out after McGraw. On my way down I lost

my left flying boot. I landed in a tree, breaking my left ankle. I saw the 'plane fall in flames nearby.

I took my parachute down and buried it and my mae west. I then removed my badges and opened my escape box. I decided to walk N.W. with the aid of my compass in the hope of ultimately reaching France. In a little while I met MacDonald. He had taken off his tunic, and was wearing a sweater. As I had great difficulty in walking, he made a pair of crutches with some sticks.

A motor cycle patrol passed quite near us, and a little later I heard some shots in the distance. About 0300 hrs, on 12 Dec, I felt I could not go on, and I suggested to Macdonald that he should leave me, and should take my escape kit to supplement his own. He refused to leave me or to take my kit. We then lay up in some bushes.

About 1100 hrs we came out of the bushes, and were seen by some peasants. About an hour later we were captured by some soldiers. They could speak French, which I can speak a little. They took us to a farm, where we were given some cognac and coffee. About noon we were taken by car to what appeared to be a Military Hospital, in a town which I cannot identify.

That evening we were taken by car to an aerodrome about 15 miles from this town, where we found Falkingham and Jeffries. I was interrogated here, and was asked some questions about the aircraft which I did not answer. I was then examined by doctor and taken to a hospital in Fossano.

On 14 Dec my leg was put in plaster. Next day the same intelligence officer described by S/Ldr. McAuley asked me similar questions, and produced a Red Cross Form containing a space for my squadron number and 'the call number' of my station. I did not complete these spaces. He also asked me whether a man called McGraw was a member of our crew. I thought that this question must imply that McGraw was still at liberty, so I denied any knowledge of him.

On 22 Dec, with S/Ldr. McAuley, I was taken by car to Fossano and later by train to Turin.

S/Ldr. McAuley and F/Sjt. Nightingale

At 2200 hrs on 22 Dec, with an escort, we left by express train for Rome, where we arrived about 1530 hrs on 23 Dec. About 1800 hrs we were taken to Poggio Mirteto about 28 mile north of Rome. This place is a decontamination and transit camp for R.A.F. P/W, and is administered by the Regio Aereonautica. We were searched on arrival, but our escape compasses were not found. We were segregated from the other P/W, but we saw the other members of our crew here, including McGraw, though we could not speak to them.

We were put in a small room together. We searched it very carefully for micrphones. We could see no signs of these, but we did not discuss any service matters. During Christmas many of our guards were very drunk, and in their cups ome of them expressed their resentment about the bombing of Turin by the R.A.F. As we were disabled, we were not, however, in a position to take advantage of their condition in order to escape, which

otherwise would have been comparatively a simple matter.

On 26 Dec a Major asked S/Ldr. McAuley similar questions to those in previous interrogations. This time the interrogator knew that we had left from Oakington. He said that he had obtained this information from some papers found in a field near our crashed aircraft. On 29 Dec we were taken by car to the Celio Military hospital in Rome.

Here McAuley was again interrogated by a man who claimed to be a scientist from the University of Rome. He could not speak English, and employed an interpreter. He brought with him a diagram of our W/T equipment, part of the navigator's log, and part of a chart used for our special equipment. These documents, he said, must have fallen from the aircraft before it blew up. He cross-questioned McAuley at some length about these papers, but to all his questions he replied 'I don't know.' He also asked him several times if he had been guided to Turin by listening to a radio call from England on the 48.7 KC metre band. To this McAuley replied that they had listened to a dance band playing from Miland and had dropped the bombs to music—whereupon he left him. Later a doctor in the hospital told him that this supposed scientist was really an Italian General.

Soon McAuley obtained some Italian/English grammars and dictionaries. We were not allowed to meet until about mid-January, but when we did meet, we began discussing escape plans in McAuley's room, of which he was now the sole occupant. About mid-Feb, McAuley found that it was possible to get out of a window in his room. About 20 Mar we knew that we were about to be moved to a P/W camp. We therefore began preparing to escape from the hospital to the Vatican City.

Capture
C.Q.M.S. Cook

In Nov 42 I was serving in Tunisia with my unit, the 1st Parachute Regt.

On 24 Nov. I was a member of a fighting patrol of my unit commanded by Capt. Stewart, reinforced by two Bren carriers and some men from the Lancs. Fusiliers, commanded by Lt. Morrell.

About 1100 hrs, with the Bren carriers in the lead, we were advancing down a road towards Medjez-el-Bab, when we ran into a German ambush.

For some reason Lt. Morrell and the Bren carriers left us. Our opponents were German parachute infantry, armed with mortars, L.M.G's and a 20mm anti-tank gun. Our party were all in an area about 70 yds by 30 yds, near a small Arab farm, and there was very little cover available.

Capt. Stewart ordered us to fight to the last man and the last round. We managed to put out of action two L.M.G.'s and inflicted severe casualties upon the enemy. (Later I heard that our fire had killed or wounded 57 Germans.) Our party, however, came under a storm of fire, and before long our ammunition was practically exhausted, and nearly all of us were killed or wounded.

Captain Stewart was killed, and of my own Bn. only five men were able to stand. I myself was wounded by a bullet through the body. All our hand grenades had been thrown.

The Germans then delivered their final assault. I can speak German fluently. When we were overwhelmed, since I fully expected that we would all be shot, I said to a German Lieutenant that I hoped he would hurry up with this unpleasant business. He seemed very upset, and actually burst into tears, saying 'How could you think that I could do any such thing.'

Lt. Cooke of the Lancs. Fusiliers was unhurt, and was the only officer remaining with us. He was at once segregated. I was able to remind the other survivors to say nothing but their number, rank and name. The Germans then told us that we must not speak until after we had been interrogated.

We were searched, but we were not carrying any private papers, and the only results of the search were three small compasses. We were then interrogated separately by a German Officer. I was asked my name, rank and number. Our treatment by our captors was very correct, and they dressed our wounds as soon as possible.

That afternoon we were taken by car to the German C.C.S. at Medjez-el-Bab. Here the wounded were given a ticket on which were printed spaces for our number, rank, name, and unit. None of us filled in the unit space.

That night we were transferred to a German Lazarett at Tunis, where a piece of bullet was extracted from my left side.

On 25 Nov we were taken by German transport plane under German escort to Naples, where we arrived about 1730 hrs. Here we were handed over to the Italian authorities, who took us to the Mental hospital on the waterfront. We were put into a verminous cell and given no further medical treatment and only a little food. Next day, 26 Nov, the Italian carabinieri removed us to the Caserta hospital near Naples.

On 29 Nov we received the first medical attention we had had since quitting Germans hands. The conditions in Caserta hospital were bad, and the place was strictly guarded.

On 31 Dec I was taken to Campo 54, Fara Sabina.

First attempted escape.

In Feb I initiated an attempt to escape from the Camp by means of a tunnel from the officers' latrine. Unfortunately this tunnel was discovered on 29 Mar, before it could be made use of.

I received an award of 30 days' solitary confinement, but on 31 Mar my physical condition was such that I was removed to hospital. Later, on the 4 Apr I was removed to Celio Hospital in Rome.

While here I learned that S/Ldr. McAuley and F/Sjt. Nightingale were also in the hospital, and were planning an escape. I resolved to join them if possible.

In a few days' time I was able to walk. Though guards were constantly in the ward, they had become very slack, and a number of them generally slept on any vacant beds in the ward.

We collected a certain amount of material for civilian clothes. Our plans was to climb out of the window of McAuley's room, and thence to get over the hospital wall and to drop into the street beyond. We had a fairly good idea of direction of the Vatican City. We were told that the Pope held audiences on Wednesdays and Saturdays, and that many people attended. This information is not in fact correct, and the audiences are held on no fixed days.

About 0225 hrs on the morning of 10 Apr (Saturday) Cook and Nightingale made up their beds to look as if they were occupied and left the ward on the pretext of going to the lavatory. They then entered McAuley's room. There we all put on the garments we had obtained, and left by the window, which another P/W closed after us. We had to leave the window in full view, but we were not observed, and we climbed the outer wall successfully. when we got to the top of the wall we realised that there was a drop of 25 feet on the outer side. This was too high for Nightingale to attempt, as his broken ankle was still weak. We therefore decided to go back and make another attempt later, when we could procure a rope. We retraced our steps, and our P/W friend inside the hospital opened the window of McAuley's room and let us in.

McAuley then collected from Red Cross boxes about 100 ft of string. This was plaited together by another P/W. The bayonet of one of the sleeping guards was borrowed in order to extract the nails from our boots. We then nailed bits of slippers on to the soles of the boots in order to deaden their noise on our next attempt.

As Cook could speak German, we arranged that if we were captured in the street we should pretend to be Germans on a visit to Rome. We also arranged that Cook should go ahead through the streets, followed by McAuley and Nightingale at suitable intervals. We planned to smoke cigarettes so that we could keep one another in view and to warn one another of danger by coughing loudly.

On 13 Apr, the day before that decided upon for our second attempt, six new patients came into the hospital, with the result that all beds were full. We were afraid that this would mean that the guards might be unusually vigilant. That morning one of the guards to our knowledge noticed that a bar to McAuley's window was missing. He was however, on bad terms with his N.C.O. so apparently he did not report the matter to him.

At 0230 hrs on 14 Apr Cook and Nightingale entered McAuley's room as before, and we all successfully climbed the hospital wall and made fast our rope to the top. We got over the wall, but on account of the presence of a carabiniere had not time to remove the rope.

Cook started off towards the Coliseum, and we followed him. We had arranged to call ourselves by Italian names so that we could address one another in Italian if we were approached by carabinieri.

At about 0345 hrs we arrived at the river Tiber near the Ponte St. Angelo. We were not aware when we left the hospital that the Vatican City was on the other side of the River. By this time there were many people about and the trams were running. Cook asked various people to direct him to the Vatican. The last man he asked seemed suspicious of his accent. Cook then addressed him in German, which the man could understand, and asked him the way to St. Peter's. The man guided him through the Porta Angelica, and the colonnades beyond it into the Square of St. Peter's, where Cook thanked him, and the man went away.

Meanwhile the rest of us were following at a reasonable distance. Cook rejoined us and we all stood and watched workmen passing through the Porta Sta Anna, into the Vatican buildings. After about ten minutes Cook again went ahead, through the Porta Sta Anna, and approached a Swiss guard who was standing on the left-hand side of the gate. Cook asked the guard in French if he was Swiss, and on receiving a reply in the affirmative, declared himself. McAuley and Nightingale followed almost directly afterwards.

We told the Swiss guard that we were three escaped prisoners of war. The gendarme asked us 'If we were three Generals?' He then took us inside the entrance, and fetched a Pontifical gendarme who conducted us to the gendarmes' barracks.

Later one of these gendarmes told us that an Italian carabiniere had come to them to ask for us to be handed over, but that his request had been refused.

On 24 Apr we were visited by Mr. Hugh Montgomery from the British Legation to the Holy See. We were given civlian clothes and shoes.

Arrangements were then put on foot for our exchange.

On 25 Apr we were received in audience by His Holiness Pope Pius XII. Cook is a Roman Catholic, but McAuley and Nightingale are Protestants. The Pope gave us his benediction and his good wishes, and presented us all with rosaries.

We left Rome by air on 7 Jun, via Barcelona and Madrid, where we spent the night. We then continued our journey by air to Lisbon, where we arrived on 8 Jun, and were taken to the British Embassy. *(L.G. 23.9.43)*

Cook, William Henry James, Warrant Officer Cl. II (C.S.M.)
6007186, 1/4 Bn. Essex Regt. (Becontree) (since killed in action) (Immediate)
During the fighting at Cassino, 15–20 Mar 44, this Warrant Officer displayed conspicuous bravery and leadership during the attack by his battalion on feature Pt. 165 (Monastery Hill) night 15/16 Mar; and during the defence of Pt. 193 (Castle) on 19 Mar.

The attack on Pt. 165 took place under conditions of great natural difficulty, owing to the darkness and rain, and soon after it had begun became disorganised by intense enemy defensive and fixed line MG fire. With complete disregard for his personal safety, CSM Cook

immediately moved round and gave major assistance to his company commander to get the operation re-organised and moving again. The services he rendered on this occasion were largely responsible for the capture of the objective.

On 19 Mar, the enemy began strong and determined counter attacks on Pt. 193 (Castle), where CSM Cook's company was waiting preparatory to attacking the monastery. His company commander assumed command of the mixed garrison and was soon wounded, and, all the other officers having become casualties, this Warrant Officer took command of his company and led it to the defence of this vital feature.

Throughout this day, he commanded the company with outstanding and gallant leadership. In the hand-to-hand fighting which developed, he was always at the most threatened spot of his sector, exposing himself fearlessly and cheering and encouraging his men. Again, as each attack was beaten off and succeeded by artillery and mortar concentrations, he moved about with cool gallantry re-organising his defences, and arranging the evacuation of casualties and replenishment of ammunition.

The bravery, devotion and leadership displayed by CSM Cook during the whole of this fighting were of the highest standard, and an inspiration to his company when much reduced by casualties.   *(L.G. 24.8.44)*

Cooke, Samuel Herbert, Sergeant
7011496, Royal Sussex Regt.
Sjt. Cooke was captured at Hazebrouck on 27 May 1940 and was imprisoned in Stalag VIII B (Lamsdorf), Germany, for the whole of his period of captivity. He made five attempts to escape before finally reaching Warsaw in the summer of 1944.

His first attempt was in November 1940; after timing the sentries, he got through the wire at night and walked 30 kms. He was recaptured the next morning and punished with 14 days' cells.

In April 1941 he volunteered to take a working party to Hindenburg, with the idea of escaping into Poland. He walked away from the cookhouse without any difficulty and hid in trains which carried him to within 5 miles of Krakow. He walked into the city to find a helper, whose address had been given him, but was halted by a German patrol asking for papers and was thus recaptured. He was again punished with 14 days' cells and bread and water.

His third attempt was made in October 1942, when with two other P/W he cut the wire. Sjt. Cooke separated from his companions outside the camp and after walking in circles was captured the following day by police.

In September 1943, while on a working party at Ratibor, for which he had volunteered in order to escape, Sjt. Cooke removed the distinguishing paint patch from his overalls and walked out of the main gate undetected. He reached Berlin by train but having no papers, was arrested by the control at the station. His punishment on return to Stalag VIII B was 21 days' cells, and he was warned that he would be shot should he attempt to escape again.

However, six weeks later Sjt. Cooke escaped for the fifth time. He and two men went to draw coal from the dump outside the main camp just before the sentries were changed. When the men returned Sjt. Cooke stayed behind in the forest. Towards evening he was apprehended by some guards off duty and was brought back to the camp.

Sjt. Cooke's final escape was effected in Apr 1944. He had obtained money by selling chocolate and cigarettes to the German guards; wearing civilian clothes acquired from Poles and carrying food given him by the British Medical Officer, Sjt. Cooke cut the wire and got away on the night of 22 April 1944. Travelling by rail and on foot, he reached the German—Polish frontier, which he crossed in dense forest. Poles assisted him on his way and, on reacing Warsaw, he went to an address that one of them had given him. Here he was well cared for, fed and given identity papers and money. Two months after his arrival there he assisted in the distribution of arms to the Resistance party in the city.

In August 1944 Sjt. Cooke decided to join the Russians, who were then advancing in the direction of Warsaw. This he did, against the advice of his host, and after long interrogations and imprisonment by the Russians, who needed a great deal of convincing that he was English, Sjt. Cooke was finally handed over to the British in Moscow on 22 September 1944.   *(L.G. 26.7.45)*

Cooke, Thomas Henry, M.M., Warrant Officer Cl. II
5199265, 5th Bn. Hampshire Regt. (Basingstoke)
Map—Italy 1/50,000, Sheet 109 IV. Coriano. 833824.

Early on the morning of 16th Sept, 1944, 'D' Coy was attacking Monte-Scudo village when they were engaged by heavy MG fire whilst crossing the open ground. No. 16 Pl. suffered a number of casualties, including the Pl. Commander and a number of NCOs. On an order from the Company Commander, CSM Cooke, although under intense MG and Mortar fire, went forward and reorganised the Pl. Later in the morning, the whole Company was subjected to violent mortar and shellfire and suffered heavy casualties. CSM Cooke personally brought in a number of casualties, completely disregarding his own safety.

By this time all three Pl. Commanders had been wounded and the Platoons were seriously depleted in numbers. CSM Cooke rallied a number of men and personally led them in a charge into the village of Montescudo which resulted in the enemy withdrawing in confusion.

Throughout the whole action he remained steadfast and courageous under most intense fire. By his resourcefulness and disregard of danger he greatly assisted his Company Commander and was an inspiration to the men, and the success of the action, in which a considerable number of casualties were inflicted on the enemy, owes

much to his gallantry.
M.M. 29.6.44   *(L.G. 8.3.45)*

Coombe, Herbert Warwick, Warrant Officer Cl. II
(R.Q.M.S.)
6133173, East Surrey Regt.
This W.O. was with his Bn. transport during the withdrawal across the R. Seine on June 8th and subsequently for a total distance of 220 miles. The transport was continually subjected to aerial attack and heavy bombing. By his fine example and coolness he did much to calm and reassure his men, and was of great assistance to the Convoy Commander.   *(L.G. 20.8.40)*

Coombes, John Latham, Lance Corporal
7915294, 40th (The King's) Bn., Royal Tank Regt.
(London, W.13) (Immediate)
On 25th September, 1943, L/Cpl. Coombes, J. L. was the Gunlayer in the leading tank commanded by a Sjt. supporting the 2/4 Hamps. Regt. in an attack at Cava de Tirreni. The tank was advancing down the main road which it was unable to leave due to the close precipitious nature of the country. As the tank advanced, it was held up by mines laid on the surface of the road. The Tank Comd got out of the tank to examine the mines when he was immediately shot by two enemy M.Gs. and fell in front of the tank in the road. L/Cpl. Coombes immediately assumed command of the tank and engaged both enemy M.G. posts, though they were difficult to locate in the close country. He then put down smoke from the tank and with great courage got out and ascertained that the tank Comd who was lying in the road was dead. He got back into his tank and informed his Troop Leader that he had taken command of the tank and again re-engaged the M.G. Posts which then remained silent. With a depleted crew, he kept his tank in action for a further three hours during which time the tank was subjected to intense mortar fire and sniping. After three hours his tank was hit by an A/Tk gun which set it on fire and killed another member of the crew. L/Cpl. Coombes again displaying sterling courage and devotion to duty ordered evacuation of the tank and still under M.G. fire and sniping, he evacuated successfully the remaining two members of the crew. His sustained courage, great coolness and fighting spirit was a magnificent example and worthy of the finest traditions of the Royal Tank Regiment.

I have the honour to recommend he be awarded the Distinguished Conduct Medal.   *(L.G. 13.1.44)*

Cooper, Hamilton Loos, Sergeant
805863, 4th Regt., Royal Horse Artillery
On 9 Dec 40, B Tp, 'C' Bty R.H.A. was ordered into action just north of Wadi el Kharuba (382301) in the open to engage enemy guns dug in around Alam el Rimin at a range of 4,500 yds and accurate enemy shell fire, B Tp remained in action engaging the enemy guns and eventually having silenced them sufficiently, continued

the advance. Throughout the action Sjt. Cooper who was the G.P.O.A. carried on his duties with complete disregard for the enemy's fire and although wounded in the head refused to leave his post until the action was over. By his gallantry and devotion to duty Sjt. Cooper set a fine example to all ranks.   *(L.G. 25.4.41)*

Cooper, John Murdoch, Lance Sergeant
2698113, 2 Bn. Scots Guards, S.A.S. Bde. (Immediate)
February 1942.

On returning from the 2nd raid against Buerat aerodrome the raiding party was ambushed by a strong and well-armed enemy force. This force was aligned along the road in an ideal position to throw grenades and to open fire with automatic weapons. The ambush was a complete surprise, but so quick was Sgt Cooper in getting his gun into action and so accurate was his aim in the face of intense fire from the automatic weapons of the enemy that the ambushers were seriously disconcerted. At least five of them were killed at point blank range by his fire. His quickness and courage on this occasion undoubtedly saved his companions. This NCO has taken part in 13 raids and performed many acts of gallantry comparable to the one described.
                                    (L.G. 26.11.42)

Cooper, Sydney George, Warrant Officer Cl. II (R.Q.M.S.)
6842786, King's Royal Rifle Corps (Winchester)
(Periodic)
During the night attack by this Bn on the Tell el Aqqaqir position this warrant officer was with the leading Coy of the Battalion. When his Coy Commander was seriously wounded at a critical moment, he immediately took over the job of reorganising the Coy on its objective. Finding the right Platoon had had very heavy casualties and both its Commander and Pl Sjt killed he reorganised it and gave it orders. Then deciding from a personal recce that the left Pl was very exposed and unsupported he moved it to a new position.

He continually moved about the Coy position under heavy machine gun fire keeping the Commanding Officer informed of the latest situations, supervising the getting away of the wounded and ensuring the supply of ammunition until he could hand over to the Coy Second in Command. He then took command of the forward Machine gun section whose Sjt had been killed and directed their fire for the rest of the day. His bearing throughout this action was worthy of the highest praise and inspired the Coy at a critical time.

Three days previous to this during the attack on Woodcock this warrant officer showed the greatest disregard for danger while he organised the evacuation of the wounded.

Again during the night 17/18 Jan during an operation his Coy was carrying out cutting the rd behind the enemy at Beni Ulid he was blown up by a mine while driving a Jeep. Although badly shocked he refused to rest but

immediately took charge of the situation taking steps to mark the minefield and divert the remainder of the Coy thereby saving many casualties and vehicles.

During the whole of this period under review this warrant officer has shown the utmost devotion to duty under every circumstance and his gallantry and disregard of danger has been an inspiration to everyone.
M.B.E. 13.6.64   *(L.G. 14.10.43)*

Cooper, Walter John Harry, Corporal (A/Sgt.)
5724708, 2 Dorsetshire Regt.
On the 28 May during the attack on Gorre Sjt. Cooper was in command of a section of carriers. At about 1100 hrs a heavy enemy attack came down and the situation was serious. Under Lt. Heron Sjt. Cooper led his carriers in a counter attack which was successful and inflicted heavy casualties on the enemy. Later a similar situation arose again and Sjt. Cooper counter attacked with great success.   *(L.G. 22.10.40)*

Coppack, Edward Tom Charles, Warrant Officer Cl. III
2060732, Royal Artillery (Leicester)
No citation.   *(L.G. 20.9.45)*

Corbett, A. B., Sergeant
7686191, 50 Div, F.S.P., C.M.P.
In the early hours of 2 June 40 Sjts. Naish and Corbett were on the mole at Dunkirk with a large number of men of various units under hy shell fire. As ships were not immediately available it was necessary to clear the mole before daybreak as otherwise hy casualties might have ensued through air and arty bombardments. These two NCOs set a great example by their courage and coolness and regardless of their personal safety persuaded many men to march back to the beach from the mole. Subsequently they assisted in embarking 159 men who would otherwise have remained in an exposed posn on the mole.
M.I.D. 29.11.45   *(L.G. 11.7.40)*

Corbett, Ralph Fenwick, Private
230522V, 1st City/Cape Town Highlanders
(Immediate)
For distinguished conduct in action

In the attack on Monte Sole on the fifteenth of April 1945 this soldier was wireless operator and runner of the assaulting platoon of the left hand company. The platoon's objective was the pinnacle of Monte Sole. Near the pinnacle the platoon ran into an extensive Schu minefield which caused numerous casualties and threatened to bar further progress and disorganise the attack. Realising how essential it was to press forward Pte. Corbett found a way through the minefield maintaining continuous wireless communication with Company Headquarters as he did so. Pressing forward to the summit the platoon was met by a determined enemy counter attack and again Pte. Corbett showed extreme bravery, killing the entire crew of an enemy machine gun himself. The platoon commander was temporarily incapacitated by mortar bomb blast and this soldier knowing that speed was essential immediately led the forward section onto its objective inspiring the men by his bravery.

Later the same night he took over command of one of the sections when the Section Commander became a casualty and organised the section to beat back a counter attack which was coming in.

Throughout the action his inspiring bravery, leadership and devotion to duty were of the highest order, and it was largely due to his unhesitating assumption of responsibility that the platoon's final objective was captured and held against counter attacks.

(L.G. 5.7.45)

Corbett, Verdun Frank, Sergeant
319399, 9th Queen's Royal Lancers (Birmingham)
(Immediate)

On 7 Dec 44 Sjt. Corbett was commanding a tank in 3rd tp C Sqn 9th Lancers who were supporting a coy of the 1 KRRC in the attack on the village of Pideura which was a key posn and strongly held. Whilst the infantry were securing a foothold in the church the other two tanks of the tp were disabled by bazookas. Further tank support was urgently required by the infantry in the church in order to silence a German strong point in the house next door. As no tank could cover him Sjt. Corbett proceeded to advance the 400 yds into the village, alone. The power traverse had been badly damaged by a bazooka the day before when infantry support during the advance had been impossible, so that he well knew that his tank was almost defenceless against any bazooka-men. Furthermore, the whole 400 yds of the road was in full view of enemy SP guns shooting from the flank. In spite of this, he continued to advance and reached the village. On arrival at the church where it had been arranged that he should meet the infantry, he was surprised to find Germans taking up posns all over the village, and no sign of our own infantry who, it afterwards transpired, had been driven out of it by a strong German counter attack.

Sjt. Corbett was able to kill one German as he ran to man his anti tank gun and then to run over the gun. By now spandau was being fired at him from all sides at 10 yds range but undeterred he proceeded to engage the house which was the German strong-point with HE fire. He now saw that more Germans were entering the house so he decided that the only way to restore the situation was to charge his tank at them. This he did, causing the front wall and top floor to collapse on top of his tank. Reversing out he found that both his 76 mm gun and his two Brownings were jammed. He now proceeded to engage the enemy with his tommy guns from an exposed posn out of the top of the turret. His gunner operator loaded one for him whilst he fired the other. He also engaged the enemy in the ditches with his hand grenades, and the rest of the crew used their revolvers out of the revolver ports. Sjt. Corbett had by now killed and wounded many Germans and had got his tank alongside the church. Standing on the turret he was able to look through the window and saw that the church was occupied by Germans. He immediately fired his tommy gun, killing several and clearing the church. Sjt. Corbett had now completely run out of ammunition, but at this critical moment the KRRCs re-entered the village and were able to enter the church and house, consolidate the posn and take several prisoners. There is no doubt that had it not been for Sjt. Corbett and the outstanding use of his tank, the German counter attack might have succeeded, and the key posn of Pideura would have remained in German hands.

Sjt. Corbett by the complete disregard for his personal safety, his exemplary offensive spirit and determination to fight his tank to the last round was outstanding in the battle at Pideura. *(L.G. 10.5.45)*

Corkery, William, Corporal
3511456, 8 Sherwood Forester
Doyle, H., Pte.
3301080, 5 Gordon Hldrs.

(1) Cpl. Corkery

I was taken prisoner by a German mopping-up party in the hills North of Lilliehammer (Norway) on 27 Apr 40, and was later taken to Oslo, by rail and ferry to Denmark, and then by ship to Stettin (Germany). At Stettin all British P/W were collected and O.R.s taken by train (cattle trucks) to camps in German occupied Poland. I was first taken to Bromberg (Bydgoszcx), where P/W were engaged on the preparation of gun ranges. As I refused to do this work I was removed the following day (7 July) to Stalag XXA, Fort 13, at Winduga, on the Vistula.

(2) Pte. Doyle

On 15 May 40 I was on outpost duty in the Saar Valley (with D. Coy. 5/Gordon Hldrs.). We had been heavily shelled for five days, and that morning the post was overwhelmed. About 75 of us were taken prisoners and removed in a lorry. Two O.R.s and I were segregated and at Comblerz were interrogated by a German General, before joining the others at the transit camp at Lindburg. From here we were taken to Stalag XXA at Thorn, and shortly afterwards, I was transferred in a party of 150 O.R.s to the working camp at Winduga.

Account by Cpl. Corkery and Pte. Doyle

On arrival all our personal belongings were confiscated, we were not interrogated but were registered. No clothing was issued to P/W. We were housed in wooden huts and the food was poor and scarce. Discipline was very strict; our quarters were searched once or twice a week. During our stay in the camp we did not see a Red Cross parcel. All our letters were censored. In spite of everything and of the German effort to convince us that the war was lost for Britain, P/W never despaired. We were obliged to work and went out daily in parties of ten or twenty under escort of two guards armed with rifles. Roll call was taken before leaving and on return to the Camp. P/W of Irish extraction were taken away soon after our arrival.

There was no recognised escape organisation amongst P/W, but individuals were constantly scheming and collecting equipment. We stole a map from the guards' canteen and had already acquired a pocket compass. It was impossible to get hold of civilian clothes, this handicap and the lack of money stopped many a man from trying to get away. The Germans had also put up a notice saying that it was useless to escape to Russia, as the Red frontier guards shot at sight. In spite of all this we decided to make a dash for it.

The guards' canteen had a door on the far side opening out of the camp, with a single wire fence beyond to negotiate. At 0430 hours on 3 Dec we went through the canteen and, when the sentry had just passed, scrambled under and through the fence and so got away. We took the river Vistula as our direction for Russian Occupied Poland and, for the first ten day, avoided meeting anybody. By then our store of food gave out, but on approaching Polish farmers, we were given food and clothing and by degrees guided to Warsaw. Here we got into touch with an Organization which helped us to the frontier at Ostroleica. Here we got through the wire and penetrated five miles beyond before we were arrested by Russians and taken to Lomsa prison for three days, then nine days at Bialostok and thirteen at Minok. At all these places the prisons were filthy and overcrowded, and we were half starved. The other inmates were chiefly Poles of whom the majority were ex-Officers. Later we were moved to a prison in Moscow, where conditions were better; this was an internment camp for political prisoners. After a fortnight we were taken, with 140 Frenchmen, to a Camp at Smolensk, where we remained from the beginning of Feb 41 until the 22 June, when the Germans attack began. We were then taken to the railway station and were all ready for our journey (rumoured to be Siberia), in cattle trucks under heavy guard, when all British P/W were suddenly ordered to leave the train. We were taken back to the camp and later to an hotel in Moscow, where we spent eight days on good rations before our release on 8 July to our own Embassy.   *(L.G. 4.11.41)*

Cornell, Sidney, Private
14635496, 7th (L.I.) Bn., Parachute Regt., Army Air Corps (St. Albans) (Periodic)
This soldier was one of the parachutists who landed behind the German lines in Normandy on the night 5/6 June 1944. During the next five weeks he was in almost continuous action of a most trying and difficult nature. Cornell was a company runner and has repeatedly carried messages through the most heavy and accurate enemy mortar and MG fire. Four times wounded in action this soldier has never been evacuated and carries on with his job cheerfully and efficiently. Very many acts of gallantry

have been performed by members of the battalion but for sustained courage nothing surpasses Cornell's effort. His courage and many wounds have made him a well known and admired character throughout not only his own battalion but also the whole brigade. Space does not permit a record of all his feats as he distinguished himself in practically every action and fighting took place daily. On 18th June 1944 his company carried out a raid on a strong enemy position in the Bois de Bavent area. The position was stronger then expected and the company was hard pressed and the wireless set destroyed. Cornell was sent back with a verbal message, he was wounded during the journey but carried on and delivered his message correctly and set off with the reply. He was wounded a second time on this return journey but again carried on and again delivered the message correctly. During the remainder of this raid, despite his two wounds, he was outstanding for his courage and dash. The courage and devotion to duty displayed by Cornell on this one occasion was an inspiration to all who witnessed it. He has performed similar runs on countless occasions and, as has been pointed out before, has been wounded twice more but is still the runner of his company and is as cheerful as before.

On 10th July 1944 his company again carried out a raid on the same area and again and as usual, Cornell's complete disregard for his own safety became the chief topic of discussion amongst his fellow soldiers. He has never failed to deliver a message correctly despite the fact that he has usually carried it through a perfect hail of enemy mortar bomb and shells and very frequently aimed MG fire as well.

He is a truly magnificent parachutist and I cannot recommend him to strongly for a decoration.
                                    (L.G. 1.2.45)

Cornell, William Evelyn, Warrant Officer Cl. III (Pl.S.M.)
6005337, Essex Regt. (Moascar)
This Warrant Officer has commanded No. 17 Platoon throughout the War in a thoroughly capable manner. He has taken exceptional pains both to train his NCOs and to get the best out of his men. In his administration of the platoon, often on detachment, he has shewn exceptional initiative and has never failed even under the most difficult conditions to feed and water his men and look after them. In addition his example of fortitude, calmness and determination has had a great moral effect on the whole company.

On or about 26 Jun 41 at Falluja
PSM Cornell led a composite platoon on a fighting patrol to a village occupied by the enemy. He was ordered by his Company Commander to withdraw owing to the heavy fire coming from the enemy positions. The enemy strength was estimated as one company. This WO withdrew his complete platoon without loss in the face of hostile fire at about 400 yards range and himself waited alone on a crest firing with a Tommy Gun until his

complete platoon were 50 yards behind the ridge. Only then did the Sergeant Major calmly rise to his feet and walk away in full view of the enemy and under their fire. His example and handling on this occasion was outstanding.

On or about 28 June at Palmyra

PSM Cornell joined with 2nd/Lieut. Grimley to form a composite platoon to make a night attack on the castle. The PSM acted as 2nd i/c the attacking force and was responsible for most of its preliminary preparations. Once more his leading of a portion of the platoon and his assistance to the platoon commander were invaluable, the PSM actually leading a party during the clearing of the surrounding moat. A great deal of the success of this operation was due to his work and leadership.

On or about 29 June at Palmyra

PSM Cornell was one of a party holding the castle before the arrival of the remainder of the company. A party of between twenty five and thirty men were seen to be occupying a neighbouring hill and were sniping an approaching MT convoy. PSM Cornell took an automatic and a number two gunner and advanced in the open towards the peak. By a series of advances and burst of fire he succeeded in driving the whole party off the peak and they retired hastily into the town. Aout six of the enemy were wounded and left behind in a ruin. The convoy was then able to proceed. Had it not been for this prompt and courageous action it would have been a very much longer task to clear the hill and the convoy would have been delayed and might have suffered casualties. *(L.G. 21.10.41)*

Cornwall, James, Sergeant
7882474, 3 Royal Tank Regt.
For gallantry, coolness and devotion to duty.
On the night of the 23rd of May Sjt. Cornwall's squadron was ordered to act as advance guard to the battalion. The squadron soon found itself in country occupied by the enemy in large numbers. Sjt. Cornwall was commanding the point tank of the advance guard. The squadron had to pass over a mined bridge defended by the enemy. An attempt was made to blow up these mines by shoting at them with a cruiser tank gun. This only exploded two of the mines which were all connected by a strip of metal along the top. On this Sjt. Cornwall, under covering fire from the cruiser tank got out of his tank and attached a tow rope to the strip of metal and then reversed his tank and withdrew the mines. This brave action secures the safe passage of the bridge for his comrades. *(L.G. 5.7.40)*

Cortis, John Fyans, Sergeant
NX 13746, 2/17 Aust. Inf. Bn.
This NCO was a sjt of the 2/17 Aust Inf Bn machine gun platoon during the operations near Alamein from 23 Oct until he was wounded on 28 Oct 42.

On the night 24/25 Oct 42 his bn had attacked; the rifle coys had reached their objectives and were being subjected to heavy enemy artillery and machine gun fire. Sjt. Cortis was moving forward with his vehicle when it came under heavy machine gun fire which set the vehicle alight and caused casualties among the personnel. Showing great coolness Sjt. Cortis took command of one sub-section of the machine gun platoon, dismounted the gun from the burning vehicle and brought the sub-section into action engaging the enemy. This resulted in some spandau posts being silenced, thus permitting the re-organisation of the coys and their consolidation of the ground won. The whole operation was made more difficult by the fact that a burning anti-tank gun portee had also lit up the area.

Sjt. Cortis later in the operation took over command of the machine gun platoon. Despite heavy casualties in the platoon he, by outstanding qualities of leadership, courage and devotion to duty was mainly responsible for most aggressive action by this platoon throughout the whole period the bn was engaged in operations. Sjt. Cortis was wounded in the execution of his duty, his conception of which was an inspiration to the men under his command. *(L.G. 11.2.43)*

Cory, Gilbert Ernest, Sergeant
NX 7864, 2/3 Aust. Inf. Bn. (Immediate)
New Guinea For gallantry and outstanding devotion to duty.

During an attack on a strongly defended enemy position on the high ground to the west of Eora Creek village on 28 Oct 42, Sjt. Cory showed exceptional courage and leadership under very heavy fire whilst commanding 14 Pl. His pl suffered heavy casualties in NCOs. Sjt. Cory moved rapidly from section to section directing operations with complete disregard for his personal safety. He received a severe facial wound, and though temporarily blinded, continued to direct the assault until evacuated. The great success achieved by this platoon was largely due to Sjt. Cory's personal effort and bravery under exceedingly heavy fire.
M.C. 21.6.45 *(L.G. 4.2.43)*

Cotterill, Richard Henry, Bombardier
NX.60163, 3 Aust. A.Tk. Regt., R.A.A.
Gallant conduct and outstanding devotion to duty whilst in action on Tell el Eisa Spur, Pt 24 (Ref: El Alemein 1:50000 square 874299) during period 11–14 Jul 42 incl. During attack on our position on 13 Jul 42, Bdr Cotterill showed extreme coolness and excellence of commanding directing the fire of his gun against 4 enemy tanks, all of which he succeeded in knocking out. On evening on 14 Jul, the enemy attacked in considerable force and although Bdr Cotterill had lost three of his crew, he again fought his gun with extreme coolness and with such command that he succeeded in destroying 3 enemy tanks before his remaining gunner was killed ad the gun put out of action. Cotterill although wounded, repaired to the nearest infantry post and acted as runner to the Coy Comd until the action had finished. *(L.G. 24.9.42)*

Cotton, Henry Edward, Corporal
6456683, 1st Bn. Royal Fusiliers (Brixton, London)
9th December 1940, at Tummar West, Western Desert

In the attack on the enemy's position Corporal Cotton's platoon commander was wounded and his platoon Sergeant was killed. He at once took over command.

His platoon was held up by fire from a machine gun post. He went forward and after reconnoitring the position, arranged for covering fire from two Bren guns while he rushed the position with two other Fusiliers. The post when captured was found to consist of five machine guns.

Corporal Cotton displayed both leadership and great courage.   *(L.G. 8.7.41)*

Cottrell, Thomas, Sergeant
4275145, 3 Recce Regt. (N.F.), Reconnaissance Corps (Newburn-on-Tyne) (Immediate)
On 7th April 1945 'A' Sqn was given the task of seizing a bridgehead over the EMS south of Lingen in order to permit the building of a bridge thus opening up an important additional route.

The operation was carried out by advancing down the east bank of the river. Despite the fact that the enemy held the bridge site in some strength the Sqn succeeded in getting two carrier troops into a position covering the north and east approaches. There still remained, however, approx a Pln of enemy well dug in covering the bridge site from the south. Efforts to dislodge them with tanks, arty and mortar fire all failed. The remaining carrier troop was then ordered to assault the position. Sjt. Cottrell in command of one of the sections was ordered to carry out the assault under covering fire from the other section.

Immediately after it had started the section came under heavy and accurate small arms fire. It continued nevertheless and succeeded in reaching the first enemy position. Sjt. Cottrell himself entered the trench and took three P.W. at the point of his sten. Still under intense small arms fire, he led his section forward again and systematically cleared several further positions.

Seeing one of his men fall wounded and lying in the open under fire Sjt. Cottrell with complete disregard for his own safety immediately started to his assistance. On his way he was confronted by a German whom he disarmed with violence and then successfully arranged the evacuation of the wounded man. Afterwards Sjt. Cottrell again led his men forward and after severe hand to hand fighting succeeded in finally clearing the enemy out of the position.

During this operation Sjt. Cottrell was personally responsible for killing six men and taking a further 8 prisoners. By his magnificent example and brilliant leadership he was responsible for his troop attaining its objective thus enabling bridging operations to commence.
(L.G. 21.6.45)

Couling, Harold Roy, Corporal (actg.)
*7384504, 16th Parachute Field Amb., R.A.M.C.
(Plymouth)*
On Tuesday the 19th September 1944 Cpl. Couling was the senior NCO in charge of a building, housing 100 patients of an MDS run by 181 Air Landing Field Ambulance. On succeeding days up to the 25th September the building was the centre of heavy fighting and frequent shelling. This NCO first organised a ration supply for his patients by going out between the opposing forces to collect stores from wrecked vehicles and abandoned buildings. When the civilian water supply was cut off he organised an emergency supply in a rubber dinghy and supervised its rationing. On many occasions each day he went out to give medical aid to, and carry in, wounded, enemy and British alike. He organised the routine of his wards and treatment of his patients in such an efficient manner that no one could have done more for them in similar circumstances. On several days shelling and small arms fire around the building prevented the visits of M.O's and Cpl. Couling performed minor operations under local anæsthetics. By 25th September 1945, 160 wounded were accommodated in his building and from 19th September until final evacuation on the 25th only one man died there. When one room was wrecked by fire from an S.P. gun this NCO rescued the patients from the debris and treated them. When injured by shell-fire on the 23rd September Cpl. Couling used an inverted floor brush as a crutch and continued in the care of his patients. Although his premises were occupied by the enemy, he made repeated journeys in the open to carry in British and German casualties and to supervise the care of his ambulance transport. When all patients had been evacuated, this NCO collected all remaining rations, medical stores and equipment, organised a truck for his orderlies and rejoined his patients to continue his work in a prison hospital. Throughout the week when he was in charge of this hospital Cpl. Couling showed great bravery and devotion to duty and his behaviour was in keeping with the highest traditions of his Corps.
M.I.D. 23.9.43 & 23.3.44   *(L.G. 20.9.45)*

Courtenay, George William, Corporal
23910745, Gloucestershire Regt.
For Northen Ireland   *(L.G. 18.12.73)*

Coventry, Donald Tudor, Sergeant
*6857923, King's Royal Rifle Corps, attd. L.R.D.G.
(Immediate)*
At Leros in November 1943 Sjt. Coventry was part of a patrol of this unit holding the Mount Clidi position. Before the battle began he showed great courage in assisting the removal of men who were wounded when a naval gun scored a direct hit. During the battle his complete personal disregard for safety was outstanding and with only two men was responsible for the capture of 17 Germans who were holding up our successful

attempt to recapture the position. During the last phase of the battle he held the forward slopes of this feature with a handful of men until finally he ordered his party to leave while he carried 2 wounded men to safety on his back. He subsequently escaped from Leros after the occupation by the Germans.   *(L.G. 14.9.44)*

Coveyduck, Walter Richard, Sapper
B27938, 5 Cdn Fd Coy., Corps of Royal Canadian Engineers
At 30 minutes past H hour on D Day—6 Jun 44—Spr. Coveyduck was in a position on the seaward side of the sea wall on the extreme left of Nan-Red beach taking cover from enemy fire from a position on the left flank. An LCI (L) touched down immediately in front of Spr. Coveyduck's position and lowered its ramps. Infantry commenced to disembark but the leaders were shot down. At the same time the action of the surf turned over the starboard ramp which then became entangled with the port ramp preventing the remainder of the Infantry from disembarking. Spr. Coveyduck, seeing the perilous position of the remainder of the troops on board the craft, with great presence of mind and disregarding enemy small arms and mortar fire, ran to the craft and disentangled the ramps, turning the port ramp right side up, anchoring it to the ground with his own weight—at the same time shouting and waving to the Infantry on board to get off quickly and remained with the ramp till the Infantry commenced to disembark.

Approximately an hour after the above incident, Spr. Coveyduck was accompanying L/Sjt. Killah in the latter's search for the remainder of his section and came upon a blazing Sherman Tank which was filled with shells and mines. A soldier was lying prone beside this tank and L/Sjt. Killah and Spr. Coveyduck noticed movement of this body. Completely disregarding the danger from this exploding and blazing tank and also enemy aimed shell arms fire, Sjt. Killah and Spr. Coveyduck picked up a stretcher, ran to the side of the tank, placed the wounded man on the stretcher and took him out of danger.   *(L.G. 19.8.44)*

Covill, Douglas Frederick, Sergeant
320318, 10th Royal Hussars (Immediate)
On April 17th, Sjt. Covill was acting as Troop Sjt. in 'A' Squadron, 10th Royal Hussars. His Troop was supporting the 24th Guards Brigade in an attack in the Fossa Marina bridgehead. His tank was hit by a bazooka and caught fire, and owing to the fact that the driver was killed it continued to move, blazing, towards the enemy. The Gunner's leg was broken, but Sjt. Covill, himself a very small man, hauled his Gunner, who was a big man, out through the turret and pushed him off the moving tank and dragged him into a ditch where he was pinned down by small arms fire. By hand signals he called up the Troop's third tank and directed its fire on to the Spandau Post and then evacuated the wounded Gunner on the back of the tank. His Troop Leader in the

meantime had been killed by a sniper. Sjt. Covill realising at once that the Troop needed reorganising, and the necessity for tank support, ran up under small arms fire and took over his Troop Officer's tank. He then reorganised the Troop, which then had only two tanks left so as to give maximum support to the infantry, which at that time was vitally necessary. He commanded the Troop until first light, having been in action since midnight of April 15th.

By his courage and devotion to duty, he set a great example and greatly assisted with his troop in the Marina Bridgehead and the forming of a bridgehead over Scolo Vol D'Albero. It is certain that if Sjt. Covill had not taken the action he did another troop would have had to take over, and the momentum of the attack would have been lost.
M.I.D. 13.1.44, M.B.E. 1.1.69   *(L.G. 23.8.45)*

Cowan, William Albert, Sergeant
530023, 8th N.Z. Inf. Bde.
For distinguished conduct prior to and during operations in the Solomon area.

Sjt. Cowan was selected to command two patrols to Treasury Islands before the landing of the 8th Bde Gp. on the 27th October, 1943. The first patrol was sent in to obtain information as to the strength of the enemy and his dispositions. The object of the second patrol was to cut a main telephone line between the enemy observation post on Laifa Point and the Japanese Headquarters, and to pass information as to enemy movements after the landing had been effected. The first patrol was carried through most successfully under difficult conditions and resulted in much valuable information being obtained. The second patrol successfully cut the telephone line at 0400 hrs on 27th October, and thus delaying information of the approach of the assaulting troops reaching the enemy. During the next five days the patrol was continuously active behind the enemy lines and much information was obtained. Throughout Sjt. Cowan showed resource and determination of a high order, and his personal example and coolness in face of considerable danger was largely responsible for the successful achievement of the mission.   *(L.G. 10.2.44)*

Cowell, William, Warrant Officer Cl. I (R.S.M.)
399176, Royal Scots Greys (Edinburgh) (Periodic)
RSM Cowell has been employed in 'A' Ech from Oct 23rd up to the present date. He has never failed to play his part every day. His duty was chiefly to ensure that no vehicles fell out and got lost, and it is greatly due to his continual energy and resource that not a single vehicle of the unit has been unaccounted for during the whole advance. He has maintained a high state of discipline and morale and his steadiness and unshakeable calm during Stuka raids and shelling have been a fine example to the men. On the evening of 5th November he was left behind with a damaged Grant Tank and the fitters who were repairing it south of Fuka. All the district was full

of roving parties of enemy and on Nov. 6th at dawn a patrol of 6 Germans blundered into the party and were captured. The prisoners said there were more enemy in the district so RSM Cowell sent the tank to beat the surrounding country and drive the enemy towards his posn. which he occupied with the fitters armed with TSMGs and pistols. In this way 70 more Italians were captured, a few hours later a convoy of 6 10-ton lorries and a General's Caravan and 2 Armd Cars appeared. RSM Cowell ordered the Grant to shell the lorries which it did knocking out the leader and the rest surrendered numbering about 250 men, the Armd Cars only making off. From Nov. 27th to Dec. 4th RSM Cowell lead the Ech. of the Light Squadron which was engaged with Swancol on patrolling activities south of Agheila. For several days the Echelon was heavily bombed, but the RSM kept the men cheerful and disciplined the whole time and never failed to send the correct packets up as ordered, leading them to the right destination in spite of inaccurate maps and difficult going conditions.

(L.G. 14.10.43)

Cowhey, Thomas Vincent Anthony, Sergeant
6913228, Rifle Brigade (Cardiff)
No citation. *(L.G. 12.2.42)*

Cowley, James Charles, Warrant Officer Cl. II
2658115, 5th Bn. Coldstream Guards (Newton Abbot) (Immediate)
On 9th September 1944 the Company of which this Warrant Officer was Company Sergeant Major was ordered to take part with another Company and a Squadron of tanks in an attack on the village of Heppen. The attack was successful, but by the time the Company had cleared its half of the village none of the officers were left, the Company Commander having been killed in the street fighting. Coming after the loss of all Platoon Commanders in the last few days fighting, the loss of the Company Commander came as a great blow to the Company and there was a moment of hesitation. At once this Warrant Officer realised that it was his duty to carry on and he at once rallied the men and consolidated the Company well forward of the objective. He then reported the situation to the Tank Squadron Leader who was the senior officer present, and continued by his personal example to encourage the men despite the fact that a good deal of shooting was still in progess. When this had been overcome and it was possible to take stock of the position it was discovered that this Company's morale was entirely restored, that the position was very satisfactorily organised and that everything that should have been done had been done.

Credit for all of this and in very trying circumstanes must be given to this Company Sergeant Major. I attach report received by me from the Squadron Leader concerned, which he asked to be allowed to send in.

(L.G. 1.3.45)

Cox, William Tom, Trooper
7888178, 2nd Bn. Royal Tank Regt. attd. 3rd K.O. Hussars
Western Desert 11th December, 1940
When 2/Lieut Duncan's Tank was knocked out and this Officer was himself wounded, Tpr. Cox, the driver of the Tank, showed great personal courage and initiative. Although surrounded by several hundred of the enemy, some of whom were still manning guns and machine guns, and none of whom had been disarmed, he jumped out of his tank, and with his revolver engaged enemy artillerymen who had fired on the tank at short range. By this action he not only saved his tank from being fired on again by enemy Field Guns, but so cowed the enemy in the vicinity, that they gave no further trouble, and surrendered. *(L.G. 25.4.41)*

Craddock, Arthur, Private
4915352, 2 South Lancashire Regt. (Hednesford, Staffs)
6th May, 1942, Antsirane, Madagascar.
This man was in No. 17 Platoon, 'D' Coy. The company was on the left of the Bn during its flank attack on the morning 6 May 42. At about 0600 hrs the Coy was advancing under heavy fire from the enemy in Bellevue Fort. No. 17 Platoon was suddenly fired at from a small building on the left flank. Private Craddock immediately rushed forward 20 yards across the open under heavy fire, battered down the door of the building and killed the four enemy snipers inside with his rifle and bayonet. By his resolute action he saved many casualties to his comrades and enabled the advance to continue. *(L.G. 16.6.42)*

Craddock, Frank Levisson, Trp
7893363, HQ Sqn., 2 Armd. Recce Bde., Royal Armoured Corps
Trooper Craddock was one of Serjt. Smith's party and displayed great courage and initiative throughout the above operation. On withdrawing it was necessary to swim a small canal in rear of their postion. Having done so Pte. Craddock saw a wounded man on the wrong side of the canal. He returned and helped the wounded man over. This attracted fire, but, having placed the first man under cover, Pte. Craddock returned again to search for more wounded, and found another man who he also helped to cover, over the small canal, this time under considerable fire. *(L.G. 18.10.40)*

Craddock, William James Edward, Warrant Officer Cl. II (S.S.M.)
399758, 3rd Carabiniers (Karachi-Sind, India) (Immediate)
Operations—Imphal Area 13 April 1944
On 13 April 44 this Warrant Officer was Squadron Sjt Major of the tanks of 3 D.G. supporting the infantry on to a strongly held hill feature. On the troops reaching their objective they came under heavy fire from further

positions and all infantry and tank officers were killed or wounded.

Sjt-Major Craddock at once took control of the tanks; and in conjunction with the infantry V.C.O. set about the re-organisation of a confused situation, made more confused by the lack of a mutual language. He very quickly reorganised his communications; and was observed moving about dismounted, seeking out centres of resistance and leading his tanks to positions from which they could more effectively engage targets.

The coolness, determination, and personal gallantry shown by this W.O. has been the subject of discussion amongst all ranks, British and Indian, of this Bn. The success of the operation was largely due to his magnificent conduct.   *(L.G. 27.7.44)*

Craggs, John Baron Kitchener, Sergeant
6139313, 2nd Bn. East Surrey Regt. (Sunderland)
On 1st Jan 42, this NCO carried out a successful counter attack with his Pl during which he showed high powers of leadership and great personal gallantry, rallying his men under heavy fire. On 2nd Jan, 42, Sjt. Craggs again led a successful counter attack and set a wonderful example to his men both in the attack and when organizing the captured position for defence. He was continually under mortar, M.G. and rifle fire, but displaying complete disregard for his own safety he kept going round from post to post giving instructions and cheering and encouraging his men. His attitude was an inspiration to all who saw him.

This NCO has commanded a Pl throughout the campaign with great success and has always shown the greatest bravery and devotion to duty. *(L.G. 13.12.45)*

Craig, Robert Hendry, Sergeant
2759260, 7th Bn. Black Watch (Glasgow) (Immediate)
During the early stages of the Akarit battle on 6 April 43, the Pl. of which Sjt. Craig was Pl. Sjt. suffered severe casualties, including the Pl. Comdr. and on reaching its final objective it was cut off from the rest of the Coy and was subjected to extremely heavy automatic fire from enemy posns holding out on its right flank. Sjt. Craig with great coolness and determination re-organised the Pl. and succeeded in getting it into suitable positions to deal with the enemy referred to. During the afternoon, two enemy tanks advanced towards the posn and as no A/Tk weapons were available, Sjt. Craig crawled forward and engaged the nearest tank with No. 36 grenades. As a result of this offensive action both tanks withdrew. Later in the day the position was attacked by four tanks followed by German infantry. Sjt. Craig allowed the tanks to pass by the position and then engaged the infantry so successfully that they discontinued their attack.

Throughout the whole battle Sjt. Craig displayed outstanding courage and powers of leadership and his conduct and bearing were a tremendous encouragement and example to the men under his command during the most trying and difficult conditions. His actions undoubtedly had a very material effect in holding off the enemy counter attacks.   *(L.G. 22.7.43)*

Crangles, Joseph Francis, Sergeant (actg.)
6088628, Queen's Royal Regt. (Rochdale)
No citation.   *(L.G. 14.2.46)*

Crawford, Geoffrey Robertson, Sergeant
NX 14899, 2/13 Aust. Inf. Bn. (Immediate)
Throughout the operations against Finschhafen Sjt. Crawford has shown outstanding qualities of leadership and courage. In particular, on 1 Oct 43, during the early stages of the final attack on Finschhafen, he was acting as a Platoon Commander when his company encountered very strongly defended enemy positions in the vicinity of Ileebe creek. Heavy fire from machine guns, sited in well dug positions on the far bank of the creek caused the company to deploy in two groups. One group, consisting of one platoon and two sections, were unable to advance. Crawford hurriedly reorganised this group and ordered it to resume the attack. Moving them to a flank under fire, calling advice and shouting orders, he determinedly led the assault up the high banks of the creek and successfully overcame the enemy in this position. At this stage another machine gun in a bunkered position switched its fire in Sjt. Crawford's direction, severely wounding him. Ignoring his wounds he again led his men in a second successful assault and personally killed many enemy. This quick and resolute action on Crawford's part undoubtedly caused the enemy in that area to break and abandon their posts.

It was not until the other wounded in his command had received medical aid that Crawford allowed himself to be evacuated.   *(L.G. 2.3.44)*

Crockett, Clarence Kenneth, Sergeant
M.35070, Calgary Highlanders
On 21 September 1944, the Calgary Highlanders took over a sector on the Albert Canal East of Antwerp and was ordered to send a fighting patrol over the canal that night, so that, if possible, a bridgehead might be secured on the far bank. A crossing had been attempted the night before but this had not been successful.

At the point where the crossing was to be made the canal is approximately 180 feet wide. About 40 feet from the near side is a small island roughly 50 feet wide. From the far side of this island, lock gates run 90 feet to the opposite bank of the canal.

At that time, a close reconnaissance of the canal by day was not possible as the enemy occupied positions on the North side and all approaches were covered by machine gun and rifle fire. It was known, however, that all bridges over the canal had been blown by the enemy except for a small footbridge from the near bank to the island. It was also known that the lock gates had been badly damaged.

Under the Calgary Highlanders plan, a detachment of 10 men from 'C' Company was to cross the lock gates silently on the night 21/22 September and establish a small local bridgehead. The remainder of the Platoon would then cross as rapidly as possible, followed successively by the other Platoons and Companies of the Battalion, enlarging the bridgehead into a firm base on the far bank.

The key to the whole venture was the initial crossing, and M–35070 Sergeant C. K. Crockett was selected to lead the detachment on their difficult and dangerous mission. At 0130 hours on 22 September, he commenced his daring and hazardous exploit. It was an intensely dark night with occasional rain. He led his party across the footbridge to the small island in the Canal, proceeding cautiously, skillfully and in complete silence, knowing that the slightest noise would be met with enemy light flares, exposing his men to an immediate hail of enemy fire.

It has been intended that the detachment would report its arrival on the island, a No 38 portable wireless set being carried for that purpose.

However, when they reached the island, the silence was so complete that the sound of a voice could easily have been heard by enemy sentries on the far bank—they therefore could not risk betraying their presence by sending the intended wireless message.

Sergeant Crockett continued to the 90 foot lock gates, which were only 18 inches wide at the top. The enemy was known to have fixed machine gun lines trained on the gates and the approaches to them. Inch by inch and step by step he led his men across the narrow pathway. After negotiating the greater part of the crossing, he found that the last 8 or 9 feet had been completely destroyed, a six inch pipe providing the only means of reaching the far bank. The crossing, which would have been hazardous by day and without the immediate danger of discovery by the enemy, was extremely perilous under the condition which existed, but he successfully overcame all the obstacles he encountered.

Finally landing on the North bank, he discovered a wire obstacle barring the path. This he slowly and cautiously moved aside, when he was challenged by a German sentry. In a matter of seconds two flares went up and, the alarm having been given, the Germans opened fire. Fire from our supporting weapons on the South bank immediately came down as previously planned.

Sergeant Crockett fired at the sentry and, while ordering his detachment to deploy in the nearest cover, quickly made his plan. There were three machine guns evident immediately covering the crossing. Selecting the one he considered the most important, Sergeant Crockett called to his men 'Okay, this is where we take them.' With magnificent courage he moved forward to the machine gun post, firing from the hip, killing the enemy crew and clearing the position. With his Piat man he stalked the second post and it was silenced with two bombs. He directed the fire of his detachment on the third position, and then led his men through all three positions to ensure that they were clear. This done, he disposed his patrol around the bridgehead, and directed their fire to neutralize other enemy points which had opened up.

The fire provided by the detachment made it possible for the remainder of the platoon to move across the gates and the first precarious enlargement of the initial bridgehead had been accomplished. Sergeant Crockett then continued to direct neutralizing covering fire to support the two succeeding platoons of his Company onto their objectives, the Company bridgehead thus being established.

The Battalion was thus enabled to establish a firm bridgehead on the far shore. The enemy launched several vicious and determined counter attacks against the position, and brought all their fire power to bear on our troops. Heavy fighting continued throughout the day and the following night before the enemy resistance was overcome and the Battalion's position consolidated.

Throughout this daring action, Sergeant Crockett displayed gallantry, determintion and judgment of the very highest order. His indomitable courage and outstanding leadership were directly responsible for the establishment of the initial bridgehead, and its subsequent enlargement. The foothold gained on the far bank by this magnificent action enabled the Engineers to construct a bridge with a minimum of delay, making possible the rapid passage of two Brigades across the Canal and the capture of the entire sector between the Albert Canal and the Turnhout Canal. His bravery and example will forever remain an inspiration to his regiment and to the Canadian Army.

Award for Gallantry

The job of our Battalion on the night of 20/21 Sep 44 was to establish a bridgehead across the Albert Canal in order to permit the building of a bridge and provide our Brigade with a firm base from which to expand. The operation had been attempted the night before by another battalion but had been unsuccessful.

Our Battalion plan was that the Battalion less 'C' Coy would provide covering fire from the south bank, and that 'C' Coy would affect the initial crossing, sending over first a small fighting patrol in soft shoes and light equipment, and then the remainder of their platoon followed by the two other platoons. As soon as 'C' Coy reported success, it was in turn to cover the crossing of 'D' and 'A' Coys. This crossing was to be carried out across a small footbridge to an island in the centre of the Canal, and from there across the lock gates to the north side.

Sergeant Crockett was selected by the Coy Comd to lead the fighting patrol. He was given all available information, but everything depended on his own ingenuity, as a detailed recconnaissance had not been possible. 0130 hours was set as 'H' hour. We moved near to the Canal around midnight. The night was pitch black, rain was falling and visibility was very limited.

Sergeant Crockett was not feeling particularly well, and had a slight billious attack, due, I think to a mild attack of dysentery from which he had been suffering. At 'H' hour he led his men onto the path leading to the foot-bridge. I was in a good position to hear what occurred as I was commanding the platoon scheduled to go across in third place. Not a sound was heard for many long minutes while we strained to follow Crockett's progress across the lock gates. Then suddenly a flare lit the Canal and enemy fire opened up. Gradually we heard the rapid fire of German automatics just across the Canal stopping and it became evident that the patrol was bringing things under control.

Very shortly the remainder of the Platoon had crossed and the remainder of the Coy followed as quickly as possible. When leading the third platoon I crossed and I found it extremely difficult due to the darkness and rain. In addition a portion of the locks on the enemy side was blasted so badly that each man had to sling arms and use both hands to cross on a girder. I visualized what a grim minute it must have been for Sergeant Crockett when he crossed that space with his hands fully occupied with his weapon and knowing the Germans were waiting within a matter of yards. However, he had kept going and as a result the whole Battalion effort was successful.

This individual bit of bravery on the part of Sergeant Crockett stands out above anything I have ever witnessed, and it gives me the greatest of pleasure to tell the story just as I saw and heard it.

(H. N. Holmgren) Lieut.
'C' Coy, The Calgary Highlanders

On the day of 21 Sep 44 'C' Coy. was given the initial job of making a crossing of the lock gates of the Albert Canal. This job had been previously given to another battalion but had been unsuccessful.

The plan was that a small fighting patrol, consisting of Sergeant Crockett, a Cpl. and eight men, was to cross the lock gates at 0130 hours and establish a small bridgehead on the other side of the Canal enabling the remainder of the Platoons to come across. On the success of the patrol the remainder of 15 Platoon was to go across and exploit this original success making a bridgehead for the rest of the Coy. The remainder of the Coy was then to cross and make a bridgehead large enough for two more Coys to follow. There was to be supporting fire from the remainder of the Coys of the Battalion.

On the night of 21/22 Sep 44 it was exceptionally dark with a light rain, visibility was practically nil, and due to moving up there was very little chance for reconnaissance. When the Coy reached the south bank of the Canal Sergeant Crockett was given his final instructions by the Coy Commander, and started out on his patrol. Two report lines were ordered, one on the island, and one when the patrol reached the other side. Communication was by 38 set.

The patrol started out and long minutes passed as we strained tensely to follow its progress either by some visible movement or sound. Everything was breathlessly quiet and not a sound was heard until Crockett sent his first report from the far bank. It turned out later that he had not sent his first report from the island due to the stillness, and he felt that any sound would betray his position. Quite unexpectedly we received the code word that meant that he had reached the far side. The Coy. Comd. then passed the remainder of the Platoon across the locks. At this time fire was heard from the far bank and immediately following the firing two flares were sent up by the enemy. Then we heard our patrol return the enemy fire. This fire grew in volume as the remainder of the Platoon reached the far side. Word was sent back by Sergeant Crockett that the remainder of his platoon was established. The remaining two Platoons of the Coy and Coy H.Q. then started across. By this time firing by the enemy had somewhat diminished.

As I was going across this narrow cat-walk which made up the lock gates, I couldn't help but marvel at the care and pains of the patrol to make such a silent crossing. Ten feet from the far bank the cat-walk itself was destroyed leaving only a six inch pipe to make the remainder of the crossing on. As we found out later, that when the patrol reached the break in the cat-walk, Sergeant Crockett went ahead to the far bank discovering a wire obstacle which he removed. He then returned and brought over the remainder of his patrol. When the patrol recced the shore they were challenged by a German sentry. Sergeant Crockett signalled his patrol into the shadows along the Canal bank at the same time telling the signaller to send back the code word. He then inched forward and shot the sentry with his sten gun. Then flares went up and M.Gs opened fire. He ordered the immediate return of fire from the patrol and taking a Piat and one man went forward to deal with one of the M.Gs. Working carefully into position he succeeded in knocking it out. He then worked back to his patrol. By this time the remainder of his Platoon had come under fire from a second gun so he ordered his patrol to destroy it while he himself drew enemy fire. The patrol then successfully assaulted the M.G. position.

By now his platoon was completely across. Carefully choosing section positions he moved his Platoon forward and directed their fire to cover the crossing of the rest of the Coy. The volume of fire laid down by his Platoon enabled the remainder of the Coy to cross with practically no trouble. Sergeant Crockett continued to direct the neutralizing fire of his Platoon to shoot both succeeding platoons of his Coy onto their objectives.

In my opinion the success of the whole operation was due to the skill, aggressiveness and excellent judgement of Sergeant Crockett, first in crossing himself, second by handling his platoon, and thirdly by enabling the Coys to cross, and throughout the action his complete disregard for his own personal safety.

M–10712 C.S.M. H. O. Larson
The Calgary Highlanders (CA(O)

On the night of 21 Sep 44 a party of ten men were picked to cross over the Albert Canal and establish the initial bridgehead on the North side, through which the remainder of the battalion could move to enlarge the bridgehead for the brigade assault. I was a bren gunner in this detachment.

It was an extremely dark night and although we knew from fire which had come from the north bank during the day that it was strongly held, there was not a sound at the time we prepared to go across.

About an hour after midnight, carrying our weapons and extra ammunition, we moved from the company position down to the bank of the canal where a footbridge connected the mainland to a small island about thirty feet out in the canal. Sergeant Crockett crossed to the island alone and then as all remained quiet returned and lead us slowly and carefully out to the island. There was still no sound and signalling us to follow he started across the top of the lock gates between the island and the north shore, a distance of about ninety feet. Feeling our way carefully so as not to make a sound we inched along until Sergeant Crockett stopped and sent back word that we were to wait where we were. He had come to a point where the lock gates had been broken away and ahead of him stretched a thin pipe about six inches in diameter. He went along this pipe until he reached the shore where he found a heavy wire barricade blocking his path. Still there was not a sound. Sergeant Crockett returned along the pipe and started forward once more, we following.

With Cpl. Harold's help he lifted the barrier and moved slowly ahead. Almost immediately I heard a sentry challenge him, then the sound of Sergeant Crockett's sten gun, followed by enemy machine gun and small arms fire from close range. We all crossed the pipe as quickly as possible and took positions as ordered by Sergeant Crockett.

There seemed to be three machine gun positions, very close, firing on us and Sergeant Crockett, firing his sten from the hip as he walked towards it, silenced the nearest one. He then crawled forward with the Piat man to a position from which they could fire on the second post with the Piat. Two bombs silenced it after which, rejoining his detachment, Sergeant Crockett directed them onto the third machine gun post. When it was silenced we moved through these positions to make sure they were cleared and were posted by Sergeant Crockett in positions forming a small bridgehead and from which we could fire on the enemy ahead of us to assist the remainder of the platoon to cross, followed by the remainder of the company and the battalion.

Sergeant Crockett, throughout this entire action, remained cool and did not at any time display the slightest hesitation or fear, neither in the deathly silent crossing nor after we reached the north bank and came under intense enemy machine gun and small arms fire which continued all that night and the following day.

M8237 G. H. Cherrington, Cpl.

I was the Piat man with a party of ten picked to cross the Albert Canal on the night of 21 Sep 44 to establish a small bridgehead on the other side of the canal, through which the remainder of my battalion and then the rest of the brigade could pass. Sergeant Crockett was the NCO placed in charge of us.

We left our company location about an hour after midnight. The night was extremely dark and you couldn't hear a thing. Making hardly no noise we made our way down to the bank carrying our weapons and ammunition. There was a small island a short way out in the canal which was joined to the mainland by a footbridge. Sergeant Crockett halted us at the bridge and told us to make no noise and remain where we were until he told us to proceed. The Sjt then very cautiously and not making any noise proceeded alone to the island. Lock gates, about 18 inches wide at the top, joined the island with the far shore about ninety feet away. Sergeant Crockett signalled for us to follow him. Going very slowly and carefully and not making any noise we began to feel our way along the top of the lock gate.

A little way along we were stopped where the lock gates had been broken and only a small pipe led from this point to the bank. Sergeant Crockett told us to stay where we were and he crawled along the pipe to the bank where a barricade stopped him. I still couldn't hear anything from the German side. Sergeant Crockett came back along the pipe and led us forward. We moved very cautiously making hardly a sound. He and Cpl. Harold lifted the barrier aside and moved ahead. A sentry challenged him immediately and the Sjt opened up with his sten. Then machine guns and rifles opened up on us. We immediately crossed the pipe as quickly as we could and were ordered to take up positions designated by the Sjt.

There were three machine gun posts very close. Sergeant Crockett charged the nearest one firing his sten from the hip. Nothing more was heard from this post. He then signalled for me to come forward. We crawled along to a position where I could fire on the second post. I fired two bombs, the second one knocked it out. We then crawled back to the rest of the party. Sergeant Crockett organised the party to attack the third post. We succeeded in knocking it out and then examined all the positions making certain it was clear. The Sjt then organised our positions so we could give covering fire as the remainder of our platoon and company crossed, followed by the other companies.

Sergeant Crockett never faltered once during the operation. He coolly told us what to do and was not at all excited. At the same time he knocked out one machine gun post himself and aided and directed the knocking out of the other two.

F33193 I. P. MacDonald, Pte.
(L.G. 10.2.45)

Crockett, William, Corporal
6141418, 2nd Bn. Royal Fusiliers (Stockport)
(Immediate)
Map Reference Italy. Sheet 100—II. NW 1/25,000.

On the night 19/20 Oct 44 the Bn crossed the R. Savio and established a bridgehead. On 22 Oct 44 the Coy was

ordered to extend their positions, which entailed the capture of 3 houses at Vla Casali 582059. Owing to casualties, Cpl. Crockett was now acting Pl Comd of No 16 Pl, the pl which was detailed to capture the houses. Cpl. Crockett fired a Piat at the first house and charged into it, followed by his men. One German was killed, but the others escaped into the second house. Repeating his tactics, Cpl. Crockett occupied this house also. The third house was now strongly held by a party of Germans armed with a 'bazooka,' at least one spandau, and rifles. With no hesitation and in spite of the enemy's fire, Cpl. Crockett after firing his Piat, forced an entry into this house also. Here 3 Germans were killed (2 by Cpl. Crockett himself) and two wounded and taken prisoner. During this action Cpl. Crockett displayed the greatest dash, vigour and personal courage, and an utter contempt for the enemy. Throughout the entire operation, from 20–24 Oct 44, by his savage and intense eagerness to close with the enemy on every possible occasion, he instilled and inspired his platoon with his own fiercely aggressive spirit, and was largely responsible for the ease with which 'Z' Coy captured and held their objectives.
M.I.D. 29.11.45   (*L.G. 26.4.45*)

Croker, Edward Vivian, C.Q.M.S.
3913773, 6 South Wales Borderers (Blackwood, Mon.)
(Immediate)
N. Burma Campaign 1944.

On 16 Nov 44 during the operations fought N of Pinwe around the Gyobin Chaung, CQMS Croker's Coy together with another Coy were cut off by enemy infiltration in rear. A strong patrol from another Coy led by the Coy Comd had managed to fight their way through to the isolated Coys with ammunition. When the patrol began their return journey, the Coy Comd was seriously wounded about a hundred yards outside the Coy perimeter. CQMS Croker left the perimeter and attempted to bring in the wounded officer, but was unable to reach him owing to intense MMG fire, and was seriously wounded in the attempt. In spite of this, he organised a rescue party and again went forward, attacking the MMG post with grenades and TSMG himself, while the rest of the party tried to reach the Officer, but once again he and his party were driven off. Although greatly weakened by his wound, CQMS Croker made a third attempt, and charging the MMG post armed with grenades and TSMG he succeeded in killing all the occupants. Meanwhile, the rescue party had been forced back by another MMG post which suddenly opened up from a flank. CQMS Croker although he was now alone, worked his way forward to the wounded Coy Comd and succeeded in carrying him to safety whilst under intense MMG fire. By his devotion to duty and superb courage CQMS Croker, in spite of his wounds, succeeded in destroying the enemy strong point and saved the life of the Coy Comd.   (*L.G. 22.3.45*)

Crompton, James, Corporal
3531408, 1st Bn. King's Royal Rifle Corps (Leigh)
(Immediate)
For extreme courage and initiative under heavy fire, setting an example which inspired his Company, while leading a Motor Section in the attack on the Traghetto 'Gap.' (Italy 1/100,000 Sheet No. 88 Imola 168636).

On the morning 20 Apr 'B' Company, 1 K.R.R.C. were attacking just north of the Traghetto 'Gap' supported by a sqn of 16/5 Lancers, with the commanding embankment of the rd. East of the PO di Primaro as their Objective. When 400 yds from the objective, the leading Pl, in which Cpl. Crompton was commanding a section, came under heavy and accurate Spandau fire on the Pl right flank and a mortar concentration. The Pl sought cover in a ditch and the advance temporarily ceased. At this critical juncture, Cpl. Crompton jumped forward entirely on his own shouting encouragement to his section, and telling them to follow him. He continued to lead the advance for the last 350 yds over completely exposed flat terrain, under heavy fire the whole way. He was first man on the objective and, on arrival, found a Spandau firing directly down the line of the Pl from the right flank. Cpl. Crompton at once led two men at the Spandau and silenced the post.

His Company Commander, who could see the whole incident, considered that this NCO's powers of leadership and determination to reach the objective, and his example at a critical moment were almost entirely responsible for the pl arriving rapidly on the objective soon after the artillery concentration, which undoubtedly saved many casualties. This example in full view of the supporting pls contributed very largely to the success of the whole Company attack.

This NCO's tireless dash and determination under heavy fire, and his shining example of courage and initiative, contributed largely to the rapid capture of the high bank dominating the 'Gap.' This enabled the 16/5 Lancers to burst out along the Reno, cutting clean across the enemy line of withdrawal.   (*L.G. 23.8.45*)

Crook, John, M.M., Sergeant
793869, 290 A.Tk. Bty., Royal Artillery (Bolton)
(Immediate)
For outstanding services and gallantry in action

At Gaungbo on the night of 25/26 February 1945 Sjt. Crook was in command of two 2 pounder Anti-Tank guns which were in support of 'A' Company 4/19 Gurkha Rifles. At about 2200 hours the position was attacked in strength and by 2400 hours both the Company Commander Major K. Faulkner and the Forward Observation Officer were killed. This left no British Officer in the position. Sjt. Crook assumed the duties of Forward Observation Officer for the Medium Battery as well as commanding his anti-tank guns. He spent the whole night touring the units in the perimeter, cheering on the Gurkhas, encouraging his anti-tank gunners. All this was done under heavy shelling and small arms fire. At the

Observation Post he directed SOS and defensive fire on to the enemy with such skill and accuracy that 19 bodies were found in a chaung together with Maps, two Officers' swords and equipment for 30 men. This NCO set a fine example of coolness and courage while under very heavy fire and at a time when both British Officers had been killed.

M.M. 22.6.44   *(L.G. 21.6.45)*

Crook, Roy Joseph, Sergeant
776642, North Somerset Yeomanry, No. 52
   Commando (21, High St., Bath)
Crete.

During operations 18th July-17th August in Crete, Sgt Roy Joseph Crooks after taking part in the rearguard action from Suda, refused to surrender and took to the hills alone.

He later joined Lieut-Cdr F. G. Pool, RNR, and assisted in collecting up troops for evacuation. During actual embarkation, on two successive nights, he volunteered to go ashore from the submarine to help marshal and embark the British troops. His initiative and masterly handling of the men contributed largely to the safe embarkation of so many men in extremely difficult conditions.

His coolness and resource in handling a most difficult situation with the local inhabitants, who were endeavouring to collect boots and clothes, is worthy of recognition.
                                                   (L.G. 23.12.41)

Crookes, Ronald, M.M., Fusilier
22525894, Royal Northumberland Fusiliers
No citation.   *(L.G. 29.6.51)*

Cross, Arthur Clifford, Sergeant
7047042, 1st Bn. Royal Irish Fusiliers (King's Norton)
   (Immediate)
On the 29 May 44 1 R.Ir.F. advanced towards the Strongolagalli Ridge and the leading company found the road and a village area to be heavily mined with tellermines and anti-personnel mines. The forward company became pinned by enemy fire and found progress impossible without the aid of tanks.

Sjt. Cross with his Pioneer Platoon at once moved forward to this area and proceeded to clear a track through the minefield. While carrying out this work the Pioneers came under intense mortar and accurate enemy sniping. In spite of three casualties Sjt. Cross coolly continued with his task until a track was cleared for the tanks to go through. Later in the evening a deep ditch prevented any form of tracked or wheeled vehicle from reaching the forward companies. Again under heavy fire Sjt. Cross assiduously set to work to make the route passable and completed a track up an exposed slope to the forward positions.

By his doggedness and complete disregard for his own safety throughout the day Sjt. Cross undoubtedly made both the taking and the consolidation of the objective possible. He showed patience, devotion to duty and courage of an outstanding quality. *(L.G. 26.10.44)*

Cross, John, Signalman
2354970, Royal Signals
In December 1941, Cross with two other signalmen, Wagstaff and Morter volunteered, with full knowledge of the dangers involved, to accompany a Major Cauvin into the Malayan jungle on a three months' trip to act as a left-behind radio/intelligence party. It was actually three and a half years before they returned.

Trained in their new duties, with two months European rations, full radio equipment, and signal plan agreed by Kranji radio station, they entered the jungle on 29th January 1942, accompanied by 25 armed Chinese guerillas. The party commenced listening immediately and calling their stations in accordance with the signal plan, but got no replies. In view of the bad news of Java and Rangoon, the expiry of the three months allowed for, and the lack of petrol for charging batteries, they reduced their daily radio watches.

For the great majority of their time, the batteries were charged by improvised water wheels involving a great deal of maintenance and a poor yield. Failing to hear from, or contact their stations, they decided to listen in to all broadcasts, and with the help of an English-speaking Chinese began to print by duplicating machine an English edition of the 'Emancipation News' in May 1943, with all editorial matter under Chinese control.

While listening to these broadcasts they received an indication that the officer with whom they had made their signal plan had fallen into the hands of the Japanese in Java. They also picked up hundreds of broadcast messages for Europeans and tried to get these into prison camps by Chinese agents of the Malay Communist Party.

Major Cauvin's health began to deteriorate seriously in August 1943, and on the 17th April 1944, he decided to leave the party and to try and contact the Tonku Makhota of Johore, or make for the Allied lines in Burma. On the 17th July, they heard that Major Cauvin had committed suicide.

In the face of every difficulty and danger the party continued in its work, and early in September 1944, decided that the English edition of their news sheet should be replaced by a non-political anti-Japanese newspaper which they called 'The Victory Herald.' They specialised on items of international news.

During their three and a half years in the jungle, under the most trying conditions, the party managed, by their high courage and general behaviour, to earn the respect, loyalty and protection of the Chinese guerillas. Had it not been for this, they would never have survived, nor would they have been able to carry out their anti-Japanese propaganda as well as explaining our view-point of the international situation to a very great number of Chinese and to the Malayan Communist Party in particular.

They suffered constantly from a lack of any sort of European food with the consequent deterioration of their health and were in continual danger of attack from the Japanese who were very active against the underground element in the district and they were obliged to move camp on more than thirty different occasions until on April 17th 1945 they joined force with Allied troops and were evacuated by them.

The party brought out valuable intelligence and a very complete knowledge of the guerilla political feelings. Cross's qualities of leadership, particularly after Major Cauvin's departure left him in sole charge of the party, were of the highest order, and it is thanks to him in no small measure that the party was eventually found alive and in a condition to pass on the important information gathered over the past three years.

It is recommended that Signalman Cross be awarded the DCM and that Signalmen Wagstaff and Morter should each receive a Military Medal. *(L.G. 25.9.47)*

Cross, Stephen John, Driver
QX 6754, Corps Troops, A.A.S.C., Australian Military Forces
During the afternoon of 18 April 1941 at Larissa, Greece, Drv. Cross was in charge of a lorry employed in carrying an infantry patrol of an officer and 16 men. When the patrol, after being under 3 hours continuous fire, was eventually surrounded by enemy tanks, Drv. Cross by superb driving and amazing coolness succeeded in bringing the lorry out over portion of a stone wall, thereby extricating the patrol from an otherwise hopeless position.

Later that day whilst the patrol was engaged in support of a 25 pdr. gun firing at enemy tanks with open sights two tanks got under the range of the 25 pdr. and concentrated shell and machine gun fire on the lorry. Drv. Cross, who had joined the patrol as support for the 25 pdr. got up from his position and going to what looked like certain suicide dodged back to his lorry and drove it to a place of safety.

By these two extremely brave acts he undoubtedly saved an officer and 16 men from death or capture on each occasion. *(L.G. 4.11.41)*

Crossling, Jonas Phillip, Warrant Officer Cl. III (T.S.M.)
547888, 274 (N.H.) Lt.A.A. Bty., Royal Artillery (Gosforth) (Immediate)
During the night of 26/27 June, 1942, when his Troop was operating in support of 293 Field Bty. RA south of Garawla Wadi, the position was surprised and over-run by German Lorried Infantry, who succeeded in capturing all the Field Gunners of 293 Field Bty., while the Troop could only get out one of the guns. Under cover of darkness, however, T.S.M. Crossling withdrew all his men, and shortly after organised and personally led a party which went in with small arms fire, beat off the enemy, and successfully brought out the two remaining guns of the Troop, and all the vehicles together with two prisoners.

But for this NCO's courage and initiative, the guns would certainly have been lost to the enemy.
(L.G. 24.9.42)

Crowhurst, Percy, Private
6200558, 1/7 Bn. Middlesex Regt. (Bromley, Kent) (Immediate)
Pte. Crowhurst was a No. 1 gunner of 'D' Coy 1/7 Mx supporting the attack of 5 Seaforths on Francofonte.

Early in the morning of the 13th Pte. Crowhurst was ordered to bring his gun into action less than 150 yds from a strong force of enemy paratroops concealed in an olive orchard. He was at once subjected to heavy mortar and M.G. fire. Quite undeterred he mounted his gun in the face of this fire and knocked out two troop-carrying vehicles which were approaching the enemy position.

Later in the morning he skilfully manoeuvred his gun to engage an enemy Spandau whose fire had pinned two inf pls to their ground. The gun was silenced and the crew killed or wounded.

By 0500 hrs on the 14th Pte. Crowhurst had dug in behind a crest. Owing to the casualties suffered by the inf and his own section the previous day, his Vickers gun was the only automatic weapon in the forward position. Any exposure above the crest immediately drew intense M.G. fire. He at once saw the inf were being forced to give ground. Without a thought for his own personal safety and acting entirely on his own initiative he moved his gun into position above the crest from where he could bring direct fire to bear upon the enemy. This action halted the enemy's advance and enabled the inf to withdraw to a more commanding feature. Pte. Crowhurst remained in this position for two hours.

Late that afternoon a strong party of enemy had worked their way round the [...] 5 Seaforths. Assisted solely by his No. 2, as the remainder of the section including their gun had become casualties, he again manoeuvred his gun with great skill. His first burst of fire had a most devastating effect on the enemy. Their advance was halted and the very sight and sound of the Vickers gun had the most heartening and encouraging effect on our inf who had been forced to give ground.

At about 1800 hrs when the situation had been restored Pte. Crowhurst immediately volunteered to rescue wounded who were lying in an exposed position under enemy observation. Under very heavy fire he worked his way forward and brought a seriously wounded man back to safety.

Pte. Crowhurst set a magnificent example of personal courage, with utter disregard for his personal safety, and devotion to duty during 48 hrs bitter fighting. His coolness and determination and the great skill he displayed in manoeuvring his gun under intense mortar and machine gun fire was, on at least two occasions responsible for halting a determined enemy advance and ensuring the safe withdrawal of the inf.
(L.G. 21.10.43)

Crowley, Bruce Joshua, Sergeant
*3617, 4th Reserve M.T. Coy., New Zealand Military
    Forces*

1. Capture

On 18 Apr 41 I took a detail of 20 vehicles to evacuate the 21 New Zealand Bn. which was fighting a rearguard action at Anglimos (?), East of Larissa, Greece. When I got there I had to wait till the troops were collected. In the late afternoon the Germans landed parachute troops in Larissa and cut off our retreat to Volos, in the Gulf of Pagessetikos. We were ordered to leave the vehicles and make our way on foot to Volos, the road being jammed full of vehicles as a result of a German road block.

I eventually ordered my men to disperse, but shortly afterwards the traffic began to move again. I had remained beside the vehicles with my driver and a few more Other Ranks, and we now tried to get across country through marshes in some of the vehicles. After driving all night we got stuck in the marshes. I had then got with only two vehicles to a blind road, and found that there were Germans on either side of us. I destroyed the vehicles and we then walked across the mountains to Volos, which we reached about 20 Apr.

Volos was by then deserted, but we managed to get an old Greek cart, two mules, and a horse and made our way towards Lamia (21 Apr). Here we found a battle raging in the Lamia Pass, and we could not get through. With the help of Greeks, however, we got a Greek schooner on which we made our way to the island of Evvoia, landing on the N.W. point just opposite Lamia. By this time we were a party of about 200, all of whom had crossed from Lamia in the schooner, most of us being New Zealanders and Australians with a few British troops.

From the N.W. point of the island about 40 of us went to Edipso, across the bay, in a motor boat. The Greek officer who took charge of the party insisted on the Greek crew taking us under threat of shooting. During the crossing there were German Stukas flying around us almost continually.

From Edipso Greeks arranged for 400 or 500 of us being taken by light schooner by night to Khalkis, which we reached on 22 Apr. Khalkis is connected with the mainland by a bridge which we crossed by vehicle, under instructions from an R.T.O. to proceed to a dispersal area. After several hous here we were sent to an entraining point, from which we were eventually taken by train to Argos (arrived 23 or 24 Apr). Here we were put in the sea evacuation area, whence we were sent to Tolo (T Beach). At Argos I was placed under the command of Lieut. Smith, 21 New Zealand Bn., having joined up with the remnants of that Bn. and various waifs and strays. I still had 16 or 17 of my own men with me.

On the first evening at Tolo we formed up on the beach, where there was a naval officer and several British officers of high rank. They were in touch with the Royal Navy by radio. We waited two or three hours on the beach till a destroyer sent in a landing craft. We were formed up into groups of six and the landing craft was filled. I was among those left behind. We were ordered back to our dispersal area just off the beach to await the next boat.

We spent the next day in the dispersal area under cover. At night we formed up again on the beach, but no ships came in. Next day at 0700 or 0800 hrs. we were told that the Germans were advancing on us and we had orders to prepare to defend ourselves. The radio set was destroyed, all communications with the Navy being thus cut off. We organised ourselves into first and second lines with the few Bren and Lewis guns and rifles we had. My men and I were ordered to the first line of defence on a ridge. In the morning the Germans (parachute troops) came down. We kept them off most of the day, and several of my men were killed and wounded. About 1500 hrs. there was a lull in the fighting, and a man bearing a white flag approached. One of our Sergeants went to meet him. He turned out to be one of our own men captured at Argos. He had a message from a German officer ordering us to capitulate by 1900 hrs., otherwise we would be bombed out from the air without quarter. We were then ordered by the Senior British officer (possibly a Brigadier) to capitulate. there were then 500 or 600 of us in the area (28 Apr).

After the wounded and officers had been removed in captured British trucks, the rest of us were marched to Nafplion, where we were put into an improvised camp in the playground of a school. We were here for two or three days, and were then removed to a camp in Corinth, where I remained till 7 Jun.

On 7 Jun I was sent by rail to Salonika, arriving 8 Jun. I was in this camp (Lager 2) till 15 Jun. Dysentery and malaria were rife, causing an average of three deaths a day.

2. First attempted escape

On 15 Jun I was one of a party of P/W who were put in cattle trucks en route for Germany. The journey was to take 10 days and we were given as rations only half a loaf of bread, 4–6 ozs. of pork, and four Greek biscuits, barely enough for one meal. By this time I had become separated from my own men, and had two men of the 21 New Zealand Bn. with me—Pte. John Smith and Pte. Kenneth Kemble, both of the H.Q. Coy. About 18 km. out of Salonika the three of us jumped from the train in the dark and lay up in a bush for the night. Next morning (16 Jun) we found we were in the garden of a farmer who had formerly served in the Greek Army. His farm was in the village of Prokhoma, on the Axioys river, about 19 miles N.W. of Salonika. The farmer gave us food and shelter. He and his friends wanted us to stay there till the end of the war, as they could not give us any help in getting out the country. At first we were, in turn, all sick with malaria, and after we recovered we worked in the fields to get fit. The whole village knew we were there and all the inhabitants helped, going without food themselves in order that we might have plenty.

We decided, however, to try to escape to Turkey, and on 23 Aug we made our own way to the village of Palga (?), just north of Salonika. Here a Greek sheltered us for two days, getting in touch with a friend in Salonika. This friend, a former Lieutenant in the Greek Army and a member of an organisation preparing for an uprising, took us from Palga to his home in Salonika. I was sent to live with a Greek Colonel, and the two others went elsewhere in Salonika.

About a month later we were handed over with eight other British soldiers, to a guide employed by the organisation. We walked over mountains for about a week till we were within about three hours' walk of Stavros. The Greek Lieutenant went with us. At first everything seemed to be prepared for our reception at the villages en route, but difficulties now seemed to develop. The Lieutenant and the guide returned to Salonika by bus to make new arrangements, promising to return within four days and our party split up. After about a fortnight the Lieutenant and the guide had not returned and Smith, Kemble and I decided to return to Salonika. We did this without a guide.

In Salonika we got in touch with the guide, who had heard nothing of the Lieutenant and was obviously too afraid to try to find out what had happened to him. Kemble, the darkest of the three of us, went with the wife of the guide to the house where he had been sheltered, and learned that the Lieutenant and a niece of the Colonel—she also had helped us—had been arrested. Both had been sentenced to death, but the sentences were later reduced—to three years' imprisonment in the case of the Lieutenant and a year in the case of the girl.

On 29 Sep we returned to Prokhoma, the village where we had originally found shelter, this being the only place where we seemed to have a reasonable prospect of getting information. Here we learned that the Germans had searched the village a week before, and had taken the farmer's wife and daughter to Salonika. Though very strictly interrogated, they had denied all knowledge of any Englishmen having been in the village, and were released. The farmer's family now put us in touch with a girl school teacher, who advised us to go to the village of Ags Demetrios at the N.W. end of the Athos (Hagion Oros) peninsula. She gave us no actual contacts there.

We walked back to the landward end of the Athos Peninsula. We arrived at the village near Stavros where the Lieutenant and the guide had left us, and got in touch with a Frenchman who had helped us when we were last there. He told us of a Greek officer who claimed to have helped Englishmen and to be looking for others to help. The snow had now begun and food was scarce, so we decided to trust this Greek, and get in touch with him through a miller in an adjacent village. Before we actually met the Greek we lived for two days in the open near the village, the miller bringing us food. Here we met two other New Zealanders, one of them Dvr. Frost, of my

unit. Later two more New Zealanders, a Scotsman, and an Australian joined our party.

The Greek officer came to see us, and showed us a list of the names of the people whom he had helped. Next night he sent two guides to take us to his village, and we were guided to a valley and told to wait. The Greek officer told us he was going to Salonika to fetch a car for us. We took this to mean a Greek four-wheeled cart. Had he said he was bringing a motor car we would have been suspicious.

The Greek officer returned that evening as arranged. We assembled and walked to the road with him. As we got close to the vehicle we saw it was a heavy lorry. Everyone but Frost and me had got in. There were two civilians standing beside the truck. Both spoke perfect English and greeted us cordially. While Frost was speaking to the civilians at the rear of the truck I went round to the side and saw a 'V' on it, which I knew was a German sign. I went to the front and saw a German soldier at the wheel. I returned to the rear of the truck and told Frost quietly what I had seen. One civilian said, 'Hop in, boys.' I said I would rather walk, as it was a cold night. Frost also refused to get in. One civilian then produced a pistol, and the other a rifle from under his coat. We got into the truck. We were taken back to Salonika. On the way we destroyed any incriminating papers and photographs we had with us. We arrived back in Lager 1 (which was also known as Frontstalag, and later Dulag 183) on 28 Oct.

3. Second attempted escape

As soon as we got back to Lager 1 we decided to have another try at escaping. There were about 70 people in the camp, all escapers except a few medical personnel. We had some maps in the camp. We got information about a tunnel which had been discovered by the Germans early in 1941, and had been closed. We located the tunnel and ripped up the floor. The top of the tunnel had been concreted over. With pieces of iron beds we prised up the concrete and dug it out. Only the top of the tunnel had been closed, but when we got down the shaft into the drive we found that the Germans had filled it with concertina wire. We cleared the tunnel of the wire and decided to go the following evening, but next morning the tunnel was found. We suspected that it had been given away as the Germans walked straight to it.

After the tunnel had been discovered a few of us who were interested in escaping got together. On 15 Nov we cut through a doorway in an empty back room. The doorway had been wired and boarded up. After we got through the doorway we had to cut through a fine mesh of barbed wire. We then crossed a road and a wall 3 ft high, and lay on a rubbish tip for some time. We next cut through another wire fence, crossed a concrete wall about 8 ft high, and went down to the road, which we reached after cutting through another fence. I was the third out of a party of 12, which included one New Zealand officer. I was accompanied by a Commando private (a Welshman). The Welshman and I went to

Tumbra (?) on the outskirts of Salonika, where we were to get in touch with Greek people whom the Welshman knew. They kept us for the night. Next day (16 Nov) we walked round the coast by the main road to Vatropheli (?) near Polyghyros. Here we met eight Australians and one Cypriot who had been to the Athos (Hagion Oros) peninsula and found it impossible to get away. We stayed here for some days, during which I had an attack of malaria. I then walked to Nea Mondania with Sjt. Donaldson, Australian I.F. We got to the village of Yarakani on the Cassandra Peninsula, where there were German-controlled schooners collecting produce. We went to a house and asked for food. While we were at the house the Greek police came and took us to the police station. The police had no option but to arrest us, as they themselves were under very strict control at that time. They treated us very well and handed us over to the Germans at Polyghyros. We were sent back to Lager 1 (Dula 183) (Salonika) early in Dec.

4. Transfer to Germany

I remained in Dulag 183 till 16 Apr 42. That I was able to do so was largely due to C.S.M. Varley, the camp interpreter, who helped me to keep off all the transports leaving for Germany. I wished to remain in Salonika, because I still hoped to escape to Turkey. Between Dec. 41 and Apr. 42 I was three times in hospital with malaria.

I left Salonika on 16 Apr. and arrived in Germany (Stalag VIIIB, Lamsdorf, Upper Silsia) on 23 Apr. 42. We had plenty of food for the journey. I was in hospital in Stalag VIIIB until the end of May 42, and then began work in the Kartei (Records office), again through the influence of C.S.M. Varley.

I left the Kartei on 16 Jul in charge of a working party of 25 men at Arbeitskommando 469, in Johannesbad, Freiheit, in the region of Trautinau (Europe air map, 1:250,000, Sheet M.33/5). I was in charge of this party till 28 Oct. While I was here nine men escaped in one night, but they did not get very far. Three men escaped on a later occasion. Th party was then broken up for the winter, the contractor having decided that he did not want any more P/W labour.

I was sent back to the Stalag where I met one of my own men, Dvr. Phelan, E. J. A., New Zealand Forces. He and I went to a saw mill at Oppeln in a working party early in Nov 42. Oppeln being a railway junction, we hoped to get help there from the Poles, but they were unable to supply us either with civilian clothes or information about escaping, and we decided to return to the camp. We were refused permission from the Control Officer, so we continued agitating and dodging work until we were sent back on 10 or 12 Nov. We were then placed in chains in common with the rest of the camp, and remained chained till 27 Jan 43.

5. Third attempted escape

On 27 Jan 43 I went to work at a paper factory between Jungbuch and Freiheit (Europe Air map, 1:250,000, Sheet 35/5). I knew this area, having been there already on the wood-cutting party, and hoped to get help. I escaped from this Commando on 13 May with Dvr. Moriarty of my own unit. The German workers supplied us with civilian clothing, food, a little money, and maps. One man in the S.S. was to help us on to a troop train going to France, but at the last moment he changed his mind, but he did not give us away. The Germans who helped us were working in the paper factory. They were Sudeten Germans and very democratic and friendly.

We escaped from the room in which we lived at the factory by taking the bars out of the window. We then walked out and away (on the night of 13–14 May). We intended to go to Yugoslavia to join the guerilla forces there. We walked across country from Jungbuch into Czechoslovakia, and thence to Miletin, Horige, and Mystere (?) near Sucha. We did not approach any Czechs for help. From Sucha we went on walking by night East to Vsestary, and then by main road to Hradec, Kralove, Pardubice, and to a point just before Chocen where we hoped to strike a railway and jump a goods train.

We got on to the railway line and just missed a train. Another was coming, but it was going too fast. We crouched down beside the railway bridge and a Czech soldier came along. He looked over the bridge and shone his torch on us. He spoke to us in Czech. I said, 'Nix verstehen.' He asked if we were German. Before I could answer he unslung his rifle. I asked who he was and he said he was Czech. I then told him we were English, but he insisted on our going with him to the orderly room at a station 2 or 3 kms away.

The other Czech soldiers here said the man who had arrested us was a young and new soldier and that any of the others would have helped us, but once we had been taken to the guard room they were unable to do anything for us. This was on 21 May.

We were then taken to Pardubice where the Gestapo interrogated us, but treated us very well. Before we left the station near Chocen, the Czech soldiers destroyed our maps and documents, including a diary, as well as some of our civilian clothes. We were five days in prison in Pardubice, and were then sent back to Lamsdorf.

6. Final escape

For my last escape I was sentenced to seven days' imprisonment but as I has been five days in prison in Pardubice I had only two days to do in Lamsdorf. On the second day I was ordered to report to the Lager Offizier, who asked if I was prepared to go to work. I agreed, hoping to be sent to a paper factory.

I was sent to the working compound, where I began to make plans for escape. In the compound I met Gnr. Edgar Harrison (S/P.G.(G)1523) and we decided to escape together. I collected maps from friends and also secured some personal papers. We also gathered as much information as we could about Breslau, the route to Stettin, and the possibility of getting a Swedish ship in Stettin. The papers we obtained were an Arbeitsdienstausweis, an Eisenbahnausweis, and a Personalausweis. We then arranged to be sent on a working party of 14 men employed in the gas works in Breslau stacking and emptying gas purifiers. We arrived in Breslau on 22 Jul (Arbveitskommando E.243).

At the gas works we got in touch with some Ukranians working there, and in exchange for cigarettes got from them civilian clothes. By the same means we got a railway time table from a Pole, and each of us bought a watch from Frenchmen. The Feldwebel found a felt hat one day in Harrison's trunk, and later a pair of civilian trousers hanging up to dry inside a pair of battle-dress trousers. After this the Feldwebel kept a close eye on us.

In preparation for our escape we packed our shaving gear, boot polish, towels, soap, socks, etc. in the brief cases bought with cigarettes from the Ukranians. We hid the cases and our civilian clothing in the vessel (purifying) house, and awaited our chance to get out.

On 22 Sep we tried to get out. We waited till an auxiliary civilian guard had passed, and made our way individually to the vessel house, where we changed, putting on blue overalls over our civilian clothes. The vessel house was near a 7 ft. wall, inside of which was a police patrol, and there were also civilians walking about. About 2 ft. from the wall was a high-tension room, and the narrow passage between the wall and the building gave us a certain amount of cover. We had stolen a small ladder two weeks before and hidden it in the vessel room. We took this ladder out and put it against the wall under cover of the high-tension room. I got up on the wall and saw a civilian truck outside. I decided to wait till it went. Ten or 15 minutes later I looked over the wall again and saw the Feldwebel and some civilians working on a cable immediately below me. We gave up the idea for that day. We were unable to take away one brief case and one parcel from under the wall and, as one of the Ukranians appropriated the attache case and the parcel, we had to start our journey with only half supplies.

Next day (23 Sep) we decided to try again. We were working on the morning shift, and had to stage our escape to catch a tram which got us to the Hauptbahnhof just in time to catch the train. As the morning was too difficult, we changed to the afternoon shift, taking the places of two of our comrades who pretended they wanted to play football. The Feldwebel was also out that day.

On 23 Sep we repeated the procedure of the previous day. We got over the wall, timing this so that the policeman had completed his patrol. I was first over with the brief case, and walked down the road to the tram stop. I caught the tram, but Harrison just missed it. This was the last I saw of Harrison till we met in Stettin.

I left the tram at the Hauptbanhof, found the platform I wanted, and then bought a third-class ticket for Glogau. I did not have to show my papers. I went on to the platform and a German soldier actually found me a seat. I changed at Glogau and booked for Reppen. At Reppen I bought a ticket for Kustrin, arriving there about midnight. My next connection was about 0600 hrs. so I walked out of the station and slept in a field till about

0515 hrs. (24 Sep). I returned to the station and bought a ticket for Stettin, which I reached about 0905 hrs.

From the Hauptbahnhof in Stettin I caught a tram to Gotzlow, having been told in the camp that Swedish ships loaded there with coal and could be boarded without help. I spent the morning in Gotzlow and had a good look at the place from a hill. It seemed quite impossible to get into the harbour and, in any case, there were no Swedish ships there.

I returned to the town and in the afternoon decided to go to the Am Dunzig where I had seen a Dutch ship. I crossed the Hansabrucke, and walked along the Am Dunzig, but I could not get into the harbour there, or round to the Freihafen. I therefore returned to the vicinity of the Arbeitsamt (labour office) near the Hansabrucke, but still on the Am Dunzig.

Here I saw three Frenchmen in civilian clothes, and black berets. I said, 'Bon jour' to them, and asked them if they were French and could speak English. They were doubtful of me at first, but were convinced when I produced a letter addressed to me in the camp, a Stalag identity disc, and a photograph of myself in uniform. They then said they had a friend who spoke Englsh, and took me to the Lager where they lived. The Frenchman who spoke English told me they worked on the Swedish ships, and would get me on board, and would look after me till they could find a ship for me. They said no Germans ever went to the Lager. I had a shave and a wash, and when I came back into the barrack room, Dvr. Harrison was standing there. He had come by another route, having missed the Glogau train.

The Frenchmen now did most of the organising for us, two of them being particularly helpful. We were in the Lager from 24 to 27 Sep. All the Frenchmen knew we were there, but none of them gave us away. A Swedish ship came in on 27 Sep and they sent us down to it in the afternoon. The ship had been loaded and we could not get on board, so we returned to the Lager.

We got on board another ship that night. Ten Frenchmen were detailed to load the boat, which was lying in the docks beside the Flughafen, near Altdamm (Germany, 1:100,000, Sheet 38). We travelled there by tram and took the places of two Frenchmen who stayed behind at the Lager. There was an air raid while we were working on the ship, so we went to a shelter for about half an hour, and then returned on board.

The two men whose places we had taken then came on the ship. By this time the cargo of coal was almost loaded, and Harrison and I began to dig ourselves in among the coal in one of the holds. The Frenchmen put us into a hold immediately underneath a ventilator. The ship was searched by the Gestapo when the cargo had been loaded, and we were told afterwards by a seaman that while the search was on one of us coughed and he stamped on the deck to drown the sound.

Before we had concealed ourselves, two drunk Swedish seamen came on board talking broken English. We decided to trust them. One of them took me to his cabin in the forecastle, where there were two other seamen. I told them who I was and showed them my photograph, letter, and identity discs, and asked them to smuggle us to Sweden. They said that they could not do this because of the German search of the ship, but that if we liked to take the risk of hiding in the coal they would not give us away.

The name of the ship was the S.S. Ludvig. One of the sailors was particularly helpful and passed us down an overcoat, coffee, cigarettes, and a letter of encouragement through the ventilator. After we had left German waters our presence was made known to the master of the ship, who treated us with every kindness.

We landed at Landskrona on 29 Sep and were handed over to the Swedish police. The Danish Vice-Consul at Landskrona who happened to be in the Police station showed us every kindness. He got in touch with our Vice-Consul at Halsingborg, stood guarantee for us with the police, and took us out to dinner. He also offered us a room in a hotel, but we refused this as we were dirty and had no suitable clothes. We returned to the Police Station, where we were locked in a cell all the following day (30 Sep) and until 1600 hrs. on the second day. We asked for a bath and a shave, but were not given permission. The Danish Vice-Consul secured our release, gave us clothes and arranged for a room in a hotel. We then went to Stockholm and reported to the British Legation.

(L.G. 17.2.44)

Crozier, Gordon Cecil, Private
C.63438, Stormont Dundas and Glengarry Highlanders (Immediate)

Private Gordon Cecil Crozier, commanding 8 section of B Company, on 15 October 1944, at Roedenhoek, so effectively neutralized enemy fire holding up his company that the Stormont Dundas and Glengarry Highlanders were able to advance and capture Roedenhoek.

As B Company was advancing on Roedenhoek, 12 platoon was pinned down by heavy and sustained 20 millimetre fire from four guns so sited as to enfilade the 300 yards of open polder country between B Company and their objective Roedenhoek, making movement impossible. Private Crozier quickly surveyed the situation and instructed his section to start moving as soon as he had neutralized the enemy fire. Private Crozier then broke cover, and with a bren gun and nine magazines made a dash for a railway cutting some 300 yards to a flank. There was no cover. As he moved to this dominating feature he was wounded by the enemy fire which swept the polder. Private Crozier, ignoring his wound, struggled to his feet and continued his advance. Moving up the steep bank Private Crozier found a fire position from which he could pin point and engage all four enemy guns; these he coolly and systematically put out of action in spite of heavy enemy fire directed against him.

B Company then continued their advance. Private Crozier remained in his position engaging enemy who appeared on the company's flank. Only after consolidation of the objective did Private Crozier withdraw. It was entirely due to this soldier's courage, determination, and spirit of self sacrifice that the battalion was able to capture its objective which enabled the brigade to complete the task of clearing its section of the Scheldt pocket. Private Crozier's gallantry, skill at arms, and example were a monument of inspiration to his comrades.

Witness's statement
C–65485 Cpl. Coulas A. F., S D & G Highlanders

At the battle of Roedenhoek on 15 October 1944, I, C–65485 Cpl. Coulas A. F. was number 2 on the Piat in number 12 Platoon. We were attempting to get into Roedenhoek when we were pinned down by 20 millimetre fire from four guns; also our supporting Wasp Carriers had been knocked out by two 50 millimetre anti-tank guns which were part of the Roedenboek defences. At this point Pte. Crozier grabbed his Bren gun and made his way under fire to the railway embankment which was also being swept by fire. Pte. Crozier engaged the enemy weapons and silenced them, allowing us to get into the position and mop it up. During this action Pte. Crozier sustained a wound across his back.

It is very doubtful in my mind that we could have got into Roedenhoek had Crozier not fulfilled the task which he took upon himself.

Witness's statement
[...]10104, Pte. Horsley J. L., S D & G Highlanders

On 15 October 1944 'B' Company was ordered to capture Roedenhoek as part of the battalion attack. I am number three rifleman of eight section. Pte. Crozier was number one on the Bren gun.

As we were advancing the company became pinned down by fire. From where I was there appeared to be four guns firing at us, one a single 20 millimetre, another on the cross road, a double 20 millimetre; on the bend of the road covering the dyke was a 50 millimetre anti-tank weapon and another 50 millimetre on the right flank of the position. Our supporting Wasp Carriers also came under fire from this position and were knocked out. Just about this time Pte. Crozier took his Bren gun. Saying that he would cover us across the open, he set out for the embankment some distance away. The ground between us and this embankment was under direct and heavy fire. However, Pte. Crozier reached this embankment. I saw that Pte. Crozier was hit before he opened fire but even this did not stop him from engaging the enemy. After the position had been cleared Pte. Crozier was evacuated and I was told that he had suffered a long wound across the muscles of his back.

We could never have got into Roedenhoek if it had not been for Pte. Crozier's action.

Witness's statement
Lt. F. [...] Groff, S D & G Highlanders

I was platoon commander of number 12 Platoon, S D & G Highlanders during the month of October.

On 15 October 1944 our battalion attacked Roedenhoek with B Company making the assault. Our first attack was held by heavy enemy fire from four 20 millimetre guns which swept the approaches to their position with accurate cross fire from both flanks. Fire from two 50 millimetre anti-tank guns knocked out our supporting Wasp Carriers.

We prepared to continue the assault with my platoon leading. Our first job was to get across the embankment which was under fire and then to move in on the enemy guns. At this point Pte. Crozier grabbed his Bren gun and ran over to the embankment and took up a fire position to engage the enemy guns in a 'fire fight.' Although Pte. Crozier was wounded early in this action he kept up his fire and neutralized the enemy guns until the whole of B Company were able to get across the embankment and on into the objective. Crozier's magnificent action undoubtedly made the capture of Roedenhoek possible. Pte. Crozier has continually shown the greatest courage in battle.

Witness's statement
G–52936 Pte. Hayward L. C., S D & G Highlanders

At the battle of Roedenhoek on 15 October 1944 I, G–52936 Pte. Hayward L. C., was Number One on the Bren gun of number 7 Section, 12 Platoon. We had been ordered to assault Roedenhoek as point section. On approaching the position our platoon was pinned down by 20 millimetre fire which enfiladed us from two directions. Pte. Crozier, who was in number 8 Section at the rear of the platoon, seeing the difficult position we were in, took his Bren gun and moved to a position on the flank from where he took on the guns that were holding us up.

We could not possibly have gone across the open ground had these guns not been put out of action by Pte. Crozier.
(*L.G. 10.2.45*)

Cruikshank, Harry Ross, Warrant Officer Cl. II (actg.)
2814746, 7th Bn. Seaforth Highlanders (Elgin)
(Immediate)

CSM Harold Ross Cruickshank was CSM of 'B' Company of this Battalion.

On 12 Feb 45, the Battalion was ordered to advance up to Cleve—Calcar road in Kangaroos. 'B' Coy was the leading Coy. Two miles outside Cleve the Company met strong enemy opposition around the village of Quaiburg, which knocked out the leading Kangaroos. The Coy 'detanked,' and was quickly involved in stiff hand to hand fighting. CSM Cruickshank was severely wounded in the head and hand in the first few minutes of the battle, but refusing any medical attention, he rallied a large number of the Company, and led them against the enemy. By a magnificent display of dash and courage he cleared several houses and captured single handed 15 enemy armed with automatics. Despite the great pain of his wounds, he continued to show outstanding powers of leadership, and for a further hour personally led assaults on several troublesome enemy MG posts. It was not until he had been hit a third time, and had been given

a direct order by his Coy Comd, that he would allow himself to be evacuated.

This Warrant Officer's gallant conduct on this occasion was an inspiration to all who saw him, and it was largely due to his leadership and complete disregard of danger and his own sufferings, that the Coy were able to capture the strong point and kill and capture over 80 enemy.
(*L.G. 10.5.45*)

Crump, Ralph, Lance Sergeant
5117061, 1 Oxfordshire & Buckinghamshire Light
Infantry (Tisbury) (Immediate)

On 7 Jan 45, 'C' Coy 43rd Lt Infty was ordered to clear the Bois de la Rochette and the Bois Spireaux of enemy; they were also to capture the Château in Sq 3281 which was known to be an enemy posn. No 13 pl, of which Cpl. Crump was pl sjt, was the pl ordered to assault the Château, and it was in a large measure due to Cpl. Crump's courage and initiative that the attack was so successful. On the approach to the objective, the pl 2-in mortarman was wounded and Cpl. Crump immediately took over the mortar and disregarding the enemy machine-gun fire, brought the mortar into action at a low angle and destroyed the enemy posn, killing three Germans and capturing the mahine-gun. Immediately after, during the assault on the Château, the leading sec came under close range hy small arms fire, and it looked as if the attack might fail; Cpl. Crump seeing this placed himself at the head of the leading sec and charged the enemy posn, getting into the château where severe hand-to-hand fighting took place; such, however, was the impetus and speed of the attack that the enemy were soon discouraged and surrendered to a tune of sixty Pz Grenadiers, in addition six were killed.

It was chiefly due to Cpl. Crump's quick appreciation, inspired leadership and brave example that the sec was able to subdue and capture an enemy posn ten times its strength.
(*L.G. 12.4.45*)

Crutchett, Frederick, Bombardier
883294, 4th Field Regt., Royal Artillery (Hounslow)
(Immediate)

At Nungshium near Imphal on 12 April 44, No. 883294 W/Bdr. Crutchett was a member of an Arty F.O.O. party in support of two assaulting coys of 3/9 Jats. The enemy allowed the forward coy very nearly to reach the first objective and then isolated them by machine gun fire from the flanks. The party crawled forward through the fire to produce the necessary artillery support. The whole area in which this coy lay was exposed to very heavy cross fire and there were many casualties. At one time some of the rear sections whose leaders were ahead, started a withdrawal movement which threatened to spread. Regardless of his own safety and under very heavy fire Bdr. Crutchett stood up and moved among these men, steadied them, and got them back into position. He then continued still under heavy fire to reorganise his O.P. signallers who had been knocked down the hill, and proceeded to an exposed position to endeavour to locate an enemy machine gun so that artillery fire might blind it with smoke. Throughout this period he was also exposed to heavy fire. When the coys were ordered to withdraw, which they were obliged to do in simultaneous rush, Bdr. Crutchett covered the withdrawal of his O.P. party, who were slightly in advance of the infantry, with his T.S.M.G.

His courage, calm and grasp of the situation were worthy of the very highest praise and were an example to all around him. By his actions he steadied the infantry and enabled very valuable covering fire to be brought down which undoubtedly prevented even heavier casualties.

On 6 Apr at Runaway Hill this NCO exposed himself to great danger from an enemy gun that was firing at our infantry over open sights. To assist his O.P. officer in observing our counter-battery fire he occupied an exposed O.P. and regardless of the enemy shells bursting on the position he passed very valuable information which assisted in silencing the enemy gun.

(L.G. 27.7.44)

Crutchley, George Henry, Corporal
4809688, 6 Lincolnshire Regt. (Skegness) (Immediate)
This NCO was commanding the left fwd pl on 22 Apr 43 when his Coy attacked Aroub Hamra (eight miles north of Bou Arada). He took forward his pl with great determination over open ground covered with enemy M.G.'s and in the final assault was always in the forefront as each enemy trench was cleared.

His example and high qualities of leadership were entirely responsible for the ultimate success his pl achieved in gaining their strongly held objective.

(L.G. 15.6.43)

Cuddie, Lloyd William, Sergeant
H26395, 27 Cdn. Armd. Regt. (Sher. Fus. R.)
(Immediate)
During the battle from 22–24 July 1944 in the vicinity of St. Andre-sur-Orne, H–26395 Sjt. Cuddie, L. W. was a troop sjt in 'A' Squadron 27 Cdn Armd Regt, which became engaged with a superior number of enemy tanks. During the course of the battle eight German Panther tanks succeeded in pinning to the ground seven tanks of this squadron at a range of 600 yards. Of the seven Canadian tanks, three were on fire, two had badly jammed turrets and a sixth could only move in bull-low. The seventh tank, that of Sjt. Cuddie was the only one fit for battle.

At this stage the enemy began an encircling movement which, if successful, would have enabled him to completely destroy the Canadian tanks. Sjt. Cuddie knocked out the leading Panther, whereupon the remainder halted and started to fire at him and at four others which were incapable of returning the fire. By the skilful use of ground and by well-directed fire, he contained the whole enemy force, thus allowing four

other Canadian tanks to move into fire positions. They, together with Sjt. Cuddie's tank, then proceeded to destroy the remaining seven enemy tanks, without further loss.

The outstanding skill, courage and aggressiveness displayed by Sjt. Cuddie was directly responsible for the complete destruction of the German tank force, which in turn enabled the advance to continue. *(L.G. 4.11.44)*

Cully, Albert, Corporal (A/Sgt.)
4745231, York & Lancaster Regt.
For conspicuous gallantry on the 28th April, 1940. The enemy had succeeded in turning the flank of the position and had been able to establish a road block to prevent withdrawal. L/Sjt. Cully was in command of the fighting patrol which was ordered to drive back the enemy infiltration. On nearing a bend in the road a road block was found. At the same time the enemy opened fire with a machine gun. L/Sjt. Cully ordered covering fire with a light machine gun while he himself advanced by the side of the road and succeeded in destroying with grenades the enemy machine gun post which was in a house covering the road block. He then cleared part of the block, returned and helped Pte. Ryan. Together they mounted a lorry carrying anti tank guns. Pte. Ryan fired his L.M.G. from the lorry and the lorry rushed the block. It was owing to the gallant action of L/Sjt. Cully and Pte. Ryan that the A.T. guns were got away safely. *(L.G. 6.8.40)*

Cunningham, George, Bombardier (A/Sgt.)
781201, 4th Field Regt., Royal Artillery (Glasgow)
Action 4th Fd Regt RA South West of Knightsbridge on 6th June 1942.

On 6th June 1942 Sjt. Cunningham was a No. 1 in 'D' Troop 4th Fd Regt R.A. The gun position was attacked and finally overrun by many enemy tanks. Throughout the action Sjt. Cunningham displayed the utmost courage and coolness under intense shell fire and machine-gun fire. Although wounded himself he continued to direct the fire of his gun until it was destroyed by a direct hit. During the action his gun destroyed 3 enemy tanks.

Cunningham, James, Driver
T/61556, No. 3 Commando
18th-19th August 1942, Yellow 2, Dieppe.
This man was outstanding throughout the operation. He showed initiative and firmness worthy of a senior NCO and set a fine example in the boat during the trying period of the Naval action. He made a toggle and eye rope to assist his comrades to climb the cliff; he was constantly alert to find the enemy's telephone wires and cut them. He was most forward when the enemy engaged us by surprise and at close range. He was the leader of a group of privates who covered the withdrawals to the beach and to the boats. Hit once on his bandolier, once on his arm, while the LCP lay off shore he coolly continued to shoot at Germans on the cliffs and certainly

accounted for some. He helped greatly to make up for the absence of NCOs in this party.   *(L.G. 24.9.42)*

Curley, Robert Francis, Sergeant
6026069, 1 Hampshire Regt. (Manor Park)
(Immediate)

At Bernieres Bocage on 14 Jun 44 a platoon was detailed to give flank protection for the bn adv on La Senaudiere. From the start progress was difficult, as enemy snipers with LMGs had prepared to bring fire upon the companies as they crossed the start line. The flank platoon was operating on its own, and from the start movement forward was difficult. Sjt. Curley, showing complete disregard for his personal safety, coaxed and led his men forward against heavy small arms fire and they succeeded in silencing several snipers. Later a wood was reached from which came heavy LMG fire. Sjt. Curley led his men with great dash and determination and together with his leading section took the first enemy post, capturing three prisoners. Suddenly a Spandau opened up at close range. Sjt. Curley dashed towards it alone, threw grenades first and fired a burst from his Sten gun. The enemy replied by throwing four stick grenades, one of which blew off Sjt. Curley's steel helmet and slightly wounded him in the neck. However, Sjt. Curley closed with the enemy killing three and taking one prisoner.

This fine example of leadership and personal bravery inspired the greatest confidence in his platoon, who were able to complete a task which was vital to the successful advance of the Battalion.   *(L.G. 31.8.44)*

D

Daley, Daniel Alexander, Lance Sergeant
NX.40585, 3 Australian A.Tk Regt.
At Tell-el-Eisa during the day 17 Jul 42 L/Sjt. Daley was in support of 2/32 Aust Inf Bn in the consolidation of ridge at 87772935 with his 2 pr gun. Despite heavy shelling and MG fire, in the enemy counter attacks he kept his gun and crew in action though lightly wounded. When enemy AFVs moved in to the attack, he was able to hit six of them even though his gunshield was being perforated by AP bullets until at last he and his gun-layer were badly wounded and the crew had to move back with the MG Section nearby to the new infantry line some 400 yds in rear. By his courage and determination he materially assisted in breaking up the counter attack, and in no small degree inspired the gunners of the troop in rear of him.   *(L.G. 24.9.42)*

Daly, John Joseph, Sergeant
6210701, Royal Artillery
No citation.   *(L.G. 9.11.44)*

Daly, Patrick, M.M., Corporal (A/Sgt.)
4039943, 10th Bn. Highland Light Infantry
  (Edgbaston, Birmingham) (Immediate)
On 27 August 44, 227 Bde was engaged in an opposed river crossing of the Seine, 10/HLI making the initial crossing on the left. Sjt. Daly was pl. Sjt. of the third pl. of 'A' Coy the leading coy in the crossing and was in charge of a storm boat loaded with half his platoon. This boat was separated from the pl comdr's boat and landed first.

When Sjt. Daly landed he found that the two leading pls had been pinned down by enemy MG fire which was inflicting casualties. He quickly located the enemy posn and armed with rifle and bayonet assaulted the posn alone. He shot the first rifleman, bayoneted the second and took the two machine gunners prisoner. The remainder of the enemy post made off. The rest of the company was then able to advance and consolidate the initial bridgehead without delay.

By his personal bravery, complete disregard for danger and speedy action, Sjt. Daly enabled the initial bridgehead to be rapidly consolidated as a result of which the remainder of the bn was able to cross without further casualties. Throughout the entire action Sjt. Daly set a brilliant example of speed in dealing with the enemy and disregard of danger which was an inspiration to all ranks.   *(L.G. 1.3.45)*

Daniel, John Henry, M.M., Sergeant
VX 9453, 2/6 Australian Infantry Bn. (Immediate)
During the present campaign in the Ma[...]k area, Sjt. Daniel, 2/6 Aust Inf Bn, has been reponsible for outstanding efforts of courage, initiative and leadership. Prior to the attack on Wombak 2, the initial recces were made by small patrols led by Sjt. Daniel and much valuable infm regarding enemy strs and disposns obtained.

On 15 May 45 the Posn was attacked, Sjt. Daniel being in comd of the flanking sec. By his daring and aggressive leadership he was responsible for the capture of vital ground which later facilitated the occupation of the whole position. Immediately following the completion of the initial phase, he aggressively led patrols into the centre of the main enemy defs, killing four enemy. His total disregard for his own personal safety, coupled with his brilliant leadership, was an inspiring example to his men and undoubtedly reduced our own casualties to a minimum. Prior to the attack on the strongly defenced enemy posn at Dombuir, on 2 Jun 45, Sjt. Daniel led a 52 hrs patrol which continually harassed and inflicted casualties on an enemy numerically far superior. Moving ahead of his sec he killed the sentry on the track and also a sniper thus enabling the sec to adv to close quarters. He crawled to the flank of the enemy and, exposing himself to hy rifle and LMG fire, succeeded in killing three enemy and badly wounding one.

Sjt. Daniel's initiative, personal courage and continued aggression finally drove the enemy from the strongly defended posn. Sjt. Daniel's devotion to duty, brilliant leadership, initiative and personal courage are an inspiration to all with whom he serves and his untiring efforts have been responsible for inflicting many casualties on the enemy.   *(L.G. 24.8.45)*

Darby, Alfred, Sergeant
46566, 76th Anti-Tank Regt., Royal Artillery
  (Birmingham) (Immediate)
On the morning of March 27th, at first light, the rear of the Divisional Arty Group which was about (T) Y 9313, was attacked by some ten tanks and four 88mm guns. Sjt. Darby was commanding a Deacon 6 pdr which was travelling near the rear of the column. The going was extremely bad but Sjt. Darby extricated his Deacon and drove straight for the oncoming tanks and 88mm guns, one of which was already in action, he wheeled his gun into action and immediately engaged the enemy, getting off some eight rounds before his gun was knocked out.

By his prompt and gallant action he unquestionably halted the whole enemy force and made them pause for a vital five minutes during which the rest of the Battery, which was strung out along the column and some distance away, was able to concentrate and engage the enemy on good terms. As a result, all four 88mm guns and four tanks were knocked out. The action was witnessed by many of his comrades who are unanimous in his praise. Sjt. Darby was wounded in this action.

(L.G. 1.6.43)

Darroch, Albert, Sergeant
2980642, Argyll & Sutherland Highlanders (69, Roxburgh St., Greenock)
No citation. *(L.G. 23.1.42)*

Darts, Frederick Joshua, Corporal
5949117, Bedfordshire & Hertfordshire Regt., S.S. Bde., No 3 Commando
Sjt. Darts was in charge of a section of 3 Cdo at Agnone in Sicily on 13 July 43.
The beach on which the Cdo landed was under heavy fire and casualties were suffered. Sjt. Dart's section was the last to pass through the wire obstacles set up by the enemy. He realised that to wait according to plan would be disastrous and therefore made a quick personal reconnaissance, discovered another gap and pushing his section through joined up with the Cdo at the appointed forming up point. This quick decision undoubtedly saved many lives in his section.

Later in the battle Sjt. Dart gathered what remained of his section and fought a rear guard action with great skill and determination. Time and again his section inflicted casualties upon the enemy by holding on till the last possible moment in the leap frog withdrawal action.

Finally the enemy began to close in and one party of German Parachutists who had worked round on the flank attempted to deceive the Cdo rear-guard by shouting out the password in English. Sjt. Dart spread out his small force and charged towards the position; in this action 12 of the enemy were killed but more enemy closed on the flanks and the section were pinned down. Under Sjt. Dart's inspiring leadership, his men held the enemy off until every round of ammunition had been fired, when they were taken prisoner. *(L.G. 28.2.46)*

Davidson, Douglas, Trooper
843717, R.A.O.C. [44 Bn. R.T.R. on AFW 3121]
Davidson was taken prisoner on 1 Jun 42 near Knightsbridge. Within the following month he made four attempts to escape; on the first occasion he crawled away from Italians who were guarding a small number of P/W sleeping in the open. Although he reached the coast, he was caught by a German patrol, and returned to the camp. The following night he made a similar escape, but was again recaptured. A few days later he and six others cut the wire surrounding Derna transit camp. Davidson separated from the others, and wearing Arab clothing given to him by friendly tribesmen, was within sight of British positions when his disguise was seen through by a German patrol.

On his return to camp with three other escapers he was made to face a firing squad; the execution was only stayed by Davidson' direct appeal to the Commandant.

In spite of this narrow escape from death, he made another attempt on reaching Benghazi camp by crawling through the wire. He was recaptured the following morning and transferred to Italy.

At the time of the Armistice he was at Monturano (Camp 70) and in accordance with the intructions of the S.B.O., took no action on hearing the news. On 26 Sep. 43, during transfer to Germany, he jumped from the train near Bologna, through a hole cut in the door of the truck. Travelling alone to Monte San Vicino, he joined a rebel band. Except for one unsuccessful attempt to cross the Maiella in Nov. 43, he remained with this group of partisans until he met advancing British troops on 6 Jun 44. Although he was not a N.C.O., Davidson was put in charge of 35 to 50 guerillas, and other escapers have praised his courage and leadership, one officer reporting that he had a reputation for outstanding courage and daring among the most reckless of the rebels, who had the most complete confidence in him. In addition, in Mar. 44 it was mainly due to Davidson's efforts that eight R.A.F. personnel were not captured when a Fascist road block was met during a drive to a rendezvous for sea evacuation. *(L.G. 26.7.45)*

Davidson, Philip Anzac, Corporal
73365, 14 Bde. Defence Platoon, New Zealand Military Forces
At Sirot on 17 February, 1944, Cpl Davidson was a member of the 14th Bde Defence Platoon which was part of a force carrying out a reconnaissance of the Island. Whilst patrolling towards the north-western coast the Pl. made contact with a party of sixteen of the enemy, who suddenly opened fire with grenades and a machine gun at a range of 30 yards. With complete disregard for his own safety, Cpl. Davidson rushed the position killed seven of the enemy and put the gun out of action. The remainder of the force were thus enabled to go forward and destroy the remaining enemy without further loss themselves. Cpl. Davidson himself continued to assist with great gallantry, in the mopping up. The conduct of Cpl. Davidson throughout the operation was an inspiration to his comrades and is deserving of the highest praise. *(L.G. 27.3.44)*

Davies, David, Warrant Officer Cl. II (Drill Sergeant)
2733197, 3rd Bn. Welsh Guards (London, E.15)
(Immediate)
10/20 Feb 44. Mt. Cerasola. Map Ref. 8604 Sheet 160/IISE 1/25,000
This Warrant Officer was on duty at advanced Bn. H.Q. throughout the operation. His courage and devotion to duty were outstanding and his action in carrying out an immediate counter-attack against enemy who had penetrated the Bn perimeter resulted in the death or surrender of all of them and in Drill Sergeant Davies sustaining a very serious wound. His cheerfulness and gallantry set at all times a high example to all ranks.
(L.G. 29.6.44)

Davies, Emrys, Sergeant
2737357, 3rd Bn. Welsh Guards (Trawsmawr,
Carmarthen) (Immediate)
25th April 1945. Castel Guglielmo 062069, Sheet 64/
III, 1/50,000 Italy.

This NCO commanded a Pl on 25 Apr 45 when the
Bn crossed the River Po and enlarged the bridgehead on
the northern bank. From first light until 1800 hrs this Pl
attacked ten farms capturing six Germans and killing
four, after fire fights at each place, and was at times over
a mile away from other elements of the Coy. At 1830
hrs the decision was taken to make a further advance at
speed. For this a Pl was needed to proceed riding on
tanks. Sjt. Daives volunteered immediately. The advance
continued northwards for 8 miles to Castel Guglielmo
062069, which was occupied by the enemy. Sjt. Davies
ordered his pl to take up a position in houses overlooking
the Canale Biancho, from where they engaged the enemy,
who replied with rifle and MG fire. Although the house
in which he stood was twice struck by bazookas and the
bridge was blown up at very close range to the pl, he
kept his men in position while the tanks backed away
from the river. Only at nightfall when ordered to retire
did he lead his pl back to safety with one prisoner.

Sjt. Davies showed powers of command, initiative
and reliability of a high order and in addition his disregard
for his own personal safety was an inspiration to his Pl
and to all those who saw him.   *(L.G. 23.8.45)*

Davies, George James, Lance Corporal
3908300, 1 South Wales Borderers (Immediate)
L/Cpl. Davies was captured on 18.6.42 with about 10
officers and 320 O.R.'s of his regiment about 45 Kms.
E. of Tobruk. The same day officers were separated from
the men and name, number and rank of every man were
taken. With the other units captured they were about 600.
The next day they were arranged in a column and
marched toward Tobruk. One truck went in front, one
by the centre and one at the rear of the column. A fourth
moved up and down the column. Each carried sentries
armed with M.G.'s.

L/Cpl. Davies and another walked off the road into
some slit trenches at about 1400 hours, and the column
marched on. They walked on by night along the coast
North of the road. Early next morning they met some
Arabs who sold them a French pistol with 5 rounds of
ammunition for a pound. They also told them that Sollum
was in British hands, and Bardia in German hands, and
gave them food and water. A few days later, about 10
miles North of Bardia a British armoured car, driven by
Germans, and two German staff cars captured them. A
senior German officer got out and went up to L/Cpl.
Davies saying in English 'You have the honour of being
captured by me,' to which he replied 'Who the hell are
you?' 'I am the Lt. General in charge of German troops
in North Africa.'

They were taken to Bardia where they were put in an
empty house. The only guard was a group of soldiers

some distance away outside. L/Cpl. Davies decided to
make a dash for it. His companion would not come, so
he went off alone. He got away unseen and went South
to Sollum. About 6 miles N. of Sollum he met a South
African with three S.A. natives. They all went South into
the desert and then East. Near Sidi Barrani, on 30.6.42
they walked into an Italian camp and were captured and
taken back to Sollum.

From there they were moved next day to a cage at
Derna. Here L/Cpl. Davies met Sgts. F. J. Walker, 32279,
I. J. Jack, 32284 and Pte. L. P. Dittberner, 32552, all of
2/Transvaal Scottish (who are being recommended for
Military Medals respectively). On 3.7.42 they escaped
together as they heard they would be moved further west
next day.

They skirted the Northern edge of the latrines in the
South East corner of the camp and crawled through the
outside wire on the East side. They had with them a tin
of Italian bully, a couple of biscuits, a tin of English
bully: each had a water bottle. They crawled across the
open ground to the ruined building. Here they had to lie
half an hour as a convoy of trucks (probably containing
more P/W) was coming down the road and pulling in to
the open space before the camp. As each one backed
and turned, its lights swept across the ground where the
escapers were lying. Then they made South to the wall
of the town. Twice they avoided walking into German
sentries as they could see that they were smoking on
duty. They went near the aerodrome and then to the road
to Tobruk. They intended to stop a truck going up the
pass into the town, get rid of the occupants and drive as
far as they could towards our lines, walking the last lap.
They found a truck which had stopped on the road. Pte.
Dittberner spoke to the driver in German while the others
went round to the back to see how many there were in it.
As it was a large party they signalled to Pte. Dittberner,
and made off without rousing suspicion. They waited
there several hours but no more trucks came.

They hid in wadis and caves for two days till an Arab
took them to where Gnr. R. H. Roper, 1528857, R.A.
(who has been awarded a DCM) had been living several
months. As they were very weak they decided to stay
with him to build up their strength. However, news of
their whereabuts reached the right quarter and they were
rescued reaching our line on 20.8.42.

L/Cpl. Davies escaped no less than three times, once
alone, and his story illustrates throughout the indomitable
spirit which eventually caused him to succeed. Though
rescued after the last escape, the party gave ample proof
of courage, forethought and determination and were
willing to take any risks in order to reach our lines. A
fine performance.   *(L.G. 11.3.43)*

Davies, Gwilyin, Sergeant (A/W.O.II)
2989309, 2nd Bn. Argyll & Sutherland Highlanders
(Cardiff) (Immediate)
Between 17–21 Sep 44 the Bn was forming part of the
brhd at Gheel. CSM Davies is CSM of B coy which was

then right flank protection on the canal bank. At all times the Coy was under very heavy and accurate mortar, long range medium and Spandau fire and a number of casualties were sustained. On 18 Sep the Coy Comd was killed and two other coy offrs wounded leaving only one junior offr to comd the coy. There was also the constant threat of a counter attack developing from the East. CSM Davies throughout the next days greatly assisted this junior offr to run the coy and his personal example under fire was an inspiration to others.

During the Bn's next action from Vleit on 25 Sep B Coy was at first in depth and at a later stage was ordered to pass through the two leading coys. During this action the Coy Comd and Coy 2IC were killed and again the coy was left with one junior offr. The country was densely wooded and when the coy had been ordered to re-organise the Coy Comd's body had not yet been brought in. It was known that he had in his pocket some marked maps. CSM Davies immediately went forward with a sgt who was with the Coy Comd when he was killed. As the Coy Comd had been killed by a spandau at very short range the task was not easy. It meant crawling fwd covered by the sgt with a bren. The spandau opened up at the slightest sound, and in addition, the enemy started to mortar that part of the wood. In spite of this, however, CSM Davies succeeded in retrieving the maps, thus denying to the enemy much valuable information. This is yet another instance of the high sense of duty, disregard of his own personal safety, and inspiring example which this W.O. has continually shown in action. In spite of the fact that CSM Davies has now had three Coy Comds killed and one wounded, he has never allowed his courage to fail him.

(L.G. 1.3.45)

Davies, Oswald, Warrant Officer Cl. I (R.S.M.)
1942533, 930 Port Construction and Repair
Company, Royal Engineers (Lymm)
Anzio—30th January, 1944:—

W.O.I Davies was in charge of diving operations at Anzio at a time when the Port was under shellfire and subject to frequent air attacks. On receiving instructions to have the harbour bed searched for delayed action mines W.O.I Davies, considering the task too dangerous for his men, undertook the job himself, and in all spent several hours crawling along the mud-stirred bed of the harbour feeling for mines. In so doing, he not only subjected himself to the danger of shell or bomb detonation which, underwater, may be fatal up to a distance of two or three hundred yards, but also to a strong possibility of detonating an enemy laid mine on the harbour bed. This self-sacrificing and courageous act was an inspiration to his diving team which enabled important diving work to be continued regardless of whether the harbour area was under shellfire or not. This work enabled many landing craft to be freed of obstructions wrapped around their propellors, thus

releasing them for further duty at a time when their services were urgently required.

It is pointed out that quite apart from the risks of war, diving always has its attendant dangers, and requires much resolution and clear-headedness. A diver must contend with possible entanglement, the cutting of an air line, physical failure of the diver through breathing difficulties under the high pressure in which he has to work, and other more technical difficulties. It therefore follows that in carrying out the task described, W.O.I. Davies displayed the very highest courage and self-discipline and is well worthy of high award.

(L.G. 21.12.44)

Davies, Richard Llewellyn, Sergeant (ActingWarrant Officer Cl. II (C.S.M.))
3765158, Cheshire Regt.
Sjt. Davies, at one stage, working for three days without sleep showed exceptional endurance and energy in the control and direction of traffic at a vital point on the main up and down road to Brussels. It was only through the resource and initiative shown by this O.R. that the hastily organized traffic in the rapid withdrawal from Brussels was able to move according to scheule on an uncongested road. Throughout nine days at this post he was untiring and an inspiring example to the remaining 60 O.R.'s.

This N.C.O. commanded a machine gun platoon throughout active operations. On 25 May 40 his platoon was detached under the command of 125 Infantry Brigade in co-operation with 5th Bn. Lancashire Fusiliers. His platoon was disposed effectively in covering the approaches to Seclin. During the afternoon, evening, and night on this date, the town was subjected to the most severe aerial bombardment. The town was partially destroyed and a majority of the buildings set on fire. Although his two sections were widely dispersed in buildings on the outskirts of the town Sjt. Davies throughout the evening continued during the air attacks to visit the gun positions and to maintain contact with the infantry troops in the area. His confident leadership and active control were an inspiration to all ranks of this platoon and formed a most effective sub-unit in support of the local infantry. *(L.G. 27.8.40)*

Davies, Sidney George John, Sergeant
553755, 4th Bn. Royal Sussex Regt. (Rustington,
Sussex)
On 28th October, 42, No. 553755: Sergt. Davies was in comd. of a tp. of A/Tk guns, which, with a few infantry were all that remained of his Battalion, after it had been attacked by enemy tanks in a very exposed and isolated position known as 'Woodcock,' and over-run. This small detachment held an advanced position just behind a low ridge at Pt. 33 (Map ref: 8669.2968). Later in the day, four enemy appeared over the ridge and brought heavy fire to bear on the detachment. Sjt. Davies, however ran to one of the guns, and, acting as No. 1. engaged them knocking out three German Mk.III Tanks., and causing

the fourth an Italian M.13, to surrender. His coolness under fire, and his gallant conduct, undoubtedly prevented the enemy tanks from breaking through the position at a spot where its consequences would have jeopardized the safety of the rest of the Brigade.

(L.G. 17.6.43)

Davies, Urias, Warrant Officer Cl. II
2733504, 1st Bn. Welsh Guards (Southampton)
(Immediate)
On 10 Sep 44 when the Prince of Wales Coy. was holding part of the village of Hechtel the enemy put in a very strong counter-attack. No. 3 Coy. who were in front were forced back through Prince of Wales Coy. and a certain amount of confusion occurred. At the time the Coy. Comd. was away from the Coy. at 'O' Gp. C.S.M. Davies did everything in his power to control the Coy. and succeeded in maintaining order. It was very largely due to his efforts that the enemy counter-attack on the Prince of Wales Coy. was unsuccessful and that the Coy. was able to hold its position. Throughout the day his leadership and example were outstanding.*(L.G. 1.3.45)*

Davies, Wallace George, Warrant Officer Cl. II (actg.)
M 15559, Loyal Edmonton Regiment (Immediate)
Reference Map Italy 1/50,000 Sheet 100 II Cesena
On the night 21/22 October 1944, the made a crossing of the Savio River. 'A' Company making the initial assault was to establish a bridgehead approximately four hundred yards deep, centering around a group of houses MR 589099. Two platoons and Company Headquaters succeeded in crossing the river and were met by severe small arms fire, which killed the Company Commander and severely wounded one of the Platoon Officers, and inflicted many other casualties. The enemy counter-attacked immediately and succeeded in forcing the remnants of the platoons back across the river.

Company Serjeant Major Davies, however, after the Company Commander had been killed, rallied company headquarters and gathering in the few men of the two platoons who were left on the enemy side, commenced to dig in and prepare to hold a position on the North bank of the river. His tiny force, consisting of ten men in all, held this position for three hours in the face of persistent efforts by the enemy to drive them off, until the rest of the Company had time to reorganize on the South bank and re-cross the river. At one time during this period they were almost overrun, but Company Serjeant Major Davies rallied them and, inspired by his personal bravery, they made a concerted effort and drove the Germans back. A few minutes later heavy shell fire began to fall on them and continued to do so for a period of almost two hours, but through sheer dogged persistence they held the ground and the bridgehead was safeguarded.

This Warrant Officer by his own personal efforts and the leadership and inspiration he gave to the small force under his command thus saved the bridgehead at a crucial moment and ensured the success of the Battalion's further operations.

(L.G. 17.2.45)

Davies, William, Warrant Officer Cl. II (C.S.M.)
3300434, 1st Bn. Highland Light Infantry
29.5.40. When a part of the Bn was suddenly attacked by enemy A.F.V.'s in an exposed position this W.O. set a high example of courage and leadership. He assisted in organising the defence and then, with complete disregard for his personal safety, he observed the fire of anti-tank rifles to such good effect that the enemy did not press home their attack. Later on receipt of orders to withdraw, C.S.M. Davis commanded one of the rear parties. By his resource and leadership he withdrew his party to safety with few casualties though they were under the fire of enemy infantry & A.F.V.s on several occasions.

(L.G. 11.7.40)

Davis, Denny, Private
5951269, 2/5th Bn. Queen's Royal Regt. (Harefield, Middlesex) (Immediate)
Ca-Menghino (Italy, 1/50,000 Sheet 109 IV 858828). 13 Sep 1944.

On the morning of 13 Sep 1944, during an attack by 'C' Company, 2/5th Bn. The Queen's Royal Regiment, on the village of Ca-Manghino, later supported by tanks, Pte. Davis before their arrival went forward alone armed with an LMG and single-handed attacked several enemy positions and dug-outs, each of which was held by at least a section of five enemy. Sometimes he was operating alone against positions as far as 300 yds ahead of the remainder of the Company.

Although wounded in the side, he insisted on continuing until he had personally [...] in all some six such positions, accounting for no less than 30 prisoners in addition to those he killed and wounded. This private soldier, in his first action, showed the most conspicuous gallantry and initiative. Without thought for his personal safety he gave such an example of individual bravery, skill and determination as to be an inspiration to the remainder of his comrades and a source of intimidation to numerous groups of well-positioned enemy.

(L.G. 8.2.45)

Davis, Herbert Arthur, M.M., Sergeant
5770827, 2nd Bn. Royal Norfolk Regt. (Manchester) (Immediate)
At Kohima, Assam—

For outstanding ability and enterprise as a platoon commander and conspicuous gallantry and devotion to duty, on 4 and 5 May 44. During the advance down Norfolk Spur and the attack on G.P.T. Ridge on 4 May, Sjt. Davis' platoon of 'A' Coy was part of the main body when the remainder of his Coy was left to contain an enemy bunker position. When the advance was checked and in danger of stopping, this N.C.O. was sent to the right flank to make a way through the jungle. Under heavy fire from snipers and L.M.G. he led his platoon into position, accounted for many enemy, and by cool and efficient leadership restored the situation and enabled the advance to continue. During the final assault on the enemy position, Sjt. Davis' personal example, when many of his platoon had become casualties, caused the remainder to carry with the bayonet 2 bunkers which were vital to the defence. On 5 May Sjt. Davis' platoon was under heavy fire and he himself was shot through the leg. He refused to go down until the situation was in hand, and continued to direct his platoon under fire with a cool disregard of danger which inspired his men to a high degree.   *(L.G. 31.8.44)*

Davis, Lewis Albert William, Lance Sergeant
60074, 7 N.Z. Fd. Coy. (Immediate)
During the battle for Cassino L/Sjt. Davis displayed determination, courage and outstanding leadership in completing several difficult and dangerous engineering operations.

On the 16 Mar 44 he made a reconnaissance for a tank route through enemy occupied parts of the town. Though he was persistently sniped and his runner killed he carried on and brought back very valuable information. This was an act of a determined and courageous NCO.

During the night 22/23 Mar 44 his platoon was engaged in replacing an assault bridge on Highway 6 in Cassino, which had been knocked out by enemy shelling. Heavy mortaring caused many casualties among whom were the Field Company Commander and the Platoon Officer. The mortaring increased in intensity and the men were driven from the site. L/Sjt. Davis realised the importance of opening this main communication and by his splendid example and inspiring leadership he soon had the party reorganised and back at work. Despite the heavy and accurate fire he held his men together and calmly went about giving assistance and directions until the bridge was completed and the route opened to tanks.

Throughout the operations in Cassino, L/Sjt. Davis has cheerfully undertaken the most hazardous engineer tasks and his steadiness and devotion to duty have been an example and inspiration to his men.   *(L.G. 3.8.44)*

Davis, Rihimona, Sergeant
25833, 28 N.Z. (Maori) Bn. New Zealand Military Forces (Immediate)
During the battle of Alamein

In the attack on Deir el Munassib on the night 3/4 Sep 42, Sjt. Davis, single handed, attacked and killed the crew of ten manning an 88mm gun. He then used the 88mm gun effectively against the enemy, knocking out two MG posts. When the enemy counter-attacked with grenades and MG fire etc, and while the Coy was in a precarious position, Sjt. Davis used a captured MMG against them effectively. His leadership and control was a potent factor in the success of the attack and the defeating of the counter-attack, and he showed courage and initiative throughout the action.   *(L.G. 5.11.42)*

Davis, Thomas, Warrant Officer Cl. I (R.S.M.)
543028, 10th Royal Hussars, Royal Armoured Corps (Wadhurst)
On 23 Jan, after the first phase of operations S.E. of Antelot, R.S.M. Davis was ordered to tow out and attach an air line to Lieut. Sloan's tank which had been damaged in action. He had connected the line and commenced to tow when the area was attacked by about 30 German tanks. Three German tanks engaged the two tanks but Lt. Sloan's tank could not fire owing to the danger of breaking the air line when traversing the turret. R.S.M. Davis's gunner was temporarily knocked out, but without support he continued the tow, loaded and commanded his tank with complete calm. He put one enemy tank out of action and damaged two others. He brought Lt. Sloan's tank to safety N.E. of Saunnu when his own tank broke down. R.S.M. Davis displayed calmness and courage of the highest degree and showed complete disregard of danger.   *(L.G. 23.4.42)*

Dawes, Byron George, Lance Sergeant
NX 15984, 2/17 Australian Infantry Bn. (Immediate)
On 3 Nov 43 Sergeant Dawes was commanding a section when his company attacked enemy positions near Jivevaneng. From the positions the enemy controlled an important sector for the Satelberg road. During the first few minutes of the attack heavy fire from enemy concealed in dense bamboo cane killed a number of his section, wounded three others and also the platoon commander. Although within 15 yards of the enemy Sjt. Dawes immediately dragged all of the casualties to a position of safety and arranged their evacuation whilst still maintaining the remainder of his section in action. A little later his section was counter-attacked by enemy estimated one platoon strength. Dawes waited until they were within 10 yards then ordered fire which he led with throwing of grenades. A number of the enemy were wiped out and the attack decisively repulsed. Dawes then established himself in a forward position—later found to be only 7 yards from the enemy. Here, despite difficult conditions of flooding rain and much enemy sniping, he continued to harass the enemy vigorously for a period of thirty six hours. During this time he himself threw some 60 grenades, and his offensive action was largely instrumental in forcing the enemy to withdraw and allow the road to be opened. Throughout the whole action Dawes, by his courage, his planned actions and untiring offensive vigour, exhibited outstanding qualities and provided a stimulating example to his Company.
                      (L.G. 23.3.44)

Day, William George, Warrant Officer Cl. II (B.S.M.)
1486714, 16 L.A.A. Regt., Royal Artillery (Maidstone) (Periodic)
At Daba Station at about 2045 hours 8 May 1942 when the station was attacked by enemy bombers, BSM W. G. Day who at that time was Troop Sergeant manned the Bren gun at Troop H.Q. An ammunition train on a

siding was set on fire by enemy action and the shells on it started to explode flying in all directions. BSM. Day continued to man his gun until a bomb exploded near by knocked him down and wounded him in the cheek. When picked up by his officer, he refused medical attention and insisted on continuing to man the Bren gun. Another enemy aircraft then dived low over the position firing its machine guns. BSM. Day showing great coolness engaged the aircraft throughout its dive regardless of further bombs, exploding shells and short range M.G. fire from the aircraft. Tracer was seen to strike the aircraft, a JU 88, which crashed and exploded, all the crew being killed. On subsequent official examination bullet holes were found in the pilots parachute which was still strapped to his back. The high degree of coolness determination and devotion to duty shown by BSM. Day under very trying conditions and his complete disregard for his personal safety, even after being wounded and badly shaken by blast, set an example which is worthy of recognition.   *(L.G. 18.2.43)*

de Nobriga, Derek John, Sergeant
6896540, Queen's Westminsters, King's Royal Rifle
Corps, No. 2 Commando (Pangbourne, Berks.)
(Immediate)
De Nobriga was embarked in HM Submarine Triumph for a Commando raid against the main Messina–Palermo railway. Triumph first attacked the Italian battle-fleet north of Messina, torpedoing the cruiser Bolzano; this was immediately followed by heavy and accurate depth charge counter attack. The submarine withdrew to carry out the Commando raid but, on approaching the shore, encountered a fishing vessel in mist and sank it, having again to withdraw since the gunfire had compromised the position. The next evening, 29th August 1941, Triumph approached and launched the raiding party in canoes. At 0320 hrs 30th August, one and a half spans of the bridge were successfully demolished, but the Commando party could not be re-embarked and were taken prisoner.

De Nobriga showed great courage, determination and resource throughout this eventful and disturbing submarine passage and throughout the successful raid. He was second-in-command of the raid. *(L.G. 11.4.46)*

de Vries, Michael Stanislaus, Private
B19518, The Irish Regt. of Canada (since killed in
action) (Immediate)
On the 24th May 1944, while the Regiment was advancing from the Hitler Line to the Melfa River and was in the area of Objective '2' Private De Vries went out on foot with Major Wallace of 8th Canadian Field Regiment R.C.A. in search of an enemy self-propelled gun. While so engaged he came upon an enemy machine gun post, which he kept under observation until at the right moment he moved in and took six prisoners. Seeing that Private De Vries was alone, five of the enemy tried to escape, at which point he seized their machine gun

and opened fire, killing all five. The sixth prisoner remained covered in the corner of the dug-out and was subsequently brought in as a prisoner by Private De Vries. From this prisoner Private De Vries learned the location of an enemy Nebel-Werfer position which he found, unaccompanied, later in the day. Opening fire, he succeeded in wounding an officer and two other ranks and killing the remaining members of the crew.

On the night of 24th May 1944, the Battalion moved up and took up positions directly behind the Westminster Regiment (Motor) at the Melfa River. On his own initiative Private De Vries went forward across the Melfa and some three or four miles behind the enemy positions. On returning at first light he reported the far bank clear of enemy infantry in any numbers and that only rear-guards of machine guns, snipers, self-propelled guns and tanks would be encountered. He also reported that the enemy was retreating in some disorder and that the main roads to the enemy rear were cluttered with discarded packs and gear. As a result of this information the Battalion was able to move forward at a greater rate than had been planned. The outstanding initiative, superb gallantry and self-sacrificing devotion to duty of this soldier were in keeping with the highest traditions of the Service.   *(L.G. 26.8.44)*

Dean, Bernard Austin, Private
14746241, 1 South Lancashire Regt. (Saltney)
(Immediate)
At Wilders-Hausen on 12 Apr 45 Pte. Dean was a member of a pl detailed to destroy a party of enemy who had cut the main axis between the bn and Bde HQ. During the assault Pte Dean showed great dash and skill in charging the enemy firing his bren from the hip and causing at least four casualties to them. A close quarter fight ensued and Pte. Dean's bren stopped firing owing to lack of amn. Two Germans closed with Pte Dean and he threw his bren at them knocking one out and causing the other to pause long enough for another British soldier to wound him. Dean retrieved his bren and salvaged four magazines from the wounded which included his comd. Pte. Dean took charge of the sec and led them to a group of houses from which the enemy had been firing. During the ensuing brisk and confused close quarter fighting he again showed great determination and coolness in leading his men and this despite the fact that he was wounded when entering the first house. Despite his wound Pte. Dean continued to lead the section, firing his bren and shouting encouragement throughout. Having accomplished his task in clearing the houses and having reorganised his section he handed over his bren and magazines to another soldier and only then did he allow himself to be taken back to the RAP.   *(L.G. 12.7.45)*

Dean, Harold, Lance Sergeant
6093662, 56th Recce Regt., Reconnaissance Corps (St.
Helens, Lancs.)
On 7 April 1943 this N.C.O. was in command of an
L.R.C. Patrol forming part of a troop whose task was to
cover the left flank of the 11 Inf Bde attack on Toukabeur.
At first light the patrol on his right came under heavy
M.G. fire from the forward slopes of the high ground in
front and was held up. L/Sjt. Dean promptly led his patrol
round the flank on to this position and captured the enemy
M.G. crew.

About an hour later an enemy sub-machine gunner
opened up from a concealed position in the vicinity.
Taking one man with him L/Sjt. Dean crawled up to
where the fire came from, surprised the enemy post and
captured five more prisoners. From these he learnt the
location of an A/Tk gun and Machine gun position further
round the hill which was firing on the carriers of the
troop.

L/Sjt. Dean reported this information to his troop
leader, Lieut Edwards, and then accompanied the latter
through heavy fire to the position. Together they captured
18 of the enemy, three heavy M.G.'s and two 50 mm A/
Tk guns. His courage and initiative played a large part
in assisting the advance of the infantry of the right.
Recommended for M.M. (*L.G. 15.6.43*)

Dean, Henry Stanley, Warrant Officer Cl. II (C.S.M.)
6346789, 6 Queen's Own Royal West Kent Regt.
(Johnstone, Renfrewshire) (Immediate)
In the action on 13 Apr 43 at Dj Bou Diss, C.S.M. Dean
showed exemplary coolness and courage as C.S.M. of
D Coy in the hand-to-hand fighting around the summit
of the objective. When the hill was taken he continued
doing valuable work during and after consolidation.

On the previous night he had been with the Coy onto
the same hill, and again the part he played was invaluable.
Three days earlier he led two pls in a counter-attack
against a party of enemy who had infiltrated to within
600-yds of our positions. The attack was entirely
successful, the enemy fled leaving two dead and seven
prisoners, without loss to the Coy.

C.S.M. Dean's untiring energy and sound tactical
knowledge, together with a cheerful disposition at all
times, make his presence in action and at all other times
a priceless boon. As a platoon Sjt he would always
volunteer for patrol work and he has been commended
for his good work on many an occasion.(*L.G. 15.6.43*)

Dean, Robert Frank, Sergeant
5435529, 5 Duke of Cornwall's Light Infantry
(Hanwell, Cornwall) (Immediate)
This NCO carried out a most remarkable patrol with one
pte soldier from 2300 hrs 28 Oct to 0500 hrs 30 Oct 44
into the Reichswald Forest. All previous attempts by
patrols to penetrate into the Reichswald Forest had failed
and it was vital that information be obtained about the
enemy defences. After a short period of careful training

Sjt. Dean with one companion at 2300 hrs on 28 Oct set
off on his dangerous mission. With great skill, patience
and cold courage he moved some 2,200 yds through
strongly held enemy positions and reached the
Reichswald Forest in the early morning of 29 Oct. Once
in the Forest Sjt. Dean spent the whole day collecting
valuable information about the enemy dispositions. Great
risks were taken to collect this information because the
south-western part of the Forest was strongly held and
there was a great deal of enemy activity in the area.

Sjt. Dean having obtained this very important information then returned through the strongly held enemy
positions. When moving down a track through the Forest
he and his companion suddenly came upon a concealed
enemy sentry, seizing an empty ration box apiece and
pretending to be a German ration party they calmly
walked past the hostile sentry. Later, when working
through the open country, the patrol was held up by an
enemy post, using grenades Sjt. Dean disposed of the
enemy and eventually arrived back in our lines at 0500
hrs 30 Oct having been in the enemy lines for 30 hrs.

This successful patrol achieved its object mainly
because of the cold courage, great skill and devotion to
duty of Sjt. Dean. I know of no man who is more worthy
of the DCM than this splendid NCO. (*L.G. 1.3.45*)

Dean, Selby, Private
VX.2002, 2/4 Australian Infantry Bn.
The above mentioned soldier during the Crete Campaign
distinguished himself by his untiring devotion to duty
without thinking of his own personal safety. Pte Dean is
a signaller in Headquarter Coy., and during heavy enemy
air action he continued repairing signalling wires which
had been severed by bombs. He also kept his communications intact with Bn while out on an isolated post under
command of Lieut Kesteven 'B' Coy and it was directly
due to his staying at his post under enemy fire that a
visual message was transmitted to Bn H.Q. giving the
condition of this platoon and information of the enemy
movements. Later it was necessary for the platoon to
stage a bayonet charge in order to avoid being cut off
from the Coy and in this charge Pte Dean distinguished
himself as a fighting member of the unit. On two nights
after this event he volunteered to go out on a dangerous
patrol and his Platoon Commander having confidence
in his courage and high ability as a signaller selected
him for these tasks. (*L.G. 30.12.41*)

Dearlove, William, Sergeant
2560755, 44 Div Sigs., Royal Signals
At both Kruisweg and Ecole D'Esteentje, this N.C.O.
displayed untiring efforts in line laying and maintenance
on the Div. lines, frequently in the face of shell fire.
During the move of the Advance Signals Group from
Esteentje to Godevaersvelde the group was attacked by
tanks near the latter place. Sjt. Dearlove had just
previously gone forward to Mont de Cats to get
instructions as to the final location for the group. Hearing

of the attack he returned to the area in which he had left the group in an endeavour to locate men and vehicles of the gp and bring them in to the Mont de Cats. At considerable personal risk he toured the ... *[continuation missing]*   *(L.G. 11.7.40)*

Deeming, Reginald William, Warrant Officer Cl. II (S.S.M.)
P1579, Royal Canadian Armoured Corps
No citation.   *(L.G. 24.1.46)*

Delebecque, Sidney, Sergeant
2614185, 6th (Motor) Battalion, Grenadier Guards (London, N.8) (Immediate)
During a night attack on the Mareth Line on 16/17 March, 1943, this N.C.O. was Commanding a Carrier Section. When his Company got seriously held up in uncharted minefields it also came under heavy machine gun fire. Sjt. Delebecque took out three carriers through the minefields and with the greatest bravery and presence of mind destroyed two machine gun posts which were holding up his Company.

Within about two hours almost all the carriers had been destroyed on mines and this N.C.O.s Company was in a most precarious position, being surrounded and attacked from all sides. Sjt. Delebecque was ordered to take up a hastily collected platoon of dismounted carrier men in order to relieve the situation. When he arrived in the position he found that only one junior officer was left alive. He with the greatest coolness and personal courage directed the action of his platoon in such a way as to enable the remnants of his Coy eventually to withdraw under extremely difficult circumstances. Had it not been for Sjt. Delebecque's inspiring example and power of leadership it is very doubtful that any of his Company would have got away at all.   *(L.G. 9.8.43)*

Demmy, William, Sergeant
P22238, Princess Patricia's Canadiam Light Infantry (Immediate)
Ref Map Italy 1/50,000 Sheet 147–I Lanciano
On the night 5/6 Dec 43, Princess Patricia's Canadiam Light Infantry attacked and captured the town of Val Roatti (MR 320097). On consolidation B Company was allotted the defence of the Northwest corner of the town.

At 0730 hours the enemy counter attacked heavily with infantry. 10 Platoon, which was under comd of Sjt Demmy, was occupying a house in the forward position of the right flank of the Company. The platoon on the right was overrun and badly cut up, leaving 10 Platoon in a very exposed position. By his personal example, and exposing himself to heavy enemy fire on more than one occasion, Sjt. Demmy rallied his Platoon around the house, despite the fact that the enemy had penetrated to his rear and on both flanks. Enemy fire was directed at his position from a distance of 75 yards from every direction; none the less the position was held and thirty enemy were killed in attempting to dislodge the platoon.

Sjt. Demmy was only able to direct the defence of this position by exposing himself at windows on the ground to heavy fire from machine guns and rifles.

At 1345 hours the enemy counter attacked again from the left with tanks. The house in which Sjt. Demmy was situated was subjected to AP and HE fire from two Mark IV Special Tanks and one A Tk gun and machine gun fire and rifle fire from following infantry. The building was almost totally destroyed. Sjt. Demmy was wounded by falling masonry and stone splinters. When the house was no longer tenable, Sjt Demmy led his Platoon out of the house and, though dangerously exposed, personally sited fire positions for his sections on the left flank. The two tanks were destroyed by our own tanks in the rear, when only 50 yards from his position. Not until all fear of counter attack had passed did Sjt Demmy report himself as wounded.

The example set by Sjt. Demmy's courage and devotion, as well as his superb leadership and determination, inspired his Platoon to hold at all costs a position that was vital to the defence of the Battalion area.   *(L.G. 20.4.44)*

Dennis, Ronald Herbert, Corporal (actg.)
14630808, 1/5th Bn. Queen's Royal Regt. (Gloster) (Immediate)
At Paarlo during the night of 29 Jan '45 the platoon to which L/Cpl Dennis belonged was holding positions in a building when the enemy launched a savage counter attack against the village. This man was in command of a Bren Group on the first floor. After several minutes the enemy fired a 'bazooka' through the window out of which his gun was firing, and wounded the two gun numbers. He assisted the two men down the stairs and into the cellar reporting to his Platoon Comd on the way. As he reached the top of the cellar steps to return to his position he came under direct spandau and bazooka fire from enemy who were actually in the building. This forced him to the bottom of the steps from where he defended the cellar for four hours, shooting up the stairs when the enemy attempted to come down. The enemy hurled many grenades down the cellar, and on several occasions this L/Cpl. was wounded by shrapnel, but he effectively held the enemy off.

During this time he was the only able bodied man in the cellar, the other occupants being wounded and awaiting evacuation. Owing to his misunderstanding an order he heard his Platoon Comd shout he thought the remainder of the platoon had surrendered; notwithstanding this his only reply to repeated enemy demands to surrender was determined fire from his sten.

By great determination and devotion to duty this L/Cpl by his own efforts prevented the enemy entering cellar, and ensured the safety of four wounded men, until a counter attack by another of our platoons restored the situation.   *(L.G. 12.4.45)*

Denvir, John, Corporal
8028, 20th Bn., New Zealand Military Forces
Captured in Greece on the 26th April, 1941 near Corinth. Held as P.O.W. in Corinth May and June. Transported to Maribor, Jugoslavia. On Sept 1st escaped to Zagreb. Was recaptured and returned to Maribor. 21 days solitary confinement. When released from sol confinement looked around for further chances of escape. One came on night Dec 10th, when Denvir, and Australian Colin Cargill from Melbourne and an English marine known only as Ginger buried themselves in a coal truck. Arrived in Ljubljana 14th Dec. Ginger very soon disappeared in Ljubljana—whether he was recaptured or escaped elsewhere Denvir does not know. Cargill was afterward captured and shot by the Italians (towards the end of Feb 1942).

In Ljubljana was told by sympathetic railway men too many Huns in other parts of the country to attempt to reach British forces and advised them to stay and fight with the Partisans (then 120 in all) in the hills. This decided upon.

After death of Cargill, Denvir—afterwards known as 'Frank' to one and all—remained fighting with the Slovene Partisans. Was wounded three times, the last time on Sept 3rd, 1943, at Mackovec near Ljubljana. For some time now Denvir has been Commandant of a Btn. *(L.G. 27.4.44)*

Derrick, Thomas Currie, Sergeant
S X.7964, 2/48 Australian Infantry Bn. (Periodic)
For outstanding leadership and personal courage in action during the initial fighting at Tell el Eisa in July 42 and devotion to duty for the period May to October 42.

Sjt. Derrick has frequently shown outstanding leadership in action and during the initial attack on Tell el Eisa in the early morning of 10 Jul 42 by his own personal courage and leadership attacked and captured three Fiat MG nests. He was personally responsible for the capture of 100 enemy by his cool determination leading his men with great dash and bravery. Later that same night in a counter attack on enemy tks and inf at the Tell el Eisa Ry Sta Sjt. Derrick was outstanding in fighting qualities. He attacked two German tks with sticky bombs damaging both and was a great factor in the successful counter attack which restored the Sta to our forces. On all occasions both in and out of action Sjt. Derrick has been exemplary in his conduct and courage. He has proved himself to be a fine leader and a brave soldier always inspiring his men to follow his example. *(L.G. 18.2.43)*

Deschene, Georges, Sergeant
D.156788, Régiment de la Chaudière (Immediate)
The 24 Apr 1945, early in the morning, Le Régiment de la Chaudière in their third day of continuous fighting, was proceeding from the village of Bunde in Germany, clearing the road leading to Diteumer Verlaat. During the stiff fighting of this day Sjt. Deschenes of 'D' Coy,

particularly distinguished himself by his personal bravery and unusually high standard of leadership.

The advance was limited to the road due to the numerous canals and ditches. The enemy had appreciated the fact and the road was under heavy fire from arty, machine guns and rifle fire. The Coy was particularly unlucky in that the coy comd, and several other officers were killed or wounded. Enemy defensive fire from artillery supplemented by machine gun fire from close range forced the new coy comd to give the order to take cover.

Sjt. Deschenes commanding 18 Pl, divided his pl in small groups and taking the lead conducted each of his grounps in turn through the enemy defensive fire and launched an attack on a series of five houses from which machine gun fire was directed at the Coy. He succeeded in cleaning out these machine gun nests, his platoon suffering many casualties. Once the position was firmly in his hands he returned cooly to Coy H.Q. asking for further orders.

This superb display of leadership on the part of this NCO, permitted the coy to attain their objective which was to secure a start line for the Bn. The initiative, coolness under fire, personal bravery and superb leadership of Sergeant Deschenes, was largely instrumental for the successes of the battalion that day.
(L.G. 22.9.45)

Devlin, George, Corporal (A/Sgt.)
7887993, H.Q. 32 Army Tk Bde., Royal Tank Regt.
Captured at Tobruk on 21 Jun 42. Sent via Benghazi to Munich for interrogation, then returned to Italy and sent via Tuturano, Altamura and Carpi to Campo 78 (Sulmona). While here he attempted in Feb 43 to escape through the main camp gate, dressed as a workman. He was discovered and awarded 30 days cells. In Mar 43 he was concerned in a tunnelling scheme which was discovered when the intending escapers were already dressed for the break-out. They were awarded 30 days cells. A few months later he and another Serjeant were in a tunnelling scheme with some officers. The tunnel was discovered when a donkey put its foot through the entrance, and Devlin received 18 days cells and was threatened with a military tribunal. After the Armistice P/W in Campo 78 were liberated, and after staying about five weeks in the hills, Devlin met three officer escapers from Campo 21, who were organising the escape of P/W and organising their billets, until the three officers were betrayed by a Fascist and had to move to Rome. During December 43 Devlin made three return journeys from Sulmona to Rome conducting parties of P/W. This work was extremely hazardous. Then he stayed in the Sulmona area till 1 Feb 44 when he joined a party of P/W who were guided by an Italian to the British lines, where they arrived on 4 Feb 44. *(L.G. 15.6.44)*

Dick, William Boyd Askings, Sergeant
841454, 1st Bn. Royal Scots (Edinburgh)
At Kohima, Assam on 7th May 1944.

Sjt. Dick displayed great courage and absolute disregard for his own personal safety. The perimeter of the battalion box came under light automatic fire from enemy snipers and Sjt. Dick's platoon was ordered to make an encircling movement and clear the area. The platoon during this action came up against an enemy attack which they themselves promptly engaged.

Sjt. Dick was immediately wounded but remained at the head of his section and, by his personal gallantry, succeeded in breaking up the enemy attack and inflicting severe casualties on them. His exemplary conduct was a superb example to his platoon.   *(L.G. 31.8.44)*

Dingwall, Leonard James, Sergeant
VX 32809, 2/24 Australian Infantry Bn.
For gallant leadership and devotion to duty.

During the attack of night 23/24 Oct Sjt. Dingwall took command when his Pl Comd was wounded and by his personal leadership in the face of very heavy fire enabled his Pl to gain the objective. His coolness and personal direction enabled the Pl to carry out the difficult re-organisation on the flank in the face of heavy fire from unattacked enemy posts on the right flank. During the attack night 25/26 Oct this NCO commanded his Pl, personally leading storming parites against two enemy posts in the teeth of heavy MG fire, killing the occupants and capturing the posts. His fearlessness and utter disregard of danger in these actions filled his men with confidence and his dashing leadership contributed to a large degree to the success of the action.

During the attack on night 30/31 Oct Sjt. Dingwall again commanded his Pl. In this action he personally led his Pl in the assault of three successive enemy strongposts and one Flak gun post capturing all the posts in the face of point blank MG fire, killing and capturing the occupants. Though wounded in this action Sjt. Dingwall continued to lead his Pl until he was unable to carry on any longer. His unhesitating decision in leadership, his cool and utter disregard for personal danger inspired his men with confidence and enabled them to follow his lead and contributed materially to the success of his Coy and Bn in the very severe fighting on the right flank.   *(L.G. 11.2.43)*

Diston, Ralph Foster, Sergeant (A/W.O.II (C.S.M.))
4448907, 9 Durham Light Infantry (Hendon,
Sunderland) (Immediate)
4448907, C.S.M. Diston, R.F. was C.S.M. of the Coy. ordered to seize the redoubt Oerzi Est in the Mareth Line on the night of March 21/22. Throughout the attack C.S.M. Diston showed a complete disregard of danger and magnificent leadership. He personally led many an assault on enemy fortified positions, clearing the numerous trenches and hideouts in the huge redoubt. His inspiring leadership rallied the dwindling numbers of his

Coy. on numerous occasions before the final surrender of the redoubt, and the capture of 120 prisoners had been obtained.

At about 1300 hrs 22nd March, German Infantry and Tanks approached the Redoubt at 200 yds range on three sides. C.S.M. Diston went around the defenders with great coolness, urging them to greater efforts. Finally, their ammunition expended, they were ordered to withdraw. C.S.M. Diston guided them through the only safe exit from the Redoubt back to the Anti-Tank ditch, where he obtained more ammunition and re-organised them.   *(L.G. 17.6.43)*

Dix, Arthur George, Sergeant
5105178, 1/7 Bn. Royal Warwickshire Regt.
(Andoversford, Glos.) (Immediate)
During an action at Butte de Chene (MR 847631) which lasted continuously from the evening of 29 Jul to the morning of 1 Aug 44, Sjt. Dix was a pl comd of 'B' Coy, 1/7 Bn Royal Warwickshire Regiment. This Coy had been ordered to capture and hold the Butte de Chene feature. The enemy position was found to be very strongly held by infantry who were protected by artillery and mortars and whose positions were heavily protected by 'S' mines laid, in depth, along hedgerows.

Sjt. Dix's pl, although suffering many casualties, captured its own objective, but only through Sjt. Dix's inspiring leadership, courage and disregard for his own safety. Sjt. Dix was severely wounded in the back and shoulders during the last stages of the attack, bu remained in comd of his pl.

During the short period of daylight left, Sjt. Dix rapidly set about reorganising and consolidating his position, a task which he carried out without the assistance of his Coy Comd who had been badly wounded. This task, already made difficult by many 'S' mines in the area, was successfully carried out despite the enemy's heavy and continuous counter fire with both mortars and Spandaus which continued throughout the night. Throughout 30 Jul Sjt. Dix's pl was subjected to intensive enemy fire both from small arms and mortars and further casualties were suffered but Sjt. Dix by his frequent visits to his Sections kept up the morale and fighting spirit of the remains of his pl.

During the night 30/31 Jul the new Coy Comd took 'B' Coy and noticing that Sjt. Dix was badly wounded gave orders for him to be evacuated. Sjt. Dix, however, again refused medical aid saying that his 'men needed his presence in order to maintain the efficiency of the pl as a fighting body as the devastating fire of the enemy tended to a certain extent to unnerve them.'

Sjt. Dix, therefore, remained with his pl, which during the night beat off further counter attacks by enemy infantry who had close heavy mortar and Spandau support. It was not until 1st Aug, when the enemy had failed to dislodge his pl, and the situation was quieter, that Sjt. Dix allowed himself to be evacuated.

There is no doubt, whatsoever, that the courage, gallantry, and high standard of leadership displayed by Sjt. Dix, coupled with his total disregard for his wounds and personal safety, resulted in this key portion of the battalion objective being captured and firmly held in our hand. *(L.G. 21.12.44)*

Dixon, Donald, Fusilier
4204835, 7th Bn. Royal Welch Fusiliers (Macclesfield)
In the bridgehead over the R Aller between Rethem and Verden. At 2230 hrs on 13 Apr 45 B Coy 7 RWF were attacking the X rds at 086772, their start line being the fwd edge of the Wood at 085763. Fus. Dixon was manning the Coy 46 set and at H hour crossed the start line with his Coy Comd. Enemy resistance was stiff and shortly after crossing the start line shells fell among the Coy and Fus Dixon was severely wounded. He had lost a leg, one eye and part of an arm. In spite of these injuries and with complete disregard of his condition he continued to operate the set.

At about this time the enemy counter-attacked with inf. For half an hour there was much confused fighting in the vicinity but with great calmness and determination Fus. Dixon still continued to operate his set. A little later when his Coy Comd who had continued forward returned to bring up the remaining elements of the Coy, Fus Dixon spoke to him. Stretcher bearers then appeared but Fus. Dixon directed them to attend to and evacuate another badly wounded soldier before allowing himself to be dealt with. Throughout the whole operation Fus. Dixon showed complete disregard for himself displaying unsurpassed devotion to duty. His great gallantry was a source of strength to those around him and an inspiration to the whole Unit.

Statement by Major W. R. Crawshay, OC B Coy 7 RWF

At 2215 hours on the night of Friday 13th April, B Coy 7 RWF advanced a thousand yards, over open ground covered by enemy fire, to capture the x rds at 086772. During the advance Fusilier Dixon operating the company WT set kept in close proximity to me. I was considerably to the fore of the company controlling the advance, 50 yards to the rear of the creeping barrage. An ill aimed salvo landed amongst the company half way to their objective wounding Fusilier Dixon most seriously: he lost a leg, an eye and half his arm. The company continued towards their objective leaving the wounded on the ground.

When the objective had been gained and the wounded were being located at about 2300 hrs, Fusilier Dixon attracted my attention by coolly saying 'Here I am Sir, I can't get contact and I'm afraid I've lost a leg.' At that moment he was trying to operate his set, and had in fact being doing so during the half hour between his being wounded and located again. When stretcher bearers came up to evacuate the wounded, half an hour later at about 2330 hrs, Fusilier Dixon who was still working his set insisted on another badly wounded man being evacuated

first. The circumstances of the battle necessitated some considerable delay in evacuating Dixon to the RAP. Throughout this period he bore his pain in a manner beyond all praise giving encouragement to the other wounded.

Statement by two Stretcher Bearers 'A' Coy 7 RWF

On the night of 13th April at approximately 2330 hours we were ordered to proceed to B Company and assist with the wounded. There, amongst others, we found one of the company signallers, Fusilier Dixon in a very critical condition. Despite his injuries he remained extremely cheerful throughout and more than once attempted to regain communication with Bn HQ. Although protesting volubly and repeatedly requesting us to go to the assistance of other of his wounded comrades we duly evacuated him to the RAP where his first thoughts were for those of his company still left behind.

Statement by Capt. W. J. W. Wolfe, RAMC, Medical Officer 7 RWF

The a/m Fusilier was evacuated through my RAP at approx 0100 hrs the 14th April 45 suffering from the following wounds:— traumatic amputation right foot, extensive SW left side of face involving left eye, compound fracture left fore arm, small SW left thigh. During his stay at the RAP his conduct was most exemplary—refusing treatment until all others he considered more severely wounded than himself were tended. *(L.G. 2.8.45)*

Dixon, Ronald Henry, Private
633741, 22 N.Z. Bn. New Zealand Military Forces
(Immediate)
During the attack towards the river Senio on the night 14–15 Dec 44, Pte. Dixon's pl sustained heavy cas from both enemy fire and minefields. At a fairly early stage in the attack the Pl Comd and all NCOs were either wounded or killed in a bloody fight for Casa Elta, a natural and well defended strongpoint. In such difficult circumstances, Pte. Dixon demonstrated outstanding qualities of courage and determination. Under hy fire he reformed the remaining personnel of the pl and though out of contact both with Coy HQ and other Pls, led the force onward to the attack. Resistance was soon encountered. Pte. Dixon skilfully deployed his men and cleaned out a defended posn. Again the force pressed on and again resistance was encountered. Pte. Dixon's natural qualities of leadership were equal to the occasion and by the time he had regained contact with the formation on his right—involving a march of several hundreds of yards over hilly and difficult country—he had led his men in the capture of two defended posn, and the silencing of three MG posts and had captured eight prisoners. As soon as contact was established, Pte. Dixon organised his men to assist in the assault on to the final posn.

Pte. Dixon at all times was in complete command of the situation. His personal courage and dash were factors

of the highest importance in the successful work of the
Pl and inspired the men in the performance of work of
unusually high quality.   *(L.G. 21.6.45)*

Dobbins, Thomas Francis, Sergeant
6466544, 5th Bn., The Buffs (Southport) (Immediate)
On the morning of 9th April 1943 whilst part of his
Company was on Pt. 667 (491439), Sjt. Dobbins took
over command of two Platoons and led them into a most
successful bayonet charge against a large number of
enemy who had advanced up the side of the hill. This
attack saved the hill from being taken by the enemy. He
was injured whilst leading this attack. Throughout the
whole battle he was a great source of inspiration to all
the men under his command.   *(L.G. 15.6.43)*

Dockerill, Arthur Harry, Lance Sergeant
940903, Royal Artillery, No. 1 Commando (Ely,
   Cambridgeshire)
On 28th March 1942, during the Commando Raid at St.
Nazaire, France.

L/Sgt Dockerill, as a member of the demolition party
under Lieut Chant's command, assisted his officers and
other members of the party who had been wounded to
climb from the wrecked bows of the destroyer, HMS
Campbeltown, on to the dock side.

L/Sgt Dockerill, carrying Lieut Chant's equipment,
a sixty-pound rucksack, then assisted him to their
objective, the pumping station of the dry dock. This was
done under enemy fire.

L/Sgt Dockerill again assisted Lieut Chant in
descending to the pumping chamber, forty feet below
ground.

His work in this pumping station was magnificent.

He stayed with the officer while the latter fired the
charges, and although the fuses were only set for a minute
and a half, he waited to assist him to climb the stairs to
the ground floor, a difficult feat, as the officer could only
move slowly and it was completely dark. He got Lieut
Chant out with a few seconds to spare before the
explosive blew up.

When the force attempted to fight out of the town
and docks, heavy opposition was encountered. L/Sgt
Dockerill, as a forward scout, armed with only a colt
automatic and grenades, assisted in leading the force
through the streets in quick time.

When he ran out of ammunition and grenades he used
his fighting knife and inflicted many casualties on the
enemy.

L/Sgt Dockerill was outstanding in his courage and
devotion to duty. Throughout the entire action he showed
a total disregard for his own safety.   *(L.G. 5.7.45)*

Dodds, George Macmillan, Sergeant
10910, 26 Rifle Bn., New Zealand Military Forces
Lieut. Midd was wounded on Nov. 24 when Sjt. Dodds
assumed command. During the attack on Sidi Rezegh
aerodrome on Nov 25 he acted with great coolness and

was an inspiration to his platoon. During the attack on
Sidi Rezegh on the night 26/27 Nov. Sjt. Dodds lead his
platoon forward under heavy M.G. fire with excellent
judgment and consolidated on his objective. He then, on
three separate occasions, personally went forward and
contacted our troops forward and on our flanks, this under
extremely heavy fire from MG and mortar. The
information he brought back was essential to his Coy.
Commander.

Throughout the campaign he showed complete
disregard of personal danger, while his one thought was
for the comfort and safety of his men.   *(L.G. 20.1.42)*

Donaghy, William, Corporal (A/Sgt.)
3771256, 6th Bn. Cheshire Regt. (Liverpool 11)
(Immediate)
Sjt. Donaghy was a M.G. Sec Comd during the attack
on Montecorvino airfield soon after the landing in the
Gulf of Salerno on 9 Sep 43. The attacking troops were
heavily outnumbered and were counter attacked by tanks
and heavy mortar and M.G. fire. Although seriously
wounded he remained with his guns, giving fire orders
with great deliberation, and obtaining excellent fire
effect. His courage and leadership were instrumental in
delaying the enemy for a considerable time, and enabling
other troops to reorganise successfully. When his own
section was ordered to withdraw, his wounds were such
that he had to be assisted from the position. In spite of
this he continued to direct the withdrawal, to encourage
the men, and organise a new section position. Throughout
the whole action he showed leadership and courage of
the highest order and exceptional devotion to duty.
                                       (L.G. 13.1.44)

Donald, James, Corporal (A/Sgt.)
2984507, 1st Bn. Cameronians (Renton) (Immediate)
This N.C.O. was in command of No. 7 Platoon 26
Column. He was ordered to counter attack a position in
'Clydeside' on the evening of 24 May against a position
strongly held by the enemy. He led the attack with dash
and determination, and although wounded early in the
engagement in the back and the arm continued to rally
his men. By his display of personal courage, the attack
succeeded in destroying one heavy machine gun, one
LMG and 20–30 Japanese.

On the morning of 19th April 1944 at Pt SC 235311
whilst the Column was engaged in blocking the road
Pinlebu—Pinbon. After the Column had made a most
successful ambush on an MT Convoy, the enemy
attacked the Column and blocked the selected line of
withdrawal for the column. Sjt. Donald's platoon
attacked this position, and by his example and complete
disregard for his personal danger, enabled the column to
make an entirely successful withdrawal, suffering no
casualties. Apart from this incident, Sjt. Donald has time
without number been an inspiration to all the Column
by his steadiness and cheerfulness under fire. He has
commanded a rifle platoon since the commencement of

operations and set a standard of military efficiency and leadership equalled only by a few officers.

Recommended for D.C.M. for conspicuus gallantry and outstanding leadership in the Field. *(L.G. 31.8.44)*

Donlan, James Michael, Lance Corporal
3454040, 9th Bn. York & Lancaster Regt.
(Manchester)
Arakan.

On the night 11/12 Jan 45, at Yoneom on the Kaladam river, L/Cpl. Donlan was stationed on the river front with the boats containing the Bn's stores: he was Signal Storeman. At midnight his area was strongly attacked by Japanese infantry from the land side, and by armed and armoured Jap naval craft from the river. L/Cpl. Donlan took over a Bren gun from a casualty. Mounting it precariously on the side of an unarmoured, grounded boat he engaged the approaching Japanese landing craft. Holding his fire until certain to kill in the darkness, he caused great execution. One of the Jap ships started to use a searchlight to pick out its targets, and brought a MMG to bear on L/Cpl. Donlan. L/Cpl. Donlan shot out the light which never lit again. He thereby certainly saved many certain casualties. He eventually became the only fire of anautomatic on the beach, and although wounded in the arm and shoulder he continued to fire calmly until the Japanese departed, and his ammunition was expended. His most resolute action prevented the situation becoming out of hand, which it threatened to occur at one moment. Furthermore his calmness under fire and disregard for his own injuries steadied his comrades in a remarkable way, despite the numerous casualties which occured among them. *(L.G. 22.3.45)*

Donnett, Allan Hugo, Sergeant
NX 42848, 2/2 Australian Infantry Bn.
For most distinguished conduct and outstanding leadership in an attack on the enemy-held village of Rindogim, New Guinea, on 4 August 1945.

D Coy of 2/2 Aust. Inf. Bn. were ordered to capture Rindogim, a native village situated on a narrow ridge rising 500 feet above the surrounding country. The only approach to the village was via a native track which followed a steep narrow spur running from the gorge to the ridge above. The leading platoon had climbed about 100 feet when they came under heavy enemy machine gun and rifle fire from concealed dug in positions.

Sjt. Donett, as platoon serjeant, was at the rear of the platoon. Immediately the enemy opened fire, without awaiting his platoon commander's orders, he moved forward and reconnoitred the position. Noticing that his platoon commander and the leading section were unable to move without being fired on he moved the reserve section to a flank and directed their fire to neutralize the enemy. Then, single-handed he charged the enemy position throwing grenades into their fox-holes and firing bursts after burst from his sub-machine gun. He killed four of the enemy and the remainder, numbering about

twenty five, fled in panic. Calling on the platoon to follow him, he pursued them, shouting orders in complete disregard for the fact that he was disclosing his position and drawing enemy fire. He continued at the head of his platoon and organised its consolidation on a knoll which dominated the village of Rindogim.

His superb courage in the face of overwhelming numbers, his outstanding leadership and unhesitating decision to maintain offensive action enabled his company to secure the heights and thus capture the objective. *(L.G. 10.1.46)*

Donovan, James Trevor, Sergeant
22770, 21st Battery, New Zealand Military Forces
(Immediate)
This N.C.O. was captured at Atlante, 25.4.41, and taken to Corinth. On 13.6.41 he escaped in transit to Salonika, but was recaptured at Volos on 26.6.41. He again escaped, this time killing his guard with a piece of wood. He was recaptured on 25.7.41 at Lamia and taken to Salolnika where he was given a period in the cells to teach him not to escape again. However, he escaped on 21.9.41 and made his way to Lanoros where he met other escapers, including Dvr. Sam War, 292 Coy., R.E. and Pte. Thomas Bevan, 1/The Welsh Regiment, who have also been recommended for recognition of their particularly fine effort. They stole a boat and after 22 days' rowing reached the island of Lemnos, where they spent two days and then rowed on to Imbros. Here they were taken by Turkish police to the mainland and eventually reached Ismir. Sjt. Donovan showed the most indomitable courage in escaping three times in the face of tremendous odds and great hardship. *(L.G. 26.3.42)*

Dooley, Martin, Bombardier (ActingSergeant)
1017735, 13th A/T. Regt., Royal Artillery
On the afternoon of 30 May 1940, Serjeant Dooley's anti-tank gun was subject to heavy and continuous small arms and mortar fire from German positions on the far bank of the canal. The position had to be held for another two days in order to cover the withdrawal and embarkation of the rest of the force. Sjt. Dooley held the position with his small detachment of five men and one bren gun, sniping every one in view till 1000 hours on the morning 1st June 1940, when penetration round his flanks made the position untenable. By his determined assistance carrying out an infantry role and by his stirling leadership Sjt. Dooley's action cosiderably influenced the whole course of the battle. *(L.G. 20.12.40)*

Dorans, Peter, Corporal
2753451, King's Regt. [Black Watch on AFW 3121]
(Callander, Perthshire) (Immediate)
At Hintha on 28th March, 1943, he was in charge of a small post holding a track along which a new attack was expected. Although he had only a handful of men with him, he considered that he would present a less vulnerable target and a more effective defence with still

fewer. He therefore, collected grenades off some of his men and reduced his party to two besides himself. When the expected attack came in, carried out by twenty to thirty Japanese, he threw grenades with great effect, carrying on with his rifle when these were exhausted, and completely broke up the attack, which was never resumed in this sector. At least eight bodies were observed to his immediate front, and more might have been seen by daylight. During the march to the Chindwin, though suffering from fever and other complaints, he remained cheerful as ever and was instrumental in encouraging weaker men not to give in. His fortitude was of real benefit to the whole column. Cheerful and tireless at all times, he was always to the fore whether in or out of action, and was of the utmost value in inspiring and controlling young soldiers. He was by common consent the finest N.C.O. in the Column. *(L.G. 5.8.43)*

Dornton-Duff, Charles Brian, M.M., Sergeant
1398040, 11 (H.A.C.) Regt. Royal Horse Artillery
Captured South of Mersa Matruh on 29 Jan 42. Sent via Benghazi, Bari and Brindisi to Campo 70 (Monturano). Dornton-Duff escaped from the column of prisoners at Mersa Matruh, but was recaptured after three days. On 12 Jul 43, in company with another N.C.O., he escaped from Campo 70. They attached themselves to a working party, hoping to escape from outside the camp; on finding this impossible, they hid inside the camp until the Guards were having their midday meal, then cut their way out through the wire. They made for Switzerland, but after walking 120 miles they were recaptured on 22 July and taken back to camp, where they were beaten up. After the Armistice P/W were not allowed to escape from Campo 70, but the Senior British Officer gave permission for Dornton-Duff and three other N.C.O.s to watch the main road for the Germans' approach. After reporting to the camp by telephone they disobeyed orders to return, and made South independently. Dornton-Duff reached British Forces at Lucera on 1 Oct 43. Sjt. Dornton-Duff is reported by Sjt. Connolly, also an escaper from Campo 70, as having displayed outstanding morale and made many attempts at escape by digging tunnels etc.
(L.G. 27.4.44)

Dowds, J. P., Flight Serjeant
553789, 83 Sqn., R.A.F.
Flight Sergeant Dowds was navigator of a Manchester aircraft detailed to bomb Cologne on 13th March, 1942. While on the outward flight, the aircraft was shot down over the Dutch–German frontier and the crew were ordered to bale out. Flight Sergeant Dowds landed in a small wood where he disposed of his parachute. Thinking he had come down in Holland, he spoke to a man standing at the door of a house and was asked in. Shortly afterwards however, the police arrived and he was arrested. He was taken to Amsterdam via Utrecht and later to a prisoners' camp at Oberursel. From this camp he was transferred to a second camp at Lamsdorf where

he made his first attempt to escape. On this occasion he and a companion were at large for seven days before they were recaptured. On his return Flight Sergeant Dowds was ill-treated by one of the German officers and sentenced to 21 days imprisonment. On being released he was chained in common with other British prisoners at that time. He remained at this camp until April, 1943, part of the time in hospital. Immediately on his release from hospital he planned and executed another attempt to escape. Posing as a Belgian worker he joined another British prisoner with whom he travelled to Brieg, where they separated. From Brieg, Flight Sergeant Dowds managed to reach Breslau by train and still passing as a foreign worker, got as far as Frankfurt-an-der-Oder. Being afraid of identity being checked in the vicinity of Berlin he then worked round by rail to Stettin where, after many hardships and setbacks, he managed to board a ship manned by a number of Danish sailors. Off the Danish coast he persuaded five of these Danes to desert, and, stealing the ship's life boat, they proceeded to make for Swedish territory. They reached Riga (Flight Sergeant Dowds remaining hidden in the forecastle) and finally left for Limhavn which they reached on 19th September, 1943. Here they were taken by the police to a gaol in Malmo. Ultimately Flight Sergeant Dowds was taken to the British Consul at Malmo and afterwards left for Stockholm, eventually returning to this country.

Dower, Sammy Joseph Edward, Lance Corporal
812051, D.M.R., Union Defence Force (Periodic)
For outstanding courage and devotion to duty at most times under fire near Acroma from 23 May 42 to 19 Jun 42. The courageous and able manner in which Cpl. Dower performed his task as NCO in charge of a gun crew of an 88 mm gun although he had not been trained in the use of this weapon is worthy of the highest praise. It was largely owing to Cpl. Dower's calmness and courage under enemy fire that several attacks of the German tanks were beaten off. During these attacks the 88 mm gun was responsible for the complete destruction of four enemy tanks and a further three were damaged and put out of action. This was mainly due to the gallantry and devotion to duty of L/Cpl. Dower. *(L.G. 19.12.46)*

Dowley, James Morrell, Sergeant
836123, 91st Field Regt., Royal Artillery
On 28th May, 1940, at St. Eloi. As only two tractors were in action so two guns had to be left behind. After our infantry had withdrawn and whilst under heavy machine gun fire, Sergt. Dowley remained alone to dismantle the breech mechanism of these guns. This he did successfully but before he could withdraw he was shot at close quarters and seriously wounded. An hour later the position was temporarily retaken by our own troops and Sergt. Dowley was brought in. Throughout the operations Sergt. Dowley set a fine example of coolness and devotion to duty. *(L.G. 20.12.40)*

Down, Alan, Sergeant
*322041, 102 (N.H.) A.Tk. Regt., Royal Artillery
(Ashington)*
Sjt. Down has been the No 1 of a 6-pr gun since the initial assault on 6 June. On night of 8 June in St Leger area the enemy were causing considerable casualties by sniping. Without orders or encouragement Sjt Down went out several times with a Bren gun, killed at least one sniper and silenced three others. In St Terre area on 9 June his gun was in support of 8 DLI when the enemy put in a determined attack with infantry and tanks and the forward infantry company was over-run, our own tanks having been withdrawn to hull-down positions. The infantry company who were in the area of Sjt Down's gun position decided to withdraw and ordered Sjt Down's gun detachment to accompany them. Sjt. Down refused as there were tanks about and his duty was to stop the tanks. He killed the only tank that appeared. Sjt Down's courage and example undoubtedly helped greatly to restore the confidence of the infantry at this critical moment, with the result that the situation was re-established and the position re-organised. On the same day Sjt. Down was ordered to take his gun forward to destroy an enemy SP gun which was causing casualties. Although commanding a carrier-drawn 6-pr whereas the enemy had a 75mm or 88mm gun in an armoured chassis, he nevertheless carried out a rapid recce, occupied a position unobserved and destroyed the gun. On 10 June when an enemy tank closed on the position under cover Sjt Down was unable to move his gun into action in a suitable place. However, not to be outdone he obtained his Piat, stalked the tank and engaged it at 30 yards range—obtaining a hit which turned the tank back.

(L.G. 31.8.44)

Downing, John Thomas, Sergeant
795225, Royal Artillery
No citation.   *(L.G. 11.7.40)*

Doyle, Benjamin Thomas, Sergeant
7880550, 7th Bn. Royal Tank Regt.
On the 21st May, 1940, the 7th Bn. Royal Tank Regt. was engaged in an action to delay the advance of the German Armoured Divisions, and to relieve the pressure on the British Garrison in Arras. Early in the action, 'B' Coy. Comdr. (myself) and Sergeant Doyle's Section (4 Matilda II Tanks in all) became heavily engaged with a German Anti-Tank Battery. All four of the enemy guns and two Matilda II Tanks, were put out of action, leaving two Matildas commanded by Sergeant Doyle and myself. Behind this German Battery, small parties of Germans with machine guns, who had been maintaining an intense fire on the Tanks, rose from cover, and retired as the Tanks reached their positions.

There must have been about 150 men in all, and they were practically all knocked out by the M.G.s of the two Matildas. The two Tanks then went to the assistance of five Matilda Tanks Mark 1, which were armed only with machine guns, and were in difficulties with four German Medium Tanks, armed with cannon. Sjt. Doyle and I, knocked out these four German Tanks, and left them burning, killing those of the crews who attempted to escape. A little later, we ran up against another German 4 Gun A. T. Battery, and these guns were all put out of action. Sergeant Doyle, under intense fire, going straight for one gun and running over it. Both Tanks now had fires in the forward tool-boxes, and had to repeatedly open the top covers, to avoid suffocation by fumes. Whilst taking a breather myself, I saw Sergeant Doyle doing the same thing with smoke pouring out of his open top cover. I also noticed that his 2 pounder gun was pointing at me, that is to his left, and surmised that his turret had been jammed by hits on the turret ring, as had my own. Shortly after this engagement, on reaching the crest of rising ground, I came on a German 88mm A.A. Gun about 20 yards from the track on which I was moving. He depressed on to me, but before he could fire, I was able to run between two high banks, which bordered the track here, for about 200 yards.

My turret was jammed with the gun pointing to the right rear and the 88mm gun was on the left of the track. As we moved out of cover my driver swung the tank and brought the gun on to the target. Almost simultan-eously Sjt. Doyle, who had appeared on the crest behind, quickly grasped the situation, swung his tank and opened fire.

He scattered the crew with his machine gun and then shelled the gun with his 2 Pounder, thus relieving, what was for me, a critical situation. I halted and opened my top cover and my tank then flared up inside and we had to get out.

Sjt. Doyle moved up and showed me his right hand which was minus the two centre fingers, these having been shot away on one of the occasions when he had opened his top cover to get air. His tank was still emitting smoke and he told me his driver couldn't stick the heat and fumes much longer. He also told me his turret had been jammed in the action with the second A.T. Battery and that all his periscopes were shattered. I gave him my map and told him to carry on to the rallying point as quickly as he could, and off he went. I met him again two days later as a prisoner at Cambrai. I consider he behaved in a very gallant manner and showed exceptional devotion to duty throughout the afternoon's battle.

(L.G. 21.6.45)

Doyle, Harold Robinson, Private
3301080, 5 Gordon Highlanders
See Corkery, William   *(L.G. 4.11.41)*

Drake, Harold Walter [Harold Walter George on AFW 3121], Sergeant
*5183848, 43rd Recce Regt, Reconnaissance Corps
(Gloucester) (Periodic)*
Throughout the campaign in North West Europe Sjt. Drake has commanded an armd car with outstanding

courage and ability. He has taken part in every battle fought by his Troop, and in Normandy in 1944 and in Holland and Germany from Feb to May 1945 was almost continuously in action. He has proved himself an inspiring leader and probably the finest sjt commanding an Armd Car in his Sqn. The following incidents are but typical of many others in which Sjt. Drake displayed great coolness and indifference to danger.

On 1 Mar 45 Drake's car was moving behind his Tp Ldr's car northwards from the village of Appeldoorn near Calcar. The Tp was moving by moonlight helped by the reflected light of a searchlight, with the task of finding out as much information as possible of the enemy positions, and of harrying the enemy in order to force him to withdraw. Suddenly the Tp Ldr's car came under heavy close-range Spandau fire. Sjt. Drake at once manœuvred his car to a flank and brought fire to bear on the enemy position enabling his Tp Ldr to withdraw slightly. Almost at once several enemy positions opened up, firing at Sjt. Drake's car. Sjt. Drake returned the fire, but his Besa jammed. Sjt. Drake at once used his Bren, firing it from the top of his car heedless that he was thereby exposing himself to the enemy fire. He continued to engage the enemy until he was satisfied that he had pin pointed the enemy positions. The accurate information obtained was of the very greatest assistance to his CO in the further conduct of the battle, and the fact that when the attack was mounted the following morning, the enemy withdrew at once, was undoubtedly due to this bold probing attack on the previous night.

On 8 Apr 45 Sjt. Drake was commanding the leading car of his Tp which was recce-ing forward along [...]men road from Lingen. As he approached the village of Bawinkel he [...] enemy position which he at once engaged. Then with his car all the [...] exposed to enemy fire, he directed mortar fire on to the position and forced the enemy to withdraw to the village. A little later the Tp moved on into the village, Sjt. Drake's car then being second. At the far side of the village the leading car was hit by a bazooka fired at close range. Sjt. Drake at once engaged the enemy position enabling the driver of the leading car to extricate his car. Sjt. Drake then, despite the fact that he was close to the enemy position in a village and liable to be stalked by a bazooka at any moment, continued to engage the enemy position until a supporting infantry platoon working round on a flank assaulted and destroyed it. This covering fire given by Sjt. Drake was a prime factor in the success of the operation and was largely responsible for the fact that the infantry suffered no casualties.   *(L.G. 24.1.46)*

Drapeau, René, Sergeant (A/C.Q.M.S.)
D51078, Royal 22e Regt., Canadian Infantry Corps
    (Immediate)
On 30 Jul 43 at Hill 204 near Catenanuova, Sicily, Sergeant Drapeau, a platoon Sergeant, was forward with the leading section which was commanded by Lance Corporal Gagnon. Under the covering fire of this section,

Sergeant Drapeau and Lance Corporal Gagnon rushed an enemy anti-aircraft post, throwing hand grenades as they went. They killed the crew who had been firing on our advancing troops and transport.

Locating an enemy 105 mm gun, which was also firing on our troops, in position 100 yards South of them, Drapeau assisted Gagnon in trying to train the anti-aircraft gun on the 105 mm, but they were unable to do so owing to limited traverse. These two Non-Commissioned Officers then advanced to within assaulting distance of the gun position, covering each other as they went. Sergeant Drapeau then skilfully furnished covering fire with his rifle, while Lance Corporal Gagnon assaulted the position. Throughout this entire action, Sergeant Drapeau was under enemy light machine gun fire. This Non-Commissioned Officer displayed coolness, bravery and determination of a high order.   *(L.G. 23.12.43)*

Drapeau, René, D.C.M., Warrant Officer Cl. II (C.S.M.)
                                                      Bar
D51078, Royal 22e Regt., Canadian Infantry Corps
Reference Map Italy 1/100,000 Sheet 160 Cassino.

On 19 May 1944, the Royal 22e Regiment attacked the Adolf Hitler line in the area MR 746179. D51078 Company Serjeant Major Drapeau was Company Serjeant Major of 'B' Company.

After the leading companies had secured the first objective, 'B' Company passed through on the left and advanced, supported by armour, toward the Adolf Hitler line. They came under intense fire and three tanks were knocked out by a 105mm gun in a concrete and steel pillbox. The company was being prepared to attack this post when the company commander was badly wounded. The three platoon commanders were also killed or wounded and Company Serjeant Major Drapeau took charge of the company. Communication had been lost with Battalion Headquarters. This Warrant Officer, unable to get instructions, went forward and reorganized his platoons which were very disorganized as a result of the heavy fire. As he was proceeding with the task, a shell landed nearby killing one man and throwing this Warrant Officer several feet.

Although badly shaken, Company Serjeant Major Drapeau continued to reorganize his company personally visiting all section positions. At this stage an enemy counter attack developed which was repelled, due chiefly to the efforts of Company Serjeant Major Drapeau who moved conbtinuously from post to post, encouraging his men and directing the fire. The company successfully held this position until communication was established with Battalion Headquarters and they were ordered to withdraw. Tired and suffering from the effects of blast, Company Serjeant Major Drapeau led the company in an orderly withdrawal to the new area. Here he was evacuated suffering from exhaustion. Throughout the attack Company Serjeant Major Drapeau set a courageous example for his men. His devotion to duty, cheerfulness and leadership were outstanding, and an inspiration to all who were with him. *(L.G. 30.9.44)*

Drew, Ronald Arthur [Leslie Charles on AFW 3121], Corporal
VX 72101, 37/52 Australian Infantry Bn. (Immediate)
On 9 Dec 43 at Tunom R map reference Fortification Point 1:25000 601750, Cpl. Drew of 16 Platoon D Company was ordered to move his section up a razorback ridge, his objective being the high ground at the top of the ridge. The precipitious and broken nature of the country made movement extremely difficult, great physical effort being required to climb to any point from which fire could be brought to bear with advantage on the enemy positions. The section was under continuous fire through out its advance up the ridge and on nearing its objective encountered the main enemy force, estimate one company strength. The platoon commander was killed and other casualties were sustained.

The enemy believing the advance to be temporarily halted counter attacked down the ridge. Cpl Drew moved forward, took the Bren Gun from the wounded Bren gunner climbed to the top of the ridge, exposing himself fearlessly to the heavy enemy fire. Firing from the hip he killed the first four enemy and succeeded in halting and breaking up the enemy attack. By the prompt and courageous action and initiative shown by Cpl. Drew the platoon was able to move forward and occupy ground vital to the attainment of its objective. *(L.G. 23.3.44)*

Drewett, Charles Eric, Corporal (A/Sgt.)
6092915, 2/6 Bn. Queen's Royal Regt. (London, S.E.16) (Immediate)
On 29 Jan, 44, 'C' Coy, 2/6 Queen's Royal Regt and 'D' Coy, 2/5 Queen's Royal Regt (under Cmd 2/6 Queen's) were ordered to attack a rocky ridge on the Ceracoli feature and then advance about 500 yds to the top of a spur. 'D' Coy 2/6 Queen's was positioned below the enemy position ready to move forward and pass through the leading coys when they reached their objective.

The two leading Coys advance was held up by stiff enemy opposition from at least four posts sited in depth in prepared sangers, so Sjt Drewett's Pl was sent off to knock out the nearer of these positions.

Sjt. Drewett moved his Pl at great speed over the extremely difficult country and by skilful use of ground was right on top of the nearest position in the matter of a few minutes. Sjt. Drewett then proceeded to lead the assault against the three sangers which opposed him. The speed at which he moved and the determination with which the attack went in completely overwhelmed the resistance, Sjt. Drewett himself killing two enemy.

Sjt. Drewett then proceeded to reorganise his Pl and take part in a general advance which was now made possible by his action. He led the left flank of this advance for about 400 yds overrunning further sanger posts and mopping up snipers.

Throughout, Sjt. Drewett showed an entire disregard for his own safety, and at the same time he manœuvered his Pl in the most skilful manner. His determination, personal courage and ability as a leader were responsible for the success of this action which led to a capture of a position which would have been of vital importance had the attack by the Bn on the right succeeded.
(L.G. 4.5.44)

Driscoll, David, Corporal (A/Sgt.)
2191210, Auxiliary Military Pioneer Corps
No citation. *(L.G. 3.9.40)*

Druce, Tazonia Dennis Edward, Sergeant
4129446, 6th Bn. Cheshire Regt. (Street, Som.) (Immediate)
On 18 Feb 44 in the Anzio beachhead, Sjt. Druce commanded a MMG section in support of 8 RF. His guns were engaging a target in their arc, when the section was attacked from the rear by a Platoon of enemy who had approached unseen through very close country. The enemy attacked with grenades and automatics from a range of about 15 yards. Sjt. Druce immediately engaged them with his rifle, killing two and wounding four others. Sjt. Druce, although wounded by a pistol grenade, continued to engage the enemy, causing them to check their advance long enough to enable the section to engage them with MMGs, when they were driven off. Sjt. Druce remained in action with his Section throughout the remainder of the day, displaying coolness and courage of the highest degree. *(L.G. 15.6.44)*

Drummond, Patrick, Warrant Officer Cl. I (R.S.M.)
3237516, 2nd Bn. Cameronians
Throughout the operations between 11th and 31st May, 1940 this Warrant Officer showed a fine example of cool leadership, and performed many duties outside his normal province. In particular near Wytschaete on the 27th May, 1940 when the Battalion was closely engaged with the enemy, he took charge of a small party of men for the protection of Battalion Headquarters which was in danger of being outflanked. On another occasion acting entirely on his own initiative he obtained and distributed a hot meal to the forward Companies at a time when the approaches to the front line were under heavy fire.
(L.G. 27.8.40)

Dryborough-Smith, Ernald Keith Norman, Sergeant
6844664, King's Royal Rifle Corps (Salisbury)
No citation. *(L.G. 20.9.45)*

Dryburgh, Thomas Henderson, Sergeant
3187762, 4 King's Own Scottish Borderers (Berwick-on-Tweed) (Immediate)
On 3 Apr 45 D Coy was fwd coy in an attack on Ibbenburen where a most determined enemy were holding strong positions in houses on the outskirts of the town. Sjt. Dryburgh was comd the fwd pl and after

moving fwd into open ground from cover of a wood, the pl was heavily engaged by small arms fire from the left front and suffered cas. At great personal risk Sjt. Dryburgh org his pl and led them through the only available cover—a very shallow ditch—towards his own objective, a group of houses firmly held by the enemy. Almost immediately the pl was subjected to further small arms fire and then came under point-blank bazooka fire which caused further cas. Owing to remainaing pls being fully committed elsewhere, no immediate sp could be given and the situation was of a nature which called for supreme leadership and the skilful use of available wpns. Sjt. Dryburgh reorg his pl with remarkable coolness and determination and, although still under very heavy enemy small arms fire, he finally assaulted and captured his objective. In spite of several determined enemy counter attacks the posn was firmly held until the pl was finally relieved. This NCOs splendid leadership and complete disregard for his personal safety was an inspiration to the men under his comd, and undoubtedly enabled the pl to secure and hold an important objective under the most hazardous conditions.   *(L.G. 12.7.45)*

Dualeh, Adan, Sergeant
1096, Somaliland Camel Corps, attd. Force H.Q.
   Signal section
Somaliland. 11th August—18th Ausut 1940. For highly meritorious service.

   This Somali N.C.O. showed great devotion to duty throughout the period of operations. During the latter stages he was in charge of the wireless set working with the Somaliland Camel Corps patrol watching the coast road from Zeila. When the enemy approached he was instructed to move independantly from the patrol. He handled his set with skill and courage, and was thereby successful in maintaining contact with both his patrol and Force Headquarters.
To be dated 11.2.41 and substituted for the award of the African D.C.M. announced in the L.G. of that date.
                        (L.G. 21.7.42)

Duddle, Joseph McPhee, Warrant Officer Cl. II (C.S.M.)
K.37029, Seaforth Highlanders of Canada
   (Immediate)
Reference Map, Italy, 1/100,000 Sheet 160 Cassino.

   On 23 May 1944, during the attack on the Adolf Hitler Line (in the area MR 7419) by the Seaforth Highlanders of Canada, all officers of 'C' Company had been killed or wounded.

   K–37029 Company Sergeant Major Joseph McPhee Duddle immediately took command of the company, reorganized it, added some leaderless men from 'A' and 'D' companies, and led it forward. As it advanced the forward elements were held up by shelling and machine gun fire from a tank located two hundred yards away on the right flank. Company Sergeant Major Duddle led two men with a Piat over open country swept by machine gun and shell fire to a vantage point thirty yards from the tank. Two shots were fired and the tank was knocked out. Company Sergeant Major Duddle then returned to the company, and again led it forward under intense mortar and shell fire to the objective MR 737192 and consolidated two hundred yards beyond it. During the advance several enemy posts were knocked out and two prisoners taken. Soon realizing that without supporting arms the company was in danger of being cut off by enemy tanks, he withdrew to the objective.

   Here he contacted Major J. C. Allan the only remaining officer of the four rifle companies, and consolidated his company. At approximately 1600 hours Company Sergeant Major Duddle was informed that there were still some 'C' company men ahead of the objective. Without hesitation he organized a party and went forward two hundred yards over ground swept by machine gun fire and found nine wounded men. He improvised stretchers from pieces of railing and web equipment and commenced evacuation of the wounded despite heavy mortar fire. At approximately seventeen thirty hours the objective was counter attacked by tanks, and as Company Sergeant Major Duddle and his party were cut off, they were forced to take cover. When the tank withdrew Company Sergeant Major Duddle found Major Allan and many of the survivors wounded, and the position completely disorganized. Ignoring the intense enemy shelling this Non Commissioned Officer organized the evacuation of the wounded and consolidated the remaining eight men on the objective.

   At approximately nineteen hundred hours he was ordered by Battalion Headquarters to return to the firm base MR 753185 which he did, attending to wounded en route and bringing back with him a seriously wounded officer of the North Irish Horse RAC. On arrival he organized a stretcher party of eight men and despite the fact that enemy snipers were still active on the Battalion front and the area was still subjected to shell and mortar fire he returned to the objective. He continued to evacuate wounded until 0100 hours 24 May 1944. The courage and leadership shown by Company Sergeant Major Duddle had a great steadying influence on his men. His cheerfulness at all times and tireless energy were an inspiring example to all ranks.   *(L.G. 30.9.44)*

Dudeck, William Edward, Sergeant
21756, 7 N.Z. Fd. Coy., New Zealand Engineers
Sjt. Dudeck as Section Sjt in a Field Coy has played an outstanding part in the Section's activities since and including Alamein. When his section had the difficult task of gapping the minefields in the Alamein attacks Sjt. Dudeck showed determination and leadership of a very high order, and when laying mines on night 26/27 Oct 42, forward of the 28 NZ Bn he was exceptionally steady in the face of continuous heavy fire. His coolness and gallantry were an inspiration to his men under the most difficult conditions.

After advancing from Alamein Sjt Dudeck was in command of the mine clearing at Halfaya Pass where he was wounded and evacuated to CCS. Before his wound had healed he was back with his section supervising and directing the clearing of mines from the Bardia—Tobruk road.

On the Nofilia—Sultan road though over 600 mines and 'booby' traps were lifted, due largely to Sjt. Dudeck's excellent supervision, and careful organisation, the work was successfully completed without a casualty.

In the move up to Tripoli Sjt Dudeck had command of the Section and as usual displayed energy and courage in lifting packets of mines at road corners, through defiles and adjacent to demolitions particularly in the Sedada—Beni Ulid—Tarhuna area. On occasions this work had to be done with all speed in the face of both heavy shelling and machine-gun fire, and it was due almost entirely to the coolness and personal example of Sjt. Dudeck that the mines and 'booby' traps were lifted to allow the advance to proceed.   *(L.G. 14.10.43)*

Dudgeon, George Sturrock, Lance Sergeant
2698547, 1 Bn. Scots Guards (Dundee) (Immediate)
For conspicuous gallantry and devotion to duty in the Argenta Gap on the 17 Apr 1945.

'B' Company made an attack at the Fossa Marina across the canal to capture some prominent occupied buildings on the North bank. Two previous attempts to force a crossing and establish a bridgehead had failed. Just as the attack started his platoon commander was wounded and L/Sjt. Dudgeon at once assumed command of his platoon.

In the face of heavy spandau fixed lines and accurate mortar DFs this NCO led his platoon across 200 yards of completely flat ground known to be heavily mined and captured his objective. He successfully mopped up the buildings taking several PW, and beat off a counter-attack which developed just in the critical moment of consolidation.

Several hours later his platoon was ordered to advance in broad daylight to the next bund. Despite heavy and accurate spandau and SP gun fire from about 500 yards range, which took its inevitable toll of casualties, he gained his objective by skilful use of the slight cover that existed.

During this action L/Sjt. Dudgeon, by his splendid example of personal bravery and devotion to duty, was an inspiration to his platoon. He rose to the occasion magnificently when his platoon commander was wounded and, despite the fact that they had not had sleep for the two nights prior to the crossing, he kept his men going for two more days under extremely exhausting and tiring conditions. He had gained the confidence of all his men and was largely responsible for the success of his platoon.   *(L.G. 18.10.45)*

Duffy, John, Fusilier
4029338, Royal Northumberland Fusiliers
Aden.

On the 20th June 1967, a Sioux Helicopter of the Queen's Dragoon Guards was detailed to remove a Royal Northumberland Fusilier picquet from Temple hill overlooking Crater. The pilot, Sergeant Ford, lifted one man out on the first run, and returned for the remaining two, Corporal Keithley and Fusilier Duffy, and their radio. Whilst taking off the second time the aircraft came under fire, the pilot was hit in the knee, shattering his kneecap. He tried to continue but lost all tail rotor control and had therefore to put the aircraft back on the ground. The aircraft slid on the flat ground and over the edge of a gully below where it burst into flames. In the crash Fusilier Duffy was slightly hurt but Corporal Keithley lost a leg, severed below the knee, and had the other leg completely shattered. Fusilier Duffy, under fire, despite the fact that the aircraft was burning, with the danger of a fuel explosion, helped the pilot out of the wreckage clear of the aircraft. He then returned to the aircraft and dragged Corporal Keithley away. He returned a third time, retrieved the radio from the wreckage, set it up and informed his base about the incident.

But for Fusilier Duffy's action, both Sergeant Ford and Corporal Keithley would certainly have perished in the wreck. His action with the radio resulted in a quick evacuation of the wounded to hospital.

By his calmness and determination Fusilier Duffy saved the lives of two soldiers under the most dangerous conditions and is worthy of recognition. *[From L.G.]*
(L.G. 31.1067)

Duke, Percy James, Sergeant
831829, 25 Fd Regt., Royal Artillery (Cramlington)
(Immediate)
On the morning of 26 Jun 44, 25 Fd Regt RA advanced behind the attacking infantry to occupy a position North of Cheux. 12/25 Bty adv party, of which Sgt Duke was one, were fired on from a wood at T.893687 in their gun area, and both officers in the area were killed while attacking the wood. In the face of rifle and automatic fire, Sjt. Duke then entered the wood alone, located the enemy and still under fire carried back the body of L/Bdr Hobson. He then collected a party of gunners from his Battery and covered by fire from two tanks, cleared the wood taking 25 prisoners. With more help a further 18 prisoners, including wounded, were rounded up, and 6 automatics and many rifles and grenades were taken. Sjt. Duke by his courage, determination and initiative saved his Battery heavy casualties and was largely responsible for clearing the way for them to get into action.   *(L.G. 19.10.44)*

Dumolo, Jack, Warrant Officer Cl. II (C.S.M.)
5248112, 1 Worcestershire Regt. (Tipton)
At Barentu when under shell fire whilst performing the duties of Platoon Commander showed great coolness.

At Keren during the Company's attack on Falestoh this W.O. was again very prominent during the withdrawal of the Company, he showed exceptional gallantry in collecting the wounded and carrying them back to the R.A.P. which was over a mile from the place of the Companys action. The following day whilst performing the duties of C.S.M. this W.O. showed untiring efforts in the reorganisation of the Company. At Teclesan this W.O. was again prominent under very heavy shell fire, and during the action showed great powers of endurance. At Amba Alagi his conduct in the field and under Mortar fire was of a very high standard. From Barentu to Amba Alagi this W.O. has been extremely gallant and has continued to set a very high standard to the N.C.O.'s and men under him.   *(L.G. 16.4.42)*

Dunbar, Robert, Private
2879107, 1 Bn. Gordon Highlanders

I was captured at St. Valéry on 12 Jun 40 and was marched via St. Pol to Béthune. We reached Béthune on 20 Jun and I escaped in company with Ptes. Harper, A. (S/P.G. (F)302) and Westland, S. (S)P.G.(F)429). We fell out on the road and hid behind some houses until the column was past. The inmates then gave us civilian clothes, and we walked back 8 miles to Auchel. We all separated in Auchel but I used often to see Harper and Westland until I was recaptured.

I spent 3 months at Auchel as the guest of a café proprietor, but a Polish girl, whose name I do not know, told a German officer that I was English. I was arrested about 20 Sep. and taken to Lille where I was tried for attempted sabotage. I was acquitted on this charge, but was sentenced to undergo 4 months solitary confinement for having escaped. I was taken to Stuttgart in a cattle-truck and driven to a camp a few miles outside the city. I never knew its name. I was in solitary confinement until the end of Jan 41 and had no chance to escape. When my sentence expired I found that the camp was full of French prisoners and that the only other Englishman was Pte. Herring, R., R.C.Sigs. (escape recorded from Front Stalag 190: date unknown). He had a French wife, a school teacher, living near Lille and she had been arrested by the Germans.

The camp was so well-guarded by wire and M.G. posts that we planned to escape while we were working outside it. We made a dash for it on 14 Feb., during the afternoon, while we were shovelling coal in a rly. siding and ran along a short curving tunnel to avoid the fire of our guards. We were fired at, but, at the far end of the tunnel, we hid in an air-raid shelter until dark. We boarded a goods train, having no idea where it was going, and hid in a truck. In the morning we slipped off and found ourselves in Holland. I cannot remember where we left the train, but we spent some weeks wandering across Holland and Belgium. We reached Lille on 12 April and Herring left me to look for his wife.

I went on alone to Auchel where I found that my host and hostess of the previous year had been sentenced to 7 years imprisonment each for harbouring me. I returned to Béthune, where another café proprietress, who knew about this, nevertheless gave me shelter and clothes and procured false identity papers for me. I stayed with her for some days. On 20 Apr I left by train for Paris assisted by a French guide. I do not know his name. I stayed 12 days in Paris and then went down to Dompierre, where I crossed the demarcation line on 2 May with the aid of a butcher's assistant. After crossing the line I was directed to Montlucon, where I was arrested and sent to St. Hippolyte.

I escaped from St. Hippolyte on 7 May but was recaptured 3 days later and given 14 days imprisonment. Early in June I escaped again and got as far as Narbonne, where I was recaptured at the beginning of July. This time I was given 30 days' imprisonment.

On 17 Aug I escaped with Gnr. Badman, A. V. (A/P.G. (F) 586) by sawing through the bars of a room near the dining-hall. We were directed to Nines, Perpignan, and Banyuls. From Banyuls we crossed the Pyrenees in a party of seven, not including a Spanish guide. It took 3 days and 2 nights to cross because the guide missed the way twice. The others who were guided across were:—

L/Cpl. Warnett, H. J. (A/P.G.(–)585)
Dvr. Dulan, J. (S/P.G.( )591)
Cpl. Donaghan, H. (S/P.G.(F)583)
Dvr. Ower, D. (S/P.G.(F)589)
Pte. Winslade, V. (S/P.G.(F)584)
Gnr. Badman, A. V. (S/P.G.(F)586)

On 27 Aug. we were arrested at Figueras and sent to a concentration camp at Miranda. I was released on 14 Oct and taken to Gibraltar.   *(L.G. 12.2.42)*

Duncan, John Kershaw, Warrant Officer Cl. II (actg.)
2880114, 14th London Regt. (1 London Scottish)
(Renfrew) (Immediate)

On the night 5/6 Apr 45 during the assault crossing of the R. Reno in square 5252 by 1 LIR, some of the boats of C coy 1 LIR were carried away on being launched. The boats allotted for the second wave of tps were used in order not to impede the momentum of the initial assault. As a result when the time came for the second wave to cross—only a matter of 8–10 minutes after the first assault—there were insufficient boats. CSM Duncan realised that it was imperative for this wave to cross quickly in order that the reserve Pl could be readily available to exploit success and that Coy HQ could control the battle. Without hesitation he dived into the river and swam across 60 yds of open water to the enemy bank. There he found a boat but no paddles, so he swam back with it pushing it in front of him. C Coy HQ embarked and CSM Duncan again entered the water and pushed the boat back across the river. By this time other boats had been mobilised to get the reserve Pl across, and CSM Duncan returned in one of these to carry on his task under the Beachmaster of ferrying other troops and stores across the river.

During the night 1 LIR suffered casualties and extra stretcher bearers were required to deal with the evacuation of wounded. CSM Duncan immediately organised a party of men, crossed the river and proceeded to the fwd Pls. He personally supervised the evacuation of over a dozen wounded men, tending to their needs whilst waiting for stretchers. Having evacuated wounded, CSM Duncan then proceeded to organise carrying parties to get amn fwd to Pls actually engaged with the enemy. On three occasions during the night he reported at C Coy HQ to see if he could be of assistance.

The behaviour of CSM Duncan, who was not a member of the assaulting Bn and in no way responsible for the tasks he undertook, deserves the highest praise. His duties were limited to organising boats and to ferrying across the river. These tasks he performed successfully but his high sense of duty and esprit-de-corps prompted him to do things entirely out of his own sphere of duty. His complete disregard for personal safety, his super-human effort of swimming three times the R. Reno and his regard for the needs of the wounded inspired all who worked with him. The fact that the river and the area beyond were continually under mortar, shell and small arms fire did not deter him in any way. His services were invaluable and most courageous.

(L.G. 23.8.45)

Duncan, Wallace Nicholson, Sergeant
VX 6589, 2/8 Battalion Australian Imperial Force
Act of Gallantry in the Field and devotion to duty in the face of the Enemy during the Battle of Veve Pass 12 April 1941.

Sergeant Duncan commanded a platoon of the Company which was not involved in the early stages of the Action and when pressure caused the centre Coy to give ground he was ordered to take his platoon to give support where it was most needed. This N.C.O. fearlessly led his men into the position indicated in the face of heavy Enemy M.G. fire. From then on he moved his platoon forward at every opportunity until he reached his position from which he was able to assist in repelling the incessant enemy attacks, and also to assist by fire several counter attacks made by the Coy on his left. Throughout the whole of the action he displayed great calmness and courage and was an inspiration and example to his men. He played a very material part in the successful holding of the position until the final withdrawal.

(L.G. 4.11.41)

Dunlea, Lewis Nesley, Corporal
60681, 37th Battalion, New Zealand Military Forces
In operations in the vicinity of Warambari Bay in Vella Lavella, this N.C.O. was a member of several patrols which were operating against concealed enemy positions. Throughout all these operations he displayed courage and resource of an exceptional character. On the 6th October, 1943, the officer commanding one of the patrols was seen to fall some distance away and in close

proximity to the enemy positions. Cpl. Dunlea with others then volunteered to go forward and bring him to safety. In spite of heavy fire from the enemy, the attempt was successful and the officer, who was found to be dead, was brought back. In performing this duty Cpl. Dunlea displayed the utmost gallantry and continued throughout the operation to give a splendid example to the men under his command.

(L.G. 9.12.43)

Dunlop, Ray Archibald, Corporal
VX4245, 2/5 Australian Infantry Bn. (Immediate)
Cpl. Dunlop commanded a section of B Company during the advance of 2/5 Aust. Inf. Bn. from Tong to the Balif—M'Bras areas during Jan—Feb 45. Throughout the operations, he displayed qualities of leadership, determination, initiative and personal bravery under fire far in excess of that demanded of him in the exercise of his duty.

Cpl. Dunlop led at least 12 successful fighting patrols against the enemy, most of which were long and arduous over difficult country. In each case his determination and tenacity secured valuable information of enemy dispositions which greatly assisted the successful advance of his Company. At Wembe on 13 Jan 45, whilst his Company was advancing, the enemy was surprised and an initial foothold was gained by one platoon on a small feature. The enemy immediately made a strong counter attack from a dominating feature a short distance away. Although under heavy MMG and LMG fire, Cpl. Dunlop calmly led his section forward and not only repelled the attack but inflicted severe casualties on the enemy. By his own coolness and bravery under fire, Cpl. Dunlop prevented heavy casualties being inflicted on his Company.

Again on 14 Feb 45, Cpl. Dunlop took part in a fighting patrol to Barangabandangi. Severe casualties were inflicted on the enemy. Heavy fire from an enemy MMG and LMGs was encountered and Cpl. Dunlop was ordered to cover the withdrawal of the remainder of the patrol. He fearlessly led his section to within 15 yards of the enemy position and brought accurate fire to bear, which enabled the patrol to withdraw. In the face of heavy fire, Cpl. Dunlop with complete disregard for his own safety then ordered his section to withdraw and remained himself engaging the enemy until all his men were safely withdrawn.

Throughout these operations Cpl. Dunlop was an inspiration not only to his platoon but to the whole Company.

(L.G. 21.6.45)

Dunn, Patrick, Gunner
887694, 106th Regt. R.H.A., Royal Artillery
(Arkwright, Liverpool)
This man has been conspicuous throughout the campaign. In particular on the 6th Feb, when his gun had been knocked out and his detachment all killed or wounded, he went, under intense fire, to take charge of another gun, whose detachment had also been knocked

out. Laying and firing the gun himself he destroyed five enemy tanks.   *(L.G. 8.7.41)*

Dunne, Joseph, Sergeant
2718336, 1st Bn. Irish Guards (Tullamore, Eire)
(Immediate)
On 26th Jan 44 this N.C.O. was in command of No. 13 Pln of No. 3 Coy, which held the left flank of the Bn's position at Garroceto. About 0800 hrs a strong German counter attack was put in. One other Pln was over-run and 2 A/Tk guns and 1 MMG were knocked out, leaving this Plns position completely exposed to the H.E., and S.A.A. fire of the enemy tanks. In spite of this heavy fire Sjt. Dunne reorganised his posn at once and beat off two determined German Infantry attacks, showing himself, complete disregard for the heavy covering fire given by the Tanks. In the night attack 29/30 Jan 44, this N.C.O. led his platoon with highest skill and determination. When his Pl was held up by a fixed line M.G., he dashed forward and destroyed the enemy post single-handed, killing the two Germans who were manning it. The following morning 30th, the Company, supported by American Tank Destroyers, carried out an offensive sweep to clear the ridge on the left flank of the Bde Salient of enemy's M.G.s and snipers. During this operation Sjt Dunne led his platoon with the greatest efficiency and courage destroying 3 enemy posts with no losses. On the morning of the 31st Jan, Sjt Dunne located a German snipers' nest. Armed with a rifle he stalked this nest and killed 5 of the six occupants during the morning. Later in the afternoon he completed the job by killing the remaining sniper who had taken refuge in Val[...] farm. On the night of the 3rd/4th Feb this Sjt. was with his company when it was over-run by a Bn of enemy. Despite being wounded he fought his way back to his own lines.

This N.C.O.'s record for skill, determination, marksmanship and personal courage during the whole of the Bn's action in the Anzio bridgehead is of the highest order and merits in my opinin the immediate award of the D.C.M.   *(L.G. 15.6.44)*

Dunning, George, Lance Corporal
5045548, 2 Bn. Lincolnshire Regt.
Taken prisoner in Belgium on 30 May 40, Dunning was sent to Stalag VIII B (Lamsdorf). During April 41 he escaped by cutting the wire, and had reached the Polish–Russian border before his apprehension five days later. Although he was punished by three months' imprisonment, he escaped again within three days of his return to Lamsdorf; this time he accompanied some Poles through a tunnel. When trying to enter Russia by a different route he was re-captured at the frontier town of Katovitch. After another term of imprisonment he was, in September 41, sent to a repatriation camp. Four months later, upon the failure of negotiations, Dunning and an officer avoided return to Germany by cutting the wire, having assured the sentries' inattention by giving them hot drinks. Dunning made his way alone to Lyons, and,

acting upon advice received, then made for Spain. Unfortunately he encoutered French Police, who sent him to Fort de la Riviere. Although he escaped from this camp during a mass break-out, he was again arrested and within a few months was sent to Carpi (Camp 73, Italy).

On 9 Sep 43, he became once more a prisoner of the Germans, when the camp was unexpectedly surrounded in the early morning. To avoid transfer to Germany, he and four others hid in a dug-out for five days without discovery, and were then able to leave the camp unmolested. Dunning went to the mountains and during the next fifty days fought with four different partisan groups. Nearing Ancona, he discovered a band which was better organised; throughout the next eight months he served with this unit, finally participating in the rebel occupation of San Severino at the beginning of July 44. When British forces arrived at Dunning handed over his arms and reported to an Amgot official.   *(L.G. 1.3.45)*

Duvanel, Randall David, Private
VX 24158, 2/4 Australian Infantry Bn. (Immediate)
For boldness, initiative and a high degree of personal bravery whilst on patrol.

In the Wewak area on 24 May 1945 Private Duvanel was forward scout of a patrol operating against Koigin, and when moving some distance in advance of the main body he was fired on by a party of six enemy at close range. Without awaiting any orders or trying to communicate with his patrol commander, Private Duvanel displayed bravery of a very high standard and a magnificent spirit of aggression by assaulting the enemy single handed. He killed or wounded five out of the six Japanese, and the sixth fled in terror.

The patrol proceeded and whilst in Koigin village two members of Duvanel's section were cutting enemy signal wires when they were charged by three Japanese bearing fixed bayonets. Unhesitatingly, Duvanel moved in and showing utter disregard of his own safety and great initiative he intercepted the enemy and killed all three.

There is no doubt that Duvenel's actions were to a large extent the cause of the patrol's success and our own light casualties. His personal bravery and the aggressive spirit he displayed was an example to the members of his platoon and indeed to the whole company.   *(L.G. 24.8.45)*

Dwyer, Desmond Francis, Bombardier
955160, 149 Anti-tank Regt., Royal Artillery
(Southport)
For conspicuous gallantry and devotion to duty during the enemy tank attack on El Ruweisat Ridge on 16 July 1942.

Bombardier Dwyer was second in command on his gun which was in the most forward position. During this action his gun ran short of ammunition. Bombardier Dwyer walked under heavy shellfire 100 yards to the portee, carried up a box of 6-pdr ammunition and engaged the enemy tanks with only one man to load.

Later in the same action he volunteered to go forward with his battery commader to look for a wounded officer forward of his position. Throughout the engagement Bombardier Dwyer set the detachment a fine example of leadership and courage. During a dive bombing attack on Ruweisat Ridge on the same day Bombardier Dwyer's gun was damaged by a bomb. At the same time a crude oil bomb burst near the gun position. With no thought for his own safety Bombardier Dwyer moved his gun ammunition from the flames of the oil bomb and threw it clear. He worked unceasingly to save this ammunition from being blown up, which would, undoubtedly, have gravely injured the members of his gun detachment and destroyed his gun. The dive bombers were still operating while Bombardier Dwyer was doing this job, and two more bombs landed near his position without in any detering him from this task. *(L.G. 24.9.42)*

Dyer, Arthur John, Private (A/Lce. Cpl.)
5568172, 2nd Bn. Wiltshire Regt.

On 23 May 40 his company was on the bank of the River Scarpe in front of Reux. During the night the village was subjected to considerable artillery bombardment for some hours. Pte. Dyer, although the only man left in his section position, which was crushed by shell fire, was still holding it by himself. He collected men from other positions and formed a section which continued to hold on under considerable fire. Later, when the enemy reached a wood on his flank, he patrolled into it with his section, and acting under orders, held another position to cover this wood, which although in the open and under shell fire, he held. On 25 May 40, when his company went forward over the river Scarpe, although most of his platoon became casualties, he brought a report of the situation over open country under heavy shell and machine gun fire to the Company Commander. He shewed similar bravery when his company occupied a position at Wambeke near the Ypres—Comines Canal. *(L.G. 22.10.40)*

Dyer, Frank, Corporal (actg.)
11405251, 2nd Bn. Rifle Brigade (Fawley, Hants.)
(Immediate)

For gallantry and devotion to duty during the attack on Tossignano 0823.

At 0600 hrs on 14 Dec 44 L/Corporal Dyer's Platoon was ordered to seize a house on the southern side of Tossignano to relieve pressure on C Coy 2 RB being counter-attacked in the Western end of the village. The entry into the house was forced and the platoon established on the ground floor which consisted of only one room. At first light the enemy counter-attacked and the Bren Gunner covering the street was killed. L/Corporal Dyer immediately manned the Bren gun and was himself hit in the leg almost at once. He refused attention and continued to fire the Bren with such good effect that the attack was temporarily stopped.

Later the house was attacked with bazookas, the ceiling blown in and the room set on fire with petrol so that the platoon was free to withdraw down the hill. L/Corporal Dyer with his pl comd and Rfn Alldridge covered this withdrawal engaging the enemy at very short range. Under cover of some rocks at the foot of the hill L/Corporal Dyer tended 3 wounded men and then on his own initiative crossed 200 yards of open ground under observed MG and mortar fire to get help from the Coy HQ at Pt.222. Smoke was put down but more men were hit near pt 222 while crossing the open ground. Seeing this L/Corporal Dyer improvised a red cross flag from a white handkerchief and the blood of a wounded man and repeatedly went forward in the face of heavy MG and Mortar fire each time helping back a wounded man.

Finally as a result of L/Corporal Dyer's determined and courageous efforts the enemy recognised the red cross flag and it was possible for stretcher bearers to collect the remaining wounded who would otherwise have spent the day lying in the open exposed to enemy fire. Altogether 12 wounded were brought in, and L/Corporal Dyer continued for 3 hours to bring in and help tend the wounded.

L/Corporal Dyer's gallantry was of the highest order and there is no doubt that by his determination and disregard for himself, he saved the lives of several men of his platoon. *(L.G. 24.5.45)*

E

Eades, Alfred Edison, Sergeant
30743, 22 N.Z. (Mot.) Bn. (Immediate)
Sgt. Eades took comd. of his pl at an early stage of the attack upon La Romola on the night of 30–31 July. His pl. comdr. was killed and there were other casualties from the heavy replies of arty., mortar and SA concs. made by the enemy to our barrage. The country was wooded and from ridges on each side of the valley of the pl's axis of advance the enemy brought to bear Spandau fire which was both heavy and accurate.

Sgt. Eades then displayed remarkable qualities of courage and natural leadership. On several occasions when the pl. was pinned down by fire, he marched along his pl. front, seeing to the welfare of his men and taking no thought for his own safety. His display of courage was undoubtedly an inspiration to his men and with him they moved forward to capture all objectives. A strongly fortified house was overcome and other positions were cleared of the enemy by his skilful direction of the attack.

Later in the advance from La Romola to the Poggiona feature, Sgt. Eades again directed his men with great skill and under some of the heaviest fire faced by the Bn. in it's Italian campaigns he captured and held his position until directed by his Coy. comdr. to retire owing to shortage of amn. and the imminence of a strong enemy counter attack.
Recommended for M.M. (*L.G. 10.5.45*)

Easter, Royden Kenneth, Sergeant
NX 18260, 2/13 Australian Infantry Bn.
During the operations of the Battalion near Alamein between 23 Oct and 6 Nov 42 this N.C.O. was in command of a platoon. In an attack made by his Battalion on the night 23/24 Oct 42 Sgt. Easter's platoon was given the task of mopping up an enemy post on the left flank of the Battalion. The post was assaulted by Sgt. Easter's platoon in company with a detachment from a battalion of the Gordons. Sgt. Easter's grasp of the situation, his initiative and the resolution with which he led his platoon into the assault resulted in the post being overcome. He was personally responsible for knocking out two Spandau machine guns and killing the crew.

On the succeeding night 24/25 Oct 42 the battalion, which on the first night had been held up short of its final objective, attacked again to complete its task. To ensure success in this operation it was necessary to gain information of the enemy dispositions. Sgt. Easter led a small patrol forward from our positions to locate the enemy. He found there was between his patrol and our own positions a party of men without his knowing whether they were enemy or some of our troops who had come in from a flank. He challenged them, discovered they were enemy and at once gave orders to

his patrol to assault. At least eight casualties were inflicted on the enemy and the patrol reached our positions without casualties. There, Sgt. Easter was able to give information concerning the enemy, on which his Commanding Officer decided to dispense with artillery support as planned, and to make a silent attack in the darkness by which the enemy were completely surprised and the battalion gained its objective. (*L.G. 11.2.43*)

Easterbrook, Robert Henry, Private
S 54670, R.A.S.C.
No citation. (*L.G. 26.7.45*)

Ebersohn, Gerrit Stephanus Scheepers, T/Sergeant
26694V, Imperial Light Horse/Kimberley Regiment
On the afternoon of 30 Jun 44 'B' Coy., in the adv. North of Aqua Viva, encountered hy enemy opposition and the Coy's right flank was halted by a nest of 3 Spandau guns. The right pl. was pinned to the ground and the adv. was halted. Enemy mortars then concentrated their fire on the Coy., causing severe casualties. Sjt. Ebersohn moved fwd. and to the right, where the Spandau nest had been located, and under intense fire reached a pt. where he was able to use his grenades. He lobbed three into the enemy strongpoint then rushed fwd. with his TMG. The post was destroyed and the adv. continued. This act required the highest order of courage and devotion to duty and was carried out coolly and regardless of personal danger. He had lost his officer, wounded early in the morning, and commanded his pl. with splendid leadership. (*L.G. 26.10.44*)

Edgell, Reginald George, Corporal
VX 120253, 39 Australian Infantry Bn. (Immediate)
On 6 Dec 42 at Gona Mission a coy. attack on the enemy's SW defences met with such strong resistance that the coy. was able to capture only 50 yards of ground at a cost of 12 killed and 46 wounded. Cpl. Edgell led the only section that succeeded in breaking through the enemy's defences. He carried on through a network of enemy post until he reached the mission village, and then finding his party was the only one to get through, decided to lead them back to another part of our front. On the way back he made a surprise flank attack on an enemy post then being engaged by a patrol from our right coy. With his Owen gun and the assistance of his Bren gunner he killed between 10 and 12 enemy holding the post and led his section safely back to our lines.

On 11 Dec 42 at the village two miles West of Gona, Cpl. Edgell commanded the leading section moving up the track to make contact with the enemy. The section was fired on by an enemy machine gun post and Cpl. Edgell received two bullet wounds in his right arm. Using his Owen gun in his left hand he immediately rushed the position killing the three machine gunners and silencing the gun. This enabled the section to establish itself far enough forward to allow the coy. to move well up to launch its attack from forward of the swamp which the enemy machine gun post had covered. In this action Cpl. Edgell had two of his men wounded. He assisted in their evacuation and reported the situation before he himself sought RAP attention.

It is recommended that he be granted the Immediate Award of the Distinguished Conduct Medal.

(L.G. 22.4.43)

Edmondson, Walter, Sergeant
7905656, 2nd Lothians & Border Yeomanry
(Edinburgh)
No citation. *(L.G. 23.8.45)*

Edwards, Charles Thomas, Corporal (A/Sgt.)
5725947, 1 Dorsetshire Regt. (Portsmouth)
(Immediate)
On 1 August 43 at Regalbuto.

Sergeant Edwards who was platoon commander of No. 11 Platoon, was ordered to cover the withdrawal of the remainder of his Company from the town after a reconnaissance had been carried out. Although surrounded by three German tanks and approximately fifty German infantry, Sergeant Edwards held his position and was himself the last to leave having successfully covered the withdrawal of the Company and beaten off at least two attacks against his position. When he eventually withdrew he and his platoon took up a position on some high ground to the North of the town. Twice the enemy supported by tanks and mortars attacked Sergeant Edwards' platoon, and on one occasion hand to hand fighting took place. On both occasions the enemy were driven back and the position was held. During the course of this action Sergeant Edwards was wounded but he fought on and encouraged his men to hold the position. Later in the action he was again wounded but still refused to be evacuated until the final attack by the enemy had been beaten off. It was entirely due to Sergeant Edwards' courage and leadership, and his absolute disregard to his own personal safety that the position was held. *(L.G. 4.11.43)*

Edwards, David John, Sergeant
3907548, 2 South Wales Borderers (Hengoed, Glam.)
On the night of 26/27 July at Croix Des Landes Sjt. Edwards was second in command of a fighting patrol ordered to bring back a prisoner for identification.

As the patrol moved down the right hand hedgerow of an orchard it was fired on by a MG from the left.

With complete coolness Sjt. Edwards placed two Bren guns in position on the right and took the Riflemen over to the left, then disregarding the enemy fire, he moved back to the Bren guns and shouted 'Charge' in order to deceive the enemy as to the direction of the assault.

Without thought of danger he himself rushed in alone from the right flank while the assaulting group of the patrol charged in from the left. Sjt. Edwards was the first man to arrive at the enemy position. He jumped into the enemy slit trench where he found two dead and two wounded Germans. He promptly hit one of the wounded Germans on the head, threw him over his should and carried him about two hundred yards back towards our own lines.

His coolness, quickness of decision and fierce agressive spirit were an inspiration to the remainder of the patrol and it was largely due to his magnificent example that an important identification was obtained without casualty to his own men. *(L.G. 21.12.44)*

Edwards, David Rufus, Private
7621381, Royal Army Ordnance Corps
Pte. Lang was taken prisoner on the 1st June, 1941, when, during the evacuation from Greece, the small boat in which he and a few others were trying to escape, was sunk by a German bomb. Pte. Edwards was captured on the same day when his unit had been surrounded by the enemy, after fighting and marching for four days without food.

They arrived at Stalag VII A, near Munich, in different parties in August, 1941, and a month later they were both transferred to the same working Camp in the West End of Munich. Here, all the prisoners of war were put to work on such tasks as repairing the railway track, clearing snow and general running the municipal services of the City.

They decided to escape by concealing themselves on the train which left Munich daily for Switzerland, and with this end in view they began collecting articles of clothing, money and food for the journey. Other British prisoners at the camp who were waiting to go to the prison in Stalag VII A for their attempted escapes, had previously told them of the exact location of the siding in which the Swiss train was made up.

In the evening of 30th March, after they had finished their work, they seized the opportunity, when the guard was not looking, of scrambling through the fence and hurrying across a field and thus reaching the public path. As they were still wearing battle-dress, they walked singly to avoid attracting too much attention from passers by, and after making a circular movement they reached a hut on the railway where they had been working before and in which they had hidden food and clothes.

At 2.00 a.m. on the following day they made their way to the siding where they knew the train was being made ready. To do this it was necessary to follow the main road for a hundred yards. After passing some women and a German soldier, a civilian regarded them very closely and seemed about to shout. They carried straight on, however, looking neither to right nor left as though they were on some official business, and the civilian walked away.

After a great deal of searching they at last found the train marked Lindau and St. Margrethen, which was standing about forty yards from the two large signal boxes, and they dived into the shadows beneath the coach directly behind the engine. At first they almost concluded that it was impossible to get a position beneath the coach, but after a time Pte. Lang, by removing his overcoat managed to squeeze himself on to a structure running parallel with one on the wheels. Throughout the journey the wheel at times rubbed against his shoe, but it did no damage. Pte. Edwards succeeded in wriggling on to a section of brake with his body lying parallel to the axle. A crouched position had to be maintained in order to keep his feet from the wheels. The weight of his body had a tendency partly to apply the brakes, and at Munich Station an engineer, fuming and cursing, worked for fifteen minutes within five yards of him. At 7.00 a.m. the train pulled out of the station, and twelve hours later, after at times having reached terrific speed, it came to rest in St. Margrethen. Here a police official noticed a part of Pte. Lang's clothing alongside the wheel and ordered him out. Pte. Edwards then emerged upon learning that they were in Switzerland.

After spending a week in prison at St. Gall, where they were very well treated by the Swiss police, they were brought to Berne and handed over to the British Legation who arranged for their repatriation to this country.   *(L.G. 18.8.42)*

Edwards, Edward Llewellyn, Private
3913961, 6 South Wales Borderers (Louth)
(Immediate)
N. Burma Campaign 1944

During the action fought to establish a block on the Sahmaw Chaung on 5 Aug, Pte. Edwards' section was leading the centre Column in the advance when they came under MMG and LMG fire from 30 yards which pinned the Section to the ground. Pte. Edwards immediately went forward and got his Bren into action, at point blank range, killing all the Japs on the first MMG position. Throughout this period Pte. Edwards was under heavy fire from unlocated MMGs and snipers. He held this position until daylight, by which time only one officer and one soldier remained in his vicinity, both of whom were seriously wounded. Seeing a patrol of another Company approaching, he crawled away in spite of heavy enfilade fire and reached them in time to give warning of another well camouflaged Jap gun which he located. He led the patrol round the flank of this position, went forward himself and killed the occupants with grenades and demolished the gun. Having disposed of this post, he returned to the wounded which he had left and succeeded in dragging them both to safety although under continuous fire with practically no cover.

By his coolness and foresight this private soldier prevented the patrol being ambushed and by his outstanding gallantry saved the lives of the wounded. In addition he personally accounted for at least 8 Japanese.
                                    (L.G. 16.11.44)

Edwards, Herbert James, Sergeant
1083895, 67th Anti-Tank Regiment, Royal Artillery
(Whyteleafe, Surrey) (Immediate)

During the enemy's counter attack with tanks and infantry on Monte Corvino aerodrome on the morning of 10 Sep 43, Sgt. Edwards was acting as No 1 of his troop. His position soon came under machine gun fire from the leading tanks. Bullets penetrated the gun shields and wounded two Gunners on St. Harrison's gun. These men collapsed and Sgt. Harrison rendered first aid. Sgt. Edwards unable to engage with his gun, crawled across the bullet-swept road and manning Sgt. Harrison's gun alone knocked out the leading tank. At this stage Sgt. Edwards was wounded. He continued to serve the gun and was joined by Sgt. Harrison. Fire was directed at the rear tanks which were hit and withdrew. During this action gun fire as well as machine gun fire was directed against Sgt. Edwards, three A.P. shells passing through the 6-pr gun shield. The courage, coolness and determination, with which Sgt. Edwards defied the enemy tanks was outstanding.   *(L.G. 27.1.44)*

Edwards, Horace Donald, Lance Sergeant
1883240, 615 Fd. Sqn., Royal Engineers (Old Hill,
Staffs.) (Immediate)
On 5 Sep 44 L/Sgt. Horace Donald Edwards was in command of a Royal Engineers reconnaissance party working under command of 'D' Squadron, 2 HCR.

The troop to which L/Sgt. Edwards was attached reached the bridge in Louvain in the face of heavy opposition and found enemy SS troops in the act of carrying out the final stages of its demolition. Despite intense and sustained enemy small arms fire directed on to the bridge from the neighbouring streets and houses, L/Sgt. Edwards immediately went forward on foot, removed the detonators from the charges and finally removed the charges themselves. By his absolute disregard for his own safety he succeeded in making safe a bridge which was vital to the subsequent advance of the Guards Armoured Division.   *(L.G. 1.3.45)*

Edwards, Thomas Emlyn, Sergeant
4123098, 2 Cheshire Regt. (Wrexham) (Immediate)
20/24 March 1943, Mareth Line.

When his Platoon Commander was sent to L.O.B. before the fighting, Sjt. Edwards was left in Command of No 9 Platoon 'B' Coy. This platoon was engaged both in the initial consolidation of the outpost position, and in the support and consolidation of the 6 Gn Howards attack on the night 23/24th. On 19th March after a daring recce in the face of enemy shelling and MG fire over very exposed ground he contrived to get his platoon into action in the only sheltered position possible in the area of high ground 623094, well in advance of the infantry, and in the only position from which he could protect the garrison of Hill 16 ('A' Coy 5 E. Yorks). He maintained his position throughout the day in the face of enemy shelling and MG fire and withdrew only to take part in the Coy harrassing shoot of night 20/21.

The following day it became necessary to support the 7 Gn. Howards on their position on Big Audrey, and Sgt. Edwards carried out a daring recce near Pt 33 in order to find a position for his platoon. *(L.G. 1.6.43)*

Eeles, Jack, Lance Corporal
2614866, 10 Armd. Div. Provost Coy., Military Police
 (Beckley, Oxon.) (Immediate)
During the passage of the minefields near El Alamein on the night of 23/24 Oct 42, it was the duty of the 10 Armd. Div. Prov. Coy. to go on ahead of the armoured troops for the purpose of marking and lighting the tracks along which the Division was to pass. The task was one of peculiar difficulty and vital to the success of the operation. The C.M.P. detachments responsible for two out of the three tracks, allotted to the Division, were commanded by Officers. Owing to shortage of officers the detachment responsible for the third track was commanded by a Sergeant.

Before the first enemy minefield was reached the Sergeant and all the rest of the C.M.P. detachment were killed or wounded except for L/Cpl. Eeles. At this critical moment L/Cpl. Eeles was left alone with the most important part of the task yet to be completed. Although this track was the one onto which the enemy concentrated the greater part of this shell and small arms fire, L/Cpl. Eeles, with the assistance of two sappers, placed at his disposal by the C.R.E. completed the marking and lighting of the track along its most dangerous and difficult portion.

The coolness and courage with which this N.C.O. took over and completed his task, his initiative and determination, are deserving of the highest praise and reflect the greatest credit on the Corps. of Military Police.
Recommended for M.M. *(L.G. 31.12.42)*

Egan, Terence John, Warrant Officer Cl. II (temp.)
2137410, Royal Regt. of Australian Artillery
No citation. *(L.G. 28.3.69)*

Eggins, Charles James, Corporal
QX3473, Australian Military Forces
No citation. *(L.G. 18.7.45)*

Ehava, Sergeant
34, Australian Military Forces
No citation. *(L.G. 19.8.43)*

Elder, Hugh McFarlane, Sergeant
2761020, 81 (West-African) Div. Recce Regiment,
 Reconnaissance Corps (Perth) (Periodic)
Led parties in the attacks on:— Alethangyaw 30th/31st Jan 44, Kanyindan 17th Feb 44, Kanyindan 11th/12th Mar 44, and on numerous patrols during the past two

months. He has on all these occasions shown a high standard of personal courage and steadiness and in particular at Kanyindan (3723) on 12th Mar 44 he gallantly led a small party of his men, including his African Tp. Sgt. in a charge across open ground, in the face of short range rifle fire from a Japanese position covering their left flank. It was largely due to his personal example and encouragement to his men that the position was carried at the point of the bayonet with four enemy killed and no casualties to his own men. By taking this position he turned the enemy left flank, this causing them, with their right flank turned by Lt. Burgess' charge to abandon their main positions. *(L.G. 8.2.45)*

Eldridge, Garnett William, Sergeant
G57535, Canadian Infantry Corps
No citation. *(L.G. 24.1.46)*

Ellin, John, Sergeant
2028054, 228 Fd. Coy., Royal Engineers
On 23/5/40 the first charge placed on a railway bridge over the La Bassée Canal produced incomplete demolition through no fault of the demolition party. Further charges had to be placed under close M.G. fire. L/Cpl. Ruthven becoming annoyed with the enemy fire, mounted the bowstring girder of the bridge, and executed a dance on it. This operation so heartened the rest of the party that the charges were completed with great energy and complete demolition was effected.

It was however due primarily to the technical ability, and to the intrepid leadership of Sgt. Ellin that the operation was successfully carried out. *(L.G. 27.8.40)*

Elliott, Charles Stanley, Corporal (Acting Sjt)
7887112, 6 Royal Tank Regt.
This N.C.O. having got called into Gallabat while working round inside the Fort with his tank broke a track and became immobile. Soon after he saw another of our tanks commanded by Sgt. Manders about 40 yds. to his left that was on fire. He got out of his tank although still surrounded by enemy and rescued Sgt. Manders and L/Cpl Wood who had been seriously wounded by an A/Tk rifle fired from the top of a building 15 yds from Sgt. Mander's tank. He laid the two wounded men between his tank and a bank and dismounted a MG and went into action with it, as owing to the position of his tank he found it impossible to man his guns properly from his tank.

I consider that this N.C.O. behaved with great coolness and resource. *(L.G. 01.1.44)*

Elliott, Edward Raymond, Private
4984378, 1st Bn. Black Watch (Peterborough)
 (Immediate)
For conspicuous gallantry and determination at the Ouadi Akarit on 6 Apl 43.

Pte. Elliot's section had taken part in a counter-attack against the enemy just before dark and had occupied a forward position well in advance of our line. At 2300 hrs. the section was attacked by an enemy patrol of not less than 25 men. Although all his section were killed or wounded, Pte. Elliot continued to hold his slit trench and to throw grenades at the enemy. When relieved by his Coy Comd shortly afterwards, Pte. Elliot was still engaging enemy and it is known that he had killed 6 of them.

By his courageous and determined action in face of overwhelming numbers, Pte. Elliot held this post single handed until assistance came.   (L.G. 22.7.43)

Ellis, John, Private
4756342, Hallamshire Bn., York & Lancaster Regt.
(Leeds 10) (since killed in action) (Immediate)
On 20 Aug 1944, the Bn was ordered to make a bridgehead over the River Touques near Ouilly Le Vicompte.

The enemy who was determined to hold up our advance, had blown every single bridge over the river, and taken up extremely strong positions on the high ground on the further side. From these positions they had a perfect field of view and field of fire on to any target which might appear on the river bank.

The Pioneer Platoon, who owing to casualties were without either an officer or a Sjt., were ordered to throw an improvised bridge over the site of one which had been blown.

The platoon were faced with two main difficulties in carrying out this task. The first was the heavy concentration of mortar and small arms fire which rained down upon them as soon as they approached the water's edge, and continued through the entire operation, the second being the fact that there was no authorised bridging material whatsoever at their disposal.

Immediately, Pte. Ellis took charge of the proceedings and looking about him quickly spotted some telegraph poles which he told his party to fetch and lay across the river to form a base for the bridge. Meanwhile he found some timber which had been used for construction of German dug-outs, and this and other improvised materials which he discovered in different places in the area, he had carried down to the water's edge.

In addition to mortar and small arms, shells were now landing all around the bridge site: Ellis however, so inspired the platoon by his own complete disregard for personal safety, that the job was completed in two hours, and the entire fighting echelon vehicles of the battalion, the heaviest weighing nine tons, were able to pass over.

Ellis's display of courage and initiative in getting this bridge built, contributed to a large extent to the Divisional advance; as the battalion being thus enabled to get forward, achieved the bridgehead which allowed the R.E. to construct the bridge over which the main body crossed.
Recommended for M.M.   (L.G. 1.3.45)

Ellis, Leslie George, Lance Corporal
B.66984, Royal Regiment of Canada
This N.C.O. landed with the first wave at Puits, during the operations in the Dieppe area, 19 Aug 42. After a gap was blown in the wire on the sea-wall, L/Cpl Ellis passed through the gap and proceeded up the hill to the right. He immobilized booby traps, explored a recently abandoned enemy post, and arriving at the top engaged an enemy post east of the beach. Finding himself alone, and seeing the second wave coming in, he returned to the wall to guide them forward. Coming across a comrade paralyzed in both legs he dragged him nearly back to the wall. Here the wounded man was killed and L/Cpl Ellis himself wounded. He succeeded in crossing the wall and was evacuated as a casualty.

L/Cpl Ellis in this action displayed the greatest initiative, skill and devotion to duty.   (L.G. 2.10.42)

Ellis, Stanley John, Corporal (A/Sgt.)
VX 106080, 39 Australian Infantry Bn. (Immediate)
During the attack on the village two miles West of Gona Mission, A/Sgt. Ellis spent three successive days (15, 16 and 17 Dec 42) in no-mans-land in an endeavour to locate and silence an enemy MMG post holding up the advance of his section. He went out before daylight each morning, dug himself a hole near the post, and throughout the daylight hours threw grenades at the enemy post, and carried on a sniping war with the enemy near him killing between 12 and 20 with his Owen gun during the course of the three days. Each night he returned to his section to plan the next days operations. At 0200 hrs on 18 Dec 42 he went out alone, wormed his way to within 10 yards of the MMG and with a shower of grenades silenced the gun and killed the crew. He then returned to his section and led it in the final assault on the enemy positions later in the day.

It is recommended that he be granted the Immediate Award of the Distinguished Conduct Medal.
          (L.G. 22.4.43)

Ellwood, William Cyril, Lance Sergeant
6019994, Essex Regt. (attd. S.S.T., No. 2 Commando)
(Paignton) (Immediate)
Gulf of Salerno 13th September 1943.

During the fighting on the 13th September 1943 on Dragone Hill the enemy attempted to come through our positions. They threw stick grenades and brought automatic fire to bear, killing one man and wounding another. Lieut Peters went forward and was also wounded. Sgt Ellwood with complete disregard for enemy fire and grenades ran forward in the open and fired magazine after magazine into the enemy from his TSMG at point-blank range. Seven enemy dead were found in this area after the action. Throughout the operations he has set a fine standard of leadership, and although hit twice by shell splinters, has continued to command his sub-section with dash and determination.
          (L.G. 13.1.44)

Emery, Alfred George, Warrant Officer Cl. II
552142, Royal Armoured Corps (Wimblington)
No citation.   *(L.G. 24.1.46)*

Emery, Douglas Elias George, Sergeant
6018298, 1st Bn. Duke of Wellington's Regt.
(Westcliff-on-Sea) (Immediate)
For outstanding bravery and devotion to duty during the attack on Monte Cece on the afternoon of 8 Oct 44 and during the night 8/9 Oct 44.

For the attack on the strongly held Monte Cece feature, A. Coy. to which Sgt. Emery belonged was allotted the task of capturing and holding the right end of the summit. The going was hard due to mud and pouring rain and the climb from the start line to the crest extremely steep. When 20 yds from the crest the leading pl. was halted by concentrated fire from four Spandaus firing from the summit. Sgt. Emery who was acting Pl. Comd., as his Pl. Comd. had been wounded, was ordered to take his pl. through the leading pl. and assault the crest. He complied with the order immediately and with himself in the van, he led the pl. on to and over the crest accounting for at least one Spandau crew either killed or wounded who fell to his own Tommy gun. The assault was entirely successful and was in a very large part due to this N.C.O.'s outstanding dash and courage in the face of withering enemy MG fire. Sgt. Emery immediately re-organised and consolidated his pl. which had suffered heavy casualties. Almost before this was completed the enemy counter attacked with some 15—20 men. Once again Sgt. Emery immediately took up a position in front of his pl. and although exposed to heavy enemy small arms fire engaged the attackers with his Tommy gun and directed the fire of his pl. to such effect that the counter attack was quickly and completely broken and the enemy withdrew leaving behind a number of dead and wounded.

Throughout the whole action which lasted until the early morning of 9 Oct Sgt. Emery displayed not only the highest qualities of leadership and devotion to duty but also showed an utter disregard for his own safety during a time of extreme danger. When not engaged actively in attacking and directing fire on the enemy Sgt. Emery was a constant source of encouragement and cheerfulness to his men moving amongst them and directing the evacuation of the wounded.

There is no doubt, that it was a very large part, due to Sgt. Emery's conspicuous bravery, that the assault on Monte Cece was a success.   *(L.G. 12.4.45)*

Endacott, Reginald, Warrant Officer Cl. II (C.S.M.)
3304449, 2 Highland Light Infantry (London, S.E. 5)
For consistent gallantry in fighting in the Sudan and Eritrea, CSM Endacott is again recommended for the award of the Distinguished Conduct Medal, particularly for his gallantry in the fighting around Jebel Shiba. Here on the 23 Jan 41, when his Coy. was held up by machine gun fire he went forward to find out the situation. In doing

so he had to cross a distance of 300 yards which was under machine gun and mortar fire.

He found out the situation and sent in a report to Bn. Headquarters. He then organised and led a party to carry forward ammunition. Having done this he collected a party from the right flank of his Coy. and led them to the left where their fire was needed. Throughout the whole action he showed great resource, courage and devotion to duty.   *(L.G. 16.4.42)*

Enderlein, Frederick, Corporal (A/Sgt.)
7902514, 4th County of London Yeomanry (Sharp-shooters), R.A.C. (New Barnet) (Immediate)
At dawn on June 30th, 1942, near Bir Umm Habib, Sgt. Enderlein was sent out on patrol with one other tank, to investigate a leaguer of approximately 60 Met. As he approached, the vehicles, which were Italian, began to move off; two anti-tank guns were unhitched and opened fire on him, together with several Breda guns, as a result of which his tank was hit several times and two of his road wheels were shot off. Sgt. Enderlein managed to cut off twenty-one of the vehicles and bring them to a halt, although his machine-gun had been hit and put out of action.

He then approached the anti-tank guns from behind the stationary vehicles and ran over them both, and the party surrendered to them. His enterprise resulted in the capture or destruction of 21 enemy vehicles and 280 casualties, either captured, killed or wounded.

(L.G. 15.10.42)

England, James Paterson, Sergeant (A/W.O.I) (Sgt.-Maj.)
Po.X.1371, Royal Marines, No. 47 R.M. Commando
(Immediate)
On 2nd November, TSM England was TSM of one of the troops of 47 (RM) Commando detailed to attack one of the strongly defended battery positions south-east of Zouteland which commanded the Scheldt estuary.

The defences included concreted casemates and pillboxes and unusually thick belts of wire covered by machine guns. The advance was over 1,500 yards of deep soft sand.

By the time the attacking troops had reached assaulting distance they had become very depleted and disorganised and it seemed as if there would be insufficient weight in the attack to storm the enemy defences.

At this critical time TSM England came under heavy fire at close range from an enemy machine gun. Seizing a bren gun lying on top of a dead marine, and firing from the hip as went, this brave NCO plodded up the soft sandy slope and charged this heavily bunkered position alone. He shot and killed two of the occupants and, running out of bren ammunition, he turned the German machine gun with good effect on three more Germans who had fled. Still alone, he worked forward to a second position 30 yards further on where he killed three more Germans, two others surrendering. Here he was later joined by men from another troop.

In a situation where the odds were strongly against him, and knowing that he was unsupported, the courage and determination of this NCO was above praise.

Later, in the growing darkness when it was impossible to give our forward troops any close support, the enemy counter-attacked and our men were driven off the enemy position on which they had gained a foothold.

The next morning another attack was put in on this enemy battery and TSM England's troop was given the task of mopping up behind the assaulting troops.

The enemy was putting up the most desperate resistance and soon attacking and mopping-up troops became intermingled. The enemy opened concentrated and sustained cross fire from the position which TSM England had rushed the previous evening and from a concrete fire control position known as the 'umbrella' on the seaward side of the dunes. On his own initiative and with total disregard for his safety he threw a smoke grenade to screen himself from the view of the 'umbrella' and rushed the machine-gun post in front of him. Killing or capturing the occupants, he continued to work through the network of trenches and tunnels.

Throughout the course of the battle for Walcheren, especially in the fluctuating and bitter fighting, his immense courage and total disregard for his safety had a decisive influence.   *(L.G. 20.2.45)*

Etheridge, Albert Edward, Pte
6913223, Parachute Regt., Army Air Corps (London, S.E.6)
No citation.   *(L.G. 20.9.45)*

Eustace, John, Sergeant
814011, 322/132 Fd. Regt., Royal Artillery (Widnes)
At Tebourba on 27 Nov 42 Sgt. Eustace was in charge of a gun when the bty was attacked by tanks. During the action Sgt. Eustace was left as the only survivor of his detachment. Although under heavy machine gun fire and gun alone. He fired in all 22 rds, destroying for certain 2 tanks and hitting others. his gun remained in action until the enemy withdrew and was the only gun saved from the day's action.   *(L.G. 11.2.43)*

Evans, Albert Frederick, Sergeant (A/W.O.II (C.S.M.))
4031694, King's Shropshire Light Infantry [1st Bn The Herefordshire Regiment on AFW 3121] (Colchester) (Immediate)
In the break out from Caumont T/7159 (Map Sheet ¼" 3A and 8) on the morning of 30 Jul 44 a depleted 'A' Coy advanced under heavy enemy mortar fire to the first objective where it had to wait for two hours pending air bombardment of enemy positions.

This first objective was in fact the enemy D.F. (S.O.S.) task and this area was mortared and shelled by the enemy consistently for two hours. During this time the Coy

endeavoured to dig in as best as they could in the open. About twenty of the Coy including all the stretcher bearers became casualties. All personnel had to make use of what little cover the ground afforded, and to move across this shell swept ground was almost certain to cause casualties.

In the midst of the heavy enemy fire, CSM Evans, with complete disregard for his personal safety, went to each of the numerous casualties, bandaging up their wounds, comforting and cheering them. Whenever there was a short pause in the enemy shell fire he collected men and evacuated the wounded. By his untiring and courageous efforts CSM Evans succeeded in moving all the wounded to a place of safety. The reserve platoon had suffered most casualties, losing their Pl Comd and Pl Sjt. After evacuating all the wounded, he then turned to this platoon and re-organised it so efficently that when the time came for the advance, they were completely ready to move forward and in good heart. He personally lead them forward with such determination that they successfully captured the next objective against stiff enemy opposition.

The fearless example of courage by this W.O. undoubtedly raised the morale of the whole Coy at this critical stage. It can be stated that it was through his personal bravery that the enemy position was overcome; and the successful attack by this Coy enabled the subsequent break through by British forces later the same day.
Recommended for M.M.   *(L.G. 21.12.44)*

Evans, Amwell Cole, Sergeant
404474, 1st The Royal Dragoons (Swansea)
No citation.   *(L.G. 19.3.45)*

Evans, Arthur Andrew, Corporal
SX.10404, Australian Military Forces
No citation.   *(L.G. 14.9.45)*

Evans, Bernard Leslie, Corporal
6206594, 1/7 Bn. Middlesex Regt.
At the battle of Wadi Akarit, Cpl Evans commanded a section of M.G.'s in support of 5th Bn. Seaforth Highlanders, who were attacking a feature, which was strongly held by the enemy. The M.G. Platoon had received orders to carry their guns and ammunition to the top of this hill, and succeeded in doing so in the face of very considerable enemy fire, which caused the Platoon Commander and eleven others to become casualties. Undaunted, Cpl Evans sited his guns over the crest on the forward slopes in the Seaforths forward positions, and opened up an accurate fire upon the enemy.

With only four men to man his guns this N.C.O. continued to fire, although the leading Infantry had been forced back over the crest, leaving him and his section alone and only some 100 yds. from the advancing enemy. By carefully conserving his dwindling stocks of ammunition, he was able to inflict many casualties upon the enemy for over an hour, during which time one of his men was wounded.

When all his ammunition had been expended he removed the locks from the guns, thus rendering them useless, and ordered his men to withdraw one by one while he gave covering fire with his rifle. ne succeeded in reaching our lines.

Throughout this operation, this N.C.O. displayed courage, initiative and leadership of a high order. Next morning his guns were found, in their positions with their full complement of belts beside them, all empty.

(L.G. 22.3.45)

Evans, David Price, Lance Sergeant (A/Sgt.)
4189858, 1 Bn. Royal Welch Fusiliers
At Ottenburg on 12th May, the platoon to which Sjt. Evans belonged was heavily shelled and then attacked and forced to withdraw to a Blockhouse from where the attack was checked. The casualties left outside the Blockhouse were 5 wounded and 4 killed together with a Bren Gun and some ammunition. Volunteers were called for to fetch in the wounded. Sjt. Evans despite heavy fire went out a distance of 100 yards each journey and recovered four of the wounded the Bren Gun and the ammunition.
Recommended for M.M.   (L.G. 22.10.40)

Evans, Douglas, Private
*4035808, King's Shropshire Light Infantry [1st Bn
    The Herefordshire Regt. on AFW 3121] (Church
    Stretton) (Immediate)*
During evening 9 Sep 44 at Helcheteren 3575 (Map Sheet 47), a Coy attack was put in to clear the eastern end of the village. The enemy held not only the houses on either side of the road with two pls, but had a third pl dug in on the NW outskirts around the windmill. these posns were in turn covered by mortar and MG fire from woods on the left and right, and a sunken lane immediately beyond, It was quite the strongest and most bitterly defended position ever attacked by this unit.

On reaching the end of the houses, Pte Evans found his pl comd and his own section comd were casualties.

Without further orders, Evans took charge of his section, reorganised it and prepared to attack the strong Windmill posn. He led them in their attack through MG and Mortar fire without fear or hesitation, and put his men into the German posn, clearing them at the point of the bayonet.

He personally captured the Bazooka which a little time previously had put one of our tanks out of action.

He then organised his section posn in the consolidation. A number of our own and enemy wounded were left in the Windmill area, but these could not be reached by the S.S., owing to hy enemy fire which then swept the area. Private Evans himself volunteered to go forward alone and evacuate these wounded. he located the wounded and personally brought back the wounded German Pl Comd. Undaunted, he organised a small carrying party and went forward again to evacuate the reaminder of the wounded. Although the area was under heavy enemy SA and Mortar fire, he organised the evacuation so successfully that no wounded were left in the posn.

The courage of this Private soldier, and his latent power of leadership contributed in no small way to the successful action of the Company.
Recommended for M.M.   (L.G. 1.3.45)

Evans, Hamwell Cole, Sergeant
404474, The Royal Dragoons (Periodic)
On August 31 1944, the Tp of which Sjt. Evans was a member approached the Southern outskirts of Grusmenil during the advance to the Somme. The village was found to be strongly held by the enemy and the Tp came under heavy fire from M.G.'s and Mortars. Sjt. Evans left the leading car and advanced alone towards the village and was able to get valuable information about the enemy. While he was returning, still under heavy fire from M.G.'s, he saw a wounded British soldier lying in the ditch. On further investigation he found and offr and 3 men, all seriously wounded who had been there for some considerable time. He applied first aid to all the wounded and then went back for a stretcher party which he guided back. During the whole time Sjt. Evans showed complete disregard for his own safety, though under constant and accurate fire. He undoubtedly saved the lives of the wounded men.

During the whole time the Regt. has been operating, Sjt. Evans has shown exemplary courage and energy on operations. On several occasions he has lifted mines and dealt with booby traps under fire, which had been holding up the advance of our infantry. On Sep 1st he led his section on foot into Picquigny where there were still a large number of German Inf. Though greatly outnumbered he fought his way to the bridge over the Somme in an attempt to prevent it being blown. He was badly wounded in the leg but continued to direct his section for some time and was responsible for killing about 30 of the enemy and causing many more to surrender in the village.   (29.3.45)

Everall, Ivor Reginald, Lance Corporal
*4105061, King's Shropshire Light Infantry [K.S.L.I.,
    1st Bn The Herefordshire Regiment on AFW 3121]
    (Leominster) (Immediate)*
North of Helcheteren 3575 (Map Sheet 47) in the weeded area 3579 on the morning of 10 Sep 44 an enemy position held by 700 or 800 men was attacked by C Coy, 1 Hereford and C Sqn., Fife and Forfar, practically all enemy being either killed or captured.

In the early stages of the attack, during very fierce fighting, 15 Pl lost its Pl Comd, Pl Sjt. and all Sec Comds. L/Cpl. Everall took comd of the platoon and under his guidance they fought their way through innumerable enemy posts to an objective 1,000 yards in depth. But for his determined and inspiring leadership the other leading platoon would have had an open flank and been subject to enfilade fire which would have stopped the attack.

When on the objective this young and junior N.C.O. properly organised the consolidation and pushed forward his contact patrols.

There is no doubt that the action of the L/Cpl. is in no small way responsible for the complete defeat of this German Para Bn.   *(L.G. 1.3.45)*

Ewell, Raymond Leslie, Warrant Officer Cl. II (temp.)
61515, Royal Australian Infantry Corps
No citation.   *(L.G. 28.3.69)*

Eyers, Francis Arthur, M.M., Sergeant
5571789, 4 Wiltshire Regt. (Salisbury) (Immediate)
On 5 Oct 44 Sjt. Eyers was in command of fwd pl North of Elst. During the previous night considerable enemy infiltration had taken place behind his platoon. Two attempts to clear this up by another platoon had failed owing to heavy MG fire from several directions. A third attempt was made and Sjt. Eyers rushed forward under enemy MG fire and silenced the nearest MG post with a grenade and Sten. Shouting to two of his section to follow him, he led them in a bayonet charge. This assault completely over ran the next enemy post and as the enemy were concentrated in a small area the platoon got well into the enemy positions. By his dash and daring the enemy were completely surprised and demoralised to such an extent that in this action 97 PW were taken by Sjt. Eyers and nine men. The success of the attack was entirely due to the outstanding courage and personal dash of Sjt. Eyers, and by his leadership and example he inspired his men to clear up a nasty situation.

(L.G. 1.3.45)

F

Fairfield, William Leslie, Lance Corporal
M.41061, Royal Canadian Regiment (Immediate)
Reference Map: 1/25,000 Sheet 371 (East) Gardenen
(East) Holland.

On the night of 14/15 April 1945, The Royal Canadian Regiment was attacking the eastern outskirts of Appeldoorn. 'C' Company was ordered to advance down the main road towards the town and to seize and hold the important cross roads at MR 803033. At 2300 hours shortly after starting the left forward platoon of 'C' Company was pinned down and four machine guns firing from the area of road junction MR 811031. The enemy called to the platoon to surrender, but instead of surrendering the platoon commander ordered the section commanded by Lance Corporal William Leslie Fairfield to move forward and clear up the resistance.

Realizing that the exact locations of these machine guns were not known and knowing full well that any movement of this section would result in casualties from intense fire, Lance Corporal Fairfield, with complete disregard for his own safety, moved forward alone and deliberately exposed himself to fire in order to obtain the exact locations of the enemy machine guns. He continued to draw the fire of these guns until all four posts had been specifically located.

Lance Corporal Fairfield returned to his section, made his plan and then led his men in a bold dash across two hundred yards of open ground to outflank two of the enemy machine gun posts. This he did with great success, killing four Germans, wounding five and taking seven prisoners. The two remaining machine gun posts were forced to withdraw as a result of this action and the platoon was able to continue its advance.

Lance Corporal Fairfield showed himself by his rapid appreciation of the situation and his complete disregard for his own safety, to be an outstanding leader of men. As a result of his daring actions 'C' Company was able to continue its advance and to subsequently reach their objective with a minimum number of casualties.
(L.G. 4.8.45)

Fairhall, William Stanley, Corporal (A/Sgt.)
*7900004, 10th Royal Hussars (Burgess Hill, Sussex)
(Immediate)*
On Nov. 2nd 42 this N.C.O. commanded a Crusader Tank which formed part of the Minefield Task Force, whose duty was to advance with our attacking infantry and clear gaps in the enemy minefields. On the morning of Nov. 2nd at about 8,000 yds. East of Tell El Aquaqir the infantry and the Minefield Task Force near were counter-attacked by 20 enemy tanks.

Other tanks close to Sgt. Fairhall withdrew, but he held his ground and fought his tank to such effect that

the enemy were halted. He definitely destroyed one German tank and damaged others.

His gallant action against heavy odds undoubtedly saved our infantry and part of the Minefield Task Force from being overrun by the German tanks, and contributed greatly to the success of the attack. By his example, he enabled the other tanks to be re-organised, and the advance to continue.

Throughout operations from Oct. 23rd to Nov. 9th this N.C.O. showed the greatest courage and initiative, and set a fine example to his Troop.
Recommended for M.M. *(L.G. 28.1.43)*

Falla, John St. Helier, Sergeant
NX 5960, 2/4 Australian Inf. Bn.
This N.C.O. has shown a consistent disregard for his own safety in dangerous circumstances and a great devotion to duty in the performance of many arduous and dangerous tasks for the furtherance of the battalion's plans. He has been persistent and untiring in the face of fatigue and unflinching in the face of danger. The following incident is related as an example of his work:—

On 15 Apr. 41 when the battalion was ordered to withdraw from its defensive position on the Aliakmon River communication with 'A' Coy. was very difficult. Sgt. Falla had spent the day reconnoitring routes to this company. He returned to Bn. HQ thoroughly tired shortly after the withdrawal order and immediately volunteered to return to 'A' Coy. with the order. The route to 'A' Coy. was extremely arduous and exhausting. Although he had approximately three miles to travel over most precipitous country and a climb of approximately a thousand feet he completed the journey and delivered the orders in less than an hour. Although almost exhausted he then guided the Coy. throughout the night and with his assistance the Coy. Comd. was able to withdraw his Coy. without loss.

Later, in Crete, Falla in the role of Intelligence Sgt. performed the duties of Intelligence Officer with outstanding merit. He made several journeys to Bde. HQ under dangerous conditions due to undetected parachute troops who had concealed themselves along roads and tracks. The Bde. I.O. personally mentioned Sgt. Falla's ability to the C.O. and complimented the C.O. on the amount of Intelligence matter which was furnished by Sgt. Falla's section.
Recommended for M.M. *(L.G. 30.12.41)*

Farnhill, Frank, Warrant Officer Cl. II (C.S.M.)
*828597, 5th Bn. Coldstream Guards (Hayes,
Middlesex.) (Immediate)*
On 23rd September 1944 the Company of which this Warrant Officer was Company Sergeant Major led an

attack on the village of Voekel.

Soon after crossing the Start Line the only officer Platoon Commander was wounded and almost immediately upon entering the village the Company Commander was killed. Despite being left without any officers and with the major portion of the operation still to be carried out, this Warrant Officer at once assumed control and by his ability and example pressed the attack through to a successful conclusion.

It was not until the final objective had been reached and after heavy fighting that it was possible for another officer to be sent up to take over command of the Company. On his arrival he found that this Warrant Officer had already re-organised the Company and had done everything that should have been done to ensure the complete success of the attack.

But for this Warrant Officer's presence of mind and personal example it is very doubtful whether the operation could have been successfully concluded.

(L.G. 1.3.45)

Farrier, Albert, Sergeant
5611662, Cheshire Regt.
No citation. *(L.G. 27.8.40)*

Faulkner, Brian, Staff Sergeant
23951692, Parachute Regt.
Colour Sergeant Faulkner, as the Regimental Aid Post Colour Sergeant during the attack by 3rd Battalion The Parachute Regiment on Mount Longdon on the night 11th/12th June, performed throughout with the utmost dedication and bravery in extreme conditions of weather and under constant, accurate artillery and mortar bombardment. He never faltered, setting a magnificent personal example of courage and competence, that was well beyond anything that could reasonably be expected. One burst of shellfire left him concussed, but he swiftly returned to his duties. One minute he could be seen consoling young soldiers, severely distressed by the experience of losing their comrades, and by the sight of terrible wounds, and then yet again he would be busy with his prime duty of tending for the casualties themselves. His personal coolness and bravery did much to calm those around him. Twice under alarm of counter attack, he forcefully rallied the Regimental Aid Post, Stretcher Bearers and those passing through the area, to form a defensive perimeter, and these actions typified his constant alertness to the tactical situation whcih overlaid his specialist reponsibilities. Once he himself led a counter attack up the ridge, to an area where he knew soldiers had been killed.

Colour Sergeant Faulkner's gallantry and example on this night, and in the subsequent two days of bombardment on Mount Longdon, were in the highest tradition of the Army, and were typical of his consistently brave and oustanding performance throughout the operation. *[From L.G.]* *(L.G. 19.9.78)*

Featherstone, Ernest, Sergeant
5043260 [3043269 on AFW 3121], 2 North
Staffordshire Regt. (Lincoln) (Immediate)
On the night of the 7/8th Feb. 44. the Bn. was holding fwd. positions in the Anzio Beachhead. Sgt. Featherstone was the N.C.O. commanding 2 Dets. of 3″ Mortars supporting A Coy. from a position in rear of the Coy.

At about 2000 hrs. 7th Feb. the Bn. was heavily attacked along its whole front and subsequently A Coy. was overrun and Sgt. Featherstone lost touch with the Coy. Comd. At the same time the enemy penetrated through the Coy. on the left. Sgt. Featherstone without orders from the Coy. Comd., continued to engage the enemy with heavy Mortar fire at gradually reducing range. His positions were attacked several times by parties of the enemy and hand-to-hand fighting took place. Each time the enemy was driven off and the Mortars continued to fire. Finally, when all the ammunition was exhausted, Sgt. Featherstone gave orders for the destruction of his two Mortars and led his two detachments back through the enemy who by this time had completely surrounded his position.

His two Mortars had fired approx. 600 rounds at the enemy during the engagement.

During previous engagements this N.C.O. had fired his Mortars from an exposed O.P. under heavy enemy MG and Mortar fire. *(L.G. 20.7.44)*

Feebery, Cyril, Warrant Officer Cl. II (S.S.M.)
2615284, Army Air Corps, 1st SAS Regiment, No. 8
Cdo 1 SBS & SAS
I have known SSM Feebery since 1941 when he was a Corporal in 'B' Battalion, Layforce.

In September 1941 he and I joined the Special Boat Section in the Middle East, and two months later we took part together in the raid led by the late Lt-Col Keyes VC. (November 18th, 1941). Our task was to guide the forces ashore and later to try to get them off again. Both these operations were rendered extremely hazardous by the very heavy seas running. Both times Cpl Feebery showed exceptional courage and coolness, and spent a long time in the water retrieving boats etc. which got washed off the submarine, and saving the men who also went overboard. He and I went ashore to try to get the party off, and were capsized in the surf twice. Our boat was damaged, and I lost my paddle altogether.

Cpl Feebery, when I decided to try to return to the ship, paddled us both back through the heavy surf. I have no hesitation in saying that his strength, presence of mind and courage on this occasion, saved us from a nasty situation.

In the next few months Special Boat Section personnel were sent out on submarine patrols from Alexandria to be put ashore at the Commander's discretion, if opportunity arose. Feebery made eight trips on submarines which included the patrol of HMS Torbay for which Lt-Cdr Miers, DSO, RN, was awarded the VC. All the submarines crew received decorations on this occasion. Reports of Submarine Commanders on Feebery's conduct and bearing on these patrols were all excellent.

Early in June 1942 Feebery (then Sergeant) was one of a small party under Major Kealy who landed on Crete. Though no positive results were obtained, Major Kealy's report—which I read—and his story which he told me personally, reflected the greatest credit on Sgt Feebery. Once again his courage and coolness in a difficult situation was excellent. In August 1942 Sgt Feebery took part in the raid on Benghazi led by Lt-Col David Stirling, and again received excellent reports. When the Special Boat Section was reformed in January 1943 under Major The Earl Jellicoe DSO, MC, Feebery was made Sergeant Major of the unit, and I have no hesitation in saying that his enthusiasm and drive played a large share in the success of the unit.   *(L.G. 3.8.44)*

Fenn, Joseph, Lance Corporal
4748318, York & Lancaster Regt. (Littleborough)
No citation.   *(L.G. 21.12.44)*

Fenton, Frank, Sapper
36392, 8 N.Z. Field Coy., N.Z.E. (Immediate)
Sapper Fenton displayed outstanding courage and devotion to duty in operating a mine detector under most hazardous conditions during the attack to the West of Tel el Eisa on the night 1/2 Nov 42. There was little cessation in the bursting of mortar shells all about him, the minefields were covered by sharp machine gun fire and Sapper Fenton, as the forward-most member of the party was being repeatedly sniped at from an uncleared enemy pocket, but not once did he hesitate or delay in sweeping for mines. He operated the mine-detector for more than two hours without relief. When it seemed certain that enemy fire would hold up operations Sapper Fenton calmly and fearlessly carried on and largely as a result of his devotion to duty and gallant example the lane was cleared without delay.   *(L.G. 28.1.43)*

Ferbrache, Stanley John, Sergeant
5503800, Hampshire Regt.
No citation.   *(L.G. 27.12.40)*

Ferusi, Selemani [Feruzi on AFW 3121], Sergeant
206183, 36 (T) King's African Rifles (Immediate)
On 3rd November 1944, during an attack on a Japanese held hill at about RU 602795 NE of Myintha, Burma. Sgt. Selemani was Platoon Sgt. of the leading platoon under C.S.M. Widdows. The platoon came under heavy L.M.G., M.M.G. and grenade discharger fire from the first. C.S.M. Widdows was mortally wounded before the platoon reached its objective. In addition, the Coy. Comd. was wounded, the Coy. 2 i/c killed, and the neighbouring Platoon Comd. killed, leaving no European in the vicinity. In spite of these adverse circumstances, Sgt. Selemani immediately took command of his platoon, and, having organised a party to evacuate his Platoon Comd.,

he at once gained control of his platoon, steadied them, and led them in to the attack onto their objective. He showed the highest qualities of leadership and complete disregard for his personal safety.   *(L.G. 22.3.45)*

Field, Frederick Charles, Corporal
2571109, 2nd Bn. Rifle Brigade
This N.C.O. accompanied Lt. C. H. Liddell on two reconnaissance patrols on the nights 2/3 and 7/8 December 1940. He and one other N.C.O. managed to crawl right up to the enemy defences which had sentries posted about 50 yards apart. He got through these and climbed over the wall of the defences and got right inside the enemy camp. He then crept back over the wall and got away undiscovered. He was thus able to bring back valuable information about the size and strength of the defences and location of the A/T mines. Again on the night 7/8 he and one Rifleman crept up to the camp on another side and found a line of tanks closely guarded by sentries. He managed again to penetrate this and got just inside. He crept back again and was able to report a gap in the defences closed only by tanks, which was of the greatest value. Both these patrols required great patience, courage and skill in locating and avoiding the enemy sentries.
Recommended for M.M.   *(L.G. 25.4.41)*

Fifer, Johannes Cornelis, Corporal (temp.)
44041, Royal Australian Infantry Corps
For Vietnam   *(L.G. 12.2.71)*

Finch, Roy Colin, Warrant Officer Cl. II (C.S.M., actg.)
3972491, 4th Bn. Welch Regt. (Lowestoft) (Immediate)
Map Ref: 1/25000 Sheet 3121 Barnstedt 049762

A/C.S.M. Finch was C.S.M. of 'C' Coy. 4th Bn. The Welch Regiment during an attack on the village of Barnstedt, Germany, on 12 April 1945.

In the first attack the Company was pinned down by very concentrated MG fire before reaching the village and was unable to move forward. it was withdrawn under cover of smoke and a new plan was made. After this attempt it was very apparent that the village was strongly held by a very determined enemy.

In the second attack the leading platoon established itself in the outskirts of the village but was then halted by a hail of MG fire from all directions. C.S.M. Finch seeing this and knowing that the enemy posts existed between him and the platoon realised that if this attack failed the village would not be taken. Without hesitation and with no thought for the personal danger to which he was exposing himself he dashed forward alone to the leading platoon. On his way he was fired at from very close range by two enemy armed with a Spandau who appeared out of a hole beside a bank. C.S.M. Finch charged this and killed both enemy with his Sten gun but was wounded in the arm. In spite of this wound he continued on his way and charged another enemy post of two men also armed with a MG who were dug in on the side of a bank. Immediately after destroying this post a grenade was thrown over the bank by an enemy post on the far side which severely wounded C.S.M. Finch, breaking his leg and blowing off the fingers of one hand. By this time he had reached to within ten yards of a Section of the leading platoon which was in a barn. He was carried inside by two men of the Section who came out to his aid. He ordered them to lay him near a slit in the wall and continually shouted encouragement to them, twice firing his Sten, which had been reloaded for him, through the slit in the wall with his remaining good arm.

Throughout the action C.S.M. Finch had no thought whatever for his own personal safety, his one aim being to assist a platoon of his Company at all cost. His devotion to duty in the face of great danger and pain was an inspiration to all who saw it. His determination to reach the platoon resulted in the wiping out, by himself, of two enemy MG posts which undoubtedly saved that platoon from being cut off, and the second attack from failing.

The extent of C.S.M. Finch's personal courage is emphasised by the fact that after the battle eighteen Spandaus and more than twelve Bazookas were picked up in the area.

Witness's Statement:

During a Company attack on Barnstedt my leading platoon was pinned down by very concentrated Spandau fire. I went forward to try to contact the platoon and C.S.M. Finch went with me. We were met with heavy fire, but, without hesitation, C.S.M. Finch dashed forward firing his Sten gun and killed two enemy manning a Spandau dug in at the side of the road. In this charge C.S.M. Finch was wounded in the arm. In spite of this wound he continued to fire at the enemy with his Sten and again charged a second Spandau post, again killing the enemy, this time with a grenade.

A grenade was then thrown at C.S.M. Finch which badly wounded him, and he lay out in a very exposed position.

C.S.M. Finch's action showed his magnificent courage and his disregard for personal safety and there is no doubt that it inspired the platoon, who were pinned down, to go forward and take the objective.

Signed W. H. Clement, Major.18.4.45

Witness's Statement:

A/C.S.M. Finch of my Coy. on the attack which we put in on the village of Barnstedt somewhere in Germany in April 1945.

On one sector of the village we were held down by enemy MG and snipers which delayed our advance for quite a while, in fact we had to withdraw to a new position under smoke.

While making new plans the C.S.M. went forward to recce the ground and reported that the village was very heavily held by MG and Bazookas.

During the second attack the platoon was again held up by MG fire, the C.S.M. Finch seeing our position and the danger we were in came forward towards us and wiped out one of the posts between us and where he

started from. He then called another section forward but they were unable to reach him as another MG post opened up on them and 'Bazookas' were fired in their direction. Seeing the danger of this section the C.S.M. came further forward with his Sten blazing and silenced the post, but while doing so was wounded very badly.

The C.S.M. was then a few yards from us and we saw how badly he was wounded, his hand and leg bleeding, in fact some of his fingers were hanging by the skin.

We moved him to a safer position and lay him on his side owing to the bad state of his leg. I remained at his side and he gave orders to the section, he carried on firing his Sten passing it to me to reload.

The remainder of the platoon advanced to our objective and we were able to remove C.S.M. Finch to a better cover where for the first time his wounds were attended.

Throughout the action the C.S.M. had no thought for himself or his own safety, his only thought being to assist his platoon and Coy. on to his objective.

Signed L. Jenkins, Pte.18.4.45

Witness's Statement:

I was commanding the leading platoon of the Coy. during the attack on Barnstedt. We advanced along the road when the platoon came under heavy fire from the front and both flanks. The tank which was advancing with my leading section was knocked out by a Bazooka and the platoon was pinned to the ground and unable to advance. A/C.S.M. Finch then came forward from Coy. HQ and dashed forward across two hundred yards of open ground which was being swept by enemy machine gun fire. He was wounded in the arm but continued to advance and located an enemy position in which there was a Spandau manned by two men. A/C.S.M. Finch killed both these men with his Sten gun and then without hesitation dashed on to attack another Spandau post. He killed the men in this post with a 36 grenade.

A grenade was then thrown from a third enemy position and this badly wounded A/C.S.M. Finch in the right leg and shattered his right hand.

Two men from my leading section, which he was now within a few yards of, left a covered position and carried him to it. He refused to have his wounds dressed and insisted that his weapon should be reloaded for him and continued to fire on the enemy. He shouted to the platoon to advance and his magnificent example rallied their spirits. They advanced and killed the remaining enemy.

A/C.S.M. Finch gave no thought for his own personal safety throughout the action and even when wounded and bleeding freely he continued to show a magnificent fighting spirit.

His action prevented the platoon from being completely outflanked to the right and he undoubtedly enabled the platoon to reach its objective without suffering more casualties than it did.

Signed J. Morgan Davies, Lieut.18.4.45

Recommended for V.C.   *(L.G. 12.7.45)*

Finlay, Nathaniel, Sergeant
6978038, Royal Irish Fusiliers
No citation.   *(L.G. 4.5.44)*

Finn, Aubrey, Sergeant
40011, 1st Northern Rhodesia Regt.
No citation.   *(L.G. 22.4.43)*

Finn, Bertram, Lance Sergeant
6205733, 56 Reconnaissance Regiment,
   Reconnaissance Corps (Ilminster, Somerset)
Since the commencement of operations in this theatre of war L/Sjt. Finn B. has continually led his patrols with courage and resourcefulness. On several occasions he has extricated his patrols from behind enemy positions, and his leadership has been a continual source of inspiration to his section.

On 17th November 1942 whilst returning to his HQ with vital information he found the road cut by enemy tanks. Faced with the alternative of taking a long safe route back or of going on and getting the information through quickly, he, without hesitation chose the latter course and by skilful use of ground and smoke he led his patrol safely through the enemy ambush and although the whole area was under heavy fire got through without loss.   *(L.G. 11.2.43)*

Fisher, Robert Wilberforce, Sergeant
14201807, 46th Recce Regt., Royal Armoured Corps
   (Stoke-on-Trent) (Periodic)
The abilities of this N.C.O. have at all times been absolutely outstanding. During the entire campaign in Italy it has been impossible to speak too highly of the leadership, courage, gallantry and devotion to duty of this N.C.O. His skill at patrolling and control at night is quite exceptional and this inevitably made him the obvious choice for the more important patrols. His work on the Volturno, Garigliano and Foligno rivers in particular deserves the highest praise and the information he obtained always proved most detailed and accurate. His conduct and self possession, after his Troop Commander had been killed during the consolidation of his troop on a feature near to Domagnano by the border of San Marino, whilst under intensive artillery, mortar and small arms fire, was quite superb. His actions materially assisted in the holding of the position and the subsequent follow through by the 6th Bn. The York and Lancaster Regt. To say that this man has been an inspiration to his comrades is an understatement. The qualities he displays are granted to few men indeed. I recommend him for a periodic award of the D.C.M.
                              (L.G. 13.12.45)

Fitt, Bertie Robert, Sergeant (A/Colour Sergeant)
5771220, 2nd Bn. Royal Norfolk Regt. (Malton,
   Yorks.) (Immediate)
At Kohima, Assam

For extreme ability and conspicuous gallantry whilst commanding a platoon on 4, 5 and 6 May, 1944.

During the attack on G.P.T. Ridge on 4 May C/Sgt. Fitt was commanding the right forward platoon of 'B' Coy. His able handling of his sections resulted reduction of three enemy bunkers in quick succession, and the maintenance of the impetus of the attack. When the position was consolidated he sited his platoon by a reconnaissance under heavy fire in such a way as to ensure the security of the right flank of his Coy. On this and the following day his personal example to his men inspired them in a manner beyond praise. C/Sgt. Fitt's platoon was again engaged in the dawn attack on 6 May on Norfolk Bunker. The attack was held up by LMG fire and grenades at a few yards range from a previously hidden post. When his Coy. Comd. was killed this N.C.O. led a second rush on the post and though shot in the face at point blank range succeeded in lodging a grenade in the post and silencing the gunner. When orders for withdrawal were issued C/Sgt. Fitt remained in command though wounded and succeeded in withdrawing what was left of his Coy.   *(L.G. 31.8.44)*

Fitzhugh, Leonard Bow, Corporal
1534766, 2nd Bn. South Wales Borderers (Liverpool)
   (Immediate)
On 4 Jan. 45, the Bn. had been ordered to attack the Bois de Hampteau, the objective including the village of Rendeux Bas. Cpl. Fitzhugh was commanding a section, and when the leading platoon of the Coy. was heavily engaged with the enemy near a road block North of the village, he was ordered to take his section round the right flank. This entailed moving over completely open snow-covered ground on a forward slope. Cpl. Fitzhugh led his section forward with great determination and dash, but when about half-way down the forward slope, the section came under heavy fire from two German tanks which were dug in on a flank and camouflaged with snow. Three men of the section were hit, but Cpl. Fitzhugh immediately led the section forward to where a slight fold in the ground offered some cover. He, himself, carried one of the wounded men to this cover and then attempted to rescue the other two. The slightest movement, however, drew heavy fire from the two tanks, a 20mm gun and riflemen. Cpl. Fitzhugh maintained this position for three hours under practically continuous enemy fire, during which time, the three wounded men died. He then decided to find a better position for his section and gave orders that he would try and find this position himself, but that if he was hit, the section was to remain where it was. He then moved forward quite alone, deliberately exposing himself to draw fire in order to determine the feasibility of the route he proposed to take. He reached a wood about 100 yards away and controlled the move of the remainder of his section, one at a time, until they had all joined him. By this time, darkness was falling and he had lost touch with his Coy., which had been ordered by the Bn. Comd. to

withdraw from the exposed forward slope on which it was engaged, preparatory to mounting a further attack. Cpl. Fitzhugh then adopted a defensive position and decided to wait for daylight. During the night, our own guns fired two very heavy programmes (Medium and Field arty.) in support of the new attack, a great deal of this fire falling within a few yards of the section's position. Most of Cpl. Fitzhugh's section were young soldiers in action for the first time, but by his calm and resolute leadership and exemplary personal courage, he maintained complete control throughout this dangerous and unpleasant time. At first light, as the second attack had failed to reach his position, Cpl. Fitzhugh personally reconnoitred a route back to the former Coy. area where he reported for duty to this Coy. Comd. with the remainder of his section.

The whole action was fought in intense cold and Cpl. Fitzhugh's magnificent leadership, bravery and skill set an outstanding example of devotion to duty which inspired his Coy., and indeed, the whole Battalion.

(L.G. 12.4.45)

Fitzpatrick, Edward, Corporal
3774526, 2nd Bn. Royal Inniskilling Fusiliers (Liverpool, 15) (Periodic)
Ref Maps—Italy—Sheet Nos 88/I–88/II–76/II–1/ 50,000, 88/I NE—1/25,000

From the time the Bn. moved to the Senio in February 1945 until he was wounded on the 21st April 1945, whilst his Company was advancing to form a bridge-head over the S. Nicolo Ferrarese Canal, Map Ref 1871, Cpl. Fitzpatrick has constantly, by his unflagging fighting spirit and courage, been an inspiration and example to his platoon.

On the Senio, this N.C.O. would, night after night, leave the dug in positions, and with either Piat or Bren gun, go up to the bank, and completely exposing himself, fire at point blank range into enemy dug-outs, that he would locate during that day. By these actions he maintained not only in his own platoon but the whole Company the aggressive spirit of defence that was so essential during these months.

On the 14th April, 1945 during the Battalion's advance to La Giovecca, Map Ref 317517, South of Argenta, Cpl. Fitzpatrick's platoon was ordered to send out a patrol to reconnoitre the ferry area across the Santerno at Map Ref 318507. This patrol was to seize any bridge or ferry that might be found there. Cpl. Fitzpatrick together with his platoon Sgt. and member of the patrol climbed up the bank, and found that the ferry had been destroyed. Seeing two Germans in trenches on the opposite side flying the white flag, they called upon them to come across. As they would not do so, the patrol waded across and Cpl. Fitzpatrick pulled them out of the trenches. Climbing up to the top of the bank, Cpl. Fitzpatrick saw a party of about twenty Germans out in the open. Firing his Bren gun, he killed three and the rest scattered.

In the early hours of the 19th April 1945 at Tomba 267621, North of Argenta, Cpl. Fitzpatrick was ordered to take a reconnaissance patrol out along the Northern bank of the Reno to ascertain the South positions of the enemy who were thought to be digging in that area. Immediately after the patrol left Tomba, our own gunners fired a very heavy and close barrage on to both banks of the Reno, to assist the advance of Commando units up the Western side of the river. During this barrage our own troops had been withdrawn from positions on the Reno bank. The patrol was called in and succeeded in regaining the house at Tomba without casualties, although shells were falling around and on the house.

Throughout this incident, Cpl. Firzpatrick remained completely calm and master of the situation, and by his demeanour and leadership, maintained the morale of his men, although they were considerably shaken. After an interval, Cpl. Fitzpatrick took his patrol out again, and leading them along the Northern bank of the river, was able to report the area clear.

On the 21st April 1945 when his Company was advancing to the S. Nicolo Ferrarese Canal, Cpl. Fitzpatrick was badly wounded by mortar fire whilst looking for a crossing place for his platoon to cross a broad dyke.

By his contempt for personal danger, this N.C.O.'s actions have been an outstanding example to men of his Company, and his leadership on patrol or where offensive action has been required, has been most outstanding.

(L.G. 13.12.45)

Flannigan, Richard, Sergeant
3186172, 2nd Bn. King's Own Scottish Borderers (Middlesbrough) (Immediate)
M.S. 196 road Allanmyo—Rangoon

On the night of 28/29 May 45 the Battalion was stretched as a cordon along the road Allanmyo—Rangoon to prevent the escape Eastwards of the Japanese from their Irrawaddy Bridgehead. Owing to the long frontage on which the Battalion was deployed the Mortar Platoon, under the command of No. 3186172 Sgt. Richard Flannigan, was responsible for a sector of the front with half their strength as riflemen as well as for applying Mortar fire with the remainder.

At about 0545 hrs. on 29th May the enemy attacked in great strength in the area of MS 196 between HQ. Coy. HQ. and the Mortar Pl.

Sgt. Flannigan ordered his men to hold their fire until the enemy were bunched in the open and then ordered the whole platoon to open fire with their rifles to stop the initial rush. This they did with annihilating effect. As soon as this was effected he at once ordered 50% back to their Mortars and proceeded to engage the enemy with 5" M fire, dropping the range till the bombs were falling within 50 yds. of his own and the HQ. Coy. HQ. positions.

The enemy were finally beaten off about 0800 hrs leaving piles of dead opposite the Mortar Pl. Throughout

the action Sgt. Flannigan with utter disregard for his own safety strolled from trench to trench and Mortar position to Mortar position—to quote the exact words of one of his platoon—'giving encouragement to some, and harsh but helpful words to the timid.' His lack of fear, his coolness and his careful organisation of his platoon to produce the maximum fire power when and where required, not only acted as a tremendous inspiration to his men, but also was undoubtedly to a large extent the cause of inflicting a heavy defeat on the enemy.
Recommended for M.M. *(L.G. 20.9.45)*

Fleck, William Paul, Sergeant
K.998, 9 Canadian Armoured Regiment (B.C.D.)
(Immediate)
On the late afternoon of 4 September 1944, 'B' Squadron 9 Canadian Armoured Regiment was to support two Companies of Cape Breton Highlanders ordered to clear and consolidate the high ground Northwest of Misano. This position was held in strength, by enemy in well-constructed positions.

The tanks were 300 yards in front of the infantry and, in the failing light, two Germans were able to knock out a tank with a Faustpatronen. In spite of the fact that the haystacks in the vicinity of the objective were fired to give more light, the crew commanders could not see the movement of enemy infantry and, as our own infantry were pinned by heavy mortar and small arms fire, it appeared as if the tanks would be forced to withdraw to them for protection.

Sergeant Fleck quickly appreciated the situation and, with his Corporal, dismounted and, armed with Thompson Machine Carbines and grenades, led his tanks onto the objective, killing at least five Germans in slit trenches on the way. On reaching the objective Sergeant Fleck and his Corporal captured eight prisoners.

Although wounded by a shell splinter Sergeant Fleck carried out a reconnaissance with his Squadron Leader. It was not until he collapsed from loss of blood that his wound was noticed and even then he refused to be evacuated.

The prompt action and aggressiveness of this Sergeant ensured the capture of the objectives, with the minimum of casualties to tanks and infantry. Sergeant Fleck has justly earned the admiration of all the men in his Squadron. *(L.G. 20.1.45)*

Flematti, Bruno, Sergeant (temp.)
54679, Royal Australian Infantry Corps
No citation. *(L.G. 28.3.69)*

Fletcher, Archibald, Warrant Officer Cl. II
3116, 6 N.Z. Inf. Bde.
In the battle of Alamein.
During the action on the night of 3/4 Sept. 42 against enemy positions North of the Deir El Angar area this W.O. acted with great coolness and courage adding determination to all those round him to carry on in the face of heavy enemy fire from mortars, machine guns and grenades. During the action the Coy. lost three of its officers and W.O.II Fletcher was left in charge of the HQ's group, which he kept going at all costs in the correct direction giving the platoons a guide to direct from and helping to maintain the momentum of the attack. He kept his signallers together and maintained wireless communication throughout the thickest of action. He and another soldier charged a strong enemy nest several times until he eventually withdrew through lack of ammunition. When the withdrawal back to the Coy. area was ordered he collected a large body of the Coy. together and arranged the carriage of many of the wounded back to our lines. He personally carried a seriously wounded man several hundred yards on his back. He also rounded up and brought back with him a large party of prisoners.

W.O.II Fletcher's calmness and leadership was responsible for bringing this party including such a high percentage of seriously wounded back to our lines through over two thousand yards under fire.
(L.G. 31.12.42)

Fletcher, Frank, Lance Sergeant
2616563, 6th Bn. Grenadier Guards (Frome)
(Immediate)
Pt. 530 Acqueedola, 6—9 Dec 43.
This L/Sgt. on Dec 7 went with an officer and two men to turn out a MG post. The going was rocky and precipitous and lateral movement limited owing to mortar and MG fire. The patrol found the enemy but the officer was fatally wounded by shots from other posts. This N.C.O. took command, killed one German and scattered the remainder. Continuing forward he located the MG post, threw a grenade which dispersed the enemy, destroyed the Spandau and threw the ammunition down the cliff. By this time MG fire was intense from covering positions so he withdrew his patrol and went by himself to try and help the officer. It was not then possible. Later he made the same journey, recovered the officer's body and again cleared the post which had been re-occupied.

This N.C.O.'s conduct under heavy fire on a forward slope was a wonderful example of courage, physical endurance and leadership of the highest quality.
(L.G. 23.3.44)

Flockhart, Cyril Bruce, Flight Sergeant
628366, 76 Sqn., Bomber Command, R.A.F.
Escaped from Stalag Luft VI (Heydekrug) via Danzig to Sweden
1. Capture
I was a member of the crew of a Halifax Mark 1 aircraft which took off from Middleton St. George about 2145 hrs. on 4 Aug. 41. We reached approximately the target area—Karlsruhe—and bombed the larger of two fires, possibly Mannheim. We were coned badly and shot up by flak, one half of the tail unit being destroyed. Sgt. Byrne put the aircraft into a steep dive and gave the order to bale out about 0200 hrs. (5 Aug.). I baled at 500 or

600 ft., and was only in the air for about two seconds. The aircraft went on, and I learned later that Sgt. Byrne had flown it alone as far as the Belgian coast, where he had been shot down by a fighter.

I reached the ground on a new road between Worms (Germany, 1:700,000, Sheet 131, 5398) and Lampertheim (6296). I sprained my knee in touching down. Two searchlights were operating along the ground near to me. I lay still for a few minutes and then gathered in my parachute, took off my harness, and hid both in a ditch. The fire at Mannheim was pretty big, and I decided it would be inadvisable to make in that direction and that it would be better to head for France. I was on the Eastern bank of the Rhine, and, as I did not feel able to swim the river, I walked North in search of a bridge. I went along the uncompleted road, which was camouflaged with grass matting. At the junction of the road with the Autobahn (Sheet 131, 565,999) I turned along the Autobahn towards Worms. When cars passed me I got into the ditch at the roadside. Before I reached the bridge I got into a wood. There was bright moonlight and good visibility, and after observing the bridge for some time, I decided to cross it, skirt the town on the South, and lie up for the day in another small wood which I could see.

I got about a third of the way across the bridge, when a guard came out of a room in the wall of the bridge. He challenged me. I tried to bluff him, but without success. He took me into the guardroom, and I was then marched, with an escort of two with rifles at the ready, to the military barracks at the North side of Worms. I was searched in the barracks guardroom. I gave my name, rank and number, and about 0400 hrs. was put into a cell.

After two or three hours the first of a number of Army and Luftwaffe officers came in. All spoke English and were very polite. I got off my bed for the first, sat up for the second, and ignored the remainder. They wanted to know where I had come down, where the aircraft was, what my target had been, and where the rest of the crew were. I did not answer any of these questions, merely repeating my name, rank and number. About a dozen officers came in between 0630 and 0900 hrs. I got very fed up and treated them with contempt. I was given bread and Ersatz coffee, and later was taken to see the commanding officer, who spoke no English. He tried to question me through an interpreter, asking me the same type of question the others had put. I refused to answer. I was taken back to my cell, where I remained for two days. There was no further interrogation during that time.

2. Dulag Luft

Two Feldwebel of the Luftwaffe took me to Dulag Luft (Oberursel, near Frankfurt). I was accompanied by Sgt. Leigh, of my crew, who had been caught near Worms about 0700 hrs. on the day on which we baled out. We arrived in Frankfurt in the evening. We were politely received at Dulag by a Feldwebel who had lived for many years in the United States. I was taken alone into a room outside the general compound, and a meal

was brought. I was asked to change into an old Polish uniform while my own, which actually had not been 'prepared,' was being examined. My collar-stud, nailfile, fountain pen, and ring were all carefully examined.

Next morning an Oberleutnant came in. He spoke excellent English, and was very charming at first. He produced a new packet of Capstans, offered me one, and put the cigarette and matches on the table. After asking after my comfort and saying I would be well treated, he said there was one formality—the completion of the Red Cross form. I looked at the form and saw that it contained a number of operational questions. I filled in my name, rank and number, and my mother's address, putting my pen through the other questions. After I had signed the form at this request, the Oberleutnant said I had forgotten to fill in some of the replies. I said I did not think the Red Cross particularly wanted the other information. He said I could not tell him anything he did not already know. I replied that, in that case, there was little point in his asking me. He showed me other completed forms, and said I was being very foolish in not doing what everyone else did. I got a bit rattled, and told him to get the Hell out of it. He became very angry and tried to bluster and bluff, but I was as angry as he was. He collected his cigarettes and matches and went away. No further attempt was made to interrogate me.

Next day (8 or 9 Aug. 41) I was put into the main compound, and was there for seven or eight days.

3. Stalag III E (Dobrilugk-Kirchhain)

When I arrived at Stalag III E (Dobrilugk-Kirchhain) (Sheet 89,0124) in a party there were already about 50 R.A.F. P/W there. During the next few weeks two more batches came in till the total strength was about 190. Food parcels did not begin to arrive there till two months later—about Oct 41.

Just before this 12 Sergeants got out by making a hole in the wall of their barrack. All were recaptured within four or five days. I was not in this party, as I was living in another barrack. As a reprisal for this escape about 50 or 60 guards were sent into the camp. All our boots were taken away and put into sacks, and we were issued with wooden-soled sandals. I was at the end of the first row, and was the first when we marched round a field at the bottom of the compound. There was a guard every twenty paces. An officer, probably a Leutnant, stood in the centre, brandishing his revolver and screaming threats in German, the import of which was that I should go faster. This I was partly unable and partly unwilling to do. I was aided by one of the guards, who had been ordered to make me march faster. He put a hand on each of my shoulders, kicked my knees forward with his knees, and trod on my heels. I still bear the marks of this. I tried to march on my bare feet, but was compelled by the officer to wear my sandals. The marching round the compound continued for two and three-quarter hours. Threats were made with rifle butts. At least a dozen of the P/W fainted and were made to rise. Where they could not walk, two of their comrades were made to assist them. During this time other guards were searching our living quarters. Food which had been saved—such as bread crusts for making puddings—was thrown about. Next morning my bungalow was punished a further hour of marching round the field, again in sandals—this time as a punishment for having been late for parade the previous evening. There were no incidents this time, as the marching was rather easier than on the day before, though most of us were in an exhausted condition.

On recapture the 12 escapers were put in a partly underground cellar. Two others who tried to escape by hiding in a latrine were also put here for five days. There was no light in the cellar, in which there were as many as five or six at one time. Except for a hot meal every fourth day they were fed on bread and water. Complaint was made to the Protecting Power, and later offenders were sent to the local police station cells.

In Jan. 42 we began to make a tunnel, with practically everyone in the camp assisting. There were several searches during its construction. One of the searches coincided with the visit of a General, who actually stood on the brick covering one of the ventilation holes. The General said the camp was not good enough for British P/W and that we would be transferred.

On 1 May 42 we discovered unofficially through an interpreter that the first party of 100 was to be moved in a week's time. We redoubled our efforts to finish the tunnel, but when I left the camp in the first party there were still 20 metres to go. I learned later that on the night before the departure of the second party they broke the tunnel and 52 men got out. After considerable search the Germans found the exit of the tunnel but did not find the entrance under a bungalow floor, till they had sent in a man through the tunnel. The engineering of the tunnel was done by Sgt. Prior, R.A.F., a Welsh miner.

4. Stalag Luft III (Sagan)
a Arrival

I arrived in Stalag Luft III (Sagan) on 8 May 42. An escape committee was organised, but escape was difficult because of the activities of the Abwehr officers. They had seismographs to detect tunnels. Several tunnels were made—none successful—from our compound. I took no part in these schemes, as I was in hospital with abscesses in the groin during the summer.

b Attempted Escape by 'Blitz' tunnel

In the early part of the winter the Germans were making large holes between the warning wire and the main wire, filling the holes with rubbish, and spreading the yellow sand on top. I discussed with Sgt. Chantler, R.A.F., the possibility of getting into one of the holes and building a 'Blitz' tunnel under the main wire. At the last moment Chantler asked me to take him with me.

We were allowed to walk till 2100 hrs. along a 'red line' between the barracks. My scheme was to crawl from between two of the barracks to a hole, about 100 metres away, carrying a spade head which I had stolen. On the night of 18 Dec. 42, Chantler and I did this. It took us

two hours to crawl, literally inch by inch, over the 100 metres. I got into the hole beside the warning wire and between two machine-gun posts on which searchlights were mounted. There was also a guard on the outside wire between the posts. The hole was about 4 ft. deep. I started working. Chantler joined me, and we took the digging in turns. We made the first part of the tunnel large enough to hold us both. I was then to go ahead, and pass the earth back to Chantler, who was to block the entrance. We had dug about two and a half metres and I was coming out with the last lot of soil before the sealing of the entrance, when Chantler signalled for silence. There was a dog on the edge of the hole looking down at us. The dog went away without making a sound. We lay quiet. Two minutes later the dog returned to the opposite side of the hole. We heard footsteps, and a terrific shouting began. A Hundmeister (one of the men in charge of the dogs) appeared. The searchlights came on to the spot. At first I refused to come out of the hole, insisting that the Hundmeister stand beside me as I came out. When we came out, we were marched with hands up down to the gate, the searchlights following us. There were one or two 'blind-spots' on the way, and we got rid of our maps and compasses. The Abwehroffizier (Major Peschel) interrogated us as to where we were going. I decided to make a joke of the whole business, including discovery of a 100-R.M. note sewn into my jacket, and succeeded. We got 14 days' cells in the camp. We had intended to jump a coal train for France in the morning, having heard of two Frenchmen from a neighbouring camp who had got on a similar train bound for Lyon.

c Second Attempted Escape

On 21 May 43 I succeeded in escaping from the camp. I joined a party of P/W going to the camp dentist. Sgt. Hale, R.A.F., who was also in the party, had made a key for the dentist's waiting-room. He opened the door for me, and locked it behind me. I went out into the corridor, dressed as a German. I was wearing well-worn R.A.F. trousers dyed to look like German working trousers, a white working jacket and an R.A.F. cap made to look like a German cap and with badges embroidered by a Pole. I carried a towel and a piece of German soap. I walked 80 or 100 yds. to the showers in the Vorlager. Here I joined a party of about 70 Germans which was forming up and marched with them, after counting, into the square in the German camp. Here we dismissed, and the party dispersed to the living quarters.

I walked into one barracks and wandered round for a little. Then I got a rake and started to rake the pathway. I did this for about an hour. I then got a plank and carried it on my shoulders to the stables, where a number of Germans were doing odd jobs. I started tidying the cart shed. The others drifted away for lunch. I went up the ladder to the hayloft, and lay down in the back of the loft till dusk. During this time I saw a signal from my compound that I had been 'covered' on the dental party (by Sgt. Menzies, R.C.A.F., a Red Cross parcels orderly who had got into the Verlager as an extra man and had joined the dental parade as it was returning to the camp)—and on parades. I was being covered on parades by Sgt. Eyles, my double in appearance, and by Sgt. Wilkie.

After dark I came out of the hayloft, made my way through the German camp, and found a bus outside the Seargents' Mess, where a concert was in progress. I thought of hiding under the back seat of the bus, but considered this impracticable. I spent the next two hours in lavatories in the German camp. At midnight I put my cap and jacket into the pit in one of the lavatories. This left me with a jacket of Harris tweed appearance made from a blanket, my R.A.F. trousers, a cap made from a duster, a pair of German Army boots, which had been given in Belgium to a Sergeant who had no footwear.

I went round the back of the lavatory, through trees close to the dog kennels, over a single strand barbed-wire fence and into a wood on the South side of the camp.

I had an address in the Warsaw area (since forgotten). I made my way on foot from Sagan (Sheet 90, 2020) to Sprottau (Sheet 91, 3714) and then by train to Glogau (Sheet 91, 7626) and Fraustadt (Sheet 79, 9041), intending to make for Lissa (Sheet 80), (64015746). On the train I travelled as a Polish workman on a false Ausweis. I had another for use in Poland. Both were forged in the camp.

From Fraustadt I walked across the Polish frontier, being unaware that there is no control on the frontier. I entered a small village a few kilometres inside Poland. A party of boys (German) in the street asked me where I was going. (It was then about 2200 hrs.) I said I was going to Lissa. They asked for my Ausweis, and I showed them the appropriate one, which had, instead of the photograph, a pencil sketch done in the camp. The sketch was good enough to pass in poor light. One of the boys was dissatisfied, but I was allowed to go. As soon as I got clear of the village I started to run along the road. A few minutes later two bicycles came along behind me. I hid in a field of barley beside the road. The cyclists were two of the boys, so I decided to cut across country.

I by-passed Lissa, walking by night and hiding by day. Two mornings later I met a barefooted boy in overalls leading a horse. I spoke to him in German, which he did not understand, so I asked him for shelter in Polish of which I had learned a few words before leaving the camp, and told him I was British. He took me back about a quarter of a mile to a middle-aged man working in a field. This man who spoke a little German said he would be glad to help. I waited with him till 0700 hrs., when the man took me to a large farmhouse. He explained to three or four middle-aged Polish women there that I was British, and I was given a meal. While I was eating a thin, shrewish Polish woman came in, and got most upset at my being there. As a result of this woman's agitation I had to leave immediately.

I went off about 0900 hrs. The man said there was a wood a few kilometres further on, and I went there. On my way through the wood I encountered parties of wood-cutters working under German gang bosses when I recognised the eagle badge of their caps. On my way through the wood I passed several of these parties, and saluted each with 'Heil Hitler.' They generally asked where I was going, and I said I was on my way to Reisen (Sheet 80, 0480) a village which I knew to be in the direction in which I was going.

I came out of the wood into heavily cultivated country where there were large numbers of workers in the fields. They also asked me where I was going, and I always gave the same answer. About 200 yds. outside Reisen a farmer wearing the Nazi party badge approached me and asked where I was going. I told him I was on my way to Reisen. He was a Velksdeutscher. He said he did not know me and asked for my Ausweis. I said I had been sent from Lissa. (My pass had been made out as from Lissa). He looked at the Ausweis and, seeing that I was supposed to be Polish, spoke to me in Polish. I said that now I only spoke German. He said that there was something funny about me and that he had better have the police. I could not break away because of the large number of people in the fields, and also because I was lame and suffering from thirst.

The farmer kept my Ausweis and sent for the police. A Feldwebel of the Gendarmerie came along and asked me the details which were contained on my Ausweis. I answered these questions without difficulty. He said I must consider myself under arrest. Handing his rifle to the farmer, he searched me and found a tin of Horlicks tablets. he asked me if the tin contained explosives. I said they were tablets to eat. He then noticed that the writing on the box was in English.

Realising that the game was up, I declared myself a British P/W. The Feldwebel's attitude changed completely to one of sympathy. On the way to the police station he bought me a bottle of beer and then gave me his bicycle to ride, telling me not to try to escape because he was a good shot. I rode to the police station with the Feldwebel walking alongside. He reported my arrest to his headquarters by telephone, and then allowed me to wash and shave. When I had finished he brought three bottles of beer in his office, and also gave me cigarettes. The two other policemen were also polite and at midday took me to lunch in a cafe in the town.

At 1700 hrs. I was taken by horse-wagon, accompanied by the Feldwebel, to the headquarters of the Gestapo in a large private house in Lissa. I was taken into a room where I was confronted by the film conception of a Gestapo agent—a pale middle-aged man with cropped hair and glasses. He sat looking at me for several minutes, and then gave an order. The Feldwebel took me to the civil prison in the castle of Lissa. I was handed over to an S.S. Feldwebel in the guardroom, thoroughly searched by him, and conducted to a cell. I was given a very small meal, and all my clothing was taken away.

At 0600 hrs. next day the Feldwebel wakened me, giving me my clothing, a slice of bread, and a cup of mint tea. At 0700 hrs. the warder returned with a Pole who carried a large hamper of hens' feathers and lengths of twine. The warder said I would have to do some work. I explained I was a Feldwebel of the British Luftwaffe and did not work. He explained what I had to do—peel the feathers and tie the stalks into bundles of 100. I refused. The warder said that if I could not work I would not eat. I insisted on seeing the Kommandant of the prison. Half an hour later the warder took me to the Kommandant, a Hauptmann. After some discussion the Hauptmann said I would not have to work, and I was sent back to my cell.

At 0700 hrs. next day I was put into a private car with two civilians, one of whom was the first person I had seen at the Gestapo headquarters. Two young boys in uniform, whom I discovered to be Ukrainians who had escaped en route to Germany, were in the car. By watching the signposts I saw we were going to Posen. At the Gestapo Hauptstelle I was taken into a room with several S.S. men and a woman interpreter, who was interrogating two men in Russian. On learning who I was, the woman spoke very charmingly in English. I was then taken downstairs to the cells.

In the office of the cells all my possessions were taken and put into an envelope. One of the S.S. people began to talk to me in German on general matters. During our talk a middle-aged Polish woman was brought in. While her possessions were being taken she fumbled and was struck in the face. She was then taken to a cell. Two Polish youths were brought in. One was rather nervous and not quick enough in handing over his possessions. He also received a blow on the face. Both Poles were taken to the cells. The officials who had ill-treated them were very nice to me.

I was taken to a cell which was crowded with civilians. I said to the official that I preferred to be in a cell by myself. He said I must go in beside the civilians. I went in. The cell was 12 ft. long, 6 ft. wide, and about 10 ft. high, with one open window about 3 ft. by 2 ft. There were already 20 men in this cell. Some sat on a wooden bed in the centre of the floor, and the rest on the floor itself. There was a latrine bucket in the corner.

I spoke to a young Pole in German. He said all the civilians were Poles. I said I was British and in a few seconds found that all the Poles spoke German. They crowded round, shook hands with me, and patted me on the shoulder. I found they were there for questioning, but they would not tell me about what. They said that after questioning people were taken to a Gestapo prison where conditions were very bad. At intervals individuals were taken from the room. At midday all the men were filed out. I was told to stay in the cell. A Pole then brought me a plate of soup and vegetables. I got at least double the quantity given to the Poles, and also a second helping which I gave to some of the Poles.

In the afternoon some of the people taken for questioning were brought back looking very nervous and shaken. One seemed to in great pain. Both his thumbs were badly swollen and blue, and he seemed to be in pain with his back, being unable to lie on it. Some of the others helped him off with his jacket, and I saw that his shirt was cut to ribbons and that there were large weals on his back. The Poles seemed to be fatalistic about this treatment.

About 1800 hrs. we all filed out into the passage, faces to the wall. Names were called out. The Poles were made to run to the office to collect their belongings. When my name was called I walked to the office. I was told to return to my place in the line after I had got my belongings. A few minutes later names were called out again and we were marched upstairs into a courtyard between a file of S.S. guards with sub-machine guns. We were put into a flat, canvas-covered Ford 30-cwt. truck. There were about 60 or 70 in the truck, both men and women. The truck was closed, and guards were put on the back. I got to the side of the truck and managed to see out of a slip in the canvas. We went through Posen to a suburb, and stopped at a Fort.

We alighted inside the gate. Names were called and we were divided into parties. I was in a party of three Polish women and four Polish men. I noted the name over the entrance to the Fort, Fort Columb. We were marched inside the Fort and made to stand in a passage with our faces to the wall. Names were called. Our personal belongings were taken away and I was searched by the S.S. guards.

An Unteroffizier was in charge. I told him I was a British P/W and must be treated as such, that I objected to being placed with Polish civilians, and that it was my right to have a cell to myself. He consulted someone on the telephone and said I would be taken to a room with German civilians, this being the best accommodation they could offer me. I was taken downstairs to a room on a level with the bottom of the moat. On entering the room I found 16 German civilians—all men. When the door closed they gathered round asking who I was, where I had come from, and why I was there. I told them I was British P/W. They were very friendly. They gave me bread, butter, jam, and Ersatz coffee. I talked with several of them on general matters—mostly why they were there. I won the confidence of some of them and found that they were there for sabotage—that is, careless workmanship or inefficiency—and several others for having been intimate with Polish women. I did a fair amount of propaganda amongst these Germans who seemed to be quite impressed.

I was two days in this cell, and at 0700 hrs. one morning taken out and convoyed with 60 or 70 others back to the Gestapo Headquarters where I was put back into the cell in which I had previously been, with about 20 other Poles.

After two hours my name was called and I was taken to a room where there were three S.S. guards. One of the S.S. guards (possibly the Leutnant) attempted to interrogate me, but I said that I understood very little German. I insisted on having an interpreter. My object in doing this was to give me time, because I understood the questions and wanted an opportunity to prepare my answers. I was made to stand at attention during the interrogation which lasted about four hours. The whole of the interrogation was taken down direct on the typewriter by one of the guards. The interpreter was also an S.S. guard who spoke imperfect English. They first asked my name. I said it was Flockhart. They said this was a lie and that my name was Wilkie. (Wilkie was one of the men who covered my absence from the camp.) I said I had never heard of anyone called by that name, except Wendell Wilkie. They did not like my answer and threatened to strike me. They continued to accuse me of lying, but eventually let this point drop.

They asked me which camp I was from. I told them. They asked me how I escaped. I told a long story of how one gets tired of prison life, and how, in desperation, I jumped over the wire and got away. They wanted to know if the guards fired on me. I made an evasive answer that I was not wounded.

They then asked many questions about the names of my parents, my birth place, and my profession. Some of the questions I answered truthfully, and others untruth-fully. They accepted all this, and then said, 'Your name is Wilkie, and you have killed a policeman, for which you are to be shot.' I maintained that my name was Flockhart, that I had not killed anyone, and that, if they 'phoned my camp, someone could be sent from the German staff to identify me positively. Their reply was that of course they would do as I suggested. They again became threatening and said that I was in their hands and that no-one knew anything about me. They said they did not believe my story about escaping or anything I had told them, and that I was in a very dangerous position. They wanted the names of those who had helped me escape, and again threatened me when I said I had jumped over the wire.

They also wanted to know how I had become a prisoner, how I had been shot down, what target I had bombed, and where the rest of my crew were. I volunteered no information beyond the fact that I had been taken prisoner at Worms.

At this stage an Unteroffizier of the Luftwaffe from the camp came into the room and recognised me. He was accompanied by a Gefreiter also from the camp. Both carried revolvers. They were told to sit in a corner.

The S.S. guard who had been acting as interpreter stuck his face close to mine and said, 'So you are a Terrorflieger who has come to bomb our women and children.' I told this guard in German exactly what I thought of him and his methods. The other S.S. guards were at first shocked that I could speak German. They then became very threatening and told me I was much too clever, and not to try to play monkey tricks with them. There was no further questioning and I was asked to sign the last of the sheets which were written in German. At first I refused to do so, but finally agreed, maintaining that I did not know what I was signing.

I was again taken to the cells for about an hour. The civilian warder asked if I was hungry and brought me sandwiches. They looked very attractive, but I did not eat them in case they were drugged. A little later the Unteroffizier and Gefreiter escorted me to the railway station in Posen, and took me back to the camp. On the train I ate the sandwiches, which were quite nice.

As soon as I got back to the camp (about 29 May 43) I was met by Oberfeldwebel Glemnitz of the Abwehr Department, a big, tough type of man who had lived for many years in the United States. He was very pleasant and gave me English cigarettes, asking how I got out of the camp. I said he could not expect me to answer that. He then talked about other things, but came back, at intervals during the next hour and a half, to my escape. I was in the cells, and when he left he gave me cigarettes, contrary to orders.

The following morning Hauptmann Brody (?), of the Abwehr Department, and Unteroffizier Flokowski, of the Lagerfuhrung (administration), tried to interrogate me. Flokowski spoke very good English. They were anxious to find out how I left the camp. My statement to the Gestapo of the date on which I had left the camp chanced to coincide with the date on which the 'cover' on me in the camp was lifted. This was about five days after I had got out, and during that period Eyles and Wilkie had covered up my absence. Flokowski said he was on duty at the office on this date and that he was in trouble, being suspected of having helped me to get out. Flokowski had for some months tried to be friendly with me and others in the camp. He traded on that friendliness now, asking me not to get him into trouble. I told the Haupt-mann it was absurd to suggest that Flokowski had assisted me, but still did not say how I had got out. They then gave up the interrogation as a bad job. I believe they thought that I went out of the camp dressed as a Russian.

I got 14 days in the cells with bread and water. Wilkie and Eyles who had covered me got seven days each. Eyles had been discovered because he could not speak German. I was already recaptured by that time.

5. Escape from Stalag Luft VI (Heydekrug)

I arrived in Stalag Luft VI (Heydekrug) (Germany, 1:100,000, Sheet 1, 2934) on 30 Jun. or 1 Jul. 43. This was a new camp with a new German staff. The camp strength when I left on 18 Feb. 44 was a little over 3,000, and the intention was to make it up to 6,000 by transfers from other camps. There are three compounds, and the camp will be overcrowded when there are 6,000 there.

I escaped alone from the camp on the morning of 18 Feb. 44. The previous day I had obtained entrance to another unfinished and partly occupied compound. About 0830 hrs. on 18 Feb. I left the wash barracks in this compound dressed in a green tweed jacket, riding breeches made from Italian pantaloons, top boots (Stiofel), a soft hat, an R.A.F. officer's mackintosh. I was carrying a canvas briefcase (made in the camp) under my arm and in my hand a rolled-up plan of the compound and environs which had been made for me in the camp by architects among the P/W. I had my hair cropped and had shaved off my moustache, and looked so like a German that one of the P/W in my own compound had actually taken me for a member of the Kriminalpolizei who sometimes visited the camp.

I walked to the warning wire, indicated to the guard that I was going to the unfinished wash barracks, inspected the wash barracks outside, and made some notes on my plan. I then went inside for a few moments. Coming out again, I walked slowly to the gate, presented my pass (a forgery) to the guard, and was accepted by him as one of the architects who had been working in the compound. I walked through the gate without being questioned.

I then proceeded to the camp sewage farm which is under construction near the river, about 200 metres from the camp. I was within full view of the watch towers. I spent about ten minutes at the sewage farm, examining the excavations, on which there was no one working, and pretending to take notes and pace distances. I then walked back towards the camp, diagonally towards one corner, and went round the outside wire. This brought me to a road which leads to the main administrative buildings. Before reaching them I turned off on another dirt track through a wood. This brought me to the main road leading to Heydekrug. Before leaving the sewage farm I had put my plan into my brief case which also contained clothing, toilet gear, and sandwiches. The pass I carried was forged and made out in the name of a Germanised (eingedeutscht) Pole.

From Heydekrug I made my way to Danzig, where I succeeded in boarding a Swedish vessel which sailed from Weichselmunde on 25 Feb. I arrived in Stockholm on 27 Feb.

Fogarty, Joseph Patrick, Lance Sergeant
WX 11396, 2/11 Australian Inf. Bn. (Immediate)
For outstanding personal courage and skilful leadership in the Wewak area.

On the 23 May 45, 13 Platoon was attacking a strongly defended enemy position in the Klewalin area. No. 1 Section, commanded by Lance Sergeant Fogarty was temporarily held up by a number of the enemy concealed in fox holes who kept up well directed fire from two machine guns and a number of rifles. Lance Sergeant Fogarty showed complete disregard for his own safety by going forward himself in the face of the enemy fire. From a standing position he engaged the enemy with Owen Gun fire killing two and forcing two Japanese officers to keep down so low as to render their fire ineffective. For fifteen minutes Lance Sergeant Fogarty remained in this position until a flame thrower was brought to bear against the enemy defences. The enemy position was then successfully assaulted. Lance Sergeant Fogarty's individual effort permitted the use of a weapon which so demoralised the enemy that the position was successfully assaulted without loss to his section.

Later on the same day, 13 platoon engaged another well concealed enemy position. The enemy held their fire until Lance Sergeant Fogarty's section was within fifteen yards of their defences. The section was pinned down and again he showed complete disregard for his own safety as he calmly organised his section, moving from one position to another under heavy, close range machine gun fire. Lance Sergeant Fogarty's section had to withdraw to permit the use of supporting fire, and although seriously wounded he refused medical aid, and insisted that he remain to give covering fire whilst the remainder of his section withdrew. When the Section had withdrawn Lance Sergeant Fogarty made his way back and then consented to evacuation.

This non commissioned officer has shown throughout this action a disregard for his own safety in the face of enemy fire. His skilful and resourceful leadership contributed largely to the success of his Company on 23 May 45.

Lance Sergeant Fogarty's courage, leadership and self sacrifice have been an inspiration to all. *(L.G. 24.8.45)*

Fordham, Philip, Sergeant
3710327, 1st Bn. King's Own Royal Regt. (Kendal) (Immediate)
During the fighting around Pideura between 7 & 13 Dec 44, Sjt. Fordham, Bn. Signal Sjt., performed his duties with superb gallantry. Line comn. to the forward Coys. was vital, and owing to the lack of experience of the existing linesmen, Sjt. Fordham insisted on going out himself on line repair works. Time and time again Sjt. Fordham took line parties forward through heavy mud and in intense shell and mortar fire. For four nights running, during which there was continuous shelling and mortaring, he spent the greater part of the night on the line.

On two occasions, when ordered to rest by the Sig. Offr., Sjt. Fordham begged to be allowed to go out, saying that unless he were there, the line would not be repaired. The forward Company Commanders all report that Sjt. Fordham went out on his work when it appeared certain that he would be either killed or wounded by shell and mortar fire. Sjt. Fordham worked throughout with the greatest coolness and, had it not been for his magnificent example, it is very doubtful if the other linesmen would have ventured out at times when line comn. was most needed.

As a result of Sjt. Fordham's work, battalion headquarters was in almost constant telephone comn. with the forward Companies and this enabled artillery and mortar DF to be brought down at times when it ws needed quickly.

Undoubtedly this not only broke up more than one enemy attack but also saved the lives of many men.
(L.G. 24.5.45)

Foreman, Henry Charles, Corporal (actg.)
NX.7852, Australian Military Forces
No citation.   *(L.G. 1.8.46)*

Forgravew, Patrick Arthur, Warrant Officer Cl. II
(S.S.M.)
P1062, Royal Canadian Armoured Corps
No citation.   *(L.G. 24.1.46)*

Forrest, Colin Grant, Corporal
A6091, The Royal Canadian Regiment (Immediate)
Ref Map Italy 1/50000 Sheet 147–I Lanciano.
On 18 Dec. 43 The Royal Canadian Regiment was
attacking the important cross-roads (MR 323142) on the
Ortona—Orsogna lateral. The attack had succeeded in
reaching the buildings at MR 314134, when extremely
heavy enemy fire temporarily prevented 'C' Company
from advancing further.

When his Platoon Commander was killed and the
Platoon Serjeant wounded, Cpl. Forrest took command
of the platoon and, with exemplary courage and skill,
led the 21 men remaining in it on under heavy fire to a
position in a gully strongly defended by the enemy at
MR 318135.

There the platoon dug in. Being unable to contact his
Company, Cpl. Forrest decided to hold the ground he
had gained until further orders were received. In spite of
numerous powerful enemy attempts to dislodge him, Cpl.
Forrest maintained his position all night and successfully
beat off all attacks.

At first light on 19 Dec. 43 he led a patrol out of his
position and succeeded in contacting battalion Headquarters. He received orders to withdraw his platoon, as
an artillery barrage was to be put down in that area in
preparation for an attack on the gully. Together with
stretcher bearers and covering party; he returned to his
platoon and, although his men were almost completely
exhausted, succeeded in withdrawing them with all their
weapons and wounded.

Throughout this action Cpl. Forrest showed courage,
great determination and leadership of the highest calibre.
His maintenance of the position in the gully denied to
the enemy the use of ground that would have been of
great assistance to him and greatly contributed to the
success of the attack later put in by the Battalion.
                                          (L.G. 20.4.44)

Forward, Askari
5594, 2nd Bn. King's African Rifles,
Somaliland.
Outstanding gallantry in the face of the enemy on
12th August in the Mirgo Pass. This young recruit
displayed remarkable coolness and courage in delivering
a box of S.A.A. to a forward platoon under heavy fire.
Although wounded in several places he delivered the
S.A.A. and returned to Coy. HQ to report.

*To be dated 11.2.41 and substituted for the award of the
African D.C.M. announced in the L.G. of that date.*
                                         (L.G. 21.7.42)

Foster, Jack Hewitt, Sergeant (actg.)
2701459, 2nd Bn. Scots Guards (Salford) (Periodic)
On 20 April 45 Right Flank was engaged in the attack
on Visselhovede. As a result of casualties the day before
L/Sgt. Foster was commanding 9 Pl.

In the first stage of the attack 9 Pl. had to advance
down the railway West of the town. This area was
strongly held and the supporting tanks were unable to
give much assistance owing to thick woods.

L/Sgt. Foster led his Pl. forward with the greatest
gallantry. During the advance all his Section Commanders became casualties, and he repeatedly crossed
open ground under heavy enemy fire to organise and
encourage his Sections. By his courage and resolution
he took his Pl. on to its objective unsupported, killing
many Germans and capturing 60.

Later in the day the Company was ordered to attack
in order to relieve Bn. HQ which was being hard-pressed
by an enemy counter-attack. L/Sgt. Foster again led his
Pl. with great dash and complete success. Capturing 50
more Germans, including 12 Officers.

Throughout a long and exhausting day L/Sgt. Foster
provided an outstanding example of leadership and skill
in handling his Platoon.

As a result of his personal gallantry and unfailing
cheerfulness he was largely instrumental in ensuring the
complete success of his Company's operation despite
many casualties.
Recommended for M.M.   *(L.G. 24.1.46)*

Fowler, David Hubert, Warrant Officer Cl. II
143188, 2 S.A. A/Tk. Regt.
23 Jan. 42. Saunnu Valley.
A Tp of 2 prs. of 8 Bty. 2 SA. A/Tk., Regt. under
command W.O. II Fowler, was detailed to remain with
21st Bty. 7 SA. Fd. Regt. in support of 9 Lancers.

Owing to extremely heavy enemy pressure 9 Lancers
were forced to withdrew under cover of 21st Bty. and
A/Tk. Tp. who were eventually overrun by German Tks.

W.O. II Fowler kept his Tp. in action and four enemy
Mk IV Tks. were destroyed and left in flames. Owing to
casualties this W.O. took over as layer on the gun, and
himself accounted for two tanks.

One section of the Tp. was forced to surrender after
covering the withdrawal of the other guns. Their guns
were destroyed by direct hits. Under the leadership of
W.O. II Fowler, one gun of the other section was
successfully withdrawn, and the firing mechanism of the
other removed.

Throughout the action W.O. II Fowler displayed
outstanding courage and determination, devotion to duty
and his fine tactical handling undoubtedly saved many
casualties and the loss of all the guns.
Recommended for M.M.   *(L.G. 12.5.42)*

Fowler, Robert Martin, Sergeant
2756619, 5th Bn. Black Watch (Glencraig)
(Immediate)

On 25th March, 1945, during the fighting in Rees, a platoon was ordered to attack with the help of tanks a strong pocket of enemy which was holding up a neighbouring Battalion. As the attack started, a Bazooka was fired at the tanks at close range, and missing the tanks, wounded Sgt. Fowler, the platoon Sergeant, in the leg. Appreciating that this post must be quickly dealt with if the tanks were not to be knocked out, Sgt. Fowler attacked this post at once. Ignoring the intense pain of his wound and paying no regard to the fusilade of shots and Bazookas aimed at him, he charged through a mound of rubble which had been a house, and on to the house, where the enemy were, followed by three men. Throwing a grenade in through the window, he charged in after it, and laid out the enemy inside with his Sten. So quickly did he carry out this important task that the attack was not held up for a moment. There is no doubt at all that Sgt. Fowler's outstanding courage and determination in the face of great danger were largely responsible for the success of the attack and for the saving of considerable casualties among the tanks. On the objective being captured the platoon came under heavy machine gun fire from enemy posts in a Bund a short distance off. Any movement was extremely dangerous as the position was open and raked by this fire. Despite this and despite the wound in his leg and considerable loss of blood, Sgt. Fowler again decided to attack these posts, as he knew his platoon would suffer casualties unless action was taken. With three men he worked his way forward to within close range of the first post, which he then rushed at the head of his men, firing from the hip as he went. Having knocked out this post he continued to deal with two other Spandau posts killing or taking prisoner all the enemy. Throughout the battle, Sgt. Fowler's bearing and complete disregard of danger were absolutely first-class, while his aggressive determination and magnificent bravery were outstanding even upon an occasion when so many brave deeds were being done. *(L.G. 7.6.45)*

Fox, Alfred, Fusilier
5507203, 8th Bn. Royal Fusiliers (Oldham)
(Immediate)

On the morning of the 9th September 1943, after the landing in Salerno Bay, 16 Platoon were in position covering a road on the Battalion axis of advance. This position was repeatedly attacked by fire from German tanks, causing casualties in Fusiliers Fox's section. Fusiliers Fox returned this fire with fire from his Bren gun thereby exposing himself.

The German tanks closed in on the position attacking with flame throwers, cannon and MG fire. Throughout this attack Fusiliers Fox stood firm returning the fire. Although badly burned Fusiliers Fox refused to leave his post, and only did so reluctantly when ordered to

withdraw. Throughout this action his conduct was of the highest standard and fine example to the rest of his platoon. *(L.G. 13.1.44)*

Frafra, Bukare, Private
19423, 3 Gold Coast Regiment (Immediate)
For continuously gallant services.

On the 18th April 1941 B company 3 G.C.R. sent out patrols to find ways over a ravine and across a tank trap both of which were well covered from an enemy position on the further slopes of a wooded hill. During the day Pte. Bukare Frafra worked his Bren Gun forward under heavy small arms fire to within fifty yards of the tank trap and inflicted seven casualties on a European working party 150 yards beyond the trap.

On April 21st his platoon put in three attacks on a hill which was the right of the enemy's outpost position. During these attacks he showed the greatest coolness and handled his gun with the highest efficiency and coolness.

On April 22nd his platoon was sent off to support an attack being made by D Company. Under very heavy fire he handled his gun with great skill until he was seriously wounded. He refused to give in until his gun was knocked out of action and he was again wounded. Throughout the last fourteen days this soldier's gallantry, devotion to duty and coolness have been a splendid example to those around him.
To be dated 30.9.41 *(L.G. 21.7.42)*

Francombe, William Henry Godfrey, Warrant Officer Cl. I (R.S.M.)
3300491, Highland Light Infantry
No citation. *(L.G. 11.7.40)*

Frankish, F., Staff Sergeant
7348884, Royal Army Med.Corps
No citation. *(L.G. 11.7.40)*

Frary, Frederick John, Sergeant (actg.)
5777736, 1st Bn. East Surrey Regt. (Norwich)
(Immediate)

Reference Italy Map Sheet 99 (iv) NW 1/25,000 Fontanelice

On the night 14/15 December 1944 L/Sgt. Frary was commanding 18 platoon, D Coy. in the area of Casino Bernardi 014282, an isolated platoon position. At about 0400 hrs one of the section posts reported that a party of Germans at least twenty five strong was close upon them, having ignored a challenge and a burst of fire. L/Sgt. Frary acted with decision and initiative. He instantly got his men to their alarm posts outside the house supported by a sandbagged LMG posn. within it. The Germans attacked fiercely with MG and other automatic fire. They made great use of Bazookas and opened fire with them from three posns. simultaneously, firing nine shots in all. A great deal of amn. was expended by the enemy and they finally made a determined attempt with loud shouting to rush the house and break in. Throughout this time L/Sgt. Frary remained in full control of his men and it was directly due to his inspiring leadership that they firmly resisted every onslaught of the enemy and returned a steady stream of fire. At the end of half an hour the enemy gave up the attack and retired in some confusion, carrying one of their number. No casualties were sustained by No. 18 platoon but a German overcoat riddled with bullets, three separate large pools of blood, and a bloodstained paratrooper's helmet were left on the ground to bear witness of those suffered by the enemy.

L/Sgt. Frary had already ensured by constant visiting throughout the night that his men were keen and alert. When the attack developed, he took command in the fullest sense and controlled the defence by his voice and personal example. He himself repeatedly fired a TMC at the enemy, and managed to send occasional reports of the course of the battle by telephone to his Coy. Comd., although he never asked for assistance.

His outstanding leadership was responsible for the defeat of the paratroops, who were definitely identified for the first time on the Bde. front as a result of this action. When they broke off contact L/Sgt. Frary, accompanied by one man, followed the retreating enemy 200 yards to the river bed to make sure that they had all gone. By his fearless and cool headed leadership, L/Sgt. Frary not only beat off a determined enemy but he produced a great moral effect in both his Company and the battalion after our first contact with 1 Para Div.   *(L.G. 24.5.45)*

Fraser, Edmund John Albert, T/Sergeant
34954, 6 N.Z. Fd. Coy. (Immediate)
On 15 Apr 43 L/Sgt. (T/Sgt.) Fraser displayed outstanding initiative and gallantry when he and two sappers went forward in an armd. car to make a recce of a minefield just South of Enfidaville with the object of finding a passage for the tanks of 3 RTR. On arrival at the minefield L/Sgt. (T/Sgt.) Fraser found an armd. car blown up by a mine and the crew all seriously injured, and a tank stationary in the field with its leader not knowing where to move or what to do. L/Sgt. (T/Sgt.) Fraser's movement was under direct observation of the enemy and the area was immediately subjected to heavy mortar and field gun fire. L/Sgt. (T/Sgt.) Fraser sent his armd. car and sappers back to cover and without assistance commenced clearing the mines to the tank which was soon able to withdraw along a cleared track. He sent for an ambulance and set about clearing a lane to the armd. car which had been blown up. Having seen to the evacuation of the wounded crew he calmly and methodically proceeded with the recce of the minefield. Despite heavy and accurate fire and almost complete lack of ground visibility due to dust and smoke of bursting shells L/Sgt. (T/Sgt.) Fraser continued searching for the limits of the field until he eventually found and marked a route to enable the tanks to bypass the mines. He reported the results of his recce to the Squadron Comd. of the Tanks and then to Bde. HQ. As a result of L/Sgt.

(T/Sgt.) Fraser's gallant action and devotion to duty wounded personnel were ensured of early treatment, an immobilised tank was enabled to take immediate part in further operations and the 3 RTR. were informed of a safe passage forward for the continuation of their advance.   *(L.G. 9.8.43)*

Fraser, William Seth Provan, Warrant Officer Cl. II (C.S.M.)
2751343, 5 Black Watch (Larbert, Stirlingshire)
(Immediate)
On 14 Aug. 44 the Battalion attacked La Bu Sur Rouvres. After passing through the leading Companies, D Company came under heavy flanking fire from several enemy machine guns, and was under heavy Mortar fire. With great courage and presence of mind, C.S.M. Fraser with a few men of Coy. H. stalked the machine guns, leading the final charge on to their position himself. He silenced the machine guns and killed or captured the crews. This gallant action made a considerable difference to the continued advance of his Company and saved many casualties. Heavy mortar fire and arty. fire was coming down but with complete disregard for his own safety, C.S.M. Fraser led Coy. H. on to the objective. Once there, he immediately organised the supply of ammunition to forward platoons, and although Stretcher Bearers had been wounded, saw personally to the evacuation of casualties. Throughout the action C.S.M. Fraser's calmness, courage and leadership were outstanding, and were an example to all ranks in his Company. His presence and example played a large part in the success of the operation.   *(L.G. 21.12.44)*

Fraser, William, Fusilier
2932798, 1st Bn. Royal Scots Fusiliers (Inverness)
(Immediate)
North Burma Campaign
      On 27 Feb. 45, Sgt. Fraser's platoon took part in a Company fighting patrol to clear enemy opposition between Sindegon and Onma. Early in the operation it encountered the enemy and came under heavy fire from a MMG and two IMG's. The Platoon Comd. and two Section Comds. were wounded. Sgt. Fraser took over the platoon and in a remarkably short time reorganised it, moving from section to section in full view of the enemy, he disposed his men to engage the enemy more effectively and to enable the casualties to be evacuated. He himself went out alone to bring back one of his wounded N.C.O.s who was in a particularly exposed position, and only desisted after extremely heavy fire had checked two attempts. He held on to his position and directed heavy and accurate supporting fire to enable another platoon to come up and engage the enemy. Under this additional support he was able to get in the casualty and so withdraw to enable the enemy to be engaged with artillery. Later in the day his platoon was ordered to go to the assistance of another platoon who were held up by heavy fire from two IMG's in position behind a

chaung bank and covered by dense scrub. Having advanced as far as possible under cover, Sgt. Fraser led his platoon across open paddy in a bayonet charge in the face of very heavy automatic fire. The platoon reached the edge of the enemy position, but was unable to charge through the sharpened bamboo fence that surrounded it. Under heavy fire Sgt. Fraser ordered the platoon to engage the enemy with grenades and by fire, which finally resulted in clearing the enemy position that had contributed to a dangerous threat to the Battalion perimeter. The courage, leadership and dogged determination to close with the enemy displayed by Sgt. Fraser were of the highest order and were an inspiration to all those under his command. *(L.G. 21.6.45)*

French, Reginald John William, Corporal
554640, 8th King's Royal Irish Hussars
(Bournemouth) (Immediate)
At Bletet El Ioela
Cpl French was in command of a Grant tank on May 27th in the first action with the 8th Hussars against the German Panzers. He had fired all his 75 ammunition and both gun traverses were out of action through direct hit.

In attempting to get out of action for repairs, he ran into Seven Mark III German tanks and was knocked out. Two members of his crew were killed and he himself hid behind a bush until the Germans had passed on. He then took command of the remainder of the crew and attended to one man who was mortally wounded and died shortly afterwards. He then made a plan to escape but met another knocked out tank of the Regiment, with two men (one wounded) lying beside it. He dressed the wounded man and taking turns to carry him, led the party for two days, in an Easterly direction until picked up by our own troops near Bir Gubi. The party had carried the wounded man for 16 miles across the desert, with no food or water except for a lucky find on a derelict vehicle. During their march they lay up all night within sight of a German dressing station. They did not proceed until the dressing station had packed up and moved on.

Cpl. French showed a complete disregard for his own safety whilst attending the wounded under fire. He also showed leadership of the highest standard in getting his party back under the most adverse conditions.

Later Cpl. French volunteered as a Tank Commander to a composite Squadron. The Squadron was in operation for ten days. During this period Cpl. French performed his duties in an excellent way. His conduct throughout was a magnificent example to all those with whom he was in contact. *(L.G. 24.9.42)*

Fricker, Arthur Aimée, Warrant Officer Cl. II
B.54548, The Algonquin Regiment (Immediate)
In Holland, on the night 1/2 Nov 44, 'A' Coy. Alg. R led the attack against the village of Bocht, in the intense fire from enemy MGs and Sp guns. Enemy mines and direct fire prevented any use being made of MM SP weapons. On the outskirts of the village the adv. was held up by

and enemy MG post. C.S.M. Fricker, acting on his own initiative, shot his way fwd. alone and succeeded in reaching the post and knocking it out. Later, while consolidation of the objective was in progress, the enemy launched a fierce counter-attack with three tks. and over one hundred inf. Coy. HQ, which had been est. well fwd., was completely cut off by the enemy force and the Coy. Comd. seriously wounded. C.S.M. Fricker org. the few remaining men for defence of the HQ but it soon became evident that the posn. could not be held and C.S.M. Fricker ws ordered to attempt to break out alone and return to Bn. HQ with all available infm. This warrant offr. again fought his way through the encircling enemy and found shelter in a water-filled ditch where he lay for the remainder of the day within a few feet of a German patrol. Finally after dark, while the area in which he had hidden was under fire from our own arty. He was able to make his way to our own lines and report to Bn. HQ. The infm. which he brought had a marked influence on the successful outcome of the attack on Welburg on the following night. The magnificent courage and devotion to duty shown by C.S.M. Fricker had a decisive effect on the final outcome of the battle and his splendid example served as an inspiration to all ranks of the bn. *Recommended for M.C.* *(L.G. 10.2.45)*

Friday, William Douglas, Private
29312, 24 N.Z. Bn. New Zealand Military Forces
For determined leadership in Infantry Section attacks, inspiring initiative and continual acts of bravery from 23 Nov 41, when his Company first went into action, culminating in a special act of bravery, when as a sole survivor of his Company, he mounted a Bren Gun Carrier and with complete disregard of heavy Artillery, Mortar and small arms fire, he directed the machine gun fire of his carrier onto enemy machine gun posts, and repeatedly shouted works of encouragement and inspiration to the defenders of an open flank. These actions undoubtedly, were instrumental in assisting to repulse the attack which was of such intensity that two Companies of the Bn. were over-run. *(L.G. 20.1.42)*

Friend, Horace, Sergeant
951064, Royal Artillery (Wisbech, Cambridgeshire)
No citation. *(L.G. 18.2.43)*

Frost, Arthur Vivian Patterson, Warrant Officer Cl. II (S.S.M.)
15571, 6 S.A. Armd. C. Regt. S.A.T.C. (Immediate)
During the breakthrough of the Italian lines by 60 Div. during night of 14/15 June 42, Sqn. Sgt. Major Frost became detached from the rest of his party belonging to a column of 60 Bde. and attached himself to a party consisting of some Cheshires and whilst heading South, ran into a party of enemy at Rotonda Mt Eifel. On being fired at, Sgt. Major Frost shot the sentry and then led a party consisting of a short thickset Sgt., a Canadian Cp. and two Ptes. all of the Cheshire Regt. They attacked

the enemy strong point, shooting many of the enemy as they came out of their dugouts. Twenty five bodies were counted and they took 2 officers and 13 O/Rs prisoners and brought them away with them. They also destroyed 8 enemy vehicles. One of the Italian officer prisoners stated that they were Div. HQ. Signallers of Bresoia Div. and that they were within 200 metres of the Div. Comdrs. tent. Sqn. Sgt. Major Frost showed great courage and initiative in immediately attacking and leading his small comd. with such skill, daring and vigour.

(L.G. 24.9.42)

Frost, Stephen, Sergeant
5380722, Oxfordshire & Buckinghamshire Light Infantry
No citation.   (L.G. 25.10.45)

Frost, William Frederick Leslie, Sergeant
D.81093, 1st Bn. The Black Watch (RHR) of Canada (Periodic)
Company Sergeant Major Frost, The 1st Battalion The Black Watch (RHR) of Canada has served in every action in which the battalion has been engaged since 1st August 1944.

In three separate battles, namely St. Andre sur Orne, 5th August 1944, Mille Brugge, 10th September 1944, and St. Leonards, 29th September 1944, all his company officers have become casualties and he has taken command of the Company. In every case he has displayed exceptional initiative, complete disregard for his own personal safety, and courageous leadership, reorganizing his Company and maintaining the control which, if lost, would have affected seriously the entire battalion.

This Warrant Officer's good judgement, leadership and confident bearing, no matter how difficult or dangerous the situation, have earned for him the admiration and respect not only of his own Company but of the entire battalion.
Recommended for M.B.E. or B.E.M.   (L.G. 17.3.45)

Froud, Stuart Lawrence, Corporal (now Sergeant)
VX 41955, 2/23 Australian Inf. Bn. (Immediate)
For conspicuous gallantry and outstanding leadership during operations North of Tarakan airstrip. On 6 May 45 Cpl. Froud's platoon was attacking a strong enemy pillbox and tunnelled position on the crest of steep jungle slope. At the height of the attack his Platoon Commander was badly wounded and Cpl. Froud led the small party which evacuated the officer under heavy fire. He then continued to press the attack with courage and determination and personally accounted for 3 enemy with grenade and rifle. His determination and courage was largely responsible for the capture of his platoon's objective. Again, as the Commander of 18 platoon he led a platoon patrol against another MG position. During the action and subsequent counter-attack Cpl. Froud was wounded but refused to be evacuated continuing to fight his platoon

in a difficult position with coolness and courage. He remained on duty until ordered by his Company Commander to be evacuated. His leadership, complete disregard for personal danger, and his aggressive spirit throughout the actions were an example and inspiration not only to his own platoon but to the whole Company.
(L.G. 3.7.45)

Fry, Algernon, Private (A/Sgt.)
5503103, 1/4th Bn. Hampshire Regt. (Greatham, Hants.) (Immediate)
On 29 Jan 44 Sjt. Fry was with his Coy. in an attack on pt 411, 8399, and was commanding a platoon. At 1430 hrs., which was H hr. for the operation, he went forward with three men, to engage 4 known enemy MG posts, leaving the rest of the platoon in fire posns. to cover his party.

Sjt. Fry rushed the first posn., threw a grenade into it and shot a German who tried to emerge. He then went to the second posn. and tried to repeat his tactics. The grenade however fell short and the occupants, two in number were dealt with by Sjt. Fry, who shot one and hit the other with the butt of his rifle.

The third posn. was then rushed and silenced, and the occupants of the fourth were taken prisoner.

Sjt. Fry next rallied a section to his left which had shown signs of wavering, and then led them forward. At this stage he was wounded in the shoulder by a bullet, but refused to go back. Later he accompanied C.S.M. McAlister on a recce to try and find a way to rush the enemy after dark, and he continued to encourage and lead his men until ordered to withdraw at about 0200 hrs. This N.C.O. displayed qualities of personal gallantry and leadership worthy of the highest regard throughout the whole action, and had finally to be almost forcibly removed to the R.A.P.   (L.G. 29.6.44)

Fuhrman, Henry Charles, Acting Corporal (Immediate)
NX7852, 2/4 M.G. Bn., A.I.F.
During AIF operations in Malaya on 10 Feb. 1942, 'C' Coy. came under command 22 Bde. 'A' Pl., which at that time was commanded by A/Cpl. H. C. Fuhrman, was ordered to defend Adv. Bde. HQ. At first light the enemy launched a very heavy attack on the forward Bn. Firing became so intense that A/Cpl. Fuhrman's posts were pushed forward. The attack increased in intensity and the forward Bn. was ordered to withdraw and take up a fresh position, with the result that the positions held by A/Cpl. Fuhrman were then in the front line.

The Japanese attacked several times during the day but each time were repulsed. During this action, A/Cpl. Fuhrman behaved in an outstanding and energetic manner. He fearlessly moved around his posts directing their fire, encouraging the men and supervising the evacuation of the wounded with complete disregard for his own safety under heavy fire. Seeing some troops on his flank about to give way, A/Cpl. Fuhrman rushed across and by his courage and example restored the position. On the 12 Feb. 1942 at Ula Pandan A/Cpl. Fuhrman again showed outstanding leadership and courage. A key point in the line had been evacuated and A/Cpl. Fuhrman was ordered to move forward with two sections and hold it. He held this position for the whole of that day until relieved and his behaviour under fire for the whole time was an inspiration to the men under his command. A/Cpl. Fuhrman's bearing and behaviour during the whole of the operations was outstanding.

(1.8.46)

Fulton, David Cameron, Private
3065961 [3065964 on AFW 3121], 1st Bn. King's
Own Scottish Borderers (Dumbarton) (Periodic)
L/Cpl. Fulton served with this Battalion in acting continuously from August 1944 until he was wounded in the battle for Bremen—Delmenhorst Rd. As a private soldier he proved himself completely fearless in the attack and tireless in his work. He has always been an inspiration to his fellowmen—always in front, calling them on to greater efforts. In the attacks South West of UDEM he was operating the 38 Set. Handicapped as he was he rushed forward in the assault, and personally took fifteen prisoners. As a Lance Corporal, he showed fine powers of leadership and was conspicuously brave on all occasions. On the Bremen—Delmenhorst Rd after house fighting for four hours he picked up his section Bren gun, rushed forward and captured a strong point of seven men. A hand grenade had seriously wounded him, but he refused to give in. He fought on with his section, they consolidated on the objective and L/Cpl. Fulton collapsed through loss of blood. He has been an inspiration and example of fearlessness and leadership to his men at all times which has always resulted in the complete over-running of the enemy.
Recommended for M.M.   *(L.G. 24.1.46)*

Fulton, Hamilton, Corporal
6347706, 8th Bn. Rifle Brigade (Paisley) (Periodic)
Cpl Fulton fought with 'H' Company, 8th Battalion, The Rifle Brigade from Normandy, June 1944 to the Baltic, May 1945, firstly as a rifleman and later as a section commander. In his first battle on June 28th, 1944 at Hill 112, Rfn. Fulton showed by his complete coolness and bravery under fire that he was admirably suited to command men in battle.

On 1st April, 1945, near Saerbeck, the platoon in which Cpl. Fulton commanded a section was clearing a wood. The right-hand section of the platoon was almost immediately held up by heavy 20mm fire from beyond the wood. Cpl. Fulton's section, which was on the left, without waiting for orders, continued the advance, and, in spite of heavy mortar fire, consolidated in the far edge of the wood and neutralised the 20mm guns. The mortaring continued, but, although his section suffered casualties and were not dug in, Cpl Fulton held his position for a considerable time, until ordered to move. There is no doubt that his initiative and coolness on this occasion was the deciding factor in his platoon's success.

On the night of 6th/7th of April, 1945, Cpl. Fulton was ordered to take his section out in front of the battalion bridgehead at Stolzenau to give warning of any approach of the enemy. So that his presence should not be revealed, Cpl. Fulton could not afford to dig his section in and the area was heavily shelled and mortared all night. In the early hours of the morning the enemy attacked, and it was due to the excellent information given by Cpl. Fulton's section that the attack was completely broken up. Throughout this action, Cpl. Fulton's gallantry and complete control of his section had a most heartening effect on the remainder of his platoon.

Throughout eleven months of fighting Cpl. Fulton has shown himself to be a brave and resolute leader and has been an outstanding section commander in every battle.
Recommended for M.M.   *(L.G. 24.1.46)*

Futter, Gilbert, M.M., Warrant Officer Cl. I (R.S.M.)
5377083, 7 Oxfordshire & Buckinghamshire Light
Infantry (Cowley) (Immediate)
On 20th January 1944 on Pt. 411 Sessa Arunca 1/50000 Map ref 8399.

At dawn on 20 Jan. 7 Oxf. Bucks were holding the above named feature. As it was beginning to get light the enemy launched a counter attack the main thrust being on Regtl. HQ. Regtl. Sjt. Major Futter personally organised and directed the fire of the comparatively few men available for the defence of HQ. Due to his personal control and example the enemy were halted approx. 100 yds. from the position and one by one killed, very few if any enemy escaped. Regtl. Sjt. Major shot 7 Germans himself and it was largely due to his personal example and initiative that the position was held and the enemy counter attack completely broken up. I consider this a very ideal example of cool courage, personal example and control at a time of crisis.
Recommended for M.M.   *(L.G. 4.5.44)*

Fyfe, Peter John, Private
61712, Royal Australian Infantry
For Vietnam   *(L.G. 1.9.72)*

G

Gallagher, Harry, Warrant Officer Cl. II
5182071, Gloucestershire Regt.
For Korea   *(L.G. 8.12.53)*

Gallagher, Joseph, Private
3054444, Royal Scots
Hodges, Daniel, Private
6396763, Royal Scots
These two soldiers were captured at Hong Kong and imprisoned in the Shamshuipo Camp. Soon after their arrival they made plans to escape and began collecting what little food they could obtain. On the 24th February 1942 at 9.30 p.m. they slipped past the sentries, through the wire surrounding the camp and out of the town and began their march to Canton which they believed to be in Chinese hands.

For two days they continued their journey, reaching the Shumchin River, which was patrolled by Japanese. On the the following day they succeeded in crossing to the Chinese side of the river. From here they struck out in a North Westerly direction and after covering some fifteen miles they met four Chinese boys who led them to the local Chinese guerillas where after questioning they were led to the Refugee Clearing Station which they reached on the 1st March. Here they decided to join up with the guerillas and the leader, a Captain Wong, posted them to one of his troops where they began training his soldiers with some British mortars and Anti-Tank Rifles which the guerillas had received in the withdrawal to the mainland.

They stayed with this troop for a week, during which time it was seen that the men were very under-trained and they then asked if they could leave. This disappointed the guerillas and after some discussion they decided to stay for another month to assist them in training. They were then moved to another troop where they taught them the use of the Vickers Machine Gun.

On April 10th, 1942, they left with a guide for Tamshai where two days later they reported to the Chinese Regular Army. Here they were supplied with identification papers and directed to the Police, who on the following day took them to Waichow where they reported to the British Authorities.   *(L.G. 29.9.42)*

Gallon, Edward, Sergeant
4453016, 9 Durham Light Infantry (Gateshead)
(Immediate)
Sgt. Gallon found an abandoned Bren Carrier on withdrawing from the Mersa-Matruh Box and having repaired it as well as they could, proceeded to Alamein, arriving on 29th June 1942. By this time Sgt. Gallon was very weary and the carrier was breaking down every half mile. Eventually, at Alamein they ran into heavy shelling and the carrier was repaired again by Sgt. Gallon, with complete disregard to his own safety. He had just withdrawn from the shelling area when he was asked if he could tow a serviceable 3 ton lorry, which was out of petrol, from the centre of the shelling area, so that it could be refuelled and used for evacuating the many troops needing transport. Without a moments thought Sgt. Gallon and L/Cpl. Ferguson drove their carrier straight to the lorry. The rate of shelling increased immediately, but Sgt. Gallon dismounted, affixed a tow rope to the lorry and towed it to safety where it was refuelled and was used to evacuate troops. Sgt. Gallon proceeded a few hundred yards when he observed that the path of a Ration Convoy, coming up the line was blocked by four immobilised 3 ton lorries which were a direct target for the enemy shelling which was very heavy. Sgt. Gallon, at once, drove his carrier to the four trucks and one at a time, with his life in immediate danger, he affixed a tow rope and managed to tow out all four lorries thus allowing the Ration Convoy to make its effort to get through the barrage. The complete disregard for his own safety under heavy and continuous shelling his devotion to duty under these conditions and in his tired state and above all his rapid appreciation of the urgency of clearing the way for the Ration Convoy, regardless of the personal cost, his patience in the unsuccessful evacuation by the abandoned Bren carrier, all showed most distinguished conduct and inspired those who were privileged to see him.   *(L.G. 5.11.42)*

Galt, Brian, Sergeant (actg.)
22321842, Black Watch
For Korea   *(L.G. 9.1.53)*

Gamble, Robert Francis, Sergeant
B.129531, 6 Cdn. A. Tk. Regt., Royal Canadian
Artillery (Immediate)
On the 16 Oct. 44, two S.P. mounts of ATp 6 Cdn. A. Tk. Regt. R.C.A. under comd. Sgt. Gamble were detailed to locate and assist a platoon missing from 'C' Coy. NSLONR.

The platoon was located at D131081 near Balhofstee and was found to be pinned down by heavy M.G. fire. As Sgt. Gamble moved his M10s forward to a position from which he could provide covering fire for the infantry, enemy M.G. fire increased and was thickened by fire from bazookas and rifles. From an exposed position in the open turret of the M10 this N.C.O. directed his S.P. mounts and engaged all visible targets including dug-outs, buildings and groups of enemy positioned behind farm implements and wood piles. At one time Sgt. Gamble was engaging approximately 80 enemy infantrymen and nine M.G. posts.

The open turret of Sgt. Gamble's M10 received a direct hit from a bazooka and painful injuries were inflicted on the gun crew and on Sgt. Gamble, who was severely burned about the head and face, one eye being partially closed and the other completely closed. Despite his wounds, this N.C.O. forged ahead with outstanding determination and continued to direct the fire of his guns onto target after target inflicting heavy casualties on the enemy until his ammunition was exhausted. As a direct result of his operations the enemy was forced to disengage and our infantry was able to take up positions dominating the area.

On return to harbour, although himself soaked to the waist in blood and almost unable to see, Sgt. Gamble's first action was to send his gun detachments for medical attention after which he began to inspect his equipments for damage. It was only after direct orders from his tp. comd. that Sgt. Gamble was persuaded to leave his guns and have his own wounds dressed.   *(L.G. 20.1.45)*

Gardner, Francis Marwood, Private
37412, 19 Bn., 2 N.Z.E.F.
The night following his capture at El Alamein in July 42, Gardner escaped from Derna. He and a companion crawled under the wire and were at liberty for three days before their recapture. Despite this failure both were caught as they tried again the next night. Gardner made two unsuccessful attempts whilst still in N. Africa. He was transferred to Italy at the end of 1942 and at the time of the Italian Armistice he was in Udine (Camp 57). After the Germans had taken over this camp, they sent all P/W to Germany. En route Gardner escaped from the moving train, in so doing injuring his head. He found help nearby at Gemona. Early in January 44, owing to increased enemy activity he joined a band of partisans in the hills, but a month later decided to organise a group of saboteurs. This he did. In exchange for stolen tobacco, Italians working for the Germans gave him explosives; with these, railway lines and power lines were cut. In November 44, when he met a member of a British Military Mission Gardner volunteered to remain behind the lines and to put his squad at the disposal of the Mission. This officer has praised Gardner's work in the following terms:—

'He built up a most efficient and reliable squad and he always led them in person till his name became almost a legend both to his friends and to the enemy.

The organising work, the courier and propaganda and supply tasks that he carried out would in themselves have been a most notable achievement. In addition he executed a significant number of derailments, sabotage actions and ambushes, cumulating in the most spectacular of all when on April 21 in accordance with prepared plans he blew up the main railway bridge over the River Orvenco, near Gemona, capturing or killing the entire enemy guard of 17 and their arms and equipment complete. This bridge had been unsuccessfully attacked 6 times in the preceding days by the D.A.F. Gardner's work was of enormous value, operationally and because his own splendid morale and high courage communicated itself to all who came in contact with him.

He did an operational and organising job in the presence of the enemy, and an administrative job after the liberation, which in normal times could not conceivably have been entrusted to less than a sergeant.'
Substituted for the award of the M.M. announced in L.G. 4.10.45   *(L.G. 1.11.45)*

Garmonsway, Ronald Francis, Corporal
5176, 22 Bn., New Zealand Military Forces
(Immediate)
On 15 July 42 Cpl. Garmonsway R.F. was a member of the platoon which evaded capture by enemy tanks on Ruweisat Ridge. He was a member of a party led by Sjt. Elliott in an attack on an enemy position. When the party came under fire from their right flank Cpl. Garmonsway led his section of 4 men in an attack on these posts over a distance of 400 yards and in the face of enemy M.G. fire. He and his section succeeded in capturing 3 M.G.'s, 1 Anti-Tank rifle, one German and two Italian Officers, one German Serjeant and approximately 60 Italian other ranks without casualty to his section.

For the remainder of 15 July Cpl. Garmonsway was in command of the remaining 16 men of his platoon and held his position on Ruweisat Ridge until relieved that night.   *(L.G. 5.11.42)*

Garner, Frederick Robert, Warrant Officer Cl. II (B.S.M.)
5932351, 2nd Royal Horse Artillery (15, Perroune St., Cambridge)
This Warrant Officer has been in charge of the ammunition vehicles of his battery, and it has been very largely due to his coolness and courage that the fire was maintained in the first three engagements on Nov. 19 and 20, and again on Dec. 1 that his vehicles were extricated without loss, directing his vehicles under fire without regard for his own safety. Throughout, this W.O. has set the most inspiring example to all.
    (L.G. 20.1.42)

Garner, Rowland Hubert, Lance Corporal
319529, 11th Hussars
Captured at El Adem on 26 Jul. 40. Sent via hospitals at Tobruk and Derna to Giovanni Berta, Sulmona and Rezanello, back to Sulmona and then to Montalbo, Lucca and finally Camp 70 (Monturano). In Feb. 41, he and another P/W escaped from Sulmona but were recaptured after three days. They were beaten up and kept for 30 days in solitary confinement in very bad conditions. In Aug. 42 Garner attempted a second escape, leaving the camp disguised as a bricklayer in company with another P/W. They were recognised and stopped by sentry and again beaten up. Garner was imprisoned for another 26 days in bad conditions.

After the Armistice P/W were not liberated from Camp 70, and the Germans took over on about 18 Sep. 43. Three days later Garner made another attempt at escape. He dyed some battle-dress trousers with a mixture of ink and water, and wearing these with a white shirt and brown gym shoes he jumped through an office window when the sentry was not looking and made off. He had been employed as an interpreter in the camp so made his way to the house of an Italian soldier with whom he was friendly and with help from this man and various others, and assisted by his fluent Italian, he made his way to the British lines.   *(L.G. 15.6.44)*

Garner, Victor Thomas Philip, Lance Corporal
2618220, 4 Tk. Grenadier Guards (London, E.11)
    (Immediate)
On 31 Mar. 45 L/Cpl. Garner was commanding a Honey Tk. which formed part of a section recceing in front of an Armd. Column directed on Greven Br., 25 miles distant. Shortly after crossing the Start Line his Sec. Comdr.'s Tank was held up by heavy enemy fire. Without hesitation this L/Cpl. looped to one side and destroyed the enemy gun and crew, and then taking the lead he set off to cover the distance in the three remaining hours of daylight. He advanced with such dash and skill that the Armd. Column destroyed or overran 40 Flak Guns and two 88mm Guns as well as much enemy transport, and all this was accomplished without the assistance of any other Recce. That the objective was successfully reached before night fall was almost entirely due to this N.C.O.'s superb leadership, tremendous initiative, entire disregard for his own safety and refusal to be dismayed at any odds against him. His conduct throughout being beyond all praise.   *(L.G. 21.6.45)*

Garratt, Edward Ivan, Sergeant
2592073, Glider Pilot Regt., Army Air Corps (Derby)
Sgt. Garratt flew as Second Pilot in a Waco CGHA glider on the night 9/10th Jul. 1943 from Sousse to Sicily. The glider landed in the correct place but before coming to rest struck violently against some object on the ground smashing the nose of the aircraft and trapping Sgt. Moore the 1st Pilot whose ankle was broken. One of the passengers was also trapped. The force of impact detonated some ammunition and as the glider was being abandoned Sgt. Garratt saw that his 1st Pilot and the injured passenger were unable to get out. He at once ran back to the aircraft and despite the exploding ammunition, he succeeded in releasing the two men, after three attempts. Just as he was succeeding in dragging the injured clear, Sgt. Garratt's right forearm was almost completely blown away, he however with complete disregard for himself completed the rescue, and was himself assisted to safety by his 1st Pilot, who was himself injured. It was 36 hours before Sgt. Garratt had any food, and two days before his shattered arm was eventually amputated. During the whole of this period Sgt. Garratt continued to behave with great fortitude,

and throughout showed the highest sense of duty. The whole glider crew were unanimous in praise of Sgt. Garratt's gallantry.   *(L.G. 24.8.44)*

Garwood, Henry James, Lance Corporal
129971, 22 N.Z. Bn. (Immediate)
On 17 Apr. 45, L/Cpl. Garwood became the comd. of a platoon at a most critical and important moment. His platoon had just captured a casa close to the eastern stop bank of the River Gainna, North of Villa Fontana when the platoon Sjt., then in comd., was wounded. Of the platoon there then remained only 17 men and from the stop bank they were opposed by a strong and extremely determined force of German paratroopers. The enemy maintained sniper, M.G. and Bazooka fire in great quantity upon the platoon position and the enemy fwd. elts were so close that they could throw hand-grenades.

To meet so difficult a situation, L/Cpl. Garwood employed only one tactic—the boldest resolution. Quickly organising his men, he brought down upon the enemy so heavy and accurate a fire that heavy casualties were caused and L/Cpl. Garwood himself was foremost in fierce encounter with hand-grenades. His disregard for his personal safety and his frequent acts of gallantry heartened his men and imbued them with an offensive spirit of such quality that they won gradually the upper hand.

At the opportune moment, L/Cpl. Garwood led his men in a dash to the stop bank and for almost an hour, until flanking support arrived, the platoon continued to engage the enemy and to consolidate the positions won. The successful est. of these positions was of considerable importance to the later fighting.

L/Cpl. Garwood's inspired leadership, his many examples of great bravery under fire, and his determination to push the attack home and to drive the enemy from his well-sited positions were factors of the highest importance to the success of the operation and they also served to weld his men into a most formidable fighting force.
Recommended for M.M.   *(L.G. 18.10.45)*

Gateley, Hugh, Sergeant
3525887, 2 Highland Light Infantry (Mossley,
    Cheshire) (Immediate)
Bir-El-Tama 5th June 1942
This N.C.O. was in command of a platoon of one of the forward companies at Bir El Tamar on the morning of 5th June 1942. At dawn his Company was ordered to withdraw to another position and, although under heavy shell fire, he stayed behind at the forward positions until every man of the Company had moved back. Later, he accompanied his Coy. Commander and another officer forward to Bir El Tamar, and when these two officers became wounded, ran back a thousand yards to the Coy. position under heavy MMG fire, gave a detailed report of the position in front asking for artillery and tank

support and finally returned to his officers and assisted the stretcher bearers party to evacuate them.

During the withdrawal of his Coy. Sergeant Gateley showed complete disregard for his own safety in his effort to bring in wounded and stragglers. At one time he stood on top of a sangar waving his Balmoral to direct stragglers during the whole of this period, but in spite of this was the last to leave the forward line and when he did, gave all the assistance in his power to the wounded at the same time encouraging the remainder of the Company.

Later in the day, the truck in which this N.C.O. was travelling was hit by a shell which killed one man and wounded himself and four others. Although wounded he did not report the fact, not wishing to discourage the men with him. He eventually succeeded in getting his wounded to an ambulance and then rejoined his unit at El Adem.

This N.C.O.'s conduct during the whole of the action set a fine example of courage and coolness under fire to all ranks, and it was entirely due to him that so many men of his Company who might not otherwise have done so, got back.   (L.G. 24.9.42)

Gaughan, John, Sergeant (actg.)
2879852, 1 Seaforth Highlanders (Glasgow, C.5)
Throughout operations against the Jap lasting over a period of five months, this N.C.O. did outstandingly well. During the whole period he showed powers of leadership, command and ability of a very high order. On 15 Apr. 44, at the village of Kasom he was in charge of a section when the whole weight of the Jap immediate counter-attack fell on his part of the perimeter. He displayed remarkable coolness and courage, and by his personal example so rallied and steadied his sec. that the Japs were held and finally beaten off with heavy casulties. There is no doubt but that for his gallantry and cool disregard for danger a critical situation was averted. He had scarcely time to reorganise, and certainly none to dig in when another wave of Japs attacked his position. By the same spirited leadership he so inspired his sec. that the second onrush was driven off more decisively than the first. All that night the Jap kept up his relentless pressure but Sgt. Gaughan was equal to every demand made on him. Time after time he rallied and steadied his men to meet the Japs as they tried everything they knew to penetrate the perimeter in the dark. His Coy. again took up the defence of the village on the night 18/19 April and again under cover of darkness the enemy made determined and persistent attacks. This time they had covering fire from 3″ mortars the bombs of which were landing in the perimeter with great accuracy, Sgt. Gaughan was wounded but with great devotion to duty insisted on remaining at his post to lead and inspire his sec. He refused all attempts to have his wounds dressed until every enemy attack had been beaten off and the position stabilised. Next morning he was evacuated to the R.A.P. where he insisted on remaining for a few days

rather than be evacuated to the rear. Later that week he rejoined his Coy. where he found that during his absence, the Pl. Comd. had been killed. He immediately took over comd. of the platoon and although inexperienced did remarkably well. He soon showed that the more responsibility he was given, the more he rose to the occasion. At Lam-Mu on 24 Apr. 44, he was ordered to make a wide detour and come in on the village from the rear. Just as his platoon formed up for the attack a hitherto unlocated enemy L.M.G. opened up on him from a nearby bunker. With remarkable presence of mind, cool skill and superb judgement he switched a sec. to deal with it, and without slowing up momentum of the attack pushed on to get to his original objective. By a display of skilful tactics he was able to dispose of what might have been a real threat to his flank. From then onwards the men in the platoon under him had the greatest confidence in his leadership. At Khongjol on 18 May 44, and on Malta on 30 May 44, he again proved himself to be a first rate leader, full of enthusiasm and the will to win through. It was however, on Nippon on 24 July 44, that he was at his best. His Coy. was the leading Coy. whose task it was to rush Nippon silently under cover of darkness and so carry the position by surprise. To do this it was necessary to march two nights through appalling jungle through heavy rain and mist. Sgt. Gaughan showed outstanding determination to overcome all obstacles of weather and terrain. It was entirely due to his personal example and leadership that the platoon was able to meet its appointed place on time. In the bayonet charge which followed he showed the same dash and gallantry and won through to his objective, inflicting heavy loss on the enemy. Throughout all these and other operations Sgt. Gaughan displayed a devotion to duty, powers of leadership and complete disregard for personal danger that merit the highest commendation.   (L.G. 28.6.45)

Gauld, George, Sergeant (A/W.O.II (C.S.M.))
2976509, 7th Bn. Argyll & Sutherland Highlanders
(Denny, Stirlingshire)
During the night attack on 26th Oct. 42 (on Nairn) just as his Coy. was preparing to charge on to the final enemy position a shell burst in Company Headquarters, wounding the only Officer left with the Coy. and knocked over Sjt. Gauld who was acting C.S.M. Although stunned and wounded in the mouth, Sjt. Gauld jumped up, rallied the men, who had gone to ground, and led them into the position, capturing a strongly held M.G. post. He then reorganised the Coy. and prepared to meet counter-attack. When a local counter-attack came, he drove it off, personally leading a section out beyond the enemy trenches. He held the position won until the arrival of another Company under an Officer, who then took command. Before the arrival of this Officer, Sjt. Gauld directed the action, moving between section positions with complete disregard for his own safety under heavy M.G. fire. For the rest of the night and the whole of the following day, he continued to move between the section

of his Company organising fire-plans, distribution of water, etc., all under frequent heavy mortar and M.G. fire.

By his prompt action in taking over command at a critical moment and his determined and fearless leadership afterwards, Sjt. Gauld not only secured the capture and retention of the objective, but gave an example which encouraged all who worked under him.

(L.G. 4.5.43)

Gay, Robert Dennis, Warrant Officer Cl. I
2613715, 156 Bn. Parachute Regt., Army Air Corps (Bristol)
R.S.M. Gay dropped with his Bn. at Arnheim on 18 Sep. 44. his coolness and courage, and a sense of discipline which no danger could divert, were of first rate importance when the Bn. found itself in action even as it began to organise on the ground. During the fighting that day and the next his leadership was conspicuous. On the second day a German A.F.V. was harassing him from a road, covered by flanking fire from a Spandau. Ignoring intense fire from the M.G. he charged the tank, attracting its attention away from Bn. HQ, and trying to put it out of action with a   but he was severely wounded in the leg, by the tank's machine gun, and subsequently made a prisoner.

His conduct as a P/W has now been reported on in terms of the highest praise. Once recovered from his wounds he was determined that imprisonment would affect within his own not any one elses. The ness high state of health and spirits, and discipline which he assisted R.S.M. Lord to produce in a prison camp is now well known and reflects most adequately the tradition of a regular grenadier guardsman and a member of the 1st Airborne Div. which R.S.M. Gay represents.

(L.G. 20.9.45)

Geiri, Alhassan, Sergeant
N.A.26389, Nigeria Regt., Royal West African Frontier Forces
No citation.   (L.G. 26.4.45)

Geoffic, Hedley Lewis, Sergeant
60894, 14 N.Z. Lt. A.A. Regt. (Immediate)
Was in command of a Bofors gun during the whole of the Egypt campaign.

He displayed exceptional personal courage, leadership and command on October 24th 1942 in the Tel El Eisa sector of the Alamein line when his detachment was ordered to a forward position through an enemy minefield which they occupied by night. At daybreak he found that he was ahead of the forward infantry who were held up and unable to advance because of a resolutely defended enemy M.G. post. Sgt. Goeffic personally located the enemy post, brought his gun into action, and manned the exposed layer's position with his bombadier. Both of them were wounded by machine gun fire, but trained their Bofors on the enemy and fired

a shot whereupon the enemy post surrendered and were made prisoners. The infantry were then able to advance.

Throughout this campaign this Sergeant has been an inspiring leader and has displayed outstanding personal courage.   (L.G. 28.1.43)

George, Charles Frederick, Corporal
6457067, 2 Border Regt., (London, W.12)
On Mar. 13, 1944 on his return journey after a long patrol in the middle of a numerous advancing enemy he spotted a carefully camouflaged office lorry. His men were tired and mostly young soldiers. Calling on them to give him covering fire, he advanced single-handed with his tommy gun on to the lorry. A Jap Officer and driver were sitting in the front seat. He shot both dead with his tommy gun in spite of the fact that they were both on the alert, and siezed a book which fell with the Jap Officer as he pitched sideways out of the front seat and also took the ignition key of the car. All this time he was being fired at from the jungle nearby. He then ran to the rear of the lorry and killed three more Japs with his tommy gun. After putting a burst into the engine of the car, he seized as many papers and books as he could carry. Finally, before he rejoined his patrol, he threw two grenades into the lorry. All this time he was under heavy, close but inaccurate rifle fire. For cool and daring bravery at a time when he was tired and hungry after a most strenuous and dangerous time on a long patrol, his action is hard to beat. The papers he took from what was obviously an important HQ appear on preliminary examination to be of considerable value.   (L.G. 22.6.44)

George, Derek Gordon, Sergeant
5776344, Royal Norfolk Regt. and 5th Bn. The Gold Coast Regt., R.W.A.F.F., (Guist, Norfolk)
Pyingyaung, Burma (6847) 24 Apr. 44
Ref. Map Burma Sheet No. 84 D/9
    At Pyingyaung, Burma (Map Ref. 6847, Ref. Map Burma, Sheet 84 D/9) on 24 Apr. 44, the gallantry of Pl/Sgt. D. G. George during an operation against the Japanese, when commanding a platoon of West African Infantry, was conspicuous.

The enemy had been located in strong, well-prepared positions at the top of a chaung. The chaung rose rapidly up a steep slope to the enemy position and the sides of it were covered with dense bamboo jungle and were impassable. In spite of heavy fire from his front and flanks Pl/Sgt. George led his platoon against the enemy position. He pushed home the assault with such vigour that the enemy broke and fled. Without delay, he organised a second assault on an enemy position to his flank and cleared it. He then collected his platoon and led them in a running fight with the retreating enemy until he had cleared the area.

During these attacks, the platoon was under heavy and accurate fire from the high ground above them. It was entirely due to Pl/Sgt. George's example of personal courage and to his outstanding leadership that his platoon succeeded in overrunning the enemy and in dislodging them from their posts.

Recommended for M.M. (L.G. 31.8.44)

George, Ivor Lawson, Sergeant
7880883, 8th Bn. Royal Tank Regt. (Wrexham, Denbighshire) (Periodic)
Sollum, Capuzzo—22.11.41—15.12.41
Bardia—31.12.41—2.1.42

In actions at Sollum, Capuzzo and Bardia he set a most brilliant example of personal leadership and gallantry. In the former two actions fighting a one tank action and time and time again saving the infantry. In all actions at Bardia on 31.12.41 and 1.1.42 he also showed a complete lack of personal safety and was responsible for the suppression of enemy strong points at point blank range.

Throughout the whole course of operations he has been a fine example to all ranks. (L.G. 9.9.42)

George, Leslie Robert, Private (A/Cpl.)
3976325, 1/5 Bn. Welch Regt. (London, S.E.18)
On 23 July 1944 Pte. George was one of the crew of a 6-pdr. A Tk. gun in 'C' Coy's area at Le Bon Repos. All four 6-pdrs. in this area had been located by the enemy and were continually under observed and accurate shell, mortar and M.G. fire, which imposed a very severe strain on the crews and caused many casualties. Throughout the ordeal Pte. George was unshaken and his cheerful bearing was an example to all.

At about 1500 hrs. on the same afternoon about a company of enemy infantry attacked the position, two sections of which charged Pte. George's gun site from its open flank. Pte. George shot the officer and wounded two of the men whereupon the remainder turned tail.

Later that afternoon a Mark IV tank approached the position. Pte. George serviced his gun alone under circumstances of the greatest difficulty, as not only were his sights blurred by rain and he was unable to load his first three rounds due to damage from shell splinters, but also he was under heavy mortar and small arms fire. In spite of this, with the first round he was able to fire, he hit the tank squarely on its heavily armoured front and caused it to withdraw immediately to a hull-down position.

Pte. George's determination to stop that tank under the conditions obtaining at the time and, in fact, his courage, bearing and behaviour throughout the whole action are deserving of the highest praise.

These incidents were witnessed by his A. Tk. Pl. Comd. and an officer from 'C' Coy, from positions close by. (L.G. 21.12.44)

Gerari, Geai, Pata (A/Aurua)
168, Papuan Infantry Bn., Australian Military Forces (Immediate)
Bougainville Southern Sector.

At 1200 hrs. on 14 Aug. 1945, an Angau native reported that a large body of enemy located in the vicinity of Hanung (MR. 082438 Musaraka) had offered to surrender and a patrol of one section under command of Cpl. Geai was sent to ascertain the strength of the enemy party and to verify the Angau Native's statement. Moving along the track towards Hanung, 3 enemy with hands upraised were encountered.

Cpl. Geai with the Angau native approached to take them P/W but when only a few yards away he observed an L.M.G. and crew in camouflaged positions covering the track and at the same time, several more armed enemy were seen moving around his left flank.

Realising that he had been trapped, Cpl. Geai called out to his section to take cover, and immediately opened fire knocking out the L.M.G. and capturing it. Intense mortar, rifle and further L.M.G. fire raked the patrol, and Cpl. Geai was wounded by machine gun burst in both the arm and hand. Even whilst injured and with a total disregard of his personal safety, he rushed forward again with his Owen gun, engaging and killing singlehanded 7 of the enemy troops. At this stage, Cpl. Geai was wounded in the leg but despite this additional severe injury, he carried on and continued to engage the Japanese and draw their fire until he was able to organize and execute the section's withdrawal, this being achieved for the loss of only one other casualty besides himself. With the enemy's treachery placing him at a seemingly hopeless initial disadvantage, Cpl. Geai's brilliant leadership and the exceptionally high degree of physical courage which he displayed in thus repeatedly exposing himself to the concentrated fire from a considerably numerically superior force undoubtedly saved the lives of many of his section, and the fact that he continued this action although thrice wounded until he had extricated the section from an extremely dangerous predicament was especially meritorious.

(L.G. 13.12.45)

Gibb, David, Warrant Officer Cl. II (C.S.M.)
3708595, 2 King's Own Royal Regt. (Aldershot)
On 21 Nov. 41 Company Serjeant Major Gibb was C.S.M. of 'D' Coy., whose objective was the Butch and Crest locality.

During the attack one platoon of the company lost its commander, killed, and its platoon Sjt. wounded. C.S.M. Gibb immediately took command and led them with skill and determination, and finally captured a strong enemy post.

During the day C.S.M. Gibb with six remaining men of the platoon held the post in face of strong automatic and Mortar fire. With captured automatics he eventually held the enemy down, and covered the evacuation of his company Comdr. and crews of damaged tanks. He then assisted in the 'Mopping up' of other enemy posts.

Throughout the action his conduct was excellent, and he displayed leadership and initiative of a high degree.

(L.G. 24.2.42)

Gibson, Malcolm, Corporal (temp.)
215712, Royal Australian Infantry Corps
No citation.   *(L.G. 19.9.69)*

Gilbey, Leonard James, Sergeant
5933104, 2nd Bn. Cambridgeshire Regt. (Cambridge)
On 14th Feb. 42, Sgt. Gilbey was holding a locality on
Hill 75 North of Braddell Rd., Singapore. During a heavy
bombardment by artillery and mortar fire he was severely
wounded. Nevertheless he continued to inspire his
platoon with a cheery confidence and held his ground in
spite of his left flank being exposed. By so doing he held
up the enemy's advance for some six or seven hours at a
critical period. He was finally carried on rifles to the
Regimental Aid Post.   *(L.G. 13.12.45)*

Gilchrist, Donald George Hugh, Sergeant
4533831, 2nd Bn. West Yorkshire Regt. (Boston Spa)
(Periodic)
Period Dec. 43 to May 44. Arakan
    Sgt. Gilchrist has served with the Bn. in all the
campaigns it has been engaged in during the present war.
During this long period Sgt. Gilchrist has proved himself
to be a gallant soldier and a resourceful and inspiring
leader. The following is a typical example of his conduct
in battle. During the operations in Ngakyedauk Pass area
Sgt. Gilchrist was comd. of a platoon of 'B' Coy. 2 W.
Yorks. On 18 Feb. 44, his platoon was ordered to clear
the enemy from a position just outside the 7 Ind. Div.
Admin. Box, into which they had infiltrated during the
night. When this task was almost completed as a result
of a bold and methodical operation, the platoon was
suddenly fired upon by an M.G. which caused three
serious casualties in his leading sec. which at the time it
was impossible to reach. Sgt. Gilchrist manouvered his
platoon to a flank and called for support from the tanks.
These supported the platoon with fire thus enabling them
to liquidate the enemy post and reach the three seriously
wounded men. At the conclusion of the operation 11
Japanese bodies were found. On this and many other
occasions Sgt. Gilchrist's leadership has been largely
responsible for successful actions by the platoon.
                                      (L.G. 8.2.45)

Gilchrist, William John, Sergeant
2717907, 2nd Bn. Irish Guards
Boulogne 23rd May 1940.
    Sgt. Gilchrist was in personal charge of an anti-tank
rifle which protected the rear of the Battalion during its
withdrawal into Boulogne on the 23rd May. For two
hours this N.C.O., with a few men, succeeded in holding
their post at a street corner, thus enabling the remainder
of the Battalion to move on unmolested.
    Although under extremely heavy machine gun fire
he showed the greatest contempt of danger and continued
to keep his anti-tank gun in action. He was instrumental
in hitting and setting on fire an enemy tank, thus blocking
a street down which the enemy were trying to move.

Later in the action he himself was wounded but refused
to leave his anti-tank rifle until it, and the Bren guns
supporting it, became jammed through over firing.
Throughout the whole action Sgt. Gilchrist showed
courage and bravery of a very high order and set the
finest example to the remainder of his platoon.
                                      (L.G. 22.10.40)

Giles, Arthur Vincent, Sergeant
NX 14674, 2/5 Aust. Fd. Coy.
During the day of 8 Jun. 41, Sgt. Giles moved through
our forward inf. positions, in front of Khirbe, which were
under heavy fire, and collected members of the section
who had become scattered amongst inf. during the early
morning attack, in order to have his men at his command
if required.
    During the attack on Khirbe, 11 Jun. 41, Sgt. Giles
with four men advanced along the road, but were
prevented from moving road blocks and mines on
account of heavy mortar and machine gun fire. When
the infantry carriers arrived fire continued and the carriers
were in danger of being destroyed. Under direct enemy
fire he coolly commanded his party in removing road
blocks and mines to clear a path for the carriers. This
party then proceeded through Khirbe and on to the
outskirts of Merdjayoun in front of the carriers, in order
to clear blocks and mines. These were encountered at
varying intervals over the whole distance. On 13 Jun.
41, Sgt. Giles commanded a party forward of Merdjayoun in removal of mines. On 11 and 13 Jun., he
supervised removal of approx. 800 French A.Tk. mines.
On night of 21 Jun., Sgt. Giles commanded a party which
moved to a position on the North Rd. from Jezzine which
was covered by enemy positions and laid a minefield.
On 28 and 29 Jun., Sgt. Giles commanded a small party
which placed a crater charge of 300lbs of ammonal in
the Jezzine—Saida Rd., at a place which was under direct
artillery fire from the enemy. Intermittent shelling of this
portion of the road was carried out by the enemy as the
charge was being laid. Throughout the campaign Sgt.
Giles by his devotion to duty and courageous example
has been an inspiration to, and earned the admiration of
his section.   *(L.G. 12.2.42)*

Giles, Edward Horace, Warrant Officer Cl. III (Pl.S.M.)
  (A/W.O.II, C.S.M.)
5721994, 2 Dorsetshire Regt.
On 19 May P.S.M. Giles was comdg. a platoon holding
a bridge South of Les Deux Acren. When the bn.
withdrew he was ordered to hold the bridge supported
by carriers. His tactical dispositions were very sound
and although in an isolated situation and pressed by the
enemy he remained perfectly calm. On many occasions
he has been an example of calmness and judgement.
                                      (L.G. 22.10.40)

Gilhespie, Desmond Stephen James, Lance Sergeant
7939451, Royal Signals
No citation.   *(L.G. 18.10.45)*

Gillan, Robert Claude, Rifleman
6895247, 2nd Bn. Rifle Brigade
For conspicuous gallantry and devotion to duty. On Jan. 21 this Rifleman was wireless operator of a command carrier patrolling forward towards the Tobruk defences under heavy shell, A/T and machine gun fire. Within 600 yards of the wire he was wounded in both legs by an anti tank shell, one leg had subsequently to be amputated. He carried on his duties as wireless operator for the next half hour sending and receiving important messages and when too weak from loss of blood to carry on, he continued to instruct the other occupant of the carrier how to manipulate the W.T. set. His coolness and gallantry under great pain were invaluable to the patrol and enabled the patrol Commander to keep in touch with his Company Headquarters throughout the patrol.
(L.G. 9.5.41)

Gilligan, Albert Edwin, Warrant Officer Cl. III (Pl.S.M.)
6281209, 4 Queen's Own Royal West Kent Regt.
For conspicuous gallantry and devotion to duty at the Foret de Nieppe between 25 and 28 May 1940.
P.S.M. Gilligan commanded his platoon for three days in action and during the subsequent withdrawal in an outstanding manner showing leadership of a high order. On several occasions his platoon was practically surrounded but counter attacked with great gallantry and finally withdrew intact through the enemy to Dunkirk.
This result was largely due to the initiative and leadership of P.S.M. Gilligan whose example inspired both his own men and some of the other units whom he took under his command. He showed throughout this period resource and leadership of a high order.
(L.G. 11.7.40)

Gilmore, John Louis, Sergeant
NGX.12, 'M' Special, Allied Intelligence Bureau G.H.Q., S.W.P.A., Australian Military Forces (Periodic)
For conspicuous gallantry in the face of the enemy while a member of an A.I.B. party operating in Japanese occupied territory of New Britain. From the 28th Sep. 1943, this N.C.O. was engaged in extremely dangerous missions, especially on the 13th Feb. 1944 when he proceeded on a reconnaissance patrol through the Torin River and Pondo, North East Britain to secure intelligence. Although the area to which he proceeded was known to be occupied by the enemy and inhabited by natives very hostile to Europeans, the former having betrayed many to the Japanese, it did not deter Sjt. Gilmore who penetrated thirty miles into the area, avoiding numerous patrols sent to capture him. Although he and his party of fourteen natives were surrounded by

the enemy, he was able by reason of his great bushcraft, to avoid capture, but was forced into the inhospitable mountain region to the South East.
He was able to warn T/Capt. Bates that the enemy was searching for him thus enabling that officer to prepare a defence. The enemy at this base was routed and a number of casualties occurred, among them being six Japanese officers killed.
On 16 Mar. 1944, while still in the mountain region and although suffering from starvation, Sjt. Gilmore began a long and difficult mountain journey in order to rescue an allied airman forced down in enemy territory behind Baien Village, Cape Orford. Sjt. Gilmore completed the mission on the 25th Mar. 1944 and had the airman (Cpl. Betz) carried to safety through enemy-patrolled territory over a hazardous and precipitous mountain route.
The fortitude and courage of this N.C.O. was a great inspiration to the other members of his particular party and the operation as a whole.   *(L.G. 19.7.45)*

Gilmour, Robert, Warrant Officer Cl. I
3122737, 4/5th Bn. Royal Scots Fusiliers (Ayr) (Periodic)
R.S.M. Gilmour has served with this battalion, as R.S.M., in every action since landing on the continent. In his special duty of keeping the forward troops supplied with ammunition he allowed no consideration of personal danger or of difficulties due to weather, ground or enemy action deter him from rendering maximum service to his battalion. At Tripsrath in Dec. 44 when line holding in very close contact, R.S.M. Gilmour personally took up ammunition to the forward companies over an exposed route nearly every day, often under heavy and accurate mortar and small arms fire. At Stein in Jan. 45, with all companies committed and no vehicles able to move, R.S.M. Gilmour personally organised and conducted carrying parties in the face of the enemy.
At all times and under all conditions his conduct, evident courage, and firm but humane handling of the men has been a most steadying and heartening influence on the Battalion in battle, and he has been an important factor in helping to sustain its fine morale throughout.
Recommended for M.M.   *(L.G. 24.1.46)*

Glenister, William Patrick, Warrant Officer Cl. III (Pl.S.M.)
6910698, Military Police
At Dunkirk on Saturday, 1st June 1940, after being engaged for three days and nights in embarkation duties at Bray Dunes during continuous heavy bombing and shelling, this W.O. volunteered to assist in the removal of wounded and was employed on this duty on the Mole, frequently under heavy fire, until he was ordered to embark at 2100 hours whereas he could have left at 1000 hours that day.
During the whole withdrawal period and whilst under heavy bombing and shelling he carried out reconnais-

sance, traffic and embarkation duties with ability. By his coolness and devotion to duty he set a fine example to the men under him and contributed greatly to the successful withdrawal and embarkation of B.E.F. troops.

(L.G. 20.8.40)

Glover, Harry Noel, Sergeant (A/W.O.II (C.S.M.))
69982068, 6th Bn. Royal Inniskilling Fusiliers
(Bangor, Co. Down)

Between 20 and 25 Dec. 42 at Goubellat J 6520 when a Pl Serjeant in a forward position, this W.O. led patrols each night, both for reconnaisance and to fight. At that time this Bn. was in its infancy in fighting, but this W.O. showed himself a leader at the early stage.

Later between 26 Dec. 42 and 10 Jan. 43 in the Mahmoud Gap J 6119, this W.O. still a Serjeant at that time, led patrols which covered distances of ten to twelve miles, always getting some result, keeping control and bringing his men back to the Bn. position intact.

On 27 Jan. 43 when C.S.M. of 'B' Coy., he went out with his Coy. to Rd. Junc. 687126 with the object of attacking high ground Argoub Hamiri 6813. When ordered by his Coy. Comd to proceed to the Southern bank of the objective with Bren guns he carried out these orders and when doing so succeeded without noise or firing to hold-up three enemy signallers from 90 Arty. Regt. whom he made prisoner.

He is brave and sure, and therefore inspires confidence in junior and newly joined officers as well as in the men of his company.   *(L.G. 23.9.43)*

Glynn, Edwin, Trooper
321863, 5th Royal Inniskilling Dragoon Guards

On night 1/2 June 1940, whilst moving along the Dunkirk beach Tpr. Glynn saw that a man had been wounded by shell fire. On his own initiative, this soldier left his squadron and under shell fire took this man to safety. He continued to rescue wounded in this way until noon on 2nd June, taking many to the boats who would otherwise have been unable to get there.   *(L.G. 11.7.40)*

Goad, Graham Henry, Private
14478, 21 N.Z. Bn.

On the morning of 29 Nov. 41 at Hill 175 Pte. Goad was company signaller of D Coy. The enemy overran the position and practically surrounded Coy. HQ the Coy. Comd. being killed. Observation was difficult for the F.O.O. and Pte. Goad observed and directed through the Bn. HQ exchange the Arty fire for over an hour although under continuous enemy fire. On several occasions he appeared to be surrounded by the enemy but managed to hold on in his slit trench. His action materially assisted in stabilising the position.

Recommended for M.M.   *(L.G. 20.1.42)*

Goddard, Gerald, Corporal
31507, 1 Imperial Light Horse, South African Forces

For outstanding gallantry and inspiring leadership in the attack on Bardia on 31 Dec. 41.

In an attack on an enemy strong point the platoon, in which Cpl. Goddard was a section commander, came under very heavy enemy M.G. fire with the result that 16 members of the platoon, including the Platoon Commander and the Platoon Sgt., were killed, and 7 more wounded. Cpl. Goddard immediately took charge of the remaining 9 men and captured the position at the point of the bayonet. He then re-organised his men and led them on to the next objective which he captured. He remained in command through the rest of the day, at all times inspiring his men with his fearless leadership.

(L.G. 3.3.42)

Goddard, Lewis Walter, Bombardier
2039296, Royal Artillery, T.A. (late 34th (The Queen's
Own Royal West Kent) A.A. Bn. R.E., T.A.)

May 29th 1940 at Dunkirk

Corporal Goddard was in charge of a detachment on board H.M.S. 'Crested Eagle' and showed exceptional initiative and coolness under fire during several aircraft attacks which finally resulted in the destruction of the ship. Corporal Goddard manned the Lewis guns after the original gunner had been wounded and the ship was on fire and assisted to keep off further attacks. He showed great courage and devotion to duty in attempting to evacuate wounded from below decks when the ship was on fire and in the process of being abandoned.

Recommended for M.M.   *(L.G. 26.9.40)*

Goldie, James Muir Lang, Private
2985254, 7 Argyll & Sutherland Highlanders
6 June 1940 Captured Abbeville

I was captured near Abbeville on 6 Jun. 40 while serving with the Battalion Bren carriers which had been sent from Battalion HQ to assist C Coy. I was captured along with Capt. Hewitt, C Coy., and ten other ranks.

Steudnitz (Arbeits-Kommando 1116)

After capture I was sent to German to Stalag IX C (Bad Sulza), and from there to the cement works at Steudnitz, near Dorndorf, about 7 miles S.E. Bad Sulza. I remained at this camp (Arbeitskommando 1116) till Sep. 41 when I was sent to the salt mines at Unterbreizbach, 10 miles S.E. Hersfeld (Arbeitskommando 147). There I was working underground.

Sep. 1941 Unterbretzbach (Arbeits-Kommando 147).

I escaped from the camp at Unterbreizbach on 21 Mar. 42 with Pte. MacFarlane, W. of my unit (S/P.G. (G) 821). The facts of our escape are as stated in Pte. MacFarlane's report, except for the following details:—

21 Mar. 1942 Escaped from Unterbreizbach.

There were four pairs of P/W in the camp who were interested in escaping, and the original plan was for the eight of us to get out together and then split into groups of two. In the end only MacFarlane and I tried. We waited for two others, but they did not turn up.

In addition to the chocolate, biscuits, sardines and tea mentioned in MacFarlane's report, we took with us in our rucksacks a change of underclothes, shirts, towels, and a blanket, as well as some soap, which we thought would be useful in paying for help. Our packs weighed about 40 pounds each.

As mentioned by MacFarlane, we secured two maps. In exchange for a greatcoat a German Communist, who worked with me in the salt mine, gave me a map of the local State. Unfortunately, I left this map behind my bed in the camp. The map which MacFarlane got from a Pole was of Western Europe. We used it to check our position while travelling by goods train to Belgium.

Railway waggons bound for destinations outside Germany bear on their side green destination labels marked 'Ausgang'.

The fastening of the sealed waggon into which we broke consisted of an iron bar and an eye with wire twisted round the eye and soldered. We broke the solder and, of course, had to replace the wire without it, but the operation was not detected.

After arriving at Hasselt we spent two days on a goods train which was marked Antwerp. When it did not move, we started walking to Louvain. We attracted a certain amount of attention on the road because of our large packs, but we made a point of keeping ourselves clean and shaven, and also cleaned our boots regularly. No one stopped us on the way.   *(L.G. 10.11.42)*

Goldman, Augustus Nathan, Sergeant
2509, 2 Royal Durban Light Infantry (Immediate)
2509, Union Defence Force (2 Royal Durban Light Infantry), Sgt. Goldman escaped from Tobruk with Cpl. C. H. Spear, No. 2587 and Pte. D. V. Borain, No. 7225 of 2 R.D.L.I. (both of whom have been recommended for a M.M.).

The party was led by Sgt. Goldman, who was I Sergeant to 2 R.D.L.I. He was able to bring back valuable detailed information about Tobruk and the route they followed.

They left the perimeter on foot and had a most eventful journey. They were fired on several times and suffered much privation through thirst and hunger.

They retained their arms and captured a German tank, killing three of the crew and forcing the fourth to drive the tank until the petrol gave out. They released the P/W and continued on foot.

Then, although weak, they tried to capture a German truck. In the hand to hand fight Sgt. Goldman had two ribs broken by a kick from a German. One German was killed and the other was captured with the truck. Although in enemy convoy they stopped to bury the dead German.

Sgt. Goldman showed very great courage as the leader of this trio and it was a remarkable feat for three men in their weak state to dare to capture a German tank—and

when that let them down, undaunted, attempt to capture yet another enemy vehicle.

It was only due to sheer determination and spirited courage that this party reached our lines.
             (L.G. 24.11.42)

Goldsbrough, Frank, Sergeant
3853977, 1st Bn. Duke of Wellington's Regt. (Preston)
(Immediate)
For courage, determination and devotion to duty on Apr 23., and May 5/6 1943.

After the occupation of Hill 174 on Apr 23 the Coy was subjected to heavy mortar and M.G. fire when digging in. Sgt. Goldsborough who was commanding his platoon, went forward by himself, attacked an enemy post with grenades and brought back a prisoner. He returned and went out again at once with two men and attacked another post with grenades. He then took out a full section himself and attacked another post. He remained a long time with little covering fire and eventually returned with 10 prisoners, Sgt. Goldsborough himself coming back several minutes after the Section. He immediately asked permission to take out another patrol but was forbidden to do so. During the whole of this time the Coy. was subjected to heavy fire and was suffering casualties. During the attack on Hill 226 on May 5/6 this N.C.O. led his men with great skill and courage, engaging the enemy in a number of strong positions until they were either killed or driven off their positions. He attacked the ridge three times before the enemy were finally overcome. His courage and determination were an example to his men, and but for his inspiring leadership it is doubtful whether the force would have reached the position on Pt. 226 that they did. Under heavy M.G. fire Sgt. Goldsborough reorganised his platoon and defended his position stubbornly against a heavy counter attack, and then drove the enemy off, inflicting severe casualties on him.

The immediate award of D.C.M. to Sgt. Goldsborough is recommended.   *(L.G. 23.9.43)*

Gomez, Darrow, Sergeant
K.15513, 3 Cdn. Anti-Tank Regt., Royal Canadian
Artillery (Immediate)
On the morning of the 30th Mar. 1945 at map ref. 973514 (sheet 4103 1/25,000) K15313 Sergeant Darrow Gomez was N.C.O. i/c a 17 pounder self-propelled Valentine gun which was part of a troop of the 105th Canadian Anti Tank Battery in support of the Royal Winnipeg Rifles. The enemy had determinedly counter-attacked the position during the previous night and with daylight came the knowledge that self-propelled guns had been brought up to support these attacks. These enemy guns had assumed a most aggressive role and were rapidly rendering unenterable the area occupied by a company of the Royal Winnipeg Rifles. Since they were deployed on high ground and at short range, any movement on the part of our infantry was extremely hazardous.

At approximately 1100 hrs. Sergeant Gomez pinpointed the location of one enemy gun after performing a reconnaissance under intense rifle and machine gun fire. Sergeant Gomez then manoeuvred his 17 pounder Valentine gun in a favourable position and succeeded in knocking out the enemy self-propelled equipment. Not content with this one success, Sergeant Gomez immediately commenced another reconnaissance in the company of 'D' company commander of the Royal Winnepeg Rifles. After considerable time, they located the position of another enemy self-propelled gun which was pinning down an entire company of our infantry. Notwithstanding the fact that the infantry company commander was killed at his side and the driver of his own equipment had become severely wounded, Sergeant Gomez fearlessly commenced to advance his gun to a suitable position. Although his own gun was twice hit by enemy shell-fire this N.C.O. attained his objective and laying the gun himself, destroyed the enemy self-propelled equipment with one round.

Shortly after this incident, a strong enemy fighting patrol attacked the position occupied by Sergeant Gomez. Although his gun was clearly exposed to this party of enemy, and at very short range, he unhesitatingly manned the machine-gun mounted on his equipment and brought fire to bear on the Infantry. One of the enemy patrol was consequently killed, seven were taken prisoner and the remainder forced to retire.

Throughout these actions, Sergeant Gomez displayed magnificent leadership and absolute disregard for his own personal safety. There is no doubt that the example he set enabled our infantry, despite heavy casualties, to hold this vital area in face of spirited enemy counter-attacks.

(L.G. 11.8.45)

Good, William Christopher Finbarr, Warrant Officer Cl. II (C.S.M.)
6282691, 1 Royal Irish Fusiliers
On 19th May during the daylight withdrawal from the very exposed posn. North of Ninove three enemy dets. with M.G.s infiltrated round the Bns. southern flank, opened fire at short range and inflicted severe casualties on D Coy.

C.S.M. Good led a party round one flank of the enemy M.G.s whilst 2/Lt. Martin led another party round their other flank. By skilful use of ground, fire, grenades and the bayonet and unhesitating courage the enemy was destroyed and put flight. The action of the party under C.S.M. Good was probably responsible for saving A Ech. of the Bns. Transport and also for saving the remainder of the Bn. from very extensive casualties.

(L.G. 20.12.40)

Gooden, Frederick Arthur, Sergeant
6020150, 1st Bn. Durham Light Infantry (Ockendon, Essex) (Immediate)
On 30 Nov. 1944 Sgt. Gooden was commanding No. 4 Platoon of 'B' Company in the attack on the three houses in the La Capanna area (415285). His task was to take the second house after the capture of the first by another platoon. On seeing the success signal from the first house he went forward and found the Platoon Commander dead, and the platoon rather disorganised. He immediately brought up his own platoon under heavy fire, organised the defence of this house and consolidated the position. As soon as he had done this, he led his platoon on to attack the second house, which was his own objective, actually going in first and clearing the building himself. The enemy then brought down heavy arty. fire on the house scoring at least two direct hits, but Sgt. Gooden coolly got two of his Brens into action and engaged the enemy who had withdrawn about 150 yds. This fire inflicted several casualties on the enemy and forced them to withdraw still further. He finally directed very accurate covering fire for the third platoon in their attack and materially helped them to gain their objective.

Throughout the whole of this action Sgt. Gooden led his platoon with considerable dash and energy. His example and disregard for personal safety under heavy fire and in frightful weather conditions was largely responsible for the success of the attack.
Recommended for M.M.   *(L.G. 24.5.45)*

Goodey, Edward Charles, Warrant Officer Cl. I
6907671, Rifle Brigade (London, N.20)
No citation.   *(L.G. 20.9.45)*

Goodyear, Cleeve William, Bombardier
QX 919, 2 Aust. A. Tk. Regt., R.A.A.
On the morning of the 16 Jun. 41 at 0530 hrs. two armd. cars accompanied by two M/Cs were observed on the road from Machrhara to Jezzine. They approached the posn. occupied by D Coy. 31 Bn. which was supported by one A/Tk. gun in charge of Bdr. C. W. Goodyear.

Bdr. Goodyear held his fire until the first Armd. car had reached a road block approx. 200 yds. in front of the gun. He then opened fire and both of the cars were hit and burst into flames. Several prisoners were taken and the two M/Cs were captured.

Shortly after this (approx. 0545 hrs.) a staff car came along the road and was also disabled. One Offr. and the dvr. were taken prisoner. At 0600 hrs. another D/R came along and was also captured.

At 0630 a third armoured car appeared moving very cautiously along the road. Bdr. Goodyear allowed this vehicle to reach a point about 600' from the gun and then opened fire. The car burst into flames.

The number of enemy personnel accounted for were approx. 7 killed and 1 Offr. and 11 O/Rs prisoners.

I wish to commend Bdr. Goodyear for his coolness in holding his fire till the last possible moment and for the good shooting which accounted for the four enemy vehs. All the credit for the disabling of these vehs. should go to this man.

(L.G. 12.2.42)

Gooley, Bede Vaughan, Sergeant
NX68829, 2/3 Australian Inf. Bn. (Immediate)
For gallantry and distinguished conduct in the field.

During an attack on a heavily defended enemy position on Longridge, Danmap area British New Guinea on 1 Feb. 45, Sjt. Gooley was acting as platoon sjt. In the initial assault his platoon comdr. was seriously wounded.

Immediately assuming command, Sjt. Gooley rallied his men and vigorously assaulted the enemy's left flank in the face of intense fire from 3 enemy L.M.G.s. One gun silenced, he led the assault into the withering fire of the remaining 2 L.M.G.'s, destroying the gun crews and capturing both guns. This resulted in the rapid withdrawal of the remaining enemy.

On a patrol 3 days previously, Sjt. Gooley's platoon encountered an enemy defended locality. Regardless of his own safety, Sjt. Gooley immediately engaged the enemy with an O.S.M.G. when an enemy L.M.G. opened fire on his left flank, he rushed forward alone and silenced the gun with a grenade.

During both actions Sjt. Gooley displayed outstanding qualities of leadership and courage of the highest order. His brilliant leadership was an inspiration to his men and largely contributed to the success of both operations.
(L.G. 21.6.45)

Gordon, Ernest Elmer, Sergeant
H.19814, Queen's Own Cameron Highlanders of Canada
Sergeant Gordon was wounded early in the attack on Dieppe 19 Aug. 42. He concealed his wounds and carried on. He repeatedly organized small parties of men and personally led them in clearing the many houses in his area. Upon the order to withdraw he personally ensured that all men of his platoon who were seriously wounded were carried back to the beach. On the beach he acted fearlessly and efficiently, going back into and through the danger zone of mortar and machine gun fire to bring aid to the wounded lying in exposed positions. Throughout the entire action this N.C.O. was cool, bold and determined, and his leadership contributed materially to the success obtained.
(L.G. 2.10.42)

Gordon, George Rousset, Sergeant (actg.)
22539314, Queen's Own Royal West Kent Regt.
For Malaya
(L.G. 29.6.54)

Gorton, Thomas Valentine, Sergeant
7929477, 12th Bn. Royal Tank Regt. (Manchester) (Immediate)
Ref. Map Italy 1:50,000 76—II Portomaggiore.

During an adv. from Portomaggiore northwards 'C' Sqn. 12 R. Tks. was in sp. of the 1st Bn. Scots Guards. (24 Gds. Bde.).

No. 14 Tp. 'C' Sqn. with a Coy. of Inf. were given the task of moving forward to secure a crossing of Cond'To Campo Grande 289762. Sgt. Gorton was acting Tp. Ldr. of No. 14 Tp. as his officer had been killed on the previous day. The tank and Inf. force on the left flank had been unable to secure a crossing on their front, but by a rapid advance and by determined and skilful handling of his tp. Sgt. Gorton managed to cross the first water obstacle and push on and seize the bridge intact over the second obstacle at 303779, which was of vital importance.

Just as Sgt. Gorton was about to cross this bridge his tp. was attacked by low flying enemy aircraft firing 20mm cannon: one tank received several hits killing the driver and putting the tank out of action.

Undaunted by this attack Sgt. Gorton carried out a quick recce on foot of the bridge as civilians had reported mines and prepared demolition charges. However, Sgt. Gorton, realising the necessity for speed and establishing a bridge-head with his inf., decided to cross at once. This he proceeded to do and took up positions with his two tanks where he could give good sp. to the inf.

Throughout the recent period of action from 9–25 Apr. 45 (both with ordinary Churchills and also with Crocodiles) Sgt. Gorton has shown outstanding leadership, and ability to control, handle and direct a troop under difficult and arduous circumstances.

His personal courage and example have been an inspiration to the men in his troop and Squadron. He has also earned high praise from the inf. with whom he has been co-operating, and when his troop officer was killed on 19 Apr. 45 showed himself perfectly capable of carrying on under trying conditions.
Recommended for M.M. *(L.G. 23.8.45)*

Gosling, Eric James, Bombardier
855881, 58 Medium Regt., Royal Artillery (Ipswich) (Immediate)
On 7 October 44, immediately after the capture of M. Farneto, A Troop OP party was ordered to establish an OP on the feature. The Troop Commander left this OP party under cover while he went forward to reconnoitre and OP. He was almost immediately killed by shell fire. Bdr. Gosling immediately took charge, and with complete disregard for his own safety, as the area was under continuous shell and small arms fire, selected an OP, and established commun–ications with his battery and the infantry he was supporting. He got in contact with the Battery Commander of 58 Field Regt. who was in support of the Battalion and reported that he was ready for any tasks.

Again with no thought for his own safety, he recovered his troop commander's body, and collected all codes and personal effects.

The enemy put in several counter-attacks on the feature, and Bdr. Gosling directed the fire of his battery with marked success until relieved by another officer.

Bdr. Gosling's coolness, leadership and courage were an example to all, and his action undoubtedly contributed materially to the breaking up of the many counter-attacks launched against the position.
Recommended for M.M.   (*L.G. 8.3.45*)

Gott, William, Sergeant
3059837, 2nd Bn. Royal Scots (Bradford) (Immediate)
On 15th Sep. 1944 Sgt. Gott was a Pl. Comdr. of 'C' Coy. who were ordered to continue the advance of the Bn. by night along the axis towards M. Paganino. On reaching Pt. 950 the leading platoon came under heavy M.G. fire. The Coy. Comdr. was wounded on going forward to contact the leading platoon and shortly afterwards the C.S.M. was wounded by mortar fire, leaving Sgt. Gott as the senior rank in the Coy. This N.C.O. took complete control of the situation and ordered the Coy. to consolidate on Pt. 950 until he could make a recce at first light. During the next 12 hours movement in the position was extremely difficult and drew fire from several M.G. positions in front and on the flanks of the Coy. Wireless communication with the Bn. had been lost owing to damage to the 18 Set and patrols sent out to try and contact the Coy. failed to do so as their position was not known and enemy fire way heavy. It was not until late in the day that contact was established. During all this time Sgt. Gott's conduct was a source of inspiration and encouragement to the rest of the Coy. and he displayed qualities of leadership of the highest order under most difficult conditions.   (*L.G. 12.4.45*)

Gouk, George, Warrant Officer Cl. II (C.S.M.)
H.19266, Queen's Own Cameron Highlanders of
*   Canada*
Throughout the entire Dieppe action, 19 Aug. 42, this Warrant Officer was an inspiration to his men and an invaluable assistant to Coy. and Bn. Officers. In the withdrawal of over two miles he was the last man to stay behind to cover the retirement of small parties of men. He was ever alert to protect the flank and rear, and his display of fearlessness in the face of heavy odds was an outstanding example of coolness, steadiness and efficiency. The comparatively small number of casualties suffered by his Coy. was, in great part, attributable to this W.O.'s gallant conduct.   (*L.G. 2.10.42*)

Gould, George James Henry, Bombardier (A/Sgt.)
2059965, Royal Horse Artillery
This Sec. Sgt. was in action close to the main Bengasi Road on the morning Feb. 6th. An enemy attack developed. The B.C. spotted an enemy gun firing straight down the road and shells were falling about 30–40 yds. to the right of a blockhouse on the road. Sgt. Gould took up a Portee to where the flash of the enemy gun was clearly seen and fired 6 rounds down the verandah of the blockhouse at 1,000 yds. The enemy gun was silenced. The Portee was then withdrawn about 40 yds. behind a small knoll and very shortly 3 enemy 'M' tanks

advanced. Two were knocked out and the other abandoned by its crew. Enemy prisoners in the blockhouse then succeeded in obtaining rifles and commenced sniping. The Portee was hit. Sgt. Gould kept very cool and ordered his Lewis gunner to engage them. The Bofors Sec. and its Lewis gun were at this time our foremost troops, except for a Cpl. Conlon of the R.B.'s and his Bren gunner who joined them, being the remnants of an R.B. section put out of action by snipers. Further, the following is a report by Capt. T. Pearson of the 2nd B. R.B. on the further good action by Sgt. Gould.

'On the morning of the 7th Sgt. Gould engaged 14 'M 13' tanks from a range of 50 yds. knocking out 4 with his first 4 shots. His gun jammed and he with crew, repaired his gun and came into action again knocking out 2 more and covering the Infantry advance on to the remaining tanks which were surrendering.'
                                                      (*L.G. 9.5.41*)

Goult, Arthur William, Sergeant (actg.)
2612007, (A/Sergeant), 3rd Bn. Grenadier Guards
*   (Immediate)*
On the night of Oct. 10/11th, Sgt. Goult was in command of four 3" Mortar detachments of 3rd Bn. Grenadier Guards, sited below Monte Battaglia (Map ref. M. 0618), and supporting the forward companies on the feature. A German patrol was heard approaching the mortar position at the same time as mortar defensive fire was being called for by the left forward company, who were being attacked. Sgt. Goult at once fired the D.F. task and reported that he was being machine gunned from the rear. He continued to fire his mortars, even though enemy grenades were falling in the mortar pits and the machine gun was firing at the mortars at close range. He was ordered to stop firing and immediately manned his position against the enemy with the Bren gun, Tommy guns and grenades. He managed to beat off the enemy, who attempted to wrench one of the mortars from its position. Finally, when daylight broke, Sgt. Goult reported that seventy Germans were in the gully 50 yards from him and wishing to surrender. No praise is too high for the way in which this N.C.O. kept firing his mortars in support of his comrades although in imminent danger himself and the gallant way in which he led the detachments to fight back at the greatly superior force, was largely responsible for the number of prisoners taken.
                                                      (*L.G. 8.3.45*)

Graham, Thomas William, Private
B.37087, Royal Hamilton Light Infantry (Wentworth
*   Regt.)*
A Bren gunner with the Protective Platoon of his OC. 1st unit during the action at Dieppe 19 Aug. 42, Pte. Bn. R.H.L.I. Graham landed on the beaches with the first wave. When, during the cutting of the second row of protective wire, two of his comrades were wounded, Pte. Graham went forward in the face of very heavy fire and succeeded in dragging them both back to safety. At a

later stage, standing up under heavy fire, he threw two smoke cannisters to cover the approach of his party to the Casino. In the Casino itself, when it was discovered that snipers were located down a passageway, Pte. Graham rushed in, threw two grenades and knocked out the snipers. Then, advancing to the town side of the Casino, with his anti-tank rifle he knocked out four machine-gun posts in the buildings on the Esplanade. When tanks later appeared on the Esplanade, Pte. Graham, although unable to communicate with them, displayed great initiative in directing their fire by firing his own Bren Gun at the walls around the enemy positions. The tanks observing his fall of shot then took over and knocked out the enemy posts. During the whole operation Pte. Graham displayed great initiative and fearless courage under fire. *(L.G. 2.10.42)*

Graham, Walter, Warrant Officer Cl. III (Pl.S.M.)
3308812, 2nd Bn. Highland Light Infantry
(Inverkeithing, Fife)
1. On 22 Jan 41 this P.S.M. was in command of No 7 Platoon of 'A' Coy. 2 H.L.I., which was ordered to clear the enemy from a strong position which he was holding in a gorge leading to Ibrahim Gub. During the last 300 yards of his approach to the enemy's position, his platoon was heavily fired on but by skilful leadership he managed to avoid casualties. P.S.M. Graham's platoon was now attacked with hand grenades but he led his men in a direct assault which ended in the capture of the enemy's position. P.S.M. Graham showed skill and leadership of a high order. (5.2.41)
2. Conspicuous gallantry and devotion to duty.
On the 15th March 1941, during the attack on Pinnacle this Warrant Officer led part of his company across a nullah: a distance of 200 yds. under heavy fire from machine guns and snipers. He then twice re-crossed this nullah to bring forward the remainder of the company. During the remainder of the operations, till he was badly wounded on Railway Bumps, he displayed outstanding courage and devotion to duty. *(L.G. 30.12.41)*

Grant, Alexander, Warrant Officer Cl. II
405651, 80th (Scot Horse) Med. Regt., Royal Artillery
(Elgin) (Periodic)
This W.O. came abroad with the regt. in Feb. 1943 a B.S.M. of 'B' Tp. 110 Bty., in Oct. 1944 he was promoted Bty. B.S.M. of 110 Bty. During the period the Regt. has been in action in Sicily, The Sangro, Anzio, Gothic Line and Senio and PO battles he has shown courage of an exceptional nature and great devotion to duty.
In the last battle from the Senio to the PO B.S.M. Grant in his capacity as Bty. B.S.M. showed great initiative and determination in maintaining the ammunition supply. All ammunition had to be ferried forward as no R.A.S.C. transport was available and although at the time he was suffering from a fractured rib he insisted on carrying on until the battle was over.

At the beginning of Sept. 1944, during the Gothic Line Battle, the Regt. was deployed below S. Clemente within 2,000 yards of the F.D.L.'s. B.S.M. Grant on this occasion showed exceptional courage and coolness when 110 Bty. suffered casualties; organising the evacuation of the wounded and helping to extinguish a fire from burning charges.
Later at the beginning of October when 110 Bty. were occupying a position on the North bank of the Marecchio he again displayed great courage in organising the evacuation of the wounded gunners when his troop was heavily shelled, carrying on through shell fire until he was himself wounded.
At Anzio from D Day onwards the coolness and courage of this W.O. were an outstanding example to his troop especially during the heavy shelling during the enemy counter attacks when he was responsible for his troop's ammunition supply: at one time insisting on carrying on after his slit trench had received a direct hit and he had been slightly wounded.
The very high morale, coolness and courage that this B.S.M. has shown since the Regt. first went into action has been of inestimable value to his battery and his example of complete devotion to duty has been outstanding.
Recommended for M.M. *(L.G. 13.12.45)*

Grant, Norman George Albert, Corporal
5670274, 4th Bn. Somerset Light Infantry (Misterton)
(Immediate)
At about 0630 hrs. on the morning of the 8th Mar. 1945, Cpl. Grant's Coy. attacked the defended approaches to Xanten. His Coy. had been pinned under heavy Spandau and Bazooka fire from the moment they came in contact with the enemy. Cpl. Grant's sec. was ordered to attack an enemy Spandau position on the far side of the anti-tank ditch. Under the heaviest fire Cpl. Grant led his sec. over 150 yds. of completely open ground to gain cover within grenade range of the enemy Spandau. He then hurled a grenade into the enemy position and charged in single handed after the explosion, many other members of his sec. having become casualties. Alone and in spite of intense Schmeisser fire he killed the entire crew of the Spandau—he, himself, being twice wounded. Despite his wounds he directed what was left of his sec. to the next objective and only when this was gained consented to be evacuated. His gallant action was the immediate cause of his Coy.'s ensuing success.
Recommended for M.M. *(L.G. 21.6.45)*

Gray, Albert, Warrant Officer Cl. III (Pl.S.M.)
6975201, Royal Irish Fusiliers
No citation. *(L.G. 20.12.40)*

Gray, Arthur James, Private
SX18206, Australian Military Forces
No citation. *(L.G. 20.4.44)*

Gray, Everett John, M.M., Bombardier (A/Sgt.)
1463728, 258 A/T Bty. R.A. of 65th (Norf. Yeo.) A/Tk.
Regt., Royal Artillery (Norwich)
For gallantry and devotion to duty in the 'January'
Bridgehead on October 25th.

Sgt. Gray was the Troop Sgt. of 'G' Troop of 258 A/
Tk. Bty. At first light on 25th October enemy armour
was seen to be grouping for an attack. The Troop
Commander himself went off to contact the tank
Commander of the tanks with which he was working,
and ordered Sgt. Gray to liaise with what was thought to
be an Infantry post of ours on the flank of the Troop.

The post turned out to be one which the enemy had
re-occupied in the night, but Sgt. Gray, quite undaunted,
went up and brought back first 6 fully armed Italian
Officers, and later about 200 Italian other ranks with the
help of one Other Rank. Whilst conducting them back
from the Troop to the rear, the party was shelled and
Sgt. Gray was wounded, and had to be evacuated, but is
now back with the unit.

The enemy post was found to contain 3 Anti-tank
guns, 3 heavy M.G.s, grenades, and rifles, and enfiladed
the Troop at close range.

By his fearless example and aggressive spirit, with
which he imbued the whole Troop, he was to a large
degree responsible both for saving the whole Troop from
a very difficult situation, and for capturing about 200
prisoners.
Recommended for M.M.   *(L.G. 11.3.43)*

Gray, Jack, Private
14781542, 5th Bn. Seaforth Highlanders (Thorpe)
(Immediate)
On 25th Mar. 45, Pte. Gray was No. 1 Bren gunner in 5
Sec. of 'D' Coy. which was ordered to carry out an
outflanking movement against a strongpoint in the village
of Groin. It was just getting light and every man knew
that speed was essential to the success of the attack. The
Sec. Cdr. attempted to lead his men along a shallow ditch
but they were soon pinned down by accurate and heavy
fire.

The Sec. Comd. then called to Pte. Gray to follow
him and together they crossed an almost completely open
stretch of ground by a series of dashes from cover to
cover, until they were within assaulting distance of the
enemy. During this manoeuvre Pte. Gray kept the
enemy's heads down by spraying their position with fire
from his Bren as he adv. His Sec. Comd. and Pte. Gray
then rose together and charged the enemy shouting and
firing. Before the position was reached both fell
wounded, but they continued to engage the enemy and
silenced the nearest Spandau post. Then after throwing
grenades at the next post, they attempted to charge once
more but were again wounded in quick succession. Even
so, Pte. Gray in spite of the severity of his injuries,
continued to pour fire into the enemy positions until the
main attack, profiting by this diversion, overran the
strongpoint.

Forty-six determined and tough German parachute
troops were made prisoner in this position, from which
three machine guns also were taken and against which
his Sec. Comd. and Pte. Gray had charged alone.

I consider that this man's determination, courage and
loyal sp. to his leader merit the highest recognition.
Recommended for M.M.   *(L.G. 21.6.45)*

Gray, Stanley, Lance Corporal
2928701, Queen's Own Cameron Highlanders, British
Troops in the Sudan Corps. (Haddington, E.
Lothian) (Immediate)
At Cheren on 16 March 1941 Lance Corporal Gray was
a section leader in the leading company whose objective
was Brigs Peak. He reached his objective in spite of
heavy casualties, and held on there for twenty-four hours,
in the face of counter attacks and heavy M.G. and mortar
fire, until he was the only man of his section left. He was
then sent back by his Coy. Commdr. to Bn. HQ with
valuable information, and returned to the front line
guiding reinforcements. Later, after 36 hours, when his
company had been relieved by troops of another
Battalion, he volunteered and took part in both daylight
and night patrols to Mt. Sanchil.

Throughout the operations L/Cpl. Gray displayed
courage, leadership and powers of endurance of the
highest order.   *(L.G. 18.7.41)*

Grayson, Arthur James, Pte. (Immediate)
SX 18206, 2/43 Australian Inf. Bn.
On 23 Nov. 43, Pte. Grayson was a member of the Tk. A
Pl., 2/43 Aust. Inf. Bn., during an attack by the enemy in
the Song River area, 620682 (Satelberg 1/25000).

Pte. Grayson and two others were holding a small
strongpost on the right flank of the position. The enemy
made several determined attempts to break through on
this flank but was unsuccessful. The enemy then put
down heavy concentration of grenades and mortars in
an attempt to annihilate the post. Whilst this was in
progress a mortar bomb fell into the pit occupied by Pte.
Grayson, between his two companions. The bomb did
not explode on impact; and, with great presence of mind
and extreme courage, Pte. Grayson placed his foot over
the bomb. It exploded immediately, causing severe
injuries to Pte. Grayson's feet and legs. By this example
of unselfish gallantry Pte. Grayson undoubtedly saved
his two companions from serious injuries and enabled
them to continue the successful defence of the post.
Recommended for M.M.   *(20.4.44)*

Green, George William, M.M., Sergeant
B.62282, Canadian Infantry Corps
Recommendation for M.M.
Sjt. Green proved a great inspiration to the men of 'A'
Company 1 Canadian Paratroop Battalion throughout the
campaign in Normandy until he was wounded at
Goustranville on 18 August 1944. His never failing good
humour and superb courage at all times endeared him to

all officers and men alike who knew him. On 18 August 1944 at 2230 hours at Goustranville, 'A' Company was given an objective in a battalion night attack on the south bridge over the eastern tributary of the river Dives. Sjt. Green was Platoon Sergeant of No. 1 Platoon and acting platoon commander on this attack. His platoon suffered heavy casualties but he reorganized it swiftly and led it on two separate assaults on enemy positions, killing and capturing well over twenty-five Germans; as he brought his platoon on to its objective on the left flank of the bridge he was badly wounded in the leg. Ignoring his wound he placed his sections in position for all round defence, got ammunition and casualty states and reported to his Company Commander. He refused to be evacuated until after every one of his men who had been wounded had been attended to.

Recommendation for D.C.M.

CSM Green landed by parachute east of the Rhine on 24 March 1945. Fire round the dropping zone was extremely heavy and it was largely due to the leadership and drive of this Warrant Officer that opposition was quickly overcome and the company collected at its rendezvous.

Immediately afterwards the company was directed on a village. A strong and determined enemy force was holding a group of fortified houses on the edge of the village. The attack was checked and success hung in the balance. In this emergency under heavy fire, CSM Green led a piat detachment up to the first house. Having organized covering fire, he led the assault himself on to the house. After capturing it, he then cleared all the remaining houses in succession. The enemy was full of fight but was worsted by the vigor of CSM Green's attacks.

This Warrant Officer's quick and determined action was of the greatest value in clearing a dangerous obstacle and restoring the impetus of the advance. His contempt for danger and eagerness to close with the enemy were an inspiration to the men.   (*L.G. 16.6.45*)

Green, Henry, Warrant Officer Cl. II
5334595, 2 Argyll & Sutherland Highlanders
   (Binfield) (Immediate)
During the adv. from Nijmegen on 8 Feb. 45 'A' Coy. was left fwd. Coy. Very soon after crossing the SL the Coy. commander was wounded and soon afterwards one of the platoon comds. killed. Later on approaching the ry. station at Kranenberg the last remaining officer was hit. C.S.M. Green took over comd. of the Coy. which came up against stiffening resistance in the station where there were many snipers and posts armed with Bazookas. A number of casualties were sustained incl. a Sergt. now comd. a platoon. C.S.M. Green, undaunted, quickly reorganised and continued the advance. He was here, there and everywhere encouraging men of the Coy. and through his complete calmness, disregard for his own safety and fine example of leadership his men were inspired to such a degree that they quickly overcame the opposition and gained the objective. Immediately C.S.M.

Green got to work to carry out consolidation and reorganisation. This was no easy matter in the fading light. He made a mental note also of casualties and where they lay. Three of his stretcher bearers had become casualties and others were already tending wounded that it was necessary to organize further carriers. This he did also and led them, in some cases, through an unmarked minefield. In spite of all these difficulties C.S.M. Green managed also to render a sit. rep. and a casualty return very soon after gaining the objective.

He accepted responsiblity at a time when the situation was most confused and comd. the Coy. in this later and difficult stage of the battle with extreme efficiency which undoubtedly influenced and contributed largely to the successful conclusion of the action by his Coy.
          (*L.G. 19.4.45*)

Green, Leonard, Private
105946, R.A.S.C. (E.F.I.)
B.S.M. Paton was captured in June 1940 at St. Valery-en-Caux, and sent to Stalag XXA (Thorn), and later to a satellite camp at Graudenz, where he was senior Warrant Officer.

Private Green captured in May 1940 between Wizernes and Boulogne, and sent to Stalag XXA. From where he went to various satellite working camps and in October 1942 to Graudenz where he met B.S.M. Paton.

They escaped from here on the 7th June 1943 after much careful preparation. They received some help from Poles (unorganized) but between the 8th and 17th June 1943 were continually on the move travelling by train to Gdynia, Danzig, Lodz, Brombert, Zoppot, and other places. On 17th June they boarded a Swedish ship at Gdynia arriving at Stockholm on 22nd June 1943.

Private Green speaks fluent German, the knowledge of which was a most important factor in this successful escape.

This Warrant Officer and Private showed the greatest courage, initiative and ingenuity. Both are recommended for awards of the D.C.M.   (*L.G. 11.11.43*)

Green, Stanley, Lance Corporal
4915273, 2 Div. R.A.S.C.
See Allan, James Snodgrass, Lance Corporal

Greenhalgh, Joseph Simmonds, Corporal
2319083, Royal Signals (Lyndhurst, Hants)
No citation.   (*L.G. 25.10.45*)

Greenyer, Walter Edward, M.M., Warrant Officer Cl. II
804771, Hampshire Regt. (Worthing) (Immediate)
After the occupation of Porselen on 25 Jan. 45 it became necessary to send fwd. a series of recce patrols to make contact with and report on the Siefgreid Line positions across the R. Roer to which the enemy had withdrawn. These 'C' Coy. were ordered to undertake and on hearing of them C.S.M. Greenyer volunteered to lead them.

On 26 Jan. 45 this W.O. accordingly led a daylight recce patrol fwd. After successfully locating and traversing several enemy minefields and crossing two streams the patrol arrived within view of three small forts. Leaving the patrol under cover C.S.M. Greenyer worked his way fwd. to each fort in turn and as all attempts to draw fire from them by exposing himself failed he approached and entered them finding them unoccupied. He then returned bringing with him much valuable information.

On 27 Jan. this W.O. again volunteered to lead a further daylight recce patrol which had as its object contact with the enemy FDLs and by drawing fire to assess their strength. Safely negotiating the minefields the patrol worked its way fwd. across the R. Wurm to within shouting distance of some occupied enemy trenches.

At this point the patrol came under heavy and accurate fire from five M.G.s and mortars from its right flank and one member of patrol was wounded. After having remained under fire for sufficiently long to locate accurately the L.M.G. positions and the bearing of the mortars, C.S.M. Greenyer skilfully withdrew his patrol and the wounded man over the open ground towards the river whilst still under heavy fire from the M.G.s and mortars. These conditions still prevailing this W.O. by drawing fire to himself managed to move his Bren group and the wounded man back across the river but, this being accomplished, found it impossible to cross with the remainder of the patrol due to the greatly increased fire then falling on the bridge. C.S.M. Greenyer then led the three remaining men of the patrol to the river and managed to withdraw by wading down it to the safety of dead ground four hundred yards further South.

Throughout the above operations this W.O. by his unshakeable coolness and supreme skill succeeded in extricating his entire patrol from an extremely dangerous situation and returned with much more valuable information.

Recommended for M.M.   *(L.G. 12.4.45)*

Gregory, Charles, Warrant Officer Cl. III (Pl.S.M.)
3123154, Royal Scots Fusiliers
This Warrant Officer Class III is recommended for the D.C.M. in recognition of the excellent work done by him during the night of May 27th and morning of May 28th on the Ypres–Comines Canal.

At about 9 pm on May 27th when Bn. HQ was almost surrounded this W.O. in company with 12 men was ordered to make a break through to the rear to keep the line of communication open. He worked his way out to a wood on the flank strongly held by enemy and made contact. He was driven back to a position on the St. Eloi Lille Rd. In the process of retirement he collected many odd stragglers together and kept them under control taking up a position on the road mentioned above, from which position he kept contact with the enemy by sending out patrols.

It is my opinion that it was due to the coolness and initiative of this W.O. that so many stragglers were safely brought back and the enemy progress slowed down.
                                           (L.G. 27.8.40)

Gregory, John, Lance Corporal
2nd Bn. London Irish Rifles (R.U.R.) (Bromley)
(Immediate)
This Rfn. displayed great courage and coolness during the attack on the afternoon of 5 Aug. 43. Under heavy fire he brought his 2" Mortar into action to engage an enemy strong point in a hut. Still under heavy fire he continued to engage the enemy till he ran out of ammunition and was ordered to withdraw. He then found a rifle and with L/Cpl. Brodie formed a centre of resistance against an enemy counter attack. He kept up continuous fire with his rifle and helped to beat off four attacks against his position. After L/Cpl. Brodie had been wounded and taken back Rfn. Gregory remained and sniped the enemy although his position was an exposed one.

His courage and disregard for personal safety were of the highest order and he was an inspiration to his company and the Battalion.   *(L.G. 18.11.43)*

Greslow, William, Private (A/Cpl.)
4914987, Black Watch [7 South Staffords on AFW 3121] (Liverpool 7)
On 8 July 44, around RM.R. 025733, a highly defended enemy position, lying between Galmanche and La Bijude.

L/Cpl. Greslow showed great gallantry in the face of intense mortar and M.G. fire which had pinned down his own platoon and the platoon on his left. His Pl. Comd. and the other N.C.O.s of his platoon having become casualties, L/Cpl. Greslow whilst still under heavy mortar and M.G. fire, rallied the remaining 10 men of his platoon and led them to the assault on the enemy position, taking it, killing the occupants and forming a firm base. From this position he opened fire on the enemy and enabled the platoon on his left to advance. The initiative, gallantry and resourcefulness of L/Cpl. Greslow restored the situation and enabled the advance to be resumed. His exemplary conduct proved an inspiration to all.
Recommended for M.M.   *(L.G. 19.10.44)*

Gretton, Abraham, C.Q.M.S. (Acting Warrant Officer Cl. II (C.S.M.))
4435724, 2nd Bn. York & Lancaster Regt. (Edgbaston, Birmingham) (Immediate)
At Herakleon, Crete on the 25th May 1941 a counter attack by 2 Coys. York & Lancaster Regt. was carried out. Though successful at first it was eventually stopped by heavy fire from enemy M.G.s and Tommy Guns and both Coys. withdrew to their starting lines. Shortly after this C.S.M. Gretton was informed by a runner from the next Company that their Headquarters had been surrounded and had had to fight its way back leaving

their Company Commander wounded in a house. C.S.M. Gretton at once organised two Secs. and personally led them to recover the Officer. The enemy were in occupation of the area of the house, but by skilful handling of this party C.S.M. Gretton succeeded in keeping down the enemy fire and brought back the wounded Officer without casualties. Throughout the whole operations at Keraklion C.S.M. Gretton who has 24 years service showed great coolness under fire and set a fine example to the N.C.O.s and men of his company.
Recommended for M.M.   (*L.G. 4.11.41*)

Gri, Armando, M.M., Sergeant
K46862, Canadian Infantry Corps
No citation.   (*L.G. 5.5.45*)

Grief, Herbert William, Sergeant
5770335, 2/5th Bn. Queen's Royal Regt. (Gresham, Norfolk) (Immediate)
Gemmano (Italy, 1/50,000 Sheet 109 IV, Sq. 8679). 10 Sep. 1944.

In the early morning of 10 Sep., Sgt. Grief who was commanding No. 10 Pl, 'B' Company, 2/5th Bn. The Queen's Royal Regiment, was ordered to attack with a view to capturing a small ridge S.W. of Monte Gemmano.

Covered by a smoke screen, he pressed his platoon, who were somewhat weak through casualties and fatigue, on, keeping them up to the artillery H.E. and smoke in order to get full value from it. The ground was very open and he was still some hundreds of yards from his objective when the smoke cleared and he came under immediate fire.

Such was his leadership, however, that his was able to keep and exercise control of his platoon, whom he disposed in what cover there was available. Throughout the day he remained pinned; but never missed an opportunity to try to work forward when opportunity offered or smoke assisted. Although out of touch with his company commander, he continued to carry on his original instructions showing great ability and presence of mind.

This N.C.O. gave a fine example of physical endurance, reliability and coolness under fire. From dawn 'till dusk he continued under heavy enemy fire to have complete control and by efficient leadership and skilful handling of his platoon he exercised considerable and successful pressure in the attack on a well-positioned enemy in some strength.   (*L.G. 8.2.45*)

Griffiths, David John, Lance Corporal
216201, Royal Australian Infantry Corps
No citation.   (*L.G. 28.3.69*)

Griffiths, Leonard George, M.M., Warrant Officer Cl. II (B.S.M.)
143j6066, 24 AA/A. Tk. Regt., Royal Artillery (Brierly, Staffs) (Immediate)
On 11 Feb 44 at about 1300 hrs. the enemy attacked 184 A. Tk. Bty. defence positions on a hill feature in 7 Ind. Div. adm. base East Mayu. W/B.S.M. Griffiths was in charge of the posn. He rallied his men against repeated attacks and himself destroyed a Jap machine gun post single handed.

At about 1400 hrs. his post was surrounded and he himself was badly wounded when the Japanese charged. He jumped up on to the parapet and shouted to his remaining five men 'Come on boys, give them a cheer'. The resulting volley broke the Jap charge.
                                          (*L.G. 18.5.44*)

Griffiths, Norman Brian, Lance Sergeant
6916117, 1 Rifle Brigade (London N.10) (Immediate)
For conspicuous gallantry and devotion to duty. On 31 Aug. 42 at about 1830 hrs. at Map Reference 42968774 his platoon was attacked by 20–30 German Tanks. He held his fire until they were at close range and succeeded in knocking out five at least, and damaging others. Although it appeared likely that his position might be over-run he continued to direct the fire of his gun in the coolest possible manner. His gallant conduct and good shooting was undoubtedly largely responsible for preventing the German Tanks breaking into the position before it was possible for our own tanks to arrive. Throughout the action which lasted for about three quarters of an hour he was continuously under heavy fire.
Recommended for M.M.   (*L.G. 5.11.42*)

Grigas, Joseph, Private
D105811, R.C.R., Canadian Infantry Corps
On 10 Jul. 43 in the vicinity of Pachino Airfield 'A' Coy. The Royal Canadian Regiment of which Pte. Grigas was a member was operating against enemy coastal defences. At 1000 hrs. the Coy. commenced an assault on a coast defence battery immediately North of Pachino Airfield. Pte. Grigas' Sec. Comd. became a casualty. Pte. Grigas took command of the section and, advancing under heavy fire managed to reach the perimeter wire. The remainder of the Coy. was by this time pinned to the ground. Pte. Grigas breached a gap in the wire and led his section through to assault three enemy concrete posts which were knocked out in quick succession. Although Pte. Grigas' section was the only section of the Coy. to enter the battery position the attack was led with such determination that it caused the immediate surrender of the garrison of approximately two hundred men and in the capture of four 9.2 howitzers and large quantities of ammunition, small arms and stores. The personal gallantry, determination and leadership of Pte. Grigas was largely responsible for the success of this operation.
                                          (*L.G. 23.9.43*)

Grigg, Ronald Francis, Lance Corporal
NX.99043, 2/25 Australian Inf. Bn. (Immediate)
On the night of 15/16 Jul 45 on a hill feature on the
Batoechampar area near Balikpapan the enemy with a
force of forty to fifty armed with light machine guns,
rifles, grenades, spears and swords ceaselessly attacked
for sixteen hours a company of 2/25 Australian Infantry
Battalion.

The darkness of the night and teeming rain made it
possible for the enemy to approach very close to our
lines. Under such adverse conditions Lance Corporal
Grigg who commanded a section where the attacks were
heaviest, exposed himself to heavy fire by moving about
amongst his section to encourage his men and maintain
better control.

Not content with repelling attacks L/Cpl. Grigg with
great daring and initiative crept forward to a fallen log,
which was being used as cover by the enemy, in a lone
effort to destroy the attackers. With only the log between
him and his foes he reduced the time his grenades would
take to burst among them by coolly retaining the grenades
to within a second of their explosion before lobbing them
over the log. In this way he annihilated the opposition
and accounted for the great majority of the twenty five
enemy dead found the next morning in front of his
section.

L/Cpl. Grigg's outstanding leadership in such inimical
circumstances, his coolness, courage and resourcefulness
set a magnificent example to his men and were mainly
instrumental in repelling the repeated attacks of a
cunning, determined and fanatical enemy.

(L.G. 14.9.45)

Grime, Sidney, Sergeant
*7896560, 'B' S.S. Sqn., Royal Tank Regt. (Werneth,
Oldham)*
May 5th 1½ miles from Antsirane.

Sergeant Grime was acting as gunner in the Squadron
Comd's tank. During the preliminary engagement of the
enemy, this N.C.O. behaved in every way as if he had
merely been taking part in a battle practice, taking on
the targets with the utmost coolness and precision.

Afterwards his tank, together with three others, was
knocked out by A.Tk. fire. Sgt. Grime assisted in the
evacuation of the wounded men to a place where they
were under a certain amount of cover from view. He
then made repeated journeys to the damaged tanks, and
assisted in the removal of a T.S.M.G., a Bren gun from
its anti-aircraft mounting, ammunition for these weapons,
water for the wounded, and a first aid box; being on each
occasion under fire from snipers and machine gunners.

Later the enemy advanced in an attempt to capture or
kill the crews who were in ground action. Sgt. Grime
assisted in engaging the enemy firing first a T.S.M.G
and later when the ammunition for that was expended,
his pistol with the result that the enemy was twice beaten
off.

Throughout these engagements Sgt. Grime remained
consistently cheerful and determined, and behaved with
the utmost contempt of danger.   *(L.G. 16.6.42)*

Grimmond, John Stanley, Warrant Officer Cl. II
(C.S.M.)
K57216, 1 Canadian Scottish Regt. (Immediate)
On 15 Aug. 1944, during this battalion's attack on Hill
168 (near Falaise, Calvados) this Warrant Officer
distinguished himself by his courage and leadership
under heavy fire.

In his capacity as acting second-in-command of 'A'
company, Company Sergeant Major John Stanley
Grimmond was ordered to set up Company Headquarters
in an orchard near the objective in order to achieve
wireless communication. Because the battalion
Commander's set had been knocked out by enemy action,
this company wireless set became the link vital to the
success of the operation, a fact which was known to this
Warrant Officer.

C.S.M. Grimmond organised his small headquarters
party, armed only with Piats and light weapons, and
attacked two enemy tanks and a number of infantry
armed with light automatics and mortars with such superb
dash and leadership that the enemy were routed and the
company Headquarters objective was taken. After having
established the vital wireless communication, the
Warrant Officer organised his men to simulate a much
larger force, and was thus able to maintain the Company
Headquarters position against all enemy attacks.

By his outstanding leadership and gallantry under
most heavy fire C.S.M. Grimmond was largely
instrumental in assuring the battalion's success on Hill
168, and facilitated the brigade breakthrough to Falaise.

(L.G. 9.12.44)

Grimsey, Arthur Edward, Sergeant (A/W.O.II
(B.S.M.))
*839909, 24 AA/A. Tk. Regt., Royal Artillery (London,
E.C.15) (Immediate)*
At about 1400 hrs. 8 Feb. 1944 the ammunition dump in
7 Ind. Div. Adm. base East Ndk came under Jap mortar
fire and a fire was started. Ammunition dumps were set
on fire and the fire threatened to spread rapidly. A/B.S.M.
Grimsey immediately and under enemy mortar fire went
to investigate the extent of the fire, visiting dumps of 25
pr and 3.7 how ammunition which were already burning
and exploding. He then placed himself in a dump of 3"
mortar ammunition close to the burning dumps and
worked there until the whole dump, estimated at 5,000
rounds was moved to safety. His example and devotion
to duty were largely responsible for the saving of this
and a great deal more gun ammunition.

On the afternoon of 9 Feb. 1944 two 5.5 gun/hows of
6 Med. Regt. came under accurate enemy gun and mortar
fire. 12 vehicles within 20 yds. of the guns were set on
fire and also a dump of S.A.A. and a dump of grenades.
A tractor being backed on to one of the guns received a

direct hit from an enemy mortar bomb. The whole area was a mass of flames and ammunition in vehicles and on the dump was exploding. A/B.S.M. Grimsey seeing one of the guns on fire at the trail end and also in danger from its tractors which was a blazing mass went out himself with a shovel while enemy mortar bombs were falling around the guns and alone extinguished with earth the fire on the trail end of the 5.5 gun and on the sight bracket.

By means of earth he also controlled the fire at the rear end of the tractor. He then organised salvage work resulting in the two guns being saved. *(L.G. 18.5.44)*

Groves, Lionel, Warrant Officer Cl. II
6348538, 6 Queen's Own Royal West Kent Regt.
(Tunbridge Wells) (Immediate)
Ref. Map Sheet No. 88 I SE (Conselice) Italy 1/25,000.

At 1930 hrs. on 13th Apr. 1945, 'C' Coy. were ordered to attack an enemy strongpoint at map ref. 288488, where considerable opposition had been met from enemy infantry supported by S.P. guns. Previous advances in this direction had been brought to a halt and casualties inflicted on our own infantry and tanks. The attacking troops had to cross 1,000 yds. of open ground in full view of the enemy and started off just before last light, with a troop of Churchills under command. When the Coy. was within 600 yds. of the objective the men came under very heavy mortar fire from the direction of Conselice and were forced to take over. C.S.M. Groves spotted the offending weapons and notwithstanding intense enemy fire dashed across to the leading tank and directed fire from the turret, thus neutralizing the enemy. He then joined the leading platoons and by his example was largely responsible for forcing the enemy to withdraw leaving two officers and several other ranks as prisoners in our hands.

On reaching the objective enemy snipers were again active, but this Warrant Officer once more located the fire and succeeded in silencing them.

Later in the night when the town of Conselice was being cleared he was always at the most dangerous point regardless of personal risk and tireless in his energy.

Without doubt this Warrant Officer, as often before, largely contributed to the success of operations by the magnificent example he set. *(L.G. 18.10.45)*

Guerin, John Francis, Trooper
SX 16061, 2/8 Aust. Commando Sqn. (Immediate)
On the night of 2 Jun. 45, Tpr. Guerin was a member of a patrol with instructions to seek out and destroy an enemy outpost believed to be in the vicinity of 075386 (Map Ref. Musuraka sheet).

Tpr. Guerin, with 2 native guides, planned and carried out a close reconnaissance in order to establish the exact locality of the outpost. With care and deliberation, he crawled to within a few feet of the enemy sentries, noting and pinpointing the enemy dispositions. He then led the patrol, with himself in charge of the main assault group,

into positions from which they could launch an attack. This involved movement within enemy hearing distance and was so successfully carried out that the Japanese sentries one of whom was only ten feet away, were unaware of the existence of the patrol.

Tpr. Guerin then led the attack against the enemy, many of whom were immediately killed. The attack was momentarily checked by an enemy machine gun firing from a covered position. Tpr. Guerin realised that swift and decisive action was vital to the success of the attack and that delay would endanger the lives of his comrades. Without regard for his personal safety he charged the enemy position, where he killed all three of the machine gun crew with his own gun. His patrol were thus enabled to press home the attack. Without loss to our own force, the raid cost the enemy eighteen counted killed, and, of the original outpost, no more than two escaped.

With success achieved, the patrol carried out an intensive search of the area and obtained many documents which were immediately forwarded to Formation HQ.

By his skilful reconnaissance and leadership, and his gallant action when faced with a situation fraught with disaster to himself and his comrades, Tpr. Guerin brought complete success to a difficult task. *(L.G. 24.8.45)*

Guise, Allen George, Corporal
6915761, 1st Bn. Rifle Brigade (Burntwood, Staffs.)
For the most conspicuous gallantry on the afternoon of 14th Jun. 42. The Anti-Tank Platoon to which this N.C.O. belonged was, after successfully fighting the German tanks for some time, put completely out of action by enemy fire and was overrun by the enemy tanks. This N.C.O. seeing the plight of his comrades, drove a Carrier forward under very heavy fire, right among the German tanks, and succeeded in bringing out from under the enemy's nose, twenty-two men of his own unit and of the R.H.A. Battery. His action, which showed the most complete disregard of personal danger, undoubtedly saved these men who must otherwise have been killed or captured by the advancing enemy infantry, and his bravery and disregard of personal danger were of the highest possible order.
Recommended for V.C. *(L.G. 13.8.42)*

Gundel, Clements, Sergeant
2717328, 1st Bn. Irish Guards (Mansfield, Notts.)
(Immediate)
In the Anzio Beach Head.

This N.C.O. has commanded a platoon of No.2 Coy. since the Bn. landed on the beaches, he has been through every action fought by the Bn. and has on all occasions distinguished himself by his skill, fine leadership and personal courage. In the night attack Jan. 29/30 made by this Bn., in repelling enemy attacks by day and by night, in hand to hand fighting with the enemy, under heavy shell and mortar and S.A.A. fire and in eliminating enemy snipers and M.G. posts, he has set an example of rugged determination and stoical indifference to the worst that the enemy could do that was an example and encouragement which the men under his command were proud to follow. On the night of Feb. 21/22 when No.2 Coy. was taking over positions from Americans, his platoon came under heavy shell fire and M.G. fire from nearby enemy posts. Sgt. Gundel kept complete control of the situation, encouraged the covering L.M.G. fire which disposed of the enemy M.G.s and led his platoon to the forward positions allotted to them. There they found there were no positions prepared so Sgt. Gundel, with 2 L.M.G. gunners protected the remainder of the platoon while they dug in, successfully beating back the German patrols which attempted to infiltrate. By dawn the platoon was successfully established and for 4 days until relieved, held their positions against constant enemy efforts to dislodge them both by day and by night. Owing to the original small numbers of the company and the daily casualties there could be little rest for anyone and none for Sgt. Gundel, but his energy and determination were as unfailing as his personal conduct was gallant. On two successive nights he went forward himself to destroy enemy snipers that had been located by day only 200 yds. from his Coy. position and by his successful elimination of them discouraged the Germans as much as he encouraged his platoon and company.

In view of this N.C.O.'s long record of devoted and gallant service in Tunisia and Italy and his particularly conspicuous gallantry during the period 21/25 Feb., I strongly recommend him for the immediate award of the D.C.M.   *(L.G. 15.6.44)*

Gurung, Dalbahadur, Warrant Officer Cl. II (actg.)
21135018, Brigade of Gurkhas
For Malaya   *(L.G. 19.5.50)*

Gutenberg, Lev, Corporal
*23211, No. 1039 Port Operating Company, Royal
    Engineers (Periodic)*
Cpl. Gutenberg was captured at Kalamata on 29.4.41 moved to Corinth P/W Camp and thence to Salonika. He was taken to Germany at the end of June, but escaped with two others by jumping from the train near the Yugoslav border.

Friendly villagers finally helped them back to Salonika, where one escaper left them because of the danger of recapture there. Cpl. Gutenberg remained with the other, however, till he obtained a passage in a caique to the Turkish coast.

They sailed on 3.8.41 and reached Khios safely, but were overtaken off the island of Inousai by a German patrol which fired on them. They were taken to Mitylene, interrogated and beaten up by the Gestapo. As a result of the ill-treatment one of the Greeks confessed that Cpl. Gutenberg and his friends were Palestinians and they were sent back to Salonika and imprisoned in solitary confinement.

They were then moved to Salonika gaol. Cpl. Gutenberg had warned his friend to say he knew nothing about their escape arrangements to avoid conflicting statements. The onus of interrogations fell on him, therefore, and he was beaten four times to try and force him to give away the names of helpers. The Germans resorted to all sorts of methods to make him confess how he came to escape. Finally, exasperated, they locked him in a disused prison latrine, with straw to lie on for about three weeks, then moved him with his Palestinian friend to a former clinic for mad people, where they were locked in separate cells. During meal times, Cpl. Gutenberg discussed a second escape with his friend; but the latter hadn't the courage or energy to escape again. Cpl. Gutenberg therefore escaped alone by climbing on to the roof from the kitchen, then slipping down a rope made by tearing up a sack which had been given him as a blanket. He sprained his ankle falling, but got away and took refuge with a Greek woman who tended his foot.

He obtained another passage in a caique to the Turkish coast in company with other British escapers. They sailed on 29.9.41 at 5 a.m., but at 10 a.m. a German patrol boat approached and as three of the Greek sailors abandoned the caique and were taken in tow by the Germans, they were convinced they had been betrayed and made for the coast. A seaplane fired at the caique, and they were machine gunned from the shore, but they slipped away into the forest.

Cpl. Gutenberg climbed a tree, as his bad foot prevented him from running. He saw a German lorry pass with troops and some captured British and Greek from the caique. In the evening he went to the beach to look for the caique but was stopped by a German soldier who asked him for his papers. He said he had left them at home and would go and fetch them. After this narrow escape he returned to the mountains as there were Germans in all the villages.

He continued to wander about, however, contacting escapers and trying to help them find boats. He was unsuccessful till in February, 1942, he heard of contraband boats sailing to Mitylene. Unfortunately the captain could only take him as he spoke Greek, but he contacted the others before he left, telling them that the captain would return for them, if the first journey succeeded.

On 4.3.42 Cpl. Gutenberg was picked up from one of the islands, and when they were a few hundred yards from the Turkish coast, he swan ashore.

This corporal not only escaped twice, once nearly reaching the Turkish coast, but was always ready to take the initiative in any scheme likely to succeed in helping escapers out of Greece. He endured great hardship and showed courage in every predicament in which he found himself.   *(L.G. 9.9.42)*

Gutteridge, Henry Brazier, Sergeant
4976548, Sherwood Foresters (Lowdham)
No citation.   *(L.G. 11.10.45)*

Guy, Harold Frederick, Corporal (A/Sgt.)
7016230, 1st Bn. London Irish Rifles (Tadworth, Surrey) (Immediate)
On the 20 Feb. 1944 in the Anzio Bridgehead, the Coy. to which Sgt. Guy belonged was ordered to attack to relieve the Bn. HQ 7 Oxf. Bucks., which was at the time surrounded. Immediately the attack began, enemy M.G.s opened fire and both shell and mortar DF tasks were brought down, with the results that in a few moments all officers and W.O.s in the Coy. became casualties. Without hesitation Sgt. Guy immediately took command. Exposing himself fearlessly he went from platoon to platoon, rallied the men and led them with such dash that the objective was reached and 7 Oxf. Bucks. were relieved. During this advance, Sgt. Guy was wounded, but this in no way deterred him from continuing to lead the Coy. Shortly after the objective was reached Sgt. Guy was again wounded, but he steadfastly continued to carry on despite the pain and loss of blood until he was ordered to the R.A.P. by his Commanding Officer. Throughout this action, Sgt. Guy displayed courage of the very highest order, and by taking command at a critical moment was mainly responsible for the success of the operation. *(L.G. 20.7.44)*

H

Hadden, Daniel, Private (A/Cpl.)
M37034, Seaforth of Canada (Immediate)
On the morning, 6 Aug 43, 'D' Coy was ordered to attack and capture a 600 foot high, rocky ridge overlooking the main road west of Aderno. The ridge was well defended, little cover was available, and the section commanded by Cpl. Hadden soon came under heavy fire from a German machine gun post, suffering two casualties. This soldier then disposed his section to give him covering fire and coolly crawled forward himself to take on the enemy post. During the 700 yard advance on the post he inflicted sufficient casualties with his Bren to keep the enemy heads down and then brought his section still further forward. Continuing on alone, still under the same heavy fire he reached grenade range, threw five grenades at the position, with his section assaulted at the point of the bayonet, and routed the enemy.   *(L.G. 4.11.43)*

Hadley, Reginald, Sergeant (actg.)
3317288, 6th Bn. Highland Light Infantry (Glasgow, N.)
On 23 Jan. 45 during a Battalion attack on Aphoven (Germany 1:25,000 Sheet 4902 — sq. 8373), Sgt. Hadley was in command of No. 16 platoon 'D' Company.

Whilst consolidating on its objective 'D' Coy. and the sub-units which were to pass through them to the final objective were held up by what was at first thought to be a sniper post. Without hesitation, Sgt. Hadley proceeded alone in an effort to destroy the post, but as a result of close reconnaissance, undertaken at great personal risk, discovered that the opposition was well-prepared strong-point which included two 7.5 cm guns.

As it was impossible to get tanks, which were supporting the attack, forward, Sgt. Hadley personally led one of his sections to liquidate the strong-point, himself killing one of the enemy at a range of only 10 yards. The enemy retaliated strongly with grenades, forcing Sgt. Hadley and his section to withdraw temporarily. After re-organising, Sgt. Hadley again went forward to engage the enemy, but by this time, he had withdrawn, leaving his guns and dead.

By his rapid appreciation of the situation and immediate and persistent offensive action, Sgt. Hadley undoubtedly forced the enemy to abandon a very strong position which might well have held up the Battalions attack at a vital stage.
Recommended for M.M.   *(L.G. 12.4.45)*

Haggard, William Alvin, Private
L.13282, South Saskatchewan Regt.
During the operation at Dieppe 19 Aug 42, Pte. Haggard's platoon was held up by a strong enemy position on the top of a hill. When the platoon Sjt. was wounded Haggard, with L/Cpl. Berthelot took over the platoon and decided on a method of attack, which was to take the form of a pincer movement, with Haggard leading a section on the left flank. This section was eventually held up in a position from which it could not see the enemy except when the latter exposed themselves to shoot. Thereupon Haggard stood up to draw enemy fire and thus bring them into view. Having killed four of the enemy by this stratagem he advanced across the open ground to wipe out the remainder with grenades, after which he continued with his section to the top of the hill to rejoin the balance of the platoon. Pte. Haggard's initiative and resourcefulness at great personal risk contributed greatly to the attainment of his platoon's objective.   *(L.G. 2.10.42)*

Haines, George Ernest, Sergeant
6141513, East Surrey. Regt., No. 2 Commando (Chatham)
On 28th March, 1942, during the raid on St. Nazaire, when the Officer-in-Command of the Headquarters' Reserve failed to make a landing, TSM Haines took command of this Group in his place.

When his party arrived at the Operational Headquarters the area was under intense fire from enemy gun positions sited on the roof of a U-boat shelter under 70 yards away.

With complete disregard of his own safety TSM Haines took up a position in the open, engaged and silenced these enemy guns with a 2″ mortar.

Shortly after this, the Headquarters Group came under enemy machine gun fire from an armed trawler inside the inner dock. Again from the open, TSM Haines engaged the new enemy, this time with an LMG. His fire caused the enemy craft to move further up the dock. This reduced the danger in the immediate area and gave the Headquarters freedom to operate.

After the attempt to re-embark had been abandoned, TSM Haines played a splendid part in a running engagement which lasted over half an hour, and in which the force fought its way to the inner dock and across the bridge into the town. The bridge itself was covered by enemy LMG fire but TSM Haines made a determined dash across the bridge and into the direct fire of the enemy weapons. Under his leadership his party managed to silence most of these gun positions, thus enabling the main force to proceed.

During the remainder of the action, in the town of St. Nazaire, TSM Haines set a magnificent example of courage and devotion to duty to all who served with him.   *(L.G. 5.7.45)*

Haithwaite, Rowland, Sergeant
781317, 5 Med. Regt., Royal Artillery (Castleford, Yorks.)

I wish to recommend most strongly the award of a decoration to the above named N.C.O. Throughout the morning of 17th March 43, A Troop gun position was continuously shelled by field and medium guns. In addition, the position was twice dive-bombed by strong formations of Stukas. The charges in a farm building were set on fire and were exploding intermittently. Without hesitation, Sjt. Haithwaite entered the building and at once commenced to remove the boxes of charges. At least two of these exploded whilst Sjt. Haithwaite was in the small building and very close to them. By removing many undamaged charge boxes, the remaining Section of A Troop which was not out of action, was kept supplied with ammuition. Sjt. Haithwaite's conduct was outstanding, and it was by his personal example of courage and disregard of danger that the remainder of the troop, who had had a bad knock, were rallied.

(L.G. 15.6.43)

Hales, Stanley Harry, Corporal
5503681, 147 Regt., Royal Armoured Corps (Hull, York) (Immediate)

During the operations of the 8th to 14th Feb. 1945, this non-commissioned officer on frequent occasions displayed the very highest gallantry and devotion to duty. On 8th Feb. 1945 this non-commissioned officer's tank became bogged and was near to a house which had been converted into a strong point immediately in front of the bogged tank. It was impossible to carry out debogging operations. With complete disregard for his own safety this non-commissioned officer got out of his tank with a Sten gun and succeeded in forcing an entry into the house and eliminating the German machine gun team, who were in position in the top storey. This he did single handed with cover from his own tank. On the 12th Feb. 1945 his tank was leading the troop when a strong enemy defence position was encountered and the track of Corporal Hales' tank was blown off by a direct hit from an enemy S.P. gun. Despite intense enemy mortar and M.G. fire Corporal Hales and his crew succeeded in repairing the damage. At this time they were within 150 yards of the enemy positions. Throughout this operation, which lasted some three to four hours Corporal Hales continued to send accurate and valuable information regarding the enemy's dispositions and movement. Later in the day when he had once more succeeded in making his tank battleworthy the enemy put in a counter-attack forcing the infantry he was supporting to give ground, and while covering this withdrawal, the tank again became bogged. Although left over 300 yards in front of infantry forward defended localities and without the close support of infantry, which is so necessary in a wood, he continued to fight his tank and through his efforts it was possible once more for the infantry to move forward and regain their original dispositions.

For these acts of gallantry it is strongly recommended that this non-commissioned officer be awarded the D.C.M.

(L.G. 24.5.45)

Hall, Alexander, Sergeant (ActingWarrant Officer Cl. II, C.S.M.)
7041717, 11 Bn. Durham Light Infantry

For conspicuous gallantry, leadership and coolness under fire.

At Bulscamps on 30th May 1940 Sergeant Hall's platoon occupied a position in a rearguard action, which it was essential to hold to ensure the safety of other Troops. Under heavy shell fire, enemy bombing and machine gun fire, he kept a grip on the situation and by his fine example and resource steadied his own and neighbouring troops at a critical moment. Having completed his task, he withdrew under orders and occupied another position in perfect order.

(L.G. 20.12.40)

Hall, Benjamin Watson Griffith, A/Sergeant
P497, Australian New Guinea Administrative Unit, Australian Military Forces (Periodic)

Since May 1942 Sjt. Hall was on outpost duty of an important and dangerous nature. He was a member of the coast watching party operating between New Britain and the Madang coast. When the party was driven from the western end of New Britain it took up a position at Saidor. From this vantage point it reported valuable information concerning the extensive enemy small craft and barge traffic that was operating between Madang, Finchaven and Lae via Saidor. The party remained at Saidor until relief was effected in Feb 43. Throughout this period Sjt. Hall carried out his task with courage and determination.

When relief was effected in Feb, Sjt. Hall sought and obtained permission to remain with the relieving party under command of Lieut. Fairfax-Ross. This action materially assisted the new party as his knowledge of the area and natives was extensive. It subsequently proved invaluable, saving both equipment and lives.

In Mar 43 the enemy established a base at Saidor using it as a regular anchorage and staging camp. The party, however, remained, signalling targets which were subsequently straffed by Allied aircraft.

Early in Apr 43 enemy patrols overran the base established by the watching party. Fighting took place and Lieut. Fairfax-Ross was seriously wounded. Enemy patrols then scouted the area intensively in an effort to liquidate them. Throughout this period Sjt. Hall remained at his post transmitting valuable information about the enemy movements. His location was behind Wilwilan approx one mile S.E. of the enemy's base at Saidor. He was surrounded by their patrols which passed within a few yards of his O.P. he remained there for six weeks thereby enabling the main party to withdraw to the hinterland. He demonstrated outstanding courage and initiative, and determination of the highest degree. His conduct throughout was most exemplary.

Sjt. Hall left the O.P. only when specifically ordered to do so by the O.C. of his party. The last signal to be received from Sjt. Hall requested permission to return to the Saidor area. It is considered that the party was then operating from Wantoat. Throughout the whole period of twelve months from May 42 until May 43, Sjt. Hall has demonstrated outstanding courage and initiative and his conduct in the field has been most distinguished.
                                              (L.G. 27.4.44)

Hall, Harry Hubert, Sergeant
3713973, 14th/20th King's Hussars (Blackpool)
(Immediate)
During the advance of 14/20 H. Gp. and 2/6 C.P. from R. Sillaro towards Medicina on 16 Apr. 45, about 1130 hrs. during a very intense Tk. action about the village of Lunoarola (152444) the Tp. Ldr's Tk. was knocked out by a Bazooka. Sgt. Hall immediately took over Comd. of the Tp. and at the same time spotting a S.P. gun shooting from area C. Novo Sillaro (146445) put his own 17 pdr. Tk. into the lead while directing his other (75mm) Tk. onto the area from which the Bazooka had fired. By very skilful handling of his own Tk. he silenced the S.P. gun (later found to be a 105mm) and then turned his fire to assist his other Tk. which was being heavily engaged from it's front and right by mortar and Bazooka fire. Almost immediately afterwards this Tk. was hit and went on fire and at the same time Sgt. Hall's Tk. was also hit by a Bazooka. Realising that the damage was not vital and that the Tk. was still manœuvrable, moved and continued to fight, destroying the Bazooka. A few minutes later his Tk. ws hit by a mortar shell, and then twice more, the third putting his 17 pdr. out of action. Again he manœuvred his Tk. and continued to give valuable support to the Tp. on his left who were also very heavily engaged and suffering Tk. casualties. Finally his Tk. was hit for the fifth time by a shell from a S.P. gun which completely removed the sprocket and drum from one side of the Tk. and immobilised it. The S.P. gun then started shelling the Tk. with H.F. and after seeing it bracketed Sgt. Hall realised that he must order the crew to evacuate so as to prevent unnecessary loss of life.

Throughout the action which took place in very enclosed country containing numerous houses and which greatly favoured the defence, Sgt. Hall displayed outstanding initiative and by his great personal courage and coolness he inspired his crew and kept his Tk. fighting to the last under circumstances of the greatest danger and difficulty.

He enabled his Squadron to complete successfully the action which was vital to the capture that evening of Medicina.   *(L.G. 23.8.45)*

Hall, Joseph, Lance Corporal
3596685, 1 Border Regt.
I was captured at Lambersart, outside Lille, 29 May 40. We were taken across Belgium by lorry to Duren (15 June 40) and subsequently to Dortmund, Westphalen-halle, Stalag VID, (29 June—20 Sep), Hemer nr. Iserlohn, Stalag Via (21 Sept—20 Oct) and finally to Strasbourg formerly Front Stalag 210, now Stalag VD, (21 Oct—13 Dec). (For account of these prisons compare S/P.G. (F) 188, 7618141 Dvr. Gaze, W., R.A.O.C.).

For the first five months I was without blankets and soap. At Hemer I was given ten days' cells for not saluting German privates. At Strasbourg we received neither parcels nor letters. We suffered greatly from our own W.O.'s, Police and Interpreters, under the charge of R.S.M. Pritchard, of the Welsh Guards. All P/W were made to work, even the many wounded. Irish P/W were frequently interviewed apart to find out their attitude to an invasion of Eire by Great Britain. At one camp 45 Irish, after interviews, were removed to a separate camp.

While at Strasbourg I forged a couple of keys with the help of two Polish P/W. I escaped at 10 a.m. on 13 Dec. From 11 p.m. until 7 p.m. I hid in a laundry run by Alsations. I left Strasbourg that night, going to Schirmeck (14 Dec 40), St. Die (17 Dec 40), Epinal (18 Dec) Vesoul (19 Dec 40), Besancon (20 Dec 40), Quingey (21 Dec). On 22 Dec I reach Villers-Farley, abut 1 Km. from the Demarcation Line which I crossed the same day.

Once in unoccupied France I got into touch with the French Police, who sent me directly to Marseilles. There I remained for 2 months at Fort St Jean. On 27 Feb 41 I crossed into Spain where I was arrested and imprisoned for about seven weeks. I was released on 24 Apr 41 and sent to Gibraltar for repatriation.   *(L.G. 12.2.42)*

Hall, Mervyn, Corporal
WX14757, 2/16 Australian Inf. Bn. (Immediate)
27 Dec 43, Shaggy Ridge, Ramu Valley
During the attack on Shaggy Ridge on 27 Dec 43, Cpl. Hall was almost entirely responsible for the success of the operation. The attack took place over precipitous ground, already made more difficult as a result of heavy bombing and shelling, which necessitated crawling on hands and knees to reach the first part of the objective— a strongly fortified pillbox occupied by five enemy with two machine guns.

Observing that his Sjt.—WX4241 Sjt. McMahon— who had crawled to within a few feet of the post was in trouble, Cpl. Hall advanced alone, in the face of a hail of grenades and machine gun fire, to the entrance of the pillbox, and killed one of the occupants with a burst from his Owen Gun. A second Jap leapt out of the post, with a knife at Cpl. Hall, but he battered the enemy with the butt of his Owen Gun, and with grenades, quickly silenced the remaining occupants.

Although almost blinded by grenade wounds, Cpl. Hall advanced ahead of his section to a second post, one hundred yards along the one man track of the razor back, and attacked with undiminishing dash and lack of regard for his safety. Only when his section were able to get forward and assist in the battle, did he consent to go back for medical attention.

Cpl. Hall's fearless leadership, and remarkable courage against almost impossible odds, enabled his platoon to consolidate on the newly won ground, and gain the objective. It is recommended that Cpl. Hall be granted an Immediate Award of the Distinguished Conduct Medal.   *(L.G. 20.4.44)*

Hall, Roy Edgar, Warrant Officer Cl. II
QX38356, 2/1 Australian Inf. Bn. (Immediate)
On 17 Feb 45, a section was sent from Nambut Peak to patrol down an almost precipitous ridge. This ridge led along a saddle and up another ridge all razor-backed, to a Knoll. Endeavouring to get forward the section came under intense automatic fire from three LMG's, which killed two and wounded four. Three wounded were exposed to enemy fire and incapable of movement. A force, commanded by WOII Hall, and including Cpl. Graham's section, sent to relieve the position, arrived at this stage. By skilful manœuvre and supporting fire Hall and Graham brought out one of the wounded. Whilst giving them covering fire another soldier was wounded. Hall and Graham returned again and brought out this soldier, whilst the Japs fired at the least movement.

The width of ridge prevented more than three men advancing at a time, and the precipitous sides precluded any outflanking movement. Hall, Graham and L/Cpl. Mould, then stormed their way upwards throwing grenades and firing their wpns. They killed eight Japs then, and drove off others. During this attack, Mould was killed and Hall wounded. Hall and Graham still under fire brought out the other two wounded and their weapons. The Coy Comd then ordered the force to withdraw. Hall and Graham were last to leave. The position was later found to contain twenty-two weapon pits and fourteen dead Japs.

Throughout the action, Hall and Graham displayed soldierly skill and coolness, courage and determination far exceeding any call of duty. By their splendid efforts with complete and absolute disregard for their personal safety, brought in the wounded & recovered the weapons.   *(L.G. 21.6.45)*

Hall, William Patrick, Lance Sergeant
2070149, 233 Field Coy R.E., Royal Engineers
(Hebburn-on-Tyne) (Immediate)
Ref Map Italy 1/50,000 Sheet 262 II Riposto.
During our advance on 14 Aug 43 one of the leading inf coys encountered a well-concealed thickly-laid belt of S-Mines in the area D 0912. Casualties were caused and the advance was halted. L/Sjt. Hall with a party of sappers was ordered to gap the minefield. The mine detectors used were not working well due to the presence of lava deposits, and the clearing party set off several S-mines. Although he was wounded by one of these mines,

L/Sjt. Hall remained in the field directing the gapping party. L/Sjt. Hall himself stood on a mine, but succeeded in warning his clearing party, enabling them to take cover and avoid injury. On completion of the gap L/Sjt. Hall returned and removed the dead from the mine belt.

By his courage and perseverance in most adverse conditions L/Sjt. Hall set an example which inspired his men in the early completion of their task and made possible the continuance of the advance.
     (L.G. 18.11.43)

Hall, William, Sergeant
784745, 55 (S.Y.) A. Tk. Regt., Royal Artillery
(Maltby) (Immediate)
1 Jul. 44 at Rauray.
Sgt. Hall was in command of a 6-pr gun detachment under comd. of 1 T.S. situated in a reserve Coy. area. Fwd. Coys. were attacked by Inf. and tanks and some of the Inf. and another gun detachment were forced to withdraw past his gun. Sgt. Hall appreciated that by manhandling his gun 350 yds. to a new position he might, with a limited arc, be able to engage enemy tanks coming round the flank of the position. This he proceeded to do under heavy mortar and M.G. fire, and, as a result, managed to destroy 5 enemy tanks. Sgt. Hall, throughout the action, showed the greatest initiative and devotion to duty, and it was largely owing to his efforts that penetration into rear and flank positions were prevented. *Recommended for M.M.*   *(L.G. 19.10.44)*

Hall, W. T., Dvr.
1927551, 107 Army Fd Coy., R.E. I Corps Tps.
I was in hospital at Camiers, with a wound in my right foot, when the Germans entered on 23 May. A week later I was forced to march, with walking wounded, to Boulogne, where we were locked up in goods station. Later we were marched through St. Omer and Haze-brouck to Lille and admitted to the French Military Hospital 'Scrive.' Five days later I was transferred to the Caserne Ste. Ruth in Lille. In the first week in June I got away in company with another O.R. (Watson, no record, recaptured at Mericourt about 30 June 40). Before this we had been given civilian clothes by a French woman visitor. We effected our escape by jumping into a moat from a sixteen foot wall. Watson and I went off independently. I made for Roubaix where I got a bicycle, as I was limping, and then obtained work for the next month at a farm near Raches.

When My foot had healed, I made for the coast, but, owing to German sentries, could not get down to the beach. I then retraced my way towards Belgium. At Rouvroy (1 July) I was arrested, as I had no identity papers, by a German patrol and taken through Lens to a prison at Loos (3 July). Here I met the writer P. G. Wodehouse. Later I was transferred to the Caserne Kleber at Lille. From here P/W were taken through Tournai and Brussels to a transit camp (a journey of nine days) about 60 kms. inside the German frontier. On

20 July, the day after arrival, I escaped alone through the wire, crossed a bridge (which was guarded both ends) and went across country to Brussels, where I had friends.

I then went on to Lille and stayed for a while at Grand Ronchin, then going on (end of Nov) to Seclin where I remained for two months. On 14 Jan 41, I sent out for the south, taking a train to Douai and St. Quentin and then towards Tergnie, which is outside the Zone Interdite. I learned on the train that a thorough inspection took place at Tergnie, so I jumped off, walked to Chauny and then took another train to Paris.

From Paris I travelled down by rail, through Lyons and Dijons to a point near Mont Chenin. From here I crossed the line of Demarcation on 17 Jan 41 with a crowd of refugees. On the advice of three French Colonial soldiers, I applied at a French Recruiting Office for a railway warrant, food voucher and an advance of demobilization money, all of which I obtained and with which I went on by rail to Marseilles. As the American Consul could not assist me, I went on to Perpignan and then across the Pyrenees into Spain. I got as far as Gerona, where I was arrested (as it was after curfew hours) and then spent several weeks in concentration camps (Barcelona, Saragosa, Miranda), until I was released on the intervention of our Embassy.

Hallam, Archie, Corporal (A/Sgt.)
4978845, 14th Bn. Sherwood Foresters (Old Brinsley,
Notts.) (Immediate)
For outstanding bravery and initiative in the fighting at San Savino on the night of 5/6 Sep. 44 and on 13 Sep. 44.

During the night 5/6 Sep., 'B' Coy. were ordered to attack San Savino. Early in the attack the Platoon Comd. and Platoon Sgt. of Cpl. Hallam's platoon both became casualties. The fighting became very confused owing to the presence of enemy tanks in the built-up area. Cpl. Hallam, however, immediately assumed command of the platoon and quickly gained control of a situation which, without adequate leadership, would have prejudiced the outcome of the operation. He quickly reorganised the platoon and commanded it with skill and initiative throughout the heavy fighting which followed.

Again, in the dawn attack on San Savino on 13 Sep., the Platoon Comd. and Platoon Sgt. of Cpl. Hallam's platoon were wounded on the S.L. Cpl. Hallam again assumed command and carried out the intricate and difficult task which had been allotted to his platoon. He assaulted and seized a key house in the village from which two enemy machine-guns were firing. The seizure of this house did much to ensure the success of the whole operation.

Cpl. Hallam then led his men to attack and capture two further houses, taking many prisoners and making a firm base from which the rest of his Company were able to complete their task with success.

The outstanding initiative and determination of this N.C.O. to hit the enemy on every possible occasion did much to ensure the success of the Battalion attack. He displayed all the best qualities of a junior leader, and his power to inspire men and to make quick decisions were an example to all.
Recommended for M.M.   *(L.G. 8.2.45)*

Hamilton, John, Sergeant
818790, 65th (NY) A. Tk. Regt., Royal Artillery
(London, E.18)
On 13th June 1944 Sgt. Hamilton was No.1 of a section of M10s in support of 8 H at Tracy Bocage. When his section was held up by mortaring at the entrance to the village Sgt. Hamilton dismounted and choosing a different route to the Tp. Comd. proceeded to stalk the enemy. So determined were his efforts that he succeeded in getting within about 15 yards of a mortar detachment, killing the firer. As they were running away, Sgt. Hamilton killed two more with his rifle.

On being held up again Sgt. Hamilton repeated the process and again killed 3 men. On returning to the 8 H a wounded man was seen. Sgt. Hamilton dismounted under heavy fire and picked him up.

Sgt. Hamilton was under heavy continuous fire for over an hour but his complete disregard for his personal safety—his determination and courage was instrumental in the success by which this very small party forced back a lot of enemy.   *(L.G. 31.8.44)*

Hammond, Henry William, Sergeant
6096867, 2/6th Bn. Queen's Royal Regt. (London,
E.15) (Immediate)
Sjt. Hammond was a platoon Sjt. with his platoon during the attack on the Ceriano Ridge on 20.9.44.

During the advance his platoon Commander was killed and the advance was temporarily halted.

With complete disregard for his own safety Sjt. Hammond armed himself with a Bren gun and against strong enemy opposition and direct small arms fire, firing the Bren gun from this hip, he led his platoon on to the objective. After the objective had been captured the enemy began to infiltrate towards the platoon position. Sjt. Hammond advanced on the enemy, throwing Mills grenades, killing one German and putting the remainder to flight. When the position was shelled and mortared, Sjt. Hammond walked about in the open encouraging his men to hold firmly to the position. Sjt. Hammond gave a splendid example to the men under his command and his personal efforts ensured that the objective gained was firmly held.
Recommended for M.M.   *(L.G. 8.3.45)*

Hampson, Henry Hare, M.M., Sergeant
7902353, 44th Bn. Royal Tank Regt. (Wigan)
(Immediate)
At 0900 hours 13 July 1943, Sjt. Hampson's troop was put under command of the 6th D.L.I. and ordered to advance with 2 Sections of carriers from Solarino 9934 along the main road to Palazzolo Accreide 8029. Soon after the advance the carriers were held up by a burning lorry across the road. Sjt. Hampson's troop took the lead and he himself pushed the vehicle out of the way with his tank. Coming round the next bend he sighted an Italian ammunition lorry and M/C and put them both out of commission. Almost immediately an R.35 was sighted and also knocked out. Sjt. Hampson then moved up to the burning ammunition lorry and sighted 8 R.35's, 4 staff cars and one truck at 956342. He was fired on and received 9 direct hits but himself knocked out 1 R.35, the four staff cars and truck. This completely blocked the road so Sjt. Hampson got out of his tank and with another member of his crew went forward on foot to find a way round, being under MG fire for most of the time. He encountered and took prisoner the Napoli Divisional Commander and half his staff and then others gave themselves up. He then organised a clearing party and removed the obstacles.

His tank had been damaged about the gun so he changed tanks and continued the advance. He had not gone far when a 105 mm opened up on him and also an anti-tank gun at 600 yds range. His Browning jammed but he knocked the guns out with H.E. Almost immediately he engaged a large number of trucks and some R.35's, knocking out 3 R.35's and several trucks. The advance then continued to Melilli and another R. 35 fell to Sjt. Hampson's gun. At Melilli he found 2 R.35's and several trucks abandoned. The advance to Palazzolo Acreide continued without further incident. The total bag of the troop, mainly falling to Sjt. Hampson's guns, was:— 8 R.35's, 5 Guns, 4 Staff Cars, 2 M/Cycles, 29 Trucks and numerous other undamaged vehicles. *(L.G. 21.10.43)*

Hann, Vernon Charles, Sergeant
5191185, 10 Gloucs. Regt. (Bristol)
N. Burma Campaign 1944.
On 17 Aug., during operations South of Thaikwagon Sjt. Hann was a platoon Sjt. in a Company ordered to capture two bridges on the Taungni—Pinbaw ry. line. At 0700 hrs. his platoon, which was leading the advance, came under heavy L.M.G. fire from a clump of elephant grass. They succeeded in reaching slight cover to a flank but the remainder of the company had suffered heavy casualties, the commander being badly wounded and the 2 i/c and remaining platoon commander killed. Sjt. Hann was ordered by his platoon commander to go back and report the enemy position to Coy. HQ. This involved a crawl of 400 yards in the open across the front of the enemy position. Under L.M.G. and sniper fire, Sjt. Hann managed to reach HQ, described the enemy positions and then crawled back to his platoon commander with orders to withdraw to a position on the left flank.

On arrival, the platoon came under comd. of the left Coy. and Sjt. Hann took over command of his platoon. An attack on the enemy position was put in almost at once and in the final assault Sjt. Hann, leading the remnants of his platoon with great dash and determination, succeeded in reaching the enemy position in spite of intense M.M.G. and L.M.G. fire. Using grenades and Tommy gun, both enemy L.M.G. posts were captured and their gun crews killed. Sjt. Hann then quickly consolidated the position with his one remaining section.

The behaviour of this N.C.O., his coolness and complete disregard for personal safety were outstanding and the rout of the enemy at this position was largely due to his gallantry and determination to succeed. *Recommended for M.M.* *(L.G. 16.11.44)*

Hanson, Albert Edward, Sergeant
3447148, Lancashire Fusiliers, T.A.
No citation. *(L.G. 3.9.40)*

Hardy, Ralph James, Sergeant
538807, Royal Air Force
About the middle of Oct. 1942 contact was established between officers at Shamshuipo Camp and B.A.A.G. officers at Waichow through the medium of Chinese overseers at the Kai Tak Airport. This N.C.O. very bravely volunteered to accompany the working party each day to act as both receiver and sender of these important messages. He displayed great initiative and daring in carrying this out under the eyes of the Japanese guard with the certain knowledge that the slightest mistake would involve him in the most severe form of punishment, if not the loss of his life. These activities were successfully carried out by him until the end of the year when working parties ceased and a new type of contact established through the Chinese drivers of the ration lorries in which he also played an important part. The value of this work for the camp cannot be over emphasised involving as it did a supply of vital necessities as well as the transmitting of constant information regarding Camp conditions to the outside.

On 1st July 1943 this N.C.O. was taken out of the Camp and conducted to the Headquarters of the Japanese Gendarmerie where he was charged with communicating with the enemy. He was subjected to the most brutal forms of torture including the Japanese water torture to compel him to disclose the names of officers associated with these activities and this he resolutely refused to do. After several hours of torture he was removed to Stanley Prison 'on remand' to await a Court Martial on a charge of espionage. The Court sat on 1st December and after the statements were read the Prosecutor demanded the death penalty but the Court awarded a sentence of 15 years imprisonment.

The resolute courage of this N.C.O. in spite of indescribable suffering and his devotion to duty provided and example of the highest traditions of the Service.

For his devotion to duty and conspicuous bravery whilst on special service during his period of captivity, this N.C.O. is recommended for the award of the D.C.M.

(L.G. 1.10.46)

Hare, Leslie Daniel, A/Corporal
VX 55687, 2/7 Australian Inf. Bn. (Immediate)
For courage, determination and dash in advancing under heavy fire 23 Aug 43.

Cpl. Hare was a sec leader of 11 pl B Coy 2/7 Aust Inf Bn during the Coy's attack up a narrow razor back ridge on Rough Hill, Bobdubi area 23 Aug. The advance was held up by the enemy occupying pits astride the track, with no possibility of encirclement due to the sheer drop on each side. With complete disregard of personal danger Cpl. Hare ran forward shooting as he went— reached the foremost weapon pits, killed the occupants and by accurate fire forced the remainder to retire. During the second stage of the advance the Coy was again held up by an enemy LMG firing along the spur. Under this heavy fire Cpl. Hare again ran forward firing a bren gun from the hip engaged the gun pit with grenades, killing the crew and silencing the gun. In these two actions performed within an hour Cpl. Hare by his personal gallantry rendered invaluable assistance in enabling his Coy to advance against a most difficult posn.

Throughout the whole engagement Cpl. Hare displayed outstanding courage and coolness eventually becoming seriously wounded in a courageous effort to silence an enemy LMG single handed on 25 Aug 43.

(L.G. 20.1.44)

Hargreaves, James, Sergeant
3520174, 9th Bn. Manchester Regt. (Ashton-under-Lyne) (Periodic)
On 13 Sep. 44, the comd. of 10 (M.G.) Platoon 9 Manch., was killed and Sjt. Hargreaves, the Platoon Sjt., took over comd. of the platoon. He remained in comd. until 9 Nov: during which period the platoon was in action from 13 Sept. to 1 Oct. and again from 11 to 20 Oct.

Between 26 Sep. and 1 Oct., the platoon was in the area 7139671, supporting a Tp. of 46 Recce Regt. which was established on the North bank of the R. Rubicone. Throughout the action, although the platoons position was constantly shelled and mortared, Sjt. Hargreaves directed its fire with complete disregard for his own safety and was largely instrumental in breaking up a series of enemy counter-attacks on another Tp. position in the area 727972. While the operations were in progress, the R. Rubcone had become flooded, cutting off the platoon from the remainder of the M.G. Coy. On two occasions, Sjt. Hargreaves, who is aged 38, crossed under fire with amn. parties and guided them to the platoon position, thereby enabling the guns to remain in action.

From 15 to 19 Oct., Sjt. Hargreaves' platoon was in action before Cesena (599042). On one occasion he was ordered to take up a fwd. position near the M. Romano feature. During his recce, he was quick to grasp the importance of siting his guns further fwd. than had been anticipated, so as to produce enfilade fire behind a ridge in front of the R. Savio. His intelligent appreciation of the situation resulted in a number of the enemy being trapped between his M.G. fire and the advancing inf. and subsequently captured.

Throughout the period during which he acted as Platoon Comd., Sjt. Hargreaves displayed courage and leadership of a very high order.   *(L.G. 28.6.45)*

Harland, Thomas, Sergeant
7905507, 1 Royal Tank Regt. (Coventry) (Immediate)
In the Mahares area (TV.2602)
This NCO displayed outstanding gallantry and skill in handling his tank in the engagement of the 8th April 1943. His sqn was advancing across open ground when it was suddenly engaged by heavy artillery and A/Tk gun fire. Sjt. Harland was on the flank of the sqn; on his own initiative he halted in full view of some of the enemy guns and laid a carefully placed smoke screen, behind which the remainder of the sqn were able to manœuvre to a battle posn. Prior to reaching this posn however the sqn met a very difficult wadi as the smoke screen was clearing away. Without hesitation Sjt. Harland made a wide sweep to his flank and drew the bulk of the enemy fire on to his tank while the sqn altered formation in order to cross the obstacle—which it succeeded in doing. Meanwhile Sjt. Harland's tank got into extremely difficult ground, where it was in danger of floundering. While still under enemy fire Sjt. Harland dismounted and led his tank on foot out of the obstacle and then mounted again. His tank was still separated from the rest of the sqn, and in trying to regain his station he ran into a 76.2 SP gun at very short range. He succeeded in engaging this gun so quickly that it was unable to fire at his tank and he subsequently destroyed it. Throughout the action this NCO displayed a complete disregard for his personal safety, and the very highest degree of leadership, tactical skill and devotion to duty. I recommend him strongly for the DCM. *(L.G. 22.7.43)*

Harmer, Reginald, Corporal
5570019, 2 Wiltshire Regt. (London, N.21)
West of Solarino on 12 Jul 43, 'C' Coy were advancing to capture and consolidate a posn between two wadis. The advance was carried out across open fields under heavy MG and Mortar fire. During this advance the Pl Comd of the leading pl was wounded and his two leading sec comds were killed. Cpl. Harmer was commanding a sec of the following pl. He appreciated the situation and led his sec into a posn from which he could give covering fire to the leading pl. He then went fwd to the leading pl and taking comd, led them to a posn under cover from which the enemy could be engaged and later destroyed.

He then himself went fwd three times into the open field under hy MG and mortar fire to bring in two wounded comrades and one LMG. It was Cpl. Harmer's swift action and courageous leadership which extricated the remnants of the leading pl from an extremely unfavourable posn and enabled the adv to continue. Cpl. Harmer was later wounded in action. Cpl. Harmer showed a complete disregard of his personal safety and gave an outstanding display of gallantry which inspired all who saw him. *(L.G. 18.11.43)*

Harmon, Derek John, Sergeant
22955109, Corps of Royal Military Police
For Northen Ireland. *(L.G. 22.5.72)*

Harmon, William Henry, Private (A/Cpl.)
3193990, 1 King's Own Scottish Borderers (North Shields) (Immediate)
On the 13th Oct. 1944, whilst the Battalion was engaged in clearing the woods SW of Overloon, L/Cpl. Harmon's Section was engaged at close range by two enemy M.G. posts. L/Cpl. Harmon immediately crawled forward under heavy fire towards the nearest enemy post, hurled two grenades into it and then rushed the post killing the two Germans with his Sten gun. L/Cpl. Harmon immediately went forward again towards the other enemy post and with a grenade and his Sten gun put the enemy post out of action. This gallant action on the part of L/Cpl. Harmon was carried out with complete disregard for his own personal safety and enabled his platoon to advance and reach their final objective. *(L.G. 1.3.45)*

Harney, James, Sergeant
4535690, 3rd Bn. Royal Tank Regt. (1, Denby St., White Abbey Rd., Bradford)
On the 25th November 1941 in the area of Bir Taieb El Essem during a movement by the Battalion to relieve pressure on a South African Bde, he came under heavy fire from thirty to forty enemy medium tanks. He ran the length of the line at close range and as a result important information was received as to disposition of enemy forces.

On the 28th November in the area Dahar Er Reian 453392 the Battalion was ordered to close with enemy tanks and during this attack Sjt. Harney prevented a serious encirclement by about 20 enemy tanks by standing fast and checking their advance.

On every occasion Sjt. Harney has shown admirable courage and coolness and has been a constant inspiration to the whole Squadron. *(L.G. 20.1.42)*

Harris, Edwin, Corporal
NX 21416, 2/17 Australian Inf. Bn.
A/Cpl. Harris was a section commander in a Coy 2/17 Aust Inf Bn during the operations near Alamein on 23 October 42 until he was wounded and evacuated on 25 Oct 42. During the attack by the bn on the night 23/24 Oct A Coy—the right forward coy—was subjected to heavy and accurate enemy artillery and machine gun fire causing considerable casualties. The coy comd ordered the right platoon to attack and silence an enemy machine gun post that was holding up the advance.

A/Cpl. Harris led his section of four men with the utmost vigour and determination against the post, killed the occupants and silenced the machine gun. During the action this NCO was wounded in the thigh and shoulder. He refused to return to the RAP and continued to lead his section throughout the attack. On the night 24/25 Oct the battalion had again attacked. During the consolidation of the objective this NCO was outstanding for his coolness under fire and ability quickly to re-organise the men of his platoon. Shortly afterwards he was again wounded by aerial bombing and evacuated. The capacity of this NCO, his courage and leadership were of a high order and did much to offset the loss of many members of his coy as casualties. *(L.G. 11.2.43)*

Harris, Wilfred, Sergeant
404148, 4th/7th Royal Dragoon Guards (Salisbury) (Immediate)
Lingevres, 15th June 1944.
Sgt. Harris was Tp. Sgt. of 4th Tp., 'A' Sqn. 4/7 R.D.G. On 15th June the task of 'A' Sqn. was to support the 9th D.L.I. across an open piece of ground to the N. of the village and then to watch the approaches to the village of Lingevres against a possible tank threat.

By good placing of his tank on the Tilly Sur Seulles road and by dismounting under fire and using his binoculars, Sgt. Harris was able first to stop an enemy tank with one round, of A.P. The infantry finished this tank off with a Piat. Shortly afterwards Sgt. Harris opened fire on a second German tank approaching the village and set it on fire with his first shot. Later in the day the infantry and anti-tank guns came up and the Squadron were relieved, but in the evening the enemy counter-attacked with tanks and destroyed the anti-tank guns, Sgt. Harris again positioned his tank admirably and by giving clear orders and remaining calm was able to destroy three more enemy tanks in very quick succession. His speed in spotting the targets, skill in positioning his tank and extreme measure of alertness for a long period resulted in him shooting five enemy Panther tanks. *(L.G. 31.8.44)*

Harrison, Cyril Edgar, Gunner
950379, Royal Artillery, att. School of Artillery (Forges), B.E.F.
1. Capture:
We had been sent out from Forges in a flying column on 16 May 40. I was acting as a truck driver. Our column was ambushed by the Germans, and I was captured just outside Albert on 20 May 40.
2. Captivity:
After capture we were taken into Albert and thence, via St. Quentin to Belgium on route for Trier. From the main distribution centre at Trier I was sent to Oflag VII

C (Laufen) and remained there till Apr 41. At this camp officers had priority in escaping. I was employed in general work around the camp and, for part of the time, as an orderly.

I left Laufen in Apr 41 for Fort 8 (Posen) attached to Stalag XXI D. This was the 'reprisals' camp, and here again officers had priority in escaping. Here I worked in the tailors' shop, having had experience of the trade as a salesman in peacetime, and helped in the making of civilian clothes for the officers who escaped from the Fort. Here I helped in a tunnel scheme, but the tunnel was not completed by the time we were all moved.

In Jun or Jul 41 I was moved to Oflag V B (Biberach). Here also I had no opportunity of escape. Again I worked in the tailors' shop, making civilian suits and also three German uniforms which were used in a successful escape from the camp. In Sep 41 I was transferred to Oflag VI B (Warburg), where I also worked in the tailors' shop. In Apr 42 I was sent to Stalag VIII B (Lamsdorf).

3. Attempted escapes:
(a) From Arbeitskommando 428 (Derschau).

From Stalag VIII B I was sent on a working party at a sawmill at Derschau, N.E. of Oppeln (Germany 1:100,000, Sheet 117). I escaped from the billet at the sawmill with a L/Cpl. in the Royal Engineers on 28 Jul 42. We collected civilian clothes. Some were stolen from the sawmill, and I had a pair of blue dungarees which my parents had sent in a personal parcel inside a pair of pyjamas. We escaped from the upper floor of a two-storey building adjoining the sawmill. We cut through the bars of the window in the afternoon with a hack-saw blade which we stole from the sawmill and covered up the cuts with chewing gum. After dark we pulled out the bars, and lowered ourselves down a blanket of ropes. We had saved food from Red Cross parcels, and I had a small map of part of Poland which I had stolen from a railway carriage. I also had a compass which I had had in France. We walked alongside the main road leading to Lodz and then struck across country for the riverMalapane, intending to head for Cracow, where we hoped to get help from Poles. We followed the river, intending to reach the railway line at Grafenweiler (Germany 1:100,000, Sheet 118). At Grafenwiler there was a thunderstorm during the night and we got thoroughly soaked. We lay up in bushes on the river bank to dry our clothes and were detected by a woman herding geese. She informed civilians who sent for the police. We were sent back to the main Stalag, and got seven days in cells. During this attempt we walked only by night and lay up by day. As we had civilian clothing, this course was a mistake.

(b) From Arbeitskommando 211 (Triebitz)

About 12 Sep I attempted to escape again, this time from Arbeitskommando 211 at Triebitz, 17 km. from Swittau. This time there were five others with me, including Pte. Morley, Australian New Zealander; and L/Cpl. Eric Egan. We had food from Red Cross parcels, but no money. I had two maps which I had copied—one

down as far as Innsbruck, and the other of the Swiss frontier. I also had a compass made from a razor blade. We left the Arbeitskommando in pairs, intending to try to reach Switzerland. Egan and I went together, and about five hours later ran into two of the others in a wood outside Zwittau. The four of us went on together for the next two days, walking across country to avoid co[...] and road blocks. We were wearing battle dress when we left the working party, but on the second night broke open a box on the railway line and each got a civilian working jacket. While walking along the railway line we encountered a Czech soldier on guard. He arrested the three others, but I managed to get away by rolling into a ditch near the line. Next night I walked to a railway goods yard from which I had heard shunting while lying up during the day. For about two hours I managed to avoid the two Czech soldiers who were guarding the yard. There were a lot of trucks in the yard, but none seemed ready to leave. Then a goods train came in on the central line, and as the train was about to leave again, I got into the brake van of a truck in the middle of the train.

After about three hours the train arrived in Brunn (Brno). This was the third day after my escape. I left the goods yard immediately, and crossed a railway bridge to the river bank, which I followed for about two miles till I found fairly good cover and lay up for the day. I started off just before dark and got on to the main Vienna road on the outskirts of the town. I walked for several nights and lay up by day.

I had left my water bottle with one of the men who had been captured, and suffered considerably from thirst. One day, in fact, I went 5 km. out of my way to a village, just to get water. There were civilians and two policemen near the village pump, but they did not pay any attention to me.

After several days' walking I stole a bicycle from an entry at a fairly large farming village on the main road, and rode on to Vienna, entering the city just after dark. I had some difficulty in getting through Vienna, as the lights went out at 2245 hrs, and I could not read the signposts. Eventually I reached the railway station at Vienna-Odling. I left the bicycle outside the station, and made my way into a goods yard, but could not find a truck bound for Linz, for which I was hoping to make.

While returning to get the bicycle I was spotted by a man, who spoke to me. To avoid him I got on to the platform. A train came in bound for Radstadt (S.E. of Salzburg), and I entered it with the passengers.

I was suffering from dysentery, and spent the journey in the lavatory. The train pulled up at the wayside station at Loebersdorf (S.E. of Vienna), out of which I got through an open gate in a goods yard. I was then in a pretty weak state, but I found cover on a river bank outside the town. During the next day I made a fire in the woods and boiled myself some cocoa, potatoes, and Oxo cubes. I was two days in the district.

At the end of the second day I returned to the goods yard, and found goods wagons labelled 'Linz.' I was taken ill again, and went into the shadow of a factory wall, where two watchmen with torches found me. This was the 13th day of my escape. I was taken to the police station, where, in view of my weak state, I was very decently treated. I was sent to Stalag XVIII A, a camp occupied by Russians and Jugoslavs. On my return to Stalag VIII B I was seven weeks in hospital.

(c) From Arbeitskommando 453 (Stramberg)

In Lamsdorf I met Pte. Oskar Scharf, a Czech Jew, who joined the British Army in Palestine, and we went out on the same working party (Arkbeitskommando 453) at Stramberg (South of Mahrisch-Ostrau), on the Czechoslovak frontier. Scharf went as interpreter. On the working party Scharf and I got in touch with Czech civilians (Communists) who were willing to take us to Budapest. We collected as much money as possible by selling cigarettes and clothing from parcels, and I had about 400 RM.

Scharf and I left the working party on 26 or 27 Apr 43. A guide met us outside the factory boundary at 2300 hrs and took us across country till we met four or five more Czechs on a road. They fitted us out with old clothing for the journey across the hills into Czechoslovakia. After crossing the hills we stayed from morning till afternoon in a village hotel. We left the hotel to catch a bus to the Slovakian border, but something seemed to go wrong with the arrangements, and we went by lorry instead. We left the lorry—Scharf, three Czechs, and myself—and while walking along a country road carrying our luggage we were overtaken by a car containing three Gestapo men. One of the Czechs got away. The rest of us were arrested. Scharf and I showed our Stalag identity discs, which satisfied the Gastapo. We were both sent back to Lamsdorf. I was sentenced to 14 days' cells, but did not serve any of the sentence, having already been 25 days in civilian prisons.

4. Escape from Breslau Gas Works:

On 23 Sep 43 I escaped from Breslau gas works. The plans for, and the execution of this escape are described in the report of Sjt. Crowley (S/P.G. (G) 1501) with whom I escaped.

I followed Crowley over the gas work wall, getting over at the second attempt, the first having been spoiled by the presence of a civilian on the street. I got over about three minutes after Crowley, and was just in time to see him catch a tram.

I walked towards the town for about ten minutes, and then got the tram to the Haupthahnhof, arriving at 1550 hrs. I spent some time looking for Crowley, who had never seen the station, which I knew fairly well. I eventually saw him in a ticket queue. I got into another queue, in which there was a delay, as a result of which I missed the train.

We had an alternative plan, however, and I took a ticket to Reppen to which I had no intention going, but which was on the way to Frankfurt. There was no train leaving immediately on this route except an express to Dresden. I took the express and changed at Leignitz, an

hour's journey from Breslau. While I was checking train times from the indicator in the station at Liegnitz a railway policeman (in blue uniform) asked me what I was doing. I said I was a foreign worker waiting for the train. He seemed satisfied, and merely glanced at the forged Ausweis which I had obtained in the camp. From Liegnits I went on to Sommerfield, and changed there for Frankfurt-an-der-Oder. Here I booked again for Stettin via Eberswalda. I arrived in Stettin at 1353 hrs on 24 Sep.

From the station in Stettin I made my way to the docks. I walked along the river bank and then out to the suburb of Gotzlow. We had been advised in the camp to go there, but I saw no sign of Swedish ships. I returned to the town and decided to seek help of Frenchmen.

The first foreigner I spoke to was a Pole working at a cement factory on the way back to town. He said there were Belgians working there, but they were all still P/W. He took me to the Lager where they lived, but I decided the place was too risky.

When I got back to the town I tried two Frenchmen wearing red white-and-blue badges. They were suspicious, though I gave them half a bar of English chocolate, and would not help. About 1530 hrs I decided to try the other side of the river. Here I spotted ome more Frenchmen. As they passed me one of them pulled out a packet of French cigarettes. I asked them for a light, and got into conversation with them, telling them who I was, and showing them my P/W disc and a letter addressed to me in the camp and stamped by the German censorship. This satisfied them and they took me to their Lager, about ten minutes' walk away. Here there was a man who spoke English. He went out, and returned with Sjt. Crowley.

The rest of my journey is as narrated in Sjt. Crowley's report.
(*L.G. 17.2.44*)

Harrison, John, Lance Corporal
550403, 10th Hussars, Royal Armoured Corps
L/Cpl. Harrison was driving a Cruiser Tank which, on coming round the corner of a wood, came face to face with a German anti-tank rifle and machine gun. His Tank Comd. and gunner were engaged at the time in firing on an enemy anti-tank gun further to a flank, so L/Cpl. Harrison at once opened his front shield and killed the crew of the anti-tank rifle and machine gun with his revolver. He then ran his tank over the German position.

His prompt and courageous action probably saved the life of his Tank Cmd, who was engaged in observing in another direction.
(*L.G. 27.9.40*)

Harrison, John Alfred, Sergeant
2613643, 6th (Motor) Bn. Grenadier Guards
(Wallasey, Cheshire) (Immediate)
During the Battalion attack on the Horseshoe feature on the night of the 16/17 March, 1943, this N.C.O. displayed extreme courage and coolness under fire. His Platoon Commander was wounded during the advance through

the enemy minefield. Sergeant Harrison got his platoon dug in the forward position; twice during the night his position was attacked by the enemy and both attacks were repulsed. At hardly any period was the position not under fire from three sides, and at times this fire was extremely heavy and many casualties resulted. It was largely owing to the devotion to duty of Sergeant Harrison and his great powers of leadership that the Company position, of which his platoon formed a pivot, was held till some four hours after daylight.   (L.G. 9.8.43)

Harrison, Walter, Lance Corporal
5831486, 2/5th Bn. Queen's Royal Regt. (Cambridge)
(Immediate)
Place of action:—Mount Stella, Salerno, Italy.

During the attack on a mountain which dominated the Divisional front, the platoon to which Pte Harrison belonged led the assault on the company objective on the top of the mountain. As the result of intense machine gun fire and grenade action by the enemy, the platoon suffered casualties and Pte. Harrison, who belonged to Platoon Headquarters, was ordered by his Company Commander to take charge of some men near him and re-organise a section post. Pte. Harrison assumed immediate control, formed the men into a section and successfully repulsed two counter-attacks on his post. In the second counter-attack the enemy infiltrated very close to Pte Harrison's post but by his determination and disregard of personal danger he beat off both attacks. The assumption of command under confused and difficult circumstances, the subsequent exercise of control and resolute action against the enemy showed qualities of leadership that were outstanding.   (L.G. 27.1.44)

Harrison, Wilfred, Warrant Officer Cl. II (C.S.M.)
5945343, 2 Bedfordshire & Hertfordshire Regt.
The enemy were shelling 'B' Coy Fwd posn at Avelghem when P.S.M. Warren was reported as seriously injured and unable to move in front. C.S.M. Harrison immediately called for a volunteer and with Pte. Peekes went out, still under shell and rifle fire, and with no regard to his own safety brought back the wounded Warrant Offr.

During the withdrawal through La Panne his Coy Comd was seriously wounded. He arranged for him to be assisted to the beach and then took charge of the Coy. He obained a Motor Cycle and under heavy shelling found an alternative route to the beaches in order to minimise losses to the Coy. He thereby managed to bring about 75 per cent of the Coy to the beaches where he had them under complete control.

Throughout the 'Flanders' withdrawal C.S.M. Harrison by displaying consistant courage and leadership was a fine example to those around him.
                          (L.G. 22.10.40)

Hart, Edward, Lance Sergeant
2736473, 3rd Bn. Welsh Guards (Leicester)
(Immediate)
28 October 1944. Map Ref. Pt. 254 045225, Sheet 99/ IV 1/50,000, Italy.

Owing to heavy casualties amongst officers and senior N.C.O.'s, L/Sjt. Hart was, on the 28 Oct. 44, in command 11 Platoon 3 Welsh Guards holding a house, in full view of the enemy on the forward slopes of Pt. 254 045225. At approximately 1000 hrs., learning from a civilian that the enemy were occupying a house 200 yds. away in La Costa 047226, L/Sjt. Hart immediately despatched a recce patrol which confirmed this report. The information he passed by telephone to the Coy. Comd. who ordered L/Sjt. Hart to prepare a plan for a night attack and submit it later by telephone for approval.

At 1300 hrs. the telephone line, the only means of communication between 11 Platoon and Coy. HQ, was out by heavy shell fire.

Acting on his own initiative, L/Sjt. Hart decided to take advantage of a heavy mist and at once put in a surprise attack. Covered only by two Bren guns, L/Sjt. Hart with one other man assaulted the enemy-held house with grenades and T.S.M.G. fire across 50 yds. of open ground. Through the speed of his attack, and the faultless manner in which it was executed, not only was the sentry surprised but all four enemy in the house were completely demoralised and surrendered without a fight. From 5 Coy. II/755 Regt., a new unit on the front, this capture was of the utmost importance to the Int. Staff. L/Sjt. Hart not only carried out far more than his normal responsibility, but acted throughout with the greatest courage and coolness, and displayed leadership of the highest order. No praise can be too high for this N.C.O. who, through his personal bravery, initiative and well thought-out plans destroyed a dangerous enemy OP and obtained a most important identification.
Recommended for M.M.   (L.G. 12.4.45)

Hart, Frederick William, Corporal (A/Sgt.)
6467931, 8th Bn. Royal Fusiliers (London, E.3)
(Periodic)
West of Teano on 30th October Sjt. Hart was platoon sergeant of his platoon during the attack. During the advance after crossing the river bed, a German sniper opened up from the bough of a tree in the middle of an open field in the vicinity of a farmhouse. Seeing that casualties were being caused by this sniper, Sjt. Hart advanced regardless of his own safety and when within 20 yards killed the German with his TSMG, thus enabling the advance to continue without a halt. Later this NCO with his Pl Comd stalked and captured a German Mortar team without giving them a chance to open fire.

The a/n NCO was i/c of a Pl during the attack on Pt 819 on the night 2/3 December. On reaching the summit, when under heavy shell and mortar fire, Sjt. Hart took his platoon to the left flank and engaged and silenced M.G. posts which were holding up the advance of the

Bn. Throughout the next five days Sjt. Hart's Pl occupied a vital position on the forward slope and throughout the period were under continual heavy shell and mortar fire. At all times he inspired his men with confidence and his display of leadership and devotion to duty at this critical period resulted in the position being firmly held. His dash and disregard for his own safety was a source of admiration and inspiration to all. Sjt. Hart has fought in every action in which the Bn has been involved since landing at Salerno and has shown great leadership and resolve. *(L.G. 24.8.44)*

Harty, John Jacob, Sergeant
K.37988, 28 Cdn. Armd. Regt. (B.C.R.) (Immediate)
At 1200 hrs., 7 Mar. 45, 'C' Sqn. 28 Cdn. Armd. Regt., with under comd. 'A' Coy. Linc. & Welld. R. and one tp. of Recce tks., was given the task of exploiting the area to the East of Veen, MR 1135 Sheet 17, 1/50,000. The particular objective was the woods at 095337. The entire area was known to be heavily mined. Lt. Carkner and Sgt. Harty, of the recce tp., were given the task of finding a route. This N.C.O. led his recce sec. fwd. to 086344 where they encountered mines across the rd. Disregarding the numerous snipers in the area Sgt. Harty dismounted from his tk. and personally cleared away the mines. The adv. continued and the woods at 095337 was reached successfully. For the first time numerous A. tk. guns started to engage the force. Sgt. Harty deliberately exposed his light tk. to enemy view and was successful in drawing their fire enabling the tk. force following to locate and destroy some of the enemy guns. At 2000 hrs. the force was given the additional task of outflanking Veen. Sgt. Harty immediately volunteered to lead the way. Darkness had fallen and the enemy was thoroughly aroused. They shelled and mortared the oncoming force relentlessly. It often became necessary for Sgt. Harty to dismount and lead the tks. fwd. by hand signals and in spite of the hail of enemy fire he did so unhesitatingly from bound to bound. When the force reached the rd. junc. at 128344 serious cas. and numerous prisoners incl. a senior enemy offr. were reported. Sgt. Harty was detailed to return to 'B' Sqn. of his Regt. and guide up more tks. He loaded his tk. with wounded men and the enemy offr. and returned. Sgt. Harty then unerringly guided 'B' Sqn. fwd. He arrived back with rfts. just as the attack was launched. This N.C.O., in spite of his task being completed, dashed into the attack and arrived on the final objective simultaneously with the leading tk. At this time Lt. Carkner was wounded. Sgt. Harty again took out cas. and carried back vital infm. on the success of the attack to RHQ. He returned again before first light with infm. and armd. vehs. for evacuating the balance of the cas. The initiative of this N.C.O., his unswerving devotion to duty, and his brilliant leadership throughout 24 hrs. of fierce action assisted materially in the eventual taking of the Bde.'s objective, Veen. His coolness under fire and utter disregard for personal safety are in the highest tradition of his regt.

and will long be a source of inspiration and example to his fellow soldiers. *(L.G. 16.6.45)*

Harvey, Leslie Hugh Patrick, Warrant Officer Cl. II (A.Q.M.S.) (A/W.O.I (A.S.M.))
1000027, R.A.O.C., L.A.D. att. 132 Fd. Regt. R.A.
(London, S.E.3)
A.S.M. Harvey's work during the present campaign has been outstanding. During the initial advance he recovered and repaired behicles belnging to eight different units. During the fighting round Medjez-el-bab and Tebourba he and his team worked day and night often being subjected to air and ground attack while recovering behicles of the regiment.

On 1 Dec 42 when the L.A.D. was attacked by German snipers he immediately organized his men into patrols to attack the enemy and himself killed two snipers with a rifle.

No job and no weather had has defeated him. He has frequently undertaken with success repairs which normally require the attention of a fully equipped workshop. The abiliy of the regiment to function and fight for a long period on reduced scales of transport was largely due to his skill and energy. Recommended for the M.B.E.
Recommended for M.B.E. *(L.G. 23.9.43)*

Harwood, Cecil Henry, Lance Sergeant
2619843, 3rd Bn. Grenadier Guards (Pontypool)
(Immediate)
Sheet 1/50,000 76 III, M 1372.

On the night 21/22 Apr. 45, No. 4 Coy., 3rd Bn. Grenadier Guards, was ordered to take part in a Battalion attack to cross the Fossa Cembalina and capture San Bartolomeo in Bosco.

During the crossing of the canal No. 4 Coy. came under heavy fire from enemy snipers and M.G.s sited to cover the crossing place. The Platoon Comd. of the leading platoon of No. 4 Coy. became a casualty and L/Sgt. Harwood assumed command of the platoon. L/Sgt. Harwood led his men forward without hesitation in the face of heavy enemy fire and by his skilful and courageous handling of his platoon succeeded in wiping out two enemy strong-points established in houses on the flanks of his line of advance, and reached the objective allotted to his Company with most commendable speed.

There is no doubt that the courage, determination and skill shown by this young N.C.O. in taking over command of his platoon at a most critical stage of the attack played a most important part in the success of the Battalion attack.

His behaviour under fire has, throughout the campaign and especially during this action, been a source of the greatest inspiration and encouragement to his comrades.
Recommended for M.M. *(L.G. 23.8.45)*

Harwood, Frank Edwin, Warrant Officer Cl. II
(B.S.M.)
1059441, 149 A/Tk Regt., Royal Artillery (Dover)
For gallantry and devotion to duty during operations at
Tobruch, Nov 26 to Dec 8 1941. During the occupation
of Wolf, where the Bty entered the position at the same
time as the infantry, his courage and coolness were
largely instrumental in the capture of one third of the
perimeter.

During the El Duda operation he manned a damaged
gun alone, and with it destroyed three enemy carriers
and throughout the ten days on El Duda his total disregard
of danger, his energy and initiative were of a very high
order.   *(L.G. 24.2.42)*

Haseley, Charles Reginald, Corporal (A/Sgt.)
4034189, 6th Bn. Durham Light Infantry (Dunnington,
Shrops.) (Immediate)
Area El Hamein.

During the Battalion attack on the night 1st/2nd
November when a Gap was formed in the enemy lines,
'D' Company was Right Forward Company of the
Battalion. No. 4034189 Corporal Haseley, C. R. was in
command of No. 3 Section of 16 Platoon and during this
attack and throughout the entire action his dash and
personal leadership were most outstanding. When the
Company came under fire of fixed lines from enemy
M.G.s Cpl. Haseley, with complete disregard for his own
safety moved about among the men of his own platoon,
leading them through and giving them encouragement
by his own personal example.

Two enemy dug in M.13 Tanks which had been
holding up the advance a short while previously were
rapidly engaged and once again Cpl. Haseley lead his
section with great dash, and himself killed the crews of
both tanks. Immediately afterwards Cpl. Haseley gave
chase to a third M.13 Tank. Cpl. Haseley was responsible
for taking many prisoners during the advance and whilst
the Company was consolidating the position gained he
led his section forward searching the ground and bringing
in two more prisoners. His leadership was of the very
highest order.   *(L.G. 28.1.43)*

Hassan, Bazabarimi, W/S Sergeant
GC 13275, 5th Bn. The Gold Coast Regt. R.W.A.F.F.
(Immediate)
Kaladan.

On 15 Jan. 45 near Teinnyo, Burma (Ref. Map 84 H/
2 1924) during operations to clear the foothills Sgt.
Hassan Bazabarimi was Platoon Sergeant of a platoon
sent to reinforce a section patrol, which had occupied an
enemy position on a spur, on which it was intended to
build up a company. On arrival it was found that the
section had been heavily attacked and forced to withdraw.
At the same time the British Sergeant commanding the
platoon was wounded and the 2 i/c of the company, who
was in charge of the operation, was killed. The enemy
were pressing in increasing strength. Sgt. Bazabarimi

took command and organised his platoon to cover the
withdrawal of the section, which had lost both of its
N.C.O.'s and personally led a party which recovered the
body of the 2 i/c and brought in all the wounded under
heavy fire. He then established his platoon on the end of
the spur and held the position against repeated attacks
for two hours, thus allowing the company to build up
behind him.

During the night 15/16 Jan. 45 the position was
shelled and mortared and at dawn, after further mortaring,
the enemy attacked Sgt. Bazabarimi's platoon. The attack
was beaten off with loss.

Later, when the company was withdrawn, Sgt.
Bazabarimi displayed the highest qualities of iniative,
leadership and gallantry and it is entirely due to his
conduct after the death of the 2 i/c that the company was
established on its objective.   *(16.2.45)*

Hassan, Mossaad, Shawish
269, No. 2 Coy. Frontier Bn. (Immediate)
On the night 27th Feb. Shawish Hassan Mossaad was
directed with his platoon onto a strong enemy force
defending a hilltop near Burye. The enemy counter-
attacked with cavalry round the flank of his platoon.
Showing great skill and coolness Shawish Hassan
Mossaad personally handled one of his Bren Guns
dropping numbers of the enemy cavalry at distances of
only ten to twenty yards from his position. His skill and
courage saved a critical situation.

On the evening of the 1st Mar. Shawish Hassan
Mossaad commanded a patrol directed to harass the
enemy positions. He approached to within 50 yds. of the
enemy camp during the supper hour and fired on the
exposed camp inflicting large numbers of casualties on
the enemy.

On the following morning on the 2nd Mar. Shawish
Hassan Mossaad was directed by El Bimb. Harris onto
the assembled rear guard preparing to withdraw from
the Lach position. He opened fire at close range, was
again attacked by the cavalry of the rear guard but
maintaining his position diverted the charge at close
range while himself under heavy fire of enemy machine
guns.

In an attack on the Addis position conducted by El
Bimb. Acland on the 24th Mar. 41 he lead his platoon
with skill and courage through difficult country at night
to within a few yds. from the enemy position. which he
bombed at close range whilst under heavy machine gun
fire and enemy bombing attacks.

Haswell, John Matthew, Sergeant
170103, 4th S.A. Armd. Car Regt. (Immediate)
Sjt. Haswell was troop Sjt. of the H.Q. Troop of C Sqn.
on 1 Dec., during a raid on the enemy line of communications in the Gazala Aerodrome District. This troop
came suddenly on a well prepared enemy position which
it engaged. The enemy opened fire with M.G.s and two
A/Tk. guns and a mortar, and the troop leader gave the

order to withdraw. In the act of turning, one of the cars was knocked out by an A/Tk. gun. M.G.s and a mortar concentrated on it. Sjt. Haswell turned his car round again, went back to the disabled car and entered it under a hail of fire. He transferred the only one of the crew still alive to his own car and although his car was repeatedly hit, he managed to rejoin his troop leader.

(L.G. 20.1.42)

Hatton, Charles, M.M., Sergeant

3390354, 1st Bn. East Lancashire Regt. (Wilmslow)

On 29th Mar. 1945 Sgt. Hatton was acting as Company Sergeant Major when his company carried out a night attack to secure a road and rail junction South-West of Bocholt at approximate map reference 214585. the enemy were known to be holding the position in some strength and the Company Commander had moved forward with a fighting patrol to make a reconnaissance of the area, prior to committing the company to battle. While the Company Commander was away, three enemy A.F.V.'s came suddenly out of a wood on the left flank and subjected the company to heavy machine gun fire at very short range. Sgt. Hatton immediately assumed command of the Company and after dispersing the platoons, he seized a Piat and, completely regardless of his own safety, worked round the flank of the tanks, quite alone, until he was able to site the weapon. Then, at almost point blank range he destroyed a Mk. IV tank with his first shot. The tank was completely burnt out four of the crew were killed inside and the fifth man who jumped out and tried to escape was shot dead by Sgt. Hatton whilst he was running away.

Later that evening, Sgt. Hatton followed up this first action by a further stalk with a Piat against an S.P. gun. This again necessitated crossing open ground under direct enemy fire.

This N.C.O. is an exceptionally cool and courageous leader. He remains calm and resourceful in the worst possible conditions and is always to be found where the fighting is thickest. He is an inspiration in battle to all who come in contact with him. *(L.G. 21.6.45)*

Hausa, Sidi, Sergeant

GC.13781, 1 Gold Coast Regt., Royal West African Frontier Forces (Immediate)

On 13th March 1945, Sjt. Sidi Hausa was in command of a patrol of ten men sent forward to cover the 'digging in' of 'C' Coy. 1 G.C.R. at Kamaunttaw on hill feature 030152.

While the position was only half dug, the enemy, some 20 strong, attacked from the North of the hill, sp. by intense M.M.G., L.M.G. and 3″ mortar fire.

Sjt. Sidi Hausa's position was exposed in the open, the only cover available being some tall trees, somewhat widely spaced. The attack was sp. from the front by fire from the automatic weapons mentioned, while the enemy attempted to envelope the patrol by approaching from each side of the hill.

Sjt. Sidi Hausa appreciating the situation and, ordering his Bren gunner to engage the enemy automatic weapons ordered five men to one side of the hill and five to the other. Then, standing up directed their efforts encouraging them and warning them of the impending approach of any target.

In this way cas. amounting to three killed and an estimated number of five wounded were inflicted on the enemy and they withdrew.

In the meanwhile the Bren gunner had been wounded, and the Bren gun damaged by a direct hit.

After a pause, the enemy moved one L.M.G. so as to give flanking fire and, led by an Officer, attempted to rush the position along the top of the hill. Sjt. Sidi Hausa, although completely exposed to the enemy fire, engaged the enemy as they rushed killing the officer and one other, and wounding four others. When the enemy came closer he threw grenades at them and drove them back.

As the enemy retreated Sjt. Sidi Hausa called upon his men to follow him and led a charge which completed the discomfort of the enemy and drove them off the hill.

This fine N.C.O.'s devotion to duty, courage, example and skill with his weapon, not only inspired his men to supreme efforts under most difficult conditions, but also inflicted heavy cas. upon the enemy, enabled valuable identifications to be obtained and enabled 'C' Coy. to dig in adequately before it became dark.

This experienced and cheerful N.C.O. is a constant example to his troops, his courage and loyalty and devotion to duty outstanding and his skill and determination a model for every soldier.

Recommended for M.M. *(L.G. 20.9.45)*

Hausmann, Fritz Sigmund, Lance Corporal

Pal/1344, R.A.S.C. (attd. S.S.T., No. 2 Commando)
(Immediate)

Island of Brac (Dalmatia) 5th March 1944. Island of Solta (Dalmatia) 19th March 1944.

In the Commando raid on Brac Island on the night of 5th March 1944 Dvr Hausmann was the leading scout of the section which carried out this raid. The section was seen approaching and two sentries opened fire with schmeiser automatics which pinned them to the ground. Dvr Hausmann dashed forward firing his TSMG and killed one sentry, but the other ran into a house. Hausmann followed, kicked open the door and threw in a hand grenade. When it had exploded he dashed in shouting to the Germans to surrender, and having killed one and wounded two more, the remaining five men gave themselves up.

On the morning of 10th March 1944 during the Commando attack on Solta Island the behaviour of this man was exemplary. In the forefront of the final assault on the village, he led a small group of men in house-clearing in an area where the German garrison was holding out, and during this operation severely wounded a German who was holding up the advance with a spandau machine-gun which was mounted in an upper window.

Dvr Hausmann is a Palestinian of German origin serving in the Commando. He has taken part in three Commando raids in these islands during the last six weeks, and in each of these his behaviour has been outstandingly bold and aggressive. He insists on being the leading scout on all approaches by day or night and is not content to await his turn for this duty. He has set a magnificent example and his conduct under fire is in the highest traditions of the Army.   *(L.G. 20.7.44)*

Haverson, Arthur Frederick, Gunner
*886387, 3 Royal Horse Artillery (120, Birchington
    Ave., Grangetown, Middlesbrough) (Immediate)*
On 21st Nov 1941 Gnr. Haversom was one of the attachment of 'J' Bty RHA near Sidi Rezegh aerodrome. His Tp was attacked by 60 enemy tanks and the remainder of the detachment were killed or wounded. Although he was under very heavy shell and machine gun fire he helped the wounded back to safety and returning to his gun manned it with his Tp Comd and Bty Comd. When his Tp Comd had been killed he brought up ammn under heavy fire and continued to man his gun until it received a direct hit and was on fire and out of action. Throughout this engagement he behaved with the very greatest bravery and courage.
                                        (L.G. 20.1.42)

Haverson, Walter Edward, Warrant Officer Cl. II
    (C.S.M.)
5766134, Royal Norfolk Regt.
No citation.   *(L.G. 22.10.40)*

Hawkins, James Hazel, Lance Corporal
553203, 3 Hussars, Royal Armoured Corps
On 11th December 1940, the tank in which this N.C.O. was travelling became bogged and was knocked out be enemy gunfire from a range of approximately 400 yards. After managing to escape from his tank this N.C.O., in spite of being under very heavy enemy fire, assisted his wounded comrades from the disabled tank. He then assisted the Medical Officer in carrying wounded back to a more covered position. He continued assisting the Medical Officer in dressing and attending wounded men, being the whole time under heavy fire from artillery and machine guns.

His gallantry is worthy of the highest praise and was the means of saving many lives.   *(L.G. 25.4.41)*

Hawkins, John, Lance Corporal
*22547183, Royal Engineers, attd. 22 Special Air
    Service Regt.*
Aqqbat Al Dhafar, Oman, 2 Dec 58 and night 27/28
Dec 58
The area of the Aqqbat at a height of just under 8,000 feet above sea level had been seized two days before by the troop of which Sjt. Hawkins was troop sergeant. Sjt.

Hawkins was in charge of an OP party of five soldiers protecting the main position. About 5 pm a group of 40 rebels with two LMGs attacked his position. The rebels were well led and used orthodox fire and movement tactics extremely skillfully. From the outset this NCO kept a firm grip on the situation and witheld fire until the enemy was 100–150 yards away. During the enemy advance bren fire had been brought down on the OP party but this was not answered until the whole group of rebels had exposed themselves out of dead ground. Very effective and accurate fire was then opened by the one bren and five FNs. 5 rebels were believed killed although rebel sources later reported that 9 had died. The remainder of the rebels then withdrew carrying their dead and wounded but keeping up sporadic bren and rifle fire. The personal example and coolness displayed by this NCO contributed greatly to the moral ascendancy of the SAS troop over the rebels in this area.

On the night of 27/28 Dec Sjt. Hawkins was again a member of a raiding party which penetrated the main rebel position 3,000 yards in front of our own FDLs. When the patrol was discovered rebel picquets commenced accurate fire from above at very close range. This NCO with little regard for his own safety stood up and threw grenade into the rebel positions causing the fire to slacken at once and finally cease.

Sjt. Hawkins has continually exposed himself to great danger and his leadership and determination has been an inspiration to all under his command.

Hayden, George William, Lance Sergeant
*5441409, 2/6th Bn. Queen's Royal Regt. (Derby)
    (Periodic)*
L/Sgt. Hayden has fought in every action with this Bn. from Salerno to the Senio. Throughout this long period his conduct in action has been marked by utter fearlessness and extreme aggressiveness.

As examples of his gallant and aggressive conduct. On one occasion in the mountains across R. Garigliano he rescued a wounded comrade pinned by enemy M.G. fire by personally smoking the enemy and carrying the man back under heavy fire. He also repeatedly went skirmishing single handed and several times killed the enemy. On another occasion at Anzio he was responsible for the maintenance of a vital position in an isolated platoon locality, personally holding the platoon strong point with a Bren gun during a Paratrooper raid.

During the Gothic Line battle, L/Sgt. Hayden again kept his tired men together by his personal example. On several occasions during the R. Lamone and Senio fighting, while a Bn. Sniper, he inspired the other snipers to greater feats of daring by his own example and his efforts led to much success.

This N.C.O.'s gallantry, aggressiveness and leadership have been of an outstanding order and have inspired those under him in most difficult conditions.
                                        (L.G. 20.9.45)

Haydon, Ernest George, Corporal
2071189, Royal Engineers, TA
No citation. *(L.G. 20.8.40)*

Hayes, Charles William, Private (A/Cpl.)
6009204, Essex Regt. (Chelmsford)
On night 29 Nov when the forward Coys were over-run by enemy tanks and infantry, and posts of various arms adjacent to that of Cpl. Hayes' started to withdraw, Cpl. Hayes held firm to his own position, and under heavy fire from enemy tanks at a range of about 400 yds in the failing light, got out of his post and rallied men of the other Coys who were starting to withdraw. He took charge of the stragglers of the other sub-units, and organised the whole into a party capable of dealing with any further enemy advance. Cpl. Hayes at the time was commanding a platoon which was somewhat detached from the rest of his Coy. Cpl. Hayes by his disregard of danger and quick grasp of the situation, held together that portion of the Coy, and definitely contributed to the successful defence of the position. *(L.G. 24.2.42)*

Hayward, William Joseph, Lance Sergeant
2035008, 225 Field Coy., Royal Engineers
    (Birmingham)
On the night 25/26 Apr 1943 during the attack by 12 Inf Bde on localities in the area of Peters Corner L/Sjt. Hayward was with a party engaged in clearing bridges across Oued Hamar of booby traps and demolition charges. Four sappers were killed when a demolition charge on one bridge was set off through some unknown cause, and the Section officer and one more sapper were wounded by a booby trap on the bridge where L/Sjt. Hayward was working. He took charge and although subjected to Mortar and M.G. fire carried on for 3 hours, partly in darkness, the task of clearing the bridge, including the heavily booby-trapped main demolition charge. His coolness and skill were largely instrumental in the bridge being cleared to enable the Inf supporting weapons to be got forward. *(L.G. 8.7.43)*

Hazle, Edmund Bryant, Private
6016667, 1/4th Essex Regt. (Westcliff) (Immediate)
At El Alamein
    On the 23rd July after an attack by 161 Bde. Pte. Hazle went forward to attend a wounded Indian soldier lying a few hundred yards from, and in full view of a snipers' post. In so doing Pte. Hazle was shot in the face and shoulder. This was the fourth man that he had hurried to attend to in this position. He knew full well the dangers of going forward but never hesitated, and his courage was an inspiration to all. Over a period of weeks this Stretcher Bearer has shown devotion to duty of the very highest order. On numerous occasions he has dressed the wounds of, and carried men from forward positions under heavy shell fire. At no time has he allowed the heaviest enemy fire to interfere with the immediate

execution of his duty, always with complete disregard for his own personal safety. *(L.G. 24.9.42)*

Hazle, Edmund Bryant, D.C.M., Lance Corporal
                                                            Bar
6016667, 1/4 Bn. Essex Regt. (Westcliff) (Immediate)
This NCO displayed most conspicuous bravery, devotion and initiative during the fighting at Cassino 19–24 Mar 44. As stretcher bearers, he and another soldier (L/Cpl. Piper) were with a company of their battalion which joined up with 1/9 G.R. on Pt. 435 (Hangman's Hill), on the morning of 19 Mar. At this time 1/9 G.R. had no medical personnel with it, and had a large number of wounded whom it had not been possible to evacuate owing to continued enemy opposition.
    L/Cpl. Hazle immediately took charge of the medical situation, and with the slender resources at his disposal (a first aid haversack) treated the wounded of both units. In very difficult conditions, to which was added a shortage of food and water; and under constant artillery and mortar bombardment; this NCO worked devotedly and tirelessly for six days, and there is no doubt that the very large number of wounded which were evetually successfully evacuated owe their lives to him.
    He arranged the collection of wounded, often exposing himself fearlessly to do so; treated them, at one time even performing an amputation; and improvised covering out of parachutes from the air dropping then being practised.
    Though at one time himself overcome by fumes from smoke shells he refused to stop his devoted work, and continued attending alike to British, Indian and Gurkha wounded.
    The magnificent service rendered by this NCO under the most grim and dangerous conditions; the medical skill he displayed; and his never faltering devotion, bravery and spirit have earned the universal admiration of the whole of the force which was isolated in this position. *(L.G. 3.8.44)*

Head, Richard Samuel, Sergeant
813847, 153 HAA Bty, 51 (Ldn) HAA Regt, Royal
    Artillery (S. Shields)
On 27 Apr 41 Sjt. Head was one of a team manning a mobile 20mm Breda gun mounted on a lorry for the protection of 3.7″ gun position North of Tobruch Harbour entrance. During a divebombing attack two bombs fell near the lorry, splinters piercing the armour plating round the gun, killing the NCO firing the gun and wounding Sjt. Head in several places. Sjt. Head lifted the dead NCO from the seat of the gun and whilst endeavouring to continue fire himself, noticed that the ammunition on the ground alongside was on fire. He attempted to drive the vehicle away but finding the controls shot away and the engine smashed, organised a party to extinguish the fire, himself setting an example by carrying boxes of ammunition from the then exploding pile. Only when the situation was under control did this NCO seek

medical aid, by which time physical exertion had weakened him considerably.

Sjt. Head's devotion to duty is an example of his character during his service, both before the war and during the campaigns in Norway and the Middle East. His gallantry, loyalty and leadership is deserving of high praise.   (*L.G. 19.8.41*)

Headon, Thomas, Sergeant (actg.)
2717158, Irish Guards (Leeds)
No citation.   (*L.G. 13.9.45*)

Hearnden, John Thomas, Corporal
1666664, Royal Engineers
No citation.   (*L.G. 29.11.40*)

Heath, George, Sergeant
6285981, Buffs (Royal East Kent Regt.) (Wapping, London) (Immediate)
Before Keren, Eritrea.

On the night of 4/5 March 1941, three Officers and 35 other ranks were given the difficult task of scaling a very steep gully running south from the heights of Beit Gabru. Their instructions were to harass the enemy position at the top where ever possible.

At 22.30 hours they bumped into an enemy post, which incidently happened to be wired and having got through the wire, succeeded in killing all the occupants of the enemy position. They straight way moved on and took up a position on top of the high ground awaiting daylight hoping then to see, what their next best move should be. As daylight broke, they were engaged by Breda, mortar and rifle fire at close range. It was evident that a considerable force of the enemy were endeavouring to surround them. At this period two men were badly wounded. The officer, realising that they were a not strong enough force to hold their position, gave orders for a withdrawal. He, Sjt. Heath and one other officer remained behind to cover the withdrawal with their Tommy Guns. The distance to the edge of the ridge where troops could take cover from fire was a matter of approximately 60 to 70 yards. This vantage point having been gained, the covering party started to withdraw themselves. After retreating some 30 yards, they came across one of the wounded man previously mentioned. His legs appeared to be paralysed.

Sjt. Heath again gave covering fire while the two officer's endeavoured to drag the wounded man to cover. They had gone but a few yards, when the officer Commanding the party was hit in the foot, At the same time, the wounded man receiving another bullet which killed him. Both men then proceeded to assist the wounded officer and again before the safety margin could be reached the O.C. party, received a second wound which laid him low, and the other officer was hit in the foot. Sjt. Heath received a graze on his left arm and stopped him from getting a wound in his hip. The Office Commanding the party's last words, were orders to leave him and for them to get away as best as they could. Sjt. Heath again gave covering fire with his Tommy-Gun. At this period, his Tommy-Gun jammed, and he managed to make the falling ground without further incident. At the same time helping back the officer hit in the foot. Sjt. Heath was the only British N.C.O. in the party. The exemplary nature of the way Sjt. Heath behaved was remarked on from all sides.

Since that date, he has continued to work with untiring energy in spite of the fact that he has had to attend sick parade daily, and has refused to be sent down on the sick list. His command has since been taken over by another officer. Both on the 15th March and 21st March 41, it attacked enemy positions advancing over very difficult and exposed ground. On both of these occasions, Sjt. Heath by his coolness determination and initiative helped very largely in these positions being gained by our troops.   (*L.G. 18.7.41*)

Hedderman, John William, M.M., Sergeant
VX.13728, 2/6 Australian Inf. Bn. (Immediate)
On 28 Mar. 45, Sgt. Hedderman conducted a recce patrol through enemy occupied territory, located and pin pointed their positions at Kilkuil and Gwanginan in the Maprik area and, on 29 Mar. 45, successfully led a fighting patrol in a carefully planned surprise attack which captured Kilkuil.

On 30 Mar. 45, as Platoon Sjt. of 16 Platoon, he assisted in the attack on Gwanginan, where he displayed cool leadership and outstanding courage.

During the early part of the attack he caused great confusion to the enemy by calling out to imaginary pls. to the left and right and in doing so, drew fire on himself.

When the leading sec. was pinned down, he quickly brought sp fire from mortar 2-in. and E.Y. rifle to bear on enemy positions, thus enabling the sec. to again move fwd.

Later when Pte. Anderson B.W.B., a member of the Platoon was seriously wounded, Sgt. Hedderman crawled fwd. under enemy L.M.G. fire to within 10 yds. of the enemy fox holes, killed two enemy with grenades and dragged and carried Pte. Anderson to safety.

In so doing he completely disregarded his own safety to save a comrade from what appeared to be certain death. While crawling fwd., his clothing was twice pierced by enemy bullets.

On placing Pte. Anderson under cover, he then continued to assist in the attack.

When the sec. comd. of the left sec. was killed, Sgt. Hedderman took over comd. and directed covering fire to enable the other two secs. to withdraw.

He then remained in position and continued firing on the enemy until every member of the platoon had been withdrawn to reorganise.   (*L.G. 5.7.45*)

Hedley, Frederick Edward, Sergeant
6853483, King's Royal Rifle Corps (attd. 1st Bn.
Nigeria Regt., Royal West African Frontier Force)
(London, N.15) (Immediate)
Arakan.

On 5 Mar. 45, Sjt. Hedley was commanding a platoon in a Company which had been ordered to cross an unfordable tidal chaung. The coy. reached its objective and Sjt. Hedley was ordered to take his platoon to a feature some 800 yds. distant from the rest of the coy. The enemy later infiltrated between the coy. position and the chaung and that evening attacked the coy. in force and overran it. Sjt. Hedley at nightfall was unaware of this.

During the night 5/6 Mar., this N.C.O.'s platoon was recced and jittered by the enemy who at 0510 hrs. on 6 Mar. made a determined attack. This attack was beaten off, four enemy dead were left on the edge of the perimeter, two others a short distance away and without doubt many more in the surrounding jungle as the sound of bodies being dragged away was clearly heard. At 0710 hrs. a fresh attack by a reinforced enemy was delivered and pressed with determination for 2½ hrs. before it was finally repulsed. After these attacks the platoon had captured one British L.M.G., five enemy rifles, much S.A.A. and again inflicted many casualties. At 1025 hrs. the enemy resumed his jittering tactics, using S.A.A. and Mortar fire, and succeeded in destroying a Bren gun with a direct hit. At noon another determined attack was made by the enemy who put in their bayonet charge with grenades, S.A. fire and savage yells, but Sjt. Hedley so encouraged his platoon that after half an hour the enemy decided to drag away their dead and give up the attack for the time. The afternoon was spent in relative quiet except for sniping and jittering until a fresh attack in strength was made at 1900 hrs. The devoted platoon repulsed this also but the enemy succeeded in emplacing two L.M.G.'s under cover from which they were able to rake the position and harass the defenders. At 1930 hrs. three flares were thrown into the position but were quickly extinguished by the troops.

The night 6/7 Mar. was quiet to begin with, but at 0100 hrs. jitter parties began in earnest and continued to probe the position until 0740 hrs. when the enemy mortared the defenders and followed up with another grenade and bayonet charge supported by the two L.M.G.'s they had successfully emplaced earlier on. A confused and furious fight took place at the end of which the enemy were again thrown back and retired to the jungle to lick their wounds, tend their casualties and drag away their dead. By 1245 hrs. 7 Mar., as no further attacks had been made Sjt. Hedley decided to disengage his platoon which he did with consumate skill and succeeded in eluding the Japanese until he neared the chaung when they again came under fire. Handling his men with great coolness he kept the enemy at bay until they reached the chaung when by good fortune he fell in with a patrol from his own unit who gave him the necessary covering fire while he got his men across. During all this period the men had no sleep, little food and no water other than that in their water bottles. Two men were drowned due to sheer exhaustion during the final crossing.

That this platoon was not destroyed was entirely due to Sjt. Hedley's cool courage and calm leadership. His great personal gallantry and encouragement of his men fired them with his own determination so that they eventually withdrew in good order and masters of their battlefield. This successful action, and the gallantry displayed, ranks equal with the highest annals of the war against Japan. *(L.G. 2.8.45)*

Hefferland, Thomas Reilly, Lance Corporal
2993345, 8th Bn. Argyll & Sutherland Highlanders
(Glasgow) (Immediate)
On the night of 25 January 1944, at Palombaro, L/Cpl. Hefferland commanded the leading section of a fighting patrol which made contact with a large party of the enemy in the area of Pt. 562. During the subsequent action L/Cpl. Hefferland received five bullet wounds in his right arm and one in his leg. In spite of his wounds and, in fact without informing his patrol commander he continued to direct the fire of his section. When the patrol eventually withdrew, L/Cpl. Hefferland and his section covered the withdrawal, and he personally covered his section out by firing his Tommy gun with his left hand. When he withdrew his section one man was missing, he then crawled back through heavy enemy fire and found that Pte. Smith had been killed.

It was largely due to L/Cpl. Hefferland's alertness and control that this large enemy patrol was surprised, and eleven Germans killed with the loss of only one man to his section. *(L.G. 4.5.44)*

Heka, Tepene, Private
67620, 28 N.Z. (Maori) Bn. (Immediate)
Pte. Heka was a member of A Coy detailed to attack and take an objective to the right of Takrouna village on night 19/20 Apr 43. Under heavy enemy shelling, A Tk, mortar and MG fire the Coy had to go to ground. Entirely regardless of his own personal safety Pte. Heka dashed from cover and attacked an A Tk post single-handed, killed the leader of the post while other members of the gun crew quickly surrendered. Then he attacked three MG posts and succeeded in putting these out of action and taking fourteen prisoners in all. By his aggressiveness, initiative and courage our troops were able to continue their advance. *(L.G. 22.7.43)*

Helliwell, Fred, Lance Sergeant
2719057, 3rd Bn. Irish Guards (London, E.5)
(Immediate)
On the night of 10 Sep. 44, L/Sgt. Helliwell was commanding the leading sec. of a platoon detailed to capture the De Groote Barrier over the Meuse—Escaut Canal, in co-operation with a tp. of tks. This N.C.O. led

his sec. with a magnificent dash across this br. which was swept with three 88mm A.Tk. guns and Spandaus, the br. itself having been prepared by the enemy for demolition. He, himself, was wounded during the assault but did not allow this to interfere with the execution of his duty to establish a firing point to secure the br. against a German counter-attack.

This N.C.O.'s great bravery and the splendid example he set to the men under his comd. cannot be spoken of too highly.   *(L.G. 1.3.45)*

Helmbright, Leonard, Private
811123, 28 N.Z. (Maori) Bn. (Immediate)
This soldier showed outstanding courage and resourcefulness during an attack on 24 Jul 44. When his section Commander was wounded Pte. Helmbright took command of the section and attacked three enemy machine gun posts. With an L.M.G. he went forward under heavy machine gun fire directed at him and wiped out single handed two of the three machine gun posts. It was this gallant deed that enabled his platoon to move forward.

Through this and subsequent actions Pte. Helmbright showed devotion to duty, courage and determination of the very highest order.   *(L.G. 10.5.45)*

Hemsted, John William, Corporal
28325, 1 Rand Light Inf.
Attack on Bardia—31 Dec 41.

This N.C.O. displayed great bravery and magnificent leadership throughout the attack on Bardia. His Pl was allotted the task of taking a strong point on the right of a gap in the outside fence. Cpl. Hemsted immediately volunteered for this duty. On the morning of the 31 December 41 he suppressed fire from this strong point and engaged it at daylight, when it surrendered, his sec capturing an offr and 26 O/Rs. During the period, the section was under heavy fire, and due to splendid leadership, stuck to their task unil it was achieved. Throughout the subsequent action, this Cpl's leadership was of the finest order.   *(L.G. 3.3.42)*

Hemstock, Norman, Trooper
7927199, 7th Queen's Own Hussars (Newark Notts.)
Throughout the operations in Burma this soldier has shown on several occasions, quite outstanding courage, coolness and devotion to duty with a complete disregard for his own safety.

At Paungde on 29 Mar 42 when the leading tank of his troop was hit and stopped, Tpr Hemstock, under heavy MG and mortar fire, dismounted from his tank and secured a tow rope to the damaged tank, thus enabling it to be towed to safety and subsequently recovered. At Shwedaung on 30 Mar 42 Tpr Hemstock saw from his tank a wounded infantry soldier lying in a clearing of the road. The wounded man's comrades told Tpr Hemstock that, owing to the heavy MG and mortar fire, they were unable to effect a rescue. In spite of this

Tpr Hemstock dismounted from his tank, ran 200 yds under heavy fire to the wounded man and carried him back, thus undoubtedly saving the man's life.

At Meiktila on 26 Apr 42 Tpr Hemstock's tank became cut off from the remainder of the troop and put out of action by gun fire. The troop leader was severely wounded. Tpr. Hemstock took charge and showing great coolness and presence of mind, destroyed the tank, and under cover of darkness, helped to carry the wounded officer to safety. This entailed a march of some 22 miles in the dark across unknown country and through several enemy pickets.

I cannot write too highly of the quite outstanding courage, resourcefulness and extreme devotion to duty shown by this soldier throughout the operations. He has done a great deal more than his normal duty and his conduct has been a magnificent example to all his comrades.   *(L.G. 28.10.42)*

Henderson, Eric Albert, Driver
46421, N.Z.A.S.C. attd. 6 N.Z. Fd. Amb. (Immediate)
This soldier was the driver of an ambulance car during the night 23/24th October and during the subsequent operations. He drove his car up the Brigade routes under heavy fire and collected wounded in the early stages of the attack and subsequently was one of the first vehicles through the gap in the mine-fields. During the first and subsequent nights he passed many times up and down these tracks where many vehicles were being destroyed by mines and his vehicle was often the only one moving in the forward areas, and under heavy fire. He used his knowledge thus gained to guide up other ambulance cars later and was thus instrumental in saving many lives.

This driver has at all times shown the greatest courage, and ability to evacuate casualties under conditions of great danger and technical difficulty. His unfailing willingness and cheerful demeanour in the face of danger was an inspiration to those engaged on similar work and to wounded under his care.   *(L.G. 28.1.43)*

Henderson, Robert, Sergeant
825210, Royal Artillery (Glasgow, S.W.1)
No citation.   *(L.G. 11.4.46)*

Henley, James Cyril, Staff Sergeant
7095, 4 (N.Z.) Field Ambulance
This NCO while under fire showed great coolness and courage at Nbeidat (Ref:[...] 441 403). On the afternoon of Nov 30th 1941, the Field Ambulance dressing station came under continuous shell fire over a period of several hours during which both patients and orderlies were killed and wounded. S/Sjt. Henley displayed a complete disregard for his personal safety during this period and continued his task of organising the reception and evacuation of patients from the theatre. He materially assisted in the case of the injured, and by his personal example encouraged confidence in his men.

A particularly high standard of work was maintained throughout the whole operations by this NCO who inspired everyone with whom he came into contact with his own contempt for danger.   *(L.G. 9.9.42)*

Herbert, Roy George, M.M., Lance Sergeant
3384201, Northamptonshire Regt., No. 3 Commando (Largs, Ayrshire)
During the operations at Vaagsö in South Norway on 27th December 1941, L/Sgt Herbert saw one of the enemy run into a dug-out. He placed his men to cover the entrance and followed the man in alone. He found the German Battery Commander. inside with some fifteen of his men whom he captured.

Later he personally bombed the enemy out of the front room of a warehouse, enabling his men to get forward without casualties. Throughout the operation he showed great determination, initiative, organising ability and powers if leadership. His personal gallantry and drive set an inspiring example to those under him.
                    (L.G. 3.4.42)

Herbst, William John, Corporal
53108, 3 S.A. Armd. C. Recce Bn. (Immediate)
On 13 Apl 42 T/Cpl. Herbst, W. J. was in command of an Armd C with a coln which was attacked by at least 15 Tanks at U8588 (ref map Ain El-Gazala). He noticed his Sec comd's Armd C moving forward under intense tank, arty and M.G. fire to pick up some infantry running in front of the advancing tanks. He moved forward to within a few hundred yards of the enemy tanks when he noticed the Sec comd's car had broken down and went to render assisance, at the same time covering both cars with protective fire from a gun mounted in his own car. He picked up two wounded infantry men and withdrew. He again went forward to pick up more of the infantry men. This N.C.O.'s action in the face of the enemy showed marked courage and devotion to duty and was instrumental in the rescue of two of his comrades.
                    (L.G. 9.7.42)

Herchenratter, August Paul Herman, Sergeant
A59661, Highland Light Infantry of Canada (Immediate)
In the attack on Buron on 8 Jul. 44, Sgt. Herchenratter was acting as Platoon Comd. of 18 platoon 'D' Coy., The Highland Light Infantry of Canada. He led his platoon in an attack on German positions in the A. Tk. ditch which cut the Vieux Cairon—Buron road. He went from trench to trench and himself wiped out one of the four M.G. posts his platoon took, when he advanced upon it alone and threw grenades into it.

From the A. Tk. ditch to the final objective in the orchard on the West side of the village he led his men through heavy mortar fire. Every time they went to ground he jumped up and dashed ahead shouting to his men to advance. He quickly organized the remnants of his platoon and set out to clear the stoutly defended orchard, wiping out most of the enemy, of platoon strength, with approximately a section of men.

On the objective he took command of the remnants of two platoons (19 men) as all the officers and other N.C.O.'s had been killed or wounded and organized the defence. So well did he do this, that a strong counter-attack was driven off. Sgt. Herchenratter's courageous fight against great odds was an inspiration to all his men and enabled his company to capture and hold the objective.   *(L.G. 4.11.44)*

Herring, David Warren, Signalman
2328065, Royal Signals, attd. 51 Highland Div. Sigs.
                    Before Capture.
Was a wireless operator in charge of wireless set in the neighbourhood of Neufchatel for 3 days. Had orders to get to the coast. On arriving at destination had orders to proceed to Viconte to establish wireless constructions from the Block watch to Divisional H.Q. This was on 10th June. At Ourville were stopped by German tanks which were in action for 7 hours. On the night of the 10th at 6.30 were surrounded and taken prisoner.
                    Capture.
The same night they slept in Ourville where they had been taken to a shed and guarded by sentries with automatic rifles. They were told to declare what they had, and were stripped, and had to give up everything. There were a large party of prisoners, mostly French.
                    Escape (1).
The next day I escaped during the journey to Rouen while marching in columns of approximately 150 down a narrow road. A lorry passed, and I broke away from the column and hid in the ditch near the road. I was by myself. After the passing of the column I proceeded to a farm I could see and was given clothing and food by the people there. This was the Mayor of Ourville, who also told me where he thought the Germans were and the best route to take. At dusk I left the farm and proceeded to St. Valery. On arriving at some cross roads in the dark I saw two people and, on asking them the way, found out they were German soldiers. They were asking for St. Valery and showed me a map where the Germans were advancing on St. Valery. This made me change my route, and I took note from the map and proceeded to Fecamp. The Germans told me it was not possible to get into St. Valery as it was surrounded by troops. This was on the evening of 11th June.

I carried on, passing Cany, which was almost demolished. At daybreak I arrived at Fecamp on 12th June. There were a number of fishing boats about, and I attempted to escape, but I was fired on by guns on the cliffs. I came back to shore and was picked up by Germans on motor-cycles. I was still in the civilian clothes I had been given by the farmer, and the Germans did not know I was an English soldier.
                    Recapture.
I was taken to a concentration camp in Fecamp, where I met troops who were captured the day before. We were

taken from Fecamp to Rouen, and there I met men of my own Company who were taken the same morning at St. Valery. They told me that nearly all my division had been captured or killed.

I immediately made plans to escape with a comrade. On the 15th June, during the march north, I and my comrade (Redman) did attempt to escape. I left Redman in a cornfield however, and he returned to the column, which consisted of roughly 2,000 French troops and 600 British troops. The French troops did not look as if they had done any fighting and had British blankets and gasmasks, and our troops had only what they stood up in.

Escape (2).

After I got away I turned south and passed Bois Guillaume. When I arrived at Rouen again I swam the Seine, and rested the night at a farm, obtaining clothes and food and necessities for the journey. On the road from Rouen, on the 16th June, I stole a bicycle and cycled past Elbeuf, Louviers and Evreux and 10 kms. past Evreux I stopped the night. The next day, 17th June, I proceeded to Paris, but on the way heard that the Germans were in Paris, so turned off towards Dreux. From Dreux I proceeded to Chartres and stopped the night at Dreux, arriving at Chartres on the morning of 19th June. I saw a German dispatch rider who was lost and who, mistaking me for a Frenchman asked me the direction, but not knowing much French I could not answer him. He then became suspicious and stopped a lorry and sent me back to Chartres.

Recapture.

At Chartres I was interrogated. The Germans told me that they were going to bomb London and Manchester, and I told them that the German soldiers were only fit to bomb civilians and that that was the way they had taken France. A German soldier lost his temper and threatened me but did not abuse me. That same night (19th June) I was taken to Evreux to a concentration camp, where I met men of the Glasgow Highlanders. The camp was in a field surrounded by barbed wire, and there was no shelter. The food was peas and beans which we got at 6 a.m. and 9 p.m. In this camp was Driver George Prince. I was here for two days. From this camp we went to Rouen and on the 24th left for Cambrai by train.

Escape (3).

On the journey the train slowed down, and I slipped out of the doors which were open, and got onto the buffer of the last truck and dived into the ditch at the side of the railway. This was about 50 kms from Abbeville. I got away and proceeded towards Abbeville, which I passed on the 30th June, and which was almost demolished. There were only a few German troops about.

Recapture.

On the evening of the 1st July I was again captured at La Hordle.

Escape (4).

I again attempted to escape by boat, which I found 50 yards from the German Guard room, but as there was an in-shore wind I could not get round the headland. (The Germans did not see me go out). I was fired on by a German sentry, and lost an oar, and when I drifted back to shore again the Germans took me prisoner.

Recapture.

They took me back to the guard room and gave me a good meal, and I slept with two German soldiers. The next day, the 2nd July, I was taken to a village along the coast where I met two other men from the Seaforth Highlanders, a Lance Corporal and a Private, who had escaped and been recaptured. After two days I was taken in the company of 3 Frenchmen and 6 British (one was L/Cpl. Dixon of the Artillery) to Rouen, where I met 20 British soldiers who had been discharged from Hospital in Rouen. On the 7th July we left Rouen for Cambrai by train. We were there for 3 days, and here L/Cpl. Dixon left to work on the railway. We were shut up in the Barracks, and guarded by sentries. We slept in the cellars which we first cleaned out. On the 11th July we left Cambrai for Tournai by lorry. We spent the night at Tournai and then proceeded towards Germany in the lorry, when I escaped from the lorry.

Escape (5).

The lorry at the rear, which was guarding us, dropped behind, and as our lorry turned the bend I jumped off into the ditch. There were about 20 in the lorry and my escape was not noticed.

I spent the night outside Tournai in a shed, and the next day, the 12th July, I proceeded to Courtrai and again stole a bicycle. I passed Ypres and arrived at La Panne on the 13th July. Here I could not find a boat available so returned inland, looking for work, and posed as a Pole to the Belgians. The man I spoke to spoke Polish, so I had to admit my nationality. He gave me a night's lodging and food and the next day (14th July) gave me 250 frs. and a map, showing the frontier between occupied and unoccupied territory. This man, who would not give his name, was the owner of a farm and Chateau about 4 kms. east of La Panne. He also helped me to pass the Belgian–French frontier at a place where it was not guarded. This place was only 3 kms. from his home and 3 kms. west of Andschoote.

I proceeded on my way passing Cassel, St. Pol and Amiens, travelling by day on a bicycle, I reached Beauvais and Paris on the 15th. Here I rested for 2 days and 3 nights with some people I discovered at Villeneuve St. George. They were French and tried to get me papers from the Spanish Consul but were unable to do so. The brother-in-law of this family is George Drummond, 51–53, Broughton Road, Edinburgh.

I left Villeneuve on the morning of the 18th July passing Fontainebleu and Meleen and arriving at Montargis at night. I was not stopped at all. I made myself a passport with a card I bought in a shop. I had by photograph taken and filled in the details and stamped it with a 2 fr. piece.

Capture by French.

I left Montargis on the 19th July, and passing Briare arrived at Nevers by night. I proceeded towards Vighy via Moulins where I arrived on the night of the 20th. Arrived at Lyons on the 21st and on the 22nd got to Andacon, where I was taken prisoner by gendarmes and kept the night in the guard room. The next day at 12 o'clock, I was taken to Tournon and entrained for Marseilles with a gendarme as escort. I was treated well.

Arrived at Marseilles on the evening of the 23rd and was taken to Fort St. Jean, and given a meal and a bed to sleep in. The next day (24th July) was taken to the British Consul and gave him my particulars. He sent me to the Seamen's Mission in rue de Forbin, where I had a meal and spent the night. The next morning (25th July) a French detective came to the Mission and asked for British soldiers. He looked English and spoke English so well that I thought he was from the Consul, and I told him I was British. He then took me back to Fort St. Jean where I was interned with 20 other British soldiers, commanded by Major Potts. Major Potts had his orders from the French. We had fatigues in the morning and evening and were not allowed out of barracks. After a week or so we were given 50 frs. a week, but I intended escaping, so asked for a month's money in advance and shortly after escaped (30th July).

Escape from Fort St. Jean.

I was walking on the ramparts about 200 ft. above the sea and climbed into a narrow ledge holding on to a rail partition topped with barbed wire. I hurried down some steps to a drawbridge and walked across the drawbridge. I went to the Seamen's Mission and said 'goodbye' to the Padre and got the fi[rst] train to Perpignan. From Perpignan I proceeded to the Spanish frontier, arriving there on the night of the 1st August. I was again taken by gendarmes when trying to cross the frontier. They would not let me go, but told me the best route to cross the frontier and the best time to go, which was at daybreak. They kept me two days at Berbere. On the 3rd August I was taken to St. Cyprien where I met Sapper Richards. On the evening of the same day we both attempted to escape by boat from the beach at St. Cyprien, but the boat sank, and we had to return. We hoped to get into Spain by passing the frontier at sea and then turn inland. On the 4th August we tried via Le Porthus to pass the Frontier but were again taken back to St. Cyprien on the 5th.

We met a Czech who, on finding out we were British, told us of his wish to return to England with us and arranged to meet us at St. Cyprien on the morning of the 8th August. He turned up, and he and I left without Richards, as Richards was ill. We met no troops at the frontier during the day, and at night we passed the mountains. We had a day and a half in the country, and at 11 o'clock we separated, as the Czech was afraid to go by road because he had been a member of the Republican Army. I arrived at Gerona at 1.30 and looked for the French Consul, but he was not available, so I continued towards Barcelona. I also enquired for the British Consul at Gerona, but could not get any information.

About 4 kilos from Gerona the railway crossed the road, and I decided to go on by rail because it was direct and there was less chance of being captured by Spanish troops. As it was only 96 kilos more to Barcelona I decided to do it in a day and a night. At 9 o'clock hat night I stopped in the railway viaduct and slept beside the track until the moon rose at 11 o'clock. I then proceeded on my way and arrived at Barcelona by mid-afternoon on the 11th, and enquired for the British Consul but could not find him. I then proceeded to the American Consul and asked him to find the British Consul and ask him to send on a man to take me to him, which he did. After giving particulars at the Consulate I was given a meal and a bath, and the next day I had some new clothes. I stayed a week in Barcelona resting my feet. The first three days I spent with Mr. Amore of the Consulate, and the last three days with Mr. Dorchy, also of the Consulate.

On the 17th I was given a passport, tickets and 50 pesetas, and a visa for Portugal, and left for Madrid. I arrived at Madrid on the 18th with the Czech, who had arrived in Barcelona three days after me. His name was Frett Von Trenk. On the 19th, the Czech left the Embassy and tried to cross the Portuguese frontier, and I did not see him again.

At the Embassy in Madrid I met L/Cpl. Donaldson and Pte. Dickson, who were also waiting to proceed to England. After 10 days, Pte. Sugg arrived at the Embassy. On the 6th September prisoners were repatriated from Spanish concetration camps and arrived at the Embassy.

On the evening of the 7th September, we left for Gibraltar. We arrived there on Saturday 8th September, and spent the following 12 days at Gibraltar as guests of the Rock. We left for England on the 19th, arriving Londonderry on the 27th September, in a destroyer.

(L.G. 29.11.40)

Heward, Herbert Samuel, Sergeant
4913149, 2 Northamptonshire Regt. (Abington, Northants.) (Immediate)
Sjt. Heward commanding 8 Pl 2 Northamptons was ordered to recapture a Platoon area which had been over-run by the enemy on May 1st in a forward sector of the Anzio Beachhead in very close contact with the enemy. The attack which Sjt. Heward was ordered to lead consisted of two waves of specially selected men, zero hour being fixed for 2230 hours on night 3/4 May, at which time the assaulting troops would crawl forward from the start line. A supporting programme of RA, and mortars, was to open only when called for.

The plan called for leadership and determination of a high order. Its success depended on elan and the spirit with which it was carried through after the initial crawl forward towards the enemy posts a few yards over a small crest.

Sjt. Heward led the crawl and assault in person. Due to his cool determination and fieldcraft he skilfully brought the assaulting waves to within 8[...] yards of the crest. He judged the moment for the assault and led the charge on the enemy post. Hardly had the men risen to their feet when they were met by a literal shower of grenades. Casualties were at once sustained and Sjt. Heward was himself severely wounded.

Showing complete and utter disregard for his wound, he encouraged his men forward in spite of the grenades and automatic fire which had now been opened at point blank range. Sjt. Heward reached the crest only to find a stretch of wire which separated him from his objective. He emptied his Tommy gun into the enemy slits, and exhorted those men who had reached the wire to do likewise.

In spite of loss of blood he returned to find another Tommy gun belonging to a dead soldier and with the second wave now going in he made a second attempt to carry out the assault. The enemy were in too great a strength and casualties among the assaulting troops were heavy—37 out of the original 50. Sjt. Heward was later found lying within a few feet of the enemy wire suffering from a broken arm and severe wounds in both legs and in the chest.

The leadership and grim determination and personal gallantry displayed by this NCO were of a remarkably high order. His dauntless courage and magnificent personal example in showing such utter disregard for his own personal safety and for his wounds, inspired his men forward and also those of the second wave, who, despite a hail of bullets and grenades, followed him—and him alone—to achieve what proved to be a task beyond the undertaking of one pl.   *(L.G. 3.8.44)*

Hewitson, George Raymond, Warrant Officer Cl. II (B.S.M.)
843963, 260 A/Tank Battery, 65th (N.Y.) Anti-Tank Regt., Royal Artillery (Waterhouses, Co. Durham) (Immediate)
On 26 Nov 41 at 0600 hours, 'J' Troop was deployed North of the Road and 'K' Troop south of the road 52 miles east of Bir el Hariga on the Trigh—Capuzzo Road, and both Troop Commanders were ordered to engage the enemy when contacted, and were told that at all costs the enemy force was to be prevented from attacking 13 Corps H.Q.

At 0630 hours, the enemy, consisting of approximately 60 tanks and 800 M.T. were sighted proceeding from ENE—WSW. B.S.M. Hewitson, commanding 'J' Troop, proceeded in his 8-cwt truck to within 200 yards of the enemy force to look them over. He then ordered his troop to open fire and with the first shots knocked out a tank, armoured car and staff car. During the general action which followed, B.S.M. Hewitson coolly directed the fire of his troop and slowly withdrew his guns when pressure became too great.

When O.C. K Troop reported to me the loss of two guns, I ordered B.S.M. Hewitson to re-inforce the right flank with a section of guns. This he did by signal and with a minimum of time lost had switched a section two thousand yards south and was in action again. The whole operation was carried out under a most intense barrage of fire. During the whole action, he displayed marvellous control of his troop, and his own bearing set a magnificent example to his men.   *(L.G. 24.2.42)*

Hewitt, Jack, Sergeant
858504, 52nd Anti-Tank Regt., Royal Artillery
For displaying great coolness, leadership and contempt of danger during the operations on the Ypres—Comines Canal.

On the 28th May, 1940, one gun was left during a partial withdrawal because its detachment, reduced by casualties, could not get it back. Volunteers to save the gun were called for. Sergt. Hewitt was one of two N.C.O.s who at once volunteered. With the remaining numbers of the gun detachment these two N.C.O.s under the command of Sergt. Hewitt succeeded in withdrawing the gun. Throughout the operations in Belgium and France Sergt. Hewitt set a high example by his coolness under fire and disregard of danger.   *(L.G. 27.8.40)*

Heywood, Albert Robert Cecil, Sergeant
5346450, 2 Royal Berkshire Regt. (Farnborough, Hants) (since died of wounds) (Immediate)
At Kaduda near Singu on the 27th Feb. 45 was ordered to take out a patrol to the village of Nattaung, and to lay an ambush on his way back. He led his patrol behind the enemy defences with great skill and as a result gained valuable information as to the location and strength of the enemy. In the ambush his patrol accounted for 10 Japs certainly, and probably more killed, with no loss to himself.

At Kabaing on the 8th Mar. 45 Sgt. Heywood was Platoon Sgt. of his platoon in a village clearing operation, in which an unknown number of Japs were concentrated in a nullah. By organizing his platoon skilfully he managed to throw grenades into the nullah, whilst a Bren gun fired down it. The platoon eventually charged the nullah firing from the hip. The result of the operation was 16 japs killed, including 2 Offrs., with no loss to the platoon.

At Mandalay on the 10th Mar. 45 during the adv. down the West side of Mandalay Sgt. Heywood's Platoon Comd. was wounded and Sgt. Heywood took over comd. During the adv. the remainder of the Coy. had to halt to clear opposition and Sgt. Heywood's platoon, continuing it's adv., became separated between bounds. The Coy. was finally halted short of its objective.

Sgt. Heywood had been ordered to push on and seize an objective 800yds to the South. He reached his objective passing through numerous small enemy localities on the way. On the objective he shot up many small parties of Japs in the area. He killed 8 Japs for certain and captured a lorry which drove towards him.

At nightfall he took up a defensive position and found his way back to the rest of the Coy. next morning having sustained only 2 casualties in the platoon.

During all recent operations Sgt. Heywood has carried out every task with great skill and daring and has shown the greatest initiative and presence of mind in dealing with the enemy.

He has proved himself a capable leader, has set the highest example of courage under enemy fire and has been largely responsible for the continual success of his platoon. He was finally wounded on 14 March.

(L.G. 2.8.45)

Heywood, George, Sergeant
4131107, 6th Bn. Cheshire Regt. (Warrington)
(Immediate)
Sjt. Heywood, on the night 29/30 Sep., was commanding No. 9 Platoon, a M.G. Platoon of 6 Cheshire, in sp of 169 (Lon) Inf. Bde. Elements of the Bde. occupied positions on the Castel Vecchio feature (715010) and orders were issued to Sjt. Heywood to take his platoon fwd. and give sp fire to a Coy. of 2/5th Bn. The Queens Royal Regiment. It was discovered that the track via La Pieta was impassable to carriers and would take some hours to put right. Sjt. Heywood went fwd under heavy fire to recce an alternative route for his platoon. On his return he led his men on a 'long carry' of 1,200 yds. through intense mortar and arty fire. Halfway to the Castel Vecchio feature his platoon was pinned down. Sjt. Heywood organised a small party of two guns and some amn., and pushed on, getting his guns into position. He then returned, still under heavy fire, to the remainder of the platoon, led up the remaining guns and amn., and, reducing the men in the gun-line to a minimum, remained in position despite the enemy's efforts to dislodge him. His platoon gave much-needed supporting fire at a very critical moment.

Throughout the whole time Sjt. Heywood displayed the highest sense of duty and complete disregard for his own safety. It was because of his personal example of courage, devotion to duty and outstanding leadership that his Pl went into action, and remained, in spite of very heavy enemy opposition. *(L.G.8.3.45)*

Hickling, Frank Albert, Lance Sergeant
806439, 11th Field Battery, Royal Artillery
On November 25th Sgt Hickling's gun was one of a section left to cover a withdrawal to Sidi Omar when tanks were expected. When about to leave the tanks appeared, the tractor of the other gun of the section was destroyed and 4 men killed and wounded. Sgt. Hickling picked up the wounded and the rest of the detachment and took his gun back to where the rest of the Regiment were in action. As he arrived there 28 tanks attacked and opened intense fire on the Battery. Sjt. Hickling was badly wounded early in the engagement but sitting on

the trail continued to control his gun until it ran short of ammunition. By then 2 men had been killed and 1 wounded. He then tried to get more ammunition but the tanks then withdrew leaving 7 destroyed. Sjt. Hickling's sustained courage, coolness and example were an inspiration to all.

Recommended for M.M. *(L.G. 23.1.42)*

Hickson, George Alfred, Lance Sergeant
A.19407, 2 Cdn Div., Corps of Royal Canadian
Engineers
L/Sjt. Hickson was in charge of a group charged with destroying the main telephone exchange in the Post Office. Finding the fire on the beach too heavy to move directly to his target, he assisted an infantry platoon in mopping up enemy M.G. positions and destroyed a 3-inch gun by detonating a 3 lb. charge on the breech. When the Platoon Commander and most of the senior N.C.O.s were put out of action, Hickson assumed command and led the platoon to the Casino where strong enemy opposition was nullified. Using explosives he blew his way through the walls to reach a large concrete gun emplacement, then with another charge blew in the steel door killing a gun crew of five. He then destroyed the 6-inch naval gun and two M.G.'s after infantry had cleared the post. L/Sjt. Hickson then re-organized his platoon and despite heavy enemy opposition led them into the town as far as the St. Remy Church. Unable to find Bde HQ and being without support, he withdrew his party to the Casino. L/Sjt. Hickson throughout the day showed determined leadership and high qualities of initiative, and was among the last group to evacuate.

(L.G. 2.10.42)

Higgins, William, Warrant Officer Cl. II (C.S.M.)
5495735, 10th Bn. Royal Berkshire Regt. (London,
S.W.18) (Periodic)
On 10/11 Nov. 43 at Calabritto, C.S.M. Higgins' Coy. was attacked several times by considerable German forces. It was during the second attack that night that the enemy penetrated the Coy's right flank and broke through to Coy. HQ. Without hesitation C.S.M. Higgins left cover and single handed faced the oncoming German machine gunners who fired as they advanced. On closing with the enemy he killed two Germans after a severe hand to hand struggle. Armed only with a L.M.G he then chased the Germans across the open and handling his weapon with the utmost fearlessness he dispersed no less than 20 Germans who broke and ran.

When the enemy attacked his Coy. again on the night 11/12 he went out to a fwd. platoon which had lost its comd. and half its strength. Under continual Mortar and M.G. fire he reorganised the platoon and when the enemy attacked stayed by the men directing their fire in an exposed position. So vigorous was the action taken by him that the enemy was successfully beaten off.

Throughout the fighting he set a magnificent example of personal bravery and his determined efforts and powers of leadership inspired the men of Coy. HQ to follow his example. Had Coy. HQ been overrun a most difficult situation would have arisen, and there is no doubt that C.S.M. Higgins' efforts were responsible for preventing this.

His action is only in keeping with the bravery he displayed on the Catanian Plain on 17 Jul 43, when with all his Offrs. casualties he rallied his Coy. and withdrew it according to plan, having first ensured personally to see that no casualties had been left behind. This W.O. has shown marked ability as a leader as well as a complete disregard of his own personal safety. His conduct and bearing throughout the campaign have been of a very high order and an inspiration to all men in his Coy.   *(L.G. 24.8.44)*

Hill, A., Warrant Officer Cl. I (R.S.M.)
5433001, Duke of Cornwall's Light Infantry
No citation.   *(L.G. 11.7.40)*

Hill, Hubert Vincent, Private
WX.12808, 2/14 Australian Inf. Bn. (Immediate)
6 July 1945 Balikpapan.

During the afternoon of the 6th July 1945, Private Hill's company captured the high ground essential to the occupation and defence of the Manggar Airstrip, whereupon it hastily dug-in during the failing light. The enemy, approximately one company in strength counter-attacked the position through Pte Hill's sector four times during the night, and in each case the attacks were halted by his courage and skill with Bren and Owen guns. During the last attack his Bren gunner was absent collecting ammunition, and Pte Hill manned both guns alternately. The enemy detected his position and charged him with spears. He killed the one in front and the one on the right hand side, but in the meantime a third had gained his position from the left and attacked him with a spear. At this stage, owing to heavy rain and mud, both weapons jammed. He grappled with the Jap with one hand and with the other attempted to right the stoppage of his Bren gun. He then jerked the Jap backwards and killed him with the Bren. In the morning nine dead Japs were counted immediately in front of his position and other dead and wounded had been carried off.

His outstanding courage, determination and coolness in extreme danger four times prevented enemy penetration in a vital sector and enabled the company to hold ground vital to the security of Manggar Airstrip.
Recommended for M.M.   *(L.G. 14.9.45)*

Hill, John Harker, Sergeant
C.5636, Hast. & P.E.R., Canadian Infantry Corps
Ref. Map Italy 1/100,000 Sheet 160 Cassino.

On 23 May 1944 during the evening assault on the Adolf Hitler line, 'C' Company the Hastings and Prince Edward Regiment was held up in its advance by withering fire from a German pillbox and dug outs at MR 737159. Quickly seeing the damage being done to his Company and the danger of delay to our advance, C 5636 Serjeant John Harker Hill of 13 Platoon personally organized and led a party of eight men on to the enemy positions. Despite the fire of light mortars, machine guns and riflemen, this Non-Commissioned Officer and his men charged the pillbox and cleared it and the dug outs of the enemy, taking fifty-three German prisoners.

It was largely due to his intrepid courage, complete disregard for his personal safety and inspired leadership, over and above his normal duty, that so many enemy were captured or destroyed with but slight losses to our forces.   *(L.G. 30.9.44)*

Hill, William Alexander, Sergeant
2693958, 1 Bn. Scots Guards (Guildtown, Perth)
(Immediate)
For conspicuous gallantry and devotion to duty near Cologna on the approaches to the River Po on night 23/24 Apr. 1945.

Sjt. Hill's platoon was ordered to advance West along the Canale Bianco and seize a bridge on the main axis approx. 2,000 yards away. As soon as the platoon started to advance it came under heavy Spandau fire from a prominent house, and was caught in the open. It was then bright moonlight. Sjt. Hill went straight into the assault with his platoon, firing his Tommy gun and cheering on his men, and the house was captured, one German being killed and several P/W taken. The advance then continued despite interference from a Spandau firing along the canal bank from a flank, and the bridge was seized and consolidated unseen by German posts within 50 yards of the bridge, on both sides. Shortly afterwards the post in front of the bridge opened fire and Sjt. Hill immediately dealt with it, taking two P/W. Then an enemy vehicle and a horse-drawn cart drove up to the bridge and were shot up by Sjt. Hill's platoon and the occupants taken prisoner.

Later on another company passed over the bridge but was soon compelled to withdraw owing to a determined counter-attack by infantry with Bazookas and supported S.P. guns. During this time and subsequently for about three hours the vicinity of the bridge was mortared incessantly. The counter-attack came in from the flank and was eventually halted just short of the bridge mainly by skilfully controlled fire from Sjt. Hill's platoon.

Although wounded early in the counter-attack Sjt. Hill remained with his platoon till the bridge was no longer in danger. Whenever a section was under heavy fire, Sjt. Hill was always there to encourage it. By his complete disregard for danger and by his unfailing cheerfulness under the most exacting conditions he was an inspiration to the whole company.

This N.C.O. has served with the same company since the outbreak of war and has been in every action with it. By his bravery and skill on every occasion he has gained the confidence of the whole company and has been a great source of strength and encouragement in every action.

Recommended for M.M.   *(L.G. 18.10.45)*

Hillier, Bert Frank, Warrant Officer Cl. II (C.S.M.)
2733893, 3rd Bn. Welsh Guards (Esher) (Immediate)
During the attack on Dj Aine El Rhorab on 9 Apr 43, all the officers of No. 2 Coy. were put out of action. C.S.M. Hillier took command of the company and organized further attacks on enemy positions in a most competent manner. He personally shot a sniper who was causing casualties to his company and throughout the operation displayed great courage and power of leadership.
(L.G. 15.6.43)

Hinchcliffe, Albert, Sergeant (actg.)
2763908, 5th Bn. Black Watch (Rotherham) (Immediate)
On 11 Feb. 45 Sgt. Hinchcliffe was Platoon Sgt. of a platoon in the leading Company attacking the town of Gennep. From the beginning resistance was stiff and the attack was slowed down. At this moment the Platoon Commander was killed. Sgt. Hinchcliffe took command of the platoon and realising that part of the enemy resistance was centred on a large group of buildings in front, he immediately collected his men and led them across two hundred yards of bullet-swept ground in a tremendous charge on these buildings. Completely disregarding the intense enemy fire directed on him, he forced an entry and almost single-handed wiped out the Germans in the building. He carried out this operation entirely on his own initiative and showed magnificent courage and leadership in its execution. When established in this position another enemy post further on engaged his Company. Quickly realising the danger of this threat to his Company's flank Sgt. Hinchcliffe immediately moved his men forward till he could get fire to bear on the enemy. There he arrayed his platoon weapons in various windows and holes in walls and engaged the enemy. To reach the enemy it was necessary to cross 100 yards of open square. Undismayed by this Sgt. Hinchcliffe again collected a few men and under a hail of bullets and grenades, stormed the building at the head of his men. Every man in the enemy post, which was a strong one, was killed or wounded, and 10, including a Captain, taken prisoner. Inspired by these successes, Sgt. Hinchcliffe's platoon, whose every move was a tonic to those who witnessed them, continued to mop up street after street, increasing their bag of enemy dead and prisoners. Throughout, Sgt. Hinchcliffe showed the most magnificent courage and aggressive determination, while his complete scorn of danger and intense enemy fire had to be seen to be believed. His outstanding action had a material effect on the success of the operation.
(L.G. 19.4.45)

Hindley, William Eric, Lance Sergeant
4197725, 4 Royal Welch Fusiliers (Llandegla, Wrexham) (Immediate)
On 22 Sep. 44, the Bn. was engaged in attacking the village of Wintelre. The M.G. fire from a group of houses some 600 yds. outside the village had held up two previous attacks. L/Sjt. Hindley and his Carrier Sec. were given the task of neutralizing these enemy posts whilst the Bn. attacked. To enable him to do this successfully L/Sjt. Hindley decided to move in his carriers to a position where he could bring the houses under Piat fire. Whilst doing this he and his sec. came under Bazooka and M.G. fire from the houses so L/Sjt. Hindley immediately closed his section to within 50 yds. of the houses and destroyed each house in turn with Piat fire. After this action 20 enemy bodies were found in one of the houses. Having completed this task this N.C.O. then found that M.G. fire was coming from a haystack some 100 yds. further down the road. Covered by the remaining carriers he took his own carrier down the road and silenced this M.G. post. This shock action undoubtedly had a considerable effect in demoralising the enemy further back in the village, who commenced to give themselves up in large numbers as soon as the attacking infantry reached them. L/Sjt. Hindley's fine leadership, initiative and disregard of danger were an example to all and contributed greatly to the successful capture of the village. His action far exceeded the task he was given.
(L.G. 1.3.45)

Hinson, James, Corporal
SX.7429, 2/48 Aust. Inf. Bn.Australian Military Forces (Immediate)
On the morning of 10 Jul 42, C Coy 2/48 Bn attacked enemy posns on Tell el Eisa Ridge. 15 Pl, as reserve Pl was ordered to attack a bty of fd guns which were holding up our adv. The attack was made without support except for 3" mortar which fired 5 bombs. Cpl. Hinson led his Sec with bayonets fixed straight at two guns which were firing point blank. He led his Sec right into the gun pit when the enemy surrendered. On the afternoon of the same day the Pl was run over by enemy tanks. Cpl. Hinson jumped out of his trench and placed a ST grenade on a tank. Later on another tank was set on fire and the crew ran away. Cpl. Hinson immediately gave chase under shell fire, captured the crew, all German, and brought them in as prisoners. Right through the day his leadership and courage was a great inspiration to his Sec and Pl, and was largely resposible for the high morale of the men being kept up.   *(L.G. 24.9.42)*

Hipgrave, Alfred Charles, Sergeant (A/B.Q.M.S.)
1068073, 32 A.Fd. Regt., Royal Artillery
When in action he was wounded and his gun disabled by an enemy shell which landed five yards away: the troop position was several times subjected to accurate counter battery fire. In spite of his head injuries he continued to serve his gun. He brought his gun out of

action as coolly as if on gun drill, while an ammunition lorry was burning and exploding within 80 yards of him. At Dunkirk with his limber gunner and driver, he swam to an empty rowing boat and rowed it, making two journeys from and to a destroyer to get all his men on board.

Recommended for M.M.   *(L.G. 27.8.40)*

Hitchin, Robert Stanley, Lance Bombardier
1091288, 172 Field Regt, Royal Artillery (London, E.7)

L/Bdr. Hitchin was a Ftr Gun in 'F' Tp Lt. Col. of 155 Bty in the action at Sidi Nsir W. D. McN. on 26 Feb 1943. He slept on the gun Graham posn and worked on No. 1 gun with Sjt. OBE, RA. Henderson, whose gun took a foremost part in stopping enemy tanks on the rd 1091209 to Maeur—Sidi Nsir. From 1100 to 1400 hrs he was under extremely heavy and very accurate mortar fire. Previous to that he was helping with amn on No. 3 gun. When No. 1 gun was knocked out in the early afternoon L/Bdr Hitchin escaped injury because he was a few yards away picking up A.P. amn. He then went to No. 2 gun. When this gun was knocked out he heard the shell coming and lay flat behind sandbags, thus escaping death when the rest of the crew were killed. He then went to No. 3 gun and helped to bring it into action. All this time he was under severe mortar and machine gun fire from guns of tanks in a hull-down position which were hitting other guns one by one and knocking them out. When it became dark and the last gun ceased firing L/Bdr Hitchin made his way behind the enemy tanks and up the hills and escaped. There was no reason why a L/Bdr fitter should serve the guns as a gun number save devotion to duty and loyalty to his comrades.

(L.G. 22.4.43)

Hobbs, Ernest William, Sergeant
10406, 23 N.Z. Bn.

During all the operations in which this unit took part in Libya Sjt. Hobbs was platoon Sjt. of the Bren Carrier platoon. His skill, dash and great personal courage were an inspiration to the whole column throughout. His resource, initiative and gallantry in several patrol actions resulted in valuable information being gained and heavy losses in vehicles, weapons and men being inflicted on the enemy.

During the heavy German attack on Fort Gapuzzo on the afternoon of 7 November 1941 Sergeant Hobbs led a carrier section in a flank counter attack. In spite of heavy enemy mortar, artillery, M.G. and anti tank fire he carried the flanking thrust with the greatest dash through the enemy attacking formation, turned and swept back to his starting point. The enemy attack was at its peak at this stage but this daring move led by Sjt. Hobbs enabled our infantry counter attack to get under way quickly and destroy the large force of German infantry that had penetrated to the centre of the Gapuzzo defences.

On the 11 December 1941, Sjt. Hobbs brought a section of carriers successfully through heavy M.G., mortar and artillery fire to support 'C' Company in their highly successful attack against enemy prepared positions on a ridge East of Gazala. His gallantry and leadership in this action are worthy of the highest praise.

(L.G. 19.3.42)

Hobson, Robert William, Sergeant
QX 1339, 2/9 Australian Inf. Bn.

At Tobruch, on night 3/4 May 41, Sjt. Hobson in company with Lieut. Noyes, attacked 3 CV3 tanks which were holding up the advance of their platoon. The first tank was forcibly opened, and a Mills bomb was dropped in. As one of the crew was able to jump out, Sjt. Hobson sat on the lids of the other two tanks to prevent the crew from escaping after the bombs had been dropped in. All three tanks were set on fire. Sjt. Hobson then led a bayonet attack by a rifle section on a nest of 7 ATk guns, protected by infantry. The whole of the enemy, numbering about 80 were either killed or wounded. The attack was carried out under intense MG and artillery fire. Sjt. Hobson displayed great leadership and daring. His coolness and determination under fire were an inspiration to his men, who secured all their objectives.

(L.G. 19.8.41)

Hoddinott, Francis Joseph, Warrant Officer Cl. II
NX 4784, 17 Aust Inf Bde.

For conspicuous gallantry and outstanding devotion to duty, in that he did, when at midday on 27 Jun 41 the enemy launched a heavy counter attack with approximately two Battalions against two coys holding Jebel Mazar feature, one French Bn moving round the Southern side and threatened to outflank D Coy on the left, W.O.(II) Hoddinott immediately organized a section with three men from Coy HQ and moved out 200 yds to the flank and forward. Using a French Hotchkiss gun and a Bren gun, effective fire was brought to bear on the enemy. The fire was so effective that the enemy were delayed for over four hours. The section was compelled to withdraw when its ammunition was exhausted but its action enabled the Coy to hold out until dark, when it withdrew without serious losses. W.O.(II) Hoddinott displayed outstanding ability, determination and devotion to duty throughout the action.   *(L.G. 12.2.42)*

Hodges, Daniel, Private
6396763, Royal Scots
See Gallagher, Joseph, Pte., 305444, Royal Scots
(L.G. 29.9.42

Hodgson, Leslie Arthur, Lance Sergeant
2734818, Welsh Guards (London, N.1) (Immediate)
2 Aug. 44. Map Ref. Terrena 031539, Sheet 114/IV, 1/ 50,000 Italy.

L/Cpl. Hodgson was a member of a recce patrol consisting of 1 Offr. and 5 O.R.s which was ordered to go out in daylight from Faella 9951 to Pran Di Sco 0253 to find out if this area was occupied. The patrol found Pran Di Sco village unoccupied but heard a civilian report that a house at 031539 was occupied by 5 Germans who were resting. The patrol advanced to capture a P/W who was much needed. When on the outskirts of the house the officer and one Gdsm. were killed by a sniper. L/Cpl. Hodgson took command at once of the remaining 3 Gdsm., took the house and captured 4 enemy; the remainder (4 and not 1 as reported by the civilian), escaped. L/Cpl. Hodgson, knowing that it would be fatal to show himself with his 4 P/W in daylight with so many enemy watching the house, (they were in the middle of an enemy Coy. position), hid his 4 P/W and his men in the attic of the house, where the enemy failed to find them, although they entered the house in some strength and shouted the names of the 4 P/W. L/Cpl. Hodgson was surrounded and could not move in daylight. As soon as darkness came, he ordered all his party to put on sacking over their boots to deaden the noise and managed to slip through the enemy. He returned to his Coy. with his 4 valuable P/W, a distance of over 3 miles. L/Cpl. Hodgson's initiative and determination to continue with his officer's intention in spite of that officer being dead and the heavy odds against him, was an outstanding performance.   *(L.G. 7.12.44)*

Hodson, Wallace Howard, Sergeant
892732, 114 (J) Fd. Regt. R.A., Royal Artillery
(Bexhill) (Immediate)
Imphal area. For conspicuous gallantry in action.
    During an enemy attack on night of 10/11 May 1944. Sgt. Hodson was No. 1 of a mortar sub-section on Scraggy Hill. Whilst engaged in firing his S.O.S. task his detachment came under heavy and accurate fire from a Jap MMG, resulting in one mortar being knocked out, all the amn. in the pit catching fire and three of his sub-section becoming casualties. He continued to fire with one mortar at the same time throwing burning and exploding boxes of amn. out of his pit and attempting to extinguish the fire by throwing blankets and greatcoats on to it. The enemy fire became intense and Sgt. Hodson was ordered away from the burning position. Under cover of a smoke bomb, he successfully evacuated his wounded men to the R.A.P. with the other wounded, where it was found that he was suffering from badly burned hands and bullet wounds in the arm. Throughout the action, Sgt. Hodson encouraged and spurred on his men, setting the highest example of coolness, courage and devotion to duty, without thought to his own personal safety.
                                            (L.G. 31.8.44)

Hogan, Norman James, Corporal
3444749, R.A.S.C.
No citation.   *(L.G. 12.5.42)*

Hogarth, Benjamin Joseph, M.M., Sergeant
546655, 1st The Royal Dragoons (Bradford)
(Immediate)
During the 4 day action when his Sqn were behind the enemy lines at El Alamein 1—4 Nov 42, Sjt. Hogarth by his initiative and complete disregard for personal danger was responsible for the destruction of many enemy vehicles. On Nov 2, when there was no longer a Troop for him to command, this NCO travelled on the outside of another Armd Car and at the first opportunity captured an Italian lorry carrying many Italians and 2x20mm Breda guns. He turned the crews off these guns and, manning one of them himself, used it to good effect on other enemy transport. When the engagement was finished he drove away the lorry and the guns. On a previous occasion when on patrol in the Alamein line on 28 Oct 42 he was unable to take his troop to a suitable lookout position owing to enemy A/Tk fire. He accordingly did his patrol on foot, returning periodically several hundred yards to his car under enemy rifle and artillery fire to make his report on the wireless. All other troops, including Infantry posts, had previously been driven from this ridge. None can fail to be impressed and influenced by the fine example which Sjt. Hogarth has at all times set.   *(L.G. 25.2.43)*

Hogarth, James McCall, Warrant Officer Cl. III (T.S.M.)
7886660, 1st Lothians and Border Yeomanry
(Edinburgh)
No citation.   *(L.G. 3.2.44)*

Hoggett, William, Lance Corporal
2326631, Royal Signals, No. 2 Commando
In recognition of gallant and distinguished services in the field.   *(L.G. 15.3.45)*

Holding, Frederick William, Warrant Officer Cl. II
WX.7386, 2/28 Aust. Inf. Bn. (Immediate)
W.O.II Holding was C.S.M. 'A' Coy. 2/28 Bn. at El Alamein in July 1942. On night of 26/27 Jul 42 in the battle of Ruin Ridge, C.S.M. Holding displayed outstanding courage and leadership. After the capture and consolidation of [...] 'A' Coy. was holding the Bn. left flank.
    At approx. 0730 hrs. 27 Jul 42 the enemy penetrated 'A' Coy area and with machine gun, mortar and infantry gun fire drove the left platoon f[...] C.S.M. Holding promptly prevented the platoon from withdrawing beyond [...] and personally lead them back in the face of heavy M.G. fire, displaying [...]ing coolness and courage in doing so. Due to casualties, this [...] with but one officer.
    W.O.II Holding, however, made up for this deficit by his tremendous [...]. Despite exceptionally heavy M.G. mortar and artillery fire, Holding moved continuously about the Coy. area leading a charmed life. Undaunted by the enemy attacks and the fact that the

Bn. was surrounded, he exh[...] ounce of resistance from the hardly pressed troops. By his bravery and meritorious leadership, he was mainly responsible for holding [...] flank and was not driven from his position until the entire Bn. [...] by tanks from the right at approx. 1030 hrs.
(L.G. 28.2.46)

Holland, Jack Frank, M.M., Warrant Officer Cl. II (C.S.M.)
6845139, 1st Bn. King's Royal Rifle Corps (Watford)
(Immediate)
For conspicuous courage, outstanding coolness and initiative under continuous and heavy fire.

This Warrant Officer was Company Sergeant Major of 'A' Company in the Battalion operations around Sidi Rezegh on November 20th, 21st and 22nd. On the 20th, he was in charge of the trucks when the Company had taken up a position on the ground. When the shell fire started to become heavy and close to his trucks he moved them under complete control and with outstanding leadership for short distances at a time, never losing contact with his Company Commander, and ending up at his original position. His conduct resulted in no truck casualties being sustained. On the 21st, during the Battalion attack, he was at rear Battalion H.Q. This H.Q. was under continuous fire. During the whole of this day, he was always at hand eager to perform any dangerous journey, tireless in his energy, an inspiration to all, officers and men alike, by his cheerful enjoyment of danger, his forgetfulness of self. On the 22nd, when the Battalion position was overrun, CSM Holland moved forward to Battle H.Q. He now proceeded to evacuate many wounded from the forward areas in a carrier, and at the end made a dangerous journey, returning with 5 men on his carrier, across ground thick with fire from enemy tanks. He was then only persuaded by a direct order, from returning to collect more men. If undertaken this journey would certainly have resulted in the loss to the Battalion of a man devoted to duty. *(L.G. 24.2.42)*

Hollands, D., Sjt.
6397264, 7 Royal Sussex Regt.
This NCO, together with an officer (2/Lt. De Manio, J.B.) displayed great courage and coolness when, at about 1100 hours, on the 20 May, 40, an enemy aircraft was shot down about one mile from Bray. Both went immediately to the place where the plane had fallen. Sjt. Holland arrived first and despite the fact that the plane was burning fiercely, that ammunition was exploding inside, and that three unexploded bombs were lying near the flames, he entered the plane without hesitation and brought the machine gun. He was about to re-enter the plane in an endeavour to bring out the pilot when he was ordered away by 2/Lt. H. C. T. Robinson, 6 R. Sussex, who had arrived at the scene. A large number of British and French soldiers were standing some distance away and 2/Lt. De Manio and Sjt. Holland set them a very

fine example of courage and coolness under extremely dangerous conditions.

Hollings, George, M.M., Warrant Officer Cl. I (R.S.M.)
6448439, 9th Bn. Royal Fusiliers (London, S.W.1)
(Immediate)
On September 10 when the Bn. was surrounded in Battipaglia, this W.O. showed a high degree of courage and devotion to duty. At a critical time when casualties were heavy and it seemed that the Bn would be over-run, with complete disregard for his own safety under heavy fire he moved continually among the neighbouring infantry and A/Tk Gunners encouraging them. This action was in a large way responsible for maintaining the confidence and offensive spirits of all troops round Bn.HQ. The same day after the town had fallen he continued to show the same courage and energy and inspiration to all troops with whom he came in contact, his gallant conduct materially helping finally to stem and stop the enemy. *(L.G. 13.1.44)*

Holmes, Frank Gibson, Corporal
4418, 1st Royal Natal Carbineers
For continuously gallant services in Somaliland (Italian) and Abyssinia during the period 5th Feb 1941—20th May 1941 and for marked gallantry in action on 22nd Feb 1941 at Gelib. Cpl. Homes was in command of a section with a Pl. on patrol. Contact was made with a strong enemy force and heavy casualties suffered. Cpl. Holmes maintained control and discipline and engaged the enemy. Though himself twice wounded he personally attended to the dead and wounded in his section. Eight of his men were killed but this NCO while in the open and under heavy fire did what he could for each one of them. He prevented the approach of the enemy and ultimately withdrew successfully with the balance of his section and would not permit his wounds to be attended to until all his men had been cared for. He showed then and throughout the campaign an exceptional example of courage and devotion to duty. *(L.G. 16.4.42)*

Holmyard, Richard George, Corporal
TX 157, 2/12 Australian Inf. Bn. (Periodic)
31 Aug 42 to 8 Sept 42
Ref Map 18 Bde Sketch (3 in to 1 mile) North Shore, Milne Bay, New Guinea, No. 3 Runaway Yo Tugalua.

The Commando Pl was detailed to give protection to Bn HQ in the eastward adv of the 2/12 Aust Inf Bn 31 Aug 42. As a Sec Comd, Cpl. Holmyard first displayed extraordinary calm and courage when his Pl proceeded to mop up enemy snipers on the east edge of No. 3 Runaway. The Pl encountered enemy sniping along the coast rd as far fwd as Rabi and without hesitation Cpl. Holmyard beat the jungle on the rd sides, outmanouvred and accounted for several snipers with inspiring dash and resolution. Cpl. Holmyard fought his sec with inspiring confidence at Gamar River throughout the night 31 Aug/1 Sept 42 when out posn was heavily attacked by large enemy forces. On the morning 1 Sept he took his sec beyond the perimeter beat the jungle for snipers again. Throughout the night 1/2 Sept Cpl. Holmyard fought through with his sec in the outer perimeter of KB Mission Sta. He led two patrols on 2 Sept 42 and was subjected to heavy rifle MG fire but with indominable spirit he fought back and secured the inf sought. Cpl. Holmyard moved fwd to a posn at Pt 124006 on 3 Sept when his pl, u/c B Coy, carried out the task of contacting the enemy to permit the 2/9 Aust Inf Bn to pass through. Strong enemy def posn was encountered at a clearing (Pt 127006) and the Commando Pl was forced to ground by intense LMG fire. One LMG post was accounted for but another took up a flank posn and maintained a most intense rate of fire. Cpl. Holmyard, accompanied by one other man, and armed with one 36 grenade rushed this enemy post across 30 yds of open ground under intense fire and routed the post—killing three enemy. His superb courage and leadership was exceptional. From 4/8 Sept 42 Cpl. Holmyard was posted at Tulagua and took part in several further patrols and carried out store protection duties.

The high degree of coolness, courage and high morale displayed by Cpl. Holmyard during ops was exceptional, and a constant inspiration to his men. He led at all times with marked vigour and great endurance.

(L.G. 28.5.43)

Holt, Leonard, Sergeant
5436422, 1 Duke of Cornwall's Light Infantry
(Handsworth, Birmingham)
At Bir el Harmat on 5 Jun 42 Sjt. Holt in the absence of the Pl Comd took comd of the carrier pl and engaged the enemy consisting of tanks, armd cars and tp carrying vehicles on two separate occasions inflicting heavy casualties and delaying the advance of the motorized infantry. When forced to withdraw he fell back on the Bn HQ position but as this appeared to be vacated he decided to move eastward with his remaining carriers. Late in the evening, on reaching a minefield on which several vehicles had already been blown up, Sjt. Holt took charge of all the vehicles he could find and personally led the way on foot through the minefield bringing these vehicles safely to El Adam. This NCO's inspiring leadership and complete disregard of his personal safety are worthy of the highest praise.

(L.G. 13.8.42)

Hopgood, Arthur Reginald, Sergeant
5493492, 2/4 Hampshire Regt. (Basingstoke)
(Immediate)
For conspicuus gallantry and devotion to duty.

During the critical period between 12 Sep and 16 Sep Sjt. Hopgood commanded the foremost platoon locality on the Bn. front—a key point of the defence. On the afternoon of 13 Sept he observed an enemy patrol which he personally stalked and destroyed—killing five and capturing two of the seven men. On the nights of 13 Sep

and 15 Sep, the enemy made determined infantry attacks supported by armoured cars and close supprt S.P. guns. Through his constant vigilance and the domination of no man's land in that part of the Sector, early warning of the mounting of these attacks was given to the Bn. Comd. On the night of 15 Sep five A.F.V.'s were within 75 yds of his position. With great coolness he reported over the air, minute by minute, the situation and disposition of the enemy. Through his cool, balanced directions the defensive fire range was shortened at great risk to his pln and three A.F.V.' were destroyed. This action of his largely contributed to the breaking up of the attack and inflicting heavy cost on the enemy. Throughout the whole of this period Sjt. Hopgood showed the greatest personal gallantry and devotion to duty and his cool, calm leadership was an inspiration to the whole of his pln.

(L.G. 10.2.44)

Hopkins, Charles William, Sergeant
5771747, 1st Bn. Royal Norfolk Regt. (Sheerness)
(Immediate)
On 6 Aug. 44, this N.C.O. was acting platoon commander during a heavy attack on the battalion position by 10 S.S. Pz. Division. Three enemy tanks and accompanying infantry penetrated his company position which bore the weight of the attack. Sgt. Hopkins' platoon was badly cut up by M.G. fire from enemy tanks but held their ground while tanks milled round inside the position. This N.C.O. was hit early on by three bullets in his leg. He refused to be evacuated and remained to command his platoon using a shovel as a crutch until he could cut himself a sapling in order to carry the weight of his 'useless' leg the better. Sgt. Hopkins then found the remnants of another platoon in his area. He immediately reorganised them and took them under his command and then carried out an excellent move to alternative positions on orders of his superior commander. Here he engaged one enemy tank with a Piat and scored several direct hits. The whole time he inspired his men with his own splendid example and cheerfulness.

I myself witnessed some of his actions and can say that his untiring efforts and devotion to duty played a great part in the eventual defeat of the enemy attack. Only after five hours, when the remnants of the enemy had withdrawn, did Sgt. Hopkins hand over his command and report to the R.A.P. *(L.G. 21.12.44)*

Hopkins, Leslie William, Lance Sergeant
6213259, Middlesex Regt. (attd. No. 9 Commando)
(Rothesay, Bute) (Immediate)
Ref Map Italy 1:25,000, Sheet 88.1. NE, Fossa Marina

During Operation Impact Royal on 13th April 1945, this unit landed from fantails on the south-west shore of Lake Commachio approximately three miles from Fossa Marina with the intention of advancing to the canal and capturing the bridges before demolition by the enemy.

On night 15th–16th April 1945 an unsuccessful attempt was made to cross the canal by means of assault boats. It was unsuccessful on account of mud, strong tide, heavy casualties among personnel, and damage to all the craft except one by shell fire. The first anxious moment occurred when this NCO's section Sgt became a casualty during the approach to the canal. L/Sgt Hopkins immediately protected this wounded Sgt with his own body, replying to the spandau fire whilst the casualties managed to crawl to safety. This was the first instance of this NCO's courageous actions. Later on during this action L/Sgt Hopkins was in charge of the leading assault boat which was to cross the canal. In spite of heavy mortar fire which almost prevented the carriage of the craft to the canal bank, L/Sgt Hopkins encouraged his men with his determination to complete the task in such a manner that his craft was successfully launched. Once they were in the water, however, enemy fire increased, inflicting casualties among his crew and also on the boat itself. Added difficulties consisted of a strong tide, waist high mud and an enemy spandau position firing at point-blank range from the opposite bank. Once his craft had been damaged, however, Sgt Hopkins immediately returned to the craft assembly area to organize further craft being brought forward and it was only due to his splendid leadership and control of the situation that this task was completed. Once again when in the water launching the craft, Sgt Hopkins was wounded in the wrist by mortar shrapnel but he remained in the water and refused to return to the bank until he had ensured that the following craft had been successfully launched and were put on the right route. He refused to be helped out to the bank until all the craft had been launched, and although he was slowly sinking in the mud and could not guarantee any assistance to help him out he remained their until ordered to be evacuated. Even at this stage, although in considerable pain, he returned to his Troop HQ and asked for another task which he would be capable of carrying out with only one arm in action. He was in such pain, however, that his Troop Leader ordered him to return to the regimental aid post.

Throughout this entire operation this NCO displayed courage over and above that which could normally be expected, both before and after being wounded. He maintained complete control of the general situation and the men under his command under appalling conditions in the canal when he himself was in grave danger of being drowned and under continual enemy fire. His coolness, fearlessness and devotion to duty were factors which contributed greatly to avert disaster when the remaining boats started to sink, and his example throughout was one of utter fearlessness and determination to complete the task assigned to him.
Recommended for M.M.   (*L.G. 23.8.45*)

Hopkinson, George Arthur, Fusiliers
22508234, East Surrey Regt. (attd. Royal Fusiliers)
For Korea   (*L.G. 9.6.53*)

Horan, Stephen, Guardsman
2718628, 1st Bn. Irish Guards (Liverpool)
On 30th Mar. 1943, No. 2 Coy. 1st Bn. Irish Guards was engaged near Medjes El Bab, Tunisia, and was ordered to carry out a raid on Recce Ridge. When dawn broke, the Coy. found itself completely surrounded. Gdsm. Horan was the Bren Gunner of his section and to enable him to inflict heavier casualties on the enemy, he stood up and fired magazine after magazine from the hip until his ammunition was exhausted in spite of shouted instructions to 'get down.'

Gdsm. Horan's gallant conduct was a magnificent example to the remainder of the Coy. and by his action a large number of casualties were inflicted on the enemy.
                                   (*L.G. 29.11.45*)

Horne, George Thomas, Corporal
7919358, 4th County of London Yeomanry
(Sharpshooters), (West Finchley) (Immediate)
On 12 June 1944, while advancing on Verrieres, Cpl. Horne, who was leading tank of the Troop, was fired on at short range by a Mark IV German tank. He got into action with great speed, and succeeded in getting a hit on the top of the turret, of the German tank. The Mk IV moved off into the village, and Cpl. Horne pursued it right through a strong infantry and A/Tk. position, and chased it round the houses. He only withdrew when ordered to do so because his position was impossible in view of A/Tk. fire.

On 13 June in Villers Bocage, his Troop was sited to fire across the main street at an advancing column of one Mk IV followed by three Mk VI. As the Mk IV passed the turning, the Troop Firefly misfired. Cpl. Horne instantly advanced and turned left into the column. He 'brewed up' the Mk IV, and before the Mk VI behind him realised what had happened, slipped out into another side street.

His Troop Leader's plan relied on this leading tank being knocked out, and by his incredibly quick and courageous decision he restored the situation caused by the misfire. All four enemy tanks were eventually destroyed, and the town held for the rest of the day.

The holding of this town prevented the juncture of Pz. Lehr and 2 Pzr. for this period, and also enabled the Tracy Bocage feature to be consolidated and held for a further 24 hours. This feature then occupied the attention of the 2 Pz., and at the same time threatened the rear of the Pz. Lehr for this period.

It is to be noted that shortly after the beginning of the action on 13 June, Cpl. Horne caught his arm in the recoiling gun, and broke it. He improvised a sling and carried on for the rest of the day.   (*L.G. 31.8.44*)

Horrigan, Denis William, Private
1736448, Royal Australian Infantry
For Vietnam   (*L.G. 21.12.71*)

Horwood, Alec George, Corporal (ActingSjt)
6089257, 6th Bn. Queen's Royal Regt. T.A
26th May 1940.

This officer and N.C.O. were taken prisoners when their post was surrounded by greatly superior numbers and after five days journey were confined in a large barn near Antwerp. On 26 May finding a window unfastened Captain Trench accompanied by Sjt. Horwood leapt out and ran for a neighbouring wood. After six days they reached Dunkirk in a rowing boat having walked over 100 miles and adopted various disguises. Both officer and N.C.O. showed great courage and considerable coolness and resource.   *(L.G. 3.9.40)*

Hosington, David, Rifleman
6842999, King's Royal Rifle Corps
Rifleman Hosington and Sapper White were taken prisoners at Calais in May 1940 and were taken to the P/W Camp Stalag XXI B at Schubin, in German Occupied Poland. Later they were transferred, in a working party, to a camp at Wlocawsk.

Conditions at both these camps were deplorable; P/W were half starved and were obliged to eat roots found in fields. As a result 75% were down with dysentery.

The working camp was enclosed by barbed wire and patrolled by sentries, but Rfn. Hosington and Spr. White nevertheless succeeded in slipping out during the night. Towards daybreak they hid in a haystack, where they were later found by two Poles. The latter informed friends, who provided food, cigarettes, money and civilian clothes and conveyed them to Krosnice. There they were put in touch with an underground Polish organization, which thencefore took charge of them.

From Krosnice they were passed on to Kutnow, whence, under the care of a Polish officer, they were taken to Dobzella. Here they had to cross the very closely watched frontier between Reichspolen and Occupied Poland. A guide then took them by train to Warsaw, travelling on the Berlin—Warsaw express in the same second class compartment as a number of German officers.

Three months were spent in Warsaw, where they were sheltered in no less than fourteen different houses, British and Eire residents being particularly helpful. From Warsaw they travelled by train via Cracow to Samok and thence by wagon via Ramanov to Barakov in Slovakia. They then went by car to the Hungarian frontier and, after a successful crossing, made their way to Budapest.

As well as passing on extremely valuable information for the use of possible future escapers, Rfn. Hosington and Spr. White brought back many items of Intelligence. These concerned, for example, German operations in Calais, conditions in Berlin and Warsaw (a street map of the city was obtained and marked to show military objectives) and, with many illustrative details, conditions in Poland generally.   *(L.G. 15.7.41)*

Hotchin, John Arthur, Lance Sergeant
4134196, 102 (Northumberland Husars) A.Tk. Regt.,
Royal Artillery (Durban)
This N.C.O. fought with outstanding courage when serving as a No. 1 of an Anti Tank gun in support of the 9th Australian Division near Sidi el Rahman on 31 Oct 42. At 1330 hrs the enemy launched an attack with tanks and our infantry made a local adjustment of their positions which left Bdr. Hotchin without cover and allowed enemy infantry to approach to within 700 yds on his flank where they opened fire heavily on him with automatic weapons. Very exposed and not yet dug in, he ordered half his detachment into a slit trench and remained himself on the gun with two other men for 32 hours under heavy fire of every kind and although wounded himself and his gun repeatedly hit, engaged enemy tanks and Anti-tank guns through-out this time until his gun was finally disabled. Never leaving his gun, he set a wonderful example to the whole of his Troop of determined courage and steady leadership which materially contributed to beating off the enemy's attacks on this vital position.
Recommended for M.M.   *(L.G. 4.5.43)*

Hough, Aubrey, Sergeant
5953381, 1st Bn. Bedfordshire & Hertfordshire Regt.
Sjt. Hough has been a mortar detachment commander since 1940, serving with 1/Beds. Herts. R. throughout.

Since the commencement of these operations he has commanded 61 Column's three inch mortar detachment. Though frequently handicapped by malarial attacks he has never neglected his duty or failed to maintain an exceedingly high standard of discipline and cheerfulness in his command. At Zigon on 24 May 1944, the leading platoon of the Column made contact with the Japanese garrison. Within a very few minutes mortars were in action, their fire being directed by Sjt. Hough by walkie talkie. In order to do this he had run forward to the leading Platoon Commander and asking for one man as escort moved to a small eminence in front of the platoon. The promptness and effectiveness of this well directed mortar fire assisted considerably in dealing with the Jap garrison later on. Subsequently on 25 May 1944 61 Coln. was ordered to take over the blocks on the Kyusanlai Pass. The 3″ mortars were distributed among each block in order to produce the maximum and most effectual mutual supporting fire. These mortar positions were connected by 'sound-power' and 'infantry assault cable.' This cable frequently broke. Owing to sickness there was great shortage of mortar personnel. Sjt. Hough carried out all repairs himself. He never failed to visit each detachment twice daily or liaise daily with each block commander though in order to do this it was necessary for him to use the main track which had been ambushed by the japs in between blocks, and was occasionally sniped.

During the attacks on Pt. 2171 near Mogaung by 16 and 61 Columns between 5—8 August 1944 it was decided to have direct air support brought down on the

Jap bunkers. In order to do this Sjt. Hough worked his way through the wire to a position from which he could identify the strongpoints. He had two men with him as escort and took a telephone and cable with the object of thus correcting the mortar fire in order that accurate smoke indication should be put down on the approach of our aircraft. While ranging his mortars the Japs heard his fire control orders. At first they merely sniped at him but when they realised the object of his task they sent a party to cut him off. Sjt. Hough ignored this party and continued to direct the mortar fire. It was not until he was thoroughly satisfied that his mortar indication was 'fixed' that he left his perilous position. By this time the Japs were so close and their fire so accurate that he was forced to leave behind his telephone. On the approach of the aircraft our troops were withdrawn 200 yards from the enemy perimeter so as to avoid casualties from our own bombs. Sjt. Hough was seen to move forward. It was only when he was given a direct order that he was not to return to his O.P. (which was within the enemy perimeter) that he reluctantly relied on his previous 'fix.' That evening it was discovered that Sjt. Hough had a temperature of 104 degrees, which he had had for 36 hours, but which he had concealed in order that he should not be prevented from participating in the attack. Throughout the campaign Sjt. Hough displayed great personal bravery, disregard of danger and devotion to duty of an exceptional standard.

Furthermore his efficiency inspired an amazing degree of confidence among troops whom he was 'supporting.'

All ranks, without exception, place the highest faith in Sjt. Hough himself and his well trained command.

(L.G. 26.4.45)

Hough, Harold, Lance Sergeant
2620559, 5th Bn. Grenadier Guards (Bolton)
(Immediate)
During the recent operations in the Anzio Bridgehead Lance Serjeant Hough was in charge of a mortar detachment. On the 25 Jan 44 during the attack on the Factory Area at Car[...]ceto his mortar was in action. The enemy opened fire on him with a 88 mm gun and three shells landed in quick succession immediately behind the mortar. Lance Serjeant Hough was wounded in the shoulder, but refusing attention, he continued firing the mortar with great accuracy until the arrival of further detachments allowed his to be relieved.

On the following day 26 Jan the enemy attacked the Factory with tanks and infantry. Lance Serjeant Hough and his detachment were in constant action and so excellent was his fire control that many casualties were inflicted upon the enemy. During that day this NCO was continually exposed to enemy artillery fire but his detachment continued to fire without a break. Throughout the action the coolness of Lance Serjeant Hough did much to encourage all around him and the accuracy of his detachment's fire played a large part in the breaking

up of the enemy's attacks. Lance Serjeant Hough was recommended for an immediate award of a Military Medal during the North African Campaign but received no recognition. His outstanding leadership and devotion to duty with complete disregard of his own personal safety was as apparent in North africa as it was throughout the recent action in the Anzio Bridgehead.

(L.G. 15.6.44)

Howarth, Fred, Sergeant
C.70214, Stormont Dundas and Glengarry
Highlanders (Immediate)
On the afternoon of 29 April 1945 Sergeant Howarth was commanding Number 8 Platoon, 'A' Company, Stormont Dundas and Glengarry Highlanders in the storm-boat assault crossing of the River Ems at Leer, Germany. By outstanding courage, leadership and initiative he led his platoon onto their objective despite stiff opposition, early losses and the upsetting of initial plans.

Sergeant Howarth, commanding the leading platoon of the left forward company, was given the task of storming the dyke 150 yards inland, and providing covering fire for other following platoons.

The river crossing proved difficult. Immediately the boats entered the main stream they came under heavy rifle and machine gun fire, suffering many casualties. The Engineer personnel manning the boats were unable to reach the planned landing point and landed the entire assault force of two companies, badly bunched and under heavy fire, in the right company area.

Sergeant Howarth lost no time in organizing and leading his men out of the confusion, deploying them on the left flank though it was from this direction that the most troublesome fire came. Despite the fire he pressed his platoon forward, using fire and movement. By leading first one section and then another, he reached one side of the dyke.

The enemy on the other side of the dyke were assaulted with speed. Sergeant Howarth was again in front, leading his men with mastery and courage. He was the first man to cross the dyke, closing with such dash and fury that he surprised one German machine gunner from behind and hurled him bodily into a deep ditch full of water. Emulating their leader, his men made short work of the enemy in their area.

The objective taken, it was soon apparent that the platoon would be short of ammunition for their fire task. Realizing this and with complete disregard for his personal safety, Sergeant Howarth went back under fire along both sides of the dyke and towards the landing point, collecting ammunition from the packs and equipment of casualties. This enable the platoon to maintain adequate fire support until the other platoons were on their objectives. Then he went out to bring in wounded. In the face of vicious sniping he organized parties to carry casualties back to a dugout on the dyke.

During the entire action the company had been suffering casualties from enemy dug-in on the left flank where the river and dyke curved away to afford enfilade fire positions sweeping the dyke and the landing area. Sergeant Howarth had detailed two riflemen to neutralize this fire, as his Bren guns were needed for the other covering fire tasks. Noticing this enemy fire gaining effectiveness, he went up the dyke under fire to find one rifleman a casualty and the other struggling with a rifle made faulty by muddy water. Sergeant Howarth replaced the casualty and, still under fire, fetched another rifle.

For the best part of an hour Sergeant Howarth scorned his personal safety to ensure the impetus and success of the attack, the best possible use of every man and weapon in his platoon, and prompt aid for the wounded. He moved through a hail of rifle and machine gun fire, unshaken, cool and competent, an inspiration to all who saw him. Testifying to the accuracy of the fire directed at him was a hole completely through his haversack and a neat slit in the shell dressing he wore under his helmet camouflage net. By his courage and exertions the operation which at the moment of landing seemed gravely imperiled, was carried through to triumph.

(L.G. 22.9.45)

Howe, Gilbert Rex, A/Corporal
Royal Marines
Far East Land Forces   *(L.G. 12.6.51)*

Howe, Stanley, Sergeant (A/Warrant Officer Cl. II
3453673, 9th Durham Light Infantry (Hyde, Cheshire) (Immediate)
On 12 Aug. 44 near La Plesses the 9 D.L.I. were ordered to attack the Pt. 262 feature. C.S.M. Howe's company was the forward company. The objective was strongly held and throughout the advance the company was heavily shelled and mortared. On arrival on the objective, one platoon was cut off, both their officer and Platoon Sgt. being killed, whilst C.S.M. Howe who was forward with the leading platoon arrived on the objective with 12 men. The situation was serious as it could be seen that a counter-attack was imminent. C.S.M. Howe made his way through heavy fire to the other platoon which was cut off. On arrival he re-organised it and with it he again fought his way on to the objective. When the enemy counter-attacked it was decisively beaten off.

Throughout this entire action C.S.M. Howe displayed personal courage and powers of leadership of the highest order and it was due to his initiative that the Coy. gained and held its objective.   *(L.G. 1.3.45)*

Howells, Harold, Sergeant
3963788, 1st Parachute Bde., Army Air Corps (Abeyan, Glamorgan) (Immediate)
For conspicuous gallantry.
On the night 2/3 February, 1943, the Battalion attacked enemy positions in area Dj. Mansour (Tunisia: sheet 41. 0.7092) Sjt. Howells was Platoon Sjt. in the Mortar Platoon. During the assault the platoon was held up by two enemy machine gun posts. Sjt. Howells immediately went forward and silenced both posts, killing the seven enemy who occupied them. By this act of gallantry he allowed his platoon to gain the top of the hill and bring down fire on to another M.G. post which was causing considerable casualties to the advancing troops. Under the cover of the Mortar fire, Sjt. Howells succeeded in working his way forward and knocking out this M.G. post. Sjt. Howells' conduct was of the highest order and he showed a complete disregard for his own safety in carrying out his duties, and was an inspiration to all.   *(L.G. 8.4.43)*

Howson, Frank, Private
4697534, 1st Bn. King's Own Yorkshire Light Infantry (Leeds) (Immediate)
On the morning of 22 Jan 44, whilst in the Minturno area, 'A' Coy 1st Bn. The King's Own Yorkshire Light Infantry, of which Pte. Howson is a member was attacked by a strong enemy fighting patrol. Pte. Howson was a No. 1 on a Bren gun and from the start of the action was seen firing his Bren accurately into the midst of the enemy and breaking up their attack. However, the enemy pressed the attack home very strongly with automatic and mortar fire and engaged Pte. Howson's posn with hand grenades. 3 hand grenades landed in Pte. Howson's slit trench one of which fell close to his leg and severed it just below the knee. Despite this most severe wound and despite the fact that the enemy were all around him, Pte. Howson continued to fire his Bren gun, reloading when necessary, and beat the enemy single handed from his position. Immediately the posn. was clear, S.B.s when up and endeavoured to pull him from his slit trench and evacuate him. Pte. Howson refused to leave his trench and continued to engage the enemy who again counter attacked. Again Pte. Howson maintained rapid and accurate fire at the enemy and beat them back from his posn. After this second attempt the enemy did not counter attack again and 'A' Coy. posn remained intact. This superb display of courage and extraordinary devotion to duty was a splendid example to all ranks in the Coy. It is quite obvious that had this Bren post fallen during either the first or second counter attack the enemy would have been able to establish a foothold in the Coy posns. Entirely due to the personal courage of Pte. Howson this was avoided. Later operations in the same area proved how invaluable it was for A Coy to have maintained their position on the right hand edge of the 172 ridge. It is obvious that this man was responsible in no small way for the successful defence of the high ground to the North of Minturno. When finally pulled out of his slit trench, he was unconscious and it was found that he had expended all amn on his person and in addition all the res stored up in the slit trench.   *(L.G. 29.6.44)*

Howsen, James Nicholson, Warrant Officer Cl. II
(C.S.M.)
4453668, 6th Durham Light Infantry (Barnard Castle)
(Immediate)
On 16th June 44 at Verrieres 'D' Coy. 6 D.L.I. advancing
behind an artillery barrage was suddenly pinned down
by M.M.G. and mortar fire from a flank. O.C. 'D' Coy.
was seriously wounded and most of Coy. HQ became
casualties.

C.S.M. Howson though severely wounded in the arm
and suffering from loss of blood took command of the
Coy., and pinpointed the enemy fire as coming from an
infantry strongpoint supported by a tank in a farmhouse.

C.S.M. Howson crawled back to the F.O.O. whom
he found dead and his signaller badly wounded, so he
himself directed the artillery on to the target and by so
doing silenced the enemy post.

C.S.M. Howson then returned to his company and
had a tourniquet applied to his wounded arm. He refused
to be evacuated to the R.A.P., although now weak from
loss of blood, until he had organised the defence of 'D'
Company.

C.S.M. Howson by his general bearing, initiative and
loyalty in battle has set an example of highest degree.
(L.G. 31.8.44)

Hoyle, Ralph, Sergeant
404685, 4th Queen's Own Hussars (Banbury)
(Immediate)
On 31 Aug near Hemeimat this NCO was in command
of a troop ordered to provide flank protection to his Sqn.
When five enemy tanks appeared on his flank he
surprised and engaged them from a range of 500 yards,
damaging one enemy tank and forcing the remainder to
halt. His prompt action and resource enabled the rest of
his Sqn to carry out their task. Later on the same day he
closed gaps in the minefield under arty and S.A. fire and
although wounded in his head in a bombing attack he
refused to be evacuated and remained in command of
his troop until dark. Throughout the day his courage,
resource and determination was beyond praise.
(L.G. 5.11.42)

Hubbard, Sydney, Warrant Officer Cl. II
5255533, Worcestershire Regt., No. 3 Commando
(Tamworth) (Periodic)
CSM Hubbard has been in 3 Commando for three years
and has consistently distinguished himself in action
throughout his career. In Normandy on D+1 during the
fierce fighting east of the River Orne he showed
magnificent gallantry by lying on a Teller mine thus
preventing it exploding and wounding many of his
comrades. Miraculously he escaped with his life,
although badly wounded. He rejoined the unit and fought
with them throughout Holland and Germany, where his
conduct has been continually of the highest order. In the
woods, during the fierce fighting subsequent to the
crossing of the River Aller, CSM Hubbard at great

personal risk so handled a section of twenty five men of
his troop that they were largely instrumental in holding
and driving back a German attack that threatened to
overrun Commando and Brigade HQ. Again during the
River Elbe crossing CSM Hubbard's troop was the first
to reach the dominating ground overlooking Lauenburg
and thus secure, without casualties, this vital feature. A
more gallant, unselfish WO it would be difficult to find
anywhere.
(L.G. 24.1.46)

Hudson, James, Private
3660867, 6th Bn. Durham Light Infantry (Bradford)
On the night of 21st/22nd March during the 151 Brigade
attack on the Mareth defences Private Hudson was with
'C' Company 6th D.L.I. On sighting an enemy Machine
Gun post he immediately led a group of men forward
with fixed bayonets and charged the position. His rifle
bolt was damaged and rifle could not be fired, but he
still led on this party relying solely on the use of his
bayonet. He succeeded in capturing the post, killing many
of the enemy personally. This action of Private Hudson's
enabled the rest of his Company to move forward onto
the position. Before leading the charge, his Company
Commander had been seriously wounded beside him.
He showed outstanding courage and complete disregard
for his own safety.
(L.G. 17.6.43)

Huffman, Albert Clare, Lance Sergeant
B126443, A. & S. H. of C., Canadian Infantry Corps
(Immediate)
At 0230 hrs. 28 Feb. 'B' Coy. A.&S.H. of C. was the
leading Coy. in the bn. attack on the high ground in the
Hochwald Forrest gap. The Coy. reached its objective
by 0400 hrs. but at 0600 hrs. the enemy counter-attacked
with a force of about one Coy. of inf. sp. by four tiger
tks. and two S.P. guns. The tks. succeeded in penetrating
the Coy. area and about half the Coy. was split off from
the remainder and forced to take cover in a house at MR
044408.

Immediately the enemy brought down intense mortar
and shell fire onto the house and several of the men
started to panic and ran from the house towards the main
bn. position. Without hesitation Sgt. Huffman rallied five
men and led them back into the house where they held
firm despite the continual shell fire. Realizing the
importance of his position in the def. of the Coy. area,
Sgt. Huffman continued to encourage his men and with
his small force was able to beat off every enemy attack.
During the ensuing 12 hrs. this small gp. of men killed
at least thirty and wounded many more of the enemy.
All day long Sgt. Huffman directed the fire of his men
and when not actually engaging the enemy he personally
maint. a constant watch even though doing so meant
exposing himself to the enemy snipers occupying the
fwd. edge of the wood. Finally one of these sniper bullets
wounded Sgt. Huffman resulting in the loss of one eye
and at least temporary blindness. Despite the intense pain
he was suffering, this N.C.O. refused to be evac. and

remained at his post for eight hrs. encouraging his men to efforts far beyond the call of normal duty. There can be no doubt that the courage and tenacity displayed by Sgt. Huffman resulted in his small force holding the key pt. of the Coy. position and preventing the entire bn. area from being overrun. His leadership and complete disregard for personal safety was an inspiration to his Coy. and a splendid example for all ranks in his bn.

(L.G. 12.5.45)

Huggins, Alfred, M.M., Sergeant
4389360, 6th Bn. Green Howards (North Ormesby, Yorks.) (Immediate)
On the night of the 25/26 Oct 42 when the Bn. attacked Point 94 in the Munassib Depression, Sjt. Huggins was Carrier Sergeant. He was in a charge led by Capt. Edwards on a very strong enemy L.M.G. post which contained 4 light automatics, 68 grenades and hand grenades. During the first attack Capt. Edwards was mortally wounded, and Sjt. Huggins left in command of the Platoon. Without hesitation he martialled two other carriers and while under heavy fire organised the next attack. He rushed over to a nearby Platoon, which was pinned to the ground by the fire of the enemy post and ordered the platoon commander to fire verey lights and flares. This exposed Sjt. Huggins to great danger. He then returned to his carrier remounted and advanced. When within five yards of the position, he landed a grenade amongst the enemy. The whole action was carried out under intense small arms fire, and his carrier was spattered with bullet marks. Once the grenade had burst the enemy surrendered. This action, which shewed such devotion to duty, and complete disregard for personal safety, was largely responsible for the final capture of the objective together with 30 or 40 prisoners.

(L.G. 28.1.43)

Hughes, Elfed, Trooper
7888901, 2nd Bn. Royal Tank Regt.
On the night of 5/6th Feb. 41 in the vicinity of Beda Fomm the Troop to which Tpr. Hughes belonged was ordered to investigate two enemy M13 tanks which had approached down a road near where his Troop was in a position of observation.

The Troop Commander was ordered not to fire unless absolutely necessary. Tpr. Hughes was therefore ordered to move forward and investigate these tanks on foot covered by the guns of the Troop.

Entirely disregarding his own personal safety Tpr. Hughes climbed on to one tank and demanded the surrender of the crew at the point of his revolver. The crew having surrendered Tpr. Hughes moved to the other tank; this crew also surrendered. Tpr. Hughes then brought back both crews a distance of 150 yards.

This very brave action enabled his Troop to remain in the same position throughout the night and later to take part in a further action. Had it been necessary to open fire the position would have been disclosed and it

would have been necessary for the Troop to change its position. thereby losing the element of surprise for further action.
Recommended for M.M.   *(L.G. 9.5.41)*

Hughes, Frank, Lance Sergeant
850427, 2nd S.A.S. Regt., Army Air Corps (Liverpool)
Cpl. Hughes was in command of a party of three men which was dropped by parachute on the night 17/18 Aug. 1944 between the rivers Seine and Risle with the object of harassing the enemy's withdrawal and causing confusion on his lines of retreat. Any petrol target was to be treated as top priority.

On 19th Aug. Cpl. Hughes observed enemy vehicles filling up with petrol from a dump near Elbeuf. Leaving his two men to give covering fire if necessary, Cpl. Hughes moved up alone to the dump and placed an explosive charge in position. This charge was seen to detonate two hours later, completely destroying the dump.

A little later this N.C.O. successfully destroyed an ammunition dump, killing a number of the enemy who were guarding it.

On another occasion this N.C.O. received information that an 88mm gun towed by a truck was in position close to a road. He decided to attack this, and under the covering fire of his two men he advanced sufficiently close to the position to throw two Mills grenades. Those of the enemy who were unharmed deserted the gun, which Cpl. Hughes captured intact.

Finally, on 25th Aug., this N.C.O. contacted a Canadian patrol to whom he handed over 14 prisoners and was able to give the officer in charge a chart of enemy minefields in that immediate area.

Throughout this operation this N.C.O. showed high personal courage, initiative and daring besides a determination to cause damage and casualties to the enemy at every possible opportunity.

His conduct is worthy of the highest praise.
Recommended for M.M.   *(L.G. 19.3.45)*

Hughes, George, Warrant Officer Cl. II (C.S.M.)
3379681, 1 Royal Northumberland Fusiliers (Colchester)
At Ed Duda on 26 Nov 41 his Machine Gun Company advanced to the attack immediately behind the tanks, and passed through to a higher feature in order to take on enemy in rear. Under intense shell fire this Warrant Officer established a Company Rallying Point and remained exposed with the recognition flag until ordered to take cover. When his Company Commander was killed he immediately visited every Platoon under heavy fire and by his coolness and complete indifference to danger set a fine example of steady discipline which was reflected throughout his Company.   *(L.G. 24.2.42)*

Hughes, Stephen, Corporal
6980586, 2 Royal Inniskilling Fusiliers (Newry, Co. Down)

On 11 July 43 this N.C.O. was commander of No. 3 Section 18 Pl which was supporting another section clearing a wood. This section struck very heavy enemy MG and Mortar fire and were unable to advance. Cpl. Hughes took his section directly into the enemy fire and vigorously attacked with bayonet and grenade.

His section destroyed 3 enemy LMG's and 4 Mortars, and were then faced by an MMG at point blank range. Cpl. Hughes went forward and threw a hand grenade, killing one of the crew and wounding two. The last man turned the gun upon Cpl. Hughes who still advanced and shot the man dead.

Cpl. Hughes then turned the MMG upon the retreating enemy with success. Throughout Cpl. Hughes showed intense offensive spirit, disregard of personal danger and yet handled his section most efficiently under difficult conditions.   *(L.G. 21.10.43)*

Hughes, William Thomas, Corporal (A/Sgt.)
VX.42434, 2/24 Australian Inf. Bn. (Immediate)

During the attack on Ring Feature 25 in the Tell el Eisa area on 22 Jul 42 A/Sjt. W. T. Hughes was in comd of No 7 Pl A Coy of 2/24 Aust. Inf. Bn. During the attack on this posn he was a constant inspiration to his Pl by his courage and example under heavy artillery, mortar and MG fire. On the objective his Pl was pinned down by the fire of two Spandaus firing from no more than 100 yds away. Sjt. Hughes crawled fwd under constant fire to a posn where he could fire on the MGs and with two shots from his rifle, put out of action the Nos 1 of each gun who were immediately replaced by the Nos 2. With his next two shots he put them out of action also. Later, under heavy fire, he turned back to bring in Cpl. Beecroft who was badly wounded and calling for assistance some 150 yds away. He had carried him some 50 yds when Cpl. Beecroft was again hit and killed outright. His conduct throughout the entire operation has been such that he has earned the respect and admiration of his Pl by his coolness and courage in all circumstances.   *(L.G. 15.10.42)*

Hugill, Harold, Warrant Officer Cl. II
820489, 88th Field Regt., Royal Artillery (Bradford)

At Kampar early on the morning of 2nd Jan. 42, T.S.M. Hugill was F.O.O. supporting the British Bn. who were holding the line at Kampar. Soon after dawn a heavy enemy attack developed which threatened the right of the Bn. A party of enemy infiltrated between T.S.M. Hugill and his main O.P. in rear. In spite of this, this W.O., who was in a forward trench with 5 or 6 men of the Leicesters. Regt. continued to observe and direct the fire of his Battery with such good effect as to be the main cause of defeating the enemy which at one time appeared likely to succeed. After the attack had been beaten off, the telephone line was cut and T.S.M. Hugill

withdrew along it towards his main O.P. together with the Inf. in his immediate vicinity. On the way they encountered an enemy party in possession of one of our M.G. posts.

T.S.M. Hugill took charge of the party and drove off the enemy with a bayonet charge, subsequently reporting himself at Bn. HQ. It was mainly owing to the skill and tenacity of this W.O. that a heavy attack was beaten off.   *(L.G. 13.12.45)*

Hull, William, Gunner
VX 11850, 2/2 Fd. Regt., Australian Military Forces

During the Cretan campaign Hull acted as Regtl D.R. and during the whole time of the enemy attack lasting 7 days he untiringly and courageously carried out his job despite all enemy action. On 21 May he was sent to No. 7 Gen Hosp to draw urgent medical supplies but was cut off by parachute troops. Whilst attempting to break through he was machine gunned and dive-bombed, and had to seek refuge behind the enemy for three hours. Towards evening he ran the gauntlet of parachute troops, and brought the supplies through safely. His coolness in the face of danger on this and many other occasions was outstanding.   *(L.G. 4.11.41)*

Hunt, Jacob Geoffrey, Lance Sergeant
NX 14892, 2/13 Australian Inf. Bn.
Tobruch—Period April/October 1941

L/Sjt. Hunt is an NCO in our Pioneer Platoon and has always been outstanding for his energy courage and resourcefulness. During this Bns tour of duty on the left of the Medauuar salient and when we were advancing our line L/Sjt, then Cpl. Hunt, was in charge of the party and went forward to wire the new position. This task was carried out despite heavy MG fire brought down on the party by the enemy. Cpl. Hunt on other nights also led parties carrying Engineer stores etc for the forward posts.

When the Bn occupied the right sector of the salient Cpl. Hunt, with one man, patrolled and located many enemy booby trap and minefields. Later he and a larger party returned to clear the area of the booby traps thus enabling our platoons to move forward and occupy the new posts. While carrying out this hazardous job the enemy brought down persistent Mortar fire on the party, killing two and wounding three in a party of eight. Displaying exceptional coolness and ability Cpl. Hunt extricated the wounded men and returned with additional personnel to continue the task.

The following night Cpl. Hunt with a new party again returned to the fwd posts to remove booby traps and again enemy opened fire, two of the party being killed and one injured. These were brought in and Cpl. Hunt, by his determination and courage set an example to his men and was able to complete the task successfully.

On other occasions Cpl. Hunt guided patrols and other parties through booby trap fields and minefields in 'No Man's Land.' Cpl. Hunt has set a wonderful example of endurance, tenacity and personal courage and there can be no doubt that his leadership and devotion to duty in completing these tasks made the subsequent forward moves of our line possible.   *(L.G. 16.4.42)*

Hunt, Kenneth, Private
5251421, 1st Bn. Worcestershire Regt. (Erdinton, Birmingham)
On June 14th 1942, in a position South of Acroma, Pte. Hunt was acting as a carrier driver when his Battalion was attacked by an enemy force of some 60 tanks and lorry borne infantry. The position eventually became untenable and at 1800 hours the order was given to retire. Pte. Hunt, completely disregarding any thoughts for his personal safety drove his carrier around various positions under heavy shell and machine gun fire, picking up personnel who were wounded and had not been brought into the R.A.P. through shortage of Stretcher Bearers. Having loaded his vehicle, he negotiated the wire and commenced to cross the minefield, which surrounded the defended locality, but realised that this would be impossible without lifting the mines, this he proceeded to do, having lifted enough to form a road, he was driving through when the vehicle was hit by a shell and brought to a standstill. Nothing daunted this soldier attempted to carry out repairs but finding this impossible, assisted the wounded to another vehicle outside the minefield, and then returned to destroy his own carrier. He then rejoined the Battalion, and although wounded by a shell splinter, carried on until an aid post was reached at Acroma. By his courage and coolness in the face of heavy enemy fire and complete disregard for his own personal safety during the entire action, this soldier not only prevented his vehicle, but also fifteen wounded men from falling into enemy hands. For his gallant action in keeping with the highest traditions of the service he is recommended for the award of the Military Medal.
Recommended for M.M.   *(L.G. 5.11.42)*

Hunter, George [Lascelles], Sergeant
3596329, 2 Border Regt. (Carlisle) (Immediate)
For highly distinguished services and gallantry in action.

On 12 Jun. 44, at MS 18, Imphal—Ukhrul road, Sgt. Hunter was chosen to lead a platoon consisting of battalion stretcher bearers with an escort from an Indian battalion, to reach the position known as Sausage, occupied by A Coy., 2 Border, some 5 miles forward of the main position, which had been attacked and subsequently invested by the enemy for some days.

There were casualties amongst the Sausage garrison who urgently required medical attention and immediate evacuation. Sgt. Hunter, by his initiative, and leadership of Indian troops to which he was unfamiliar, led his force over difficult country through the Jap cordon without incident.

The following day Sgt. Hunter led his party, which was carrying four stretcher cases, back to the battalion,

over the same route, and regained the main position without being discovered.

On 14 Jun., A Coy., were without rations. Although still fatigued from his previous exploit, the N.C.O. volunteered to lead a ration party of Dhotial porters, with small escort, to Sausage. He was again successful in reaching the position without casualties, though being spotted and consequently mortared by the enemy. Although not arriving until 2000 hrs., after a 5 hour trek, he started back to the battalion early next morning, and arrived back safely for the second time.

On 25 Jun. 44, B & C Coys. escorted a relieving company of the 14 F.F.Rif. to Sausage. Sgt. Hunter was again selected to guide the leading platoon of B Coy., by his route, now known as 'Hunter's Track' to Sausage. This he did, and it was due to his invaluable knowledge of the ground that the leading Coy. reached the feature unopposed, and passed through the relieving convoy safely, with only some shelling en route.

Whilst on the position during the changeover, enemy mortars opened up and Sgt. Hunter was severely wounded in the left arm. He was quickly bandaged up, but it seemed inevitable that he would lose his arm. Although he was suffering from loss of blood, it was with difficulty that he was persuaded to lie on a stretcher for the return journey. The Japs sprang an ambush on the way home, and Sgt. Hunter again displayed great courage and devotion to duty in rising from his stretcher and giving orders to those around him. He was in a state of collapse when the column reached HQ.

Sgt. Hunter, in leading his parties along this route, which afforded the enemy many opportunities for successful ambush, showed courage, endurance and extreme devotion to duty. In completing successfully his three missions, he is an outstanding example of a very gallant man.   *(L.G. 4.1.45)*

Hunter, Irving, Lance Sergeant
3190527, 2nd Bn. King's Own Scottish Borderers (Southwick, Dumfries) (Immediate)
Nakyo-Aing 24 February 1945.

On 24 Feb. 1945 No. 3190527 L/Sgt. Irving Hunter was commanding a Section in a Rifle Company engaged in an encircling attack against the South of the strongly held enemy position in the village of Nakyo-Aing.

His Section was opposed by a strong enemy bunker, but, using their own weapons they charged it with such determination and skill that they annihilated the seven enemy holding it without loss to themselves.

A little later in the action L/Sgt. Hunter himself attacked in rapid succession four smaller bunkers and destroyed the enemy occupants with grenades and Tommy gun fire.

Later, seeing a flanking platoon held up by heavy enemy fire, he crossed an area of open ground swept by enemy M.M.G. fire to a Tank, to whose Commander he explained the situation and secured his urgently needed co-operation in support of the other platoon.

The action of this N.C.O. caused a break through of the outer system of the enemy's defences, and was to a large extent responsible for the success of the whole action at Nakyo-Aing which resulted in the capture of the Village and the infliction of a severe defeat on the enemy.

Throughout the operations lasting some five hours L/Sgt. Hunter displayed exceptional courage and leadership and a complete disregard for his own personal safety that acted as an inspiration to All Ranks.

(L.G. 21.6.45)

Hunter, James Richard, Private
5781377, 1 Suffolk Regt. (Barking) (Immediate)
During the attack by his Battalion on Colleville-sur-Orne on 6 Jun. 44, this soldier individually attacked an enemy pillbox which was holding up the attack of his Battalion. Carrying a Bren gun he worked forward under heavy M.G. fire until he was able to fire into the pillbox loophole. A fierce exchange of shots took place, during which Pte. Hunter was hit in the head. Suffering severely and blinded by blood, this soldier bandaged himself and then carried on with the fire fight, finally destroying the enemy in the pillbox. He then carried on with his platoon during the remainder of the action until finally ordered to the R.A.P.

Throughout the whole of the action this soldier conducted himself in a most gallant way, showing splendid behaviour and was a magnificent example to his comrades.
Recommended for M.M.   *(L.G. 31.8.44)*

Hunter, Leopold Arthur, Sergeant
4450411, 5th Bn. Sherwood Foresters (South Shields) (Immediate)
This N.C.O. was Platoon Sgt. of Lt. Wright's No. 9 platoon 'A' Coy in the attack upon the high and bare feature 'West of Monte Vecchia 9473; this feature had first to be captured before the attack on the village could go in.

On arrival on this feature, what remained of the platoon was subjected to intense Mortar and M.G. fire. The Platoon Comd. dealt with two M.G.'s whilst Sgt. Hunter with five men charged the other two; he himself killed four of the enemy and this small party led with outstanding bravery, liquidated the remainder.

Throughout this last ten days of continual fighting Sgt. Hunter has displayed powers of leadership far beyond that expected of a N.C.O. and has infused all his subordinates with such a spirit of aggressiveness and disregard of danger that he has in no small measure contributed to the magnificent success of the Bn.

(L.G. 8.2.45)

Hunter, Wallace John, Lance Sergeant
920830, 129th Field Regiment, Royal Artillery (Stanraer) (Immediate)
On 2nd March 1945 during the attack by 63 Bde. on Meiktila West, L/Sgt. Hunter was acting as O.P. assistant to Captain M. I. Roy, R.A. whose Battery was in support of the 7/10th Baluch.

In the course of the attack the Company which Captain Roy's O.P. was with became held up by heavy enemy fire from bunkers while in an exposed position, suffering a number of casualties including Captain Roy who was killed.

The enemy then formed up for a counter-attack but L/Sgt. Hunter remained at his post and with the utmost coolness and efficiency brought down accurate and sustained artillery fire which broke up the attack and dispersed the enemy to cover. During the whole of this time L/Sgt. Hunter's vicinity was subjected to intense fire from small arms and grenade dischargers.

L/Sgt. Hunter subsequently remained in the same position for a further two hours directing harassing fire on the enemy and making use of smoke until the withdrawal of the company and their wounded had been completed, being continuously subjected to fire from the enemy positions and from tree snipers in the vicinity.

In the words of the Infantry Company Commander:—
'L/Sgt. Hunter by his gallantry and devotion to duty in remaining in an exposed position under intense fire and continuing to direct the fire of the guns after his O.P. officer had been killed beside him, not only saved the company from further casualties but was a stirring example to my men which will not be forgotten.'
Recommended for M.M.   *(L.G. 20.9.45)*

Hunter, Winston, Warrant Officer Cl. II (B.S.M.)
409615, 80th (Scottish Horse) Med. Regt., Royal Artillery (Aberdeen) (Immediate)
In the Anzio Beachhead
On the afternoon of 3rd February, 1944 'D' Troop came under heavy enemy shell fire. During this period B.S.M. Hunter showed the greatest devotion to duty, organising the supply of ammunition and later the repair of a gun, which had gone out of action. On the same night when 'D' Troop moved to an alternative position B.S.M. Hunter organised the move of his troop, there being no Troop Leader, and later the supply of ammunition in the new position, during a time of intense firing. This entailed over two thousand rounds being brought to the new troop position within eighteen hours. For the organisation of this B.S.M. Hunter was largely responsible.

By his example, devotion to duty, and inspiring leadership this Warrant Officer performed a service of outstanding value.   *(L.G. 15.6.44)*

Huntly, George Cedric, Lance Bombardier
905802, 129th Field Regt., Royal Artillery
(Edinburgh)
905802 P/A/L/Bdr. Huntly G. C. carried out the duties
of Assistant to the Field F.O.O. during the attack on the
enemy bunker position at MS 22 in the Chin Hills on
26th February 1944.

When the F.O.O. Captain D. G. Lewis R.A. was hit
by a sniper from a nearby fire position, L/Bdr. Huntly
who was with him at the time, took over the duties of
F.O.O. and unhesitatingly made a fire plan to neutralise
the enemy fire which was causing casualties to our troops.
Throughout the whole of this time this NCO was under
heavy enemy mortar and small arms fire.

When his position became untenable owing to
intensity of the enemy fire, L/Bdr. Huntly coolly and
confidently led his party to a safer place and installed
them there. He then found and consulted the Infantry
Company commander and when it was clear that
Artillery support could not be given due to the confused
nature of the fighting returned to his party and sent a
wireless message back to that effect together with a
detailed & valuable account of the progress of the battle.

L/Bdr. Huntly then organised a stretcher party from
the infantry and again under heavy grenade, mortar and
small arms fire attempted the rescue of Captain Lewis.
When the stretcher party themselves became casualties
L/Bdr. Huntly went on himself and in the face of fire
from an enemy bunker only forty yards away succeeded
in dragging Capt. Lewis into a shell hole where he found
him to be dead.

L/Bdr. Huntly then organised the rescue of another
wounded officer and succeeded in bringing him to safety.
He then returned to his F.O.O.'s party and carried on
until relieved later by another officer.

Throughout the action L/Bdr. Huntly under fire for
the first time, shewed devotion to duty of a high order.
He coolly accepted the extra responsibility thrown on
him by the loss of the F.O.O, showed outstanding
leadership in command of the F.O.O. party, and great
gallantry in the face of enemy fire.   *(L.G. 18.5.44)*

Hurwitz, Samuel Moses, M.M., Sergeant
D.26248, 22 C.A.R. (C.G.G.), Canadian Armoured
Corps (Immediate)
On 20 Sep. 44, 3 Sqn. 22 Cdn. Armd. Regt. (C.G.G.),
with under comd. one rifle coy. and the carrier Scout
Platoon of the Alg. R., was ordered to seize and hold the
railroad station at Sluiskil (MR270036). A force made
up of one inf. platoon, one sec. of three carriers and the
tk. tp. comd. by Sgt. Hurwitz was ordered to assault an
intermediate strong pt. which consisted of slit trenches,
ditches, and a number of houses on the road to the station.
Upon reaching the objective the enemy was found to be
in str. and a fierce close quarter combat ensued in deep
ditches and houses where the tks. could not be used to
advantage. Sgt. Hurwitz quickly appreciated that more
men were needed on the ground and leaped from his tk.,

taking with him two crew members. Under covering fire
of his tk., Sgt. Hurwitz and two men with him cleared
three buildings and two elaborate trench systems. Sgt.
Hurwitz then personally charged two machine gun posts.
His only weapon was a pistol but his daring and
determination unnerved the M.G. crews and the positions
were silenced. A total of twenty-five prisoners were taken
by him and his crew. This determined and gallant action
by Sgt. Hurwitz enabled his tp. to move into a dominating
fire position which covered the objective of the main
force and enabled it to move forward and seize the
railroad station where an additional 150 prisoners were
taken and a large amount of valuable equipment captured.
Recommended for M.M.   *(L.G. 13.1.45)*

Huskisson, James Septimus, Sergeant
2214892, 507 Fd. Coy., Royal Engineers
At the Canal du Nord on the 18/19 May 1940 the Coy.
was destroying bridges under very trying conditions
owing to enemy action. Sjt. Huskisson by his leadership
cheerfulness, courage and technical ability, inspired his
section to great efforts and in no case by rapid action
retrieved a failure and successfully blew his bridge in
the face of the enemy.   *(L.G. 11.7.40)*

Hussein, Ali, Ombashi
3350, Sudan Def. Forces
No citation.   *(L.G. 9.8.41)*

Hussey, Frederick, Signalman
2322622, 42nd Divisional Signals
28th May 40 to 2nd June 40
Sigmn. Hussey F. was a wireless operator at
Divisional H.Q. Although his vehicle was shelled
continuously by the enemy, he showed great courage
and devotion to duty and continued at his post throughout
the final stages of the operation.

Hutchinson, C., Warrant Officer Cl. II (B.S.M.)
757664, Royal Artillery
For devotion to duty and personal example at Dunkirk
on 27th May 1940.

By his personal bravery and coolness in the face of
enemy bombing inspired and controlled large numbers
of men on the beaches prior to evacuation. He showed
initiative and powers of organisation above the ordinary
under difficult and dangerous circumstances and
spontaneously assumed command of and organised a
large mixed force and thus enabled orderly embarkation
to take place.

There is no doubt that the control exercised by B.S.M.
Hutchinson was directly responsible for the small number
of casualties incurred at that particular part of the beach
and for the discipline maintained there. He showed fine
powers of leadership and a total disregard for his own
safety.   *(L.G. 11.7.40)*

Hutchinson, Henry Frederick, D.C.M., Sergeant

Bar

318883, 11th Hussars, Royal Armoured Corps
(Salisbury)

First Citation

At Gabr Saleh on 24th August this N.C.O.s Troop Leader and another man were separated from the cars by a 100 yards of impassable ground, when 10 enemy aircraft attacked also bombing and machine gunning the two men. Sergt. Hutchinson, to detract the enemy, withdrew the cars, but when this failed he, manning the A/A Gun himself made five separate attempts under severe air attack before rescuing the two men whose lives were undoubtedly saved by the skill and great gallantry of Sergt. Hutchinson. He has consistently done good work in the field.

Second Citation

On 26 Nov 41 Sjt. Hutchinson was in command of his troop of three armoured cars when he ran into a convoy of 30 ro 40 lorries protected by three M.16 tanks. This convoy was carrying petrol and supplies from El Adem to a force N.W. of Gobi. It had, though, lost its way and was attacked by Sjt. Hutchinson's troop South of Gobi. He waited till most of the column had passed him and then attacked the rear, knocking out the last three lorries. The column then split up in complete disorganisation, the three tanks disappearing in a Westerly direction. In the ensuing action 18 lorries manned by Germans using A/T guns from the ground were knocked out and other damaged, many prisoners were taken including the officer i/c the convoy. The quick appreciation and dash of this NCO was entirely responsible for no part of this convoy reaching its destination. On the morning of 25 Nov 41 this NCO carried out a reconnaissance in the Ghirba area.

Owing to the information he gave and owing to the fact that he held off an enemy threat, two 'C' and 'A' Sqns of this regiment were able to break through between two large enemy columns and rejoin H.Q. in the South when it looked as if they were both going to be encircled. Since the start of the present campaign this NCO has been responsible for the destruction of 58 enemy lorries and the capture of an unknown number of prisoners and enemy material. This NCO has performed the arduous and exacting duties of troop leader in an armoured Car Regiment since June 1940 and his leadership and courage has been an inspiration.

I strongly recommend that he be awarded a bar to his DCM.   *(L.G. 19.3.42)*

Hutchison, Robert David, Private (A/Cpl.)

2762486, 1st Bn. Black Watch (Dunfermline)

During the night advance on Gerbini on 19 July 1943, 'C' Coy. was ordered to take up a position astride the cross-roads at Crociata Jannarello. When the leading platoon was nearing the objective it came under heavy fire from the front, and was pinned to the ground. It was therefore necessary for the two remaining platoons to work round and attack the enemy position from a flank. The way was however, barred by a German S.P. gun which started firing at the Coy. at point-blank range. Cpl. Hutchison, realising that the success of the operation depended on the elimination of this gun immediately went forward alone, under very heavy fire, particularly from another A.F.V. from a flank. He worked his way right up to the gun, which was being fired on by our own troops, and succeeded in throwing a grenade inside from a few feet. The burst hit and disabled the gun, and caused the gun crew to jump out, where they were dealt with by the L.M.G.s of the Coy. The silencing of this gun was a determining factor in the success of this operation. The initiative, courage and determinaion of Cpl. Hutchison then, and during the rest of the operation, were of the very highest degree, and an inspiration to all around him.
(L.G. 23.9.43)

Hutton, George Francis, Warrant Officer Cl. II
6012900, Essex Regt., No. 2 Commando
In recognition of gallant and distinguished services in the field.   *(L.G. 15.3.45)*

Hutton, Henry, Corporal
2716327, 2nd Bn. The Monmouthshire Regt., South
Wales Borderers (Liverpool) (Immediate)
On 4 Jan. 45, the Bn. had been ordered to attack the German positions in the Bois De Hampteau, the final objective including the village of Rendeux Bas. When the greater part of the Bois De Hampteau had been secured against some opposition, Cpl. Hutton's Coy., in which he was commanding the leading section, was launched against the village of Rendeux Bas along the main road from Hampteau. On rounding a bend in the road, a well-sited road block was encountered with a steep cliff on one side and some open ground and a mill on the other. Cpl. Hutton was ordered by his Platoon Comd. to search the mill and at once led his section forward through the road block, which included a thick anti-personnel mine field. On entering the mill, the section immediately engaged some enemy on the road to the South with their L.M.G., killing three of them. The enemy replied at once from a dug-in and camouflaged tank, obtaining six direct hits on the mill building with a 75 mm gun. Cpl. Hutton decided that he could carry out his task better from outside the building and moved his section forward, continuing to engage the enemy while the section itself was under intense fire from several Spandaus. A few moments later, yet another Spandau opened fire from a flank, and every member of the section was wounded, including Cpl. Hutton who had his leg broken by a bullet. In spite of intense pain and sustained enemy fire, Cpl. Hutton manœuvred his Bren gun into a fresh position, maintained fire on those enemy positions which he had located, and then dressed the wounds of his men. At this time, the section was in position in a frozen stream, up to their waists in water and ice, while the remainder of the platoon were getting

in position to support a further attack by the remainder of the Coy.

The enemy then sent out a party of about eight men armed with Bazookas and Spandaus, presumably with the object of stalking three tanks which were supporting the Coy. They had succeeded in knocking out one of the tanks before being observed by Cpl. Hutton. Although suffering terribly from the pain of his wounds and the cold, Cpl. Hutton immediately engaged the enemy party with his Bren and three remaining rifles. The enemy at once withdrew. Cpl. Hutton, by this prompt action, undoubtedly saved the remainder of the troop of tanks, which was not then in a position to manœuvre.

Cpl. Hutton's section remained in position for a further four hours, half submerged in icy water and yet continually engaging the enemy whenever opportunity offered. Cpl. Hutton inspired and encouraged his men throughout this time, tending the wounded as best he could, though one died later of his wounds. Cpl. Hutton's conduct throughout this action showed courage, leadership and determination of an outstandingly high order. His bravery has become a by-word and has inspired not only his Coy., but the whole Battalion.

(L.G. 12.4.45)

Huxford, Herbert George, M.B.E., Warrant Officer Cl. II
310799, 9th Queen's Royal Lancers (Dorking)
(Immediate)
Ref. Map Italy 1/50,000 Sheets 88I (Argenta) 76II)Porto Maggiore.

W.O. II Huxford is S.S.M. of 'B' Squadron, 9th Lancers, and by his initiative and enterprise has contributed greatly to the success of his Squadron. He commands a 105mm tank and always supports one of the leading troops. In the advance North of Fosso Benvignante on 18th Apr., the Squadron was held up by 2 batteries of 88mm guns. S.S.M. Huxford was ordered to deal with the battery to the left front. By great speed and accuracy, under A.P. and H.E. fire shot over open sights at short range, he engaged each gun in turn, knocking out 2. As a result of this, the tanks and infantry were able to advance to the objective. On the same day the Squadron was held up by a fosso. This W.O. brought forward the Fascine, and, under heavy H.E. and small arms fire, supervised the crossing operation which resulted in the capture of other bridges intact and the consequent havoc in the enemy gun lines. On 24th Apr., North of Ferrara, S.S.M. Huxford was supporting the leading troop which was held up by 3 Mk. IVs and an 88. The only cover available—the Signal Box—was occupied. So regardless of great danger, he moved his tank up and down in the open under exceedingly accurate fire, and engaged the 88 from every angle, displaying the keenest determination and gallantry, which was an inspiration to the whole Squadron. After an hour of such treatment the gun destroyed itself. This action greatly assisted the Squadron in reaching their objective. His

energy, cheerfulness and enthusiasm have been a magnificent example to his Squadron. *(L.G. 23.8.45)*

Hywood, William Carson, Corporal
SX24447, '2' Special Unit, Australian Military Forces
(Periodic)
From 3 Mar. 45 to 16 Aug. 45 this N.C.O. displayed leadership, gallantry and cold-blooded courage of the highest order.

On 3 Mar. 45, Cpl. Hywood was a member of a small party of 4 officers and 3 N.C.O.s who entered British North Borneo well knowing:—

(a) That there was a large price on the head of the leader of the party as a result of his previous mission into the area (Enemy posters were found bearing his portrait and offering a reward of 15,000 dol. for him dead or alive).

(b) That having left the submarine there was no chance of withdrawal.

(c) That the coast was strongly held by the enemy and continuously patrolled by land and sea.

The landing was made by rubber boat and canoe midway between two strong enemy posts at Tegahang and Pura Pura 3 miles apart. Owing to the hostility of the natives, 250 miles were travelled by canoe at night before finding a friendly contact enabling the party to move inland. The cold-blooded courage required to make a landing of the type above described is worthy of the highest commendation.

Whilst in the interior this N.C.O. did magnificent work in gathering intelligence, organising native guerillas and harassing the enemy, capturing considerable quantities of Japanese equipment and killing numbers of the enemy.

In addition, on 21 May 45, this N.C.O. was extracted by Catalina with his party leader and when further information was required on behalf of 9 Aust. Div. he volunteered to enter Borneo again. On 29 May 45, with his party leader and another N.C.O. and one native, Cpl. Hywood was inserted by Catalina into the strongly held Beaufort area near Brunei Bay.

After reconnaissance of the situation on 31 May 45, the party leader discovered that the railway stationmaster at Bongowan was a Chinese named Ah Lee, known to him in pre-war days. In a particularly daring operation in which it was necessary for Cpl. Hywood to crawl to the fringe of the jungle within 10 yards of the railway station building in order to provide fire cover if necessary, this station master was extracted in broad daylight from the station which was staffed and guarded by Japanese.

From 29 May 45, to 7 Jun 45 this small party operated in the heart of the most strongly held area in British North Borneo, necessarily on the alert 24 hours of the day.

On 7 Jun. 45, this N.C.O. with the party was extracted by Catalina and a few weeks later returned to the interior of Borneo where his work continued to be of great value and earned the highest praise of his commander.

(L.G. 6.3.47)

I

Ibrahim, Wadai, Serjeant
NA/32204, 2nd (W.A.) Bn. The Nigeria Regt.
On 23 Jan 45, this NCO was the African Sergeant of a fighting patrol sent from Kinzeik to Myohaung. When the patrol attacked a party of Japanese who were trying to demolish a bridge over a chaung, Sjt. Wadai Ibrahim stalked a detachment of them and killed three. At about this time the patrol came under heavy machine gun and mortar fire which continued intermittently for two days and nights, but during this period he accounted for three more Japanese. On 25 Jan, when part of the enemy had withdrawn, he went forward alone to repair the damage the enemy had done to the roadway. This he succeeded in doing although enemy snipers were firing at him. He finally crossed to the far bank, bayonetted a sniper & then called over the two secs under his command who effectively dispersed the remaining enemy and thereby eliminated the threat to the bridge. His great courage, devotion to duty and cheerfulness throughout these two days and nights in an exposed position had a most marked effect upon the members of the whole patrol.
(19.4.45)

Ilala, Sergeant
British Solomon Islands Defence Forces
S.W.Pacific   *(L.G. 6.6.44)*

Illingsworth, Stephen, Private
24579367, Parachute Regt.
In the early hours of 28th May 1982, the 2nd Battalion The Parachute Regiment launched an attack on enemy positions in the area of the Darwin and Goose Green settlements on the Island of East Falkland. The enemy were thought to be entrenched in battalion strength. In the event, their numbers were far greater and fierce fighting ensued all day.

Private Illingsworth was a member of 5 Platoon, which was the depth platoon in B Company's advance. At one point the advance came under heavy and accurate enemy fire, and OC B Company attacked the enemy position with his leading platoons, leaving 5 Platoon to provide covering fire. Dawn was growing stronger and it became clear that 5 Platoon was in fact exposed on a long forward slope without protection and very vulnerable to increasingly heavy enemy machine gun and rifle fire. Its position became untenable and it was ordered to withdraw back over the crest. It was during this manœuvre that one of their number was hit in the back.

Private Illingsworth, who had already reached comparative safety himself, immediately rushed forward in full view and fire of the enemy, accompanied by another soldier, to help their wounded comrade. In an effort to locate the wound they removed his weapon and webbing equipment, and having administered First Aid, dragged the soldier back over the crest line, despite a hail of enemy fire which miraculously missed them. Once in a position of safety, Private Illingsworth continued to tend the injured man's wounds.

The fire fight continued intensively, and 5 Platoon began to run short of ammunition. Remembering that he had left the webbing equipment, with ammunition in it, lying on the exposed forward slope, Private Illingsworth decided to go forward alone to collect it. Disregarding the enemy fire, which was still extremely heavy he broke cover and advanced once again down the forward slope. As he did so he was killed.

In these two acts of supreme courage Private Illingsworth showed a complete disregard for his own safety, and a total dedication to others. While his action in coming to the help of a wounded soldier may have been almost instinctive on seeing the plight of a comrade, his move forward to collect much needed ammunition for his beleagured platoon was a display of coolly-calculated courage and heroism of the very highest order.
[From L.G.]   *(L.G. 19.9.78)*

Imms, Edward, Warrant Officer Cl. III (T.S.M.)
398934, 5th Royal Inniskilling Dragoon Guards
On Thursday 23rd May, 1940, T.S.M. Imms' tank troop was blocking a gap between two squadrons near Lynd, which was strongly held by enemy who had artillery and anti tank weapons. With complete disregard of his personal safety this W.O. pressed the enemy over nine hours and thereby prevented the enemy from splitting these squadrons. Again on May 27th 1940, his troop was cut off from its squadron by six enemy heavy tanks whilst on patrol near Neuve Chappel. By his inspiring leadership and coolness in a desperate situation he succeeded in leading his troop through the enemy lines with small losses, thereby saving them from annihilation.
(L.G. 20.12.40)

Ison, Bertram Talbot Scott, Lance Sergeant
852192, 67 Fd. Regt., Royal Artillery
During operations on River Dyle he maintained his communications through prolonged bombing and gun fire on his O.P. He kept closely in touch with the Infantry and was responsible for much valuable liaison work. He later collected 16 men who were lost and marched them over ten miles to safety. He showed complete disregard for his personal safety and was a fine example to all throughout all phases.   *(L.G. 11.7.40)*

J

Jackman, Kenneth John, Sergeant
14463612, Cameronians
For Malaya   *(L.G. 4.1.52)*

Jackson, Alfred William, Sergeant (A/W.O.II (C.S.M.))
3241839, 2nd Bn. Cameronians (Birmingham)
(Immediate)
Between 15th and 21st March 1944 in the Anzio beachhead the company of which CSM Jackson was CSM was holding a forward position only a few yards from the enemy. The country was covered in thick scrub; visibility was extremely limited and an aggressive enemy made constant attempts to infiltrate. The whole company area was kept under almost continuous mortar fire during daylight. In these trying circumstances the aggressive spirit shown by CSM Jackson was beyond praise. He went constantly from post to post, regardless of mortar fire and enemy snipers, seeking for OP's from which he could see and engage the enemy. He organised and led harrassing parties with LMG's, Piats and 2″ mortars which inflicted casualties on the enemy.

His total disregard of personal danger, his zeal for battle ad his determination to engage the enemy were major factors in enabling our forces to retain hold of a most important sector. He gave an outstanding display of how a warrant officer can operate in battle.
M.M. 2.8.45   *(L.G. 20.7.44)*

Jackson, Clifford, Lance Sergeant
5348543, 9th Bn. Royal Fusiliers (Bedworth,
Warwick) (Immediate)
On the night of 21/22 Jan 44 this NCO was acting as Pl. comd holding a defensive locality over the River Garigliano. On the morning of 23 Jan a shell landed near his sanger and partially blinded him with the blast. A quarter of an hour later his platoon was heavily counter-attacked, and his men started withdrawing. He immediately rejoined his men and led them back under heavy automatic and mortar fire to their original positions. He kept them there, by his personal example and control, and inflicted heavy casualties on the attacking enemy. This man's personal example and fine leadership at a critical time restored a situation which might have become completely out of control: and his tenacity and courage in refusing to leave until the danger was over, when he eventually had to be led back to the R.A.P. still partially blinded, were beyond praise.
Silver Star 14.5.48, M.M. 8.12.53   *(L.G. 4.5.44)*

Jackson, George, Private
6021512, 1/4th Bn. Essex Regt. (Finsbury)
(Immediate)
This soldier displayed most conspicuous bravery and devotion during the operations of 5 Ind Inf Bde in the area Djebel Garci (Emfidaville Line) 19 to 23 Apr 43.

He was one of a patrol of fourteen men, under an officer, which set out on the night of 19/20 Apr to penetrate the enemy lines and create a diversion during the main attack. During the night the patrol was discovered by the enemy, and after a hazardous journey was located at first light in a wadi well inside the enemy lines.

The officer in charge of the patrol went forward some fifty yards under enemy observation to make a reconnaissance. While doing so he was severely wounded, and the enemy immediately brought down intense machine gun fire on the [spa]ce separating him from the patrol.

The NCO in charge of the patrol asked for a volunteer to go to the officer's assistance, whereupon Private Jackson immediately went forward to where his officer was lying. Finding that further assistance was necessary, he returned to the patrol for dressings and, taking the officer's batman with him, went back to the wounded officer. While attending to the officer the batman was killed. Undeterred Private Jackson completed his attentions to the officer under what was now concentrated machine gun fire, reinforced by snipers, and went back to the remainder of the patrol to report to the NCO.

The NCO wanted some orders from the officer, so Private Jackson again returned to him and apart from receiving the orders attempted to carry the officer back to cover. The officer refused, however, to let this be done owing to his apparent mortal wound, and Private Jackson returned to the patrol with the orders for its movement.

Before the patrol moved off down the wadi, the officer called out for someone to collect his compass and binoculars. Private Jackson thereupon immediately returned to his officer for the fourth time, subsequently rejoining the patrol with the equipment.

In making these four journeys across some fifty yards of ground swept by intense cross machine gun fire, and in full view of the enemy Private Jackson appeared to face certain death, and it was indeed a miracle that he survived unscathed. His action in facing these journeys; not in the heat of the battle but knowing the risks involved; disclosed bravery, devotion and loyalty to his officer beyond all praise.
Statement by 6011533 Pte (T/L/Cpl) Patrick, C.
I went out with a patrol commanded by Lieut. C. Hailes which left our lines on the night April 19/20. When we were well behind the enemy lines Lieut. Hailes was shot. At the time he was about sixty yards out in front of the rest of the patrol, which was in a shallow wadi. When Lieut. Hailes did not return, Cpl. Thompson asked for a volunteer to go and find out what was wrong. Pte. Jackson at once went out, and came back saying that Lieut. Hailes had been hit in the stomach and needed dressing. He

returned with Pte. Marsh. A little while later he crawled back and said Pte. Marsh had been shot and killed, but he had managed to dress Lieut. Hailes' wound. I heard Pte. Jackson tell Cpl. Thompson that Lieut. Hailes would not let him move him, so Cpl. Thompson asked him to go back and get orders. All the time the machine gun fire was very heavy indeed. Pte. Jackson returned once again to Lieut. Hailes, and came back soon after with orders to move. Just as we were moving off I saw Pte. Jackson crawling out again, and he came back with a pair of binoculars and a compass. All the time we were there the machine gun fire was very fierce, and the snipers were always having a go.

Statement by 6030727 Pte. Sykes, A.

I was one of a patrol of fourteen which went out on the night 19/20 April under Lieut. C. Hailes.

During the night, when we had passed through a lot of enemy positions, Lieut. Hailes was shot. As he was fifty yards out in front of the rest of the patrol, Cpl. Thompson asked for a volunteer to go out to Lieut. Hailes and find out what was wrong with him. Without giving anyone else a chance, Pte. Jackson crawled out under very heavy machine gun fire. I was crouching by Cpl. Thompson when Pte. Jackson got back, and I heard him say Lieut. Hailes was bad and needed dressing. I saw Pte. Jackson and Pte. Marsh, Lieut. Hailes' batman, go out together. After a time Pte. Jackson crawled back alone and said Pte. Marsh had been killed. Pte. Jackson went out again through all the fire to get orders from the officer, and brought them back, and later when we were moving out he went back a fourth time to get Lieut. Hailes' binoculars and compass. The machine gun fire was very bad and Lieut. Hailes was lying in an exposed position.

Statement by 6021944 W/Cpl. Thompson, H.

I was 2 i/c of patrol when Lieut. Hailes was shot and wounded. I called for a volunteer, Pte. Jackson. G. immediately came forward. He crawled forward to Lieut. Hailes to investigate his wounds, he returned and reported to me, again Pte. Jackson G. crawled forward to dress Lieut. Hailes' wound, he was accompanied this time by Pte. Marsh. Pte. Marsh was shot and killed. Pte. Jackson G. again returned and reported situation to me. Pte. Jackson G. once more crawled forward to receive orders for myself. Pte. Jackson G. returned with these, telling us the route back. Again Pte. Jackson. G. crawled out to get Lieut. Hailes' binoculars and compass. During the whole of this time, the area in which Pte. Jackson G. moved in was under very intensive and accurate machine gun and rifle snipers fire.

Statement by 6021448 Pte. Hounson, E.

I was a member of a patrol which set out on the night of April 19/20, under Lieut. Hailes.

When Lieut. Hailes was shot he was about fifty yards ahead of the rest of the patrol. Cpl. Thompson called for a volunteer to go out to Lieut. Hailes to see how bad he was. Pte. Jackson went out and came back saying he needed a shell dressing as the wound was serious. He returned to Lieut. Hailes accompanied by Pte. Marsh,

batman. Pte. Marsh was killed by machine gun fire, which was going on terrible all the time. Pte. Jackson came back and said Lieut. Hailes wouldn't let him move him as the wound was too bad. Cpl. Thompson asked if he had given any orders, so Pte. Jackson went out to Lieut. Hailes and returned with orders to move on. Just as we were moving Lieut. Hailes called out for someone to come and fetch his binoculars and compass. Pte. Jackson went out for the fourth time, and got back all right. The machine gun fire and snipers were very intense the whole time.

Recommended for V.C.   *(L.G. 22.7.43)*

Jackson, James, Lance Corporal
VX 14220, 2/5 Australian Infantry Bn. (Immediate)
For outstanding bravery under fire and inspiring leadership:

Cpl. Jackson was section commander of 3 Sec during 'A' Coy attack on Mt Tambu on 16 Jul 43. He ably supported his Pl Comd—Sjt Taylor—and by his fearless disregard of danger was an inspiration not only to his section but to the whole platoon. With three grenades he attacked an automatic weapon and destroyed it single-handed. He attacked another enemy pillbox with a TSMG and wiped out the three occupants.

During an enemy counter attack, whilst his section was consolidating, Cpl. Jackson went forward for fifty yards alone and covered their consolidation. He was instrumental in beating off the eight enemy counter attacks on his platoon during the night 16/17 Jul.

During an attack on 18 Jul Cpl. Jackson was again instrumental in the gaining and consolidation of the forward slopes of Tambu's South Pimple and his untiring direction of his section's steady fire resulted in the successful extrication of another section—No 8.

Again during incessant enemy counter-attacks on 19 Jul Jackson himself inflicted approximately 30 casualties on the enemy. His example, demeanour and resolute leadership contributed largely to the capture and consolidation of the Mt Tambu feature. *(L.G. 4.11.43)*

Jackson, Joseph, Corporal
3781177, King's Regiment, No. 2 Commando
In recognition of gallant and distinguished services in the field.
Recommended by S.A.C.-in-C. Meditteranean
        (L.G. 15.3.45)

Jackson, T., Warrant Officer Cl. II (C.S.M.)
3377300, 1st Bn. East Lancashire Regt.
This Warrant Officer has been the mainstay of his Company during the period 17th May to 2nd June, 1940. In Tournai he showed complete disregard for enemy shell fire and brought ammunition up to the forward posts despite heavy shell fire. His general conduct gave the troops great confidence and his example was undoubtedly a great help to young soldiers. At Rousbrugge Maringe, this Warrant Officer was left in charge of the rearguard

of his company. We were in very close contact with the enemy (probably 50 yards) and when the last platoon was ready to leave it was found there were still some men left behind with the transport. This Warrant Officer remained behind until he was able to collect the last few men but he allowed the platoon to withdraw. I consider that this was a brave action as the enemy had been extremely active on the company front. *(L.G. 11.7.40)*

James, Samuel, Warrant Officer Cl. III (Pl.S.M.)
4796142, 2nd Lincolnshire Regt.
On the afternoon of the 28th May 1940 P.S.M. James led his platoon in a local counter attack in order to fill a gap between 'D' Coy and the Regiment on the left of the Battalion. In spite of strong opposition and in the face of heavy shell and mortar fire, elements of the enemy who had penetrated the position were driven out and the line re-established. P.S.M. James displayed the utmost coolness and courage and handled his platoon skilfully. His example was invaluable in inspiring his platoon and constituted greatly to the success of the operation. During the whole course of the operations in Belgium and Flanders this W.O. has set a high standard of courage and devotion to the Platoon under his command.
(L.G. 11.7.40)

James, William Rowland, Warrant Officer Cl. II (B.S.M.) [now Lieutenant on AFW 3121]
853841, 2nd Regt., Royal Horse Artillery (Ashton-under-Lyne)
This W.O. has got 6½ years regular service in L/N Battery 2nd Regiment R.H.A. At the outbreak of War he was promoted from L/Bdr. to L/Sjt. and went out to France in this Regt. He fought then in Belgium and in France. He was recommended for an immediate award for his gallant action as Troop BSM in a sharp engagement at Mont Des Cats, when his conduct won him the high opinions of all ranks as follows:—

'A Brigade of the 44 Div rallied during the night at the Mont Des Cats. L/N Battery was the only Artillery present. It was impossible to get a covered position as the roads were blocked by abandoned vehicles. [...] guns were got into action and succeeded in silencing the fire of some 8 Mortars. A German Battery then started to fire at our guns. They were engaged by the remaining two guns until these two were finally knocked out by direct hits. B.S.M. James showed the greatest courage and ability throughout this action, finally going on to a gun himself after the whole detachment had been wounded.'

He remained B.S.M. to L Troop L/N Bty during the operation in Greece where his ability—coolness under fire and high example to all caused his name again to be forwarded by the Formation Commander for an immediate award of the D.C.M. Once again his conduct was unrecognized.

On return from Greece this W.O. became Battery Sergeant Major and served with his Battery on the Libyan Frontier. On 14 Sept 41 the enemy carried out a reconnaissance in force with 200 Tanks. L Troop advanced, the better to be able to reach the enemy with their fire. Their subsequent withdrawal at the last minute in the face of a heavy attack [was due] largely to the coolness and ability of B.S.M. James, [...] this he was again put in for an award and again failed to get one.

Throughout the operations from Nov 18, 1941 to March 42, the actions of the Battery have been marked by the distinguished conduct of this W.O. at all times. He carried out the duties of Tp Gun Position Officer for long periods, after casualties had been received. He carried the duties of Tp O.P. Officer in support of Armour with conspicuous success. He earned the very high opinion of the Tank Bn Comdrs, whom he supported and his conduct was noted by the Brigade Commander and also by the Divisional Commander on several occasions during this period. During this campaign he surpassed all others in his splendid enthusiasm, his fighting spirit and tactical ability and without question was deserving of an award before any in the Regt. Again he was given 1st priority for an immediate award and failed to have one granted. He was then put up for a periodical on the recommendation of higher authority. His case was cited at length. This list has now been published and his name is once more absent. He has since been made a Lieutenant on an immediate emergency commission. I wish to press very strongly indeed for this W.O. to receive recognition. I request that very special consideration may please be given to the award of the D.C.M. I wish this award to take first priority in this Regiment.
M.I.D. 24.6.43 *(L.G. 18.2.43)*

James, William Sidney, Warrant Officer Cl. II (R.Q.M.S.)
1423930, 12th Royal Lancers
This W.O. acted as Qr.Ms. to the Regiment throughout the period 10–31 May and it is due to his excellent common sense, personal disregard for bombing, and exceptional continuous efforts that the Regiment never lacked for supplies, ammunition, or petrol, although constantly on the move during this period. The Armoured Cars of the Regiment covered in some cases 2000 miles and the Regiment was attached to nine different formations for operations so that the magnitude of his task will be readily appreciated and yet without those supplies the Regiment would have been immobilized.
Duplicated in L.G. 22.10.40 *(L.G. 5.7.40)*

Jarvis, Edward Henry, Warrant Officer Cl. III (Pl.S.M.)
6912609, 2nd Bn. Rifle Brigade
For cospicuous gallantry. At Sidi Saley during the night 6/7th Feb., this Warrant Officer was commanding an isolated platoon on the beach when attacked in the moonlight by two enemy medium tanks. Accompanied by one Rifleman, he ran up to the tanks on the move and fired through the slits with his rifle, wounding the crews.

One of the officers fired at him with a pistol from the door of the tank and he thereupn hit him over the head with the butt of his rifle. The crew then surrendered.

(L.G. 9.5.41)

Jarvis, Heigham Owen, Warrant Officer Cl. III (T.S.M.) (A/W.O.II, B.S.M.)
800598, 3rd Corps, R.H.A., Royal Artillery
On May 23 T.S.M. Jarvis assumed command of the Bty, the only officer present being wounded. During this time the troop was heavily countered by enemy guns, and attacked by low flying enemy aircraft. T.S.M. Jarvis continued to fire against the enemy until ordered to withdraw. Whilst limbering up, the troop came under intense artillery fire, shells landing amongst guns and detachments. By his conspicuous gallantry and coolness, this warrant officer succeeded in withdrawing three out of his four guns, the other gun having been put out of action by hostile fire. He set a fine example to all ranks.

(L.G. 20.12.40)

Jeffrey, Clarence, Sergeant
6286764, 5th Bn. Buffs (Royal East Kent Regt.)
(Riseley, nr. Reading) (Immediate)
During the advance of 5 Buffs to its start line on 8 Apr 43 the Coy. was surprised West of Mergueb Chouach by a German ambush. Sjt. Jeffery was ordered by his Pl. Comd. to go round the right flank of the enemy and deal with them. He went round followed by two others, crawled round the back of a sniper and made him surrender, then went straight for a Mortar Position held by seven men. These also surrendered with their weapon intact; thus these three men brought back eight prisoners on their own together with a Mortar, an M.G. and half-a-dozen rifles.

His Acting C.S.M. was injured on the 9th of Apr and this N.C.O. took over the job. From that moment he was a great inspiration to his men in the Coy., and he worked untiringly throughout the whole of the time his Coy. was on Pt 667. His conduct and gallantry throughout the whole of the operation was of the highest standard.

(L.G. 15.6.43)

Jemson, Cyril, Trooper
305317, S.A.S. Bde, 1st S.A.S. Regt., Army Air Corps
(Preston) (Immediate)
On the night 15/16 July 1944 Tpr. Jemson was one of an operational patrol commanded by Lt. Wellstead whose task was to blow the Digoin—Paray le Moniel railway line some 70 miles S.W. of Dijon. In order to get to the line it was necessary for the patrol to cross bridges over the river Bourbice and over a canal. Tpr. Jemson was left on the causeway between the two with a bren gun, to cover the canal bridge and protect the line of with-drawal of the patrol. His orders were not to open fire whatever happened until the enemy opened up. While the rest of the patrol was working on the railway line German patrols came down both banks of the canal and

one bank of the river. Hearing our patrol at work, they proceeded to prepare an ambush between the two bridges and all round ... *[continuation missing]*

(L.G. 21.12.44)

Jennings, Arthur, Warrant Officer Cl. I (R.S.M.)
4442560, 8th Bn. Durham Light Infantry (York)
(Immediate)
During the night withdrawal from the Gaurawla Nulla 28th June a column was surprised at the head of the Nulla, and became heavily engaged. The coln became divided by heavy machine-gun, mortar and A/Tk fire, and further advance was held up. This W.O. took command of the situation, organised covering fire from Bren Guns, and personally observed fire of the 2″ Mortar and the Brens and in doing so was almost continually exposed to heavy fire. The enemy fire was sufficiently neutralised to enable the successful withdrawal of the coln to continue. He was the last to leave the posn, having seen everyone clear, and it was largely due to his action and personality that the party was successfully withdrawn. *(L.G. 24.9.42)*

Jennings, Thomas Douglas, Corporal (A/Sgt.)
7016326, 5th Bn. Black Watch (London, E. 14)
(Immediate)
On the night of 24/25th March, 1943, the Bn was ordered to attack and capture area forward of the Mareth Line occupied by the enemy. One Coy. was very heavily shelled indeed while forming up on the Start Line. The shelling accounted for 75% of the Coy., either killed or wounded. A small party, including Sjt. Jennings, forced its way forward to the objective, still under intense artillery fire and considerable small arms fire. Sjt. Jennings was first on the objective and dealt with considerable numbers of the enemy. All round, Italians were jumping out of their trenches and giving themselves up, and the situation was very confused. Sjt. Jennings assisted in the reorganisation of the small part of the Coy. now remaining and continually encouraged and exhorted his men to hold on to the position which was very precarious. the enemy brought accurate Mortar fire to bear, killing and wounding many more. Eventually a counter-attack developed and at first was successfully held off. During the whole of this time, Sjt. Jennings had shewn complete disregard for his own safety, and a strong determination to hold the position won at any cost, all amidst intense enemy fire. Not until when ordered by one remaining Officer to withdraw, would he consent to do so, and throughout, his first thoughts were for the rest of the party and not for himself. Sjt. Jennings showed courage and devotion to duty of a most remarkable kind and helped materially in destroying large numbers of the enemy, and taking a good few prisoner.

(L.G. 17.6.43)

Jesse, James Henry, Warrant Officer Cl. II
QX 3097, 2/9 Australian Infantry Bn. (Immediate)
During the action Cape Endaiadere 18/22 Dec 1942.

This WO was a platoon commander in C Coy. From the outset and during the whole period he distinguished himself. In the early stages W.O. Jesse led his platoon ably with courage, determination and skill. Later he was commanding the remnants of the company for a few hours and never once faltered in his judgment or leadership. After Captain Griffin had been killed and no other officer was to hand, the remnants of the Coy were being shelled badly and there appeared to be a danger of them becoming disorganised. WO Jesse effectively took charge and continued the attack. Later Major Parry-Okeden was sent up. This WO showed remarkable leadership, judgment, coolness and courage throughout and will make a future senior officer.   *(L.G. 22.4.43)*

Jessome, Patrick Jerome, Lance Sergeant
F.89382, 2 Cdn. Fd. Coy., Royal Canadian Engineers
  (Immediate)
On the night of 24/25 October the leading Infantry advancing into South Beveland were stopped by a road block of mines and wire obstacles covered by heavy fire from a dyke commanding the area M.R. 537203. An infantry company attack followed by an artillery concentration, followed by a second Company attack failed to secure the road block. There was no possible diversion due to flooding. At 0530 hrs. 25 Oct 44 a small party of Sappers was chosen to attempt to clear the road block which was threatening the advance of the Division. L/Sjt. Jessome specially requested to be included in this task. He personally removed most of the wire obstacles which were being swept by vicious machine gun fire. He then proceeded 100 yds beyond the road block to ensure that there were no more mines in the road.

This mans leadership and complete contempt of danger provided a steadying example for the entire Sapper party and the obstructions were completely removed in quick time. The rapid advance of the Division was thus maintained.   *(L.G. 13.1.45)*

Jessup, Geoffrey Alfred, Lance Corporal
1951864, 77 Aslt. Sqn., Royal Engineers
On the evening of 25 Mar 45 No 1957864 L/Cpl. Jessup G. and No 6409984 Spr. Chappel J. were acting as skeleton relief crew, as Dvr & W/Op/Comd respectively on LVT No 5822157 supporting the assault of the 1 SS Bde on Wesel. When returning upstream from the far bank of the Rhime near Wesel at approx 1945 hrs the engine of the LVT failed and it drifted rapidly downstream out of control.

American troops mistaking the Buffalo in the gathering darkness, for an enemy craft apparently attempting to sink the bridges downstream, opened fire with Bofors guns. Despite shouting, the firing continued. L/Cpl. Jessup immediately ordered the three passengers to empty the two petrol jerricans, and to prepare them for use as Life-floats. He showed them the two kapok floats in case it should be necesary to abandon craft. At this stage Spr Chappel was seriously wounded in the shoulder. L/Cpl. Jessup went to administer morphia to him and on returning found that the three passengers had abandoned the craft, taking with them one of the only two kapok floats. Left alone with the wounded man, L/Cpl. Jessup tried to get the anchor to hold when the craft later drifted into shallower water. The craft began to make water and he decided to abandon it. With almost unbelievable skill L/Cpl. Jessup contrived to get the wounded man overboard and on to the remaining kapok float. At the same time he scuttled the craft by opening the ramp door, to prevent it drifting into the bridges downstream.

He then swam downstream with the float until they were again fired on, this time by British Troops. L/Cpl. Jessup was twice wounded, once in the arm and once in the leg. The filling was ripped out of the float, and it rapidly became waterlogged and useless.

After drifting a further distance downstream the two wounded men were recognised by an RA Sjt, who swam out with a line and helped them ashore, where they both received medical attention. L/Cpl. Jessup displayed great gallantry and consistent disregard of his own personal safety throughout. By his courage and sheer determination he was able though himself twice wounded, to save the life of a comrade and to prevent damage to the bridge at a critical stage of the operation, in circumstances that were far beyond the call of duty.   *(L.G. 20.12.45)*

Jobes, Edward, Corporal
K57492, 1 C. Scot. R., Canadian Infantry Corps
After showing exceptional gallantry throughout the beach assault, and subsequent advance ino the hinterland as section leader, Cpl. Jobes found himself on the morning of 9 Jun 44, acting Platoon Sjt. As forward platoon on the railway embankment beside Putot-en-Besson, his platoon found themselves subjected to terrific fire from Tiger Tanks, 'hulled-down' MG and rifle fire. Despite this fire, this NCO, showing terrific drive and initiative moved among the platoon ordering, advising and collecting valuable information and taking it to Coy HQ, all of which was subject to the same fire. Finally the enemy attempted to left-flank the Coy and covered the advance by increased fire, forcing the coy to take cover. Picking up a Bren gun, Cpl. Jobes leaped to the top of his slit trench and under withering fire sprayed the enemy infantry. Inspired by his example, many others braved the fire and despite casualties forced the enemy to retire, thus saving the situation until friendly armour could be brought up.   *(L.G. 19.8.44)*

Johns, Stuart Louis, Lance Corporal
A.118218, 22 Cdn. Armd. Regt. (Immediate)
On 24 Apr 45, in the initial stages of the breakout across the Kusten Canal, No 1 Troop of No 2 Squadron 22 Cdn Armd Regt, under command 'A' Coy, Lake Sup R (Mt), was advancing along the road from MR 141025 to MR 131031. About three hundred yards from a road block which dominated the objective the Troop Commander's

tank and that of his Troop Sjt were forced to draw back because of mechanical difficulties. L/Cpl. Johns took command of the remaining two tanks on the instant and moved steadily forward in the teeth of point blank panzerfaust fire from position on the right flank. It soon became apparent that a further advance was suicidal. The panzerfaust fire became more intense as the enemy closed on the right flank and a heavy machine gun concentration from the vicinity of the road block pinned our own infantry to the ground, depriving L/Cpl. Johns of essential protection on his right. From his commanding position in the turret of his tank, L/Cpl. Johns appreciated the predicament in which our infantry found itself, and at the same time noticed a covered avenue of advance which was apparently not visible from ground level. Without a moment's hesitation he scrambled out of his tank and made his way back to the infantry through a hellish concentration of machine gun fire. He guided the infantry forward to a suitable covering position, and then, again fully exposing himself to the merciless fire, climbed back into his tank and continued the advance. So skilfully did he direct the fire of his two tanks and of the Badger flame thrower which he had called up in support that the positions in the vicinity of the road block were over-whelmed, the enemy on the flanks were forced to withdraw and 'A' Coy was firmly established on the objective. The initiative, dash and powers of leadership displayed by L/Cpl Johns on this occasion were largely instrumental in assuring the successful breakout from the bridgehead. The complete disregard for his personal safety displayed by this NCO was an inspiration to all ranks of the small force concerned, and will long remain a model of conduct for the 22 Cdn Armd Regt.

(L.G. 22.9.45)

Johnson, Harold, Warrant Officer Cl. III (Pl.S.M.) (A/ W.O.II (C.S.M.))
5043330, 2nd North Staffordshire Regt.
P.S.M. Johnson shewed conspicuous devotion to duty and set a very fine example to his Platoon throughout operations from the river Dyle to Dunkirk over the period 13th May to 1st June 1940. This Warrant Officer's Platoon held forward positions both on the river Dyle and river Escaut and, owing largely to the example set by P.S.M. Johnson, the Platoon never faltered in the holding of its exposed positions despite the intense bombardment and small arms fire at close range to which it was subjected on numerous occasions.

P.S.M. Johnson with his Platoon also did excellent work during an attack by the Battalion on the Lys Canal on 27th May 1940.   *(L.G. 27.8.40)*

Johnson, Herbert Hume, Corporal
NX.2470, 2/1 Australian Infantry Bn. (Immediate)
Recommended by Commanding Officer for DCM, for most distinguished conduct and gallantry in the face of the enemy.

Cpl. Johnson commanded a section in a vital forward position on the key height commanding the Retimo airfield. At about 1630 hrs on 20 May a large force of paratroops landed on this vital hill completely surrounding Cpl. Johnson's section. After fierce fighting our troops in front of and on either side of Cpl. Johnson's section were either over run or forced to withdraw. As the hill was completely covered with 2 foot high vines and Germans were able to creep up close to Cpl. Johnson's post and, as his post was halfway down the hill, the enemy could command it from their position on the hill top. Despite being under continuous mortar, grenade and small arms fire from all sides he maintained his isolated position most gallantly all through the remaining daylight of 20 May, that night and the next day until, finally the Germans were driven from this vital hill. To my mind Cpl. Johnson's gallant stand greatly hindered the German paratroops in their most determined effort to capture this vital hill.

The abovementioned action of Corporal Johnson was of the finest spirit of determination and courage which could be asked of any soldier.   *(L.G. 25.9.47)*

Johnson, Raymond Anthony, Corporal (A/Sgt.)
6285732, 2/5th Bn. Queen's Royal Regt. (Kingston-on-Thames) (Immediate)
Farneto (Italy, [...]0,000 Sheet 109 IV 862793) 10/11 Sep 1944.

Sjt. Johnson was in command of No. 15 Platoon, 'C' Company, 2/5th Bn. The Queen's Royal Regiment, during an attack by his company on he village of Farneto on the night of 10/11 Sep 1944. With weak numbers and under heavy fire he led his platoon to the assistance of another who were having great difficulty in the mopping up of enemy positions. The operation became one of clearing houses and dug-outs, which, under Sjt. Johnson's leadership was most brilliantly carried out. This move was effected with the greatest precision and without hesitation; and it was this skilful decision and display of initiative which alone produced immediate and decisive success, inflicting heavy casualties on a well-placed enemy in greater strength than the attackers.

This NCO showed throughout this action a very high standard of command and personal example. He was most intelligent in his appreciation of the assistance he could give and further exploitation of the position by speed and initiative. The success of the attack was largely due to his efforts and leadership.
Recommended for M.M.   *(L.G. 8.2.45)*

Johnson, Sidney James, Corporal (A/Sgt.)
B.73005, Highland Light Inf. of Canada (Immediate)
Following an assault landing on the south bank of the Schelde, Sjt. Johnson was in charge of a section of 3″ Mortars under command of 'B' Company, The Highland Light Infantry of Canada. At 1400 hrs, 10 Oct 1944, 'B' Company was assaulting an enemy strong-point near Paviljeon. The enemy position consisted of dug in

machine gun posts and 20 mm guns, and had held up our advance for the past 36 hours.

In order to observe properly, and correct his section's mortar fire, it was necessary for Sjt. Johnson to take up an exposed position that was being swept by enemy machine gun fire. In that position he was wounded, but stayed at his post and continued to direct his section's covering fire on 'B' Company's assault. He was wounded a second time, and then a third time, but still continued at his post directing mortar fire of his section.

Only when the objective was captured, consolidated, and all danger of immediate counter attack was past did he permit himself to be removed from his post and his wounds to be dressed.

Through his superb handling of his section and complete disregard for his own safety, Sjt. Johnson inflicted heavy damage upon the enemy and enabled the infantry to capture its objective, thus securing the battalion beachhead, permitting the landing of supplies.
(L.G. 20.1.45)

Johnson, William Gervase, Warrant Officer Cl. III (Pl.S.M.)
3906108, 2 South Wales Borderers (Immediate)
During the withdrawal operation on the neighbourhood of Hopen and of Bodo on the 30th and 31st May and 1st June, P.S.M. Johnson in charge of Bren Carriers was ordered to cover the retirement of 1 S.G. This he did in a most cool and efficient manner. As enemy cycle patrols approached he immediately advanced towards them, dispersing them with his Bren gun fire and inflicting several casualties. Once when one of his carriers was damaged by mortar fire he took immediate steps to destroy it. His actions throughout had a heartening and inspiring effect on the troops he was covering, and he was largely responsible for the fact that the Scots Guards were able to embark in an orderly manner.

The Officer Commanding 1 S.G. and the officers of H.M.S. 'Echo' have paid testimony to the fine actions of this Warrant Officer. *(L.G. 6.8.40)*

Johnstone, James Stewart, Lance Sergeant
14002580, 5th Bn. Black Watch (Galashiels)
(Immediate)
On 11 Feb 45 the Bn attacked the town of Gennep and fighting continued for some 36 hours. L/Sjt. Johnstone was commanding a section in a Company engaged on clearing the main street. There were enemy in many of the houses and cellars, and considerable resistance from enemy snipers and machine-gun nests. Halfway down the street about a dozen enemy advanced towards his section firing their weapons. Without a moments hesitation Sjt. Johnstone charged them alone, firing his Sten gun, and completely broke up their attack, killing two of them. Then a house at a multiple road junction—a key point in the town—was seen to hold an enemy post. Quickly realising the importance of this position, which dominated communications in the town, L/Sjt.

Johnstone collected his section and disregarding the intense enemy fire up the street, led his men in a magnificent assault up the street, rushed the house and forced an entry. The enemy fought fiercely from room to room, but L/Sjt. Johnstone rushed each room in turn and wiped out the enemy to a man. Within minutes more enemy reformed and advanced on the house under heavy bazooka fire and grenades. Sjt. Johnstone was everywhere in the house encouraging his men and directing their fire and was completely regardless of exposing himself to the danger of very close contact. The enemy were driven off, suffering several casualties. Shortly after, the enemy again reformed for the attack and after preliminary bazooka fire, rushed the house and gained a footing in one room. Sjt. Johnstone rushed there, killed two men with a grenade and the remainder were quick to get out. By his magnificent courage and devotion to duty in the face of intense enemy fire, Sjt. Johnstone succeeded in capturing and holding this important position, and his action had a material effect on the advance of 1 Gordons through his Company area. His inspiring leadership and cheerful and determined agressiveness through several hours of street fighting were an example to which his men were quick to re-act.
(L.G. 19.4.45)

Johnstone, Leslie Milne, Sergeant
2766113, 1st Bn. Black Watch (Forfar) (Periodic)
Throughout the campaign in N.W. Europe, since early June 1944, this NCO has either led a section or acted as Platoon Sjt, on occasion commanding a Platoon. Throughout, he has displayed absolutely outstanding courage and leadership. In Holland, in October, after the crossing of a river, he personally led an assault on an enemy post and killed the occupants, and later used an abandoned wasp flame thrower with great effect. At Laroche in January he peronally led an assault across bullet swept ground to clear a strongly held house, the capture of which was vital to the attack. After the Rhine crossing, he took over a Platoon and held out in a house for several hours against the most determined enemy attacks accompanied by bazookas and S.P. guns. At one time, he personally climbed onto the roof in full view of the enemy, and from this position was able to shoot and kill a bazooka party who were infiltrating and endangering the whole position. During the whole campaign, it is difficult to speak too highly of this NCO's conduct. Throughout his entire company, his courage is a bye-word, and it is difficult to overestimate the tremendous value of his splendid example to the men around him.
M.I.D. 9.8.45 *(L.G. 24.1.46)*

Jones, Benjamin Vaughan, Marine
Ply.X.100514, 23rd Light A.A. Bty., Royal Marines
At his gun position south-west of Canea on 21st May displayed outstanding courage, by shooting down an enemy aircraft by firing a bren gun from the shoulder. Later in the day he made a lone bayonet charge against

seven parachutists armed with sub-machine guns who had landed in a glider close to the gun position. He was wounded in this action. This prompt action displayed great bravery and was a fine example to all ranks.

(L.G. 4.11.41)

Jones, Charles Reilly, Private
3060843, 1st Bn. Black Watch (Edinburgh)
Pte. Jones has acted as Coy. Runner throughout the operations from El Alamein to Tripoli. His example of great personal bravery has been an inspiration, not only to his own Coy., but to the Bn. as a whole. His action at Homs on 19 Jan 43 was particularly praiseworthy. His Coy. on this occasion closed to within short range of the enemy rear-guard. Coy. HQ and all pls were in very exposed positions and any movement at once brought down very heavy and accurate M.G. and L.A. fire from the enemy. In spite of these conditions, Pte. Jones repeatedly carried messages to forward pls. under very heavy small arms fire and eventually made his way back to Bn. HQ with the information that the enemy's withdrawal had started.
M.M. 20.12.45   *(L.G. 4.5.43)*

Jones, David John, Sergeant
2733460, 2nd Bn. Welsh Guards
This N.C.O. was one of the few senior Sgts. left behind in the closing stages of the Battle of Boulogne in May, 1940, after the main body had been withdrawn during night of May 23rd. All through the very testing and trying 36 hours that ensued until Saturday, May 25th, Sjt. Jones worked with indefatigable energy and exhibited extreme courage under the worst possible conditions.

He assisted in organising the defences of the harbour railway station where the final stand was made; twice he climbed over the breastworks to help remove ammunition trucks which had been hit by enemy fire and were exploding, although all the time he was exposed to accurate German small arms and [...] fire. When efforts were made to establish contact with the other side of the harbour to obtain help, this Sjt. volunteered to cross in a small row boat. This he did, accompanied by a Frenchman. They were nearly successful in their mission when their craft was hit by enemy fire, sank and they were forced to return as the Frenchman was wounded. Sjt. Jones helped him in the water to the safety of dry land.

He was seldom absent from the front line defences, and his cheerfulness was infectious, although the position was always utterly hopeless. The soldiers under his command were deeply infected by this N.C.O.'s bravery, cheerfulness and great devotion to duty, and were themselves inspired to perform their duties with fortitude and energy.

The reason why this citation has not been previously submitted, is because the initiator was informed that Sjt. Jones had died on the line of march 'en route' to Germany as a prisoner-of-war. The initiating officer has just returned from B.A.O.R. to discover that this N.C.O. is still alive.   *(L.G. 28.2.46)*

Jones, Emlyn, Lance Sergeant
2732412, Welsh Guards (London, S.E.27)
B.E.F. (POW Pool)   *(L.G. 13.9.45)*

Jones, Ernest, Warrant Officer Cl. II (B.S.M.)
768834, Royal Artillery
No information available.   *(L.G. 27.9.40)*

Jones, Frederick Todd, Warrant Officer Cl. II (R.Q.M.S.)
2732115, 2nd Bn. Welsh Guards
During the fighting at Boulogne this Warrant Officer showed great courage and coolness when under fire and despite a strong attack by the enemy he went up to the foremost line and supervised the removal of rations and stores from a lorry which had been damaged. As a result valuable food and stores which were urgently required by the battalion were saved. On completion of this work R.Q.M.S. Jones at once assisted to re-organise the defence by posting his men at a position which was being attacked and so helped to stop penetration of our defences.   *(L.G. 22.10.40)*

Jones, George Wilford, Sergeant
4128975, 6th Bn. Cheshire Regt. (Romiley, Ches.)
(Immediate)
On 16th September 1943, No. 8 Pl, 6 Cheshire (MMGs) was occupying a defensive position in the locality of 2/5 Queens. Sjt. Jones commanded a section of this Platoon, which was in position on a railway cutting. The troops were very tired as they had been continuously in action since 9th September 1943. Shortly before dawn the enemy attacked on the front of 2/5 Queens with armoured cars and infantry. The enemy pressed their attack strongly against the particular locality in which Sjt. Jones' section was established. Owing to enemy infiltration very close to the Platoon's position, one of Sjt. Jones' guns was put out of action. He continued the fight with great determination with the remaining gun and the moment there was a slight lull in the battle he got his second gun into action again with great success. Subsequently, when his Platoon Commander became a casualty, he continued to fight the Platoon with energy and determination and the action of this Platoon contributed very largely to the successful repulse of the attack on the front of 2/5 Queens.

Sjt. Jones himself was very exhausted but he never allowed his efforts to flag and he set a fine example of energy and devotion to duty under the most difficult circumstances and his conduct had an inspiring effect on the troops around him.   *(L.G. 27.1.44)*

Jones, John Elwyn, Guardsman
4194198, 2 Bn. Welsh Guards

1. Capture:

I was ordered to France with my Battalion about 22 May 40. When midway across the Channel we were told that our task was to defend Boulogne. On reaching Boulogne my Company (No. 3) was ordered to take up a position outside the town on what I think was the Boulogne—Desvres road (N.W. Europe 1:250,000, Sheet 1, G 84). Our platoon (No. 9) commanded by 2/Lt. Perrins, was ordered to hold a cross-roads about 5 km. from Boulogne.

About 0500 hrs (about 23 May) we were attacked and there was heavy fighting. In the afternoon we were ordered to make our way back to Boulogne, every man for himself. Nine of us, including 2/Lt. Perrins, L/Cpl. Williams, L/Cpl. Wilcox, Guardsman Roberts, Guardsman Kay (other names not remembered), deployed into a house quite near our original position. The Germans shelled the house and it was burned down. We crawled in to a hen-coop in the yard, but the Germans trained a field gun on to this and shouted out that they would blow it to pieces if we did not come out. We then had no option but to surrender.

We were led a few hundred yards to a company headquarters, where some German officers attempted to interrogate us. We refused all information, and the interrogation was not pressed. We were marched along the road to Montreuil (G 72), stopping the first night in a village and sleeping in a church. The following day we were marched to Montreuil. We were kept in the square which was wired off and converted into a temporary P/W cage. On the second day all officer P/W were moved off. On the morning of the third day we were marched, having been given no food, through drenching rain to Hesdin (G 91). This was about 27 Mar. At Hesdin we slept in a field. There were by now thousands of us. We had a plan of rushing the guard and trying to break away, but it proved hopeless. The following day we were marched to Frevent (H 10) where we slept in a sort of factory.

2. First Attempted Escape:

Our route next day was via Doullens, and a few kilometres along the Doullens—Arras road I told L/Cpls. Price, Coope and Peadle that I was going to try and break away. The Germans had guards going up and down the column all the time on motor bicycles. When two of the guards were not looking I darted into a hedge. This was about 1500 hrs on 29 May. I remained in the hedge until 2200 hrs. I then headed S.W. walking by the stars. I slept most of the next day, continuing again that night. I avoided all main roads. I eventually reached Amiens at 0500 hrs on 1 Jun and, hoping it was still occupied by our own troops, peered into some houses. I was just about to knock at a window when I saw that German soldiers were asleep inside. Their motorbicycles were parked in the yard. I walked out of Amiens and was actually passed on the road by a German convoy of about 50 vehicles.

The troops in the convoy looked at me, but took no notice, although I was still in British battle-dress. I immediately took to the fields, but about half an hour later ran into a German N.C.O. who levelled a Tommy-gun at me and rounded me up.

The following day I was marched via Doullens to Cambrai. Here several of us were entrained and taken to Belgium (place not known). We were marched again for several days and eventually entrained on 9 Jun (place not remembered) for Trier. We were in Trier for about two days in a sort of transit camp (a military barracks) and then entrained for Lamsdorf, arriving there on 13 Jun.

At Lamsdorf there was as yet no British camp. There was a Polish camp, but we were not accommodated with the Poles. We slept, some in stables and some in the open. We were given no clothes and no covering and very little food.

3. Working Camps: Laband, Piltsch, Bauerwitz:

After a week at Lamsdorf about 500 P/W, including myself, were detailed to go to the working camp at Laband (Germany 1:100,000, Sheet 118, 4478). We were employed for the first year on steel erection and our job was transporting iron girders. The Germans were erecting several factories on this site. About Jun 41 we were detailed to new work making roads. During this period there had been several attempts at escape. Men would walk away from their working parties, but they were invariably caught.

In Nov 41 Pte. Robert Steward, Cameron Highlanders, and I managed to make contact with two Polish girls who were working nearby under German compulsion. We were able to arrange a meeting with them in an empty house. Stewart and I were able to break out of camp on several occasions between Dec 41 and Mar 42 and meet these girls. Poles were given leave to go home periodically by the Germans and we were hoping to influence the girls to take us to Poland when they next went on leave.

Our method of getting out of the camp was watching the sentries and merely climbing over the wire, which was single-stranded, returning the same way in the morning. We could easily have escaped this way, but had no intention of doing so as yet. We wanted the girls to procure us civilian clothes and make all preparations until the time should be ripe to get away. About Mar 42, however, we were detected returning to the camp and were punished with extra parades. In Aug 42 Stewart was moved from Laband. In Oct 42 I myself was sent to Piltsch (Sheet 127, 9440). On reaching Piltsch I found that there were only 14 P/W there in the working party. We were employed on loading sugar beet into trucks. Our stay at Piltsch was terminated by an incident when I struck the overseer, a soldier temporarily released for labour service. No charge was brought against me, as the guard was absent, having been bribed by us with chocolate and cigarettes to let us work at our ease.

About Nov 42 we were moved to Bauerwitz (Sheet 127, 9958) to work in a sugar factory. I decided to try and get returned to the main camp at Lamsdorf, as it was impossible to escape from Bauerwitz and went sick the first day. There was no M.O., and I managed to persuade a civilian doctor that there was T.B. in my family. Without very much examination he returned me to Lamsdorf.

4. Second Attempted Escape:

On 3 Dec I was sent out again in a working party to Munsterberg (sheet 116, 3208). We were employed on loading coal at a cement works.

Here Pte. Bell, Norfolk Regiment; Guardsman Mill, 2 Bn. Welsh Guards; and myself planned to escape. We were billeted with some German guards in a house. We were locked in at night and there were bars over the windows, but we discovered that there was a door which enabled us to get access to the roof next door. This had an iron bolt across it, bu we found that we would be able to cut out the wood and remove the bolt. We had removed the lettering ('Kriegsgefangener') which was stamped on our working overalls and sewn on a patch made of pyjama material dyed with an indelible pencil. I had also been able to procure a compass from one of the German civilians working in the factory.

On 24 Apr 43 one of the P/W kept watch. We removed the iron bar, got on to the roof and dropped down into the road at about 2100 hrs. We had planned to go South to Jugoslavia. We crossed the river Nwisse at Glatz (Sheet 116, 0490), continued walking South, and lay up by day. We took the route Habel-Schwerdt (Sheet 116, 0474)—Mittelwalde (Sheet 126, 6405 5557) and crossed the Czechoslovakian frontier.

At Sternberk (Czechoslovakia 1:75,000, Sheet 4158, 17°17′E 49°44′N) we were accosted by a gamekeeper, who asked us for our papers. We said we were Bulgarians who had been working in Germany and were returning home. He did not believe us and took us to the Mayor, keeping his rifle trained on us. The Mayor, who was inclined to believe our story at first, sent for the police and we eventually had to admit our identity.

We were taken to Glatz and from there sent to a punishment camp in a quarry at Konigswalde (Germany 1:100,000, Sheet 116, 5600 5611) for a fortnight and then back to Munsterberg. Here I refused to work. The Germans gave me no food for three days, but I stuck it out and they eventually sent me back to the main camp (Lamsdorf) and I was given 14 days' cells.

After this I was sent (early Jun) to work at a sawmill at Sandowitz (Sheet 118, 3404). I saw no chance of being able to escape from here, and about Jul I feigned sickness and was sent back to Lamsdorf.

5. Third Attempted Escape:

In Aug I was sent out to work again at a sugar factory at Ratibor (Sheet 127, 1250), where a Pole and I planned to get away. The Pole obtained some German money. When the plans were maturing he fought shy of the attempt, but gave me 100 R.M.

Two others—Marine Roberts, H.M.S. Gloucester and A.B. Jenkins, H.M.S. Bedouin and I then planned to use the German money to escape. It was the custom to be handed over to a German civilian overseer to start the day's work, and we three managed to slip away at 0630 hrs in the darkness in Nov 43, when the hand-over was taking place, and jump over the factory wall into the road.

We walked to Ratibor station and bought tickets first to Heydebreck (Sheet 117, 1578) then to Gleiwitz (Sheet 118, 4474) and then to Kattowitz (Sheet 118, 7370). From Kattowitz we went by tram to Sosnowiec (Sheet 118, 8273). Here we tackled two young Poles in the street, and after chatting to them told them that we were British P/W and asked them if they could help us. They took us to a camp in which French civilian workers were living. We were put up here for the night and advised by the two Poles to go to Nyszkow (Poland 1:300,00, Sheet 74, 19°22′E 50°34′N). We tackled a man in the street here, and he took us to his house. We stayed here till dark and then continued walking in the direction of Warsaw.

When we arrived at a village called Drzymbice we approached a farm and said we were Frenchmen. The people spoke fluent French and soon discovered that we were not Frenchmen and we eventually had to admit our identity. The man went out and returned with another man who said he was a Polish officer. He put test questions to us to see whether we were really British, and, being satisfied, said he would send an escort for us. The idea was that we were to join the Polish partisan army. Four days later four Poles and two British soldiers (Cpl. Richards, R.E. and an Australian (name not known), both captured at Crete), came to take us away. We were taken to a place called Lelow (Poland 1:300,000, Sheet 74, 19°36′E 50°41′N) and waited here five days for another escort. Whilst we were here another Polish officer (a M.O.) made contact with us. Richards and the Australian told him that they did not intend to fight with the partisans, and they left that night to follow up a contact they had made at Cracow.

On the fifth day the escort collected us and we were being taken to a place between Radon (Germany 1:100,000, Sheet 55, 1658) and Kielce (Poland 1:300,000, Sheet 75, 20°47′E 50°54′N). On the way we ran into a band of Germans. There was a short engagement in which several of the Poles were killed and wounded. Two Poles and we three managed to get away. On the advice of the Poles we were making our way back to Lelow when, after two days' walking we were picked up by some Germans at Sawiercie (Sheet 74, 19°13′E 50°28′N) on about 5 Dec.

We were taken to the police station, then to Oppeln for five days, and then back to Lamsdorf where we got 17 days cells.

6. Fourth Attempted Escape:

On 11 Jan I was sent to another working camp at Freihermerscorf (Sheet 127, 7634). This was a slate quarry. After a few days I again feigned sickness so as to get back to Lamsdorf. About 28 Jan I was sent to Peiskretscham (Sheet 118, 4485) where we were employed digging foundations. There were already several R.A.F. personnel working here. A naval P/W (A.B. Peascod, W., H.M.S. Bedouin) and I planned another escape. We dyed our battle-dress trousers with indelible pencil and had managed to steal a civilian jacket and a lumber jacket. There was already a pair of wire-cutters in the camp and on 2 Feb at a favourable opportunity when the sentry was away from the position on his beat, we cut the wire and got out.

We walked to Bleiwitz, reaching it that night. We bought tickets to Kattowitz, went by train to Sosnowiec, and back to the French civilian camp which I had visited on the previous occasion. Next day we made contact with the same two young Poles whom we had met before. We told them that this time we did not want to join the partisan army, but wanted to take a train to Danzig and attempt to board a Swedish ship. They collected 150 German R.M. for us. We had already bought tickets for Danzig and, having just missed a train by about 30 seconds, were waiting on the platform. We thought we would enter the lavatory to be less conspicuous and were just about to do so when we were hailed by two Gestapo men. We told thm we were Frenchmen working at the Osthutten factory and stopping at the Osthutten-Gesellschaftslager (The French civilian camp), but they checked up on this, found it was untrue, and we had to reveal our identity. We were taken to Teschen, the new Stalag VIII B, on 7 Feb and given 21 days' cells.

Early in Mar I was sent on another working party to a working camp No.763 (Gross Peterswald), where I was a week and from where, after again feigning sickness, I got sent back to Lamsdorf (now Stalag 344).

7. Escape from Derschau:

At Lamsdorf I managed to get into touch through a friend of mine with the R.A.F. people in the camp who are preparing escape identity cards. The condition was that if I were given a card, I should take an R.A.F. P/W with me. Cards were made out for F/Sgt. Cowell and myself, and we were given 100 R.M. between us by the escape committee.

We went out on a working party to Camp 428, Derschau (Sheet 117, 0113), on 5 Apr. I had obtained a pair of R.A.F. trousers and a lumber jacket. We found it impossible to procure a second suit of civilian clothes and, as I had a better chance of getting away owing to my knowledge of German and previous experience, we agreed that I should go alone.

At the camp at Gross Peterswald I had procured from a Czech and, been able to secrete, a hacksaw blade. With this I half sawed through two of the bars in the room in which we slept, and on the night of 17 Apr I pushed out the bars and let myself down with a rope, which we had made by tying some skipping-ropes together.

I walked to Oppeln (Sheet 117, 9615), took a train to Breslau, changed here and went on to Frankfurt. On the train Breslau—Frankfurt my identity card was examined and passed. At Frankfurt I took a train to Stettin, reaching Stettin at about 1400 hrs (17 Apr). In Stettin I accosted some Poles in the street and asked them where I might be able to make contact with some Swedish sailors. They gave me the address of a brothel in the harbour district. I asked a girl here if she knew any Swedish sailors, and she said she had an appointment with one that evening. A meeting was arranged, and the Swedish sailor took me that night straight back to his ship. A German guard who was on the quayside chatted with the Swede and for some reason did not ask me for my pass, and we rowed out to the ship, which was lying amidstream.

When we got aboard I found that the ship was not sailing for at least a couple of days. The sailor put me into his own bed, sleeping on the floor himself. There was another man in the cabin, and he was the only other person who knew of my presence that night. The next morning one other member of the crew, the mess man, who brought my food down to the cabin, also got to know that I was aboard.

That day I heard a rumour that the ship was not sailing for a month, and began to think that I had better make a move to board another ship. I remained in the cabin, however, as one of the men thought the rumour could not be true. On 20 Apr the ship moved to the coaling quay to take on coal. This took about 24 hours. On the morning of 21 Apr we knew that we would be sailing that day and my friends moved me down to the water ballast tanks at about 0500 hrs. A manhole was opened on the top of the tank and I got in. There were a couple of inches of water at the bottom, in which I had to sit. The manhole cover was screwed down again and I was told to remain there till they fetched me. I was in the ballast tank until 2200 hrs that night, when they came for me. We had sailed at about 1630 hrs.

I heard later that the Germans had searched the ship for about two hours. My sailor friends told me that the search was a particularly thorough one, as the Germans appeared to think that somebody was on board.

I went from the ballast tank back to the cabin and remained here till the early morning of 23 Apr, when I was taken to the stoke-hole, where I hid underneath the boiler, as the ship was nearing Stockholm, where a customs search would take place. I was anxious to reach the British Legation without any Swedish authorities knowing I was on board.

We docked at Stockholm at about 1500 hrs on 23 Apr. That night at about 2200 hrs I came back to the cabin and did not leave the ship till the evening of 24 Apr. I was given civilian clothes and a passprt by my friends and taken ashore. One of the seamen accompanied me to the British Legation, and the following day I reported to the British Military Attaché.

(L.G. 3.8.44)

Jones, John Michael, Warrant Officer Cl. II (C.S.M.)
4192380, 4th Bn. Royal Welch Fusiliers (Newtown, Mon.)
During the night of 17 Jul 44 during the Bn attack on Evrecy the 4 offrs of his coy were killed and he came up to take over. The coy was under very heavy fire and very scattered. The CSM organised a party of all available men and continued with the attack. He pushed forward a further 800 yds. He came under very heavy fire and owing to casualties was forced back. He reorganised and attacked again with a second party. During this attack, whilst under fire, he climbed on to a Churchill tk and conversed with his comd. The second attack, owing to enemy opposition and the smallness of his party, was unable to proceed very far. He then proceeded, whilst personally under fire, to get back what wounded he could. He got back 6 and attended to as many men as he could find during darkness who were too badly wounded to get back. He was then forced, owing to the tactical situation, to withdraw.   *(L.G. 19.10.44)*

Jones, John, Sergeant
3650892, 1 South Lancashire Regt.
When the Officer commanding the Carrier Platoon was wounded his N.C.O. took and retained Command throughout the Battle of Nieuport on 30/31 May and 1st June 1940. He used his Carriers with the utmost dash, resolution and determination and by his leadership held up and inflicted many casualties on the enemy. Throughout the battle he maintained close touch with all his Carriers and his Commanding Officer and directed the actions of his Sections without regard for his personal safety, thereby setting the highest example to those under his Command. His devotion to duty, coolness, reasoned orders and dispositions were of the highest possible order, and were instrumental in stemming more than one enemy rush.   *(L.G. 20.12.40)*

Jones, Percy, Warrant Officer Cl. II (C.S.M.)
5567817, Wiltshire Regt.
Middle East   *(L.G. 29.11.40)*

Jones, Reginald Llewellyn, Warrant Officer Cl. II
34888, Royal Australian Infantry Corps
For Vietnam   *(L.G. 10.12.68)*

Jones, Robert Owen, Sergeant
3385592, 2 Royal Welch Fusiliers (Caernarvon)
Antanambao, 6th May, 1942.
   This N.C.O. was part of 'A' Coy, 2/R.W.F. who advanced in the night attack under Command of 6/ Seaforths. On reaching the Pill Box Area, several men both of 6/Seaforths and 'A' Coy 2/R.W.F. fell, but Sjt. Jones continued his advance and entered the Machine Gun Pill Box single handed when he immediately killed three men who were working the gun, whereupon 12 other men who were sheltering in the Pill Box, having come in from the trenches, surrendered to him. This

N.C.O. showed dash and determination and disregard for his own safety.
M.I.D. 9.3.46 & 19.9.46   *(L.G. 16.6.42)*

Jones, Ronald, Sergeant (A/W.O.II
5053218, 5th Bn. Wiltshire Regt. (Rhyl) (Immediate)
This WO was CSM of 'D' Coy, who, on the night 1/2 Oct 44 were occupying a defensive posn North of Elst. During this night the enemy put in a Bn attack against his Coy. All four Offrs of the Coy were wounded and an additional Officer sent from another Coy was also wounded. CSM Jones then took Comd of the Coy and rallied them, despite the fact that considerable enemy infiltration had taken place and that the posn was under direct fire from an enemy tank. As a result of this WOs leadership and personal courage the enemy were eventually driven off and suffered very heavy losses, and 'D' Coy retained a firm hold on their defensive posn.
(L.G. 1.3.45)

Jones, Thomas John, Sergeant
4076321, Royal Welch Fusiliers
No citation.   *(L.G. 3.9.40)*

Jones, Wallace, B.E.M., Lance Sergeant
2323922, 70th Div. Sigs., Royal Signals (Oldham)
For conspicuous gallantry and great devotion to duty at Tobruk on the night of 21 Nov 41 and on the following days. L/Sjt. Jones was in charge of a line party detailed to lay a line to a forward position reported to have been captured by our own troops. In complete darkness L/Sjt. Jones laid the line to the position, which he found to be still occupied by the enemy. His cable truck was immediately put out of action by enemy fire, he and his party were surrounded and captured, and he was disarmed and searched. The Officer conducting the search turned aside to examine a jack-knife and taking advantage of this momentary diversion, L/Sjt. Jones pushed aside the sentry's rifle and made good his escape despite heavy enemy machine gun fire which was opened. Before finding his way back L/Sjt. Jones took steps to ensure that the line he had laid was made useless as a possible source of information to the enemy.
   On the following days, L/Sjt. Jones displayed great courage and initiative in laying lines under heavy enemy machine gun and shell fire, and on 27 Nov 41 he volunteered to lay and laid with a party of young soldiers the line through the corridor, which enabled communication to be maintained with Ed Duda from the time of its capture. Throughout the operation L/Sjt. Jones' unfailing cheerfulness and devotion to duty were an outstanding example to all with whom he came ino contact.
B.E.M. 30.12.41, No citation   *(L.G. 24.2.42)*

Jones, William, Lance Sergeant
1120624, 12 Para. Bn., Army Air Corps (Wargrave)
(since killed in action)

L/Sgt Jones was in charge of a bren group in a very exposed posn. His gp was attacked by two pls of inf supported by SP guns. By skilful handling and great persnal bravery he held off this attack until all around him had been killed. *(L.G. 28.9.44)*

Jordan, Friedrich Gustav, Private
Pal/13869, No 12 Palestinian Company, The Buffs
(Periodic)

Pte. Jordan was captured at Areopolis at the beginning of May, 1941. He was in Corinth P/W camp for about a month and then taken to Athens en route for Salonika, but escaped by jumping off the train in the Lamia valley. He spent a month in the Mount Olympus area learning Greek, then walked to Salonika. Here he obtained a Greek Identity card from a policeman and walked to Stavros, but, finding it impossible to enter Turkey, retraced his steps to Agionorus.

Here he met two W.O.'s, with whom he remained some time as they were both sick with malaria and unable to escape. He put them in touch with a doctor from Neo Marmora in Sithonia and also told them of an escape organisation, by means of which they subsequently left Greece. Pte. Jordan reached Skyros from Sithonia, via Kassandra, Skopelos and Allonysos.

At Skyros he met Cpl. Abbott (who has also been recommended for recognition) and a number of escapers. He obtained a boat for them for 500,000 drs. in which they proceeded to Turkey, the fare being paid there—not known by whom.

This Private, besides effecting a very good escape on his own, was instrumental in enabling quite a large number of escapers to reach neutral territory. He kept his wits about him, and was undaunted by hardships and disappointments when plans failed.
Recommended for B.E.M. *(L.G. 9.9.42)*

Joubert, Ferdinanc Burger, Trooper
173393, South African Forces
Madagascar *(L.G. 22.12.42)*

Joyce, Christopher, Private
14401848, 79 Coy., Pioneer Corps (Westmeath, Eire)
(Periodic)

On Sugar Green Beach at 05-00 hrs 9.9.43 Pte. Joyce who with his section was making his way to Amber Beach, spotted a M.G. post. Without waiting for instructions he dashed forward, entered the post, and at the point of the bayonet captured the gun and its crew of 4 gunners. Throughout the rest of the day engaged on the extremely important work of laying Sommerfeld track on Amber Beach under continuous mortar fire, this soldier continuously set a fine example of energy and courage which was of immense value to the others engaged on this work. *(L.G. 24.8.44)*

Joyce, Kenneth Donald, Warrant Officer Cl. II
VX 40737, 2/23 Australian Infantry Bn.
Tel El Eisa—28/29 October 1942

For conspicuous personal gallantry, and magnificent leadership, during the attack by 2/23 Aust Inf Bn on the night 28/29 October 1942. Warrant Officer Joyce was CSM of A Company, the forward Company, in the assault with tanks on strong enemy positions North of Trig 29. The attacking force came under intense anti tank, mortar and machine gun fire immediately after crossing the start line, all officers in the Company became casualties, and many tanks were knocked out. Warrant Officer Joyce gathered together surviving members of his Company, and gallantly led them without tank support, on to the Company's objective. The enemy were finally driven off after a fierce hand to hand engagement, in the course of which some 40 prisoners were taken by the Company. This gallant Warrant Officer then proceeded to re-organise and hold the ground he had gained. He moved freely around his Company area adjusting dispositions, and inspiring and encouraging his men by his fine example.
M.I.D. 24.6.43 *(L.G. 11.2.43)*

Julian, Roy Ernest, Warrant Officer Cl. II (B.S.M.)
790344, 116/118 Fd Bty, Royal Artillery (Immediate)

On 15 Dec, at Pt 204, this W.O. was acting as Troop BSM of 'B' Troop, 116/118 Fd Bty RA. Throughout the action the position was under heavy M.G. and shell fire. In the course of the action BSM Julian was ordered by a Capt to try to run some ammunition through to 105/119 Fd Bty RA which at the time was also under heavy fire. BSM Julian personally took three trailers across, only to find that 105/119 Bty position had by then been overrun by tanks. His vehicle was knocked out in his efforts to get back to his own troop. He made his way there on foot, however, and immediately assisted to man a gun whose detachment had suffered several casualties.

Later his Capt gave this W.O. orders to bring what vehicles he could from the wagon line in an effort to save some of the guns. BSM Julian took drivers and having collected sufficient vehicles he led them personally to the position which was still under heavy fire. To assist the drivers, he carried and waved a flag thus drawing increased fire on himself. He left the position in the last vehicle with his Capt and when this vehicle was finally knocked out he assisted to carry Capt who was seriously wounded in the leg, five miles back to the A.D.S.

Throughout the action this W.O. set a splendid example of coolness, devotion to duty and disregard of personal danger. *(L.G. 24.2.42)*

K

Kane, Francis, Private
QX 33906, 15 Australian Infantry Bn., (since died)
(Immediate)
On 7 Jul 45 while on patrol, Pte Kane was acting as forward scout. Contacting a party of 15 enemy at 108360, he immediately fired killing the leading three with his OSMG and at the same time was fired on by an enemy LMG from a range of 30 yds. With complete disregard for his own safety, Pte Kane stood his ground and coolly placed the other scouts into position, then directed the fire of his patrol with the result that four more enemy were killed. Pte Kane's actions were undoubtedly responsible for the success of the patrol.

On 9 Jul 45 while leading his section in the attack at 110336, Pte Kane showed outstanding courage in continually exposing himself to enemy fire in order to obtain the best results from the fire power of his section. His actions were responsible for locating and killing at least five enemy. In leading his section in the final stages of the attack, Pte Kane was seriously wounded but continued to encourage and command his section until he lost consciousness. This soldier's fearlessness and courage while acting as forward scout for his section, during actions in New Guinea and in the Solomons, together with his firm determination always to close with the enemy, have proved a fine example to his fellow soldiers. Died of wounds 10.7.45   *(L.G. 28.9.45)*

Kapatula, Sergeant
79 [77 on AFW 3121], 1st Northern Rhodesia Regt.
Somaliland. For conspicuous gallantry on Aug, 15th when the area of his pl posn was over-run by the enemy Sjt. Kapatula kept the men of his section under control in the face of very heavy fire. Waiting until dusk he led his section from the posn and passing through enemy held country reported to the Bn 50 miles in rear. It was entirely owing to Sjt. Kapatula's resource that this small body of men were enabled to fight their way clear and rejoin.
To be dated 11.2.41 and substituted for the award of the African D.C.M. announced in the L.G. of that date.
(L.G. 21.7.42)

Kasap, Jechel Usher, M.M., Sergeant
PAL/12300, Palestine Regt.
Spec Ops. Middle East
M.M. 11.3.43   *(L.G. 23.3.44)*

Katchanoski, Philip Peter, Lance Corporal (A/Cpl.)
K.79724, 1 C. Scot. R., Canadian Infantry Corps
(Immediate)
On the 17 February 1945, during the battle for possession of the high ground (Heselen Field) at the approaches to Calcar, Corporal Katchanoski showed courage and leadership above and beyond the call of duty. During the reorganization on the objective, his platoon Officer ad platoon Sergeant became casualties. Corporal Katchanoski then took charge of the remainder of number 8 platoon, and personally sited fire positions and saw that his men were dug in. This was in the face of terrific mortar and machine gun fire. When darkness came, acting under orders from his Company Commander, this NCO gathered his platoon and moved them into a new position on the exposed flank. There he again saw that his men were properly sited and dug in. In the next five days, three of which he was in command, his platoon successfully beat off counter-attack after counter-attack. During this time Corporal Katchanoski seemed by continually visiting his men's positions to be everywhere at once, lending encouragement to his platoon and by his actions inspiring them to deeds of heroism. Though sniped at from all directions, and intermittently mortared unmercifully he was completely oblivious of his own personal safety. His actions are in keeping with the highest traditions of the Regiment and of the Canadian Army.   *(L.G. 26.5.45)*

Kay, William Frederick, Corporal
U1853, 48th Highlanders of Canada (Immediate)
I have the honour to recommend U.1834 Cpl. Kay, W.F. for an immediate award for conspicuous gallantry in action. On 18 Jul. 43 while 'D' Coy., 48th Highrs of Can. were occupying forward positions on a hill they came under fire from enenmy snipers and machine guns. 16 and 17 Pls. were sent out around the right flank to engage them and soon came under heavy concentrated fire from numerous positions on top of a ridge in front of them. An attack was immediately sent in and two sections were pinned by fire. Cpl. Kay immediately sized up the situation and led his section of five men around through some dead ground and attacked the highest position. This position containted three machine guns and about seventeen Germans and appeared to be the main position. The section led by Cpl. Kay advanced in the face of M.G. fire and grenades and Cpl. Kay, though wounded in the arm, tossed two 36 grenades in the midst of the enemy and followed in with his Tommy gun blazing. He personally accounted for [....] Germans and the section took care of the remainder. When this enemy position fell, the remainder of the enemy abandoned the rest of the ridge and fled. It is estimated that there was about a full Company of Germans along the ridge.
(L.G. 23.9.43)

Kay, William Henry, Corporal
320331, 1st King's Dragoon Guards (Hull)
   (Immediate)
On 21 July '44 at 403346, Cpl. Kay was leading point of
an Armd C patrol recceing a route to Anghiari (427410).
On encountering an enemy position held by four coys,
he jumped out of his [...] and stormed, single-handed,
four enemy weapon pits with a bren gun. He silenced all
four, but after silencing the third his bren gun was shot
out of his hand, so he finished the fourth off with
grenades. After using all his grenades he ran back to his
[...] and seizing a tommy gun proceeded to knock out
four bazookas inflicting many more casualties on the
enemy who were completely disorganised by his
courageous act. Upon seeing his Troop Leader wounded
he rushed to his assistance pulling him under cover whilst
under withering fire from the enemy. This Cpl set a fine
example of coolness and courage to the rest of his troop
and it was largely through him that the engagement was
brought to a successful conclusion.   *(L.G. 7.12.44)*

Kearns, Thomas Joseph, Corporal (actg.)
5255255, 1st Bn. Leicestershire Regt.
On 18 Jan 45 Cpl. Kearns was in command of a section
standing patrol on the right flank of his Coy which was
defending Zetten. The sectioin was about 150 yards from
the remainder of the platoon and being separated from it
by several houses, was absolutely isolated. Cpl. Kearns
had eight men in his section. None of his men were over
20 years of age and several were under 19. None of them
had been in action before. Shortly after 0500 hrs 18 Jan
45 enemy approached his post. After informing his
platoon commander by telephone he opened fire. The
enemy attack developed against the centre and right and
left flanks of the Company about 0600 hrs. At least a
platoon was directed against the right flank held only by
Cpl. Kearn's section. From 0600 hrs until 2030 hrs
repeated efforts were made by the enemy to reach Cpl.
Kearn's post. The enemy penetrated into the houses in
front, to the sides and behind, and the post was subjected
to machine gun and Bazooka fire. Some 30 Bazooka
bombs hit his post or neighbouring houses. Attempts
were made to relieve Cpl. Kearns several times during
the day, but the intensity of the machine gun fire made
this impossible for infantry and the presence of Bazookas
in the surrounding houses made it almost suicidal for
tanks. Throughout the day Cpl. Kearns and his section
repelled repeated attempts to rush their post. Ten enemy
dead were afterwards found lying round the post and an
unknown number of wounded were removed by the
enemy or removed themselves. During the latter part of
the action the telephone was cut and Cpl. Kearns knowing
that several attempts to relieve him had failed might well
have despaired. It was not until well after dark when the
enemy had withdrawn that relief reached him. In this
action fought with very young soldiers, Cpl. Kearns
showed as a junior NCO leadership determination and
courage over a long period, of a quite exceptional order.

It was through the inspiration of his personality and
courage that these young soldiers prevented the enemy
from overwhelming the right flank of the Company.
      (L.G. 12.4.45)

Keating, Arthur Oscar, Bombardier
25641, 7 N.Z. Anti-Tank Regt. (Immediate)
On 9 Apr. 43, Bdr. Keating was No 1 of a 6 pr A. Tk
Gun, one of a Troop providing flank protection to the
Gun line of 4 NZ FD Regt. When he was putting his gun
into position a group of about 13 enemy tanks which
had been by-passed by our armour made a sudden dash
from a wadi nearby, against the soft vehicles behind the
screen of armour. The enemy tanks spotted the gun going
into position and opened up with MG fire wounding one
of the crew. Bdr. Keating promptly swung into action
and engaged a Mk IV Special Tank on which he scored
one hit when a tank shell mortally wounded his layer. In
an endeavour to save this man's life he then ordered the
remaining two unwounded men to carry the wounded
back for medical attention. He himself took over the gun
entirely and continued laying, loading and firing at the
advancing tanks, putting one out of action and registering
at least one hit on a Mk VI. The attack was halted and
our own tanks then arrived to drive the enemy off. The
prompt and cool action and tenacious devotion to duty
of this NCO contributed largely to restoring a very critical
situation. Furthermore the sheer gallantry of his attempt
to save the life of a comrade by remaining alone at the
post of danger was an inspiration to all. *(L.G. 22.7.43)*

Keelan, John, Sergeant
840508, 515 Fd. Bty. att. 83/85 Fd. Bty., Royal
   Artillery (Shildon, Co. Durham) (Immediate)
During the action at Ruweisa Ridge on 2 July this N.C.O.
behaved with great coolness and showed an excellent
example to his detachment. His Troop was shelled
severely for several hours and finally attacked by enemy
tanks. He controlled his detachment and supervised the
fire of his gun with great steadiness and determination
and set a splendid example to all around. When a shell
killed four of his detachment he continued to fire his
gun alone until the last round was expended. Although
wounded and still under heavy fire from tank cannon
and machine guns when the troop was ordered to
withdraw he brought his gun safely to the rear.
      (L.G. 24.9.42)

Kelly, Cyril, Sergeant
3855935, 2nd Bn. Royal Inniskilling Fusiliers
For most conspicuous gallantry on the night of 23rd May,
1940 near Plouvain when acting as senior Serjeant of
the Carrier Platoon. Sjt. Kelly ably assisted 2/Lt.
Cocksedge the officer in charge of the Carrier Platoon
in holding off determined frontal and flank attacks by
the enemy on the Reserve Company's position. When
orders were given to withdraw at dawn on the 24th May,
this N.C.O. repeatedly led his Carriers forward under

heavy Machine Gun and Artillery fire and thus enabled the forward Platoons to withdraw under cover of their fire. It was entirely due to the action of these Carriers that the Reserve company was extricated. When the Officer i/c Carriers was wounded on 27th May this N.C.O. commanded the remnants of the Platoon until the B.E.F. was evacuated.   *(L.G. 20.12.40)*

Kelly, Frederick, Warrant Officer Cl. II (C.S.M.)
3651274, 1st Bn. London Irish Rifles, Royal Irish Fusiliers (Oldham)
On 2 Mar 44 this Warrant Officer was C.S.M. of D Company, which was ordered in the evening to clear the enemy from a Wadi at about 823303, in the area N.W. of the Flyover bridge, in the Anzio bridgehead. This was partially done but owing to darkness, the thickness of the scrub, and casualties from shellfire, it was not possible to finish the job that night. The next day the remnants of the Company went forward to complete the job. Almost immediately the Company Comd. received wounds from which he later died & C.S.M. Kelly received a bullet wound in the chest. Although by now there were only about 15 men left in the Company, C.S.M. Kelly carried on, saw the task completed and remained to see that the position was held until it was possible to get reinforcements under cover of darkness. Although wounded and under constant fire he remained cheerful to the end, and his gallantry and devotion to duty was of the highest order, and ensured that all the enemy were either killed or captured, and the situation completely restored. His example of courage and his determination to see the task completed, under the most trying conditions, were beyond praise.
M.B.E. 1.1.54   *(L.G. 15.6.44)*

Kelly, Patrick Edward, Sergeant (actg.)
5884593, 1st Bn. Northamptonshire Regt. (Ramsey, Huntingdon)
On the Silchar Track from 15 May 1944, until he was wounded in the area of Dog Picquet on 24th June 1944, Acting Serjeant Kelly, the Battalion Sniper Sjt, rendered continuously gallant service. Day by day, sometimes accompanied by his sniper half section, Pte. Brown, but more often alone he would move out from the battalion position to kill Japs. With complete confidence and cool calculation he would plan his daily forages. He would move out on to the precipitous slopes of Pt. 5846, to the ridge immediately above the Silchar Track and across to the 3/8 Gurkha Rifles on Wireless Hill. His bag of thirty three Japs killed until he was himself wounded when on one of his forages, testifies no doubt that his bold action was a real menace to the Jap forces who were fighting all out to block the Silchar Road. On one of his forages, he was able to establish that the Japs had pulled out from one of their positions on Gun Spur, and as a result of this it was possible to plan a raid to hasten their pulling out from other positions in that area. This information was obtained entirely through the resource

and ingenuity of Sjt. Kelly who with complete disregard for his personal safety and alone, worked his way up the steep slope to the enemy position and in the dense jungle worked through and round a small enemy post to establish the fact that the enemy had gone from one of his positions commanding the Silchar Track. His actions set a fine example of devotion to duty to his comrades.
                                            (L.G. 28.6.45)

Kelly, Peter, Corporal (A/Sgt.)
3768563, 2 King's Regt. (Manchester) (Immediate)
During the action of crossing the River Gari 11/12th May, 1944, this NCO took over command of a platoon when the Platoon Commander had been killed. He organised his platoon quickly and with determination under heavy enemy machine gun and Mortar fire. Throughout the following 36 hours his leadership was of the highest order and he was an inspiration to his men under conditions of great strain. During the action many casualties were sustained by his Company and other sub-units nearby. They were lying in and around enemy minefields in very distressed conditions. Morale was becoming low, stretcher bearers had become casualties, communications with the river bank had broken down. It was at this stage of the battle that Sjt. Kelly, on his own initiative, volunteered to fetch medical aid. He crawled four hunderd yards to the river bank in broad daylight whilst under heavy mortar and machine gun fire, and in full view of the enemy. He swam the river which was flowing very fast (8 knots) fully clothed, and returned to the wounded who received immediate attention from the medical personnel he brought back, and evacuation of the casualties proceeded. This action put new life into all the troops, and their morale rose at once. This was illustrated by the manner in which they immediately fought back at the enemy and managed to hold on to the ground they had gained. After this Sjt. Kelly, although wet through and in a state of fatigue rejoined his platoon and continued to fight back at the enemy with great determination and leadership. There is no doubt that Sjt. Kelly's conduct throughout these two days of battle was of the highest order. His actions certainly affected the conduct of the battle and he was instrumental in saving the lives of at least fifteen of his comrades. At no time did he 'let up' on his duty which was carried out to the full, quite regardless of fatigue and his own personal safety.   *(L.G. 26.10.44)*

Kelly, Stephen, Sergeant
7015604, 2nd Bn. London Irish Rifles, (R.U.R.)
(London, N.W.10) (Immediate)
Ref. Map. Torino di Sangro, 1/50,000 Italy Sheet 148 iv & Map. Lanciano 1/50,000 Italy Sheet 147–1.
   On 30 Nov during the attack on Fossacessia (MR 396036) Sjt. Kelly personally accounted for three enemy posts which were holding up the attack. On entering the town the leading tanks became divorced from the infantry, Sjt. Kelly quickly appreciated the situation &

led his pl. to their support clearing a way for them through the town. This enabled the tanks to take up dominating posns on the further side of the town. On 2nd Dec on the Treglio Ridge (MR Lanciano 3607) Sjt. Kelly led his pl. under heavy M.G. fire in a bayonet charge dislodging the enemy from their posns & consolidation. Here although running short of ammunition the Pl. beat off a determined enemy counter attack. During this counter attack Sjt. Kelly was wounded but refused to leave until the position was firmly established. Throughout Sjt. Kelly has shown great powers of leadership & complete disregard for personal safety. His example has been an inspiration to all. I strongly recommend the award of the D.C.M.   *(L.G. 23.3.44)*

Kelman, Murray McDonald, Driver
59948, Royal Engineers (Edinburgh)
145 Inf Bde, P.O.W. Pool.   *(L.G. 25.10.45)*

Kemble, Arthur John, Lance Sergeant
5340081, 1st Bn. Royal Berkshire Regt. (London, E.2)
In the early morning of 28 Apr 44 the Japanese made a determined attack on our perimeter. L/Sjt. Kemble, A Coy, 1/R. Berks R. was in command of a fwd sec post and received the brunt of the attack. The post was surrounded for approximately four hours and at daylight between 40 and 50 Japanese dead were lying within a radius of 20 yds of the post. It was undoubtedly due to the example of this NCO, who, in spite of casualties amongst his sec, held his post firm and was without doubt instrumental in causing the failure of the Japanese attack.
(L.G. 31.8.44)

Kemp, James Patrick, Warrant Officer Cl. II (C.S.M.)
4439323, 9 Durham Light Infantry
For outstanding service during the counter attack on the Bulscamp posn. He displayed initiative throughout and when the left half of the Coy came under heavy rifle fire before reaching the objective he rallied the N.C.O.s and men and led them forward and entered the village on the left where he successfully maintained his posn in spite of heavy fire.   *(L.G. 20.12.40)*

Kemp, John, C.S.M.
K.62419, 1 Canadian Parachute Bn. (Immediate)
24 Mar 45, Diersfordter Wald.
    Immediately after the parachute drop, CSM Kemp's company had to storm a strongly fortified enemy position covering the Rhine approaches. The coy came under heavy enemy mortar and MG fire and several of its officers were killed. CSM Kemp immediately assumed command of the men in his area and speedily re-organised them. With complete disregard for his personal safety he led the attack on the enemy LMG positions which were holding them up. Again under heavy fire he stormed and captured the houses which formed the backbone of the defence of the positions. By his readiness to assume responsibility and by his inspiring conduct

under fire, he achieved the early capture of a vital objective.   *(L.G. 2.6.45)*

Kemp, William John, Warrant Officer Cl. III (Pl.S.M.)
7811727, 1 Bedfordshire & Hertfordshire Regt.
(Worthing) (Immediate)
P.S.M. Kemp was in comd of a pl which was attacking a strong enemy posn outside the Eastern Perimeter of Tobruch Fortress on 22 Nov 41. This W.O., from the outset of his Pl's advance over a long exposed approach to the enemy's posn was in advance of his men, continually encouraging them.
    On arrival at the enemy's defensive wiring this WO stood, completely regardless of his personal danger, in an exposed posn, directing the secs of his pl through the gaps he had found. His coolness and courage had an enormously steadying influence on his pl. The care with which he directed his pl through the wire and on to the various objectives (enemy posts) ensued the success of the attack. When the objectives had been taken, this W.O. in spite of his wounds, crawled between the sangars in which his pl was disposed in order to cheer his men. Throughout this period the area was being heavily shelled and mortared by the enemy. The area was also under enemy machine gun fire. Throughout the attack the conduct of this WO was of an exceptionally distinguished order in face of the enemy.   *(L.G. 24.2.42)*

Kendall, Leslie Anderson, M.M. [Arthur on AFW 3121], Sergeant
6199876, 6 Queen's Own Royal West Kent Regt.
(London, E.18) (Immediate)
For conspicuous gallantry and devotion to duty.
    Whilst Sjt. Kendall was in command of a sec of M.G.s attached to VI Cdo. during the action fought at Djebel Azzag on 5.6.7 Jan 43 his section had to carry their guns and 4,000 rds of amm over a mountainous and muddy country in pouring rain continuously for twelve hours before reaching their posn. He then played an invaluable part in holding Djebl Azzag against repeated enemy counter attacks supported by M.G.s and mortar fire. Sjt. Kendall kept his guns in action until the enemy were within 25 yards of his gun, then on both guns being hit and disabled, and upon being ordered to withdraw, he removed the firing locks from both guns, while grenades were being thrown at him and succeeded in withdrawing his men, including one wounded man, to safety. All through this action Sjt. Kendall's high courage and determination was a fine example to the men under his command and an inspiration to all those around him.
M.M.:8.7.43   *(L.G. 23.9.43)*

Kennedy, Robert Francis, Corporal
SX 7092, 2/48 Aust Inf. Bn. (Immediate)
For outstanding leadership and bravery in leading his Section in the attack on Trig 29.
    On the night 25/26 Oct 42 Cpl Kennedy was in command of a section in the attack on Trig 29 (Miteiriya

Ridge), which was strongly held by Germans. Kennedy displayed great coolness throughout the action and his own personal bravery was an inspiration to the men of his Section. He attacked and killed two Germans who were holding up his Section from a post and later bayoneted Germans opposing his Tommy gunner who was out of ammunition. He was quick to reorganise to hold the ground gained and later when badly wounded continued to control his Section instructing them in their tasks and ensuring that all necessary works were carried out. Cpl. Kennedy's control and leadership played a great part in the success of the operation and his personal courage and bravery set a fine example to the men of his Section.   *(L.G. 11.2.43)*

Kennedy, Thomas, Corporal (A/Lce. Sgt.)
4120967, Cheshire Regt.
No citation.   *(L.G. 22.10.40)*

Kenny, Ronald Michael, Warrant Officer Cl. II
22502533, King's Regt.
For Northen Ireland   *(L.G. 1.5.73)*

Kent, Stanley Thomas, Warrant Officer Cl. I
12128, Royal Australian Infantry
WO Kent saw active service during the Second World War with the Australian Imperial Forces from 1939 to 1945 and re-enlisted in the Australian Regular Army on the 29th of June 1951. Before being posted to South Vietnam, WO Kent served as an instructor to National Service trainees and with the Citizen Military Forces as a member of a regular army cadre.

Upon arrival in Vietnam on the 16th of March 1965, WO Kent was assigned to the province of Quang Tri as an advisor to the Vietnamese Regional and Popular Forces.

On the 28th of May 1965, the 912th Regional Force Company and the Sector Intelligence and Reconnaissance Platoon were occupying a blocking position outside the hamlet of Van Van in Quang Tri Province. These units had been in contact with the enemy all day as the Viet Cong were attempting to break out of a cordon established by regular Vietnamese troops and Regional Forces troops.

Viet Cong pressure on the blocking force increased and at this time the Vietnamese Commander was mortally wounded. WO Kent initially assisted this officer to a more secure area. When the troops saw that their Commander had been wounded and was being evacuated, they began dropping back from the blocking position in a state of confusion. WO Kent quickly assessed the situation and immediately and voluntarily returned to the most forward positions, where he exposed himself to hostile fire and to direct observation by the Viet Cong. He moved about freely reassuring the Vietnamese troops by his presence and urging them to return to their firing positions. This they did. His actions trascended the normal requirements of an advisor as he personally imposed leadership directly upon the Vietnamese troops at a time, when had he not done so, the situation would have completely deteriorated. As a direct result of his actions, the blocking force held its position thus containing the Viet Cong. At the same time reasonable security was provided for the medical evacuation helicopter landing area, enabling casualties to be evacuated quickly.

WO Kent's conduct reflected great credit upon himself as a professional soldier and was in the highest traditions of the Australian Army. *[From L.G.]*
                                          (L.G. 18.3.66)

Kenyon, Frederick Bradshaw, Sergeant
A.303, 6 Cdn. Armd. Regt. (1H.) (Immediate)
On the 14 Aug 44, Sjt. Kenyon was in command of 4 Tp of a Sqn, 6 Cdn Armd Regt in the attack across the river Laizon and on the wood MR 1443 (France Sheet 714). From the SL to the river crossing, a distance of 3000 yds, he successfully led his troop through heavy shell and anti-tk fire and in doing so over-ran and destroyed the crews of 3 enemy guns. His tank was the first in the Sqn to reach and cross the river but his motors, soaked by the crossing, started to cut out and he had difficulty in moving forward. Despite this handicap he pushed on with his troop through a village and into the fields beyond where he was met by heavy enemy fire from 75 mm a/tk guns. He took up a fire position and killed or dispersed the crews of four of these guns. He was then ordered to withdraw his tp to an orchard for re-organization, which entailed re-crossing the river. Here his own tank and one other became mired, but though under heavy small arms fire, he immediately dismounted and was successful in digging his tank out and rejoining the unit to press on the attack. The outstanding skill, courage and aggressiveness displayed by Sjt. Kenyon was directly responsible for the destruction of 7 enemy guns. His acts were an inspiration and an example to all ranks. *(L.G. 13.1.45)*

Kerr, William Thomas Western, Lance Corporal
31683, New Zealand Military Forces (Periodic)
L/Cpl. Kerr was taken prisoner fifteen miles south of Lamia on 25.4.41. He stayed a week at Lamia and was then sent to Chalkis where he spent a fortnight. From here he was sent to Larissa. After a week, on 25.5.41, he escaped by means of a rope made from pack-straps. He walked to Katerini and travelled from there by the regular sea service to Salonika. He then walked to Stavros via the villages of Rnear, Alimbeathy. Here he turned North East towards the Bulgarian border, intending to escape via Turkey. Hearing this was impossible, he turned back and reached Salonika on 30th May. He was taken by the Greek police to the American Consul who introduced him to a British agent. Accommodation was arranged for him, and through the agent a boat had been bought, which was to pick him up with a number of other escapers at Oros.

On 8th June he set off for Oros with a British W.O.II, a Greek nurse, a Greek officer and the latter's fiancé. But the Germans learnt of the scheme and those who were bringing the boat round were arrested, including the agent. L/Cpl. Kerr remained at Oros with the rest of the party, sheltered by the monks till the 1st July. He then walked to near Stavros, where he met two more escapers. The three hid in the fields round Stavros from the 3rd to 26th July. They then walked back by easy stages via Olympiatha, Stratiotos, Ierissos and Phosphori to Eviron. Here they bought a boat from the monks on the promise of £50 and left for Turkey on 4.8.41.

The boat called at Imbros and Tenedos, but they were not allowed to land. They succeeded in doing so on the Turkish mainland only after their boat had been sunk.

L/Cpl. Kerr did an excellent escape by himself and afterwards, in his unflagging efforts to leave Greece, showed great courage and endurance. He was undaunted by failure, long marches and was consistently enterprising.
M.I.D. 30.12.41   *(L.G. 9.9.42)*

Keys, Herman Cyril, Corporal
L10216, Canadian Infantry Corps
Dieppe   *(L.G. 9.2.46)*

Khattri, Sob Bahadur, Havildar
8288, 9th Gurkha Rifles, Indian Army
Recommended by A.L.F. S.E.A./N.E.I.
Subsequently cancelled (see L.G. 30.6.47). Awarded I.D.S.M. L.G. 25.7.47.   *(L.G. 28.11.46)*

Killalea, Henry, M.M., Lance Sergeant
VX 17880, Sigs. 1 Aust Corps
At Rail Siding near Levadia, Greece, on 20 Apr 41 three trains loaded with petrol, gun ammunition and anti-tank mines were set alight as the result of heavy bombing and maching gunning by enemy aircraft. Amm was exploding and it was considered by senior Officers present too dangerous to attempt salvage.

L/Sjt. Killalea M.M. with Driver McDonald (NZ Div Sup Col) on their own initiative managed to drive a locomotive without having any knowledge thereof and as a result saved 28 trucks of petrol and amm by shunting them down the line to a safe distance. They then again on their own initiative proceeded to load oil on supply vehicles and salvage 25 pounder amm, A/Tk mines, etc., which were stacked no more than 20 feet from blazing trucks where 25 and 60 pounder shells were exploding at frequent intervals.

But for the initiative and courage of L/Sjt. H. Killalea, M.M. and Dr McDonald considerable valuable supplies of amm and petrol (of which at that time a serious shortage existed) would have been lost. *(L.G. 4.11.41)*

Kilpatrick, Bernard, Sergeant
3251866, 6th (Lanarkshire) Bn. Cameronians (Motherwell) (Immediate)
At Alpon on 9 Mar 45, Sergeant Kilpatrick was in charge of the two rear sections of his platoon whilst the platoon commander went forward with the leading section. This section came under heavy enemy small arms fire. Sergeant Kilpatrick deliberately exposed himself in order to draw fire and, succeeding, directed bren gun fire in return though hit for the first time; subsequently he remained in the open directing 2" mortar fire and refused to go back to have his wound treated. Subsequently extremely heavy fire was directed on the platoon who were in very open country. He was given a message to take to Coy HQ and was hit twice again whilst crawling back but made the shelter of a shell hole. The platoon now began to withdraw to a covered position. This NCO again directed the 2" mortar on the enemy and rallied the men as they came back until the platoon commander was able to get back and take over. The Platoon was then divided into two groups over one of which he took command and succeeded in getting his group under cover where they remained pinned under heavy fire, and bearing his wounds uncomplainingly until the platoon were relieved by a further attack at 1930 hrs. His fortitude, courage and coolness in a very critical position were of the greatest encouragement and example to the men.   *(L.G. 21.6.45)*

Kimberley, John Henry, Private
B.83344, Royal Hamilton Light Inf.
1. Capture
I was captured on 19 Aug 42 after the Dieppe raid. The boats which should have taken off my Battalion were unable to approach owing to heavy enemy fire, and the men waiting for them were surrounded and captured. I had received at that time two flesh wounds.
2. Camps in which imprisoned
Camp Verneuil, South of Rouen: 23 Aug—4 Sep 42
Stalag 344, Lamsdorf: 8 Sep 42—1 Mar 44
Stalag II D, Stargard: 1 Mar—3 Aug 44
3. Attempted escapes
(a) First attempted escape
On 20 Aug 42, although suffering from three flesh wounds, I made an attempt to escape while we were marched to our first prison camp. During a rest on the march I slipped through the low hedges and, after the column had marched off, struck back towards the beach and from there set off in a Northerly direction. After 18 hours of freedom I was discovered while sleeping by a patrol and recaptured. I was taken to Rouen and from there to Verneuil, where I spent three weeks in a hospital while my wounds were being attended to. Early in Sep I proceeded by train to Stalag 344 (Lamsdorf).
(b) Second attempted escape
At the beginning of Mar 43 I made another attempt to escape. I exchanged identity with a British P/W Rfmn. Wastle, Rifle Brigade, P/W No. 10661, whose home

address is 104 Windermere Road, London. I adopted his name and went on a working party from which I escaped. The working party at that time was in the city of Breslau. I hid in a railway goods train and went from there to Dresden. I carried supplies of food with me. In Dresden while the train was stopped the brakeman came and discovered me in the truck. I was taken back to Stalag 344, where I received 10 days' detention. When I was taken prisoner and when I returned to the camp I still was believed to be Wastle, the British soldier. In this attempt I received no help and was not provided with any papers of any kind.

After I came out of detention Rfmn. Wastle, with whom I had exchanged identities, wanted to escape himself, so I resumed my real identity and my chains again.

(c) Third attempted escape

On 4 Aug 43 I again exchanged identity with 2045290 Gdsmn. Rowles, T., Royal Horse Guards, whose home address is Rawley Gardens, London. This time I made for Switzerland, in the hope of getting out from Switzerland through France to Spain. Again I escaped from a working party at Stramberg, which was close to our camp. I travelled on foot across country for the first two nights. I crossed the border into Czechoslovakia on the night of 6 Aug. With me I had a New Zealander, Dvr. Wilson, J., P/W No. 23851 (believed still a P/W in Germany). On 8 Aug we reached Valis, a Czech town. There we were picked up by partisans, who have been hiding out in that hilly country. We stayed with them until 26 Aug. They are organised into regular parties. The leader spoke English. We lived in the hills all the time and killed game, which we exchanged in unguarded villages for bread and other essentials. No sabotage work was done in this area, as the partisans simply were hiding in the hills waiting for the day of liberation to come.

On 28 Aug we left the partisans and went to Bistritz (Germany, 1:100,000, Sheet 69, 9934). We by-passed Hullein, a fairly large town, as there was a concentration of Gestapo there. We now travelled by day, as we were dressed in civilian clothing. We moved across country to Ostrokow. On the way we were helped by local people, who supplied us with food, shelter, and guides. From Ostrokow we moved South towards Austria, by-passing Goding. We then followed the Slovakian border along the river Morava. While we were on the frontier of Slovakia and Austria, near Bratislava, we were caught by the German Border police on 7 Sep. We were at liberty altogether for 34 days.

After recapture we were taken to Goding on 7 Sep and imprisoned there for one month until 7 Oct. All that time we were in the hands of the Gestapo, who interrogated us four times. We were not ill-treated physically, although they tried to starve us. The information they tried to get was names of partisans and their helpers and about arms smuggling across the German—Czecho-Slovakian border. After they could find out nothing, they turned us over to the military

authorities in Goding. We remained there until 15 Oct, when we were returned to Stalag 344. We did not get any more detention, as the Camp authority felt 30 days with the Gestapo was sufficient. Both of us were physically very run down, and we were unable to make another attempt for some time. I remained at Stalag 344 until 4 Mar 44, when all the Canadians were moved to Stalag II D (Stargard), 35 kms. from Stettin.

(d) Fourth attempted escape

On 2 Jun 44 I left Stalag II D on papers describing me as a French mechanic and authorising me to travel from Posen to Stettin. When I came to Stettin, which journey I made very comfortably by train, I slept the first night in an air-raid shelter. On 3 Jun I contacted a French radio mechanic, who was forced to work in one of the radio stations in Stettin. He took me to a French civilian camp near the city of Stettin, where I stayed 14 days. I was trying to contact a Swedish boat, but at that time there were none available. I was, however, informed that I could be taken on board a Finnish boat which was due to call at a Swedish port, provided that I was able to bribe certain members of the crew with sugar. In order to obtain the necessary sugar, I decided to barter cigarettes, and was obliged to return to Stalag II D in order to get these cigarettes. I used as an intermediary, a French P/W who supplied me with the cigarettes. However, when I arrived on the railway station of Stargard to take my train back to Stettin I was stopped by a policeman who wanted to see my papers. At that time there were about five or six hundred people on the station. My papers were in good order. This made me believe that I had been betrayed by the French P/W, who had brought me 1500 cigarettes. I was captured again on 17 Jun and taken back to Stalag II D, where I remained in solitary confinement until 12 Jul.

4. Escape

On 3 Aug 44 I went on a working party inside the town of Stargard. The guarding of these parties was very slack. I therefore decided to make another attempt to escape. We took along little boxes in which we had our lunches, and I distributed my civilian clothing in the boxes which were carried by different members of the working party. Our work at that time was sacking grain. While no-one was looking I slipped away into a nearby wood and changed into my civilian clothing. Nearby there was a French civilian camp. I approached a Frenchman who was a truck driver and bribed him for 250 cigarettes to take me to Stettin. He did so on 4 Aug, after I had spent the night in a bush nearby.

In Stettin I visited a brothel and contacted a Polish girl (killed in a bombing raid). It was a brothel reserved for foreigners. I was therefore quite safe as far as Germans are concerned. This girl claimed that she was engaged to a British Intelligence Officer who was posing as a Belgian worker. She was very anxious about him because she had not heard from him for four months. She promised me that she would put me in touch with a Swedish sailor the next day.

On 6 Aug I returned to the brothel, where I met this man. After making satisfactory arrangements with him he promised that he would help me to get on a Swedish ship. During the same night I went through the dock yards and swam to the ship, which was anchored about 30 yards off-shore. I was hidden in a dry tank which enabled me to evade any possible search by the Gestapo.

On 7 Aug I was joined by another escaped P/W who was trying to go back to Sweden. He claimed to be an escaped Canadian P/W, but I found out later that he was a Frenchman and not a Canadian. Only two sailors on that boat were acquainted with our presence. We were fed on board ship for five days until 11 Aug. On that day, while the ship was passing the town of Dalaro close in shore, we jumped overboard and swam approximately three quarters of a mile to the shore. We landed wearing only trunks, and when questioned by civilians we claimed that we were British residents in Stockholm whose canoe had capsized during an outing. However, this story did not impress the local authorities, and we were interrogated in a very general way by the local police. They treated us very well, provided us with the necessary minimum of clothing, and sent us to Stockholm on 12 Aug, where we went to the British Legation.

5. Camp Conditions

At Stalag VIII B all the prisoners who were captured in Dieppe were roped from 8 Oct 42 onwards. After two months chains were substituted for the ropes. The punishment for interfering with the ropes was that the offender was made to stand with his nose and toes touching a wall for periods up to eight hours at one stretch. When the chains, which were in the form of hand-cuffs with a long connecting chain, were produced it was found that they were extremely easy to pry open. The guards did not enforce the wearing of chains very strictly, and the men were therefore able to take them off for quite long periods.

The food in that camp was very bad, and we more or less lived under starvation conditions. We were grateful for the Red Cross parcels, which kept us more or less alive. There was a Russian camp nearby. Many of the Russians, who were not supplied with Red Cross parcels, died during that winter. They were trucked out by wagon loads and buried in large trenches. From time to time we were able to smuggle in some food to this camp after bribing the guards with cigarettes.

7. German Morale

The morale of the German people as far as I was able to observe during my stay in camps and my attempted escapes is changing. The belief that the Army is invincible has completely vanished, and the German people seem to feel that they are in danger. However, there is a great faith in the effectiveness of V.1 and everyone believes that Southern England is in flames. At the beginning of the invasion of France everybody hoped for an early peace, because they thought that the Allied Armies would be defeated in an early stage of the offensive. In recent times, however, just before I left

Stalag II D, these hopes have vanished. All there is left behind is disillusionment, and people seemed to have very little hope for the future. *(L.G. 24.3.45)*

King, James, Sergeant (A/W.O.II (C.S.M.)
3244021, 6 Seaforth Highlanders (Wigan)
During a company attack on an enemy locality in a wadi on 19 Mar 44, CSM King showed conspicuous gallantry and devotion to duty. Throughout the attack which lasted for 6 hours he personally directed the supply of ammunition to the forward elements, and, going forward himself with the carrying parties across ground which was constantly under enemy fire, showed a magnificient courage and example to all ranks. In addition CSM King showed throughout a spirit of aggression which deserves the highest praise, and from an exposed position he personally sniped at least 3 of the enemy. During the whole course of the attack his conduct was an inspiration to all ranks and the greatest assistance to his Coy Comd.
(L.G. 7.12.44)

King, James, Sergeant
2733681, Welsh Guards
Throughout the fighting at Boulogne this N.C.O. showed the utmost coolness and courage. Acting as Medical Sergeant at the Battalion R.A.P. he never spared himself for a minute. On several occasions he went out himself and carried in wounded under very heavy shell fire until he fell exhausted, having strained himself by his exertions. At all times he was a great encouragement to others and by his example and devotion to duty a large number of wounded men were brought in who otherwise would have been left behind and taken prisoners.
(L.G. 22.10.40)

King, John Thomas, Sergeant
H16295, Canadian Infantry Corps
N.W. Europe
M.I.D. 10.1.46 *(L.G. 24.1.46)*

King, Reginald James, Sergeant
6405684, 4th Bn. Queen's Own Royal West Kent Regt. (London, W.4) (Immediate)
At Kohima from 5–20 April 1944 Sjt. King was commanding the Mortar Platoon. His det posts were widely separated and owing to the nature of the ground were in very exposed positions and impossible to conceal adequately. All his positions were accurately pin-pointed by the enemy. During this period Sjt. King was continually visiting his mortar positions although under fire, and when commns had gone he himself went from pit to pit bringing down close and accurate D.F. fire on hard pressed positions on his own initiative and undoubtedly doing much to break up enemy attacks before they developed. Early in the battle Sjt. King was slightly wounded but continued at his job. Later, on 19 Apr. he was again wounded by a sniper when directing fire from an exposed position. Sjt. King throughout the

battle was a fine example by his cheerfulness and complete disregard for his own personal safety and an inspiration not only to his own platoon but to all those who saw him on his frequent visits to every ... *[end missing]*.
M.I.D: 5.4.45   (L.G. 27.7.44)

King, Robert George, Corporal
6292313, 1st Bn. East Lancashire Regt. (London, N.W.10)

On the evening of 1st March 1945 the company in which Cpl. King was a section commander was ordered to attack an enemy strong point in the area of Bussenhof at 972378 East of Weeze. The attack went in in the face of very heavy enemy machine gun fire both from the objective itself and from other enemy localities on the flanks. In addition the whole area was being heavily mortared by the enemy and a large number of casualties were caused in the company. About halfway to the objective Cpl. King's platoon sergeant and platoon commander were both wounded. Immediately, this NCO took over command of the platoon, rallied the men and, still under heavy fire of all kinds, led them on towards the objective. During the approach to the objective Cpl. King himself was wounded three times in the neck, back and leg, but despite his wounds he managed to carry on and, by his determined leadership and brilliant example, succeeded in capturing the objective after close hand-to-hand fighting with grenades and stens. Ten Germans were killed in this area. Later Cpl. King was told by his company commander to hand over his platoon which was to move on to a further objective, and to allow himself to be evacuated. Cpl. King however refused to be evacuated until his platoon was safely dug in on the final objective, some three hours later. This NCO set a very high example of devotion to duty and of quite outstanding courage under very heavy enemy fire. Not only did he display leadership of the highest order but although wounded he inspired his platoon at a time when the absence of a more determined leader would have had dire results for the success of the attack. It was due to his efforts alone that this strong position which was held by enemy parachute troops, was eventually captured in close quarter combat and in the face of the fiercest resistance from a determined enemy.   (L.G. 21.6.45)

King, Robert, Corporal
2979592, Argyll & Sutherland Highlanders (7, Hamilton St., Clydebank)
Malaya   (L.G. 23.1.42)

Kinghorn, Alan James, Gunner
TX.2238, 8 Aust Rd. Regt.

On 11 July, 42, Gunner Kinghorn A. J. was acting as O.P.A. to Capt. J. S. Elder, 'D' Tp. Comd. Elder was ordered to move fwd. from the Trig. 33–P. 24 ridge to the Pt.s 24 feature, West of Tell el Eisa Sta. This he did and, at approx. 1100 hrs., he was wounded. In accordance with Gunner principles but with no experience in shooting with live amn. Kinghorn took over and shot his troop and when necessary, his bty., until relieved by Lieut. T. D. Smith, a period of 4 hours. T. C. Smith was wounded in the head 2-hour later and Kinghorn took over again. On this occasion, he shot the tp. and bty. for a period of 3 hrs.

Continually, during the total period he was in control, the enemy attacked with tanks and inf. assisted by fire. These attacks were beaten off, to a great degree, by the arty fire Kinghorn assisted to put down. Major G. F. Copeland, 3 A/Tk. Regt., formerly a field gunner officer in Militia, was able to observe some of the results of Kinghorn's shooting and states it was excellent. He was struck by Kinghorn's coolness under heavy fire and his determination to keep his tp. and bty. firing while there was a target to shoot at. As the C.P. manned by Kinghorn was the only one supporting 24 Bn. in the area and the only one from which certain of the attacks could be seen, Kinghorn's control of his bty. and his passage of information enabling regimental concentrations to be put down, undoubtedly were a big factor in the defeat of the enemy.   (L.G. 24.9.42)

Kingston, Gerald Elwood, Corporal
C 65591, Loyal Edmonton Regiment (Immediate)
Reference Map Italy 1/25,000 Sheet 100 II NW Cesena

After crossing the Pisciatello River on the night of 17/18 October 1944, 'C' Company of the Loyal Edmonton Regiment with one troop of tanks in support was ordered to extend its bridgehead into the enemy's defensive position the following afternoon. Number 13 Platoon was commanded in this action by C65591 Corporal Gerald Kingston who had taken over when his officer was wounded during the river crossing. Number 13 Platoon was ordered to occupy a group of houses—C Strrighi (MR 627066)—which was thought to be held by the enemy. As 13 Platoon approached its objective it came under intense machine gun and grenade fire from well concealed and dug-in enemy positions which were screened from the view of our supporting tanks. Corporal Kingston with complete disregard for his own personal safety called on his men to charge the enemy and led them across fifty yards of open ground to engage the enemy weapon pits. A German officer attempted to halt the charge by throwing grenades until Corporal Kingston killed him with a burst from his Thompson Machine carbine from a range of only five yards. The remainder of the enemy were driven into their dugouts and quickly disposed of by hand grenades.

Although wounded, Corporal Kingston continued to lead his platoon until the houses had been completely cleared of the enemy. With the houses cleared, the remainder of the company was able quickly to complete its task. In the houses taken by 13 Platoon twenty-one of the enemy were captured and four killed. Among the prisoners was a German officer with a wireless set who had been directing heavy and accurate artillery fire all day on the only spot in the battalion area where vehicles could cross the Pisciatello River. Throughout this operation Corporal Kingston, although wounded, conducted himself in a most commendable manner. His courage, initiative and leadership were of the highest order and it was largely owing to his gallant action that his Company's attack was successful. His capture of the enemy observation post and wireless set enabled supporting arms to cross the river and thus ensured the breaking of the enemy's defences in the battalion sector.

(L.G. 17.2.45)

Kinnear, Forbes, Warrant Officer Cl. II (C.S.M.)
3047077, 1st Bn. Infantry (Edinburgh)
At Donbaik, Burma on 19th March 43.

At 0200 hrs on the morning of 19th March 1945 'B' Coy, The Royal Scots, carried out an attack by moonlight on two enemy strong points known as S.M.10 and S.M.11. Shortly after leaving cover very heavy enemy mortar and M.G. fire was opened on the Company either killing or wounding all the officers almost immediately. CSM. Kinnear, though himself wounded, took command and for the remainder of the action rallied and controlled the Company until, owing to heavy casualties, it became impossible to complete the task. CSM. Kinnear showed outstanding courage and devotion to duty under intense enemy fire and, though wounded, he was almost the last man to return when the action could no longer be maintained. *(L.G. 1.6.43)*

Kirby, John Williamn, Sergeant (T/W.O.II)
27758, Royal Australian Infantry
WO John William Kirby was the Company Sergeant Major of D Company Sixth Battalion The Royal Australian Regiment during the battle of Long Tan in the Republic of South Vietnam on 18th August 1966. WO Kirby showed outstanding bravery throughout the three hours of the battle, during which time the Company area was being swept with machine gun and small arms fire and subjected to continuous attacks by superior Viet Cong forces. In an area where virtually any movement resulted in a hail of fire from the enemy, he continually moved around the company and platoon areas, distributing ammunition and organising the collection of the wounded and their movement of the Company Aid Post. At times he went outside the perimeter to assist the evacuation of the wounded from the forward platoons. At one stage he personally destroyed a heavy machine gun post being set up 50 metres from the perimeter.

He organised the resupply of ammunition by helicopters and continued with the distribution of ammunition and movement of the wounded until the Company was relieved. Then, when most of the Company could relax, he continued working at full pressure for another five hours, organising and supervising the loading and evacuation of the casualties.

His gallant performance, without any thought for his own safety inspired and assisted D Cmpany to defeat an enemy force much larger than the company. *[From L.G.]*
(L.G. 10.1.67)

Kirk, Victor David, Lance Sergeant
7921, 20 Bn., New Zealand Military Forces
Throughout the operations this N.C.O. showed exceptional gallantry, coolness and skill. He was in the leading platoon during the Attack on Maleme on May 22 and with his section fought his way forward in continuous fighting for over two miles, displaying the utmost resolution, and repeatedly rushing and destroying M.G. posts. He then accompanied an officer on a very dangerous journey through 600 yards of enemy occupied ground, shooting a German on the way and bringing safely back about 100 men who would otherwise have been cut off. At Galatos on May 25 when his company was out flanked he organised a party and led a counter attack which was completely successful, 44 Germans being killed of whom Kirk accounted for 11.

Being separated from his Company he then with his party joined in the counter attack on Galatos made by the 23 bn., disposed of a large number of the enemy and remained in position on the outskirts of the village until 0530 hours next morning when finding that all other troops had withdrawn some hours before he skilfully led out his party and rejoined his unit. *(L.G. 4.11.41)*

Kirkham, Henry Edgar, Corporal (A/Sgt.)
7887180, 6th Royal Tank Regt.
Sjt. Kirkham was commanding a Light Tank co-operating with the Free French Forces at Bardia on 3 Jan 1941. Whilst leading the French forward the tank was hit and the elevation and telescopic gear of the gun was put out of action. He reported this and continued to advance. Later, when he heard that the Troop Commander's tank was hit, he moved his tank over to tow him out. On the way he discovered another tank commander trying to mend his track under heavy fire. As the track was found to be beyond repair, he towed his tank away, which was within 600 yds of the enemy defences, and under point blank intensive fire. Finally he volunteered to go back and tow another disabled tank. I consider Sjt. Kirkham to have displayed exceptionally high qualities of bravery and devotion to duty and that his action saved a Light Tank and its crew from destruction. *(L.G. 9.5.41)*

Kirkhope, William Adamson Forbes, Signalman
7662003, Royal Signals (attd. S.S.T.), S.S. Bde. Signal Troop, No. 2 Cdo. Bde. (Dunfermline)
Gulf of Salerno 13th September 1943

On the 13th September at SS Brigade HQ on the Vietri–Salerno Road Sgmn Kirkhope volunteered to repair a vital line to one of the forward units which had been cut by shell fire.

After proceeding along the line the break was found, and as the enemy was mortaring the area heavily Sgmn Kirkhope had to perform the repairs under conditions of extreme danger.

On the return journey Sgmn Kirkhope visited a relaying station where he found the operator exhausted from long hours on duty under fire. He at once relieved the operator and himself continued to operate the station though he had had no rest since the assault landing five days earlier. He continued on duty all day.

A few hours later the line was again cut by enemy fire during the ensuing battle on Dragone Hill. In spite of very heavy mortar fire and his great fatigue Sgmn Kirkhope continued to man the relaying station which now served as the only link forward.

Throughout the operation this man showed the greatest willingness to undertake all tasks however dangerous and his unflurried efficiency and technical skill under fire ensured the maintenance of communications during a critical period of 24 hours.   *(L.G. 13.1.44)*

Kirkland, Stuart Bennett, Corporal (A/Sgt.)
A50491, Essex Scottish Regt., Canadian Infantry Corps (Immediate)
On the 13 Aug 44 the Battalion was ordered to attack the feature point 184 and the woods 0544. B Company, with Sgt Kirland as A/CSM, was the right forward company. The forming up position had not been mopped up by the troops preceding, with the result that the coy became committed before crossing the start line. As a result of this, direction was lost and the company's axis of advance was interpreted as being towards Tournebu. On the outskirts of Tournebu the only two officers in the coy were wounded by heavy MG fire from the hedges which pinned the company down. Despite the loss of about 30 men from a company of 90, Sjt Kirkland immediately took hold. Placing himself at the head of the remaining riflemen, he ordered the Bren guns and mortars to give covering fire while he led a bayonet charge against at least two machine gun posts in the hedge on the outskirts of the village, resulting in the destruction of the enemy position and the capture of about 30 prisoners of war. Following the assault, Sjt Kirkland carried on the attack against the buildings on the outskirts of the village, directing the fire and leading his men in to clear the houses and took more prisoners. Having completed this he consolidated the company about the houses, despatching a runner to report to Battalion Headquarters. Then he started arranging the collection and evacuation of the wounded. During the whole of this action, communications over the wireless with Battalion Headquarters were spasmodic and he was left to his own resources. The fact that the company overcame the opposition which had pinned them to the ground was due entirely to the initiative and the gallant and spirited leadership of Sjt Kirkland who, discarding any thought of personal safety, placed himself at the head of his men for the assault. His display of courage and singleness of

purpose to come to grips with and destroy the enemy was a source of inspiration to his men and is, and will be, an example to the Regiment for all time.
                                                  (L.G. 4.11.44)

Kiyanga, Maziku, Sergeant
60118, Kings African Rifles
To be dated 30.9.41   *(L.G. 21.7.42)*

Knapp, Arthur Cyril, Sergeant
5667019, Royal Sussex Regt.
For exceptional determination, coolness and courage demonstrated on several occasions during the fighting 23/29 May 1940. On one occasion at Strazeele on May 27th he went back in the face of intense enemy shelling and machine gun fire to find a fellow Sgt. who had been hit and carried him back. At Mont Des Cats on 29th he dragged four wounded men to safety and tended them during heavy shelling and dive bombing.

Throughout he shewed complete disregard of his peraonal safety, and was an example to those under his command. When the shelling was hottest he was seen playing a mouth organ to encourage his men.
                                                  (L.G. 11.7.40)

Knapp, Leonard Stanley, Warrant Officer Cl. II (T/Sgt.-Maj.)
1061601, 13 A/T. Regt., Royal Artillery
At 9-30 p.m. on 16 May 1940 T.S.M. Knapp was order to withdraw one of his guns, which was within 500 yards of the enemy positions in order to conform with a general withdrawal to a prepared position in the rear. During the operation the gun-towing vehicle overturned. Serjeant Toplass, L/Bdr. Smith, Gunner Hancock, Gunner Robson, Gunner Poole and Driver Dockery then manhandled the gun a distance of three miles to the appointed rendezvous, coming under machine gun and shell fire during this move. The first mile of this distance was along a very rough lane which made the task of manhandling the gun very arduous and difficult. Although it took three hours to reach the rendezvous and it was highly probably that the rest of the battery would have moved off, T.S.M. Knapp carried on in the hope that he would be able to make contact or find a vehicle capable of towing the gun to the rear position. The successful recovery of this gun was entirely due to the initiative, determination and example set by T.S.M. Knapp, and the wholehearted devotion to duty of the detachment.
M.I.D. 23.5.46   *(L.G. 20.8.40)*

Kneen, Edmund Clarence, Private
NX.8507, 2/1 Australian Infantry Bn. (Immediate)
Recommended for distinguished conduct and gallantry in face of the enemy.

On the afternoon of 21st May 1941 Pte Keen was a member of a fighting patrol ordered to clear the beach North of Retimo Aerodrome. The patrol went further than was ordered, and was cut off by a party of 25–30 of the enemy, who suddenly appeared in their rear. There ensued a fierce clash during which two of the patrol were killed and three wounded. It appeared that the whole patrol would be wiped out but for the calm action and bearing of Pte Kneen, who kept the enemy at bay with a sub-machine gun, at great risk to his personal safety, while the remainder of the patrol made off safely.

The wounded were unable to escape during daylight as two of them had foot injuries, so Pte Kneen, again by drawing fire on himself, made it possible for them to crawl to a nearby hole, into which he himself dashed when they had reached it safely. In this hole the party discovered two enemy wounded, and Pte Kneen dressed all the wounded, at the same time keeping a sharp lookout lest the enemy should attempt to rush them. When darkness came Pte Kneen successfully covered the withdrawal of the whole party, a necessarily slow one, and brought all the wounded to our own lines without further casualty. During enemy action Pte Kneen has displayed the greatest coolness and courage.

(*L.G. 25.9.47*)

Knight, Edward Albert, Sergeant
L.35252, 17 Can. Field Regt., Royal Canadian
Artillery (Immediate)
On the night 16/17 April 1945 at Otterloo when the enemy attempted to break through the town and rejoin his main forces, this Non-Commissioned Officer was in command of his gun detachment in 60 Battery. This battery was sited in rear of the other two and during the early stages of the attack, although subjected to intense mortaring and machine-gun fire, did not have the enemy actually on the gun position, and as a result was able to maintain a terrific concentration of fire to assist the other two batteries who were heavily engaged in fighting the enemy.

While 60 Battery guns were still firing the enemy did reach his position. With contempt for the mortar bombs and machine-gun bullets which were landing all over the position, Sergeant Knight, realizing his gun must continue firing, shot the first enemy to approach his gun. Then a second German appeared and as this Non-Commissioned Officer attempted to deal similarly with him, his weapon jammed. Again with no thought of personal consequences and displaying valor and a sense of duty far beyond the normal call, Sergeant Knight disposed of the next German with his bare hands. While all this was going on he still continued to pass fire orders to his gun, which remained in action the whole time. His courage and coolness in a situation which seldom confronts the gunners kept his detachment on the gun and continued to produce the essential fire required by the other batteries.

Later on, 'tank alert' was ordered when information was received that tanks were entering the town from the North, Sergeant Knight, again with utter contempt for the mortars and machine-guns, moved his gun up into the town to a position where he could cover the main cross-roads, so that he could engage any tanks which might threaten the battery position. During the whole engagement this Non-Commissioned Officer's conduct was almost beyond comprehension. His cool, stout-hearted steadiness and courage, the example he set for his detachment and the rest of the unit undoubtedly kept the remainder of his battery in action until the attack was successfully repulsed.

(*L.G. 22.9.45*)

Knight, Victor Henry, Corporal
NX.16912, 2/2 Aust. M.G. Bn.
On 12 Jul 42 at pt 33, 87543017, West of El Alemein, Cpl. Knight was A/Sec Comdr of No 1 Sec No 2 Pl, A Coy, 2/2 Aust M G Bn. On the evening of 12 Jul 42, this Pl had been attached to 24 Aust Inf Bn and the posn they were occupying was attacked strongly by the enemy. Cpl. Knight with utter disregard for his personal safety controlled the fire of his Sec with such coolness and deliberation that his guns on the right flank of the posn, remained in action and were largely responsible for repulsing the counter attack. During the action he moved his guns seven times in the face of heavy enemy MG and Mortar fire, so that they were never pin pointed by the enemy. He stood up and observed enemy movement and directed his fire with the utmost nonchalance, and his actions had the greatest effect on the morale of all the troops in the area. Attached is a report by the Inf Coy Comdr on the spot.

(*L.G. 24.9.42*)

Knight, William John, Sergeant
6286258, 1 Buffs (Royal East Kent Regt.)
(Portsmouth) (Immediate)
On 7 Nov 1942 when 8 Armd Bde cut the enemy's line of retreat at Galal (811315) Sjt. Knight was in command of a Motor Pl. This Pl was defending one of the flanks of the R.H.A. Bty and he successfully mopped up an enemy pocket of resistance. At one moment he found himself alone well out in front of his Pl in a captured Fiat car doing a reconnaissance when suddenly from the East a large enemy column headed by 20 tanks, approached his position and was engaged by our forces. He was in the line of fire of both sides. He tried to open fire with a captured Breda L.M.G. but it failed to function; undaunted he made a quick decision and drove toward the enemy tanks which were now halted. The engine of his vehicle stalled so he jumped out and ran toward the leading enemy tanks. Whereupon the crews of two of the tanks promptly surrendered to him and he escorted them back, still under heavy fire from both sides, to our own lines. The coolness and bearing shown by this N.C.O. on this occasion was of the highest order and was a magnificent example to all around him and was, I am convinced, instrumental in persuading these tanks which had not been knocked out to surrender. Sjt. Knight has commanded this Motor Pl ever since the Pl Comdr was wounded and he has done so remarkably well. During periods of heavy shelling and bombing when the

men have been visibly shaken he has held them together and set them a magnificent example and has led them with good judgement and determination on all occasions. I strongly recommend him for award in view of his outstanding conduct in action when in command of a Platoon.

M.M. 17.6.43   *(L.G. 28.1.43)*

Koen, Gunther Rene, Corporal
546662, South African Forces
See Coehn.

Krawa, Momadu, C.S.M.
NA/25164, 3rd Bn. Nigeria Regt.
During the period under review 16 Feb 45 to 15 May 45, this ANCO has displayed exemplary qualities of leadership and disregard to his own personal safety. On 25 Mar 45 in the Letmauk area this ANCO personally got to the top of the feature known as Helen although it was strongly held by the enemy. He remained there and pin pointed the enemy positions thus enabling considerable casualties to be inflicted upon them; thus driving them off.

At Alegyun on the night of 28 Feb/1 Mar 45 during an enemy attack on the perimeter, he collected, organised and led a scratch force of batmen, cooks and carriers and beat off two determined attacks. On this occasion his leadership and disregard of danger restored a critical situation. He is always ready to volunteer for dangerous duties and is constantly an inspiration to his troops who have the greatest confidence in him. He is a gallant and fearless soldier.

Recommended for M.M.   *(L.G. 17.1.46)*

Kreger, Lionel, Trooper (A/Cpl.)
K4519, 14th Cdn. Armd. Regt. (Immediate)
During the advance to Foiano (MR229096) on 2 Jul 44, the Recce Tp of 14 Cdn Armd Regt was acting as the vanguard of an Inf Bde. Upon finding the direct route to Foiano impassible due to demolitions one sec of the Recce Tp was sent to find a possible entry around the unexplored right flank. A/Cpl. Kreger was the crew commander of one of the two tanks in this sec. When the alternative route was reached it was found that the road ran at right angles through the high banks of a canal. In order to avoid exposing his tk in these narrow defiles, A/Cpl. Kreger dismounted three times in spite of heavy small arms and mortar fire to inspect three bridges. Later, when the second tk had gone back to bring up engineers, A/Cpl. Kreger, quickly appreciating that his tk gun was useless because of the high bank, again dismounted to prevent enemy demolition squads from approaching the bridge. Realizing the importance of securing the bridge intact, A/Cpl. Kreger, in full view of the enemy and under continuous fire, held the bridge for half an hour until the main body arrived. This route was for a period of two days the only Bde route open. Subsequently at a canal crossing Southeast of Monte S. [...]ino (MR R157184), A/Cpl. Kreger denied the approach to a bridge by dismounting with a Bren gun. He was again prevented from using his tk because of the high canal banks but with a complete disregard for his own safety and although within the enemy's defences he tenaciously held the bridge, only retiring to his own lines when outflanked and wounded. By this time the tks of the leading sqn were within sight of the bridge. By his initiative and courageous and determined action A/Cpl Kreger held open on two occasions what was to become the main Bde axis with the resultant speed-up of the Div advance.

(L.G. 21.10.44)

L

Lacey, Charles, Sergeant (A/W.O.II (C.S.M.))
2656975, Coldstream Guards (Ipswich)
No citation. *(L.G. 27.1.44)*

Lacourse, Benoit, Sergeant
D57655, Le Régiment de Maisonneuve (Immediate)
In the afternoon of the 23rd July 1944, Le Régiment de Maisonneuve was ordered to capture Etavaux.
    D57655 Sgt. Lacourse, B. was acting platoon commander of 15 Platoon 'C' Company, which was on the right of railway line. In the heat of the battle, all his men except four went with 14 Platoon on the left. Sgt. Lacourse coolly appreciated the situation and realized that enemy machine gun posts on his right would jeopardize the whole operation as they were sweeping the approaches of Etavaux. With great dash and determination, he led the four remaining men to the attack in the face of intense enemy fire and personally destroyed three machine gun posts with grenades. There is no doubt that this fait d'armes, done with complete disregard for his personal safety, enabled his company to attain its objective successfully. *(L.G. 7.10.44)*

Lafleur, Conrad, M.M., Sergeant
D.62077, Fusiliers Mont-Real
Sgt. Lafleur was a Private in the Fusiliers Mont-Real at the time of the Dieppe raid, where he distinguished himself by his conduct under fire. He was taken prisoner by the Germans and succeeded in escaping to this country, for which he was awarded the M.M. On arrival here, he volunteered for secret service, was trained as a wireless operator and went to France in July 1943 with a R.A.F. officer. Their mission was to form an organisation for the evacuation, by Lysander aircraft, of Allied airmen and to provide them with means of getting to Spain. In this job they achieved considerable success. 17 Allied airmen were sent out by air and a much greater number were passed out by land routes to Spain.
    In January of this year the Gestapo surrounded a house where Lafleur was working a wireless transmitter. Some of the Germans entered his room but after shooting four of them he succeeded in escaping. Unfortunately, the R.A.F. officer was subsequently arrested and committed suicide. Lafleur was thus obliged to return to this country and, with other members of the organisation, he crossed the Spanish frontier and returned here via Gibraltar at the beginning of March 1944.
    Throughout the period of his work abroad, Sgt. Lafleur has shown great technical skill as a wireless operator. He has maintained successful W/T communications over a long series of difficult operations. In addition to this, we learn from a report of the R.A.F. officer, who paid a short visit to this country before his death, that Lafleur has shown great courage and initiative in difficult circumstances. Although not a native of France, he has been successful in incorporating himself into the life of that country and has always shown a good sense of security. An example of his courageous attitude is to be found in the circumstances of the attempted arrest by the Gestapo mentioned above.
M.M. 22.12.42 *(L.G. 15.6.44)*

Laidlaw, Archibald, Corporal
22218758, King's Own Scottish Borderers
For Korea *(L.G. 30.11.51)*

Laing, John Augustus, Sergeant
28764, 7 N.Z. A. Tk. Regt. (Immediate)
At Mitieriya ridge on 26th Oct. 42 28764 Sgt. Laing, J. A., penetrated beyond the F.D.L.'s of the 22 N.Z. Bn. by night and destroyed two Fiat and one German 3.7 cm Anti-tank guns. During this period he encountered and eluded an enemy patrol and then removed the firing mechanism of abandoned British Anti-tank guns which had been used during the day by the enemy.
    On 27th Oct. 42, at 1630 hrs. after an almost direct hit from a mortar on his gun pit, he personally removed a wounded man, under fire, to a disused mortar pit, subsequently crossing the exposed ground, while continuously under fire, to minister to the casualty until nightfall when stretcher bearers were able to evacuate the wounded. During the whole period of the occupation of the forward slope by 'G' Troop he served the weapons of abandoned tanks within the F.D.L.'s and put them in fit condition for snipers to operate by moonlight.
(L.G. 28.1.43)

Laing, John Ramsey, Warrant Officer Cl. II
403240, 15th/19th King's Royal Hussars (York)
BEF 1940 (P.O.W. Pool).
M.B.E. L.G. 8.6.50 *(L.G. 14.2.46)*

Lake, Hugh, Lance Sergeant
1880512, 9th Field Company, Royal Engineers (Air Force), Airborne Div. (Immediate)
On 20th Sep. L/Sgt. Lake accompanied a party ordered to defend Heveadorp flying ferry. During the night 20th/21st the ferry was heavily attacked and the protective party forced to withdraw. L/Sgt. Lake, however, lay up near the ferry on the waters edge, half submerged. He loosened the cables and prepared to disable the ferry should the enemy attempt to use it. He remained on his own under fire within 200 yds. of the enemy without food or water until the early morning of 22nd Sep., when he rejoined the unit wounded and exhausted with detailed

information of the enemy's movements and dispositions on the river bank.

On the evening of 22nd Sep., less than 10 hours after his return, L/Sgt. Lake volunteered to accompany a party which was to ferry the Poles across the river Neder Rijn. His knowledge of the river bank materially assisted the ferrying operations. During the return journey L/Sgt. Lake was again wounded—this time in the neck.

During 22nd Sep. the unit was running short of food and water. On his own initiative L/Sgt. Lake organised a foraging party and with two sappers carried water through intense mortar fire to the company position.

On the night 25th Sep. L/Sgt. Lake led a party of R.E. which fought its way through enemy opposition to the river bank. L/Sgt. Lake, though badly wounded a third time in the shoulder and back, saw all his party safely into boats before he allowed himself to be carried aboard.

During the whole period of operations L/Sgt. Lake set a magnificent example to his men and his complete disregard for danger was a continuous inspiration to those near him. His initiative and energy materially assisted the various operations in which he took part and his determination not to give in, though thrice wounded, certainly led to the safe withdrawal of the men under his command.   *(L.G. 9.11.44)*

Laloge, Emile Jean, Sergeant
K 52168, Calgary Highlanders (Immediate)
In the early morning of 1 Nov. 1944 the leading company of the Calgary Highlanders suffered heavy casualties after being subjected to enemy fire of all types as they were proceeding across the causeway to Walcheren Island. 'D' Company was ordered to proceed through and the leading platoon No. 18 was commanded by Sergeant LaLoge. The platoon fought its way to within 25 yards of the enemy end of the causeway when they were pinned down by severe enemy machine gun and 20 millimetre cannon fire which swept the open causeway.

When his runner had failed to reach company headquarters Sergeant LaLoge made his way back through the intense fire. After arranging for artillery support he returned to his platoon. With the aid of artillery fire the platoon succeeded in reaching its objective after heavy fighting.

The right flank of the platoon position was very close to the enemy's position and three times Sergeant LaLoge picked up enemy grenades which fell near his men and threw them into the water. When one of his Bren gunners was killed and the gun slightly damaged Sergeant LaLoge repaired and manned the gun until one of his men was able to relieve him.

A counter-attack was developing and he called for fire from the Piat only to find that the Piat man was wounded and unable to operate the weapon. Sergeant LaLoge immediately took over the weapon and successfully broke up the counter-attack by accurate fire.

The successful accomplishment of his company's task in which over sixty prisoners were captured, one 20 millimetre cannon and two medium machine guns were knocked out, and many enemy killed and wounded, was directly due to this N.C.O.'s magnificent courage and leadership. His complete disregard for his own personal safety and his cool and efficient manner in handling his platoon under continuous heavy fire inspired his men to face and overcome the terrific odds against them.
M.M. 31.5.45   *(L.G. 10.2.45)*

Lamb, Charles Phillip, M.M., Sergeant
554456, 11th Hussars, Royal Armoured Corps
On December 14th during an air attack by 12 Fighters on his Troop Sgt. Lamb, whilst firing his gun, saw his Troop Leader, 2/Lt. Reid Scott, had been wounded in the head.

He handed his gun over and proceeded on foot to Lt. Reid Scott to see the situation as his car being the wireless is the 'Parent' car. One other man was wounded as well as 2/Lt. Reid Scott. The Bren rifle had been put out of action. He attended the two wounded men, returned to his car and carried on firing his Bren rifle and took immediate charge of the Troop. All three cars had been hit and damaged. He then evacuated one badly damaged car and the wounded men and carried on with the two remaining cars though he had been wounded himself early on.

Sgt. Lamb's personal bravery and cool headedness under fire and most severe conditions was a fine example to his men and the fact that the Troop was so quickly reorganised and ready for further action was entirely due to him.

Sgt. Lamb has previously shown outstanding courage, ability and skill in the face of air attacks and on two occasions he has brought down two enemy aircraft.

I recommend he be awarded the D.C.M.
M.M. 1.4.41   *(L.G. 25.4.41)*

Lambert, Joseph Alfred Germain, Lance Sergeant
D51289, Les Fusiliers Mont-Royal (Immediate)
During the attack of 'D' Company of Les Fusiliers Mont-Royal on the Church of St. Martin Fontenay on 1 Aug. 1944, Lance-Sergeant Lambert was commanding one of the two assaulting platoons. During the first stage of the attack, the officer in charge of the assault became a casualty. Using his own initiative, L/Sgt. Lambert took charge of the assault. He led the men inside the church yard in spite of strong M.G. fire coming from the left flank. Once inside the yard, a fierce hand to hand battle took place. Showing no regard for his own safety, L/Sgt. Lambert stood in the middle of the yard and directed every section to its post. Then an enemy M.G. opened fire from a corner of the wall. There again ignoring the danger, L/Sgt. Lambert organized the mopping up of the enemy dugouts and weapon pits until all enemy fire inside the yard had been annihilated. As soon as the consolidation took place the new position began to be

heavily shelled by enemy mortar fire. L/Sgt. Lambert was seen running to every section post ensuring that each of them was properly sited. Then he came back inside the wall which was subjected to a very heavy concentration of enemy fire. There he himself organised the evacuation of the casualties, giving first aid to those needing it. His actions during these two hours of fierce fighting was real inspiration for all the men of 'D' Company. During the next 24 hours, during which the Company was under violent mortar and gun fire, L/Sgt. Lambert displayed a great sense of duty and a fine example of leadership. His coolness and his courage under enemy fire played a great part in the success of this operation.   *(L.G. 4.11.44)*

Lancaster, John Moss, Sergeant (actg.)
14473928, King's Own Scottish Borderers
For Korea   *(L.G. 28.12.51)*

Lang, David, Private
VX 6693, Australian Military Forces
See Edwards, D. R.   *(L.G. 18.8.42)*

Langan, Arthur Anthony, M.M., Private
3383646, 5/7th Gordon Highlanders (Manchester)
    (Immediate)
On 30 Aug., 'D' Coy., 5/7th Bn. The Gordon Highlanders was advance guard to the Battalion. The leading platoon, after beating off an enemy counter-attack, was pinned down by heavy Spandau fire. Private Langan's platoon was then ordered to attack in co-operation with a troop of tanks. The number of trees and banks hindered the advance of the tanks and in consequence they were not able to neutralise the enemy fire. The fire came at the platoon from nearly every direction and it appeared for a moment that the attack would be stopped.

Private Langan rose the occasion; taking command of his section he led the platoon forward, being at times as much as fifty yards ahead of it. Whenever the enemy Spandau fire came especially close he stopped and, using his Bren from the hip, he shot it out with the enemy. He disposed of two Spandau's in this way.

Later that day the Company went into action a second time and attacked a village through a thick pine wood. During the advance through the wood Private Langan's platoon came under withering fire from a Chateau on the fight flank. The whole platoon took cover. Private Langan stood up and raked the Chateau with Bren fun fire. Under cover of his fire another platoon, charging down the slope at top speed took the objective.

It was largely due to the valour and magnificent leadership of Private Langan, (now a Sergeant) that these two attacks resulted in such rapid success.
M.M. 19.10.44. Recommended for M.M.
                                   (L.G. 21.12.44)

Langford, Ernest Leslie, Warrant Officer Cl. II (actg.)
5780501, 1st Bn. Royal Norfolk Regt. (King's Lynn)
    (Immediate)
During the attack on Lingen on 5 April 45 the leading platoons of the two ass. Coys. were held up by a party of enemy in well placed positions. One of the Coy. Comds. was hit and could not temporarily be recovered. Sjt. Langford, who commanded the only available Wasp, was ordered to move up to the enemy strongpoint and flame it so that an ass. party could go in and the wounded Coy. Comd. be recovered. Although fire was directed at and into his carrier, with complete disregard for his own safety Sjt. Langford moved it close to the enemy position which he flamed so accurately that the Spandau team was burnt alive. The remaining occupants of the post were either wounded or surrendered. The Coy. Comd. was then recovered and the ass. party consolidated the position. Whilst this was in progress a further enemy Spandau opened up from the flank. Using his own initiative and with great promptness, Sjt. Langford directed his carrier at this post knowing full well that there was no inf. covering fire sited to sp. him. Refusing to be cowed, the enemy kept up his fire. Once again, however, the skilled handling of his carrier and the direction of his flaming decided the issue and the occupants of the post were ejected screaming. Later on Sjt. Langford was ordered to repeat these tactics against a second similar strongpoint in a cellar. The route to this was covered by snipers firing from upper storeys. Between them the enemy were temporarily frustrating all attempts of our leading elts to get fwd. Manœuvring of the carrier could be done only with the greatest difficulty. In spite of this and the accuracy of the enemy snipers' fire, Sjt. Langford successfully ran the gauntlet to within point blank flaming range of the strongpoint. Although under Spandau fire from 20 yds. range, the skill and accuracy with which this N.C.O. completed his task was in no way impaired. In a space of seconds the objective was a sheet of flames, the enemy were bolted and 8 out of the 10 killed or captured. This N.C.O.'s supreme disregard of danger, his tactics and his infectious confidence completely turned the scales in a very difficult town fighting operation. Thanks to him and his skilful use of his Wasp, the morale of the enemy was completely undermined.   *(L.G. 12.7.45)*

Langley, Albert Pretoria, Warrant Officer Cl. III (Pl.S.M.)
533123, King's Royal Rifle Corps (London, N.W.5)
K.R.T.C. 1941, 1st L.N.B. Yeo., Calais (Repat. P.O.W.)
                                   (L.G. 3.2.44)

Langtry, John Osborne, Sergeant (now Lt)
VX 101703, 24 Australian Infantry Bn. (Immediate)
South Bougainville.

For great personal courage, inspiring leadership and devotion to duty in determined attacks against strong enemy positions.

On 21 June 45, Sergeant Langtry, 15 Platoon Commander, 'C' Company, 24 Aust. Inf. Bn. (A.I.F.), displayed superb qualities of leadership when he led his platoon three times against strongly held enemy positions in the Katsuwa–Kingori area South Bougainville.

Returning with his platoon to the company in the Katsuwa area after a three day patrol, Sergeant Langtry located a strong enemy position astride the Commando Road near Kingori. He attacked immediately but, although causing the enemy at least 10 casualties, his platoon had not sufficient numbers to hold the ground won.

Displaying great initiative, Sergeant Langtry telephoned for artillery support and although he was not trained in this arm he fearlessly moved forward to a position in close proximity to the enemy and registered the target. He then directed an accurate concentration onto the area at considerable danger to himself.

Leading a fighting patrol forward to follow up the artillery fire, Sergeant Langtry found the area even larger than he had anticipated, and after a sharp fight in which further casualties were inflicted on the enemy, he bypassed and continued on towards his company.

There he found the remainder of the company being fiercely attacked by a strong enemy force. Leaving one section to guard his stores, he led the remainder of his platoon in an encircling move to reinforce his comrades. Reaching the company area he assisted in the defence of the position in which 18 enemy were killed, and then led another patrol back to repair telephone wires cut by the enemy and to contact the section guarding his stores. Darkness overtook the party but the Sergeant pushed on through the jungle until he found his men.

Starting back for his company area on the morning of 22 June he observed the Japanese in the act of cutting the telephone lines. Once again Sergeant Langtry led his men into the attack and after a fierce fight drove them off killing two enemy and wounding several. He then rejoined his company.

This N.C.O. who has commanded a platoon since 16 April in continuous operations against the enemy has at all times displayed outstanding qualities of aggressive leadership. His fighting spirit, initiative and splendid handling of his men enabled him to successfully attack forces much larger than his own. His capable and shrewd leadership was responsible for inflicting many casualties on the enemy with little cost to his own men.
(L.G. 12.10.45)

Lasgourgues, Leopold, Lance Corporal
NX 53016, 2/3 Aust. Indep. Coy. (Immediate)
At 'Woody Island' in the Wau Valley on 3 Feb. 43 Spr. Lasgourgues L. was a member of an attacking force of one section led by Major Warfe.

Heavy enemy opposition was encountered and the section came under fire from 6 L.M.G. and 1 H.M.G. plus rifles from a range of 50 yards. During this action Sapper Lasgourgues charged single handed and captured

an L.M.G. killing the crew of 2. He then took over the captured weapon and firing from the hip killed 4 more of the enemy.

Heavy fire was directed at him and he sustained a serious wound through his chest. After being wounded he continued to fire with deadly effect until weakness caused by loss of blood compelled him to drop the L.M.G. When lying on the ground surrounded by the enemy he then threw 2 grenades before losing conciousness. His gallant and determined action prevented our small force from being surrounded and annihilated and enabled an orderly withdrawal.

It is considered that the action Spr. Lasgourgues was far beyond the normal call of duty and has been an inspiration to the whole Company during subsequent operations.
(L.G. 19.8.43)

Laurie, Donald Cairns, Sergeant
VX 7410, 2/23 Australian Infantry Bn. (Immediate)
In the Singaua Plantation during operations East of Lae. For fine leadership devotion to duty and outstanding personal gallantry. Sgt. Laurie commanded a lightly equipped platoon which was sent fwd. At last light on 5 Sep. 43 to picquet a river crossing 6,000 yds. fwd. of the fwd. elements of the Bn. HQ failed and for 36 hours he fought and maintained his platoon in their isolated position. He intercepted a force of approx. 60 enemy who were attempting to rejoin their main forces further West and resisted six separate attacks against his platoon position between 1400 hrs. and last light on 6 Sep. 43. Although the situation of the platoon appeared at several stages to be hopeless, his cheerful courage and fine personal example inspired his men to continue their resistance. With grenades rifle and bayonet he was seen by six members of his platoon to kill 10 enemy and in addition he is known to have accounted for others during the hrs. of darkness. Throughout the engagement he carefully conserved his platoon's slender supplies of ammunition, moving continuously between his sections and fwd. positions and directed the action with coolness, courage and fine judgement.
(L.G. 13.1.44)

Lawrence, Edward, Warrant Officer Cl. II (Sq. Ajt-Maj)
*390399, 1st Lothians and Border Yeomanry
(Edinburgh)*
R.A.C. 1941, B.E.F. (Repat P.O.W.)
(L.G. 3.2.44)

Lawrence, John Kingston, Sergeant
2245, 6 N.Z. Field Coy. (Immediate)
When clearing a gap in enemy minefields forward of our F.D.L.'s on Miteiriya ridge on the night 24th/25th Oct. 42, Sgt. Lawrence displayed outstanding devotion to duty and inspiring leadership in holding his Section together and completing the task under very trying and hazardous conditions, and after his Field Coy. Commander had been fatally wounded. The clearing of this gap to allow armour forward was considered of such importance that the Coy. Commander himself took

charge. Enemy mortar fire and machine-gunning was so intense that progress in lifting mines was slow, and to add to the difficulties the Coy. Commander became a casualty. Sgt. Lawrence immediately assumed control, rallied the men and pushed on with the work. When our own artillery fire came down on this minefield in preparation for the advance of the armour the gap was still incomplete. Under our own artillery barrage and also enemy fire Sgt. Lawrence encouraged and directed his men and completed the gap just in time to pass the advancing tanks through. It was in considerable measure due to his vigourous leadership and gallant example that the gap in the minefield was completed and lighted to allow the 2 N.Z. Div. Cavalry and the 9 Armd. Bde. to move through without delay or hindrance.

(L.G. 28.1.43)

Lawrie, James Chisholm, [Laurie, Hamish on AFW 3121], Sergeant
3061871, 12 Royal Horse Artillery (Peebles)
(Immediate)
For conspicuous gallantry and devotion to duty at Thala on 22nd Feb. 43. Sgt. Laurie was No. 1 of one of the 25 pdr. guns of 'F' Bty. At about 2000 hrs. night 21st/22nd Feb. the enemy succeeded in penetrating the position with tanks followed by Inf. and supported by artillery fire. Some seven of these tanks penetrated as far as the gun positions. Three reached Sgt. Laurie's gun position. He at once brought his gun into action himself and in spite of the half-light succeeded in destroying one tank, and turning others back. He loaded, layed and fired the gun himself, while under heavy enemy fire.

During the rest of the night and throughout the following day Sgt. Laurie's gun was in a most exposed position and was constantly shelled and machine-gunned.

Sgt. Laurie's conduct throughout was outstanding and an inspiration to his detachment.   *(L.G. 8.4.43)*

Laws, Leslie Arthur [Robert], Driver
2195978, 127 (Dorset) E. & M. Coy., Royal Engineers
Laws was captured at Kalamata, Greece, on 29 Apr. 41. Later he was transferred to Austria and sent to Wolfsberg (Stalag XVIILA) and subsidiary working camps.

During the autumn of 1943 he began a series of attempts to locate partisans with a view to arranging a mass escape. Eventually, in August 1944, three partisans promised to bring a liberating force. A fortnight later, as this plan had not materialised, Laws obtained a guide who took him and a small number of P/W to a partisan encampment several miles away. The next day Laws and a N.C.O. returned to the camp with a guerilla force. The remaining P/W, numbering 80, were released, guided through Yugoslavia and on 17 Sep. 44 evacuated by air to Italy.

All who escaped with him have paid tribute to Laws' courage, determination and ceaseless efforts to effect their release.   *(L.G. 1.3.45)*

Lawson, Stanley Edward, Trooper
81425, 19 N.Z. Armd. Regt. (Immediate)
In the Liri Valley action on the night of 16/17 May the tk. of which Tpr. Lawson was operator hotly engaged the enemy from 1830 hrs. to 2000 hrs. when the tk. comd. was wounded by shrapnel and collapsed in the turret but not before he had ordered the crew to keep on fighting. Tpr. Lawson took comd. while still loading and operating the set and continued to fight his tk. to good purpose. Just after last light Tpr. Lawson's crew picked up four wounded men from another tk. which had been knocked out. With these and his own wounded sergeant aboard Tpr. Lawson carried on engaging targets until darkness precluded further action. By this time the tp. comd. had been killed and his tank burned. None of our inf. had been sighted for about an hour and Tpr. Lawson found himself totally lost with no sp. in sight in enemy territory. He apprised his sqn. comd. of his predicament and suggested the use of flares as a guide but these could not be distinguished and Tpr. Lawson decided, in spite of the risk involved, to fire flares himself and thus indicate his position. This proved to be a slow process but firing flares at intervals, and being re-directed by wireless by his sqn. comd. after each flare he was eventually guided to his own lines about 0300 hrs. During the most unnerving period between 2145 hrs. and 0030 hrs. when he had already been continuously in action since 1830 hrs., or lost in almost total darkness and surrounded by an active enemy to whom he presented a good target, and with five wounded men in his tk. Tpr. Lawson's courage proved an inspiration to those with him and his voice over the air never faltered. At intervals in the light of his own and enemy fires, as he was guided home he engaged the enemy as he saw them with the co-ax gun. When the tk. finally reached our own lines Tpr. Lawson was quite cool, insisted on removing the wounded and gave a concise and coherent account of the action as he had seen it, with valuable information regarding our own and enemy activity forward. By his resolution, courage and intelligence Tpr. Lawson was undoubtedly mainly responsible for keeping his tk. in action, bringing it home and saving the lives of his crew and four other wounded men with him.   *(L.G. 26.10.44)*

Lawton, Frederick Gourlay Price, T/Corporal
30866, Transvaal Scottish (V) (Periodic)
For individual and associated acts of bravery and devotion to duty in the field.

Cpl Lawton has been on active service with this unit for the past twenty-six months, has proved himself a good leader, and has always been an example to the men who served under him.

On the 2nd Dec. 41 he was wounded in a dive-bombing attack, but, realising the number of other casualties to be attended to, he immediately rendered all the assistance he could to other members of his section. Only when all had been attended to did he allow his own wounds to be dressed.

Another example of his N.C.O.'s spirit and determination presented itself when on the night of 6th/7th Mar. 42 he was in comd. of a patrol in Wadi Belfarais, in Cyrenaica. An A/P mine was exploded, wounding all five members of the patrol. After the detonation, a German patrol appeared. Although badly wounded in two places, Cpl Lawton, displaying great presence of mind and fortitude, succeeded in evacuating the wounded men—two of whom had to be carried—and led them safely back to our lines.

Although, as a result of his wounds, he now possesses a permanent disability, Cpl Lawton returned to the front line at the first opportunity, and continues to give the most valuable service in an active capacity.
M.I.D. 15.12.42   *(L.G. 18.2.43)*

Laybourne, Henry Donald, Sergeant (actg.)
2368822, Royal Signals, Attd. No. 1 Special Force H.Q., S.O.(M.), C.M.F. (Immediate)
Sjt. Laybourne was parachuted into North East Italy in Sep. 1944, as wireless operator to his Mission. After crossing to the West of the Tagliamento River the Mission and the partisan forces in that area were subjected to constant harassing by the enemy and finally to a large scale offensive which resulted in the dispersal of the partisan forces.

Throughout these operations, always on the move and constantly under fire, Sjt. Laybourne by his coolness and courage was able to maintain constant contact with Base and to pass much valuable intelligence to the Allied Armies. On many occasions when forced to disperse suddenly by enemy attacks, Sjt. Laybourne remained behind until the last to ensure that all his equipment was safe and that his link to Base was not interrupted.

When the enemy attacks became so great that the partisan forces were compelled to disperse he accompanied his Mission Leader up the 6,500 ft. high Monte Raut where in the middle of winter, suffering from frostbite, hunger and privation, he continued to maintain constant contact with his Base. When his Mission Leader, in order to re-organise the partisan forces, decided to proceed to the plains in civilian clothes, Sjt. Laybourne volunteered to accompany him although unable to speak the language and fully realising that his capture in civilian clothes would mean his instant death.

Despite the almost continuous efforts of the enemy to locate his set and the necessity for his having to be constantly on the move to avoid detection, he maintained constant contact with Base as a result of which the most valuable information and intelligence was made available to the Allied Forces.

On 23 Feb. 45, after almost six months continuous service in enemy occupied territory under the most rigorous conditions, he was offered the opportunity of returning to the Allied Lines when his Mission Leader was ordered to return to Base. Sjt. Laybourne, realising that his withdrawal without a replacement would result in a break in the passing of intelligence from this part of

the Field, voluntarily elected to remain with the partisan forces until a replacement could be found.

Throughout, this N.C.O. displayed exceptional courage, coolness and devotion to duty in the face of constant danger.   *(L.G. 2.8.45)*

Layton, Douglas, Lance Sergeant
1890359, 276 Field Coy., Royal Engineers (Horsfield, near Leeds) (Immediate)
On the morning of 23 Oct. 44, 1890359 L/Sgt. D. Layton was going forward with his Pl. Officer on road clearance task, in the attack for Schijndel and Shutsboom Map Ref. 398388, when the Pl. Officer was wounded. L/Sgt. Layton, in the absence of his Pl. Sgt., took over command of this party. He at once dispersed the Sappers in their road clearing and marking task, and went forward with a recce party into the outskirts of Schijndel. There being slight opposition, L/Sgt. Layton, on the spur of the moment, decided to take full opportunity to recce the route forward. He took his recce party in a H/T right through Schijndel and Shutsboom to the point which he knew was to be the limit of the Bde. attack.

Having marked the route open to that point, he decided to return since it was obvious that the enemy were still in the towns behind him.

After passing back all the information over the air he started to make his way back when some very close fighting developed. L/Sgt. Layton led his party in such a manner and with such encouraging example that they managed to get back and join the remainder of his road clearing party, who he found fighting at the other end of Schijndel. The enemy were beaten off and a wounded sapper recovered by L/Sgt. Layton who then brought his entire party back, under orders from his O.C.

Information was passed back by L/Sgt. Layton continuously throughout this exploit. It was due to his rapid snatching of the opportunity, which allowed that information to be got and passed to higher formations.

During the whole exploit L/Sgt. Layton's efficiency in taking over from an officer, courage and enduring cheerfulness was a leading factor in his men achieving their success.

This recce was carried out over 1,000 yds. ahead of leading troops.   *(L.G. 1.3.45)*

Leach, R. L., Sergeant
6087, Armoured Car Coy., Federated Malay States Volunteer Forces
On or about the 24th Jan. 42, this N.C.O. was in command of 'D' Troop and was patrolling the road from Benut to Senggarang. He first of all encountered the enemy about 1 mile South of Senggarang. At this place three of our trucks were drawn up on the side of the road, and the troops sheltering in a ditch from heavy M.G. fire. After observation Sgt. Leach discovered the fire was coming from a small Kampong on the side of the road. He brought his Troop into action and silenced the enemy machine guns, inflicting heavy casualties. The

column then proceeded but again came under M.G. and mortar fire 200 yards South of Senggarang. On reaching Senggarang our own troops were contacted and a party organised to rescue the wounded at the scene of the ambush. On approaching this place the truck for the rescue of the wounded was fired upon and ditched. Sgt. Leach gave covering fire and the crew of the truck took cover on the lee side of the Armoured Cars. The Troop then moved to the scene of the original ambush, where eleven wounded men were found. The Troop was halted and gave heavy covering fire when Sgt. Leach dismounted and placed two severely wounded men in his car. Four more wounded men clung to the lee side of the car, while five others walking wounded sheltered on the lee side of the cars. The Troop then proceeded at walking pace and all the wounded were safely brought to Benut Dressing Station in spite of being engaged by low flying aircraft. The whole of this action was carried out under heavy M.G. fire and the coolness and gallantry of this N.C.O. was most marked.

There is no doubt that it was due to the personal example and great courage of this man that the operation was successful and the eleven wounded rescued.

(L.G. 13.12.45)

Leach, Richard Owen, Sergeant
851795, 31st Field Regt., Royal Artillery (London, W.13) (Immediate)
During the period the Regiment was in action, for six weeks East of Cassino, Sgt. Leach was Bty. N.C.O. i/c Sigs. On the night 13/14 he started to lay a line from his position to Tactical HQ of the Regt. in the mountains North of Cassino.

This line he completed the next night. Throughout the two nights the line laying party was shelled, mortared and in danger from enemy patrols.

On the night 23/24 Feb. it was necessary to lay another line. This line took three nights to get through and on each night the line laying party was again shelled and mortared. On the morning of the 26 Feb. the line was completed but heavy shelling at once smashed it. Although Sgt. Leach had had little sleep for three days and no food since 1700 hrs. the night before, he at once went back down the line to mend it, and when in the vicinity of the Italian Barracks came under M.G. fire from the direction of the Monastery. He then carried out a reconnaissance having got across a minefield for an alternative route, as he decided the way the line had been laid the night before was too vulnerable. The line was then relaid. During these operation Sgt. Leach always carried the heaviest load, did the maximum amount of work himself, set a fine example of cheerfulness and resource, refusing to be daunted by any misfortune. The whole Artillery support of 7 Ind. Inf. Bde. depended on communications being got through successfully.
M.I.D. 15.12.42; B.E.M. 1.1.67   *(L.G. 24.8.44)*

Leadbetter, William, Corporal (A/Sgt.)
4105843, 2/5th Bn. Leicestershire Regt. (Birmingham) (Immediate)
At Mondaino 9374 (Italy 1/50,000 Sheet 109—IV Coriano) on the night of 31st Aug./1st Sep. 44 L/Sgt. Leadbetter was Pl Sgt. of 9 Platoon 'A' Coy. 2/5th Bn. The Leicestershire Regiment. The Coy. was advancing on Mondaino village after days of hard fighting. While a recce was being carried out by the Coy. officers, heavy M.G. and mortar fire was directed on the Coy. position. L/Sgt. Leadbetter was ordered to take a party round the left and eliminate two of the M.G.'s which were pinning the Coy. to the ground, so that an attack in force could be launched.

Without hesitation, still under heavy fire, he organised a small party and led them to the assault with great dash and personal courage, knocking out both M.G. positions and killing or capturing one officer and seven men.

His quick action undoubtedly saved the lives of many of his comrades, while his disregard for personal danger, his dash and ability, not only succeeded in demoralising the enemy, but was a magnificent example and inspiration to all around him.   *(L.G. 8.2.45)*

Lear, Percy Cardinal, Lance Corporal
231061V, 8 Fd. Sqn. S.A.E.C., South African Forces (Immediate)
On 29 Apr. 45, at MR G268617, L/Cpl. Lear was returning from a br. recce with Major Rocyn-Jones who was O.C. 8 Fd. Sqn. S.A.E.C., and 4 other details. The party ran into a pocket of the enemy, approximately 140 strong, who opened up with small arms. On instructions from Major Rocyn-Jones the party dispersed covered by L/Cpl. Lear who manned the machine gun on the Humber, firing until the magazine was empty. During this time he was wounded, losing two fingers of the left hand. The Humber was then hit by Bazooka and brewed up. L/Cpl. Lear tried to crawl away but was taken prisoner. He spoke to the enemy in Italian, telling them that they were completely surrounded by tanks and that there was no chance of escape. The enemy, who appeared to be in a state of nervous tension, accepted this story and spiked their A.Tk. guns, broke their Bazookas, killed the draught animals and burnt all personal papers. Of the remainder of the party, Major Rocyn-Jones and another detail had been killed, two had escaped and one other taken prisoner. L/Cpl. Lear was taken to a farm house, and when the enemy group moved off, taking the other detail with them, two Germans were left to guard him with instructions not to leave him for two hours.

L/Cpl. Lear, speaking to them in Italian, persuaded them to surrender to him and took them back some distance to one of our tanks.

An ambulance was sent for, but L/Cpl. Lear insisted on returning to Sqn. HQ., despite his wound and loss of blood, in order to report the result of the recce and to state what Major Rocyn-Jones' intentions had been.

As a result of his determination and courage, invaluable information was obtained from the recce and a large amount of enemy equipment destroyed.

(*L.G. 23.8.45*)

Leatherland, Alan Wilfred, Sergeant (A/W.O.II)
5824964, 1st Bn. Suffolk Regt. (Holbeach)
(Immediate)

During that attack on Overloon on 12 Oct. 1944 'A' Company met very heavy opposition from the flanks. The Company sustained many casualties from continuous shelling and from small arms fire. The Company Commander was killed. Both Officer Platoon Commanders were wounded in trying to resume the advance. All the senior N.C.O.'s were casualties.

Under heavy fire, C.S.M. Leatherland went forward in the open to the leading troops, detailed three of the remaining Lance Corporals as acting Platoon Commanders and then personally led the Company forward again towards the objective in the face of heavy fire from dug-in enemy positions. He overcame the enemy on the objective and consolidated it under continuous fire from M.G.'s on the flanks and shell fire until the remainder of the Battalion later reached their objectives. C.S.M. Leatherland personally accounted for several of the enemy dead. The Company captured some twenty prisoners in this action.

Throughout C.S.M. Leatherland was exposed to heavy fire of all kinds. Regardless of his own safety he coolly walked about in the open directing platoons during their advance and personally indicated to the supporting tanks the targets which were holding up the Company. He displayed courage of the highest order and proved himself a first class leader under the most trying conditions.

His cool determination and inspiring example were entirely responsible for the success of the attack by this Company.   (*L.G. 1.3.45*)

Lee, George William, Private (A/Cpl.)
4689721, 1/4 Bn. King's Own Yorkshire Light Infantry (Dewsbury) (Immediate)

On Sun. 16 Jul. 44 Cpl. Lee was in command of No. 1 Section of 16 Pl.

He led his men to the objective with great dash and skill being amongst the first to arrive at Barbee Fme.

Having cleared the buildings and killed two of the enemy with a grenade this N.C.O. took his section over to the left flank to some houses about 200 yds. away (856652) to deal with some enemy snipers who had been firing at the remainder of the platoon.

Cpl. Lee cleared these houses and proceeded in a Westerly direction through the orchard behind them. He got his section into the next field and on arriving at approx. 851652 Cpl. Lee observed an enemy officer and an enemy soldier working on a telephone line.

After ordering his Bren gunner to cover them he called out to them to surrender. The officer made as if to grab

his weapon and so he was shot, whereupon the other rank surrendered. This latter man later gave some very useful information.

Cpl. Lee and his section then continued to search the area to the West & SW of Barbee Fme for further enemy.

They went much further than ordered and ensured that this flank of the Coy. position was clear of the enemy.

Cpl. Lee then returned to the main Coy. position at Barbee Fm with his section and the enemy prisoner. He reorganised his section near to the West edge of the wood by Barbee Fm. This was carried out with speed and efficiency under heavy mortar and shell fire.

Later snipers infiltrated into the position and the area in the vicinity of Cpl. Lee's section became a 'hot spot.'

This N.C.O. kept his men together by his superb leadership and accounted for a number of the enemy. Cpl. Lee found time to cross fire-swept ground to report to his Coy. Comd. on the situation. The information he gave was of the greatest value.

In returning to his section Cpl. Lee was severely wounded.

Although in considerable pain his fine fighting spirit was unaffected and he was a splendid example to other wounded men.

This N.C.O. has displayed outstanding leadership and an utter disregard for his own personal safety particularly on patrols.

His section left the wood complete except for one man killed by a sniper under the Sec. 21C and their morale was as high on withdrawal as it was in the attack.

This I attribute to Cpl. Lee's magnificent example.

(*L.G. 19.10.44*)

Lee, Kenneth William, Corporal (A/Sgt.)
556058, Nottinghamshire Yeomanry (Retford, Notts.)

On the morning of 29th Oct. as the Sherman Squadron was taking up position, Sgt. Lee's tank struck a mine, damaged a bogey wheel and was thereby rendered immobile. The position in this sector was obscure, but it was soon realised that the enemy had guns of all calibres concealed in the sand dunes in our immediate vicinity and it was decided to draw back the line of heavy tanks some 400 yds. to a position from which they could get better observation and not run unnecessary risks of being knocked out. This was carried out and Sgt. Lee's tank was therefore left some 400–500 yds. in front of the main line. I sent for a Scammel and Recovery Vehicles, but these did not immediately appear. At 1700 hrs. reports began to come in from Sgt. Lee that Infantry in fairly large numbers were advancing towards him with the obvious intention of capturing the tank and he was subjected to heavy attacks from mortars and hand grenades. Sgt. Lee engaged the Infantry with his Browning and also with H.E. from his 75mm gun, thereby killing some 30–40 of them. At this time the Recovery Section arrived and this N.C.O. under intense small arms fire jumped out of his tank and assisted in fastening the tow rope. While this was in progress, a

tank attack developed, the main objective being apparently to destroy this Sherman Tank. Sgt. Lee remounted his tank and again vigourously engaged the enemy. The result of the action was that 5 M.13's were destroyed. By his initiative, courage, leadership and entire disregard for his own personal safety, Sgt. Lee destroyed a considerable number of the enemy, saved his tank, which was in action again on the following day and by his actions set the highest example to all ranks of courage, tenacity and devotion to duty.
Recommended for M.M. *(L.G. 25.2.43)*

Leech, Arthur Alexander, Sergeant
64102, 21 N.Z. Bn. (Immediate)
On the evening of the 9th Apr. 45 after the initial successful crossing of the R. Senio, Sjt. Leech's platoon was held up by enemy strong posts situated in depth. Although wounded and bleeding profusely, this N.C.O. refused to be evacuated and led his section in a succession of gallant attacks against well entrenched posts succeeding in every case in either capturing or destroying the positions thus enabling his Company to move into position behind the barrage. Without doubt Sjt. Leech by his great courage, determination and leadership played an outstanding part in opening the way for the following successful advance. *(L.G. 18.10.45)*

Leeks, Ronald, Corporal
6026470, 2 Somerset Light Infantry (London, E.12)
(Immediate)
Map Ref. Sheet Italy 99/I 50,000.
On 23 Nov. 44 at the crossing of the R. Cosina (364191) Cpl. Leeks was commanding a section in 'C' Company which company was ordered to pass through 'B' Company to enlarge the bridgehead.

While passing across the river, Cpl. Leeks platoon came under heavy enemy shell fire which wounded the platoon Sergeant. Cpl. Leeks having got his section across, came back and assisted the Platoon Commander in passing across the other two sections.

During the subsequent advance both leading sections came under heavy enemy S.A. fire and were pinned down in the open. The other section commander was killed. Cpl. Leeks then took command of both sections and directed their fire, personally exposing himself both to pinpoint enemy positions and to a wounded man back.

Cpl. Leeks then manœuvred both sections to a covered position from which a successful assault was made.

Throughout the action, Cpl. Leeks displayed a very high standard of personal courage and leadership, but for which it is unlikely that his platoon would have gained their objective. *(L.G. 26.4.45)*

Leeson, Herbert Thomas, Corporal
QX.3026, 2/32 Australian Infantry Bn.
Cpl. Leeson was a member of 13 Platoon 'C' Coy. and took part in the attack on Pt. 22 in the vicinity of Tell El Eisa on 17th Jul. 42. After consolidation he asked to be

allowed to use a captured 20mm Breda. During the first two enemy counter-attacks, under heavy M.G., A. Tk. and mortar fire, he single-handed destroyed 2 and probably 3 enemy vehs. before the gun was put out of action by a direct hit from an A Tk. shell, which knocked Cpl. Leeson out of the pit and wounded him in the face. However, despite the injury he immediately repaired the gun and continued to engage the enemy.

Later, on hearing of a wounded man lying exposed to fire out in front on the right flank, with complete disregard to his own safety and in the face of heavy M.G. and shell fire, Cpl. Leeson left the pit and went to the assistance of this man, and carried him in safely. In this act, Cpl. Leeson sustained a more serious wound in his hip, but disregarding his injuries, he immediately returned to his gun and commenced fire at low flying enemy aircraft.

The initiative, courage and devotion to duty displayed by Cpl. Leeson throughout were an inspiration to his men. *(L.G. 24.9.42)*

Legg, Leslie Roy, Private
VX 47870, 2/24 Australian Infantry Bn. (Immediate)
Pte. Legg was a Bren Gunner in 7 Platoon, 'A' Company during an attack on Japanese positions astride the Bonga—Wareo Road covering a track junction leading to Lakona on 12 Dec. 43.

During the initial stages the attack was brought to a standstill by heavy automatic fire from both flanks rendering further progress impracticable without heavy casualties.

Pte. Legg showed splendid initiative and courage in advancing alone for 20 yards and bringing fire to bear on the first of the two enemy L.M.G. posts on the right flank. Single handed he fought his way forward through heavy fire killing three Japanese with his Bren gun and grenades and capturing the L.M.G. Pressing further forward he fought his way to a position from where he brought fire to bear on a second L.M.G. post completely neutralising the gun and killing all the occupants.

By Pte. Legg's individual action the Company was able to maintain it's advance and eventually succeeded in capturing the objective resulting in the opening of the Bonga—Wareo Road.

Throughout the whole action, lasting six hours, Pte. Legg showed magnificent courage and was in the forefront of the Company advance and the first to gain the ridge which was the final objective. *(L.G. 23.3.44)*

Legge, Percy David, Sergeant
2321944, Royal Signals
During the 6th, 7th and 8th June, in the Bosc Bordel, Buchy area, this N.C.O. and other ranks (under Lt. J. J. G. Harvey) worked ceaselessly, and with complete disregard to their own safety, in repairing the telephone cables in the 'B' Bde. area, which were continually cut by enemy bombing. Largely as a result of their efforts telephone communications were maintained right up to

the moment of the withdrawal on the evening of 8th June.
(L.G. 20.8.40)

Leisegang, Ralph Theodore, Sergeant
1665, U.M.R., Union Defence Force (Immediate)
On 8th June 42 Sgt. Leisegang was acting as platoon commander the left half of a company attached to a force know as 'Guycol' which was operating against the enemy between Barrels 11 and 13 four miles South West of Strickland in the Gazala Line of the Western Desert.

This company was engaged in an attack on a very strongly held enemy position. During the action this platoon became separated and Sgt. Leisegang displayed the highest qualities of leadership and initiative under heavy enemy fire. With great dash and vigour he personally led his platoon in a highly successful bayonet charge which materially helped in taking the position together with 460 prisoners and considerable booty.

His was a brilliant achievement under most trying conditions.   (L.G. 19.12.46)

Leitch, Alexander Ritchie, Lance Corporal
3192726, 4 King's Own Scottish Borderers (Mussel-burgh)
On 24th Jan. 45 a battalion of the King's Own Scottish Borderers was ordered to clear the German town of Heinsberg. L/Cpl. Leitch was a company signaller in 'B' Company, which was deployed to protect the flank of the attack.

The company began to dig in during darkness, but when daylight came it was found that they were in a very exposed position and were completely overlooked by the enemy from a ridge only 250 yards away. From dawn onwards the whole company area was subjected to heavy shelling, and mortar and small arms fire.

Many casualties occurred, and as any movement brought renewed fire from the enemy, the stretcher bearers were unable to attend to the wounded. At 1300 hrs. it was therefore decided to put down an artillery smoke screen in front of the company position, so that they could reorganise and evacuate the wounded. No artillery forward observation officer was then available and L/Cpl. Leitch manned the company wireless set to pass range corrections to the guns.

The Company HQ soon after received a direct hit from a mortar bomb which seriously wounded the Company Commander and Company Serjeant Major and killed the Second in Command, leaving no officer in charge. L/Cpl. Leitch was himself wounded. His right leg had been so severely shattered that it had later to be amputated: he had also a large wound in his hip.

Nevertheless L/Cpl. Leitch remained at his post, realising the importance of the smoke screen. For 45 minutes he continued to observe and direct the fire of the gunners, so that the area was successfully smoked and it became possible for the wounded to be evacuated, and the company to be re-organised. During all this time he was alone and suffering intense pain.

Not until he was sure that his work had been completed did he disclose that he had been wounded.

Owing to the extent of the enemy fire, it took a further 30 minutes for stretcher bearers to reach him, and during that time he continued to give directions over his wireless set and bring down fire accurately on the enemy position.

The actions of this N.C.O., under critical circumstances, alone at his Coy. HQ, and gravely wounded, were a splendid example of courage and devotion to duty. By his bravery and indifference to his own wounds, L/Cpl. Leitch saved his company's position and the lives of many of his comrades.
Recommended for V.C., Recommended for M.M.
(L.G. 12.4.45)

Leng, John, Lance Sergeant
4390815, 4 Green Howards (Middlesbrough)
Ualeb—Gazala Line—27 Mar. 42—1 Jun. 42.
Sgt. Leng as Sec. Cdr. Carrier Pl. during five days of battle displayed outstanding devotion to duty. On the morning of 28th May 42, he led his Sec. to occupy an important feature overlooking the main Trigh Capuzzo mine gap. The ridge was occupied by a small enemy force and one carrier was knocked out. Sgt. Leng led his remaining two carriers and drove off the enemy force. He personally engaged enemy machine gun and directed a second carrier which successfully put out of action an Anti-Tank gun. He successfully held the ridge until the arrival of the Officer Commanding the Standing Patrol. On the 2nd Jun. 42, Sgt. Leng had been captured by the enemy and during his being transported he knocked out a German guard and with a party drove back and successfully rejoined our lines.   (L.G. 8.11.45)

Letendre, Samuel John, Rifleman
M.31085, Regina Rifle Regt., Canadian Infantry Corps (Immediate)
On 6 Oct. 1944, in the area of Moerhuizen, Belgium, during the battle for the South side of the Scheldt Estuary, M 31085 Rifleman Samuel John Letendre, 1st Battalion The Regina Rifle Regiment, was in the section of his company on the extreme left of the Brigade front holding a bridge-head over the Leopold Canal. This section position was considered to be vital to the security of the bridge-head.

During one of the numerous enemy counter-attacks the section leader was killed, the section became disorganized and its position precarious. Without hesitation and without orders Rifleman Letendre took command. With complete disregard for his own safety he moved about under fire, organized the section and encouraged the men. Several counter-attacks by the enemy followed. So completely had Rifleman Letendre re-organized the section that all counter-attacks against the position were beaten off and many casualties inflicted on the enemy.

The courage, initiative and fighting spirit exhibited by Rifleman Letendre were an example to all ranks who rallied under his leadership and held a vital position under most difficult circumstances.

Recommended for M.M. (L.G. 10.2.45)

Letts, John Aubers Ridge, Private
5882681, 1st Battalion, The Northamptonshire Regt.,
On 9th Sept. 1937, Private Letts was one of a piquet overlooking the Marai Narai for the purposes of road protection. The piquet was under continuous, close, and accurate rifle fire from 8.00 am until 3.20 pm hours. Private Letts was wounded in the left chest. He insisted on remaining with the piquet until ordered down at about 4.00 pm. Before and after being wounded, he was conspicuous for his acts of bravery and devotion to duty.

For instance—after he had been wounded, he perceived a Jemadar Royal Artillery who was wounded and fell in an exposed position. Private Letts immediately dashed out and brought the Jemadar to safety. In doing so, he narrowly missed being hit again. He rendered the greatest assistance to his piquet commander in locating the dispositions of the enemy, which often necessitated exposing himself to enemy fire. (12.11.37)

Levene, James, Private
*3777022, 1st Bn. King's Regt. Infantry (Dingle,
    Liverpool)*
On the 3rd of June 1944, Pte. Levene was Bren gunner of the point section of the King's Coy. (attd 1/Bn. The Lancs. Fusiliers) moving towards Loihinche (Map Ref. 92C/SE 6632). The column had halted at the base of Pt. 1094 (Map Ref. 92C/SE 655301) where the track split into 3 branches. Pte. Levene suddenly spotted the enemy lying in wait on the right of the track some 15 yards away. He fired a full magazine at them inflicting several casualties before they replied. There is not doubt that but for Pte. Levene's quick observation and prompt action the enemy would have inflicted heavy casualties upon his platoon. He then crossed a track covered by enemy fire and drove an enemy L.M.G. from our right flank saving further casualties to our tps.

On the morning of the 18th June Pte. Levene's platoon was leading the assault on Naungkaiktaw ref sheet 92C/ 15/9 & 6—637356. During the advance, ignoring heavy fire, he was always in the front. When his platoon was eventually halted owing to the platoon on the left being held up, he ran forward on to a bunker in an exposed position and killed six Japs as they attempted to withdraw. He then remained in this position cutting off one of their two lines of withdrawal and killed several more. There is no doubt that his gallant action enabled the platoon to advance.

Later in the morning of 18th June Pte. Levene and his section were sent to reinforce a platoon which was attacking and clearing Naungkaiktaw and had suffered casualties. He was quite unshaken by earlier experiences and was keen to engage and kill more of the enemy. He set an excellent example by his cool and fearless conduct throughout. He showed complete contempt of danger

and exposed himself freely to enemy fire in order to use his Bren to the best advantage and was invaluable in clearing further strongpoints and eventually putting surviving enemy to flight. (L.G. 26.4.45)

Levesque, Rosario, Warrant Officer Cl. I (R.S.M.)
D.61000, Les Fusiliers Mont-Royal
R.S.M. Levesque, a veteran of the Great War, saw action once again at Dieppe, 19th Aug. 42. Landing with the 2 i/c of the battalion, R.S.M. Levesque, at great personal risk obtained for him all possible information as to the progress of the operation. He remained with the 2 i/c until the latter was severely wounded and then crawled through heavy fire to inform the commander of HQ Coy. of what has happened and assisted him in directing further operations. During the withdrawal his coolness and initiative in directing men to the boats were invaluable.

Throughout the action R.S.M. Levesque performed gallant service and more than once risked his life to look after the wounded. (L.G. 2.10.42)

Levy, Edmund Sidney, Sergeant
37178, Royal Australian Armoured Corps
For Vietnam (L.G. 21.12.71)

Lewis, Arthur Henry, Lance Sergeant
*A22019, 8 Cdn. Recce Regt. (14 C.H.), Canadian
    Armoured Corps (Immediate)*
Late on the afternoon of the 22nd of February 1945 'C' Squadron 8 Canadian Reconnaissance Regiment (14 Canadian Hussars) was ordered to reconnoitre the main road Moyland—Till in Germany.

At Moyland, the Squadron was stopped by mines and blocks of trees felled across the road some thousand yards in depth. The Squadron was withdrawn to await first light, and the removal of the obstacles by the Engineers. A Section of the Assault Troop, led by Serjeant Lewis was left in Moyland to assist in this task.

After darkness had fallen it was found that the Engineers could not be made available, Serjeant Lewis, acting on his own initiative, under heavy mortar and shell fire, removed the mines and road blocks. This entailed the hauling of felled trees from the road and the directing of the vehicle that was so employed. This necessitated repeated backing on to the road verges, in every case Serjeant Lewis tested the verges for mines. In addition Serjeant Lewis personally lifted fourteen mines, which required the use of a small flash light, the use of which attracted heavy machine gun fire. This dangerous and difficult task had to be carried out under close range observation and fire from enemy positions. The enemy were, at this stage, most alert and keen to discover any forward movement in the area, and machine gun fire on fixed lines commanded the road.

It was through Serjeant Lewis' devotion to duty, disregard for his personal safety and cheerful leadership and encouragement to his men carrying out a most difficult and dangerous task, that it became possible for elements of the Squadron to occupy Till that night, and as well allowed them to secure the left flank of their Divisions advance towards Calcar some twelve hours sooner than would have otherwise been possible.

(L.G. 12.5.45)

Lewis, George Henry Floyd, Warrant Officer Cl. II
1069543, Royal Artillery
For Malaya   *(L.G. 19.5.50)*

Lewis, James Frederick, Warrant Officer Cl. II (A.Q.M.S.)
1425952, 8 Armd. Bde. Gp. Wksp., R.E.M.E.
(Periodic)
This W.O. has, from the outset of the campaign, displayed outstanding devotion to duty and has never hesitated to carry out the recovery of all types of equipment including A.F.V.s in the face of the enemy.

On many occasions he has taken recovery vehicles under shell and mortar fire to disabled tanks and vehicles and by his skill and coolness under fire has organised and supervised their immediate recovery.

On the night 22nd/23rd Apr. 43 he supervised the recovery of 6 tanks and one Scorpion under direct shell fire from the minefields to the North of the Takrouna feature near Envidaville.

On the night 23rd/24th Apr. 43 he again recovered 2 tanks from the same minefield as the previous night and also 2 more tanks from the West of Takrouna.

On the night 24th/25th Apr. 43 he supervised the recovery of 2 tanks from the North West of Takrouna and personally went on hands and knees to investigate another tank under shell fire so intense that no vehicle could get near to it. To do this he had to cross a field known to contain booby traps and mines. Several subsequent attempts were made to recover this one remaining disabled tank and finally on the day of 1st May 43 he succeeded in doing this under shell fire, first of all taking a welding equipment to the tank to cut away very badly jammed tracks which had rendered previous recovery impossible.

These are but a few examples of the outstanding initiative shown by this W.O. which have proved a fine example and inspiration to all ranks who have worked with him in his recovery section.
Recommended for M.M.   *(L.G. 25.11.43)*

Lewis, Leonard, Corporal
3961349, 6th Bn. Lincolnshire Regt. (Carmarthen)
(Periodic)
On 1st Sep. 1944, 'C' Company were ordered to attack the Western End of Monte Gridolfo Ridge (MR 960752 Italy, Sheet 109/4, 1/50,000.

Cpl. Lewis was in command of one of the forward Sections. The platoon came under intense small arms fire as it came into the open, moving down the forward slope and suffered a number of casualties. Cpl. Lewis

and his Section never faltered but doubled forward into a gully and from here worked up to the objective. Covering 800 yards in 12 minutes Cpl. Lewis was the first man into the village, and engaging the enemy at close range, caused several casualties to them and captured the first of the prisoners. During the whole attack his leadership and personal gallantry were of the highest order and an inspiration to his men, and greatly influenced the success of the attack.

On 10th Sep. 1944, 'C' Company's task was to attack between 'B' and 'D' Companies. The Company was shelled all day and suffered casualties. Cpl. Lewis was conspicuous for his steadiness and deliberateness in all moves and his grip and command of his men was most apparent. When the company attacked at dusk his personal gallantry was outstanding as he led his men to the enemy position. This Section reached the first enemy M.G.'s and a hand to hand fight took place, casualties being inflicted on both sides. During this Cpl. Lewis could be distinguished firing his T.M.C. and urging his men on. His leadership and bravery throughout the day was outstanding.

On 19th Sep. 1944 at Monte Lupo (MR 8086) Italy, Sheet 109/4, 1/50,000, Lieut. Stockdale's platoon, of which Cpl. Lewis was a member, was ordered to occupy Pt. 244 consisting of a farmhouse on a bare ridge some 600 yards to the West of our positions, supported by a troop of tanks. The approach to the objective was completely devoid of cover with both flanks open. The Tanks moved forward supported by artillery and smoke, and with great dash, this N.C.O. and his men followed their officer at the double. Before they had gone many yards a salve of heavy calibre shells dropped amongst them, killing five men outright and wounding others. Out of this Cpl. Lewis, Lieut. Stockdale and three O.R.'s dashed on towards the objective. They covered 300 yards, passed the tanks and then paused for breath, but came under M.G. cross fire from the left of the objective and from the right rear, wounding a N.C.O. and killing one man. Nothing daunted this N.C.O. and his Officer went straight for the objective and by grit and determination reached it and as they did so a stream of about 20 enemy retreated from the farm. Those that remained—about 10—were engaged by this N.C.O. and his Officer in the building with T.M.C. and Grenades. At this juncture, Lieut. Stockdale was killed and Cpl. Lewis wounded and taken prisoner. The forward movement of the tanks caused the enemy considerable confusion; taking advantage of this, Cpl. Lewis escaped although wounded in the head, and making his way back over the ground over which he had come, reached his company position in a state of collapse.

Throughout these and other actions this N.C.O. has invariably displayed the greatest courage and steadiness. His sense of discipline and duty have been a very fine example to those under his command and enhance the fine qualities of leadership he has always shown.

(L.G. 28.6.45)

Lewis, Percival Albert Henry, Corporal (A/Sgt.)
7912525, 50th Bn. Royal Tank Regt. (Bristol)
(Immediate)
During the fight for the bridgehead across the Mareth Line on 22nd Mar. 43, Sjt. Lewis was commanding one of the tanks supporting our infantry on the most forward defended locality. Under very heavy shelling and machine gun fire, this N.C.O, repeatedly left his tank to contact the infantry and get information for his Squadron about the approach of the enemy and to give first aid with his tank kit to wounded on the front. When attacked by tanks and inf. of 15 Pz. Div., his tank was hit and he fought it until he was forced to evacuate. He took his Bren gun and T.S.M.G. and fell in with the infantry defending the Wadi, remaining there until 23rd Mar., after the remainder of the Bn. had been withdrawn. Sjt. Lewis' action as a soldier in falling in line with the infantry when his tank had been knocked out had a very great influence on them at a most critical stage in the operation. When this happened Sjt. Lewis had been forward under fire without rest for over 48 hours. His cool courage and determination to do more than duty demanded of him was an inspiration to all.
Recommended for M.M.   *(L.G. 1.6.43)*

Lewis, Samuel, Corporal (A/Sgt.)
4854847, 4th Bn. Gordon Highlanders
On 26th May 1940 this N.C.O. was Section Corporal of a M.G. Section which was occupying a position in the Gapaard area, near Commines. During the late afternoon heavy enemy pressure caused the Infantry on the left front to withdraw and at the same time a platoon of Machine Gunners also withdrew, leaving their guns. In the confusion of the battle, Cpl. Lewis had lost touch with his Section Commander but immediately took control himself, rallied the survivors of the withdrawing Machine Gun Platoon and under heavy fire went out and collected the abandoned guns. Two of these guns he immediately put into action with his own Section and he then kept all guns in action until the morning of 27th May. This had a considerable effect in delaying the enemy advance. This N.C.O. displayed courage, initiative and devotion to duty of a very high order and his services are deserving of suitable recognition.
(L.G. 27.8.40)

Leyland, Adam, Corporal
3861072, 1 Loyal Regt. (Wigan) (Immediate)
On 21st Apr. 43, Cpl. Leyland took part in a counter-attack on Pt. 250 of the Kesskiss feature.

Through his leadership, example and aggressiveness he inspired his section to capture its objective, and seek out, kill or capture 10 Germans and at least 1 M.G. 34.

On 23rd Apr. 43, during a counter-attack on Pt. 156 of the Guiriat El Atach feature, Cpl. Leyland led his section through intense machine gun and mortar fire. He captured the position on the slope facing the enemy, and for nearly 12 hours all attempts to dislodge his section

failed. On several occasions he crawled over the hill under machine gun and mortar fire to give information to his platoon commander. He was wounded three times, and refusing offers of help, led his section back in good order when relieved by another Coy.

The gallantry and leadership displayed by this N.C.O. on 21st Apr. and 23 Apr. materially affected the success of the operations in which his Bn. was concerned. I consider his action an outstanding example of leadership and inspiration to all.   *(L.G. 8.7.43)*

Liddell, Robert, Sergeant
3187413, 1st Bn. Royal Scots Fusiliers (Ulverston)
On 3rd Oct. 1944 in North Burma, Sgt. Liddell was Platoon Sergeant of the left leading platoon of his company which was advancing on Mawlu across open paddy. At about 1230 hrs., when 200 yds. from the edge of the village, the right forward platoon was held up by L.M.G. and rifle fire from the left. Sgt. Liddell's platoon pushed on into a slightly wooded and overgrown area to their left front which afforded some cover. Sgt. Liddell was moving with the Platoon HQ close behind the forward section, when he saw a Japanese in the doorway of a builidng a hundred yards away. He immediately went forward to warn the leading section, from whom it was screened, of the presence of a Japanese post and ordered them to stand fast while he reconnoitred. He crawled to a mound within 25 yards of the building from where he exchanged shots with a Japanese Officer who withdrew into the building shouting orders. A medium machine-gun near the building and on the flank of the platoon opened fire at 75 yards range, as the platoon resumed its advance, forcing it to take cover and re-opening fire at every attempt to advance. Sgt. Liddell remained in his exposed position which was now attracting fire, with complete disregard for his personal safety, and attempted to eliminate the machine-gun with his grenades, at the same time waving to the platoon to advance. The Platoon Comdr. at this stage ordered the platoon to withdraw and Sgt. Liddell remained to cover this operation, engaging and driving to cover three Japanese who attempted to reach fire positions. He then rejoined his platoon and assisted his Commander to reorganise for a second assault. When the attack was resumed, Sgt. Liddell led two sections against the area where he knew the enemy to be. The attack was met by heavier fire than before but, though the sections were forced to take cover, Sgt. Liddell continued to advance urging them on. The Platoon Comdr. now decided that heavier support was required and recalled the sections. Sgt. Liddell was then close up to the enemy and remained there in an exposed position for a further five minutes, trying to locate the enemy's detailed dispositions, before he returned to his platoon.

Later in the evening, after the opposition had been neutralized by artillery fire and the company was able to reach its objective, Sgt. Liddell coolly assisted his commander in organising the consolidation under fire from snipers and grenade dischargers. When his commander was mortally wounded he immediately took command and moved amongst his men encouraging them without regard to his own safety.

Throughout the action Sgt. Liddell showed the utmost courage, coolness and initiative and his conduct was an inspiration to all.
Recommended for M.M.   *(L.G. 22.3.45)*

Light, Harold, Warrant Officer Cl. II
1055722, 53rd Field Regt., Royal Artillery
May 19th to 30th.
This N.C.O. acted as liaison officer between Regtl. HQ and his Bty. Throughout the fighting from Tournai to Dunkirk he maintained touch when all other form of communication had failed. He was frequently subjected to very heavy shelling, bombing and M.G. fire both from air and ground, but continued to carry out his duties without loss of time and with the most admirable coolness and steadiness. His reliability under fire and his disregard for danger made him of greatest assistance to his Regimental Commander.   *(L.G. 11.7.40)*

Lightfoot, Houlton St. Clair, Corporal
30891, 1 T.S., South African Forces
At Gobuen in Italian Somaliland when the Bn. was being heavily shelled by the enemy guns, a call went out for stretcher bearers to go forward to collect wounded. No stretcher bearers were present and Lightfoot with complete disregard to his own safety, volunteered to go fwd. under the heavy fire and bring in the wounded. He assisted in bringing in three of the wounded.

Under heavy fire at Agi Ali he volunteered to carry amn. over open ground to a platoon which was running short of amn. This hazardous feat he accomplished carrying many hundreds of rds. of amn.

At Combolcia he volunteered to go fwd. with Capt. Briscoe under enemy fire to see what aid could be given to 'B' Coy. who were pinned down by the enemy. During the move fwd. Capt. Briscoe was mortally wounded and Lightfoot was wounded in the back. In spite of his own wound Lightfoot remained in open ground under enemy fire with Capt. Briscoe dressing his wound, and only moved to cover when he realised that Capt. Briscoe was dead.

This man is the finest type of fighting soldier.
Recommended for M.M. M.M. 28.6.45   (L.G. 16.4.42)

Lightfoot, Richard, Sergeant (A/W.O.II (C.S.M.))
3602167, 1 Seaforth Highlanders (Maryport, Cumberland)
At Kasom, Assam (Map Ref. Assam & Burma 83 L/NW 1/2″ to 1 mile 692830) on the nights 15/16 April 1944 and 19/20 April 1944, during continuous attacks by the enemy, the conduct of this W.O. was of the highest order. By his coolness under heavy fire he was an inspiration to all the men of his Coy. When casualties occurred he was immediately on the spot, and personally

attended to the wounded until they could be taken over by the M.O. During both nights whilst the fighting was at its fiercest, he continued to move from one part of the perimeter to another to encourage the men. Throughout, he showed unflinching courage and devotion to duty.
                    (L.G. 8.2.45)

Limbu, Bardhoj, Sergeant
21146536, 10th Princess Mary's Own Gurkha Rifles
For Malaya   *(L.G. 21.10.52)*

Limbu, Barmalal, Sergeant
21135475, 2nd Bn., 10th Princess Mary's Own Gurkha Rifles
Having placed half his force in ambush some 2,000 yards distant Sergeant Barmalal was, with 10 men, in a temporary resting-place. At 1500 hours he received warning from one of his sentries that a very large enemy force was about to attack a longhouse near his position. Although the enemy were unaware of his presence, he placed the need to protect the defenceless civilians in the longhouse before the security of his own small party and unhesitatingly ordered that the enemy be engaged.

During the four hours before nightfall over 120 regular troops supported by mortars and at least three medium machine guns made three separate, determined but unsuccessful attacks on our position. In each case their vastly superior numbers and the weight of small arms fire concentrated on the defenders carried them to within yards of their objective before being beaten back. Throughout the whole battle Sergeant Barmalal, regardless of his own safety, moved amongst his men, personally re-siting some, adding his own fire to positions under the greatest threat and encouraging all by his calm and commanding bearing.

When a strong group of enemy were seen to be forming up for their final assault in dead ground dangerously close to his position he took four men with him and crawled forward to a position from which he was able to drive this party off with grenades.

The third attack was launched through scrub which afforded a covered approach up to his position. Ordering the light machine gun and four men to cover the open approaches, Sergeant Barmalal led the remainder to a detached position from which he could better meet this new threat. For thirty minutes this small group, inspired by their commander, waged an intense battle in the undergrowth at point blank range. At one stage the enemy actually penetrated his position before being driven back, Sergeant Barmalal accounting personally for at least two of the casualties.

With his ammunition all but exhausted he nevertheless asked to remain when ordered to break contact and withdraw. He continued to hold his position until the enemy withdrew under cover of their supporting fire at 2100 hours, taking with them their casualties. Searches on the following day showed these to have been heavy.

Throughout six hours of battle, fought with the utmost ferocity and determintion by both sides, the premediated bravery, professional skill, aggressive leadership and selfless example under fire displayed by this junior Sergeant were unquestionably responsible for the successful tactical defeat, by a small force, of an enemy who outnumbered them by twelve to one. Sergeant Barmalal's conduct on this day was in the highest traditions of his Race, his Regiment and the British Army. *[From L.G.]* (L.G. 22.6.64)

Limbu, Bhaktabahadur, Sergeant (actg.)
21141665, 10th Princess Mary's Own Gurkha Rifles
For Malaya (L.G. 1.5.53)

Limbu, Lalbauhadur, Sergeant
21138005
For Malaya (L.G. 7.2.50)

Limbu, Narprasad
21136894, 10th Gurkha Rifles, RFN
For Malaya (L.G. 15.9.53)

Linton, A. C. G., Bdr.
1443995, Royal Artillery
1443995 L/Sgt. A. C. C. Linton who is at present attached to 'C' Troop of this Bty. was in position near Qincampoix road block on the Rouen—Forges road.

On the afternoon of the 8th June, an enemy attack developed and when the infantry of Syme Bn. withdrew his gun acted as reaguard, protecting the infantry from A.F.V.'s.

His detachment is known to have accounted for two light tanks, one field gun, and one aeroplane, and six parachutists.

During the whole action he showed considerable courage and cheerfulness, and was a perfect example to his men.

I strongly recommend that his action be rewarded with a D.C.M. 20.12.40

Linton, Andrew Conrad Greene, Bombardier
1443995, Royal Artillery
Lister, Ernest Evelyn, Corporal
T/106085, R.A.S.C., 51 Div.,
14th June 1940 Capture Neufchatel.
My Unit, 508 Petrol Coy. R.A.S.C. was withdrawing from Metz in the first half of June 40. On about 14th June I was taken prisoner, near Neufchatel, while blind from a wound in the face and suffering from loss of memory. I did not recover my sight for three weeks after my capture.

Jul/Sep. Stalag XIII A Nurnberg.
During this time I was taken through St. Die and Colmar to Stalag XIII A at Nurnberg, where I was in hospital until the end of July, during which time I was trepanned. After discharge I was transferred to the camp and on and after 15th Aug. given the task of cleaning out the open latrines, together with a gang of other P/W, all Jews. I was the only British P/W, the others being chiefly coloured French Colonial troops.

21 Sep. Escape.
I had planned with five Frenchmen to escape. One, who came from Alsace and spoke G, was employed in the Power house, where he worked at the Dynamos which supplied current for electrifying the wire fence round the camp. Through him we learned that every day between 1700 and 1705 hours the current was interrupted while dynamos were switched over.

Making use of this information one of our party, on 20th Sep., cut the wire during the five minutes interruption of current. Other P/W crowded round and so the work was done without the guards noticing. The cut was then covered with P/W washing and at 0130 hours next morning our party crawled through at ten minutes interval between each man. We had obtained civilian clothing from some Spanish 'Red' P/W, who were lodged in the camp.

Once out we made for the railway goods yard and hid up on an adjoining hill, for three days, while we watched the railway traffic to make sure which train would serve our purpose, namely to make for France. During this time one of the Frenchmen would leave us at night and steal food for the party.

On the third night (24th Sep.) we decided to travel on a train composed of petrol wagons which we found out, by the labels, was going in the right direction. We were able to scramble under the wagons and hide up on top of the bogeys. We travelled this way for three nights, leaving the train before daylight and then waiting until nightfall to board another train. On the early morning of 28th Sep. we got as far as the Eastern bank of the Rhine, opposite Strasbourg. Leaving the train we sought a place from which we were hidden and yet could watch the river traffic. From the spot selected we saw four motor boats moored alongside each other, bows end on to a wooden jetty. Between the jetty and our hiding place was a hut used by the boats' crews as their quarters when off duty. We lay hidden for three days and noticed that:—

(a) Each boat took in turn to patrol a length of the opposite.

(b) In the daytime there was half an hour's lapse patrols.

(c) At night from 2100 hours there was a lapse between patrols.

On the third night we decided to seize one of the boats the Rhine the crew of the hours and had entered the hut, we dashed down to the jetty, sank their boats by pulling out the plugs and then started up the fourth (which had just come in and so had a warm motor. I acted as the mechanic as I had had previous experience of motors).

The noise of the motor attracted the guards who covered the river with a searchlight and opened fire on us with a M.G., killing or mortally wounding three of our party of five, who were standing amidships. The remaining Frenchman however replied with a M.G.

mounted forward and the German fire ceased and the searchlight went out.

Meanwhile I steered in the dark for the far side and, when nearing the bank, my remaining companion and I jumped for it, allowing the boat to carry on to some piles, where it crashed and sank.

We scrambled ashore through some reeds and got clear away, heading West, without any apparent pursuit. After about seven days travel we got to Rombas, where I had been previously with my unit. We were sheltered in the attic of a house, belonging to Mme. Bourget (?). Three days later, while we were hiding, a German patrol entered the house, shot Mme. Bourget and raped and maltreated here daughter before leaving. The girl died a few hours later and we buried her, in a blanket, in the garden. A neighbour next door was a witness and the facts were recorded at the Mairie of Rombas.

Oct. 40. Recapture nr. St. Pol and escape after 4 days.

We left immediately afterwards and went our way Westwards to Arras, beyond which towards St. Pol we were recaptured on betrayal by a peasant, who was given a reward at the Kommandandatur, in our presence.

After four days in a transit camp, we got away by hiding in a lorry which drove out of the camp. Once outside we jumped clear and made off, heading South for Epinal, where we laid up for three weeks. We then continued on to the demarcation line which we crossed (where I cannot remember) and then got to Macon, where we were arrested and escorted to Fort St. Jean at Marseilles.

30th Nov. (about) Marseilles.

I got away from Fort St. Jean soon after Christmas and went to Cannes, where I was given shelter by various British residents until the end of April.

I was then picked up by French plainclothes detectives and taken to St. Hippolyte du Fort, where later I was passed by the Mixed Medical Commission and repatriated through Madrid and Gibraltar.

I should add that my French companion, who escaped with me from Stalag XIII A can be traced through Lieut. Marquis, 4ieme Bureau, 'Etat Majeur,' Caserne St. Martin, Perpignan.   *(L.G. 20.12.40)*

Lister, Ernest Evelyn, Corporal
T/106085, R.A.S.C.
See Linton, A.C.G.   *(L.G. 4.11.41)*

Littlefair, John Andrew, Sergeant (actg.)
2886369, 1 Gordon Highlanders (Stockton-on-Tees)
(Immediate)
On the night of 23 Mar. 45, 'D' Coy was the leading Coy. of the Battalion crossing the Rhine and had been ordered to capture as an initial objective, a large farm building. This they successfully accomplished but the enemy managed to set the farm alight with an incendiary, thus showing up all our positions to his intense and accurate Spandau fire. The adjoining platoon to Sgt. Littlefair's lost their Comd. and Platoon Sgt. and so he,

seeing that the situation was deteriorating, went across regardless of the heavy enemy fire and the open (and now well lit up) ground, to rally this platoon. His initiative, the great example and the encouragement he gave on this occasion were immediately responsible for this platoon proceeding with great dash to capture a further objective. It is doubtful but for this N.C.O.'s voluntary actions whether it would have succeeded otherwise.

As the Coy. proceeded into the rubble and ruins of Rees, the example set and display of superb personal bravery by this N.C.O. were quite exceptional. His Platoon Comd. had been killed by his side on entering the town, yet he led himself each action so that the young soldiers in the platoon, many had not been in action before, should be given every chance.

His conduct in the face of heavy and accurate Spandau and Bazooka fire and very considerable mortar and artillery fire was an inspiration to his platoon and Coy.; it is impossible to pick out the clearing of any one area more than another—in all he was in the lead, showing the highest degree of initiative, resourcefulness and energy. His personal bravery under appalling conditions after 36 hrs. continuous street fighting, his determination to evict a very stubborn enemy, his standard of leadership and initiative and his constant regard for his men were all worthy of superlative tributes. The number of enemy he must have personally killed is high and never did he hesitate even though his platoon by the end had suffered 50% casualties. Throughout, he was fighting German paratroopers who asked for, and gave no quarter, and the resistance was at this time tougher than anything previously met in this campaign.

His cheerfulness, the confidence he gave and the magnificent coolness he displayed, were largely responsible for the remarkable success this Company had. Without the supreme efforts of this N.C.O. Rees would have taken a much longer time to clear and many more casualties would have resulted.   *(L.G. 12.7.45)*

Lloyd, Ronald Cecil, Lance Corporal
7910346, 4 Royal Tank Regt.
On Jun. 17, 41, L/Cpl. Lloyd was driver of Lt. Cole's light tank when orders were given for that officer to engage the enemy armour in order to gain time for the withdrawal of the battalion of infantry occupying a position along the top of the escarpment just East of Halfaya Pass. (Ref. Map Egypt, 1:50,000, Sheet 5136 Saloom.) The light tank was accompanied by one Matilda tank which being slow and a large target was soon put out of action, leaving the light tank to engage some three sixwheeled armoured cars and several heavy tanks alone. The fight lasted about an hour, and the success of the engagement lay in avoiding close action, to do which it was essential that the utmost use was made of the light tanks powers of acceleration, speed, and handiness in ground which while difficult for the light tank was extremely bad for heavier tracks, and out of the question

for wheels. To get the utmost out of the vehicle in such circumstances required in a driver a very high standard of skill and concentration. The tank was continually hit by small arms fire and near misses from the heavier weapons were frequent, but L/Cpl. Lloyd interpreted every order passed down to him from Lt. Cole with the greatest alacrity. Only the firer could really select the actual path the tank was to traverse, and a too sudden turn among boulders or ridges will tear off or break a track. Often Lloyd opened his front flap the better to see quite regardless of his own safety. When on one occasion his engine stalled due to a 'stoppage,' he on the instant leapt out and set to work to rectify it which he succeeded in doing with the help of Lt. Cole, getting away again just as fire was brought to bear on them. That this crew succeeded in achieving its purpose against such odds, and eventually return to our lines was obviously due in a very great measure to the skill courage, and devotion to duty of the driver—L/Cpl. Lloyd.

It is remarkable to reflect yet an incontestable fact, that upon the driving-skill and coolness in action of one Lance Corporal, depended many of the lives—indeed possibly the fate of the whole unit, which without any other support effected a daylight withdrawal under the very noses the enemy armour.   (*L.G. 25.9.47*)

Lloyd, Thomas, Lance Sergeant
4192000, 1st Bn. Royal Welch Fusiliers (Wrexham)
(Immediate)
Imphal Operations. 20 May 1944.

During an attack on Kuki Picquet, Cpl. Lloyd's platoon was held up by extremely strong enemy opposition.

Cpl. Lloyd, under very heavy fire from enemy snipers and three enemy machine guns, worked his way forward to within fifteen yards of the Japanese machine gun post which he put out of action himself with his section's L.M.G.

When his company was subsequently ordered to withdraw this N.C.O. was cut off by himself and unable to withdraw for six hours. During this time he kept enemy snipers engaged and it was entirely due to his action that his company was able to withdraw with but few casualties. When night fell Cpl. Lloyd succeeded in rejoining his company bringing with him the L.M.G. and his own Bren gun.

Some days later during an attack on his position by the Japanese, Cpl. Lloyd, in face of enemy fire, rallied his men and engaged the enemy himself with a 2" mortar at very short range.

This N.C.O.'s devotion to duty, individual leadership and courage have been of a very high order and an inspiration to all around him.   (*L.G. 22.3.45*)

Lloyd, William Richard John, Lance Corporal
3963811, 8 Bn. Sherwood Foresters
1. Capture.

I was captured at Lillehammer (Norway) on 22 Apr. 40 while manning a road-block alone. I was equipped with an anti-tank rifle, but the ammunition was of reduced charge type and failed to penetrate enemy A.F.V.'s. I was surrounded and captured. I believe that my C.O. and most of my battalion were captured about the same time.

2. Camps in Poland.

Stalag XX A, Fort 13 (Thorn). Early May 40 for about three weeks.

Working Party at Bishofsberg. End May till 18 Dec. 40.

Stalag XX A, Fort 13. 18 Dec. 40 till Jul. 41.

Farm at Laskowitz (Germany),1:100,000, Sheet 42, 3031). One day in Jul. 41.

Stalag XX A, Fort 13. Jul. 41 till Oct. 41.

Stalag XX A, Fort 15. Oct. 41 till Feb. 42.

Surveillancelager 39 (Falkenburg) (Sheet 56, 0698). Feb.42 till about Oct. 42.

Surveillancelager 88 (?) (Gross Wolz) (Sheet 42, 5440). Five days in Oct. 42.

Stalag XX A, Fort 15. Oct. 42 till Apr. 44.

Surveillancelager 56 (?). Exact location uncertain. Apr. 44 to 19 May 44.

3. Attempted Escapes.

(a) From Danzig in Aug. 40 with L/Cpl. Smith, Manchester Regt. and Pte. Kelly, regiment unknown. We walked across country and succeeded in getting into Congress Poland. Kelly was caught two days before Smith and myself. We were captured at Liehe, after about ten days, at night, when we ran into a German convoy on its way to Russia. We were sent back to Fort 13 and did about six weeks in the cells.

(b) In Jan. 41 from Fort 13 (Thorn) with Pte. Burfield (S/P.G. (P) 1977) and Pte. Dimmock, Sherwood Foresters. We walked out of the Fort without difficulty and were at liberty for seven to eight days. By jumping goods trains we got to the vicinity of Bromberg and were caught there in a railway yard. We were sent back to Fort 13.

(c) In Aug. 41 from Lascowitz (Sheet 42, 3031) with Burfield. We ran away from a farm on the first day working there and were caught sleeping in a barn near Stargard (Sheet 27, 3581) after about 14 days. We were sent back to Fort 13 and were confined to the Stalag after serving a sentence of 21 days.

(d) In Dec. 41 from Fort 13 with Burfield and Pte. Gilliland, who belongs to a Scots Regiment. We managed to steal three bicycles and got as far as Posen, where we were caught by the police.

(e) In May 42 from Fort 15 with Burfield. We scaled the camp wall, a set of railings, and a barbed wire fence by means of a rope ladder. We were caught the same day about 20 km. outside Thorn. We did a sentence of 21 days in Forst 16 and were then sent back to Fort 15.

(f) In Sep. 42 from Fort 15 with Burfield. We again got out by using a rope ladder. We were caught in Nakel (Sheet 56, 7489) after a few days. We had travelled most of the time by passenger trains and had no identity papers.

(g) In Dec. 42 from Fort 15 with Burfield. On this occasion we got out of the camp concealed in boxes. We travelled by passenger train and got as far as Strasbourg where we were caught at a railway station because we had no identity cards.

(h) In Mar. 43 from Surveillancelager 36 at Falkemburg (Sheet 56, 0698) with Burfield. We got out at the back of the camp while the guard was being changed at the front, and travelled by passenger train without identity papers to Berlin. In the station in Berlin we were apprehended because of our shabby clothes. We received 21 days' cells, the normal punishment for escaping.

(i) In Aug.43 from Falkenburg with Burfield, again at the back of the camp. We were caught at Derschau, near Danzig, having travelled there by passenger train without papers. We were arrested in Derschau because we were out after curfew, and again our shabby clothes attracted attention.

(j) In Nov. 43 from Gross Wolz (Surveillancelager 88) (Sheet 42, 5440) with Burfield. Thirteen others got out at the same time through a hole in the wall. Burfield and I were re-captured in Danzig the following night, having travelled their direct. We were caught while trying to find a barn in which to sleep on the way to Gotenhafen (Gdynia). After having done 21 days' cells for this attempt, four of us—L/Cpl. Howie, D.L.I., Pte. Smith, Burfield and myself, were kept together in a room in Fort 16 and were interrogated by German Army Officers at the Stalag HQ in Thorn. We admitted having helped to make the hole in the wall through which we escaped, and were asked if we had had a notice read out to us that offences like this were to be regarded as sabotage. Burfield and I denied having seen the notice, but the two others admitted having heard it read out. We were kept for a week in Fort 16 and then sent to Fort 15. Six or seven weeks later we were called to the Stalag and told that we had been tried by proxy in Berlin, and that while we would not receive a sentence of imprisonment, we were liable to disciplinary punishment. We were given seven days' cells in Fort 16.

(k) After serving our seven days we were sent back to Fort 15. Burfield and I escaped from Fort 15 again, about Jan. 44, by walking out of the camp. We went by passenger train to a town North of Graudenz (Sheet 42, 5028), where we were caught at the station. We did the usual 21 days in Fort 16.

4. Escape.

On 3 Apr. 44 Burfield and I were moved to Surveillancelager 56 (?) about 20 kms. from Thorn. (Note:— Both Lloyd and Burfield are uncertain of the location of this camp, but think it was probably on the East bank of the River Vistula near Szarkomizna. (Germany, 1:100,000, Sheet 57, 6159). They state that the name of the camp is Weichselgard, but there is no village of that name.) This was a camp for incorrigible escapers. During our first week at Weichselgard nine men escaped. All of them were recaptured. Burfield and I were not in this party.

On the night on which the nine men escaped I was taken back to the hospital at Fort 14 (Thorn) suffering from a poisoned arm. I was in the Fort for about a week, and on discharge from hospital was sent to Fort 13.

In Fort 13 I made final arrangements for our escape with three friends who were not members of the Escape Committee. I arranged that, if possible, Burfield and I would escape from the camp at Weichselgard and return to Thorn, where, by assuming the identities of two of our friends, we would be able to enter and leave Fort 13. Neither our friends nor ourselves were in touch with any Polish organisation.

On 19 May, about a week after my return to the camp at Weichselgard, Burfield and I escaped with Pte. W. Charleton, who belongs to a Scottish regiment; Pte. G. O. Russell, D.L.I.; and Pte. Young, D.L.I. The camp is approached from the outside by a gate at which two guards are posted. When P/W return from work it is the custom for the guard to patrol the outside perimeter of the camp as soon as the working party has entered the gate. To facilitate our escape we arranged that two of our comrades should start a fight outside the gate so as to distract the attention of the guards. The guards were so interested in the scuffle between these two men that they failed to begin the patrol of the wire, and the five of us were just able to enter the camp, go into our barrack-room, and immediately get through a back window without being observed. We then passed through a gap which had been forced in the wire fence with wedges of wood. We had already obtained civilian clothing by theft from the store at Fort 16, where the Germans kept clothing which had been used by escapers who had been recaptured. About 50 yards outside the wire there were a few trees beside a stream, and here the five of us changed into our civilian trousers and jackets. Our party then broke up and we did not see the three others again.

Burfield and I walked to a small railway station (no name) some distance from the camp, and from there got a slow train to Thorn.

On arrival at Thorn, about three days after our escape, we went from the railway station to the Kommandantur of Stalag XX A. We went to the back of the Casino which is use by the Germans as officers' mess, and here met two of our friends who were working in the Kommand-antur. They went into the Casino and obtained, from a Polish girl who works there, the key of a back room.

In this room we were visited by Spr. Hayhurst, R.E., who said that he was intending to escape and had a contact in Thorn. It was agreed that, in order to enter the camp, Burfield should assume Hayhurst's identity. Burfield went into Fort 13 that day as Hayhurst and made enquiries about obtaining identity cards. He got in touch with a P/W who said he would get us Werkausweise by that night. Burfield came back to the Casino after dinner and remained there that night, while I went into Fort 13. I saw the P/W who had promised the cards, and he said he would produce them by next day. I then went to see another P/W who works at Stalag headquarters. He said that at dinnertime next day he could photograph Burfield and me in the camp. I spent the night in Fort 13, and went out next morning. Later in the morning Burfield and I returned to Fort 13 where we were photographed. Burfield came into the camp in the name of a private who stayed out. We borrowed uniforms in order to enter the Fort.

That day we left the Casino and went to a house near the Kommandantur occupied by a Polish woman whom we had know previously. She allowed us to stay there for two days. On our second day there our Werkausweise were brought to us from the camp. They were genuine documents, probably supplied by Poles. When we got them the photographs were attached and stamped, only personal details being left blank. We filled in the papers ourselves, assuming the fictitious identities of 'einge-deutschte' Poles. These Werkausweise are in general use in that district without any other identity card.

After two days we moved to a house just outside Thorn occupied by a Pole, whom we had known since our first arrival in Thorn. We stayed here for two or three days till we left for Gdynia on 29 May. We travelled by passenger train via Graudenz, Marienburg, and Danzig, buying fresh tickets at each of these stations. Short distance trains in that region are not controlled. We missed our connection in Graudenz and had to wait for five hours, which we spent in the town.

We arrived in Gdynia between 1800 and 1900 hrs. on 29 May. We immediately went to the docks near the station, and after cutting down a flight of steps, reached the Swedish dock, at the entrance of which there was no guard. At this dock we found three Swedish ships. While watching the ships we met a Pole who advised us to wait till it was dark before trying to get on board. He told us that the gates of the docks were all guarded except the one at which we had entered.

We left the docks and hung about in a public house nearby till 2300 hrs. We then returned to the docks, but it was still too light to attempt to board a Swedish ship, as a sentry was now patrolling the entrance to the dock, and a German destroyer with sentries posted lay alongside the ship which we had selected.

Accordingly, we waited till 0300 hrs. (30 May), hiding under some trucks close to the ship. At 0300 hrs. we took off our boots and, while the sentry was at the other end of his beat, we walked up the gangway. I went up first, followed a minute later by Burfield. When we got on board we went to the officers' quarters where we disclosed our identity to two of the officers, who immediately expressed their willingness to help us. We were hidden in a large tank in the bilge of the ship. The two officers unscrewed a manhole to let us in, and then screwed down the manhole on top of us. They gave us a

torch and food and water. It was agreed that the captain should not be informed of our presence on board.

The ship sailed on the morning of 31 May. It was searched twice before it left the dock, but we were not disturbed.

On the afternoon of 1 Jun. the officers fetched us from our hiding place, as the ship had by then reached Swedish waters. We went to live in the crew's quarters, and the captain was informed that we had been hiding behind a boiler.

We were landed at Sundsvall at 1200 hrs. on 3 Jun, being taken ashore by a policeman. After we had been given a bath and a change of clothing we were interrogated by a Swedish policeman. We had previously asked to be put in touch with the British Consul, but were told that the Acting British Vice-Consul was not then in Sundsvall. We were in Sundsvall in a hotel till 4 Jun., and arrived in Stockholm early in the morning of 5 Jun. *(L.G. 3.8.44)*

Lloyd, William, Sergeant
319036, 9th Queen's Royal Lancers (Swindon)
(Immediate)
On 29th May his troop leader having been killed in action, Sgt. Lloyd assumed command and, on many subsequent occasions, led his Grant Tank Troop with the greatest courage and determination. In particular, on 17th June at Sidi Rezegh, when the regiment was attacked by superior numbers of Pz. K.3 Tanks, the determined resistance offered to the enemy by Sgt. Lloyd's troop was largely responsible for beating off the enemy attack. On July 22nd, South of El Ruweisat ridge, Sgt. Lloyd again showed great courage and determination in leading his squadron, single file, through a gap in the enemy's minefield. From the moment Sgt. Lloyd reached the gap the squadron was subjected to the heaviest fire from tanks and anti tank guns directed from both flanks as well as the front. Sgt. Lloyd continued through the gap, reporting locations of enemy tanks and guns. Subsequently, when it became necessary to withdraw the regiment through the minefield, Sgt. Lloyd covered the movement and was the last to come back. His determination, courage and complete disregard of personal safety have earned him the admiration of all officers and other ranks of his squadron. *(L.G. 15.10.42)*

Lock, Albert Ronald George, Warrant Officer Cl. II
13926, 26 N.Z. Bn. (Immediate)
In the vicinity of Enfidaville on the night 24th/25th Apr. W.O. II Lock was C.S.M. of a Company which attacked and captured Terhouna ridge. During the consolidation the Company Commander was mortally wounded and W.O. II Lock took command of the Company temporarily. As the main route to the Company was under fire W.O. II Lock reconnoitred an alternative route back to Battalion, advised them the Company was consolidating on their objective and then guided the supporting arms to the Company area where he handed over to the

senior platoon commander who had reported to Company Headquarters at the request of W.O. II Lock. The following morning as one of the forward platoons had not reported their consolidation W.O. II Lock, on his own initiative, set out to try and locate them. He had proceeded some distance forward over open ground when he was fired on by an enemy machine gun post. He successfully withdrew and later, in a Bren carrier, again went forward and contacted the missing platoon which had been isolated in their area by enemy fire.

Throughout the whole operation this N.C.O.'s personal courage and coolness was an example to everyone and his initiative and determination were largely responsible for the successful consolidation and defence of Terhouna ridge. During all operations in which this Battalion has taken part W.O. II Lock has performed with outstanding ability and courage carrying out his duties without regard for his personal safety and often assisting others where the firing was heaviest.

M.I.D. 24.6.43. M.M. 14.10.43   *(L.G. 22.7.43)*

Locke, George Leonard, Sergeant
6026479, Reconnaissance Corps and 82 (W.A.) Recce Regt. (Chelmsford) (Periodic)
Arakan. 16 Feb.—15 May 45.

At Kolan Chaung on 11 and 12 Apr. 45, was a Troop Commander in a Squadron which was holding a vital hill. The enemy made determined attacks on this position with a considerable force supported by heavy weapons.

Sjt. Locke's coolness, leadership and control over his troops, was responsible for the repulse of their heavy attacks during the night and the following day.

By moving amongst his men when they were under mortar and M.G. fire, he steadied them and broke up a Jap attack at extremely short range, inflicting heavy casualties.

On 13 April he took an active part in the rearguard action of his Squadron.

Twenty-four hours later, on the 14 April, when his Squadron was ordered to attack enemy positions forming a road block at Shaukchon, Sjt. Locke led his troops into the attack and was the first to reach the enemy position.

He has in all occasions shown a high devotion to duty, great courage and outstanding leadership in action and his skill as a leader of African Troops has resulted in his troops carrying out their duties very efficiently at all times.

Recommended for M.M.   *(L.G. 17.1.46)*

Lockhead, George Lambie, Lance Sergeant
8282, 20 N.Z. Bn., Australian Military Forces
On the morning of 23 Nov. 41 Sjt. Lockhead was platoon Sjt. of one of the forward platoons in the attack by the 20th battalion on the Blockhouse, Zoffran. The Battalion reached its objective but when ordered to dig in found it was not possible to bring the Coy. transport with the necessary tools closer than some 400 x owing to heavy M.G. fire. Whereupon Sjt. Lockhead, under constant fire

the whole time, and moving over exposed ground in full view of the enemy, returned to the trucks and collected and distributed to his platoon, the necessary tools for digging-in.

Two hours later, on the order to retire, Sjt. Lockhead formed the rearguard, carrying out his task coolly and with distinction, enabling the Coy. to withdraw successfully. Later on, when checking his platoon, Sjt. Lockhead found that Pte. G. S. Low was missing. Without hesitation Sjt. Lockhead went forward of the F.D.L.'s and advancing over ground that was still being swept by heavy M.G. and mortar fire he located Pte. Low, who was wounded, and carried him back to safety.

On the afternoon of the 24 Nov. Sjt. Lockhead took over command of 11 Platoon 'B' Coy. and on the morning of 25th, during a two Coy. ('B' and 'D') attack against a German M.G. Bn., he led his men with exemplary bravery and by incomparable example. Then for six hours, under constant heavy fire from mortars and M.G.'s, he moved among his sections encouraging his men and dressing all the wounded. Ordered to withdraw at dusk, Sjt. Lockhead brought out all his men, including the dead and wounded.

In all actions of this Campaign Sjt. Lockhead was conspicuous for his outstanding leadership and this, together with his complete disregard for his personal safety while under fire, made him an inspiration to all who fought with him.

Recommended for M.M.   *(L.G. 29.11.45)*

Lockie, William Stewart Inglis, Warrant Officer Cl. I
2966866, Argyll & Sutherland Highlanders (Letchworth, Herts)
51st H.D., P.O.W. Pool.
M.I.D. 20.12.45   *(L.G. 11.10.45)*

Lockwood, Walter George, Warrant Officer Cl. I (R.S.M.)
6079585, 2/7 Queen's Royal Regt. (Guildford, Surrey) (Periodic)
On the occasion of the assault landing by 2/7 Queens on the Salerno beaches R.S.M. Lockwood acted as assistant U.L.O. His cool courage in laying tapes and directing the troops across the mined beaches and later in organising the replenishment of ammunition in face of very heavy shell-fire were deserving of the highest praise. He was continually in the forefront during the operations culminating in the attack and capture of Mt. Stella and showed great gallantry under extremely difficult conditions. During the crossing of the R. Garigliano R.S.M. Lockwood was in charge of the rowers and despite continuous heavy shell-fire he maintained an uninterrupted service for three days.

During the whole period between the assault at Salerno in Sep. 43 and the present operations to force a crossing of the R. Garigliano R.S.M. Lockwood has shown the highest qualities of personal bravery. The cool efficiency with which he has carried out his numerous

duties often under the most difficult conditions has been an inspiration and example to the whole Bn.
M.I.D. 5.8.43 *(L.G. 24.8.44)*

Lodge, Robert, Sergeant
550157, Army Air Corps
NW Europe.
MID 15.6.44 *(L.G. 19.3.45)*

London, Brian Kent, Sergeant
214650, Royal Australian Infantry Regt.
For Vietnam *(L.G. 2.4.70)*

Long, Ernest Henry, Warrant Officer Cl. II (actg.)
5442253, 5 Duke of Cornwall's Light Infantry (New Biggin-by-Sea) (Periodic)
This W.O. was the Bn. Sniper Sjt. during the operations in Normandy and France 24 Jun.—2 Aug. 44. During the actions of Cheux and Hill 112 his courage and coolness were outstanding. It was a large extent due to his excellent leadership of the Bn. snipers that the Bn. was able to obtain sniper superiority on Hill 112. In addition to this he led several sniper F.O.O. patrols into the reverse slope positions of the enemy on Hill 112 enabling the artillery to do great execution. The F.O.O.'s had the greatest confidence in his ability to get them to good O.P.'s in the face of the gravest risks. In fact was a sort of mother to them.

During the bitter fighting at Jurques (Tiger Hill) on 3 Aug. 44 it was a sniper scout patrol led by Sjt. Long that destroyed the small rearguard detachment of the enemy and got back the vital information that the enemy had fallen back from this important feature.

During the fighting on the railway embankment at Driel rnhem, 24–28 Sep. 44 and in the woods at Mook in Oct. 44 Sjt. Long led his snipers with great courage and skill inflicting heavy losses on the enemy.

In the action of Hoven, 22 Nov. 44, in spite of being wounded he refused to go to the R.A.P. until he had completed his task and he could hardly move when eventually evacuated.

Later Sjt. Long was promoted to C.S.M. As C.S.M. he continued to give sterling service, notably on the escarpment at Goch where suffering badly from blast he refused to be evacuated until his Coy. was relieved.

His smiling quiet courage has always been a tonic to everyone in the Bn. *(L.G. 24.1.46)*

Longmore, Walter Stanley, Sergeant
4918979, Hallams, York & Lancaster Regt. (Dudley, Worcs.) (Periodic)
Sjt. Longmore has served with this Bn. since 30 Aug. 44, having originally landed in Normandy with 59 Div. During this time he has commanded a platoon, and occasionally acted as C.Q.M.S. and C.S.M.

At Nieuwkerk in October two Coys. of the Bn. were holding a salient which for 36 hours was subjected heavy shelling and which with few intervals was attacked from

3 different directions by inf. and tks. Sjt. Longmore's platoon bore the brunt of these attacks, but all ranks retained their cheerfulness and not one inch of ground was given up, until the party was finally ordered to retire.

Again during the four months from Dec. to Mar. on 'the Nijmegen Island' he was always first to volunteer for any particularly difficult or dangerous patrol. During this time, it is known that he himself killed four Germans and it is thought many more. He was responsible more than anyone else for retaining that superiority by night in 'No Man's Land' which was so essential during that difficult period. One night when out with a small recce patrol he encountered 30 Germans walking straight towards him. He held his fire but the Germans spotted his patrol too soon, but not soon enough however to avoid incurring heavy casualties from his two Bren guns: in the confusion which resulted he was able to withdraw his patrol which was outnumbered by 5 to 1, without loss.

His imperturbability, his coolness under fire in all circumstances and his fine understanding of his responsibilities as a leader, have been an inspiration to the whole Coy. His courage is unquestionable and the fact that he has come through the campaign unscathed is due, not to this endeavours but to the generosity of a kind fate.
Recommended for M.M. *(L.G. 11.10.45)*

Lord, Stuart Victor, Sergeant
20460, 21 N.Z. Bn. (Immediate)
On the night 14th/15th Jul., when his Coy. was advancing on the El Ruweisat Ridge, tanks were encountered which were holding up the advance. Sjt. Lord led a small party toward one tank took the crew prisoner and disabled it with grenades. A second tank nearby opened fire on the party. Sjt. Lord immediately made for it, killing the commander and again using grenades to disable the tank.

Sjt. Lord set a worthy example to his fellows.
Recommended for M.M. *(L.G. 24.9.42)*

Loryman, George Henry David, Corporal (A/Sgt.)
5503704, 1 Reconnaissance Regt. R.A.C.
(Peterborough) (Immediate)
This N.C.O. was the commander of a medium armoured car in the area of road 899328. The left of this position was held by 10 R. Berks. until they were driven out on the night 7/8 Feb. 44. Sjt. Loryman was then left unsupported and faced by an enemy of nearly 75 men. In the moonlight he manœuvred his car from fire position to fire position and managed to control the lines of approach so successfully that the enemy could not advance. Throughout the night Sjt. Loryman harassed the enemy, at day break he found himself surrounded and a target for a large close support gun and 88mm gun.

Sjt. Loryman continued to move his car about despite the enemy efforts to destroy him by shell fire and engaged the enemy killing over 20 by Besa fire. At 1030 hrs. on 8 Feb. 44 he decided to break out of the enemy circle by cutting across country. This he succeeded in doing but the car became bogged when only 600 yards clear.

Loryman instructed his gunner to continue engaging the enemy and he himself went across country for a mile to collect six boxes of ammunition. He returned to his car and continued to engage the enemy preventing further penetration.

At approximately 1700 hrs. the same day Sjt. Loryman and the driver started to dig out the car's wheels whilst the gunman kept the enemy infantry down. During this time the car had been hit four times by mortar fire and once by a shell which put the 37mm Besa out of action. At 2130 hrs. approximately the car was clear of the mud and with his remaining Besa still engaging the enemy Sjt. Loryman withdrew and rejoined the squadron. During the whole period an observer from a flanking armoured car estimated that over 60 enemy were killed or wounded and one vehicle set on fire.

By his determination Sjt. Loryman prevented the enemy from penetrating behind 'C' Squadron area at 903333 and so gaining the objective.   *(L.G. 15.6.44)*

Loudon, William, Sergeant (A/W.O.II (C.S.M.))
2981316, 7th Bn. Argyll & Sutherland Highlanders
(Larbert, Stirlingshire) (Immediate)
On 20.7.43 during the battle at Gerbini, 'C' Coy. was engaged in heavy fighting and suffered severe casualties including, all their officers. C.S.M. Louden immediately took command of the remnants of the Coy. and the supporting weapons placed under its command. With energy, confidence and determination he reorganised these troops, collected any stragglers from other companies and placed them in sound defensive positions. For 22 hours this Warrant Officer held this isolated position against repeated enemy counter-attacks and in face of heavy shelling. Throughout this period he controlled his force with skill and resource; personally led his Coy. in local counter-attacks, organised the evacuation of wounded and was seen carrying ammunition to his forward sections under heavy fire. His cheerfulness and determination to hold the position were infectious.

Later in the battle when asked whether he required assistance or reinforcements, he replied that other Coys. must be as hard pressed as his and that he would hold the position to the last man.

Despite the fact that his was an isolated position and that on several occasions after heavy shelling his Coy. was surrounded by the enemy, C.S.M. Louden held this vital position until ordered to withdraw. He then extricated his Coy. in good order as a formed force: the result was that morale remained at the highest pitch and little equipment was lost.

The courage of this warrant officer was an inspiration to the men under his command and his leadership and cool resourcefulness under the most difficult conditions worthy of the highest praise.   *(L.G. 4.11.43)*

Loughlin, James, Bombardier
820805, 68 (SM) Field Regt., Royal Artillery (Fife)
(Periodic)
Throughout the period 27 June to 18 Sept., and from 1st Oct. to date, this N.C.O. has shown exceptional powers of leadership and devotion to duty when he has been N.C.O. i/c line laying parties for 269th Fd. Bty. R.A.

On 30th June the Bty. was in action at Torchuagno in a very exposed position and was very heavily shelled. During the shelling line communications failed and Bdr. Loughlin under extremely heavy fire repaired the line on at least two occasions. His example to others and his disregard for his own safety were exceptional and he succeeded in establishing communications at a most critical time.

On 26 July he was in charge of a line-laying party during a night attack on the Anghiari ridge. The line had to be laid across a very open valley subject to very heavy M.G. and mortar fire. Again showing exceptional powers of leadership he led his party through this area and brought the line up to the O.P. When the line was broken by shelling he himself returned and repaired it on numerous occasions, often under heavy mortar fire.

On continuation of the advance on 27th July this N.C.O. was again ordered to reel out the line behind the leading Coy. on to their objective. By choosing the shortest route in order to save wire, he was unable to follow the Coy., but he had communications established on the objective as soon as the Coy. reached it. Again he and his party were under considerable shell fire and had to take the risk of running into parties of Germans en route. Again Bde. Loughlin's superb example of leadership and foresight enabled the line to be got through at a most critical stage.

From 3rd to 8th August during Operation 'Vandal,' he was in charge of a line maintenance party on M. Castello. During the whole of this period the cable route was under exceptionally heavy shell fire. One portion of the line had to run along a ridge which was seldom free from shell fire. This particular part of the line had to be relaid six times owing to continual breaks, but Bde. Loughlin never failed to re-establish communications in the shortest possible time. His complete disregard for his own personal safety and the way in which he led the men through this period were of the very highest order.

Finally during the period 3rd Oct. to 10th Oct. in the operations which terminated in the capture of M.Farneto, Bde. Loughlin, again in charge of a line laying party, laid and maintained the better part of a line some 15 miles long, in the very worst conditions of rain and weather. The cable was perpetually being cut by tanks and shell fire, and for a period of three consecutive nights and days he himself had no sleep and was almost continually out on the line. Again he kept communications through and again he led his men with superb example.

The conduct of this N.C.O. under the very worst conditions of battle has been exceptional, and his work as N.C.O. i/c line-laying parties has been absolutely vital to the course of battle.

Recommended for M.M.   (*L.G. 19.4.45*)

Lovegrove, Hubert, Private
6137165, 4 Gordon Highlanders
19th May 1940. Capture. Asche.

I was attached to 'C' Coy. HQ near Asche (Belgium) when on 18th May 40, we were overrun. Six of us managed to get away and, as we were then cut off from our own lines, decided to go forward and rejoin by making a circuit. We put up that night at a farm, but were betrayed to the Germans, who collected us next morning.

Bocholt Stalag VI F.

We were marched through Brussels, Tirlemont and across Holland to Bocholt (Stalag VI F), from where, after a week, I was taken across Germany in a cattle truck to Thorn, Stalag XXA, which was the central camp for British O.R. P/W, and had dependent upon it several working camps situated in a series of old Polish forts nearby.

On arrival at Thorn I was admitted, for ten days, to the Camp Hospital, suffering from exhaustion and debility. On release I was photographed, registered and my finger-prints recorded, but not interrogated. No issue of extra clothing was made, and discipline was severe. My room mates were sailors from H.M. Submarine Seal. During my stay at Stalag XXA (June/July 40) I did not see a Red Cross parcel. The camp was well guarded and the sentries did not talk to P/W. Although at this time, there were no attempts at escape, P/W were unfailingly cheerful. At night the whole camp was a blaze of lights.

July 40. Gruppe School for Parachutists.

At the beginning of July 40, when P/W were sorted out into their trades, I was taken in a party of 200 to Gruppe (Grupa), some 35 miles North of Thorn. This was a school, in the course of construction, of elementary instruction for parachustists (paratroops) and had accommodation for 16,000 men. I was employed in my own trade as ornamental plasterer. As the only one on this work I enjoyed a certain amount of liberty and had an opportunity of talking with German soldiers.

I watched them training and they seemed very sure of themselves. During fighting practise, they used wooden bullets. I collected some of these, but was seen doing so, and had to give them up. Escape from Gruppe was an easy matter but the problem was to collect food for the journey. I heard that Red Cross parcels were due to arrive—and decided to wait. On 27 Aug. one parcel arrived which was divided up amongst the 200 of us and I thought it was no use waiting any longer.

28th Aug. 40. Escape.

Pte. John Finley, Queen's Royal Regt. (West Surrey), and another private (name and regiment unknown) agreed to escape and join me at a selected rendezvous. On 28th Aug. I knocked out the solitary guard, who was watching me working, walked through the barracks and across the roads into some woods, from where I made

for the rendez-vous and found my two companions waiting. We had as equipment a map and compass, given to me by a Polish professor, who was employed as a labourer by the Germans.

We cut across country to the Vistula, but here my companions lost courage and left me, as they had decided that it was impossible to swim across the river. This however I managed to do and, having dried my clothes, then went on, heading for Russia.

Before my first meal at Lwalle, I went three days without food or water. At Lwalle I stayed two days at an address given me by the Polish professor who supplied me (at Gruppe) with a map and compass. My journey from that point, towards the Russian frontier, was approximately Soldau, Groudenz and Ostrelenka to the river Bug.

Russia.

I found the frontier heavily wired with a sentry posted every 1,000 metres. At dusk I managed to get through the wire but a few hours later was picked up by a posse of Cossacks. I spent the next 5 months in one prison or another, under appalling conditions.

Feb. 41. Smolensk. June 41. Moscow.

In Feb. 41 I was interned at Smolensk and remained there until the end of June, when I was taken to a hotel in Moscow and, a week later, handed over to our Embassy.

I suggest that escapers should carry a token easily recognisable by the Russians.   (*L.G. 4.11.41*)

Lovelace, George Victor, Corporal (A/Sgt.)
2659111, 3 Coldstream Guards (London, N.1)
(Immediate)

On July 1st 1944, No. 1 Coy. 3 Coldm. Gds. was leading the advance Guard of 24 Gds. Bde. On arrival at the Southern outskirts of Trequanda an attack had to be staged to brush aside opposition. Sgt. Lovelace, whole Pl. Comdr. had been wounded in a previous action, commanded his platoon and in spite of Spandau fire, took the objective, killing five Germans without loss to any of his platoon. He then, without any further orders, exploited another 500 yards into the town itself, because he considered that the enemy might be withdrawing. This proved correct but through his initiative he took another two prisoners.

On 2nd Jul. 44, No. 1 Coy. had one of its platoons pinned to the ground on a hill 4,000 yds. North of Trequanda by HE fire from a Mk VI Tank. Several casualties were incurred, whereupon, Sgt. Lovelace, oblivious to his own safety and disregarding the fact that it was another platoon, crawled out under heavy fire and brought a badly wounded man back on his back.

During the whole of this period, 1st/2nd July, Sgt. Lovelace was an inspiration to others, both in efficiency, as a leader, and as a saviour of men's lives. He worked continuously during this period either to destroy Germans or save his comrade's lives.

Recommended for M.M.; M.I.D. 11.1.45

(*L.G. 7.12.44*)

Low, John, Private
M57061, Edmn. R., Canadian Infantry Corps
The Edmn R. was ordered to attack point 736, a high feature North of Regalbuto, 2nd Aug. 43. The only cover in the three mile approach to the objective was that afforded by boulders and crevices in the rock and forward movement in the face of the enemy fire was hazardous and possible only by skilful use of ground.

'B' Coy. advanced some 2,000 yards, when the intensity of the enemy fire across the path of advance caused casualties and made a reorganization necessary.

A call came for stretcher bearers and from 'D' Coy. some 500 yards to the rear, Pte. Low and Pte. Colbeck volunteered.

Crawling from boulder to boulder, from hollow to hollow as they advanced up the slope, machine gun fire was seen to concentrate upon them, they were caught in snipers cross-fire, but still carried on.

After advancing 150 yards, Pte. Colbeck was wounded. Pte. Low stopped, in full view and fire of the enemy dressed the wounds of his comrade, and then dragged him behind a small rock that allowed some cover.

To his comrades, the further advance of this soldier could only end in sudden death, but to their amazement he continued on towards the wounded men. German fire appeared to centre around him. Bullets were seen kicking up the dust along the line of his path, but Pte. Low showing intense devotion to duty and conspicuous bravery, successfully crawled the remaining 300 yards and reached the wounded men.

In the open and what seemed to his platoon murderous fire, he dressed the wounds of each of the three in turn, found cover for them, and carried and aided them to it. Such was the nature of the wounds of these men, that it was later found that their injuries would have been fatal without his assistance. Pte. Low having completed his task returned under the same continuous fire to 'D' Coy. and resumed his first aid work.

Through the valour, conspicuous bravery and courage of Pte. Low, these three wounded soldiers were rescued.
Recommended for V.C.   *(L.G. 23.12.43)*

Lowman, Stanley Frederick, Sergeant
6454940, 1/5 Bn. Queens Royal Regt. (Godalming)
   (Immediate)
Sgt. Lowman has shown conspicuous gallantry in command of his platoon on all occasions, but particularly on two. First, on 16 Oct. 43 he led his platoon by assault boat and wading across the River Volturno and attacked an enemy M.G. post with such vigour and dash that the rest of the company were able to cross the river in safety and eventually clear the enemy from the river. His courage and determined leadership were exemplary.

Second, on 1 Nov. 43, when his company was attacking the S. Anna ridge, the enemy suddenly opened fire with M.G.'s from the right flank and rear. Sgt. Lowman quickly manoeuvred his platoon to deal with this and by his rapid and determined action enabled the company to attain its objective. During this action he showed conspicuous gallantry in the face of machine gun fire, and by his courage and determination enabled his platoon to overcome the enemy's resistance.
Recommended for M.M.   *(L.G. 24.2.44)*

Lucas, Daniel Lewis, Sergeant
1117663, 105 Anti Tank Regiment, Royal Artillery
   (Sidmouth) (Immediate)
At 0400 hrs. on the morning of 9th Jul. at 'Bexhill' R. 093255, the enemy launched a strong infantry counter-attack and forced our infantry back past the M10 commanded by Sgt. Lucas, leaving Sgt. Lucas with his M10 and 2 Canadian tanks to face the thrust.

Sgt. Lucas noticed a German machine gun spraying our troops and promptly engaged it with H.E. putting it out of action. He then engaged the enemy infantry with his Tommy gun and Browning. As there appeared a danger of being cut off he dismounted under heavy rifle and machine gun fire and cleared the M10 tracks of the splinter cover. He then returned to his post, rallied the infantry, and continued engaging the enemy with Tommy gun and Browning. He noticed a German firing a Bazooka 50 yds. off, this Bazooka put out one of the tanks. Sgt. Lucas fired H.E. at it and killed the operator. Meanwhile the surviving Canadians from the tank had 'baled out.' Sgt. Lucas again left his M10 under heavy fire and carried one of the wounded Canadians over to his M10 and put him inside.

Undoubtedly Sgt. Lucas' coolness and handling of his M10 saved a breakthrough and possible occupation of a very important post from which the Germans would have overlooked the axis Rd.

Sgt. Lucas' M10 was on its own, the other M10 having been set alight previously. He had been continually under mortar, 88 SP gun fire and 'stonks' for 14 days. The 'positions' of the M10s were over-looked by an enemy OP and the approach under direct observation. The M10 is very vulnerable to infantry attack.

Throughout he has shown coolness and by his bearing has set a very good example to his crew.*(L.G. 7.12.44)*

Lumsden, Walter, M.M., Sergeant
2694174, 2nd Bn. Scots Guards (London, S.E.3)
   (Immediate)
During the day attack on the Tobacco Factory near Battipaglio on 10 Sep. Sgt. Lumsden showed great coolness, gallantry and initiative under heavy enemy fire. At one time he drove off some German grenade throwers with 36 grenades although outranged by stick grenades. Shortly after he personally with a Bren knocked out a Spandau post which was inflicting casualties on the platoon, bringing his gun into action under heavy fire. He then saved the life of a tank gunner at great risk to his own by attracting his attention to the correct way of escape, again exposing himself to enemy fire. Finally

when the position became untenable he and his platoon Commander had to cross a 6 ft. spiked gate under the fire of about 6 Spandaus; his platoon Commander became suspended from the spikes by his trousers and was unable to cut himself loose. Sgt. Lumsden calmly produced a knife, cut his platoon Commander's trousers off him, and both got safely away still under heavy fire. Throughout the battle this Sgt.'s courage and daring were an inspiring example to his platoon.
MM. 18.5.43. Bar to M.M. 23.3.44   *(L.G. 27.1.44)*

Lundie, Ronald Thornhill, Warrant Officer Cl. II (C.S.M.)
2318534, Royal Signals, 2nd Corps
This W.O. rendered the most valuable assistance on La Panne beach. His work under trying conditions, including heavy bombing, was of a high order.   *(L.G. 20.8.40)*

Lush, Lawrence, Corporal
5572085, 2 Wiltshire Regt. (Andover) (since killed in action)
This N.C.O. comd. a sec. of a Coy. holding the Pt. 201 feature (8096). On 20 Jan. 44 the enemy attacked this feature and this N.C.O.'s sec. was attacked from three sides. He fought his sec. until all except himself were killed or wounded. He personally rushed the enemy killing five of them with his T.S.M.G. and scattering the remainder, before withdrawing to his alternative position.

    This N.C.O.'s bravery, coolness and devotion to duty are beyond all praise and his leadership and personal example were an inspiration to all around him.
                         (L.G. 29.6.44)

Luyt, Richard Edmonds, Sergeant
L.F.1916, East African Forces (attd. 2nd Ethiopian Battalion)
In the action on the motor road between Gigga and Dambacha that took place on 6th Apr. 41, Sgt. Luyt was commanding his platoon at a point in ambush near the road. He was attacked by superior forces of the enemy, but in spite of this continued at his post until his ammunition was exhausted. His platoon suffered very heavy casualties, and towards the end of the engagement Sgt. Luyt took over the management of his machine-gun himself and continued to fire it until all ammunition was expended. He then withdrew his M.G. and succeeded in avoiding capture. In this action he displayed the greatest coolness and courage and undoubtedly he and his platoon inflicted more than 200 casualties upon the enemy. His escape with his life was almost miraculous, as he was under continuous heavy fire for some hours without adequate cover.   *(L.G. 30.12.41)*

Lyle, Henry, Corporal
3126021, 2nd Bn. Royal Scots Fusiliers (Mauchline, Ayr)
During the night attack on Antsirane 5th May 1942, this N.C.O. was leading his section which was fired on from

a Pill Box on the East side of the road. He showed conspicuous gallantry and disregard of danger in entering the Pill Box and capturing over a dozen prisoners.
                         (L.G. 16.6.42)

Lymer, John, Corporal
3445531, Lancashire Fusiliers (London, W.14)
France 1940 (from P.O.W. Pool).   *(L.G. 11.10.45)*

Lynch, Desmond Thomas Lee, Sergeant
2718820, 1st Bn. Irish Guards (Birtley, Co. Durham)
(Immediate)
Attack on Pt. 212 & 214 April 27th—May 1st.
    The 1st Bn. Irish Guards were right hand Bn. in a Bde. attack on Apr. 27th. No. 4 Coy., in which Sgt. Lynch is a Pl Sgt., was leading with its objective Pt. 212 & 214. The company came under very heavy fire at the start line and had considerable casualties inflicted on it. The company comd. and 2 platoon comds. were wounded or killed and the C.S.M. killed. Sgt. Lynch looked after his wounded Pl. comd. and then took charge of the company or what was left of it. When the advance continued he organised his coy. and assaulted and gained his objective. Throughout the period of 28th–30th when the force was being continually attacked he remained in command of No. 4 Coy., except for a brief period when Captain Ismay was there. He was throughout an outstanding figure and his smart soldierly appearance under the most difficult circumstances created an impression amongst the men equalled only by his constant calm and bravery. No. 4. Coy. held the West of the ridge forward towards Pt. 214 and was continually under shell and mortar fire even when infantry attacks were not in progress. That the men never wavered under the fire was largely due to his example and in particular to his prompt action at the beginning. At 1100 hrs. Wednesday 28th, enemy 88mm guns opened up on the W of the ridge with a violence that was as unexpected as its effects were unpleasant. Casualties were caused and some of the men badly shaken. Sgt. Lynch was at the time at Force HQ without hesitation he ran up through the heavy fire to his Coy., held the men steady in their positions, moved a Bren gun forward, at great personal risk to meet the first infantry assault and gave the first fire order. The initial success gained by this Sgt. in beating back the first German assault raised morale to the highest possible peak by proving conclusively by his own example that the fiercest fire could be endured and a determined attack broken by S.A. fire. This Sgt. consistently showed the greatest devotion to duty and even after when half blinded by blast on Friday 30th, he continued to command and encourage his rapidly dwindling Coy. I strongly recommend this Sgt. for gallantry and good example.
M.B.E. 11.6.60   *(L.G. 8.7.43)*

Lyons, John Joseph, Private (A/Cpl.)
4798597, 6th Bn. The Lincolnshire Regt. (Lincoln)
(Immediate)

In the Salerno Sector on the morning of 23rd Sep. 43 this N.C.O. was in command of No. 2 Section of 'D' Company of 6th Bn. The Lincolnshire Regt. which had been ordered to capture the Costa Piano feature 6133. While forming up on the start line in the dark the Coy. came under very heavy M.G. fire which caused considerable disorganisation. At this time the Coy. Comd., two Pl Comds. and C.S.M. all became casualties. Captain Tyler who rallied all the men he could then ordered Corporal Lyons to lead the Company with his section straight for the Water Tower feature which was part of the Company objective. This he did in the face of intense mortar fire leading his Section with great determination and with complete disregard for his own safety. On arriving at his objective he held it until the remainder of the Company (30 men) arrived. 15 minutes later this N.C.O. heard a German officer trying to rally some of his men in the woods on the reverse slopes of the hill. Corporal Lyons at once proceeded to the spot and fired his T.M.C. at the officer, hit him, and compelled him to surrender. Throughout the action the conduct of this N.C.O. was an example and an inspiration to his men.   *(L.G. 13.1.44)*

Lyons, Richard, C.Q.M.S.
3852167, 1st Bn. Loyal Regt.

At Bergues on June 1st 1940, during a counter-attack on the enemy this N.C.O. set a very fine example to the men of his Company by working his way forward under heavy M.G. fire and engaging the enemy. During the subsequent withdrawal he again did much to keep up the morale and discipline of this Company. His determination and initiative was of the highest order.
                    (L.G. 27.8.40)

M

Maangi, Pita, Private
68097, 28 N.Z. (Maori) Bn.
Pte. Maangi was a member of a forward platoon of a forward Coy. during the attack on Scola Fratturo on 11th April 1945. During the attack both forward platoons were forced to ground by heavy machine gun and mortar fire, both platoons receiving heavy casualties. The wireless sets with the platoons were knocked out of action and there was no means of communication to HQ other than by runner. Every burst of enemy MG and shell fire was inflicting casualties on the two pinned down platoons. Pte. Maangi realising that any further delay without support would mean more casualties to his comrades acted on his own initiative and walked across the area swept with MG and mortar fire to an area where he knew that there were tanks available to support them. During the whole time that Pte. Maangi was walking across the danger area the enemy increased his fire but Pte. Maangi regardless for his own personal safety walked on. Contacting the tanks he walked ahead of the armour guiding them to the two pinned down platoons. The enemy on seeing the tanks approaching increased the rate of his mortar fire to such an extent that nothing could be seen due to dust and smoke. As the dust and smoke cleared Pte. Maangi could still be seen walking on in front of the tanks and by this time was only one hundred yards away from the enemy strong points. By directing the fire of the tanks on to several of the enemy's dug in positions and MG nests many of the enemy either surrendered or were killed. The advance was then resumed and the objective taken, Pte. Maangi taking part in the charge with a forward section. Throughout this operation Pte. Maangi displayed courage and devotion to duty and initiative of the very highest order. This courage and devotion to duty was an inspiration to all those who fought with him.   *(L.G. 18.10.45)*

McAleer, Frank, Sergeant
6976983, 6th Bn. The Royal Inniskilling Fusiliers (Aldershot)
On 24th February 1943 No. 6976983 A/Sjt. McAleer at about 0800 hours proceeded from Minefield Fm. 657058 to Pt. 286 (6506), a hill known to be occupied by enemy with strength about one Platoon. His military mission was information, but his own object was to obtain revenge for the loss of a patrol on night 23rd/24th February 1943. He spotted a M.G. post, went to the flank of it, surprised the crew of two, collected the M.G. and doubled the two prisoners a matter of 1,000 yards back to Minefield Fm. This was in broad daylight. The daring act resulted in obtaining information, which when later used, caused about 30 casualties to the enemy.
(L.G. 22.4.43)

McAlister, Arthur Alexander, Colour Sergeant (A/ W.O.II (C.S.M.))
5494881, 1/4th Bn. Hampshire Regt. (Upper Chute, Hants.) (Immediate)
On 29th January 1944, during an attack on pt. 411, 8399 the officers of 'D' Coy. 1/4 Hamps., and of 'B' Coy., became casualties.

C.S.M. McAlister organised the two companies into one, and led them in repeated attempts to capture the objective. When it became dark, he went forward with Sjt. Fry to make a recce so as to find an approach and a position from which to rush the enemy. In doing this he was wounded by a grenade but after attention from a stretcher bearer he returned to his command and again tried to capture the hill.

This W.O. displayed a very high standard of personal courage and leadership throughout.

He later withdrew under orders with 'B' and 'D' Coys., refusing further medical attention until the withdrawal had been effected.

The attack began at 1430 hours and the Coys. withdrew at about 0200 hours.   *(L.G. 29.6.44)*

McAllan, Alexander, Trooper
7923068, 3rd County of London Yeomanry (Arbroath) (Immediate)
Tpr. McAllan on 5th June 1942 was acting as Commander in a Honey tank which accompanied 3 Crusaders of 3 C.L.Y. acting as escort to 15 Amn. lorries endeavouring to reach a Box which was surrounded at Bir Aslagh by enemy Infy. and tanks.

Such was the strength of the enemy Infy. and A/Tank guns, and the extremely close range of 400 yards at which the German tanks engaged our convoy on their 3 mile run from Knightsbridge, that all the Crusaders were hit several times and disabled.

The crew of one of these commanded by 2/Lt. Sale was forced to abandon their tank and take cover in a slit trench from the concentrated fire from all arms which was then sweeping the battlefield.

Tpr. McAllan, with utmost coolness and gallantry halted his tank, which had already sustained one hit, and evacuated 2/Lt. Sale's crew to the Knightsbridge Box. In the process the Honey was hit 5 more times and after being calmly and successfully navigated through the narrow gap in the Knightsbridge minefield, finally failed on the edge of the mined defence.

Tpr. McAllan remained with his vehicle and during a fierce infy. attack on the Box next day, fought his immobilised tank as a pillbox, with himself acting as loader to a Guardsman gunner.

On several occasions during this action, when the Honey was receiving especial attention from enemy A/

Tk. guns, he left the tank with his gunner to take cover in slit trenches, only to again fight his tank whenever the opportunity occurred.   *(L.G. 24.9.42)*

McAllister, Edward William, Lance Corporal
SAP/196908, 2 S.A.P., South African Forces
For conspicuous bravery when leading his section in the attack at Salum on 11th and 12th Jan 42. On the latter occasion when fierce mortar and machine gun fire were directed at his men from enemy strong points sited in camouflaged caves cut out of the rock above Salum Pier, he and Cpl. Otto rushed forward and by a resolute hand grenade attack overcame all enemy resistance, bringing about the surrender of 1 Officer and 40 other ranks. His coolness and courage were an example to all.
                    (L.G. 19.3.42)

McAllister, Thomas Francis, Signalman
QX 3889, Signals, 9 Aust. Div.
This soldier worked as a linesman throughout the operations near Alamein from the night 23rd/24th October until he was wounded on 29th October 1942.

In this work he showed the greatest courage and persistance under most dangerous and difficult conditions.

On the night 23rd/24th October 1942 he was a member of a line team laying a line to a Bn. Headquarters, when their truck came under heavy shell fire which wounded the N.C.O. in charge. McAllister at once took command of the team and completed the laying of the line. He with his team then laid other lines under heavy fire. During the ensuing days shell fire and traffic caused the lines to be continuously cut. Despite the great dangers and discouragements of his task McAllister worked painstakingly and persistently under fire at the repair and maintenance of lines, going for long periods without any sleep. He was seriously wounded when a vehicle in which he was travelling in the performance of his task was blown up on a minefield.

The work of this soldier in the maintenance of communications was outstanding as line communication, even though it could only be maintained for short periods, was of the utmost value and a considerable factor in the success of the operations.   *(L.G. 11.2.43)*

McArthur, Alexander Howden, Warrant Officer Cl. II
1500854, 4th Bn. Royal Welch Fusiliers (Glasgow)
    (Periodic)
C.S.M. McArthur landed in Normandy with the Bn. and was then a Sgt. commanding a rifle platoon. On numerous occasions this W.O. has displayed a very high standard of leadership and disregard to his own personal safety. For example, on one occasion his platoon suffered many casualties, Sgt. McArthur quickly reorganised the platoon and led them on to his objective. At s'Hertogenbosch when ordered to clear a wood of Spandau posts, he personally led the forward section and against considerable automatic fire captured his objective. In Holland,

this N.C.O. led a very successful patrol deep into the enemy's lines on the North side of the Wettering Canal. Throughout the above period and particularly during these latter months since his promotion to W.O., C.S.M. McArthur has shown a very high standard of leadership. His example within the Bn. and particularly to his Coy. has been far higher and the shouldering of his responsibilities has exceeded the normal expected of a W.O. even in the field.   *(L.G. 21.6.45)*

McAughtrey, Thomas Conit, Sergeant
7902406, North Irish Horse (RAC) (Portrush)
    (Periodic)
This N.C.O. has been in every action with 'B' Sqn. N.I.H. during the period 1st September—31st December 1944.

On 22nd September he was commanding 2 Tp. He led the successful last light attack on S. Guistina 785988 and his tks. were the first on to Route 9. During the night he remained in the 1 Somerset Light Infantry F.D.L.s and drove off repeated enemy counter-attacks. On the 10th his tks. drew exceptionally heavy shelling but Sjt. McAughtry spent the day in and out of his tk., liaising with the Inf. Comd. and fighting his tp. in an exemplary manner until relieved at last light.

On 15th October he was leading tk. in a most difficult stream crossing at 603975(W) R. Just short of the far bank he broke a track. Under fire and up to the waist in water and mud Sjt. McAughtry, assisted by his crew, repaired the track and got across.

This N.C.O. has proved himself to be an outstanding Tp. Ldr. Throughout the period he fought consistently well and in the five months continuous fighting (up till 3rd December) he has gained much honour and glory for himself and his Regt.

Sjt. McAughtry has a splendid fighting record both in N. Africa and Italy and I very strongly recommend him for the D.C.M.
M.B.E. 8.6.68   *(L.G. 28.6.45)*

McAuley, Melvin Foster, Private (A/Sgt.)
L86683, 1st Cdn. Special Service Battalion
    (Immediate)
On the morning of 27th February 1944 on the Anzio Beachead, Italy, the enemy opened up with an all out Artillery and Mortar barrage as a prelude to an attack against one of our positions along the Mussolini Canal.

During the barrage our L.M.G. covering the enemy advance was put out of action. The crew seeing the enemy within 100 yards abandoned the gun with a warning to Sgt. McAuley that a break through was imminent.

With two riflemen, Sgt. McAuley immediately ran to the machine gun position in full view of the enemy, and in the face of machine gun and machine pistol fire from three sides stripped the gun, readjusted the headspace and brought fire to bear on the enemy who were now within 30 yards of his position. The enemy withdrew leaving several of their comrades.

Sgt. McAuley's exceptional devotion to duty and complete disregard of his own personal safety was an inspiration to the other members of his company and was a material factor in turning the tide of battle.

(*L.G. 21.10.44*)

McAuley, Vincent Cronkite, A/S/Ldr.
J.4761, 7 Sqn, Bomber Command, RAF
See Cook, William.

McBeath, Duncan, Private
2825830, 5th Bn. Seaforth Highlanders (Strathcarron, Ross-shire)
El Hamein.

This N.C.O. showed great initiative and leadership on the night of 1st/2nd November 1942. After all the senior N.C.O.'s of his platoon had been killed and although separated from his company this N.C.O. took command of the remnants of the platoon which he succeeded in leading to the final objective where he collapsed on reporting to the officer present. He succeeded in doing this in spite of being badly wounded early in the attack. Except for the unexampled courage and leadership of this N.C.O. it is doubtful if the remainder of the platoon would have won through.

(*L.G. 14.1.43*)

McBride, Robert Frank, Warrant Officer Cl. II
90208, 2 S.A. A/Tk. Regt., South African Forces
23rd November 1941. 1 Mile North of Sidi Omar.

'I' Tp. under command Troop S/M McBride was detached from the Bty., to protect Bty. 4.5≤ Gun Hows. under command Maj. Trench, R.A. at 1200 hrs. 19 German Mk IV & Mk III tanks attacked the Bty.

The tanks opened up heavy fire, and attacked from South and East in outflanking movements. S/M McBride skilfully and courageously manoeuvred his Troop, under heavy fire, and was able to drive off the German attack, and destroy 5 tanks, thus saving the Bty.

Throughout the action, S/M McBride displayed conspicuous courage and distinguished tactical handling, that enabled his 4 guns which were on portees and very exposed, to drive off the attack.

Not only did this W/O's brilliant handling of A/Tk. guns save the R.A. Bty., but it also saved his troop many casualties.

Note. At time of this action, the 2 S.A. A/Tk. Regt. was under command 4 Ind. Div. at Omar Nuovo.
Recommended for M.C.   (*L.G. 19.3.42*)

McBride, William, Corporal (actg.)
14671256, 7th Bn. The Black Watch (Cupar) (Immediate)
On the night 25/26th March 1945 L/Cpl. McBride, then a Pte. soldier, was in the leading platoon which, on the successful capture of the Bn. objective at Empel, was ordered to cross the bridge which was found to be unblown and to endeavour to seize it and hold it intact.

Very shortly after the platoon had crossed the bridge it came under heavy fire and very serious casualties were sustained including the Pl. Comd. and most N.C.O.s. L/Cpl. McBride immediately took command of the men nearest to him and, showing the utmost determination and resourceful leadership, he cleared the enemy from the immediate vicinity of the bridge and succeeded in establishing a small bridgehead to cover it. During the remainder of that night and throughout the following day the enemy made repeated and insistent attempts to return to the bridge in order to demolish it but these were all driven back by L/Cpl. McBride and the small force under his command. As a result of L/Cpl. McBride's splendid and most courageous action this important bridge was still intact when a further attack was launched against the enemy positions the following night and this had a very material bearing on the development of the whole divisional plan.

During the whole of the period described L/Cpl. McBride displayed the highest possible standard of courage and personal example and the initiative and leadership displayed by him were quite outstanding.

(*L.G. 21.6.45*)

McCallum, Charles Reginald, Private (A/Cpl.)
VX 15241, 2/14 Australian Infantry Bn. (since died of wounds) (Immediate)
For two days to 29th August 1942, at Isurava, the 2/14 Aust. Inf. Bn. had repulsed attack after attack by the Japanese on our positions. Heavily reinforced after the initial stages, the Japanese attacks became heavier and more fierce each time. On 29th August instns. had been issued to 2/14 Aust. Inf. Bn. they must deny the area to the enemy, while 39th Bn. and elements 53rd Bn. were extricated. The instns. included the order that the enemy would be held off at all costs. 'B' Coy. 2/14 Aust. Inf. Bn. was in a fwd. position, on slightly raised ground overlooking the L of C. Four times during the day the Coy. had been off this ground and each time they had counter-attacked and recovered the positions. VX15241 Pte. Charles Reginald McCallam had participated in all these operations and at 1730 hours had been wounded three times, but was still manning his Bren L.M.G. and a T.S.M.G. he had acquired from a wounded comrade. At this stage the enemy launched a particularly heavy attack, the fighting becoming extremely savage and the fwd. posts being lost and won again. Finally the weight of the enemy reinforcements prevented us from regaining the ground lost and our tps. were becoming extremely exhausted. Pte. McCallam continued to provide covering fire with his weapons, and, when at last the order came to withdraw, he remained behind to cover the withdrawal of his Platoon. He had his T.S.M.G. on his left shoulder, and with his Bren stalled off enemy rushes, and, when the magazine ran out, the enemy rushed him but he swung the T.S.M.G. fwd. with his left hand and sprayed the advancing enemy, checking them while he placed a full magazine in the Bren with his right hand. Having emptied

the T.S.M.G., McCallam brought his Bren into action again and continued firing until all the tps. in the platoon area were clear. The enemy were so close in one of their rushes on the position, one of them tore his utility pouches off as he wrenched himself away. Finally, members of his platoon called to him they were all clear and McCallum came back bringing both his weapons with him. Altogether it is estimated he alone killed at least 25 Japanese.

At all times in action, McCallum was admirably calm and steady. On this occasion his utter disregard for his own safety and his example of devotion to duty and magnificent courage was an inspiration to all our tps. in the area. His gallant stand and the number of casualties he alone inflicted checked the enemy's advance and allowed the withdrawal to proceed unhindered and without loss.

Recommended for V.C.   *(L.G. 4.2.43)*

McCambridge, Peter James, Sergeant
7012426, The Parachute Regt., Army Air Corps
    (Shrule, Co. Mayo)
This N.C.O. was one of the parachute troops who landed behind the German lines in Normandy on the night of 5/6th June 1944. During the fighting for Benouville bridge on 6th June, McCambridge's platoon was responsible for holding the village of Le Port. At one period his section became detached from the platoon and the fighting, which went on for 21 hours almost without pause, was particularly fierce. McCambridge noticed that one house dominated the scene of the fighting. By skilful use of a smoke grenade and displaying the greatest dash he got his section across a road swept by enemy M.G. fire and into the house. He used anti-tank grenades to smash open the garden gate and the door of the house. Once inside the house he was completely cut off from the rest of his company, who actually had withdrawn slightly, but he was in a dominating position and became the target for the enemy who greatly outnumbered his section and were surrounding him. So well did he dispose his men however and so splendid was his leadership that he held this isolated house until the seaborne troops eventually entered the village from the other end, several hours later. At times the enemy were close enough to try and beat down the door by beating it with their rifle butts—McCambridge dealt with such attacks by having grenades dropped on them from the upper windows. There is no doubt that the holding of this dominating house seriously weakened the enemy attacks and greatly assisted the bn. to carry out its job of holding the bridge. On 20th June at Bois de Bavent during a company attack Sgt. McCambridge, together with another N.C.O., saved the life of his platoon comd., who had been wounded and whose phosphorus bomb was burning in his pouch. Between them they extracted the burning bomb and dragged the officer to cover despite heavy and accurate mortar and M.G. fire.

McCambridge has shown himself throughout three weeks continuous fighting to be a truly magnificent N.C.O. He is calm, cheerful and always reliable.
                                        (L.G. 19.10.44)

McCarron, Philip, Private
2883301, 5 Bn. Gordon Highlanders
McCarron was captured on 12th June 1940 at St Valery-en-Caux and was imprisoned at Lamsdorf (Stalag VIII B) and various working camps attached.

While in the forestry working camp at Althammer in March 1943, McCarron escaped through the wire into the forest, but was recaptured after 7 hours.

His second attempt was made with two other P/W in June 1943 from a working camp at Ilnau. Having acquired civilian clothes and a supply of chocolate, they made for Breslau, but were arrested by the police at Bernstadt.

On 8th October 1943 he made his third attempt. With one companion he escaped from a working party at Bedzin. For eight days they were sheltered at Czeladz by a Polish woman, who also arranged their journey to the border of Poland proper. Receiving casual assistance from Poles, they reached the Hungarian Frontier, where Ukranian guards, believing that they were attempting to avoid labour service, put them on a train returning to Lwow. However, they managed to jump out of the train and cross the border into Hungary. After travelling some distance through the Carpathian Mountains, coming to the end of their resources, they gave themselves up to Hungarian soldiers at Uzsok. They were treated very badly and sent via Komarom and Budapest to a working camp near Szigetvar.

On 19th March 1944, when the Germans occupied the district a Dominions officer forbade escape attempts as he hoped to be able to arrange for all the P/W to join a guerilla force.

However, this plan did not mature, and the P/W were sent to Zemun in Yugoslavia in transit for Germany.

On 2 April 1944 McCarron was removed to a German hospital in Belgrade. About a fortnight later, escaping through a window of the hospital, he met a Serb who put him in touch with Chetnik forces. An escort was provided for his journey to Kostinci where he met members of a British Mission on 18th May 1944. On the night of 29/30th May 1944 he was flown to Bari, Italy.
                                        (L.G. 3.8.44)

McCarvell, Robert Francis, Bombardier
838057, Royal Artillery
Special Operations. Middle East.   *(L.G. 1.6.44)*

McClelland, William, Corporal
7017382, 18th London Regt. (1 London Irish Rifles/
    R.U.R.) (Belfast) (Immediate)
On the night 5/6th April 1945 Cpl. McClelland was N.C.O. i/c 2" Mortar and Piat group in 15 Platoon 'C' Coy. 1 L.I.R. During the initial assault across the R. Reno

in square 5252 the Platoon Comd. and Platoon Sgt. were wounded and Cpl. McClelland took temporary comd. of 15 Platoon. Shortly afterwards he himself was wounded in the leg, but despite this he carried on encouraging and leading his Platoon under the most difficult conditions. His leadership inspired the platoon to hold the ground they had gained despite heavy enemy machine gun fire and mortaring, and it was not until at least an hour had passed that Cpl. McClelland was relieved by an officer. Later the platoon adv. a few hundred yards and got out of wireless touch with its Coy. HQ. Cpl. McClelland, who had refused to be evacuated, volunteered to act as runner to Coy. HQ. Twice he took back messages across fire-swept ground, running and crawling in water-logged ditches, to Coy. HQ. Both of these messages enabled the Coy. Comd. to take action to help the platoon.

On 6th April 1945 15 Platoon assisted in an attack with tank support, and throughout Cpl. McClelland displayed great courage and cheerfulness especially under heavy mortar fire. During the night 6/7th April Cpl. McClelland offered to carry out a vitally important contact patrol with the Coy. on the right. Despite enemy fire and minefields this patrol was successfully accomplished twice during the night.

On the morning of the 7th April, when his platoon was being relieved, Cpl. McClelland was severely wounded by an A/P mine. Even then he displayed great cheerfulness. The success of the severely handled and much reduced 15 Platoon throughout the whole action was due to the courageous example and excellent leadership displayed by this N.C.O.
Recommended for M.M. (*L.G. 23.8.45*)

McClew, David, Sergeant (actg.)
4751946, 5 Queen's Own Cameron Highlanders
(Westcliff-on-Sea) (Immediate)
During the attack which cut the main Cleve—Hekkens road through the Reichswald on 11th February 1944, Sgt. McClew started as a Pl Sergeant in 'C' Coy. The Coy., which was leading the advance, met heavy enemy opposition from trenches behind one of the forest clearings. Sgt. McClew's platoon commander was wounded as the platoon started its assault over the open stretch of a hundred yards to the enemy line. Sgt. McClew immediately took command, and moving up and down amongst his men rallied the platoon which had received some twelve casualties from M.G.s and Mortars. This entailed moving about completely exposed with bullets passing him from every angle.

Having rallied his men, he led the remnants of his platoon against the enemy. More of his men fell wounded around him, but Sgt. McClew charged on shouting encouragement and firing his Sten gun as he went. He reached the position at the head of a section and completely cleared the position. Sgt. McClew and his section accounted for twenty enemy killed and wounded—twenty who between them had been manning and firing five machine guns.

Throughout the operations since 9th February, Sgt. McClew has displayed the highest qualities of leadership and courage. His actions have been an inspiration to his men. (*L.G. 10.5.45*)

McCloskey, Aleck Bruce, Warrant Officer Cl. II (temp.)
29779, Royal Australian Infantry
Award dated 13.8.70; Vietnam (*L.G. 8.9.70*)

McCloy, James, Corporal
4270213, 1 Royal Northumberland Fusiliers
(Dunston-on-Tyne)
In the attack on Dalby Square on 23rd Nov 41 this N.C.O. led his Machine Gun Section into action in trucks immediately behind the tanks with great dash and courage. By his initiative he was able to destroy many of the retreating enemy. When the enemy counter-attacked his Section held their ground and destroyed enemy in vehicles and two light tanks. In the operations at Ed Duda on 25th Nov this N.C.O. drove through intense enemy fire and got his Section into action on the far side of the feature. From here he was able to direct his guns onto large enemy convoys and concentrations, and although cut off the next day by enemy action, he fought his guns with skill and resolution without losing a single man. (*L.G. 24.2.42*)

McClurg, Lenard Thomas, Corporal
6947, 22 N.Z. Bn. (Immediate)
In the battle of Alamein at Numassib.

During an enemy tank and infantry attack directed against the 22 N.Z. Bn. on the morning of the 4th September, Cpl. McClurg was in charge of a mortar section in the right forward Coy. The enemy approached to within 3/400 yards in this sector, where they were halted by the accurate and intense fire of Cpl. McClurg's section until the artillery S.O.S. fire dispersed the attack.

This was achieved by Cpl. McClurg's determination and complete disregard of his personal safety. Throughout the action he repeatedly moved back and forward over a distance of one hundred yards under heavy fire directing and observing the detachments' fire.

During a second attack Cpl. McClurg was wounded in three places while directing the fire of his section, but carried on his duties until this attack was also beaten off.

His action was an example and inspiration to those in the vicinity, and responsible for their vigorous defence of the sector. (*L.G. 5.11.42*)

McConchie, Philip Andrew, Sergeant
9743, 20 N.Z. Bn.
On Saturday 27th June Sgt. McConchie was in charge of a 2 pr. A/Tk. gun attached to 'A' Coy. He led a crew who had never manned or had experience with A/Tk. guns previously. From the very start of the action this N.C.O. displayed coolness and confidence. When action started he held his fire and by doing so destroyed a portee,

(killing the gun commander), a small tank, a troop carrier and two Tpts. His gun was subjected to heavy mortar fire—No. 2 was wounded and the firing mechanism broken. The gun was then useless and the position of the crew very critical. Sgt. McConchie held the crew together by his coolness and example. During a lull he walked out to the damaged portee, retrieved the firing mechanism and got his gun into action again. When his officer arrived he accompanied him out and towed the other portee back. During the withdrawal before the move Sgt. McConchie had trouble getting his gun onto the portee and eventually had to tow his gun out. At one of the heaviest stages of the fighting he went out some 20 yds. under heavy fire to retrieve water and tobacco for his men. Sgt. McConchie's coolness and efficiency under fire were outstanding and undoubtedly the gun could not have been held in action without him.   *(L.G. 13.8.42)*

McConville, Warrant Officer Cl. II
7010702, Royal Ulster Rifles
For Korea   *(L.G. 17.7.51)*

McCormac, Charles Edward, Sergeant (now Flight Lieutenant)
520544, Royal Air Force Volunteer Reserve, attd.
   Convoy Pool Operating Army
Escaped P.O.W.   *(L.G. 31.8.45)*

McCormick, William, Sergeant
2976691, Royal Artillery (Campbeltown)
From 51st Highland Div. P.O.W. Pool
                                           (L.G. 11.10.45)

McCracken, C. H. K., Fusilier
7043029, 2nd Bn. Royal Inniskilling Fusiliers
For most conspicuous gallantry when acting as the sole remaining Stretcher Bearer at Hollebeke 27th May, 1940 and at Oosttaverne 28th May, 1940. In both these actions when under very heavy shell fire, he continually dressed and evacuated wounded single handed. He showed complete disregard for his own safety and set an excellent example to the remainder of his Company.   *(20.6.40)*

McCree, Arthur Wilford, W/Cpl.
2621280, A/Sgt., 3rd Bn. Grenadier Guards
   (Immediate)
(Sheet 1/100,000 76 M 0198)
   On the night 24/25th April 1945 the 3rd Bn. Grenadier Guards made an assault crossing of the PO. No. 3 Coy. were to land on a separate beach and protect the Bn.'s flank. Sgt. McCree was in command of the leading platoon which was to cross the river in a Dukw.
   As soon as the Dukw came out of the water it came under heavy and sustained fire from four posts on the floodbank about 200 yds. away. The situation was critical as his platoon was dispersed, and until the posts were put out of action it was impossible to land the remainder of the Coy. Sgt. McCree realised this and with superb

disregard for his own safety stood up and called his section commanders together and got the attack organised in an extremely short time. The platoon, as it advanced in the bright moonlight across the sand, came under heavy fire all the way, but Sgt. McCree led them up the floodbank with such dash that the first two posts were overwhelmed and the enemy killed before the enemy had time to defend themselves. The remaining two posts caused a temporary hold up, but Sgt. McCree and Platoon HQ accounted for one with a bayonet charge and the other surrendered before this onslaught. In 10 minutes Sgt. McCree's platoon had killed 6 and taken 16 prisoners, thus enabling the remainder of the Coy. to land unopposed.
   Sgt. McCree throughout this action displayed courage, dash and initiative of the highest order in the face of severe handicaps, and it is entirely due to his leadership that the initial Bn. assault was successful, as it would have been impossible to land the remainder of the Bn. with enemy in their original positions.
Recommended for M.M.   *(23.8.45)*

MacCrudden, John, Trooper
7893115, Royal Tank Regt. (Thorpe, Surrey)
Tobruk 1942 (from P.O.W. Pool)   *(L.G. 11.10.45)*

McCuish, David Allan, Sergeant
H.800021, 2nd Bn., Princess Patricia's Canadian
   Light Infantry
For Korea   *(L.G. 4.1.52)*

McCulloch, George, Private
2760444, 1st Bn. Black Watch (Dundee)
During the night of 23rd/24th November 1942, Pte. McCulloch's company had just captured its second objective, the enemy strong point 'Killin,' when it came under close range M.G. fire from its front. At this time, the shelling was very heavy. Two companies were already on the objective and the two reserve companies were forming up to continue the advance.
   As soon as Pte. McCulloch had located the enemy M.G., he ran forward and attacked the post, single handed, until the rest of his platoon came up.
   Pte. McCulloch's prompt and brave action was not only an inspiration to his comrades, but was instrumental in preventing the enemy M.G. from taking a heavy toll from the Battalion.
Recommended for M.M.   *(L.G. 31.12.42)*

McDaid, Patrick, Colour Sergeant (A/W.O.II (C.S.M.))
1st Bn. London Irish Rifles (E. Stanley, Co. Durham)
   (Immediate)
On the night of 5th September 1944, 'D' Coy., 1/LIR, was strongly counter-attacked after capturing a feature North of Il Tribbia. The enemy attack was made in three waves each of a strong platoon strength and pressed home with the utmost determination by fanatics who knew the ground. There followed a hand to hand fight round a

house which lasted some 1½ hours. In the fighting the Coy. Comd. was killed and C.S.M. McDaid had to take over command of the Coy. until another officer could be found. He conducted the fight with the greatest skill and determination keeping a steady control of the situation, yet not sparing himself to move up immediately to deal with any enemy infiltration on the cordon. On several occasions he went forward and dispatched five enemy single handed with his T.M.C. His coolness and steadiness in a fast and hectic fight was the inspiration of all ranks. After 1½ hours ammunition was low, generally to the last magazine and C.S.M. McDaid decided to withdraw to the rd. behind the feature. Coolly giving orders and maintaining covering fire to the last, he successfully achieved the withdrawal and saw to the evacuation of the wounded. On arrival back at Bn. HQ he volunteered to go up again with another Coy. and retake the position. C.S.M. McDaid's conduct was of the highest order and the successful withdrawal of the Coy. was largely due to his actions. His courage, resourcefulness and coolness under fire, without thought of personal safety was an inspiration and example to his Coy.
Recommended for M.M. (*L.G. 8.2.45*)

McDonald, Allexander, Private
5887774, 2 Northamptonshire Regt. (Old Tupton)
(Periodic)
In every action Pte. McDonald has been responsible for maintaining communication with forward Coys. He was always irrepressibly cheerful and showed a very high order of courage.
At Anzio in March 1944 during a Bde. attack, Bn. HQ and the route to forward Coys. was shelled and mortared most heavily throughout the day. Crossing this ground many times attracting observed machine gun fire and constant mortar fire, Pte. McDonald, disregarding personal safety, had but one aim, to keep the line through. During the critical attacks and counter-attacks in the 'Fortress' area at Anzio on May 1st, the wadi joining Bn. HQ to the 'Fortress' Coys. was subjected to continual arty and mortar DF. Pte. McDonald spent eight hours in an inferno of shelling and mortaring, constantly mending the lines.
On 28th April 1945 at Neu Darchau on the Elbe the battalion took part in a deception plan which drew heavy enemy artillery fire throughout the night. Once again Pte. McDonald was out mending lines to forward Coys. under heavy fire. He gave no thought for his own danger, he thought only of the forward Coys., who relied on the line for arty support. His matchless courage and distinguished conduct have inspired his platoon in battle and made command possible. No greater combination could be given by one man.
M.I.D. 19.7.45; Silver Star (U.S.A.) 25.3.49
(*L.G. 24.1.46*)

McDonald, Edward, Sergeant
2928608, Queen's Own Cameron Highlanders
(Edinburgh)
No citation. (*L.G. 24.2.42*)

MacDonald, Duncan, Sergeant
QX 4060, 2/32 Aust. Inf. Bn.
L/Sgt. MacDonald was platoon sgt. of 9 Pl 'A' Coy. 2/32 Bn. in the attack on the Ry Blockhouse 870303 Sidi Abdel Rahman on night 30th/31st October 1942. During the attack the platoon was fired on from the right by two enemy M.G. posts. L/Sgt. MacDonald immediately organised a party consisting of himself, Pte. Davidson and two others to attack these posts. As they closed in the two others mentioned were both wounded. L/Sgt. MacDonald took up a Bren dropped by one of the wounded men and continued the attack with Pte. Davidson, each taking one post. He fired on both posts while advancing and then attacked one himself, killing the four occupants, while Pte. Davidson attacked the other. The gun was then turned on parties of enemy seen by light of flares. He then endeavoured to contact the res. platoon to obtain an escort for prisoners taken by Pte. Davidson but was unable to do so. He returned and together with Pte. Davidson destroyed the guns and took the prisoners back to a group in rear before rejoining the platoon.
So fine an example of leadership, personal courage, and cool determination in the face of the enemy was an inspiration to his Coy. (*L.G. 11.2.43*)

MacDonald, Edward, Sgt.
2928608, Camerons
This N.C.O. was one of a small raiding party with Lt. Mayne, who, at Sirte on the 12/13th Dec., destroyed 24 aeroplanes, bomb stores and petrol stores. This N.C.O. was conspicuous throughout for his utter disregard of danger—his coolness and steadiness when faced by a superior number of the enemy. The example set by this N.C.O. was an inspiration to all, and was instrumental in the success of this operation. (*24.2.42*)

MacDonald, Enoch Charles, Sergeant
4857535, 1st Bn. Leicestershire Regt.
(Wolverhampton)
Sgt. MacDonald set a fine example of personal courage during the fighting at Kampar on 1st, 2nd & 3rd January 1942. His position was several times attacked and intermittently subjected to intense mortar fire and on all occasions Sgt. MacDonald remained cool and determined and it was largely his cheerfulness and encouragement which rallied his men to holding on.
On 3rd January 1942, one of his men was so severely wounded that he was unable to move from where he was lying in an exposed position in the valley. Sgt. MacDonald made his way to this man under heavy rifle fire and when he found it impossible to extricate the man gave him water before he died. This N.C.O. only got

back to his position with great difficulty, owing to the enemy fire.

His conduct throughout the operation has shown him to be a very good leader and a very brave man.

(L.G. 13.12.45)

MacDonald, George Edward, Sergeant
6584837, Royal Artillery (London, N.4)
B.E.F. 1940 (from 1 Armd. Div. P.O.W. Pool)
(L.G. 8.11.45)

McDonald, James, Warrant Officer Cl. II (C.S.M.)
3757247, Green Howards
C. in C. Home Forces. (Rec Authority)   *(L.G. 7.1.41)*

MacDonald, Michael Bernard, Sergeant
F 54680 (P54680 on AFW 3121), The Cape Breton Highlanders (Immediate)
On the night 30th April/1st May 1945, Sgt. MacDonald was a Platoon Sergeant in 'D' Coy., the Cape Breton Highlanders, who were attacking the key strong-point in the defences of the port of Delfzijl.

The strong-point was sited on the top of a dyke 30 feet high and its guns commanded all approaches across the flat open ground. The strong-point consisted of four 105 mm guns, two 20 mm guns, many machine guns and 300 infantry. Some of the enemy infantry were firing from concrete pillboxes at the foot of the dyke.

Sgt. MacDonald's platoon, at dawn, had fought its way into the centre of the enemy position, and had cleared and occupied a trench within 50 yards of the 105 mm gun positions. The enemy were then firing at the platoon from all sides, with every weapon that could be brought to bear on the trench.

Sgt. MacDonald, with five of his comrades, disregarding the intense enemy fire dashed forward a further 25 yards and occupied another enemy trench. Here they were subjected to the direct fire of a bazooka and two machine guns fifty yards away. Enemy entrenched on the top of the dyke threw grenades down into the trench. Two of Sgt. MacDonald's comrades in the trench were killed and a third was mortally wounded. In the confusion of the exploding grenades and bazooka bombs two of the enemy crept up unnoticed and reaching the edge of the trench demanded surrender. Sgt. MacDonald and his two remaining comrades, with their ammunition exhausted and covered by the enemy's weapons appeared to have no alternative but to surrender. As they climbed out of the trench Sgt. MacDonald said to his comrades, 'While the rest of the Company is still fighting, we won't give up, make a break for it,' upon which Sgt. MacDonald knocked down the nearest enemy with his fist, seized his rifle and put the second German to flight. As a result of this act the enemy in the pill-boxes again opened fire and Sgt. MacDonald fell, seriously wounded in both legs. With great fortitude he crawled back to the trench in which his two comrades had already taken up positions and remained with them for more than seven hours.

Sgt. MacDonald's daring attack, unarmed, on his armed captor allowed his comrades to reach safety. His supreme courage and cheerfulness during the long hours when he lay, wounded, in the trench encouraged his comrades to hold their well nigh untenable position until they were relieved seven hours later.   *(L.G. 22.9.45)*

MacDonald, Peter Daniel, Sergeant
2978172, Highland Light Infantry (Johnstone, Renfrewshire)
N.W. Europe 1944. (P.O.W. Pool)   *(L.G. 11.4.46)*

MacDonald, Stewart, Sergeant
F64934, Cape Breton Highlanders of Canada
On 3rd January 1945 the Cape Breton Highlanders advanced in a Northerly direction from the Lamone River astride a high dyke. At approximately 0500 hours 'A' Coy. on the right attained the objective at Fatta Brocchi.

At 0615 hours an enemy force, estimated at sixty in strength, launched a determined counter-attack against the platoon on the right flank commanded by Sgt. MacDonald. The attack was made in two waves. The first of which, led by a Captain, came in from the right and the second, led by a Company Sergeant Major, came in from the left. The enemy approached to within 50 yards of the position unobserved, fired two shots into a house in the platoon area and rushed the position.

During the initial stages of the assault Sgt. MacDonald, in full view of the enemy and under heavy small arms fire ran from slit trench to slit trench encouraging his men and directing and co-ordinating their fire. The enemy pressed on with determination and when only fifteen yards from the most forward platoon position the Bren gun which was sited there jammed. Realizing the desperate situation Sgt. MacDonald immediately ran forward towards the advancing enemy and under a hail of bullets and without cover of any kind held off the enemy with his Tommy gun while still shouting fire orders to his platoon. This gallant N.C.O. personally killed the German officer and two other ranks and seriously wounded the Company Sergeant Major, and his platoon, having killed or seriously wounded twenty of the enemy and captured ten, forced the remainder to withdraw in complete disorder.

The gallantry, determination and inspiring leadership displayed by Sgt. MacDonald was directly responsible for routing the enemy counter-attack and enabled the Battalion to continue its advance to the Reno Canal with the subsequent capture of San Alberton, the Brigade objective.   *(L.G. 7.4.45)*

McDonnell, John Joseph, Sergeant
3447097, 3rd Bn. Parachute Regt., Army Air Corps (Lowestoft) (Immediate)
For most conspicuous gallantry and devotion to duty on 26th February 1943 at Ragoubet El Araan, Bou Arada (Tunisia Sheet 41 7097). During a strong attack by the enemy who had overrun one of our positions, Sjt.

McDonnell went forward alone, under heavy machine gun fire, and recaptured the post, capturing five of the enemy together with the M.G. Meanwhile another party of the enemy had worked round his right flank to surround him. Indicating the target to his section, who pinned them to the ground, he dashed forward and killed all except one whom he took prisoner. Continuing up the hill, he led his section under intense M.G. fire and captured another M.G. post, turning the captured M.G. onto Pt. 375 from which at least 3 M.G.s were firing. Without hesitation he attacked this nest with grenades, silenced the M.G., and killed or captured all the occupants, thereby enabling the counter-attack force to continue and regain all positions. Observing large numbers of enemy withdrawing, he doubled his section down the hill, and although suffering losses from heavy enemy fire, he succeeded in compelling large numbers to surrender in spite of the fact that by this time his ammunition was exhausted.

Previously on 24th February 1943 in the same area his platoon was attacked by a strong patrol which was driven off. As soon as he saw that the patrol was withdrawing this N.C.O. without hesitation and entirely alone, at point blank range, jumped our wire and ran after them and compelled two to surrender. The bravery and initiative displayed by this N.C.O. on these and other occasions have been an inspiration to all ranks.

(L.G. 22.4.43)

MacDougal, Bruce Halkister, Warrant Officer Cl. II
NX 572, 2/3 Bn., Australian Military Forces
For conspicuous gallantry and devotion to duty during the Battle of Tobruch on 21st January 1941. The officers of this N.C.O.'s company became casualties during the morning of the battle and WO II MacDougal took command of the company, re-organising it and leading it successfully in the ensuing fighting. He led his company in the face of heavy enemy fire from a strongly defended post and personally rallied and led a platoon against a part of the post in the race of heavy fire. WO II MacDougal has shown absolute fearlessness and complete disregard for personal safety in all actions in which he has been concerned, and provides an outstanding example to the men under his command.

(L.G. 9.5.41)

McDougall, Robert, [Roy on AFW 3121], Sergeant
2928612, 3rd Bn. Parachute Regt., Army Air Corps
(Immediate)
For unexampled bravery and devotion to duty on 26th February 1943 at Ragoubet El Araan, Bou Arada (Tunisia Sheet 41, 7097). This N.C.O. was in command of a forward section post and a heavy attack was launched against him. He repelled the attack and the enemy withdrew and attacked once more; again such was the fire of his section that they were again forced to withdraw. By this time Sjt. McDougall had lost all but two of his section but he still stood fast. For the third time an attack

was made and this time the Sjt. was himself shot through the neck and mouth, but he continued to fire the Bren himself at twenty yards range. Another section worked round to a flank and their fire, combined with Sjt. McDougall's forced the enemy to retire. This N.C.O. was then ordered to withdraw and it was found that he had been wounded so badly that he was in a very bad way and could only just crawl. The bravery and tenacity of this N.C.O. prevented the enemy's strong central thrust from penetrating the company position, his conduct being an inspiration to all ranks. *(L.G. 22.4.43)*

McElhatton, James, Private (A/Cpl.)
5627682, 1 Devonshire Regt. (Hebburn, Durham)
(Immediate)
For most conspicuous gallantry in action.

Cpl. McElhatton was in command of a section of Coy. 1 Devon which was holding a post called Crete West at Tengnoupal. Throughout the night of May 6th and 7th 1944 following very heavy and concentrated bombardment by enemy medium and field artillery two very determined attacks and six minor attacks were put in on the position. The wire was cut and penetrated, and trenches were blown in. Cpl. McElhatton's section took a major part in beating off all these attacks and it was due to his magnificent leadership, complete disregard of his personal safety, and fine example that his section not only held firm but inflicted very severe casualties on the enemy. He himself in spite of intense and close grenade fire went forward three times out of his position into the open the better to see the Japs and mow them down with his Tommy Gun. Wherever the fight was thickest, he was there, completely regardless of his own personal safety, moving up and down his section during the night long attacks and spurring his men on to put forth their maximum efforts. This N.C.O. is most strongly deserving of the award now recommended. *(L.G. 31.8.44)*

McElroy, Arthur, Corporal (A/Sgt.)
2716645, 3rd Bn. Irish Guards (Enniskillen)
On the afternoon of 15th September 1944, this platoon Sgt. was a complete inspiration to all the men in his platoon during the counter-attack on the enemy in the woods at 336976, near De Groote Barrier. Though wounded in the foot during the attack, he showed complete disregard for his injuries and his offensive example was no doubt directly responsible for his platoon reaching their objective. He personally shot and bayonetted several Germans and all the time shouted encouragement to the section comds. and Gdsm. of his platoon. After consolidation his company commander ordered him to return to the R.A.P. for treatment as he was fighting with one boot on one foot and a shell dressing and one sock on the other. Though he left the area of company headquarters, he was later found to be still with his platoon and had to be forcibly evacuated. This N.C.O.'s high conception of duty to the men under

his immediate command and his personal bravery cannot be spoken of too highly.   *(L.G. 1.3.45)*

McEvoy, Keith Albert, Corporal
WX 11335, 2/3 Aust. Indep. Coy. (Immediate)
Near Salamaua.

During the attack by his Company on Ambush Knoll on 15th July 1943, Cpl McEvoy showed dash and courage of the highest merit, materially assisting the success of the operation. His section led the main advance on the position. The enemy were driven from their forward weapon pits but, from their main position, brought fire to bear on our line of approach. Sections moved to each flank and Cpl McEvoy and five men remained in the centre. Cpl McEvoy gave orders for an assault and, moving directly into the enemy's line of fire, leaped over a barricade of bamboo across the ridge. However at this moment four of his party were wounded by enemy grenades and only the one remaining man joined him across the barricade. Undeterred, Cpl McEvoy pushed forward and engaged the enemy at very short range, forcing them to withdraw from a portion of their forward trench. This enabled other troops to move forward under cover and bring heavy fire to bear on the enemy position. In the face of considerable enemy L.M.G. and rifle fire and grenades, Cpl McEvoy continued his action all the afternoon and maintained harassing fire during the night. The following morning it was found that the sustained attack in which Cpl McEvoy had played such a gallant part had forced the enemy to withdraw, leaving the position in our hands.
                    (L.G. 20.1.44)

McEvoy, William Henry [William Henry Montgomery on AFW 3121], Sergeant
7260085, R.A.M.C., 1st Bn. The Queen's Own
    Cameron Highlanders (Edinburgh)
On the night 24/25th February 1945 Sgt. McEvoy was Medical Sergeant of the 1st Bn. The Queen's Own Cameron Highlanders. The Bn. had been ordered to force a crossing of the Irrawaddy River from Myittha, about 25 miles West of Mandalay and to form a bridgehead on the South bank. Another Bn. was crossing on the right flank. It was estimated that enemy opposition would be light and in view of this the crossing was to be silent using light rubber boats paddled by hand, in an attempt to effect complete surprise.

Sgt. McEvoy was in the first flight in a boat containing the Medical Officer and bearers. As the flight approached the South bank, it came under machine gun fire and heavy casualties were sustained in Sgt. McEvoy's boat — the Medical Officer and four stretcher bearers being killed — and in the boats around him. The men momentarily wavered but Sgt. McEvoy immediately took control, rallied the men and urged them forward through the fire. His magnificent leadership and personal example enabled the boats to land, and while the assault troops pressed inland, Sgt. McEvoy organised the collection of

wounded, and himself set a magnificent example of coolness and courage under fire.

Sgt. McEvoy worked throughout the night and following day doing work far above his station until another Medical Officer arrived. The Officer commanding the ADS which received the casualties stated that this N.C.O.s treatment of them could not have been more skilful had it been performed by a Medical Officer.

It transpired that heavy opposition had prevented the right flanking Bn. from landing and it was through the bridgehead formed by Sgt. McEvoy's Bn. that the Brigade passed. This N.C.O. made a tremendous contribution to its success and his conduct throughout was beyond all praise.

Separate report by Medical authorities is attached.
        Report by Major K. D. G. Abbott.

At approximately 1000 hours on the morning of February 25th, 1945, casualties from the 1st Bn. Cameron Highlanders were evacuated across the Irrawaddy to the A.D.S. at Myittha. These casualties had been wounded at various times between 0245 hours and 0600 hours and had remained on the beach on the South bank of the Irrawaddy until approximately 1000 hours owing to there being no boats to evacuate them. These casualties, consisting of wounds of the head, shoulder, arm, buttock, back, thigh and leg arrived at the A.D.S. in excellent condition. The wounds had been well dressed and all fractures and cases in which a fracture had been suspected had been extremely well splinted at the R.A.P. Morphia had been given to all patients and all details had been most completely entered on their Field Medical Cards. All this excellent work had been done by Sgt. McEvoy under very difficult conditions.
B.E.M. 30.12.60   *(L.G. 12.7.45)*

Macey, Clifford Norman, Sergeant
P3515, 2nd Canadian Armoured Regiment (Ld.S.H.)
    (Immediate)
On 24th May 1944 a force of all arms based on 2nd Canadian Armoured Regiment (Ld.S.H.) (R.C.) commanded by L/Col. P. G. Griffin was given the task of pushing through a gap established in the Adolph Hitler Line and capturing a crossing over the River Melfa. A portion of the reconnaissance troop of the Regiment under Lieut. E. J. Perkins was ordered to precede the main force and seize a crossing over the River Melfa. Sgt. Macey acted as troop Sergeant of this detachment. The troop reached the crossing of the River Melfa at approx. 1500 hours and Lieut. Perkins and Sgt. Macey successfully reconnoitred a crossing of the river and then jointly carried out the hazardous task of getting their force of three tanks and thirteen men over a very difficult crossing. It was then found necessary to widen the track on the far side. This was done partially with explosives but mainly with pick and shovel by personnel of the party. During this highly hazardous operation, in the course of which the small force was protected only by two Bren

gunners, the personal example and leadership of Sgt. Macey were beyond all praise.

A party of five, including Lieut. Perkins and Sgt. Macey rushed a large house at the top of the bank from an unexpected direction capturing eight paratroop prisoners including one officer and one N.C.O. without loss to themselves. Sgt. Macey then returned over the river to guide 'A' Squadron across. It was found that 'A' Squadron had suffered heavy casualties and the attempt to get them across was abandoned as overly hazardous. The reconnaissance troop was then ordered to hold if possible, pending the arrival of 'A' Coy. Westminster Regt. (Motor). Until 1700 hours this tiny force of thirteen held the crossing under a constant threat of attack by three Panther tanks which were approx. 600 yards away and which shelled and machine gunned the position frequently.

During this time Sgt. Macey was completely calm and established confidence wherever he went. At approx. 1700 hours the bridgehead was strengthened by the arrival of 'A' Coy. Westminster Regt. (Motor). Following this the bridgehead was attacked twice by Panther tanks. During both of these attacks Sgt. Macey set an example of coolness by standing up in his reconnaissance tank to fire his point five Browning at the oncoming Panthers.

During the night the position was heavily shelled by mortars and Nebelwerfers and it was largely due to Sgt. Macey's energy in driving the men, now thoroughly tired, to dig deep slit trenches, which prevented any casualties from this source. In the early morning the enemy started to threaten a counter-attack. Sgt. Macey, although entirely without sleep and under the greatest strain for more than twenty-four hours continued to be an example of coolness and leadership until the troop was ordered to withdraw at 1200 hours 25th May 1944, following a successful attack by the Irish Regt. of Canada and the Westminster Regt. (Motor).

The qualities of leadership demonstrated by this N.C.O. throughout the operation were outstanding. By his example of coolness, cheerful obedience to the orders of his troop officer, and above all by his driving force which overcame all obstacles, he rendered invaluable assistance in the execution of a hazardous and highly successful operation.   (*L.G. 29.7.44*)

MacFarlane, William, Private
2977912, 7 Argyll & Sutherland Highlanders
6th June 1940. Captured Abbeville.

The whole of our Company was captured in the town of Abbeville on 6th June 1940, when the whole battalion had been surrounded and the order given to surrender. We were marched through Northern France into Germany and, after passing somewhere near Brussels, we arrived at the Rhine, and about the end of June were put on barges. After a journey of three days, during which we had no food, we were disembarked and sent to a holding camp at (?) Sagenheim. From there we were sent

five days later to Stalag IX/C (Bad Sulza). I was only two days there before being sent on a working party to the cement works at Steudnitz, near Dorndorf about 7 miles S.E. of Bad Sulza. There were 70 men in this work camp (Arbeitskommando 1116), and we all lived together in two rooms near the factory. I was among those who worked in the quarry filling waggons with chalk.

In September 1941 I was transferred to the salt mines at Unterbreizbach, about ten miles S.E. of Hersfeld, (Arbeitskommando 147) where I was employed in the turning shop. Again there were about 70 men in the camp, which was about 10 minutes' walk from the mines.

About the beginning of 1942 I began planning to escape with Pte. James Goldie of my unit, with whom I had been since capture. We saved chocolate biscuits and tea from Red Cross parcels and discussed ways of getting out of the camp. The mines were worked in two shifts. I worked from 0600 to 1800 hours, and Goldie from 1400 to 2200 hours. We decided to escape on the night of 21st March. This was a Saturday, and we reckoned there would be a chance of our not being missed on the Sunday. I made a jemmy in the turning shop and burst open the gate on the East side of the camp which was only used by the guards and the women working in the kitchen. We were locked up at 2100 hours in our huts, and the doors were not opened again until 2245 hours, when the second shift came in from work. There were two sentries and four women who worked in the cookhouse. After the women finished at 1900 hours the two guards became responsible for the feeding of the second shift when it came off work. One of them ought to have remained on guard outside, but we knew that they both generally went into the dining room. I broke the lock of the gate about 2030 hours and the gate remained open till 2245 hours, when Goldie and I left. Two other men of our regiment were to have come with us, but they did not turn up, though we waited ten minutes for them.

The following is a summary of our equipment and plans:—

Clothes: We wore ordinary battle dress on top of which we had blue overalls with 'K.G.' in red on the back. We were able to conceal these letters with rucksacks which we made out of sacks.

Food: We had collected sufficient chocolate and biscuits for ten days, six tins of sardines, and about six lbs. of tea. Our idea was to use the tea as bribes.

Maps: We had two maps of Germany and adjacent countries, one of which Goldie had got from an anti-Nazi German working underground with him in the mine, and the other of which I got from a Pole who worked at the head of the shaft. I told the Pole I was going to escape, but did not tell him how or when.

Plan: There had been a number of other attempts from the camp, but none of the men had tried to escape otherwise than on foot, and they had all been recaptured. We decided to try to jump on railway waggons at Gerstungen, about 12 miles N.E. of Unterbreizbach.

We took six days to get to Gerstungen walking in a circle to avoid detection. We walked at night, avoiding villages, and slept in the woods by day. There was snow on the ground up to our knees, and quite frequently we had to use melted snow instead of water. On our second night out we left our hiding place rather early and were crossing a main road near a village when we were stopped by a German. We told him we were Frenchmen going to Gerstungen and when he asked us why we did not speak French we admitted we were English. By giving him cigarettes we persuaded him to let us go, but we suspect that he reported our presence to other villagers, because we were chased very shortly afterwards. We managed to hide in a wood and our pursuers did not come after us.

We reached the goods station at Gerstungen on the night of 26th March. We broke the lead seal of a closed salt waggon and entered by the door. We then opened a window, came out by the door—which we resealed— and got in by the window. There were quite a few railwaymen about, but no one saw us. We had plenty of room on top of the sacks of salt inside the waggon. Unfortunately, the train only moved for a few hours at a time and then lay up for half a day or a day, so that the journey to Belgium, which would have taken about two days' normal travelling, lasted eight days. We had neglected to take water with us, and did not leave the waggon during the numerous stops for fear of being seen. We suffered terribly from thirst, and during the last few days were unable to eat the food we had brought with us. We knew the waggon was bound for Belgium as we saw the destination (Hasselt) written in German on the notice on the side of the truck. In Belgium a French notice was substituted for the German one.

We were able to check our position on one of our maps by watching the names of the stations we passed through. On Good Friday (3rd April) we arrived in Hasselt. We remained in the waggon all day and most of the night, and then dropped out about 0400 hrs (4th April). We walked to a stream on the outskirts of Hasselt, where we washed and made tea in tin cans picked up on the road. We then walked to Tirelmont, the journey occupying two days. We had to walk by day because we could find no cover for hiding. We were still in our blue overalls over battle dress, but, though we walked on the main road, no one challenged us. On 5th April we approached a house in Kessel Loo and asked for water to make tea, speaking in broken German, which the people understood. An old woman took us in and kept us for the night. Early next morning we were taken by bicycle to Louvain, where we were sheltered for six weeks by people who belonged to a Belgian patriotic organisation. We then went to live with another family who put us in touch with an operation which arranged for our return to the U.K.   *(L.G. 10.11.42)*

McGarrigle, Ernest Morland Walker, Lance Sergeant
2657234, Coldstream Guards
This soldier was taken prisoner in Belgium in 1940. He soon escaped but was recaptured on his way back to the Lille area where he had hoped to find members of his unit. He again escaped, although under close observation by the enemy, and reached Lille, having obtained civilian clothes from friendly Belgians.

Here he heard of the capitulation of Belgium, and after waiting for possible opportunities to rejoin his unit, he decided to return to the U.K. via Spain.

With Belgian and French identity cards he made his way with great ingenuity and perseverance, experiencing a third capture and escape, to Perpignan at the end of 1941, when largely because of lack of funds he was persuaded to abandon his project of crossing the Pyrenees.

Early in 1942 he joined a resistance group in the Haute Loire when he greatly assisted in the reception of supplies by air and gave arms instruction to the Maquis groups.

After D-Day he commanded a platoon before and during the battle which led to the capitulation of the enemy garrison numbering over 2,000 at Le Puy. He also undertook a number of ambushes, as a result of which German troops were only able to advance 15 kms in eight days towards the fighting zone.

Guardsman McGarrigle had shown great courage in endeavouring persistently to rejoin his unit. He was quick-witted and resourceful in his escapes and was doggedly determined to continue the fight. He was of immense value to the maquis group and played a very courageous part in attacks on the enemy—all the above voluntarily and without special training. He did much to raise morale in French Resistance circles by his very fine example and it is recommended that he be awarded the Distinguished Conduct Medal.   *(L.G. 21.6.45)*

McGee, Michael John, Private
14216814, 7 Para. Bn., Army Air Corps (Aughnacloy, Co. Tyrone) (since died of wounds)
The above named soldier was one of the parachutists who landed behind the German lines on 6th June 1944. His Coy. was in continual action for 21 hours during most of which time it was cut off from the bn. and attacked by superior numbers of inf. and tanks and S.P. quns. On one occasion Pte. McGee by engaging a Panther tank at point blank range with his Bren gun fired from the hip, caused it to stop at a point when his comrades put it out of action with a ha[...] bomb.

This soldier's complete disregard for his personal safety was largely responsible for the successful and gallant action fought by his Coy.   *(L.G. 22.3.45)*

McGibbon, William, Lance Sergeant
2754256, 2nd Bn. Black Watch
Somaliland.

For conspicuous gallantry in the action at Barkasan on the 17th August, 1940. When No. 18 Platoon was heavily engaged by greatly superior forces and all but surrounded this N.C.O. observed an enemy M.G. section coming into action. Without hesitation and heedless of danger he armed himself with 3 grenades and crossed 40 yards of bullet swept ground and killed the crew of the M.G. section and destroyed the gun. He then returned to his post. His action at a critical period was an example of the greatest courage and initiative to the men of the platoon.   *(L.G. 29.11.40)*

McGilvery, Mark Leonard, Private
L. 41106, Lake Superior Regt. (Motor) (Immediate)
On 4th May 1945, No. 8 Platoon of 'B' Coy., Lake Superior (Mot), was acting as vanguard of the 4 Cdn. Armd. Bde. column. At MR 292195 the leading elements came under fire from an enemy battle group made up of an anti-tank gun and supporting infantry in the wood at MR 290200. No. 8 Platoon was ordered to destroy the gun and clear the wood. After advancing for about 100 yards through the heavy brush, the anti-tank gun was sighted. Pte. McGilvery worked his way carefully forward to get a clean shot with his Piat. Unfortunately he was observed from the flank and came under heavy automatic fire, the monopod of his weapon being shot away. Unshaken by his narrow escape and by the enemy's heavy fire which was becoming more intense, Pte. McGilvery inched his way forward, covered by his number two. Having reached a position from which he was sure of a kill, he supported his damaged weapon on a fallen log and obtained a direct hit on the piece with his first bomb, rendering the gun useless. At that moment his number two was gravely wounded by automatic fire from a machine gun post in the immediate area of the gun. Showing remarkable steadiness, although his cover from the rear had been removed, he took deliberate aim and, with his second bomb, killed three of the members of the gun crew. While he was now subjected to point blank machine gun fire, Pte. McGilvery did not waver for a moment but calmly turned his weapon on the machine gun post and silenced it with his third bomb. He then rushed the post, killing the two remaining machine gunners with a grenade. His task completed, he turned back to his wounded comrade and carried him to safety. The cool courage displayed by Pte. McGilvery and the devastating effectiveness of his individual action broke the spirit of the Germans remaining in the wood. No. 8 Platoon quickly carried through normal mopping up which resulted in a bag of forty prisoners of war. The road was once more open and the 4 Cdn. Armd. Bde. column resumed its advance.
Recommended for M.M.   *(L.G. 11.8.45)*

McGrath, Jack, Corporal (actg.)
H17820, P.P.C.L.I., Canadian Infantry Corps
   (Immediate)
Ref Map Italy 1/25,000 Sheet 89 III NW.
   On the night of 19th December 1944, in the final phase of the advance to the Senio River, 2 Cdn. Inf. Brig. was ordered to advance and encircle Bagnacavallo from the North. The Princess Patricias's Canadian Light Infantry was to be right forward battalion and to execute a wheeling movement, striking West through the area MR 4041—3941 and then South towards Bagnacavallo. The Bn. plan called for the securing of four objectives in the general area MR 4041—3941, as a first phase, and a subsequent exploitation Southwards.
   In this first phase, 'C' Coy., P.P.C.L.I. was given as objective a group of houses at MR 402411 (Code name Maroon). This position turned out to be the key to a group of strongly held enemy localities in this area, and in fact the advance of the whole Brigade was held up until it was captured. 15 Platoon of 'C' Coy. in which H–17320 Pte. (A/Cpl.) McGrath was a section leader, was given the task of providing right flank protection for this operation.
   During the attack the leading platoon came under fire from a M.G. post and Cpl. McGrath was detailed to wipe out this interference. Without hesitation he led his Section forward a distance of 75 yards over bullet-swept ground, under heavy shell and mortar fire, to within a short distance of the enemy post. From there he led a bayonet charge assaulting the post and personally killing three of the enemy; the post was eliminated. His Section was immediately fired upon by another enemy M.G. post, in a flash, Cpl. McGrath led a charge against this well dug-in position and successfully dealt with the enemy, himself killing two and wounding another. While engaged in the attack on this second post one of the men in his Section was wounded. The Section now came under fire from an enemy tank on the objective in addition to the mortaring and shelling. Having completed his task Cpl. McGrath directed the successful withdrawal of his Section to their platoon position, under fire the whole time, himself carrying the wounded man on his back. During the return a mortar bomb landed directly behind him killing the wounded man and hurling Cpl. McGrath to the ground. Despite his dazed condition and suffering from severe bruises, he made his way back to his Platoon. On arrival there this gallant soldier volunteered to search out yet another M.G. position which he suspected to exist and again went forward with one of his men. Still under heavy mortaring and shelling, and fire from the enemy tank, he searched out this third M.G position and with the other soldier charged and cleared it, taking three prisoners. He refused to be evacuated that night, in spite of his dazed condition, and next morning took part in yet another assault on an enemy post.
   In this action Cpl. McGrath, under the heaviest fire of all types, displayed courage, initiative and devotion to duty of the very highest order. He personally killed five and wounded one enemy, and took three prisoners. By his outstanding gallantry and individual effort, he destroyed three well dug-in M.G. posts and, attracting as he did practically all the enemy's attention, made possible the gaining of the Company's objective with a minimum of casualties. As a result of this successful

action the enemy was forced to abandon the area, and the whole Brig. was able to exploit rapidly to the Senio river.   *(L.G. 10.3.45)*

McGree, Arthur Wilford, Sergeant (actg.)
2621280, Grenadier Guards (Loughborough)
No citation.   *(L.G. 23.8.45)*

MacGregor, Robert, M.M., Warrant Officer Cl. II
408246, 1st Royal Tank Regt. (Elgin) (Immediate)
On 30th September 1944, S.S.M. MacGregor was in command of a tp. of tks. which was ordered to attack Middelrode village (MR 3942 Sheet S'Hertogenbosch) in conjunction with a section of carriers and a platoon of infantry.

As soon as the advance started the enemy brought down heavy observed shellfire on the attacking troops and after 300 yards the infantry and carriers were brought to a halt by M.G. fire.

Realising that the whole attack was in danger of being held up and knowing full well the risk attached to advancing in such close country without infantry support, S.S.M. MacGregor moved fwd. with his tp., destroyed the M.G.s holding up the infantry and one A.tk. gun which he met face to face at 50 yards range and reached the centre of the village. The infantry then came up and S.S.M. MacGregor moved to a position from which he could shoot the enemy withdrawing from the village and observe the enemy's main position. He remained in this position under continuous shellfire and mortar fire and sniping for 7 hours directing arty fire on to the enemy guns.

During this action S.S.M. MacGregor's troop destroyed 2 A. tk. guns and 2 M.G.s and took 20 P.O.W., besides killing a number of enemy and forcing 200 to withdraw from the village.

This W.O.'s coolness, courage and judgement were entirely responsible for the success of the action and had it not been for his leadership and handling of the situation, both his own troop and the infantry would have undoubtedly suffered severe casualties without reaching their objective.
M.M. 31.12.42; Recommended for M.M. (L.G. 1.3.45)

McHardy, William, Sergeant
550636, 11th Hussars (Immediate)
Early on the morning of April 8th, Sgt. McHardy was commanding one of the leading Armoured Car troops in the hills West of Skhirpa. An enemy column headed by two lorries towing guns appeared crossing his front along a track. Realising that if they were not stopped quickly the whole column might go into action or make its escape, he immediately attacked and knocked out the two leading vehicles, thus stopping the column.

Without waiting to collect the prisoners, he went straight on amongst the rest of the column, capturing a total of 7 lorries, 5 105mm guns, 1 6-pdr and not less than 100 prisoners. By his prompt decision and swift

action he took the enemy by surprise, thus preventing them from putting up resistance or making their escape.

Since Alamein he has had several successful engagements, capturing many prisoners and lorries, and on one occasion putting out of action and capturing the crew of a Semovente tank. I recommend that he be awarded an Immediate D.C.M.   *(L.G. 22.7.43)*

McIvor, James Ivan, Sergeant
H40964, Canadian Infantry Corps
C.F. N.W.E.   *(L.G. 24.1.46)*

Mack, Charles Wilbur, Sergeant [W.O. II on AFW 3121]
30795, N.Z. Div. Cavalry Regt.
On the 29th November at Zaafran Sergt. Mack's squadron had been heavily engaged with the enemy and had suffered a number of casualties in both men and vehicles. Sergt. Mack got word that there were four American tanks which had apparently been abandoned through their crews becoming casualties, on a ridge near the enemy positions. He collected four men as drivers— took them forward and recovered the tanks. He then organised 'scratch' crews from amongst the men he had with him, including several who had never been in a tank before—gave them half an hours instruction in how to operate the guns, etc., and took them forward again to attack the enemy. He came under heavy shell fire from an enemy position but by skilful manœuvre and aggresive action he succeeded in destroying the enemy tank which was observing for their artillery. This enabled him to go forward again until he was attacked by a number of enemy tanks. He held his ground and destroyed two more tanks and a number of transport vehicles, and succeeded in killing at least sixty of the enemy. For two hours he held the enemy at bay during the whole of which time he was in action and subjected to ceaseless attacks from vastly superior enemy forces. He was finally withdrawn by his squadron leader. By his inspiring leadership and sound tactical skill Sergt. Mack not only inflicted heavy casualties on the enemy but also undoubtedly prevented an attack from developing on the rear of N.Z. Divisional Headquarters.

None of the men whom Sergt. Mack led into action had ever seen an American tank before that day.
                                          (L.G. 19.3.42)

McKay, David Playfair, Sergeant
*4270544, 1 Royal Northumberland Fusiliers
(Newcastle-on-Tyne)*
This N.C.O. has shown consistent gallantry and devotion to duty throughout the eight months of the Defence of Tobruk and in the break out, commanding a Machine Gun Section through this long period. He showed outstanding leadership in the attack on Dalby Square when he led his Section into action on truck in the face of the enemy at close range. Later when the enemy counter-attacked he held his ground and when under fire

from the Tanks he dragged a gun into action in the open and engaging the infantry prevented them closing in. He showed the same fine fighting spirit in other engagements especially at Ed Duda where he fought his Section until surrounded by Tanks and then succeeded in extricating nearly all in the darkness saving his locks and instruments.

These are typical examples of his constant bravery and determination to get to grips with the enemy.

(L.G. 9.9.42)

McKay, David Thomas, M.M., Lance Sergeant
73454705, 185 Fd. Amb., R.A.M.C. (Periodic)
This soldier during his service with this unit overseas has consistently shown exceptional zeal in carrying out his duties. His conduct and outstanding bravery have at all times been an example to his comrades and to patients under his care. He has on numerous occasions volunteered for hazardous and extremely dangerous duties, often outside the normal scope of his duty. During the initial landing in Italy, the fighting round Salerno, the crossing of the Volturno and in more recent engagements his conduct has been outstanding and his zeal an inspiration to everyone associated with him. He has been recommended on three separate occasions for immediate award of the Military Medal, and I consider his personal safety and devotion to duty are such that he should be recommended for a M.M. as a periodical award rather than for a B.E.M. for his outstanding work in every other direction befits him.
Recommended for M.M. Originally Gazetted M.M. Amended to D.C.M. 24.8.44   *(L.G. 2.11.44)*

Mackay, Robert Weir, Lance Corporal
C 58039, 21 Cdn. Armd. Regt. (G.G.F.G.) (Immediate)
On 10th April 1945, L/Cpl. MacKay was acting as crew comd. of a light tank in No. 3 Section of the Reconnaissance Troop of 21 Cdn. Armd. Regt. This section was operating in front of the advance guard of 4 Cdn. Armd. Div. on the divisional centre line. The section came under heavy enemy machine gun and anti-tank fire from the vicinity of the road junction at MR 895711 and the section leader's tank and the third tank were hit and set on fire, their crews being forced to abandon them. These crews were pinned to the ground by fire from three 20 mm guns cited in the immediate area of the road junction. Realizing that the unhorsed crews could not hope to get back without fire support, L/Cpl. MacKay ordered his tank to swing clear of the protection of the burning vehicles and took up a position in the open to shield them from observed fire. The three 20 mm guns immediately concentrated their attention on this one tank. Undeterred, in the face of this point blank fire, L/Cpl. MacKay carried straight on knocking out one gun with his 37 mm and crushing another under the tracks of his tank before it was finally immobilized. Although now a sitting target which was receiving repeated hits, L/Cpl. MacKay continued to fight his tank until the third gun was put

out of action. As his vehicle was now burning he ordered his crew to bail out and make their way back. On leaving the tank L/Cpl. MacKay received a bullet wound in the stomach. Although in great pain and unable to stand, he worked his way into a nearby ditch and engaged the advancing enemy infantry, who threatened the escape of his crew, with a Sten gun, driving them to ground. He continued to command the area until infantry elements of the advance guard working forward on the flanks, were able to overrun the enemy thus held in the open. Throughout this entire action this junior N.C.O. displayed the greatest heroism and devotion to duty. The intense and accurate fire he directed from his tank and while lying wounded on the ground was instrumental in saving the lives of his comrades and in enabling the infantry to move steadily forward. The carefully sited rearguard position was swept aside and the divisional advance continued uninterrupted.   *(L.G. 11.8.45)*

McKenna, James, Sergeant
331113, 1st Bn. Highland Light Infantry (Nairn)
(Immediate)
On 22nd October 1944, this N.C.O. was in command of No. 12 Platoon of 'B' Coy. During the phase of the Bn.'s advance from Helzenhoek to Mariaburg, Sgt. McKenna with his platoon led his Coy's advance from track junc. 403494 to the objective at 392486 all this area being heavily wooded and entrenched. He had been ordered to push on as quickly as possible and seize the objective by-passing opposition which did not directly threaten his axis. He carried out these orders with exemplary exactitude despite heavy Spandau fire which swept his route at several points. He thrust forward disregarding the enemy's fire and reached his objective in the minimum of time possible. Throughout this advance in extremely difficult country he showed the highest degree of leadership, initiative and skill. On several occasions he personally led his assault section across the open spaces that intersperse the woods, when these were covered by M.G. fire, at all times disregarding his own safety.

Finally when a very short distance from his objective his platoon came under a heavy mortar concentration, which inflicted 10 casualties – over a third of his platoon in a matter of seconds. Regardless of the fact that every member of his Platoon HQ had been hit around him, he retained complete control and seized his objective. He next personally tended all his casualties that were still living as all the Coy. S.B.s had become casualties except one, who was busy elsewhere. Sgt. McKenna's magnificent courage and example enabled the objective to be seized before the enemy had time to withdraw across the road and establish a fresh position. This N.C.O.'s disregard for his own safety and calmness in a critical situation undoubtedly largely contributed to the successful conclusion of the operation and are worthy of the highest praise.   *(L.G. 1.3.45)*

Mackenzie, Donald, Private
19139393, Seaforth Highlanders
For Malaya   *(L.G. 13.12.49)*

McKenzie, Gregor, M.M., Sergeant
2748467, Black Watch
M.E. 1942. P.O.W. Pool.
M.M. 15.5.42   *(L.G. 11.4.46)*

MacKenzie, Murdo, Sergeant
2817888, 4th Seaforth Highlanders
While his Battalion was holding forward positions in
the Moyenneville—Behen Sector during the period 30th
May to 1st June, Sgt. Mackenzie gave invaluable service
as Signalling Sergeant.

Heavy and frequent shelling made the maintenance
of telephonic communication between Battalion Headquarters and the forward companies a continual and
hazardous task, but by his untiring energy, his devotion
to duty and the splendid example he set, contact was
maintained almost entirely throughout.

This N.C.O. was wounded by shell fire while repairing
lines on the 1st June but he carried on without telling
anyone until his task was completed.
Recommended for M.M.   *(L.G. 18.10.40)*

McKenzie, Noel, Sergeant
NX 35589, 2/43 Australian Infantry Bn. (Immediate)
On 2nd October 1943, Sgt. McKenzie was in command
of a section of the Bn. Tank Attack Platoon, as part of a
fighting patrol against a large party of enemy at 632710
(Ref. Map. Satelberg 1/25,000).

When contact was made Sgt. McKenzie immediately
encircled boldly with his section. He personally led the
attack from the flank, against very heavy fire, with
coolness and great courage. When his section was
engaged by an L.M.G. on the right flank, he with
complete disregard for his own safety, advanced through
its fire and silenced it with his Owen gun, finally leading
his section to its objective. Although heavily outnumbered, this section, very largely due to Sgt.
McKenzie's example of personal courage and disregard
of danger, drove the enemy from the position, inflicting
many casualties. This engagement lasted for two hours.

On 3rd October 1943, Sgt. McKenzie commanded
his section as part of the platoon defensive area at 626684
(Ref. Map Satelberg 1/25,000), astride the coastal track.
In the face of repeated enemy attacks, of which there
were no less than six, over a period of nine hours, Sgt.
McKenzie, by constantly moving from section to section
with a cheery, confident and aggressive spirit, did much
towards the ultimate success of the engagement.
                                             (L.G. 30.3.44)

MacKenzie, Peter, Warrant Officer Cl. II (C.S.M.)
6142452, 1/6th Bn. East Surrey Regt.
On the 6th May 1943 during the attack on Frendj this
W.O. went forward under fire alone to bring in a wounded

man, at the same time locating an enemy post which he
silenced with a Bren gun. He saw a section held up by
fire on a flank, and finding it to be strong he directed the
fire of a tank on to the nearest post, collected a party of
four men, fixed bayonets and firing from the hip, killed
one Bosche, wounded two and captured about thirty who
surrendered. This W.O. displayed initiative of a very high
order throughout the action and considerable determination.   *(L.G. 22.7.43)*

McKinnon, Alexander, Sergeant (A/W.O.II (C.S.M.))
2981109, 8 Argyll & Sutherland Highlanders
(Kilkenzie, Argyll) (since killed in action)
On night 19th/20th November 1942 Sgt. MacKinnon was
in action with No. 15 Platoon during a raid carried out
by 'X' Coy. 8 A. & S.H. on a wood occupied by German
tanks and infantry. After the attack the platoon was
ordered to move to a R.V. some two miles off and were
subjected to machine gun fire which caused casualties.
Sgt. MacKinnon was last to leave and picked up a
wounded man 2986941 Cpl. Reid some 20 yards from
the enemy positions. Reid was hit in the chest and legs
and could not walk. Sgt. MacKinnon carried him back
to safety at the R.V. Cpl. Reid subsequently died in
hospital.

On 28th November 1942 8 A. & S.H. were engaged
in action against the main German position on road Sed
Jenane—Mateur. Sgt. MacKinnon was commanding No.
15 Platoon when 'X' Coy. moved right flanking in
support of the Van Gd. pinned down by machine gun
fire. Led by Sgt. MacKinnon 15 Platoon forced out two
German machine gun posts and then attacked a strong
point in a farm which dominated the centre of the valley.
His skilful leading and determination drove the enemy
out and with one section Sgt. MacKinnon occupied this
farm under enemy M.G. fire from both sides. He held it
for some time but was forced to withdraw. He prevented
the enemy recovering the farm and reoccupied it with
his platoon at dusk.

At Medjez-El-Bab on 28th/29th December 1942 Sgt.
MacKinnon took out a patrol of 25 men to hold a ridge
in front of Grenadier Hill. At 2300 hours approx. 60
Germans were seen moving onto this ridge which
provided excellent observation all round. Sgt.
MacKinnon ordered his patrol to hold their fire until at
20 or 30 yards. Fire was opened at short range and
approx. half were hit and fell. Sgt. MacKinnon went
forward with a section and captured an officer and two
men with a wireless set. The Germans withdrew leaving
a number of dead including one officer. Our own
casualties were one wounded. Valuable information was
obtained from prisoners.

Throughout the North African Campaign Sgt.
MacKinnon has shown coolness and courage of a high
order. His leadership, good judgement and control set
an example to all section and platoon commanders.
                                             (L.G. 23.9.43)

McKnight, William John Ross, Sergeant
C6078, Hast. & P.E.R., Canadian Infantry Corps
(Immediate)
'D' Coy. Hast & P.E.R., during the attack on Valguar-Nera, 17th July 1943, after an advance of 5 miles over mountainous country, occupied by night a position on a height overlooking the town. When dawn broke enemy machine gun fire from a feature 400 yards to the South caused casualties and made a reorganization necessary before the advance could continue.

The Coy. Comd. gave the order, but before it could be communicated, Sgt. McKnight with Tommy gun and Cpl. Lawson with rifle, on their own initiative started toward the enemy post. Utilizing the little cover available, they crawled down the hill, crossed at the run a 100 yard stretch of open ground in the valley and started the almost sheer ascent. Bursts of enemy machine gun fire struck the ground around them as they advanced.

Hauling themselves up hand over hand they ascended until within grenade range. Sgt. McKnight and Cpl. Lawson, skilfully throwing grenades, charged the post and cleared it with rifle and bayonet. Ten Germans were dead and two machine guns captured.

Through the initiative, courage and gallantry of Sgt. McKnight and Cpl. Lawson the company reorganized without loss and the advance continued.

(L.G. 23.12.43)

McKue, Douglas, Warrant Officer Cl. II
3052736, 2nd Bn. The Royal Scots Fusiliers
(Leamington Spa) (Periodic)
C.S.M. McKue has served with this Bn. since it joined the B.E.F. in 1939, and has seen action in France, Madagascar, Sicily, Italy and Germany. In the Anzio Beachhead he not only had charge of gun positions, but used to come up with the carrying parties night after night bringing food and amn. to the fwd. troops. At all times he has proved himself more than equal to every emergency which arose and with his long experience and knowledge of the enemy has been a tower or strength to platoon and Coy. Comds.

During the advance on the Elbe when only two offrs remained in the Coy. C.S.M. McKue controlled Coy. HQ and the reserve Platoon. During the attack on Hohenzeethen he showed the utmost dash and initiative and contributed largely to the success of that operation. In addition he found time to organise the evacuation of the wounded and the many P/Ws taken and to see to the replacement of the considerable amount of amn. expended. During the attack on Neu Dachau when the Coy. Comd. was wounded and the other offr. was separated from the rest of the Coy., C.S.M. McKue found himself in charge. He quickly and successfully consolidated in the town despite the darkness and the attacks of the enemy with mobile flak guns. He was able to assure the Comd. Officer when he arrived that the town would be held and instilled that determination into all the men about him. Again he found time to evacuate the wounded and P/Ws and to see that the amn. was distributed.

C.S.M. McKue represents the finest type of Warrant Officer. As Platoon Sgt. in a rifle Coy., A. Tk. Platoon Sgt. and C.S.M. in many varied actions he has proved a tower of strength to his officers and his own fine and fearless spirit has inspired his men to reach the high standard he has always maintained.

Recommended for M.M. *(L.G. 24.1.46)*

McLachlan, Horton Ford, Corporal
QX4934, 2/15 Australian Infantry Bn.
During an attack carried out by 2/15 Aust. Inf. Bn. on enemy positions at West Point 23 near Tel el Eisa on 1st September 1942 Corporal McLachlan showed great courage, dash and leadership.

McLachlan, who was in command of the rear section of his platoon, was ordered to attack an enemy post which was firing at his platoon from the right. Leading his section into the attack he bayoneted three enemy and subdued the post. He then took a Thompson sub machine gun from a wounded man in his section and led a further attack, in the face of Spandau fire, on another post 100 yards ahead which was enfilading his company. With his section he cleared out this position, himself killing the enemy machine-gunner and three others with his Thompson sub machine-gun.

Moving forward with the only two of his men left, McLachlan, assisted by covering fire from the right, assaulted another enemy post 200 yards ahead, throwing two grenades, which killed four enemy. Having by this time exhausted all his ammunition, he threatened four enemy (the crew of a Spandau) with his Thompson sub machine gun used as a club. One of these men seized McLachlan by the leg, but McLachlan got free by kicking him in the face, at the same time calling on one of his section to throw a grenade into the pit, which disposed of the four men in it.

The determination and fighting spirit of this N.C.O. were largely responsible for enabling his company to get on to its objective. *(L.G. 5.11.42)*

McLaughlin, Richard Osborne, Sergeant
NX.41139, 2/5 Aust. Cav. (Cdo) Sqn. (Immediate)
On 4th July 1945 near Balikpapan a troop of 2/5 Aust. Cav. Cdo. Sqn., was ambushed in a water course North of Sepinggang Airstrip by an enemy force of approximately forty employing light and heavy machine guns.

The two forward sections were trapped in this cross fire and Sjt. McLaughlin commanding another section instantly led his section to a flank and skilfully disposed them so that fire could be brought to bear on the enemy positions. For ninety minutes his section engaged the enemy at point blank range and thus permitted the other sections to withdraw.

During the engagement one of his men was wounded within twenty yards of an enemy machine-gun position. Sjt. McLaughlin advanced in the face of fire from three enemy machine guns, replying with bursts from his Owen sub-machine gun as he ran and carried his wounded comrade back to the safety of his own lines.

When the enemy attacked his position they were repelled with heavy losses. When the complete force had been extricated from the trap Sjt. McLaughlin fought a successful rearguard action for eight hundred yards across difficult country.

Sjt. McLaughlin's fearlessness, his control and his determination were an inspiration to his men in a situation fraught with great peril and requiring the highest leadership.
Recommended for M.M. B.E.M. 1.1.54 (L.G. 14.9.45)

McLean, Adam Kennedy, Corporal (A/Sgt.)
10602763, 46th Recce Regt., Reconnaissance Corps (Coatbridge)
On 26th August 1944 during the initial stage of the advance to the Gothic Line, Sgt. McLean was a member of a Scout Tp. which was given a line of hills as its axis of advance. The approach to the high ground was difficult and the Tp. sustained casualties from mines and shell-fire. They fought their was on to the Monte Bianco feature, where they came under heavy M.G. fire. By this time there was only one Heavy Armoured Car left and this with steering so damaged that it had been left further down the hill. Sgt. McLean realized that the fire power from this car was necessary and ran down the hill for it. By skilful driving he managed to get forward from one fire position to another and thus engage the enemy. Although by this time the shell fire was being directed towards himself. The Tp. eventually reached the top of the feature and were immediately counter-attacked; Sgt. McLean once more drove the car even closer to the top of the hill in order that its guns could be used against the enemy. Thus the attack was beaten off.

During the next day part of the Sqn. was in a harbour area waiting to go forward when heavy shell fire was brought on to them, causing casualties and setting alight two vehicles; both of which contained some ammunition. Disregarding the continued shelling and the exploding ammunition, Sgt. McLean carried several casualties into a nearby house, and then drove away seven other vehicles from the danger area.

Throughout both days, Sgt. McLean's conduct, skill and courage were an inspiration and an example to all, and deserving of the highest praise.
Recommended for M.M.   *(L.G. 8.2.45)*

MacLean, John Archibald, Sergeant
2824467, 5th Bn. Queen's Own Cameron Highlanders (Conon Bridge, Ross-shire) (Immediate)
During the heavy fighting against German troops on 14th July 1943 at Francofonte, Sergeant McLean consistently showed the highest personal courage and initiative in leading his platoon in battle. His bravery and disregard for danger culminated about 1700 hours, when the whole of his company was temporarily held up by an enemy

position consisting of two anti-tank guns, and infantry gun and light automatics. Sergeant McLean at once set about the engagement of this post by the fire power of his platoon. This done, he personally led the attack and went into the final assault himself with the bayonet, leading the charge and encouraging his men with the war cry of the Clan McLean.

As a result of his dash and bravery, the surviving enemy abandoned their position, leaving eight prisoners and all their weapons in our hands.

Quite apart from this specific act of gallantry, Sergeant McLean's leadership and distinguished conduct during the recent fighting in Sicily has been of the highest traditions of the Cameron Highlanders. *(L.G. 23.9.43)*

Maclean, John Somerville, Sergeant
2692917, 4 Border Regt., T.A.
Recommended for the award of the D.C.M. for conspicuous initiative and inspiring leadership.

Sjt. Maclean's Coy., carried in lorries, suddenly came under flanking fire at short range from houses in the village of Saveuse. The men immediately dismounted and took cover, but as sub-units had been split up to make the most of the transport accommodation some tactical disorganisation ensued.

Sjt. Maclean, quickly appreciating that heavy casualties could only be avoided by immediate offensive action, collected a handful of men, charged the nearest enemy with the bayonet at point blank range, and put them to flight with the loss to them of some prisoners.

Sjt. Maclean's unhesitating offensive, his coolness and his courage formed a fine inspiration to his men and were in great measure responsible for averting a very dangerous situation.
(L.G. 23.8.40, duplicated L.G. 22.10.40)

McLean, Norman, Warrant Officer Cl. II
D.16016, Fus. Mont Royal
After his capture during the Dieppe raid, McLean was sent to Stalag VIIIB (Lamsdorf), where he became the leader of the Escape Committee. Between July and October 1943, under his supervision, a tunnel 50 yards long was constructed, and through this fifteen P/W escaped at the beginning of October. In order to conceal the existence of the tunnel, the wire round the camp was cut.

On 21st October 1943 another fifteen P/W, including McLean escaped in the same manner, and after their exit the tunnel was to be closed until the following spring. Each of the escapers prior to his departure had been provided with forged documents and civilian clothing.

McLean travelled by train to Budapest, arriving on 26th October 1943. Here he found other P/W and, acting upon the instructions of an officer, arranged that all should be constantly ready for immediate evacuation by air.

When the Germans occupied Hungary of 19th March 1944, McLean was interned by Hungarian police at

Szigetvar. He escaped but was re-arrested and taken to Dulag 172 at Zemun. During the next month several unsuccessful attempts were made to get through the wire, but on 17th April 1944 with two other P/W he escaped from his German captors. After three months' service with the partisans, McLean finally encountered Allied forces on 20th July 1944.   *(L.G. 24.3.45)*

MacLennan, Duncan, Warrant Officer Cl. II (C.S.M.)
2816336, 4th Seaforth Highlanders T.A.
On 15th/16th May this W.O. showed great initiative and daring in getting withdrawal orders out to the several posts in different parts of a village. Enemy elements were in the village at the time and bombing and sniping made movement in the darkness very difficult. C.S.M. McLennan showed most commendable initiative and complete disregard of all danger. It is largely due to him that the withdrawal of his company was successfully effected.
Mid 11.10.45. (DCM announcement duplicated LG 22.10.40   *(L.G. 5.7.40)*

MacLeod, Alexander Ross, Sergeant
B.19629, 6 Cdn. Armd. Regt. (1H) (Immediate)
On 13th April 1945, 3 Troop of 'A' Sqn. of 6 Cdn. Armd. Regt. was supporting the leading Coy. of the West Nova Scotia Regt. in an attack aimed at securing the approaches to Apeldoorn. B 19629 Sgt. MacLeod was a crew comd. in this troop.

The attack was strongly opposed by HE and AP fire from several enemy SP guns and tanks as well as machine gun fire. In the initial stages of the attack the troop leader's tank was knocked out by AP fire and Sgt. MacLeod took over command of the troop. He immediately laid down smoke which allowed the troop leader and his crew to be safely evacuated from their burning tank. When at this point the attack bogged down, Sgt. MacLeod without hesitation, went forward on foot in the face of heavy shelling and machine gun fire to make a personal recce. Displaying great courage he went from spot to spot until he had pinpointed the enemy strong points which were holding up the advance. Upon returning he was able to so position his tanks that they were able to destroy the enemy positions and thus allow the infantry to continue their advance. During this phase this N.C.O.'s tank was hit by AP fire. Disregarding his personal safety he pressed forward to engage and destroy an A/Tk. gun and its supporting SP. His initiative at this point enabled the tank advance to be continued with a minimum of delay.

Later in the same attack our infantry were held up again at the fringes of Apeldoornshch Wood by an enemy tank. Although it was already last light and the tank gunners could no longer satisfactorily distinguish their targets, Sgt. MacLeod, displaying an utter disregard for the danger involved, again dismounted and crawled forward to within 150 yards of the Panther to determine its exact position. Returning to his own tank, he led it to

a position where it outflanked the enemy tank. By arranging a clever diversion with the other tanks in his troop he was able successfully to engage and destroy the enemy tank. The infantry were then able to move forward and make firm their final objective.

During this whole action Sgt. MacLeod displayed great initiative and determination. His outstanding display of courage was an inspiration to all ranks and as a result of the destruction he inflicted on the enemy the infantry were able to capture their objective with the minimum number of casualties and with the minimum of delay.   *(L.G. 21.7.45)*

MacLeod, Donald, Sergeant
2818541, 4th Bn. Seaforth Highlanders
This N.C.O. showed the greatest gallantry and devotion to duty in the attack against the Abbeville Bridgehead on June 4th. After his Platoon Officer became a casualty in the early stages, Sergeant McLeod led the platoon forward in the face of withering machine gun fire. As they advanced, every man fell but Sergeant McLeod carried on alone until severely wounded. He had then reached his objective.

During the two days and nights that followed this N.C.O. showed the greatest grit and determination in working himself back through enemy positions until he reached a point where he could be evacuated.
(L.G. 18.10.40)

McLeod, James Ronald, P.O.
J.89683, Royal Canadian Air Forces
Gazetted by Air Ministry   *(L.G. 12.6.45)*

McLoughlin, Michael, Sergeant (A/W.O.II (C.S.M.)
4340914, 7 Green Howards (Galashiels) (Immediate)
Mareth Line. Northern Sector.
On the night of 20th March 1943, Sjt. McLoughlin was A/C.S.M. to 'B' Coy., the forward Coy. in a Battalion attack on a strongly held enemy position.

The Company was held up at a minefield whilst the R.E. parties cleared a gap and bridged the Anti-Tank ditch and enemy shell and mortar fire was intense. Sjt. McLoughlin, regardless of his own safety was everywhere rallying the men and inspiring them with his indomitable spirit.

The heavy fire was again encountered across the Anti-Tank ditch, but Sjt. McLoughlin pushed on undeterred, shepherding his party through to the objective.

When the Company had rallied on the objective, Sjt. McLoughlin was again around among the men under heavy fire exhorting them and inspiring them with courage and confidence. He was everywhere he was wanted, continually urging them to greater efforts.

When day broke the Company was in an exposed position and still subjected to heavy shell, mortar and M.G. fire, but throughout the day Sjt. McLoughlin was an inspiration to all who saw him with his cheerfulness, courage and confidence.   *(L.G. 1.6.43)*

McMahon, James Thomas, Bombardier
NX.40595, 3 Aust. A. Tk. Regt.
Gallant conduct and outstanding devotion to duty.

Whilst in action in vicinity of Pt. 33 (Ref. Map El Alamein, 1:50,000, square 875 301) on 10th July 1942, during an enemy counter-attack on our positions, Bdr. McMahon, then a Gunner acting as No. 1, towed his gun fwd. to Pt. 33 and engaged enemy tanks.

Although 3 members of his crew were wounded and he himself wounded in the leg and with two fingers injured by the recoil of the gun, he fought his gun with superb courage and spirit under extreme difficulty and succeeded in destroying 2 enemy tks. He continued to fight until the enemy was repulsed and stayed with his gun until eventually relieved and ordered to the nearest R.A.P.   *(L.G. 15.10.42)*

McMahon, Norman John, Private (A/Cpl.)
B.132561, Royal Canadian Regiment
Ref. Map 1/50,000 Italy Sheet 101 – III Rimini

On 16th September 1944 during the battle of the Rimini Gap, The Royal Canadian Regt. attacked the Northwest corner of the Rimini airfield (MR 8793). Private (Acting Corporal) Norman John McMahon was commanding 1 Section, 16 Platoon, 'D' Coy. This section was the leading section of the company attack, the objective being a house (MR 878935).

On approaching the objective, the company came under heavy M.G. fire from another house (MR 877934). Immediately on his own initiative, Corporal McMahon with his section assaulted this house. Leading his men across ground completely swept by fire of the enemy, estimated at one platoon in strength, and despite their stubborn resistance, cleared the house. Twelve Germans were killed, two were captured and the remainder fled in disorder. Corporal McMahon personally killed five or six of the enemy with his T.M.C. and showed himself to be a fearless leader as he assaulted the house at the head of his section. Corporal McMahon then pushed on to the company objective, where he again succeeded in killing six or seven more of the enemy and took a key position where he engaged the enemy until the remainder of his company consolidated.

His initiative, personal bravery, outstanding example and skill in handling his section contributed largely to the subsequent success of the operation. As on three previous occasions the gallantry of this N.C.O. has been an inspiration to his men and he has upheld the best traditions of the Canadian Infantry.   *(L.G. 27.1.45)*

McMahon, Robert Allan, Lance Corporal
B127987, Calgary Highlanders (Immediate)
On 8th February 1945, 'A' Coy. of Calgary Highlanders, the right forward company in the initial phase of the attack to capture Wyler, Germany, was given the task of clearing the village of Vossendahl with, as final objective, sealing off the enemy's escape route from Wyler.

The section led by Lance Corporal McMahon ran into an unmarked area, heavily mined with Schumines and all, except this N.C.O., became casualties from mines and enemy mortar fire. The task allotted the section was to clear two buildings on the edge of the village of Vossendahl. Realizing that if these buildings were not cleared the success of his company's effort would be jeopardized, L/Cpl. McMahon went forward alone through the remainder of the minefield, cleared the buildings, killing and wounding a number of the enemy and taking prisoner one officer and twenty-two other ranks. Had he not succeeded, it is doubtful if his company could have reached it objective without great loss of lives and time.

Being alone he had to evacuate the prisoners himself. One of the prisoners, an officer, attempted to stir up insurrection but this Corporal McMahon stopped with his fists. He marched the prisoners back through the minefield, handed them over and returned once more through the minefield, rejoined his platoon and went with them to the final objective.

L/Cpl. McMahon displayed great courage, initiative and unselfish devotion to duty throughout the entire operation and set an example which was an inspiration to his company.
Recommended for M.M.   *(L.G. 12.5.45)*

McManus, Thomas, Corporal
63336, 21 N.Z. Bn. (Immediate)
On the night 23rd/24th October at Miteiriya Ridge after both Platoon Commander and Sjt. had been wounded, he rallied the remainder of his platoon and led them under very heavy fire. Held up at one stage by an M.G. post, he went resolutely forward and captured the gun killing the crew. When his Coy. moved forward to exploit success, Cpl. McManus with his section captured 30 prisoners and demolished three enemy field guns. Throughout the entire action he was a fine example and inspiration to his men.   *(L.G. 28.1.43)*

McMillan, William, Warrant Officer Cl. III (Pl.S.M.)
(A/W.O.II) (C.S.M.)
3308515, 2nd Bn. Highland Light Infantry (Maryhill, Glasgow) (Immediate)
During the attack on Sanchil, on 17th March 1941 when the company came under heavy fire, this W.O. was wounded and severely shaken by a shell which burst very close to him: nevertheless he remained at duty and gave the men a magnificent example of determination and indifference to danger.

During the attack on Railway Bumps on the 25th March 1941 A/C.S.M. McMillan was again conspicuous. Finally in the seizing of Plateau during the Battle of Massawa, this W.O. was an inspiring example to all in his dash and determination to close with the enemy, when his company seized its objective capturing many prisoners and Machine Guns.   *(L.G. 18.7.41)*

McMillan, William, Warrant Officer Cl. III (Pl.S.M.)
2747338, 1 Queen's Own Cameron Highlanders
On 21st May this W.O. showed great courage and set an example to his men when organising the withdrawal under heavy machine gun fire of his platoon. He was the last to leave the position having organised evacuation of his wounded.   *(L.G. 22.10.40)*

McMullen, Senaca Lent, Sergeant
H.19165, Queens Own Cameron Highlanders of Canada
1. Capture.
I was captured at Dieppe on 19th August 1942.
2. Camps in which imprisoned:
Verneuil (N.W. Europe 1:250,000, Sheet 7, R 0039) from shortly after capture till 28th August 1942.

Stalag VIII B (Lansdorf) (Germany 1:100,000, Sheet 117, 6900) from 1st September 1942. I went into hospital with dysentry on 6th September, remaining till 23rd October, when I was put into Block 6. On 7th March 1943 I changed indentities with a Private and went out on a working party.

Working party at Bedzin (Sheet 118, 8177). Here I worked in a coal mine. On 30th April 1943 I made an attempted escape. I was captured on 5th May.

Stalag VIII B (Lansdorf) from 6th May till 20th July 1943.

Working party at Glatz (Sheet 116, 0590). At Glatz I made an attempted escape on 26th November 1943. I was recaptured on 27th November and sent back to Glatz, remaining there till 19th December.

Stalag VIII A (Gorlitz) (Sheet 102, 9968), from 19th December 1943. On 5th January 1944 I declared my true identity.

Stalag VIII B (Lansdorf), from 5th January till about 18th February 1944.

Stalag II D (Stargard) (Sheet 38, 0312), from about 18th February 1944. On 28th May I again changed identities with a Private and was sent on a working party.

Working party at Teschendorf (Sheet 39, 3033), from 28th May 1944 till escape on 9th June. I escaped with Pte. Nelson (S/P.G.(G) 2056), who had also changed his identity at Stargard.
3. Camp Conditions:
(a) Stalag VIII B (Lansdorf).
I had my hands tied for 12 hours daily, with a break of one hour at noon for soup from 23rd October 1942 till 2 December 1942. The ropes were then replaced by handcuffs and chains, which I wore until I changed my identity on 7th March 1943.

I was punished in early November 1942 for having loosened the ropes around my wrists. The punishment was that I had to stand with my nose and toes touching a wall for two hours. My hands were tied behind my back during this time.

A week later I received eight hours of the same punishment with a break of 15 minutes for soup. I was punished because I had visited another compound,

contrary to orders. During the time I was standing against the wall, I was twice struck across the shoulders with a bayonet because I was not actually touching the wall.

It was usual to see at least a dozen men at a time being punished in this way during October and November 1943. Despite the hardships, morale in the Camp was very high.
(b) Stalag II D (Stargard).
The Russian P/W at this Camp were ill-nourished and subjected to severe beatings. An average of three or four died each day as a result of malnutrition and ill-treatment. The treatment of British P/W was reasonable. Morale against the Canadian, French, Serbian, and Polish P/W was very high. Italian P/W were very despondent.
4. Attempted Escapes:
(a) On 30th April 1943 Sgt. Adams, Royal Regt. of Canada, Pte. Gledhill, Queens Own Cameron Highlanders of Canada and I climbed over the fence of the enclosure of the working camp at Bedzin (Sheet 118, 8177). Sgt. Adams and I had changed our identities with Privates at Stalag VIII B in order to get on the working party at Bedzin. We walked across country after our escape. We skirted Bedzin to the South, and on the night of 2nd May we got on a goods train East of Bedzin. We passed through Samkowize (9183) and at daylight hid in some woods until the following evening (3 May). We got on another goods train and continued towards Warsaw for a distance of approx. 20 kms. We hid in a wood until the following evening, when we again got on a train, but were discovered by a railway employee. We succeeded in getting away. Later that night we got on to another goods train and travelled a short distance. At daylight on 5th May a Polish railway employee entered the compartment where we were. He informed us that he was a member of the Polish underground movement. He brought us bread and water. He also gave each of us 300 zlotty. He said that he would help us to get to Turkey as railway workers, and advised us not to attempt to get to Danzig alone, as we had intended. At this time we were still in uniform. He told us to remain in the railway compartment, the train being in a siding, until that evening, but shortly after he left us an engine moved the coach in which we were for a distance of approx. five or six kms., where it was left in a siding. About 1100 hrs a gendarme entered the coach and discovered us. We were searched and taken to the police station, but after a few hours we were moved to a Russian camp in the neighbourhood and put into a cell, where we remained until the following day (6th May). On this day we were taken to Stalag VIII B (Lansdorf). We were punished with 14 days' solitary confinement, with bread and water. We maintained our false identities, and upon release from cells we were put into the Arbeits compound.

(b) On 20th July 1943 I was sent to Glantz (Sheet 116, 0590) on a working party. On 26th November I left the camp by climbing over the fence at night. I got on a goods train travelling towards Vienna and was discovered by a railway employee about 100 hrs next day. I was handed over to the police and taken back to Glatz. I was punished with seven days' solitary confinement.

5. Escape:

On 9th June 1944, Cpl. Nelson and I escaped from the house where our working party was accommodated at Teschendorf (Sheet 39, 3033). We got into the enclosure after dark by loosening the bars across a window. We then cut through the enclosure fence, which was patrolled by sentries. We walked along the main road to Freienwalde (Sheet 38, 2225) where we arrived at 0600 hrs on 10th June. As we had a wait of two hours for a train to Stargard, we decided to hid in a wood on the outskirts of the town. At 0745 hrs. we started walking to the railway station, and on the way we were stopped by a policeman. He had noticed that our boots were wet, and he wanted to know who we were and where we had been. We showed him our false identity papers, which indicated that we were Swedes working in Germany, and told him that we had just come through the woods from the farm where we were working, and also that we were going to Stargard (Sheet 38, 0312) for a day's holiday. He appeared to be satisfied , and I asked him at what time the train departed for Stargard. He told me, and we continued on our way to the station, where we arrived without further incident. I bought two single (third class) tickets to Stargard and we got on a train a few minutes later, arriving in Stargard about 0930 hours. We walked around the town for about half an hour and then went back to the station, where I purchased two tickets (third class) to Stettin. We then went into the waiting room and we remained there until the arrival of the Stettin train at 1100 hrs. We got on the train and had our identity papers examined by an Army Feldwebel shortly afterwards. He asked for our authority to travel, and we showed him our travel permits. He then enquired whether any other occupant of the carriage could speak Swedish, but no-one was able to do so. He then left us.

The train on which we were travelling did not go into Stettin, but by-passed it. I discovered this after a time. We got off the train at a small station (place unknown), where I purchased two tickets to Stettin. The train arrived within a few minutes, and we travelled (third class) to Stettin, where we arrived at 1430 hrs.

On arrival at Stettin we had to show our Ausweise at the station barrier. We passed through without trouble and walked around the town for about 15 minutes, and then returned to the station, where I purchased two tickets (third class) to Pasewalk (Sheet 37, 3331). We then went into the station cafe and I bought some beer. We waited in the cafe until 1615 hrs, when we got on the train for Pasewalk and arrived there at 1730 hrs. We walked into a park in the town and sat there until 1830 hrs., when we went back to the station and I purchased two tickets (third class) to Swinehunde (Sheet 22, 5176).

The train for Swinehunde left about 1900 hrs., and we arrived in Swinehunde at 2130 hrs. We walked to the Western outskirts of the town and hid in a wood until 0800 hrs. on 11th June. We then walked into the town and wandered around until 1100 hrs., when we met a French P/W who directed me to an address which I had. We followed his directions and arrived at a place where we were given food and shelter until 14th June. During these three days we made daily journeys to the water-front in search of a suitable ship for Sweden. On 14th June we went on board a ship, and arrived in Trelleborg near Malmo, Sweden, on 1st July 1944. (L.G. 28.9.44)

MacNab, Donald George, Sergeant
2124, 6 N.Z. Field Company (Immediate)
S/Sgt. MacNabb was the leader of an organised escape party which left Greece for Turkey in October. Every detail of the escape was carried out by S/Sgt. MacNabb himself. He managed to hire a boat, the money for which he obtained by collection from various Greek helpers. He collected together a party of escapers and sailed for Turkey. The skipper of the boat endeavoured to betray them and MacNabb took charge. He navigated the boat and reached Turkey successfully.

The party unfortunately landed in a closely guarded Military Zone. By skilful manœuvring and forced marching he managed to get his party right through the military area before being captured by the Turks.

Whilst in Greece S/Sgt. MacNabb ran an 'Intelligence Bureau' in Athens for the collection of military information. On leaving Greece he collated all this and concealed it inside the lining of his clothing. It was discovered by the Turks during a thorough search and confiscated. MacNabb later managed to get the papers back and eventually passed them to the Military Attaché. Through the enterprise and inititative of this N.C.O. a great deal of valuable information reached G.S.I., Middle East.
M.C. 23.11.44   *(L.G. 26.3.42)*

McNea, Ernest, Warrant Officer Cl. II (C.S.M.)
4611239, 1st Bn. Duke of Wellington's Regt. (Halifax)
(since killed in action)
On 4th February 1944, 'B' Coy., 1st Bn. D.W.R. was holding a position on the left flank of the battalion in the left sector of the Anzio beach head. From 0300 hours until 1630 hours the enemy put in continued attacks on this Company's position. These attacks were successfully repulsed, until finally No. 4 Platoon was overrun with the loss of the Platoon Comd. This enemy success opened to the them the Coy's position, and if not dealt with promptly, would have allowed them to dominate another rifle company and battalion HQ, with possibly very serious effect.

At this time the O.C. 'B' Coy. was engaged with the enemy away from his HQ and no other officer remained with the Coy. C.S.M. McNea appreciated the gravity of the threat, and immediately organised a counter-attack drawing the personnel from his own Coy. HQ, a much depleted platoon of his own Coy., and men from other units in the vicinity. He personally led the attack, which he conducted with skill and great determination, finally driving the enemy from their recently won position, inflicting severe losses upon them.

Later, the battalion was ordered to withdraw, and had it not been for this action by C.S.M. McNea, the ability of the rifle Companies and Battalion HQ to do so may have been rendered impossible by the presence of the enemy behind them.

By his initiative, coolness and high personal courage, C.S.M. McNea inspired his men and undoubtedly prevented an enemy success which may have had serious and far reaching results. *(L.G. 15.6.44)*

McNulty, Alan Barry, Sergeant
3411264, Royal Australian Infantry Regt.
For Vietnam *(L.G. 2.4.70)*

McParlan, Joseph, Warrant Officer Cl. II (C.S.M.)
3649956, [...]th Bn. (Lancs) Parachute Regt. Army Air Corps (London, E.4)
He was dropped in error 10 miles from his D.Z. Unperturbed he collected other men also dropped astray and organised them into an effective fighting force although cut off from all possible help. He carried out raids on the enemy area, captured many prisoners while causing great disorg–anisation.

With complete disregard to his own safety he disguised himself in civilian clothes and though speaking no French or German, passed through the enemy lines and brought invaluable information to his battalion headquarters and organised help for his party.

He returned and directed a raiding party on to enemy A.F.V.s but found that his force had dispersed in his absence. Still in plain clothing he again returned safely though the enemy lines and reported for duty with his battalion.

All this time he was without rest or sleep.
Recommended for M.C. B.E.M. 8.6.44 (L.G. 19.10.44)

McPhee, Albert Roy, Warrant Officer Cl. II (C.S.M.)
B54652, Algonquin Regt. (Immediate)
On the night 26/27th February 1945 Alq Regt. with under comd. 29 Cdn. Armd. Recce Regt. was ordered to seize and hold the high ground in the Hochwald Forest gap at 036407. The attack was to be completed by first light and the adv. to the objective was to be made over boggy ground, through one of the main enemy def. lines. On the way to their F.U.P. 'B' Coy. was pinned down by intense enemy M.G. fire and it appeared that the adv. would be delayed. Without hesitation C.S.M. McPhee left his cover and on foot led one of the sp. tks. fwd. over 300 yards of open ground to a position from which neutralizing fire could be brought down on enemy positions. He then returned to his Coy. mounted the leading tank and led the force through heavy enemy fire over three prepared anti-tk. obstacles onto the objective. There can be no doubt that the initiative and leadership

displayed by this N.C.O. greatly aided in the successful capture of the objective without loss of valuable time. C.S.M. McPhee's courage and complete disregard for personal safety was an inspiration to all ranks in his Coy. and a magnificent example to the entire bn.
Recommended for V.C. *(L.G. 12.5.45)*

MacPhillips, Patrick, Warrant Officer Cl. II (C.S.M.)
2973389, Argyll & Sutherland Highlanders
No citation *(L.G. 30.1.40?)*

MacPhillips, Patrick, D.C.M., Warrant Officer Cl. II (C.S.M.) **Bar**
2973389, Argyll & Sutherland Highlanders
At Alam el Dab near Sidi Barrani on 10th Dec. 1940 CSM McPhillips, by his complete disregard for his own personal safety, set a fine example of courage to all ranks of his company. During an attack on a heavily defended position CSM McPhillips was the first of his company to reach the enemy lines. Wounded early in the action and suffering considerable pain he remained at his post and by his cheerful spirit and entire disregard of danger was an inspiration to his company.

When the battalion objective was taken CSM McPhillips in spite of his wounds came forward and made a personal report to his Commanding Officer. He was then sent back by his C.O. to have his wounds attended to. After his wounds had been dressed he again returned to his post and remained with his company until finally ordered to the rear by his C.O. at 1100 hrs. the following day. *(L.G. 25.4.41)*

McQueen, Edward James Everitt, Sergeant
21828, 7 N.Z. Field Coy.
Throughout the Libyan battle until his evacuation was ordered Sgt. McQueen displayed outstanding courage and inspiring leadership as a result of which heavy casualties and transport losses were prevented. On 3rd Dec 41 when he was in charge of road work near Menastir the 22nd Bn. was attacked and the transport was being rushed down the road. Heavy artillery and machine-gun fire was encountered and drivers were leaving their trucks, control was being lost, and the road was becoming blocked with lines of vehicles. Sgt. McQueen realising the seriousness of the position immediately took control and, displaying a total disregard for personal safety and refusing to leave when himself was wounded, soon had some of the drivers back and damaged trucks were quickly moved aside to allow the remaining traffic to pass and disperse. He then turned his attention to wounded personnel. Despite his wound he carried on and again on the following day was responsible for saving transport under almost similar conditions between Menastir and Capuzzo. Sgt. McQueen was at all times an example and an inspiration to all who came in contact with him.
Recommended for M.M. M.I.D. 30.12.41
(L.G. 19.3.42)

MacQueen, John Hugh, Warrant Officer Cl. II (C.S.M.)
F55611, Canadian Infantry Corps
N.W.E.   *(L.G. 24.1.46)*

McQuillan, Vincent Daniel, Sergeant
QX 4682, 6 Aust. Cav.
On 5th January 1941 at Bardia Sgt. McQuillan showed
great courage and coolness in an attack on a strong post
in the Southern defences. He captured 60 prisoners at
pistol point and showed great dash and initiative
throughout the action. The success of the attack was
largely due to his resolute leadership and entire disregard
of danger.   *(L.G. 9.5.41)*

McQuoid, William James, Lance Corporal
6460926, 2nd Bn. Royal Fusiliers (London, S.W.17)
During the attack on the strong point at Sidi Abdullah
on 19th April 1943, the Coy. met intense opposition in
the way of A/Tank Gun fire, machine guns and grenades
from well constructed fortifications. Without hesitation
L/C McQuoid dashed forward towards an enemy
machine gun and first fired at the crew with his rifle,
killing at least two men. He followed up this charge by
standing on the parapet and lobbing a grenade down into
the trench. He withdrew slightly and took another
grenade from one of our injured men, then returned to
the parapet and hurled it amongst the enemy. Immediately after this he was wounded by another grenade
which was thrown at him from a nearby trench.

L/Cpl. McQuoid's action silenced the Machine Gun,
gave the Company a moment's respite which enabled it
to recover and sweep along the right flank and get into a
position from which we were able to drive out the enemy
from the remaining trenches and later consolidate our
position. In the opinion of his Coy. Comd. it would have
been almost impossible to achieve this had it not been
for L/Cpl. McQuoid's heroism, and many more men
would certainly have lost their lives.
Recommended for V.C.   *(L.G. 22.7.43)*

McRae, Martin Tetakhi, M.B.E., Warrant Officer Cl. I
39098, 28 NZ (Maori) Bn. (Immediate)
During the attack on Cassino WO I McRae displayed
outstanding bravery and devotion to duty during the
whole operation.

On one occasion he personally rounded up several
prisoners in daylight under heavy machine gun fire and
then, calling up a tank, he advanced with one of his
English speaking prisoners and through the prisoner
called out to all enemy in the block of buildings to
surrender or he would have them blasted out. Over 60
prisoners were taken without loss.

On other occasions he supervised the replenishment
of ammunition to all Coys. under heavy enemy fire and
still under fire was directly responsible for the removal
of a number of our wounded to safety.

In all operations he has shown the utmost bravery,
determination and devotion to duty.

M.B.E. 1.1.43   *(L.G. 3.8.44)*

McTier, Donald Nelson, Lance Corporal
7901807, 4 Royal Tank Regt.
On November 23rd 1941, during the fighting after the
break out from Tobruk, L/Cpl. McTier was gunner of
Capt. Gardner's tank when that officer went to the
assistance of two armoured cars of the K.D.G.s. These
cars were halted near an enemy strong point known as
'Wolf,' and were being shelled to pieces at close range.
(Ref. Map 1:250,000, Egypt & Cyrenaica, Salum—
Torbruch, Sheet 3, about 426417). Capt. Gardner directed
his tank up to one of the cars, and dismounting, set about
fixing a tow rope to pull the car away. Finding the officer
commanding the car lying beside it desperately wounded,
he lifted him into the car and gave the signal to tow. As
the vehicles moved away the towrope shot away. Capt.
Gardner therefore returned to the car and removing the
wounded officer from it carried him to his tank where
he placed him on the outside and drove away holding
the wounded officer on. During this time Capt. Gardner
was wounded in two places. For this operation Capt.
Gardner was awarded the Victoria Cross. During the
above operation L/Cpl. McTier as gunner replied to the
enemy fire which was intense. Both small arms and anti-
tank fire plastered the Matilda tank. Then the loader, who
is also the wireless operator was killed. There was
nobody in the tank now except the driver and McTier.
The orders from Capt. Gardner outside the tank had to
be passed to the driver who, being closed down and with
the rear of his tank to the car for towing, was unable to
see Capt. Gardner's signals. McTier appreciated the
situation rapidly and disentangling himself and the
microphone leads from the dead operator, and covered
with blood, he reared himself up into the open cupola
where he saw for the first time exactly what was going
on outside. There he remained, head and shoulders
exposed with complete indifference to his own safety,
in order to attend to his tank commander's directions.
With so grim an object lesson at his feet, a less hardy
soldier might have had some misgivings, but Capt.
Gardner told me he saw McTier in the cupola,
microphone in hand, acknowledging his signals with a
wave of the other as he passed them down to the driver,
and all the time Pandemonium reigned. It was thus that
a classical example of towing was carried out under the
most trying possible conditions, yet with a facility
reminiscent of a drill operation. L/Cpl. McTier, by his
cool courage gave the essential and unfaultering
assistance required by his tank commander at a time
when every moment was vital. Indeed, McTier's
courageous disregard for his own safety coupled with
his skill in directing his tank into the most convenient
positions for the operation in hand bore an influence on
that operation which cannot be exaggerated, and at the
same time set an example which will rank high in the
annals of his Regiment and of The Service. Again, on
December 15th 1941 L/Cpl. McTier was wireless

operator to Lt. Pope, who commanded one of twelve tanks supporting the Buffs in an all day battle at Pt. 204 about ten miles S.W. of El Gazala. The enemy stood back and shelled with artillery and tanks for some time during which time Lt. Pope was killed when the cupola of his tank was blown off. L/Cpl. McTier then took command of the tank and fought it with conspicuous success for the rest of the day although the crew was now only three and the cupola was gone. Just as the position was about to be overrun, the OC Buffs ordered the three surviving tanks to fight their way out if they could, McTiers was one of those which succeeded in doing so entirely due to this young N.C.O.'s untiring energy and skill.

Throughout the operations November 21st–December 16th 1941, L/Cpl. McTier set a high standard of initiative, courage and skill backed by a fearlessness in hot corners which was a fine example for any A.F.V. crew.   *(L.G. 25.9.47)*

MacVeigh, Frederick, Sergeant
D. 26538, 22 Cdn. Armd. Regt. (Immediate)
On 4th April 1945, Sgt. McVeigh, commanding a force of 4 light tanks, was given the task of reconnoitring a possible bridgehead into the town of Almelo. The town was known to be strongly held and defended by self-propelled guns. He proceeded to the West side of Almelo and, under a hail of machine gun and small arms fire, personally reconnoitred the site of two blown bridges. He maintained covering fire on the bridges and so aggressive was his display that the enemy shifted his major strength to this sector and another force was enabled to enter the East side of the town. He then proceeded to a bridge on the N.E. side of Almelo. Barring his route were several strong points and anti-tank positions. Sgt. McVeigh pressed on through a terrific concentration of fire. Utilizing a railway bridge and a partially demolished bridge over two water obstacles, he coolly circumvented the worst of the anti-tank fire. Within sight of his objective, two of his tanks were knocked out by anti-tank guns and he came under the most intense fire from a building used as Gestapo Headquarters. Sgt. McVeigh instantly dismounted and organised the tank crews in a ground role. Under intense fire, he crossed open ground to bring forward his covering tanks and attacked the enemy with such verve that the Gestapo HQ was reduced and many prisoners taken, including the Comd. Offr. and second-in-command. Throughout, this N.C.O. was constantly exposed as he moved in the open, exhorting and directing his troops. Sgt. McVeigh then quickly sighted his force to cover the bridge. He called down fire from the heavy tanks in daring proximity to his own position, but this succeeded in destroying the defended houses on the far side of the canal and driving off the self propelled guns. Under determined counter-attacks he maintained his position for four hours until support arrived. As a result of his action the A. & S.H. of C. were able to establish a

bridgehead and the impetus of the brigade advance was sustained. Had it not been for the determination, initiative and inspiring bravery of this N.C.O., an infantry attack would have been necessary to establish this bridgehead, with resultant heavy casualties and loss of vital time.
M.I.D. 9.8.45   *(L.G. 11.8.45)*

McVeigh, Patrick, Sergeant (actg.)
3853876, Loyal Regt., No. 4 Commando (Kilmarnock)
At Flushing on 1st November 1944, this NCO in command of a sub-section, went to the assault of the Naval Barracks, defended by approximately 60 enemy. With great skill and pertinacity L/Sgt McVeigh harassed the enemy while searching for a means of breaking in. When engaged from the houses surrounding the barracks he detached himself and disposed of a least two enemy pockets of three to six men with machine-guns, thus paving the way for the break-in to be made. He then led the assault on the barracks which he cleared, accounting for 25 enemy killed and wounded and taking between 30 and 40 prisoners. L/Sgt McVeigh showed personal bravery to an outstanding degree, and by his cunning leadership attained his objective at the cost of only one man killed, though fighting throughout against great odds.   *(L.G. 22.3.45)*

Mahoney, L., Warrant Officer Cl. II (C.S.M.)
3440518, 6th Lancashire Fusiliers
During the temporary absence of his Coy. Comd., he took command of HQ Coy. and organised the position at Marquaine for defence. During the counter-attack on the Canal North of Tournai he discovered a German post and with the assistance of Major Crux captured four prisoners and a light machine gun. Later he undertook a general recce with Capt. Easton, the Adjutant, and then organised a support post behind 'B' Coy. which he fed and supplied with amn. in a very able manner. During the final operations preceding the withdrawal from the Escaut he held these posts until 0500 hrs. the following day, and then withdrew his men and guns intact at the time he was ordered to withdraw. His activity and cheerful bearing was conspicuous throughout the whole engagement, and were a fine example to his men.
(L.G. 11.7.40)

Maidens, Donald Hayes, Corporal (actg.)
*A.44319, P.P.C.L.I., Canadian Infantry Corps
(Immediate)*
Ref. Maps: Deventer 1/25,000 Sheet No. 3702, Zutphen 1/25,000 Sheet No. 3803.

On 11th April 1945, Princess Patricia's Canadian Light Infantry made an assault crossing of the Ijssel River. The two assaulting companies, 'D' Company right and 'C' Company left, successfully reached their objectives in area of MR 936024 forming a small bridgehead through which it was planned that 'A' Company and 'B' Company would pass. A44319 Private

(A/Corporal) Maidens was acting platoon sergeant of 15 Platoon, 'C' Company.

In order that 'A' Company and 'B' Company could reach their objectives quickly it was essential that the routes they were to take be cleared of the enemy. Volunteering to clear the route to be taken by 'B' Company, which was to pass through to 'C' Company, A/Corporal Maidens went forward alone, in daylight over the flat open country and for a total distance of no less than 1,000 yards under fire from snipers and machine guns to capture 2 machine gun posts and a total of 12 prisoners. A little while later, A/Corporal Maidens and another Corporal charged and captured a machine gun post which was bringing down intense fire on 'D' Company area and 'A' Company forming-up place. A/ Corporal Maidens personally killed the machine gunner and took 2 snipers prisoner. By these gallant actions, in addition to almost single-handedly accounting for 3 machine gun posts and 14 prisoners, A/Corporal Maidens made it possible for 'A' Company and 'B' Company to get on to their objectives quickly and thus maintained the momentum of the assault.

At approximately 1700 hours on 13th April 1945, P.P.C.L.I. attacked to the South West with the object of breaking out of the bridgehead. As 'C' Company were advancing to their objective (MR 894005) they came under very heavy machine gun fire. A/Corporal Maidens moved a section into a right flanking position from where he led an assault over 300 yards of ground, swept by heavy machine gun fire, to overcome the strong point and enable the advance to proceed. A/Corporal Maidens personally killed one officer and two other ranks and captured three prisoners during the attack on this well defended position before he himself was severely wounded and evacuated.

During the period of time from the crossing of the Ijssel until he was wounded, A/Corporal Maidens was an inspiration not only to his platoon but to the whole company. The complete disregard he showed for his own safety, and his leadership under fire, contributed greatly to the success of both the operations described. His courage was of the highest order and his actions in the face of the enemy completely fearless, and in keeping with the finest traditions of the service. *(L.G. 23.6.45)*

Maidment, George, Private
WX 4227, 2/16 Australian Infantry Bn. (Immediate)
On 30th August 'A' Coy. and 'B' Coy., of which Pte. Maidment is a member, were ordered to clear the Abuari ridge where the enemy were strongly established and from which two Coys. of 53 Bn. had been unable to dislodge them on the previous day.

The attack had to be made up a steep wooded slope against carefully prepared and camouflaged positions.

Maidment's platoon encountered a very strongly defended Japanese position and was held up.

Casualties began to mount and Maidment's section leader was killed.

Disregarding heavy automatic rifle and machine gun fire, Maidment coolly collected grenades from the pouches of his dead section leader and dashed up the slope towards the enemy positions. He was badly wounded in the chest and lung almost at once but destroyed several of the near machine gun posts and continued his onslaught until all his grenades were used and he was ordered to rejoin his platoon.

The enemy immediately began to press forward. Maidment then picked up his section leader's Tommy Gun and, showing an entire disregard for cover and for his own safety, he held up the enemy with accurate fire until his amn. was exhausted.

This action allowed his platoon time to withdraw and reform, and was directly responsible for the infliction of severe casualties on the Japanese and the prevention of what seemed inevitable and heavy losses on our side.

It was only after all his amn. had been expended that Maidment was prevailed upon to rejoin his comrades.

Although suffering from loss of blood and exhaustion he refused all assistance to the rear. On arrival at the R.A.P. he collapsed and was evacuated to Hospital as a stretcher case.

Maidment's unsurpassed courage, fortitude and devotion to duty were an inspiring example.
Recommended for V.C.   *(L.G. 4.2.43)*

Maier, James, Private
A.21509, Essex Scottish, 4 Cdn. Inf. Bde.
Operation Jubilee—Dieppe Area—19th August 1942.

In a day filled with incidents of heroism, Pte. Maier set a fine example of courage and initiative and soldierly leadership. Under heavy fire he engaged enemy positions with an L.M.G. Although wounded he persisted in his attack. Wounded a second time, more seriously, he nevertheless used an A.Tk. rifle with telling effect against two posts which had defied small arms fire.

Both of these silenced, he continued to snipe successfully with this weapon until the time of withdrawal, when he collapsed from wounds and loss of blood. Believed to be dead, he was thrown overboard, but recovered and was picked up from the water by another craft. His actions throughout showed the highest devotion to duty and were an inspiration to his comrades.
(L.G. 2.10.42)

Maile, Edward, Sergeant
320533, 10th Hussars, Royal Armoured Corps
At Huy on 27th May, 1940, Sgt. Maile found his tank unable to be manœuvred to attack enemy in position. He therefore dismounted and on his own initiative engaged an enemy machine gun post with his revolver, killing and scattering its crew. Subsequently Sgt. Maile volunteered to return to an abandoned tank which had its starting equipment damaged. He returned to it under fire, repaired the damage, and brought the tank out of action.
Recommended for M.M.; M.M. 28.1.43 (L.G. 27.9.40)

Main, Donald Alan, Corporal (A/Sgt.)
6968295, 7th Bn. Rifle Brigade (London, N.5)
(Immediate)
Sjt. Main was a member of the Coy. of 7 R.B. ordered to capture the pass North of El Hamma between DJ Haidouch and DJ Zemetel Beida before first light on 31st March 1943. The Company came under heavy M.G. fire soon after the commencement of the advance and was temporarily held up by a M.G. post 50 yards to the right flank. Sjt. Main on his initiative led his Section to the attack and silenced the gun, being wounded in the thigh. He then continued successively to silence four more M.G. posts, killing most of the crews in each case, which were causing casualties on the right flank. Throughout Sjt. Main acted entirely on his initiative without waiting for orders from a superior officer. He continued fighting with his company in spite of his wound until ordered to withdraw.
M.C. 7.12.44 *(L.G. 1.6.43)*

Major, Leo, Private
D.106190, Le Regt. De La Chaudière (Immediate)
On 13th April 1945, Le Regt. de la Chaudiere was deployed and in position preparatory to launching an attack on the town of Zwolle in Holland.

To save as many Dutch lives as possible, it was necessary to know exactly the location of the enemy positions, many of which were not known. D106190 Pte Major and a corporal from the scout platoon volunteered to enter the town and contact the underground movement to obtain the necessary information.

At the entrance of the town, was a road block guarded by a small group of enemy. The patrol was discovered and the Corporal killed. Pte Major killed two Germans and scattered the others. Undaunted by the death of a friend and comrade, he continued the patrol alone for 6 hours, contacting the underground and formed patrols of local Dutch civilians, with the result that by morning the enemy garrison menaced from inside and from outside, were forced to withdraw as their position became untenable. To urge them on Pte Major had the Gestapo HQ set on fire.

Around 0500 hours 14th April 1945, this gallant soldier, waded across a canal, after posting numerous patrols of the Dutch Resistance Movement at strategic points. On his way back, though wet and tired, he picked up the body of his Corporal and brought it in.

The gallant conduct of this soldier, his personal initiative, his dauntless courage and entire disregard for his personal safety was an inspiration to all. His gallant action was instrumental in enabling the mopping up on the 14th April 1945 to be done successfully without a shot being fired. *(L.G. 11.8.45)*

Major, Leo, D.C.M., Corporal Bar
D.800999, Royal Canadian 22e Regt.
For Korea *(L.G. 12.2.52)*

Major, William Blyth, Sergeant
5111310, Royal Warwickshire Regt.
B.E.F. *(L.G. 20.8.40)*

Majozi, Lucas, Private (Stretcher-bearer)
N.17525, S.A.M.C., South African Forces
For individual acts of bravery and distinguished services whilst under enemy fire.

On the night of 23rd/24th October 1942, Pte. Majozi accompanied his Coy. into action as stretcher-bearer. In the later stages of the action, when within 100 yards of the enemy and under heavy fire, he, without thought of personal safety, continued evacuating casualties, assisted by a co-bearer.

He was then wounded by shrapnel in the leg, hip, buttock and neck but continued evacuating wounded and when told by the Medical Cpl. to go back to the R.A.P., replied that there were many wounded men still in the minefield. He went back there and with the assistance of other stretcher-bearers brought back more wounded. After his co-bearers had become casualties, he did not waver, but alone carried wounded men back to the R.A.P. on his back.

When he was eventually told by his Coy. Comd. to go back, he smilingly refused, and remained on duty, working incessantly until he collapsed the next morning through sheer exhaustion, stiffness and loss of blood.

His extreme devotion to duty and gallant conduct whilst under continuous enemy fire throughout the night saved the lives of many wounded men who could otherwise have died through loss of blood or possibly further wounds.
Recommended for M.M. *(L.G. 31.12.42)*

Makewell, William Robert, Warrant Officer Cl. III (Pl.S.M.)
6189463, 1/7 Middlesex Regt.
For conspicuous gallantry and leadership in the Field. On 28th May 1940 P.S.M. Makewell was given a position to occupy on the canal bank at Comines. The position was under heavy fire the whole time but P.S.M. Makewell managed to get the whole platoon into action as ordered, by personally positioning each man and gun. This platoon was then able to inflict severe losses on the enemy, disabling an enemy A. Tk. gun and clearing a row of buildings of the enemy. P.S.M. Makewell inspired his platoon by his fearlessness and devotion to duty. He was wounded whilst getting his platoon into action, but continued to carry out his duties until his task had been completed. *(L.G. 22.10.40)*

Maloney, James, Warrant Officer Cl. I (R.S.M.)
4534959, 2nd Bn. West Yorkshire Regt. (Maltby, Yorks) (Immediate)
On 8/9th February 1944, R.S.M. Maloney was in charge of three composite rifle sections of 2 W. Yorks. These had been formed from Bn. administration personnel of 'B' Ech, and were holding the South face of the Bde.

'B' Ech area, near the East end of the Ngakydauk Pass, Arakan. During the night the enemy kept up a steady fire on their positions which was suddenly increased at 0615 hours and supplemented by rifle grenades. At the same time a large party was seen moving down a chaung in the rear of the positions in close formation. With great speed and presence of mind R.S.M. Maloney reorganized his fire plan to cover this chaung. By moving freely amongst his sections was able to hold their fire until all sections could engage the enemy with all weapons at approximately 30 yards range in a bend of the chaung. On being engaged with small arms, those of the enemy who remained alive replied with L.M.G.s and grenades, whereupon R.S.M. Maloney delivered a shower of grenades on them in the nulla. This was so effective that the great majority of the enemy were killed and the remaining few fled in disorder. At the conclusion of this engagement 44 Japanese dead were found in the Chaung, including one officer.

Recommended for M.M. M.I.D. 26.10.54(L.G. 22.6.44)

Manahi, Haane, Lance Sergeant
39009, 28 N.Z. (Maori) Bn.

On the night 19th/20th April 1943 during the attack upon the Takrouna feature L/Sjt. Manahi was in command of a Section. the objective of his platoon was the pinnacle, a platform of rock right on the top of the feature. Early in the advance his platoon came under heavy enemy fire which caused many casualties, including the Platoon Commander. First light on 20th April 1943 found the platoon reduced in strength to ten and pinned to the ground a short way up the feature by heavy Mortar and S.A. fire. The platoon continued the advance towards their objective, L/Sjt. Manahi leading a party of three up the Western side. During this advance they encountered heavy M.G. fire from posts on the slope and extensive sniping by the enemy actually on the pinnacle. In order to reach their objective L/Sjt. Manahi and his party had to climb some 500 ft. the last 50 ft. being almost sheer and during the whole time they were under heavy fire. L/Sjt. Manahi personally led the small party and silenced several M.G. posts in turn. Eventually by climbing hand over fist they reached the pinnacle and after a brief fight some 60 enemy, including a O.P. officer, surrendered.

They were there joined by the remainder of the platoon and the pinnacle was captured.

Within a short time the small area was subjected to intense Mortar fire from the considerable enemy force still holding the village of Takrouna and the Northern and Western slopes of the feature, and later to heavy and continuous shelling. The platoon Sjt. was killed and other casualties reduced the party then holding the pinnacle to L/Sjt. Manahi and two Ptes. An Arty. O.P. offr. who had arrived ordered L/Sjt. Manahi to withdraw but he and his men remained and held the feature. This action was confirmed by Bde. HQ as soon as communication were established.

The end of the morning, 20th April 1943, found the party short of amn., rations, and water. L/Sjt. Manahi himself returned to his Bn. at the foot of the feature and brought back supplies and reinforcements, the whole time being under fire.

During the afternoon the enemy counter-attacked in force some of them gaining a foothold. In face of grenades and small arms fire L/Sjt. Manahi personally led his men against the attackers. Fierce hand to hand fighting ensued but eventually the enemy were driven off.

Shortly after this the party was relieved.

On morning of 21st April 1943 urgent and immediate reinforcements were required and L/Sjt. Manahi again led up a party consisting of 15 men. At this time the enemy had once more gained a foothold on the pinnacle.

L/Sjt. Manahi led one of two parties which attacked and drove back the enemy. This attack was made under concentrated Mortar and heavy M.G. fire. All that day the feature was heavily shelled, Mortared and subjected to continual M.G. fire from in and about Takrouna.

Late in the afternoon of 21st April 1943 L/Sjt. Manahi on his own initiative took two men and moved round the North Western side of the feature. In that area were several enemy M.G. and Mortar posts and two 25 prs. operated by the enemy. With cool determination L/Sjt. Manahi led his party against them, stalking one post after another and always under shell and M.G. fire. By his skill and daring he compelled the surrender of the enemy in that area.

This courageous action undoubtedly led to the ultimate collapse of the enemy defence and the capture of the whole Takrouna feature with over three hundred prisoners, two 25-prs., several mortars and 72 M.G.s.

On the night 21st/22nd April 1943, L/Sjt. Manahi remained on the feature assisting in the evacuation of the dead and wounded and refusing to return to his Bn. until this task was completed. During that time the area was being heavily and continually shelled.

Throughout the action L/Sjt. Manahi showed the highest qualities of an infantry soldier. His cool judgement, resolute determination and outstanding personal bravery were an inspiration to his men and a supreme contribution to the capture and holding of a feature vital to the success of the operation.

65184 Pte. Grant, Hinga of 28 N.Z. (Maori) Bn. on oath states

On the night 19th/20th April 1943, I was a member of the section led by L/Sjt. Manahi. During the advance upon Takrouna our platoon sustained heavy casualties and at first light there were only some ten of us left. We were then pinned to the ground by mortar fire and heavy M.G. fire coming from the slopes of the feature and the pinnacle.

I was one of a party of four led by L/Sjt. Manahi up the slopes. We were trying to reach the pinnacle. On the way up we were fired on by enemy from posts below and on the pinnacle. L/Sjt. Manahi was always in front of us and personally attacked and captured M.G. posts.

To get on to the pinnacle itself we had to climb up almost sheer rock face and hand over hand. After brief fighting there, the enemy surrendered and we took approximately 60 prisoners. We were there joined by the remainder of the platoon.

After capturing the pinnacle we came under heavy mortar and shell fire and also fire from M.G.s sited in and about Takrouna below us. Towards the end of the morning our party holding the pinnacle had been reduced to three. L/Sjt. Manahi returned to the Coy. and brought back supplies and a few reinforcements. In going down and up the hill he was under fire the whole time.

In the afternoon further reinforcements arrived, this time from 21 N.Z. Bn. The enemy counter-attacked and some of them gained a foot-hold on the feature. L/Sjt. Manahi led an attack against them. There was fierce hand-to-hand fighting but eventually the enemy withdrew.

All the remainder of that day we were subjected to steady fire. After dark I returned to my unit with L/Sjt. Manahi.

Of the original party from my platoon who attacked the pinnacle on 20th April 1943 L/Sjt. Manahi and myself are the only ones not casualties.

2978 Lieut. Ian Henry Hirst of 21 N.Z. Bn. on oath states

On night 20th/21st April 1943 I was one of a party of two officers and forty-five other ranks who relieved a section of Maoris who had been holding the pinnacle feature above Takrouna village. I was not there at the actual relief and the Maoris had returned to their unit when I arrived. The pinnacle was a flat ledge of rock barely a quarter of an acre in size and covered by native houses with small winding alley-ways between. About 100 feet directly below was the village of Takrouna. While I was on the feature, the village and the Western slopes were strongly held by the enemy.

At about 2200 hours enemy troops fired on us from some of the houses on the pinnacle. It was later found that they had gained a foot-hold by using a secret and covered approach. Fierce fighting ensued and the position was desperate. Reinforcements were asked for and at about 0800 hours 21st April, L/Sjt. Manahi in charge of fifteen Maoris arrived. I discussed a plan of attack with him. This included bringing our own arty to bear on the feature. After a concentration during which we took cover, L/Sjt. Manahi personally led four men in an attack on some of the houses. They came under the heaviest mortar fire we experienced there and also considerable M.G. fire but the attack was a complete success. The enemy withdrew by the same means as they had used earlier to gain a footing and the entire pinnacle feature was once again in our hands. Following this we were heavily shelled and mortared and fired on by M.G.s from in and about Takrouna.

Later in the afternoon of 21st April L/Sjt. Manahi and one or two of his men, on their own initiative, moved out from cover on the pinnacle and I saw them stalking enemy section posts on the North Western slopes of the Takrouna feature. They stalked post after post capturing them in turn. When I saw the number of enemy surrendering I realised they were cracking and took a party down to the village which was captured. But for the action of L/Sjt. Manahi and his men, the capture of the whole feature would have been delayed considerably. During these operations L/Sjt. Manahi and his men were continually under shell and small arms fire.

The number of enemy who finally surrendered exceeded three hundred, including eighteen officers. Two 25-prs., several mortars and seventy-two M.G.s were captured.

12331 Cpl. Wilfred Lawson Richards of 21 N.Z. Bn. on oath states

I was with the party from my Bn. which, on the afternoon of 20th April 1943 reinforced the Maoris holding the pinnacle feature above Takrouna village. We arrived there at approximately 1500 hours. The Maoris appeared to be commanded by a Serjeant whom I now know as L/Sjt. Manahi. As far as I remember there were eight Maoris there.

Shortly after we arrived the enemy gained a foothold on the pinnacle. I do not know how many were there. Heavy fighting ensued with considerable S.A. fire and grenades by each side. A counter-attack was ordered by our officer, Lieut. Shaw. Not long after this Lieut. Shaw was wounded and evacuated and Lieut. Hirst arrived to take over. I can remember seeing L/Sjt. Manahi preparing his party for the attack. I do not remember seeing him during the fighting that ensued. I was myself too busily engaged with my own section. When we moved off to the attack we came under some of the heaviest Mortar fire we experienced during the whole time we were on the pinnacle. There was also heavy small arms fire. The fighting lasted about half and hour before the area was cleared of enemy. I myself saw Maoris engaged literally in hand to hand fighting, some of the enemy being thrown over the cliff by them. The situation at the time was so confused with fighting in and out of buildings that I am unable to swear to having seen L/Sjt. Manahi as being one of the Maoris. All I can be certain of is that he was in the fighting.

On the afternoon of 21st April 1943 I was still on the pinnacle and L/Sjt. Manahi and Maoris were there also. We had been subjected to heavy and continuous shelling and Mortaring and also M.G. fire from in and the vicinity of Takrouna village. There was practically no period, even by night, when we were not under heavy fire. Communications were difficult for the route up and down the feature was exposed and subjected to continual fire. Evacuation of wounded was difficult. The enemy showed no signs of giving in. We were suffering constant casualties.

At approximately 1700 hours 21st April 1943 I remember particularly noticing L/Sjt. Manahi. With the assistance of him and other Maoris some enemy who had regained a foothold on the pinnacle the previous night and remained in the buildings all day were driven back. I then saw L/Sjt. Manahi and another Maori leave the pinnacle and move down round the North Western slopes. They had said they were going to have a look at what was there. This was from where a lot of the Mortar and M.G. fire had come. I saw them disappear in the direction of the enemy positions and before long there was the sound of considerable fighting. Being engaged in placing my section in new positions I did not actually see what went on. I know that as a result of the action by L/Sjt. Manahi and the other Maori the enemy positions in that area were cleared and many prisoners captured. Not long after this the enemy in the village surrendered to us and the Takrouna feature was captured.

After the capture of the feature the intensity of the shelling increased. Heavy concentrations fell all round the area we were occupying. This lasted most of the night and we were expecting a counter-attack at any time. Over this period I remember seeing L/Sjt. Manahi helping to carry out his dead and wounded Maoris. All this was done under fire.

Recommended for V.C.   (*L.G. 22.7.43*)

Manning, Arthur David [Alfred David on AFW 3121], Sergeant
6201417, 1st Middlesex Regt. (London, E.10) (since died)
During the whole period of hostilities this N.C.O. displayed the best and finest characteristics of a highly trained junior machine gun commander. He showed outstanding coolness, courage and resourcefulness during many nerve racking periods. On 22nd December 1941 when ordered to vacate his pill box and proceed to Stanley he acted with perfect judgement in the collection of his machine guns and equipment, organization of his crew for withdrawal, making sure that nothing was left to the enemy. This was done under heavy rifle and machine gun fire. Due largely to his skill and loyalty to his superior officer he succeeded in reaching his destination. In spite of great fatigue and pain from lacerated feet he and some of his crew went out almost immediately into action and engaged the enemy at short range in the withdrawal of the force from Stanley Village to the Fort. This N.C.O. was a perfect example to his men throughout. Every task given him was carried out in the strictest order. He was fearless under fire and his men looked to him as a leader to be followed. This N.C.O. is one of the best type of men that the army produces.
(*L.G. 4.4.46*)

Mansfield, Hugh, Corporal
4863900, 1st Bn. Leicestershire Regt. (Rothley)
On the night of the 18th January 1945 the village of Zetton was attacked. Cpl. Mansfield, Carrier Comd. of No. 1 Section, Carrier Pl was ordered with his Bren group to take up a position in a house and to cover the rear part of the building. The front part of the house was defended by a rifle section of 'D' Coy.

In the early hours of the 19th January several Boche gained entrance to the front of the building and wounded three men also taking several prisoners. Cpl. Mansfield and three men armed with a Bren and rifles succeeded in driving the Boche from the building.

During this phase the Boche were trying their utmost to dislodge this valiant group by firing bazookas at the house accompanied by threats of 'We will shoot the prisoners we have already taken if you do not surrender.'

Disregarding both fire and threats, this N.C.O. with five badly shaken men and three wounded ones, hopelessly outnumbered and surrounded, gallantly rallied his party and caused the Boche to withdraw from the area of the building.

It was now getting light and the enemy again commenced attacking, Cpl. Mansfield appreciating the seriousness of his position, and that help was very badly needed, then, with complete disregard for his personal safety, dashed out into the road which was being subjected to a murderous fire by both our own troops and those of the enemy, and succeeded in reaching Coy. HQ a 100 yards away.

By this very gallant action this N.C.O. was able to get a section of Infantry back to his position. This was successful in stopping the enemy from overrunning the position. He was also able to give the Coy. Comd valuable information regarding this sector.

After settling the relief section in position, this N.C.O with his Bren group continued to man his gun beating off several enemy attacks until dusk, when he was ordered to proceed with the Coy. to reserve area, as another Coy. was taking over.

Cpl. Mansfield's Bren Carrier was now between the enemy and our own tps. His driver was already wounded and evacuated. Ordering his men to remain in their positions he again went forward, knowing full well that he could be plainly seen by the enemy, as the area around was lit up by burning buildings. Despite this, he successfully retrieved the vehicle, returned to his position, got his men on the vehicle and drove to the previously arranged reserve area.

During this action Cpl. Mansfield displayed courage, initiative and leadership of an outstanding order. It was due to his enterprise, energy and bravery that eight men, three of whom were wounded did not fall into the enemy's hands and through his magnificent efforts a serious threat to the Company HQ and the communications of the defending forces was thwarted.
Recommended for M.M.   (*L.G. 12.4.45*)

Mant, Douglas Edward, Corporal
PO X.2992, 40 Cdo., Royal Marines
No citation.   (*L.G. 13.7.57*)

Marlow, Geoffrey John, Warrant Officer Cl. II (B.S.M.)
6341806, 4th Regt., Royal Horse Artillery (Orpington, Kent)
This W.O. has been B.S.M. of 'C' Bty and has been present since the commencement of hostilities. In my opinion his example and powers of leadership has had a great deal to do with the very high standard which has been reached in the Bty. By means of his coolness and resource, on one occasion he saved ammunition lorries from falling into enemy hands. I consider him quite the most outstanding senior N.C.O. I have met during this war.   *(L.G. 8.7.41)*

Marriott, Maurice, Warrant Officer Cl. III (Pl.S.M.)
4340408, 2 East Yorkshire Regt.
On the 29th May when commanding a platoon of 'A' Coy. which was holding a bridgehead on the Yser Canal. Although severely wounded in two places, P.S.M. Marriott continued to command his platoon and readjusted his position when the enemy threatened the right flank.
Only when loss of blood caused him to lose grip of the situation did he leave his command, which continued to maintain a heavy fire on the enemy.
By his courage and disregard of personal danger this Warrant Officer set an example to all ranks and inspired them to further effort in the defence of their position.
O.B.E. 3.6.35 [?]   *(L.G. 11.7.40)*

Marriott, Roy Hammond, Private
VX 20960, 2/5 Aust. Fd. Amb. (Immediate)
23rd/24th October 1942.
From Goodenough Island to Gili Gili.
Pte. Marriott was a stretcher-bearer of 2/5 Aust. Fd. Amb. Light Sec. att. to 2/12 Aust. Inf. Bn., during action on Goodenough Island. He strengthened the morale of the troops by his prompt evacuation of wounded from the front line under heavy machine gun fire. Although wounded twice in the back, he continued to help the orderlies in the R.A.P., and had to be restrained from going back to bring out more wounded.
On 24th October 1942, the motor vessel McLaren King left Goodenough Is. with wounded soldiers. Pte. Marriott was the only A.A.M.C. man aboard. At about 1230 hours the ship was attacked by 3 enemy aircraft and strafed for approximately 20 minutes. In this attack 4 wounded men received further wounds, and 2 members of the crew wounded, including the Ship's engineer who received a bullet through his leg resulting in a fracture. During the strafing Pte. Marriott showed great fortitude by attending to those freshly wounded while under fire. In spite of his own wounds, which seriously hampered his movements, and exhaustion due to haemorrhage, Pte. Marriott improvised splints and splinted the engineer's fractured leg. He continued to attend all wounded until the ship arrived at Gili Gili wharf several hours later, where the patients were handed over to A.A.M.C. personnel. Pte. Marriott then insisted on all other wounded men being treated and taken to hospital before receiving any treatment himself.   *(L.G. 30.3.43)*

Marshall, Francis Michael Joseph, Lance Sergeant
24172, 24 N.Z. Bn. (Immediate)
On the night of the 23rd/24th October 1942 during the attack on Miteiriya Ridge (874292) L/Sjt. Marshall showed great leadership in urging his platoon forward in the attack and keeping it close up to the arty barrage. Although wounded, L/Sjt. Marshall took over command of the platoon when the Pl Comd. was wounded and evacuated, and by his courage and leadership brought his platoon safely through a minefield thick with mines, wire and booby traps and covered with fire by enemy automatic weapons and mortars. He carried on until wounded a second time and his courage and leadership during the action is worthy of recognition.
Recommended for M.M.   *(L.G. 28.1.43)*

Marshall, Wilfred [William on AFW 3121], Lance Corporal (Stretcher Bearer)
3318605, 6th Bn. Highland Light Infantry (Rochdale) (Immediate)
On 4th April 1945, during a Battalion attack in the Dortmundems Canal bridgehead South West of Ibbenburen, a platoon of 'B' Coy. 6th Bn. H.L.I., was heavily counter-attacked by determined enemy troops, and suffered considerable casualties. Regardless of intense enemy small arms fire and grenades, L/Cpl. Marshall tended to the wounded without once seeking cover. When the area in which he was working was overrun L/Cpl. Marshall continued ministering in the open, to our own and German casualties, even when it came under our own artillery defensive fire, until he himself was wounded. Thereafter, as the only person possessing the necessary medical knowledge and despite his painful injury, he supervised the splinting, bandaging and care of all casualties and in addition to saving the lives of at least Cpl. Spence and Pte. Harding of his own Coy., earned the admiration of a German Officer who, before withdrawing with his troops, commented on L/Cpl. Marshall's gallantry to one of our own P.W. When the situation had been restored he organised the successful evacuation of all the wounded.
By his devotion to duty and complete disregard for his own personal safety, L/Cpl. Marshall undoubtedly alleviated the suffering or saved the lives of a large number of wounded.
M.I.D. 9.8.45   *(L.G. 21.6.45)*

Marshall, William Chrichton, Warrant Officer Cl. II (S.S.M.)
544652, 7th Queen's Own Hussars, Royal Armoured Corps (Durban)
Showed outstanding coolness, initiative and courage throughout tank engagements on 21.11.41, 23.11.41 and 24.11.41. In particular 21.11.41 when his tank had been hit six times and the driver had fainted S.S.M. Marshall

got out under heavy fire, entered the driver's compartment, and drove the tank for the remainder of the day. On 24.11.41, when attacked in Leager at night S.S.M. Marshall's tank was hit at point blank range by gunfire. The tank disintegrated and S.S.M. Marshall who was mounting the tank at the time was hurled back semi-unconscious. He was taken prisoner and carried away, on the back of a German tank. On recovery, S.S.M. Marshall knocked out the German soldier guarding him, jumped off the tank and after walking all night joined his unit next morning. The unfailing courage, initiative and cheerfulness in times of stress of the Warrant Officer have been invaluable in maintaining morale of all troops associated with him.

M.B.E. 2.1.56   *(L.G. 20.1.42)*

Marshall, William Keith, Sergeant
32714, 25 (N.Z.) Bn. (Immediate)

Sgt. Marshall was sergeant of a platoon. During the night attack on 23rd October 1942 on Meteirya Ridge his Platoon Commander was wounded and evacuated early in the evening and this sergeant immediately took over command of his platoon and continued as commander for the subsequent eleven days of the campaign.

In the subsequent attack on the night of the 26th October 1942, the platoon under command of Sgt. Marshall attacked an extremely strong enemy position and through his capable leadership and devotion to duty his platoon captured over 50 P/W without casualties to his own men.

Under most trying circumstances he held his platoon and by his fine qualities of leadership his initiative and his cheerfulness he kept the morale of his men particularly high.

Throughout the whole campaign Sgt. Marshall has been an inspiration and a fine example to his men and his capable leadership contributed largely to his platoon's success under very difficult conditions.

Recommended for M.M.   *(L.G. 28.1.43)*

Martell, Thomas Kleen, Private
F40151, West N.S.R., Canadian Infantry Corps

During an encounter between forward elements of 'D' Coy., West N.S.R. and the Germans near La Rosamarina at approx. 1400 hours on 2nd August 1943 the number one and number two of the Bren in Pte. Martell's section were put out of action, the number one being killed and the number two being seriously wounded, both by heavy M.G. fire. Pte. Martell, a rifleman, without hesitation picked up the loads of these two men, weighing approx. 60 lbs, a Bren and utility pouches filled with ammunition, in addition to his own rifle ammunition and haversack, and carried them forward 100 yards over open ground continuously swept by M.G. and rifle fire to his section who were in an advanced position and isolated without an automatic weapon. By so doing he succeeded in making his sections position on a hillside tenable. Pte. Martell was forced to travel in short bouts because of

the weight of the three loads which proved so heavy that he was forced to crawl the last 100 feet over bullet swept ground, but he managed to reach his section safely and to deliver his loads, then taking up his position and engaging the enemy with his rifle. Pte. Martell showed distinct coolness, complete disregard for his own safety, courage of a high order and initiative in […] without a moments hesitation and taking orders from no one he seized up the loads of two other men and carried them forward to the remainder of his section who were in an isolated position and in danger of being wiped out.

In my opinion Pte. Martell has more than fulfilled the duties expected of a private soldier to such a degree that his courage and initiative are deserving of recognition and I hereby recommend him for the D.C.M.

(L.G. 4.11.43)

Martin, Alfred Charles, Corporal
1876945, 54th Fd. Coy. Royal Engineers (Hacheston, Suff.) (Immediate)

On 21st Nov 41 in the attack on Tiger from the Tobruk perimeter, while attached to The Black Watch, Cpl. Martin showed most conspicuous gallantry and devotion to duty. With his Sec. Comdr. he controlled the making of a 50 yard gap in the enemy minefield on the left of the intermediate objective of Jill.

This lengthy task was successfully completed under intense artillery and small arms fire, and although previously wounded in the arm, this N.C.O. remained until the work was finished, and proceeded to guide tanks through the gap until ordered back to the R.A.P.

His courage and determination were an example and inspiration to his subordinates.

Recommended for M.M.   *(L.G. 24.2.42)*

Martin, Charles Cromwell, Warrant Officer Cl. II (C.S.M.)
B.63919, 1st Bn. The Q.O.R. of C., Canadian Infantry Corps (Periodic)

B63919 C.S.M. Martin, Charles Cromwell, landed with the assault Coys. on D Day and has taken a leading part in all engagements in which this battalion has been committed since that date. He has been subjected to the heaviest shell, mortar and M.G. fire on many occasions, and at all times his coolness under fire and in actual contact with the enemy has been a source of help and encouragement to the men under his command. He has personally accounted for many enemy casualties both dead and prisoners. His utter disregard for personal safety has upon many occasions been the means of saving lives of many of his men, while his leadership ability has been the means for the success of many actions undertaken by 'A' Coy. during the past five months.

M.M. 21.6.45   *(L.G. 17.3.45)*

Martin, E. A. K., T/Warrant Officer Cl. I (R.S.M.)
1447648, 60th A.A. Regt., Royal Artillery
T.S.M. Martin showed great devotion to duty throughout the period of hostilities, and his example when his section was being bombed and machine gunned on numerous occasions was outstanding. He commanded the section on many occasions during the enforced absence of the Section Commanders and as such was responsible for bringing down several enemy planes.   *(L.G. 11.7.40)*

Martin, Harry Redfearn, Sergeant
31635, 25 N.Z. Bn.
Within half an hour of the opening attack on Hill 175 on Sunday 23rd Nov. when his platoon commander was killed, No. 31635 Sgt. Harry Redfearn Martin took over command of his platoon and remained in command for the succeeding eight days of action. During the afternoon of the 23rd when his platoon was enfiladed with heavy M.G. fire from the left rear and right front and also from enemy tanks, this N.C.O. by most skilful use of fire and movement succeeded in pushing home a series of local counter-attacks and in consequence succeeded in neutralising enemy opposition in a strong M.G. position. His leadership, courage and self sacrifice was an inspiration to his platoon and it was due to his skilful handling that his casualties were minimised without in anyway reducing the effectiveness of the attack.

(L.G. 20.1.42)

Martin, James Allan, Corporal
3191176, 8 Durham Light Infantry
Captured 2nd June 1940. Escaped 13th July 1940. Left Gibraltar 17.10.40. Arrived U.K. 29.10.40.

Capture.

Cpl. Martin was wounded near Moeres at about 1600 hours on 31st May 1940 and was taken to a C.C.S. at La Panne. On 1st June he was taken to another C.C.S. in the chateau du Moulin Rouge near Dunkirk. There he was attended by R.A.M.C. personnel and on June 2nd was taken prisoner about 1600 hours by the advancing German troops. A number of R.A.M.C. officers and O.R.'s volunteered to remain with the wounded and they too fell into the hands of the Germans.

On June 5th Cpl. Martin was taken to Zuidcote Hospital in an English ambulance under German guard and there he stayed for 5 days. On June 10th he was transferred to the 17 General Hospital at Camiers near Le Touquet. A number of British R.A.M.C. Officers were there and the hospital was run by an R.A.M.C. Colonel named Wilson to whom all British arrivals reported. There was apparently very little supervision of the hospital by the Germans and apart from guards posted outside and an occasional visit from a German officer there was practically no control.

While in bed was informed by others that five British officers tried to escape from Camiers, two were shot and killed and three got away successfully. The two officers, killed by the guards' shots, were buried in the grounds of No. 17 General Hospital at Camiers. Cpl. Martin was briefly interrogated in hospital by a German officer who astonished him by saying that he knew Martin was in the Intelligence Section of the 8 D.L.I. Martin had been very careful not to reveal his regiment or his duties and is certain that he had no incriminating documents on him. The only explanation he can offer for the knowledge shown by the German Intelligence Officer is that either one of the R.A.M.C. orderlies, who knew his regiment, had been induced to pass the information on, or else extremely clever deduction by his immediate captors based on other prisoners captured in the same district. Otherwise the interrogation was very brief and no attempt to force him to make a statement was made. The interrogator spoke 'perfect English with an Oxford accent.'

Martin remained at Camiers for about 3 weeks and was then taken to a clearing station in Lille. He reports that it would have been possible for an active man to have escaped from the Lille clearing station and he was about to try his luck when an R.S.M. stopped him going. His explanation of this is that he thought the R.S.M. felt that if anyone got away vengeance would be wreaked on the nuns who had apparently taken responsibility for looking after prisoners at the station. Martin said that similar conditions also existed in a P/W camp at Seclin.

From Lille he was moved to Tournai and thence to Brussels and then to a small village over the German frontier near Aachen. By the time he reached there he had been discharged from hospital, although he was not completely fit.

Escape.

The P/W camp at this village consisted of a very large farm house in big grounds surrounded by a high wall. Martin spent 13 days observing the habits of the guard, timing the changes of the guard, etc., and found that at a ceremonial changing of the guard at 1530 hours there were a few minutes when the grounds were not under close observation. On the 14th day he determined to scale the wall and having escaped detection in getting through the grounds, which were wooded, he was given a leg up by an R.A.F. observer and got away unnoticed. As there was only one roll call per day—at 0900 hours—his escape may very well have remained unnoticed until the following morning. His first act was to lie up in the woods near a small house. He watched the inhabitants of this house go out and when they were clear of the house (having obligingly left the door open) he went in and stole a suit of civilian clothes which fitted him fairly well and buried his khaki in a hole in the wood. At dusk he set off to walk into Belgium (about 25 kilometres). As there were no frontier guards he had no difficulty in gaining Belgian soil, but he was careful to avoid any village or main road until he was sure that he was well in Belgium.

He struck the main road leading West and skirted Liege and other towns walking only at night or for an hour after dawn and sleeping in barns by the way. Martin speaks French fluently and asked permission from farmers to lie in barns etc. explaining that he was a refugee.

He walked through Tournai and was not stopped or questioned. He entered France via Roubaix and made his way to Haubordin near Lille where he stayed for 4 weeks with an Englishman whom he had met when his battalion was stationed there. He said that the airports near Lille were busy with German aircraft starting off for flights to Britain. He also said that there were a number of heavy guns and A.A, in the Foire Commercials at Lille at that time. While he was in Lille the civilian population were evacuated from Camiers and district and at first it was thought that Britain had invaded that part of France. He stated it as his opinion that the French population would help the British in an attempt at invasion although such help would be of a discreet nature owing to the fear of reprisals.

The general attitude of the French was very helpful to him and he was surprised at their readiness to assist in his escape regardless of extremely heavy punishment if caught. This was especially so in the North of France where British troops had been previously, where a British victory was considered their only hope.

His friend in Lille provided him with 600 francs and a bicycle and on August 16th after visiting Gondecourt where he had previously been stationed, he set out for Spain on his bicycle. His friend had given him two good maps and he was able to buy food without suspicion as his French was fluent. When he was in Gondecourt he heard that 6 men of the Middlesex Regt. (probably 8th Middx.) were hiding in the area. They did not wish to compromise him by making contact with him. He believed that there were hundreds of British soldiers hiding in France at that time and that they would gradually straggle across to this country.

Before leaving Lille he took the precaution of providing himself with an identity card which he found to be essential. It was actually an old one belonging to his friend and which he had, with an ink eraser, deleted his friend's name and substituted the French version of his own name, i.e. Jacques Martin. A point to remember is to practice the new signature until it becomes natural. He gave another bit of advice, viz. the age to be included on the card should be outside the military grade, i.e. in the case of a young man, below 18, in the case of an older man, over 45.

Although he did not realise this at the time his indiscretion in giving his correct age (22) nearly landed him into trouble and he had to explain that he was born in America and had not done military service in France. On the card he suggested that the average escaping prisoner should describe himself as a labourer (main d'ouevre) but to comply with this the hands should be roughened and the muscular development compatible with that of a labourer. Another description for a 'white-collar worker' would be architect (architecte) or student (studiant). Only a knowledge of French is necessary for any prisoner attempting this means of escape.

At Hendaye Martin was arrested by French Gendarmerie who thought he was a deserter from the French Army. He was, however, set free on the next day and swam the river to Arun in Spain. He walked to San Sebastian where he reported to the British Consul. Next day he was arrested and put in prison because he had no papers. He was released after 24 days and proceeded to Madrid with the assistance of the British Consul. He still had no papers and was arrested there again and imprisoned in the Direction De Seguridad where he was kept for 9 days. He was then released at the instigation of the British Embassy where he stayed for several days and was put on the train for Gibraltar, thus eventually reached England recently.

There were many other useful tips given by Martin as follows:—

(i) If you can speak French even moderately well you can probably get away without detection if you produce an identity card in France which is in order. The government stamp must be carefully copied on tracing paper and forged on the card and the Mayor's signature must be forged. It is essential to have an identity card from which to copy but it is not difficult to obtain these from well-wishing French civilians but care must be taken that they are not seeking to entrap you and report you afterwards.

(ii) Possession of money is important, but if it is impossible to get any, get food sent through the usual channels in tablet form.

(iii) Simple labourer's clothes are the best disguise and can fairly easily be 'acquired' (without payment).

(iv) A bicycle is by far the best means of transport and is easily 'lifted.' Bicycles are supposed to be licensed but the license is not often checked and this risk one must take.

(v) You may be advertised for in the local papers. It is, therefore, desirable to try and obtain glasses or to alter the shape of the face in some way.

(vi) Belgium is, or at least was, not so full of German troops as France and any escape from German might well be made through Belgium where a bicycle could fairly easily be acquired.

(vii) The best time to escape is from hospital, where supervision is at a minimum. It is possible to make out that one is more incapacitated than is actually the case.

(viii) In the space for town of registration on the identity card put a town which has been wrecked by bombardment e.g. St. Valery or Amlens, where the records could not be checked.

(ix) If challenged as to reason for travelling in France say you are a refugee going to stay with relatives in the South.

(x) When trying to cross the frontier into Spain the river should be swum out of sight of villagers or others. There are plenty of places.

(xi) If arrested in Spain try and gain time until you can contact the British Consul. Refuse to answer questions without an interpreter.

Cpl. Martin brought back some information on enemy intentions etc. which, although now out of date, is of interest. He states that he gave to the British Consul in San Sebastian as much information as he could about German gun emplacement and airports which he saw during his journey.

He said that although it was forbidden to listen to the B.B.C. many people in France did so. The Germans tried to make English prisoners believe that they had complete control over the air but those with Martin refused to believe it.

He said that he saw many German uniform troops in San Sebastian including a large number of officers. The Spanish papers reported that Franco reviewed 50,000 troops in San Sebastian and Martin thinks that these were all German. This was on 23rd August.

A German soldier, who shared a cell in the Madrid gaol with Martin, said the troops were going to La Linea. This German had been put in gaol for being drunk and assaulting a Spanish policeman.

He said the Spanish were detective-minded. He was imprisoned for 3 days in a darkened cell in Spain for refusing to say 'Viva Franco' and give the Fascist sign. His worst experience was in the underground prison of the Direction De Seguridad where he met prisoners of many nationalities including a nightporter of the British Embassy in Madrid, who incidentally had been in the D.C.L.I.

The Spaniards would not allow Martin to communicate with the British Consul but a released prisoner did so for him.

When at San Sebastian he heard that there was German Artillery on the Rock above the prison there and was told that the Germans had brought it with them when they came.

He estimates that Spanish feeling vis-à-vis Britain is mixed, the Communists being 100 per cent pro-British.

His general treatment by the Germans in the concentration camp was decent, but he only had one meal a day consisting of cabbage, soup and black bread. Extra rations were offered as a bribe to prisoners who would perform manual labour in the camp. The camp was very lightly guarded. He thinks there were only six men on guard at a time. In this connection it must be remembered that this was shortly after the great German push and that camps in Germany proper will be different. Martin stressed, however, that the chances for a prisoner who speaks German to escape are 'very favourable' (he puts it at 5 to 1 on) and provided the camp is not too far from the Belgium frontier he thinks that even non-German speaking prisoners could, with luck, make it.

(L.G. 7.3.41)

Martin, William John, Driver
1439369, 140th Fld. Regt., Royal Artillery
Account of escape.

Captured about 2nd June 1940. Escaped about 7th June 1940. Left Gibraltar 7th Dec. 1940. Arrived London 14th Dec. 1940.

Prior to capture.

My Unit was attached to the 3rd Division, and on the 1st June left Cassels, having first destroyed our guns. On the following evening we dismantled our lorries and went on on foot with our small arms.

Capture.

Between Cassels and Hazebrouck we came under fire, and, at first, thought that it came from infantry, but a few moments later fire grew heavier and we were surrounded by German tanks. Our Major was wounded and the others, carrying the wounded, sheltered in a house nearby. Soon afterwards the house was surrounded by Germans and the Major, realising our desperate position, told us to surrender. Five minutes after giving this order he died of his wounds. When the roll call was taken, it was found that 200 soldiers had been killed and wounded.

We were not able to destroy our pay-books, and these were, in some cases, taken from us.

On capture I was marched in the column to Cambrai, our route was a circular one with the idea of impressing the inhabitants. I reached Cambrai about the 7th June and was put in a railway truck to be taken on to Germany.

1st Escape and Recapture.

I managed in the darkness to jump out of the truck and got away. I obtained civilian clothes soon afterwards, but, two days later, was recaptured at Hirson. At first I was taken for a spy, but on producing my pay-book established my identity and was put in the prison camp there, where I stayed for five weeks.

2nd Escape and Recapture.

I managed to escape again and made for Epernay, here I swam the river Marne and went on another 15 kms. to a small village, where I was re-arrested by the Germans.

I was taken back to Epernay, where I spent three weeks in prison.

3rd Escape

I managed to get away again by scrambling over the wall and headed South by way of Troyes, Auxerre, Clamercy, Chateauroux, Limoges and so to Marseilles.

I should mention that at St. Pol there is a large Aerodrome, and, at Epernay, a munition dump and what appears to be a training centre for German recruits; there were about 1,000 of the latter, chiefly young boys, some of them were not even in uniform. I understand that they had only recently arrived from Germany.

I crossed the line of demarcation at Tourchampault, 8 kms. from Nevers.

At Marseilles I was sent to the internment camp at Fort St. Je and my subsequent journey was that of the party headed by Major Potts. *(L.G. 7.3.41)*

Mason, Edward Richard, Warrant Officer Cl. II (actg.)
4039085, Royal Welch Fusiliers
No citation.   *(L.G. 30.4.57)*

Mason, Geoffrey George, Lance Sergeant
60106, 21 N.Z. Bn. (Immediate)
During the fighting in Cassino from 20th March 1944 until he was wounded on 21st March 1944 L/Sjt. Mason showed outstanding personal bravery, initiative and leadership.

On the morning of 21st March 1944 the platoon, of which he was Platoon Sjt., was heavily counter-attacked. In the early stages of the fighting the Platoon Comd. was wounded. L/Sjt. Mason at once assumed Comd. The position of the platoon at that stage was precarious and the enemy were pressing home their attack supported by heavy fire. Coolly and without care for his own safety L/Sjt. Mason went from post to post and quickly re-organised the defence. As a result the position was held firmly and the enemy forced to withdraw. L/Sjt. Mason himself led a party of his men against enemy who had gained a foothold driving them out with heavy casualties and capturing 10 P/W. Towards the end of this action L/Sjt. Mason was himself severely wounded.

There is no doubt that by his own example of courage, resource and determination at a very difficult and dangerous time L/Sjt. Mason was largely responsible for the safety of his platoon and the holding of an important area.   *(L.G. 3.8.44)*

Mason, George Harry, Sergeant
4612227, 6th (Pnr.) Bn., King's Own Royal Regt.
On 26th May 1940, at Merville Sgt. G. Mason showed great daring and initiative when he successfully lead a patrol resulting in the capture of 12 enemy prisoners, 3 armoured troop carriers, 4 motor cycle combinations and 1 anti-tank gun.

On 27th May, also at Merville, Sgt. Mason showed great bravery and leadership in maintaining a position with two sections in the face of intense enemy bombardment, thus preventing the enemy from penetrating into the Town. His leadership and personal bravery were outstanding.   *(L.G. 22.10.40)*

Mason, John, Sergeant
3446337, 2nd Bn. Lancashire Fusiliers (Bournemouth) (Immediate)
On 24th April 1944 Sjt. Mason was commanding a M.M.G. sec. on a ridge facing Cassino monastery. Although the position was overlooked from the monastery in front and Monte Cairo in the rear, Sjt. Mason never hesitated to engage the monastery area offensively, although accurate and heavy fire was invariably returned. His position was heavily shelled from the rear and a direct hit was registered in one of his posts, killing and wounding half his section. Despite this continued shellfire and regardless of his own safety, Sjt. Mason immediately dressed the wounded and organized

their difficult evacuation down the rocky and precipitous slope to the R.A.P. He then resumed his position at the gun and manned it himself until a reserve section could be sent up. Sjt. Mason showed courage of the highest order and his example and leadership held the platoon together in a very difficult and critical situation.
                                    (L.G. 24.8.44)

Massey, Louis George, Driver (A/Cpl.)
T/125117, R.A.S.C.
I escaped from Winduga in Poland on 2nd December 1940 at 5.30 a.m. through the canteen window with Cpl. Corkery and Pte. Doyle. The escape was not difficult. We did ten kilometres before daylight and hid in a wood for the day. We decided to follow the North bank of the River Vistual travelling only by night and making a detour round every town. On 3rd December we set off in a snow storm and reached Wloclawek before morning. There was a big concentration of German troops here billetted in hospitals, etc. We made a detour to avoid the town and slept in a straw stack. We carried on in this way for 10 or 11 days and on the 11th morning, our food having run out and it being too cold to sleep at night, we decided to take a chance and speak to someone. Luckily the man we spoke to was a Polish workman. He took us to his house, fed us and gave us a place to sleep. This was near Modlin. Next morning we were handed over to another Pole who gave us money and a compass. In this way we carried on in a North Easterly direction, sometimes helped by Poles and sometimes on our own. We crossed the River Bug, which was frozen over, on the night of 23rd December and found shelter with a Pole. Next day we crossed the frontier through the wire near Ostroleka where we forced our way into a house. While we were talking one of the men fetched the frontier guards. They treated us very roughly and knocked us about. Then they took us off to a barrack where we stayed the night. Next day (25th December) we were taken to Womza prison. We were there about three days. Conditions were extremely bad. On the 28th we were taken to Bialystok. Here we were put in one room with 120 other prisoners. It was impossible to lie down. They left us here for 10 days and from there we were taken to Minsk prison. Conditions here were indescribably bad. After 10 days in Minsk we were taken to Moscow where we were put in Lubianko for one night and then moved to the state prison.

We were in the State prison until 5th February 1941. We were questioned continually and the Russians kept on insisting that we were German spies. Apart from this we were treated well and given good food and books to read. We stayed here until 5th February when we were moved to Michourin, near Tula. We arrived here on 8th February. The place was an internment camp and conditions were very bad. There were a number of French soldiers in the camp. We soon decided to go on hunger strike to get better conditions and to demand to be allowed to communicate with the British Authorities in

Moscow. As a result of our strike, conditions improved a great deal and we were finally very well treated. We worked in the forests and were given tobacco and cigarettes.

On June 28th, after the outbreak of war with Germany, we were sent back to Moscow where we were lodged in a house outside the town and eventually handed over to the British Authorities on 6th July. *(L.G. 2.12.41)*

Mataira, Joseph William, Sergeant (now Second Lieutenant)
802053, 28 N.Z. (Maori) Bn. (Immediate)
In the attack on Cassino on the night 18/19th March 1944, Sjt. Mataira displayed outstanding initiative and determination. He led his platoon in the attack on the Western side of the town, engaged in a hand to hand struggle with the enemy of whom he killed at least two, and then became cut off from his men and was taken P/W behind a wall guarding an enemy position. Completely disregarding his own safety, and despite having already been wounded, he repeatedly called out to his men to hurl grenades over the wall. They finally complied, wounding several of Sjt. Mataira's captors and scattering them. Sjt. Mataira then picked up a T.S.M.G. and accounted for two more of the enemy before rejoining his men. *(L.G. 3.8.44)*

Matpi, Sergeant
417, 1st Papuan Inf. Bn., Australian Military Forces
On 16th February at Ruange Pte. Matpi in company with another native killed thirty (30) Japs in a running fight to Ruance. This deed was witnessed by NGX146 Lieut. R. I. MacIlwain. On 18th February at Tapen Pte. Matpi and the other native soldier told their OC Captain H. P. Hitchcock that a large number of enemy were escaping at the far end of Tapen village. On receiving permission to pursue the enemy, they did so, knowing that this act would be of great personal risk to themselves. Pte. Matpi and the other native then pursued the enemy killing forty-four (44) Japs including two (2) Officers. The two officers put up a stubborn fight to protect their men. This deed was most outstanding. After running out of ammunition these two boys killed the remaining six Japs with the butts of their rifles. At Kwembung on 20th February Pte. Matpi again with the same boy raided the village and accounted for another six (6). At Wandabo on 22nd February Pte. Matpi with the same boy raided Wandabo and killed eleven (11) Japs. After this action during which the other boy was wounded, Pte. Matpi carried on with his section and accounted for another nineteen (19) Japs in the gardens of area Wandabo and Kwembung. Since then Pte. Matpi has increased his total of enemy killed by him to one hundred and ten (110). *(L.G. 9.5.46)*

Matthews, Alfred, Rifleman
6844118, King's Royal Rifle Corps (London, N.15)
Calais 1940; P.O.W. Pool *(L.G. 20.9.45)*

Matthews, James Boyd, Corporal
H165, 2 Cdn. Armd. Regt. (Ld.S.H.)
During the action at the Torrice Crossroads, Highway 6, on the 30th May 1944, after enemy tanks had been located by the Reconnaissance Troop of the 2nd Canadian Armoured Regiment (Lord Strathconas Horse), 1st Troop, 'B' Squadron under command of Lieutenant Black was ordered forward to engage. Almost immediately the Troop Sergeant's tank threw a track leaving the remaining two tanks under Lieutenant Black and Corporal Mathews to continue on their fire positions. During this time the troop was coming under well-directed and accurate fire from the enemy tanks as well as heavy enemy shell and machine gun fire. Lieutenant Black's tank was hit and burned but undaunted and entirely alone, Corporal Mathews pressed on and continued the fight against heavy odds. By dint of outstanding initiative and determination and still being exposed to the same heavy enemy fire, he manoevred from position to position and succeeded in destroying a Mark V Panther tank, a 75 mm self-propelled gun and a Px KW IV tank. Only after firing all his ammunition did this N.C.O. break off the engagement in order to refill from a disabled tank nearby.

During this refilling Corporal Mathews assisted in evacuating casualties while under heavy enemy machine gun fire and, having refilled, went forward to cover the right of the crossroads. En route the clutch gave out and the tank bogged in the heavy going, where upon he dismounted the crew and dug in on the threatened flank, standing to all night against the expected counter-attack.

By his courageous leadership and dogged determination Corporal Mathews was responsible for turning the tide at a moment when the situation was critical, as it was impossible to manœuvre more tanks into position at that time owing to the nature of the ground and the advantageous and commanding positions held by the enemy. *(L.G. 7.10.44)*

Matthews, Peter Glyn, Sergeant
2733864, 2nd (Armd. Recce) Bn. Welsh Guards (Swansea) (Immediate)
On 27th April 1945 this N.C.O.'s Tp. was supporting an Inf. Coy. in an attack on Kirchtimke, a village known to be strongly held by Inf. and SP guns belonging to 15 Pz. Gren. Div.

Two SP guns were dealt with by his Tp., but shortly afterwards, the Tp. Ldr. was wounded by shellfire. Sjt. Matthews, well knowing that the third SP gun had withdrawn into the village, advanced down the main street in support of the Inf., firing into the houses from which small arms firing was coming.

Half way down the street, this Sjt's Tk. was fired upon by the SP gun at short range. The first shot made a large hole in the track of his Tk., whilst the second blew off a bogey wheel.

Sjt. Matthews maneouvred off the road, engaged the SP gun, and destroyed it.

In the meantime, the other Tks. in the Sqn. were held up by extensive minefields and bad ground. Sjt. Matthews' two Tks. were the sole remaining ones which could support the Inf. to their objective.

When they had done this, Sjt. Matthews patrolled forward on his own, shooting up enemy Inf. who were attempting to withdraw. Eventually his damaged Tk. broke down, but he himself remained under very heavy shellfire in his Tk., covering the main road.

Throughout this engagement, this N.C.O. was under enemy mortar and shellfire, and small arms fire of intense fierceness. He had exhibited an outstanding devotion to his duty, whilst his calm demeanour in face of danger had inspired those who had witnessed his actions.

His vigour, and adroit handling of his small command had destroyed many enemy, including one SP gun and had caused considerable panic in their ranks. In face, if it had not been for the help of this N.C.O. and his two Tks., the Inf. would have suffered far heavier casualties, and might never have succeeded in capturing the village.
(L.G. 23.8.45)

Matthews, Wesley John [William on AFW 3121], Sergeant
6351472, 9 Cameronians (now Royal Irish Fusiliers)
(Bexley Heath) (Periodic)
Sjt. Matthews joined the battalion in September 1944 and shortly afterwards was promoted Sniper Serjeant. He has taken part in all the battles since.

On 19th November 1944, 'A' Coy. was ordered to cross the Van Deurne Canal. Prior to this patrols had probed the defences on the enemy bank of the Canal. Sjt. Matthews took part in these patrols. The crossing of the Canal was completely successful and 'A' Coy. pushed forward and took up a defensive position. Orders were again given for further patrolling to contact the enemy who were thought to be occupying the village of Helenaveen. Sjt. Matthews volunteered for the patrol. The patrol task was to visit approx. ten areas and ascertain the strength and disposition of the enemy forces. The patrol was out for four hours and gained much valuable information. About 1500 hours it bumped into a strongly defended enemy post in the centre of Helenaveen and was heavily engaged by small arms fire and had to withdraw. Casualties were inflicted on the enemy, Sjt. Matthews accounting for three. During the withdrawal of the patrol the signaller carrying the 18 set was wounded in the back and had to be carried by the other members of the patrol. All this time the ground was being swept by enemy small arms fire and it seemed impossible that with the wounded man any of the patrol would escape alive. Sjt. Matthews with great bravery and coolness seized a Light Machine gun, and dashed across the open ground to a position from where he could fire. This fire was accurate, causing the enemy to take cover, thus enabling the remainder of the patrol to withdraw out of range.

On th 28th April, Sjt. Matthews was again attached to 'B' Coy., leading company of the battalion during the Elbe crossing. 'B' Coy. task was to clear the battalion assembly area. Sjt. Matthews went out with a patrol detailed to search houses and enemy positions. One position contained a German mobile gun well dug in. Sjt. Matthews repeatedly sniped at the Germans around this position, and in doing so crawled forward in front of the leading platoon, regardless of his own safety. He constantly exposed himself in order that his fire would be more accurate. His efforts resulted in the killing of three Germans. He then took a patrol and captured the remaining 18 Germans and captured the post. His personal bravery during this action resulted in the enemy being denied the use of the dug-in gun, thus saving casualties in 'B' Coy., which during this time was in a very exposed position.

On the 11th April 1945 Sjt. Matthews was attached to 'B' Coy. At 1930 hours 'B' Coy. was ordered to attack a crossroads South of Celle. Approx. two hundred yards short of the objective heavy opposition was encountered, and one platoon commander was wounded and the company serjeant major killed, and the remaining platoon serjeant wounded. Sjt. Matthews immediately started to reorganise the company and finally took command of one platoon. His actions during the hours of darkness were a great inspiration to the men, and he continually reconnoitred forward of his platoon area to stop enemy infiltration.

Sjt. Matthews has shown himself to be an excellent sniper and a fearless leader throughout the campaign. He was invariably to be found in the most dangerous positions and endeavouring to accompany any patrol in order to come to grips with the enemy. This was so to such an extent that he had to be ordered by Headquarters only to go out on patrols when ordered to do so by HQ and not on his initiative. His unfailing cheerfulness and quick action in dangerous situations have done much to maintain a high morale in the companies to which he has been attached. He has at all times shown courage and leadership of a high order which have been a constant source of inspiration to all ranks in the battalion.
Recommended for M.M.   *(L.G. 24.1.46)*

Matlock, Thomas Arthur, Warrant Officer Cl. II (C.S.M.)
4739803, 5th Bn. East Yorkshire Regt. (Immediate)
C.S.M. Matlock is C.S.M. of 'B' Coy. On the evening of the 14th June 1942, during the breakout through enemy lines the company was under terrific fire from artillery, M.M.G.'s and Anti Tank guns. C.S.M. Matlock, accompanied by a Private soldier, attacked and destroyed the whole crew of an enemy M.G. post which had been holding up his company's advance. C.S.M. Matlock then advanced on another post. He was wounded in the face and arm by a Breda bomb but in spite of this he accounted for this post and on the way back took a prisoner who attempted to stop him.   *(L.G. 24.9.42)*

Maxey, Grederick Henry John, M.M., Warrant Officer Cl. II (actg.)
2765150, 5th Bn. Black Watch (London, E.1)
(Immediate)
On the night 26/27th February 1945 the Battalion attacked South from Thomashof. Sgt. Maxey, commanding a platoon, was given the task of capturing three small houses near the river. On the way forward, he came under heavy Spandau fire from a well dug in position on the bank. Realising the need for dealing with this post quickly, if his Company was to avoid heavy casualties, Sgt. Maxey immediately went forward with one man. Scorning the heavy fire, he rushed the post and knocked out the enemy in it with the butt of his weapon. He then rushed on to the house, which was alive with enemy, cleared a way in with his Sten, and wiped out the enemy in the room to a man. By now his platoon was up with him, and inspired by his terrific dash and leadership the other houses in the area were soon dealt with also. It was very largely due to Sgt. Maxey's magnificent courage and unflinching devotion to duty, that this strong enemy position was captured quickly, and that the remainder of the attack was able to proceed. Sgt. Maxey then saw that the platoon on his left was in difficulties. Going far beyond the requirements of duty he went to it, and finding that the Officer had been killed, took command. The enemy were in a strongly held pill-box. Piat bombs made no impressions on it, so Sgt. Maxey charged the doorway alone, taking no heed of the stream of bullets directed at him, killed the enemy in the doorway, and threw a smoke grenade inside, whereupon the enemy gave up. Once again the capture of this post was due almost entirely to Sgt. Maxey's great dash and resoluteness. Throughout the battle his inspired leadership, courage and devotion to duty were of outstanding value, and up to the highest traditions of the Highland Division.
M.M. 21.12.44   *(L.G. 24.5.45)*

May, Neville, Corporal
WX 8755, 2/28 Australian Infantry Bn. (Immediate)
At 1800 hours on 9th September 1943 when 2/28 Aust. Inf. Bn. was undertaking an opposed crossing at the Busu River Cpl. May led his section across the river as part of 19 platoon 'B' Coy., the assaulting Coy. During the crossing he did everything in his power to keep his section together and by his superb tenacity succeeded in bringing them intact to the hostile bank. On arrival there he found that an enemy M.G. post about 100 yards from the sea beach and not far into Kunai was causing casualties. Although he was exhausted from his efforts during the river crossing, he without hesitation proceeded to advance alone on the M.G. post. He located it 150 yards from the river bank at approx. Map Ref. 74302 Malahang 1/100,000, and attacked it single handed with grenades and Owen gun fire, wiping out the post.
    By his determined effort and great courage and stamina Cpl. May not only saved his Bn. many casualties,

but set an example which inspired his Company throughout the action.   *(L.G. 20.1.44)*

May, Terence John Henry, [Terence John Emery on AFW 3121], Private
14673987, 1 Gordon Highlanders (London, S.E.15)
(Immediate)
On 24th March 1945 this soldier's company was approaching the NW outskirts of Rees, having been under continuous mortaring, shelling and Spandau fire for the last eight hours. Pte. May's Platoon Comd. and two Sec. Comds. had become casualties and he, by his own initiative and energy, had assumed responsibility for the survivors of two sections, which he proceeded to lead with the utmost skill and daring.
    The leading platoon had got a footing into the town, but was held up by very heavy fire; an attack upon the rear of the Coy. HQ then started, but Pte. May seeing the situation, quickly on his own got his section Bren gunners into position where they successfully silenced the attack, killed a German paratroop officer and four soldiers. The enemy, however, did not withdraw, so Pte. May organised an attack which drove these determined enemy off.
    Throughout this operation heavy fire of all types was being directed at his section and although they were mostly untried recruits fighting in action for the first time, the coolness, determination and confidence Pte. May gave was of such high quality that his men never had any doubt of success, even against so determined an enemy.
    The same bravery, the same disregard for intense fire and the same high example this soldier continued to set for the next 36 hours, during which he led his section with great cunning and dash. Their job was as difficult as it could be—clearing suicidical paratroopers from prepared positions in ruins, yet never once did his heart waver, his cheerfulness die down nor his utter contempt for danger fail him. In one particular street his personal actions in carrying out a reconnaissance in the face of intense Spandau fire, then leading his men across this fire to take a heavily defended post from the rear, showed skill and powers of leadership of a kind normally expected from an experienced officer.
    This private during 50 hours continuous fighting carried out the duties of a senior N.C.O. exceptionally well, and to him must go much of the credit due to his Company for their part in clearing a major portion of Rees. Without his initiative, leadership, drive and supreme devotion to duty, this platoon would have accomplished little. The standard he showed throughout was superb.   *(L.G. 7.6.45)*

Mayanja, Zafaniya, Warrant Officer Cl. II (C.S.M.)
U/283, King's African Rifles,
To be dated 30.9.41   *(L.G. 21.7.42)*

Mayne, William Arthur, Sergeant (A/W.O.II (C.S.M.))
5496094, 1st Bn. Hampshire Regt. (Bexley)
(Immediate)
At Agira on 26th July 1943, his Company were heavily counter-attacked on the objective taken the night before. The Company had many casualties including all Officers except the Company Commander. C.S.M. Mayne took immediate command of two platoons and by his energetic action stopped the enemy's attack. He reorganised their positions under heavy mortar and M.G. fire. When later a withdrawal under a second attack became necessary, he remained with the rearguard until his position was almost surrounded. Then with a few men he fought his way out and rejoined his Coy. Commander.

By his instant assumption of responsibility and his disregard of personal safety under heavy fire he set a fine example to the men under his command and rendered great help to his Coy. Commander in a difficult situation.
(L.G. 18.11.43)

Maziku, Kiyanga, A/Sgt.
60118, 1/6 K.A.R.
For highly distinguished services and gallantry in action.

In the action at Billate River on 19th May A/Sgt. Maziku displayed the greatest courage and leadership. When his Officer was wounded, this N.C.O. immediately took over command of the platoon and skilfully directed its attack on the strongly defended enemy position.

Finally he was wounded, but before being evacuated conveyed valuable information to his Coy. Comd. and indicated the main centres of enemy resistance.

The indomitable spirit displayed by this most gallant N.C.O. was in large measure responsible for the success of the action.
Award backdated to 30.9.41 *(L.G. 21.7.42)*

Meadows, Walter, Guardsman
2613804, 2 Armd. Bn. Grenadier Guards (Manchester 21) (Immediate)
This Guardsman took part in some of the bitterest street-fighting in the Battle for Nijmegen on 19th September 1944. During the course of this fighting one of the tks. of his own tp. was knocked out and the men who evacuated it were seriously wounded by enemy Spandau fire. At the same time, a section of Infy. closely supporting this tk. were fired on by 2 other Spandaus and 3 were seriously wounded. Summing up the situation, this Guardsman dismounted from his tk., and under this intense enemy fire, ran across the street and carried back one of the wounded men, then although he himself was wounded in the hand, he again crossed the street and rescued a second wounded man from the middle of the road, which was still under a hail of enemy bullets. Once again, in spite of being wounded a second time, he crossed the road, forced a German Spandau man to surrender by jumping down on top of him in his trench and at the same time he carried back a third comrade who lay wounded near the knocked out tank. He was for the third time wounded, this time in the neck, and it was with the greatest difficultly he was persuaded not to attempt to rescue a fourth wounded comrade as the condition of his own wounds was becoming serious. His amazing courage and undaunted devotion to duty saved the lives of three of his comrades and inspired all around. The great bravery of this action speaks for itself.

Regardless of all danger, though three times wounded, he went back three times to save his wounded comrades, and thus set an unparalleled example of devotion to duty, and extreme bravery in the face of very heavy and intense enemy fire. *(L.G. 1.3.45)*

Measey, George, Sergeant
5106143, 7th Bn. Duke of Wellington's Regt. (Birmingham) (Periodic)
Sgt. Measey has been with the battalion in action since D plus 4 except for a short time when he was wounded. For a good proportion of this period he has been a platoon commander through the shortage of officers and several times has acted as Sergeant Major.

When acting as a platoon commander in the fighting around the Depot de Mendicitie in early September 1944, Sgt. Measey was wounded in the head but though in great pain he completed the engagement before obeying the order to have his wound attended at the R.A.P.

In September 1944 at Schanker (7423) the company after a first class assault were counter-attacked by a self-propelled gun and 40 enemy and ammunition ran low in one platoon which was temporarily isolated. Sgt. Measey led a relief party with further ammunition through very heavy shelling and his example undoubtedly saved an extremely delicate situation.

In the following week Sgt. Measey again led an ammunition party to his forward platoons which were isolated and pinned down in the flat open ground around the anti tank ditch at Roosendaal. Later in the day he personally crawled 300 yards while being sniped to take up 2″ mortar smoke ammunition required to allow the platoon to disengage.

During the four and a half months on the 'island' salient across the Rhine at Nijmegen Sgt. Measey was constantly employed on standing and fighting patrols in the most difficult conditions and here as on countless occasions his bravery became a legend and an example to the many young soldiers in his company.

Sgt. Measey's courage, calmness, interest in his men and his constant cheerfulness have made him a proud landmark in the battalion and the guide for many inexperienced soldiers when action was particularly fierce.
(L.G. 24.1.46)

Medley, Albert, Sergeant
551386, 4th Queen's Own Hussars (Welford, Northants.) (Immediate)
Crete.
This N.C.O. was captured during the battle of Crete,

after twenty minutes he succeeded in eluding the guard and took to the hills where he remained at liberty for a year, assisting other stragglers and greatly assisting in keeping up the morale until he was evacuated with another party which he organised. Immediately after his arrival in this country he volunteered to return to Crete and guide a party of saboteurs to Maleme aerodrome, landing from a submarine and guiding across very rough and dangerous country. The mission successfully accomplished, he guided the party back and embarked them aboard the submarine in very bad weather and the party reached Alexandria without loss of a man.
Recommended for M.M.   *(L.G. 15.10.42)*

Medley, Albert John, D.C.M., Warrant Officer Cl. I
                                        Bar
551386, 4th Queen's Own Hussars
M.E. (No citation)   *(L.G. 9.8.45)*

Meldrum, George Hastings, Corporal
H19299, Canadian Infantry Corps
Dieppe   *(L.G. 9.2.46)*

Meldrum, Robert, Lance Sergeant
2757795, 6th Black Watch (Crail, Fifeshire)
(Immediate)
Ref. Map:— Italy 1/50,000 Sheet 113/1.

On the evening of 29th July 1944, 'A' & 'B' Coys. ran into an ambush on the side of a very steep hill (pt. 788 897533) and extremely thickly wooded country. It was pitch dark. 2 platoon., of which L/S Meldrum is Platoon Sjt., were on the left flank, and suddenly, without warning 4 M.G.s and several Schmeissers opened up and enemy rifle grenades were fired. This enemy attack was concentrated on 2 Platoon from the front and left.

L/S Meldrum, with utter disregard of his own safety, ran from man to man and put them into fire positions and saved the situation by stopping a break-through which would have endangered the complete force of 'A' & 'B' Coys.

Thereafter the attack intensified and the platoon was completely pinned down. However, once more L/S Meldrum, with great courage and devotion to duty under very heavy enemy fire went from section to section and once again held the flank firm. By doing so he formed a firm base enabling the remainder of the force to carry out flanking movement on a key position.

On the morning of 30th July 1944, L/S Meldrum and his platoon were again involved in wood fighting and suffered casualties. Again he saved the situation by his grand leadership and courage, and when eventually the platoon had to withdraw – the enemy being too strong – he dashed out under M.G. fire without regard for his own safety and brought in two badly wounded men.

On the evening of the same day a small force of two platoons was detached to hold a dominating feature, and commanded by two officers. In the course of the evening one officer was killed and the other wounded, having to

be evacuated. L/S Meldrum took command and rallied the men, which was no easy task as shelling and mortaring were extremely heavy and there were numerous counter-attacks going on, on the remainder of the Coys. 400 yards away.   *(L.G. 8.2.45)*

Meller, William, Lance Sergeant
1541951, 11th Bn. Royal Scots Fusiliers (Manchester, 20) (Immediate)
On 10th March 1945, the company of which Cpl. Meller was a member took part in a water-borne raid on the enemy South East of Haalderen after landing from assault craft.

On beaching, the company came under Spandau fire from either side of the bund road to the North West wounding the N.C.O. in charge of one of the assaulting sections and dispersing the section in the consequent confusion. The second section of the platoon went into the attack across the bund and owing to casualties and heavy fire was lost to the platoon for the remainder of the action.

The third section of the platoon commanded by Cpl. Meller was now the only section left and had to clear the enemy from their well constructed positions dug into the bund and search six houses, a task which had been given to the whole platoon.

Cpl. Meller led his section for the next two hours with great bravery and dash, with complete disregard for his own personal safety and it was his leadership and example which enabled his section to complete a task which would normally have required a platoon.

Although leading his section in these attacks under Spandau fire at close range and from many directions he never once faltered or hesitated and it was due in great measure to him that the remains of the platoon were able to fulfill their task and successfully withdraw after killing some twelve of the enemy and capturing six.

This N.C.O.'s performance during the action rose to a level far and away above that consistent with his normal rank and appointment.   *(L.G. 7.6.45)*

Melling, Herbert, Sergeant
549835, 17th/21st Lancers (Ashford, Kent)
(Immediate)
Sgt. Melling has served for seven years with the 7th Hussars.

At the outbreak of war he was recalled to the Colours and posted to the 17th/21st Lancers. He saw active service in Norway.

Since the landing in North Africa he has served with distinction in every battle in which the Regiment has taken part. On April 9th, 1943, at Fondouk, Sgt. Melling was commanding a two tank tp. on the right of the gap, he was ordered forward to cover the withdrawal of the remaining five tanks of the Squadron. He went forward and when the other tank of his troop was knocked out, he silenced the gun and engaged the machine guns and snipers who were picking off the dismounted tank crews.

When ordered himself to withdraw, he again advanced to collect another dismounted crew and then circled round picking up other men as he went.

He finally returned with 23 men on his tank.

As soon as he had brought them to safety he unhesitatingly returned to the battle, attaching himself to 'A' Sqn. as there was nothing left of his own Sqn.

The initiative and bravery of this N.C.O. saved many mens' lives and was an inspiration to the remainder of his Sqn. I consider his action should receive an award. *Recommended for M.M.*   *(L.G. 15.6.43)*

Melvaine, Morris, Private
NX 40814, 2/3 Aust Inf. Bn.
For conspicuous gallantry and devotion to duty on 27th Jun 41 during an attack on Jebel Mazar an enemy machine gun well concealed opened fire on the company. Pte. Melvaine without hesitation made straight for the gun which then directed its fire onto him, continuing to fire until he was within a few yards. He killed the gun crew and captured the gun, thus allowing the advance to continue and prevented further casualties in the company. Pte. Melvaine displayed remarkable courage and determination in his action.
Recommended for M.M.   *(L.G. 12.2.42)*

Mendes, James Albert, Guardsman
2723989, 2nd Armd. Bn. Irish Guards (Birkenhead)
On 21st April, 1945, the Troop in which this Guardsman was serving, was ordered forward into an isolated position in the village. Comd. of Wistedt, covering the flank of the Squadron/Company Group at Elsdorp. Almost immediately after taking up position a sharp counter-attack developed against the Squadron/Company Group which entirely enveloped this forward Troop. The Troop position was assaulted with determination by about one Company of enemy supported by S.P. guns.

The Troop Leader, when unable to contact his Sherman 17-pr by wireless, accepted Gdsm. Mendes' voluntary request to be allowed to make his way on foot to the Sherman Vc to deliver an order or, alternatively collect the tank himself. This he did in the face of enemy encroachments from three sides.

Gdsm. Mendes found that the Sherman Vc had been hit on the cupola and that the commander had been killed. Gdsm. Mendes at once jumped into the drivers seat and drove the tank, which was under enemy fire, to a covered position. Reorganising the crew and acting as Tank Commander himself, he brought the tank back into action and fought it with great determination until ordered by the Troop Officer to bale out as the tank was on fire.

On baling out, he seized a Bren gun and continued to cover the withdrawal when the Troop Commander ordered a 'break out' from the surrounded position.

His action did much to make a 'break out' possible and was the direct cause of the survival of the party who finally returned to our lines. This determined fighting diverted the enemy from their main objective and helped

materially in the defence of the Squadron/Company Group area.   *(L.G. 12.7.45)*

Mensah, Kwaku, Private
18389, 3rd Gold Coast Regt.
For very gallant services in action

On 22nd April 1941 D Company 3 G.C.R. attacked an unexpectedly strong enemy position a Wadarra. No. 18389 Kweku Mensah was the carrier of the 18 set at Coy HQ when at about 1100 hrs the Company came under very heavy L.M.G. and artillery fire. The Company Commander and several soldiers, including the operator of the 18 set were seriously wounded.

At about 1230 hrs the Coy began to withdraw and some time later it was discovered that the wounded operator was not the Company HQ. Pte Kweku Mensah went forward again to try to find him. Under heavy fire he passed through the withdrawing forward platoons, found the wounded operator and brought him back to Company HQ. On his arrival there he found that a number of seriously wounded men had been collected and that there were no more stretchers available. The Company Commander was seriously wounded and there was no other European to whom he could report. He decided to go back to Bn:HQ to report; a distance of about 12 miles over very difficult country some of which was under heavy fire. On arrival at Bn:HQ a stretcher party was collected which he led back to the place where the wounded had been collected. He then collected his 18 set and led the stretcher bearers back to the R.A.P.

Throughout the day this soldier displayed gallantry, initiative and fortitude under heavy fire and trying conditions and his conduct must have been a great example to those around him.
To be dated 30.9.41   *(L.G. 21.7.42)*

Mercer, John Edward, Fusilier
3325056, 2 Royal Scots Fusiliers (Leeds) (Immediate)
On 31st March 1944 at about 0800 hours the Bn. was holding a defensive position in the Fosso Della Ciocca. Fusilier Mercer was occupying a slit trench in the fwd. platoon area of 'B' Coy. which was the fwd. company of the battalion with two other Fusiliers. A German attack was impending and heavy fire from automatic weapons was being directed at his trench and at all other trenches in the platoon area. Suddenly Fusilier Mercer saw a German about 20 yards away, about to throw a stick grenade. Ignoring the intense fire and the stick grenade which burst just outside the trench, Mercer raised his L.M.G. and shot the German. Immediately afterwards an egg grenade thrown by another German, landed on the parapet and started to roll into the trench. Shouting, 'Watch yourselves, Lads,' to his two companions Mercer swung his foot up and jammed it on top of the grenade, thus preventing it rolling to the bottom of the trench at the same time shielding his face with his greatcoat. The grenade exploded under his foot wounding Fusilier Mercer in the head and leg. By his extreme gallantry,

and total disregard of the inevitable effect on himself, Fusilier Mercer undoubtedly saved his companions from the consequences of the explosion of the grenade. Later when his two companions had applied field dressings to his wounds, he refused to be evacuated on a stretcher and despite serious injuries to his leg, insisted on walking back to the R.A.P. in order that other more seriously wounded men might take his place on a stretcher. His last words to his companions as he walked off were, 'Sorry to leave you now, lads.'

His example was an inspiration to the whole company which had suffered severely in this attack. Statements by No. 3196646 Fus. W. Carson, No. 14382915 Fus. K. Squires and Lieut. C. B. Boyle are attached. An additional statement by Lieut. J. T. M. Barnetson is attached.

Statement by Lieut. C. B. Boyle

When Fusilier Mercer was wounded, his two companions applied Field Dressings to his wounds. Some time later when stretcher bearers arrived to evacuate the wounded, Fusilier Mercer refused to be carried away, but walked off, saying 'Sorry to leave you now, lads.'

Statement by No. 3196646 Fusilier Carson, W.

On 31st March 1944 at about 0800 hours I was in a slit trench with Fusilier Squires and Fusilier Mercer in the forward platoon of my company. A German attack was impending and heavy Spandau fire was coming across the top of the trench. Suddenly Fusilier Mercer spotted a German about 20 yards away about to throw a stick grenade. Ignoring the Spandau fire and the stick grenade which burst beside the trench Fusilier Mercer raised his Bren and shot the German.

Almost immediately afterwards an egg grenade landed on the parapet and started to roll into the trench. Shouting, 'Watch yourselves, lads,' Fusilier Mercer swung his foot up and jammed it on top of the parapet preventing it rolling into the trench, at the same time shielding his face with his greatcoat. The grenade exploded under his foot, wounding Fusilier Mercer in the head and leg.

Had Fusilier Mercer not acted as he did the other two of us would undoubtedly have been hit.

Statement by No. 14382915 Fusilier Squires, K.

On 31st March 1944 at about 0730 hours I was having breakfast in my slit trench with Fusilier Carson. The third occupant, Fusilier Mercer, was on duty by the Bren gun. Suddenly he fired a burst into a bush about 30 yards away saying that he had seen a German who might have been on a recce. About half an hour later the Germans opened up with heavy, concentrated and accurate machine gun fire and we suspected an attack. Fusilier Mercer spotted a German about 20 yards away and, shouting a warning to us, he killed the German with a burst from his Bren gun. We 'stood to' and once again Mercer's warning of grenades coming at us enabled us to take cover. One egg grenade came over our heads and landed on the edge of our slit trench which was sloping downwards and was of hard baked earth. Fusilier Mercer shouted, 'Watch yourselves, lads,' and I turned round in time to see him jam the grenade against the edge of the trench with his foot. The grenade would undoubtedly have rolled in amongst us had Mercer not taken this action. There was an explosion, but not a sound from Fusilier Mercer whose face was now bleeding profusely and whose leg was also wounded. I offered him a Field Dressing which he refused, and told him to lie down while we attended to him. He would not do this and would not even lie on a stretcher when he was eventually evacuated, walking by himself to the Aid Post. During the whole action he kept cheery and encouraging and never complained of his wounds. He assisted in distributing ammunition and by his general behaviour kept morals at a high level. When he left eventually he cried, 'Keep it up, lads. Sorry to leave you.'

Statement by Lieut. Barnetson, J. T. M.

On the morning of 31st March 1944 at about 0730 hours, I hear a burst of Bren fire coming from the direction of Fusilier Mercer's trench, which was quite the most exposed in the platoon area. The Germans had previously attacked on his position and he knew the importance of his sector. A German attack developed, and throughout the action Fusilier Mercer's voice could be heard exhorting and encouraging the others in the platoon and shouting challenges to the enemy. I also heard him asking how the ammunition was going and encouraging everyone generally. His cheerfulness and courage in the face of danger was an example to all. When the attack was over I checked my platoon and found that Fusilier Mercer had been wounded by a grenade: he was told to lie down on a stretcher but refused it as he said others more seriously wounded than he might require it. Though bleeding from head and leg and undoubtedly suffering from loss of blood, he walked off to the Aid Post by himself and left the area calling, 'Keep it up, lads' and, 'Sorry to leave you now, lads.'

Recommended for V.C.   *(L.G. 20.7.44)*

Meredith, John Clifford, Sergeant
24103698, Parachute Regt.

Sjt. Meredith was a Platoon Sergeant in D Company 2nd Battalion The Parachute Regiment during the 24 days of the Falkland Islands campaign. He was a dedicated and devoted leader, encouraging and steadying the younger soldiers under fire and inspiring the Platoon by his personal example. In the battle for Port Darwin and Goose Green on 28th 29th May 1982, during the later stages of a long and demanding day, his Platoon Commander was killed while advancing on an enemy position which it was assumed had surrendered. Five men, including one wounded, survived in the Platoon Commander's party but were in a perilous and exposed position. With conspicuous gallantry and presence of mind, Sergeant Meredith rapidly assumed command of the Platoon, organised covering fire for the trapped men and stabilised the situation. He then personally took a machine gun and moved forward under heavy enemy fire to where he could neutralise the remainder of the

enemy and give directions to extricate the trapped men. Subsequently the Platoon under his direction captured the enemy position. Later in the campaign, with a new and inexperienced Platoon Commander, he again showed conspicuous bravery, professionalism and leadership at the battle for Wireless Ridge on the night of 13th/14th June 1982. At a critical moment, when the Platoon's assault on this 1000 metre long ridge looked as if it might flounder, he moved forward to assist his Platoon Commander in leading the Platoon forward in the face of heavy machine gun fire. These two incidents typify Sergeant Meredith's outstanding skill and gallantry throughout the campaign which were in the very highest tradition of the Parachute Regiment. *[From L.G.]*
(L.G. 19.9.78)

Meredith, John Thomas, Warrant Officer Cl. I
4852785, 1st Bn. Leicestershire Regt. (Quetta, India)
On 11th February 1942, the remnants of the Bn. were holding a perimeter position astride Jarang Road at about 8½ M.S. together with some Indian Troops of different Bns. and Bdes., and some Aust. A.S.C. Personnel. The enemy attacked this position from the West, S.W. and South while the Bn. was awaiting the arrival of the 3/16th Punjabis from the N.W. prior to an enemy withdrawal towards Bukit Timah. As the enemy pressure from the S.W. increased R.S.M. Meredith on his own initiative organised a local counter-attack with about 20 men of different units which he led with intrepidity and determination, advancing about 300 yards. The enemy were temporarily driven back several hundred yards leaving 14 dead on the ground. R.S.M. Meredith killed several himself both with revolver and rifle during the attack. He brought back two enemy Tommy guns.

The example of absolute fearlessness set, and the powers of leadership shown, by this W.O. were of the highest order on this occasion as on many others. Without his bold and well timed action which relieved the enemy pressure on the S.W. at a critical moment it is doubtful whether the force would have been able to make a successful withdrawal to the S.E. since the enemy at this time began to attack the position from the direction of Bukit Timah also. Whenever enemy bombs, artillery, mortar, MG or rifle fire came down on troops anywhere nearby, R.S.M. Meredith was always walking coolly about steadying and encouraging the men and attending to wounded.

His example really has been an inspiration to all at all times of stress.   *(L.G. 13.12.45)*

Meredith, Percy, Lance Corporal
2655736, Coldstream Guards
B.E.F.   *(L.G. 11.7.40)*

Merrin, Bertie, Warrant Officer Cl. III (T.S.M.)
397654, The Queen's Bays (Dragoon Guards), Royal Armoured Corps
On May 24th, 1940 near rinoy T.S.M. Merrin was in command of a troop of three tanks, two of which were put out of action by anti-tank gunfire. T.S.M. Merrin dismounted from his own tank under heavy fire and rescued the wounded man who was the only survivor from the other two tanks.

On June 8th, 1940, near La Hallotiere, T.S.M. Merrin was ordered to carry out a reconnaissance of the enemy positions. This time all his tanks were put out of action. He dismounted from his tank and continued to carry out his reconnaissance on foot. He engaged enemy infantry who tried to capture him with his revolver. He then reported to his squadron with valuable information which was instrumental in enabling the squadron to carry out a successful action against the enemy. As soon as he had given in this information T.S.M. Merrin collected his crews and brought them safely back from behind the German lines. On the way he also rescued eight infantrymen who were also cut off.

During this action T.S.M. Merrin displayed gallantry, resource, and determination of a very high order.
(L.G. 27.9.40)

Metheringham, John, Sergeant
4449491, 10th Bn. Durham Light Infantry
On 27th May the Battalion Transport was heavily bombed and machine gunned by hostile aircraft. Five men were buried under debris, and this rescue was due to the non-commissioned Officer, who led a rescue party under fire. His example of coolness and courage was outstanding. During the withdrawal to Dunkirk from the Arras Area, this non-commissioned Officer set a magnificent example of courage and determination in carrying out his duties, carrying out many journeys during day and night in country known to be investigated by hostile A.F.V.s, and subject to hostile Air Attack.
Recommended for M.M.   *(L.G. 11.7.40)*

Michie, Norman, Corporal (A/Sgt.)
3190644, 2nd Bn. King's Own Scottish Borderers (Galasbiels)
22nd February 1944. On a feature East of Mayu Ridge.

The Coy. attacked a Jap position with a precipice on one side and a deep Chaung on the other. Sgt. Michie was the Platoon Comdr. of the platoon which was ordered to move round by the right via the Chaung and to come up behind the jap position on the top of the ridge. Sgt. Michie led his platoon with great determination in face of enemy fire and succeeded in coming out at the right place, thus enabling the Coy. to take the position. I then ordered Sgt. Michie to attack and to try to occupy the next feature. He succeeded in getting himself and a few men on to the position in spite of enemy fire but with the remainder of the platoon was held up about half way.

Sgt. Michie though wounded in the leg continued to engage the enemy with fire and to hold the ground gained.

Throughout he showed great determination and courage.

Recommended for M.M. (*L.G. 18.5.44*)

Micklewright, Douglas William, WS/Cpl.
6462571, 2nd Bn. Royal Fusiliers
Ref Map:—1/25,000 109 IV NW.

On 14 Sep 44 'X' Coy 2 Rf advanced to attack pt 113 863884. Cpl. Micklewright was commanding the leading Sec of No 12 Pl. He advanced rapidly across country, drove the enemy from some houses at 870881 and chased them to the foot of pt 113. From there he led a dash to some houses at 863884, and caught a party of Germans as they were emerging from their shelters. The enemy surrendered and Cpl. Micklewright pushed on to the crest of a house on the right flank, at 862886. Undaunted by the hail of bullets, he led his Sec in a quick assault down the hill to the enemy positions. The slit trenches forward of the house were overrun and the enemy surrendered. Jumping over the surrounding fence, Cpl. Micklewright dashed round the side of the house, where he was met by a burst of machine gun fire and wounded. He threw a 36 Grenade through a window and again tried to enter the house, but was again badly wounded in the head by a Mortar Bomb. By this time every member of his Sec had been killed or wounded, and Cpl. Micklewright ordered the remnants to withdraw under covering fire from his TSMG. Not until every member of his Sec was safely under cover did Cpl. Micklewright himself withdraw, still firing his TSMG. He was wounded for the third time by fire from an enemy tank.

Although by the time he reached Coy HQ on a stretcher he was very weak from loss of blood and only semi-conscious, he accurately described the position of 3 enemy MMG positions, which were then knocked out by Arty Fire. Throughout this actiohn Cpl. Micklewright showed superb personal courage and dash, and it was largely due to this and to his inspiring leadership, initiative and drive that the Coy were able to capture and hold their objective.

(Originally gazetted 8.3.45 as Ricklewright, amended LG 22.3.45 to Micklewright)

Middleton, Norman, Sapper
839960, 170 Tunnelling Coy., Royal Engineers
1. Capture
I was captured together with a number of my platoon, while on night patrol at Wimereux, near Bologne (N.W. Europe 1:250,000, Sheet 1, G 6858) at the end of May 1940. We were marched across France and into Germany. We took about fourteen days and went via Luxemburg. The first place I remember stopping at was Trier (Germany 1:100,000, Sheet 119B, 4613) and here we were put on trains for Limburg (Sheet 108, 3484). At Limburg we remained for about three days and we were then sent to Stalag VIII B (Lansdorf) (Sheet 117,

6801) where we arrived about the second week in June 1940.
2. Camps in which imprisoned.
Stalag VIII B (Lamsdorf) (now Stalag 344) June 1940—5th September 1944.
3. Attempted Escapes.
I remained at VIII B the whole time I was in Germany, but while there, I was constantly sent out on working parties and made the following attempts at escape:—
(a) First Attempt.
This was made immediately after I arrived at the camp. I had no food, no German papers of any kind and was wearing a blue French naval uniform from which I had removed all marks. I was working with a party of six in a garden at the very edge of the camp, and separated from a park by an iron fence. While the others engaged the guard in conversation I jumped over the fence and ran into the trees. As I crossed the road beyond the park, I was seen by the sentry at the main camp, and the alarm was sounded. I managed to evade capture, however, and made West for the range of mountains along the Czechoslovakian border. I avoided everybody and lived by stealing food where I could. I managed to do this for four days. By that time, however, I was getting very exhausted and I decided to take a risk and sleep under cover in a windmill. Unfortunately I must have been discovered by the farmer, for when I woke up the German police had surrounded me. I was sent back to VIII B and given 28 days' solitary confinement.
(b) Second Attempt.
I made a second attempt while I was on a working party at a camp at Reigersfeld (Sheet 117, 1771) in September 1940. On the fourth day I was there, Pte. Hardy, S.E., Gloucester Regt., P/W No. 12639 and I decided to try and get away by jumping the camp wire while the guards were engaged on the evening roll call at 2000 hrs. On the day we planned to escape, the guards were drunk, and the roll call was altered to 1800 hrs. We managed, however to jump the wire successfully, but were detected almost at once and recaptured about two hours later. We were taken back to the camp, and the whole camp was brought out on parade. We were stripped and beaten up with rifle butts by the guards. My nose was broken and I lost four teeth. Pte. Hardy had his arm fractured. We were then pushed into the camp cess pool and locked in a cupboard, and left without food or clothes or medical attention for about thirty hours. At the end of that period we were taken out and sent back to Lansdorf. The camp authorities there, were told that we had accidentally fallen down some stairs.
(c) Third Attempt.
This was made in September 1941 while I was on a working party at the mines of Knurow (Sheet 128, 4765). The camp was in the pit yard, and was surrounded by a single strand fence of barbed wire. I decided to escape with Pte. Donovan, Pioneer Corps. We got civilian clothes and a pair of wire cutters from some Poles in the mine, and we saved food from Red Cross parcels and

our rations. We cut the wire at night and made our way through the yard and out. We walked by night passing through Kattowitz (Sheet 118, 7370) and continued down the road towards Jablunkov (Czechoslovakia 1:75,000, Sheet 416) in Czechoslovakia. Unfortunately we were not prepared to find the frontier guarded, and walked on to it unexpectedly. We were stopped by the guards. By this time I could speak a bit of German and tried to bluff it out. I told them we were going to Cadca (Sheet 4261) near Jablunkov, and gave an address there. We were then asked for papers and I pretended to have forgotten them. I think we might have got away with this, but the guard saw our parcel of food, and opened it. When he saw Red Cross chocolate and other food, he at once accused us of smuggling and took us to the frontier post. Here we admitted our identity and were handed over to the police at Istebna (Sheet 4162). We remained there three days and were then taken to Stalag VIII D (Teschen). After about four days we were returned to Lamsdorf. We were each given 21 days' solitary confinement.

(d) Fourth Attempt.

In May 1942 I made another attempt while working on Party E.51 at the mines at Klausburg (Germany 1:100,000, Sheet 118, 5678). I was again accompanied by Pte. hardy. We obtained civilian clothes from foreign workers, and we changed into these at the Lager and pinned the legs of our khaki trousers over the civilian ones, and put on our greatcoats. When we paraded for night shift, we looked fairly normal. We were marched down to the mine, and our plan was to slip away with the help of the rest of the shift, while the guard walked forward to open the gate and turn on the light at the entrance. It was three days before a suitable occasion arose. The people behind then took our coats, while we tore off the legs of our trousers and walked off down the street as the others turned into the yard. We took a train into Hindenberg (5475) and walked from there to Kattowitz (7369). We made for Jablunkov by my old route and crossed the frontier in the dark hours off the road. We passed through Zvolen (Czechoslovakia 1:75,000, Sheet 4562) and crossed Czechoslovakia making for Hungary. After we had been walking for about three weeks, stealing food and avoiding all contacts, we began to near the Hungarian frontier. Our clothes, however, had been getting pretty ragged and we could not shave properly as hour razor blades were giving out.

Near Leva (Sheet 4761) our appearance excited suspicion and we were arrested by the Hungarian frontier police. We were taken to Leva and handed over to the Slovaks. We were then taken to Bratislava (Czechoslovakia 1:75,000, Sheet 4758), and imprisoned there for 30 days.

At the end of that period we were handed back to the Germans and taken to Stalag XVII A (Kaisersteinbruch) near Vienna. About July 1942 we were sent back to VIII B. We were given 28 days which was automatically cancelled since we had already served it at Bratislava. We were, however, put into the Straf Company with other escapers. In September 1942 we had our hands chained as part of the reprisals for Dieppe. Later in December 1942 I was sent for nine months to work in the granite quarries at Alt Wette (Germany 1:100,000, Sheet 117, 5473). After I had finished this I was allowed back on to ordinary working parties again.

(e) Fifth Attempt.

In August 1943 we were sent to a work camp at Sternberg (Czechoslovakia 1:75,000, Sheet 4158) where we were engaged in hay pressing. We had an enormous dump collected near the camp. The camp was surrounded by a single strand fence and the guards were very lax. We found we could use our hay tools to cut the wire and we were able to loosen and unscrew the bars of one of the windows of the hut. Following this, we decided to try and destroy the dump of hay. On 27th October two members of the Pioneer Corps., one of whom was a Pte. Cremona and I managed to get out of the camp and set the hay dump alight by means of greased rags. The whole thing burnt to the ground. Although we got back into the camp and covered up all the traces we felt we might be suspected and decided to try and get out. We used the same method to leave the camp a few nights later. We had managed to get some dye for our uniforms and had saved some food. We got away, but were arrested about thirty-six hours later outside Prostejov (Sheet 4258). We were taken to the German HQ at Hohenstadt (Sheet 4058) and then sent back to VIII B. We got two days confinement.

(f) Sixth Attempt.

In June 1944 I was again sent to the work camp at Sternberg, near Olomouc. I managed to cut the wire again using some cutters out of the cobbling kit of another P/W. I was also helped by a German woman at Sternberg who gave me civilian clothes, money and a ration card. She gave me this in return for coffee but I think she wanted to get 'even' with one of the guards who disliked her. This time I walked to Olomouc and got the train to Brno (Sheet 4357). From Brno I went to Vienna and here I got on to the Strassbourg train. I found however they were searching the train so I got off at Salzburg (Germany 1:100,000, Sheet 156, 9896) and got on to a train for Innsbruck (Sheet 159, 5436). At Innsbruck I got a train for Landeck (Germany 1:250,000, Sheet M 48, V 44) intending to make for Switzerland. Before we arrived I was caught by the Gestapo. I was taken to Stalag XVIII C (Markt Pongau St. Johann). There I was given a week in jail, and then sent back to Lamsdorf, where I got fourteen days in confinement.

4. Escape.

I managed to escape with Rifleman McGlone (S/P.G. (G) 2615) on 5th September 1944. This escape was not planned in advance and we had no special kit with us. We heard on the morning of 3rd September that the repatriates were being mustered in the hospital compound prior to departure. We decided to try and join them and managed to leave our compound with a working party which was going to another part of the camp. When the party passed the place where the repatriates were being lined up, we managed to leave it and entered the hospital grounds. We jumped the low wire fence and joined the queue of repatriates without being detected. The Germans were checking each man by his identity card and we joined a party which had already been done. By carrying other people's luggage we avoided looking conspicuous and were marched off to a tent to be searched. This was not very thorough and we got through it successfully. After the search we were all marched out of the camp to a field outside. At this point the Germans naturally discovered that they had two extra leaving the camp and they decided on a second card check. This was very stringent, the repatriates were made to dump their luggage and then were carefully checked man by man. With the help of Cpl. Jarvis, L., we managed to hide under some piles of kit which were not searched. The Germans decided the count at the camp gates was erroneous, and we were marched to the station. Here the repatriates were mustered in groups of fifty and we again avoided detection by lying under the kit. We then boarded the train. On the train we were checked again, but we hid under the seats. By this time, however, the Germans had found that two men were missing from the camp, and naturally suspected we were on the train. They, therefore, came down in force and did a thorough search, coach by coach. By now it was dark and when the guards were about half way down our carriage we climbed on to the roof by means of the ladder at the end of the coach and crawled across. After allowing them time to get clear, we entered the coach from the other end. A further search was made later in the night, Rfmn. McGlone managed to hide under the seat, while I hid behind the lavatory door, I was not discovered because another man was in with me, and after checking his card, the guards passed on. At Sassnitz (near Rugen) (Germany 1:100,000, Sheet 10, 1243) where we embarked for Sweden a further check was made on the quay and we again hid under the kit. We then marched on to the boat without further difficulty and landed at Tralleborg. We were then taken to Goteborg and there we were put on board S.S. Arundel Castle on 8th September.

After the ship had sailed we reported to the Orderly Room. We were told by the captain that we would have to return to Sweden. We returned in the pilot boat to Goteburg and from there we were sent to Stockholm, arriving on 11th September. We left Stockholm for U.K. by air on 24th September 1944.   *(L.G. 26.7.45)*

Milburn, Frank, Sergeant
4343040, 12 Parachute Bn., Army Air Corps
(Greenside, Co. Durham) (since killed in action)
Sgt Milburn was in charge of fwd. position in front of his Coy. When attacked by two Platoons of German inf. supported by three SP guns he held his fire and controlled his section until he was able to engage the enemy at point blank range. Afterwards he led an assault on one of the SP guns under heavy fire from the other two.

This N.C.O.'s courage and leadership were of the highest order and contributed to the success of the airborne operation on 6th June 1944.   *(L.G. 28.9.44)*

Millard, Reginald James, Warrant Officer Cl. II (B.S.M.)
1068242, 3rd Corps Tps., Royal Artillery
For conspicuous gallantry in man handling guns under rifle and machine gun fire so as to enable them to knock out enemy posts. He set a splendid example to all ranks. *M.I.D. 6.4.44; M.B.E. 8.6.50*   *(L.G. 27.8.40)*

Miller, Albert Edward, Lance Sergeant
6201283, 1st Middlesex Regt. (London, N.9)
For most outstanding coolness, courage, resourcefulness and devotion to duty during the action at North Point Electrical Power Station on 18th & 19th December 1941.

This N.C.O. formed part of the mobile MG Platoon sent to reinforce the garrison at that point. Although wounded at the outset when driving a 15 cwt truck this N.C.O. at once organised his men for action and himself carried out a recce to ascertain the whereabouts of the enemy fire which had caused considerable damage to the three vehicles approaching the locality. He succeeded in locating an enemy gun and by accurate bombing put it out of action with hand grenades. This accomplished he returned at once to help in organising the local defence of the power station and showed commendable foresight and clear headedness in placing his weapons in the most advantageous positions, so much so that not one was put out of action by the enemy. Early on 19th December he located an enemy Machine Gun which was causing much damage, engaged it single handed and put it out of action. His disregard for danger and his great courage and resource enabled his men to put up a most determined defence and after destroying his arms he was forced to surrender when only one of his party remained unwounded. It is certain that but for the action of this N.C.O. extending over the better part of a day the enemy would have made much more rapid advance on the part of the front.   *(L.G. 4.4.46)*

Miller, George William Ernest, Sergeant
7896779, 1st Northamptonshire Yeomanry (Daventry)
     (Immediate)
At Honnerpel on 23rd March 1945 during Operation 'Plunder,' Sgt. Miller was commanding a Troop of 'Buffaloes' in the absence of this Troop leader. His Troop was carrying the 'carpets' for the exits of the 'D.D.' Tanks from the R. Rhine. He had been mainly responsible for the special training of his Troop, as well as leading it in the actual assault, where his was the first 'carpet-laying' craft across the River.

On the far bank he assisted the 'D.D.' Tank Recce Officer in recceing suitable exits for the Tanks and organised the landing and laying of the 'carpets.' Furthermore he had to remain on the bank without cover until all the 'D.D.' Tanks had landed — a matter of several hours. All this time he was under periodical mortar and shell-fire, and amongst other things arranged for the evacuation of the Recce Officer, who had been wounded by it, thus leaving him in charge. He also assisted in the salvage of several 'D.D.' Tanks, which had become stuck in the mud, or the rescue of their crews.

Throughout he set a wonderful example of coolness, efficiency and courage to the rest of his Troop during a very difficult and unpleasant period. His conduct was undoubtedly the chief reason for the efficient landing of the 'D.D.' Tanks in this sector.

M.I.D. 10.5.45   *(L.G. 12.7.45)*

Miller, George, Warrant Officer Cl. II (B.S.M.)
1056050, 12/25 Field Battery, Royal Artillery
(Tonbridge, Kent)
The above was B.S.M. of 12/25 Bty. R.A., 25 Fd. Regt. R.A. When this Regiment fought its last action in Tobruk on the 19th June 1942. When all 'A' Tp's guns had been knocked out by shell and M.G. fire and both officers had been wounded, he took command and evacuated all wounded and survivors from the position. In doing so he showed utter disregard for his own safety although the area was at all times under heavy fire of all sorts.

Later this W.O. took command of 'B' Tp's 2 remaining guns—the G.P.O. having been killed—and brought them into action alongside the S.A. Artillery.

At all times this W.O. showed great initiative and resource as well as great courage. It was largely due to him that eventually 40 men of the Battery were able to escape from Tobruk.

I strongly recommend this W.O. for an award.
                    (L.G. 15.10.42)

Miller, John Auston, Warrant Officer Cl. II (actg.)
K.R. 4072, Kenya Regt.
No citation.   *(L.G. 19.7.55)*

Miller, Stanley George, Staff Sergeant
NX 9615, 2/1 Australian Infantry Bn. (Immediate)
New Guinea.
On 20th November 1942 2/1 Bn. were held up be enemy forces approx. 2 miles North of Soputa. 'B' Coy. endeavoured to move round their left and succeeded in driving in the enemy flank a short distance, but the Company was eventually held up by strong Jap forces and suffered very heavy casualties. The Jap positions were only 20 to 35 yards apart from our own. (Distances subsequently measured).

S/Sgt. Miller is the Coy. Quarter Master Sgt. and was in position at Coy. Headquarters with the Coy. Comd., Lieut Prior. No rations having arrived he had no definite duty to do.

At approx. 1100 hours, it was reported that Pte. Lollback was severely wounded in the shoulder and could not move without assistance. S/Sgt. Miller went forward and brought Lollback out under heavy fire.

Later an Aust. N.C.O. was shot through the stomach in a forward and exposed position and as the area was under heavy fire and the approach was across an area bare of cover it was considered by the Coy. Comd. impossible to help him during daylight. However his cries of agony were demoralising to our troops and must have been giving satisfaction to the enemy and S/Sgt. Miller volunteered to the Coy. Comd. to try and reach him and administer morphia. He then went forward under heavy rifle and L.M.G. fire and reached the N.C.O., gave him the morphia and dressed his wounds. He then came back, had a stretcher made and with a stretcher bearer (Cpl. Kemsley) and dragging the stretcher slowly and arduously, crawled for 20 minutes back to the N.C.O., and brought him out despite the enemy fire. Later in the day the N.C.O. died at Ads. Soputa.

At 1700 hours Cpl. Ward was wounded in the knee and S/Sgt. Miller again went forward under fire and helped him out.

On all the above occasions and during the whole action, S/Sgt. Miller showed a complete disregard for his personal safety, and conspicuous gallantry and courage in the face of enemy fire far beyond the call of his personal duty as a C.Q.M.S. His conduct was an inspiration to all and his actions are worthy of the highest praise.

All the wounded men were subsequently evacuated in hours of darkness on night 20th/21st November.
Recommended for M.M.   *(L.G. 22.4.43)*

Milligan, David Tait, Warrant Officer Cl. III (Pl.S.M.)
2926314, 1st Queen's Own Cameron Highlanders
On 21st May this W.O. was leader of a patrol. By his skill and leadership two enemy machine guns and 15 prisoners were captured; the same night he took part in an attack and though wounded five times continued the advance. His courage and leadership showed a splendid example to his men.   *(L.G. 22.10.40)*

Milligan, Roger Edwin, Lance Corporal
2555, 5 N.Z. Fd. Pk. Coy. (Immediate)
As a bulldozer operator L/Cpl. Milligan has displayed outstanding gallantry and has performed valuable work. At Nofilia he continued to work with energy and without hesitation in repairing heavily mined roads even though one bulldozer operator was fatally wounded and then another seriously injured by 'S' mines.

It was, however, at Sedada on 17th January 1943 and Beni Ulid on 19th January 1943 where his work in operating the bulldozer on heavily mined craters was of such outstanding value.

Dismayed by the explosion of several mines and the occurrence of casualties among adjacent personnel he rapidly cleared a track down the defile into Sedada and as a result both the 7 Armd. Div. and the 2 N.Z. Div. were able to continue their advance without delay.

At the demolished roads and mined craters through Beni Ulid he again rushed through highly dangerous road repairs despite bursting mines and numerous casualties. He was well aware of the risk that he was taking. It was very considerably due to the energy, coolness and bravery of L/Cpl. Milligan that the road repairs were completed in good time for the passage of 2 N.Z Div.

(L.G. 18.5.43)

Millington, Robert Edward, Private (A/Cpl.)
3653499, 2nd Bn. Gloucestershire Regt. (Liverpool)
(Immediate)

Cpl. Millington was commanding the leading sec. of 7 Platoon 'A' Coy. in the attack on the outer defences of Le Havre on 10th September 1944. His platoon was working with a tp. of tks., Crocodiles and Avre, leading the assault on Post No. 3 of the position.

There was a hold up passing through the gap due to one 'Croc' going up on a mine and Cpl. Millington found his sec. on the enemy side of the gap with the armoured support not yet through.

He had been ordered to push on as fast as possible and to get fullest effect from the concentrations.

Without further orders and with great dash he led his sec. without immediate support straight for his objective against a line of Spandau posts he had to traverse 300 yards of open country in the face of heavy DF and small arms fire. He reached his objective and neutralised the posts.

By his outstanding bravery, determination and complete disregard for his personal safety, Cpl. Millington was a great inspiration to the men under his command. His prompt and fearless action maintained the momentum of the Bn. attack and was responsible for him reaching his objective and capturing twenty prisoners who only gave themselves up when faced by a section of determined men with fixed bayonets.

(L.G. 21.12.44)

Millroy, Robert, Sergeant
408489, Reconnaissance Corps (Kingston-on-Thames)
No citation. *(L.G. 1.3.45)*

Milner, Thomas Edward, Sergeant
M.51023, 29 Cdn. Armd. Recce Regt. (8 Alts. R)
(Immediate)

On 24th April 1945 'C' Squadron 29 Cdn. Armd. Recce Regt. was advancing up the main Garrel—Oidenburg road to drive the enemy from dug in positions in the wood at MR 263904 (1/25,000 Sheet 2914 Germany). On reaching the edge of the wood the leading troop, commanded by Sgt. Milner, was engaged by enemy machine guns and Panzerfausts firing from strongly defended positions inside the wood. Realizing the difficulty of clearing the enemy without infantry support, Sgt. Milner withdrew his tanks out of range of the anti-tank weapons and engaged the enemy positions with intense direct fire from his own guns, indirect fire from a supporting squadron and a regiment of field arty. He then launched a second attack under this covering fire

but was again driven off by the heavy enemy fire which had not been reduced by the arty concentration. As it was impossible to advance in tanks until the Panzerfausts were driven out, Sgt. Milner ordered his tanks to provide covering machine gun fire while he went forward alone on foot carrying a shell casing full of petrol, a Verey pistol and some phosphorus grenades. Moving direct under the supporting fire, he worked his way to the closest trench, poured the petrol into it and ignited it with the Verey pistol and a grenade. Two of the enemy immediately surrendered. Using these two as a screen Sgt. Milner moved on towards the other enemy positions. Almost immediately the remaining enemy either surrendered or ran back out of the woods. Within a matter of minutes Sgt. Milner and his troop captured twenty German paratroops and moved on through the woods without loss of a man. The magnificent gallantry and leadership displayed by this N.C.O. in the face of fanatical opposition undoubtedly enabled his troop to clear a position that could easily have delayed the advance of his entire regiment until infantry support could be obtained. His initiative and complete disregard for personal safety were an inspiration to all ranks in his regiment. *(L.G. 22.9.45)*

Minchin, Robert Fraser, Private
TX 9149, 15 Aust. Inf. Bn. (Immediate)
Ref. Map Mivo River 1/25,000 (Revised 6th July 1945)

On 16th July 1945 Pte. Minchin was a member of a fighting patrol which left 'C' Coy. at 108337 and proceeded East across the Mivo River. At 114338, a party of enemy, far superior to the patrol both in numbers and firepower, were contacted, and the patrol was immediately fired upon by at least three enemy LMGs. The patrol was in a very critical position, and was forced to withdraw after suffering seven casualties.

At the time of the encounter, Pte. Minchin was forward scout, and, because of enemy fire could not withdraw with his section, but was forced to remain concealed behind a log. When the patrol withdrew, the enemy advanced and Pte. Minchin, quick to take advantage of the situation, immediately engaged the enemy with his OSMG, forcing them to take cover and preventing them from pursuing the patrol. He killed at least four enemy attempting to outflank him. By his determined single handed action, Pte. Minchin undoubtedly saved the remainder of the patrol from suffering many more casualties.

Pte. Minchin remained in the vicinity of 114338 for nearly two hours after his own patrol withdrew, engaging any enemy movement with OSMG fire, although two enemy LMGs were searching his area with fire. Later, when our own artillery fire was brought down on the area causing the enemy to withdraw, Pte. Minchin followed the enemy through the area and slept the night 16/17th July in the jungle just East of the enemy position.

On the morning of 17th July Pte. Minchin moved back through the enemy position and made observations of the defensive layout and the terrain North and East of the position. He recrossed the Mivo and joined his company and passed on the information he had collected together with details of the effectiveness of our own artillery fire and the enemy's reaction to it. Throughout the entire action right to the time of rejoining his company Pte. Minchin displayed great courage and coolness although isolated and under heavy fire from the enemy and from our own artillery. His offensive spirit and capable collection of information under conditions of great difficulty and danger have proved a very fine example and an inspiration to his fellow soldiers.

(*L.G. 12.10.45*)

Minnigin, George, M.M., Lance Sergeant
5501826, 5th Bn. Hampshire Regt. (Southampton)
(Immediate)
Italy. 1/50,000—Salerno.
　'White Cross Hill' 682322 and S. Nicola Sq. 6730.
　During the whole of the fighting round 'White Cross Hill,' 12th/21st September 1943, Cpl. Minnigan has shown outstanding leadership and devotion to duty, and has carried out tasks far above those which it was his duty to do.
　On September 15th, after the enemy had captured 'White Cross Hill,' Cpl. Minnigan was with a section of carriers which remained in S. Nicola village to watch and delay any enemy attempts to penetrate Southwards round the right flank of the Bn. Throughout the day the section was under continual M.G. and mortar fire. Cpl. Minnigan took over command and by his fine example and leadership kept the section together and remained in the village until dark.
　On more than one occasion during the day he went up onto the slopes of 'White Cross Hill' and brought back wounded and stragglers who had been left there after the Company which had counter-attacked the hill had been withdrawn.
　On the next day he went back to the village and brought in a wounded Italian from the area of the Pimple. On the same day he recovered an ambulance which had been fired on by the enemy and abandoned on the road to S. Nicola. It was impossible to turn the ambulance round on the road so Cpl. Minnigan drove it into S. Nicola village where he was able to turn it round.
　On the 17th an Italian reported that there was a wounded 'commando' in S. Nicola church. Cpl. Minnigan at once went out. He found the man but had insufficient dressing to bind up his wounds. He returned to collect some and then went back to the wounded man. He dressed his wounds and remained with him until it was possible to evacuate him after dark.
　On the nights 18/19/20th September, the carrier platoon was ordered to find standing patrols in S. Nicola village. Cpl. Minnigan at once volunteered to lead these patrols which he took to the village on all three occasions, remaining there throughout the night.

The example which this N.C.O. has set and the tireless energy he has shown have throughout been an inspiration to the whole platoon.
M.M. 22.4.43 　　　　　　　　　(*L.G. 13.1.44*)

Minns, John, M.M., Corporal
6847226, 2nd Bn. King's Royal Rifle Corps (London, S.E.15)
At Djebel Satour on 7th May 1943 Corporal Minns was sent out on a daylight patrol into the enemy F.D.L.s. The patrol consisted of one officer, Corporal Minns 2 i/c, and five others. Immediately after clearing a path through an enemy minefield, heavily booby trapped, the patrol was fired on by three enemy snipers and an L.M.G. at 80 yards range. In attempting to engage and destroy the opposition the officer was killed and Corporal Minns took charge. He at once made further efforts to stalk the enemy at closer quarters during which the patrol became pinned to the ground, where all members of the patrol including Corporal Minns became casualties. Undeterred by the enemy superiority, the loss of his commander and a very heavy artillery concentration Corporal Minns succeeded in working the patrol back under cover. Continuing to observe throughout the day he was able to fix the location of an enemy infantry position, two mortars and a 75mm gun. After dark he led back the patrol through the minefield and the fire of enemy L.M.G. fixed lines and report the valuable information he had gained in time to alter the plans of a Company detailed to move forward that night into the area he had patrolled.
　By his individual and most determined efforts to carry out his orders and despite his three wounds Corporal Minns turned what had begun a disastrous patrol into one of the greatest value. His gallant leadership throughout that most hazardous patrol resulting in all but one of the wounded returning safely to our lines.
M.M. 22.7.43 　　　　　　　　　(*L.G. 9.8.43*)

Mitchell, Frank Chalais, Sergeant
6457889, 1st Bn. Royal Fusiliers (20, Sherard Road, Eltham, E.9) (Immediate)
On the night 14/15th June 1941, Sgt. Mitchell was in charge of a section of carriers under the command of O.C. 'B' Coy. 1/R.F. who was holding a position immediately South of Saassa. At 0300 hours 'B' Coy. was attacked by at least 12 AFV's and a large number of infantry. Heavy fire compelled 'B' Coy. to withdraw. Sgt. Mitchell was ordered to cover the withdrawal. This he did with the greatest skill and the utmost gallantry. In the final stage he alone in his carrier held up the entire enemy force and although enemy tanks approached to within 50 yards of him and he was under a fierce fire, both small arms and guns, he held his ground until he was certain that all vehicles had withdrawn. He then extricated his own carrier and brought it out of action carrying 10 of 'B' Coy., some of whom were wounded.
　Again at Kuneitra on June 16th 1941, Sgt. Mitchell with a Bren Carrier and an anti-tank rifle was guarding a

road block which was attacked by two French medium tanks. After the road block was forced and the anti-tank rifle knocked out Sgt. Mitchell salvaged the Bren gun and collected grenades. He then went off 'tank hunting' in an endeavour to put grenades under the tracks of a tank. Having failed to damage the tank he returned to 'D' Coy. HQ and proceeded to use his Bren gun on enemy advancing on the Damascus road block. He maintained his gun in action until ordered to retire from the building. Throughout the actions he fought with the utmost determination and vigour and showed a total disregard for his own personal safety. His continuous aggressive action was a magnificent example of courage to all around him. He finally escaped from capture.
Recommended for V.C.　　　　　　　*(L.G. 2.12.41)*

Mitchell, Frank Patrick, Sergeant
NX 102436, 'M' Special Unit, Australian Military Forces
For conspicuous gallantry and leadership in operations within enemy territory.

On 5th February 1945 he was instructed to take five native troops to the native village of Jgitakua to clean out a number of enemy reported as ten. On arrival, he found this number reinforced to sixty; but he decided to carry on as instructed. (This operation was to coincide with a drop mission, to prevent news of our proximity to the enemy being reported to enemy HQ.) In the ensuing fight, during which the Japs used several Type 89 grenade discharges, one type 96 LMG, one Juki type 92 HMG, one SMG and several rifles (against Mitchell's one Bren and five Owens) twenty-eight enemy were killed or wounded, some dying later from wounds. Known dead were confirmed and graves later inspected. Mitchell brought the whole force back without single casualty.

In face of seemingly overwhelming odds this N.C.O. displayed extreme coolness, courage and devotion to duty in attacking and destroying 50% of the enemy force in this village. It is recommended that this act of bravery be rewarded with the award of the D.C.M.
　　　　　　　(L.G. 12.10.45)

Mitchell, George MacKenzie, Warrant Officer Cl. II (C.S.M.)
B46319, A. & S.H. of C., Canadian Infantry Corps
(Immediate)
On Friday, 8th September 1944 at about 1800 hrs. 'C' Coy., A & S.H. of C. was forming up preparatory to making an improvised crossing of the canal at Moerbrugge, Belgium. Fierce enemy fire upon the position reduced the Coy. str. from 63 to 46 and imperilled the success of the crossing. With utter indifference to direct shell fire at 300 yards range C.S.M. Mitchell aided the two remaining Coy. offrs. in organizing boat positions, rallying the men and attending the cas. The crossing was successfully made and consolidation effected largely due to this W.O.'s efforts. At first light on 9th September 1944 the enemy in approximate str. of one bn. attacked

the 'C' Coy. position and succeeded in surrounding it. The Coy. was without comns. and reduced to reliance on rifle and L.M.G. fire since it's Piat and mortar men and their eqpt. had been cas. during the crossing. The C.S.M. continually visited positions, encouraging the men and personally broke the most determined enemy assault by firing Bren gun and grenades from a second story window while fully exposed to enemy fire from houses directly across the narrow street. At about noon the enemy renewed the attack against the Coy. which by now was even more depleted in str. The C.S.M. in the interval had worked strenuously and unceasingly in reorganizing the position, strengthening it, attending to cas. and reallocating weapons and amn. Greatly outnumbered in the face of the new attack which was supported by six 20 mm A.A. guns, M.M.G.s and three 8 cm mortars, the Coy. continued to hold its position. C.S.M. Mitchell again personally broke the back of the attack by forcing the enemy out of their most menacing position using 36 grenades. At about 1500 hours the Coy. still isolated and under fire was reduced to 37 O.R.s with the Coy. Comd. as the only offr. A strong fighting patrol had failed to break through and relieve the pressing shortage of amn., food and water. C.S.M. Mitchell took out a party and returned with all of these as well as an M.O. who gave the wounded the first expert attention they had received. Throughout the entire operation C.S.M. Mitchell was an inspiration to all the men in his Coy. By his coolness and courage under fire and his complete disregard for personal safety he was undoubtedly, both by leadership and personal example, a decisive influence on the successful est. and maintenance of the br. head by the bn.　　　　　　　*(L.G. 9.12.44)*

Mitchell, Henry James, Sergeant
867330, 2 Grenadier Guards
This N.C.O. commanded a platoon on the extreme left of the Brigade Sector near Furnes. During 30th May, troops further to the left were seen to be retiring from the Canal bank, consequent, upon very heavy shelling and the loss of all their Officers. Sjt. Mitchell proceeded from his position to intercept these troops and by his determination and posers of leadership led them back to their positions. He then took charge and distributed ammunition and collected wounded, walking along the canal bank regardless of enemy fire. His initiative and gallantry undoubtedly restored a very difficult situation.
Duplicated entry L.G. 22.10.40　　　*(L.G. 11.7.40)*

Mitchell, Peter, Sergeant
2698385, 2 Special Air Service Regiment, Army Air Corps
Serjeant Mitchell was one of a detachment of 2nd S.A.S. Regiment which was dropped in daylight by parachute in the area of Chieti on 2nd October 1943, with the object of collecting escaped British P.O.W. for embarkation under 'A' Force arrangements.

On landing the party was fired on by the enemy who had seen the descent, but they managed to make good their escape. During the next week the party aided a total of 300 P.O.W. to the evacuation beach R.V.'s.

After the 12th October no more landing craft were available but the party suceeded in finding a further 250 P.O.W. and putting them on to the best route to the Allied lines.

Between the 20th and 30th October two German convoys were attacked by this party inflicting damage and casualties on the enemy.

For the next two months further P.O.W. were assisted by the party, and a number of Fascists who were actively assisting the Germans were killed.

On 4th January 1944, Sjt. Mitchell, in company with another N.C.O., was in a house and found himself surrounded by approximately a company of the enemy. Sjt. Mitchell shot his way out of the trap and continued firing until all his ammunition was exhausted.

He made good his escape and finally, after lying up and changing into civilian clothes, he succeeded in crossing the line near Guradiagrele early in March 1944. He brought with him some 20 ex-P.O.W. whom he had collected en route.

Sjt. Mitchell was active behind the lines for six months. During this period he was largely responsible for the successful return of a considerable number of British ex-P.O.W.s, and continually showed a fine offensive spirit.

His devotion to duty during this period is worthy of high praise.   *(L.G. 9.11.44)*

Mitchell, Wayne Robert, Private
M.800148, Princess Patricia's Canadian Light
*   Infantry, Royal Canadian Infantry Corps*
For Korea   *(L.G. 9.10.51)*

Moat, Jack, Sergeant
7887542, 1 Royal Tank Regt. (Canterbury)
*   (Immediate)*
Sgt. Moat was in command of a Sherman tank during an action to clear the enemy from the area of Corso near S'Hertogenbosch on 30th September 1944.

Sgt. Moat's tank was in a position of observation directing arty fire when it was observed by an enemy OP and heavy and accurate mortar fire was quickly brought down on it. Sgt. Moat was hit in the head by splinters from a mortar bomb which burst against the tank aerial and the tank refused to start up. Sgt. Moat then climbed out of his tank and attempted to hitch the tow rope of another tank on by himself. He was unable to do this and so he collected two members of his crew to help him, both these men were killed by mortar fire while attempting to fix the tow rope and so Sgt. Moat finished the job himself. By this time a Spandau had opened up on him as well as the mortar fire so he climbed back into his tank and engaged the Spandau himself with his Browning and destroyed it. He then ordered the tank

to be towed away and went forward on foot to try and deal with the mortar OP.

He located the OP and captured it himself taking 12 P/W. This action put a stop to the mortar fire and undoubtedly saved many lives. This N.C.O.'s aggressive spirit and cool courage were an inspiration to his troop and by his action he opened the way for the advance to continue.
Recommended for M.M.   *(L.G. 1.3.45)*

Moffat, Thomas, Warrant Officer Cl. II (actg.)
740392, 2nd Bn. Loyal Regt. (Preston)
During the operations in Johore and Singapore in January and February 1942 this warrant officer displayed great gallantry under fire and by his example inspired those around him with a determination and aggressive spirit. In the fighting West of Singapore during the later stages he was responsible, in some critical periods, for directing controlled fire which resulted in considerable casualties to the enemy, and materially affected the local situation. He invariably showed little regard for his own safety and proved himself a courageous leader in the field.
                    (L.G. 13.12.45)

Mohamed, Abukr, Ombashi
40602, Sudanese Defence Forces
No citation.   *(L.G. 29.9.42)*

Mohammed, Jamaluddin bin, Corporal
1319, Malay Regt.
For Malaya   *(L.G. 7.7.50)*

Mohammed, Musa, Bashshawish
Sudanese Defence Forces
No citation.   *(L.G. 5.11.42)*

Moir, Thomas, Sergeant
1481, 4th Field Regt., New Zealand Military Forces
*   (Periodic)*
Sgt. Moir was one of the party of nine, including L/Bdr. Johnston and Ptes. McKergow and Collins, who have also been recommended for recognition, which arrived recently from Crete.

They were all captured immediately after the fighting and escaped within a month.

Like the other odd P/W at liberty on Crete, they wandered in twos and threes from village to village living as long as they could in each place—generally in the district West of Maleme.

They found a boat—only to discover it was not seaworthy. They tried a second time, but this time the weather defeated them. They then heard of two diesel-engined and several sailing boats at the village of Mesoyia. They stole the best looking sailing boat as the owner might have removed a vital part of the diesel engined boat and the noise it made might attract the Germans. There was also the problem of petrol.

They spent the next two days collecting olives and bread from their friends in the hills—but many others must have known they were going because they were caught as they set off. Though the Cretans were sympathetic, robbery was not taken lightly: protests and warnings of bad weather and certain shipwreck were flung at them. But nine determined men, hardened by months of rough living were not easily thwarted, and they sailed on the 8/9th April 1942 at midnight.

They had little water and put in a sheltered creek where they knew of a brackish but drinkable well in the hills above and left again that night hoping to reach Mersa Matrouh.

Two days later the mountains of Crete could still be seen about sixty miles away. German aircraft passed by but paid no attention.

Sgt. Moir had had some experience of navigation and L/Bdr. Johnston had done some sailing.

On 14th April they landed at Sidi Barrani with about 16 days' supply of water, a few olives and three loaves of bread in hand.

There seems to have been no question of leadership of this party. Their problems were resolved by discussion, but credit for their safe crossing must go to Sgt. Moir and L/Bdr. Johnston.

This party, in view of their long stay on the island under the most trying conditions and in constant danger of recapture, experienced an extraordinarily difficult time behind the enemy lines on Crete, and their final escape from the island required great courage and determination.

Undaunted by all they have been through, however, Sgt. Moir, with L/Bdr. Johnston and Ptes. McKergow and Collins, has now volunteered to return to rescue the remaining escapers on the island.
Recommended for B.E.M. M.M. 20.6.46 for Crete 1941 (P.O.W.) No citation. (*L.G. 9.9.42*)

Monaghan, Peter, Warrant Officer Cl. III (T.S.M.)
1065892, 13 A/T Regt., Royal Artillery
Throughout the operations in Belgium and France T.S.M. Monaghan showed conspicuous courage, foresight and initiative. As a result of his determination all four guns of his troop reached the Dunkerque area intact and in full fighting order. Finally at daybreak on 2nd June after orders had been given for embarkation and a hitch in the supply of boats had occurred T.S.M. Monaghan found a sailing boat containing food but no crew. He took charge of the boat and sailed it across the Channel, without charts, with nearly 200 officers and men on board. The boat was located by the Dover Patrol 24 hours later and brought safely into harbour. (*L.G. 20.12.40*)

Monkhouse, John William, Corporal (actg.)
14209568, A/Cpl., 1st Bn. East Lancashire Regt.
  (Seaton, Cumberland)
This N.C.O. commanded a sec. in the leading Coy. during the advance through the Reichswald on 11th February 1945. The Coy. was held up by an enemy position of Coy. strength well dug in and concealed in the thick undergrowth in the forest. Cpl. Monkhouse's platoon came under fire from enemy M.G. positions some 200 yards to the right of the axis of advance. While the leading sec. returned the fire, the remainder of the platoon went to cover and worked into fire positions. While this was being done, another enemy M.G. opened fire some 50 yards away to the front of the platoon and strong parties of enemy commenced infiltrating between the left flank of the Coy. and the track along which the Bn. was advancing. Seeing this, Cpl. Monkhouse at once got his Bren gunner into a position to give him covering fire and then on his own initiative, in spite of heavy and accurate fire from enemy small arms, he dashed forward and assaulted single-handed the enemy M.G. position. During this advance, Cpl. Monkhouse was under continuous fire but regardless of his own danger he carried straight on until he reached the enemy weapon slits, where, using his Sten and throwing grenades, he personally killed five Germans and captured the gun.

This N.C.O.'s inspiring example of personal gallantry and initiative enabled the remainder of the Coy. to carry on with the main attack on the enemy Coy. locality.
(*L.G. 10.5.45*)

Monks, Charles Edward, Corporal
2329993, Signal Company, 50th Parachute Bde.,
  Royal Signals (Warrington)
For Conspicuous gallantry and coolness in action.

At the position known as Red Hill near Buri Bazar on 28th May 1944, the 3/1st Gurkha Rifles were ordered to make a Bn. attack to clear the enemy from the South Eastern portion of the hill. Each company was allotted a British Signaller from 50th Parachute Brigade HQ with a light R.T. set, as this Bde. HQ had the Bn. under command at this time. At the start of the attack the C.O., Adj. and three Rifle Coy. Comds. were all killed or wounded. Cpl. Monks was with one of the two forward Coys. which were under close and heavy fire from the enemy from small arms, grenades and a Bn. gun. When their British Officers were all killed these Coys. wavered and started to fall back. Cpl. Monks however rallied them and stopped the movement to the rear. He then passed back accurate and clear information over the R.T. and by his cheerfulness and complete disregard of personal danger persuaded the Gurkha officers to organize a second attack on the position. This was done and Cpl. Monks again went forward with the attacking troops. He continued to pass back information clearly and calmly and it was in very great part due to his courage and example that the attack, which was in great danger of failing with heavy casualties succeeded in the end. This was all the more noteworthy as Cpl. Monks could not speak any Gurkhali so that all he did was accomplished by signs and personal example. All the Gurkha ranks and the only British Officer left at Bn. HQ could not give enough praise to this gallant and resourceful N.C.O.

This citation is written on the report submitted by the 3/1 Gurkha Rifles themselves.   *(L.G. 22.3.45)*

Montgomery, Walter, Guardsman
2718746, 1st Bn. Irish Guards (Belfast)
This Guardsman took part in the successful night attack by No. 1 Coy. on the night 29/30th January on the left of the main axis Anzio—Albano road. On reaching the objective, the ground was found to be covered by enemy tanks who attempted to prevent the Coy. digging in by putting up flares and firing M.G.s on the digging parties. All through the night this Gdsn. gave what covering fire he could to his comrades by firing at the enemy tanks with his Bren gun. This covering fire could not be very effective, but it did force the enemy tanks to limit their vision by shutting down their Visors and exposed this Gdsn. to the continued attention of the enemy. When morning 30th January came and no supporting arms or British ranks appeared, the Coy. position was untenable and the Coy. was ordered to withdraw to another position on the flank. With great coolness and fine courage this Guardsman, accompanied by Gdsn. Taylor, set up his Bren on the top of the railway cutting and gave covering fire to the remainder of the ... *[continuation missing].*
(L.G. 15.6.44)

Moody, John James, Sergeant
5627323, 1st Bn. Somerset Light Infantry (London, S.E.16) (Immediate)
On Pyinshe Kala Ridge.
    28th February/1st March, Sgt. Moody was in comd. of the fwd. platoon of his Coy. at the Southern tip of this very narrow ridge. On night 28/29th February the platoon holding the main position in rear of and overlooking his position, was driven out by the enemy leaving him isolated. For the next 15 hours Sgt. Moody held his position under continual harassing by arty mortars and snipers, and hit back inflicting casualties on the enemy reinforcing and supplying their tps. in his rear. The enemy sent a bogus V force agent with orders for him to retire, who was suitably dealt with. Attempts to contact Sgt. Moody's platoon failed. Towards evening on 29th February, the mortar fire became so accurate on Sgt. Moody's position that he moved his platoon to an alternative one. His men had only their emergency ration left but Sgt. Moody had not allowed this to be consumed. Under cover of darkness on 29th February, Sgt. Moody evacuated his position and returned to Coy. HQ on the morning of 1st March. He showed throughout courage and leadership of a high standard and continued to act offensively at every opportunity.   *(L.G. 18.5.44)*

Mooney, Benjamin, Sergeant
4864164, 1st Leicestershire Regt. (Leicester)
    (Periodic)
Sjt. Mooney took over command of a platoon in July 1944. He has commanded that platoon until now.

At Le Havre, when his Coy. were putting in an attack to capture a hill, a Spandau was holding up the advance of his platoon by its accurate fire. Sjt. Mooney personally led a sec. against this Spandau and silenced it killing two, and capturing another of the team.

By his magnificent bravery and complete disregard for his own personal safety in attacking and silencing this Spandau Sjt. Mooney enabled his platoon to reach their objective.

At Merxplas Sjt. Mooney again led his platoon with great dash and again personally led a sec. against a Spandau team and captured it. Having reached the objective he ordered the platoon to dig in and although the platoon were being fired on by numerous Spandaus and one SP gun he walked round his platoon position organising the defence of his area and encouraging the men.

At Stone Br near Wustwezel, although attacked by 4 tks. and approx. 100 infantry and although his platoon were almost surrounded, Sjt. Mooney refused to be downhearted and continued to lead, organise, and encourage his men to hold on and beat off all attacks until the enemy eventually withdrew.

At Brembosch he led his platoon over an A/Tk. ditch, which was covered with fire and filled with water, and captured his objective and 30 prisoners.

At Roosendaal he again led his platoon over an A/Tk. ditch which was covered by fire and filled with water. Having reached his objective Sjt. Mooney found that a party of the enemy had got into a farm house approx. 200 yards in front of his objective and were bringing heavy fire on his men.

Sjt. Mooney personally led a party which attacked and captured the house and brought back under very heavy fire approx. 20 prisoners.

During the 4 months period on the island near Nijmegen, he never relaxed his discipline over his platoon. At this time he took out at least 10 patrols. He always achieved more than he was told to do and always gained valuable information for future attacks.

Sjt. Mooney's platoon has done as much under his command as any other platoon in the Bn.

This has been due almost entirely to Sjt. Mooney's inspired leadership, his perpetual cheerfulness, his great sense of humour and above all to his wonderful example of courage, bravery and complete disregard for his own personal safety.
M.I.D. 9.8.45   *(L.G. 24.1.46)*

Moore, Alfred George, Corporal (A/Sgt.)
6143807, East Surrey Regt. (New Malden)
Italy.
M.I.D. 20.12.40   *(L.G. 26.10.44)*

Moore, Archibald, Lance Corporal
3192988, 5th Bn. King's Own Scottish Borderers
(Stevenson) (Immediate)
On 21st January 1945 at Waldfeucht Pte. Moore was the loader of a six pounder anti-tank gun which was in position in the open when two enemy Tiger tanks approached. Pte. Moore, inspite of being under heavy and accurate small arms and shell fire, carried out his duties with coolness and efficiency. When the N.C.O. directing the fire of the gun was wounded Pte. Moore took over his duties and directed the fire of the gun until the tank was destroyed and the crew tried to escape. Pte. Moore then took over the Bren gun from a comrade who had been killed and engaged the escaping tank crew and some infantry in the area.

His personal disregard of danger and his coolness, efficiency and initiative were largely responsible for the destruction of two enemy Tiger tanks at very short range and his example was an inspiration to all members of his gun crew.   *(L.G. 12.4.45)*

Moore, Horace, Sergeant
406289, 10th Royal Hussars (Birmingham)
(Immediate)
On the morning of 23rd November 1944 near S. Lucia, Sgt. Moore was commanding a tank supporting the Infantry Bn. which had crossed the river Cosina during the night. The Inf. had captured intact the only remaining bridge over the river, and were holding a very small bridgehead beyond it.

It was vital for the success of the operations of the whole Div. that this bridge be held. The enemy realised this and made every effort to recapture and destroy the bridge.

Sgt. Moore got his tank across the bridge just before first light. He pushed forward in the most determined way in the half-light, and in conditions which confined his movement to the roads, which he knew would be covered by Anti-tank fire. By his determination and disregard for danger he advanced several hundred yards and thus enabled the infantry to enlarge the all important bridgehead.

Enemy defensive fire by guns, mortars and nebel-wefers was very heavy, and eventually forced the Inf. to withdraw a short distance. Undaunted by this, and by the fact that his vision and field of fire were very greatly impeded by houses and the close nature of the country, Sgt. Moore held his ground. Although he knew that enemy snipers and bazooka men might well be stalking him he dismounted from his tank and went into the upstairs window of a house to get observation. From there he spotted an enemy Tiger tank manoeuvring into position 400 yards from him. Whilst he was endeavouring to engage this another enemy tank appeared, approaching at a fast speed down the road. With the greatest coolness and speed he engaged this and knocked it out, thereby effectively blocking the road to other enemy tanks. As a result the enemy soon abandoned his counter-attack with tanks, and the remaining tanks withdrew. Twenty-one enemy infantry then surrendered to Sgt. Moore, some of them from positions in his rear.

This N.C.O. showed the most outstanding skill and initiative in very awkward conditions, and by remaining in his most advanced position alone he stemmed the enemy counter-attack in this vital sector. His coolness and example were a magnificent encouragement to the infantry he was supporting and probably was decisive in enabling the bridgehead to be held.   *(L.G. 10.5.45)*

Moore, Robert Henry, Private
6141948, East Surrey Regt. (London, S.W.2)
On February 26th at Goubellat, 12 Platoon was ordered to counter-attack Fort MacGregor. After traversing some 1,000 yards of very flat country and when some 400 yards from the enemy, the platoon was pinned to the ground by very heavy M.G. fire. Pte. Moore, then acting as a runner, at great risk to himself, ran the gauntlet of fire and brought a message to the effect that the platoon would withdraw. He stayed until all the platoon had withdrawn and then helped back the Platoon Commander who was wounded.

Although forbidden to do so, he returned to the platoon position under heavy fire to bring back a Bren gun. The gun was jammed and although he was being sniped at he took the gun to pieces, rectified the trouble, and then turned it on the sniper whom he killed. He then went across and obtained papers and photographs from the body.

During the rest of the day this man worked continually with the carrier platoon bringing in wounded prisoners.

Throughout he showed utter disregard for his own safety and was an inspiring example to those around him

This man could not be recommended for immediate award before owing to the fact that his platoon officer, Lt. Louis has only just returned from hospital.
     (L.G. 8.7.43)

Moore, Ronald Joseph, Trooper
1248, 2nd N.Z. Div. Cav. Regt., Long Range Desert
Group.
After the engagement at Gevel Sherif South West of Kufra on 31st January 1941, Tpr. Moore and three other private soldiers were 'missing, believed killed'; in reality they were hiding from enemy aircraft and ground troops, their trucks and weapons having been destroyed, and did not see the retirement of their patrol which was made according to orders. Moore was wounded in the foot, one of the others had a bullet wound in the throat and third suffered from an internal injury of long standing.

Next morning, 1st February, they collected one 2-gallon tin of water, but no food, from one of the British vehicles which had been destroyed and burnt, and under the leadership of Moore started to walk South Westward along the tracks by which the patrol had retired towards the French outpost of Tekro 300 miles away. Soon afterwards they picked up one small tin of jam which was soon eaten.

They walked for 10 days and covered 210 miles of sand desert, with no further supplies of water or food, before they were picked up by the French. One man died soon afterwards.

That any of them survived this amazing journey is entirely due to the efforts of Moore, who eked out their tiny store of water, supported the other weaker men by his own example leadership, and kept them on the correct route which had for long stretches been obliterated by a sand storm. In addition he showed a remarkable combination of tact and firmness in dealing with one of the men who, younger and less intelligent than the other two, had soon become mentally deranged.
M.I.D. 8.7.41   *(L.G. 25.4.41)*

Moorin, Aaron, Gunner (A/Bdr.)
1436449, 190th Field Regt. Royal Artillery (Glasgow)
On 29th June 1944 this man was at an O.P. at Cheux with his Bty. comdr. as an O.P.A. The position had been counter-attacked heavily and was later being continuously and heavily mortared. The B.C. sent Moorin to the HQ of the Bn. supported for information as to the position and on his return he found the B.C. killed and the signaller seriously wounded. Moorin at once reported this to the C.O. by wireless and was ordered to continue in the position, and report the situation by wireless. This he did under continued heavy fire passing valuable information. Later when the Bns. wireless broke down orders for the Bn. were sent to him by the Bde. Comdr. over the R.A. wireless net. These he delivered and then sent back their replies and information. Each of these meant a journey of 50 yards under heavy fire. He continued to do this for over 4 hours until relieved by another party under an officer. During that time he was the only R.A. representative with the Bn.

I consider that this Junior N.C.O. displayed a very high degree of courage and determination to ensure support of the Infantry in the most adverse circumstances and regardless of personal danger.   *(L.G. 19.10.44)*

Mordin, James Edward, Sergeant
855505, 98 (Surrey and Sussex Yeomanry Q.M.R.)
  Field Regt., Royal Artillery
Acting as 'E' troop B.S.M. detached from his battery in the defence of Hazebrouck, 27th May observed eleven tanks proceeding across his front. This N.C.O. immediately engaged these tanks with 'E' 2 gun which came under heavy fire from one tank which 'hulled down.' 'E' 2 fired about twenty rounds and several hits were scored, the remaining tanks dispersed and withdrew. It was only when 'E' 2 gun was completely wrecked and four of the detachment killed or wounded did Sergeant Mordin, who although wounded, make arrangements for the withdrawal of the detachment before he collapsed. Throughout this engagement, Sergeant Mordin's conduct was an inspiring example to all.   *(L.G. 20.12.40)*

Morgan, Arthur Stephen, Lance Sergeant
4189542, 1st Royal Welch Fusiliers (Newport, Mon.)
  (Immediate)
On 13th march 1945, 4189542 Cpl. Morgan was in command of a sec. of 13 Platoon 'C' Coy., 1 R.W.F.

The task of the coy. was to adv. with one sqn. of tks. in sp. along the axis of the Ava Rd. from MS 10 to occupy the village of Thinban.

On reaching the area of thick scrub about 250 yds South of the gp. of pagodas at 432453, the two leading pls. of the coy. came under extremely heavy and accurate automatic and sniper fire from a number of well concealed enemy positions to their front and on their flanks.

Although held up on the right, 13 platoon continued to adv. on the left in face of withering small arms fire. Cpl. Morgan led his sec. in front of the tp. of tks. and, with utter disregard for his own personal safety, adv. to within a yard of the enemy positions, killing the Japanese where they stood in their fox-holes with his Sten gun and hand grenades. As the tks. adv. Cpl. Morgan himself walked in front of them and, by dropping smoke grenades into the entrance of Japanese fox-holes, although he himself was within point blank range of enemy fire, indicated the positions so well to the tks. that the latter were able to destroy the positions completely.

When he ran out of grenades, Cpl. Morgan continued to indicate targets to the tks. by going up to the positions and pointing them out.

During the whole of this time, Cpl. Morgan was continually under very heavy enemy fire and, apart from positions which were destroyed under his directions by the tks., he himself destroyed no less than five Japanese positions.

Throughout the engagement, this N.C.O.'s conduct was beyond all praise. He displayed outstanding initiative and his personal courage and exemplary bearing were an inspiration to all ranks. It was entirely due to his efforts that the enemy in these positions were so successfully eliminated.   *(L.G. 2.8.45)*

Morgan, Dewi Meurig, Sergeant (A/T.S.M.)
Ply X.4501, Royal Marines
For Malaya   *(L.G. 11.1.52)*

Morgan, Eric, Warrant Officer Cl. II (C.S.M.)
3596878, Border Regt.
No citation.   *(L.G. 20.12.40)*

Morgan, George Moscrip, Lance Corporal
2758665, 7 Black Watch (Rutherglen, Lanarkshire)
On the morning of 21st January 1943, 7 Black Watch put in an attack in order to get astride the main road East of Corradini and cut off the enemy rear guard. L/Cpl. Morgan was with the Bn. compass party and during the early stages of this action, just after daybreak, he succeeded in getting his Bren gun into action, notwithstanding heavy M.G. and Mortar fire. At this time the

compass party were on a completely exposed and bare hill face under heavy fire. L/Cpl. Morgan succeeded, however, in temporarily silencing two enemy M.G.s by the fire of his Bren, and by so doing he enabled the compass party to get forward into the cover of a small wadi.

At this point the Officer i/c Compass Party had to return to Bn. HQ to report upon the situation. Any movement from the wadi drew intense fire from enemy M.G.s and the officer was wounded almost immediately he left the cover of the wadi. L/Cpl. Morgan realised there was no hope of the officer reaching Bn. HQ unless the enemy M.G.s were engaged more closely still. He again succeeded in bringing his Bren into action, from a new fire position, though this was devoid of all cover. Here, in addition to being fired at by M.G.s he was subjected to very heavy and accurate mortar fire. He kept his gun in action, however, and undercover of his fire the wounded officer got back to Bn. HQ and made his report. He continued to keep his gun in action until his whole amn. supply was exhausted. Throughout this action L/Cpl. Morgan displayed the greatest coolness and courage. He took the most deliberate risks in order to safeguard his party and his gallant action undoubtedly saved a very difficult situation and was noted by many at the time. It also provided the means of getting back information to his Commanding Officer which was of the greatest value to him subsequently in making his plan.
Recommended for M.M. (L.G. 22.4.43)

Morgan, James, Private
2823589, 4th Bn. Seaforth Highlanders
During the attack on the Abbeville Bridgehead on the 4th June 1940, Private Morgan was wounded by machine gun fire. He lay out under full and close observation of the enemy from 4.30 in the morning until about 10.00 pm.

As he began to move back under cover of darkness, he found a man too badly wounded to move. Although himself suffering considerably from several bullet wounds about the arms and shoulders, he lifted his comrade on to his back and carried him nearly two miles to the Regimental Aid Post.
Recommended for M.M. (L.G. 18.10.40)

Morgan, William, Corporal (A/Sgt.)
4188023, 1st Bn. Royal Welch Fusiliers
On 24th May, at Calonne Sur Lys, the advance was held up by enemy armed with Tommy Guns and a Machine Gun Post. Cpl. Morgan successfully disposed of these Germans armed with Tommy Guns taking them prisoners, then went forward himself and put the Machine Gun post out of action with a hand grenade.
(L.G. 22.10.40)

Morgans, Maldwyn Richard, Lance Corporal
2078514, 245 Field Coy., Royal Engineers (Neath)
(Immediate)
L/Cpl. Morgan was in a mine clearing detachment detailed to clear gaps through enemy minefields on the Moletta River immediately in front of the assaulting infantry in the attack on enemy positions in the Sandhills on 23rd May 1944. In the move up with an infantry covering party his Platoon Officer was killed and several wounded by an 'S' mine exploding. L/Cpl. Morgan immediately assumed command and reorganised the remainder of the mine clearing party and successfully cleared a path through the minefield which was under continuous enemy fire. He then went back and brought forward the infantry covering party through the gap and into position where scaling ladders were placed to enable the infantry to cross the Moletta. He then withdrew his party and went back along the route to contact the Inf. Coy. moving up to the assault. It was largely due to this prompt and effective action and to L/Cpl. Morgan's outstanding bravery and leadership in the face of determined enemy fire that the task was completed, which enabled the infantry to reach their objective according to plan. (L.G. 21.9.44)

Moriarty, Maurice, Lance Corporal
2710497, 1st Bn. Irish Guards (London, N.12) (since killed in action) (Immediate)
This L/Cpl. was stretcher bearer to No. 2 Coy. During the night attack 29/30th January 1944, the Coy. suffered heavy casualties when it came up against a belt of defensive fire, laid by 8 enemy M.G.s in the narrow strip between the Anzio—Albano road and the railway line running parallel to it. Cpl. Moriarty worked tirelessly and unsparingly all night, dragging wounded men from under M.G. fire with complete disregard for his own safety. During the preliminary arty conc. and subsequent enemy night attack on night 3rd/4th February, this Cpl. again showed himself completely fearless in attending to the wounded and taking them to positions of comparative safety. After the attempt to form a strong point round the road, cutting and railway bridge had been abandoned, Cpl. Moriarty remained behind by the road, tending the wounded, ignoring the shells and bullets which were now falling and flying directly up the road from enemy positions on the high ground on the other side of the Anzio—Albano road. Single handed, under heavy fire, this Cpl. collected up to a dozen wounded men and put them between the bank and some carriers. The position was overrun by the enemy who ordered this Cpl. to march off to the rear as a P.O.W. This, Cpl. Moriarty refused to do, although threatened, with a revolver, and had not a German soldier fortunately been wounded at this moment, he would probably have been shot. He remained with the wounded all the rest of that day and night and the following day, refusing to leave our wounded, although the whole position was subjected to heavy and accurate shelling by our 25-pdrs. and

medium guns. The following night, with remarkable resource and initiative, he seized the opportunity to load the wounded on to two carriers, and together with another man, drove them away suddenly in a successful dash for the Scots Gds. lines. The tireless devotion of the Cpl. to his wounded comrades and his complete disregard of his personal safety or the consequences to himself of his courageous actions are an exceptional example of gallantry, self-sacrifice and resource.

I strongly recommend Cpl. Moriarty for the immediate award of the D.C.M.   *(L.G. 15.6.44)*

Morland, Peter Douglas, Warrant Officer Cl. II (C.S.M.)
3655808, South Lancashire Regt., attd. S.S.T., No. 2 Commando (Wallasey) (Immediate)
Spilje Bay, Albania July 28th–29th 1944 Operation 'Healing II'
This Warrant Officer went into action in the role of a Section Officer. Throughout the whole action Morland showed a complete disregard for his own safety, initiative and great powers of leadership. On the first attack, his section came under heavy machine-gun fire and suffered casualties. He rallied his men and led the charge clearing the ridge. On the second attack his section again came under heavy fire causing many casualties, but armed with a pistol, he by his gallantry and leadership, pressed home the attack and cleared his objective. He then immediately gave first aid to the wounded, arranged their evacuations, and made two attempts to get over the crest of a ridge, and rescue two men, after three other attempts had been unsuccessful. In the latter stages, his section was reduced to a mere handful of men. Seeing that the other section was in difficulties, he collected men of different troops and another regiment, put in an attack and enabled the other section to withdraw. In the last stages of the battle, having no men, under heavy mortar and machine-gun fire, he helped evacuate the wounded to the regimental aid post he had formed and thence back to the beachhead. His example, fine and untiring energy throughout were an inspiration to all. This Warrant Officer has consistently shown great courage in previous actions in Norway, Scaletta and Salerno, and on other Commando raids on the Yugo-Slav islands.   *(L.G. 5.10.44)*

Morris, Alec Henry, Warrant Officer Cl. I
12840, Royal Australian Infantry Corps
Award dated 23.4.68. For Vietnam   *(L.G. 10.12.68)*

Morris, Frederick Benjamin, Guardsman
2735425, 2nd Bn. Welsh Guards (Swansea)
This man has been the Turret Gunner in a Tk. ever since fighting in Normandy.

In the Battle of Hechtel on 10th September 1944 he knocked out an 88 mm gun. In order to get a proper vision of this gun, he and his Tk. Comd. dismounted and sawed off the branch of a tree in full view of the enemy before destroying the 88 mm gun.

Just beyond Nijmegen on 21st September 1944, he knocked out two enemy Tks. within 10 minutes. In this action he displayed the greatest coolness, as his own Tk. was on a raised causeway and in a very vulnerable position.

On the evening of 26th April 1945, his Tp. was ordered to seize the high ground North of Kirchtimke. It was impossible to get off the road, owing to heavy going.

The leading Tk. was knocked out by a German SP gun firing from the high ground, and the Tp. Ldr. got out of this Gdsm's Tk. to help rescue the crew of the damaged Tk. In the absence of the Tp. Ldr., this Gdsm. took charge, backed his Tk. to get a Hull-Down position, at the same time returning the enemy fire. Three SP guns were now firing at him, and a shell hit and penetrated his Tk. and blew his foot off.

This Gdsm. got out of the Tk., but, although unable to walk, refused help until another wounded man had been evacuated. He has lost his leg above the knee as the result of this action.

Throughout the entire campaign this soldier has produced a very high standard of Gunnery, and has at all times exhibited a great devotion to duty, perfect coolness under fire, and complete disregard of his own personal safety.   *(L.G. 24.1.46)*

Morrison, Edward John, Sergeant (temp.)
3/1967, Royal Australian Regt.
For Korea   *(L.G. 14.4.53)*

Morrison, Edward John, D.C.M., Warrant Officer Cl. I
                                                  Bar
31967, Royal Australian Infantry
WO Morrison served overseas with the 2nd/1st Machine Gun Battalion during the Second World War from 1941 to 1945 and re-enlisted in the Australian Regular Army in 1951. He was decorated on two occasions for gallantry with the 3rd Battalion of the Royal Australian Regiment in Korea. In 1964 he was selected as an advisor with the Australian Army Training Team in Vietnam and was appointed a Battalion Advisor to the Vietnamese Armed Forces.

During the night 8th/9th December 1964, head-quarters personnel of the 3rd Battalion of the 3rd Regiment of the Army of the Republic of Vietnam, supported by two field guns, were in a defensive position on Hill 159 in Quang Tin Province. With this force were Lieutenant B. K. Skinner of the United States Army and WO Morrison.

At approximately midnight, a Viet Cong force estimated as a reinforced battalion attacked the hill. During the attack, although severely wounded by grenades, WO Morrison by leadership and example, sustained and rallied the small group in defence. Eventually, at 0330 hours with the defence pushed back by overwhelming numbers he organised a withdrawal to the artillery position where further defence was made with small arms and with the artillery firing at point blank range.

Lieutenant Skinner had also been wounded in the early stages of the attack and when their wounds could no longer be neglected both the advisors were temporarily moved to a nearby sheltered position for treatment.

As dawn was breaking, the artillery position was [...] and at extreme personal risk both the advisors reconnoitred the Viet Cong disposition on top of the hill for counter-attack. During this reconnaisance Lieutenant Skinner was killed and WO Morrison again wounded.

The defence by this small force was sufficient to delay the Viet Cong and permit the arrival of a relief column which, with daylight, retook the hill. The whole operation resulted in most severe losses to the Viet Cong and permitted highly successful follow-up action.

Although severely wounded, WO Morrison displayed outstanding qualities of leadership, bravery and devotion to duty. *[From L.G.]*   *(L.G. 27.7.65)*

Morrison, Thomas, Sergeant (actg.)
410298, Lovat Scouts, 2 Polish Corps (Sunderland)
(Periodic)
On August 11th, 1944 Sgt. Morrison carried out a forceful fighting patrol in the Ponte-Alla-Peira area for 36 hours which resulted in the capture of 8 P.O.W. On August 30th 1944 he took a patrol to the Selpa Donica area: this patrol captured one prisoner and wounded two of the enemy. On September 4th, 1944 he carried out a successful patrol across enemy occupied territory to Ciano to contact 'F' Recce of 6th Armd. Div. approximately 12 miles away to the left flank. On September 12th he led a fighting patrol to ambush a party of enemy close to the Gothic Line N.E. of Stia. The result of this patrol was two enemy killed and two wounded, with no casualties to his own patrol. On September 15th he was again sent out on an ambush in the above area to obtain an identification and he personally cut off and captured one P.O.W. On October 11th he was Tp. Sgt. of the Tp. which captured Cornio when two enemy were killed and 19 surrendered: he himself was wounded in this operation. This N.C.O. was in sole command of his Tp. from August 8th to September 15th when he led them on all occasions with vigour and determination.
Recommended for M.M. M.I.D. 19.7.45 (L.G. 28.6.45)

Morse, William Thomas, Sergeant
VX 3680, 2/5 Aust. Inf. Bn.
On 3rd January 1941 at Bardia Sgt. Morse was comd. of No. 9 Platoon. After the attack by 2/5 Bn. had been driven back he showed courage and skill in moving and placing his platoon to support a flanking move by Capt. W. B. Griffiths, beating off an attack by tanks in doing so. His disregard of danger and fine leadership were largely instrumental in restoring a dangerous situation, and contributed materially to the final success of the attack.
(L.G. 9.5.41)

Morton, Robert McDonald, Sergeant (now. Second Lieutenant)
22884, New Zealand Military Forces
Spec. Ops. M.E.
M.C. 6.3.47. No citation. S.W. Pacific.   *(L.G. 4.5.44)*

Moshi, Sidiki, Sergeant
GC22266, 5th Bn. The Gold Coast Regt., Royal West
African Frontier Forces (Immediate)
Kaladan.
On 17th January 1945 near Teinnyo, Burma (Ref Map 84 H/2 1924) Sgt. Sidiki Moshi was Platoon Sgt. of 11 Platoon 'D' Coy. during an attack on a strongly held enemy position on a steep ridge. The Platoon Comd. was wounded and Sgt. Sidiki Moshi took command, leading the platoon towards the objective in the face of determined resistance.

The Coy. came under heavy mortar and machine gun fire and suffered heavy casualties, including four out of the five Europeans, but Sgt. Sidiki Moshi continued to press forward with great determination in an attempt to complete the final assault. It became evident, however, that the position had become untenable. Casualties were mounting, many wounded were lying exposed in front of the enemy, and orders were therefore issued to withdraw.

At this point Sgt. Sidiki Moshi also took command of 12 Platoon, whose Platoon Comd. had been wounded. Reorganising both, he organised and led personally a further attack made to cover the evacuation of the wounded. Not until all except one man had been brought out did he start the withdrawal, in which he exercised perfect control of both platoons.

Throughout this action Sgt. Sidiki Moshi displayed outstanding personal gallantry under heavy fire, and it was entirely due to his magnificent example and skilful leadership that the casualties were evacuated and the two platoons successfully extricated from an awkward situation.   *(L.G. 19.4.45)*

Moss, Ronald Kenneth, Private
SX 20339, 2/6 Australian Infantry Bn. (Immediate)
During ops. on Observation Hill in the Mubo area Pte. Moss was a member of 9 Pl 'A' Coy. 2/6 Aust. Inf. Bn.

On 7th July 1943 an attack was made on a located enemy post and Pte. Moss was outstanding in the accuracy of his covering fire.

The enemy launched a small counter-attack from a flank. Pte. Moss appreciating the danger, ran fwd. and dispersed the attack alone, killing four of the enemy in doing so.

At this stage all the N.C.O.'s in the platoon had been either killed or wounded and the platoon forced to withdraw. Pte. Moss assumed the duties of platoon sgt. and personally covered the withdrawal of the fwd. elements and then carried out one of our dead while returning under heavy fire.

On 9th July 1943 Pte. Moss volunteered to recce a strong enemy post and crawled fwd. past the fwd. enemy weapon pits in doing so. Although observed and fired on, he completed the recce and returned with an outline plan for a flank attack, which was later successful.

On 11th July 1943 he led a demonstration against the enemy and pinned them down for two hours while an attack was launched from a flank. On the enemy realising the position and attempting to reinforce their flank, Pte. Moss, under heavy fire, led an attack into the position, causing the enemy to evacuate it.

During the entire action his coolness, sound judgement and courage were outstanding and had a most beneficial effect on the Coy. *(L.G. 4.11.43)*

Mossaad, Hassan, Shawish
269, No. 2 Coy. Frontier Battalion, Sudan Def. Forces (Immediate)
On the night of 27th Feb. Shawish Hassan Mossaad was directed with his platoon onto a strong enemy force defending a hilltop near Burye. The enemy counter-attacked with cavalry round the flank of his platoon. Showing great skill and coolness Shawish Hassan Mossaad personally handled one of his Bren Guns dropping numbers of the enemy cavalry at distances of only ten to twenty yards from his position. His skill and courage saved a critical situation.

On the evening of the 1st Mar. Shawish Hassan Mossaad commanded a patrol directed to harass the enemy positions. He approached to within 50 yards of the enemy camp during the supper hour and fired on the exposed camp inflicting large numbers of casualties on the enemy.

On the following morning on the 2nd Mar. Shawish Hassan Mossaad was directed by El Bimb. Harris onto the assembled rear guard preparing to withdraw from the Lack position. He opened fire at close range, was again attacked by the cavalry of the rear guard but maintaining his position diverted the charge at close range while himself under heavy fire of enemy machine guns.

In an attack on the Addis position conducted by El Bimb. Acland on the 24th Mar. 41 he led his platoon with skill and courage through difficult country at night to within a few yards from the enemy position which he bombed at close range whilst under heavy machine gun fire and enemy bombing attacks. *(L.G. 9.8.41)*

Moultrie, George, Warrant Officer Cl. II
2868419, Gordon Highlanders (Culter)
From 51st Highland Div. P.O.W. Pool *(L.G. 11.10.45)*

Mulholland, James William, Sergeant (A/W.O.II) (C.S.M.)
3596406, 5th Bn. Border Regt.
On 27th May, during the withdrawal of the Brigade, enemy armoured fighting vehicles came into contact with the Brigade column; an enemy machine gun was mounted and opened fire on to our troops crossing an exposed area of road of approximately five hundred yards. C.S.M. Mulholland spotted the point from which the enemy's light automatic was firing and seizing a Bren gun dashed thirty yards across a bullet swept area to take cover inside an outbuilding. From there he engaged the enemy post which promptly ceased firing. This prompt action enabled his company column to resume its advance and to gain the shelter of the first houses of a village. Throughout all active operations between 16th May and 1st June, this C.S.M. has done untiring and excellent work and has set a very high standard of fearlessness and energy to the men of his Company. *(L.G. 22.10.40)*

Mummery, Alfred Henry, Warrant Officer Cl. II
6008074, 5th Bn. The Essex Regt. (Saffron Walden)
He has taken part in all the actions fought by this battalion since it landed in Italy in September 1943. During the Italian campaign, on his own initiative, he twice took command of platoons whose commanders had been killed. By his immense cheerfulness and complete disregard of his personal safety under very heavy fire, he was responsible for extremely successful attacks by these platoons. On 12th January 1944 at Castel Vezzani in Italy, a party of Germans with three MGs, broke into his company area. He went out alone to locate them and succeeded in destroying two of the gun teams single handed. He then led a section which knocked out the third team. He arrived in B.L.A. in March 1945 and took part in the rapid advance from Uelzen to the Elbe and on to Lubrek between 21st April and 5th May 1945, as C.S.M. of his company. His conduct under fire was magnificent. The example of his fine bearing and personal courage, coupled with his continual cheerfulness and untiring work, has been an inspiration to his company and of outstanding value to the whole battalion.
M.I.D. 11.1.45 *(L.G. 24.1.46)*

Murdoch, James, Sergeant
3129532, 1st Bn. Royal Scots Fusiliers (Bridge-end, Ayrshire)
North Burma Campaign.

On 11th February 1945, Sgt. Murdoch was platoon sergeant and 2 i/c of a platoon reconnaissance patrol which encountered a strong enemy position in the area of a bridge over the Nansit Chaung on the Mongmit road. The forward section and the platoon commander crossed the chaung which was about 20 yards wide at this point, when the enemy opened up on them at ranges varying from 15 to 30 yards. Sgt. Murdoch who was in the middle of the chaung, immediately rushed forward to join his platoon commander on the enemy side of the bank. Throughout the action Sgt. Murdoch was of the greatest assistance to his platoon commander as he constantly exposed himself to close range fire from the enemy in order to fire back at them and to encourage the other men to do likewise. When the platoon commander ordered the withdrawal of the section under a smoke screen, Sgt. Murdoch was the last to leave the enemy side of the chaung. On reaching the other side of the chaung, Sgt. Murdoch remained on the bank in full view of the enemy. *(L.G. 1.11.45)*

Murdoch, James, Warrant Officer Cl. II (actg)
3189012, King's Own Scottish Borderers
For Korea *(L.G. 10.10.52)*

Murphy, Edward, Sergeant
3853118, 1 Loyal Regt. (London, S.W.12)
For conspicuous gallantry on 29th April 1943 on Pt. 212 of the Dj-el-Asoud feature.

On 29th April 1943, Sjt. Murphy commanded 18 platoon, 'D' Coy., when the Coy. reinforced the Irish Guards on Pt. 212 in order to hold the position against tank and infantry attacks.

During the whole of the day Sjt. Murphy displayed great personal gallantry and magnificent leadership.

Pt. 212 was attacked five times by enemy infantry supported by tanks and heavy mortar fire. Again and again Sjt. Murphy, by his example and leadership, inspired his platoon to beat off the attacks. At one stage 18 platoon temporarily ran out of ammunition, but Sjt. Murphy not to be outdone, hurled stones at the enemy, and his men seeing this astonishing sight again beat off the attack, with stones and rifle butts.

Apart from his personal courage and tenacity, it was Sjt. Murphy's example which enabled his men to hold fast, and at no time did they yield an inch of ground.

I was present on Pt. 212 during the action in which 'D' Coy reinforced the Irish Guards, and I could not help noticing the magnificent manner in which Sjt. Murphy led his platoon.

At all times he showed exceptionally good leadership and held his platoon together by his devotion to duty under heavy mortar and M.G. fire in the face of repeated and determined attacks by the enemy. His manner was a fine example to the men under his command.

At one time during the action his platoon were short of ammunition, but Sjt. Murphy carried on the defence by throwing stones at the enemy until more ammunition was available.

At all times he showed complete disregard for his own safety and was a shining example to his platoon. *(L.G. 22.7.43)*

Murray, George John, Sergeant
6528126, 9th Bn. Royal Fusiliers (London, S.W.8)
(Immediate)
On the night 17/18th January 1944, when the Bn. Crossed the Garigliano, Sgt. Murray was in command of his platoon. Having led his men to the Coy. R.V. he was then ordered to resume the advance to the Bn. objective. Sgt. Murray had by then only twenty men left, owing to the enemy M.G. posts already encountered: but during the advance five more Spandau posts were met, and

successfully dealt with by Sgt. Murray himself advancing to the enemy positions under cover of fire from his platoon, and killing the enemy by throwing grenades and firing his T.S.M.G. His courage and his prompt action whenever opposition was met inspired his platoon throughout the advance: and when he had finally taken the objective, with fourteen men remaining, he remained, although wounded in the head, to beat off two fierce counter-attacks made by the enemy. Sgt. Murray was responsible for the death of many of the enemy during this action, and it was undoubtedly largely due to his devotion to duty and complete ... *[continuation missing]*. *(L.G. 4.5.44)*

Murray, Gordon John, Sergeant
48265, 21 N.Z. Bn. (Immediate)
On the 4th April 1945 Sjt. Murray's platoon attacked the enemy held stopbank of the R. Senio and attempted to dig in near the top so that control of the river might be obtained. Close fighting with grenades took place and Sjt. Murray, realising that certain enemy-held positions must be taken for the platoon to be able to continue, personally attacked and took two such positions immediately placing his men in to hold them against counter-attack. He himself took a major part in beating off the counter-attack and maintaining our foothold.

On the 8th April Sjt. Murray again succeeded by fearless leadership in beating off a determined enemy attack on his positions and so enabled us to retain the control so vital for the breaking of the Senio line. This N.C.O. by his outstanding leadership and devotion to duty has been an inspiration to the whole of his Coy. and, indeed, to the Bn. *(L.G. 18.10.45)*

Murray, John, Fusilier
3131938, 6th Bn. Royal Scots Fusiliers (Saltcoats)
(Immediate)
At Derlyck on 7th September 1944 Fusilier Murray was the Gunner of a Bren gun carrier covering the road into the town. When darkness fell, the carrier itself was drawn across the road to act as a block to prevent the enemy from driving convoys through the town.

During the night the enemy attempted to drive two columns through the town. The second column approached down the street covered by Fus. Murray's section. Fus. Murray opened fire when the column had got to close range and was himself entirely responsible for the destruction of the first two enemy vehicles and the men they were carrying. A third enemy vehicle then by-passed the first two vehicles and charged the carrier next to which Fus. Murray had taken up his post. The impact of the enemy vehicle threw the carrier against the wall and pinned Fus. Murray between the wall and his carrier. Both his legs were broken.

Nevertheless, he dragged himself into a new position and fired his gun at the enemy vehicle, killing the driver. Though helpless from the waist down and in great agony, Fus. Murray still stuck to his gun and when 15 minutes later three more enemy vehicles tried to approach his post he agained opened fire at short range. The vehicles were stopped and put out of action, several enemy killed and twelve prisoners taken.

Altogether Fus. Murray remained at his post keeping his Bren gun in action for half an hour after Fus. Murray's legs were crushed by the carrier. Throughout he made no mention of his injuries until on the point of contact he was evacuated.

By his efforts he accounted for some twenty enemy killed, wounded or taken prisoner, and by his superb courage and selfless devotion to duty all attempts by the enemy to penetrate into the town were prevented and the battalions position secured.   *(L.G. 1.3.45)*

Murray, John, Warrant Officer Cl. III (Pl.S.M.)
3049400, 1 Royal Scots
On 21st May near Calonne on the R. Escaut when his platoon was overrun and his platoon comd. wounded he rallied his platoon and took up a position from which he covered the withdrawal of the remainder of his Coy., and the evacuation of one wounded officer and two wounded O.R.'s. Throughout this operation this Warrant Officer displayed exceptional bravery and resource.
(L.G. 20.12.40)

Murray, William, Marine, T/Corporal
PO/X.106801, Royal Marines, No. 41 RM Commando
Pachino Peninsula 10th July 1943
This NCO was in a leading assault group of 'B' Troop whose duty it was to clear enemy machine gun positions from the cliff edge in area 8889. Having cleared two posts without much difficulty he encountered considerable opposition from a third post some distance away. As no supporting fire was obtainable because they were on the waters edge, Corporal Murray charged the position with fixed bayonets. Before reaching it he received a hit from a splinter of a hand grenade which penetrated his left eye. He showed an exceptional high sense of duty throughout, continuing to lead the assault, bayoneting two of the enemy himself and then clearing the area capturing four prisoners. Full well knowing that he had lost his eye, his subsequent undaunted courage cheered on his subordinates and is worthy of the highest praise.
(L.G. 7.12.43)

Murray, Wlliam Patrick, Sergeant (actg.)
2655211, (W.R.) Reconnaissance Regt., Royal
Armoured Corps (Cheshunt) (Periodic)
Since he landed in Normandy this N.C.O. has led a section of an Assault Troop in every operation in which his Sqn. has been engaged. On every occasion he has not only displayed outstanding tactical skill and the most aggressive and spirited attitude but, by his personal courage and indifference to danger, he has inspired his men to achieve many notable successes against the enemy.

At Dodeward, Holland on 26th February 1945 he led a daylight fighting patrol into a factory where a British officer had been wounded and taken prisoner. At great risk to himself he led his section into the close area of the buildings until contact was made and the enemy vigorously engaged. Another patrol, operating on a flank, had meanwhile located the main enemy position and had attempted to rush it. The intense fire of the enemy killed or wounded all but the leader of this patrol, who was left isolated, and in close contact with the enemy. Sgt. Murray realised that immediate retaliatory action must come from him, but as he was unable to disengage his own section now busily engaged, he ran across the open space himself and reaching cover, immediately engaged the enemy with his own weapon. He was then able by shouting to guide a small party round cover to his position. By his own accurate fire he had inflicted such casualties upon the enemy that he was able to establish a firm base in very close proximity to them. This he maintained until ordered to withdraw.

On the next day, when operating in the same area, Sgt. Murray spotted a strong enemy patrol attempting infiltration. He at once attacked it, and without loss to his section, dispersed it. Three enemy dead were recovered, and it was afterwards proved that a German Captain had also become a casualty in the same action. Three days later, lying in ambush with his section for six hours in the bitter cold, Sgt. Murray accounted for five more enemy dead.

On another occasion Sgt. Murray was the senior N.C.O. in the assaulting party of a fighting patrol which crossed the Waal in LCA and attacked the village of Ochten. The assaulting party he commanded completely destroyed a strong point and inflicted casualties, bringing back one enemy dead for identification.

Throughout the campaign this N.C.O. has maintained an extremely high standard of skilful and vigorous leadership, and has a long and uninterrupted record of courageous action and first class soldiering to his credit.
(L.G. 24.1.46)

Musa Mohamad, Ba[...]
S.D.F.
E. Africa   *(5.11.42)*

Mutale, Private
286, 1 Northern Rhodesia Regt.
15th August 1940. Br. Somaliland
At Tug Argon, British Somaliland heavy enemy attacks were made on the position held by 'A' Coy. 1/N.R.R. and attacked M.G.'s of S.C.C. between Aug. 10th and Aug. 14th. All these attacks were repulsed. On Aug. 15th the position was bombarded by six enemy batteries continuously between 2.00 pm and 4.00 pm. During this bombardment Pte. Mutale's Sec. post was wrecked by shell fire and he withdrew under his Sec. Comdrs. to other cover further up the slope where his European Pln. Sgt. was. About 4.00 pm the bombardment slackened

and the enemy infantry came into the assault supported by Mortar and very heavy M.G. fire—Sgt. Duff (Pte. Mutale's Pln. Sgt.) continues:—

'Pte. Mutale ran forward at once again with me, to a point, from which we could fire on the enemy. Seeing the enemy advancing in great numbers through gaps in the Zareba, and realising that they presented a good target for the Lewis Gun which had been left in the wrecked post, Pte. Mutale on his own initiative ran forward towards the enemy, under extremely heavy fire from two machine-guns and a number of light automatics.

He reached the post, secured the gun and amn. and was running back through a storm of fire, when (as was inevitable) he was wounded, in the neck and mouth.

He crawled back to me and continued firing beside me with a rifle until he became too weak from loss of blood to continue. He only went back when I ordered him to get under cover. He was later captured by the enemy.'

I consider this man showed initiative and great courage in his efforts to retrieve the Lewis gun and great devotion to duty in fighting on in an exposed position after being seriously wounded.   *(L.G. 16.4.42)*

Mwaleza, Lance Corporal
510, 1st Northern Rhodesia Regt.
Somaliland.

For continuous gallantry and devotion to duty at Hargeisa on Aug. 5th and seq. This N.C.O. in charge of an A/T rifle was completely cut off by the quick advance of an enemy mechanized column. In unknown country he made a wide circle of some 50 to 70 miles, collecting 3 more stragglers on the way and finally 48 hrs later, brought his whole party complete with A/T rifle, ammunition, etc. into Bn. HQ at Tug Argon, which his Coy. had orders to reach on their withdrawal. To do this he had to avoid large bodies of enemy troops and his personal example of resourcefulness must have had a great effect on his comrades.
To be dated 11.2.41 and substituted for the award of the African D.C.M. announced in the L.G. of that date.
          (L.G. 21.7.42)

Mwamba, Corporal
281, 1st Northern Rhodesia Regt.
Somaliland.

For conspicuous gallantry on the afternoon of Aug. 15th when Observation Hill in the Tug Argon position was captured by the enemy. After helping his det. Comdr. to fight his mortar to the end, Cpl. Mwamba regardless of his own safety carried a badly wounded companion through heavy fire to a place of safety 15 miles back. To do this, this N.C.O. had to cover large tracks of country held by the enemy and only his skill and devotion enabled him to do so successfully.
To be dated 11.2.41 and substituted for the award of the African D.C.M. announced in the L.G. of that date.
          (L.G. 21.7.42)

Myers, Stanley, Lance Sergeant
3446805, 2 Bn. Lancashire Fusiliers (Clitheroe)
Tourabeur.

On 15th April 1943, during operations in the mountains, the Germans attacked Djebel Bettior by night under cover of a heavy mist and penetrated to the rocks immediately above Bn. HQ of the 2nd Bn. The Lancashire Fusiliers.

No. 3446805 L/Sgt. Myers, who was commanding the Pioneer Platoon, rallied personnel of HQ Coy. who had fallen back under a shower of grenades and seizing an L.M.G., returned the enemy fire. Leading two or three men with rifles and automatic weapons he helped to restore the position and forced the enemy to withdraw. With complete disregard for his own safety, L/Sgt. Myers fetched ammunition to maintain his gun, and, by firing fuses to Hawkins grenades which he threw at the enemy inflicted casualties and caused them to fall back. Although constantly under fire he showed complete disregard for his personal safety and by his determination and courage was an inspiration to those around him.

It was largely due to his courage that a serious situation was averted. I consider this N.C.O.'s conduct to be of a very high order and strongly recommend him for an immediate award.   *(L.G. 15.6.43)*

Myers, Thomas, Sergeant
4455621, 9th Durham Light Infantry (Spennymoor)
(Immediate)

At St. Joost on the evening of 21st January 1945, Sgt. Myers was platoon Sgt. of a platoon engaged in clearing the village. The platoon had cleared several houses when Sgt. Myers was sent back to company HQ to report on the situation. The enemy was at this time on three sides of the company and the position was confused. After leaving company HQ this N.C.O. was informed that approximately 20 Germans were between him and his platoon coming in his direction. He immediately ran some twenty yards across bullet swept ground to the corner of a house where he waited for the enemy to appear. He allowed them to approach within fifteen yards and then opened up with his Sten, killing and wounding eight or nine. The remainder took cover behind a house. The N.C.O. waited for developments and saw a German with a M.G. leading the enemy from behind the house. He again waited until they were all in view, and then threw three or four grenades at the party inflicting more casualties and causing the rest to disappear. Sgt. Myers then continued on his way to his platoon. On the way he encountered two more enemy at point blank range whom he shot and killed.

Sgt. Myers thus single handed inflicted over a dozen casualties on the enemy, and by his courage and determination fought his way back to his platoon, preventing the enemy from completely encircling his company, and enabling them to be withdrawn without fighting their way out.
B.E.M. 13.6.64   *(L.G. 12.4.45)*

Myles, Thomas James, Sergeant
7519992, R.A.M.C., 72 Ind. Inf. Bde. (Ballyshannon,
   Co. Donegal) (Immediate)
Mayu Range, Arakan. 26th March 1944.

On the 26th March 1944 during an attack on enemy positions near the Maungdaw—Buthidaung road, this N.C.O. was in command of attached section 69th Indian Field Ambulance. During the attack he moved with the leading platoon and immediately went forward treating and evacuating each casualty as it occurred. He dressed one N.C.O., within five yards of an enemy held bunker from which the enemy were throwing grenades. During the final attack on the last feature a private soldier had one leg blown off by a grenade. Sgt. Myles immediately went forward under considerable fire from snipers, and although shots passed through his equipment he still continued to treat the private soldier. Throughout the action he showed complete coolness and absence of fear.
Recommended for M.M.   *(L.G. 22.6.44)*

N

Nabarro, Derrick David William, Sergeant
999513, 10 Sqn, Royal Air Force
I was second pilot of a Whitley which took off from
Leaming at 2100 hrs on 28 Jun 41 to bomb Bremen. We
reached the target and bombed it, but on the return
journey were shot down by Flak at 0030 hrs on 29 Jun
41 over Kiel. We baled out and came down in the Baltic
Sea. The rest of the crew were:— Sjt. Gregory, (pilot),
(P/W); P/O Watson, (rear Gunner); and two P/O's,
(names not known), believed P/W.

We were picked up by a German minesweeper at 0630
hrs, and were treated very considerately. They allowed
us to wash and gave us a blanket, coffee, and cigarettes,
although they were rationed to three a day themselves.
We were taken to army barracks in Kiel the same day
and put into separate rooms. I had my head treated here.
There was no interrogation or questioning. Two hours
later we were moved on to a G.A.F. Station just outside
the town by the side of the harbour. We were all
interrogated here in a friendly manner during a meal.
We were asked how we were shot down, make of aircraft,
and squadron number. We just gave our name, rank and
number and said we were not allowed to say anything
more. They said they knew we were a Wellington crew
and what bomb-loads our various aircraft carried. Their
estimate was 1,000 lbs short however. They did not
persist in the interrogation. We were then taken to another
G.A.F station and interrogated separately by a friendly
Major. They used the rolling stone method, beginning
with unimportant questions, such as father's christian
name, and gradually increasing the tempo, finally asking
the number of my squadron. When I did not answer that
the interview came to an end.

In the evening we were taken by train to Frankfurt
Am Main. On the journey a German, who was very
friendly and said he had been to Newcastle before the
war, came in to talk to us. He provided a bottle of
lemonade and apologised for not having any beer. Only
the Army personnel were asked for papers on the train,
which were strictly controlled. We left Kiel at 1800 hrs
on 29 Jun and reached Frankfurt at 1100 hrs on 30 Jun.

We were taken from the station to Dulag Luft about
15 kms N.W. of Frankfurt, just to the North of the railway
going from Frankfurt to Oberursel. I was interrogated
here by Eberhardt, the official interpreter who asked the
type of aircraft I was flying and length of my R.A.F.
service. He seemed to be more interested in my squadron
number than base. When I refused to speak, he took down
some particulars such as home address for Red Cross
purposes, and then left after quarter of an hour. Later on
another man came in, who said he was a history
professor. He tried to start a discussion, but I did not
encourage him and the conversation did not last very
long.

Next day, 1 Jul, I was taken to hospital in a wood 2
[...]ms away. We occupied the top floor with three beds
to a room. I was with two other British P/W, and we
were very careful not to discuss service questions. I was
two weeks in this hospital where the treatment was very
good. While I was there they brought in the false Red
Cross form, on which I just filled in my name, rank,
number and home address.

I went back to the camp for two days before being
taken to Stalag IX C at Bad Sulza about 15 July. I
remained there in the main camp, till I escaped in Nov
41. They took my fingerprints here, but there was no
interrogation. The living conditions here were bad; 150
of us lived, ate and slept in a room about 120 ft by 60 ft.
Apart from French, Belgian and Serb P/W, there were a
large number of British wounded from Dunkirk. Morale
was high among all, but especially among the British
wounded. There was an unofficial escape club, the
nucleus of which was made up of people who had already
attempted to escape.

I escaped first in Sep 41 with Sjt.-Pilot Hall. We had
food for a fortnight, a compass and map tracings of the
route to the Italian–Swiss frontier provided by a
Frenchman. There were watch towers at the four corners
of the compound, but the sentries on these could not see
each other, nor could they see immediately below the
tower. In broad daylight we climbed over the wire up
against one of these towers and out of sight of the sentry.
Some one in the camp signalled to us when the sentry
was looking the other way, and we dashed away into a
ditch. Unfortunately two Serbs saw us, and by their
excitement roused the suspicions of the guard who looked
in our direction and saw us crawling along the ditch.
When they re-captured us they found our map tracing,
but not the compass which Hall hid between his legs
with a bit of sticking plaster.

We were given 24 days in the cells, but were turned
out after a week to make room for other escapers. While
in prison I talked to a Major in the next door cell who
had been in charge of the escape club at Oflag X C
(Lubeck) and he told me about the Schaffhausen route.

My second escape was made in Oct 41. I was in the
potato cart cleaning it out, when the guard, getting
impatient, drove off with me still inside. When we got
near a wood I jumped off and hid in it. On this occasion
I happened to have with me a week's supply of Vitamin
tablets. I then jumped two goods trains, but three days
later was caught asleep in a waggon at Apolda. This time
I was sentenced to 21 days in the cells but I only
completed 15. I had by now made two dozen keys for
the window of the cell and we were always able to keep
anyone in them provided with food.

I then set about making preparations for escape with
a Belgian, whose christian name is Godefroi; he found

out the times of the train, and I got sixty marks, a pair of slacks, and a leather jacket from a Frenchman in return for a fountain pen, a wrist watch, and an Army greatcoat. He also provided maps. I improved my French by conversation with a Corsican.

We escaped on 25 Nov by going up to the guard at 0630 hrs and saying we were going to clean out the Commandant's office, which was outside the main wire. He let us through without fuss, as he had been on duty for three hours and was due to be relieved. We had then only a single strand of barbed wire to negotiate and this presented no difficulty. We went to the next village and caught a local train towards Berlin. Godefroi spoke German and throughout the journey bought the tickets without exciting comment. We changed at Naumburg and went out into the country till 1600 hrs when we caught a train for Apolda arriving there at about 1730 hrs. We walked about the town for an hour and then caught a train to Kassel at about 1900 hrs. We did not go about together, but met in the station Lavatory to make our plans and decide which trains we were going to take.

I carried a lot of 10 pfenning pieces in order to be able to lock myself in the lavatories and avoid being seen hanging about stations. It was also a convenient place to shave. The train to Kassel was very crowded but we managed to get seats. There was an R.A.F. raid during the journey and the train stopped for three hours. Through this we missed our connection and had to wait 15 hours at Kassel. We walked about the town and then went into the buffet and slept the night there near some German soldiers. We bought beer and Ersatz coffee but no food. Our chocolate and vitamin tablets, provided by Red Cross, kept us going for a week.

The following morning we caught a train a 1100 hrs to Koblenz arriving at 1700 hrs. We had to wait over night and caught a train on the morning of 30 Nov to Gerolstein about 50 kms from the Luxembourg frontier.

At Gerolstein we were caught leaving the station. It was Sunday, which is strictly observed in this Catholic part of Germany, and our unusual appearance attracted attention. The station police asked for our papers, but our forged documents purporting to belong to Belgian workers did not deceive them. We were taken to a cell underneath the police station where we found a French escaped P/W. We all escaped the following morning by going to the washing place, knocking out the guard and getting out of the window. We then ran across country due South for about 12 kms. At about mid-day we hid in some woods beside a railway and river. We started off again at night by full moon. It was very cold and our shoes were waterlogged. We went due West and arrived at Prum the following morning (2 Dec). We hid in a little copse, forded a river that evening, and carried on all night. The following morning (3 Dec) without realising it we crossed the frontier into Luxembourg (near Trois Vierges). We went on by day to Houffalize in Belgium, where we stayed the night at a cafe, the proprietor of which recognised us as escaped P/W. It

was the first place we tried and the people were extremely sympathetic. We saw no guard on the frontier, except the Customs Post at Trois Vierges. but we realised we had got out of Germany by the fact that people looked so much more cheerful.

Godefroi knew this part of the country and we went by tram to Bastogne and then on by train to Libramont. We stayed the night at Godefroi's home near here.

The next day I went on by train with the Frenchman via Namur and Charleroi to Erquelinnes on the Belgian–French frontier. We walked over the frontier to Jeumont without being stopped. Godefroi's father had given me 600 Belgian francs which enabled me to reach Paris by train. We travelled first to St Quentin, crossed the red line on foot near Montescourt without being stopped and went on by train to Paris.

I then decided to get to Rouen to see if I could find a friend of mine, Pte. Jim Sumner, R.A.S.C. whom I believed to be in Heilag Rouen, to see if I could help him. However I could find no trace of him. A Frenchman in Stalag IX C had given me his home address in Rouen, and I went there and his parents put me up for the night. The next afternoon I went to Paris and stayed the night with a gendarme, the brother of another Frenchman in Stalag IX C.

I then went to Nevers by train to find the Frenchman with whom I had escaped from Gerolstein. He told me how to get across the Demarcation Line, wrongly as it turned out. I was caught by the Germans just South of Nevers, when I was crossing back to Occupied France by mistake after having already crossed once in the other direction. I told them I was trying to get into the Occupied Zone, and they sent me back to Unoccupied France. I thought this might be a trap, and so walked down the road towards Sancoins. I thought the Germans were probably watching me and would recapture me if they saw me trying to hide. The result was that I was captured by the French.

I was sent to Toulouse and there interrogated by the Air Force. Apart from telling them what I knew about Germany I gave them no other information. I was then sent to St Hippolyte on 18 Dec 41 and transferred to Fort de la Revere in Mar 42.

The story of my escape from Fort de la Revere is the same as that of F/Lt. Barnett (M.I.9/S/P.G.(–)887).

(L.G. 19.1.43)

Nadeau, Guy, Warrant Officer Cl. II (C.S.M.)
E19022, Canadian Infantry Corps
N.W. Europe   *(L.G. 24.1.46)*

Naismith, Alan Kenneth, Corporal
VX 4838, 2/7 Aust Inf Bn. (Immediate)
For outstanding leadership and personal bravery throughout the enemy attacks against the vital position of Old Vickers Ridge held by A Coy during period 1—5 Aug 43.

Cpl. Naismith in command of 8 pl A Coy, the only NCO in the pl, was occupying the right forward sector of the Coy position and instructed to hold the ground at all costs. Commencing on 1 Aug 43 the enemy launched his first attack—directed against 8 pl. Despite the fact the strength of the pl was only 12 all ranks this attack was repulsed but this was followed up by stronger and more determined attempts by the enemy to capture the posn. For four days and nights this pl was subjected to continual and intensive fire from MMGs Mortars LMGs and snipers. Twelve separate and determined attacks were successfully repulsed during this period. On one occasion during a night attack with the bayonet the enemy succeeded in reaching 8 Pl's position. Only after fierce hand to hand fighting were the enemy driven out. Due to the nature of the ground, grenades were used extensively during the fighting. In order to ensure an adequate supply as each Jap attack was repulsed Cpl. Naismith moved forward under fire from snipers and collected grenades from enemy dead and from dumps they had left in the area. In this manner Cpl. Naismith collected and used over 200 jap grenades. On one occasion he surprised a party of five enemy, priming grenades. He killed all of them and took the grenades back to his pl position. In several sorties of this nature he personally accounted for another 10 enemy—eventually being wounded himself.

Throughout the whole of this gallant action Cpl. Naismith displayed the highest qualities of leadership and courage. His amazing coolness and contempt of enemy fire—his steadying influence during the night attacks and his countless acts of personal bravery inspired the pl with confidence and determination which assisted them to withstand all enemy attacks. This enabled Old Vickers Position to be used as a firm base for further successful operations. *(L.G. 20.1.44)*

Nankiville, Herbert Ernest, Lance Corporal
WX 13372, 2/28 Aust Inf Bn. (Immediate)
On 19 Oct 43 D Company was ordered to clear the Katika track of the enemy at 638682 (Satelberg 1/25000).

L/Cpl. Nankiville showing outstanding courage and determination led his section up a steep slope under heavy grenade and rifle fire and drove the enemy from the ridge. Reorganising his section on the ground captured. This action permitted his platoon to inflict heavy casualties on the enemy.

Again on 20 Oct 43 he led his section with skill and vigour against an enemy position on high ground in a successful attempt to locate their posts. Despite strong opposition from machine guns and grenade fire, he pressed home the assault, his section suffered casualties and this NCO was himself seriously wounded several times, but he continued to lead his men until it was possible for the company to be reorganised. He has since had his right eye removed.

This NCOs leadership, courage and complete disregard of personal danger was an inspiration to his fellow men who hold him in the highest regard.
(L.G. 2.3.44)

Napier, Walter John, Warrant Officer Cl. II (C.S.M.)
6335249, 4th Queen's Own Royal West Kent Regt.
For conspicuous gallantry and devotion to duty in the Foret de Nieppe between 25th and 28th May 40, especially on 28 May 40. C.S.M. Napier's work was outstanding. He fought resolutely for three days never losing a position, even when his right flank was turned. He set a fine example to the men. He was constantly in action with his Company H.Q. supervising the distribution of ammunition and controlling fire with marked success. During the retirement on the night of 28 May when intercepted he showed the greatest bravery, twice charging and killing enemy at short range with the pistol and contributing greatly to the operation of breaking through the enemy lines. When no officers were left C.S.M. Napier took over command of the Company and brought the remainder of it through to Dunkirk. A gallant Warrant Officer whose example inspired the men and whose personal disregard of danger was outstanding.
(L.G. 22.10.40)

Napoli, Julius Joseph, Fusilier
24441110, 2nd Royal Fusiliers (Gibraltar)
Ref Map—Italy, Sheet 121 II 1/50,000
On 1 Jul 44, 'Y' Coy attacked an enemy strongpoint at Terrarassa 299001. Fus Napoli's Pl Comd and Sec Comd became casualties, and he personally took charge of 12 men and led them, in spite of heavy MG fire, to some buildings. The remainder of his Coy were unable to reach the buildings owing to the enemy's fire, but Fus Napoli rallied and organised the 12 men, beat off with small arms fire three determined counter-attacks, and hung on to the position for six hours until relieved. In between these counter-attacks Fus Napoli, always under heavy and accurate fire and with complete disregard for his own safety, on several occasions left the cover of the buildings and brought in wounded men. It was chiefly due to Fus. Napoli's initiative, powers of leadership and splendid example of personal bravery, that the position was held. *(L.G. 7.12.44)*

Narvey, Joseph Paul André, Lance Corporal
D.801889, Royal Canadian 22e Regt.
For Korea *(L.G. [..].2.52)*

Natt, A. H., Sjt.
Australian Military Forces
S.W. Pacific *(L.G. 6.3.47)*

Naylor, Robert Benjamin, Guardsman
D26479, 22 Cdn Armd Regt (CGG) (Immediate)
At 1400 hrs 26 Feb 'B' Coy A & SH of C with under comd No 2 tp of 3 sqn 22 Cdn Armd Regt (CGG) was ordered to capture the village of Mechelshof MR 995453:11/25000 sheet 4203. To achieve the objective

it was necessary to dispose of an enemy strong pt at MR 997458. The enemy here were well dug in and had a variety of automatic weapons and bazookas. Very soon after the attack was launched the tp leader and one tk became cas. Gdsm Naylor, gunner in the tp leader's tk, appreciating that if the inf were left without tk sp success would be unlikely, immediately took comd of the remaining two tks and ordered the co-dvr of his tk to take over his gun. He then brought such effective fire to bear on the enemy posn at MR 997458 that the inf were able to close and clean it out. The attack on Mechelsof then commenced. Gdsm Naylor exhibited great qualities of leadership boldly using the two remaing tks.

(L.G. 12.5.45)

Ndalama, Saimon, Private
DN/5428, King's African Rifles,
To be dated 11.2.41 and substituted for the award of the African D.C.M. announced in the L.G. of that date.

(L.G. 21.7.42)

Neall, Oliver Zachariah, Private
VX 9024, 2/8 Bn., Australian Military Forces
Act of gallantry and devotion to duty at Battle of Tobruch on 21 Jan. 42.

During the approach of his Company to Fort Pilastrino, they were attacked by a number of enemy tanks. Private Neall ran over 200 yards in the face of heavy machine gun fire to get the anti tank rifle and ammunition from another member of his section who had been wounded. He then opened fire on the tanks and succeeded in accounting for three tanks. He was the object of fire from all tanks during this action and the success of his fire caused the remaining tanks to withdraw. Throughout the remainder of the action Private Neall continued to display similar courage and initiative and assisted in no small measure to bring victory at the end of the day. *(L.G. 9.5.41)*

Neilson, Evan Garth, Corporal
QX 21829, 2/3 Aust Indep Coy. (Periodic)
Bobdubi—Salamaua Area Mar—Sept 43

Cpl. Neilson has given most valuable services under fire in many operations, including the Jap Track in February, Bobdubi in May, Goodview Junc and Ambush Knoll in July, Bobdubi Ridge and Feature Ridge L of C in August, and Arnold's Crest in September. His resoluteness and fearlessness have been an inspiration to his comrades. Cpl. Neilson played a very distinguished part during operations against the Graveyards on 17 Jul. His section advanced from Namling up the steep slopes of the Graveyards ridge and by a surprise assault gained their objective. Cpl. Neilson moved with great dash using his TSMG with devastating effect. He accounted for eight of the enemy himself and cleared many weapon pits. A force from another unit did not gain their objective as planned and throughout the night Cpl. Neilson's section was subjected to counter-attacks from both sides along

the ridge. By coolly holding fire until the enemy were within a few yards range, Neilson's party broke up all assaults on his sector of the perimeter, inflicting many casualties on the enemy. On 29 Jul, during the attack by his platoon on Timered Knoll, Cpl. Neilson's section commander was killed. Cpl. Neilson, although then only a private, immediately took command of the section. He continued to press the attack though subjected to heavy MMG and LMG fire and suffering numerous casualties and led the section forward with great dash to exploit after the main enemy position had fallen. When his unit attacked Feature ridge on 25 Aug, Cpl. Neilson's section came under cross fire from two strong enemy positions and several of the section were wounded. One of these was unable to move and was lying in an area which was coming under very heavy enemy grenading and LMG fire. Immediately upon seeing this Cpl. Neilson threw himself over the wounded man protecting him from fire until other members of section had dragged him to safety.

(L.G. 27.4.44)

Nelson, Charles, Warrant Officer Cl. II (C.S.M.)
2309537, H.Q. Transportation Bde, G.H.Q. Div, 1st
Echelon, No. 2 Docks Group Royal Engineers,
Supplementary Reserve
On the 18th June this Warrant Officer under heavy bombing carried out the dangerous task of removing a quantity of grenades and explosives which were a source of considerable danger while on the quay.

(L.G. 27.8.40)

Nesling, Stanley Gordon, Corporal (A/Sgt.)
7946362, Nottinghamshire Yeomanry (Stanmore)
(Immediate)
Sjt. Nesling commanded a 17-Pr Tank in C Sqn who were sp 6 DLI in the Gheel bridgehead over the Albert Canal on 11 Sept. His tp were the first to go through the centre of Gheel which was at the North end of the bridgehead. Owing to enemy action, the other two tanks in his tp were knocked out by an SP Gun firing from some woods about 400 yds from the village. In spite of being constantly engaged himself by this SP Gun he remained alone at the North end of the village to prevent enemy infiltration into the village. However, an enemy Infantry patrol managed to infiltrate and engage his tank from the cover of a house to his rear. Sjt. Hesling however, instead of attempting to rejoin the Sqn, immediately made a plan to deal with this Bazooka patrol who were engaging him. In spite of firing his 17-pr and Browning into the house, which he considered was affording protection for the patrol, he was unable to dislodge the enemy. He therefore dismounted and stalked the enemy with his Bren Gun giving orders to his gunner to cover him from the tank. He eventually sighted the enemy position, opened fire with his Bren, wounded the Section Leader and killed several others. The remainder fled in disorder, leaving behind them 2 Bazookas.

He then proceede [...]ear the rest of the street on fo[..] his Bren Gun, with his tank giving [...] covering fire. He remained at the North end of the village for the rest of the day and in spite of numerous attempts on the part of German Infantry, he prevented them from entering from the North end of the village. His initiative in dealing with enemy Infantry, working alone on foot and armed only with a Bren Gun, and his complete disregard for his own personal safety, aroused the admiration of, and inspired confidence in all those who were under his command during a very critical period. *(L.G. 1.3.45)*

Neville, Daniel John, Warrant Officer Cl. II
11448, Royal Australian Infantry Corps
For Vietnam *(L.G. 10.12.68)*

Newhouse, Henry Ernest, Gunner
876868, [...] Regt., Royal Horse Artillery (High Bentham, Yorks.) (Immediate)
On October 28th in a position forward of El Alamein near Point 33 map ref. 866296 Sig. Newhouse was wireless operator on the armoured OP car. In the early morning the OP car was under constant shell fire and machine-gun fire, and while operating his set Sig. Newhouse was hit in the neck by macine gun bullets, one passing under his spine. He had a Field Dressing put on and continued to operate his set.

Later in the day his car hit a mine and Sig Newhouse salvaging his set, walked into the Battery position and put his set in a new OP car, refusing further medical aid. Early the next morning the same OP was ordered to support the 2 RB in an attack. The vehicle was hit and disabled by machine-gun fire from an enemy strong point.

Sig. Newhouse again salvaged his set in full view of the enemy, and again walked into the Battery, although in this engagement he had been hit in the back by machine gun bullets.

When he arrived at the Battery position he had his back dressed, and then went out again in a third OP car, although advised by the MO that he should be evacuated.

During all this time he behaved with great bravery, operating his set and passing important fire orders with complete disregard for his own safety. *(L.G. 28.1.43)*

Newland, Eric Henry, Sergeant
11003975, 1 Airlanding Light Regt., Royal Artillery
Sjt. Newland of 2 Bty was ordered on 21 Sept to man a gun of 'B' troop 1 Bty near Oost[...] Church with a scratch detachment consisting of Bdr Roall[...], Gnr M[...] and Bnr Batsden from 2 Bty as the original 1 Bty detachment had all been killed. Soon after he had taken over the gun the position came under heavy fire from two tanks at a range of under 300 and from German Infantry who had infiltrated into some buildings which overlooked the position at a range of about 150.

One of the tanks was eventually stopped by a shot from a Piat at a range of about 100 from the position,

but it continued [...] heavy fire on the position. No gun could be brought to bear on this tank from its position in its pit. Sjt. Newland was ordered to [...] his gun out into the open in order to engage the tank with direct fire. The gun was hooked [...] a jeep and driven into a position in the open at a range of about 100 from the tank which was still firing fiercely. Sjt. Newland then laid the gun himself with great coolness and scored a direct hit with his first round. Not content with this he fired two more rounds at the tank until it was ablaze before he withdrew himself and [...] detachment under cover.

Throughout the whole of this engagement carried out under heavy fire Sjt. Newland showed complete disregard for his own personal safety and his courage and determination were an inspiration to his men.
(L.G. 9.11.44)

Newlove, Douglas Leighton, Warrant Officer Cl. II
273243, 21 NZ Bn. (Periodic)
WOII Newlove was CSM of C Coy during the period on the Senio when the Battalion was engaged in hard fighting for the stopbank. The Coy had gained their positions on the bank and were digging in when the enemy suddenly attacked and a fierce grenade fight ensued. Although Coy HQ was some distance from the stopbank WOII Newlove hastened to the Pl position which was being attacked and personally took charge of a section, which he led in a brilliant counter-attack against the enemy. In the grenade fight which followed WOII Newlove, with total disregard for his own safety, stood up on top of the stopbank and caused terrific havoc amongst the enemy with grenades. After the action the enemy laid a heavy mortar concentration over the whole Coy area but WOII Newlove, knowing that ammnition would require replenishing, walked freely around the positions and personally carried supplies to the posts which required them. WOII Newlove has over a long period of time, shown courage of the highest order. His constant devotion to duty has been an inspiration to all in the Coy and in all actions he has shown himself to be a fine leader of men.
M.I.D. 29.11.45 *(L.G. 13.12.45)*

Newman, Harold, Private
5247965, 1st Bn. The Worcestershire Regt. (Quarry Bank, Staffs.)
On the 14th June 1942, Pte. Newman, a member of the Intelligence section had been posted together with another man, in an advanced O.P. on an exposed ridge about one mile outside the Battalion perimeter, south of Acroma. During the day, the Battalion was heavily attacked by tanks and lorried infantry supported by artillery. Throughout the morning Pte. Newman kept Battalion H.Q. very accurately informed of the enemy dispositions on our front, at a time when the situation was very vague. In the face of heavy shell fire the two soldiers remained to man their exposed position, continually being severed; and even when the enemy

tanks had passed over their O.P. Pte. Newman continued to telephone through information, until 1230 hrs when the last message received was that six tanks were over his post, one 30 yards away, and he feared that the telephone line would reveal his hide-out. Nothing is known as to what finally occurred to the men manning the O.P. after this, their last message. For his devotion to duty and courageous behaviour in continuing to remain at his post when it had been completely surrounded by the enemy, Pte. Newman is strongly recommended for the award of the Distinguished Conduct Medal.

(L.G. 31.12.42)

Newman, Sidney, Sergeant
4073460, 4th Bn. The Black Watch, T.A
On 13th May, 1940, Sjt. Newman gave a fine example of courage and endurance under heavy enemy fire. During each successive enemy attack he preserved complete calm and was a source of inspiration to all the men in his post. He himself with total disregard of danger, moved his L.M.G. from one position to another and by his accurate fire did much to repel the repeated attacks on his post.   *(L.G. 5.7.40)*

Newman, Stuart Samuel, Sergeant
4073460, Black Watch
No citation.   *(L.G. 22.10.40)*

Newman, William, Corporal
*7888553, Royal Armoured Corps (4 Royal Tank Regt.)
(E. Grinstead, Suss.)*
This N.C.O. was a gunner on the tank commanded by Captain Austin. During the action at Pt. 206 on the morning of June 15th, the tank was set on fire by enemy gunfire. The Tank Commander ordered evacuation, and he and the operator dismounted, Captain Austin was at the time wounded. The fire burned fiercely but Cpl. Newman ordered the driver to carry on driving slowly, while he himself proceeded with his bare hands to extinguish the fire. He succeeded in extinguishing it and then commenced to load and fire the gun by himself while the tank continued to harass the enemy. Naturally he was in considerable pain at the time from the burns he had sustained on his face, arms and legs. Finally a shell immobilised the tank, and this particular action having been beaten off, the crew were captured by the enemy, as were also Capt. Austin and the operator. Later in a counter attack by the same Sqn. Cpl. Newman and the driver Tpr. Robertson were liberated when Pt 206 was captured.

The devotion to duty displayed by Cpl. Newman in extinguishing the fire, and unaided, loading and firing his gun and continuing to fight his tank despite the grave nature of his wounds and the intense pain he was suffering, is deserving of the highest praise, and sets an example as high as any in the history of the Service.

(L.G. 21.10.41)

Ngakete, Tukaki, L/Cpl. (T/Cpl.) (Immediate)
65332, 28 NZ (Maori) Bn.
This soldier showed outstanding courage and resourcefulness during the attack on Pt 29 on the night 1/2 Nov 42. When his Sec Comd fell wounded, he took control in an attack on enemy MG posts. Annihilating the fwd elements of the enemy with hand grenades and bayonets, he led his men further to the next line of pits. His whole sec ultimately became casualties and he then joined other members of his Coy, and boldly led them forward again. It was his courage, determination and brilliant leadership that enabled his Coy to gain its final objective.

Nicholson, Jack Turner, M.M., Sergeant
3056933, Royal Scots (Immediate)
For gallantry and devotion to duty during Operations on the islands of Santorin and Paros. This Sjt. was the senior NCO of the SBS Patrol which attacked the garrison at Santorin on the night 23 April 1944. Together with one Officer and ten other ranks he entered the building occupied by approximately 30 of the enemy, an intense close quarter engagement followed. Under Sjt. Nicholson's direction the doors of the living quarters were kicked in and grenades thrown into each room, followed by fire from SMG and Bren. The enemy replied vigorously, killing two of the SBS. Aroused by the noise, an enemy patrol arrived on the scene and commenced firing from the street through the main entrance, of the building, causing further casualties. They were, however, driven off by Sjt. Nicholson with a Bren. The attack was continued until this NCO had established that all the occupants of the building were either killed or wounded. The Patrol then withdrew, covered by Sjt. Nicholson who again neutralised enemy fire from close range. On the night 16/17 May 1944 this NCO was ordered, together with two men, to attack the house in Paros Town occupied by the Garrison Commander and two German O.Rs. Although the general alarm had been given, and all the enemy in the vicinity were standing to, he carried out his task killing the O.Rs and capturing the Officer. On the way back to the RV however, and whilst still in the town, they were engaged by an enemy patrol, and the German Officer was wounded in the neck. Later, a number of hand grenades were thrown at the party and the Officer killed. Sjt. Nicholson therefore left the Officer and returned to the RV with his men. On both these occasions and previously during the attempted invasion of Simi in Oct 1943, the coolness, example and personal disregard of danger of this NCO was of the highest order.
M.M. 14.9.43   *(L.G. 4.1.45)*

Nicholson, Samuel James, Guardsman
2720987, 1st Bn. Irish Guards (Belfast) (Immediate)
This Guardsman was wounded on the afternoon of Tuesday 27th April 43 in the attack on pt 212, but continued on with his company, and his self-dressed wound was only discovered on Wednesday morning, when he was sent back to the R.A.P. He re-appeared on

the hill on Thursday night (29th April) having, on his own initiative, made his way back to the Bn's position. On the way he had to pass through enemy occupied territory and past their tanks. He came across a company of the 1st Loyals, who had been overrun and separated from the remainder of their Bn. He took charge of this coy, and gave it instructions not to move till he returned. He then set out alone to find a way up to the Bn—an extremely difficult feat in the dark, without a map and in the midst of the enemy, but he achieved it. Reporting to an officer, he asked him if he would [...] some Loyals, because, if [..] he could provide some. On learning that they would be acceptable, he went back, found the company of Loyals, and led it up to the Bn. The following morning he acquired a Tommy Gun and took an active and leading part in the subsequent fighting, urging on the Loyals, for whom he considered himself in some way responsible.

The initiative and daring shown by this Guardsman was of the highest order and, in my opinion, quite extraordinary. Officers, with maps, in daylight and with no danger from the enemy, lost their way trying to reach pt 212, while this Guardsman, with no maps, only a very general idea of the Bn's position, and the pitch dark succeeded in bringing a company safely up to the Bn through the enemy lines and within 200 yards of their tanks.

I recommend this Guardsman for gallantry and initiative. *(L.G. 8.7.43)*

Nicol, William, Warrant Officer Cl. II
23867615, Scots Guards
WO2 Nicol was the CSM of Left Flank, 2nd Battalion Scots Guards throughout the campaign in the Falkland Islands. During this time he maintained exemplary standards of personal courage and leadership which inspired similar standards in all members of his company. Three particular occasions stand out: On 6th June, after a 6 hour sea voyage at night in open boats in which most men were completely soaked, the Battalion was ordered to occupy defensive positions on high ground in freezing rain and sleet. Due to CSM Nicol's efforts, although a number of exposure casualties were taken in other companies, none occurred in Left Flank.

On 8th June some 12 enemy aircraft involved in an attack on shipping at Fitzroy flew in three sorties at low level over the Company's position at Bluff Cove. No warning of the enemy aircraft was received but, despite his CSM Nicol so rapidly and skilfully organised and controlled his company in firing rifles and machine guns, moving from sangar to sangar with no thought for his own safety, that 2 or 3 enemy aircraft were brought down by the Battalion.

On 14th June at Tumbledown Mountain, his company were ordered to take a strong enemy positin as part of a Battalion night attack.

After the initial assault, the company came under constant and devastating machine gun and sniper fire.

One of the platoon sergeants was wounded, and CSM Nicol went forward under accurate sniper fire to rescue him. Wounded in the hand while doing so, he continued to tend the dying sergeant.

He remained cool and calm under heavy fire encouraging and exhorting his men and, at the same time, advising one of the young platoon commanders how to defeat a seemingly impregnable enemy position.

He remained unperturbed by the weight of enemy small arms, artillery and mortar fire thus instilling great confidence in men who might well have been frightened. He refused to be evacuated himself, until all the other casualties in the company (26 in all) had been evacuated. CSM Nicol's distinguished conduct and conspicuous personal bravery throughout the campaign and in particular on the three occasions described proved an inspiration and example to all ranks and have made an outstanding contribution to his company's exceptional achievements. *[From L.G.]* *(L.G. 19.9.78)*

Nicoll, David, Private
2762701, 7th Bn The Black Watch (Tayport, Fife)
During the Sferro Hills battle on the night 31 July/1 Aug 43, Pte Nicoll was acting as runner to the officer commanding the left forward Coy of this Bn. The Coy's objective included the top of a ridge—the approaches to which were extremely preceipitous. During the early stages of the attack on this ridge the Coy Comdr was going forward to the leading Pls to ascertain their positions and to let them know how the other Pls were getting on and while doing so was fatally wounded. Pte. Nicoll was also wounded in the face and head but notwithstanding this and entirely on his own initiative he made his way forward to the Pl which had the next senior officer in it in order to report to him that his Coy Comdr was a casualty so that he could take over the Coy. Pte. Nicoll then proceeded under heavy fire, to visit the other two Pls to let them know what had happened and to get a report from them on their positions. He then made his way back to Coy HQ and was able to supply the acting Coy Comdr with most valuable information regarding the Coy's position.

After the Coy had secured its objectives on the ridge it was heavily counter attacked and the position of the fws Pls on the ridge, who were by this time very weak in numbers, became extremely precarious. At this stage the Coy Comdr was informed by the C.O. that he had arranged for a Coy from a Bn on the left to work its way along the ridge in order to assist the fwd Pls and it was very necessary that this information should be got to these Pls as quickly as possible. Pte. Nicoll immediately volunteered to go forward with this message and although he had considerable difficulty in seeing on account of his face wound he insisted on doing so as he knew where the forward Pls were. He again made his way up to the top of the ridge in face of enemy opposition who threw grenades down at him and succeeded in delivering his message to both Pls.

Pte. Nicoll showed most outstanding courage and initiative and his efforts very materially contributed to the securing and retention of his Coy's objective.

(*L.G. 18.11.43*)

Nightingale, Frank Lewis, Corporal
Ch.X.101330, No. 41 RM Commando, Royal Marines
At 1545 hrs. on 5th November 1944, Y Troop 41 (RM) Commando as part of a Commando attack, assaulted Battery W.18 at Domburg on Walcheren which contained some 200 Germans.

During the fighting in the battery, Cpl Nightingale was forward with his section officer and one other marine. They were heavily engaged by enemy machine-gun and rifle fire from the surrounding woods, and the marine was killed and the officer seriously wounded. Cpl Nightingale attempted to carry on the fire-fight with his bren gun but this fired only a few rounds and stopped. Cpl Nightingale seized a captured German MG 34 and continued to fire this until the enemy was forced to withdraw. After a while the enemy counter-attacked in a determined manner but Cpl Nightingale once again drove them to ground and alone held on to this flank until the remnants of his section were able to advance and join him. Through this NCO's personal disregard for safety, and his determination to kill the enemy, the troop was able to hold on to the position.

(*L.G. 20.2.45*)

Nightingale, Frederick Kitchener, F/Sjt.
618551, 7 Sqn, Bomber Command, RAF
See Cook, William, CQMS.

Nimmo, James Little, Warrant Officer Cl. II (C.S.M.)
K.62193, 1 C Scot R., Canadian Infantry Corps
(Periodic)
CSM Nimmo of 'B' Company 1st Battalion the Canadian Scottish Regiment, has consistently performed his duties with outstanding courage and shown excellent leadership in the face of heavy enemy opposition. On the night of 18/19 February 1945 during the taking and holding of the high ground (Heselen Field) at the approaches to Calcar, Germany, in the face of strong enemy resistance CSM Nimmo showed extreme bravery and coolness in reorganizing his Company, and beating off four determined enemy counter attacks.

In the early evening his company commander was called to attend an Orders Group and owing to the enemy's harrassing fire and the difficult terrain was unable to rejoin the company until just before first light. All platoon commanders had become casualties during the days bitter fighting and CSM Nimmo took over command. It was his energy and utter disregard for his own personal safety that inspired the men to fight through the long night. When dawn came it was discovered that the enemy had dug in about 100 yds in front of the company position. It was estimated that they were about 80 strong and the company strength at this time was 53 men, of which 24 were holding a blockhouse 300 yards away. This left 29 men opposing the enemy.

The Company Commander appreciated that reinforcements were needed to meet this new threat and that the battalion headquarters must be advised of the situation. CSM Nimmo volunteered to try and get back to the battalion command post. To do this he had to cross 300 yards of flat ground, in full view of the enemy, before he came to any cover. He made it, although it seemed incredible that anyone could live through the hail of machine gun and rifle fire that the enemy laid down. The information which the Sergeant Major brought back enabled the Battalion Commander to re-group his forces to meet the new threat and to supply the badly-needed reinforcements to 'B' Company. Company Sergeant Major Nimmo with the reinforcements again made the hazardous journey and arrived at the Company without the loss of a single man. His actions this day were worth of the highest tradition of this Regiment and the Canadian Army.

Belgian Croix de Guerre 1940 with Palm:LG.16.1.47
(*L.G. 22.9.45*)

Nimmo, James, Corporal
21124374, Argyll & Sutherland Highlanders
For Malaya   (*L.G. 21.3.50*)

Nolte, Hendrick Christian, T/Warrant Officer Cl. II
74654, 3 S A Armd Car Regt (V) S A T C., South
African Forces
Area Bir el Abd, 8529, on 4 Nov 1942 Sjt. Nolte was ordered to take his own and two other Armd Cars to the Southern flank of the Trento Division with a view to harassing the enemy. Although heavily shelled in doing so he moved up to within a mile of the main enemy position. There he shot up an Infantry post, capturing 30 (thirty) PWs and a truck. In order to dispose of these he had to send back one armoured car as an escort. Having done so he moved forward slowly with the other Armoured Car and by skilful use of ground and cover he brought his car to within 1,000 (one thousand) yards of the enemy's main gun positions which contained 4 x 105 mm, 4 x 25 Prs and 4 x 75 mms. These he immediately engaged with his own 20 mm and the 47 mm in the accompanying car. Although under heavy shell fire he shot it out with the enemy over open sights and succeeded in knocking out 1 x 75 mm and 1 x 105 mm. Reinforced at that stage by two other cars he charged the position under covering fire from his 47 mm. Sweeping through the whole enemy position with his three Armoured Cars he silenced the guns with machine gun fire, capturing or killing the crews. Sjt. Nolte's gallantry, skill and devotion to duty in annihilating these gun positions enabled the remainder of his Squadron to attack the remaining enemy positions and capture over 1200 prisoners, 10 Field Guns, more than 50 A/Tank guns and 117 Machine Guns.

The action lasted one and a half hours and during the whole of that time Sjt. Nolte showed the outstanding valour, skill, devotion to duty and disregard of danger.

This N.C.O.'s conduct inspired and encouraged his men, throughout an engagement which might but for his daring have necessitated a larger scale operation and considerable loss of life. *(L.G. 31.12.42)*

Norden, Richard Leslie, Private
2412437, Royal Australian Infantry Corps
For Vietnam *(L.G. 10.12.68)*

Norman, Frederick George, Rifleman
7018331, 1st London Irish Rifles (Hoverhill, Suff.)
(Immediate)
Rifleman Norman was Signal operator with D Coy who occupied positions North of Lorenzo during 18–26 Jan '44. On 24 Jan '44, the Coy was subjected to very heavy mortar and arty fire followed by a strong enemy attack. During the early part of the enemy bombardment the Coy Comd, CSM and one signaller were wounded and another man of Coy HQ killed in close proximity to Rfn Norman. He himself was severely wounded in the arm and leg and his wireless set put out of action by shell splinters.

At once he realised the vital need of maintaining the only means of communication with Bn HQ and crawled from one slit trench to another to get another set. He found this set also out of action from shell fire but crawled back with it, still under heavy fire and calmly stripped both sets until he had made the necessary repairs to get one set in working order again and re-establish communication. During the greater part of this time he was working alone, his arm severely damaged and giving him great pain, the other members of Coy HQ dead or wounded around him but he refused to allow his own wounds to be attended to until he had re-established communication.

By his coolness magnificent courage and complete disregard of personal safety he regained touch with Bn HQ and then calmly passed information of the situation thereby enabling the Bn Comd to take the necessary measures to deal with it.

Finally, he was relieved at Coy HQ but on return to Bn HQ seeing there was a shortage of signallers he insisted on remaining at duty there and was again wounded when Bn HQ came under heavy shell and mortar fire.

I consider his devotion to duty and gallantry under fire of the very highest order. *(L.G. 20.7.44)*

Nott, Allen Henry, Sergeant
VX135885, Australian Military Forces
No citation. *(L.G. 6.3.47)*

Nuttall, Capel Malyneaux Bertram, Warrant Officer Cl. II
3440495, Lancashire Fusiliers (Bury)
B.E.F. 1940 (from P.O.W. Pool) *(L.G. 11.10.45)*

Nwinya, Silika, Warrant Officer Cl. II (Platoon Comd.)
12077 [12087 on AFW 3121], 2nd (NY) King's
African Rifles (Immediate)
For conspicuous gallantry and outstanding leadership.

On the afternoon of 27th October 1944, P.S.M. Selika received orders to attack and attempt to capture a feature known as Longstop Hill, near Chinmagala, Burma, as part of a two Coy. operation.

P.S.M. Selika formed up his platoon in dead ground behind a bank and decided to attack under smoke cover. He led his platoon forward at the charge, broke through the enemy wire and was engaged by an L.M.G. from a strong point on higher ground. He himself engaged the with a Bren while his platoon attempted an outflanking movement. When P.S.M. Selika found his ammunition running low he withdrew his platoon under cover and refilled magazines.

He again led his platoon to the assault from a fresh approach and succeeded in getting so close to the strong point that he was himself able to drop several grenades into the position and silence the L.M.G. Heavy and concentrated enemy fire was coming from several directions and P.S.M. Selika decided that he must have more grenades before resuming the fight.

When fresh supplies arrived from Coy. HQ he again rallied his platoon and, showing the utmost determination and outstanding leadership, once more went forward with grenade and matchet. The platoon's rush brought them to the top of the strong point where some four enemy bodies were found lying. At this stage showers of grenades and heavy enemy fire blasted several of the leading men off their feet and wounded P.S.M. Selika.

Showing complete and absolute disregard for his personal safety, P.S.M. Selika arranged his platoon in a defensive formation and organised the collection of his wounded whilst informing his Coy. Comd. of the situation.

Time was getting late and his Coy. Comd. ordered P.S.M. Selika to break off the action so that mortars and artillery could be brought to bear on the enemy position. Despite his wounds P.S.M. Selika successfully broke off the action and withdrew his much depleted platoon with the wounded.

P.S.M. Selika's devotion to duty, unsurpassed courage and high qualities of leadership were an inspiration to all officers and men of the battalion. Throughout the history of the King's African Rifles there can have been no finer example of gallantry displayed by an African rank.

The original entry was amended. See L.G. 19.7.45
(L.G. 22.3.45)

O

Obbard, Arthur Sidney, M.M., Corporal (A/Sgt.)
6345039, 6th Queen's Own Royal West Kent Regt.
(Lenham, Kent) (Immediate)
On the night of 13/14 Nov 43 near the mouth of the Sangro river (Map Ref Sq 3999—Italy 1/100,000—Sheet 148—4) Sjt. Obbard, MM, was in command of a fighting patrol ordered to destroy enemy positions on the slopes of the escarpment 22 miles from our forward positions. In bright moonlight he led his men safely through enemy minefields along a covered line of approach to a point a few hundred yards in rear of the enemy. From here the patrol advanced swiftly through scattered cover, on to the nearest slit trenches, and wiped out the garrison. Surprise lost, Sjt. Obbard then switched the direction of advance and swept through a series of trenches and diggings, putting the enemy to flight. Once again he changed direction, and thrusting along the lower slopes even heavier resistance was met. The whole patrol fought valiantly until all positions in the neighbourhood had been liquidated.

The close fighting lasted at least twenty minutes, and all this time Sjt. Obbard was rallying his men, changing his plan of action as further situations arose, and showing personal valour of the highest order. It was entirely due to his leadership that the patrol was an unqualified success, and the excellence of his tactics kept casualties in the patrol to a minimum. The ... *[continuation missing].*
M.M. 18.11.43 *(L.G. 9.3.44)*

Obbard, Arthur Sidney, D.C.M., M.M., Sergeant
Bar
6345039, 6th Bn. Queen's Own Royal West Kent Regt.
(Lenham, Kent) (Immediate)
Ref Map Italy 1/50,000 Sheet 99 IV (Casola Valsenio)

During the fighting near Monte Spaduro 028269 it was essential for future operations to establish what enemy troops were defending the Salara ridge 035262, and so to discover the exact boundary between two German divisions. Thus, on the night 24/25 Nov 44 Sjt. Obbard was sent in command of a fighting patrol of ten men, to obtain identifications from German positions located on these slopes. The approach was a very open one, and was subjected to constant harrassing fire. In addition, the patrol at an early stage passed through an uncharted minefield and detonated two mines which failed to explode, but in spite of these difficulties Sjt. Obbard moved his men to close quarters unseen. Before reaching the located positions, however, he sensed a German sentry a few yards to his front, and halted the patrol. At this time they were not fully deployed for the assault and Bren guns had not been placed in position. Creeping forward a short way himself, Sjt. Obbard and the sentry saw each other simultaneously, but Sjt. Obbard

fired first and as his opponent fell more of the enemy opened fire. Shouting to the men following to rush them, he threw a grenade straight into one trench, and destroyed another MG post before the remainder of the patrol reached him. In spite of further resistance they overpowered the entire outpost garrison in a matter of seconds, killing three and capturing five, two of whom were wounded. Sjt. Obbard rapidly reformed his patrol and withdrew with all five Germans, carrying one of the wounded bodily.

The patrol was only out for forty minutes, covering a distance each way of approximately 500 yards, and returned without casualties and with most valuable identifications and information. This operation had been attempted before unsuccessfully, and the enemy knew that there was only one possible approach to the positions. On this occasion its complete success was entirely due to the lightning action, outstanding personal bravery and brilliant leadership of Sjt. Obbard. His complete contempt for the enemy, his utter disregard for his own safety, and his exceptional powers of leadership have a great influence on all those who serve with him.
(L.G. 10.5.45)

O'Brien, Cornelius, Corporal
3393801, 1st Bn, East Lancashire Regt. (Dublin)
Cpl. O'Brien's coy attacked and captured a posn astride the X-tracks 893484 on the evening of 11 Feb 45 during the advance through the Reichswald. As a result of his Pl Comd becoming a casualty Cpl. O'Brien found himself commanding No. 9 Pl. The enemy had been reinforced in this sector and launched an almost unbroken series of counter attacks during the night 11/12 Feb and throughout the whole of the following day. Cpl. O'Brien's pl was slightly fwd of the remainder of the coy and was subjected to incessant sniping, mortaring and shelling in addition to the counter attacks already mentioned.

On the evening of 12 Feb 45 a very determined counter attack in at least coy strength supported by arty came in from the SE end of the Reichswald. Owing to poor visibility and the close country large parties of enemy were able to approach unseen until they were almost on top of Cpl. O'Brien's posn. While the pl were engaged in repelling this counter attack a party of approx 12 Germans were seen working round the flank of the pl into some thick undergrowth to their right. Without hesitation, Cpl. O'Brien immediately leapt from his slit trench and still under heavy mortar and [...], led a handful of men to engage the enemy at close quarters. With his own Sten gun Cpl. O'Brien killed 7 Germans. Others were wounded, and the result of this prompt and audacious sortie held up the enemy counter attack long enough to enable the Coy Comd to restore the situation.

During this respite Cpl. O'Brien went round his pl posns, which were still being heavily shelled and mortared, encouraging his men and ensuring that amn was adequatley distributed.

Later the same day the enemy again counter attacked—this time they were some 200 strong—and again Cpl. O'Brien's pl received the full weight of the assault. Using all their weapons the pl stood firm and repulsed every attempt by the enemy to over-run the posn by sheer weight of numbers. The determined resistance which was offered by this pl under Cpl. O'Brien was very largely instrumental in frustrating the continuous and determined counter attacks made by the enemy on the coy posn during this period.

Cpl. O'Brien set the highest example of coolness and leadership under heavy fire. His conduct is quite exemplary and is an inspiration to all who serve with him. *(L.G. 10.5.45)*

O'Brien, John Francis Patrick, Corporal
SX 1603, 7 Aust Div, Australian Military Forces (Immediate)
K.B. Mission Action, Milne Bay, New Guinea, night 27/28 Aug 42.

For conspicuous gallantry and devotion to duty on the night 27/28 Aug 42.

During the withdrawal of our own troops from K.B. Mission after 42 hours fighting of enemy tanks and infantry, Cpl. O'Brien played a magnificent part in attempting to prevent further exploitation by the enemy. Enemy tanks and infantry had commenced to advance along the road. Cpl. O'Brien, who had shown initiative in obtaining an anti-tank rifle with considerable trouble, manned the gun in an exposed position on the road. It was pointed out to Cpl. O'Brien that the task would be a suicidal one, but this did not deter him. When the tanks approached he fired at the first one at a range of 10 yds and stopped it, but the tank was now in a position in which to fire on him. Despite this, and under fire from the tank and also mortar fire from the infantry, he attacked a second tank, stopping it with 2 shots from his anti-tank rifle. During this encounter he received a bad wound in the arm from a hand grenade thrown from the tank. Several enemy infantry were also killed. Injured in such a manner, he took part in a subsequent 3 days' march through thick jungle country without rations. He had a section of men under his command and by his example inspired them. His general conduct throughout the entire action was courageous and exceptional. *(L.G. 4.2.43)*

O'Brien, John Peter, Private
VX 56822, 2/24 Aust Inf Bn.
For conspicuous gallantry and devotion to duty at El Alamein 25 to 31 Oct 42.

On the night 25/26 Oct C and D Coys of this unit had to attack along the length of the enemy defensive posns and in doing so became involved in hand to hand fighting of the most severe nature, resulting in loss of check on

distance and the objective was over-run. When it became necessary for these Coys to withdraw and re-organise on their proper objective it was found that a number of men had fought their way well fwd of the rest of the Coy and had run into a heavily wired and defended enemy strongpost and had suffered heavy casualties.

Pte. O'Brien went fwd of the Coy in the face of very intense fire of all natures from this post and moved from one to another of these men dressing their wounds and then brought them out, still under heavy fire making repeated trips through this fire till all the wounded were got back to the re-organisation area.

On the night 30/31 Oct all other stretcher bearers with C and D Coys but Pte O'Brien became casualties. During this attack it became necessary for an offrs patrol to go into a very strong defended locality known as 'Thompsons Post,' instead of as reported, this locality was found to be strongly held and the patrol was ambushed by very intense fire at short range, suffered casualties and was forced to withdraw.

Pte. O'Brien, with complete disregard for his personal safety, moving fwd through terrific fire, entered Thompsons Post and brought the wounded out from right inside the post.

As the depleted Coys were moving back from the post to link up with 2/32 Bn, three aerial bombs sited as anti-personnel mines were exploded killing twelve and wounding sixteen. Pte. O'Brien, though still under heavy fire from Thompsons Post and in danger of the aerial bombs being repeated went fearlessly to all the wounded dressed the whole sixteen and organised PsW carrying parties. Though wounded himself in this action, Pte. O'Brien would not pause to dress his own wound but completed the dressing and evacuation of the others before accepting attention himself.

The cool efficiency and utter fearlessness of this man saved many lives and inspired the men with confidence in the knowledge that if wounded they would receive immediate attention no matter what the circumstance. *(L.G. 11.2.43)*

O'Brien, Richard, Lance Sergeant
5340890, Royal Berkshire Regt. (attd. S.S.B., No. 2 Commando)
Sgt O'Brien was one of the detachment of 2 Commando on Operation 'Musketoon.' This highly successful operation resulted in the destruction of the important electric power plant at Glomfjord in Norway on the night of the 20th October, 1942. Sgt O'Brien throughout showed great skill and resolution. He helped reconnoitre the difficult mountain crossing from the landing place to the objective and personally laid the charge which destroyed the pipe-line. He then made his escape, spending, in all, twelve days in enemy-occupied country. When suffering from sickness, privation and exhaustion he showed remarkable endurance and determination.
M.M. 13.1.44 *(L.G. 9.3.43)*

O'Connell, Daniel, M.M., Warrant Officer Cl. II
3443480, 2nd Bn. Lancashire Fusiliers (Burnley)
    (Periodic)
Ref Map: Italy 1/50,000 Sheet 88 II Imoia and Italy 1/
25,000 Sheet 88 I NE Argenta
    For conspicuous gallantry and devotion to duty during
the period 1st April—2nd May. Throughout this period
CSM O'Connell has been CSM of a rifle company of
2nd Bn The Lancashire Fusiliers and has taken part in
all actions which made up the advance from the R Senio
to the R PO. He has been responsible for organizing Coy
HQ, controlling the Coy in the absence of the Coy Comd
and arranging stretcher and ammunition parties, many
of which he led personally under extremely heavy enemy
fire. He has never hesitated to expose himself in the
course of his duties and has carried out all tasks with the
utmost speed and efficiency. By his personal courage,
cheerfulness and powers of leadership he has inspired
the men of his coy and has maintained a very high
standard of morale. The success of the Coy in these
operations may be attributed very largely to his
personality and the respect felt for him by all ranks. CSM
O'Connell has served with the Bn for seventeen years
and since 1939 has taken part in all engagements of the
bn in France, N Africa, Sicily and Italy. He was promoted
CSM of 'D' Coy at the close of the Tunisian campaign
and has remained with that Coy ever since, leading and
serving his men with skill and devotion. Since his
previous award in October 1943, his gallantry and
devotion to duty have been conspicuous and his example
an inspiration to the whole Bn.
M.M. 23.9.43   *(L.G. 13.12.45)*

O'Connor, Owen George John, Lance Corporal
N 454252, 24 Aust Inf Bn. (Immediate)
South Bougainville.
    For Most conspicuous bravery, superb leadership and
devotion to duty in the face of heavy enemy fire.
    In the Hongorai river area, on 13 May 45, L/Cpl.
O'Connor was second in command of a patrol of eight
men, with the task of locating enemy dispositions, and
denying to the Japanese information regarding our
preparations for a major attack on the enemy positions
along the Hongorai River. During the forward movement,
the patrol was attacked by a party of 50 Japanese. In the
hail of fire which was directed at our patrol, the patrol
leader was wounded, falling into the enemy fire lane.
The leading Owen gunner also fell wounded.
    L/Cpl. O'Connor rapidly appreciating that bold and
decisive action alone could retrieve the situation,
immediately took control. Under withering enemy fire
he rallied the remaining members of his patrol and
reorganised them into positions to withstand the
onslaught of an enemy force numerically vastly superior
to his own. He then dashed forward without hesitation
and with complete disregard for his own personal safety
and reached his patrol leader. While in the act of dragging
him back, three Japanese with fixed bayonets charged at

O'Connor and the wounded man. Standing guard over
his comrade, O'Connor killed all three enemy with his
Owen gun. Then despite intense enemy fire which riddled
his clothes and equipment, O'Connor, with heroic
determination continued to cover the extrication of his
comrade while another soldier dragged him to safety.
    O'Connor again faced the murderous hail of fire and
dragged the wounded Owen gunner to a position of
temporary security. His grim determination and courage
undoubtedly deterred the enemy from annihilating his
small party.
    O'Connor then reorganised his men who, under the
inspiration of his gallant leadership, fought on until the
enemy were finally driven off. L/Cpl. O'Connor's
determined stand with his small force, in the face of
overwhelming odds, prevented the enemy from
penetrating and disrupting our preparations for what later
culminated in a successful major assault on the enemy's
strong defences along the Hongorai river. His unselfish
heroism and devotion to his wounded comrades has
inspired the whole battalion, and instilled confidence and
example into all that wounded men, still in danger of
their lives, will be fought for and not abandoned in these
vicious patrol clashes of the jungle.   *(L.G. 10.1.46)*

Odong, Yoweri bin, Warrant Officer Cl. II
N 158, King's African Rifles
No citation.   *(L.G. 22.3.45)*

Office, Selemani, WS/Cpl.
DN 9419, 26 (EA0 Bde, 11 (EA) Div, 33 Corps, 22
    (NY) K.A.R. (Immediate)
At approx 1500 hrs on 26th Oct 1944, an attack was
made on the strongly defended position known as Dick
Hill, part of the Jap defences of Kantha, Burma. Prior to
this Cpl. Office had reported sick and had been marked
C.I. His Coy Comd was informed that Cpl. Office was
not fit to accompany the coy. Cpl. Office approached his
Coy Comd and stated he would like to go with the coy
as he wanted to lead his section. He had several boils on
his back and said he would be alright if he did not wear
equipment. This was agreed.
    When the main enemy position was encountered and
18 Pl did a right flanking attack, Cpl. Office lead his
section with great courage and although wounded by a
grenade, continued on. When 18 Pl were pinned down
he organised his section and controlled his section fi[...]
extremely well. 18 Pl again attempted to attack the
position and Cpl. Office was wounded again but still
carried on, shouting words of encouragement to his
section. The attack was pinned down again and Cpl.
Office, now wounded twice, crawled up to his section
and organised them. When the coy had returned to its
firm base Cpl. Office insisted he stay with his section
after having had his wounds dressed. On the following
day when being evacuated, the S/B party, carrying Cpl.
Office and one other man, which had lagged behind
slightly, suddenly decided that they heard some enemy

and dropped both stretcher cases and sought cover. Cpl. Office immediately took over the situation and got the party under way again.

Ogden-Smith, Bruce Walter, M.M., Sergeant
682661, East Surrey Regt., COPPs
In spite of feeling in bad physical condition, Sergeant Ogden-Smith showed courage, coolness and ability in assisting Major Scott-Bowden to carry out the first experimental beach reconnaissance from 'X Craft,' which entailed amongst other things swimming on to vigilantly defended enemy beaches and moving about there 'under the nose' of sentries on two consecutive nights, the 18th and 19th January 1944. Recommended for the award of the DCM.
M.M. 2.3.44   *(L.G. 15.6.44)*

Ogle, Richard Davidson, Lance Sergeant
4383645, Black Watch (Gateshead)
B.E.F. 1940 (from P.O.W. Pool)   *(L.G. 14.2.46)*

Oldford, Joseph Winston, Warrant Officer Cl. II (C.S.M.)
F54818, Canadian Infantry Corps
N.W. Europe   *(L.G. 24.1.46)*

Oliphant, Rosslyn Ernest, Sergeant
C.R.3008, Rhod. Regt. (attd. Somaliland Camel Corps.)
No citation.   *(L.G. 11.2.41)*

Oliver, Ralph, Corporal
4448623, 1st Bn. The Durham Light Infantry (West Hartlepool)
At Tobruch on the night 7/8th December, 1941, 'C' Coy carried out an attack on the left of the Battalion on PT 157. Cpl. Oliver became separated from the rest of the Coy in the dark. He collected seven men, carried out two assaults on enemy M.G. positions, captured two machine guns and twenty prisoners and then organized a defensive position with enemy captured weapons on the flank of his Coy. He showed great courage during the operation and was an excellent example to his men.
(L.G. 24.2.42)

O'Neill, James, Corporal (A/Sgt.)
2824426, 1st Seaforth Highlanders (Port Glasgow, Renfrewshire)
When in command of a patrol of two sections suddenly encountered a company of Japs at Nampamaung S.F. 2628. on 20th April 43. He coolly and skilfully conducted the withdrawl of his two sections, covering movement with fire and delaying, and inflicting casualties on the Japs. One of his sections was thus enabled to withdraw southwards along the Chindwin and cross intact at Nanthanyit S.F. 2321. but he and the other section eventually had to swim the Chindwin (600 yds wide) at Taungbola (SF.2525) under fire. Despite covering fire

from the other section and from a patrol on the West bank three were killed whilst swimming, one drowned and one missing. At least 20 Japs were killed in the engagement. His placing of his other section in a position whence it could withdraw intact whilst himself remaining at the point of danger to cover its withdrawal are in the best traditions of leadership.   *(L.G. 30.9.43)*

O'Neill, James, Warrant Officer Cl. II
3251512, Cameronians & 3rd Bn Nigerian Regt. (Dumbarton)
On 24 Feb 45, during ops between the ME and Dalet Chaungs, a coy of 3 N.R. attacked the hill feature at 926337. On first contact with the enemy, a number of the leading troops came under accurate LMG fire and several were hit, including the Pl Comd who was mortally wounded. The enemy fire was now heavier and the loss of their Pl Comd had an adverse effect upon the men. CSM O'Neill immediately went forward rallied the platoon and disregarding the enemy fire led them straight to their objective which they captured and consolidated. The following day, a N.C.O. was wounded in a patrol encounter and lay in the open 100 yards from an enemy post. CSM O'Neill went forward, again under fire, and brought the wounded man back to safety.

On both these days this W.O. displayed complete disregard of his personal safety and the standard of his leadership was the highest. Both during the attack and a subsequent counter attack by the enemy his calmness under fire and cool courage were an inspiration to the troops of the platoon he was commanding.
(L.G. 21.6.45)

O'Neill, William, Sergeant
WX13036, 2/5 Aust Ind Coy. (Immediate)
At Mubo on 1 Oct 42. For conspicuous and outstanding bravery.

During a raid by Kanga Force he single handed held up the advance of a large body of Japanese who were trying to cut our troops off from a bridge the only avenue of escape. During this action he killed twelve Japanese who endeavoured to pass his position, wounding many others. Sjt. O'Neill stayed until all other troops were clear and he was forced to abandon his position owing to the lack of ammunition.   *(L.G. 30.3.43)*

Onions, George Robert, Corporal
558597, 5th Royal Tank Regt. (Wolverhampton) (Immediate)
On 28 Sep 43 'B' Sqn 5 R Tks was ordered to seize the bridge over the river Sarno at Scafati MR N4438 which was known to be the only bridge which was at that time left intact. Cpl. Onions was driving his troop leader in the leading tank of the Sqn. The troop leader, an officer, was wounded on approaching the bridge and evacuated. Cpl. Onions quickly appreciating the situation, took over command of the tank himself. He crossed the bridge and took up a position on the enemy side of the river and

held off many enemy counter-attacks put in at last light and during the night. He was shelled by German Mark III Tanks and sniped by the enemy who were in houses all around him. He stayed in position all night with no support against an enemy tank counter-attack, no anti-tank guns being able to be brought up and placed for his protection.

During the night he ran short of ammunition, and organised a party of infantry who were in the house parallel to his tank, to assist in going back over the bridge and carrying up the necessary ammunition. He was under intense enemy fire throughout the whole period, the streets being illuminated like daylight, owing to a vehicle being set alight by enemy shelling on the bridge. By his initiative, bold and resolute action and complete disregard for his personal safety, the bridge which was vital for the advance of the 5th Army was kept intact from numerous enemy counter-attacks during the hours of darkness.   *(L.G. 27.1.44)*

Opie, Leonard Murray, Warrant Officer Cl. II (temp.)
4/400006, Royal Australian Regt.
For Korea   *(L.G. 14.10.52)*

Ord, Robert Edward, Lance Sergeant
319449, 16th/5th Lancers (Colchester) (Immediate)
Sjt. Ord was the tank commander of a Sherman tank on 15 May 44 during the attack on a heavily defended position, when his Sqn was supporting the 6 R Innisk Fusiliers on to Ridge at 834775. He was the left hand tank of the left leading troop, when his tank was blown up in the middle of a minefield, sited on the same ridge as the enemy positions with the mines hidden in deep grass. Thinking his tank had been hit by an AP shell, he ordered his crew to evacuate, but when he saw he had been blown up, he immediately re-manned the tank.

He stayed in his tank from 1300 hrs to 1930 hrs that day. During this period he was continually being sniped, engaged by AP fire and heavily shelled, as he was in full observation of an enemy OP in a house 350 yards away. He was also completely unsupported by any other tanks, all of which had been forced to withdraw slightly down the ridge and were some 250 yards behind him.

In face of this intense enemy fire, Sjt. Ord acted as OP for the rest of his Sqn and the supporting Artillery the whole time he was in the position and directed fire on to the enemy infantry 300 yards in front of him. He also mended the traversing gear of the turret which had been damaged by the explosion of the mine, so that he could fire his guns, which he did to such good purpose that he knocked out one of several Mk IV Tanks, and SP Guns that were advancing on to his position, thereby halting their advance. In addition he was able to observe and report on the enemy on the left flank, who were holding up the advance, and gave valuable information of a farmhouse not 350 yards from him, which was an enemy strong point and housed an OP. The reports which he passed back over the wireless were of the highest order, clearly given in such a calm voice that it was impossible to believe he was continually under the heaviest enemy fire.

He finally abandoned his tank only when ordered to do so by his Squadron Leader, when the deteriorating light was preventing further observation and the fire from an SP Gun brought up to deal with him became so accurate that it appeared to be only a matter of a few minutes before his tank received a direct hit. On re-joining his Squadron, he insisted on taking over another tank at once, which he commanded for the remainder of the day and in the subsequent advance.

By his action, Sjt. Ord undoubtedly prevented many casualties in the tanks and infantry, besides inflicting heavy losses on the enemy. Throughout, his courage and calm tenacity was an inspiration to his crew and the whole Squadron.   *(L.G. 26.10.44)*

O'Reilly, Bernard, Private
19038608, King's Own Yorkshire Light Infantry
For Malaya   *(L.G. 5.7.49)*

O'Reilly, Cornelius, Corporal
7020028, 2nd Bn The Royal Ulster Rifles (Brighton)
  (Immediate)
This NCO was in command of a Rifle Section during the attack on Cambes. His Pl Comd was killed and the Pl Sjt. was wounded. During the fighting considerable confusion arose, and this NCO gathered the men around him and led them with outstanding bravery and leadership. On reorganising he took over command of the Pl, leading them during a difficult period of mortaring on the objective, with determination and leadership which inspired and kept them steady. Cpl. O'Reilley is recommended for the immediate award of the DCM.
                    (L.G. 31.8.44)

O'Reilly, James Francis, Sergeant
18176, 26 NZ Battalion (Periodic)
Near Empoli on the night 10 Aug 44 18176 Sjt. O'Reilly J. F. commanded a platoon protecting the right flank of his company during an advance on Avane and St. Maria. During the advance a German fighting patrol estimated 60–70 strong contacted Sjt. O'Reilly's platoon and he immediately attacked them inflicting casualties. At first light, with still a number of the enemy behind his position, Sjt. O'Reilly moved his platoon to a better position and again attacked. Through Sjt. O'Reilly's leadership and personal example casualties were inflicted and prisoners taken and only a third of the enemy force got back to their own lines. In this and previous operations Sjt. O'Reilly's qualities of leadership, command and initiative have been outstanding and an inspiration to all with whom he came in contact.
M.I.D. 29.11.45   *(L.G. 21.6.45)*

Organ, Patrick Joseph, Corporal (A/Sgt.)
5883032, 2nd Northamptonshire Regt. (Limerick)
(Immediate)

At 1000 hrs 1st May 14 Pl 2 Northamptons, occupying a most forward position in the Anzio beachhead, was overrun by a strong enemy force, later known to have consisted of between 40 & 50 men. Sjt. Organ's Pl was immediately ordered to carry out a counter-attack. Hardly had the Pl fixed its bayonets and were ready to charge the 200 yds uphill than the Pl Comd and Pl Sjt became casualties.

Without a moments hesitation and showing a complete grasp of the situation, Sjt. Organ reorganised the Platoon and led them personally into the attack. The last 120 yds of ground was very open and was subjected to intense enemy mortar, machine-gun and small arms fire. This intense fire broke up the attack.

Sjt. Organ re-organised his men in the meagre cover that was available and once again led his men in to the attack. Led personally by Sjt. Organ the remnants of the Platoon reached the enemy trenches, and more able to inflict casualties on the enemy in the bitter hand to hand fighting which ensured. The main force of the counter attack had, however, once again broken up by the intense fire which the enemy was able to bring to bear on the last 120 yds of ground leading up to the crest. Realising it was impossible to retake the position almost single handed, Sjt. Organ brought a mere handful of men back to the Rear Pl Area.

At 1545 hrs a third and more deliberate counter-attack was launched supported by RA and 3″ Mortars. Sjt. Organ, now with a different pl was again ordered to counter-attack. Again he reached the crest with his men, only to find the withering enemy fire from exceedingly close range, had broken up the attack. At 0015 hrs the following morning a night attack was put in. Its success depended upon a patrol covering a gap in the wire through which the assaulting troops must pass. Sjt. Organ crawled out with his patrol, and remained in the position guarding the gap within 120 yds of the enemy until zero hour.

The quite outstanding powers of leadership and gallantry shown by this NCO throughout a bitterly contested battle, which never really abated for 16 hrs, were beyond all praise. The complete indifference to his own personal safety under intense and most accurate enemy fire at very close range, and the determination with which he led and pressed home his counter-attacks were a magnificent inspiration to all ranks who came under his command that day. *(L.G. 3.8.44)*

Orton, Reynold Arthur, Sergeant
1880080, Royal Engineers
For Korea *(L.G. 10.7.51)*

O'Shea, Michael Patrick, Guardsman
2717837, Irish Guards

During the withdrawal from Vensmoen on the 26th May 1940, a party consisting of Irish Guardsmen and men of an independent company came to a fast flowing river. Guardsman O'Shea assisted the whole party of 25 men to cross through this water by means of a belt of web straps. Many times he was nearly pulled back into the water himself, which would have meant the loss of several lives. On one occasion he ran 25 yards down stream and pulled a man out who had been carried away by the current.

Further back he carried a man of the Independent company who had fainted, for a mile to safety. Owing to these acts of gallantry he missed the ferry and with a few others had to walk 25 miles to rejoin his unit.

During the whole time his unfailing courage and sound advice were an inspiration to the officers and men of the party and were probably a main cause of its escape. *(L.G. 6.8.40)*

Ostara, Ernest Barrington, Warrant Officer Cl. I
214406, Royal Australian Infantry

WO Ostara served with the Australian Imperial Forces during World War Two and saw active service with the 2/6 Australian Commando Squadron from 1943 to 1946. He enlisted in the Australian Regular Army in September 1947. Before being allotted for duty with the Australian Army Training Team in South Vietnam he served with the First Battalion Royal Australian Regiment in Korea in 1953 as well as in a number of instructional posts including appointments with cadets, commandos and the Infantry Centre. WO Ostara commenced his tour of duty with the Australian Army Training Team, Vietnam, on the 10th November 1963, his first assignment being that of Advisor to the Vietnamese National Training Centre at Dong Da.

At 1500 hours on the 7th January 1965, the Reconnaissance Company, with WO Ostara as Senior advisor, was in refresher training at Dong Da Training Centre. An operation was in progress to the Northern end of the training area where a 'Tiger Company' (a heliborne reaction force) was clearing a Viet Cong company from a nearby village. The Viet Cong broke clear and moved South across undulating scrubby country in plain view of a group consisting of Australians and Vietnamese troops. Under the guidance and with the assistance of the Australian members of the Training Team, the Vietnamese troops blocked the Viet Cong move with machine gun fire inflicting seven casualties on the Viet Cong and forcing them to take cover and move into a narrow steep sided water course. At this stage the group of ten Vietnamese troops who were being instructed by WO Ostara, under his direction quickly took up an intercepting position further up the water course. The advancing Viet Cong on meeting this group threw grenades which caused panic among the Vietnamese troops under training. Quickly assessing the seriousness of the situation and to protect the troops under his care WO Ostara single-handed attacked the Viet Cong force. With his personal carbine he shot down the leading element of two who proved to be a senior Viet Cong Commander and his orderly. Rounding a bend to follow up, he found no remainging enemy. His actions made a tremendous impact on the force to which he was attached, which on succeeding days undertook further successful operations. WO Ostara's action was a splendid individual effort and is in the highest tradition of the Australian Regular Army and reflects great credit upon himself. *[From L.G.]*   *(L.G. 27.7.65)*

O'Sullivan, John, Warrant Officer Cl. III (T.S.M.)
808244, 13th Anti-Tank Regt, Royal Artillery
At St. Vanant on 27th May 1940 T.S.M. O'Sullivan was directing the fire of one of his anti-tank guns during a heavy enemy attack which was accompanied by Tanks. Under intense M.G. fire and small arms fire the gun succeeded in accounting for a number of Armoured Fighting vehicles until the No. 1 and one man of the detachment were killed and two others wounded. T.S.M. O'Sullivan though himself hit in the arm, with one other unwounded man continued effectively to fire the gun until the remaining unwounded man was hit. T.S.M. O'Sullivan then manned the gun alone and destroyed at least one other tank before a shell from a tank put the gun out of action, and again wounded T.S.M. O'Sullivan.
(L.G. 20.12.40)

Otis, Howard Glenwood, Private
A105661, The Royal Canadian Regt. (Immediate)
Reference Map Italy 1/50,000 Sheet 89 III Ravenna W
On the night 17/18 December 1944, The Royal Canadian Regiment was ordered to form a bridgehead across the Fosso Vecchio. 'A' Company reached its objective astride the Via Bondellino and consolidated with 7 Platoon forward, at a house at MR 390367. A105661 Private Howard Glenwood Otis was Piat man with 7 Platoon.
At 0615 hours, 18 December, 7 Platoon was heavily counter attacked by two tanks and infantry estimated at between 50 and 60 in strength. The Platoon Commander ordered Private Otis to go forward with him and hold off the tanks while the platoon moved to a more favourable position. Private Otis worked his way forward to a commanding position under heavy enemy shell and small arms fire and waited until the tanks were approximately 30 yards away. He then opened fire with his Piat,[...] out of action. He then fired on the leading

tank and hit it, but [...] failed to explode. The enemy infantry were meantime closing in on the position, but Private Otis coolly reloaded and fired again, the bomb hit the rear of the tank and killed seven or eight of the enemy who had apparently been sheltering behind the tank and were just preparing to rush him. His Platoon Commander then ordered him to rejoin his platoon. As Private Otis was carrying out this order he came across another soldier from his platoon, shot through the leg and unable to move. In spite of very heavy enemy fire, this brave soldier stopped and picked up his wounded comrade, and carried him back to the Platoon and safety.
In the action Private Otis, showing total disregard for his own personal safety, caused substantial losses to the enemy, and rescued a helpless comrade from capture. As a result of his determination the counter attack collapsed and 'A' Company was able to continue its consolidation. His conduct upheld the highest traditions of the Canadian Infantry.   *(L.G. 7.4.45)*

Otto, Carel Jacobus Stephanus, Corporal
SAP/196405, 2 S.A.P., South African Forces
For conspicuous bravery when leading his section in the attack at Salum on 11 and 12 Jan 42. On the latter occasion when fierce mortar and machine gun fire were directed at his men from enemy strong points sited in camouflaged caves cut out of rock above Salum Pier, he and L/Cpl. McAllister rushed forward and by a resolute hand grenade attack overcame all enemy resistance, bringing about the surrender of 1 officer and 40 other ranks, although wounded in the process. His coolness and courage were an example to all.   *(L.G. 19.3.42)*

Oxley, Leonard Ernest, Sergeant (A/W.O.II (C.S.M.))
2610093, 1st Battn, The Parachute Regt., Army Air
   Corps (Immediate)
During the airborne operation at Arnhem, Sept 17th–25th, 1944, this Warrant Officer showed magnificent powers of leadership, and on every possible occasion displayed the most conspicuous personal gallantry. On Sept 23rd, when commanding a much depleted company, his sector was heavily attacked by two Tiger Tanks, a flame-thrower, and a superior force of infantry. Judging the exact moment for counter-attack, he personally led his men with such skill and daring that one tank and the flame-thrower were destroyed and some thirty enemy killed outright. His personal initiative and reckless courage in this action were an inspiration to all and were entirely responsible for turning the enemy's attack into a rout and preventing his sector from being overrun.
(L.G. 9.11.44)

P

Page, Frederick Cyril, Private
5683268, 1/4th Bn The Hampshire Regt. (Southend-on-Sea)
On 31 Aug 44 at approx 2300 hrs 14 Pl 'C' Coy were attacked whilst holding the eastern part of the village of Monte-Gridolfo (Map Sheet 109 IV—Pesaro 1/50,000, 946752). When the pl comd found that the enemy had infiltrated into some of the houses in his area he asked for a volunteer to go back to Coy HQ and report the situation. Pte. Page immediately volunteered and although the streets were under heavy MG fire from the enemy he made his way back to Coy HQ. The Coy Comd ordered him to stay at Coy HQ but he asked permission to return as his pl were in need of every man. On his way back he took a Bren gun from a wounded man and seeing 6 enemy approaching up the street he ran straight towards them firing the Bren from the hip, killing two and wounding one other. The enemy retreated. He then informed his pl comd that the message was through to Coy HQ and continued mopping up the enemy in the streets with the Bren gun. During this street fighting he was badly hit in the leg by a mortar splinter, but he continued to man his gun and fire at the enemy. Eventually he fainted at his post through loss of blood. Pte. Page's unselfish devotion to duty and very great bravery was an inspiration to the whole of the pl. His courage was beyond all praise. *(L.G. 8.2.45)*

Page, Robert Dudley, Warrant Officer Cl. II
5886493, 61 Recce Regt., Reconnaissance Corps, RAC (Wellingborough)
SSM Page was in command of 'C' Squadron HQ vehicles when the Sqn crossed the Albert Canal at K071843 South of Gheel on 9 Sep 44 in offensive operations. The vehicles immediately came under heavy fire and three were hit. SSM Page quickly organized the HQ behind some houses, being continually under MG fire while doing so. Soon after, the first Sqn casualties came in. The bridge over the canal by now had been broken and rendered useless by enemy shellfire, but SSM Page got them across by boat, still under constant and heavy fire. After two hours of fighting, the forward troops required ammunition. Owing to the bridge being broken the ammunition truck was still on the far side of the canal. SSM Page organized the transport of ammunition in a small boat, and himself took it forward to the armoured cars. The route was under enemy observation, and he was under heavy mortar and MG fire the whole way. His truck was hit three times. Nevertheless he maintained the ammunition supply throughout the whole day until the troops were relieved at dusk.
By his energy, enterprise and great personal courage SSM Page played a large part in the Squadron's success;

his outstanding devotion to [...] and example being a great inspiration and encouragement to his comrades during a very t[...] day. *(L.G. 1.3.45)*

Page, Walter William, Warrant Officer Cl. II (R.Q.M.S.), A/WOI Supt Clerk
Royal Signals
This W.O. is superintending clerk to S.O. in C. He was sent from Premesques late on 26 May in charge of 10 other ranks to report to an officer at Dunkirk. For various means the rendezvous miscarried and R.S.M. Page tried to reach the Signal office in Dunkirk. Being prevented by burning buildings in this object, he went to the Docks in search of an officer. There he found an officer of the Mercantile Marine in command of a supply ship to be unloaded. He collected about 150 men of various arms and departments in the dock area and kept them at work unloading through the 27th under heavy bombing attacks, until an ammunition ship alongside was bombed and set on fire about 2200 hrs. He showed resource, initiative and determination to a high degree. *(L.G. 11.7.40)*

Paice, Michael Francis, Private
NX73320, 55/53 Aust Inf Bn. (Immediate)
He displayed outstanding bravery whilst a member of a fighting patrol which attacked Jap positions on Smith Hill in the Pieaterapaia area, Bougainville on 8 Feb 45. Pte. Paice was in the position of third scout in the patrol when the patrol came under heavy fire of MG, SMG, rifles and grenades from the Jap positions. The leading scout being killed, Pte. Paice went forward under fire, killed two Japs and silenced a Jap post with his OSMG and then attempted to get out the body of the leading scout, but his patrol comd, Lieut. Ryan being seriously wounded, he went to his assistance and brought him back whilst he himself was still subject to heavy Jap fire from extremely short range. Pte. Paice's courage and determination assisted materially in the result achieved by the patrol in killing 5 Japs and inflicting heavy casualties on the remainder.
(L.G. 21.6.45)

Palfreeman, James William, Sergeant
4447140, 9th Bn. Royal Northumberland Fusiliers
This N.C.O. was the Platoon Sjt of a Platoon moving to occupy a bridge at Aire on the 24th May 1940. On the way the Platoon met the enemy in superior force and were hard put to it to hold their own. During the action this N.C.O. crawled to the platoon truck which was under fire to get a Bren Gun which he used with considerable effect against enemy infantry. Later, one of his men was wounded by a Mortar bomb and this N.C.O. with a Fusilier crawled out and brought the wounded man in.

Later when the Platoon was ordered to withdraw Sjt. Palfreeman carried the wounded man back to a truck. This N.C.O. set a very fine example to his men.

(L.G. 20.12.40)

Palin, William Henry, Warrant Officer Cl. II (C.S.M.)
3447324, 2nd King's Regt. (Rochdale) (Immediate)
During the crossing of the R. Gari on 11/12th May, 1944, the conduct of this Warrant Officer was of the highest order and a steadying influence to troops who might easily have become thoroughly disorganized.

During the initial crossing of the River his Company was subjected to intense Mortar and Machine gun fire. Many casualties were sustained and the loading of boats was becoming disorganised until CSM Palin rallied his men and personally checked each man into his boat. In consequence his Company made a successful crossing of the River under very heavy Mortar and machine gun fire.

During the forty hours that followed his Company was the only one of the Battalion to hold on to the ground it had gained and there was considerable confusion around him. CSM Palin organised stragglers and ammunition supply and enabled his Company to fight back at the enemy whilst under continuous Mortar and Machine gun fire.

During the action he made a forward reconnaissance under fire to locate wounded whom he could hear. He succeeded in this by crawling one hundred yards forward to some ditches, found the wounded including his Commanding Officer. He was able to report this and enable evacuation to take place therefore saving the lives of some of his comrades. Apart from this CSM Palin was a tower of strength to his Company Commander, Major Tuohy, and his conduct throughout the battle was an inspiration to all ranks. Under conditions of the greatest strain and without regard for personal safety, he was in a large way responsible for the successful action of his Company.   (L.G. 26.10.44)

Palmer, George Henry, Sergeant
6988, 22 NZ (Mot) Bn. (Immediate)
On the afternoon of 17 Oct 44, Sjt. Palmer was in comd of a pl ordered to attack and capture Casalini, south of the R. Pisciatello and west of Saia, and a posn known to be held in strength by the enemy. A tp of tks was in spt of the pl and to it Sjt. Palmer directed one of his secs with instructions to make a feint frontal demonstration several hundred yds southward of the posn. He himself led the remaining two secs to the right flank and by the exercise of very good control and excellent use of cover, he brought the force to within striking range of the enemy before the alarm was raised. As the first bursts of enemy automatic fire fell among his men, Sjt. Palmer called to them and led them in a charge across open ground and under fire with such dash that two MG posns were quickly over run and the crews killed or captured and the remaining enemy in the posn put to disorderly flight.

Sjt. Palmer immediately consolidated the posn and by bringing fire to bear against enemy pockets still in the rear he inflicked cas and within a short time had est complete superiority over the ground. The posn had been held by Paratroopers. Five were killed and four captured. Sjt. Palmer's coolness of judgment, personal courage and energetic and determined leadership inspired his men and his tactical appreciation of the situation was a copybook demonstration of the values of speed and surprise.

At a subsequent stage of the advance, on the night 21 Oct 44, Sjt. Palmer was ordered to occupy with his pl a house situated within a short distance of the enemy. As the Sjt. led his men towards the posn, a strong force of enemy was seen approaching it from the other side. Again demonstrating remarkable qualities of judgment, Sjt. Palmer ordered his men fwd and in a rush the posn was gained with leading elements of the enemy force less than 20 yds away. Notwithstanding that the enemy force was of skilled and capable Paratroopers who fought vigourously, Sjt. Palmer so quickly and capably organised the defence that several enemy attempts to gain possession were repulsed by hy and accurate fire, and after suffering many cas the enemy withdrew. In large measure the success of the defence depended upon Sjt. Palmer and the inspiration drawn by his men from his courage and extreme colness in a difficult situation was a signal factor in the success of the operation. *[continuation missing].*   (L.G. 10.5.45)

Pals, Laurens Klass, Sergeant
H.16444, Canadian Intelligence Corps
For gallant and distinguished services in the field
(L.G. 15.6.46)

Pannell, John Leonard, Private
6769459, Queen's Own Royal West Kent Regt.
For Malaya   (L.G. 22.1.52)

Parfitt, Desmond, Lance Sergeant
320087, 9th Queen's Royal Lancers (Calne, Wilts.)
Sjt. Parfitt was commanding the third tank in 2nd Troop 'B' Squadron 9th Lancers during the attack by the regiment on the San Savino feature South of Coriano on 5 September 1944. He led his troop under very heavy fire down into a very steep and rough wadi and up the other side into the enemy FDLs, when he was fired on by a bazooka from a house. The bomb struck the back of the tank and blew off some bridging equipment. Sjt. Parfitt destroyed the house with H.E. His Troop Sergeant's tank was then knocked out by a bazooka from very close range. Sjt. Parfitt went on towards the objective. He had, in the meantime, got separated from his Troop Leader by a sunken road, and when he got up to his Troop Leader, some 10 minutes later, he found his tank had been knocked out and was blazing. The same gun then opened up at him and just missed the turret. He reversed very quickly back, and, looking over his

shoulder, he saw a bazookaman part the bushes behind and level his tube at the tank. He shouted 'traverse left,' and his gunner traversed 180 degrees at full spped and blew the German to bits with a H.E. round. He then saw five men stalking him with what looked like sticky-bombs, and he shot all of them before they could attack. Shortly afterwards, as he was reversing, he saw a lot of Germans lying at the bottom of their slit-trenches. He shot one, and the rest came out with their hands up laying two bazookas and their arms on the ground. He waved these back toward the squadron position. A face suddenly appeared at an upstairs window of one of the farms, and a moment later a grenade exploded on the top of the turret, smashing the periscope and temporarily blinding Sjt. Parfitt in one eye with dust and very small particles of metal. More Germans then appeared running about and, although he could not see properly, he told his gunner to traverse backwards and forwards as the tank drove out at full speed straight through a barn which was in the way, back to his squadron just behind.

Through this single-handed action, Sjt. Parfitt showed the greatest gallantry against very great odds. On his return to the squadron his eye was bandaged and, although in great pain, he refused to be evacuated and came up into the line again when he was shortly despatched with an infantry section to mop up some Germans in a vineyard. He remained in action until his squadron was withdrawn some time after dark, dealing with continuous sniper and bazooka attacks on the squadron. Sjt. Parfitt killed a great many Germans, and was responsible for acconting for four bazookamen. He very greatly assisted the squadron to hang on to this important feature and showed the very greatest courage, resource and devotion to duty throughout the whole action.   *(L.G. 8.2.45)*

Park, Frederick George, Sergeant
2564780, 27th Lancers, RAC (Cardiff) (Immediate)
9 Dec 44 Ref Map Italy 1:50,000 Sheet 89—I
At MR 588480 on the morning of 9 Dec 44 Sjt. Park was commanding a tp holding the br over the Fozzatone. His main posn was in a house 50 yds from the br with section posts on the canal bank and fwd of the canal. The woods came down to the canal astride the rd. No. 3 tp was on his left in a house used as an OP: this house was surrounded on three sides by floods. On the right a group of Partisans were watching the canal.

At 0900 hrs the enemy attacked in strength of approx 60. Fire from Sjt. Park's tp halted them on the edge of the wood, killing at least 10. His fwd sec had, however, been overrun and the two Browning gunners killed. As the remainder of the sec withdrew to the main posn, Tpr. Edwards fell wounded on the br. Sjt. Park at once ordered a fire plan to give cover, and he himself ran fwd and carried Edwards back to the house; he was under hy Spandau fire.

The partisans had by now vanished, and the enemy was infiltrating over the canal to the East. The tp was under constant mortar and shell fire.

Owing to bridging difficulties no reinforcements could be expected for 3 hrs, and the ground in the rear of the posn was completely open. Sjt. Park's Sqn Leader spoke on the wireless and asked him if a withdrawal would be possible should the enemy surround him. Sjt. Park replied that he might succeed in withdrawing his own tp, but that he had now 7 cas (4 being stretcher cases) and that the left hand tp would not be able to withdraw and would be isolated. He therefore intended to hold the posn. At 1300 hrs Air reported enemy reinforcing and a further attack was mounted at 1500 hrs. By this time a tp of tks with a PPA patrol had arrived at the br and the situation was restored, the enemy withdrawing leaving his dead.

This NCO displayed outstanding personal courage and fine leadership throughout the action.

(L.G. 24.5.45)

Parker, Benjamin Herbert, Sergeant
1464377, 52nd Anti-Tank Regt, Royal Artillery
For distinguished conduct when acting as Troop Commander during the operations South of Ypres, 26th—28th May 1940, and the subsequent withdrawal to Dunkirk. Sergeant Parker took over command of his troop when his Troop Commander became a casualty. In the face of heavy enemy shell fire and mortar fire, and dive bombing, he kept his guns in action until ordered to withdraw to a fresh position. Throughout this period and the subsequent withdrawal to Dunkirk this N.C.O. by his coolness, judgment and complete disregard for his own personal safety, was a great example to all ranks.
O.B.E. 1.1.60   *(L.G. 27.8.40)*

Parker, Charles Terance, Private
QX.11509, 2/26 Bn., Australian Military Forces
On 29th January 1942 during a daylight attack on a hill feature near the 30th mile stone on the main North road his platoon was held up by an enemy machine gun which was inflicting heavy casualties. Pte. Parker showed outstanding courage and gallantry by charging forward alone and throwing a grenade, disabling the crew to such an extent that he was able to go in and kill the remainder with the bayonet. This action enabled the platoon to advance and to capture its objective. As a platoon runner he showed courage and determination on all occasions and was always an inspiration to his comrades.
(L.G. 10.1.46)

Parker, Clifford Ronald, Sergeant
550304, 11 Hussars (PAO), Royal Armoured Corps (Barnes)
On Dec 12 1941 when his Sqn was operating with Col. Currie's coln, the tp of which he was in comd left the leaguer at dawn to gain contact with the enemy. After proceeding half a mile he encountered a stationary enemy

coln of 30 vehicles. He could not see in the half light
what they were. He remained in observation until further
troops were placed in posn for an attack. He then carried
out a successful attack. Immediately after this he was
ordered South to watch the South and South-East flanks
of Col. Currie's coln. After going half a mile he
encountered two enemy colns each consisting of a
hundred and fifty vehicles moving across the South flank
of Col. Currie's coln. One of these colns was turned back
by another tp. Sjt. Parker then engaged this coln causing
great confusion to the enemy, who replied with anti-tank
guns. He accounted for 18 prisoners, 3 field guns, 2 anti-
tank guns and 4 lorries besides leaving considerable dead
on the field. Previous to this date he had captured 4
vehicles and 6 prisoners. From 21 Nov to 7 Dec his Sqn
was attached to the 22nd Armd Bde and subsequently
the 4 Armd Bde. During this time his tp was continually
on patrol and he invaiably gave accurate and valuable
information in spite of being frequently under fire. Brig.
Scott-Cockburn personally spoke very highly of this
N.C.O.s actions.

This N.C.O. has taken part in the entire Libyan
campaign since June 1940. On one occasion in April
1941 his tp was heavily attacked by 11 M.E. 110s,
machine-gunning and bombing; all the personnel,
including himself, were wounded. Two of his cars had
become separated, but despite the fact that he was
wounded he removed the wounded from his car, placed
them in a slit trench and then drove the car 400 yds away
and kept wireless watch till assistance arrived. His calm
manner and cheerful disposition at all times set a fine
example to all ranks under him. I recommend strongly
that he be awarded the Distinguished Conduct Medal.

(*L.G. 24.2.42*)

Parker, John Arthur, Corporal
NX 3653, 1 Fd. Coy., Royal Aust. Engineers
After the evacuation of Greece I was stationed at Souda
Bay, Crete, with the survivors of my company (190 out
of 263), our duty being to unload incoming vessels. On
20 May 41 parachutists were dropped at Canea, and on
26 May we received orders to retire to the village of (?)
Neon. From there we continued to retire, and I reached
the evacuation point on 29 May. Here we were organised
into parties of from 50 to 100, each under an officer. On
1 Jun Major Travers, of 8 Fd Coy., who was in charge of
my party ordered us to surrender. We had had no rations
for four days.

The Germans, who treated us fairly, took us back to
Canea, where we were kept in the old Italian enclosure
(Skines' camp). On 24 Jun 60 of us Australians left Souda
Bay in a Greek ketch with an escort of parachutists. We
reached Port Piraeus on 26 Jun, and were kept in barracks
in Athens till 2 Jul, when we were marched through the
streets to the railway station and entrained. Next day we
had to walk about 30 miles from Bralo to a staion to the
West of Lamia, as the railway line was out of use as a
result of demolitions which had been done by my own

company. We reached Salonika on 6 Jul and were
quartered in an old Greek barracks. Two days later we
were moved to another camp in Salonika.

On 13 Aug a batch of 1000 British prisoners entrained
for Germany. We travelled in wagons. The actual journey
lasted six days, and during that time we were only once
allowed out of the train—for about ten minutes at Zagreb.
We arrived at Stalag VIIA (Moosburg, Bavaria) about
20 Aug.

Working parties were sent out to the Munich area.
The work consisted mostly of improvement schemes,
railway track maintenance, and street sweeping. With
escaping in view two friends and I volunteered for
working, having got considerable local information from
French P/W. At 1750 on 26 Nov we left our work and
went to a park near the railway marshalling yard. Here
we waited till about 0200 hrs on 27 Nov when we went
to the yard where the train for St. Margrethen (Switzerland) was formed up. We were discovered and one of
my friends was, I believe, recaptured. As a result of the
alarm my other friend and I left the yards. We spent the
day in some shrubs on the outskirts of Munich, returning
to the yards at night. In the darkness I lost my friend. I
reached the carriage labelled St. Margrethen and waited
some time. Then I strapped a ladder, which I found on
the side of the train, underneath the carriage. The train
left Munich staion at 1800 hrs (27 Nov) and reached St.
Margrethen at 1900 hrs on 29 Nov. I travelled the whole
distance resting on the ladder underneath the train.

I went to a carpenter's shop. A British-born woman
was sent for, and on her advice I handed myself up to
the local police. After two days in the cells at St.
Margrethen I was taken to St. Gallen. Three days later I
was removed to Zurich and Berne, and next day was
handed over to the British Military Attaché.

(*L.G. 12.2.42*)

Parker, William Charles, Sergeant
4031468, 1 Reconnaissance Regt. (Blackwood, Mon.)
(Immediate)
Action in the Anzio bridgehead.

From 25th January 1944 until 17th February 1944 in
the Anzio bridgehead, Serjeant Parker has shown
outstanding leadership and courage. His aggressive determination to kill the enemy has inspired the men under
his command and during the above period his section of
12 men have inflicted heavy casualties to the enemy.

On a patrol on 1st February 1944 at 898340 Serjeant
Parker and three troopers carried out a night reconnaissance patrol which penetrated behind an enemy position
of some 80 strong. Exact and detailed positions of the
enemy automatic weapons and mortars were pin-pointed.
The enemy discovered this patrol and surrounded it. By
skilful leadership Serjeant Parker was able to break
through the enemy and remained within a few yards of
the enemy gaining full information. At day break the
patrol regained its own lines and our artillery were able
to destroy the enemy position.

For 8 days this NCO held a small section post against three enemy attacks. On four nights he led successful night patrols against enemy forward positions, causing casualties and confusion. On 5th February in daylight Serjeant Parker and four men surprised an enemy O.P. at 899343, [...]ed three enemy and brought back three prisoners. On night 16th/17th February Serjeant Parker led a small fighting patrol of 10 men to drive an enemy platoon away from one vehicle which had been overrun. He cleared the enemy away from the armoured car and so allowed the recovery party to repair same and get it back into our lines.

On 12th February Parker and one man equipped with an 18 set worked forward to within 300 yards of the enemy position of Buonriposo feature and from there directed our artillery fire on to the enemy and prevented them from digging in. For six hours he remained in his O.P. and conducted many successful shoots for the 2nd Field Regiment, R.A.   (*L.G. 15.6.44*)

Parkin, Percy Guest, T.S.M.
404454, 4th/7th Royal Dragoon Guards (Breaston)
(Immediate)
On 18 Nov 44, 2nd Troop 'A' Sqn, commanded by T.S.M. Parkin had the task of closely supporting the Infantry of 7 S.L.I. on to the objective at Neiderheide, and then to assist in the shoot on to another target to enable phase II of the operation to be carried out.

When the operation commenced, T.S.M. Parkin led his troop across country. He came to a marked enemy minefield, and as there was no way round and the Infantry were badly in need of his close support, he led his troop straight through it. His troop did not suffer casualties although two other tanks on his right were blown up.

He then led his troop through a thick wood, silencing two spandau positions, enabling his Infantry to get through. From here, when the Infantry of 1 Worcs were again held up towards Richsden, he took the lead right up to the village in face of many enemy weapons and without anyone to protect his flank.

Next morning at 0715 hrs. T.S.M. Parkin reported that three Panther tanks and Infantry were approaching his position. This confirmed the expected counter attack. He immediately adjusted the position of his troop in the face of heavy artillery fire, and succeeded in stopping this enemy move, knocking out one Panther tank and killing a number of infantry.

This success was immediately attributable to his cool and determined leadership in his troop. I consider he led the troop most gallantly throughout the operation, with complete disregard for his own safety, using a great deal of determination and setting a fine example to his troop and to all.   (*L.G. 22.3.45*)

Parkinson, Ronald Carne, Lance Bombardier
1139455, 52nd Field Regt, Royal Artillery
(Rossendale, Lancs.) (Immediate)
During the attack on the Gothic Line NE of Vicchio by 21 Ind Bde, L/Bdr. Parkinson was an OPA with an Foo party attached to 3/15 Punjabis. On the evening of 17 Sep 44 D Coy reached their first objective and their advance was being held up by heavy concentrations of our own artillery from a number of regts unregistered on tasks owing to lack of time. L/Bdr Parkinson, on his own initiative, finding that communication was impossible from his position, moved his wireless set out on to higher ground in a completely exposed position in the shelled area so that it was no longer screened. He got through and stopped the fire thereby saving many lives, enabling the advance to continue and setting a fine example to all around him of coolness, initiative and disregard of danger.

Later the same evening the advance was continued by C Coy towards Pt 1073. The objective was rea[...]ed without opposition about [...] hours. However, about 4 mins after the Company had arrived, there was a loud shout of 'Heil Hitler' from a distance of 15–20 yards and heavy small arms fire was poured into the Company position from three sides. Bullets were spattering the ground all around but once again the courage displayed by L/Bdr. Parkinson in reaching a telephone which, in the confusion, had been kicked downhill towards the enemy, enabled heavy artillery fire to be brought down within 3 mins. on the direction from which the enemy was approaching. As a result, the counter-attack was finally repelled. To reach the telephone, L/Bdr. Parkinson had to pass right through the line of both our own and the enemy's fire.

The following day the enemy were detected trying to re-occupy Pt 1019 which they had previously evacuated and it was decided to prevent the re-occupation by means of observed artillery fire. It was not, however, possible to obtain satisfactory observation from our own Fdls and it was decided that the gunner party should go with infantry protection to a shell crater some 250 yds from our own lines. The enemy had, however, advanced further than had been supposed and as the leading elements of the party reached the crater, accurate fire was opened by 2 enemy medium machine guns. L/Bdr. Parkinson was at this time some 50 yds behind the main party and entirely without cover. Ordered to abandon his wireless set and crawl to cover, he refused, and for 10 mins. under constant MG and mortar fire, he endeavoured to call for artillery fire on the enemy. Eventually he got through and the party was able to withdraw safely under cover of an artillery smoke screen. Thus 3 times in 24 hours L/Bdr. Parkinson showed great initiative and ability carrying out these feats with a complete disregard for his own safety and setting a fine example to gunner and infantryman alike. His action on all occasions must have had an important bearing on the

operation which was in fact the breaking of the Gothic
Line.   *(L.G. 12.4.45)*

Parkyn, Harry, Sergeant
999193, 71st A/Tk Regt, Royal Artillery (Bedfort)
   (Periodic)
This NCOs courage and leadership have been outstanding since the beginning of the BLA campaign. The
following instances are cited:—
   On 2 July 44 his Tp Comd was killed at Rauray. Sjt.
Parkyn immediately took charge of the deployment of
the Tp in heavy and continuous shell-fire. One gun had
to cross terrain swept by German machine gun fire. Sjt.
Parkyn himself recced the route on foot and himself took
the gun into action riding on the bonnet of the towing
vehicle. He visited all his guns at a time when any
movement was extremely dangerous, personally laid
telephone wire over open country to each of his guns
and took charge of the line party when the line was cut
by mortar fire.
   This was his Tp's first experience of action in such
circumstances and beyond doubt Sjt. Parkyn's confidence
and steadfastness had an immeasurable effect on the
morale of his men. The Tp Officer who came in
replacement was wounded and Sjt. Parkyn again
commanded the Tp. In the battle for Cahier, he had to
effect a night deployment of his Tp through mist followed
by enemy air action. In spite of all dangers and difficulties
he maintained his objective and had succeeded in
deploying all his guns by daybreak. In Antwerp he was
wounded but remained with a gun until satisfied that it
had neutralised an MG post on the far side of the docks.
In the Ardennes he again had to take over comd of his
Tp and once more showed the same courage under fire
and the same qualities of leadership. Finally in the
Bonninghardt Forest, when acting as Tp Sjt his guns were
held up by an SP which destroyed 2 Inf carriers just
ahead. An alternative route was quickly recced and
notwithstanding the destruction of a carrier on a mine,
he assisted the Tp Comd in the immediate deployment
of the Tp in the required area.
   Throughout the campain, Sjt. Parkyn has exerted the
greatest good influence on those around him. He
maintained his cheerfulness under extremely trying
circumstances and his complete disregard of his own
safety inspired his men to rise above tremendous
difficulties. When in charge of the Tp, he always
commanded the respect and admiration of the Inf Comds
when he was called upon to support.
M.I.D. 8.11.45   *(L.G. 24.1.46)*

Parrott, Godfrey George, Staff Sergeant
7873283, R.E.M.E. (London, W.14)
ME 1941 (from P.O.W. Pool)
M.I.D. 22.12.39 and 1.4.41   *(L.G. 14.2.46)*

Parsons, Charles James, Sergeant
VX.38874, 4 A/Tk Regt, Australian Military Forces
On 14 and 15 Jan 1942, during the operations at Gemas
Sjt. Parsons performed valuable work in the supply of
ammunition under fire and in the destruction of a gun in
difficult circumstances, after he had made every possible
effort to withdraw it intact. On 20 Jan at Muar Sjt. Parsons
engaged four enemy tanks, allowing them to approach
within thirty yards before opening fire, destroying three.
He then went forward and destroyed the fourth tank with
grenades single-handed. On 21 Jan Sjt. Parsons showed
similar courage and initiative in the successful extrication
of his detachment after it had been cut off by a road
block.   *(L.G. 10.1.46)*

Parsons, William Henry, Sergeant (actg.)
2737136, 2nd Bn Welsh Guards (Birmingham)
On 9 Apr 45 the Squadron to which this NCO is attached
was advancing towards the bridge over the Hase Canal.
The Medical Half-Track which is under command of
this NCO was sent to collect some wounded Guardsmen
who were advancing with the leading troop of the
Squadron. The area, which was thickly wooded, was full
of the enemy. Sniping and Spandau fire was so intense
and accurate that leading Tank Commanders were
reporting to their Squadron Leader that it was unsafe to
look out above the turret, even for a moment. Under these
circumstances the Squadron Leader forbade the Medical
Half-Track to go forward until things were quieter.
Having heard this discussion, however, this NCO decided
to take the law into his own hands, slipping up the column
without the Squadron Leader noticing. On arrival with
the leading troop, this NCO dismounted, and with the
aid of another Guardsman, lifted into the half-track two
wounded men who had been lying unattended in a ditch.
the leading Troop Leader reported that it was one of the
bravest things he had ever seen, as Spandau fire at that
time was extremely heavy. The wounded owe their lives
entirely to the gallantry and unselfish resolution of this
NCO and the Medical Orderly who was with him.
   On the next day, 10 Apr 45, this NCO performed an
equally brave deed under similar circumstances. The
Squadron was forming up for an attack in support of a
Company of the Scots Guards on Menslage when a heavy
and accurate concentration of enemy shellfire came down
upon Squadron Headquarters. The vehicle in front of
the Squadron Leader's was hit and caught fire and the
Squadron Leader's own tank immobilised by shellfire.
The third tank, just behind the Squadron Leader's,
received a direct hit and caught fire. The crew of this
last tank bailed out, badly shaken, only to be hit by the
next shell as they ran for a ditch. Every member of the
crew was a casualty, and the Medical Half-track was
sent for. Despite the fact that the immediate area was
being plastered by shells every minute, this NCO, with
his Medical Orderly, calmly dressed the wounded men,
and drove the Half-track away.

For sheer coolness and efficiency under fire this incident must rank unparralleled. It is quite true to say that this NCO was only doing his duty, but on this particular occasion it was about the worst job in the world to have to do. Had this NCO not ordered up the Half-track when he did, the wounded men would certainly have been killed, because a few minutes after they had been evacuated, two more enemy shells landed exactly where they had been lying in the ditch. *(L.G. 24.1.46)*

Partridge, Percy Ambrose, Warrant Officer Cl. II (actg.)
5880594, 2nd Bn The Royal Norfolk Regt. (Peterborough) (Immediate)
At Saye, Central Burma.

On 20th February, 1945 during the Battalion's assault on the village of Saye, the reserve company while mopping up ran into a strongly entrenched enemy L.M.G. post. The leading platoon commander was wounded attempting to knock out the post. A troop of tanks returning to harbour were passing the scene of this encounter at the time and CSM Partridge immediately signalled them to the platoon's assistance and then reorganised the platoon. Covered by fire from the tanks himself, he then approached three times the mound on which the bunker was and threw several grenades over the top, rushing over the top after the third approach. His sten gun jammed, and showing complete disregard for his personal safety, he changed magazines. The gun again failed to fire. CSM Partridge became so infuriated at this that he rushed back down the slope, threw away his sten gun, grabbed a rifle and bayonet and once again rushed over the top. He bayonetted two Japs and shot one, his grenades having previously silenced two others. Two L.M.G.s were captured in the position which was wiped out largely due to the determination and speed of CSM Partridge's assault which was a great inspiration to the men of the platoon.
Recommended for M.M. *(L.G. 24.5.45)*

Passmore, Leslie Ross, Private
VX 19811, 2/8 Bn., Australian Military Forces
Act of Gallantry and devotion to duty at Battle of Tobruch on 21 Jan 41.

During the advance of his Company to its first objective on the morning of the day of the battle, his Company was held up by a counter attack by enemy tanks. Private Passmore seized the Boys anti tank rifle from his comrade who had been wounded, and dashing to a forward position brought the rifle into action under heavy fire from all quarters, during the counter attack which lasted about an hour. He accounted for three enemy tanks eventually despite the fact that other tanks were making him the target for their fire and were firing amongst other weapons 2 lb. shells towards him. Throughout the remainder of the day, with a Bren Gun, Private Passmore exhibited similar dash and cool daring, and his bravery and initiative were an inspiration to his comrades and of invaluable assistance in the forward advance of his Company. *(L.G. 9.5.41)*

Paton, Angus, Warrant Officer Cl. II (B.S.M.)
1668842, Royal Artillery
Green, L., Pte.
105946, R.A.S.C. (E.F.I.)
B.S.M. Paton was captured in June 1940 at St. Valery-en-Caux, and sent to Stalag XXA (Thorn), and later to a satellite camp at Graudenz, where he was senior Warrant Officer. Private Green captured in May 1940 between Wizernes and Boulogne, and sent to Stalag XXA. From where he went to various satellite working camps and in October 1942 to Grandenz where he met B.S.M. Paton.

They escaped from here on the 7th June 1943 after much careful preparation. They received some help from Poles (unorganized) but between the 8th and 17th June 1943 were continually on the move travelling by train to Gdynia, Danzig, Lodz, Brombert, Zoppot, and other places. On 17th June they boarded a Swedish ship at Gdynia arriving at Stockholm on 22nd June 1943. Private Green speaks fluent German, the knowledge of which was a most important factor in this successful escape. This Warrant Officer and Private showed the greatest courage, initiative and ingenuity. Both are recommended for awards of the D.C.M. *(L.G. 11.11.43)*

Paton, Frederick James, Sergeant
3308169, 1st Bn The Highland Light Infantry (Livingston) (Immediate)
On the 22 Sep 44, this N.C.O.s Coy was ordered to advance through another Coy to seize rd junc 274215. No. 10 Platoon commanded by Sjt. Paton led the Coy into the attack. He had been ordered to clear all the houses on the right of the road, seize the x-rds and push on at least 50 yards up the main street. Heavy opposition was immediately met. Sjt. Paton led his platoon through very difficult going, consisting of small gardens and orchards, keeping complete control at all times. On several occasions, when held up by Spandaus, he personally led an assault section to overcome them completely disregarding his personal safety. His dash and initiative enabled the objective to be secured in the shortest, possible time. Finally his coy was held up by an Infantry gun, he personally shot one of the gun crew whereupon the rest fled, then while leading his men forward again to capture the gun he was wounded by a sniper. Throughout this action, Sjt. Paton, showed the highest degree of skill and initiative and by his personal courage and disregard of danger set his men a magnificent example. *(L.G. 1.3.45)*

Payne, Percy George, Sergeant (A/W.O.II (C.S.M.)
6976361, 1st Bn The Royal Irish Fusiliers (Neath) (Immediate)
Italy 1/25,000 160 II NW 8119.

CSM Payne was Acting CSM of 'C' Company, 1st Bn The Royal Irish Fusiliers during the attack from the

Rapido bridgehead to Highway 6 on 17th May 1944. 'C' Company was right forward company and combined in the attack with a squadron of tanks.

Shortly after crossing the Start Line, the company commander was killed and CSM Payne was entirely responsible for the command and control of the company until the senior platoon commander arrived at company HQ. During this period they experienced extremely heavy enemy mortar and small arms fire and CSM Payne showed great coolness in handling the company.

Once onto the objective a great deal of liaison was necessary within the company and CSM Payne moved fearlessly between platoons under enemy shell and mortar fire until the consolidation was completed.

His fine conduct during an extremely heavy action was to no small measure responsible for the success of the company.   *(L.G. 26.10.44)*

Peacock, Clarence, M.M., Warrant Officer Cl. II
2653740, 1st Bn. Green Howards (Catterick Camp, Yorks) (Immediate)
On the evening of 1 May 45, 1 Green Howards attacked the rly junc at Buchen. B Coy, of which CSM Peacock was a member, was the left fwd coy of the Bn.

Before actually gaining the objective, the Coy Comd and two offrs were wounded. CSM Peacock immediately assumed command and, in spite of failing light, (2100 hrs), he personally controlled the right fwd pl. By his initiative and leadership the pl was successfully est on the objective. He then went back to his Coy HQ where the wounded offrs were lying and arranged for their evacuation, personally carrying one of them on his back seventy yards to a place of safety.

Throughout the action, snipers and well-concealed MGs were bringing accurate fire to bear on all gaps between buildings and approaches. The successful establishment of the Coy on the objective was vital to the effective deployment of the res Coy. CSM Peacock's quick appreciation of the tactical situation, his immediate assumption of control of the Coy, and his personal initiative and complete disregard for his own personal safety, were an inspiration to his men, and largely instrumental in ensuring the success of the whole Bn attack.
M.M. 14.2.39; Norwegian M.C. 11.8.42; M.I.D. 20.12.40 & 2.10.50 (backdated 18.9.50)   *(L.G. 2.8.45)*

Peacock, John William, M.M., Sergeant
318961, 11 Hussars (PAO), Royal Armoured Corps (Hayes End)
At about 1500 hrs on Dec 10 1941 Sjt. Peacock was in charge of his tp keeping observation on an enemy bivouac in the area 7 miles West of Acroma. His tp was subjected to intense enemy shell fire and was attacked by anti-tank guns. He held on to his posn and then advanced, capturing 5 anti-tank guns and fifty odd prisoners causing the enemy to withdraw one mile, thus allowing our O.P. to take up a posn from which he could bring his gun-fire to bear on the enemy.

I consider that by this N.C.O.s brave action the enemy were forced to withdraw to a less favourable posn in which intense gun-fire could be brought to bear on them. This N.C.O. has, during the past four weeks shown the utmost bravery and initiative which has resulted in some of the most important information being obtained.

This N.C.O. has been through the entire Libyan campaign since June 1940 during which time he has performed the exacting and responsible duties of tp leader in a manner beyond praise. In view of this I recommend that this N.C.O. be awarded the Distinguished Conduct Medal.
M.I.D. 1.4.41, MM: 8.7.41   *(L.G. 24.2.42)*

Pearce, Peter Lancelot, Gunner
K8085, 6 Cdn Fd Regt., Royal Canadian Artillery (Immediate)
K8085 Gnr. Pearce, P. L. was acting as Observation Post assistant during the attack by Camerons of Canada on Fontenay Le Marmion which commenced on the night 7–8 Aug 44. His officer was wounded, but was able to carry on until hit a second time at about 1100 hrs. From then, until relieved about eight hours later, Gnr. Pearce took command of the Observation Post and maintained communication with the guns, engaged many hostile targets, kept contact with the infantry and throughout kept his regimental commander informed of the tactical situation. These duties of an O.P. officer were performed by Gnr. Pearce under heavy and continuous machine gun and mortar fire, often under direct observation by the enemy. For several hours the position of Camerons of Canada was completely surrounded, and all their means of communication had been put out of action. The fact that Gnr. Pearce remained at his post and kept contact with his regimental commander, was the sole means by which the Brigade Commander was enabled to learn of the desperate situation and plan the steps necessary to restore it.

The performance of Gnr. Pearce, was an outstanding example of the greatest courage, presence of mind, and ability to take responsibility in a most critical and dangerous situation. It was in keeping with the highest traditions of the Service and earned the admiration and gratitude of all ranks of the infantry, for whose ultimate safety he was largely responsible.   *(L.G. 4.11.44)*

Pearce, William George Ernest, Bombardier
872737, Royal Artillery (London, E.1)
S.W. Pacific 1942 (from P.O.W. Pool)   *(L.G. 14.2.46)*

Pearton, Arthur Max, Sergeant
547637, 12th Royal Lancers R.A.C
On 21 May in the area of Avesnes the Armoured Car in front of this N.C.O. was stopped by fire and overturned in a ditch 100 yds. in front of his car. He then advanced and although his gunner was killed beside him, silenced

the fire of the enemy's M.G. post, killed several of the enemy, rescued Sjt. Murden and Tpr. Fowles from the leading car and brought them back safely into dead ground behind.

Although Sjt. Pearton's car was hit twice by A/T Gun fire his brilliant marksmanship when under fire, his determination and the inspiration which he gave to the remainder of his own car crew carried this exploit through to a successful conclusion.

This N.C.O. was frequently in the leading car of his troop and never lost his dash. He finally lost his car when inflicting heavy casualties on the enemy and through his very fine leadership was able to withdraw his crew to safety in spite of the enemy's fire.

(L.G. 5.7.40 and 22.10.40)

Peck, Desmond John, Private
VX.9534, 2/7 Bn., Australian Military Forces
On 4 Jun 41, three days after his capture in Crete, Peck and eight other Australians walked out of the P/W enclosure at Sfakia, Crete. Two months later Peck was recaptured and sent first to Canea prison and then to a camp at Galatos. Again on 20 Aug 41 he climbed through the wire and was at liberty almost four months before being re-arrested. Cretan villagers released him within two days. For the fourth time he came into German custody on 28 Apr 42, but on 15 May 42, with six companions, he knocked out a guard and escaped from the military prison at Rodi. Although the party succeeded in securing a boat, this capsized in a storm, and Peck was rescued by an Italian destroyer.

Imprisoned in Italy, Peck left a camp at San Germano Vercellese, where he had been employed on agricultural work, by climbing the wire. A fortnight later he was apprehended once more.

At the time of the Italian Armistice he was released from Vercelli prison, and immediately formed a small organisation to care for P/W and send them to the partisans. When, at the beginning of October 43, the Germans dispersed the guerilla force, Peck arranged to evacuate P/W to Switzerland. Early in November, because more funds were required, Peck got in touch with the Committee of Liberation. Under their auspices he toured many districts to convince P/W of the sincerity of the scheme, and during December, induced the Committee to reorganise and improve their machinery for helping P/W.

On 12 Feb 44 Peck was arrested by the Gestapo. After three months' imprisonment he escaped from a working party employed at the Lambrate marshalling yards; when the guards took shelter during an air raid, Peck ran in the opposite direction. Making his way to Intra he met members of the organisation and with their assistance reached Switzerland on 22 May 44.   *(L.G. 1.3.45)*

Peel, Edward Robert, Lance Sergeant
VX 1356, 2/2 Fd Coy., Australian Military Forces
On 5 Jan 41 at Bardia prior to the attack by the infantry Bde. this NCO was ordered to make a crossing over the anti-tank ditch and cut the wire. This task completed on his own initiative he led forward his sub-sec and cleared an area of A/Tk mines under shell fire.

Later, whilst reconnoitring forward of his sub-sec he came on a dug-out which had been missed, with two others he attacked the post with his pistol and cleared the position. At night-fall leaving his sub-sec under cover, he went forward with one Spr. to locate his Sec. Officer. He noticed B Coy of 2/7 Bn. pinned down by heavy fire in front of post 16. He returned and successfully directed D Coy in the darkness to the relief of B Coy. Throughout the day, L/Sjt. Peel handled his men with great coolness and showed fine courage under fire.   *(L.G. 9.5.41)*

Pegler, Herbert Ronald Douglas, M.M., Corporal
555266, 7th Queen's Hussars, Royal Armoured Corps (Calne, Wilts.) (Immediate)
This N.C.O. was operator-gunner of a light tank during the raid on the western exits of Fort Capuzzo on the morning of 17th April, 1941. Early in the action his tank sustained a direct hit on the front of the turret from an enemy A/Tk gun. In spite of this he continued to keep up such a rapid and accurate fire that he is known to have knocked out a large enemy armoured car, several vehicles and set fire to an ammunition dump. Throughout the action his tank was under heavy M/G, A/Tk gun and artillery fire. Regardless of his personal safety he continued to serve his guns with telling effect until his Squadron was finally withdrawn. This N.C.O. set a fine example, in the face of enemy fire, which should be a lesson to all ranks. Recommended for an immediate award of the Distinguished Conduct Medal.
M.M. 24.9.40   *(L.G. 18.7.41)*

Pegler, Leslie Arthur, Lance Corporal
5681550, 1st Bn The Somerset Light Infantry (Barnet) (Immediate)
Arakan

On the night 29 Feb/1 Mar. 44, L/Cpl. Pegler was a section commander in one of the leading platoons in a Coy attack on Pyinshe Kala ridge. The attack was made up a steep hill against a strong enemy posn. The troops came under fire soon after they had started, but continued to crawl upwards through thick undergrowth. The Pl Comd and Pl Sjt. became casualties and L/Cpl. Pegler took command of the platoon, encouraging his men and urging them up the hill. He himself was amongst the foremost men. Enemy LMG fire and grenades caused further casualties in the pl & L/Cpl. Pegler located an enemy LMG. He ordered up a Bren gun and directed fire against this enemy post. The gunner became a casualty and the gun jammed. L/Cpl. Pegler stripped the gun and got it firing again when it was able to silence one of the enemy LMG. By this time further casualties had occurred & the pl was ordered to withdraw. L/Cpl. Pegler was personally responsible for bringing down three wounded men to the stretcher bearers & then made two journeys back up the hill under enemy fire to retrieve a Bren & Thompson sub MG. belonging to men who had become casualties. L/Cpl. Pegler did not finally come off the hill until he assured himself that all wounded & all automatic weapons had been brought down. He received slight wounds during the operation but took no notice of them. This N.C.O. showed great courage & determination during the engagement & displayed initiative & powers of leadership when considerable responsibility devolved upon him.   *(L.G. 18.5.44)*

Pelletier, George Gerald, Private
B67589, Canadian Infantry Corps
Dieppe   *(L.G. 9.2.46)*

Peni, Satuata, Sjt.
Fiji M.F.
S.W. Pacific   *(L.G. 21.9.44)*

Penn, Joseph, L/Cpl.
4748318, Hallamshire Bn Y & L Regt
At 0415 hrs on 25 June 1944, the Hallamshires took part in a Divisional attack on Fontenay. During the attack, a heavy fog reduced visibility to a maximum of 5 yds. When this lifted, it was found that the Bn was at very close quarters with German SS tps. Its left flank was exposed to fire from enemy Panther tks, as the bn on the left had not been able to reach its objective.

As a result of this, the wounded on the open slopes to the North of the town and on the left of the Bn position were exposed to aimed enemy fire from Panther tks and spandaus at very close range. In addition, the whole bn area was under heavy mortar and shell fire throughout the day.

L/Cpl. Penn was in command of a section of stretcher bearers operating in this very exposed area. Throughout the day, L/Cpl. Penn worked with complete disregard for his own safety and set a magnificent example of devotion to duty. On twelve occasions he brought in wounded men under aimed spandau fire at about 100 to 200 yds range. He was undeterred by the deaths of two members of his section. In all, he brought in 32 wounded men before himself seriously wounded in the late evening. Though hardly able to [...] he refused medical attention until he had helped to bring in the [...] known wounded man in the area—his thirty-third in the day.

By his unequalled gallantry and devotion to duty, he was an inspiration to the other members of his section and to all those around him. He was directly responsible for saving the lives of many of those he brought in. His survival was a miracle. His courage was superb.

Penn, Montague Scott, Warrant Officer Cl. II (B.S.M.)
1065529, Royal Artillery
For great gallantry and devotion to duty during the assault and defence of El Duda (Tobruch) on Nov 27 and 28 1941.

His disregard of his personal safety during heavy shell and M.G. fire was an inspiration to his troop. He took the place of his wounded men during an attack by heavy German tanks and served that gun himself till it was destroyed by a direct hit and himself wounded, the nearest tank being then 25 yds away.   *(L.G. 24.2.42)*

Percival, Geoffrey Norman, Sergeant
5386921, 7th Oxfordshire and Buckinghamshire Light Infantry (Canterbury) (Immediate)
Map Italy 186 II 7330.
For conspicuous gallantry and devotion to duty.

When in command of an A/Tk gun in a vital defile West of Salerno on 15 Sep a strong German tank and infantry attack developed against this position. In the course of the battle five German tanks were knocked out some 60–100 yds from his position. No. 2 of the team was wounded and two others killed. Sjt. Percival immediately took over the duty of loader and at the same time engaged the enemy infantry with his rifle, killing a number. His gun was then damaged and Sjt. Percival continued the action with small arms. The German infantry then moved round his right through thick country. Sjt. Percival immediately attacked them personally with grenades and Tommy gun and drove them back. He repeatedly led small parties through the undergrowth against the Germans. All tps in his area placed themselves under his command, and such was his inspiring leadership, example and gallantry, that every German attempt to penetrate his position was defeated.
(L.G. 13.1.44)

Perkins, John Sinclair, Sergeant
38269V, Imperial Light Horse/ Kimberley Regt. SAAC (Immediate)
At M. Salva[...]o, Pt 826, M.R. L739264 on the 23 Oct 44 the Bn was engaged in an attack on a commanding and well defended mountain peak. As they advanced casualties in the platoon were heavy and the Platoon Officer was killed. Sjt. Perkins immediately took command of the platoon and under heavy enemy machine gun and mortar fire moved amongst his men, rallied them and fearlessly led them in the final attack. His outstanding leadership at a critical time resulted in the attaining of an important objective and the annihilation of the enemy position where many dead were strewn. The prompt assumption of command and the bravery of Sjt. Perkins was directly responsible for the success of the attack.
(L.G. 10.5.45)

Perry, Jack, Sergeant
4918912, 1st South Staffordshire Regt. (Longton, Staffs)
During the action at Henux on March 17th 1944 throughout the day this N.C.O. showed remarkable courage and initiative of the highest order. In the attack on Henu Hill, he was well in front leading his platoon. He was an excellent example to his men attacking the enemy where they were found and leading his men at an M.M.G. post and ultimately capturing it. He went into the village throwing his grenades and firing his sten, oblivious to all dangers, he went right into the enemy position and rescued one of our own N.C.O.s who was seriously wounded. This action was carried out under the very noses of the enemy who were firing at him.

This NCO was a great inspiration to his men throughout the whole day. In the counter-attack he was wounded but refused to come back until the hill was consolidated.

During the attack on our positions from 12th April 1944 until the 15/16th April, this NCO continually did excellent work. During the final attack in which the enemy, penetrated the position held by this NCO, he held his ground despite enemy superiority of numbers and continued to fire and throw grenades always moving from Section to Section inspiring his men and issuing reserve grenades and ammunition. At all times he showed complete disregard for his own safety despite very heavy enemy fire which was concentrated on his position. This Platoon in this last action killed approx 100 Japs with a loss of 3 B.O.Rs killed and 10 wounded. It was partly due to this Platoon Sjt. that the position held until a counter-attack was put in.
Recommended for M.M. (*L.G. 27.7.44*)

Pester, Frank Ernest, Sergeant
1875129, 77 Ind Inf Bde, 4th Corps, Royal Engineers (Leicester)
Operations in Burma, February—May, 1943.

This N.C.O. was Platoon Serjeant of the Sabotage Squad of his Column. He turned to good use his experience in previous campaigns and led with a sure hand the younger soldiers in his squad. On 6th March, 1943, he was in technical charge of the blocking of the Bonchaung Gorge. Working in the darkness without the assistance of moonlight, on a railway which had already been attacked at many points that day, and in close proximity to an enemy who had already been thoroughly roused, he brought down hundreds of tons of soil and rock on to the line, completely blocking it. On 28th March, 1943, he played a leading part in clearing Hintha village at its western end, killing several Japanese with his own hand and eliminating at least two machine-gun posts at close quarters. He was engaged in hand to hand fighting for two periods of at least five minutes. He set a fine example of utter fearlessness in danger, and an example no less valuable and more rare of complete

cheerfulness in adversity over a long period of hardship and privation. (*L.G. 16.12.43*)

Pethick, William Cyril, Corporal
5439092, 1/7th Bn The Queen's Royal Regt. (Pengelly) (Immediate)
At Vallee on 6 Aug '44, this NCO was in command of a section which occupied a position on the road running west from the village. This position was only 80 yards from the enemy and came under very heavy spandau fire, but Cpl. Pethick with extra ordinary courage and self sacrifice, crept forward himself under the hail of fire and wiped out an enemy post with hand grenades.

The whole area was subjected to continuous heavy shell fire, and three vehicles were 'brewed-up' within ten yards of their slit trenches. He held his position with his section for three days, during which time his example and devotion to duty was unsurpassed. It was entirely due to his courage that his men were able to hold to their position for so long. (*L.G. 21.12.44*)

Pettinger, John Stuart, Sergeant
24159222, Parachute Regt.
Sergeant Pettinger is a Patrol Commander D (Patrol) Company 3rd Battalion The Parachute Regiment. On the nights of the 2nd 3rd June Sergeant Pettinger was Commander of one of a number of patrols tasked to gain information about enemy forces holding Mount Longdon on East Falkland Island.

Sergeant Pettinger's mission was to recce routes onto Mount Longdon with the aim of placing a rifle company in the best possible position for a night assault later. This meant closing with the enemy who at times were only a few metres away in order to gain his information. This he did with great success on four occasions over the two nights, displaying a high standard of skill and coolness, knowing that capture would lead to the compromise of the battalion plans. The information gained led to him being able to produce accurate descriptions of routes onto the objective, detailed information on enemy strengths and locations, and on the night of 8 June to lead a platoon along the assault route in a rehearsal for the planned attack. Once again he closed with the enemy, gained further information, and cleared more routes, again with great coolness. On the night of 11th/12th June, Sergeant Pettinger acted as guide for B Company for their part in the battalion night attack onto Mount Longdon and was able to place them in such a good starting position that the attack came as a complete surprise to the enemy. Once the battle had commenced he was a constant source of information and advice to the Company Commander, while acting with dash and determination during the many assaults against strong points that night, killing at least three enemy. During the preparation for the attack on Mount Longdon Sergeant Pettinger completed six close target reconnaissances against the objective. He displayed the highest standards of professional skill, alertness, accuracy of reporting, coolness in the face of the enemy as well as courage during the actual assault. *[From L.G.]*   *(L.G. 19.9.78)*

Pevalin, Sidney Walter, Corporal
6913438, 2nd Bn. The Rifle Brigade (Worcester Park, Surrey)
On 18th June 1942 this N.C.O. was in command of a patrol of carriers of 'B' Coy. 2 Rifle Brigade, S.W. of El Adem , when his platoon commander ordered him to engage a German Mk. III tank and a troop carrier advancing towards him. He led his carrier round behind the tank, dismounted and with another Rifleman jumped on to the tank. He was able to fire through a slit at the crew as they were about to fire on the platoon commander's carrier, wounding three of the crew and capturing the whole party. The leadership resource and courage of this N.C.O. saved his platoon commander and enabled this valuable capture to be made.
(L.G. 13.8.42)

Phillip, Percy William, Warrant Officer Cl. I (R.S.M.)
2308424, Royal Signals
B.E.F.   *(L.G. 11.7.40)*

Phillips, Arthur Hubert Gordon, Sergeant
2734495, 1st Bn. Welsh Guards (Neath) (Immediate)
When on 7 Sep No. 4 Coy. took up a defensive position on the outskirts of Beeringen, his Pl. was placed on the main road running west from the town. At about 2100 hrs. whilst his platoon commander was at an 'O' Gp. Germans were reported to be coming down the road in half-track vehicles and M/C combinations.

Sjt. Phillips ordered his Platoon to their trenches and himself stayed with the forward section near the road and armed himself with the P.I.A.T. The leading two vehicles were a large half track and a two-ton truck with about seven Germans in each. Sjt. Phillips allowed them to draw level before opening fire and blowing up the second vehicle. The section was then heavily fired upon from the leading truck, which had halted, with grenades and machine pistols. Sjt. Phillips reloaded the P.I.A.T., crawled out of his trench and blew up this vehicle at 15 yds range. No Germans got out of either vehicle. Since the exploding ammunition was proving dangerous, he then withdrew the section about 50 yds and returned to Platoon Headquarters where he manned the two inch Mortar and himself, though under continuous M.G. fire knocked out one of two machine guns which had opened up at 200 yds to his front. The enemy then withdrew. It was later discovered that the enemy strength had been some six half track vehicles and ten M/C combinations: these had been entirely routed as a result of his gallantry and determination.   *(L.G. 1.3.45)*

Phillips, Peter Donald, Lance Sergeant
2328498, 1st Airborne Div. Signals, Royal Signals (London, N.W.6) (Immediate)
For one month the above mentioned NCO performed extremely gallant service behind the enemy lines. His initiative and endurance under extremely difficult conditions whilst living in the Div. areas of 3 German Divisions would be highly creditable to an experienced officer. He moved about in uniform and civilian clothes carrying a wireless set and constantly sent back reports of POWs and enemy positions, and it was only by extremely bad luck that his information, which was received correctly, could not be successfully acted upon. He fully realised his fate if he was caught by the Germans with a W/T set. At length, having realised that sea evacuation of POWs was impossible, he personally recce'd a route through the enemy lines and every night during the next week he ferried no fewer than a total of 481 POWs through the lines. To cross and recross the enemy lines this number of times, alone deserves especial mention. It may be added that the greatest number of POWs produced by any individual officer put in prior to L/Sjt. Phillips was 23. The gallantry and initiative displayed by L/Sjt. Phillips is an example which all may look up to.   *(L.G. 20.4.44)*

Philp, Reginald John, Colour Sergeant (A/W.O.II)
5437087, 5 Duke of Cornwall's Ligh Infantry (Bude) (Immediate)
At approximately 1900 hrs on 22 Sep 44 the abovenamed WO was travelling in a carrier in the bn coln during the op move from Oosterhout to Driel. A gap had been caused in the coln owing to the picking up of marching personnel and as a result CSM Philp found himself to be in the leading veh. Whilst he was endeavouring to close this gap he ran into five Tiger tks approaching from the opposite direction. Both parties drew aside to allow passage and it was not until the third tk was approaching that CSM Philp realized that they were enemy tks, whereupon he immediately stood on top of his carrier and opened fire with a German Spandau in his possession, which resulted in the killing of the tk comd. The tk then opened fire and sprayed the carrier and its occupants were forced to jump from the veh and take cover in ditch. CSM Philp then made his way back along his original route and contacted the soft vehs in the rear. His infm thus enabling a detour to be made avoiding the tks. His coy comd met the remaining convoy and CSM Philp joined the coy comd on a tk hunting expedition, his infm again enabling a trap to be set for the returning tks, which was responsible for the destruction of four of the enemy tks. During the whole of this op he showed complete coolness and disregard for his personal safety and all this time he was suffering from wounds in the face received from arty fire.   *(L.G. 1.3.45)*

Phythian, Ellis, Private
3447678, Cheshire Regt.
Private Phythian was captured wounded near Tournai, Belgium, on 19th May 1940. In mid-September 1940 he was transferred to Germany, and later to Poland, where he made an attempt to escape from a working party near Posen in June 1941.

On 31st March 1943 he escaped from a working party in Posen. The Sergeant, who was to have accompanied him and who had their maps and food for the journey, did not turn up at the agreed rendezvous. Private Phythian, however, decided to carry on alone and boarded a goods train near Posen, which took him across Germany to Nancy, France. For four days he remained hidden in a brake van in this train without food or water. From Nancy he started walking to Paris. After walking for six or seven days he reached S[...]-Ste-Croix, near Vithy-le-François, where he contacted an organisation which helped him to continue his journey. After reaching Spain he was imprisoned and interned for about seven weeks before being released to the British authorities.
(L.G. 9.12.43)

Pickens, Murlin Joshua [Murlin Joseph on AFW 3121], Lance Corporal (A/Cpl.)
A11701, Perth Regiment, Canadian Infantry Corps (Immediate)
Ref Map Italy 1/50,000 Sheet 141–II Ortona
On 17 Jan 44 The Perth Regiment put in an attack against strong enemy positions South of the Arielli River in the area MR 2917.

During the assault, Cpl. Pickens was acting platoon serjeant of No. 17 Platoon, D Company. When his platoon came under heavy machine gun fire, Cpl. Pickens went forward alone in order to reconnoitre new positions and the best route to them and then led the platoon into these positions, thus avoiding casualties. One man in his section was however wounded; Cpl. Pickens pinpointed the fire and by skilful use of cover stalked the enemy post and disposed of it single handed.

A few minutes later the leading section came under heavy mortar, machine gun and sniper fire, as they came over the crest of a slope, Cpl. Pickens was at the time at Platoon HQ. Quickly appreciating the situation and realising that the momentum of the attack must not be lost, he dashed forward and shouting 'Follow me, there's nothing to it,' led the section on. He then returned and brought the remainder of the platoon forward in the same manner, inspiring the men by his gallantry and drive to continue the advance in spite of intense fire.

The courage and leadership displayed by Cpl. Pickens were of the highest order. By his dash and elan he inspired the platoon to drive forward in the face of bitter resistance until the enemy fire was sufficiently neutralised to enable the remainder of D Company to occupy their intermediate objective.
(L.G. 6.5.44)

Pickett, Arthur, Corporal
NX 4293, 16 Aust A.Tk Coy
During an attack by six enemy M.11 tanks on 2/3 Bn, H.Q. in Wadi Gerida vicinity of Bardia on 3 Jan 41, a gun crew of 16 Aust. A Tk Coy., under Cpl. Pickett came into action at a range of less than 200 yards in the open, the remaining guns being further back. In spite of M.G. and 2-pounder fire from the tanks the crew kept their guns in action at point blank range and put four tanks out of action. The fifth tank hit the portee with a shell and blew the crew off, damaging the portee, killing NX 5409 Pte. W. Dawes and wounding NX 4986 Dvr. E. Grant. The remainder of the crew immediately got the gun into action again against this tank, which was put out of action when a shot from the sixth tank set the portee on fire. The action of the NCO and the gun crew was an outstanding and inspiring example of conspicuous gallantry.
(L.G. 9.5.41)

Pickett, Charles Stanley, Corporal
2615311, 2nd Bn. Queen's Own Cameron Highlanders
On Saturday the 20th June 1942 after the Bn position had been cut off from the remainder of the Tobruk Garrison the Bn Commander ordered all companies to move up to the forward positions of the bn. Cpl. C. Pickett of the A/T Pln was ordered to sight his gun in the area of 'B' Coys H.Q. position; on the morning of the 21st June 1942 the bn sector was heavily attacked from both front and rear. At about 1000 hrs seven enemy tanks were observed forming up. Cpl. Pickett held his fire until the tanks were well within effective range; he then opened fire and maintained complete control of his team as a result of which each tank was successfully engaged and destroyed. By this cool and gallant action under intense Artillery and Small Arms fire Cpl. Pickett smashed an enemy tank attack, which, if it had been allowed to develop fully would have involved the Bn in a most critical position.
M.I.D. 15.6.44 *(L.G. 15.6.44)*

Pinkney, George, Warrant Officer Cl. III (Pl.S.M.)
4438949, Durham Light Infantry
For gallant conduct in action with the enemy.
(L.G. 20.12.40)

Piper, Richard, Trooper
3715768, King's Own, Royal Armoured Corps (Cleator Moor)
Ref Map 1/25,000 Sheet 24 N.W. Brecht. Place of action Map Ref 747191
On 21 Oct during the attack on Nieuwmoer by 107 Regt RAC Tpr Piper was co-dvr of the Tp Ldr's tk on the leading Tk Tp. Enemy S.P. guns were known to be defending the village of Nieuwmoer, and on crossing the road running East and West through the village the Tp Ldr's Tk was engaged from close quarters by an enemy S.P. hidden amongst houses to the left rear. The

first round hit the Tk and set the engine compartment on fire. Two more rounds followed in quick succession severely wounding the Tp Ldr, Dvr and Gnr. The Tk immediately caught fire.

Tpr Piper evacuated his seat in the forward compartment of the Tk and in spite of the danger from the burning Tk which might cause amn to explode at any moment and the accurate enemy small arms fire directed at his tk from close range, he proceeded to lift his Tp Ldr from the Tk and drag him to safety. He then returned to the Tk which was still under enemy small arms fire and lifted the wounded Gnr from the Turret and dragged him to safety. The Tk by now was burning fiercely and risk from exploding Amn and petrol tks was even greater than before.

In spite of this and the stream of enemy small arms fire which was by now continuously directed at his Tk, Tpr Piper returned across the open ground for a third time and extricated the Dvr and dragged him under cover. He then rendered first aid to his Tp Ldr who was in danger of losing his life from loss of blood and applied a tourniquet to his shattered leg. Next he applied first aid to the wounded Dvr, but on turning his attention to the Gnr he found that he had already died from wounds. He remained with them still under small arms fire until the enemy were driven back and his Tp Ldr and Dvr could be evacuated.

Tpr Piper by his complete disregard for his own personal safety in returning repeatedly to his blazing Tk whilst under accurate enemy fire undoubtedly saved the lives of his Tk Comd and Dvr. His gallant and unselfish conduct in most adverse circumstances is beyond praise.

Statement by WS/Sjt. Corker, W.—107 Regt. R.A.C.

(King's Own)

On the 21st day of October, 44, I Sjt. Corker was acting in the capacity of Tank Commander in N. 4 Troop, 'A' Sqn. The troop had been sent in support of No. 2 Troop to the left of the centre line near the village of Nieuwmoer. On reaching the road running East to West, I observed a tank burning about 100 yds North of the road. I also saw 3715768 Tpr Piper R. dragging away from the tank a body. Machine gun fire was coming down all around him, and for this reason I put down 2 inch smoke to cover them. The fire was coming from the N.W. I knew there was an enemy S.P. down the road to the left and up till then had not been knocked out but was being engaged. My own and the troop leader's tank (Lt. R. Webb) then ran in close to assist and give cover from the enemy fire. We found in a ditch some 20 yds away Tpr Piper who was attending to the very severe wounds of Lt. Mitchell and Tpr Plant, to whom he had affixed very good tournaquets and had given them morphia. In my opinion Tpr. Piper paid utter disregard to his own safety in pulling his Tk Comd and crew out of the tank in as much as the tank may have exploded and enemy machine gun bullets may have killed him.

Statement by 7[...]60535 P/U/L/Cpl. Curno D.

I certify on 21st Oct 44, I saw Tpr Piper rescue under fire Lt. Mitchell and Tpr Plant from a burning A.F.V.

(L.G. 22.3.45)

Platten, Charles Henry, Lance Corporal
T/225565, 49 Gen Tpt Coy., R.A.S.C. (Wells, Norfolk)
(Immediate)
On 28 Jan. 42 this N.C.O. was on Tp. carrying duty south of Benghasi when the town was cut off. After immobilising his vehicles he made his way with help of senoussai towards our lines and was picked up by a tp of the South African Armoured cars on 4 March.

He provided valuable information regarding enemy dispositions he had seen during his journey, and produced information which appeared worthy of further investigation. Before returning to Div. HQ he volunteered to lead a party back into the enemy lines to investigate further the enemy laager which he had passed. Accordingly arrangements were made for him to guide a party of 5 back the way he came and he did this with such accuracy that he was able definitely to recognise places he had seen before and confirm all reports that he had previously made. A sa result of this reconnaissance, our air forces were guided onto and successfully bombed very important concentrations of enemy troops.

Throughout the 35 days journey of approximately 250 miles back to the lines of 1 Armd Div and during the subsequent patrol which he led, this N.C.O. displayed courage, determination, initiative and physical fitness of the highest order under conditions of the greatest hardship. *(L.G. 12.5.42)*

Plummer, Charles, Sergeant
4916775, 3 Monmouthshire Regt., South Wales
Borderers (Wolverhampton) (Immediate)
On 30 Nov 44 Sjt. Plummer commanded the res pl of 'C' Coy whose objective was the village of Broekhuizen. The two leading pls came under intense SA fire from the village, and also arty and mortar fire from their right flank across the R Maas.

At the outskirts of the village the Coy Comd and the two leading pl comds were killed, leaving no offrs except the 2IC who was behind the area of the battle. Sjt. Plummer, seeing the remnants of the Coy go to ground, immediately led his pl fwd and took complete control of the situation. Under very heavy shell, mortar and MG fire he personally reorgniased the remainder of the Coy to form a strongpoint. He then continued to comd the Coy with skill and determination until the arrival of the 2IC one hr later, twice visiting exposed positions with complete disregard for his own safety.

His coolness and courage under conditions, in which it was almost certain death to move in the open, were an inspiration to all around him. There is no doubt that he was responsible for restoring and reorganising his Coy into fighting shape. *(L.G. 1.3.45)*

Pollak, Joseph, Private
12872, R.A.S.C. [PAL/12872, Pioneer Corps on AFW 3121]

Captured in Greece on 29th April, 1941, Private Pollak escaped from Corinth P/W Camp about six weeks later. After spending two months in Corinth he moved to Athens, where he was arrested by Germans on 14th September, 1941. For eight days he was imprisoned at Everoff, but with the help of two doctors he was transferred to the Public Hospital, from where he escaped. He returned to friends he had previously made a Kalamaki, and remained with them until, in December 1941 he took a party of 28 escapers to the island of Antiparos. However all were captured on 14th January, 1942, and taken to Syros. Transferred via Rhodes to Italy, he was ultimately imprisoned in Camp 78 (Sulmona).

Released on 12th September, 1943, owing to his knowledge of languages, including Italian and German, Private Pollak was employed by British officers in helping other P/Ws in the district. During October he was sent with a message to Allied authorities but, failing to get through owing to German activity, returned to Sulmona and continued his former work there. Early in December he accompanied the heads of the Sulmona organization to Rome, where he was again employed as a runner.

On 5th January, 1944 Private Pollak was arrested by Germans and taken via Bussi to Civitaquana. After many interrogations his captors recognised him as a P/W and sent him to Aquila. On 3rd March, 1944 he was entrained for Germany and, although his boots had been removed, he jumped from the moving train near Arezzo. Six days later he reached Rome where he recommenced his duties with the organisation. On 4th June, 1944, when the Allies entered Rome, he directed armed guards to vital points to prevent sabotage. *(L.G. 9.11.44)*

Pollock, James Taylor, Sergeant
7894505, 1st Fife & Forfar Yeomanry (Lundin, Lincs) (Periodic)

Throughout the period 1 Feb—10 April 1945 Sjt. Pollock has been Tp Sjt of 3 Tp, 'A' Sqn, 1 FF Yeo. His all round excellence in the field and control of his Tp is beyond praise.

At Gennep on 12 Feb when his Tp were supporting 152 Bde of 51 (H) div in the attack on the town, his Tp Officer was knocked out and Sjt. Pollock continued to fight the Tp with great skill and daring. Having successfully 'flamed' the objective he was required to extricate his Crocodiles through the narrow and heavily mined streets. Although under heavy and continuous fire he withdrew his Tp to rear rally without further loss.

While supporting 7 Bn BW, 154 Bde at Hassum, Sjt. Pollock again assumed command of the Tp when his Tp Ldr's tank was bogged in a crater. Again he successfully flamed his objective allowing the infantry to take the position. Near Goch on 19 Feb 2 Bn Seaforths suffered casualties and were forced to withdraw, Sjt. Pollock was

ordered to go out with his Crocodile and an infantry section to recover the wounded and dead. On approaching the area, artillery, mortar and machine gun fire became very heavy so Sjt. Pollock signalled to the infantry section to withdraw and pushed on alone. On reaching his objective he refused to allow any of his crew to dismount from the tank owing to the concentration of fire but himself got out and unaided lifted the casualties on his flame trailer and returned to our lines.

Sjt. Pollock has consistently shown the highest courage and daring. His willingness to accept responsibility and his coolness and initiative at all times have made him a magnificent example to his men and an invaluable N.C.O.
M.I.D. 9.8.45   *(L.G. 11.10.45)*

Pook, Idris Lloyhd, Warrant Officer Cl. II
5191254, 10th Gloucestershire Regt. (Bristol) (Immediate)

In NE Burma 1945.

At about 0800 hrs on 26 Feb, the leading pl of CSM Pook's coy were ambushed while crossing Nwa Sakan chaung, near Myitson. They came under heavy machine-gun fire from the front and both flanks. The Coy Comd and five men were wounded instantly and there was momentary confusion in the [...] pl. Without awaiting orders, CSM Pook immediately took forward the reserve platoon to close the gap on the threatened left flank. This area was under the heaviest fire, but CSM Pook organised a defensive perimeter, selected positions and personally led each section into its area. Three men had meanwhile been wounded whilst attempting to bring in our casualties, lying in the fire lanes of the enemy LMGs. CSM Pook, skilfully using cover, crawled forward, and succeeded in dragging them one by one to safety, killing two Japs who attempted to interfere. Meanwhile, the Coy Comd was lying wounded and unable to move fifty yards outside the most forward section. CSM Pook decided to try and get him in, as he alone knew the exact location. [...] crawled forward, found his Coy Comd and crawled back under LMG fire from two directions with the officer slung over his shoulders.

Throughout the action, the personal courage, and outstanding leadership of this WO was an inspiration to the depleted coy. In spite of casualties to many NCOs and most of his key personnel, CSM Pook encouraged his men and re-organised and consolidated his position. It was largely due to his determination to hold on to the ground already won that eventually forced the enemy to withdraw. *(L.G. 12.7.45)*

Poole, David, Sergeant
5043426, 1st Bn The Leicestershire Regt. (Stoke-on-Trent) (Immediate)

On 29 Sep 44 'D' Coy 1 Leicesters carried out a silent dawn attack on the compound of the Belgian State Institution at Merxplas. Sjt. Poole was in command of the right forward pl. To reach the compound the platoon had to cross 250 yds of open ground, cross a moat 20 ft wide and 5 ft broad with 5 feet of water in it and a bank 5 ft high in which were enemy positions.

The platoon came under heavy fire as it reached the moat from a post in front of the moat. With great dash Sjt. Poole led his platoon against this post and took it.

The platoon now came under heavy fire from the far bank of the moat. Without hesitation Sjt. Poole plunged into the moat followed by his platoon and succeeded in liquidating the enemy positions on the far side of the moat. He then re-entered the water and still under fire from the flank assisted three men who had got into difficulties in the water to get out.

After crossing the dyke the Coy was at [...] 1000 yards from its objective. Numerous buildings which were held by the enemy had to be cleared. Sjt. Poole led his platoon forward with the greatest dash and determination. Throughout the morning the platoon, constantly under fire from machine guns and rifles, continued to fight in this maze of buildings many of which were large and formidable.

Shortly after 1300 hrs Sjt. Poole was himself wounded by a sniper, but the platoon had now reached its objective. Throughout a long, dangerous and difficult action Sjt. Poole by his disregard for his personal safety kept complete control of his platoon and was master of every situation. Throughout this action he displayed the very highest standard of skill, courage and leadership. The success of his Coy in reaching its objective was very largely due to his outstanding leadership.*(L.G. 12.4.45)*

Poole, Ernest William, Corporal
L800192, Royal Canadian Army Medical Corps
For Korea   *(L.G. 18.4.52)*

Pope, Glyn Haddy, Sergeant
SX 6915, 2/48 Aust Inf Bn. (Immediate)
For outstanding courage, personal gallantry and leadership of the highest order during operations on Tarakan.

On the 6 May 45 C Coy 2.48 Bn was ordered to capture a small but important feature known as Sykes Hill which dominated the road and Tarakan town. The enemy were well dug in on the crest and reverse slopes and the flanks were covered by fire so that the only approach to the feature was frontally up a precipitous slope.

14 Pl commanded by Sjt Pope was halted some 50 yards from the top by heavy MG, rifle fire and grenades. Showing great determination and under the inspiring leadership of Sjt. Pope the Pl struggled up the slopes and had almost reached the crest when the enemy threw down grenades and 75mm fused shells at close range and they were forced to withdraw. Sjt. Pope reorganised the Pl at the foot of the feature and again attacked up the hill but the enemy with grenades and accurate rifle and MG fire forced him to withdraw slightly. Again for the third time the Pl attacked and due to the outstanding

courage of the Pl as a whole and in particular of Sjt. Pope they gained the top of the feature inflicting severe casualties on the enemy and forcing the remainder to witdraw.

Sjt. Pope was always well to the fore and though wounded in the ch[...] and leg led the attack personally destroying three enemy posts and when his rifle was damaged he continued to fight with grenades. When the initial part of the feature had been taken he reorganised his Pl which was now reduced to eight men and continued the fight along the ridge until his wounds caused him to black out and he had to be evacuated.

This NCO's utter disregard for personal safety his outstanding courage and leadership and his refusal to admit defeat in what seemed an impossible situation was largely instrumental in the feature being captured and has inspired the whole Coy and earned admiration of every officer and man in the Bn.   *(L.G. 3.7.45)*

Porter, David, Corporal (A/Sgt.)
2156419, 1 Demolition Sqn. P.P.A. Royal Engineers (St. Helens) (Immediate)
On 29 Jun 44 at Castel San Pietro, Italy, Sjt. Porter, in charge of a patrol of three, was ordered to reconnoitre a track leading to the village of Castel San Pietro. Finding the village apparently deserted, he entered it and in one of the houses he surprised a German Post. Two of the enemy were killed and a third one captured. When they came back into the street Sjt. Porter's patrol came under heavy fire from three Spandaus concealed in the hillside above the village and also from a patrol of eight men armed with automatic rifles. With great gallantry and considerable skill Sjt. Porter beat off the enemy who were attempting to cut off his retreat, and after two hours rejoined his own positions without suffering any casualties and brought back with him a prisoner and a German wireless set.   *(L.G. 8.2.45)*

Portsmouth, Clifford John, Private
144837, 1st Royal Natal Carbineers (Immediate)
For conspicuous gallantry in action on the 8th April, 1942 in an action designed against Trig 112 (U835915) in the Gazala area. Pte. Portsmouth as Pl runner repeatedly carried messages to and from forward sections under very heavy fire. He located a heavy machine gun position which was holding up the advance, indicated the target and was instrumental in destroying it. He killed no less than seven of the enemy by rifle fire and after finding a number of infantry hiding in a rock cistern destroyed them with hand grenades. He destroyed an enemy vehicle and anti-tank gun. In mopping up operations he gave valuable assistance to his officer in maintaining communications, thereby ensuring a successful completion of the action. At this stage he located and collected a large number of prisoners. Throughout the action he showed splendid courage and initiative, his disregard of danger and desire to get to grips with the enemy being quite unexcelled.   *(L.G. 9.7.42)*

Potterill, Frederick Roy, Private
31897, Transvaal Scottish (Immediate)
For conspicuous gallantry in action.

At Huberta Pass near Dire Daua on 27 Mar 41. Pte. Potterill, with complete disregard for his personal safety, rescued two badly wounded comrades lying in the open. Going forward under heavy fire he carried the two men to cover. *(L.G. 21.10.41)*

Potts, Edward, Warrant Officer Cl. II
3384774, 1st Bn, The East Lancashire Regt. (Belfast)
On the night 8/9 Feb 45, 'B' Coy attacked the first and second trench systems of the Siegfried line posn in the area 830520. The leading pl had just reached its objective and No. 11 Pl had started moving to the right towards its objective at 829518. Just short of their objective, enemy MG fire from two Spandaus opened up at 30 yds range. The Pl Comd and three others were wounded and three men were killed. In the darkness this caused some disorganisation and the pl failed to capture its objective. Hearing of this, and without reference to the Coy Comd who was otherwise engaged, CSM Potts on his own initiative went fwd in the dark and with great difficulty succeeded in collecting together and reorganising the remainder of this pl. He was under heavy close range enemy small arms fire during this time as the enemy fired long bursts of Spandau at all movement.

Having eventually collected the pl together, CSM Potts then personally led them in a determined assault against the posn. After fierce hand-to-hand fighting with grenades and stens, he succeeded in capturing the pl's objective. At least six enemy were killed, many were wounded and some 15 prisoners were taken in this assault.

After capturing the objective, CSM Potts sent fwd a patrol in front of his posn. This patrol was ambushed some 50 yds fwd of the area. Three of the men were wounded and could be heard in the darkness calling for assistance. Regardless of his personal danger and knowing full well that the enemy knew the exact spot where the wounded men were located, CSM Potts deliberately and voluntarily went fwd three times in succession and quite alone to bring in these wounded men. Each time he carried back one of them. This was done with the enemy no more than 50 yds away and in spite of the frequent bursts of fire at every movement the enemy could hear in the dark.

This WO's behaviour throughout the whole of this operation has been beyond praise. He is a cheerful, stout-hearted and inspiring leader and is always to be found wherever the fighting is thickest and most dangerous. In the worst of conditions he remains quite undaunted and retains an aggressive spirit which is inspiring to all who come in contact with him. In this operation, as in every other operation, he was in no small measure responsible for the high morale of his coy. His enthusiasm is infectious. *(L.G. 19.4.45)*

Povey, Frederick Richard, Lance Sergeant
6347091, 6th Bn The Queen's Own Royal West Kent Regt. (Northfleet, Kent)
For conspicuous gallantry and devotion to duty at Djebel Abiod on 17 Nov 42 when commanding an A.tk gun.

At 1330 hrs L/Sjt. Povey saw a German column consisting of approx 18 tanks and some lorried infantry approach his position. With great coolness and gallantry, L/Sjt. Povey and his men waited until the leading tank was within 100 yards and then opened fire, setting the tank alight. His gun then came under most heavy fire, but he continued to engage the other tanks which were within range, until they moved to a hull-down position. On being told that he could withdraw he refused, and remained in his position until dark. L/Sjt. Povey's personal bravery was an example to his detachment throughout the action. *(L.G. 11.2.43)*

Powell, Edward Joseph, Sergeant
1859585, Royal Engineers
B.E.F. *(L.G. 11.7.40)*

Powell, Ernest, Sergeant
4122491, 2nd Cheshire Regt. (Lymm, Warrington) (Immediate)
Sjt. Powell was the Pl Sjt. of a M.M.G. Pln. ordered to support the 9/D.L.I. on March 20/21 during the attack on the Mareth Line. After the wounding of his Pln. Comdr. on the morning of March 21/22, he took command. He maintained his position firing his pln. from a forward position on the left flank until the difficulties of replenishment under very fierce fire from enemy artillery and tanks necessitated his withdrawal behind the A/Tank ditch. Here he took up a position on the right flank and kept his guns in action almost continuously throughout the night of March 22/23 with harassing and defensive fire, breaking up at least two counter attacks. Later, when two of his M.M.G.s were out of action he obtained a Bren gun to increase the fire power of his pln.

Sjt. Powell showed splendid leadership, much resource and fine devotion to duty in most difficult and dangerous circumstance. The successful maintenance in action of his pln. during the hazardous night of March 22/23 greatly assisted the defence of the A/Tk ditch position beyond the Wadi Zigzaou. *(L.G. 1.6.43)*

Powell, Samuel, Private
538967, 7th Bn Oxfordshire & Buckinghamshire Light Infantry (Oxford) (Immediate)
During the first attack by 7th Oxf & Bucks on Point 819, 950074 (Italy 1:50,000 Sheet 160 (ii) Cassino) on 11 Nov 43 Pte. Powell was in the right forward company. Early in the advance from the start line three Spandaus fired on this company from the base of the Razorback and Pte. Powell's Platoon was ordered to destroy them. In the course of this operation, Pte. Powell, with a Bren gun and two Mills grenades, by climbing up a steep rock face ten yards ahead of the rest of his section, succeeded

single-handed in killing all of the three Germans manning one of the Spandaus, which he then rendered useless.

The platoon, on rejoining the Company, was then ordered to clear a small ridge in the basin between Pt. 819 and the Monastery Hill. The Company had already suffered many casualties on this small feature and Pte. Powell's platoon came under heavy fire at point blank range as they attacked it. With complete disregard of danger and in the face of heavy machine gun fire, Pte. Powell, again leading his section by at least ten yards, charged a Spandau post and, by the use of a Mills grenade and then firing his Bren gun from the hip, destroyed single-handed this second post, killing two Germans.

By his initiative and speed in action he saved many lives, and by his personal example of fearlessness and the offensive spirit he inspired all those around him with the same courage.   *(L.G. 23.3.44)*

Powell, Stanley William, Trp
7899689, Royal Armoured Corps (Hussars)
No citation.   *(L.G. 27.9.40)*

Poynton, Joseph William, Private
WX 12552, 2nd Independent Company, Australian Military Forces (Immediate)
During the operations at the Dilly Aerodrome on the night 19/20 February, 1942, Pte. Poynton together with three others, fiercely attacked Japanese troops crossing a small bridge leading to the Dilly Aerodrome and by his example, coolness, daring and total disregard of danger he very materially prevented two attempts to take the Aerodrome Hangars. He fought the Japanese at close quarters with his Tommy gun inflicting several casualties.

In subsequent action, on the following day, when Ptes. Poynton and Growns took up an ambush position, Growns very quickly inflicted one Japanese casualty, Poynton, with great determination and daring went into action and silenced a Lewis gun nearest him with the Thompson machine gun. He then obtained some hand grenades from a Dutch soldier, rushed forward to a nearby tree, threw three grenades, the third of which blew up the gun and 4 of the crew, and this resolute and daring action enabled Lieut. McKenzie to continue the manœuvre.   *(L.G. 4.2.43)*

Pradham, Bhaktabahadur, Sergeant
21139002, 7th Gurkha Rifles
For Malaya   *(L.G. 29.6.54)*

Pratt, George, Lance Sergeant
6919921, 8th Bn The Rifle Brigade (London, N.19) (Immediate)
On 10th September in the attack on Helchteren Corporal Pratt was commanding a section in the leading platoon. Shortly after crossing the start line his platoon Serjeant was killed. The platoon then came under heavy mortar and machine gun fire and the platoon commander was wounded. Corporal Pratt immediately took command of the platoon and with great courage led them to their objective. The objective was captured, many Germans were killed and several taken prisoner. Corporal Pratt consolidated on the objective and reorganised the platoon which had suffered many casualties. Throughout the action Corporal Pratt showed a complete lack of fear and set a fine example to his platoon. There is no doubt that his initiative in taking over the platoon at a critical time contributed greatly to the final capture of the whole position.   *(L.G. 1.3.45)*

Pratt, Robert Donaldson, Sergeant
2688669, 13th London Regt. (1st Bn. Princess Louise's Kensington Regt.), Middlesex Regt., T.A
During the withdrawal from the Ligne de Contact on the evening of 15th May 1940 Sjt. Pratt's M.G. section located in Wolscher Wood was withdrawing to Remeling. In the course of this withdrawal O.C. 'C' Coy 5th Gordons asked this N.C.O. if he could give his company covering fire to enable him to get across the open ground. At least three German M.G.s were in action against 'C' Coy 5th Gordons at that time.

Sjt. Pratt unhesitatingly got his section into action and immediately silenced at least one enemy M.G. and continued firing on the remaining guns until the Gordons passed through M.G. section position. This action drew the enemy fire on to himself with the result that only one man of the Gordons was wounded during the encounter. O.C. 'C' Coy 5th Gordons personally congratulated Sjt. Pratt on his gallant action.

Sjt. Pratt handled his section with great skill and determination and set a magnificent example to his men. His conduct and initiative was all the more praiseworthy as his instructions were to get back to Remeling without occupying any intermediate positions. *(L.G. 22.10.40)*

Pratt, Robert Donaldson, Sergeant
2688669, 1st Bn. Princess Louise's Kensington Regt., T.A. (The Middlesex Regt)
15th May, 1940, Sjt. Pratt's M.G. section was ordered to withdraw to a rear locality without occupying any intermediate position. During the course of the withdrawal a company of a neighbouring Bn. had to withdraw across some very exposed ground which was being swept by enemy M.G. Fire. Sjt. Pratt unhesitatingly got his M.G. section into action and although by doing so he drew the enemy fire to his own position he so successfully engaged the enemy that the neighbouring unit withdrew with only one casualty. Had it not been for the initiative, skill and determination of Sjt. Pratt, heavy casualties would undoubtedly have been suffered.   *(L.G. 5.7.40)*

Preece, Frederick Amos, Trooper
404153, 101 Troop, No. 2 SBS & Royal Armoured Corps (Dragoon Guards)
On the night of 11th–12th April, 1942, Captain Montanaro, accompanied by Trooper Preece, entered

Boulogne harbour in a canoe which had been taken by a Motor Launch to about 1½ miles from the harbour entrance. Successfully avoiding detection by the breakwater forts, and a number of vessels which were active in the harbour, they manoeuvred the canoe alongside an enemy tanker to which eight explosive charges were attached below water. They withdrew still undetected and commenced their return across channel without great expectation of being picked up until daylight some four hours later. Their canoe had suffered some damage during the operation and the sea conditions were deteriorating so that it was fortunate that as planned the motor launch was able to make contact and pick them up an hour after they had left Boulogne harbour by which time they were 2 to 3 miles clear of the enemy coast.

Subsequent air reconnaissance has established that the tanker was damaged and beached.

Trooper Preece contributed his share in the success of the operation by carrying out implicitly the orders of Captain Montanaro and by showing courage and endurance over a long period spent in imminent danger of discovery by the enemy.　　　　(*L.G. 16.6.42*)

Preece, Harold, Lance Sergeant
5047654, C.R.E. Bde, Sickle Force Div, Royal Engineers
On the morning of the 27th April a road crater had been prepared beside the left forward company position of the York and Lancaster Regt. It was to be fired at 10[...] when the withdrawal had started. L/Sjt. Preece accompanied by one sapper went forward from Kola to carry out the task of firing the crater. He approached to within a few yards of the crater when an enemy machine gun opened fire, both men were wounded. Although wounded in the chest and head L/Sjt. Preece crawled forward to attempt to fire the charge but was unsuccessful. He was later picked up and evacuated by the stretcher bearers of the York and Lancaster Regiment. This N.C.O. showed courage and determination all through the operations and set a fine example to his men.
　　　　(*L.G. 6.8.40*)

Prendergast, John, Sergeant
3957274, 1 Bn. The Welch Regt.
After serving in Libya my unit went to Crete in Feb 41 and were in the Canea and Suda area. We were on the beach at Suda Bay at the time of the capitulation. With four others from other units I managed to get into the hills, where we remained for four days. We then returned to Suda Bay and marked out a boat in which we hoped to get away. We went into a wood near the bay to await nightfall, but the Germans surrounded the wood and we were taken prisoner (4 Jun).

We were taken to Canea and kept for three weeks in an improvised prison camp where our rations were one bowl of rice soup a day. We left this camp on 27 Jun, and 3000 of us were sent to Salonika in a cargo boat. There were 1000 packed into the hold where I was. Our only rations for the voyage were a tin of bully beef and a packet of biscuits each.

We arrived in Solonika on 1 Jul and were put into a prison camp in a former Greek barracks. We were badly overcrowded, and had to sleep on the floor without blankets. There were about 100 sleeping in a room large enough to hold about 30. Food was very short. We were issued with soup generally once, but sometimes twice, a day and with one loaf of bread a day for ten men. This gave each man about one ounce of bread. We were all very weak from lack of food, and the Germans used to keep us standing for hours on the square in the sun waiting for roll call. The guards used to fire if more than two or three went to the lavatory at one time. The treatment, however, was not so brutal as we had received in Crete. While we were being taken from Suda to Canea the Greek women set out buckets of water for us, and our German guards frequently kicked the buckets over and hit the women. One British officer fell exhausted. A German picked him up by the coat and, when he collapsed, kicked him. I called the guard a swine and he drew his revolver, but I stood close to him and he did not fire. At that moment another guard kicked me from behind.

After four or five weeks we were transferred to Germany. Before leaving Salonika 190 of us, who were either born in Ireland or had Irish parents, were separated. As I was born in County Cork, I was included in this party. The party travelled separately to Stalag III D (Westermarck, near Berlin), where we were put in a special camp, No. 717. We travelled in horse wagons, 42 men to the wagon. The journey lasted ten days and was made via Belgrade and Austria. The only food we had was one loaf of bread and a tin of meat each issued in Salonika. We arrived at Westermarck on 11 Jul.

Accommodation at our camp was fairly good, and at first food was at least edible. For five months we received no clothing we were wearing tropical kit for the best part of the winter—and no Red Cross parcels. The N.C.O.'s refused to work, but the men were employed moving sand from pits and filling up holes in waste land near the camp. An attempt was made to make the men work on the railway, but they realised that this was helping the enemy's war effort and they succeeded in running a train off the rails and down an embankment. Three or four trucks of ammunition were derailed near Westermarck, and the line was blocked for three or four days. After this the men were taken from the railway to work in the sand pits again, and in the winter they cleared snow from the railway and streets.

At the end of Nov no clothing had yet been issued and the whole camp struck work. We were put on half rations for a week as a punishment. A German officer was then sent from the Camp H.Q., and we explained the reason for the strike. I was in charge of the party which went to the Stalag III D stores in Wilhelmstrasse, Berlin. The Feldwebel ordered the storekeeper to issue us with British battle dress, but a German lieutenant countermanded the order. All the British clothing was returned to stores, and we got French uniform.

At the end of Mar 42 we were still wearing French uniforms, although we knew there were ample stores of British battle dress in Berlin and that the French P/W were actually wearing these British uniforms in Stalag III D. The camp again struck work and one morning we were ordered to pack and were moved to a French camp (Stalag IIID/700) at Falkensee, near Spandau.

At Camp No. 717 we were all interrogated by a Leutnant Dr. Reinald. His interrogations began about a week after our arrival. At my interrogation he asked me why I was in the Army, and I replied, 'Because I like it.' He asked why I had left Ireland and I told him that I had lived and worked in England and that if a country was good enough to live in, it was good enough to fight for. This annoyed him, and he did not interrogate me further. Those of us who were interrogated first warned the others what to expect, and Leutnant Reinald did not get any information. None of the interrogations lasted more than five minutes. Leutnant Reinald was very hot-tempered, which made it easy to get out of answering him. He spoke very good English, was aged about 45, grey-haired, short and stout. He wore uniform. Most of us told him we wanted to get to a British camp and did not want to be in a special Irish one.

On one occasion Leutnant Reinald brought a number of propaganda sheets in English containing stories about the arrival of British and American troops in Northern Ireland and of friction between Britain and Eire. I appropriated the copy which was pinned on the notice board and lit a fire with it. The Unteroffizier was very angry and threatened to stop rations. He told a German officer, who asked me why I had burned the paper. I replied, 'You don't expect us to believe that.' He walked away without answering. There was no anti-British lectures in the camp, and I saw no other instances of propaganda, apart from 'The Camp.' There was no anti-British sentiment among any of the Irishmen in the camp.

A factor in maintaining morale in the camp was a wireless set on which we got the B.B.C midnight news. Just before Christmas 41 I was in charge of a party which was doing a job on the railway. I was in one of the railway sheds and managed to get a small wireless set from a consignment of five or six. I put the set in a sack and piled wood on top. As we were allowed to take wood into the camp the guard noticed nothing amiss. The set was in perfect order except that it lacked one valve, but a Polish workman bought a valve for us outside and we worked the set from the electric current. We used to get the midnight news because at other times the presence of the guards made listening too dangerous. We wrote a bulletin every night and read it in the rooms in the morning. The existance of this bulletin was a means of keeping down camp rumours. The guards once heard the wireless and next morning our room was searched. The Germans failed to find the set, although they actually moved the coal box in which it was hidden. The set was in use till Mar.

I escaped from Stalag IIID/700 on 25 Apr 42 with Sjt. Bryan, John, R.A.F. Our bungalow was in the centre of the French camp. There was a guard at each end of our building. I worked out a plan for getting out of our room as soon as possible after 2100 hrs, when the guards called the roll and locked us up. During the day I loosened the bar with which the outside shutters of the window were secured. After we had been locked in I slipped a table knife through the crevice between the shutters and lifted the bar, which was unlocked. We then opened the shutters and got out about 2200 hrs. It was a moonlight night with some cloud. We made our way through the French camp in uniform to an empty bungalow next to the German guards' billet. We got into this bungalow and hid for about an hour. We then took off our uniform, below which we had civilian clothes of a kind, and left them in the lavatory.

We had made the following preparations for escape:—

Clothing:— I had British battle dress trousers which we had dyed. We got the dye from a Pole at Stalag IIID/717 who was working outside. The dye was supposed to be black, but the trousers turned out brown. I had a battle dress blouse and a white trench coat which I had picked up in Crete and which I had been allowed to keep, having said it was an Army coat. I was wearing Army boots. Bryan also had battle dress trousers dyed brown, an R.A.F overcoat with black buttons, and Army boots.

Food:— I had ten 4-oz bars of chocolate, two packets of ginger snaps, and a water bottle full of Ovaltine made very thick with plenty of sugar. Bryan had chocolate and two packets of biscuits. We carried out food in canvas bags which we had got in the camp.

Maps:— In the camp I had charge of a map of Western Germany, Belgium, and France which a P/W had found in a rubbish tip. A P/W named Frank Stevens, R.A., made a number of copies of this map showing differing routes out of Germany, and I had one of his copies and another which I had made myself. Our idea was to check possible destinations on the map with wagon labels from the side of railway trucks.

We got out of the empty bungalow through the window nearest the wire, which at that point was about 30 yds away. There was a sentry in an elevated box, about 50 yds from us, at the corner of the wire. (There were six of these boxes at intervals round the camp with a searchlight and a machine gun mounted on each). Once we got out we made our way in the shadow along the side of the bungalow towards the box, which was so placed that the sentry could not see us. I went across to the wire first, and out an opening sufficiently large to let us through. The wire was of small diamond-shaped mesh. Bryan followed when I had got through. A yard and a half further on there was another wire fence of the same kind. I cut an opening through this fence. Beyond it there was a third fence of barbed wire and steel netting. Bryan joined me as I was cutting an opening in this last fence. We could hear the sentry coughing and laughing above us, but he did not see or hear us.

Outside the wire we used cover again and crossed a field for about 100 yds. It was impossible to go further, as there were Flak positions about 400 yds further on. We then turned West and, after crossing a road, continued towards Westermarck, taking our directions from the stars. It was about 2200 hrs when we left the camp, and when I looked at my watch after crossing the road, it was 2310 hrs. We kept on across country. At one stage we had some difficulty at a railway crossing where there were a number of policemen and civilians. After about ten minutes a train pulled in and blocked the road. Once the road was clear of people on our side we started walking towards the level-crossing. The train pulled out before we reached the crossing and we walked straight on, passing a number of Germans, including two Gestapo policemen in green uniforms. Bryan and I spoke to each other in German, and they took no notice of us.

We went on across country, following tracks. At one stage we got into some wired allotments, but we simply cut our way out with our wire cutters. We met no-one before reaching Westermarck station at 0100 hrs. (26 Apr).

We took up a position near where goods trains were pulling in. I took off my white coat, as it was showing in the bright artificial lights of the goods yard. I then left Bryan and reconnoitred the train. I crawled and rolled forward across the line to where the trains had pulled in. I walked along a goods train, partly under the trucks and partly in the shadows alongside. My objective was to collect a number of wagon labels so as to find a truck bound for a suitable destination. I collected four labels and returned with them to the embankment where I had left Bryan with the case. We got under a lamp-post and examined the labels which were marked, respectively, Cologne, Luxembourg, Essen, and Antwerp. We buried these labels and returned to the part of the train from which I had got the Antwerp wagon labels. We found another wagon also marked Antwerp and set about getting into it. There was a railway guard walking up and down all the time. We had chosen a large closed truck, the door of which was sealed with wire and lead. I nipped the wire on the inside of the bar, and we opened the door. Bryan got in and I closed the door and put on the seal again. As the break in the wire was on the inside of the bar, it could not be detected. Bryan then opened a window near the roof. I climbed in, and we locked the window from the inside. I had got inside just in time, for the railway guard came along with a lamp, and through a crack in the door we could see him examining the seal.

The train left Westermarck at 0800 hrs on Sunday, 26 Apr. It travelled via Hanover and Essen. Essen was the last station we saw before reaching Antwerp on Tuesday morning, 28 Apr. We were shunted into a big goods station at the docks which was completely enclosed, partly by a high wire fence and partly by a wall. We got into the station about 1900 hrs. We could see a number of Germans in top boots and full equipment, apparently standing by for something. We waited in the truck till dark (about 2200 hrs), when we decided it was time to get out, as we were afraid of being caught in the town after curfew. I got out through the window to make for an air raid shelter about 30 yards away, where I was to wait for Bryan. On my way to the shelter a German guard saw me and called, 'Hallo, hallo' after me. I took no notice and walked quietly on to the shelter. I stood near the door. The guard followed me and came into the shelter. I was standing in one of the blast protection slip-ways, close against the wall. The guard had a torch in one hand and a revolver in the other. I waited till he got level with me and hit him under the chin, knocking him out. I put him in the far corner of the shelter. I waited some time for Bryan, but he did not come.

I then left the shelter and went round the back of it to a high wall. By climbing an electric light pole which was flat against the wall, I was able to get to the top and drop into the street. I made my way along the street to the main thoroughfare of Antwerp. There were a good many people about, and I decided to get out of the town quickly. I got my direction from the shadow of the moon, and left Antwerp from the S.E. side. On the outskirts I came to a bridge over a main railway. When I was about 20 yards from them I saw two German sentries on the bridge. I was on the far side of the road and I walked over to them as if to speak to them. As I approached them I raised my hat and said, 'Gute Nacht.' They saluted me and let me go on.

After crossing the bridge I got off the road and for the rest of the night walked across fields. About 0500 hrs (29 Apr) I hid in a small store-house near a farm. About an hour later I saw a light in the house and went to the door and asked for water. The man who came to the door asked me who I was, and, when I replied that I was English, he told me to go away. I went into a wood and washed and shaved with the kit I carried with me. I walked for a few hours more through the fields and came to a house, where I saw people having breakfast. They gave me coffee without asking who I was. The man asked later, and, when I told him, he allowed me to finish my coffee. Then he said I must go away, saying they were frightened of the Germans in the district.

I continued on foot, sometimes following roads and sometimes going across country, keeping my direction by the sun and using my watch as a compass. I slept in woods by night, I passed through Contich and Malines, and about 3 May I arrived in Brussels, through which I passed without difficulty. I had no help during this time, and lived on my chocolate, eating a bar a day. I followed a canal from Brussel, and after a day's walking reached Hal.

From Hal my route (as far as I can remember it) was:— Soignies, Mons, Erquennes, Chambry, Laon, Cerny, Fismes, St. Giles, Cohan, Courmont, Le Charmel. I walked most of the time on by-roads and across country.

I am not certain where I crossed the Franco–Belgian frontier, but it was at a village (probably near Erquenes) through which the boundary ran. I found it easy to cross, as there appeared to be no guards. On the evening of 7 May I got to within 2 kms of Charteves, near Chateau-Thierry. As I was walking along the road I met a man who looked at me very hard and asked in French where I was going. I replied in German that I was going home. He walked on about 100 yds. Meanwhile a man on a bicycle passed me, and the first man spoke to him, got the bicycle, and followed me. He said to me in English, 'Are you English?' 'I am a friend if you are English.' I admitted I was, and he took me to a village, where I rested for three days. My helper brought a French ex-P/W who took me to Paris and provided me with an identity card. Three weeks later the ex-prisoner took me by train to St. Pierre-le-Moutier, South of Nevers. From there we went to a hut in a wood and waited about four hours till 2100 hrs. During that time a number of French ex-P/W and one woman and her son arrived. After dark our party, numbering 14, walked through fields and woods to the river Allier, which we crossed by boat. After a meal at a hotel we walked to a village about 8 kms away, and about 0600 hrs we got a taxi to the bus route, about an hour's journey away. The bus went through Vichy to a big station some distance to the East, whence we got a train to Nimes (3 Jun). In Nimes I was handed over to an organisation.

§   §   §

We interrogated 2957274, Sjt. J. Prendergast yesterday. As the men's representative at Work Detachment 717 of Stalag III D he appears to have defended the prisoners of war's interests with determination and perseverance, especially in maintinaing his demands for adequate clothing. He organised two strikes, after the second of which the detachment was closed down. We hope that his conduct will receive suitable recognition.

(L.G. 10.11.42)

Price, William John, A/Corporal
22187869, 1st Bn. Suffolk Regt.
For Malaya   *(L.G. 27.7.51)*

Prichard, Ronald James, Private
601363, Royal New Zealand Infantry Regt.
For Vietnam   *(L.G. 12.11.68)*

Prince, Wilfred Charles, Sergeant
318897, 11th (Prince Albert's Own) Hussars, Royal
*   Armoured Corps*
On 21st June, 1940, T.S.M. Howarth's Troop was sent to Bir Gubi to reconnoitre. After the troops arrived, Blenheims bombed a patrol dump, when the troop approached it was heavily shelled. Enemy planes also bombed and machine-gunned each car. TSM Howarth's car was wrecked and Sjt. Prince's and Cpl. Emery's were put out of action. Sjt. Prince burried maps, Bren and Boy's rifles, etc. Aeroplanes set car on fire. Troop walked during the night and rested during the day. By midday water was exhausted. Sjt. Prince was suffering from blindness and not able to focus properly. He set off in search of and found a car which they thought they heard, being rescued after 3 days and nights in the desert. He showed initiative, coolheadedness and leadership considerably above the average of his rank and he saved the lives of Trprs. Spencer and Driver. *(L.G. 29.11.40)*

Prince, William Ronald, Sergeant (A/W.O.II
4190471, Royal Welch Fusiliers (Wrexham)
At s'Hertogenbosch on the 26th October 44, Sjt. Prince was command a Pl of C Coy. A Coy. of another Bn. had succeeded in crossing the R. Dommel establishing a small bridgehead. Sjt. Prince's Coy. was ordered to cross the river and reinforce this bridgehead. By this time, however, the enemy had reacted strongly and the bridge came under fire from enemy infantry and from a tank. None the less, Sjt. Prince by his spendid leadership and complete indifference to enemy fire succeeded in getting his Pl. across and into a large building on the far side. A portion of the remainder of the company succeeded in crossing, but the enemy reaction was becoming increasingly strong, and the remainer of the battalion was ordered to cross by bridge which had been secured further down the river.

Meanwhile Sjt. Prince had discovered that the majority of the company from the preceding battalion were in the block of houses on the other side of the main road leading from the bridge, with which communication was now impossible as the road was swept by enemy fire. The CSM, who was at the time in command of the company had been severely wounded in [....] assumed command of all troops in this block of buildings, and [...] about organising this force, which consisted of about two platoons of his own company and one platoon of another battalion, for a resolute defence of the bridgehead. Under his inspiring command, this force dominated the enemy in the neighbourhood for about ten hours, until the remainder of the battalion, having fought its way up from the other bridge, succeeded in joining up with them.

By his inspiring leadership and resolute defence Sjt. Prince contributed very materially to the success of the operation in that his efforts undoubtedly helped to divert a considerable part of the enemy strength from the main bridgehead.
M.I.D. 23.3.45   *(L.G. 1.3.45)*

Prinsloo, Jan Hendrik, Private
36131V, Witwatersrand Rifles / de la Rey Regiment
*   (Immediate)*
For outstanding bravery and courageous personal initiative in probing enemy lines.

On the morning of the 19th Oct 1944 Pte. Prinsloo accompanied his platoon into the attack on Pt. 806. His platoon had been ordered to send forward a clearing party to clear the bush in front of the platoon position, after the occupation of the feature.

While clearing the forward slopes, the patrol heard movement of enemy ahead of them. Pte. Prinsloo crawled forward on his own and located the enemy positions, pin-pointing the M.G. positions. He then returned to the patrol and led them on to the enemy post, and was instrumental in wiping out the enemy positions.

The patrol continued and later captured some P.W. Returning with these P.W. the patrol had to withdraw fast, owing to enemy reinforcements being brought up and they came under very heavy M.G. and rifle fire. On nearing our lines it was found that one section commander was missing. Prinsloo returned immediately and crawled through the enemy positions located the N.C.O. and attended to his wound (Cpl. Nieuwoudt having been badly wounded) Pte. Prinsloo then crawled back through the enemy lines and on reaching our lines reported to the Pl Comd and asked for a stretcher party. This he led back to where the N.C.O. was, picked him up, and led the party back again safely to our own lines.

During the night 19/20 at approximately 2400 hrs the platoon position was heavily counter-attacked and Prinsloo's section was over-run. Prinsloo himself however stuck tenaciously to his trench and refused to give in. Eventually he was forced to withdraw approximately 15 yards and he again took up position and fought back the enemy who were pressing hard.

At first light the following morning it was found that the enemy had practically surrounded the section and it was in extreme danger of being cut-off completely. Prinsloo then crawled through the cordon of enemy and reported the position to his platoon comd, who was able to bring in reserves and restore the position, pushing the enemy back over the crest. But for the initiative and courage of Prinsloo, the rest of the platoon would have been cut-off and surrounded, and a break-through in our lines been effected by the enemy.

His devotion to duty was outstanding and his coolness and courage in the face of heavy odds exemplary.

Statement by No. 173765V Lieut. P. J. Dreyer

I am Pl Comd of No. 14 Pl D Coy WR/DLR Pte Prinsloo is a member of No. 3 section. On the morning of the 19 Oct 44 I was ordered to clear the forward slopes of Pt 806. Pte Prinsloo accompanied his section on this task being leading scout of his section. While moving forward Pte. Prinsloo located an enemy M.G. nest which he engaged, putting the gun out of action and then directed the patrol on to the remaining enemy, which we were able to wipe out. On completion of this mission the patrol returned with PsW. We were fired on from the right flank whilst disarming the PsW. The patrol had to withdraw hurriedly from the position and during the period one of my N.C.Os was badly wounded and lying in the open. Prinsloo alone crawled back through the enemy to attend to Cpl. Nieuwoudt and placed the N.C.O. under cover and in a comfortable position. He, Prinsloo then returned to me and reported the state and the position of the wounded N.C.O. A stretcher party was called and Prinsloo led this back through the enemy and brought in Cpl. Nieuwoudt.

During the night 19/20 Oct 44 my platoon was heavily counter-attacked, the section post in which Prinsloo was, being over-run. Prinsloo manning the Bren Gun and keeping the enemy back remained in his position until forced back by overwhelming numbers. He then crawled back about 15 yards and again took up a firing position. This he held until first light the next morning, when he crawled through the enemy and reported to me, he then took forward a section with which he fought the enemy back and occupied his original position.

Statement by No. 307650V Cpl. Perrin D. A.

I am section commander No. 1 Section, 14 Platoon, D Coy, WR/DLR. On the night of 19/20 October 1944, my section was holding a position on Pt. 806. At approximately 23.00 hours the enemy heavily counter attacked on our platoon front. Heavy firing broke out on my right flank opposite No. 2 Section. This went on for about a quarter of an hour, when I realised the enemy had broken through our lines. Through all this firing I heard a Bren being fired on my right. Shortly afterwards Pte. Prinsloo reported to me and told me the enemy had broken through. He then took up a firing position on my right flank from where he continued firing keeping the enemy back and killing many of them. At approximately 2400 hours I sent Prinsloo to report to Platoon H.Q. He came back and told me he could not get through as the enemy were between us and Platoon H.Q. At first light the following morning Prinsloo succeeded in crawling through the enemy positions and went to Platoon H.Q. Shortly after Prinsloo brought up another Section in support and leading them they wiped out the enemy and took up his old position.

Statement by No. 572651V Pte. Dold J. D.

I am a member of No. 3 section 14 Pl. I was the No. 2 on the Bren Gun fired by Pte. Prinsloo. On the night of the 19/20 October 1944 the enemy heavily counter-attacked on the platoon front on Pt 806. Slightly to the right of Pte Prinsloo and myself heavy enemy small arms fire broke out, deafening the shouts for help from one our men. At the same time enemy firing opened up from behind us about 15 to 20 yds away. We realised then that our section position had been over-run by the enemy. Prinsloo, however kept the enemy on the right, where they outnumbered us three to one, at bay with his bren gun, until forced to withdraw for about 15 yards where Prinsloo after making contact with the section on our left again took up a firing position. Prinsloo held his ground all night, fighting back all the time and so preventing the Germans from advancing any further. At first light he crawled through the enemy who had come in behind him and informed the Pl Comd of the situation.

Leading back a section he cleaned up the enemy using his bren gun and restored the section to its former position.　　　　*(L.G. 8.3.45)*

Proffitt, Norman, Sergeant
7886900, 1st Derbyshire Yeomanry (Derby)
Sjt. Proffitt has been in command of a Troop for the past four months and has carried out his duties in a very gallant manner. On several occasions undeterred by enemy artillery and light automatic fire he has obtained the most valuable information, most noticeable during the withdrawal from Gafsa on Feb 16th, when he was able to give continuous valuable information regarding the enemy advance.

On two occasions he has personally cleared of mines long stretches of road and track, in particular during the advance from Thelepte on Mar 2nd, when he cleared one mile of mined track through an important pass, thus obtaining observation onto the Cafsa—Feriana road. Sjt. Proffitt, by his wonderful courage and gallant actions, has inspired his Troop with a fighting spirit totally unsurpassed by any other and by his untiring energy and true devotion to duty has been an example to all.
(L.G. 23.9.43)

Prouse, Franklin John, Sergeant
7883485, 7th Royal Tank Regt.
Bardia 3 Jan 41.
Commander of Tank 'Givenchy.' After his tank was stopped by direct hits from enemy guns he continued to give most effective covering fire enabling the Infantry to continue to advance. His tank was stationary under artillery and anti-tank gun fire for 4 hours but despite this he and his crew repaired the tracks and brought the tank out of action. Sergeant Prouse was slightly wounded when his cupola received a direct hit. His devotion to duty and gallantry were exemplary and were responsible for recovering his tank in conditions of great danger and difficulty.
(L.G. 9.5.41)

Pryor, Walter Edward, Sergeant
SX.7338, 2/48 Aust Inf Bn. (Immediate)
For leadership, courage and resourcefulness in holding his Coy together in the attack for 15 hrs after all the Coy offrs had been killed or wounded.

On 22 Jul 42 at Tell El Eisa Sjt. Pryor was acting as CSM for B Coy during an attack on strong German posns. By 0700 hrs the Coy Comd was wounded, two Pl Comds killed, and the third Pl Comd and his Pl out of contact with the remainder of the Coy which had received heavy casualties.

Sjt. Pryor assumed comd of the Coy, and in the face of intense enemy fire of all arms led it fwd to within 150 yds of the enemy posts. Throughout the day he organised and controlled the Coy's operations. With great coolness and determination, and by personal example he encouraged his men to hold on and fight until 2200 hrs, when in the dusk enemy action indicated that his now very small force would be surrounded and he fought his way back in good order, bringing wounded men with him.

This splendid act of initiative and courage has made a profound impression on B Coy and the whole Bn.
(L.G. 24.9.42)

Pugh, Evan Victor, Bombardier
872789, 7 Medium Regt, Royal Artillery (Ramsgate)
On 15 January 1941 outside the Tobruch perimeter Bdr. Pugh as assistant OP officer went foward under MG and artillery fire and located an enemy strong point containing MGs and light artillery. On his return Bdr. Pugh gave a very clear and accurate account of the target and how it could best be engaged. At daybreak on 16 January 1941 Bdr. Pugh lead an OP party forward with a small infantry escort and the target was successfully engaged. During the move forward the party was engaged by enemy MG and artillery fire but due to Bdr Pugh's [...] and determination the [...] OP was found and occupied. This NCO has shown outstanding courage and ability during the whole of the operations in [...] and the western desert.
(L.G. 8.7.41)

Pugh, Peter John, Sergeant (actg.)
5949801, Gloucestershire Regt.
For Korea *(L.G. 8.12.53)*

Pun, Birbahadur, Rifleman (local Lance Corporal)
21148065, 2nd King Edward VII's Own Gurkha Rifles (Sirmoor Rifles)
On 2nd August 1965, Lance Corporal Birbahadur Pun, Support Company, 2/2nd Gurkha Rifles took part in an ambush operation near the Sarawak—Indonesian border. Lance Corporal Birbahadur was a general purpose machine gun gunner and also the left flank man of his ambush group. The ambushers were lying in the thick alluvial mud beside a track and had been in position for two days. Eight Indonesian soldiers appeared on the track moving from right to left of the ambush. Lance Corporal Birbahadur allowed the enemy to approach to within ten feet of his position. He then opened fire and in the space of a few seconds had accounted for all the enemy. His high standard of camouflage and his expert marksmanship were the factors which contributed most of the completely successful outcome of this operation.

On 2nd September 1965, Lance Corporal Birbahadur accompanied his company on another ambush operation in the same general area as before. On this occasion a stream was being ambushed and he was Section 2nd in Command with a flank protection group. The Indonesians came along a parallel track in company strength, not less than 100 strong, towards Lance Corporal Birbahadur's position. Once fire had been opened by our troops, the enemy assaulted boldly under cover of heavy machine-gun fire in an attempt to overrun the position. At this stage, on his own initiative, he detonated a Claymore mine which threw 2 enemy light machine-gunners, who were supporting the attack, into the stream, killing them instantly. In addition, the mine wounded numerous other enemy soldiers. In spite of this set-back, the Indonesians continued to press home their assault. Determined to stem the enemy's rush, Lance Corporal Birgbahadur leapt to his feet and, regardless of his own safety, hurled M.26 grenades at and sprayed the charging enemy groups with his small machine gun, killing or wounding many Indonesians. At one stage, when his light machine-gun gunner was changing magazines, the enemy made a rush to capture the gun. Whereupon, this courageous young Non Commissionbed Officer dashed forward, firing his small machine gun and broke up the enemy attack with further casualties, thus saving his light machine-gun and its gunner.

In the second action his bravery and audacity, his fearless conduct in the face of exceptionally heavy fire against overwhelming odds contributed very largely to the successful outcome of the battle. *[From L.G.]*
(L.G. 24.5.66)

Pun, Mangahadur, Colour Sergeant (actg.)
21132119, 2nd King Edward VII's Own Gurkha Rifles
No citation.   *(L.G. 28.5.57)*

Purdon, Arthur Henry Jason, Warrant Officer Cl. I
NX.67447, 2/30 Bn., Australian Military Forces
  (Immediate)
During AIF operations in Malaya, the 2/30 Bn AIF was attacked on 16 Jan 42 in the area of Gemas by an overwhelming enemy force in a number of positions. In these withdrawal operations, WO Purdon RQMS 2/30 Bn was the last person to leave the battlefield. He remained behind to ensure the evacuation of wounded. He showed exceptional gallantry by repeatedly assisting wounded personnel while subject to heavy small arms and mortar fire from enemy in close contact at short range.

WO Purdon consistently distinguished himself by his courage in taking ration parties forward daily despite severe bombing and shelling and he always succeeded in getting through to the most forward troops. At all times during the whole of the operations in which his unit participated WO Purdon showed exceptional courage and devotion to duty under heavy enemy fire. *(L.G. 1.8.46)*

Purdon, Reginald Keith, Lance Corporal
1165, [...] N.M.R., South African Forces
For highly distinguished services in action.
During the fighting at Dadaba on 13 May 41, L/Cpl. Purdon with great determination and personal courage led his section against an enemy arty battery which was engaging him over open sights. Killing or capturing the bulk of the gun teams he took all the guns of the battery. Carrying on, his section took several M.G. posts at the point of the bayonet. His devotion to duty and gallant leadership did much to break the spirit of the defenders.
(L.G. 21.10.41)

Purvis, Joseph, Fusilier
4270748, 7 Bn. Royal Northumberland Fusiliers
Following his capture at St. Valery-en-Caux on 12 June 40, Purvis was transferred to Germany, where he was imprisoned at Stalag XX C, Stalag IX C and subsidiary working camps. When employed in salt mines at Volkerode during Sep 41, he made his first attempt to escape; with one companion he emerged from a mine-shaft, collected their hidden store of food from the baths, climbed through a window and over the fence. Although after three days' freedom his companion was compelled through illness to give himself up, Purvis continued alone towards Switzerland. On the tenth day of his solitary journey, he was discovered by a hunting party and handed over to the authorities.

Transferred to Merkers in Dec 42, he participated in a mass break-out but was recaptured within fortyeight hours. At the beginning of Feb. 43, Purvis planned an escape with another prisoner employed nearby. On 29 April 43 the details were complete, and, whilst two other prisoners attracted the guard's attention, Purvis climbed the 12' wire fence. In anticipation of being joined by his companion, he remained in the locality for three days, but on 2 May he hid in a waggon and covered himself with salt. Half an hour later the truck was sealed. After travelling thus no less than five days Purvis heard both French and German spoken, and getting out he discovered that he had reached Switzerland.

For fourteen months he remained there before he was evacuated to France. When the arrangements for the remainder of the journey broke down he was compelled to join the Maquis. Before reporting to a British officer at Decize on 30 Sep 44, he took part in four battles against the Germans in the area South West of Toulouse.

This solo escape into Switzerland by a private soldier was a first-class performance.   *(L.G. 26.7.45)*

Q

Quaife, Walter, Sergeant (A/W.O.II (C.S.M.))
*5344959, 10th Bn The Royal Berkshire Regt.
(Dorking) (Immediate)*

In the operations involved to supply his Coy in the La Cogna Wadi, Sjt. Quaife shewed the most conspicuous gallantry in his capacity as A/CQMS. On the night 25 Feb 44, he was in charge of his Coy's supply vehicles. On being informed that the route was clear, the column proceeded to move up: meanwhile the enemy counter-attacked in strength and recaptured the house which commanded the supply route. As the house was approached, the enemy opened fire and attacked the column. Fierce hand to hand fighting ensued, in which two vehicles were immobilised and several of our men hit. Sjt. Quaife, quickly taking stock of the situation, shouted to the drivers to turn their vehicles round; then, without thought of personal danger, he ran towards the enemy and engaged them with his TSMG, in the first surprise knocking out the MG, killing one and wounding two of its team. He remained in position engaging the enemy to the left, and then when his vehicles had turned round led them back. It was undoubtedly owing to his prompt action and selfless courage that the vehicles and supplies were prevented from falling into enemy hands.

The following night it was decided in any event to dump the supplies near the house, so that they could be secured by a fighting patrol, should the enemy still be in possession. On arrival Sjt. Quaife went forward himself with one man to discover if the house was in our hands. As he approached a group of Germans sprang for him. He forced himself free and jumped into a ditch, and opened fire with his TSMG. He ordered the man with him to return to the vehicles and tell them to go back without him, when all the supplies were dumped. He himself with the greatest selfless courage remained by the house, firing at the enemy with intent to draw attention to himself, to allow the supplies to be dumped and the vehicles to get away. Only when satisfied that this was done, did he move back himself alone on foot.

On these occasions, which are typical of his conduct throughout the recent fighting, Sjt. Quaife shewed a constant undauntable courage, and complete willingness to sacrifice himself to further the success of the object in hand. *(L.G. 15.6.44)*

Quill, Ernest Jack, Corporal
6847254, 1st Bn King's Royal Rifle Corps (London, E.18) (Immediate)

For outstanding courage and determination in assuming the duties of Platoon Commander after being wounded. On 1 Jan 45, Cpl. Quill's Pl was holding a posn in and around a house at MR 482462 Italy 1:25,000 89 III NW. Cpl. Quill's section was responsible for a bren posn in the farmyard. At about 0300 hrs the area was mortared, the listening post driven in and the posn surrounded by a strong enemy raiding party. Cpl. Quill was badly wounded in the shoulder by a spandau bullet but continued firing his bren gun with the utmost determination and prevented any enemy entering his sector. However the outside posts on another flank were neutralised and enemy entered the farm yard and bazooked the house, which collapsed except for a small part of the ground floor. All the posts in the house ceased firing and it was clear that unless they could be brought into action again the whole posn would be over-run with the possible exception of Cpl. Quill's gun post. The only way in was across the open farm yard, which was brightly lit by burning haystacks, and through the door, which was under constant fire. Cpl. Quill entered the building, where he found that the Pl Comd, Pl Sjt. and several Riflemen were wounded, one section Comd and two Riflemen were missing, Cpl. Baptist and the few Riflemen still in action were dazed and injured by debris, most of the weapons and amn were damaged or buried under debris. Helped by Cpl. Baptist he rallied the Pl and organised the fire posns and treatment of the wounded. As soon as the posn in the house had been restored he again crossed the open yard with one Rfn to occupy an outside post, from which he enaged the enemy until they withdrew. After a relieving force and arrived, Cpl. Quill completed the re-organisation of his Pl and stayed at his post until ordered back to the RAP by an officer, when the full severity of his wound was discovered. This NCO's fighting spirit and self sacrifice were a magnificent example to his Pl. His courage and initiative saved a very ugly situation. *(L.G. 21.6.45)*

R

Rackham, Hugh Arthur, Sergeant
5774879, 4th Bn Royal Norfolk Regt. (Wymondham, Norfolk)
This NCO was acting 2nd i/c carrier Pl from the start of the action along the Bukit Timah in Feb 42, and was prominent in several minor skirmishes with the enemy, and took command of the Pl when the officer was killed. On 13th Feb the enemy made a determined attack on the Bukit-Adam Rd cross roads supported by mortar and shell fire and the unit astride this cross roads started to give way. Sjt. Rackham immediately took the carrier Pl to the area being attacked and put them in position to fire up the main road, and in spite of being wounded in the back by shrapnel in the early stages, he continued to fire himself and encouraged his Pl to keep firing for over an hour until the attack was repulsed. It was entirely due to this NCO's bravery, initiative and devotion to duty that the attack on this point was repulsed and the line kept intact. He was evacuated to hospital and had the shrapnel removed but refused to stay and returned to his unit to render what assistance he was able.
(L.G. 13.12.45)

Radcliffe, Edward John, Warrant Officer Cl. II
4269977, Royal Northumberland Fusiliers
For Korea   *(L.G. 10.7.51)*

Rae, Colin David, Sergeant
68074, 21 NZ Bn. (Immediate)
On the 5th of April 1945 Sjt. Rae volunteered to take a party to clear a strong enemy post between the railway and the Senio stopbank. It was essential to the success of the assault across the Senio that the position be taken as it entirely dominated D Coy's positions and made it impossible to continue with the necessary preparations. It was due mainly to the dash and determination of Sjt. Rae that, inspite of Schu mines the post was taken and new positions dug in under continuous bazooka, mortar and grenade fire. Again on the 9th of April, Sjt. Rae led his men with outstanding ability in the assault across the Senio, playing an important part in the mopping up of the enemy positions and when later his Pl Comd was wounded, he led the platoon with initiative and skill. Sjt. Rae's courage and leadership is of the highest order.
(L.G. 18.10.45)

Rai, Birbahadur, Rifleman
22145085, 10th Princess Mary's Own Gurkha Rifles
For Malaya   *(L.G. 7.5.54)*

Rai, Dhanbahadur, Corporal
21141660, 10th Gurkha Rifles
For Malaya   *(L.G. 15.5.51)*

Rai, Hardam, Sjt
21141359, 10th Princess Mary's Own Gurkha Rifles
For Malaya   *(L.G. &.8.51)*

Rai, Hindupal, Rifleman (Local Lance Corporal)
21140375, 10th Princess Mary's Own Gurkha Rifles
On 25th March 1966, Lance Corporal Hindupal Rai was commanding a section of 10 Platoon D Company 1st Battalion 10th Princess Mary's Own Gurkha Rifles near the Sarawak border covering a complex of tracks to prevent the withdrawal of an enemy incursion party. Visibility was about three to ten yards.

At 1030 hours, approximately 25 regular Indonesian troops approached 10 Platoon's position, seven of them passing Lance Corporal Hindupal's post from right to left at a range of three yards. Coolly he allowed them to pass towards platoon Headquarters and a general purpose machine gun on his left. As the machine gun opened fire Lance Corporal Hindupal and his rifle group engaged three enemy to their front killing two. Within second, two more enemy advanced towards Lance Corporal Hindupal's position firing bursts. He shot them both dead at point blank range. Heavy automatic fire was now directed towards Lance Corporal Hindupal's section and a fierce fire fight ensued. By shouted fire orders, personal example and by crawling to the various groups of his section Lance Corporal Hindupal was able to prevent the enemy's approach to the platoon position from along the main track. The order was then given to break off the engagement. He ordered his light machine gun group to move first while he covered them. The sound of this movement attracted further well-directed automatic fire which wounded the light machine gun Number 1. Lance Corporal Hindupal at once engaged the enemy, silencing them temporarily and continued to cover the withdrawal of the light machine gun party. Now ordering the rifle group to withdraw, first one and then a second Rifleman were killed within a few yards of him as they moved to the rear. He again took on the enemy single handed and so ensured the safe withdrawal of the remainder of his men. He was the last man to leave the position and was in the act of changing his magazine when an enemy advanced towards him firing an automatic weapon. Lance Corporal Hindupal shot him dead at two yards' range.

He now withdrew to the Company rendezvous, and reported that since he had been forced to leave two of his dead in the ambush position while extricating the rest of the section, he wanted to go back to get them. In spite of the now confused situation and continued enemy fire aimed at the ambush area, he personally led two sections of his platoon back to his post to recover the bodies. It seemed at the time, and in retrospect still does, that this act called for the greatest courage of all.

In the action 13 enemy were killed; D Company lost 4 killed and two wounded. Lance Corporal Hindupal personally killed 5 enemy and dominated the action on the right flank of his platoon. His leadership, control, personal example, coolness and, above all, his courage throughout a fierce engagement at point blank range were outstanding. *[From L.G.]*   *(L.G. 13.12.66)*

Rai, Jasbahadur, Corporal
21145403, 2nd Bn., 7th Gurkha Rifles
For Malaya   *(L.G. 1.9.50)*

Rai, Pancnaraj, A/Sergeant
21139042, 7th Gurkha Rifles
For Malaya   *(L.G. 19.10.51)*

Rai, Purnabahadur, Sergeant
21146867, 7th Gurkha Rifles, Brigade of Gurkhas
For Malaya   *(L.G. 20.6.50)*

Rai, Rabibahadur, Sergeant
21141438, 10th Princess Mary's Own Gurkha Rifles
For Malaya   *(L.G. 27.4.51)*

Rai, Rabilal, Lance Corporal (actg.)
21144926, 7th Gurkha Rifles
For Malaya   *(L.G. 24.4.53)*

Rai, Ramsur, Sergeant
21134202, 6th Gurkha Rifles
No citation.   *(L.G. 10.1.56)*

Rai, Sherbahadur, Lance Corporal
21146023, 1/10 Princess Mary's Own Gurkha Rifles
For Malaya   *(L.G. 16.5.50)*

Rai, Tulbahadur, Warrant Officer Cl. II
21145402, 7th Gurkha Rifles
No citation.   *(L.G. 8.5.56)*

Raistrick, Sam, Corporal
7886103, 44th Bn. Royal Tank Regt. (Doncaster)
At Tel El Eisa on 17th July Cpl. Raistrick was the driver of one of three tanks ordered to carry out a recce towards the Quatara Road. His tank came under very heavy fire from A/Tank guns and was knocked out and set on fire.

Cpl. Raistrick was seriously wounded in the lower left leg which was practically severed and has since been amputated. He struggled out of the driving compartment of his Valentine Tank on to the turret where he remained in spite of his very severe injury, until he had helped the Commander and the gunner out of their seats in the turret of the burning tank and on to the ground. The Commander had both legs practically severed and the gunners clothes were on fire. Cpl. Raistrick did his best to beat out the flames. Before a tank rescue party could be organized and moved, under cover of smoke, through intense fire, the gunner died. The Commander died a

few minutes after the arrival of the party. Cpl. Raistrick's heroic action took place under continuous heavy shell and machine gun fire, which was directed at the tank. But for his magnificent courage and his complete disregard for his own life, the gunner and Commander must have been burnt to death in the tank.
                                            (L.G. 15.10.42)

Rakena, Pou, Corporal
801845, 28 NZ (Maori) Bn. (Immediate)
During the crossing of the Senio River on the night 9 April 1945, Cpl. Rakena's platoon sjt was mortally wounded. Being the senior section leader he took over the platoon. The platoon came under very intense small arms fire. With complete disregard for his own personal safety he charged two enemy spandau posts single handed killing the entire crews. The remaining spandau posts surrendered. After having rallied his men the enemy began to bazooka them. Displaying outstanding courage Cpl. Rakena went forward firing his bren gun from the hip, capturing the bazooka and killing the crew. This opposition having been eliminated the whole coy advanced. During the whole advance to Massa Lombarda this NCO showed courage of the highest order and was a constant source of inspiration to his coy. The success of his coy was due in no small measure to his initiative and superb leadership.   *(L.G. 18.10.45)*

Rana, Balbahadur, Corporal (actg.)
21132235, 2nd Gurkha Rifles
No citation.   *(L.G. 8.5.56)*

Randall, Donald Charles, Lance Sergeant
2929382, Queen's Own Cameron Highlanders, No. 2
Commando (Halewood, Liverpool)
On 28th March, 1942, during the Commando Raid at St. Nazaire, France, Sgt Randall was a member of an assault force commanded by Capt Roy. The second in command of this force was wounded in the leg and unable to land, and Sgt Randall, showing great initiative immediately took charge of the section and led it to its objective. On arriving at the objective both his section and the remainder of the force were seriously depleted owing to wounds and it was found impossible to carry out the written orders. Realising this, Capt Roy immediately called for a volunteer to assist him to destroy two gun positions which were on top of the pumping station some 20-feet high at the top of a two-storey building. Sgt Randall immediately volunteered. With Capt Roy, in the face of heavy plunging fire, he reached the top of the building with a scaling ladder and with amazing coolness forced the enemy gun crew to withdraw and placed the charge on the guns and brought about their total destruction.

On completion of this task, Sgt Randall went straight to the bridge where he took up a position without cover with an LMG, and, with total disregard for his own safety, gave covering fire to the remainder of the force which had to cross the bridge.

Throughout the whole action this NCO's individual bravery and total disregard of his own personal danger was an example to all and worthy of the highest traditions of the British Army. His cool courage is worthy of high recognition.
Chevalier of the Legion of Honour (French), award dated 1.3.49, approved 16.7.53 *(L.G. 5.7.45)*

Ranford, Robert Frank Gordon, Sergeant
SX 7410, 2/48 Aust Inf Bn. (Immediate)
For leadership and great determination in destroying enemy posts holding up the advance of his Coy during a Bn night attack.

On the night 30/31 Oct 1942 South East of Sidi Abd El Rahman during an attack several thousand yards behind the enemy lines, Sjt. Ranford took command of his Pl when his Pl Comd was wounded and silenced an enemy post which was holding up the Coy advance. Sjt. Ranford's Pl was then subjected to intense fire from a nearby 88 mm gun and machine guns. With great initiative and dash he organised his Pl and stormed the enemy posts killing 14 enemy and destroying the 88 mm gun and two machine guns.

Sjt. Ranford was badly wounded during this attack but he gallantly continued to lead his Pl, now reduced to seven men, forward to continue the advance. Later his Coy was again held up and Sjt. Ranford immediately went forward to clear the opposition to allow his coy to continue when he was again badly wounded and evacuated. Sjt. Ranford throughout the whole operation showed great personal courage and initiative. His determined leadership in the face of heavy oppostion destroyed the enemy in several posts and allowed his Coy to continue the advance. These fine qualities were a great inspiration to his men and despite their small numbers they fought successfully, almost yard by yard, against a well dug in and larger enemy force.
M.I.D. 30.12.41 and 8.3.45 *(L.G. 11.2.43)*

Rankin, Donald Colin, Corporal
NX 2613, 2/1 Aust Inf Bn.
On 4 Jan 41 several enemy posts had surrendered during early stages of 2/1 Bn attack on centre of Bardia defences. 8 Pl, 'A' Coy, of which Cpl. Rankin is a member was depleted by detachment of prisoner escorts. On approaching heavily defended sangars at about point 51434002 (ref map Bardia 1/50,000) and when the pl was 150 yards from the Sangar, the enemy opened fire with light artillery and small arms.

The enemy was at least 5 to 1 and under cover, whilst 8 pl was in the open. Cpl. Rankin showing no regard for his personal safety, charged the right of the post, followed by the remaining three men of his section, and set up his L.M.G. on the enemy side of the sangar wall thus taking the enemy post in enfilade and silencing the light artillery. The post then surrendered to the Pl. It is thought that by

his action and example Cpl. Rankin saved serious casualties to his Coy. *(L.G. 9.5.41)*

Ransfield, David P[...], Lance Corporal
40532, Royal New Zealand Infantry Regt.
For Vietnam *(L.G. 29.8.69)*

Raphael, Lance Corporal
7632, 2nd Bn. The King's African Rifles,
Somaliland. For conspicuous and continuous gallantry in the face of the enemy in the Marko Pass Area from 11th–15th August, 1940. This young NCO displayed remarkable qualities of coolness and devotion to duty, while firing his Bren Gun inflicting heavy casualties on the enemy. On the 12th August when his platoon was forced to withdraw he returned to his gun position with an Askari to retreive a box of Bren Gun magazines left behind by his section.
To be dated 11.2.41 and substituted for the award of the African D.C.M. announced in the L.G. of that date.
(L.G. 21.7.42)

Rapps, Leonard, M.M., Lance Corporal
4625825, 1 West Yorkshire Regt. (Bridgend, Glam.)
(Periodic)
From the time the company was sent off to Richmond Park and Victory Bastion during the Tonzang action on the Tiddim Road, this NCO time and time again showed dash and courage of the highest order. The climax was reached at M.S. 103 area on 28 Mar 44 where his coy was ordered to capture an enemy occupied feature. After this feature was captured the coy was ordered to take the 5805 feature to reach which the coy had to go through dense jungle in rapidly fading light and subsequently in the dark. It was known that at least one enemy company occupied the saddle between the first and second objectives and the coy had to move extended and L/Cpl. Rapps was in the front ranks of the leading platoon. He moved well ahead of his platoon and as was expected ran straight into an enemy fixed line. Although seriously wounded he engaged the enemy at very close range and succeeded in killing two of them whilst he also enabled his platoon to move back from a very difficult position to a previously arranged R.V. L/Cpl. Rapps then crawled back and most certainly by his action saved what may well have been very heavy casualties.
M.M. 30.6.42 *(L.G. 8.2.45)*

Rattew, Ronald Frederick, Lance Sergeant
5729787, 2/7th Bn. Queen's Royal Regt. (Rhondda)
(Immediate)
On 3rd March 1945 Cpl. Rattew was a section leader of 'D' Coy on 2/7 Queen's attack to clear the enemy from the East side of the flood bank of the River Senio.

During the Coys advance through very heavy mortar and shell fire all Cpl. Rattew's section became casualties, but he continued alone to his objective. On arrival at the Pl objective without waiting for orders he was immediately active assisting the Platoon Commander to reorganise the platoon. He distributed ammunition and stores and un-deterred by steady and accurate enemy fire he continued to visit all posts encouraging and directing the men. He himself dug a pit for a wounded comrade before digging his own.

The very weak platoon held its position for six hours against determined and continuous attempts by the enemy, who held prepared positions on the far side of the same bank, to dislodge it. Throughout this period Cpl. Rattew was continuously in action inspiring his comrades by his own gallantry and cheerfulness.

When the platoon was eventually relieved Cpl. Rattew at once set about organising and delivering supplies to the forward platoons in face of intense enemy fire.

Throughout this action Cpl. Rattew displayed a magnificent fighting spirit, very great initiative and powers of leadership far above those of a junior NCO. His outstanding personal example and gallantry inspired his comrades and undoubtedly had a decisive effect on the success of the action.   *(L.G. 5.7.45)*

Rattigan, Michael, Lance Corporal (A/Cpl.)
23738257, Royal Green Jackets
For Northen Ireland   *(L.G. 24.7.73)*

Raw, Joseph Dennis, Corporal
4274, 1 Royal Natal Carbineers (Immediate)
For conspicuous gallantry in action at Combolcia Pass on 22 April 41. After an MG Post had been silenced, two other MGs opened fire. Cpl. Raw attempted to dislodge the gun crews with bombs, and when this failed, he stalked the positions and shot the crews. This action saved his company many casualties.   *(L.G. 21.10.41)*

Rawcliffe, William, Sergeant
2706856, 5th Bn King's Own Royal Regt.
During the action at Bourghelles, on 27th May, Sjt. Rawcliffe led his section of Carriers with great gallantry through the village which was then occupied by the enemy and was thus largely instrumental in checking the enemy advance. Later that day, by holding out with his section in the village of Cysoing, in spite of heavy shelling, he effectively covered the withdrawal of the remainder of the rear guard which was otherwise in danger of being outflanked. At all times this NCO has shown exceptional coolness, leadership and personal bravery.
M.I.D. 20.12.40   *(L.G. 22.10.40)*

Rawling, George Ernest, Sergeant
6201202, 2nd Bn The Middlesex Regt. (York)
Sjt. Rawling was Pl. Sjt. of a M.G. Pl. which landed on D Day—June 6th, 1944. The task of his Pl. was to protect the right flank of the KSLI during their attack towards Baen. In order to carry out this role, the Pl. took up an isolated posn on the right and were at once subjected to extremely heavy Arty and M.G. fire, which killed the Pl

Comd. and his Rangetaker. Sjt. Rawling took over Comd. of the Pl. and successfully supported an attack by a Coy. of the KSLI on a Lt Gun Bty which was holding up their advance. He then moved the Pl. fwd on the right flank of the foremost Inf localities around Bievielle. From this posn the Pl., under Sjt. Rawling's direction, engaged an enemy M.G. posn which was firing on the KSLI, killed 10 of the Gun numbers—the remaining one man coming fwd to surrender. The following morning the Pl. were continually sniped from a chateau to their left rear. Sjt. Rawling, taking with him a Cpl. and one O.R. made his way to the chateau entered the building from the rear, personally killed three German soldiers, and threw grenades into the cellar. While withdrawing a stick grenade was thrown at Sjt. Rawling's party from an outhouse and he was wounded in the back. Though in great pain he insisted on being carried back to the Pl. where he appointed his successor, ensured that Gun pits were properly dug and camouflaged and that all ranks realised that the posn was to be held to the last round and to the last man. Only then did Sjt. Rawling allow himself to be evacuated. His example was, and remains, an inspiration to his men.   *(L.G. 31.8.44)*

Rawlins, Lawrence John, Sergeant
5496658, 8th Bn The Gold Coast Regt & Hampshire Regt. (Bitterne Park, Southampton)
At Chathang (Map Ref:— 928638 Burma 84 C/16) on the 15 Feb 1944 Sjt. J. Rawlins went to the assistance of an ambushed patrol that had suffered casualties including the European patrol leader who was lying in the paddy. On reaching the scene of the ambush Sjt. Rawlins and his section came under the same heavy enemy fire and suffered casualties. The seriously wounded patrol comd of the previous patrol was lying in the pen paddy and his every movement brought down searching enemy fire. The surrounding bush had been fired by the Japs and flames were sweeping across the paddy towards the wounded European. Regardless of his personal safety and thinking only of his wounded comrade, Sjt. Rawlins together with one African, Cpl. Mama Dagomba GC 22066 crossed the open paddy and carried the wounded European to safety.

Again at Palegaing (Map Ref:—930321 Burma 84 D/13) on the 2 Mar 1944 Sjt. Rawlins was taking part in a night patrol to an enemy posn. The patrol was ambushed and split, the Offr comd the patrol becoming cut off. Sjt. Rawlins assembled the patrol, then went alone in search of the offr. Clambering over the area, he was over-powered and disarmed by 3 Japs and escorted to their HQ. Taking the Jap Comd completely by surprise despite his escort with raised bayonets, he lashed out, kicked the Jap comd in the stomach and made his escape. That night he spent evading capture in the enemy posn and returned the following day able to give accurate and valuable information of the enemy posn and strength.

Sjt. Rawlins in both actions showed supreme courage devotion to duty and above all self sacrifice for the safety of his comrades. *(L.G. 8.2.45)*

Ray, Sidney, Warrant Officer Cl. II (C.S.M.)
6595888, 1st Bn. Highland Light Infantry
This W.O. was with his company when it came suddenly under heavy fire from enemy A.F.V.'s. The two officers in his sector were killed and he took command, showing a splendid example of coolness and leadership. In withdrawing from the position C.S.M. Ray displayed skill and resource in bringing his party intact to a rear position. *(L.G. 11.7.40)*

Raynor, Leslie, Lance Sergeant
2658372, 2nd Coldstream Guards (Swinton, Yorks.)
(Immediate)
Sidi Brahim 26 Apr 43.
On 26.4.43 this NCOs Pl came under very heavy machine gun and mortar fire from hills overlooking their position. After suffering casualties the Pl withdrew leaving L/Sjt. Raynor and his section behind. He showed great coolness and courage under very difficult circumstances and reorganised the defence of the area. He on several occasions went across open ground swept by fire to fetch ammunition. This NCO has repeatedly displayed great courage in action throughout the North African campaign, and has been an inspiration to all under his command. *(L.G. 23.9.43)*

Reace, George Arthur, Warrant Officer Cl. II
2881169, 14th London Regt. (London Scottish) (attd. S.S.T., Att. No. 9 Commando) (London, S.W.4)
(Immediate)
Ref: Maps Italy Sheets 13 and 19, Sqs (w) M55, 56, 65 & 66
In Operation Roast which took place from 1st–4th April 1945 the task of this unit was to carry out an opposed landing on the western side of the spit of land between Lake Comacchio and the Adriatic and destroy or capture all enemy troops and material in this area. This task was completed, resulting in the capture of 100 prisoners of war by the Commando Brigade and elimination of the entire enemy force in this area. The early part of this operation consisted of a most exhausting journey over Lake Comacchio in stormboats which had to be pushed or paddled most of the way due to engine breakdowns or shallowness of water. All craft had to be pushed approximately 2,000 yds before shore could be reached and everyone almost without exception was physically exhausted before the actual battle began.
Not only in this operation but in all previous actions in which this unit has taken part this WO has carried out his duties as a CSM most efficiently, conscientiously and courageously. During this particular operation his Troop HQ was, at many times, left in a very isolated position in completely open country and in enemy-held territory whilst sections were detached mopping up enemy strong points. At one stage when he and three men of his HQ were guarding approximately 80 prisoners of war the HQ was counter-attacked and stonked by a battery of enemy mortars. Not only did he retain his control over the prisoners of war but he also drove off the counter-attack with only two other men under his command. Had the counter-attack penetrated his position it would have resulted in his troop being split. His general coolness, skill and devotion to duty whilst advancing to the final objective resulted in a total bag for his troop of 100 prisoners of war which would have had to have been abandoned during the advance had he not kept his head at all times. Earlier in the operation the Troop HQ was heavily mortared and he was seriously wounded in the groin, but he continued to advance with his troop and did not report his injuries to his Troop Commander until the operation was completed as it would have entailed reorganization within the troop and possible failure in capturing the final enemy positions had the enemy been given time to reorganize. When he was finally ordered to be evacuated he refused to do so as there was no other NCO available to take over his duties and in great pain he continued throughout the operation for the next eight hours to assist his Troop Leader and to control another section when its officer became a casualty.
CSM Reace has at all times shown outstanding ability, bravery and courage. His utter disregard for safety and determination to complete all his duties has always been of the highest order.
M.I.D. 11.1.45 *(L.G. 5.7.45)*

Reay, Allan Hutchinson, Corporal
7904602, 3rd Bn. Royal Tank Regt. (Ashington)
At Aqaqqir on 29 Oct 42, Cpl. Reay, a tank gunner was, owing to casualties, appointed tank comd. His tank was detailed to carry out a very hazardous and most important special reconnaissance in the face of strong enemy opposition. In the execution of his task his light tank was opposed by a German Mk III Special operating under cover of at least six anti-tank guns. He attacked the German Tank and although his own tank was hit by both the enemy tank and anti-tank guns he continued to attack until he had destroyed the enemy tank. Though his own tank was crippled he cleverly avoided the hostile anti-tank guns and completed his task. Throughout the day he continued in his hazardous position of observation.
The boldness, initiative and skilful handling of this young NCO was an example to all and procured most important information which was urgently required by higher authority. *(L.G. 28.1.43)*

Redgrave, Ernest Albert, Private
QX 12408, 2/31 Aust Inf Bn. (Immediate)
Pte. Redgrave is a member of B coy and during the bns attack on Vardu on 10 Nov 42 his pl encountered heavy fire from two MG posts as a result of which three of his section became casualties. Pte. Redgrave ran fwd over open ground and silenced each enemy post with his

TSMG, thus allowing his pl to go fwd. In a further attack in morning of 11 Nov 42, his section leader became a casualty, and he took over control of the section. Shortly afterwards the Bren gunner was killed and Pte Redgrave ran over and operated the LMG directing his fire on an area strongly held by the enemy, thus interfering with their fire and enabling his pl to move fwd. Later that afternoon the Bn attacked enemy positions at Gorari with support of two coys of 2/1 Bn. The latter, and also HQ Coy of this Bn were pinned down by very heavy fire from many enemy poitions on the right flank.

Pte Redgrave charged one of these positions with his TSMG, killed four enemy, wounded others, disorganised the defence and enabled the attack to proceed to a successful conclusion. By his complete indifference to his own personal safety, his initiative, and quick grasp of the situation, he has been a source of inspiring leadership to his fellow men.   *(L.G. 22.4.43)*

Redican, Peter, Private
13030449, 5/7th Gordon Highlanders (Billingham-on-Tees) (Immediate)
In Lisieaux on 22 Aug 44, 'C' Coy, 5/7th Bn. The Gordon Highlanders were holding the line of a street. They were ordered to send forward a patrol to the line of the railway which was held by enemy S.S. troop. When the patrol had reached the objective, the enemy opened up at point blank range both with spandaus and with grenades. Under intense fire half the patrol managed to reach a ruin. The enemy fire then increased in violence and movement towards the objective seemed quite impossible.

At this stage, Pte. Redican, entirely on his own initiative, seized a bren gun and leapt into the open under a hail of enemy fire. Standing up completely exposed to the enemy he started firing at them from the hip, burst for burst. Very shortly he was hit in both legs. He fell to the ground but again seizing his bren, he reloaded and continued firing although seriously wounded and in great pain.

This great act of gallantry drew the attention of the enemy on him and him alone. Taking advantage of it, the remainder of the patrol moved to a flank and neutralised the enemy's fire. Pte. Redican's heroism and utter contempt for death could not have been surpassed and undoubtedly saved the lives of his comrades.
          (L.G. 21.12.44)

Redington, Reginald Victor Gordon, Gunner
893567, Royal Artillery (10, Cameron Road, W. Croydon)
No citation.   *(L.G. 23.1.42)*

Redpath, Ernest, Warrant Officer Cl. II (B.S.M.)
721558, 74th Field Regt., Royal Artillery (South Shields) (Immediate)
At Mrassas on 15 June 42 when his Troop was engaging Tanks BSM Redpath showed great coolness under fire, and by his efforts prevented much valuable equipment from falling into enemy hands. He not only directed the fire of one gun for some time but also helped to man another with his Tp comdr till it was knocked out and the Tp Comdr wounded. After carrying the latter back under heavy fire from Tanks he collected and saw to the evacuation of other wounded, mobilised men and vehicles to withdraw the guns out of action and saw them safely across a shell-swept wadi. He recrossed the wadi to help in saving equipment from a damaged truck and from a gun whose tractor had been set on fire. He finally saw that all abandoned vehicles were destroyed before he left the position.   *(L.G. 24.9.42)*

Redpath, John Alexander, Sergeant
30836, 19 Army Troops Company, New Zealand Military Forces (Immediate)
Sjt. Redpath was captured by the enemy during the operations in Crete, and escaped soon ater capture from a prison camp in the neighbourhood of Canea. With a few companions he made his way first to the area of Suia (South West Crete) but being unable to find any craft there and encountering small German patrols they took to the hills. Here they heard of a clandestine organisation for the repatriation of Cretans operating through the Northern tip of Cape Spathia Peninsula, and therefore made their way to that area.

From Crete, Sjt. Redpath and his comrades managed to get across to the area of Cape Mallea, (South East Peloponnese), arriving there early in August. They were unable to make arrangements for their escape from here and hid in the hills in this area. During their stay here they were joined by other Imperial Service personnel, who had succeeded in escaping from prison camps in Crete, and who had made their way to the South East Peloponnese. Finally a party of seventeen men had collected there. This party was organised and led by Sjt. Redpath and it is mainly due to his powers of leadership and their initiative that they were able to survive.

While Sjt. Redpath was hiding in the South East Peloponnese he tried by every means possible to obtain a boat in which to sail, with his party, to British territory. He was unable to find any suitable boat until Mid-October, when a Greek caique, carrying a cargo of figs, put in to the coast in that area. Seizing the opportunity, Sjt. Redpath and his party forced the crew of this boat to take them on board, after all peaceable means had proved ineffective. Once on board, the Greeks proved unwilling to carry out the orders of Sjt. Redpath, so he took over the command of the boat, sailed and navigated her himself, and brought the party safely to the coast of North Africa. During this voyage the caique at first flew the German flag until bombed by a British Blenheim aircraft. They were three times attacked by enemy aircraft and machine-gunned.

On arriving at G.H.Q., Sjt. Redpath at once volunteered to return to Greece in order to help in the organisation of escapes for further Imperial Service personnel still in hiding in the Southern Peloponnese.

His previous experience as an escaper and his foresight in making careful and detailed note of the location and situation of Imperial personnel there, have made him a most useful organiser. This, coupled with his powers of leadership, courage and initiative, single him out above others and a number of successful escapes are the result of his work.

M.M. 4.5.44 *(L.G. 26.3.42)*

Reed, William Gerald, WO
Aus.402479, Royal Australian Air Force, 460 Sqn.
Bomber Command, RAF

I was a member of the crew of a Wellington aircraft which left Breighton on 2 July 42 at about 2315 hrs to bomb Bremen. We reached the target and bombed it, but on the return journey were hit by Flak. After an unsuccessful attempt to right the aircraft the pilot gave us orders to bale out about 0235 hrs.

I landed in a clearing in a wood with a dislocated shoulder. I remained where I was and attempted unsuccessfully for about four hours to reduce the dislocation. I destroyed my parachute and buried my harness under a bush. I then approached a farmhouse to ask for help. I said 'Dutch?' and they said, 'Ja, Deutsch.' I took this as confirmation that I was in Holland and asked if they would bring a Dutch doctor, instead of which they apparently rang up the police, as a Corporal of civil police and a Bergermeister came and took me prisoner. I was compelled to show them where my harness was, and was made to walk one and a half miles, in spite of my dislocated shoulder, accompanied by one policeman, whilst the others travelled in a car.

The Germans took the harness. I was then taken in the car to the Burgermeister's office in a small village (name not known), where they attempted to interrogate me. I was then taken to an aerodrome, where I was well-treated by the German Hauptmann M.O., who gave me gas and reduced the dislocation, and then taken back to the Burgermeister's office, where I found Radke and Wyllie. Wyllie had a strained back, and Radke a sprained ankle. We were all three taken in a car by Luftwaffe M.Ps to a gaol in Rheine, abut 20 kms away. On arrival we heard about the fate of the remainder of our crew. We stayed at Rheine one night and were taken next day by two Luftwaffe M.Ps to Dulag Luft by train.

I was in solitary confinement for about five days, and the usual attempts were made at interrogation, the usual Red Cross forms being presented. I was eventually moved into the main camp at Dulag Luft, where we were kept for about 14 days, and then moved to Stalag VIII B (Lamsdorf) arriving there on 4 Aug 42. All R.A.F. personnel (at that time about 300) were kept in the 'Straf' compound.

2. First attempted escape

In Sep 42 a New Zealand rear-gunner (name not remembered), a Sergeant Pilot Smith, W., and I devised the following plan of escape. We had acquired a map of that sector, which was already in the camp, collected about 35 or 40 marks, a haversack of food (supplied by ourselves and the M.O.) and two compasses. I had remodelled my Australian battle dress to look like a skiing jacket, and Smith had some overalls. The New Zealand rear-gunner was to go through with us through the two sets of double wire to the outside wire, and return with the cutters.

We were to cut our way through two strands of wire, enter a disused compound, cut a further two strands of wire and, if all went well, make our way to Brieg (sheet 105, 6335), steal bicycles, or get on a goods train to Breslau, there try to steal an aircraft from an aerodrome of which I knew, and, failing this, take the train to Stettin.

At certain times sentries stopped patrolling and were then, as we thought, sent off duty. On 20 Sep 42 we cut our way through the double wire and crossed the disused compound, but before we had a chance to get through and cut the final wire the sentry in a sunken observation post spotted us and opened fire with a rifle. The alarm started to ring, searchlights came on, and we had to go back. The holes in the wire were discovered the following day, but we managed to secrete our escape kit. The Germans never identified us as the two who had made the attempt.

Shortly after this attempt the chaining of Ps/W took place, ad it was impossible to attempt to escape.

3. Second attempted escape:

About the end of Mar 43 I approached an Army Private with the suggestion that he should change identities with me so as to enable me to get into a working party with a view to escaping. This was Harold Bagshaw, R.E. P/W No. 133884. I had also met a Viennese boy called Egon Blumenthal, who was impersonating an Australian R.A.F. Sergeant called Hayes.

I wanted to take Blumenthal with me in my escape to facilitate travelling, and had to find someone to take Blumenthal's place as Hayes. I found a New Zealander called Sutton who was willing to take the risk. We then changed identities. I became Bagshaw. Blumenthal, posing as Hayes, changed identity with Sutton.

Blumenthal and I, now as Sutton and Bagshaw, were then sent out in a working party at a quarry about 15 kms East of Neurode (Sheet 116/6393/5606). This was 10 Apr 43. Blumenthal had been getting friendly with a German sentry with a view to acqiring train time-tables and money. On 17 Apr Blumenthal heard that he was to be moved next morning back to the Stalag, becuase his triple change of identities had been discovered. It was, therefore, essential that we should make our attempt that night, although we were still unprepared. I wore R.A.A.F. pants with a civilian sweater, and Blumenthal wore R.A.F. pants with an R.A.F. sweater. We had smuggled these clothes out of the Stalag.

We managed, with the help of two others, to wrench some bars and frame complete from a back window of the billet under cover of an improvised band concert. We went to the quarry, broke into the place where the civilian working clothes were kept, and stole coats. We moved on foot, crossing the Czech border twice, and eventually, on 19 Apr, reached Glatz (Sheet 116/0490) where we got a train to Breslau. We had papers (blank forms, but owing to the haste in getting away we had not filled them in. We borrowed a pen from a man in the waiting hall in Breslau and Blumenthal filled in the papers. They were scrutinised in the station by a civilian policeman and passed muster. We proceeded by train to Frankfurt-an-der-Oder, where we had to spend two hours in the station. A severe Gestapo check took place here, but through the extreme skill of Blumenthal, who was almost insolent to the Gestapo scrutinisers on the occasion of two separate checks, the situation was saved.

We reached Eberswalde (Sheet 52/2056) on 20 Apr where we changed on to the Berlin—Stettin express. We reached Stettin station at about 1015 hrs. Here I left Blumenthal and looked for an exit, about which I had heard. I found it and we passed through it, a small exit at the back, and found ourselves in the streets of Stettin.

We made our way to the Bollwerk, where we studied a map of the town. We had something to eat, went to a cinema, and then went to the Kleinoder Strasse, where we tackled a Swede and told him who we were, but he refused to help us. We then caught a tram at the Baum Brucke for Gotzlow (suburb of Stettin) and slept in the shrubbery just North of Gotzlow. That night (20 Apr) there was a severe air raid.

We went back in the morning by ferry boat to the Baum Brucke. After a shave and a walk round to inspect the raid damage, we went back to the wharf beyond Gotzlow and walked back behind the harbour towards Gotzlow, where we had seen two Swedish boats. I tackled a Frenchman, who offered to help, and we made an appointment to meet again at 2100 hrs. He turned up in French battle dress and showed us a way to get round the wire into the wharf. He said he would like to try to escape with us.

We boarded a boat, and the Frenchman, who did not think the captain would help, suggested that we should get into a life boat and go down to the engine room next day. Whilst we were asleep in the life boat a Swedish sailor lashed the canvas cover down so that we were imprisoned. We decided to try and conceal ourselves in the gear and were in the boat for three days, till the morning of 24 Apr, but when the German search took place we were discovered. We had to admit that we were P/W. I secreted my papers in the life boat, and Blumenthal managed to destroy his on the way to the Gestapo Headquarters.

We were kept here till 29 Apr, were very badly treated, and were then moved to a military prison. Here we met a Pte. O'Brien who had made an escape from Ratibor and been caught in a station control at Stettin.

We were all three taken back via Berlin a fact which proved to my advantage later, as I noted the Berlin underground stations, to the main camp, which we reached about 8 May 43. Here all the facts of the change of identities came to light, and we received 14 days' cells.

4. Third attempted escape:

For my third attempt I had planned to change identities with a Jew and be attached to a Jewish working party. In those supervision was very slack, and I also wished to be with Blumenthal. Blumenthal could then go out under his own name. At the gate Blumenthal was, however, stopped, owing to his two previous change of identities. I passed through as J. Minski, a Palestinian Private, with whom I had changed places.

We went to Gleiwitz (OST) (Sheet 118/4474) on 3 Jul 43 on railway work. After much effort, extending over three weeks, I eventually found a Jew who was willing to take the chance to escape with me. I needed him for his language knowledge for the journey to Stettin, in case of any hitch or difficulty. He was a Strasbourg Jew called Tiffenbrunner. I had clothes and all travelling necessities, and when Tiffenbrunner, who was about 6 ft. 2 ins. in height, had managed to get a suit, we escaped from the working place. We went into the hut in which tools, etc. were kept and came out, having assumed our disguises inside.

We walked to a tram connecting Gleiwitz and Hindenburg (Sheet 118/5475) (27 July), took the tram via Hindenburg to Beuthen (6680), where we caught the train to Breslau. We reached Breslau at about 1330 hrs, and after spending 12 hours in the town caught the midnight train to Berlin. We negotiated the underground stations, which I had memorised on my previous return under guard, and safely got the train to Stettin. We arrived about 1030 hrs on 28 Jul. We went through the usual procedure of trying to get into touch with Swedes, but all attempts failed. We then got into touch with some French workers, who took us to their Lager in the Finow Weg, where we got a pass to get into the Freibezirk harbour. After two or three ships turned out to be too small to hide in, we boarded a larger boat, but were ordered off by the first mate.

There was nothing for it but to return to Gotzlow as on the previous occasion. Tiffenbrunner became discouraged and did not want to take the risk of going round the wire, so I agreed to meet him next morning at 1100 hrs if my attempt was not successful. I boarded a boat, but found it was a Finnish one and was useless. I had to stay on the wharf all night, as loading was in process and the wharf was illuminated.

I met Tiffenbrunner next morning as arranged. He had intended to wait for an 'organisation boat' which was known to the French. We had hardly walked down the street, when we were accosted and arrested by a harbour patrol policeman. We discovered that the first mate who had turned us off his boat had sent in a police description of us.

After a great deal of trouble with the Gestapo, owing to my changed identities and to my having been caught with my papers on me, we were eventually returned to camp.

5. Escape:

In Jan 44 I decided to make another attempt to get away. All my attempts between Jan and Apr to join working parties were frustrated by my being recognised and turned back. I had met Pte. Toch, R.E. a Jew (S/P.G. (G) 2073) in Jan, and decided to take him with me in the same capacity as my previous companions. I grew a moustache, cut my hair very short, removed my false teeth, and managed to get out of the gate in a working party on 10 May as Pte. Elykim Wald. The party included Toch, and we were to work in a mine (at the Hohenzollern Grube) at Beuthen (Sheet 118/6680).

Our escape was held up for two months because of a Gestapo search following the shooting of two men, who had escaped. In this search our civilian clothes and money were found. I always carried my papers on my person, so that they were safe. I had to send to camp for cigarettes etc. to get sufficient money to buy more clothes.

On 11 Jul at about 0930 hrs Toch and I left our respective working places and changed our clothes in an underground tunnel. We walked into Beuthen, caught the tram to Kattowitz (7570). I had found it advisable on each occasion to go, at the beginning of the journey, in the opposite direction to that intended, and then double back on our own tracks.

We returned by train to Beuthen and then went through Gleiwitz to Breslau. We encountered a Gestapo check before reaching Breslau, but got through it successfully, although we had not got the 'special travelling pass for foreign workers.'

At Breslau we found there were no normal trains to Berlin owing to bomb damage, so we made our way by slow train via Frankfurt to Kustrin and then to Stettin. Stettin was hardly recognisable after a year's bombing.

After another unsuccessful trip to Kleinoder Strasse we met an Englishman and an Irishman (Spr. Johnson, S/P.G. (G) 2066) who were also attempting to escape. We fought shy of these, however, and I told Toch, after we had had a Gestapo check in a cheap eating house, that we must make an attempt that night, even if without help. We went by tram again to Gotzlow, waited till dark, went as previously round the wire, and boarded a Swedish boat. I put Toch into the engine room and went up to the quarters again, woke a man, and asked if he would help us. This man sent me to the forecastle, where the men suggested that we should hide ourselves. I returned to Toch in the engine room and about 10 minutes later a Swede (the third engineer) hailed us in English and said he would help us.

We concealed ourselves under the false bottom of the engine room and had to remain there for 10 hours. The boat sailed at about 0700 hrs on 15 Jul, and it was not till we had passed the second check at Swinemuende that we made our way out. About an hour later our friend showed up and took us to his cabin. Our presence was only known to two others.

We reached Trolleborg on the evening of 15 Jul and finally docked at Solesborg at Mid-day on 16 Jul. We were taken to the Consulate at Malmo in a taxi and eventually, having seen the police, were taken to Stockholm. *(L.G. 1.12.44)*

Rees, Philip, Lance Sergeant
3957743, 6th Bn. The Royal Scots Fusiliers (Llanelly)
On 5 November 1944 Corporal Rees commanded a section of the leading platoon of 'B' Company, 6th Battalion The Royal Scots Fusiliers in the attack on Schans. Soon after leaving the start line the tanks which were supporting the company ran into a mine field and were unable to proceed with the infantry. Corporal Rees however continued to advance with his section over very exposed and open ground which was being heavily shelled and mortared at the time. An enemy MG post then opened fire and held up both forward companies inflicting many casualties. Corporal Rees with complete disregard for the heavy mortar and MG fire and despite the fact that the area contained many anti-personnel mines left his section where they had been halted and alone stalked the MG post. When within range Corporal Rees threw a grenade at the post and rushed in with his Sten gun putting the whole post out of action. He then went on to round up some fifteen prisoners from the houses in the area which he brought back single handed.

This outstanding action resulted in both forward companies being able to continue their advance and consolidate their position. Throughout Corporal Rees showed the most superb bravery and gallantry and was an inspiration to all the troops pinned to the ground in that area. *(L.G. 1.3.45)*

Reesby, Gilbert Henry, Sergeant
44892, 30 Bn. New Zealand Military Forces
At Green Island on 20th Feb 1944 Sjt. Reesby was in temporary command of a platoon of 30th Bn which was engaged in liquidating an enemy post on the coast in the vicinity of Tanaheran Village. Under heavy fire, and with complete disregard for his personal safety, he led his platoon to within 30 yards of the enemy and killed some of them in doing so. This action enabled the remainder of the Coy to encircle the enemy and to approach within assaulting distance. When the signal for the assault was given Sjt. Reesby led his platoon with great dash; was the first man into the position and killed several more of the enemy. Throughout the operation he displayed outstanding courage, and set a splendid example to the whole of the company. *(L.G. 27.3.44)*

Reeves, Sims Edgar, Sergeant
NX 8060, Australian Military Forces
S.W. Pacific *(L.G. 8.3.45)*

Renwick, Gilbert Usher, Sergeant
H19744, Canadian Infantry Corps
Dieppe
M.I.D. 8.11.45 *(L.G. 9.2.46)*

Revel-Burroughes, Herbert William, Warrant Officer Cl. III (T.S.M.)
1426200, 5th HAA Bty., Royal Artillery
On the afternoon of May 15th 1940 the gun position at Montbre was attacked by four Dornier 17's flying in line astern formation. Only one 3.7 gun and one Bren gun were in action. TSM Revel-Burroughes the G.P.O. at the time ordered his Command Post detachments to 'Take Cover.' At the same time he joined the gun detachment and took cover behind the gun. As the first plane passed the crossing point firing on the section, he gave the order 'action' to the gun detachment, took over the duties of No. 5 and laid the gun on a future bearing and angle. He fired the gun himself at an estimated moment. At the second burst the plane was seen to crash. He then engaged the second plane. This plane appeared to be hit and began losing height. The other planes changed course and flew away from the position resourcefulness and initiative in this action, particularly since his gun had no open sights and his section was being machine gunned at the time.   *(L.G. 20.12.40)*

Reynolds, James Boyle Curran, Guardsman
24549305, Scots Guards
On the night of 13th/14th June 1982, on the Island of East Falkland, the 2nd Battalion Scots Guards attacked well entrenched enemy positions on the craggy ridge feature of Tumbledown Mountain, seven kilometres to the west of Port Stanley.

During the attack, Guardsman Reynolds' Platoon came under fire from a group of enemy snipers. His Platoon Sergeant was killed instantly. A confused situation developed and his Section became separated. Guardsman Reynolds immediately took command. Having located the enemy snipers he silenced several of them himself.

That done and showing a complete disregard for his own safety, he moved forward to render first aid to a wounded comrade. He himself was wounded in the hand by enemy sniper fire, but continued to aid his colleague. Whilst doing so, he was killed by enemy mortar fire.
[From L.G.]   *(L.G. 19.9.78)*

Richard, Francis Joseph, Private
H.46459 [B–466459 on AFW 3121], The Lake Superior Regt.
On 31 Oct 44, during the adv of 4 Cdn Armd Bde towards Steenbergen (6337) 'C' Coy, Lake Sup R (M) was ordered to secure a brhead over the stream at 633353. The line of the stream was held in considerable str, and the area where the crossing was to be made was under very hy and accurate fire from enemy SA, arty and mortars. The assault was to be made with two pls. On the right the pl to which Pte. Richard belonged was ordered to cross and secure a rd junc at 635357. The crossing was successfully made at 2300 hrs, but during the approach to their objective Pte. Richard's pl came under hy enemy defensive fire as a result of which both

the pl comd and the last remaining NCO became cas. The pl very quickly became disorganised and the adv came to a halt. At this pt, and in spite of the enemy fire, Pte. Richard assumed comd of the pl, rallied it and led the men fwd to their objective, where they dug in and prepared to hold the ground they had gained. When daylight came, the pl came under observed fire from enemy SA weapons, as well as almost continuous mortar and arty fire. Despite the enemy fire, Pte. Richard retained complete control of the pl going about from post to post encouraging his men and supervising the defence of the posn until relieved at 1900 hrs, 1 Nov 44. The initiative, quick assumption of responsibility well above what might reasonably be expected of him, and leadership displayed by Pte. Richard in the face of hy enemy fire undoubtedly played a great part in the success of this operation. The brhead thus secured was subsequently used by 10 Cdn Inf Bde for their assault on the town of Steenbergen itself.   *(L.G. 20.1.45)*

Richards, Harry, Private
WX.1944, 2/11 Bn., Australian Military Forces
On 29 May 41 at Crete Pte. Richards assisted and half carried Sjt. Kilpatrick a hospital patient across the island to the Beach at Sphakia. When invited by the Beach Staff to go off with Kilpatrick and be evacuated, he refused saying that he would go back and get someone else who could not walk. On 1 June having been left behind after the evacuation Pte. Richards recovered an invasion barge which had been abandoned by the Navy, collected a party of 50 including two Marine officers, took charge (with the concurrence of the officers) laid in supplies of food and water at Cavdos Island, [....] after the barge had been damaged on a reef, travelled 80 miles until the petrol gave out, rigged a sail with blankets, navigated to Sidi Barrani and landed the whole party in good heart and condition on 9 June. Pte. Richards is a farmer.
                                   (L.G. 30.12.41)

Richards, Robert, Corporal
D157727, Régiment de Chaudière (Immediate)
On 17 September 1944, during the attack on the Boulogne fortress 'D' Company Regiment de Chaudiere was ordered to attack a fortified enemy position West of Denacre, North East of the town of Boulogne. The position consisted in series of about ten reinforced concrete dugouts, sited on the forward slope overlooking the regiment's axis of advance. These dugouts were joined together by an intricate system of communication trenches. Both the concrete position and the trenches were manned by over one hundred Germans firing a variety of small arms. The approach to the position was barred by a minefield containing both anti-tank and anti-personnel mines.

D157727, Corporal Robert Richards, was in command of one of the leading sections in the forward platoon. As he crossed the starting line, Corporal Richards was wounded in the hip by shrapnel from a mine which exploded in front of him. Ignoring his injuries and refusing to have his wound dressed, Corporal Richards led his section into the attack and although considerably hampered by his wound was successful in capturing the objective. Only then did he consent to have his wound dressed by the Stretcher Bearer. He refused however to be evacuated and carried on for 2 days during which time he took part in another attack, again leading his section in an exemplary manner. He was eventually evacuated by order of the Medical Officer.

The qualities of leadership, exceptional courage and determination displayed by Corporal Richards were of the highest order. His distinguished conduct throughout the whole operation was an inspiration not only to his sec but to the platoon and the company.
(L.G. 30.12.44)

Richards, Ronald Francis, Warrant Officer Cl. III
(Pl.S.M.)
3907897, South Wales Borderers (Immediate)
On the Ankenes Peninsular on 1st May 1940, No. 3907897 PSM R. F. Richards was with his platoon in an advanced billet. When the platoon was heavily shelled and ordered to withdraw, together with his Platoon Commander he organised the withdrawal, the former and two other ranks were wounded. As soon as PSM Richards had seen the rest of the Platoon to safety, he returned to the wounded men, dressed thir wounds, and then dragged them one by one to safety, a distance of some [...]00 yds. During this period he was continually under shell fire and showed a complete disregard for his own safety. Subsequently on 2nd May, 1940, when his Company was attacked by the enemy this W.O. exposed himself fearlessly in organising the defence of his post, and was largely responsible for the defeat of the enemy on the sector held by his platoon. *(L.G. 6.8.40)*

Richards, Roy, Warrant Officer Cl. II (C.S.M.)
5722253, 1st Bn. Parachute Regt., Army Air Corps
(Cheshney)
For conspicuous gallantry and devotion to duty on 8 March 43 in the Tamera Sector (Tunisia Sh 10). CSM Richards was a member of a counter-attack force which had to attack a strong position on which the enemy had established himself. Whilst gaining their objective the force came under heavy shell and mortar fire and the force commander was killed. CSM Richards immediately rallied the men, who were considerably shaken, and took the objective. He then sent the remainder of the force to assist another platoon which was in difficulties, while he himself mounted a machine gun and held the position by himself for three hours. He caused severe casualties to the enemy who were trying to regain the position. CSM Richards showed a complete disregard for his own safety and by his courage, coolness, and initiative under fire, undoubtedly saved a vital position from falling into the hands of the enemy. *(L.G. 18.5.43)*

Richardson, Harry Llewellyn, Lance Sergeant
2733752, Welsh Guards (Deinolen, Caernarvonshire)
B.E.F. (from P.O.W. Pool)
M.I.D. 1.11.45 *(L.G. 13.9.45)*

Richardson, John Henry, Sergeant
SK 12487, Princess Patricia's Canadian Light
Infantry
For Korea *(L.G. 23.1.53)*

Richardson, Thomas Smith, Corporal
4854736, Leicestershire Regt.
On 10th Dec. 1940 Cpl. Richardson was a sub-section commander in the Carrier Platoon. In the attack on an enemy position near Sidi Barrani he led his carrier with great courage in the face of heavy fire. He went straight for an enemy MG post and destroyed it totally with grenades. Throughout the battle he behaved with the greatest determination. *(L.G. 25.4.41)*

Richardson, Walter Thomas, T/Warrant Officer Cl. I
(Sgt.-Maj.)
835578, 21st A/Tk Regt., Royal Artillery
During the advance to east of the river Dyle and during the withdrawal to the river Senne while working with the Divisional Cavalry Regiment also during the subsequent operations culminating in the withdrawal to the coast he commanded his Troop of Anti-Tank guns with skill and initiative. He volunteered at Bray-Dunes to remain behind with the Bren guns of the battery which remained for A.A. protection of the beach and cover the evacuation. Throughout the operations he set a fine example by his coolness and efficiency.
(L.G. 27.8.40)

Richmond, James, Warrant Officer Cl. II (C.S.M.)
2692726, Scots Guards (Loanstroon, Ayrshire)
This Warrant Officer is CSM of 'G' Coy Bn Scots Guards. On 16th June 1941 he was present with his company during the attack on Salum Barracks, which started at 1130 hrs. The company debussed from their 3-tonners about 600 yds from the barracks and advanced on foot. Considerable light mortar and small arms fire was brought to bear on the Coy H.Q. during the movement forward, and after they had reached the nearest buildings. CSM Richmond saw a sniper on the roof to his right flank. Although he was under cover he stood up in full view and threw a hand grenade, which put the sniper out of action.

Shortly afterwards he used his rifle to snipe an enemy post covering the main gateway to the barracks until such time as a Bren Gun was brought into the position. He then joined in to the assault on the post and was conspicuous for his leadership and coolness. The post was captured and consisted of 30 Italians with L.M.Gs and an infantry gun. Later he repeatedly exposed himself leading small parties into dug outs and ruins in search of enemy known to be hiding.

In this action the company captured 11 officers and 209 other ranks, besides killing or wounding some 30 others. During the whole action, CSM Richmond set a magnificent example of bravery and coolness in difficult moments, and contributed in no small measure to the eventual success.   *(L.G. 21.10.41)*

Ricklewright, Douglas William, Corporal
See Micklewright

Ridley, David Greenwall, Sergeant
4459243, 1st Bn. The Durham Light Infantry (Pelton Fell, Co. Durham)
On the night 14/15 Dec 44 Sjt. Ridley was in command of No. 3 Platoon 'A' Coy in a night attack on to Pt. 168 and Casa Bianca (254229). No. 3 Platoon was in reserve. No. 2 Platoon, the left leading Platoon, ran on to a Schu minefield, suffered several casualties and withdrew to the reserve Platoon area. Sjt. Ridley personally went into the minefield three times to bring out casualties. This he did in spite of considerable mortar and Spandau fire. No. 3 Platoon was then ordered up on the right to exploit behind the right forward Platoon which had gained a foothold on Pt. 168. The enemy were holding positions less than 100 yds away, but No. 3 Platoon dug in successfully. They were under constant Spandau and grenade fire from very close quarters, but due to the inspiring leadership of Sjt. Ridley stuck to their posns. All other NCOs were wounded and eventually he was hit also, but he continued tirelessly to visit his pits and encourage the men with complete disregard for his own personal safety. He personally accounted for three enemy, and would not go back to the R.A.P. until 24 hrs later when the Platoon had been relieved.
                    (L.G. 24.5.45)

Riedy, Arthur Reginald, Lance Corporal
QX21198, 2/3 Aust Pioneer Bn. (Immediate)
For outstanding bravery and gallantry in action at Tarakan.
On 12 May 1945 when his coy was attacking a feature east of Tarakan L/Cpl. Riedy was a member of 16 platoon 2/3 Aust Pnr Bn. His section leader led the platoon in the attack with Riedy following him when they came under heavy fire. These two men charged the first LMG position and after grappling with the enemy Riedy killed them both. They then charged a position six yards to the right, killed the occupants and silenced the gun. On his left front was yet another position which he attacked with grenades but failed to silence the gun and under covering fire by Riedy the section leader again charged but was killed on the edge of the weapon pit.
A stretcher bearer arrived but owing to enemy fire could not reach Cpl. Mackey who was thought to be still alive. Reidy then went forward, dragged his body clear of the enemy and continued to engage the remaining positions until he himself was wounded and evacuated.

By his outstanding bravery and complete disregard for his own life L/Cpl. Riedy's actions saved his platoon from a great deal of enemy fire and enabled it to hold onto the ground for more than three hours.
                    (L.G. 20.9.45)

Rigby, Hubert Edgar, Sergeant
4545006, 1st West Yorkshire Regt. (Leeds 6)
(Immediate)
Sjt. Rigby has served with his Company throughout the period covered by this citation in the capacity of Pl Sjt. and for long periods as Pl Comd. He has throughout the whole campaign, proved himself to be a leader of the highest calibre; cool, courageous and resourceful in action.
On April 6th, at Yindaw, a village held in considerable strength by the Japanese, Sjt. Rigby was Pl Sjt. of the right hand forward Pl of the Company which had been ordered to obtain a footing in the village in order that tanks could be used. The left hand Pl of the Company came under extremely heavy fire from the enemy positions and suffered casualties. It was decided to withdraw the left hand Pl but when the evacuation of wounded started it was found that the Japanese had the whole area so covered by L.M.G. and sniper fire that additional casualties were suffered.
Sjt. Rigby immediately took command of two sections of the right hand Pl and covered by the fire of the 3rd section he pushed further into this strongly held village until such time as he found positions which could dominate by fire those enemy bunkers which were interfering with the withdrawal of the left hand Pl. He himself adopted a very exposed position from which he see the withdrawal of the left hand pl, and at the same time his own sections on his right so that he could direct the covering fire to the maximum advantage. He remained in this exposed position under heavy fire without regard to his own safety until such time as the Pl on his left had retired.
At a later date Sjt. Rigby's Coy had been ordered on a sweep to pick up escaped British and American P.O.W.s. During the course of this sweep information was received that there was a considerable number of Japanese in the village of Naungpattaya. The Coy Comd issued orders for the attack. During this attack Sjt. Rigby's Pl was held up by a bunker containing 5 Japanese. He placed an L.M.G. in a position from which it could cover the bunker, and selecting a few men to accompany him Sjt. Rigby crept up to it from a flank and destroyed the enemy with grenades. In doing so Sjt. Rigby was wounded in the leg by a grenade thrown from the bunker and although he was given permission to retire from the battle he declined to do so but continued to command his men until the whole village was cleared. A total of 42 Japanese were killed in this action.
By the end of the day Sjt. Rigby's wound had become so aggravated that walking was a physical impossibility. Although he must have suffered great pain Sjt. Rigby

stuck to his post with the same courage and tenacity and indominatable spirit which he has always displayed in action.

These are but two instances of Sjt. Ribgy's capacity as a soldier and as a leader. His conduct throughout the campaign has been an inspiration to the men of his Pl and he has, by his tenacity and personal examples of bravery and leadership, set a standard hard to equal.

(*L.G. 17.1.46*)

Riley, Charles George Gibson, Sergeant (A/W.O.II (C.S.M.))
2656281, 3 Bn. Coldstream Guards, 'L' Det SAS Bde.
(Immediate)
This NCO led a party on the first Buerat raid Feb 1942. The party placed demolition charges on many heavy enemy transport vehicles and on various dumps. By skilled and daring leadership he succeeded in bluffing the enemy sentries. Thereby he avoided giving any alarm which would have interfered with the work of other parties operating in the same area. He has shown the greatest gallantry and the highest qualities of leadership in other raids at Slonta and Nofilia in March, April 1942.

(*L.G. 26.11.42*)

Rimmer, George Leonard, Lance Corporal
104053, 49 General Tpt Coy., R.A.S.C. (Birkdale)
On the night 29/30th Jan. this NCO was driving the only four wheeled drive 3 ton lorry with the Bn then part of Goldforce making the move to escape encirclement in Bengasi. On this particular night the force was due to cross the road Antelat—Agedalia where it was thought enemy opposition might be met. A mile or two short of this road about 15 of the bn. troop carrying lorries got stuck in soft ground. Regardless of the fact that the force was disappearing into the darkness this NCO turned aside and was responsible for towing 11 of the lorries out of the soft ground and sending them on to catch up with the force. The remainder were pulled out with his help by the Bn. carriers. It was not until all the lorries were clear that he came on himself. This devotion to duty at a critical moment and in unknown country where his action might well have led to his being lost and falling into eney hands was most marked.

M.I.D. 23.5.46 (*L.G. 23.4.42*)

Rippin, Thomas, Sergeant
4799923, Lincolnshire Regt. (Liverpool, 7)
(Immediate)
During the Battalion attack on Herouvillette on 8 July 44 'B' Coy was the leading Coy in the assault. On arrival on the objective, Sjt. Rippin's platoon infiltrated forward under the leadership of the platoon commander. Shortly afterwards, the platoon was cut off and the platoon commander was seriously wounded. Sjt. Rippin immediately took command, and under continuous machine gun and mortar fire organised the resistance and beat off several determined enemy counter-attacks, although the platoon was completely surrounded and cut off from the Bn. This Pl, although finally reduced in numbers to 10, held on under the inspired leadership of Sjt. Rippin until finally relieved. By his personal courage and bravery, this NCO inspired those of his platoon that had not become casualties to hold on to their position under the greatest difficulty. The forward position held by this platoon undoubtedly prevented the enemy from working round and infiltrating into the main Battalion position. Sjt. Rippin showed complete disregard for his own personal safety and was an inspiration to his men.

(*L.G. 21.12.44*)

Ritchie, Robert John, Sergeant (A/W.O.II (C.S.M.))
2818099, 6th Seaforth Highlanders (Carrbridge, Inverness-shire)
Sjt. Ritchie was acting CSM of 'D' Coy during the assault crossing of the R Garigliano on 17/18 Jan 44. During the actual crossing, which was accomplished under heavy shell fire, Sjt. Ritchie's magnificent coolness and leadership played a decisive part in getting the company across and quickly re-organised on the opposite bank. During the night his company fought its way forward mopping up 3 enemy posts, and when dawn came had reached its first objective. Throughout the night and during the sustained counter-attacks which followed the next morning Sjt. Ritchie's skill and bravery were of the greatest possible assistance to his Coy Comd and an inspiration to the whole Coy. As a result of his counter-attacks the enemy succeeded in cutting the Company off from the remainder of the Bn. When the greater part of the company had been killed or captured, Sjt. Ritchie taking personal comd fought his way back with a small remnant of his Coy and rejoined the Bn. Throughout the operation Sjt. Ritchie displayed magnificent qualities of leadership, and a coolness and courage of the highest order.

(*L.G. 29.6.44*)

Rix, Derek Everard, Corporal
H.6235, Winnipeg Grenadiers
Cpl. Rix was in command of a section of the Winnipeg Grenadiers at Hong Kong in December 1941. At dawn on 19 December when the Japanese attacked the Wong Nei Chong area, Cpl. Rix and his section were cut off from their platoon. They worked their way from their open position on the hillside above the Blue Pool Valley to join a section of the Hong Kong Volunteer Decence Corps who were holding Pill Box No. 2 on the slope of Jardine's Lookout and cooperated in the defence of the pill box during the remainder of the morning. At about noon a patrol of Japanese succeeded in reaching Pill Box No. 1 (about fifty yards further up the steep hillside) and heavily engaged the crew, who were soon in a very difficult situation. After an unsuccessful relief attack by some of the crew of Pill Box No. 2, Cpl. Rix with a mixed party of Winnipeg Grenadiers and Hong Kong Volunteers made another attempt. They were under fire from across the valley and had to climb a steep hillside

in the face of the enemy, but succeeded in wiping out the surviving Japanese around Pill Box No. 1, thereby retaining control of both Pill Boxes for some hours longer. As Pill Box No. 1 was no longer of use due to the machine guns being damaged, and the loopholes being under continuous close range rifle fire, Cpl. Rix took up a very precarious position close to Pill Box No. 2 for treatment. Later when enemy pressure increased and there was no sign of relief, the Hong Kong Volunteer Defence Corps officer in command gave leave to walking wounded to retire, but Cpl. Rix preferred to stay and see the action through to a finish. Cpl. Rix proved himself an able and courageous NCO and his conduct throughout was a credit to his Unit and the Canadian Army.

(L.G. 2.4.46)

Rixon, Derek Edwin, Gunner
206285, Royal New Zealand Artillery
For Korea   *(L.G. 18.3.52)*

Roach, Horace, Sergeant
7535247, 26th Ind Field Ambulance, R.A.M.C.
(Karachi, India) (Immediate)
Sjt. Roach displayed conspicuous bravery, devotion, and initiative during the fighting at Cassino 20–24 Mar 44.

As as result of enemy counter-attacks on 19 Mar, the route by which casualties had previously been evacuated from the battalion became occupied by the enemy. This isolated battalion had a mounting list of casualties denied proper medical attention. A medical officer succeeded in getting through to the battalion, and returned to report that these casualties must be evacuated.

Sergeant Roach, thereupon, volunteered to take with him a picked party of stretcher bearers to bring the wounded back. To do this he had to make his way over a route of great natural difficulty, on which any movement was at once subjected to close-range sniping and MG fire and which was constantly being shelled and mortared both by ourselves and the enemy.

Taking advantage of an early morning mist on 21 Mar and of the smoke which was being put down, Sergeant Roach gallantly and skilfully led his party over this route and returned with a proportion of the more severely wounded. He also guided and directed many who were able to walk or crawl back. Again on 22 Mar Sergeant Roach offered to repeat this feat since some more wounded remained.

Again he accomplished it successfully, though during the course of this journey he was taken prisoner temporarily by the enemy; who, however, released him with a warning against repetition, because of his Red Cross safe-conduct.

As a result of the brave and devoted efforts of Sergeant Roach, and of his skill and initiative in accomplishing so hazardous a journey on two occasions, seventy casualties were successfully evacuated from this isolated position. In all his other actions throughout the battle, he displayed the same outstanding qualities of

bravery and devotion, under heavy and constant fire, in his efforts to treat and evacuate the wounded; at all times exposing himself fearlessly and without any consideration of personal risk.
M.I.D. 24.6.43   *(L.G. 24.8.44)*

Roach, Reginald Edwin, Sergeant
SX 4152, 2/27 Aust Inf Bn. (Periodic)
2/27 Aust Inf Bn of which Sjt. Roach is a member, was engaged in repeated attacks on enemy defences at Gona, New Guinea between 29 Nov 42 and 9 Dec 42. During this period Sjt. Roach took part in many attacks and led two patrols which were sent out. On these two occasions Sjt. Roach showed outstanding courage and leadership. On 1 Dec 42 during a dawn attack he displayed gallantry of a high degree in carrying to safety WOII Halligan who had been badly wounded. This act was carried out under hy fire. On 3 Dec 42 he was ordered to lead a night patrol with the object of destroying an enemy MG post. On the way to this objective he destroyed an enemy listening post of two men and a standing patrol of 6 men. He also obtained valuable infm about the foremost enemy strong posts.

On 5 Dec 42 he led fwd a raiding party which succeeded in reaching the enemy MG post and silenced it with hand grenades. In spite of hy enemy return fire Sjt. Roach's patrol suffered no casualties. As a result of these patrols the infm gained was of extreme value in the success of subsequent attacks. It is recommended that he be granted the Periodical award of the Distinguished Conduct Medal.   *(L.G. 23.12.43)*

Road-Knight, Charles Thomas Arthur, Warrant
    Officer Cl. II (B.S.M.)
2691562, Royal Artillery (Broomgate, Lanark)
Malaya   *(L.G. 5.3.42)*

Roberts, Charles William, Sergeant
Ex.1689, Suda Sector, Crete, Royal Marines
At Canea on 19th May whilst in action at his gun position was hit in the abdomen by an explosive bullet. Although knocked to the ground he continued to give orders until he became unconscious and collapsed. His devotion to duty and example to all ranks deserves the highest praise.
(L.G. 4.11.41)

Roberts, Frederick John, Sergeant (temp.)
215875, Royal Australian Infantry
No citation.   *(L.G. 16.1.70)*

Roberts, Reginald Vernon, Sergeant
NX.25805, 3 Aust A Tk Regt RAA
Gallant conduct and outstanding devotion to duty whilst in action on Tell el Eisa Spur, Pt 24 (Ref: El Alamein 1:50000 square 874299) during period 11–14 Jul 42 incl. During an attack on our position on 13 Jul Sjt. Roberts manned a Bren Gun and rendered assistance to the infantry in repulsing the attack, which was unsupported

by tanks. During an enemy attack on evening of 14 Jul again unsupported by tanks, he fought his Bren gun with vigour, and when the 'Tanks alert' was sounded he directed the fire of his A Tk gun with extreme coolness and accuracy and succeeded in knocking out 2 enemy tanks. During the same day he also knocked out 2 light enemy field guns which were shelling our position, with his gun. During the night of 14 Jul an enemy tank succeeded in penetrating our positions and Sjt. Roberts and another Sjt, because of heavy casualties to the crew, manned the gun and though the sights were damaged, showed initiative and resourcefulness in method in laying the gun. During the withdrawal of our troops from these positions that night, Sjt. Roberts marshalled and controlled Anti Tank Gunners in such a manner as to be an inspiration to the Gunners and infantry on the near vicinity. *(L.G. 24.9.42)*

Roberts, Richard Ievan, Sergeant
7913161, 46th Bn. Royal Tank Regt. (Blaenan[..], N. Wales) (Immediate)
On 26th January, 1944, Sjt. Roberts was ordered to command one of two tanks whose task it was to drive enemy infantry who were supported by several S.P. guns, from a group of houses. While proceeding down a narrow road towards their objective, the leading tank hit a mine and was unable to move further and, at that moment, three enemy S.P. guns appeared from a sunken road on their left flank. Without hesitation, Sjt. Roberts ordered his tank to advance, drove past the disabled tank, which was unable to protect itself, and engaged the three S.P. guns at point-blank range. Sjt. Roberts then controlled the fire of his tank with such accuracy that two of the enemy guns were put out of action, whereupon the third attempted to escape. Enemy spare crews immediately came forward to man the two guns, whereupon Sjt. Roberts ordered his driver to ram the escaping S.P. gun, at the same time firing all his guns to prevent the enemy bringing the other two S.P. guns into action. This was accomplished so successfully that all three S.P. guns were detroyed. By this time, the other tank had become fit for action and they continued the attack together. Sjt. Roberts then destroyed a Mk IV tank. Throughout this action Sjt. Roberts fought entirely on his own and his gre[...] dash and complete disregard for his [...] safety were entirely instrumental in saving his Squadron Leader's tank from destruction and in the complete annihilation of the enemy's position around the houses, which our infantry were able to occupy soon afterwards.

The following morning, Sjt. Roberts was again ordered to advance forward in rear of an officer's tank, which was soon hit by a H.E. shell and set on fire. Sjt. Roberts immediately ordered his crew to leave their tank and take fire extinguishers to assist in putting out the fire. Although the burning tank was in full view of the enemy and subjected to both artillery and small arms fire, Sjt. Roberts climbed on to the tank and turned on the emergency extinguished inside the turret, despite the fact that ammunition was already exploding inside. All this was done with such promptness that the tank was saved from destruction and was able to continue in action.

Throughout these and other operations, Sjt. Robert showed great courage and was an inspiring example to the men of his Squadron.
M.I.D. 24.6.43 *(L.G. 15.6.44)*

Roberts, Robert James, Lance Sergeant
43465, 6 NZ Field Coy. (Immediate)
During the recent operations from the Senio to the Piave L/Sjt. Roberts has displayed outstanding efficiency and gallantry. He has performed engineer tasks requiring organising ability and leadership much beyond what could be expected from him.

On 11 Apr 45, while in support of 28 NZ (Maori) Bn, L/Sjt. Roberts organised his Platoon and directed the construction of a Bailey bridge across the Santerno. The bridge site was under observation of an enemy machine-gun post out to the flank and the area was frequently sprayed with bullets. The casualties were light, but it was not easy to keep his Platoon working at maximum efficiency under such conditions. He placed a Sapper with a Bren gun clear of the bridge, and each time the enemy opened fire the Bren gunner fired long bursts in the direction of the enemy post, with the result that some of the enemy fire was diverted and the bridge area suffered less interference. L/Sjt. Roberts rallied his men to such good effect that, after all, the bridge was completed in good time for the passage of tanks.

Again on the night 15/16 Apr 45 L/Sjt. Roberts was in charge of the construction of Sydney Bridge over the Sillaro. Especially in the early stages, the bridge site was subjected to mortar and some small arms fire, but he held his men together and the support weapons were allowed to pass before daylight. L/Sjt. Roberts always inspired confidence and was on every occasion a great help to his officers. *(L.G. 18.10.45)*

Roberts, Sidney, Warrant Officer Cl. II (C.S.M.)
3245109, Cameronians (Featherstone, Yorks.)
For sustained courage, outstanding leadership and devotion to duty throughout the operations.

At Pegu on 6 Mar 42, the H.Q. of West Yorks Regt to the SW of the town was practically surrounded by the enemy. No Tps were then available to counter-attack. CSM (then CQMS) Roberts got a 2≤ Mortar and heavily engaged the enemy with accurate fire. He constantly moved his posn to avoid enemy mortar fire and to deceive the enemy as to our actual strength. His action undoubtedly prevented the HQ from being overrun before sufficient tps could be collected to counter-attack.

During the attack on Padigon Wood on 29 Mar 42, the attack on Shwedaung Wood on 30 Mar 42 and subsequent withdrawal on 30/1 Mar.

In particular, in the attack on Shwedaung, while clearing the wood, C Coy lost touch with the Coy on its left, A Coy attacking astride the Road had suffered severely and had failed to capture an L.M.G. and Mortar post situated close to the Road which had escaped the Arty preparation. Subsequent shelling subdued these two posts, but they again opened up and prevented the clearing of the Tpt through the Southern Rd. block. CSM Roberts C Coy was sent to gain touch with A Coy. While attempting to do this at a time when the guns were shelling the approximate area of these posts, CSM Roberts spotted a Culvert under which several Japs were sheltering, obviously the Mortar and L.M.G. dets. Although he had only one bomb, he stalked and successfully bombed the culvert. He then went back to his Coy HQ about 1000 yards away to collect more bombs, returned and again bombed the culvert and destroyed the mortar. This action enabled the Tpt to get through. Throughout the 48 hours fighting CSM Roberts set a great example of courage and leadership. During all operations CSM Roberts keeness, ability and disregard of personal danger have been an inspiration to the men of his Coy.   *(L.G. 28.10.42)*

Roberts, William John, Private
4457717, Durham Light Infantry
No citation.   *(L.G. 4.11.41)*

Robertson, Alan Charles Tuarea, Sergeant
11687, 26 NZ Bn.
Throughout the action of the Battalion in Libya Sjt. Robertson showed outstanding qualities as a leader, his intrepid bearing and coolness at critical stages being a constant source of inspiration to the men of his Company. After all Officers of the Company had become casualties he showed great initiative and it was due to his prompt action and leadership that the remnants of his Company were saved.

On the afternoon of Sunday, 23 Nov 1941, in the Battalion's first engagement S.E. of Sidi Rezegh Sjt. Robertson's Company was severely pressed, and when the supplies of ammunition were becoming exhausted, he, on his own initiative, and under continuous and heavy machine gun fire, procured and distributed replenishments to platoons and sections. This action made possible, and his personal example encouraged, so fierce a counter-attack by his Company that the enemy was forced to retire and the Battalion's front was consolidated.

On the night 26/27 Nov 1941 at Sidi Rezegh the Battalion again attacked under intense machine gun fire. Sjt. Robertson's example of cool personal courage was an inspiration to his Company, which, despite several casualties completed the advance to the objective. In this advance his leadership was outstanding.

Subsequently, he led a party under heavy fire and brought out all the Company's wounded, his prompt action undoubtedly saving a number of lives. On the afternoon of 30 Nov 1941, in the same area, the Battalion was attacked by a strong force of tanks supported by infantry, and the forward troops were over-run. At the

last possible opportunity before being completely surrounded, and only after reporting to the nearest Company Commander and receiving orders, he organised and executed an orderly withdrawal thereby saving the lives not only of his Platoon but of several members of another unit who were in the area.
M.I.D. 24.6.43   *(L.G. 9.9.42)*

Robertson, Harold, Corporal
837, S.A.T.S.C., South African Forces (Periodic)
This NCO was in charge of 'C' Sqn. mechanics throughout the campaign. He at all times was most conscientious in his work and by his fine example and leadership of the mechanics under his charge was instrumental in maintaining the Armoured cars of his Sqn., many of which had done 10,000 miles, in a condition to carry on. No car was ever abandoned except through conditions beyond his control. He further displayed great coolness, courage and initiatie when on Jan. 10, 1942 in the Wadi Faregh, 10 miles West of El Haseat he with two other mechanics in an armoured L.A.D. accompanied Lt. Hall of the K.D.Gs and one of their Sqn. Echelons to repair one of the K.D.G. armoured cars, that had been blown up in a mine field. En route Lt. Hall's car was blown up in a minefield. Cpl. Robertson took this officer's armoured car in tow with his L.A.D. which was then itself blown up. Whilst in this predicament, two enemy armoured cars attacked them. Lt. Hall and Cpl. Robertson enegaged these cars with their Boyes rifles. Cpl. Robertson fired 7 magazines from the Boyes which he was firing from his shoulder over the bonnet of his car. Lt. Hall had a leg almost completely severed by a 22 mm shell, and when the enemy cars were 150 yds. away, he ordered Robertson to cease fire. The enemy left two of Lt. Hall's men to care for him and took the remaining men and vehicles. Cpl. Robertson escaped, returned to the wounded officer, rendered first aid, repaired a vehicle the enemy had been unable to start, placed the officer in it, and started back with the vehicle which was blown up on another mine. He took the injured officer out, and stayed with him, at the same time sending the two Ptes. off on foot to seek assistance. The officer died later that night, but Cpl. Robertson remained with the damaged vehicle until found by a search party the next day.   *(L.G. 9.9.42)*

Robertson, Struan, Lance Sergeant
2121805, 252 Field Company, Royal Engineers
  (Thornliebank, Renfrewshire) (Immediate)
On the night 23/24 Nov 43 No 3 Pl of 252 Fd Coy RE were engaged on a bridging operation over the Fiume Zittola MR 077497 the task being to construct an 80' D/ S Bailey Br. 2121805 A/Sjt. Robertson was the senior NCO present and responsible for the detailed construction of the br. An attempt during daylight 23 Nov had failed owing to heavy and accurate enemy shell fire. Weather conditions were appalling and the working party had been exposed to rain and cold for some 8 hrs prior

to the night work commencing. Enemy interference commenced about 2100 hrs with accurate shell fire followed by mortar fire. This continued for about 32 hrs at 15 or 20 min intervals. Throughout this period A/Sjt. Robertson set an excellent example to his men by his coolness and utter disregard for enemy fire continuously organising and encouraging his men under very difficult conditions. This undoubtedly led to the successful completion of the task in hand by 0700 hrs 24 Nov.

(*L.G. 6.4.44*)

Robertson, William Malcolm, Warrant Officer Cl. II
2695566, 1st Bn. Scots Guards (London, S.W.5)
(*Periodic*)
This CSM served in Right Flank (Coy), 1st Battalion Scots Guards, as a CSM from March, 1944, during which time he has never missed an action except for one month when he was in hospital with a small wound. During this period his behaviour was magnificent. During uncomfortable moments he invariably showed less concern for the shells and bullets and for his own safety than anyone else. This he did deliberately to encourage the rest of the company. This occurred many times with the result that he had a big effect on the company.

On the occasion when he was wounded near Monte Catarelto, although he was told by the Medical Officer to go back immediately he insisted on staying with the company for another two days until the company was relieved. He then went to hospital for a month. He felt that it might have a bad effect on the company if he was to leave during this period which happened to be very unpleasant owing to as heavy shelling as the company had ever experienced.

In addition to consistent gallantry over this period he has shown quite exceptional efficiency in the many difficult administrative and tactical problems that he has had to deal with. His Company Commander always felt that he could [...] over his company to this CSM at any time.

At Porto Garibaldi when the Battalion attempted to cross the Valetta Canal, CSM Robertson's company had the task of giving covering fire from the near bank of the canal. On the way up to the canal banks the company was subjected to a heavy DF. The Company Commander was slightly wounded. When the leading platoons reached the bank they were subjected to very accurate and heavy spandau fire from the opposite bank, a distance of approximately 30 yards. Any movement on our bank was immediately observed and engaged by the Germans, owing to the artificial moonlight. One of the platoons was in a particularly uncomfortable position for about three hours. Twice during this period this CSM volunteered to visit this platoon, because the Company Commander was slightly incapacitated and although it was not strictly necessary to do so as wireless communications were working with the platoon. At this time it was known that the approaches to this platoon were particularly well covered by spandaus and any

movement had been immediately engaged. In fact during his first visit he had some very narrow escapes. He was quite unperturbed by this and shortly afterwards, and on his own initiative, went again. Finally, when the order was given to withdraw, he again volunteered to go and ensure that this order was received by all the groups of men who were on the river bank and to whom it was very difficult to communicate owing to the spandau fire. The CSM's behaviour on this occasion had a great moral effect on the leading platoon and on the company as a whole.

Throughout the final offensive and at all times CSM Robertson has performed the most valuable services to his company, since the greater part of the company administration has fallen on his shoulders. At no time of the day or night has it been too much for him to attend to company administration and supply details which would assist anyone, however, tired he might be. By sheer personal example under dangerous conditions and by his drive and thoroughness out of the line he has maintained absolute discipline within the company and has earned the everlasting admiration of all ranks.

(*L.G. 13.12.45*)

Robey, Kennery Douglas, Sergeant
2581303, 133 MEF Bde., Royal Signals (Immediate)
Sjt. Robey was dropped to the Olympus area of Greece on 12 June 43. During all the time he has been in the country he has shown indomitable courage, and devotion to duty of the highest order. In particular, on 16 Apr. 44 when a strong enemy patrol managed to evade the Andarte guard and approach his station, they opened fire at a range of 800 yds. Robey, with utter disregard for his personal safety, succeeded in saving his W/T set. The British Liaison Officer in charge of the station states:—

'I saw all was lost and ordered Robey to save his W/T set at all costs, leaving behind a useless set as decoy. He carried out my orders and waded through deep snow with the set. At the moment he left H.Q. bullets were actually raining on the doors. As he emerged he was fired on and was under fire till he was out of sight of the Germans. He buried the set in the snow and then returned to H.Q. under even more intense fire, to rescue the gold, ciphers and records. Owing to the fact that deep snow lay all around, speed was impossible and he was therefore an easy target for enemy fire. Despite this, he carried out his task and got away safely.'

Two months later Sjt. Robey again managed to save his W/T set during a sudden enemy drive. His superb courage and resource had an inspiring effect on all members of the station, as a resut of which they showed coolness and confidence under very trying and hazardous conditions. Sjt. Robey's health has suffered owing to the hard life he has had to live and the M.O. attached to the station has ordered his evacuation.

For his outstanding bravery and devotion to duty he recommended for the Immediate Award of the DCM.

(*L.G. 4.1.45*)

Robino, Pasquale, A/Sergeant
QX3703, 2/3 Aust Fd Amb. (Immediate)
For gallantry and extreme devotion to duty under fire.

During the occupation of Pabu by 2/32 Aust Inf Bn Sjt. Robino was in charge of stretcher bearers from the supporting Ads. Throughout the vigorous action his conduct was so courageous and outstanding that largely due to his example, no casualty was left unattended for a moment, irrespective of the intensity of enemy fire prevailing at the time. On 26 Nov under intense gun and mortar fire he personally dressed and carried wounded personnel from both on and inside the perimeter back to the Ads. On the peremeter in full view of the enemy, a target exposed to their direct fire and whilst all other personnel were in slit trenches he despite warnings from all around him to seek cover splinted a compound fracture of the leg and then carried the patient over the crest to cover. Whilst carrying this out mortar bombs and shells were hitting the trees directly above his head and landing all around his position. On the same day under the same conditions he carried at least 5 patients from exposed positions to the comparative shelter of the Ads. At all times during the bombardment of the position, by his own example and absolute disregard of danger he maintained the morale of the SB's at a high level and inspired the high standard of work done by them. When 2/32 Bn was relieved by the 2/43 Bn and volunteers were called to remain for a further 48 hours he was the first to volunteer to remain.   *(L.G. 23.3.44)*

Robinson, A. G., Gunner
1486290, Royal Artillery
No information available   *(L.G. 27.9.40)*

Robinson, Alfred Lampton, Warrant Officer Cl. II
NGX 263, Australian New Guinea Administrative Unit, Australian Military Forces (Immediate)
WO Robinson was the first Australian soldier to land at Momote, Los Negros, on 29 Feb 44. Immediately after the landing Robinson volunteered to carry out recce patrols through the enemy lines. Accompanied by native members (2) of the RPC, he succeeded in penetrating the enemy lines on 4 occasions and each time brought back much valuable intelligence. A veteran of the fighting at Rabaul of Jan 42, Robinson quickly proved himself an efficient and daring scout. On the 11 Mar 44, he volunteered to act as guide to a party of 35 officers and men of the 302 Recce Troop which was to attack and capture Hauwei Is. Major Waden of the 39 Fd Arty accompanied the platoon. Covered by a Naval PT boat, the small force landed at Hauwei Is at 1000 hrs. The enemy commenced firing from concealed positions with mortar, MG and rifles. The landing craft Vehicular in which the party landed was subjected to heavy fire from enemy pill boxes. Some of the landing party retreated back to the vessel which put off into deep water. Robinson and his native guide together with other US soldiers were still on the beach. The PT boat had

withdrawn having suffered casualties, and the party had no vessel to support them. The LCV put back to the beach and the remainder of the US troops and Robinson went aboard. WO Robinson half carried one American soldier back to the landing craft. Robinson obtained bandages for the wounded man and guided the craft in its third attempt to get the wounded away. By this time enemy fire had become more intense. As the vessel backed away a mortar bomb landed on the water line and the vessel began to sink. Robinson took to the water with the American soldier. Despite heavy enemy fire and risk of sharks, Robinson continued to support the wounded man for approx 5 hours. It was necessary to swim all the time as a strong head wind threatened to take them back to the island. Robinson and the wounded American soldier were picked up later in the afternoon by a Naval craft. On the following day Robinson again volunteered to act as guide to a stronger force that was to attack Hauwei Is. Despite the fact that he was suffering from exposure cramp and sunburn, he accompanied the force that ultimately captured Hauwei Is.

During the period 14 Mar to 14 May Robinson was in charge of a small native (RPC) patrol which operated on the South coast of Manus. With great skill he organised a system of native espionage throughout the SE portion of Manus Is. where the Japanese forces were endeavouring to concentrate. On receipt of reports of enemy troops, WO Robinson immediately proceeded to the area with his native force and attacked the Japanese force found there. WO Robinson organised and led the patrols in person and received no assistance from other troops. These attacks were carried out at: Malai Bay—5 Japanese killed (entire force); Wari village—5 killed, 4 prisoners (entire force); Patusi village—5 prisoners (entire force); Loi village—18 killed, 3 prisoners (entire force); Patusi village—13 prisoners.

In all these operations WO Robinson showed great skill and courage and in all operations not a single enemy escaped. On 16 Mar when enemy prisoners were urgently needed by HQ, a party of 4 were captured by an Angau patrol led by Major J. K. McCarthy. En route to base, one of the enemy jumped overboard from a PT boat in mid-ocean and attempted to commit suicide by drowning. WO Robinson jumped overboard fully equipped and overcame and rescued the prisoner.

It is considered that WO Robinson displayed great courage, initiative and skill in the above mentioned incidents. With scant regard for his own life, he was a constant volunteer and was outstandingly successful in each venture he undertook.   *(L.G. 23.8.44)*

Robinson, Arthur, B.E.M., Warrant Officer Cl. II
2412487, Royal Regt. of Australian Artillery
No citation.   *(L.G. 28.3.69)*

Robinson, Bert, Sergeant
4077693, 3rd Monmouthshires, South Wales
Borderers (Newry, Co. Down) (Immediate)
On 19th July, during the attack on Bras Sjt. Robinson's Coy came under extremely heavy mortar and shell fire, with the result that all his offrs were killed or wounded, and the strength of the Coy reduced to approx a pl. By his own personal bravery, initiative, and efficiency, he reorganised what was left of the Coy, and completed the capture of the objective and subsequent mopping up. He then consolidated his posn during a most critical time, when flanking fire was brought to bear on his Coy as well as short range fire from the front and periodic shell and mortar fire. During the whole of this time, he kept cool and kept me informed of the situation, being the senior member of the Coy. This was a very critical time, as this flank was very open and I was extremely nervous of what might happen should a counter attack come in. However, he dealt with the situation admirably, organised the mopping up of all enemy posts immediately to his front and continued in command until relieved by an offr with another pl. Before effecting this relief, I had previously organised another offr with his pl to do the same, but this party was badly shot up before it was able to do this job. Subsequently and throughout the whole period, his efficiency and personal disregard for his own safety was the talk of his Coy. *(L.G. 19.10.44)*

Robinson, Frank, Warrant Officer Cl. II (actg.)
5767863, Royal Norfolk Regt. (Clapham)
51st Highland Div, P.O.W. Pool   *(L.G. 11.10.45)*

Robinson, George, Sergeant
7879797, 1st King's Dragoon Guards R.A.C. (Seedley,
Salford) (Immediate)
On 29 Mar 43 at Wadi Merteba, 'A' Sqn KDGs were leading the centre of the 'left hook' directed on Gabes. Wadi Merteba was found to be strongly held by enemy infantry well dug in. The Sqn, supported by 4 guns, attacked these. Sjt. Robinson was Troop Leader of the right tp. While the centre tps and guns were engaging the enemy, Sjt. Robinson worked round the enemy flank unobserved and attacked them in the rear. He did not open fire until he was right amongst the enemy dug-outs, when he opened up on 4 a/tk guns knocking out the crews. He threw hand grenades into the dug-outs from his turret. This defended locality, with over 200 men taken completely by surprise, surrendered to him. He then engaged the adjoining posts who also surrendered. In about three hrs 35 officers and approx 1,000 ORs complete with their guns and equipment were captured. Sjt. Robinson played a great part in this victory by capturing the first strong point. It was not known the enemy were Italian until the post surrendered. He showed initiative, gallantry and skill of exceptionally high order. This NCO has served in the field for just under two and half years. *(L.G. 17.6.43)*

Robinson, Henry, Lance Sergeant
4386986, 1st Bn. The Green Howards (Darlington)
(Immediate)
On the night of 7/8 February 1944 a recce patrol consisting of L/Sjt. Robinson and two men was sent out to locate and estimate the strength of the enemy positions on Pt. 165, North of Minturno. Whilst moving up the Southern slopes of this feature the patrol heard movement further up. Almost immediately, a German grenade thrown from above burst in front of L/Sjt. Robinson severely wounding him in the face and eyes and inflicting deep cuts in his shoulder and leg. At the same time the enemy opened fire with two machine guns from the ridge of Pt. 165. Undeterred by the intense pain he was suffering from his wounds L/Sjt. Robinon sent one man back to give immediate information to his Coy comd, whilst he himself remained to complete his task of pin pointing the enemy MG position.

L/Sjt. Robinson continued his recce until the effect of the blast on his face completely closed his eyes. It was only with the greatest difficulty and as a result of a dogged determination that he regained his unit lines at all, over 15 hours later in a completely exhausted condition and totally blind. In this condition in the Regimental Aid Post he passed his information to his Company Commander, thus finally completing the tasks allotted him. L/Sjt. Robinson's conduct showed a tenacity of purpose worthy of the highest traditions of the British Army. *(L.G. 29.6.44)*

Robinson, John Murray, Sergeant
54159, Royal Australian Infantry Corps
For Vietnam   *(L.G. 12.2.71)*

Robinson, John Robert, Warrant Officer Cl. III
(T.S.M.)
37237, 5th Royal Inniskilling Dragoon Guards
On May 17th, 1940, TSM Robinson was ordered to hold the main approach to the important village of Chappelle St. Vlrich. Before he had time to take up his position, his troop was attacked and outnumbered by enemy armoured cars and motor cycle troops. By his outstanding leadership and coolness under fire this Warrant Officer enabled a dangerous situation to be restored.
(L.G. 20.12.40)

Robinson, Lorimer Lane, Sergeant
7887757, 12th Royal Lancers R.A.C. (Kilmarnock)
(Immediate)
On May 30th 1942 round Knightsbridge, a large number of men were seen walking about between the enemy and our position, who were identified as our own escaped prisoners, who were in an exhausted condition, most of them unable to walk. Sjt. Robinson was instructed to go out and bring them into our lines. Throughout the afternoon he made at least 20 journeys under continued shell fire and brought in at least 200. He was at times shot at by the enemy over open sights. I was at the time

2/i/c 4th County of London Yeo. and watched this armoured car during part of the afternoon and after many enquiries found it to be commanded by Sjt. Robinson 12th Lancers. On May 31 he located an Italian column of met South of Bir Harmat, which was subsequently shelled by us. The lorries were then pursued and 78 Italians surrendered to Sjt. Robinson and another armoured car.
M.I.D. 15.12.42   (L.G. 24.9.42)

Robinson, Peter Thomas, Sergeant
2613912, 2 Armd. Grenadier Guards (Poole)
   (Immediate)
Sjt. Robinson was in command of a tp of No. 1 Sqn, 2nd Armd Bn. Gren Gds which at about 1600 hrs on Wed 20 Sep 44 was ordered to assault and cross the br at Nijmegen. The br is approx 700 yds long and has an embankment of equal length on the far side which makes it impossible for tracked vehs to get off the rd even when across. The br was known to be prepared for demolition and as the far side was in the hands of the Germans it could be blown at any time. This Sjt. started to lead his tp across the br and had just reached it when A/T Guns opened up from the far bank. Showing great coolness, Sjt. Robinson quickly withdrew his tp to Hull Down positions and engaged the enemy. At this stage it was reported to him that it was thought that the rd across the br was mined. As the light was failing, he was ordered to make a dash across the br at all costs with his Tp Sjt. leading. This was successfully done under heavy fire from 88 mm, A/T guns, and firing from the other bk and from an SP A/T gun firing down the br. Enemy small arms fire from the br itself in the girders of the br, as well as bazooka fire directed at the Comdr made this extremely hazardous. On reaching the far side of the br Sjt. Robinson took the lead on his own initiative and knocked out the SP gun which was firing down the rd. He then continued down the rd for 1500 yds under very heavy A/T & bazooka fire until contact was made with the American Paratroops. This Sjt. showed outstanding bravery and initiative in crossing such a formidable obstacle against such defence and there is no doubt that but for his courageous action the br might not have been captured intact.   (L.G. 1.3.45)

Robinson, Raymond Edward Lawrence, Sergeant
7894701, 2nd Fife & Forfar Yeo., Royal Armoured
   Corps (Hove)
This NCO has commanded a tank from the landing in Normandy to the capture of Lubeck. On every occasion in contact with the enemy he has fought his tank with the utmost vigour. On one occasion, when the other three tanks of his troop had been knocked out, he remained alone in a position exposed to enemy Anti-tank gun fire, six hundred yards ahead of the remainder of his Squadron. He stayed in this position for seven hours observing the enemy and engaging targets, until darkness fell.

On 5 April 1945 his troop ran into an SS Bazooka party manning a road block at Glissen. The leading tank got through, but was cut off. The Troop Leader in the next tank was bazookaed and the commander killed. Sjt. Robinson took immediate control of the troop, which was well ahead of the Squadron, and together with his fourth tank attacked the enemy at very close range in a built up area of houses and trees.

His aggressiveness and spontaneous action was so successful that the majority of the enemy were killed or taken prisoner. This allowed him to regain contact with his point tank and recover the crew of the knocked-out tank. He continued to lead his troop with great success for the next fortnight. His determination, courage and disregard for his personal safety throughout the whole campaign has set a fine example to the whole squadron.
                                           (L.G. 24.1.46)

Robinson, Robert, Warrant Officer Cl. II (actg.)
7046161, Royal Irish Fusiliers (Enniskillen, Co.
   Fermanagh)
Italy   (L.G. 12.4.45)

Robinson, William, Sergeant
4264669, 143 Special Service Company, Durham
   Light Infantry (Shiremoor, Northumberland)
   (Immediate)
Sjt. Robinson commanded a section of three men who were part of a covering party on an R.E. enterprise at Maungdaw (then in enemy hands) on the night 16/17 May 1943. It was Sjt. Robinson's party who withstood an enemy bayonet charge after the enemy had sustained heavy casualties in their MG positions. The bayonet charge was made with the greatest ferocity and was met by firing from the hip with LMG's. In the subsequent proceedings two of Sjt. Robinson's men were bayonetted but their assailants in each case had their skulls battered in by other members of the party. It finally ended in unarmed combat which resulted in two more of the enemy being destroyed by various methods, making a grand total in that affair of twelve or thirteen dead Japs and only two survivors. At that stage Robinson was ordered to embark, but as the launch had been destroyed he took his wounded with him and searched for and subsequently found a sampan in which they all reached Teknaf in safety. Sjt. Robinson's part in the operation was simply outstanding. When he wasn't killing Japs he was laughing in sheer enjoyment, and the reliance his men have in his personnal courage, quick appreciation and decisive action ensures the success of any future enterprises under his command.   (L.G. 22.7.43)

Robson, George, Corporal (A/Sgt.)
2819343, 1st Field Squadron, Royal Engineers
   (Hetton-le-Hole, Durham) (Immediate)
On 25th Oct 1942, at Alamein, Sjt. Robson with two sappers was detailed to accompany the Queen's Bays in their advance through the last two enemy minefields

during the afternoon. After getting through the minefields the Queen's Bays were heavily engaged and lost several tanks, but succeeded in damaging one 88 mm and 2 Mk IV German Tanks. This NCO immediately went forward by himself on foot, under heavy fire, carrying his charges and succeeded in demolishing the 88 mm and both tanks. Again, on the morning of the 26th Oct, he volunteered to go with a party of Inf carriers who were attacking the 'Kidney' feature, to demolish any guns which were over-run. On reaching the feature the Carriers came under heavy fire and were forced to withdraw. Sjt. Robson in his carrier continued on to the feature, where he captured and demolished one 50 mm A/Tk gun. While fixing the charges to this gun he was under fire from enemy infantry in slit trenches at a range of 20 yds. On the completion of this task he withdrew to rejoin the infantry carriers.

Sjt. Robson's example of bravery and determination, in the face of heavy fire, was a great encouragement to all ranks until he was wounded on the morning of 27th Oct 1942.   *(L.G. 11.3.43)*

Roby, Christopher William James, Sergeant
5378376, Oxfordshire & Buckinghamshire Light Infantry
No citation.   *(L.G. 20.8.40)*

Rochberg, Samuel, Lance Corporal
PAL/601, 285 Coy. R.A.S.C.
In June 1941 Rochberg escaped from Corinth prison and from then until his recapture in August 1942 he worked on an Escape Committee and lived amongst the Greeks.

After a few months of hiding in the hills Rochberg was employed by the Germans as a foreman on rock blasting, and making stones and sand for road making. In the status of foreman he had to sign contracts and vouchers for petrol and dynamite. By manipulating his books he was able to obtain for the saboteurs a little petrol and dynamite every week. Later he was able to obtain a considerable quantity by bartering with the Germans. He refused to take an offer of going to Germany as an Engineer but stayed behind helping the saboteurs to cut telephone wires each night.

In August 1942 he was betrayed by a compatriot to the Italian Secret Police who handed him over to the Germans. For the next 3 months he was moved from one Interrogation Centre to another before being finally sent to P/W Camp in Italy, where he was employed by S.B.O. on Intelligence work.

After the Armistice it was decided to evacuate the camp. Rochberg and 2 Sergeants were sent to connect up the camp with an outside telephone wire. Later, posing as a German workman he was able to give the camp plenty of warning of the impending invasion of the camp by the Germans. Rochberg and another P/W made their way south and crossed our lines into safety.

This is an outstanding achievement and I thoroughly recommend him for an immediate award for his great service to the Allied Cause.   *(L.G. 24.8.44)*

Rochester, William Turnbull, Warrant Officer Cl. II (C.S.M.)
444793, 11th Bn. Durham Light Infantry (Birkley, Co. Durham) (Immediate)
At Rauray (8865) on 28 June 44 and again on 1 July 44 this Warrant Officer showed the highest standard of devotion to duty and example. He was CSM of a very young Company who took their objective after suffering heavy casualties. Throughout this period his example and steadiness, in face of determined counter attack instilled great confidence in his company. His company Commader was killed and the acting Company Commander was wounded. All the subalterns were wounded but with this W.O. present the company remained cheerful, stood firm and held on.
(L.G. 19.10.44)

Rocks, Felix, Sergeant
3318787, 1st Bn. The Glasgow Highlanders (Highland Light Infantry) (W. Bromwich) (Immediate)
Sjt. Rocks was on 4/5 Apr a pl comd, when the bn crossed the Dortmund—Ems Canal and adv towards Drierwalde. While his pl was crossing the Canal in aslt boats under hy shell fire, his organising abilities and control of the men were exemplary and had a great influence on those under him. When a pl comd was killed and the plan of attack had to be changed at the last minute, Sjt. Rocks took over the task of the leading pl, and his leadership and high example—particularly to the young soldiers in the pl—got the pl fwd to its objective, under very hy SA fire, incl fire from 20-mm guns.

Although wounded twice during this attack, with a magnificent disregard for the pain he was in, Sjt. Rocks carried on until a NCO could be found to relieve him. Sjt. Rocks refused to be evac until he had given his relief a clear account of the situation. The aggressive spirit of Sjt. Rocks and his complete disregard of personal safety were most meritorious, and his cheerful disposn, even after he was wounded, set a very high example to all who were in contact with him.
M.I.D. 9.8.45   *(L.G. 12.7.45)*

Rodger, James Mason, M.M., Sergeant
3319295, Reconnaissance Corps and 81 (WA) Div Recce Bn (Glasgow) (Periodic)
In the campaign in the Kaladan Valley
During the period under review, 16 Nov 44—15 Feb 45, this NCO has for most of the time commanded his platoon. He has personally led a minimum of thirty separate long range offensive patrols of platoon strength and on every occasion has produced the most valuable results. Frequently, he has used his initiative to obtain information and attack enemy parties outside the initial scope of his patrols. At all times in face of the enemy he displayed powers of coolness, bravery and determination of the highest order. In particular in the middle of Nov 44 at Ahkang in the Arakan, he cleared a party of enemy from the route along which his coy was moving causing

a number of casualties. On 22 Jan 45 near Kanzeik when holding a bridgehead, he ambushed and sank an enemy M.L.C. causing many casualties and capturing much equipment. On this action he was completely separated from the rest of his coy and within 1000 yards of an enemy Bn. concentration. His contempt for the enemy even when completely outnumbered and far from his base has been a magnificent example to his platoon.
M.M. 13.9.45   *(L.G. 15.11.45)*

Rodriguez, Ferdinand Edward, Signalman
2187745, Royal Signals
Signalman Rodriguez volunteered for work in France when he was serving with the Royal Signals in the Middle East in March, 1942. After the necessary preliminary training in the United Kingdom he went to France by Lysander on 26th October, 1942. His mission was to organise wireless transmitter communications for a large network of agents. This group of agents was capable of producing first rate intelligence but was without any efficient means of communication. The transmitters were dropped by parachute. Signalman Rodriguez arranged for the sets to be installed close to places of military importance. Considerable ingenuity was required for their efficient transportation and installation.

After Signalman Rodriguez had been in the field for about six months there were about 30 wireless transmission stations working from widely separated areas, for which he had recruited and trained the operators locally. Several hundreds of messages of high operational value to all three servies were received by these lines, which were so well established that they continued to work satisfactorily, still manned by the same operators, long after Signalman Rodriguez' had been captured and imprisoned. He was caught while operating a set from the tower of a village church, by Gestapo men who asked to see the contents of his suitcase. By way of reply he thrust the case containing the set into their outstretched arms and fled amid a hail of revolver fire, remaining in hiding with peasants in the vicinity until he was able to move on. Later he took personal charge of the group's communications Headquarters in Paris. He maintained good relations with his French colleagues who admired the courage, skill and good temper with which he carried out his hazardous duties.

After a years work in the field he returned to U.K. for leave. He returned to France but was immediately arrested by the Gestapo. Questioned for a fortnight by the Gestapo, Signalman Rodriguez revealed nothing of his work. He was kept in solitary confinement for many months in Germany on low rations and was eventually tried by a German court martial and sentenced to death.

After he had been in prison for 18 months and under sentence of death for 7 months, it was possible to negotiate his exchange for a German officer and he arrived back in this country on 2nd February, 1945 in good spirits in spite of his poor physical condition due to malnutrition and long confinement.

Throughout all his long period of service in enemy occupied territory Signalman Rodriguez showed outstanding qualities of courage and leadership.
(L.G. 21.6.45)

Roe, Edward Augustus [George on AFW 3121], Gunner
860176, [...] Bty 3/Royal Horse Artillery (5, Cunnington Rd., South Farnborough)
On the 22 Nov 1941 at Sidi Rezegh Dvr Roe was driver of a 2 pr Portee of 'D' Bty RHA which was defending the aerodrome area. In an attack by a large number of enemy tanks his gun was hit and the detachment Comd wounded. Dvr Roe immediately took over the duties of No. 2 on the gun and when later the No. 3 was wounded he laid the gun himself. Finally when the remaining NCO of the detachment was wounded, he took Comd of the gun and kept it in action until the enemy tanks were driven off. During the whole action the gun was under heavy fire from enemy tanks and arty. Dvr. Roe showed great courage and presence of mind by taking charge of the gun when both NCOs had been wounded, although he himself was not a gunner, and by keeping the gun in action he was able to inflict further damage on the enemy and prevented them getting into his part of the position. His courage and initiative was a fine example to the rest of his Tp.   *(L.G. 20.1.42)*

Rogers, William Barry, Sergeant (T/W.O.II)
214091, Royal Australian Infantry Corps
Warrant Officer Class II William Barry Rogers enlisted in the Australian Regular Army on the 6th June 1961 and was allotted to the Royal Australian Regiment. He volunteered for duty in Vietnam and joined the Australian Army Training Team on 3rd January 1967.

He was posted to the Mike Force (Reaction Force) of 5th Special Forces Group (Airborne) where he was given command of a platoon of indigenous soldiers in 11 Company. On 19th February 1967 the company conducted a cordon and search of Ban Co Village in Quang Ngai Province where W.O. II Rogers and his platoon were ordered into the attack position, while the other two platoons cordoned the village. During the move into position five armed enemy moved towards the attacking platoon, were fired upon with no results and escaped into the village. The company was then ordered to attack the village quickly, and soon all platoolns came under intense small arms fire from the North-west and North-east sections of the village. As the company moved to secure the high ground on the North-east of the village they came under more heavy fire and the troops halted and took cover. W.O. II Rogers on the right flank saw the company halt and ordered his platoon to attack the North-west portion of the village; followed by only two members of his platoon he moved across 200 metres of open ground covered by enemy fire and assaulted the enemy position in the woods on the edge of the village. This aggressive move unnerved the enemy and they tried to escape, and W.O. II Rogers personally killed three of them. Seeing two more enemy fleeing from the village he chased them and exchanged fire with them until they escaped into the jungle. The company was then able to move in and search the village. During the search a vast tunnel complex was found and the indigenous soldiers, fearing booby traps, would not search them. W.O. II Rogers then unhesitatingly entered the tunnels, searched them and destroyed several hundred kilogrammes weight of rice and found several boxes of small arms ammunition.

By his daring actions W.O. II Rogers broke the resistance of the enemy ambush in the village and, his personal bravery and leadership set a strong and enduring example to the inexperienced soldiers of his platoon when he searched the tunnels by himself. By these courageous actions he has brought great credit on himself, the Australian Regular Army and the United States Army Special Forces. *[From L.G.]*

(*L.G. 26.9.67*)

Rolfe, Alfred John, Private
NX 86223, 2/13 Aust Inf Bn. (Immediate)
On 1 Oct 43, during the final attack on Finschhafen, elements of the forward company of Pte. Rolfe's battalion came under heavy machine gun fire from a strongly defended enemy position in the viciity of Ilebbe Creek. Whilst Pte Rolfe's platoon was being re-roganised for a further attack he climbed the bank of the creek nearest the enemy and in full view of their positions commenced to engage the nearest post by firing his bren from the hip. Orders were given for his platoon to continue the attack. They again came under fire from several enemy automatic weapons on their flank and suffered many casualties. While the further forward movement by his whole platoon was temporarily held up, Pte. Rolfe coolly pressed forward by himself towards the nearest enemy machine gun position and engaged it at close quarters by fire from his bren gun, killing the enemy gun crew and thus silencing the post; continuing to advance firing from the hip he rushed another strong post and inflicted further casualties on the enemy. During this gallant action, Pte. Rolfe was severely wounded in the chest by fire from a third enemy post. The courage and determination of this soldier enabled his platoon to overcome the strong enemy position on their flank and this was a direct factor in the final success of the action.

(*L.G. 2.3.44*)

Rolston, Andrew, Warrant Officer Cl. II
6976413, 2nd Bn. Royal Inniskilling Fusiliers
    (Oxford) (Immediate)
Map Ref 214735—Sheet 76 II S.W. Italy
At 0130 hrs on 21st April, 1945, 'C' Company was the leading company of the Battalion in an attack to form a bridgehead over the Canal at 214735 (Sheet 76 II S.W. Italy). As the company crossed the Canal they came under very heavy shell fire. All the officers were wounded

and the company suffered severe casualties, and in consequence were badly disorganised. CSM Rolston took over command and skilfully reorganised the company, and formed and held the bridgehead thus enabling the rest of the Battalion to pass through.

Under heavy shell fire he maintained the company in position by his personal example, until relieved by the arrival of an officer from another company.

It was entirely due to the personal courage and initiative of CSM Rolston, that the company was able to complete its task, in spite of the loss of its officers and the natural confusion and disorganisation caused by this and the numerous casualties suffered in the company.

(*L.G. 18.10.45*)

Romaines, James Richard, Sergeant
2324204, 97th Field Regt, RA Signal Section, Royal
    Signals (E. Jarrow, Durham)
Sjt. Romaines showed conspicuous devotion to duty at all times, but especially during the operations in the Western Desert, June 4th to July 2nd 1942. In the night of June 18/19th, when his section was surrounded by the enemy and many outlying trucks were captured, he succeeded in bringing his men, vehicles and equipment intact through heavy fire, hotly pursued by enemy armoured cars or tanks. At Matruh from June 25th to 28th he was out night and day laying lines and maintaining communications. No task was too arduous for him. His unfailing cheerfulness, keenness and competence was an inspiration to his whole section who were suffering from lack of sleep and irregular meals. At Deird Sheen on the 1st July when the box he was in was attacked and finally overrun by enemy tanks and infantry he organised the defence of RAQ by his section and finally personally blew up a 6 pdr gun under the noses of the enemy infantry who were then in the position.
M.I.D. 20.12.41   (*L.G. 18.2.43*)

Ronald, Askari
13678, 2nd Bn The King's African Rifles,
Somaliland. For outstanding gallantry during the period 12–15th August, 1940 as a member of the Mortar Detachment. Under heavy artillery fire he remained at his post and continued to bring forward mortar ammunition showing complete disregard for his own safety and setting a fine example to the other African Troops. In the latter stages of the battle when only one British Rank was available Askari Ronald was responsible for maintaining the gun in action while the European was in the O.P.
To be dated 11.2.41 and substituted for the award of the African D.C.M. announced in the L.G. of that date.
(*L.G. 21.7.42*)

Ropati , Yaca[...], [Private]
Fijian Forces
S.W. Pacific   (*L.G. 7.12.44*)

Roper, Reginald Herbert, Gunner
1528857, 170 Lt AA Bty, 57 Lt AA Regt, Royal
Artillery (Bournemouth)
On 2 Feb 42, Gnr. Roper was a gun no. in a Lt AA Tp operating with a rear gd of 5 Ind Inf Bde near Carmusa. Their gun tractor was hit and destroyed and Gnr. Roper's gun covered the withdrawal of our tps engaging enemy inf and AFV's at short range until the gun and most of the det were knocked out by a direct hit. Throughout the action Gnr. Roper, although seriously wounded in the knee, had carried out his duties with exemplary coolness and courage. When the posn was finally taken by the enemy, he managed to evade being captured by struggling to a wadi where he collapsed. He was taken by friendly Arabs to a cave near Derna where he remained hidden for about 5 months. For 3 months his leg refused to heal and he suffered from blood poisoning. At the risk of losing his leg or worse, Gnr. Roper steadfastly resisted the temptation to give himself up to the enemy where medical treatment could be expected, and by operating on his leg with his clasp knife, he finally removed the shell fragments and his wound healed. Learning that four British soldiers had escaped from Derna he persuaded the Arabs to bring them in and hide them while he made plans for their escape. Having acquired a knowledge of Arabic, he got news of a British patrol operating near Mechili. He set off with his companions and they joined it after a forced march of some 50 miles through the Gebel. Gnr. Roper eventually rejoined his regiment after an absence of 72 months.

By his fortitude, endurance and resolution, Gnr. Roper not only succeeded himself in rejoining his Unit but organised the escape of his companions and he has set a fine example of courage and faith.
M.I.D. 11.1.45   *(L.G. 31.12.42)*

Rose, Clifford John, Warrant Officer Cl. II (C.S.M.)
(A/W.O.I (R.S.M.)
6010523, 1/4 Bn The Essex Regt. (Ilford, Essex)
(Immediate)
This Warrant Officer displayed conspicuous bravery, devotion and leadership during the fighting at Cassino 15–20 Mar 44.

On the evening of 15 Mar, his battalion took over Pt 193 (Castle) preparatory to securing further objectives on Monastery Hill. RSM Rose was placed in charge of the forward Administrative Post, the main function of which was the supply of ammunition. Owing to the natural difficulties, this post had to be on the outskirts of Cassino itself, and because of the continued enemy resistance was subjected to constant and intense enemy defensive fire by artillery and mortars.

Through four days and nights, RSM Rose maintained this forward post in spite of heavy casualties which were occurring amongst his command, and by his own personal example of cool continuous bravery, and utter disregard of enemy fire, ensured its efficient functioning throughout. On many occasions fires started amongst the

ammunition, and whenever these occurred, this Warrant Officer personally led parties to extinguish them.

On 19 Mar, particularly, when the enemy were counter attacking Pt. 193 (Castle) all day, the situation regarding ammunition supply became critical, and the enemy fire had become intensified. Again RSM Rose met the situation magnificently, and his personal initiative and organisation under conditions of extreme hazard ensured an adequate supply of ammunition to the forward troops and their supporting weapons. This played a decisive part in the defeat of all enemy attempts to obtain this vital objective.

The bravery, devotion and leadership displayed by RSM Rose during all this time, and in fact, on every occasion his battalion is in action, are a magnificent example and merit the highest praise.
M.I.D. 24.6.43   *(L.G. 25.11.43)*

Rose, Clifford John, D.C.M., Warrant Officer Cl. I
(R.S.M.)   **Bar**
6010523, 1/4th Bn. The Essex Regt. (Ilford) (Periodic)
Throughout the operations in Tunisia in which the battalion has been engaged from 15 Mar to 15 May 43, this Warrant Officer, whose primary operational task has been organisation of ammunition supply, has displayed outstanding bravery, resource and devotion to duty.

The success of these operations in difficult and hilly country has depended essentially on rapid re-organisation of captured objectives, and in this ammunition supply has been a vital factor. In the Matmata Hills, 24 to 28 Mar., RSM Rose organised the supply on a narrow road under heavy artillery bombardment, and personally led trucks forward to the front line on repeated occasions and in spite of the additinal risk of enemy mines.

At Akarit, 6 Apr 43, when the battalion was [...] from its wheels, he organised the supply into the hills, and again led it to the forward troops under intense bombardment and small arms fire. Finally, at Djebel Garci, 19/23 Apr, where ammunition trucks had to run the gauntlet of enemy observation and intense artillery and mortar concentrations, RSM Rose personally took forward ammunition over and over again; on one occasion his own truck being hit and the driver killed.

At all times cool, devoted, and entirely regardless of his own personal safety, this Warrant Officer has provided a magnificent example to all ranks of his battalion; and his devoted service played a considerable part in the success of its operations. Throughout all previous operations in which the unit has been engaged, RSM Rose has displayed the same outstanding qualities.
                                                 (L.G. 24.8.44)

Rosemond, Robert, Warrant Officer Cl. II
3326139, 6th Bn. Highland Light Infantry (Leeds)
(Periodic)
Both in his capacity of Pl. Sjt. and later in his present rank, CSM Rosemond displayed great courage and initiative in all the major actions in which his Coy was

involved, during this Unit's 9 months campaigning in the N.W.E. theatre of operations.

He particularly distinguished himself on 30 Dec. 44 at Rischden, North of Geilenkirchen, when his Coy went to the relief of another Unit of the Bde, whose fwd elements had been over-run. During his Coy Comds absence for orders, there being no other Officer with the Coy, he re-organised it in preparation for a counter-attack while under sustained small arms and shell-fire. Due to his resource, an immediate attack which the situation demanded was able to be launched as soon as orders were received, and the situation restored. Later on the same day this W.O. successfully handled a situation when the fwd elements of the Coy were threatened with being cut off.

In the Dortmund—Ems Canal bridgehead South of Ibbenburen on [...] Apr. 45, during an attack, in the initial stages of which his Coy Comd was killed, CSM Rosemond took over command at Coy HQ until such time as he was relieved by the only surviving Officer in the Coy. Rarely was there a second in command in the Coy and CSM Rosemond invariably had many administrative duties to perform in addition to his combatant ones. These he always discharged with the zeal, resource and ability which were characteristic of him in action.

(L.G. 24.1.46)

Ross, Alexander, Warrant Officer Cl. II
2814737, Seaforth Highlanders (since commissioned)
51st Highland Div, P.O.W. Pool
M.I.D. 20.12.40 *(L.G. 11.10.45)*

Rothwell, Herbert, Sergeant (actg.)
3851880, 2 Recce Regt., Reconnaissance Corps R.A.C.
(Bolton) (Immediate)
At Ngazun
On the 8th March 1945 Serjeant Rothwell was a Section Commander in a Carrier Troop commanded by Lieut. Sutton. This troop was ordered to attack and penetrate known enemy positions, with a view to establishing their strength, and to bring back enemy identifications if possible.

At 0830 hrs the patrol met and destroyed an outpost of two men on their first bound, and at once came under heavy mortar and shell fire, which kept up unceasingly until the conclusion of the action over an hour later. After a pause on the first bound, Serjeant Rothwell's section was ordered to advance to the next feature, which, it is now known, was held by at least an enemy company. On seeing them approach the enemy opened up with LMGs, rifles, and grenade dischargers. Sjt. Rothwell with great coolness stood up in his carrier to control his section and personally directed the return fire, which caused the enemy several casualties. He then drove his own carrier right into the enemy position and engaged them at close quarters with grenades. During this time he wiped out an LMG post, consisting of an officer and two men, and halted the carrier alongside the

trench whilst one of his crew got out and recovered the LMG and a satchel of documents carried by the Jap officer, both of which were brought back to our own lines.

Not satisfied with this, he attacked another foxhole, killing one occupant and wounding the other with a grenade, and dismounting himself, despite very heavy fire directed against his carrier, he dragged the second Jap out of the foxhole and hoisted him on to the front of the carrier in an attempt to bring him back alive. Unfortunately, whilst withdrawing from the position, the prisoner commenced to struggle and, falling off the carrier, was run over by one of it's tracks. Meanwhile, Sjt. Rothwell was called upon to assist his Troop Comander, who, with the second section, was also heavily engaged with the enemy. Rallying his section, which was still being shelled and mortared, he supported the other section's withdrawal before finally disengaging himself.

Serjeant Rothwell's brilliant leadership and the example he set of aggressiveness and complete disregard for his own safety undoubtedly contributed more than anything else to the successful completion of the patrol, which obtained all the information required about the enemy positions, inflicted at least 12 casualties, and captured a LMG and documents all without loss to themselves. *(L.G. 12.7.45)*

Rourke, Floyd Orin, Lance Corporal
M.105583, The Calgary Highlanders (Immediate)
On 26 April 1945 the Calgary Highlanders were ordered to capture Gruppen-Buhren, Germany. 'A' Company was detailed to secure the first objective to serve as a firm base for the battalion attack.

To reach this objective 'A' Company had to cross 1200 yards of open, flat ground completely devoid of cover and to assist them a smoke programme was laid on. Unfortunately, due to a sudden change in wind, the smoke cleared and the Company, now exposed, was subjected to most intense 20 mm, LMG and small arms fire which killed the platoon commander of number nine platoon, the leading platoon, and caused many other casualties.

L/Cpl. Rourke, realising that he was now the senior NCO in the platoon immediately took over command of the platoon and skillfully led the men over the remaining 700 yards of open ground, through the barbed wire entanglements and enemy crawl trenches and into the final and successful assault of the objective.

Once on the objective, L/Cpl. Rourke quickly reorganised the platoon and made a further bound to attack an 88 mm gun which was knocked out and the crew captured. A group of enemy now appeared on the platoon left flank and L/Cpl. Rourke immediately moved his men over and engaged them capturing a further twelve prisoners.

This junior NCO, by his initiative, good judgment and complete disregard for his personal safety, not only was directly responsible for the capture of an enemy gun and sixteen prisoners but also caused by his bravery and splendid leadership the collapse of enemy resistance in the area which resulted in the complete success of the company attack.   *(L.G. 22.9.45)*

Routledge, Ronald John, Sergeant
P.7541, Royal Canadian Corps of Signals
Recommended by: PW Far East Can Mil H.
                                          (L.G. 15.6.46)

Rowe, Kenneth Medcalf, Lance Sergeant
A.11385, The Perth Regt., Canadian Infantry Corps
(Immediate)
On 31 August 1944, during the assault on the Gothic Line, the Perth Regiment captured Feature 204. At about 0145 hours 1 September, the enemy launched a strong counter-attack on the Regimental position. The main force of the attack came through a platoon commanded by Lance Sergeant Rowe. In the early stages of the attack some of the section positions were overrun and the platoon suffered heavy casualties, Lance Sergeant Rowe himself being wounded in the head, refusing Medical attention at this critical juncture he rallied what remained of his platoon and personally led three successive charges in a gallant effort to regain these lost positions. The first two attempts were beaten back after being bitterly contested but Lance Sergeant Rowe led a third and successful assault during which he personally rushed a machine-gun post with great daring and cleared the position at the point of the bayonet. In the course of this bitter fighting 20 Paratroopers were killed and 10 captured. As on many other occasions, the cool determination and courageous leadership displayed by Lance Sergeant Rowe were a real inspiration to his men and it was due to his personal gallant efforts in this critical situation that the counter-attack on his company failed and the Battalion position was held.   *(L.G. 20.1.45)*

Rowlinson, John Sumner, Corporal
7931598, 51st Bn., Royal Tank Regt. (Stockport)
In an action on 28 Feb 43 North of El Aroussa this NCO displayed outstanding courage and devotion to duty. His tank was set on fire through penetration by 75 mm anti-tank gun which set his amn on fire and he himself suffered severe burns of the face and hands. After giving orders to abandon tank and extricating himself he found that three members of his crew had not followed him. Despite his own injuries and the heat of the burning cordite he re-entered his tank twice and helped out two seriously wounded men and subsequently carried them under heavy enemy M.G. and Mortar fire 30 yards to the shelter of a ditch where he applied first aid and continued with no thought for himself to sustain them until the conclusion of the action. This NCO showed complete disregard for his own personal safety, thereby saving the lives of two of his crew.   *(L.G. 4.5.43)*

Rowlinson, William Josiah, Corporal (temp.)
2/400239, 3rd Bn., Royal Australian Regt.
For Korea   *(L.G. 25.1.52)*

Rowlinson, William Josiah, Corporal (temp.)   Bar
2/400239, 3rd Bn., Royal Australian Regt.
For Korea   *(L.G. 4.3.52)*

Roy, Robert, Sergeant, Pipe Major
2216942, 2nd Black Watch (Glasgow)
On 21 Nov 41 Pipe Major Roy displayed the most exceptional and outstanding gallantry and devotion to duty in the attack of the bn on Tiger from the Tobruch Perimeter. From the start line to the German Bn posn commanding the objective, he played his pipes with the foremost tps almost continuously throughout the advance of 22 miles, under heavy enemy fire of all kinds for the entire distance.

When collective movement ceased, and while the enemy posn was being reduced, the Pipe Major crawled round to the wounded men near him, dressing wounds and giving them water, when any movement brought down a hail of enemy fire.

In the vicinity of the objective he was ordered back to the R.A.P. having been wounded three times. His bravery and example of complete disregard of personal danger was an inspiration to the advancing tps and had a direct bearing on maintaining the impetus of the attack. This NCO previously distinguished himself in the defence of Crete where he was again wounded and captured by the enemy. On recovery, he escaped from a P.O.W. camp in Greece and at considerable personal danger made his way to Syria where he rejoined the bn.
Recommended for V.C.; M.I.D. 15.12.42; M.B.E. 31.5.56
                                          (L.G. 24.2.42)

Royston, Frederick, Private
6284264, 2 Bn. The Buffs (Royal East Kent Regt.)
Towards the end of May 40 I had charge of a section outside Pradelles, South-east Cassel. We stood out as long as possible against the advancing Germans and then made our way to Bn. H.Q., where I found the Commanding Officer and 10 men. Shortly afterwards Bn. H.Q. was over-run, and I and some others made for Dunkirk by lorry. Ultimately the road became impassible because of a French convoy, and we continued on foot. We met an officer, and with seven men I dug a position on his orders, but we were forced to withdraw on the approach of German tanks, and after that it was every man for himself. With two companions I got to within about 7 miles of Dunkirk. There I was wounded in the groin. and on my orders the men left me alone. I was found by a German medical officer who dressed my wound and I was taken to a farm occupied by the German Medical Corps (30 May). From there I was moved by car to Mons, where I was kept for one day in a private house, and to Courtrai, where the wounded were four days in a hotel which was being used as a hospital.

From Courtrai I was sent to a hospital in a country house, seven or eight miles from Koblenz. There my wound began to give me trouble, and I was kept in the hospital for three months, when I was told I was to be moved to North Germany. I decided to try to escape. I was allowed to go walking in the grounds every afternoon and discovered a probable way out through the latrines. The hospital was a sort of clearance camp for wounded, and my hour for walking was from 1600 to 1700 hrs. each day, when I was unguarded except for the ordinary sentries.

On 23 Sep I went out to the latrine about 1600 hrs and began cutting through the wire fence with a pair of joiner's pliers which I had found in the hospital. The fence was about 3 yards wide, and it took me a considerable time to cut through. Having cut a passage, I remained in the latrine until dusk, and then crawled through the gap in the wire on my stomach. I lay in the bushes outside for about two hours, and then started walking.

I knew the way by which I had been brought from Belgium to Koblenz, and I followed this in the reverse direction, keeping to the fields. I walked for three nights and lay up during the day. I had brought only one piece of bread with me from the hospital, and I had no other food except some carrots which I stole from gardens.

When I reached the frontier I hid in a spinney and watched the German sentries during the afternoon. The furthest points of the sentries' beats were about half a kilometre apart and the two met in the middle and then retraced their steps. At dusk I crept to within about 30 yards of their meeting place, and when they separated I crossed a small road into a wood. A dog, which ultimately turned out to be locked up in a hut in the wood, began to bark, and I had to lie low for a bit until it had quietened. I then took off my boots and what remained of my socks and circled the hut, only to find myself on the wrong side of the road. I remained hidden all day until dusk, when I began walking over the fields. By this time I was just about all in, but I met a farm hand in the fields who took me to a farm. I am not certain where this farm was, but I think I arrived in Belgium well South of Courtrai. I was very well treated at the farm, being given food, civilian clothes and a 100 franc note, with the advice that I should keep to by-roads till I reached the French frontier.

I arrived at the frontier at Le Seau, between Bailleul and Armentieres. Near the frontier I met a Belgian who said that it wuld be quite easy to get across. He gave me a 100 franc note to give to the Customs officer. At the frontier the official asked for papers. I said, 'Anglais,' and gave him the 100-franc note. Speaking to me all the time in French, he escorted me over the frontier past the German guards. Before he left me he advised me to try to get to Lille, where he said there was an organisation. It took me about a week to reach Lille via Merville. I stayed at farms during that week. Just outside Merville I met a woman who took me to her home in Lille, where she was already sheltering two British soldiers L/Cpl. Green, R.A. (whom I believe to be in Fort de la Revere) and Pte. Taylor, J., Ox. & Bucks L.I. (Fort de la Pevere).

After I had been there two days Major Lowden, York & Lancaster Regt., and Captain Wright, 9 Queen's Royal Lancers, arrived from Loos, where they had been in prison. Just afterwads a Lieut. Salt arrived, also from Loos. On the advice of Major Lowden and Captain Wright, I found an outlet through a glass panel in the roof of the house, in case we should be raided by the Germans. About this time there was a certain amount of dispute among our helpers as to which of them should get us away, and one evening one of them, a woman, arrived in a very bad temper because we had favoured someone else's scheme. She said that she would not help us any more and would not be coming to visit us again. I noticed that she left at 1700 hrs exactly, and I suspected that we might have trouble that night.

At 2240 hours there was a banging at the front door. I went to Major Lowden and Captain Wright in their bedroom and warned them to get dressed. The front door was burst open, and I just had time to get Green and Taylor out through the roof and into the attic of the next house, which it had already been arranged was to be our hiding place should we be raided. At 0500 hrs next day the owner of the attic came up, brought us civilian clothes, and told us to report to a cafe in Rubaix. I took Green and Taylor there by tram, and on the way I saw Major Lowden, Captain Wright, Lieut. Salt and the woman who had been sheltering us under an escort of one German officer and four soldiers.

From Roubaix we were taken to Tourcoing, where I was sheltered in a cafe while Green and Taylor were housed in the other end of the town. My hostess tried to get in touch with an organisation, but when a week had passed with no developments I asked if I could try alone to get to Unoccupied France, and she agreed. Seven hundred francs were collected by French friends for my journey. I left Tourcoing on the 0515 train on a Friday morning just before Christmas 40 and travelled to Bethune via Lille. From Bethune I went to Abbeville where I was supplied with false identity papers for crossing out of the Zone Interdite. I crossed the boundary by the main bridge at Abbeville, where my papers were examined by two German sentries, and caught the train for Paris, whence I went to Bordeaux. I could get no assistance there for crossing the Line of Demarcation, but was advised to go to a place near Tours. I crossed the Line there with the assistance of a cafe owner whose brother met me on the other side and took me to a small barn, where I stayed the night.

Next morning I went by train to Marseilles. There I went to a mission, and the following morning detectives took me to the police station and said I had to sign an internment form, but promised that I would be allowed a certain amount of freedom. On my return to the mission, however, I learned that I was to be interned the next day. I accordingly stayed that night at a hotel, and next morning was advised to go to Perpignan. There I was arrested at the station and sent to St. Hippolyte.

On my second day at St. Hippolyte I got out alone and travelled with two other British soldiers from Toulouse to Tarbes, whence I carried on alone to Pau. I stayed about two weeks there and in April 41 tried to cross the Pyrenees alone without a guide. I had to give up because of the snow, and, returning to Pau, surrendered to the Prefect of Police, who set off with me and two gendarmes for St. Hippolyte. I escaped at the station at Nimes and went to Perpignan, where I was arrested and sent back to St. Hippolyte.

About this time the French were tightening their control at St. Hippolyte at the instigation of the German Commission, and when I told 2/Lt. Hewitt I still wanted to get to Spain he said any further attempts would be punished with 30 days' solitary confinement. Two days later I got out again, but was arrested after five hours and was given the sentence of 30 days' solitary confinement.

After doing 25 days in prison I complained to the doctor that my wound was troubling me and he sent me to Nimes for x-ray treatment. I was two weeks in hospital. Two French soldiers then came for me and said we would be leaving on the 1730 train that day. They allowed me, however, to visit some friends in Nimes, on the understanding that I should meet them on the station. This I did not do. Instead I went alone to Perpignan, where I was advised to go to Laroque, near the frontier. I set off by bus and got off two villages before Laroque where a Frenchman showed me a pass into Spain. I walked along a main road, and after 252 hours I got as far as 3 km. past Figueras. There a Civil Guard asked me for papers, and I had to admit I had none and that I was British. He asked if I had any money, and I said I had 1275 pesetas. I was arrested and sentenced by a special commissioner for having contraband money, the judge saying that I would remain in prison 'until the Consul got me out.' I was in prison in Figueras from 31 Jul to 29 Nov. I shared a cell with one Frenchman and two Belgians and was well treated. I was then sent, via Barcelona and Saragossa to Miranda where I was interned from 7 Dec till early in Apr 42. While I was in Miranda the Gestapo used to visit the camp each Wednesday and ask for volunteers from among the German Jews, Poles, and Spaniards to return to Germany. The German Jews were most ready to go and some Spaniards went. The Poles on the other hand, did not volunteer. When F/O Milroy Gay (S/P.G.(–)674) left Miranda I took over the British group., I was released from Miranda, and after a fortnight in Madrid was sent to Gibraltar at the end of April for repatriation.

(L.G. 16.6.42)

Rudge, William Francis, Sergeant
3654948, South Lancashire Regt. (attd. S.S.T., No. 2 Commando) (Warrington) (Immediate)
Gulf of Salerno 13th September 1943

On the 13th September 1943 on the Dragone Hill, Sgt Rudge, one of the six survivors of the forward section of 22, showed outstanding bravery whilst in close contact with the enemy. After being mortared and shelled for two and a half hours and during a period of close confused fighting he twice rallied the men near him and repeatedly drove off the enemy. He also organised a party to go forward, under enemy machine gun fire, to retrieve a Vickers gun (whose crew were all casualties). The gun was used afterwards and inflicted casualties. Sgt Rudge carried back on three separate occasions badly wounded men, always returning immediately to the firing line, and his behaviour under a most severe concentration of mortar and machine-gun fire for a period of about three hours was an inspiration to the section.

(L.G. 13.1.44)

Rudman, William Arthur, Corporal
6403538, 2nd Bn. The Devonshire Regt. (Burwash)
During the period 6 Jun 44 to 8 May 45, Cpl. Rudman has shown conspicuous bravery and devotion to duty on many occasions. In Jun 44 as a private soldier he was in a platoon attacking in the Hottot sector. His Section comd became a casualty. Rudman straight away assumed command in a critical situation, rallied his men and led them on to their objective under very heavy fire. In Aug 44, at Cond Sur Noireau, Cpl. Rudman's section was fired upon from close quarters. This NCO immediately dashed into the ruined house throwing a grenade. He killed two Germans and caused the surrender of the remaining five. On 10 Jan 45 when acting as Pl Sjt. at Bakenhovern, his platoon was attacked at night. His wireless communication had failed. He therefore decided to cross over the small canal and pass his information through a neighbouring platoon. This entailed coming under very heavy enemy MG fire on every occasion. His information was of vital importance and led to the bringing down of an artillery DF task which materially affected the outcome of the battle. On 18 Jan 45 at Schilberg, he again assumed command of the platoon in the middle of the battle, encouraging his men by his own personal example and his complete disregard for safety. At all times this NCOs devotion to duty and inspiration to all ranks has been of the very highest order.

(L.G. 24.1.46)

Russell, Croslyn Holmes, Sergeant
5619215, 2nd Bn., The Devonshire Regt. (Bristol) (Immediate)
At Les Forges, on 14th August, 1944, Sjt. Russell's Company was sent out to mop up enemy pockets of resistance. He was commanding a Platoon, consisting of only two sections. His Platoon cleared a small village, taking three prisoners and then, owing to the very close country, lost contact with Company H.Q. Sjt. Russell decided to resume his advance. As light was failing, his Platoon encountered an enemy Post, but before the enemy had a chance to open fire, Sjt. Russell led his

Platoon into the attack, killing two, wounding two, and taking seven prisoners. As it was then too dark to continue the advance, Sjt. Russell reorganised his Platoon, in case of counter-attack, placing the prisoners in the centre. At daybreak, he managed to contact his Company H.Q. and proceeded to help the Company to take all their objectives. Through this NCO's drive, leadership and bravery, he saved his Platoon from suffering any casualties and greatly contibuted to the success of his Company's attack. *(L.G. 1.3.45)*

Russell, Douglas Haigh, Sergeant
DX 87, 2/3 Fd Regt., Australian Military Forces
On 12 Apr 41 at Kleidi Pass Sjt. Russell was No 1 of a gun which remained in action to cover the withdrawal. His gun was ordered to remain in action and be the last to withdraw. For some time prior to withdrawal his detachment was under MG fire and he displayed great coolness and control in eventually getting his gun away with the enemy inf only about 600 yds away. By maintaining his gun in action to the last he was largely responsible for the other 9 guns being got away.
(L.G. 4.11.41)

Russell, Harold Cecil, Warrant Officer Cl. II (C.S.M.)
M.63, 1 Gold Coast Regt.
For marked gallantry in action.
On 10 May on Black Shirt Ridge 9 miles N.W. of Uadara this Warrant Officer set an inspiring example to his Company during an engagement lasting 22 hrs. Under heavy M.G. and Arty fire he was instrumental in bringing in three badly wounded men, thereby saving their lives. Later he led the Mortar Platoon forward, and brought them into action. He was always to be found where the fight was thickest encouraging the men and setting a magnificent example of courage and devotion to duty. This Warrant Officer has previously shown utter disregard for his own safety under fire, and his conduct is the admiration of the Africans in his Company.
M.I.D. 30.12.41, 19.9.46, 1.1.55, M.C. 17.1.46
(L.G. 30.12.41)

Russell, Lawrence Elgin, Corporal
K.74053, North Nova Scotia Highrs. (Immediate)
K.74053 Corporal Lawrence Elgin Russell, 15 Platoon, 'C' Company, North Nova Scotia Highlanders, on a dyke South East of Hoofdplaat, on 9 October, 1944, showed outstanding bravery and initiative when leading his section to trap and destroy a party of 18 enemy, then, taking over command of the remnants of his platoon after the platoon commander was killed and sergeant wounded, he successfully repelled a strong enemy counter attack.
On the morning of 9 October, 1944, 'C' Company was ordered to move West along the dyke South of Hoofdplaat Polder. Some enemy were seen on a transverse dyke ahead. Corporal Russell quickly seized the initiative and by rushing his section around the corner

of the dyke was successful in killing 16 and wounding the other two members of the enemy patrol, quite a number of whom fell by fire from Corpral Russell's sten gun.
The company occupied a position further along the dyke and were heavily shelled causing the death of Corporal Russell's Platoon commander and wounding the platoon Sergeant. The platoon strength was down to eight when a strong enemy counter attack formed up on his platoon front. Corporal Russell displayed cool personal courage of the highest order by moving around in the open and reorganising his fire positions to meet the counter attack. He then communicated with company headquarters to call for artillery fire and returned to encourage his men.
Corporal Russell's quick seizure of the initiative and confident manner in a position of great personal danger, resulted in his few men holding a forward position which later became a base from which to move the battalion forward and was instrumental in the clearing of the Breskens pocket. His display of bravery and leadership was of a very high order. *(L.G. 10.2.45)*

Russell, Neil Hamilton, Sergeant
QX 2047, 2/12 Aust Inf Bn.
On the night 11/12 July, 41 this non-commissioned officer was in command of a fighting patrol which co-operated with other detachments from 1/12 Aust. Inf. Bn. in a raid on the enemy who was established in earthworks two miles from the perimeter of Tobruk defences. The enemy position was protected in front by rows of booby traps and vehicle mines.
Sjt. Russell lead his patrol to the assault in a particularly cool and efficient manner passing without hesitation through the mine-field and penetrating the enemy localities. At this stage he sustained wounds from booby traps, which he tripped in leading the patrol forward, but continued in action and closed with the enemy. In the subsequent fighting he was again wounded with grenade splinters but continued to deal vigorously with the enemy, inflicting casualties and securing prisoners. On the withdrawal signal he extricated his patrol and on ascertaining that one man was missing due to severe wounds he immediately returned some distance to the locality of the raid with a stretcher bearer. This action was carried out in moonlight under severe machine gun fire from the enemy on the flanks. The wounded man was located and although almost beyond aid assistance was given and endeavour made to move him to safety. Only when the stretcher bearer had been mortally wounded and nothing further could be done did Russell relinquish his attempt. His leadership, devotion to duty and personal indifference to danger were an example to all. They contributed in the largest degree to the success of the raid and set a high standard of soldierly conduct. *(L.G. 21.10.41)*

Ruthven, A., L/Cpl.
See Ellin, J.

Rutter, John Richard, Warrant Officer Cl. II (B.S.M.)
797866, B Bty. 1st Regt. Royal Horse Artillery
(Eighton Bank, Co. Durham) (Immediate)
BSM Rutter was BSM of Downman's Troop, B Bty
RHA, 1st Regt RHA during the tank action near Elwet
Tamar on the evening of 2 Jun 42 when the Bty was
attacked by 60 tks. He took charge of a section of guns
and got them into action on three different occasions
firing on the flank where the threat was greatest. On the
last occasion the range was 400 yds and he was covering
the withdrawal of the Bty and he put one German tank
in flames. Throughout the action he showed great
initiative and complete disregard to his own personal
safety. He set the very highest example to all those who
were with him. After the last action when the quad and
gun were set on fire by MGs he immediately got the
crew on to other vehicles, despite the fact that he himself
had been wounded in two places.
M.I.D. 8.7.41   (*L.G. 13.8.42*)

Ryan, Denis, Corporal
3452615, 2nd Bn., Lancashire Fusiliers (Ashton-
under-Lyne) (Immediate)
On the 10.4.43 'B' Coy 2 L F., were ordered to advance
from behind Pt 512 to Toukabeur. When the two leading
platoons had cleared the shoulder of the hill, they came
under heavy fire from 2 MG's and 1 88 mm gun, and
were pinned down. Cpl. Ryan crawled forward, located
the MG's shouted to his pl to engage them with fire and
then called to Cpl. Nuttall and L/C Newsham to
accompany him in an assault on the 88 mm gun 150 yds
away. The three NCO's then assaulted the gun with
'Tommy' guns and a bren, killed one member of the
crew and captured the rest. They then turned their
automatics in the direction of the MG's and shouted to
their sections to continue the advance uner cover of their
fire. Their fire was speedily effective and the enemy
MG's were almost immediately silenced. The company
was then able to continue its advance without further
opposition.
    I consider that these three NCO's by their swift and
courageous action, and their skilful team work,
admittedly saved their company many casualties and are
all deserving of an immediate award.
M.M. 23.9.43   (*L.G. 15.6.43*)

Ryan, George Alexander, Lance Sergeant
5344360, 9th Bn., Royal Fusiliers (London, S.E.1)
(Immediate)
On 25 April 1945 Cpl. Ryan was leading a section of X
Coy 9th Bn Royal Fusiliers. The company was engaged
in hard fighting to clear the enemy who were holding
the South bank of the river Po, in order to enable the
remainder of their forces to ferry across the river. The
enemy were determined and well entrenched and the

slightest movement on the flood bank brought down an
immediate hail of MG and rifle fire.
    Cpl. Ryan seeing some 50 of the enemy attempting
to ferry the river, and acting entirely on his own initiative,
decided to assault the positions from the rear. In order to
do so he had to expose himself to intense and accurate
fire, but with complete disregard for personal safety, he
rallied his section together, and covering the movement
across with his T.S.M.C., led them round the left flank.
From this position he led the assault on the enemy HQ,
a house which had been made into a strongpoint. In the
face of heavy fire he captured the house, and accounted
personally for three of the defenders. This done he
organised his section on the top floor of the building and
opened fire at the enemy from the flank. The action
completely demoralised the enemy and 40 of them
surrendered.
    Next Cpl. Ryan fought his way down to the river bank
itself and ignoring enemy fire, coolly established his
section there. From this position he engaged targets on
the opposite bank with Bren and rifle fire, and by so doing
enabled the Coy to put a platoon across the river and
force a bridgehead.
    Throughout the whole action Cpl. Ryan's, courage,
coolness and aggressive spirit was an inspiration to his
men, whilst the initiative and skilful leadership which
he continuously displayed were of considerable
advantage to the Company.   (*L.G. 18.10.45*)

Ryan, Michael, Bombardier
900091, Royal Artillery (Preston)
M.E. 1942 (from P.O.W. Pool)   (*L.G. 13.9.45*)

Ryan, Robert William, Private
SX 13321, 2/6 Aust Inf Bn. (Immediate)
Pte. Ryan was a member of a fwd sec which was heavily
attacked by the enemy on Lababia Ridge on 21 Jun 43.
All but three of this sec were killed or wounded and Pte
Ryan took comd. His deadly LMG fire and coolness
staved off the attack. On being reinforced, he quickly
and efficiently reorganised in time to repel the next attack.
During dusk on 22 Jun 43 he fired with devastating effect
until his amn was almost exhausted and then kept the
enemy off with grenades, running from pit to pit to do
so. During the whole action his conduct was of the
highest order. He proved a splendid leader and his
courage and coolness inspired his sec to hold on in the
face of what appeared to be impossible odds.
                                (*L.G. 7.10.43*)

Ryan, William Martin Patrick, Warrant Officer Cl. II
    (Local)
2325915, I.S.L.D. (No. 11 (U) Section), Royal Signals
CSM Ryan was dropped by parachute into Yugoslavia
in October 1943 as a W/T operator to the ISLD party at
Croat Partisan Headquarters. He at once established his
W/T station and since that date has single handed carried
a great volume of intelligence traffic. For 6 months he

also handled the operational traffic for the British Mission in that area. This work involved being on the keyboard every day for many hours at a stretch and not once during the whole period did CSM Ryan miss a scheduled contact. When on several occasions the Headquarters was attacked by the enemy CSM Ryan displayed courage and tenacity of a high order. One example of this was when 5 Stuka aircraft made a direct attack on the W/T building while CSM Ryan was transmitting a most immediate operational message. He refused to take cover, and successfully completed the signal.

Taking into account the constant danger of working in enemy occupied territory CSM Ryan showed a very high technical excellence and maintained an exceptional standard of courage and devotion to duty over a long and trying period. *(L.G. 2.8.45)*

Rycroft, Francis Arthur, M.M., S.Q.M.S. (A/W.O.II (S.S.M.))
7886155, 6th Royal Tank Regt. (Immediate)
On 22/7/42

This Warrant Officer discovered the existence of an enemy strong point within 500 yards of our forward positions South of Ruweisat Ridge. This strong point consisted of tanks hidden beneath the edge of a depression and anti-tank and machine-guns, the whole surrounded by wire and a minefield. SSM Rycroft went forward on foot to within 300 yards of the enemy and mapped all the defences. Subsequently he personally directed the fire of the Regiment on the various targets by standing on top of his tank. In the course of this he was wounded, but returned into action immediately his wounds had been treated. The whole action resulted in the total destruction of eight German Mk III or IV tanks and several guns without loss to the Regiment, and this success was in great measure due to the resource and disregard of personal safety by this Warrant Officer.
M.I.D. 1.4.41, M.M. 25.4.41, M.C. 23.3.44

(L.G. 24.9.42)

S

Sabin, George William, Sergeant (actg.)
*551503, Warwickshire Yeomanry, Royal Armoured
Corps (Moreton-in-Marsh)*
Advance on Cita Di Pieve—14th June 1944.

After the capture of Orvieto on 14th June 1944 the advance continued towards Cita Di Pieve with Sgt. Sabin's Troop leading. Some opposition was encountered from a 88mm gun which was knocked out, and mortar fire, but the Troop found a way round a bridge which had been destroyed, shot up enemy infantry running away from it and were finally held up by a strong point in a farm on the left of the road. The leading tank was twice hit by A/Tk. gun but Sgt. Sabin saw the flash and knocked it out, killing several of the crew. He continued firing until the strongpoint was silenced, and it was afterwards found that he had destroyed two other A/Tk. guns and two M.G.s. He then moved on up to a ridge and engaged a concentration of enemy vehicles, destroying or damaging many of them, including an 88mm gun.

Advance from Panicale up Route 71—19th June 1944.

At the S.W. corner of Lake Trasimeno on 19th June Sgt. Sabin's Troop was leading the advance from Panicale up Route 71. They pushed on through Macchie which was strongly held by the enemy, many of whom they drove out into the open country beyond. There the leading tank was destroyed by an A/Tk. gun and Sgt. Sabin's tank was set on fire by a Faustpatrone. Both crews baled out but Sgt. Sabin engaged the enemy infantry with his T.S.M.G. and killed a sniper who was trying to shoot his Troop Ldr.

The Troop Ldr. was then wounded in the head and his tank went back. Sgt. Sabin, seeing that all the dismounted men had been taken prisoner hid in the corn and escaped notice. He hid there all that day and night and gained valuable information about the strength and disposition of the enemy. About 300 passed him (within a few yards) and in the morning he contacted our infantry and gave them information which led to the capture of a considerable number of the enemy.

Advance on Cita Di Castello—13th July 1944.

During the advance to Cita Di Castello, the Sqn. supported the attack on Monte Sante on 13th July. Very heavy shelling and mortaring went on all day and one shell landed on Sgt. Sabin's tank, blinding him with the blast. He was persuaded to go back to the R.A.P. but an hour later insisted on returning on foot to his tank. That afternoon it became vital to find out if a bridge N. of the town had been blown, and Sgt. Sabin's Troop was sent to find out. In spite of heavy shell fire and mortaring, Sgt. Sabin in the leading tank reached the bridge which was found to be blown, and engaged the enemy while the troop returned with the necessary information.

Advance down the Talla Road—6th August 1944.

North West of Arezzo, during the advance down the Talla Road on 6th August 1944, Sgt. Sabin's tank was leading. He gave invaluable support to the infantry who were held up by M.G. fire, and continued to push on until his tank blew up on a minefield. He successfully got the tank off the road and in spite of enemy fire salvaged all the tank equipment before having to abandon it.

In every action in which Sgt. Sabin has taken part he has shown consistent bravery, coolness and resourcefulness which have been an inspiration to all who have worked with him.   *(L.G. 19.4.45)*

Saint, Basil Gilbert, Trooper
*7906260, 4th County of London Yeomanry, Royal
Armoured Corps (Yeomanry) (15, Cambridge Ave.,
Greenford, Middlesex)*

On 23rd November during the enemy attack on the South African Brigade Tpr. Saint took his Scout Car into the middle of the tank versus tank battle and personally collected sixteen men from disabled tanks under very intense fire. He succeeded in leading these men through the enemy lines and in rejoining his Unit early the following morning. His courage and devotion to duty in all actions from 19th to 29th November have been an example to all ranks.   *(L.G. 20.1.42)*

Salmon, George Scores, Lance Sergeant (A/Sgt.)
2217940, 505 Fd. Coy., Royal Engineers

On 22nd May 1940 this N.C.O. was detailed with a party of 8 sprs. to complete the demolition of a bridge over the La Bassee canal at Givenchy which had been partially blown up by another unit.

L/Sgt. Salmon with his party arrived on site at 1900 hrs. and in spite of continuous shell fire from the enemy throughout he successfully completed the task and blew the bridge at 2030 hrs.

On several other occasions this N.C.O. has performed excellent work under difficult and dangerous conditions, e.g., the carrying out of the demolition reconnaissance of the main road bridge over the R. Dendre in Ath whilst it was being bombed by enemy aircraft.

    (L.G. 22.10.40)

Salter, Harry, Sergeant (actg.)
*883359, 85th Anti-Tank Regt., Royal Artillery
(Oxford)*

At dawn on Sunday, 15th February 1942, 'D' Troop 251 A/Tk. Battery was taking up position in support of 4 Suffolks who, considerably disorganised, had withdrawn to Mount Pleasant Rd. during the night. Sgt. Salter was given his gun position by Lt. Carpenter and was leading his gun into it when he was suddenly attacked by a party of the enemy who came up a slope on his left. Considering on his own initiative that his Anti-tank role was now of less importance he proceeded to wheel his gun into a better position to engage these enemy infantry on his left. This he did under heavy enemy machine gun fire and sniping from trees close by, ordering the remainder of his detachment to take up fire positions and engage the enemy with small arms fire. As the fight continued it became apparent that a certain house held enemy machine guns and snipers. On his own initiative and at great personal danger he returned to the gun and without assistance loaded and fired six rounds into the house which caused the enemy to cease firing temporarily. The gun was now engaged by enemy mortars and after one of the detachment had been wounded Sgt. Salter withdrew it temporarily.

Later at 12.00 hrs. 4 Suffolks reported to 54 Inf. Bde. that a party of Japanese were holding another house on Mount Pleasant Rd. in strength with machine guns. These were causing considerable casualties amongst the infantry in the neighbourhood who were unable to drive them out. The position was extremely serious as the infantry were desperately fatigued and disorganised and any further penetration into the Mount Pleasant Rd. position then would have been fatal. Orders were given to Sgt. Salter to engage the house. Showing the utmost coolness and complete disregard of his own safety Sgt. Salter wheeled his gun forward to within 40 yds. of the house under point blank machine gun fire from it. In spite of the heavy enemy machine gun fire, Sgt. Salter doggedly continued to fire at the house until the machine guns were silenced and the house burst into flames. This caused the enemy to run out of the back of the house where they were shot by a party of 4 Suffolks. The situation was thereby completely cleared and the road reopened for movement of troops. Throughout this action Sgt. Salter kept his head and displayed a most superlative bravery which had a great effect on the tired and disheartened troops by whom he was surrounded.

On the previous day on the Bukit Timan Rd. Sgt. Salter destroyed an enemy light tank with his gun, in face of heavy enemy fire. *(L.G. 13.12.45)*

Samari, Osuman, Sergeant
NA/29985 [NZ.29935 on AFW 3121], 1 Bn. Nigeria Regt.

Sjt. Osuman Samari was the Sjt. of the platoon which was involved in more action than any other in the Bn. He led his men in three major attacks and two fighting patrols, in which they, themselves, inflicted nearly sixty casualties on the enemy. The consistent success and invariable reliability of this Pl, was very largely due to the courageous and outstandingly efficient leadership of Sjt. Osuman Samari. Two instances may be cited of his qualities.

On the 14 Dec 44, Sjt. Osuman Samari's Pl was ordered to seize a feature in order to give flank protection to the remainder of the Bde. Within a few minutes of arrival at the objective, the Pl Comd discovered that he was astride a track, along which a force of at least a Coy of enemy was withdrawing. Simultaneously the enemy saw the Pl, and quickly took up positions on three sides of the feature. One machine gun position was screened from our fire by trees, so a rifle bomber was ordered to operate in the open. Sjt. Osuman Samari, on his own initiative, immediately took a bren gun, and moved into the open with the rifle bomber, to give him covering fire. He successfully engaged a number of enemy who rushed from the machine gun position, when one of our grenades scored a direct hit, and then, when the rifle bomber was wounded by a sniper, he shot the sniper out of his tree. Continuing to fire in the open, Sjt. Osuman engaged the other two machine gun positions, and finding many targets bunched in the open, he fired to such effect, that he was largely responsible for the fifteen casualties, which the Pl Comd estimated had been inflicted. The news of this action occurring as it did on the first day of the campaign, was not fully credited, until subsequent intelligence reports, confirmed both the number of the enemy, and their casualties. Again, on the 12 Apr 45, Sjt. Osuman Samari's Pl and one other, were ordered to drive the enemy from a feature at Letmauk which overlooked the water point. His Pl led the attack, and within a few minutes of crossing the start line, they came under heavy fire from four machine guns. Sjt. Osuman Samari immediately led a bayonet charge, but when within twenty yards of the enemy, the accurate fire had killed the officer in comd of the operation and wounded the Pl Comd and a number of Africans. The Pl was then forced to take up immediate positions at this short range. Sjt. Osuman Samari dragged back the wounded to safety, and, on his return, himself crawled to one of the flanking machine gun posts and destroyed it with a grenade. Subsequently, he silenced another to his front. This Pl was forced to lie thus, at twenty yards range for some three hours, before a flanking move relieved them, and during this time they inflicted fourteen casualties. Throughout, Sjt. Osuman crawled from Sec to Sec, encouraging and enheartening his men. The high morale which sustained this Pl throughout this action was undoubtedly inspired by Sjt. Osuman Samari. *(L.G. 6.6.46)*

Sander, Norman, Sergeant
831831, 31 Fd. Regt., Royal Artillery (Carlisle) (Periodic)

Sgt. Sander was Signal N.C.O. of his Troop. At the battle of Capuzzo (515376) in June 1941 he closely followed up our tank attack in an unarmoured truck, and laid a line from the OP to the Bty. position. In the evening his Bty. was seriously engaged by tanks and ammunition was short. Without waiting for orders he immediately went to the wagon lines and next appeared leading up ammunition lorries in spite of heavy enemy fire.

During the months of September, October and November 1941, Sgt. Sander's Troop maintained a sniping gun and OP in front of Halfaya. The positions were very exposed but the communications were always maintained.

On 15th December 1941 the Regt. was heavily attacked by tanks. Sgt. Sander again brought up ammunition on his own initiative although the gun positions had been overrun by the enemy before he arrived. He then tried to evacuate a gun, but no sooner was it limbered up than it was destroyed by a direct hit. Undeterred Sgt. Sander set to work on another—this he brought out—the only gun of the Regt. to be saved—and on the way he picked up many more wounded men.

This N.C.O. has always shown an entire disregard of personal danger and a ready resource under the most trying circumstances. Not only has he carried out his own tasks with great efficiency but he has shown himself always eager to do that 'little bit extra' which means so much. *(L.G. 9.9.42)*

Sanderson, Charles Frederick, Sergeant
QX11361, Australian Military Forces
Recommended by Gov. Gen., Australia *(L.G. 6.3.47)*

Sandford, John Grant, Sergeant
775188, Royal New Zealand Infantry Regt.
No citation. *(L.G. 30.9.69)*

Santi, Edward William, Bombardier
20311, 5 Fd. Regt. N.Z.A.
Bdr. Santi was gunlayer throughout the action on No. 3 gun. In the action at Thermopalae this gun was the most forward 25 pr. and was acting in the anti-tank role. During the attack by German tanks on the afternoon of 24th April 1941, by his skill at laying and extreme coolness in action Bdr. Santi destroyed nine tanks. The gun was shelled by tanks and continually bombed and machine gunned by planes. When all the ammunition had been expended, orders to withdraw were received. The gun crew prepared to destroy the gun by firing it with a long lanyard. They retired to the end of the lanyard and pulled it but the gun failed to fire. Bdr. Santi went back to the gun under fire and refixed the lanyard, then came back and fired it. He then went to the gun again to make sure it was destroyed before thinking of his own safety.

These action were witnessed by 2/Lt. Parkes who was Section Commander and in charge of No. 3 gun during the action. *(L.G. 4.11.41)*

Sargent, William, Sergeant
827399, 129th Field Regt., Royal Artillery (Edinburgh 12)
Kennedy Peak—11th March 1944.

An outstanding example of courage and devotion to duty and an inspiration to all ranks. For 20 consecutive days the Battery in which Sgt. Sargent was No. 1 of a 25 pdr. gun was subjected to periods of heavy shelling both by day and night causing casualties. Sgt. Sargent's gun was straddled on many occasions and his position finally

hit. Throughout this whole period Sgt. Sargent showed complete indifference to enemy shell fire and by his example of continued fearlessness exerted a most encouraging and steadying influence on the whole Battery under trying circumstances.
M.I.D. 4.4.52 *(L.G. 8.2.45)*

Saunders, Gordon Lawrence, Lance Sergeant
880972, 1st Medium Regt., Royal Artillery
(Birmingham) (Immediate)
During the night of 19/20th March 1944 L/Sgt. Saunders was a member of an O.P. in sp. of 'A' Coy. 16/10 Baluch on the ridge West of pt. 614. (8 miles S.E. of Maungdaw). During the night 19/20th March the position was attacked by the enemy in strength. The attack was repulsed but the F.O.O. was killed and L/Sgt. Saunders took charge.

During the 20th the Coy. moved to a new position where they were harassed throughout the day and night.

The only comms. were the O.P. 48 set which was worked by L/Sgt. Saunders and Gnrs. Slater and Wellstead. The Inf. were out of touch.

On morning 21st March the O.P. received orders to withdraw and L/Sgt. Saunders decided to get what remained of the Coy. out with him.

After sending a patrol to ascertain whether there was anyone left alive in the Coy. Comds. position, L/Sgt. Saunders organised the defence of the remainder with the Coy. Subedar. He first brought down two bty. concs. and thereby silenced two enemy posts on pt. 614. He then arranged with his regt. a fire plan which enabled the Coy. the march down to the blind side of the ridge where he decided to remain rather than risk a night march.

During the night 20/21st March the enemy made repeated efforts by trick to draw fire but, as a result of his explicit orders which he made the Baluchis understand, no shot was fired and the position was undiscovered. At first light, he led the Coy. with all arms and amn. down to a nullah and into the Bn. position.

Throughout these days L/Sgt. Saunders set a high example of unfaltering coolness and courage and it was due entirely to his leadership that the remnants of the O.P. and 'A' Coy. of 16th/10th Baluch were extracted without further loss.

§ § §

I thoroughly endorse the remarks of Lt. Col. Fairlie Comd of 16/10th Baluch. L/Sgt. Saunders carried out magnificent work over a period of three days continuous fighting. There is no question but that his work inflicted many casualties on the enemy and saved many of our own troops. His courage and leadership were an example to all.

This bn. had just come into action for the first time. L/Sgt. Saunders virtually took charge of the Coy. there being no British officer in it and the Indian Coy. Comd. having failed. Strongly recommended. *(L.G. 22.6.44)*

Saunders, Wilfred, Private (A/Sgt.)
6460005, 1st Bn. The Northamptonshire Regt.
(Northolt) (Immediate)
At Pt. 5846 on the Silchar Road on 27 April 1944 4 Coy.
were ordered out of the box to attack and dislodge some
enemy who had established a gun on a nearby spur. Sgt.
Saunders, Cook Sgt. to the Bn. joined this Coy. as it
passed by the jungle water point and volunteered to carry
out any task ordered by the Coy. Comd. When the Coy.
in the late afternoon put in an assault on the enemy who
had got into a position commanding the road at mile 22,
Sgt. Saunders with the Coy. Comd. joined the assault.
Sgt. Saunders and five others only from the platoon
assaulting succeeded in reaching the enemy position
through showers of grenades and accurate L.A. fire.
Although wounded through the right arm Sgt. Saunders
by his example and quick assumption of comd. held on
to the ground gained in the enemy position and succeeded
in forcing the enemy to pull out slightly. His tenacity
and bravery coupled with splendid leadership were
directly responsible for the success of the next assault
carried out by another platoon which cleared the enemy
off and secured the position. Sgt. Saunders then brought
out the Coy. Comd. Capt. Eales White who had been
wounded through both legs whilst under fire and got him
back to the Bn. Box. 800 yards away and up a steep path
for over 1,000 feet. This is the second time Sgt. Saunders
has displayed great gallantry and power of leadership.
The first at Kyaukchaw when a Private soldier earned
him a certificate of gallantry and the second individual
act of gallantry did to my mind prove the key action
which ensured success and the death of some 25 Japs.
Recommended for M.M. M.I.D. 5.4.45   (L.G. 31.8.44)

Saunders, William Richard, Lance Corporal
B55128, Irish Regt. of Canada (Immediate)
On the morning of 2nd January 1945, the Irish Regt. of
Canada launched an attack on Conventello. At the start
line 'C' Coy. came under extremely heavy shell, mortar
and small arms fire and suffered heavy casualties. Despite
the fact that the enemy fire continued L/Cpl. Saunders
not only personally carried five of his wounded comrades
to safety but assisted his Coy. Comd. to re-organize the
company for a fresh assault and by his fearless example
encouraged all ranks to further action.
In the opening phase of the assault, L/Cpl. Saunders
was painfully wounded in the foot by enemy small arms
fire but carried on and led his section onto the platoon
objective five hundred yards in front of the start line.
Here the platoon was engaged by a well sited enemy
machine gun which dominated the position from a range
of 50 yards. While still under heavy fire this N.C.O.
skilfully worked his way forward and silenced the gun
with grenades and Tommy gun fire killing three of the
enemy, wounding four and taking two prisoners.
On returning to his platoon position he allowed his
wound to be dressed. Before this was completed enemy
mortar fire killed a Bren gunner who was covering the

advance of the platoon on the left flank. Without
hesitation he seized another Bren gun and, running
forward to a suitable position, continued the covering
fire thereby enabling the platoon to reach the objective.
Throughout the entire action the initiative, bravery
and leadership of the N.C.O. was a source of inspiration
to his comrades and enabled the Coy. to attain and hold
the objective and to continue its advance later in the day.
(L.G. 7.4.45)

Savage, John, Corporal (A/Sgt.)
5955846, 2/4 Hampshire Regt. (Luton) (Immediate)
On 22nd July, 'C' Coy. were ordered to capture Pt. 253
ref 9445 (Ref Map: Italy: 1/50,000 Sheet 114–IV) which
entailed an assault up a steep hill in the midday sun, of
about 1,000 yds. The Officer in charge of No. 13 was
wounded crossing the S.L. Sgt. Savage, who was acting
as Platoon Sgt., took over command, and at once led
them forward with such great dash and determination to
their objective through heavy M.G. and shell fire that
they completely over-ran the enemy defences, killing
and capturing many Germans as they went forward. On
the objective, a German Mk IV tank was sited, together
with an 88mm gun. Quite undeterred by this, Sgt. Savage
dashed forward with his platoon at such speed that both
were captured intact, together with a number of prisoners.
On the capture of the objective his platoon and No.
13 platoon were reduced to about 10 men each, with no
officer.
Sgt. Savage quickly re-organised them into one
platoon, consolidated, and was ready for the counter-
attack which came in within five minutes, about 40
strong. This was beaten off, leaving the ground strewn
with enemy dead.
Recommended for M.M.   *(L.G. 7.12.44)*

Savill, Albert William Frank, Sergeant
3957422, Welch Regt. (Downpatrick, Co. Down)
Crete 1941 (from P.O.W. Pool)   *(L.G. 11.10.45)*

Savours, Norman Robert, Lance Bombardier
910203, 144th (Surrey & Sussex Yeo.) Army Field
Regt., Royal Artillery (Swansea) (Immediate)
On 16th and 17th March 1941 after the capture of Fort
Dologorodoc L/Bdr. Savours was O.P. telephonist and
for many hours manned a telephone in an exposed
position under heavy shell and mortar fire.
On the morning of 17th our Infantry attacked again
and L/Bdr. Savours manned a lamp under fire and in full
view of the enemy in an attempt to maintain communication with the F.O.O. until information was received
that the F.O.O. had been wounded.
At 1700 hours when our Infantry made a further
attack, he laid a cable forward to the F.O.O. single-
handed and when the cable ran out, went back under fire
and fetched more.
At 2000 hours a counter-attack was made on the
company in whose area the F.O.O. was situated. The

wire was cut and L/Bdr. Savours went out to mend it, again under heavy mortar fire, but could not find the break in the dark. He then got a rifle and bayonet, took ammunition forward to the Infantry and helped in the defence. While doing so he was wounded but remained at his post.

On the morning of the 18th, although he had then been on duty continuously for 48 hours and had been wounded, he again accompanied the F.O.O. forward laying a cable, and when this had been done, volunteered to take a message back to the Infantry Bn. HQ., collapsing when he delivered it. When he had recovered he returned to the forward O.P. mending breaks in the line as he did so, all this being done under heavy mortar fire and while being sniped.

Throughout this operation L/Bdr. Savours showed the utmost devotion to duty and it was largely owing to this endurance and example that communication with his Battery O.P. was maintained at a time when nearly all other communication in the area had failed.

(L.G. 18.7.41)

Sawyer, Harold Victor, Corporal
B37591 [D37591 on AFW 3121], R.H.L.I., Canadian
Infantry Corps (Immediate)
Cpl. Sawyer of the Royal Hamilton Light Infantry was a section leader in number 7 platoon on the morning of 25th July 1944 during the attack on Verriers.

As the Coy. neared the line of hedges to the North of Verriers they came under heavy machine gun fire from tanks on their right flank and machine guns in the hedges to their front. The German machine guns to their front were causing particularly heavy casualties and had made it impossible for the Coy. to advance. Cpl. Sawyer led a party of three other men from his section against the machine gun positions. With great daring and still under heavy machine gun fire from the tanks and machine gun posts he and his party attacked along the right flank of the battalion objective and destroyed four of the enemy machine gun posts which were holding up the advance. He was wounded during the course of the action.

This daring and courageous action enabled the Coy. to continue its advance to the objective. *(L.G. 7.10.44)*

Sawyer, William Henry, Sergeant
1874065, 79 Assault Sqn., Royal Engineers
(Barrowby, Lincs.) (Immediate)
This N.C.O. was in command of a lone Avre, Churchill loaded into an L.C.T. (A) H.E. in the assault flight on 'D' Day. His craft made an incorrect landfall and Sjt. Sawyer was unable to join the gapping team, which was to clear the mines in front of him.

He was carrying on his tank the Bobbin device, which reduced his armament to one Besa M.G., but despite this he decided with great boldness and initiative to risk the mines and to secure a beach exit into the strong point C.O.D. alone. This he succeeded in doing and he

continued under continuous fire to prepare further exits and to rally another troop that had lost both its officers.

The same afternoon he displayed especial courage as a tank comd. in the capture, by ten unsupported Avre, of the Ouistreham Lock gates defences where 6 officers and fifty one prisoners were taken from the concrete emplacements and dugouts.

On the morning D + 2 his tank together with three other Avre supported 41 R.M. Commando in the reduction of the strong point at Lion Sur Mer where he made bold use of his Besas' fully conscious of the dangers he ran in operating beyond the range of his main armament the petard.

In this operation Sjt. Sawyer assumed command of the Avre det. after the only officer had been killed and two of the Avre had been destroyed.

On D + 3 he took part with four other Avre in the attack by 2 R.U.R. on Cambes. Again the role of Infantry Tank was forced upon the Avre by the course of events and with great courage Sjt. Sawyer rendered valuable support at a critical time by determined use of his secondary armament until his tank was hit by an anti-tank gun and burnt out.

This N.C.O. throughout the four days displayed the highest standard of courage and stamina, undaunted by his unit's heavy losses during this period and the complete disintegration of his own troop.

His coolness is made all the more praiseworthy by the fact that on D—3 he had been rendered unconscious by an explosion, which occurred during the loading of an explosive device on his Avre and which resulted in the death of one man and the wounding of eight.

The example set by this N.C.O. throughout was exceptional.   *(L.G. 31.8.44)*

Sayle, Eustace MacDonald, Corporal
3246105, Cameronians (Ramsey, Isle of Man)
(Immediate)
For conspicuous gallantry during period 4–7th March which set a splendid example to the rest of his company.

At Payagyi on 4th March 1942 Cpl. Sayle formed part of an Officers patrol which entered the village during the night of 4/5th March. He spotted a party of enemy cooking by a fire. He crawled up to them and fired on them at close range with a L.M.G. killing 5. This fire caused a M.M.G. to open fire on him—he immediately stalked the M.M.G., threw a grenade which knocked over the gun and knocked out the crew of three.

At Mazin, just South of Pegu it was reported to me that the HQ of 1st West Yorkshire Regt. was surrounded. I ordered 'B' Coy. to clear a wood to enable them to withdraw. A patrol under Cpl. Sayle was sent out to locate this HQ. He found that their rear was covered by an enemy M.G. which prevented their withdrawal. Cpl. Sayle ordered 2 men to cover his advance, stalked this post and threw two grenades into it, killing 4 enemy and capturing the gun.

On 7th March at about Kyadsku, during the afternoon although the road block was cleared and enemy fire to a great extent silenced as carriers had not been fired on, it was not certain whether 'soft' transport would be fired on. Cpl. Sayle volunteered to got through on a motor cycle. He was fired on and wounded in the face.

(L.G. 23.4.42)

Scaife, Herbert Matthew, Lance Sergeant
2118916, 82 Assault Squadron, Royal Engineers
L/Sgt. Scaife was comd. of an AVRE which landed on Le Hamel beach at H hour on 6th June 1944. His AVRE was one of a half-troop of three. The plan for this half-troop was to proceed, under comd. of the Tp. Officer as soon as they had got through the beach minefield to Le Hamel and Asnelles in close support of the assaulting infantry.

In the event, L/Sgt. Scaife's AVRE was the only one to get clear of the beach minefield in the early stages of the assault. Observing this, L/Sgt. Scaife, without waiting for further orders, proceeded at once to the scene of the fighting in Asnelles and Le Hamel where the assaulting infantry were being held up by fire from the buildings at the top of the beach, particularly the Sanatorium buildings. On the way he noted that a gun in a thick concrete emplacement at the eastern end of the Sanatorium which enfiladed the beach was still firing.

L/Sgt. Scaife brought his Avre close in to the Sanatorium from the rear and fired a Dustbin from his Petard at 50 yards range. This destroyed a M.G. post and induced large numbers of the German defenders to surrender, besides allowing the infantry to get in and mop up. L/Sgt. Scaife then attacked the gun emplacement, scoring a direct hit through the rear opening with his first shot, completely wrecking the gun and killing the crew. He then proceeded through Le Hamel with a party of 1 Hamps. destroying M.G. nests which were holding up the mopping-up party with close range fire. L/Sgt. Scaife displayed great initiative and personal courage, in addition to the most soldierly qualities, in thus tackling single-handed and without hesitation a task which had been allotted to three AVRE under command of an Officer. He did so, moreover, knowing that his only offensive weapon was the Petard, only recently issued and fitted to the AVRE, whose potentialities he did not know since he had had no previous opportunity of firing it at a substantial target. *(L.G. 19.10.44)*

Scales, William Ernest, Warrant Officer Cl. III (Pl.S.M.)
5946522, 2nd Bedfordshire & Hertfordshire Regt.
When 'B' Coy. were under heavy shell fire at Burgoyne farm, 10 Platoon lost its officer and sustained about 50 per cent other casualties P.S.M. Scales re-organised the platoon and posted the Bren guns in effective positions while maintaining control over his own platoon. This effort enabled the Coy. to hold the enemy attack which followed and during the action P.S.M. Scales' fine example of courage and leadership created a feeling of confidence in the men of both platoons and was largely responsible for the successful withdrawal, carried out in contact with the enemy, which was ordered that night.
Recommended for M.M. *(L.G. 22.10.40)*

Scanlon, Joseph Hughes, Warrant Officer Cl. III (Pl.S.M.)
4264033, 8th Royal Northumberland Fusiliers
As Platoon Comd. he showed unquestionable courage, bravery and leadership during operations from Deval to Dunkirk, and particularly in the defence of Arras, where, by his own conduct he set his men an example and encouraged them under enemy fire and aerial bombardment. *(L.G. 20.12.40)*

Scheele, David Willem, Sergeant (temp.)
54901, Royal Australian Infantry Regt.
For Vietnam *(L.G. 2.4.70)*

Schroder, Stanley William John, Private
10855, New Zealand Military Forces
Special Ops. M.E. *(L.G. 23.3.44)*

Schwegmann, Victor, Warrant Officer Cl. II
90530, 2 A/Tk. Regt. S.A.A.
T.S.M. Schwegmann was in command of 1 Sect. A/Tk. guns with an Inf. post at Bir el Silqiya.

At about 0720 hours on 24th December 1941 an enemy force of one captured 'I' Tank, 4 light Tanks and infantry, covered by heavy Artillery fire launched an attack on this post with the object of regaining possession of the wells there.

T.S.M. Schwegmann displayed considerable coolness and judgement in the control of his section of A/Tk. guns.

Fire was not opened on the 'I' Tank until it was within 300 yards of his position. Though the 'I' Tank was hit over 30 times between ranges of 300 and 60 yards it managed to withdraw on fire.

The fire of A/Tk. guns was then directed on the 4 light Tanks, all of which were destroyed in seven rounds.

The action was carried out under heavy hostile shell and M.G. fire, and the fact that the attack was successfully beaten off was entirely due to the coolness and judgement displayed by T.S.M. Schwegmann in the handling of his section of A/Tk. guns. *(L.G. 3.3.42)*

Scobie, William Melville, Corporal (Lance Sergeant)
2928024, 2nd Queen's Own Cameron Highlanders
This N.C.O. was a member of the Pioneer Pl. of the Q. O. Cameron Highlanders, during the attack on Nibeiwa Camp on 9th December 1940. This platoon assisted the assaulting Coy. and later the Coys. engaged in mopping up centres of enemy resistance in the camp. Throughout these operations, this N.C.O. conducted himself extremely gallantly and showed complete disregard for his personal safety. Later in the day, this N.C.O. was ordered by his Commanding Officer to remove certain enemy A/T mines from a minefield in the vicinity of the

Camp, so as to allow some damaged 'I' Tanks to extricate themselves. The pattern of the mine and its mechanism, found in this minefield was unknown to this N.C.O., who refused to allow any of his men to commence work on the mines until he had successfully removed some himself.

His conduct and devotion to duty in this act set a fine example to his comrades.   *(L.G. 25.4.41)*

Scott, Alfred, A/Corporal
VX 4310, 2/31 Aust. Inf. Bn. (Immediate)
A/Cpl. Scott was a stretcher bearer with 'D' Coy. in its attack on enemy positions at Edwards Plantation at 1515 hrs. on 15th September 1943.

Shortly after the attack commenced Pte. Rowe of 18 Platoon was caught in the open clearing and badly shot through the throat and arm. On any member of his section endeavouring to go to his assistance he was immediately fired on. A/Cpl. Scott came up threw off all his equipment with the exception of his R.A.P. haversack and rushed into the clearing to Pte Rowe under heavy fire from L.M.G. and rifle. He wrapped a field dressing on Pte. Rowe's throat to staunch the flow of blood and while doing so, Pte Rowe was wounded again, this time in the right foot. Holding the dressing in position he picked up Pte. Rowe and carried him back under intense fire to the shelter of the trees on the edge of the clearing.

A/Cpl. Scott went on, immediately leaving Pte. Rowe to be picked up by other stretcher bearers and in succession and again under fire in the open clearing, dressed the wounds of, and carried to safety, Ptes. Watts and Symons who were severely wounded. He also tended Lieut. Hamilton who was wounded by a grenade.
(L.G. 20.1.44)

Scott, John Aitchison Kennedy, Sergeant
311324, Royal Australian Infantry Corps
No citation.   *(L.G. 19.9.69)*

Scott, John, Corporal
6978128, 1st Bn. The Royal Iniskilling Fusiliers
(Culmore, Co. Londonderry) (Immediate)
At Donbaik, Mayu Peninsular, Burma on 19th January 1943.

The Carrier in which Cpl. Scott was gunner was damaged on the open beach by enemy A/Tk. fire, but was able to return to its harbour. Cpl. Scott immediately volunteered to go out in another Carrier to tow in a Carrier from the beach which had been damaged by enemy fire, and was on fire, this latter Carrier was in full view of the enemy, and was under intense fire from both the A/Tk. gun and automatic weapons. On reaching the blazing Carrier Cpl. Scott dismounted and adjusted the tow chain, it was a lengthy business, as on two occasions the tow chain came off the burning Carrier. On both occasions Cpl. Scott dismounted in full view of the enemy and re-adjusted the tow chain, with the result that the damaged Carrier was saved from falling into enemy hands.

Recommended for M.M.   *(L.G. 8.4.43)*

Scott, Kenneth Alec John, Sergeant
6897910, Royal Signals
Middle East   *(L.G. 9.8.45)*

Scott, William McGee, Sergeant
7892111, 2nd Fife & Forfar Yeomanry (Dundee)
(Immediate)
On 6th August Sgt. Scott was acting as Troop Leader and was in reserve in the area of the high ground South-East of Burcy. A strong German counter-attack was put in; 2 Tiger tanks with infantry advanced down a sunken lane; knocking out 2 of our tanks which were covering that approach. Sgt. Scott was ordered to move up and engage the enemy. He placed his tanks in position, visibility being extremely bad as the enemy were approaching with the sun behind them. Although under intense M.G. fire he stood up on the top of the tank to direct fire, then moving out on his feet about 50 yds. to observe the effect. He destroyed one of the Tigers and damaged the other, so that it withdrew. Throughout he displayed the very highest courage and complete disregard for his own safety, and it was entirely due to his inspiring leadership that the enemy tanks were destroyed before they could do further damage.
(L.G. 1.3.45)

Scrutton, Samuel Thomas, Sergeant
B65569, Queen's Own Rifles of Canada (Immediate)
On 11th June 1944 'D' Coy. Q.O.R. of C., while serving under comd. 'B' Sqn. 6 Cdn. Armd Regt. attacked enemy positions in and around the villages of Le Mes-Nil-Patry and Les Saullets. Very heavy casualties were suffered at the outset. Lt. H. G. W. Bean, Comd. 17 Platoon, was severely wounded three times, and Sgt. Scrutton was ordered to assume comd. During all the heavy action Sgt. Scrutton had backed up his Platoon Comd. to the utmost. He continually encouraged and assisted the members of the party. When he took over comd. he withdrew the party successfully to their own lines whilst continuously under heavy enemy fire. Throughout the action Sgt. Scrutton showed no regard whatsoever for his personal safety and accounted for and killed 12 to 15 Germans. By his leadership, determination and coolness, Sgt. Scrutton was an outstanding example to all ranks.
Recommended for M.M.   *(L.G. 19.8.44)*

Seall, William Francis, Sergeant
5722194, 2nd Bn. The Dorsetshire Regt. (Merfield,
Yorks) (Immediate)
On the night of 9/10th March 1945, Sjt. Seale was comd. 15 Pl 'C' Coy. The Bn. carried out a difficult and arduous night infiltration into the enemy posns. near Kyauktalon.

When daylight broke the platoon came under very heavy fire from enemy M.M.G.s and L.M.G.s which had been unlocated during the hours of darkness, and the situation became critical.

The Coy. Comd. saw that there was a dominating posn. on the left flank and he ordered Sjt. Seale to move his platoon there.

Sjt. Seale, although wounded in the leg when fire had first been opened, carried out this difficult operation in brilliant fashion. He laid on a fire and smoke plan with his platoon weapons, extricated his casualties and moved his platoon across the open to the new position without any more casualties being incurred. All this took place under heavy fire, and it was necessary for Sjt. Seale to move about in full view of the enemy in order to organise and supervise the operation.

This successful manoeuvre enabled his Coy. to consolidate their posns and later inflict a crushing defeat on the enemy.

Sjt. Seale's powers of command and tactical handling of his platoon were quite outstanding, and his great gallantry inspired his men to carry out an extremely difficult operation which turned a critical situation into a brilliant success.
M.I.D. 19.7.45   *(L.G. 2.8.45)*

Seaman, Leonard Frederick, Lance Sergeant
249108, 22 N.Z. Bn. (Immediate)
The platoon of which L/Sjt. Seaman was acting as Sjt. during the attack from Rinaldina toward the river Senio on 14/15th December 1944 was one of a Coy. detailed to capture and occupy Casa Elta, a position situated on a high, bare feature and manned in formidable strength and with many automatic weapons by the enemy.

Two attacks were launched by the Coy. against Elta and each was repulsed in fighting of great severity involving many cas. to the Coy.

In an area bombarded by German arty and swept by SA fire, L/Sjt. Seaman rallied fifteen men, the remnants of two pls., and at their head worked in bounds to the left flank. Maintaining excellent control, he led them quietly and skilfully up hill and at the strategic moment a charge was made through a line of enemy posns. and around to the rear of Casa Elta.

Rallying his men once more, L/Sjt. Seaman led them in a sustained charge which over ran enemy M.G. posns.—he himself killed or captured the defenders of two—and on into the posn. itself. Eighteen enemy were taken P/W. A count of 15 dead was later made, and among the enemy equipment captured were seven M.G.s.

As L/Sjt. Seaman headed the final assault, he was shot at close range and severely wounded in the chest, but although bleeding freely and in great pain, he refused all attempts at field dressing until the position had been consolidated, and during the mopping-up stage, when many enemy were being encountered, he continued to direct the op. calmly and without thought of his personal comfort. Only when he had seen to the proper disposition of his force against possible counter-attacks would he consent to the dressing of his wound.

The capture of the Elta position was entirely due to L/Sjt. Seaman's judgement and leadership. Whether under the heaviest of fire or the most severe pain, he remained master of the situation, unflurried, completely courageous and superb in his judgement and appreciation of a situation.   *(L.G. 21.6.45)*

Searle, Clifford Frederick, Lance Sergeant
14241831, Royal Armoured Corps, No. 9 Commando
Operation 'Roast'—Lake Comacchio 'Spit'—2nd April 1945
This NCO came abroad as a private. He has twice been promoted in the battlefield. During extremely heavy and accurate sniping which had pinned the troop to cover, his Section NCO was hit. L/Sgt Searle made a 30-yd dash, under full view of enemy snipers, and, ascertaining that his superior NCO was killed, he calmly knelt and took map and compass and other necessary articles from the body, receiving a bullet through his steel helmet in the middle of his operations. He then took over the section and led his men through a thick smoke screen which obliterated both own troops and enemy. This smoke was subjected to heavy 3≤ mortaring but Searle kept the men going by voice control although he suffered a further three casualties. He led the final charge and overran two spandau positions capturing two 75-mm howitzers. Immediately following this the area was covered by defensive fire task and the troop suffered a further 15 casualties. L/Sgt Searle now infiltrated with two men on the troop right flank, and silenced a spandau which was firing on and holding up the advance of the troop on the flank. Under a further accurate defensive fire mortaring of the troop, bringing the total casualties to 29, L/Sgt Searle rallied three men and started to lead them over an open space to the next objective. All the party were wounded by shrapnel or automatic fire and Searle, although badly wounded in the chest assisted in dragging one other to safety. He then reported to his Troop Leader and would not be helped back to the regimental aid post until he had furnished a full report. Under continuous mortaring, shelling and small arms fire which inflicted 35 casualties out of 58, L/Sgt Searle's behaviour was outstanding in his complete disregard for his own personal safety, and his coolness and excellent leadership in controlling his men under the hardest possible conditions.
Recommended for periodic M.M. M.I.D. 18.10.45
                                    (L.G. 13.12.45)

Searle, John Edward, Sergeant
NX 21876, 2/13 Aust. Inf.
This N.C.O. is recommended for a decoration for his actions during the recapture of Ed Duda on night 29/30th November 1941.

Sgt. Searle commanded the right forward platoon during the counter-attack and his outstanding example of coolness under fire and his control of his platoon enabled the Coy. Comd. to change the direction of the counter-attack on reaching the first objective.

During the period of exploitation and mopping up, a party of twelve German infantry came in from the right rear of the advance and captured two Coy. Stretcher Bearers, Ptes. Smith, B. and Perkins who were attending to enemy wounded on the first objective. Sgt. Searle saw this enemy party moving away to the South West and with five of his men he captured the entire party at the point of the bayonet. During this engagement one German soldier ran behind a disabled German cruiser tank and commenced to fire on the party. Sgt. Searle quickly moved to the rear of the tank and dispatched this German with his bayonet.

At about 0800 hrs. on the following day, 1st December, two German infantry tanks approached the small sangars which Searle's platoon had built on the South West slope of feature Ed Duda. These tanks came up to 50 yds. of the platoon position and with their guns trained on the sangars called on the platoon to surrender. Owing to the fact that Sgt. Searle had previously ordered his men to hold fire until ordered, these two enemy tanks moved away and evidently reported that our position was not occupied as the top and not the slope of the feature was then subjected to heavy shell fire.

Later in the day, by the same means, Sgt. Searle organised the capture of a German six wheeler truck, five German signallers and much valuable equipment. As his devotion to duty, his coolness under fire and his outstanding example to his men was definitely one of the decisive factors in the success of the counter-attack on, and the subsequent retention of this important feature, Ed Duda, Sgt. Searle is recommended for suitable recognition of his services.   *(L.G. 24.2.42)*

Seaward, Michael Darwen, Sergeant
7892946, 4th County of London Yeomanry, R.A.C. (Yeomanry) (Old Chellows, Rusper, Suss.)
At El Gubi on 19th November 1941, whilst in the middle of the enemy position, he dismounted from his own tank under intensive enemy fire to fasten tow ropes on to a disabled tank, which he succeeded in towing out of action, returning himself to the action. Throughout all operations extending from 19 to 29th November 1941 his complete disregard of danger has been an inspiration to all ranks.   *(L.G. 20.1.42)*

Seccombe, Garth Turow, Warrant Officer Cl. II
22769, New Zealand Military Forces
Dieppe.   *(L.G. 14.2.46)*

Seekings, Albert Reginald, Lance Sergeant
5933155, Cambridgeshire Regt., 'L' Det. S.A.S. Bde. (Immediate)
This N.C.O. has taken an important part in ten raids. He has himself destroyed over 15 aircraft and by virtue of his accuracy with a Tommy gun at night and through a complete disregard of his personal safety he has killed at least ten of the enemy. He particularly distinguished himself on the raid at Benina in June 1942.

M.M. 18.11.43. M.I.D. 8.11.45   *(L.G. 26.11.42)*

Seggie, Norval James, Corporal
33443, 1 Rand. Light Inf. (Immediate)
For outstanding courage and leadership in a night patrol operating from Ain-El-Gazala on the night of 13/14th May 1942.

The platoon of which this N.C.O. was a Sec. Comd., was ordered at very short notice on night 13/14th May 1942 to endeavour to obtain a prisoner which was urgently needed by higher authority.

The platoon of which he was a part were blown up in a truck approaching the enemy posns., and was badly shaken. His Platoon Sgt. and 3 other men were injured. The platoon nevertheless carried on on foot for 8 kilometres, and Cpl. Seggie with his sec. by good sec. leading, crossed a minefield and stalked to within 15 yards of an enemy post, when they made their assault killing 4 Germans and capturing one.

The success of this patrol was due in no small measure to this N.C.O.'s courage and skill in handling his section.
Recommended for M.M.   *(L.G. 4.8.42)*

Selemani, Feruzi, Sjt.
206183, (EA) Inf Bde, 11 (EA) Div, 33 Ind Corps, 36 (TT) King's African Rifles (Immediate)
On 3 Nov 1944, during an attack on a Japanese held hill at about RU 602795 NE of Myintha, Burma, Sjt. Selemani was Pl Sjt of the leading pl under CSM Widdows. The Platoon came under heavy LMG, MMG and grenade discharger fire from the first. CSM Widdows was mortally wounded before the pl reached its objective. In addition the Coy Comd was wounded, the Coy 2 i/c killed, and the neighbouring Pl Comd killed, leaving no European in the vicinity. In spite of these adverse circumstances, Sjt. Selemani immediately took command of his platoon, and, having organised a party to evacuate his Pl Comd, he at once gained control of his pl, steadied them, and led them in to the attack on to their objective. He showed the highest qualities of leadership and complete disregard for his personal safety.

Selemani, Office, Corporal
DN 9419, King's African Rifles
No citation.   *(L.G. 22.3.45)*

Self, George Henry, Sergeant
4452660, 8th Durham Light Infantry (Ushaw Moor, Co. Durham) (Immediate)
On 8th September 1944 near Gheel, Sgt. Self was Platoon Comd. of the assault platoon which was detailed to making the initial crossing over the Albert Canal. During the crossing all the Officers of his Coy. were either killed or wounded but together with the Sgt. Major, he succeeded in taking the objective against heavy opposition and taking a number of prisoners. Having taken up their position they were subjected to heavy mortar and machine-gun fire. Sgt. Self himself, taking a

couple of men, went out and silenced two Spandau nests. During the night they were heavily counter-attacked. During this very difficult period by his own personal example he held his men together when out of touch with the remainder of the Bn. and defended his position with great skill although suffering many casualties. The enemy was driven back leaving many dead on the field. The next day the Coy. was moved forward and the Acting Coy. Comd. was taken prisoner. Sgt. Self at once took command of the Coy. and although over-run by tanks and large numbers of enemy infantry, he inflicted heavy losses on the enemy and succeeded in getting the majority of his men back through enemy lines to safety, where they took up defensive positions and helped repulse the strong enemy counter-attacks. Sgt. Self was an inspiration to all those around him by his complete disregard for his own personal safety and calmness in very trying circumstances when he suddenly found himself in command of the Company.   (*L.G. 1.3.45*)

Semark, Albert Arthur, Sergeant
2734436, 1st Bn. Welsh Guards (Kings Lynn)
(Immediate)
During the attack by the Prince of Wales Coy. 1st Bn. Welsh Guards on the village of Houssemagne on 11th August, this N.C.O. owing to shortage of Offrs. found himself in comd. of No. 3 Platoon, the left fwd. platoon. They were continuously engaged with the enemy from shortly after crossing the SL at 0745 hrs. until after 1700 hrs. During the initial stages this platoon successfully attacked a number of M.G. posts. Whilst clearing the village they came upon considerable opposition which was overcome. At the end with only two weak sections left this N.C.O. led his platoon on a wide flanking movement to destroy some M.G. posts which were still holding out. In the case of one post he crawled forward himself with two men and knocked out the enemy M.G. He then crawled back and gathered the remains of his platoon to complete their task. There is no doubt that the success of No.3 Platoon was to a great extent brought about by the courage, leadership and initiative of this N.C.O. which were of the highest standard.
Recommended for M.M.   (*L.G. 21.12.44*)

Seton, Carden Wyndham, Sergeant (now A/Lieutenant)
NX 91635, Australian Military Forces
S.W. Pacific   (*L.G. 8.3.45*)

Setuata, Feni, Sergeant
638, Fiji Military Forces
No citation.   (*L.G. 21.9.44*)

Sexton, Donald, Sergeant (actg.)
6266608, 1st Leicestershire Regt. (London, N.9)
(Periodic)
A/Sjt. Sexton joined 'D' Coy. 1 Leicesters six months ago as a private soldier. He immediately showed great personality, knowledge, leadership and bravery.

As a Cpl. he led numerous difficult patrols with great bravery and complete disregard for his own safety. On one occasion he commanded two sections in a house which was completely surrounded by the enemy for 24 hrs. By his coolness and leadership he kept off all enemy attacks and also broke up numerous enemy counter-attacks by fire, which he could see forming up to attack other positions.

When he was wounded at the end of April A/Sjt. Sexton was in command of a platoon.

Throughout his service as a N.C.O. in this Bn. A/Sjt. Sexton has shown unflagging energy and enthusiasm and has carried out his duties in an exemplary manner and without any consideration for his own comfort or convenience.

As a leader he has proved himself cool and courageous and has the complete loyalty and confidence of his men.

He has been an example of selfless devotion to duty to N.C.O.'s and men alike.
Recommended for B.E.M.   (*L.G. 11.10.45*)

Shackleton, John Henry, Sergeant (A/W.O.II (C.S.M.))
4534747, 2nd Bn. The West Yorkshire Regt. (Hull)
(Immediate)
On 13th February 1944 Sgt. Shackleton was A/C.S.M. of 'B' Coy. 2 W. Yorks., which had been ordered to clear certain road blocks in Ngakedauk Pass in conjunction with Tanks. On their return from this operation the leading platoon and Coy. HQ were ambushed by the enemy. In this ambush the Coy. 2 i/c, who was temporarily in-charge of the Coy., was killed and the leading Platoon Officer seriously wounded. Sgt. Shackleton immediately took charge of the situation and succeeded in extricating the leading platoon and Coy. HQ from a difficult situation without further loss. Having done this he returned to the scene of the ambush which was still under heavy fire from 2 L.M.G.'s and personally carried 2 wounded men to safety being himself wounded in the process.   (*L.G. 22.6.44*)

Sharkey, William John, Sergeant (A/Colour Sergeant)
7010920, 2nd Bn. The Royal Ulster Rifles
(Coatbridge)
On 20th July 1944 the Battalion occupied high ground on Escoville—Troarn road. Sjt. Sharkey was in command of a platoon, his Platoon Comd. having been killed earlier in the day.

A task had been set this platoon of clearing an avenue of trees in conjunction with two tanks. As the platoon advanced on each side of the avenue, covered by a tank moving on the road, an enemy machine gun post opened fire at about 30 yards range. The tank was unable to engage the machine gun and four men of the leading section were wounded. With great initiative, Sjt. Sharkey, partially using the tank as cover, dashed to within 20 yards of the machine gun; moving quickly from behind the tank and with no regard for his own safety he personally attacked the machine gun post and with his Sten gun shot the crew of the gun. The task was successfully completed.

Later in the day, the Bn. captured the road junction a short distance to the North West of Troarn.

Sjt. Sharkey's company was the leading company of the attack. The forward platoon came under heavy machine gun fire and was pinned down. The leading tank was also knocked out by an anti-tank gun. Sjt. Sharkey, with his depleted platoon, worked round the right flank to deal with the anti-tank gun but came under machine gun fire from the right.

In co-operation with two tanks, he pushed forward with great determination and captured the enemy post of six men. On the objective, he cleared a sunken lane which contained many slit trenches. Setting an outstanding example of courage and leadership he dashed from slit trench to slit trench, firing bursts from his Sten gun. A number of the enemy were killed and another six of the enemy were captured.

Owing to his splendid leadership and determination to kill the enemy, his platoon did great work throughout the day. His initiative, dash and bravery was a great inspiration to his platoon.
Recommended for M.M.   *(L.G. 21.12.44)*

Sharples, Geoffrey Corbett, Sergeant
2654058, 2nd Coldstream Guards (Fullham, S.W.6)
During the attack on Long Stop Hill on the night of 24/25th December 1942 this Sgt. displayed the highest qualities of courage and devotion to duty. His Coy. found themselves pinned on a hill top completely dominated by German mortars and M.G. fire. The Coy. Comd. and Sgt. Major had both been wounded and this N.C.O. took over the duties of Sgt. Major. Throughout the night, which was bright moonlight, he was tireless in carrying amn. to the forward posts under enemy observation, mortar and M.G. fire. His personal example was of the greatest encouragement and inspiration to the whole Coy., and he appeared utterly unconscious of his own safety throughout the whole action. He was subsequently severely wounded.   *(L.G. 18.3.43)*

Shaw, Ashley George, Driver
T/106298, 5 Lt. Fd. Amb., R.A.S.C. (Farnham, Surrey)
(Periodic)
On 16th December 1941 Dvr. Shaw was on duty as Ambulance driver with the strongpoint column, North West of Bir El Gubi. At about 1600 hrs. the point was subjected to an intense 'Dive Bombing' and M.G. attack. Shaw saw there were casualties from the first attack and immediately ran his ambulance to the spot and, with the aid of his orderly, loaded up 5 cases and took them back to the Medical Post. The ambulance was being bombed and machine gunned all the while. The cases were seriously wounded and after attention were reloaded into the ambulance and at 1730 hrs. Shaw moved off for the

nearest A.D.S. being given only a compass bearing to drive upon for approx. a distance of 21 miles. He drove this distance in the darkness but encountered no A.D.S. At 2100 hrs. 1 case died in the ambulance the others being in a very serious condition. He halted and with his orderly re-dressed wounds and gave what comfort was possible to the cases. At first light on 11th December he drove on and after 12 miles met a Fd. Amb., but the cases were [...]sed as the Fd. Amb. was moving. He carried on and encountered another Fd. Amb. where a Medical Officer looked at the cases and directed him straight to the nearest C.C.S., which he reached at 1030 hrs. and the cases were taken off.

Without any rest he immediately drove back to his place of duty with the strongpoint column.

Dvr. Shaw has been one of the outstanding Ambulance drivers in the Western Desert for the past 8 months. From July 1941 to the present he has only rested in HQ when his Ambulance needed attention. He has practically been continuously on duty with forward columns. On November 14th, 1941 he left the HQ and joined the 51st Field Regt. Since then he has done forward Ambulance work continuously. On 18th December his name was mentioned to me by the Officer Commanding C.C.S., and a strong letter of praise came from the Regimental Medical Officer. I gradually gathered together facts of the episode on which I have based my recommendation.

I may mention that his name was put forward for notice after the French campaign of 1939–1940 for magnificent work both before and at Dunkirk.
Recommended for M.M. M.M. 27.1.44. M.I.D. 19.7.45.
(L.G. 9.9.42)

Shaw, Bertram John, Private (A/Cpl.)
14586565, 2nd Bn. The Essex Regt. (Sittingbourne)
(Immediate)
On 27th September 1944 at Ryckevorsel 'B' Coy. were responsible for defending the left flank of the Bn. area. In the early morning the enemy launched their third counter-attack against the Coy. The attack was preceded by heavy mortar and shell fire and it was later discovered that the strength of the enemy was approx. 3 Coys., with 3 armd. cars. Cpl. Shaw was commanding a section in the forward platoon of 'B' Coy. After an hour and a half of the attack, the platoon HQ and the rear section had been overrun, thus causing the remaining two sections to be cut off from the remainder of the Coy. Cpl. Shaw, who commanded one of these sections, immediately assumed command of them both. He co-ordinated the fire of the Bren gun and positioned the riflemen to form a firm base. The first wave of enemy, attacking frontally, were killed or wounded from approx. 80 yards range. By this time only one Bren remained in action and ammunition was running low. The enemy then attacked his left flank with 3 armd. cars, whilst enemy infantry infiltrated to the rear to within grenade range.

There was no more Piat amn. left so Cpl. Shaw directed the remaining Bren at the 3 armd. cars, blowing the tyres on one and causing the withdrawal of all three. The enemy infantry were held off with grenades. Throughout this engagement Cpl. Shaw personally directed the fire of all weapons and it was undoubtedly through his fine example and determined leadership that the two sections held firm to their positions until the arrival of tanks, fighting patrols and ammunition eased the position for them. His courage was an inspiration to all who worked with him.   *(L.G. 1.3.45)*

Shaw, Thomas Stewart, Sergeant
2818683, 6th Bn. The Seaforth Highlanders
On the 27th May 1940, at Zillebeke, while defending the exposed left flank, Sgt. Shaw handled his carrier with great skill and bravery, keeping his gun in action under heavy artillery, mortar, and M.G. fire. Thereafter, when ordered by his Coy. Comd., he displayed great bravery in rescuing wounded men, returning time and again for wounded. In the evening, he covered the withdrawal of the left Coy. most bravely, collecting two abandoned L.M.G.s and ammunition.
On the 28th May 1940, he again showed great resource in recconnoitring up to the position of the 2nd Royal Scots Fusiliers' position under very heavy fire, and also when the enemy had penetrated behind Bn. HQ on the St. Eloi—Messines Road he held the entrance to the village, and returned thrice for wounded men under heavy fire.   *(L.G. 27.8.40)*

Shaw, Walter, Warrant Officer Cl. I
4799610, 2nd Bn. The Lincolnshire Regt. (Leicester)
On the 14th October 1944, the Bn. was committed to an attack on a wooded objective which involved the crossing of about 800 yards of very open ground. C.S.M. Shaw was C.S.M. of 'D' Coy. the left forward Coy. On crossing into the open ground, the forward Coys. came under most accurate and intense defensive fire from guns of all calibre, mortars and machine guns. Many casualties were caused, but despite the Coy. Comd. falling mortally wounded, and the Coy. becoming split up, C.S.M. Shaw rallied the men around him and led them cheering into the attack which proved highly successful. C.S.M. Shaw fell very seriously wounded in the lung in the latter stages of the advance, but although hardly able to talk he refused help and continued to direct his survivors in consolidation. He had to be forcibly evacuated, protesting against it continuously and there is no doubt that his fortitude was largely responsible for the spirited rally of the depleted Coy. on the objective.
I strongly recommend that this W.O. be awarded the D.C.M.
Recommended for M.C.   *(L.G. 1.3.45)*

Shead, Walter, Sergeant
135569, 3 S.A. Armd. C. Recce Bn. (Immediate)
I have the honour to submit the name of 135569 Sgt. Shead for consideration of the award of the D.C.M.
From the commencement of active operations against the enemy with 5 S.A. Inf. Bde., Sgt. Shead has exhibited soldierly qualities of the highest order and his conduct in the face of the enemy has at all times been an example of courageous determination.
On 23rd November 1941 (D 7) 1 Coy. was picketting enemy Met. and Tank forces in the vicinity of 5 S.A. Inf. Bde., South of Sidi Rezegh. At about 1100 hrs. an unidentified force was observed in the distance. Sgt. Shead proceeded in his armd. car to investigate. He made for the centre of the column and upon reaching it found it to be a German Panser force. He raced towards the rear of the column coming under fire in the process. At the end of the column he found three tractor propelled panser replenishment vehicles lagging about 200 yds. behind. Sgt. Shead placed his a/car between these and end of column and compelled them to surrender, turn about, and drive their vehicles into 5 S.A. Inf. Bde. lines. The prisoners totalled eleven.
On the following day when the remaining a/cars of 1 Coy. were operating with a support group under Brig. Campbell Sgt. Shead went with his section to the right flank to investigate movement there. He came across enemy tanks which were proceeding parallel to the support gp. column and wirelessed the information. He was pursued by three tanks and fired upon. While being pursued Sgt. Shead noticed a motor cycle several hundred yards ahead of the panser column. He immediately cut over and upon finding the motor cyclist to be a German D/R took him prisoner, before making his getaway.
Whenever Sgt. Shead's section has been called upon to make any investigation, Sgt. Shead has proceeded in person to the task. His devotion to duty and disregard for personal safety while in search of information has been most marked.   *(L.G. 20.1.42)*

Sheldon, Benjamin Eyre, Lance Sergeant
4752630, 7th Bn. Royal Tank Regt. (Sheffield)
On 10th July 1944 Cpl. Sheldon was in command of a tank which formed part of a supporting troop of tanks. The troop of tanks in front was engaged on the '112 feature' SW of Fontaine Etoupefor and entirely destroyed by German Tiger Tanks, thus making it necessary for the supporting troop to take over. Having taken over the position, the troop Comd.'s tank and the troop Sgt.'s tank were promptly destroyed, leaving Cpl. Sheldon's tank alone against apparently overwhelming odds. Without paying any regard to the apparent hopelessness of the situation, Cpl. Sheldon not only held his ground, but by a combination of skilful commanding, brilliant gunnery, and total disregard for his own safety, actually destroyed 3 Tiger tanks at close range despite intense enemy fire.
This magnificent piece of work was largely responsible for securing the left flank of the objective, inflicting

heavy losses on the enemy and setting a wonderful example to the remainder of his Sqn. *(L.G. 19.10.44)*

Shelford, Charles, Private
39159, 28 Maori Bn. (Immediate)
At Gazal Box 14th December 1941.

I wish to recommend Pte. Shelford for an Immediate award. During a night attack by this Bn. on the 14th December 1941 the first line of positions at Gazala he showed outstanding heroism and courage.

After the first entrenchments had been taken his Section carried on with the Platoon Comd. for a distance of 300 yds. to a ridge. The Platoon Comd. then discovered that his section was now isolated from the extreme left flank of the Bn. and was being fired on from the right rear and from their left flank. Pte. Shelford volunteered to cover the 300 yds. to the enemy firing from the rear and clean it out. Meanwhile the enemy on the left flank were sweeping the area with Anti-tank gun, M.M.G.s and L.M.G.s as well as rifle fire. Notwithstanding the intensity of the enemy fire from his flank and his front Pte. Shelford covered the 300 yds. walking and running and firing his Spandau M.G. from the hip.

When he was about 20 yds. from the trench he was hit in rapid succession by 3 grenades in the legs. Badly wounded and dazed he attempted to bring his Spandau into action but that had been hit and the butt smashed so even though he was suffering intense agony he threw a mills bomb into the trench. This brought out the enemy and by this time his Platoon Comd. and Section arrived and took charge of the prisoners. Altogether 4 Officers and 36 O/Ranks came out of the trenches in the vicinity including the Commander of the enemy positions. The surrender of the Commander started the collapse of the entire position and ended the enemy resistance in that area. Pte. Shelford's conduct was outstanding even in action in which deeds of bravery were numerous and in my opinion and the opinion of the Platoon Comd. certainly merits the Award requested. *(L.G. 24.2.42)*

Shelton, J., T/Warrant Officer Cl. I (R.S.M.)
4066190, 2nd S/L Regt., Royal Artillery
T.S.M. Shelton set a splendid example of coolness and efficiency. With his Troop he was attached to an Infantry Bn. on May 24th and organised a defensive position which succeeded in holding up the enemy.

His action throughout six days inspired confidence and he finally brought all the survivors of his troop to England. *(L.G. 11.7.40)*

Sheppard, Leslie, Warrant Officer Cl. III
4856611, Leicestershire Regt. (Market Harborough)
Norway & France (from P.O.W. Pool) *(L.G. 11.10.45)*

Sheriff, Horace, Sergeant
3854714, 1st Bn. The Loyal Regt.
On May 22nd 1940 at Pont A Chine his Coy. was in a defensive position on the canal. Two enemy M.G.s continuously harrassed the position from 400 yards distance. Sgt. Sherriff spotted their position and with one man crawled forward to within 200 yards of the enemy posts. He then stood up and by resting a Bren gun on a wire fence opened fire and silenced both enemy guns. He showed great courage and devotion to duty, and his action saved many lives. *(L.G. 22.10.40)*

Shorthouse, Raymond David, Corporal
24128884, Royal Regt. of Fusiliers
For Northern Ireland   *(L.G. 1.5.73)*

Sibbald, John Edmund, Sergeant
2615057, 3rd Bn. Grenadier Guards (London, S.W.6)2612007 (Immediate)
During the counter-attack on Monte Battaglia (MR M.0618), on the morning of October 11th, Sgt. Sibbald was in command of the left forward platoon of No. 1 Coy. 3rd Bn. Grenadier Guards, holding the western slope of the hill. His platoon was strongly attacked before light by a Coy. of enemy, a platoon of which managed to work its way into Sgt. Sibbald's position. By his control and skill, he was able to throw the enemy back down the hill with heavy losses, causing several casualties himself; both with close range Tommy gun fire when his slit trench was rushed by four Germans and by hurling grenades at the retreating Germans. During this desperate battle, Sgt. Sibbald was throughout, giving an accurate account of it over his platoon wireless set to his Coy. Comd. He also calmly reported yet another German company forming up on his left flank. This information was as accurate as it was vital and passed over the wireless in the heat of a hand to hand struggle. The result of it was that an artillery concentration was at once put down on this German company, breaking up their attack and causing them to run for safety to a position from which the entire Coy. was taken prisoner when daylight came. *(L.G. 8.3.45)*

Sibson, Harold, Sergeant
4863949, Leicestershire Regt.
Recommended by A.F.H.Q. Greece. *(L.G. 10.5.45)*

Siely, Walter James, Driver
5977, Div. Petrol Coy., 1 Div., New Zealand Military Forces
Report of escape.
Siely was captured in Crete on 1st June 1941. From a temporary camp at Glataos he thrice attempted to escape, only to return to camp each time on seeing the reprisals taken by the Germans on Greek helpers.

From Salonika, in October 1941, Siely was transferred to Stalag VIII B (Lamsdorf), Germany, where he posed as a Corporal to get out on working parties. In the summer of 1943 he helped 32 P/W to escape from a party at Stranberg, having obtained maps from a Czech girl, but was frustrated in his own attempt by being arrested as an agitator. After serving his sentence of 7 days' cells,

Siely was sent to Arbeitskommando 399 (Oberwich-stein). He escaped from here by filling a window bar in his billet, and was at liberty for four days.

On his recapture, he was sent via Stalag VIII B to a working camp at Freiwaldau, from where he escaped again in January 1944 with two companions. They got out of a trapdoor in the theatre of their Lager and had reached Olmutz in Chechoslovakia by train before being recaptured by the Gestapo.

Siely's third attempted escape from Germany was made from a working party attached to Stalag VIII A (Gorlitz) engaged on railway repairs at Parschnitz. At the first favourable opportunity, he and two other P/W went to a shed nearby and got out of the rear window. They walked across the Czech frontier, but were recaptured at Kipel, having asked the wife of a Sudeten German for help.

They were eventually returned to Stalag VIII A, from where, whilst on a working party at a cement factory in Munsterberg, Siely and a British P/W made their final escape. Their preparations were more thorough, and Siely had obtained identity documents for them from the main camp.

On 13th July 1944 they pulled a bar from the window of a washhouse adjoining their billet, and at 0515 hours on 14th July 1944 they got out through the window and walked to the station, where they caught a train to Breslau. They reached Stettin by train via Frankfurt and Eberswalde, their identity papers having passed muster at booking officers. In Stettin they approached a Frenchman who his them in his Lager, and with his aid they met two Swedish sailors who eventually agreed to help Siely, his companion and two Frenchmen to get on board their ship. On 24th July they got aboard and were hidden in the airshaft of the main funnel for five days, after which time the Captain was informed of their presence and they were put ashore at Kalmar, Sweden. They reached Stockholm on 1st August 1944.

Account of Escape.
1. Dvr. Siely.
(a) Capture.

I was captured in Crete on 1st June 1941, the day of the British capitulation to the Germans.

(b) Camps in which imprisoned.

Galatos (Crete), three months in a temporary camp. Here conditions were very bad. I made three attempted escapes from this camp. On each occasion I got out through the wire with a friend and got in touch with Greeks who hoped to be able to get us away by boat. This, however, was difficult to arrange, and on each occasion, seeing the reprisals taken by the Germans on Greeks who helped escapers, we returned to the camp.

Salonika, six weeks. From Salonika we were sent to Germany in cattle trucks—40 men to each truck—with only four loaves of bread each for a journey which lasted about 12 days. My first camp in Germany was:—

Stalag VIII B (Lamsdorf). I was here for seven months. From Lamsdorf I went to work on a building

job at Novy Jicin (Neutitschein) in the Czechoslovak Protectorate South of Mahrisch-Ostrauk. At Lamsdorf I had signed on as a Corporal to get on this party. In Novy Jicin I met a Czech girl who spoke English. She told me of the existence of a Czechoslovak organisation which might be able to help me if I could escape, but advised me to learn German and some Czech before I made a serious attempt. I did not escape from this party.

I was next employed at a sugar factory at Troppau (Germany 1:100,000, Sheet 127, 9333) from which there was no chance of escape. From Troppau I went to another party at Belton (not traced) in the same area, and to a third party at Stranberg, near Sternberg (11 miles North of Olmutz). In the summer of 1943 no fewer than 32 P/Ws escaped from Stranberg. I helped them all by getting maps from the Czech girl. I had intended going out myself, but on the day I had chosen for my attempt I was arrested by the Germans who had heard of my activities. The Commandant said he could not charge me with having helped my comrades to escape, but that he would charge me with being an agitator and influencing the men on the job. On this charge I received seven days' cells.

I did my time at Jagernsdolf (Sheet 127, 7950) the HQ of the guards i charge of the working parties in the district. Hauptmann Gross, who had sentenced me, asked if, after my sentence, I would like to go out on a working party, as there was then an epidemic of typhus in the camp. I agreed, and just before winter set in in 1943 I was sent to Arbeitskommando 399 at Oberwichstein (not traced). I had signed a paper promising to be a 'good boy' and not cause trouble.

(c) First attempted escape.

I had been about a year and a half in Germany when I made my first attempted escape. After I had been about a week at Kommando 399 I escaped with a Londoner (Cpl. Cushion). We filed a bar in a window in the billet at the Lager and got out. Four days later we were recaptured and taken to Jagernsdorf, where I 'did' 14 days.

(d) Second attempted escape.

After I had served my sentence I was sent back to Stalag VIII B. A short time later I went out on a working party at a Holzwolle factory at Freiwaldau (Sheet 126, 4366). I was among those who came under suspicion when the factory and several adjoining farms was burned down, and in January 1944 I escaped with Cpl. Verner, No. 3 Commando; Pte Eagan, The Buffs; and Sgt. Wagstaff, a Canadian. We got out of a trapdoor in the theatre of our Lager. We went from Freiwaldau to Goldberg (not traced) by passenger train without identity papers. In this district we met a party of Czech partisans at Schonau (Sheet 103, 6454) with whom we spen 24 hours. We told them that we intended to try to link up with the organisation about which the Czech girl had told me. The partisans fed us and conducted us to the railway station. They told us they had an Englishman with them, but they would not let us see him. We continued by train to Olmutz (Olomouc). Unfortunately, the map we had showed the German and Czech names of this town some distance apart, and when the train stopped at Olmutz we did not realise that we were already at our destination. As a result, we were late in leaving the train and were stopped and arrested by the Gestapo. During this escape we wore Army overcoats and trousers dyed blue.

We were taken to Olmutz gaol, where we were interrogated. Ten days later we were transferred to Prague, and spent 11 days in the Wehrmacht prison.

When captured I had inside my stocking a scrap of paper with the address of a Communist living near Brno, in Czechoslovakia. This scrap of paper was found. Lieut. Miller, Royal Canadian Engineers, was in my cell in the Wehrmacht prison, and advised me what to do when interrogated, telling me not to reveal where I had got the address. We were all interrogated separately by Dr. Krugen, who was specially flown from Berlin to investigate our connection with the partisans. I was taken alone to the Gestapo HQ in Prague for interrogation by Kruger. I was kept waiting for two hours before Kruger asked me to sit down. I refused saying that they would 'belt' me if I did so, and that if they hit me, I wanted to get in one at them. Kruger said to the others in German: 'We will have to change our tactics'. He then shook hands with me and said that he was an international lawyer and would get me out of the 'spot of bother' I had got into. Throughout the interrogation Kruger was very smooth, taking the line that he was trying to help me. He wanted to know where I had got the address, where I had crossed the frontier, and how I had travelled. I said I had found the scrap of paper in the corridor of the train. In the end he said I had cleared myself satisfactorily, and I was sent back to the Wehrmacht prison/

At the end of 11 days we were all sent back to Lamsdorf. For our escape we were sentenced to 21 days' cells, which we had already served.

After I had served my sentence I volunteered for another working party and went to Marschendorf, near Trautenau (Sheet 115, 6403). I had with me a copy of a foreign worker's Ausweis, obtained in Lamsdorf, which I hoped to be able to get copied. On this party I met L/Cpl. Evans.

2. L/Cpl. Evans and Dvr. Siely.
(a) Escape Preparations.

When we were sent back from Marschendorf to Stalag VIII A Verner, and we two each sold a battle dress and personal clothing such as Jerseys and underclothing. The cigarettes we obtained for the clothing were bartered for chocolate, which in turn was bartered with Serbians for civilian clothes. We were unable to obtain anything in the way of identity papers.

We chose a working party of N.C.O.s and Privates which was engaged in railway repairs and based at Konigshan (Sheet 115, 6916). We could not escape from the Lager at Konigshan as the Unteroffizier in charge watched us too closely.

(b) Attempted Escape from Parschnitz.

After six days we were sent to work at Parschnitz (Sheet 115, 6704). On the journey we wore our civilian clothes under our uniforms. We had collected a store of biscuits, chocolate and cigarettes, which the other members of the party, all of whom were keen to help us get away, carried for us in their pockets. Verner and we two each had an Italian Military rucksack obtained in the Stalag from Italian P/W. These rucksacks we left in a shed near our working place in the railway at Parschnitz, and a friend surreptitiously packed them with our food. We found later, however, that he had not had an opportunity of completing the packing, and we were short on biscuits.

We were unloading a train and when it pulled into a siding at the sation at Parschnitz to allow and express to pass, we three made for the shed. There were three Czechs in the shed, but we turned them out, removed our battle dressed, picked up our bags, and got out of the rear window.

We headed for Czechoslovakia, hoping to make contact with the Czechoslovak organisation of which Siely had heard on a previous attempted escape. We waited till nightfall in a wood near Parschnitz, and then got on to the railway track, along which we walked. On this walk we crossed the Czech frontier, which we knew to be patrolled by Grenzpolizei, but, although we heard dogs, we saw no sign of patrols. Next morning we reached the village of Schwadowitz (Sheet 115, 7400). We spent the day in a wood. In the evening an old woman, who told us there were no trains running, directed us to Eipel (Sheet 115, 7197). As we had had no bread since we set out, we went to a house at Eipel (after listening at the window to make sure the people were Czech). There were a woman and her daughter in the house. We told them we were British escapers, and they appeared ready to help us. At this stage the woman's husband arrived, and we gathered that, while the wife was Czech, he was a Sudeten German. He said he would lose his head if he gave us food. The wife and daughter broke down and cried at this. We left the house quickly and, as we were very fatigued, we went to sleep in a haystack near the house. About 0300 hrs. 16 Czech policeman headed by one Gestapo man came along armed with bayonetted rifles and pistols, and woke us with shouts of 'Raus'.

(c) Imprisoned in Konigsgratz and Prague.

We were taken to the gaol in Eipel. After a few hours we were moved to the Gestapo political gaol in Konigsgratz (Hradec Kralove), where we were detained for ten days. Here we were interrogated separately, by a civilian, through an interpreter, Siely being taken first. We had agreed beforehand that, in the event of capture, we should say that we were soldiers, that it was our duty to escape, and that we were heading for Italy. We were asked how we had obtained civilian clothing. We said we had got it from friends, and when we were asked for the names of these friends, we said they had been repatriated. We were well treated by the Feldwebel who seemed to be in charge of about 30 Gestapo men in the gaol. There were officers there, but we never spoke to them. Our interrogation seemed to be a joint one for the Staatspolizei and the Kriminalpolizei. Our fingerprints were taken.

From Konigsgratz we were sent to the Gestapo prison in Prague. The three of us were put into a cell, across from which was another Englishman (Pte. York, R.A.S.C.) who had escaped from a working party attached to Stalag IV C (Colditz). He had been seven weeks in gaol. In the same prison were an R.A.F. officer and a Czech pilot serving in the R.A.P. Later the R.A.F. officer was sent back to Stalag Luft III, but the Czech was kept back. We never saw either of them.

Treatment was very bad in this prison. We had to be up at 0600 hours every day and had to scrub the floor of our cell. The food was damnable. At 0600 hours we got coffee and 150 grammes of bread; at 0900 a very thin soup; at 1600 hrs. coffee; and nothing more for the rest of the day. On arrival we had to stand facing the wall while our particulars were being taken, and those prisoners who did not clean their rooms got from one to four hours of this punishment. We also had to do everything at the double, and had to do strenuous exercises, also at the double, in the prison yard. Siely refused to do the exercise. We complained, and the Commandant was brought. He said that we had been sent in as political prisoners and that he did not know anything about our being soldiers. In the prison all prisoners are shaved once a week, by a barber who is allowed about one minute to shave each man and has to do 72 men with one safety razor blade. The S.S. guards threatened to knock us down when we answered them back. We saw them kick many prisoners, but we personally were never kicked. We stood on our dignity, and they showed respect for us. When we were entering the cell for the first time a Czech guard took a packet of cigarettes which Siely had managed to secrete during the search. When asked in Czech to return the cigarettes, the guard gripped Siely by the throat and later fetched an S.S. trooper who also gripped hold of Siely. The incident closed with the Commandant being fetched. We were eight days in the Gestapo prison and were not interrogated.

From the Gestapo prison we were transferred to the Wehrmacht gaol, also in Prague. Here we were put into a room with nine Russians and ten Englishmen. Conditions were very bad. There were only six straw paliasses in the room, which was lousy. The food was good, but short. The Russians were very generous and shared with us what they had. This gaol was also used for German deserters, of whom there were thousands, including officers. We were here for ten days awaiting transport. We were not interrogated. All the other Englishmen left when we did.

(d) Lamsdorf and Gorlitz.

We were sent from Prague to Stalag 344 (Lamsdorf), and spent 14 days in the Lager gaol. The Lamsdorf Commandant refused to try us as escapers, as we now belonged to Stalag VIII A. In time R.S.M. Sheriff, who is one of the finest Englishmen in Germany, got us transferred to the Straf compound where we spent 21 days.

About 14th June 1944 we were sent to Gorlitz, where we were interrogated and tried by the Gerichtsoffizier for escaping. We got 21 days' cells, which, however, we had already served.

(e) Escape.

On our arrival at Stalag VIII A (Gorlitz) we decided on a more serious attempt at escape, and realised that we would require to equip ourselves with identity papers. Before our previous attempt Siely had left with a N.Z. friend the copy of the foreign worker's Ausweis. This Ausweis had been copied and used. Siely had now obtained, in the Straf compound in Lansdorf, three much more up-to-date documents—a Dienstausweis, certifying that the foreign holder was in employment by a German firm; a Personalausweis (or identity certificate); and an Eisenbahnausweis permitting the holder to travel by train. We now obtained copies of these documents for both of us, and also had the documents stamped with a replica of the Breslau police stamp. The Personalausweis bore photographs. (Siely had a proper identity card photograph. Evans' was cut from a larger photograph which he had had with him when captured.) We managed to get, through a friend, from Frenchmen in the camp two civilian suits, and to have ourselves put on a working party near a railway line. A route to Stettin was worked out for us.

The working party was at a cement pipe factory at Munsterberg (Sheet 116, 3208) about 60 km. from Breslau. This Privates' party numbered about 32 and was working about 12 hours a day. We went as N.C.O.s and were detected straight away, which meant that we were closely watched. On the journey to Munsterberg we wore our civilian clothes under our battle dress, and on arrival (6th July 1944) hid them in the straw of our paliasses. We worked for only a few days, and had trouble with the Germans because we were not working hard enough.

On 13th July we pulled a bar from the window of a wash house attached to our billet, which adjoined the factory. At 0500 hrs. on 14th July the guard came in to our sloping quarters and shone the light in our faces to make sure we were there. At 0515 hrs. we got up, dressed (with our civilian suits under our battle dress) and went out to the wash house, crossing a corner of the yard to do so. The guard had not noticed the window from which we had removed the bar. In the wash house we took off our battle dress, which a comrade was to take away at once so that the Germans should not know we had escaped in civilian clothes. We got out through the window, being partly screened by bushes from the guard who was patrolling the yard of our billet. We crossed a private garden, jumped a fence on to the road, and walked past the main entrance of the factory to the station. We each carried a small attache case which we obtained in the Stalag for 150 cigarettes. The train for Breslau left at 0555 hrs, and we caught it with about two minutes to spare. We had no difficulty in getting our tickets, and did not have to produce our identity papers.

(f) Journey to Stettin.

We had three hours to wait in Breslau and sat in a public park, where we ate our breakfast. We had brought a loaf and some German margerine from the Lager so that if we had to eat in public—as for example, in the train—we should not be conspicuous. We had also brought French cigarettes to smoke on the journey, as we were travelling as Belgians. We re-booked to Frankfurt-An-Der-Oder, leaving Breslau at 1000 hrs. There was no incident on this stage of the journey.

At Frankfurt, Siely was asked to show his identity papers when getting a ticket to Eberswalde. The girl booking clerk pointed out that the documents said that he was travelling to Stettin. When he explained that he wanted to spend the night with friends in Eberswalde, she produced a ticket. As Evans' photograph was not as good as hi, Siely produced his own card at another booking office and got another ticket for Eberswalde.

We arrived at Eberswalde about 2200 hrs. On the journey Siely asked a German soldier if it was necessary to change en route for Eberswalde. The soldier said, 'Parles vous Francais?' Siely replied that he was Flemish, and the soldier merely told him in German that the train went direct to Eberswalde. We spent the night in the open near the Eberswalde aerodrome. It rained during the night.

(g) Search for ship in Stettin.

At 0745 hrs. next day (15th July) we caught the train for Stettin, arriving without incident about 1100 hrs. Leaving the station, which shows signs of bad bomb damage, some passengers showed identity cards. Others did not, and we followed the example of the latter. We crossed the Bahnhof Brucke, but soon returned. We had no information about Stettin and walked all round the centre of the town. After a time we met two Poles who wore the 'P' sign, by which we knew they were not Germanised and therefore could safely be approached. Siely spoke to them in Polish, telling them who we were and asking to be taken to a brothel frequented by foreign sailors. The Poles showed us a brothel in the Kleinodor Strasse, but, as it was morning, the house was closed. The Poles then took us to a Swedish sailor whom we had watched coming off a ship at a quay near the Wesen Strasse. The sailor could not understand us, and we got no satisfaction from him.

At this time we noticed two Germans looking at us suspiciously, and we thought it would be a good thing to get rid of our attache cases. We left the two Poles, and made our way on foot through the town to a public park, probably North of the Westend Sec. (Pharus Plan of Stettin, C 4). This was a big public park in which there is an S.S. barracks. Here we hid our cases.

We were now getting desperate, as it was raining and we had nowhere to sleep. We saw French workers, who were obviously on their way back from work to their Lager, and followed them. Siely stopped one, saying 'Parlez vous Anglais?' and showing a Stalag identity disc and a letter from home on a P/W card. The Frenchmen took us to his Lager, which is probably beside the building marked 'Stadtkuche' on Fabrik Strasse (Pharus Plan C 4). He took us in and fed us.

There were about 20 Frenchmen living in the room into which we were taken. They fed and sheltered us for a week. By day we slept in the air-raid shelters at the camp. At night we went into the town, accompanied by two Frenchmen, to visit the brothels and Gasthauser in search of a Swedish soldier. The two Frenchmen who accompanied us gave us French workers' papers. One of these men had been hiding in another camp from the Gestapo for a year. Both the men accompanied us to Sweden.

At the end of seven days (on 22nd July) we had to move to another French Lager at the Zuckersiederei adjoining the Neue Speicher (Pharus Plan, G 8). We lived here in a bombed house, coming out at night to join the Frenchmen. One of them lived in the Lager, while the other lived at the Opel Works, where he was employed.

On 22nd July we went out to the Flughaven (Sheet 30, 7516) and had a look round the shipping, but could not get in touch with any Swedes. Siely and one of the Frenchmen then travelled one stop back towards Stettin on the tram, getting off when they saw ships flying the Swedish flag. Near here Siely met two Swedish sailors on their way to church. He asked to see their papers and they produced their ship's books. Siely immediately disclosed his identity, asked for help in getting on to a Swedish ship, and invited the sailors to go to the French Lager to discuss the matter. One of the men spoke English. Evans and the other Frenchmen now joined the party, and we all went back to the lager at the Zuckersiederei. here we said that if we were caught we would be shot; also that if they got us to Sweden, the Swedes could collect certain money. The English speaking Swede said it would be very hard to get us on board.

(h) Voyage to Sweden.

For two nights this Swede came to the Lager and spoke with us. His ship was lying at the quay on the Stettin side of the Reihewerderhafen, which is the port where Swedish vessels load coal. Their cargoes of iron-ore are discharged at the quay where the ship was lying. The ship was at the outer end of the quay and was anchored some distance off the quay. On the night of 24th July we went form the Lager to the landward end of this quay. After getting off the tram we hid in bushes beside the road till 2300 hrs. Keeping to the bushes, we skirted the West side of the quay till we had reached the seaward end, still on the West side. (By doing this we avoided the watchman's post on the landward end of the quay and a Gestapo post further up the quay.) We were accompanied by only one of the Frenchmen. At the end of the quay the English speaking Swede joined us, having swum from the ship—a distance of 400 or 500 yards—with a lifebelt for the Frenchman, who could not swim. The four of us then swam out to the ship, which we boarded by a ladder let down by the other Swede. Next morning the boat moved to the coaling harbour and the first Swede went ashore for the other Frenchman, who got on board by using a Swedish passport.

The Swedes hid us in the airshaft of the main funnel of the ship, entrance being gained through a cleaning manhole. In the airshaft we had to lie on a ledge about a foot broad. As the chimney itself got red hot, the atmosphere in the ventilation shaft was stifling, and we were unable to eat the food which was lowered to us. We were, however, kept plentifully supplied with water. On one occasion Siely lost consciousness and fell to a wider ledge about 20 ft below, hurting his head and arm superficially. After this our helpers were forced to report our presence to the Captain, and we came out early on the morning of 29th July, having been five days in the airshaft.

By this time we were off Kalmar in Swedish waters. On learning we were English; the Captain said he would put us ashore in the pilot boat. This was done, and next day the local newspapers reported that two Englishmen and two Frenchmen had swum ashore from an unknown vessel. We were well treated by the police in Kalmar and allowed to report to the British Vice-Consul, who got us clothes and sent us to Stockholm. We arrived at the British Legation on 1st August.   *(L.G. 9.11.44)*

Simpson, Derrick Bell, Gunner
6098896, 11th (H.A.C.) Regt., Royal Horse Artillery (Wembley) (Immediate)
On 13th June 1942 Gnr. Simpson was layer on a gun in action near Knightsbridge. During the day the troop had to occupy four successive positions in the open to meet successive enemy attacks and was heavily shelled in each position.

Gnr. Simpson was wounded early in the day but refused to leave his post. During a lull he received first aid but returned to his gun during the hottest bombardment when all the other numbers had become casualties. Then with another wounded man and two borrowed ammunition numbers he got the gun into action and served it until the Troop evacuated the position.

He was sent to the R.A.P. during the move but refused to be evacuated and returned to the layers' seat for the rest of the day.

His courage and devotion to duty were an inspiration to all his comrades.   *(L.G. 15.10.42)*

Simpson, Eric Edwin, Sergeant
789776, Royal Artillery (Nottingham)
145 Inf. Bde. P.O.W. Pool   *(L.G. 25.10.45)*

Simpson, Harry, Warrant Officer Cl. II (actg.)
2756332, 7th Black Watch (Crewe) (Periodic)
C.S.M. Simpson has, throughout the campaign, shown himself to be an outstanding and extremely gallant leader. There are many specific cases of gallantry to the credit of this W.O. who has been wounded 5 times and has, on more than one occasion, got off a stretcher to return to fight after being wounded. In Normandy in August 1944 he was detailed as Carrier Sgt. to cover the flank of a Bn. attack. This attack was held up and showed signs of faltering when C.S.M. Simpson, finding his carriers could not proceed further, dismounted the crews and put in a very skilful and dashing attack on the enemy's flank, enabling the Rifle Coys. to get on and saving many lives and taking many prisoners. At the village of Breedeweg on 8th February 1945 severe enemy opposition was encountered and the Platoon Comd. of C.S.M. Simpson took over the platoon and personally led and assaulted no fewer than three enemy strong points and eventually gained the objective by most outstanding gallantry and leadership, being wounded, but remaining at duty, early in the proceedings. Shortly after the crossing of the Niers River, this W.O., now a C.S.M., performed an almost similar outstanding performance in taking over a platoon whose Comd. and others were hit and taking the platoon through to its objective. He was again wounded in this action. At the crossing of the Rhine his bravery and inspiration were outstanding. His Coy. holding the left of the 21 Army Gp. Bridgehead was heavily counterattacked and a number of enemy succeeded in infiltrating into the widely held Coy. positions. The situation at times became tense but whenever and wherever things looked most grim there was C.S.M. Simpson generally engaging the enemy single-handed with Sten and grenades, and rallying and supplying with amn. all the platoons in the Coy. His behaviour on this occasion, as on many others, was an inspiration to all, a fact which has very frequently been expressed by the men in his Coy. who regard C.S.M. Simpson's bravery and leadership as something seldom, if ever, equalled.   *(L.G. 24.1.46)*

Simpson, Henry, Sergeant
4611795, 7th Bn. The Duke of Wellington's Regt. (Oldham) (Immediate)
During a strong enemy attack on Haaldaren 7566, a key point in the defence of the Nijmegen Bridge, on December 4th Sjt. Simpson was in command of a section of carriers which was ordered to place a stop across a line of buildings to halt the enemy house clearing operations. That this difficult mission was soon completed in the darkness was due to Sjt. Simpson's great leadership. Shortly afterwards Sjt. Simpson was told to clear the enemy from a school from which Bn. HQ was being threatened.

Under the cover of Bren fire, this N.C.O. led three riflemen immediately towards the door of the School in the face of the concentrated fire of six Spandaus. Sjt. Simpson was seriously wounded in the leg and fell, but in spite of great pain, he remained on the ground directing the assault, shouting encouragement and refused to be taken to safety until his men, fired by his great example, rushed the door and forced the enemy garrison of 14 men to surrender.

This N.C.O.'s decision to assault a greatly superior force and the inspiration he gave his men when wounded saved Bn. HQ from encirclement with the eventual result that a counter attack was planned which entirely eliminated the enemy force.   *(L.G. 5.4.45)*

Simpson, John Stanislaus, Warrant Officer Cl. II
4748429, Hallamshire Bn. York & Lancaster Regt.
    (Wigan) (Periodic)
C.S.M. Simpson has served with this battalion throughout the whole campaign as C.S.M. of a rifle company. In June 1944, during the battle of Fontenay, which began in thick fog, C.S.M. Simpson was mainly responsible for saving his company from getting lost and finally reached the objective with the leading troops. Following this his company bore the brunt of the very heavy shelling which was experienced for three weeks at Tessel Wood, and Simpson's cheerfulness and behaviour under fire inspired the company and maintained their morale at a high level.

In August 1944, at Chicheboville, C.S.M. Simpson was advancing with company HQ and the reserve platoon, when it came under heavy and accurate shell fire. Five men of company HQ were hit, as was the platoon commander and platoon sjt., and the men were badly shaken. C.S.M. Simpson was unperturbed and reorganised first the platoon, nominating new leaders, and then company HQ, enabling the advance to be continued almost without a check. Only then did he report that he, too, had been hit in the back by a piece of shrapnel, for which he had later to be evacuated.

Later, at Merxplas, his company was acting as advance guard after the battalion had crossed the Turnhout Canal. Approaching the village the company was met by intense shell and mortar fire, and in the first ten minutes a dozen casualties including one officer had been received. Orders were given for the company to consolidate as further advance was impossible, and the stretcher bearers started to collect the wounded. The task was a formidable one and C.S.M. Simpson completely ignoring his own danger, went forward into the shell fire and personally carried three seriously wounded men back to company HQ. He undoubtedly saved their lives.

Again, in October, his company repelled a determined enemy counter-attack at Aerle.

Throughout these and other actions C.S.M. Simpson's bearing under fire and his cheerful imperturbability have always had a steadying influence on the men of his company, with the result that their morale has always been of the highest quality. Amongst the other ranks of the battalion he stands out as the one man who, in action, and out, has set the best example, won the truest loyalty,

and maintained most consistently the fighting qualities of the men under his command.   *(L.G. 24.1.46)*

Simpson, Rayene Stewart, Sergeant (T/W.O.II)
24492, Royal Australian Infantry
WO Simpson served with the Australian Imperial Forces from March 1944 to January 1947. He re-enlisted in January 1951, serving with the Royal Australian Regiment during 1951 and in Malaya during the emergency.

WO Simpson was assigned to the first Australian Army Training Team Vietnam in August 1962 and returned to Australia in August 1963. He volunteered for a second tour with the Australian Army Training Team Vietnam and was assigned to the training team on the 13th July 1964, from the First Special Air Service Company.

He was immediately posted to the advisory group with United States and Vietnamese Special Forces in the mountainous jungles of the North West. Shortly after his arrival, he took a major part in the establishment of a new patrol base at Tako, designed to control border infiltration; and thereafter his task was to provide advice in the training and operations of Vietnamese patrols from that base. On one such patrol, led by a Vietnamese Special Forces Officer the platoon size group was intercepted by a superior Viet Cong Force. The Vietnamese leader was an early casualty. WO Simpson was severely wounded by rifle fire in the right leg. Despite his wound, he rallied the platoon, formed a defensive position, contacted base by radio, and, by personal example and inspiring leadership, held off repeated assaults by the Viet Cong force, until, with ammunition almost exhausted, and himself weak from loss of blood, the relief force he had alerted arrived at the scene. Even then, not until he was satisfied that the position was secure and the troops of his patrol adequately cared for did he permit himself to be evacuated. [From L.G.]   *(L.G. 29.10.65)*

Sinasac, Milton Douglas, Lance Corporal
A.20191, Corps of Royal Canadian Engineers
A member of Lieut. Ewener's party, L/Cpl. Sinasac proceeded with his commanding officer as far as the Casino during the action at Dieppe, 19th August 1942. When Lieut. Ewener, due to wounds was unable to carry on, he led the demolition party of 6 men from the South door of the Casino across the M.G.-swept Esplanade towards the Rue Duquesne Road Block. Fire was so heavy he could not reach this objective but managed with two other men to attain the Rue Syngoyne Road Block where he left the men while he dashed back to the Casino to bring up more wall charges. In returning he was wounded, but with the assistance of Spr. Laur carried back two more charges through the enemy fire. At the Road Block he fired the charges, but due to the heavy M.G. fire had to withdraw his party and was not able to observe the extent of the damage. He was again wounded,

but managed to return with his group to the Casino. While being evacuated his L.G.A. was sunk but L/Cpl. Sinasac was able to swim to a nearby craft. Throughout the operation this N.C.O. showed exceptional personal bravery and determination. *(L.G. 2.10.42)*

Sinclair, Allan, Sergeant
3060504, 7/9th (H) Bn., The Royal Scots (Cornsay Colliery) (Periodic)
This N.C.O. has commanded a platoon almost continuously throughout the campaign. Possessed of unbounded energy and cheerfulness, he has been a fine example and great leader of his platoon.

At Soltau on 19th April 1945 his Coy. was pushing East to gain a line of railway dominated by some high wooded country. This area was known, from reconnaissance the previous day, to be held by the enemy. The leading platoon had been held up by Spandau fire from the railway line. Sgt. Sinclair was ordered to destroy the Spandaus holding up their advance. To gain the railway, 300 yards of flat and completely open ground had to be crossed.

Sgt. Sinclair quickly made his plan, personally leading two sections forward, under cover of the third section and smoke from his 2″ mortar, he went straight for the railway. Several men of his force were wounded and one killed, before the railway was reached. Undeterred, Sgt. Sinclair pushed on and, gaining the objective, drove off the enemy, who left behind two Spandaus and other weapons. He quickly reorganised his remaining few men and secured and held the objective until the remainder of his platoon arrived. By this action he enabled a second platoon to come forward without casualty and so secure other ground from which a further advance could be made.

Always cool and determined under fire, and possessed of accurate judgement, he was always keen to tackle any task, however formidable. His aggressive determination and cheerfulness have at all times been an outstanding example to all those with whom he came in contact.
(L.G. 24.1.46)

Sincup, Arnold William, Lance Sergeant
4035009, King's Shropshire Light Infantry (attd.
S.S.T., No. 1 Commando) (Winchester) (Immediate)
Arakan 1945
On the 31st. January 1945 at Hill 170 near Kangaw L/Sgt Sincup was section Sgt of a platoon counterattacking the enemy. When his platoon officer was wounded he took command of the two leading sections of his platoon and attacked an enemy post, personally killing five of the enemy of whom one was an officer. He then rallied the sections, evacuating five of his men who were wounded and made two attempts to bring in another wounded man who was covered by enemy machine-gun and sniper fire. He then took up part of the defence of the forward right flank and by his leadership and personal example held this flank, helping with other

troops to break up determined enemy attacks. He remained with his sections in this position constantly engaged with the enemy for ten hours, until relieved by another unit. *(L.G. 19.4.45)*

Skeates, Thomas William, Corporal (A/Sgt.)
4740867, 6th Bn. The York & Lancaster Regt.
(Pontefract) (Immediate)
For outstanding bravery and devotion to duty.

Sgt. Skeates was ordered to take a strong fighting patrol of one platoon to Corpo Di Carva on 22nd September 1943. He moved out by night and on reaching Corpo Di Carva early morning was fired on by Germans. He manoeuvred and took 5 prisoners. Again he was fired on and took another 6 prisoners. He locked all prisoners in a room, destroyed the 88mm gun and made a strong point of the Eastern approaches.

Without food and wounded he remained for 24 hours with his platoon and held the village despite being attacked by two German tanks. He returned after 48 hours on being relieved by the D.L.I. and reported to Bn. HQ.
(L.G. 13.1.44)

Skingley, Arthur Thomas, Sergeant
5882195, 1st Dorsetshire Regt. (Canning Town)
(Immediate)
At Vizzini on 14th July 1943 Sgt. Skingley's platoon was ordered to attack a located enemy position. The position was gained and the majority of the enemy holding it were accounted for. During the course of this action Sgt. Skingley's Platoon Comd. was killed and Sgt. Skingley immediately took over command. Enemy fire was then directed on to the platoon from both flanks and in accordance with the instructions Sgt. Skingley commenced to withdraw his platoon, but not until he and his platoon had accounted for the enemy position on the top of the feature the platoon had attacked. During the withdrawal, which was harassed by heavy fire from both flanks, Sgt. Skingley showed great skill and calmness in extricating his platoon which he did with few casualties until he was finally wounded. Although the wound was severe and causing great pain Sgt. Skingley still continued in command of the platoon and carried out a fighting withdrawal. Finally he collapsed and insisted on being left with a Tommy gun saying he would look after himself as he did not want to be a burden to the remainder of the platoon. Sgt. Skingley was eventually picked up by a search party and brought back to HQ. He showed leadership of the highest order and his desire to extricate his platoon even at the cost of his own life showed the greatest courage. *(L.G. 4.11.43)*

Skinner, Duncan Gordon, Lance Corporal
K53850, The Seaforth Highlanders of Canada
(Immediate)
Rimini 101–3 1/50,000.
On 20th September 1944 'C' Coy. of the Seaforth Highlanders of Canada was ordered to secure the

crossroads at C Des Vescovo (MR 830953) (code name Cockstown). After a night approach march the Coy. came to within 300 yards of the objective at approx. 0730 hours, when the leading section, under command of L/Cpl. Skinner came under heavy machine gun fire from dug in positions on the face of a 70 foot cliff on the edge of a draw to the left.

L/Cpl. Skinner immediately placed his Bren gun crew in position to give covering fire, and continued to advance in front of the Coy. with the rest of his section. Within 150 yards of the objective, L/Cpl. Skinner signalled his Bren crew forward, but they were unable to advance due to very heavy machine gun and mortar fire, which had now been brought to bear from other enemy positions on the right.

Ordering his section to follow, L/Cpl. Skinner led his men in a dash to a house occupied by Germans on the far side of the draw. This N.C.O. by skilful handling of his men, and although without his Bren gun crew, cleared the house with hand grenades and rifles, killing eight of the enemy, the total number of German occupants.

From this position L/Cpl. Skinner was able to give right flank protection for his Coy., which had to proceed along a semi-sunken road, and he received orders to hold his position at all costs. The position was immediately counter-attacked, and was subjected to heavy mortar and machine gun fire. One German soldier came to within a few yards of the house with a Bazooka and opened fire. L/Cpl. Skinner crept out of the back of the house alone and armed with a Tommy gun, crawled into a position from which he killed the German soldier.

For a period of three hours, from 0830 hours to 1130 hours, L/Cpl. Skinner and his men held this half ruined house, beat off three counter-attacks, and under heavy enemy fire made it possible for the Coy. to pass through on the left and outflank the enemy. In this operation 'C' Coy. captured 86 prisoners and counted 30 German dead. All objectives were taken, and as a result when this success was exploited, the enemy was finally driven from the whole ridge.

By his outstanding bravery and leadership under the most difficult conditions L/Cpl. Skinner was largely responsible for the success of the operation.

(*L.G. 20.1.45*)

Skipper, Louis, Sergeant (A/Com.QMS)
6459115, 9th Bn. Royal Fusiliers (London, W.1)
(Immediate)
On the 10th September at Battipaglia this N.C.O. assumed command of his platoon when his officer was captured. By about 1500 hrs. Sgt. Skipper found that his platoon was completely surrounded. With determination, inflicting casualties on enemy infantry, he extricated his platoon and joined 'D' Coy. who were still holding the bridge.

His courage and skill in leading his platoon through the enemy was of a very high order and enabled the

platoon to resume the action a few hours later with renewed determination. (*L.G. 13.1.44*)

Skittrall, William Joseph, Sergeant (actg.)
14207071, 2nd Bn. The Essex Regt. (London, E.15)
(Immediate)
During the battle of Zetten on 20th January 1945, Sjt. Skittrall was leading two assault sections of his platoon. During the initial part of the action his party captured five houses, constituting a well defended strongpoint, killing and wounding twelve enemy and causing another 15 to withdraw. Throughout this part of the action Sjt. Skittrall personally fired the platoon Piat with deadly effect. During the fierce close quarter fighting his two sections had lost heavily and owing to enfilade fire from another group of houses Sjt. Skittrall and his seven remaining soldiers were cut off. He did not have enough men to cover all approaches and after a fierce fight the enemy entered the same house that Sjt. Skittrall's party were defending.

Immediately he blew a hole in the wall separating the enemy from his party and entered the same room, accompanied by one other soldier. On entering the room he blazed away with his Sten and killed four enemy personally and single-handed captured the remaining three, the soldier with Sjt. Skittrall having by this time been wounded.

In the next half hour two more counter-attacks were put in on his position but he held firm, causing casualties to the enemy. He then turned his attention to the houses which enfiladed the approach to his position and moving out himself under cover of a smoke grenade opened fire with his Piat from close range causing the enemy to withdraw and thus allowing another Coy. to go through and take their objective.

Later in the same day he personally stalked and killed two enemy snipers.

His personal coolness and courage and his inspired leadership played a very large part in the eventual success of the Battalion's battle.

M.I.D. 10.5.45. Croix de Guerre, Bronze approved 3.4.45
(*L.G. 12.4.45*)

Slack, Harry Repton, Gunner
892399, 98th Field Regt., Royal Artillery (Shoreham-by-Sea) (Immediate)
Map Square W.3788.
On 28th June 1944, Gnr. Slack was O.P.A. in a Tk. O.P. with 'B' Sqn. 12 C.A.R., in support of 2 Som. L.I. The tanks crossed the stream N.E. of Vaiano, on to the ridge beyond, but the infantry were held up at the stream by heavy small arms fire. The ridge was covered with wheat, from which enemy infantry began to counter-attack the tanks with Bazookas and L.M.G.'s, so the Sqn. Comd. decided to withdraw 300 yds. As Gnr. Slack and his Tp. Comd. were entering their tank from their ground O.P. the Officer was hit with a burst of M.G. fire and fell

dead inside the turret. Almost immediately a Bazooka bomb penetrated the tank just behind the co-driver.

The driver and co-driver were wounded and baled out. Gnr. Slack was hit in the foot and two fires were started in the tank.

In this demoralising situation, and in spite of the pain of his wound, he acted with the most remarkable courage, resource and skill. First he put out the fires, then he went back 300 yards through wheat raked with M.G. fire to look for the missing members of the crew, contacted a Platoon HQ and asked them to look out for the men, then he returned to his tank, now alone in front of the others in an area full of enemy infantry firing at close range, opened up on the wireless and asked his B.C. for instructions. Asked if he could drive the tank back he said he would try. He drove the tank back a mile across country and 2 miles by road to Strada, contacting Coy. HQ on the way and reporting by wireless that one of the missing men had come in. At Strada his wound was dressed and he was evacuated to M.D.S.

Single-handed, he had saved his tank from brewing up, recovered the body of his Tp. Comd., traced a missing man, and driven the tank back though the controls were damaged and he had little experience of driving. All this was done with a painful, undressed wound. It was a feat of amazing bravery, coolness and resource.

(L.G. 7.12.44)

Slack, Robert Hodgson, Sergeant
777283, 21 Anti-Tank Regt., Royal Artillery
On 19/20th May 1940, he commanded a Troop of Anti-Tank guns which was ordered into action on the Escaut Canal itself. Enemy infantry crossed the canal and our own infantry fell back. Sgt. Slack fought the enemy with Bren guns and rifles of his Troop, succeeded in getting one gun away, destroyed the others and got away the gun detachments, many of whom were wounded.
(L.G. 20.12.40)

Slack, Sydney Joseph, Warrant Officer Cl. III (Pl.S.M.)
2733239, 1st Bn. Welsh Guards, Attd. Brig. Norman's Force,
For personal courage, resource and initiative. On 29th May 1940 near Vyfeg, South of Bergues, the position held by P.S.M. Slack's platoon was heavily attacked by tanks and infantry. One tank halted behind a hedge three yards away from P.S.M. Slack. He immediately threw a grenade under the track. The turret of the tank was opened and a German appeared with a revolver. P.S.M. Slack immediately threw a second grenade which burst inside the turret and put the crew out of action. Later he showed the greatest coolness and resource when his platoon was ordered to withdraw in close contact with the enemy and it was largely owing to his resource and personal leadership that the operation was carried out successfully.
B.E.M. (Civil) L.G. 11.6.66   *(L.G. 27.8.40)*

Slater, Eric, Staff Sergeant
23514790, Cheshire Regt.
For Oman   *(L.G. 7.12.76)*

Slatter, Arthur Frederick, Warrant Officer Cl. III (Pl.S.M.)
4029775, 1st King's Shropshire Light Infantry
For conspicuous gallantry and marked ability in leadership of the Carrier Platoon during the period 14–22nd May 1940.
He fought a succession of highly successful Rear Guard actions in close contact with the enemy and never once did he lose his grip on the situation and on his men. It was entirely due to his personal example that his entire platoon was brought back safely as far as Tournai.
(L.G. 11.7.40)

Sleeth, Herbert, Lance Corporal
6200387, 1/7th Bn. Middlesex Regt. (South Shields) (Immediate)
Battle of Alamein—23/27th October 1942.
On the night of October 23rd, during the advance, L/Cpl. Sleeth was hit in the back by a piece of shell casing which knocked him off his feet. Although carrying four belts of ammunition and a box of spare parts, he carried on for a further two miles and successfully delivered his load to the gun line. The platoon was shooting during the whole of the following morning and came under Mortar fire. L/Cpl. Sleeth was again hit, this time in the left arm but refused attention. That evening the platoon accompanied two Coys. of 5/7 Bn. Gordon Highlanders which went forward to reach the final objective. During the following day, October 25th, the platoon was under heavy Mortar and shell fire and L/Cpl. Sleeth was hit once again in the left arm. By October 26th the position was cut off and the platoon had no food or water and very little ammunition. The inf. wireless was out of order and no contact could be made to the rear. L/Cpl. Sleeth volunteered to go back and bring up supplies by carrier. He set off in the afternoon through minefields and over ground swept by shell and M.G. fire and successfully reached Coy. HQ.

He returned at first light to the position with supplies of food, water and ammunition.

He was subsequently injured by a grenade explosion and had to be evacuated.

The conduct of this N.C.O. throughout the complete operation was of a very high order. His steadiness under fire and the calm and determined manner in which he carried out his duties, in spite of being wounded several times, were an inspiration to the remainder of his platoon.
(L.G. 4.5.43)

Smart, William Godfrey Danvers, Private
19451, Cape Town Highlanders (Immediate)
On the night of 23/24th October 1942, Pte. Smart went into action with Coy. HQ as one of the intelligence personnel attached to the Coy. Early in the Battle his

Coy. Comd. was wounded, and also two of the 3 Pl. Comds. In the dark, the third Platoon Comd. could not be contacted. For 2 hours Pte. Smart took charge. He directed the Coy. onto the first objective, undaunted by shell and machine gun fire. On the first objective he carried out reorganisation. During the whole period he kept in contact with Bn. HQ, sending back the correct messages and information.

It was through his courage and initiative that the Coy. was able to carry out its task. He continued to direct the Coy. until he was seriously wounded and evacuated. *Recommended for M.M.*   *(L.G. 31.12.42)*

Smelt, William Henry, Sqn. Q.M.S.
7884356, 1st East Riding Yeomanry (Hull)
B.E.F. 1940 (from P.O.W. Pool)   *(L.G. 11.10.45)*

Smillie, Walter, Corporal
14314520, 2nd Bn. The Seaforth Highlanders
  (Glasgow) (Immediate)
On 21st April 1945 a section of the Carrier platoon was ordered to patrol into the outskirts of Ganderkesee. Cpl. Smillie was the N.C.O. with this patrol. On approaching the village the patrol left their vehicles and proceeded on foot. They were almost immediately fired on by M.G. fire. The patrol went to ground, while Cpl. Smillie alone proceeded to stalk the post from the rear. This was successful Cpl. Smillie killing one of the enemy and capturing another. The Patrol then proceeded and Cpl. Smillie was instrumental in assaulting another post and taking a further nine prisoners. The patrol was then held up by heavy fire and was ordered to go to ground. Almost immediately 40 fanatical Germans formed up and shouting and screaming advanced on the patrol, firing as they came. Cpl. Smillie seized the only Bren left working and fired at the advancing enemy. He killed seven. The main body of the patrol were then ordered to withdraw, while Cpl. Smillie remained to cover their withdrawal. This he did, lying in the open, moving frequently from place to place, always under fire and in very close contact. The patrol then established itself, and Cpl. Smillie rejoined, and in doing so was wounded. No sooner was the patrol established than the enemy attacked again. Although in great pain Cpl. Smillie again seized the Bren and the replenished magazines, and continued to fire at the enemy who this time surrounded the post. Coolly and cheerfully and in spite of great pain, Cpl. Smillie remained at his post – refusing to have his wound dressed. So well did Cpl. Smillie handle the Bren— moving from place to place again and again in the very teeth of the enemy that they were forced to retire having suffered a number of casualties.

This N.C.O. throughout this action displayed in the highest degree qualities of courage and inspiring leadership. His bearing was beyond praise and only after the patrol had been relieved by a Coy. would he consent to being carried away and evacuated.   *(L.G. 12.7.45)*

Smith, Allan Joseph, Private (A/Cpl.)
VX 54564, 2/6 Aust. Inf. Bn. (Immediate)
During an enemy attack on our defensive positions on Lababia Ridge in Mubo area on 21st June 1943, A/Cpl. Smith led three patrols into enemy areas and attacked a party of 25 Japs. A/Cpl. Smith personally shot five of these when his rifle was shot from his hands and he received a slight wound. Grasping the rifle of a wounded comrade, he continued firing until he was able to pick up the wounded man, whom he carried back to his sec. post while under fire.

Later, when the enemy assaulted his post with the bayonet. A/Cpl. Smith led the riflemen of his section in a bayonet charge. This halted the enemy and they were all killed by L.M.G. and S.M.G. fire.

During all attacks this N.C.O. was an inspiration to his section and his courage and determination saved their part of the defensive sector.   *(L.G. 7.10.43)*

Smith, Arthur Edward, Corporal
6094692, 9th Bn. Royal Fusiliers (London, E.17)
  (Immediate)
On 25th April 1945, following a rapid advance by the Brigade, 9 R.F. reached the South bank of the River Po. At this stage the enemy was in some disorder, and it was essential in order to achieve complete and rapid success that he be given no time in which to organize himself in his already well prepared positions on the North bank.

With this in view, 'Y' Coy. 9 R.F. were ordered to cross the river and establish a bridgehead without delay. The crossing was to be made in stormboats, but, owing to the speed of the advance, only a very limited number were available.

The attack was launched at 1700 hrs., the leading stormboat immediately coming under heavy MMG fire, one Fusilier being killed outright and the navigator wounded. With its engine damaged by the enemy fire, the boat grounded on a sandbank sufficiently near the far bank to enable the section to jump out and wade ashore, though they suffered two further casualties in doing so. The wounded navigator was now in great difficulties; he had left the boat and was sheltering behind it as some protection from the intense fire still coming from the enemy who were obviously trying to deny us further use of the boat.

Seeing this, Cpl. Smith, whose company was giving covering fire from the near bank, without the slightest hesitation or regard for his personal safety, though knowing well the risk he ran, stripped off his clothes, jumped into the river and swam towards the boat.

From the moment he entered the water he came under accurate MG fire. The distance to the boat was about 300 yards, the current strong and the water icy cold. After battling with the current, Cpl. Smith reached the far bank 150 yards below the grounded boat and was then subjected to a veritable hail of bullets as he ran along the completely open bank to the boat. With the assistance of the wounded navigator, he refloated the boat, and swimming behind pushing it, started for the near bank.

Enemy fire was now so intense that the water around the boat was at times lashed white with spray from the bullets, and it seemed a certainty that Cpl. Smith must be hit, but he carried on, and by sheer grit and determination reached the near bank.

The swim back from the far bank with the boat had taken him 40 minutes altogether; including his swim out and the refloating of the boat his action had lasted over an hour, but, despite his state of now almost complete exhaustion, his first action on reaching the near bank was to help the wounded navigator to safe cover. Then, after only a brief rest, he rejoined his platoon and quietly dressed ready for the next fight.

Cpl. Smith's brave action not only retrieved the much needed boat, but it inspired his comrades, who had watched the exploit with breathless admiration, to press home the crossing with vigour. The early establishment of the 9 R.F. on the far bank, to which Cpl. Smith so notably contributed, was a major factor in accelerating the advance of the Division.

Statement by Witness – W/Lieut. W. D. Rees. (265856)

'Y' Coy. were about to cross the Po in stormboats. One boat had been launched and two sections of 'Y' Coy. were in the process of crossing when Spandau fire of some intensity opened up on the boat and 'our' bank. The boat however reached the far bank, and the sections made for cover. Some casualties were observed. The operator of the boat was seen clinging to the side of the boat, wounded and with Spandau fire hitting the water around him. He unsuccessfully tried to swim the boat back keeping the boat between him and the enemy, but the current kept him to the enemy bank. Next I saw Cpl. Smith, nude, swimming furiously across the river. He had been observed, and little spouts of water indicated that he was under accurate and heavy machine gun fire. He reached the shore about 150 yards downstream of the boat, and ran along the bank to the stormboat, still under heavy fire.

He went in the water again, and with the operator helped to swim and push the stormboat to 'our' bank, which took them about 40 minutes to so do, being subjected the whole while to machine gun fire. He then helped the injured operator to the shore and assisted him to cover.

Statement by Witness—W/Lieut. R. P. Duthaler, M.C. (314293)

At 1700 hrs. on 25th April 1945, 'Y' Coy. of 9th Bn. Royal Fusiliers were attempting to force the crossing of the River Po in stormboats. The first stormboat crossed the river, but the enemy Spandaus immediately opened fire on it. One man was killed outright in the boat and the man operating it was wounded. The boat grounded on a sandbank and two more men were hit whilst crossing from there to the far bank of the river. The wounded operator was unable to start the engine and tried to gain some protection from the heavy fire by clinging to the front of the boat and keeping it interposed between himself and the enemy bank. Owing to the strength of the current he could make no headway and was forced to ground again on the bank.

Cpl. Smith, seeing this, without the slightest hesitation or regard for his personal safety, stripped himself and swam out across the river. The two enemy machine guns fired on him continuously but he reached the far bank. From there, still exposed to heavy fire, he ran out along the sandbank to the grounded stormboat, and immediately assisted the wounded man to bring it back. During the whole crossing, which took him three quarters of an hour the river was swept by a hail of bullets. At times the water around the boat and around Cpl. Smith's body was lashed white with Spandau bursts. But he carried on regardless, reached the other side again, and helped the wounded man up the bank and into safety. The courage and tenacity of Cpl. Smith not only in the first swim across, but also in the exhausting and protracted struggled back in icy water and against a strong current was beyond all measure.

Cpl. Smith after a very brief rest rejoined his platoon.

Statement by Witness—Lieut. Col. J. R. Cleghorn, D.S.O. (63475)

At about 1700 hrs. on 25th April 1945 'Y' Coy. were in the process of crossing the River Po in stormboats. One of the stormboats suddenly came under intense Spandau fire. In spite of this opposition the occupants carried on towards their objective, leaving the pilot of the boat. The pilot was wounded, and jumped into the water, placing the boat between himself and the enemy, being unable to operate the boat by himself.

Seeing this Cpl. Smith whose company was giving covering fire from the near bank, immediately stripped, jumped into the water, and swam out to the boat, some two to three hundred yards, all the time coming under fire. On arrival at the far bank, he ran along the sandbank to the boat, having himself been carried downstream by the current.

He assisted the navigator to get the boat afloat, and by swimming behind the boat, pushed it back to the near bank, taking some forty minutes to do so. On reaching the near bank, Cpl. Smith assisted the wounded man under cover and rejoined his section in spite of being completely exhausted.

Throughout the whole of this action, Cpl. Smith was being fired at, some periods of which the water around him gave the appearance of boiling with bullet splashes.

Only the highest sense of duty, bravery and complete disregard for his personal safety, impelled this N.C.O. to carry out this gallant action.

Recommended for V.C. (*L.G. 18.10.45*)

Smith, Donald Newstead, Sergeant
7928447, 23rd Hussars (Acomb, Yorks) (Immediate)
On 6th August 1944 on the high ground at Le Bas Perrier Sgt. Smith took over 4th Troop from the Tp. Leader who had been killed. During the afternoon he was ordered to

take his Troop forward to support the Infantry in Le Bas Perrier. Despite the fact that he was suffering from minor injuries and shock caused by a bomb landing next to his tank Sgt. Smith took his Tp. forward. On arriving at the Inf. position Sgt. Smith found his Tp. reduced to 2 tanks. Despite this he went forward to locate a Tiger tank that was menacing the Inf. The other tank then broke down but Sgt. Smith continued. He manoeuvred into such a position as to prevent the Tiger coming forward and eventually compelled it to withdraw. Despite his being surrounded by enemy and under continual fire Sgt. Smith remained in his position until ordered to return to his Sqn. He refused to do so until he was able to recover his other tank. This he did by dismounting from his own tank and under small arms fire attached a tow rope to this other vehicle in order to give it a tow to start.

(L.G. 1.3.45)

Smith, Dudley Edward, Sergeant (tem. St.-Sergeant)
169864, 3 S.A. Armd. C. Recce Bn., South African
   Forces (Immediate)
For gallantry, determination and devotion to duty.

On 5th June 1942, S/Sgt. Smith was Sec. Comd. of Sec. of armd. cars that co-operated under comd. of Lt. Hugo with a coln. from 151 Bde. Proceeding West from U9664 and forming a screening patrol for the Inf. and Arty. in the coln. the armd. c's located an enemy dug-in Inf. position at U9563. S/Sgt. Smith leading his Sec. in the attack on this position with marked courage and coolness and with complete disregard of personal safety, assisted in the capture of the position and the taking of 2 20mm guns, many machine guns and 300 prisoners.

Shortly afterwards an enemy battery was reported by the armd. c's 1 mile further South. Again S/Sgt. Smith led his Sec. in an attack that resulted in the position being taken together with 3 Offrs. and 26 O/R's. The patrol was later attacked by 14 enemy fighter aircraft and S/Sgt. Smith was wounded in the buttocks and legs. With complete disregard of his own injuries he proceeded from armd. car to armd. car ascertaining whether any of his men had been wounded and rendering what assistance he could.

His conduct throughout the operations was an inspriation to his men and his courage, tenacity and devotion to duty contributed largely to the success of these operations. *(L.G. 13.8.42)*

Smith, Eric Oswald, Lance Sergeant
2578997, 4 Corps Signals, Royal Signals (Mitcham)
   (Periodic)
L/Sgt. Smith has served on the 4 Corps. front for the past two years. Between 24th March and 1st April 1944 he was N.C.O. in charge of a Line Maintenance party in Moreh. During this period our lines were repeatedly cut by the enemy; despite continual artillery and mortar fire and interference from enemy patrols L/Sgt. Smith repeatedly took out small parties to effect line repairs. These parties were always liable to be ambushed or cut

off by the enemy, but largely owing to the resource and leadership of this N.C.O. the linemen under his command never failed in their task. On one occasion when the Signal Office sustained a direct hit from an enemy shell and many men were killed and wounded he rallied and encouraged the remaining men and quickly restored communications.

When a withdrawal from Moreh was imminent he volunteered to remain behind to ensure that maximum damage was carried out to deny line facilities to the enemy. During the subsequent withdrawal to Shenam he accompanied the Rear Guard and repeatedly exposed himself to enemy fire in his endeavour to maintain line communication with the remainder of the force. He has always set a very high example to his linemen and his outstanding courage and leadership throughout the recent operations are deserving of recognition.
M.B.E. 31.12.60   *(L.G. 8.2.45)*

Smith, Ernest Frederick, Corporal
6461769, 2nd Bn. Royal Fusiliers (London, W.1)
   (Immediate)
Ref. Map Sheet 100—II Cesena 1/50,000.

On the night of 19/20th October 1944 the Bn. crossed the R. Savio South of Cesena and advanced Westwards to establish a bridgehead. Cpl. Smith was commanding the leading section of 12 Platoon in 'X' Coy. and his immediate objective was a house at 584665 occupied by the enemy. On approaching the road junc. at 584064 his section came under intense enfilade M.G. fire from houses at 584068, pinning the section out in the open. Cpl. Smith decided that the only hope of extricating his section was to press home the attack and capture his objective. Ignoring the enemy fire, he dashed towards the front of the house killing one German with a burst from his T.S.M.G. and wounding another, who surrendered.

First throwing a grenade, Cpl. Smith followed through the stable into the house, where he met a German N.C.O. whom he shot dead. By this time, other members of Cpl. Smith's section, inspired by his aggressive spirit, had reached the house, and under Cpl. Smith's direction completed the clearing of the house, including the capture of three more Germans who by this time were cowering in the cellar.

It was entirely due to Cpl. Smith's daring, initiative and complete disregard of danger, that the house was taken. The capture of this house, covering a double road junc. was vital to the security of the bridgehead, and the entire credit goes to Cpl. Smith.   *(L.G. 26.4.45)*

Smith, George, Fusilier
846213, 6th Bn. Royal Scots Fusiliers (Sheffield)
   (Immediate)
On 16th April 1945, the Carrier Platoon of 6 R.S.F. was ordered to occupy the village of Niendorf, to the SE of Uelzen, and it was of the greatest importance to subsequent operations that two bridges in the village

should be captured intact. First reports indicated that the village was not occupied by the enemy.

As the carriers approached it became obvious that this village was, in fact, held in some strength and it was then decided to rush the foremost enemy positions. But, on reaching the bottleneck formed by the two bridges, the leading carrier came under fire from bazookas and machine guns sited in nearby buildings.

Fusilier Smith, who was a member of the crew of the second carrier, immediately leapt out and, without any orders, charged the German defences. Completely regardless of rifle and machine gun fire, he ran fifty yards to the first bridge and hurled grenades into the enemy posts, wiping out two bazooka teams and killing an officer manning a machine gun.

This prompt action, carried out entirely on Fusilier Smith's own initiative, enabled the carrier platoon to rush the bottleneck and to capture all their objectives. Fus. Smith displayed great disregard for his own safety throughout the period and it was largely due to his personal courage and vigorous offensive spirit that this local action, so vitally important to the full scope of future operations, achieved immediate success. *(L.G. 2.8.45)*

Smith, Harold, Sergeant
822907, 159/53rd Light A.A. Regt., Royal Artillery
(Hyde) (Immediate)
Night 11/12th August 1943. Lentini L.G., Sicily.

On the night of 11/12th August 1943, the Lentini L.G., which was being defended by Sjt. Smith's Bty., received a sharp attack from enemy A/C. Towards the end of the engagement an Anti-Personnel Bomb exploded by the Sjt's Gun Pit, wounding 2 of his gunners, and very seriously wounding himself in the chest. Despite the fact that he was in great pain and could only talk and breathe with difficulty, Sjt. Smith continued to maintain complete control of his Detachment. He directed the fire of his gun until the end of the attack by which time he only had 7 rounds of H.E. Amn. left. He then ordered that the Bren gun be made ready in an A.A. Role and supervised the carrying out of this instruction. He made the wounded gunners as comfortable as possible and then started towards the gun position nearest to his own to obtain help and to find out more about the amn. situation. However, the heavy smoke from two burning haystacks nearby and the smell of cordite overcame him and he collapsed before reaching his objective.

Fortunately Sjt. Smith was quickly found and taken to the nearest C.C.S. where he remains on the D.I. list.

Throughout the action he thought only of his duty and of his Detachment, and conducted himself in a manner which was inspiring by its selflessness and heroism. *(L.G. 18.11.43)*

Smith, Harry Whittaker, Trooper
19039549, 4th Queen's Own Hussars
For Malaya   *(L.G. 4.3.49)*

Smith, James Reginald, M.M., Sergeant
613614, Royal Air Force
On 8th January 1944, in Albania in the mountains above Kostenje, Brig. Davies and Major Chesshire of the Allied Military Mission were wounded in a battle with Nationalists fighting on the side of the Germans. Sgt. Smith at once went to his officers' help. As the conditions in the snow were freezing, he moved them to a sheep fold 500 feet down the mountain, while under heavy fire, and dressed their wounds.

After some hours, a heavy attack was made from all sides on the sheep fold by about 200 Nationalists. Sgt. Smith went into the open at great risk to himself in an endeavour to stop the attack. Failing to achieve this, he returned to the sheep fold where the wounded were collected in a small hut. The Nationlists then charged the hut. Sgt. Smith blocked the only door with his body and fought these wild mountaineers off with his fists until he was borne in by weight of numbers. He then rushed to protect the wounded and standing across the Brigadier's body held the attackers at bay until their leader arrived to take control. Had it not been for the gallantry and clearheadedness of this N.C.O. both officers would have lost their lives. The party was taken prisoner and Sgt. Smith was repatriated 15 months later.

It is recommended that Sgt. Smith be awarded the Distinguished Conduct Medal.
M.M. 16.5.44   *(L.G. 8.3.46)*

Smith, John Frank, Sergeant
808677, 10 Fd. Regt., Royal Artillery
On the evening of 29th May when left with a forward gun to defend the bridgehead, Sgt. Smith showed great courage keeping his gun in action under heavy machine gun and rifle fire. In this action he accounted for two tanks at point blank range and held up the enemy infantry for a considerable period, only withdrawing when large enemy forces were within 200 yards of his gun.
M.I.D. 19.9.46   *(L.G. 20.12.40)*

Smith, Linus Patrick, Sergeant
5179689, 1st Gloucestershire Regt. (London, S.E.13)
At Shwedaung on 29th March 1942 this N.C.O. was in charge of the Unit Ambulance, and wounded, owing to enemy road blocks in the village. The Ambulances were under fire and dive-bombing attacks. Sgt. Smith organized the removal of the wounded to shelter, and when his Ambulance, with other transport, was destroyed, he obtained another vehicle and drove it out with all his wounded, through streets under machine gun and mortar fire. But for his initiative and determination many of his wounded would not have reached hospital.

Later, at Yenanyoung, on 17th April 1942, this N.C.O. again distinguished himself by removing a wounded officer to safety under fire at a road block. In doing so he injured his leg. Unable to get the officer away by road, he attempted to carry him to the river. On the way he again came under fire, and hearing an enemy patrol approaching he dragged the officer into a culvert where he remained hidden with him until C.Q.M.S. Biggs found them. With the later assistance the wounded officer eventually reached hospital.　　　　　*(L.G. 28.10.42)*

Smith, Malcolm, Private
2928537, 2nd Queen's Own Cameron Highlanders (Stranraer, Wigtown)
For conspicuous gallantry in action before Cheren.

On 3rd February 1941 this private soldier was acting as a Section Commander and during the attack on enemy positions showed conspicuous gallantry by silencing two enemy M.G. posts single-handed with the use of hand grenades after stalking the occupants of the posts, alone and on his own initiative.

Later by his example and leadership he was responsible for driving off three enemy counter-attacks, during the night.

Throughout the whole action he set a high example of courage and determination, until he was finally wounded.　　　　　*(L.G. 18.7.41)*

Smith, Robert William, Warrant Officer Cl. II (A/W.O.I)
2653987, 5th Bn. Coldstream Guards (Romsey, Hants) (Immediate)
At last light on Thursday 14th September 1944 when the Bn. was in a defensive position North of the Merse/Escaut Canal, one of the two Bn. ammunition lorries was hit by a salvo of German shell fire. It at once caught fire and the ammunition started to explode.

Without hesitation and with a very full realisation of the risks involved, R.S.M. Smith walked up to the second lorry which had just been placed alongside the first for a certain purpose and drove it away well clear from the burning one.

During his walk to the lorry, his efforts to start it, and whilst driving it away he was in imminent danger of being blown to pieces either by an explosion from the burning lorry or by his own exploding also.

There is no doubt that but for this example of courage and devotion to duty the whole of the Bn. ammunition reserve might have been lost and a very much heavier toll of life taken place at Bn. HQ than in fact happened.
M.B.E. 1.1.51　　　　　*(L.G. 1.3.45)*

Smith, Robert, Sergeant (Electrician)
3049215, 1st Lothians & Border Horse Yeomanry, T.A
For the operation in the vicinity of Nieuport 28/30th May, I placed him in command of an improvised section consisting of 1 A.T. Rifle, 1 Bren gun, 8 Riflemen. He himself and all his men were inexperienced in infantry tactics. Selecting him for his personality and character, I ordered him to hold an exposed position on the canal bank just East of Wulpen. This was a critical place as it commanded the main road, Nieuport—Wulpen and the Eastern portion of Wulpen. He was in this position from 1500 hours 28th May, until nightfall 29th May.

Throughout 29th May his section were under heavy S.A. and mortar fire, and, for a part of this time, under arty fire as well, and during this time the Germans made constant efforts to cross the canal in his vicinity, using various subterfuges such as advancing between horses or cattle, and adopting various disguises, including dressing as nuns, all of which, however, were spotted and dealt with. Sgt. Smith was wounded early in the afternoon but insisted on remaining in command of his section until it was relieved by other troops, about 2100 hrs. that day.　　　　　*(L.G. 18.10.40)*

Smith, Ronald Arthur George, Lance Sergeant
6472861, 8th Bn. Royal Fusiliers (London, N.15) (Immediate)
On the night 6/7th September 1944 'W' Coy. 8 R.F. was ordered to attack the enemy and consolidate the position in the vicinity of the village of Croce. L/Sgt. Smith was Platoon Sgt. of the leading platoon. On his own initiative he went forward of his platoon with a small party of men, overran many of the enemy and cleared up a large area of enemy resistance. Alone, showing complete disregard for his personal safety, he attacked an enemy M.G. post and killed the crew with his T.M.C., captured the M.G. and returned to his platoon.

Later, now single handed, he went forward to another M.G. post, he captured the enemy gun crew and with their weapon brought them back to our line. Had these enemy M.G.'s not been silenced they would have taken very heavy toll of L/Sgt. Smith's Coy. which in turn might well have prejudiced the security of the whole of the Croce feature.

Apart from these two outstanding incidents L/Sgt. Smith set a very high example of leadership and military qualities and his whole conduct was in the very highest tradition of the service.　　　　　*(L.G. 8.2.45)*

Smith, Sidney Thomas, Private
4860844, 1st Bn. West Yorkshire Regt. (Leicester)
Ningthoukong—Night 6/7th June 1944.
During the night 6/7th June the Japanese put in a heavy attack against the fwd. positions of 1 W. Yorks. in Ningthoukong. 'A' Coy., which held portions of the perimeter, and of which Pte. Smith was a member, came in for particularly strong assaults by the enemy. Pte. Smith was one of three Bren gunners manning fwd. posts in bunkers. The enemy's attack was so strong that two of these three L.M.G.'s were put out of action and Pte. Smith's was the only one left firing. All the remainder of his section had become casualties and the enemy had entered bunkers on his right thereby enfilading him. Notwithstanding these facts, coolly and completely undaunted, despite the enemy's intense frontal and flanking fire he stuck to his gun, was determined not to yield an inch, and did not. He held his bunker from 0100 hrs. to 0400 hrs. and during that time inflicted many casualties on the enemy. He was such an obstacle to their attacks that the enemy eventually singled him out for

special attention by throwing large numbers of grenades at his bunker. Still he fearlessly held his position. At last three grenades fell inside the bunker. With great courage he managed to throw two of them back on the enemy, but the third blew up in the bunker and severely wounded him. His continued and stubborn resistance was a most vital factor in the ultimate repulse of the enemy. His endurance and courage were of the highest order, culminating in great individual gallantry and devotion to duty. *(L.G. 5.10.44)*

Smith, Stanley Duncan Gilbert, Sergeant
1874998, 275th (H) Field Coy., Royal Engineers
(Periodic)
This N.C.O. has on many occasions been entrusted with an officer's responsibilities and by his fine leadership and outstanding courage has never failed to complete his task.

On the night 23/24th October near El Alamein he commanded 'A' gap through the first enemy minefield which, owing to the large task allotted to the unit, was not visited by an officer until after it had been completed. He successfully completed this gap in spite of continuous mortar and artillery fire. The next day he wired in the enemy minefields, again under fire, and set a fine example by personally carrying back a badly wounded L/Cpl. of his party. On the night 2/3rd November he commanded a party which picked up our own minefield between our own F.D.L.'s and those of the enemy. He carried on this work and completed it while the barrage was falling on his right to allow the 9th Aust. Div. attack to go through.

Between 3rd and 8th December 1942 he was in command of a 2,500 yd. sector of minefield at Mersa Brega. Again by himself he successfully sited and laid a mixed field of over 1,000 Teller, French, British Mk IV and the dangerous Italian N.S. mines by night and in contact with the enemy.

On the 14th and 15th December after the break through at Mersa Brega he commanded a night road clearance pty. engaged in clearing mines (incl. A.P. mines) from the road. This difficult and dangerous task he accomplished without casualties to his party.

Again, on 21st January 1943 and 22nd January 1943, his fine leadership rallied his tired section which filled in one large crater on the Corradini Pass under long range artillery fire and later that night completed a difficult detour round a demolished bridge at Corradini which he kept going all next day.

His courage and leadership have always been a magnificent example to his men, and have come always to the fore on the difficult and dangerous occasions when these qualities are most needed. *(L.G. 14.10.43)*

Smith, Thomas, Sergeant
2877443, 2nd Bn. The Gordon Highlanders (Periodic)
Sjt. Smith served in 'C' Coy. since landing in Normandy on 20th June 1944. He has at all times been a example

of courage and devotion to duty and has shown leadership and courage of a high order throughout the campaign.

On 30th June 1944 his platoon Comd. was wounded with several other numbers of his platoon. Sjt. Smith then became A/Platoon Comd. While under very heavy shell and mortar fire, Sjt. Smith moved about and reorganised the platoon and encouraged his men.

On 15th July 1944 during the attack on Hill 112, Baron, he was commanding 14 Platoon on the morning of the 16th it was found that the Coy. was surrounded. This was discovered by Sjt. Smith whose prompt action in quickly switching his platoon to protect the rear of the Coy. and by his aggressive action saved them from being completely over run. In the subsequent action which followed he showed courage and resourcefulness and devotion to duty of the highest order.

On 5th August 1944 his Coy. was leading Coy. on the attack on Estry Cross Roads on the morning of 6th while the attack was still going on, the other two Platoon Commanders were wounded. Sjt. Smith reorganised what remained of his own and No. 13 Platoon, both having had heavy casualties, and formed a strong defensive position. This was done under extremely heavy shell and mortar fire. During the night and the day and the night of 7th he was chiefly responsible for keeping the men awake and alert as they were continually under fire and threatened by counter-attack. To do this he had to move about exposed to fire all the time. He did this unhesitatingly and showed great courage and endurance. He refused to rest himself and only did so after being directly ordered to by the Coy. Comd.

He remained with No. 14 Platoon throughout the following actions—Seine, Escout Canal, Gheel Bridgehead and Best Woods. At the latter he was himself wounded while his officer was killed. He reorganised his platoon under heavy M.G. and sniper fire and on orders from higher authority withdrew the remnants to safety.

During the attack on the woods at Goch he was almost completely blinded by blast from a shell. He continued to lead his platoon to their objective and was only evacuated after being directly ordered as he was completely blinded in one eye, being admitted to hospital.

He rejoined the Coy. after the Rhine crossing and took part in the advance to Celle, Ulzen and the Elbe crossing. He continued to show the same high standard of courage, example and devotion to duty. He has in all, been wounded 4 times.

Sjt. Smith's conduct in battle has always been an example for all to copy.
Recommended for M.M. *(L.G. 24.1.46)*

Smith, Thomas Geoffrey Oliver, Private
NX 173075, 2/5 Aust. Inf. Bn. (Immediate)
On 4th July 1945 in the Ulum area, Pte. Smith was a member of a patrol which came under heavy fire and was held up.

Pte. Smith on his own initiative dashed to a flank, and hurling grenades as he ran, he silenced an enemy pill box. He then rushed forward and firing in the open killed the crews of two other enemy strong posts which were holding up the advance.

Again on 12th July 1945 at Ulum, Pte. Smith's platoon was engaged in an action which lasted five hours. At one stage of the attack the adv. was held up by L.M.G. and rifle fire. Pte. Smith moved forward and silenced several enemy pits and then skilfully stalking the L.M.G. he killed the crew and captured the gun. This courageous action enabled the position to be captured after fierce resistance by a fanatical enemy rear guard action.

During both of these actions Pte. Smith showed exceptional courage, coolness and dash, with complete disregard for his own safety under heavy fire.
Recommended for M.M.   (*L.G. 12.10.45*)

Smith, Walter John, Sergeant
10075, 23 N.Z. Bn. (Immediate)
During the attack on Takrouna on the night 19/20th April 1943 Sjt. Smith was separated from his platoon and at first light found himself at the foot of Takrouna Hill which dominates the surrounding country. He reconnoitred a track up the steepest part and then collected and led a party to the top. There they captured an enemy observation post and took over a hundred prisoners.

During the daylight he and his handful of men broke up several counter-attacks and Sjt. Smith made several trips down the cliff-face and across the open, bullet swept and heavily shelled ground to get reinforcements. His courage, determination and disregard for his personal safety made possible the capture and holding of this most important feature.   (*L.G. 22.7.43*)

Smithers, Gordon Otway, Corporal
QX 8348, 2/15 Bn., Australian Military Forces
On the morning of 16th May 1941 Cpl. Smithers commanded a sec. in a fighting patrol led by Capt. A. E. de Lacy Peek and at approx. 0130 hrs. he led his sec. into attack under heavy fire at approx. position 39624268.

Cpl. Smithers had instructions to destroy a medium tank that was reported on the patrol's left. He moved out, halted his sec. approx. 40 yds. from the tank, the night being so dark it was nearly impossible for the enemy in the tank to see them.

He went forward about 20 yds. himself to investigate and found an old truck 15 yds. to the right of the tank and so decided to make use of it for cover for the covering fire he would want to attack the tank.

The Bren gunners went forward to the right, crawled under the truck and awaited developments, being told not to fire until the enemy commenced, to enable the attack to have as much surprise as possible.

Cpl. Smithers then led the attack on the tank in all throwing four ST grenades. Immediately after the first ST grenade hit the tank, four men climbed out and quite a large number of men in the vicinity rose from the

ground, apparently having been asleep there—the tank was seen by myself later to be burning.

There were also two heavy M.G. posts, one approx. 50 yds. to the left and another about the same distance half left from the tank, these were both firing by this time so Cpl. Smithers split his sec. and under cover of half his men's rifles plus the Bren led the attack using hand grenades to such good effect that both guns were silenced and did not open fire again.

It was during the attack on the 2nd M.G. post that he received a burst of bullets as a result of which he lost his arm. He then called his sec. to withdraw and was helped back by one of his men as were the other wounded.

In all the casualties were, one man missing and three wounded. The patrol was in all approx. 2½ hrs. getting back and distance was 15 kilos. each way.

The general behaviour of Cpl. Smithers throughout was a shining example to his men.   (*L.G. 9.8.41*)

Smy, Charles Lacey, P/A/WO II (C.S.M.)
3rd Bn. Coldstream Guards, 201 Guards Brig., 56 (Lon) Div., 10 Corps.
On the 25th September 1943 this W.O.'s Coy. took part in an attack upon enemy positions at Point 270, a hill, North of Salerno. C.S.M. Smy was left near the foot of the hill in charge of Rear Coy. HQ. Casualties from the two assaulting Coys. were heavy and had all to pass through the area of Rear Coy. HQ en route for R.A.P. Owing to enemy sniping machine guns it became impossible to evacuate them further than this position. C.S.M. Smy immediately organised an impromptu First Aid Post. Without any doctor and with no skilled help other than the Coy. Stretcher Bearers he dressed the wounded and tended to their needs.

From 1400 hrs. 25th September and on throughout the night and following day he worked unceasingly and unsparingly single-handed save for a few runners and signallers and two stretcher bearers. During that time wounded men passed through his hands, all having to wait at his position until dark and thereafter until stretchers became available for their further evacuation. Throughout the whole of this time his position was continually under heavy enemy shell and mortar fire and, until dusk fell on 25th September, continuously sniped from two enemy sniping M.G. posts. C.S.M. Smy worked on. He dressed the wounded, fed them, cheered them. In addition he organised the replenishment of food, water and ammunition to the forward Platoons, maintained W.T communication between Coy. HQ and Bn. HQ and arranged for his local protection.

In this work he never paused. Except on one occasion when the sniping Spandau was particularly troublesome, he himself with one other man stalked it, shot at it, and drove it temporarily away.

He showed complete disregard of all shells, mortars or snipers. When others took cover he went on with the work in hand. His tireless and unsparing energy, his bravery and his infectious cheerfulness under the most trying conditions were an example and an inspiration to all who passed his way. And by his prompt help and care of the wounded, in spite of the danger to himself that every movement involved, many lives among the men he cared for must have been saved.

M.B.E. 12.6.58 (L.G. 27.1.44)

Smyth, David, C.Q.M.S.
6977274, 6th Bn. The York & Lancaster Regt. (Kells, Co. Antrim)
For outstanding leadership and devotion to duty.
During the advance on the Mine near Sedjenene on 29th march 1943, C.Q.M.S. Smyth was with his Coy. detailed to capture a hill feature that dominated the mine. The Coy. succeeded in capturing the feature but during the German counter-attack all officers were either killed or wounded. C.Q.M.S. Smyth took charge, rallied the remainder and succeeded in holding the hill and stabilizing the situation although the company was reduced to less than forty.

His action and rallying power went a long way to assist in the defeat of the Germans. *(L.G. 1.6.43)*

Snape, Frank, Corporal (A/Sgt.)
5952486, 2nd Bedfordshire & Hertfordshire Regt. (St. Albans) (Immediate)
This N.C.O. showed outstanding qualities of leadership and personal courage throughout the operation over the Gari from 11th to 18th May 1944.

As Platoon Sjt. his calmness and indifference to danger did much to steady his platoon during the first two days and set a magnificent example.

After his Platoon Comd. was wounded he commanded the platoon in the attack on Hill 50, his leadership and courage being an inspiration to his platoon.

After the capture of Pt. 50 and while his platoon was digging in an enemy M.G. opened up from a position to their rear. Sjt. Snape went off alone, crept up to the position and assaulted single-handed, throwing a 77 grenade and then rushing in to kill the four occupants with his pistol.

His own account of the action was that 'nothing much had happened". This action was only known after discussion with his platoon when he admitted it to be true. *(L.G. 26.10.44)*

Sneesby, George Henry, Private
4800749, 4th Lincolnshire Regt. (Grantham) (Immediate)
On 25th June 1944 during the Bn. attack on Fontenay the a/m soldier, a pioneer by trade, was attached to one of the assault Coys.

Under extreme difficulties of opposition and obscurity this Coy. made good its objective. As it was reorganising a party of Germans, mounted in six half-track vehs., endeavoured to break out of the position and escape. Thick mist overhung the vicinity. Pte. Sneesby, who was nearby, realised at once that an individual act on his part

alone would prevent their escape. As the leading veh. drove up towards him the six Germans inside rained a hail of Smeiser fire down the track to their front. In full face of this fire Pte. Sneesby ran up to the leading half-track armd. car and threw a grenade into the driver's compartment. At this stage he was wounded in his thigh and his back by fire directed at him from the following vehicle. In spite of this he whipped out another grenade and threw it into the back of the leading truck—disabling the occupants. Having silenced this party he 'brewed' the engine with another grenade, thereby blocking the exit for the following vehicles. Refusing to be deterred by his severe wounds, Pte. Sneesby then in a most determined manner advanced against the occupants of the second vehicle. So cowed were they by this man that they surrendered to him. It was not until he was joined at this stage by more men from the Coy. that Pte. Sneesby allowed himself to be treated. He is still in hospital as a result of the wounds received.

By this superb act of individual gallantry, Pte. Sneesby himself accounted for the capture or death of some 10 Germans and was entirely responsible for preventing the escape of the six vehs. and their 30 occupants.

This magnificent example of courage had a high morale effect on the Bn.

M.I.D. 22.3.45 (L.G. 5.4.45)

Snell, Frederick William, Corporal (A/Sgt.)
H.16019, P.P.C.L.I., Canadian Infantry Corps (Immediate)
Ref. Map Italy 1/100,000 Sheet 160 Cassino.

On 23rd May 1944 Princess Patricia's Cdn. Light Inf. was ordered to penetrate and capture a sector of the Adolf Hitler line in the area MR Square 7419, 'B' Coy. was ordered to advance and consolidate on the right flank. Cpl. Snell was section comd. of 3 Section, 11 Platoon of this Coy.

His platoon commander was killed during the attack and the platoon badly disorganised in front of a belt of mined wire. Cpl. Snell took command and under heavy accurate fire from all arms, ran from man to man rallying the platoon, and allotting positions. Having reorganized his force, Cpl. Snell noticed that his men were suffering casualties from sniper fire. Observing movement in a tree to his front, Cpl. Snell ran forward alone across ground covered by deadly fire, a distance of about thirty yards, located two snipers up the tree, and standing coolly in the open, shot down the two Germans with his TMC. Before returning to his position, Cpl. Snell was fired at by another sniper to his right. He advanced alone through the same fire and killed this enemy.

By his action Cpl. Snell undoubtedly saved the lives of many of his comrades and contributed to the advance of his Coy. His bravery and initiative were of the highest order. *(L.G. 30.9.44)*

Snell, John Alfred, Driver
2912, 4 Res. M.T. Coy. N.Z.A.S.C.
For outstanding example of initiative and courage on night 18th April 1941. When proceeding from a position NE of Larissa where a portion of convoy had been waiting to pick up the 21st Bn. it was ambushed by the enemy. After running through the first of these troops the convoy stopped to decide its action and to pick up the wounded. Dvr. Snell crawled forward under fire to some Bren carriers which apparently had shown no inclination to engage the enemy. He obtained there a number of hand grenades. The officer in charge of the carriers decided to try and break through the ambush. A driver was obtained for Dvr. Snell's lorry and he (Dvr. Snell) stood on the running board of the vehicle where the fire was most intense and when moving forward he threw the grenades, silencing at least two enemy machine or Tommy gun positions. The Australian soldier who volunteered to drive Snell's truck was shot and the vehicle crashed into a ditch. Dvr. Snell then jumped into another truck and carried on with the rest of the party until the road was absolutely blocked and all personnel had to abandon their vehicles and take to the open country.   *(L.G. 4.11.41)*

Snudden, James Morrison, Lance Corporal
B142193, A. & S.H. of C., Canadian Infantry Corps (Immediate)
On 28th February 1945 A. & S.H. of C. was holding a high ground in the Hochwald Forest gap L/Cpl. Snudden J. M., was in comd. of a sec. sited along the edge of the woods in the North side of the gap at approx. 044408 1/25,000 sheet 4304 Xanten. At 0600 hrs. the enemy counter-attacked the Coy. position with a force of about one Coy. of inf. sp. by four tiger tanks and two SP guns. The enemy attack succeeded in penetrating the Coy. position and driving back the majority of the Coy. to more sheltered positions. Acting on his own initiative L/Cpl. Snudden maint. his sec. in their position from which they could constantly threaten the flanks of the attacking force. For the following twelve hours this sec. continued to harass the enemy and despite intense fire directed onto their position by enemy M.G.'s, mortars and tanks, this N.C.O. encouraged his men to hold out. Frequently in order to direct the fire of his men it was necessary for L/Cpl. Snudden to expose himself to the enemy fire but he never hesitated and his magnificent direction resulted in such heavy casualties to the enemy that their main force was eventually forced to withdraw. On one occasion an HE shell from one of the enemy tanks landed within a few feet of his position and blew him out of his slit trench. Although badly stunned and shocked he returned to continue his efforts with increased vigour. During the entire period he was constantly moving about his area encouraging his men and inspiring them to efforts far beyond the call of normal duty. Finally at 2200 hrs. his amn. was running low and the Coy. str. had been greatly depleted. L/Cpl. Snudden volunteered

to go back to Bn. HQ for assistance and despite the fact that enemy had infiltrated behind his position he succeeded in getting though and leading fwd. a small group of rfts. to his Coy. The courage and leadership displayed by this N.C.O. undoubtedly was a major factor in the successful defence of the position. His splendid devotion to duty was an inspiration to all ranks in his Bn.
Recommended for M.M.   *(L.G. 12.5.45)*

Snyman, Louis Jakobus, Sergeant
85417V, 12 Fd. Sqn. (V), S.A.E.C., South African Forces (Immediate)
For cool courage, leadership and devotion to duty.

On the night of 4/5th July 1944, Sgt. Snyman was in charge of a Sapper Recce Party sent out to report on mines and demolitions along the road from Palazuolo to pt. R.065207 and hence towards Rapale. The infantry FDLs were just West of Palazuolo. About 3,000 yards out Sgt. Snyman halted the party and went forward alone to a wood pile out of which he brought 2 German soldiers who had been manning an L.M.G. They were taken along on the recce. On approaching a farmhouse some 2,000 yards further on the prisoner showed signs of nervousness and Sgt. Snyman went forward with Sapper Pye to investigate the house. Proceeding very stealthily they surprised a German soldier in the barnyard and captured him. He told them that his comrades were in the house and Sgt. Snyman called on them to surrender. Three more came out and surrendered. A shot was then fired from the window of the house wounding Sapper Pye in the shoulder. Sgt. Snyman with complete composure returned and silenced the fire. While doing so one of the prisoners made a break to escape. Sgt. Snyman killed him in mid-air as he was clearing a low hedge. The party now set off on the return journey with Sgt. Snyman and one infantry man in the lead assisting the wounded man. As they approached a farmhouse they came under M.G. fire which wounded the infantry man at Sgt. Snyman's side. Sgt. Snyman laid the wounded man he was assisting in a ditch, then stalked and killed the two German M.G. operators at close range with his T.S.M.G. He then returned, picked up both wounded men, and set off down the road assisting them. Having proceeded some 100 yards the M.G. again opened on them from the rear, killing the previously wounded infantry man in Sgt. Snyman's arms. Apparently a third number had taken over the dead men's weapon and was firing it. Sgt. Snyman again laid his wounded charge in the ditch and returned and silenced the fire and then lead the patrol back to camp to render the report on his recce. By his cool daring and outstanding leadership he was responsible for the killing of 3 Germans, capturing of 5 others and a most valuable recce report.

On 15th January 1944, during the adv. on Allerona, Sgt. Snyman with a small Engr. party was leading with the fwd elements of Witwatersrand Rifles/De La Rey Regt. He was detailed to proceed fwd with three sprs. to

reconnoitre for mines in the road. The road was under heavy enemy Mortar and small arms fire and one of the three sprs. was shot and killed immediately by snipers. Sgt. Snyman, nevertheless, with the greatest courage, continued to go fwd alone, completed his mission, and then attacked the nest of snipers and killed one of them. Throughout this op., Sgt. Snyman displayed outstanding courage and determination with complete disregard for his personal safety.
Recommended for M.M.   *(L.G. 26.10.44)*

Souter, John, Sergeant
790258, 2nd Royal Horse Artillery (Stockport)
   (Immediate)
On April 12th 1941, the exceptionally gallant and skilful handling of his troop inflicted extraordinarily severe casualties upon the enemy, and played a very material part in preventing what might have been a serious disaster, after the enemy had broken into our position. Though wounded himself, and under heavy close range M.G. and rifle fire throughout most of the time, he continued to fire his gun over open sights enabling the other three guns of his troop to be safely withdrawn, after which he managed to extricate his own. Throughout this critical afternoon he displayed the highest qualities of leadership, courage and presence of mind.
M.I.D. 20.12.40   *(L.G. 21.10.41)*

Sparks, George Frederick, M.M., Sergeant
549913, 12th Royal Lancers (Portsmouth)
   (Immediate)
On 2nd November 1942 Sgt. Sparks was commanding a troop of Armd. cars. A car of a troop on his left had been knocked out by a 50mm A/Tk. gun, and the same gun had also hit Sgt. Sparks' second car. Sgt. Sparks proceeded alone to try and locate this gun. As he advanced over a slight rise, he saw a M.13 tank coming across towards our Infantry positions. He engaged the tank with his 2 pdr., and it tried to turn back, but was hit, and stopped. He then saw a large half-tracked vehicle come up to the tank. This he engaged, and knocked out with his first shot. Both enemy crews 'bailed out' and stretcher parties were seen taking the wounded away. Strong enemy infantry positions and mines in front of him prevented him from advancing and capturing the crews. Sgt. Sparks then went back, and with the assistance of a 6 pdr. A/Tk. gun, the tank and half-tracked vehicle were finally and completely destroyed. Sgt. Sparks has shown outstanding powers of leadership during these operations.
Recommended for M.M. M.M. 18.2.43 *(L.G. 25.2.43)*

Speake, Arthur Spencer, Corporal
4034649, 1st King's Shropshire Light Infantry
   (Shrewsbury) (Immediate)
On the night 4/5th October 1944, Cpl. Speake led his section in their attack on the summit of Monte Cece. As they approached their objective they came under heavy fire from an enemy Spandau post at short range. With great dash Cpl. Speake led his section in a bayonet charge on this post. Several of the enemy were killed and the rest fled in the moonlight.

His section then came under fire from a second Spandau post. Firing from the standing position as the ground made any other position impossible, with complete disregard for his own safety he went forward with a Bren gun in a direct fire fight, silenced the Spandau, killing three enemy in the post. The rest fled in the moonlight. Immediately afterwards a third enemy Spandau post opened up on his platoon from a position slightly in the rear. He advanced on this post with one other man and disposed of it with grenades. He then reorganised his section as part of his platoon in consolidation and his cool judgement and fine leadership ensured that two enemy counter-attacks were repulsed with further loss to the enemy.

Throughout this action Cpl. Speake showed the highest degree of leadership, devotion to duty and contempt for personal danger and there is no doubt that his fine example was a great contribution to the success of the engagement.
Recommended for M.M. M.I.D. 23.9.43 (L.G. 12.4.45)

Spence, Colin John, Private
NX33552, Australian Military Forces
Recommended by Gov. Gen., Australia   *(L.G. 6.3.47)*

Spencer, George Grenville, Sergeant
SX 1193, 2/10th Aust. Inf. Bn. (Immediate)
For conspicuous gallantry and bravery during Buna Aerodrome action.

On 26th December 1942 Sgt. Spencer took over command of 15 Platoon 'C' Coy. 2/10th Bn. when Lieut. McDougal was wounded during an attack on a Japanese Pill Box.

Through Sgt. Spencer's action in withdrawing part of 15 Platoon from a dangerous position and then himself occupying a hazardous but more advantageous fire position, covering loopholes in the pillbox, he finally silenced the opposing automatic fire and was personally largely responsible for the success of the attack.

Further, on 29th December 1942 during the Coy's unsuccessful attack on the coconut grove Giropa Point, Sgt. Spencer walked out across open ground and in the face of deadly fire from enemy positions, set up and operated himself, his platoon 2" Mortar, causing casualties to the enemy and appreciably reducing their fire, thereby enabling our wounded to be withdrawn and considerably reducing casualties to our own troops.

Sgt. Spencer's leadership and judgement since he has commanded his platoon has been of the highest order.

His courage at all times was a great inspiration to his platoon and his Coy. He was always found in the most dangerous position in his platoon and had a complete disregard of his own safety to attain success for his unit.
B.E.M. 1.1.69   *(L.G. 22.4.43)*

Spendlove, Norman Joseph, Corporal (A/Sgt.)
VX106341, 24 Aust. Inf. Bn. (Immediate)
Ramu Valley Area.

For distinguished conduct in action.

During an attack on positions in precipitous country near Saipa on 24th January 1944, A/Sgt. Spendlove rallied his platoon and led them on after they had suffered casualties and shock from moving too closely behind their supporting artillery.

Although himself dazed and shaken, under heavy fire from the enemy, he led his platoon in three unsuccessful attempts to capture the enemy platoon position, situated on a narrow razor-back with unscalable flanks.

While still under heavy fire, he reorganised his platoon, and led them in a bayonet charge which captured the position. He was the first man to reach the objective.

His success allowed the rest of his company to move up the defile and pursue the enemy.

Before the assault he led a reconnaissance party to examine the position. Although ambushed at point blank range, he coolly extricated the party and its wounded.

Throughout the day's operations, his conduct was distinguished by complete disregard of his own safety in pursuing his objective, and his determination and courage were an inspiration to his men.
Recommended for M.M.   (*L.G. 30.3.44*)

Spiers, George William Vernon, Bombardier (A/Sgt.)
841284 [241284 on AFW 3121], 3rd Indian Light
  Anti-Aircraft Battery, Ind. Artillery, Royal Artillery
  (Portsmouth)
On a number of occasions during the campaign in Burma he distinguished himself for his resource and coolness under fire. At Moulmein, on 31st January 1942 his gun position was attacked by a superior force of enemy infantry. Although heavily outnumbered he engaged the enemy with rifle fire, organised local resistance from his trench and inflicted casualties during the evening bayonet encounter. This resistance enabled survivors to warn the gun detachment early. At Prome on 30th May 1942 his good judgement was instrumental in beating off attack after attack by enemy fighters.

At Shweygin, on May 10th 1942 he was responsible as detachment commander for destroying an enemy field gun. He never failed in his consideration for his detachment, insisting on marching with them to India, although he himself was very ill.   (*L.G. 9.3.43*)

Spiller, Jack Arthur, Sergeant (A/C.Q.M.S.)
2615794, 3rd Bn. Grenadier Guards (Northampton)
  (Immediate)
For outstanding courage and leadership.

During the attack on Perugia by 3rd Bn. Grenadier Guards between 18th and 20th June 1944, Sgt. Spiller was commanding No. 7 Platoon in No. 3 Coy. He led his platoon with great dash in an attack on the evening of 18th June and on the 19th June was ordered to attack a vital road junction with a troop of 16/5 Lancers. Two tanks were knocked out by 75mm early in the attack, but Sgt. Spiller, with great skill, managed to outflank the enemy gun position. Although under intense M.G. and Spandau fire he led his platoon on to the objective and consolidated. The enemy put in a counter-attack which was held. He then went forward with stretcher-bearers to bring in some wounded men. On approaching them he was subjected to more M.G. and sniping fire. However, waiting for the opportunity he managed to crawl forward and extricate the wounded men one by one until they all reached safety. It was entirely due to the great personal courage and devotion to duty of this Sergeant that the objective was reached and held. Sgt. Spiller has been Platoon Sgt. or acting Platoon Comd. on active operations since December 1942 and on every occasion has shown himself as an outstanding leader, whose courage, skill and utter devotion to duty has never yet received recognition.   (*L.G. 7.12.44*)

Squire, Albert, Sergeant
7881824, 7th Royal Tank Regt.
This N.C.O.'s tank received 28 hits from guns of varying calibre during the attack on Tummar West on 9th December. The tarpaulin and camouflage nets caught fire. Sgt. Squire got out and cut the burning gear adrift while under fire. He rallied his tank and during the night of 9th December got it sufficiently fit to take part in the attack on gun positions W of Sidi Barrani in the forenoon of the 10th December when his tank was again repeatedly hit but managed to crawl to the rallying point. Throughout the action he handled his tank with skill and dash. This N.C.O. showed exemplary bravery and devotion to duty in keeping his tank in action on 10th December after the severe handling it received on 9th December.   (*L.G. 25.4.41*)

Stainton, Thomas F., Sergeant
Hong Kong Volunteer Defence Corps
For conspicuous gallantry, initiative and devotion to duty. This N.C.O. was a member of No. 2 Coy. H.K.V.D.C. all of whom fought with great gallantry and amongst whom he was outstanding. Throughout hostilities he was an example of coolness, courage and enterprise and at the same time showed complete disregard for his personal safety. In particular on the morning of 22nd December at Repulse Bay, Sgt. Stainton endeavoured to dismount a machine gun from a disabled Bren Carrier whilst in full view and under heavy enemy fire. That afternoon he took a fighting patrol to Violet Hill to locate enemy snipers, arrived within a short distance of the enemy position and then successfully fired the undergrowth to dislodge them. On 23rd December when his platoon was heavily attacked on Stanley View two sections suffered severe casualties but he and his section maintained their position and so enabled all the wounded to be withdrawn to safety. On 24th December he was severely wounded at Chung Am Kok but despite this made his own way back to Stanley.   (*L.G. 4.4.46*)

Standish, Colin Alden, C.Q.M.S.
E.29812, Canadian Infantry Corps
Standish was C.Q.M.S. of 'C' Coy., Royal Rifles of Canada at Hong Kong in December 1941. During the night of 18/19th December at Lye Mun Gap he showed conspicuous bravery in maintaining a constant supply of ammunition to the forward positions of his Coy. which were heavily engaged with the enemy. During the course of his duties he came under extremely heavy mortar and rifle fire. His vehicle received a direct hit during the course of the action, but despite this, he made necessary repairs under fire to maintain his supply. In an endeavour to cut the supply line, the enemy had infiltrated behind out lines, submitting supply personnel to heavy and constant sniping fire. This did not stop Standish from travelling back and forth over this dangerous ground to keep forward positions supplied. During intervals of unloading vehicles in the forward area, Standish took an active part in the action. His conduct was an inspiration to all ranks, and due to his gallantry and efforts it was possible to hold this position until the order arrived to withdraw. This N.C.O. never relaxed in his duty, and was conspicuous in his bravery during the entire campaign in securing and delivering food, water and other supplies to the outposts under fire and against heavy odds. At times when transport was not available he carried rations on his back, taking time off to hunt snipers who were a constant threat to all personnel. During the whole period as a prisoner of war he carried on with the same spirit of self-sacrifice, and although quite ill, he always saw that his men received all that was available to reduce the misery of Japanese camp life.
(L.G. 2.4.46)

Stanley, Gordon Arthur, Sergeant
5105857, 42 W/T Section, Royal Signals
For courage and devotion to duty in Flanders during the period 14–28th May 1940. On one occasion particularly when the unit HQ at Cost—Capelle were being bombed and machine gunned from the air, he manned a M.G. which he had taken from a derelict lorry belonging to another unit and disabled an enemy aeroplane.
Recommended for M.M. *(L.G. 11.7.40)*

Stansfield, Kenneth, Sapper
2072164, 210 Fd. Coy., Royal Engineers (Rusholme, Manchester)
Spr. Stansfield was attached to the standing patrol responsible for closing a gap through our minefield in case of emergency. At about 0600 hours on 1st September he was given orders to proceed forward to the sec. comd. and instruct him to close the gap. As he was passing these orders to Cpl. Barson the sec. comd. six enemy tanks appeared making for the gap and opened fire on the party. Cpl. Barson ordered Spr. Stansfield and another man to accompany him forward to the end of the gap nearest the tanks and lay the mines which were placed there in readiness. This party laid their mines in face of heavy M.G. fire and successfully closed the gap. All the members of the Inf. Sec. were killed or wounded during this operation and Spr. Stansfield was the sole unwounded survivor. A little later he helped to bring in the wounded and later again lifted and relaid and thickened up the mines previously laid. During the whole of these proceedings the area was under intermittent shell fire or threat thereof. Throughout the whole time Spr. Stansfield showed complete disregard of danger, and cheerfulness and resource of a high order. His bearing and example have been a constant inspiration to all around him. He continues to volunteer cheerfully to lead out patrols through the minefield or undertake any other action required of him. *(L.G. 5.11.42)*

Stanton, William Randle, Lance Sergeant
3647447, 3rd (Cheshire) Fd. Sqn., Royal Engineers (St. Helens) (Immediate)
At about 2315 hours on night 23/24th October this unit was starting to clear a gap in the first enemy minefield at about 87452920. The gap to be cleared was being swept by M.G. fire from a post some 400 yards distant, which had not been mopped up, fire being drawn by a pilot vehicle halted on the near edge of the minefield.

While the vehicle was being driven away, L/Sgt. Stanton the N.C.O. i/c Reserves, came forward and led the tape-laying party across the minefield under a heavy fire in which several casualties were incurred, thus allowing work to commence.

At about 0445 hours on the same night, while the unit was clearing a gap in the second enemy minefield at about 87232910 forward of the Miteriya Ridge, a Spandau opened up from the left flank, and the mine detector party were pinned to the ground, several being wounded. L/Sgt. Stanton again came forward and taking a mine detector from a wounded man, stood up and swept to the end of the lane. On his example the remainder of the party recommenced work and completed their task 300 yards long in spite of further casualties.

L/Sgt. Stanton's courage and complete disregard of personal safety was a magnificent example to his Sappers throughout the night, and his action did much to ensure the success of the nights mine clearing operation.
M.I.D. 30.12.41 *(L.G. 25.2.43)*

Stapleton, Cornelius, Warrant Officer Cl. II (C.S.M.)
A21463, Canadian Infantry Corps
No citation. *(L.G. 9.2.46)*

Steele, Albert McCort, Private
B.65037, 1 Bn. R. Regt. C., Canadian Infantry Corps (Immediate)
Pte. Steele was a member of 17 Platoon 'D' Coy. 1st Bn. The Royal Regt. of Canada on 24th April 1945 when the Coy. lead the bn. in a series of attacks and clearing operations from Kirchatten to Dingstede.

Opposition was scattered but each enemy pocket fought fanatically to slow down our advance. Throughout the operation the platoon was without an officer and short of N.C.O.s. Pte. Steele was acting as platoon runner. On one occasion he noticed a section somewhat disorganised after the loss of an N.C.O. Without hesitation he rallied the men and making skilful use of the section's Bren gun to cover their movement, led the section around in a flanking attack thereby cutting off a large number of enemy. Those who were not killed or wounded, surrendered, approx. forty taken prisoner.

With complete disregard for his personal safety he engaged two enemy posts single handed and succeeded in wiping them out, one with his Sten gun and the second with a grenade.

The operation was most difficult, through heavily wooded areas. As a direct result of the presence of mind of Pte. Steele in disposing of these determined enemy pockets the success of the platoon operation was assured, and the Coy. was able to complete the clearance of the enemy's main defences flanking the road.

The initiative and courage displayed by Pte. Steele in the face of heavy fire from enemy automatic weapons was an inspiring example to the entire platoon.
Recommended for M.M.   *(L.G. 22.9.45)*

Steele, Kenneth, Bombardier
3051609, 32nd Lt. A.A. Regt., Royal Artillery (Edinburgh) (Immediate)
This N.C.O. is the detachment commander at a Light A.A. gun position in the Grand Harbour area. On 21st April 1942, during a heavy raid, many bombs fell around the position. Bdr. Steele kept his gun firing against the diving aircraft and displayed great coolness. One bomb fell about 20 yards from the gun position on the bastion wall, and he and four members of his team were wounded. He kept his gun in action against more diving aircraft and refused to hand over his duties until ordered to do so.

Bdr. Steele's devotion to duty on this and many other previous occasions has been most marked and his leadership has set the highest example to the men of his detachment.   *(L.G. 14.7.42)*

Steele, William Henry, Warrant Officer Cl. II
2657536, 1st Bn. Coldstream Guards (London, S.W.14) (Periodic)
Throughout the whole campaign this W.O. has shown himself to be entirely without fear. On the 9th March 1945, in the battle near Wesel a direct hit killed or wounded all the HQ personnel, including the Coy. Comd., of the infantry Coy. which he was supporting. S.S.M. Steele dismounted from his tank and, in spite of very heavy Spandau and shell fire which killed two members of his crew proceeded with the utmost coolness to deal with the wounded and prisoners. On one occasion single-handed he entered the house on his own initiative and came out with six prisoners and a Spandau. On another occasion a Guardsman of his Sqn. trod on an Anti-personnel mine and was badly wounded. This W.O.

immediately led two stretcher bearers into the minefield. Both the bearers stepped on mines and were wounded. S.S.M. Steele, by himself bound them up. Another party came out to his aid but another mine was set off and he received the full blast in his face, half blinding him. Quite unperturbed he helped the wounded to safety. His conduct at all times has been an inspiration to all ranks.
(L.G. 24.1.46)

Steiner, Leonard August, Lance Sergeant
64225, 21 N.Z. Bn. (Immediate)
On the night 19/20th April 1943, during the attack on the Takrouna front, L/Sjt. Steiner was in command of a section of one of the forward platoons. Throughout the advance he displayed able leadership in controlling his men and when opposition was encountered, his personal courage and vigour in attack was an inspiration to those around him. On nearing the objective, L/Sjt. Steiner took over the platoon when it was found that his Platoon Commander had become a casualty, and immediately came under intense machine gun fire. Without hesitation he launched a final attack on the enemy and succeeded, with a depleted platoon in silencing five machine gun posts. L/Sjt. Steiner personally accounted for two of these posts. The positions were well entrenched but this failed to deter him as he attacked with Tommy gun and grenades. Never at any stage did he lose control of his platoon and immediately after his assault, he withdrew them slightly to a favourable position and contacted the remainder of his Coy.

Further to this, L/Sjt. Steiner took command of a party which volunteered to recover the wounded, which they succeeded in doing in spite of the fact that the area was still under heavy machine gun fire. Their difficulties and danger increased as dawn broke, but L/Sjt. Steiner with complete disregard for his personal safety continued in his dangerous work and was responsible for the saving of several mens lives. Throughout the entire action, this N.C.O.'s leadership, courage and determination were of the highest merit.   *(L.G. 22.7.43)*

Stenning, William Henry, Warrant Officer Cl. II
VX 1883, 19 Aust. Inf. Bde., Australian Military Forces
Act of gallantry and devotion to duty at Battle of Tobruch on 21st January 1941.

During the attack WO Stenning assumed command of a platoon in his Coy. after the Platoon Commander and Platoon Sergeant had been wounded. When his Coy. was held up by stationary tanks well entrenched, WO Stenning displaying initiative and bravery, personally took forward an anti tank rifle in the face of heavy machine gun fire from the tanks and under artillery fire and was successful in silencing and capturing the crews of five tanks. Later in the day, when his platoon became separated from their Coy., they were attacked by three medium tanks and the platoon under the leadership of Stenning held their position and put all three tanks out of action. WO Stenning was wounded in the shoulder during this engagement. His gallantry and devotion to duty acted as an inspiration to all under his command and served as a fine example to the men he led, encouraging them to advance under the most adverse circumstances. *(L.G. 9.5.41)*

Stephenson, James, Private (A/Sgt.)
*5046681, 1st Bn. The Gordon Highlanders
(Ballykinlen, Co. Down) (Immediate)*
El Alamein.
On the night of 27th October 1942, A/Sgt. Stephenson located an enemy sniper and accompanied by an officer, stalked and killed him. The following morning A/Sgt. Stephenson discovered that another sniper had moved up to the same position and was firing at the Coy. on his right. Without hesitation and regardless of his own safety, A/Sgt. Stephenson jumped from his trench and crawled across 100 yards of open, bullet swept ground, and shot the sniper with a Tommy gun. This was in broad daylight and despite the fact that the sniper continued to fire at him. *(L.G. 14.1.43)*

Stephenson, Leslie Norman, Signalman
2581346, Royal Signals
Spec. Ops. M.E.
M.I.D. 6.4.44 *(L.G. 13.7.44)*

Stevens, Eric George, Staff Sergeant
*7373608, 16 (Parachute) Fd. Amb., R.A.M.C. (Barnet)
(Immediate)*
For conspicuous gallantry and devotion to duty.
On 17th March 1943 the A.D.S. was at Tamera (G.S. Map 4225—Nefza Sheet 10 1/50,000—099737). The surrounding area was being not only shelled constantly but was also dive-bombed eight times during the day. At the end of the day (during which over 100 cases were treated) there was not a square yard of the A.D.S. site left untouched by splinters of bomb or shell. Staff/Sgt. Stevens was N.C.O. on duty throughout the whole of this period and on one occasion he was assisting Captain J. W. Logan to amputate a badly mangled arm when a dive-bombing attack took place. Although all personnel were ordered to take cover, Staff/Sgt. Stevens remained with Capt. Logan and assisted him until the amputation was finished in spite of the fact that one bomb exploded about fifty yards away and shells were bursting all around while this operation was in progress.
Staff/Sgt. Stevens has on two occasions during the campaign served with the French units and has assisted in liaison work between French and British as well as rendering medical attention to French wounded. He served with 2/9 R.T.A. in the Beja sector and took part in the attack by 1 Thabor (Goums) in the advance in the Djebel Abiod—Sedjenane Sector (Tunisia Sheet 10). This N.C.O. was also in charge of the medical detachment which flew out from England and dropped at Bone at the beginning of the North African Campaign.

Throughout the whole of the campaign Staff/Sgt. Stevens by his coolness and courage has set a very high standard to all of the Parachute Field Ambulance.
M.M. 23.12.43. No citation—Sicily. *(L.G. 15.6.43)*

Stevens, Harry Lewen, Warrant Officer Cl. III
6909125, Rifle Brigade (Andover)
Calais 1940. P.O.W. Pool *(L.G. 20.9.45)*

Stevens, Robert James, Private (A/Cpl.)
V 265240, 24 Aust. Inf. Bn. (Immediate)
During the action in New Guinea at Markham Point 4–9th September 1943 A/Cpl. Stevens under heavy enemy fire, on 4th September maintained his own fire to cover the withdrawal of his Platoon Comd. who was wounded in both legs. Under fire, he then carried his Platoon Comd. Orders to a neighbouring Section and returned under fire. Under withering fire, he dragged a wounded comrade to safety through the enemy barricades. He then led a neighbouring platoon to support his own position. When the enemy overwhelmed the position, he led patrols through the enemy lanes of fire in search of wounded and missing men. His conduct throughout was distinguished by a complete disregard of his own safety in the service of his platoon and comrades. *(L.G. 18.11.43)*

Stevens, Victor George, C.Q.M.S. (actg.)
6098655, 1st Seaforth Highlanders (Sutton)
During the course of operations just concluded this N.C.O. showed himself to be an outstanding leader. He acquitted himself with much credit on a number of occasions. During April and May 1944, owing to the shortage of offrs. this N.C.O. at the time, a Sgt., was in comd. of a platoon which position he filled with the highest credit and success. During the night 16/17th April 1944, his platoon was part of the defence of Kasom village. He was in comd. of a platoon which consisted almost entirely of untried men. The position had been hastily prepared and owing to the rocky nature of the terrain it was practically impossible to dig in. The men were thus very exposed and the Jap made repeated and determined attacks to capture the village. C/Sgt. Stevens' platoon was occupying part of the perimeter which the Japs were determined to penetrate. Time and again they hurled themselves against his platoon but each time he repulsed them with heavy loss. C/Sgt. Stevens kept moving from one section to another with great coolness and daring, steadied the men under him and by sheer force of personal example and complete disregard for his own safety held his ground. There is no doubt that under his inspiring influence, command and leadership a critical situation was saved. Again at Lam-Mu on 24th April 1944, after his Coy's successful attack on the village C/Sgt. Stevens' platoon occupied a most exposed section of the perimeter. This task was specially given to him by the Coy. Comd., who now had the utmost confidence in C/Sgt. Stevens' ability to hold on. Time after time the enemy put in spirited counter-attacks with

heavy covering fire, but again C/Sgt. Stevens showed the same courage, devotion to duty, and calm leadership and beat off every attack. Again at Scraggy on 31st May 1944, and Mitlong Khunou on 24th June 1944, this young N.C.O. showed courage and conduct of the highest order. His ability and leadership were such as to merit the entire confidence of the men under him, and he personally contributed in no small measure to the unqualified success of his Coy.

M.I.D. 5.4.45   *(L.G. 28.6.45)*

Stevenson, Joseph, Warrant Officer Cl. II
5382330, 2nd Oxfordshire & Buckinghamshire Light Infantry (Belfast) (Immediate)
C.S.M. Stevenson landed by glider East of the Rhine on 24th March 1945. The same night he was placed in comd. of a platoon, of which the Platoon Comd. had become a casualty. The platoon was on the East bank of the River Issel. The enemy was very close, and was supported by SP guns. It was quite obvious that the position would rapidly become untenable unless the platoon could impose its will upon the enemy.

Throughout the night and following day C.S.M. Stevenson took all forms of offensive action, directed to the domination of that part of the battlefield. He succeeded so well that his position was held against heavy odds. The enemy made several attempts to break in, but all were defeated. Small parties which did infiltrate were promptly destroyed. In order to draw the enemy's fire and to manoeuvre them on to his own killing ground, C.S.M. Stevenson repeatedly exposed himself without thought of personal safety.

His courage and cheerfulness inspired the whole platoon. It was very largely due to his infectious leadership that a most important position was held under great difficulties at a critical time.

Recommended for M.M. M.B.E. 2.1.65 (L.G. 21.6.45)

Stevenson, Leonard, Sergeant
4985522, 5th Bn. The Sherwood Foresters (Old Chilwell, Notts.) (Immediate)
When first contact was made with the enemy on the Gothic Line across the River Foglia on 30th August 1944, Sgt. Stevenson's platoon was pinned to the ground by heavy M.G. fire from houses about 946728. After an advance over some 800 yards of open and mined ground enfiladed from both sides by batteries of enemy M.G.s, the platoon reached a house where it was pinned by further M.G.s on both flanks. This N.C.O., followed by a small group of men, displaying courage of the highest order, charged at one house occupied by another enemy M.G.; he himself killed both members of the crew. He then collected one of the Sections of the platoon and charged two more strong M.G. positions, again killing and capturing every one of the enemy. Sgt. Stevenson, throughout the period of fighting from 26th August 1944 to 5th September 1944 has shown unsurpassed courage and leadership which has in no small way contributed to

the outstanding success of the breach of the Gothic Line.
(L.G. 8.2.45)

Stevenson, Robert, Corporal
2754743, 1st Bn. The Black Watch (Prestonpans) (Immediate)
During the advance on Gerbini on 19th July 1943, 'C' Coy. was ordered to take up position astride the cross-roads at Crociata Ja Jannarello. During the advance, a German S.P. gun was firing on the Coy. from the right flank. Cpl. Stevenson's platoon made a detour to the left to get on the enemy's flank. Close to where they made contact, an enemy armoured car opened up with two automatics causing casualties in the Coy. This, and the fact that the S.P. gun was firing over on the right, made Cpl. Stevenson realise the seriousness of the situation and the urgent necessity of silencing the armoured car. Disregarding the heavy fire in this area, and the fact that our own troops were firing at the armoured car, Cpl. Stevenson worked his way right up to the armoured car and put a grenade inside it through a small opening below the gun. The car burst into flames and was thus silenced. This action enabled the Coy. to gain its objective. Cpl. Stevenson's complete disregard for his personal safety was an inspiration to all ranks with him. His courage and determination to kill the enemy were of the very highest order, and beyond praise.

Recommended for M.M.   *(L.G. 23.9.43)*

Stevenson, Robert, Warrant Officer Cl. II (C.S.M.)
6976089, 6th Bn. The Royal Inniskilling Fusiliers (Omagh, Co. Tyrone) (Immediate)
Ref Map Italy 1/100,000 Sheet 148. Crossing of R. Trigno. 3rd November 1943.

On the morning of 3rd November 1943 the battalion attacked S. Salvo position from across the R. Trigno.

By the time that the advance from the first objective had started, all the officers in 'A' Coy. had been killed. C.S.M. Stevenson then took command of the company and without further orders directed it on towards the final objective.

Although the company was attacked by enemy tanks when it was in open country and suffered further considerable casualties C.S.M. Stevenson successfully retained control of the company and subsequently led it on into the attack on S. Salvo, which was ultimately occupied.   *(L.G. 10.2.44)*

Steward, James, Warrant Officer Cl. II (C.S.M.)
6285245, 21st Independent Parachute Coy., Army Air Corps
Arnheim.
On 22nd September 1944 the above W.O. who was acting as liaison between Coy. HQ and Troops under command worked continuously under fire during the nine attacks made on one position that day. Late in the afternoon of the same day he proceeded alone to ascertain whether Troop movement by our left flank was our own

or enemy troops. When heavily fired on by the enemy he returned with the information.

On the morning 23rd September 1944, whilst carrying out his liaison duties, he was fired on by the enemy from a house into which they had infiltrated into the Coy. position over night. he at once attacked it single-handed with 36 grenades and destroyed the four enemy in occupation.

On 24th September 1944 the C.C.S. who occupied by the enemy, and the position in the Coy's left flank became obscure. I sent C.S.M. Steward to try and find out if the enemy were infiltrating through the grounds of the C.C.S. He entered the grounds where he met two armed sentries who told him he was a prisoner. Having neutralised this opposition he returned with the most valuable information. His complete disregard of personal danger throughout the action was a fine example to all the troops under my command and the value of the information he supplied was of the utmost importance.

(L.G. 9.11.44)

Stewart, Alistair Buchanan, Lance Sergeant
22318 [22368 on AFW 3121], Under Comd. from 32 Bty., 7 N.Z. A.Tk. Regt.
During the attack on Fort Capuzzo in the afternoon of 27th November 1941 Sgt. Stewart's gun was brought into action against enemy A.F.V.'s, M.T. and Artillery. After knocking out several vehicles the portee carrying his gun was set afire. In spite of heavy S.A. fire Sgt. Stewart and his crew quelled the blaze and continued to work the gun with further success. The portee was again set on fire and the three members of the gun crew were wounded. In spite of his wound and the blazing portee, assisted by a Bren gunner of his crew Sgt. Stewart continued to engaged successfully. Owing to ammunition exploding under the portee Sgt. Stewart was finally forced to abandon the gun taking with him the sights and firing mechanism. He and his crew then continued the action with Bren guns and rifles until surrounded by enemy A.F.V.'s and infantry. Through this and consideration for his wounded he was obliged to give in. However, he and the survivors of his crew succeeded in escaping and rejoining their troop.

Throughout this and other actions nothing but cool courage and utmost gallantry and determination have been shown by Sgt. Stewart. *(L.G. 19.3.42)*

Stewart, Donald, Signalman
6216249, 1 Airborne Div. Signals, Royal Signals (Harrow) (Immediate)
Sigm. Stewart is very strongly recommended for the M.M. In company with L/Sjt. Phillips this man for one month performed excellent service behind enemy lines on the 8th Army front in Italy. In uniform he acted as operator of a wireless set which passed most valuable information. He then assisted L/Sjt. Phillips in passing 481 P.O.W.'s actually through the German lines. This necessitated crossing the lines 10–12 times. it would have

been impossible for L/Sjt. Phillips to have done his job without the help of Sigmn. Stewart, and the gallantry and nerve displayed by this man is an example to all. *Recommended for M.M.* *(L.G. 20.4.44)*

Stewart, Farquhar, Sergeant
2813322, 6th Bn. The Seaforth Highlanders
On 27th May 1940, at Zillebeke, when all three officers of his Coy. had become casualties, Sgt. Stewart took command of the Coy. He showed great coolness, resource, and personal courage in maintaining his Coy. position under very heavy artillery, mortar, and machine gun fire, sending back valuable information. He inspired the men by his example and from 11.00 am till late afternoon held on to his positions with the remnants of his Coy. until the Bn. was ordered to retire into reserve, when he conducted the withdrawal with great skill under heavy fire. *(L.G. 22.10.40)*

Stewart, Jack, Warrant Officer Cl. II (C.S.M.)
B.36973, Royal Hamilton Light Infantry (Wentworth Regt.)
C.S.M. Stewart, 'B' Coy. R.H.L.I., displayed great courage and power of leadership during the operation at Dieppe on 19th August 1942. In company with Capt. A. C. Hill, 2 i/c of 'B' Coy. R.H.L.I. he cleared not only the Casino and cinema, but penetrated into the town to a greater extent than any of the other elements of the 4 Cdn. Inf. Bde., Throughout he led his men with great skill and initiative. C.S.M. Stewart set an excellent example of courage and leadership. After assisting in the withdrawal from the beaches, he himself swam for two miles before being picked up. *(L.G. 2.10.42)*

Stewart, James Duncan, Sergeant
2929422, Queen's Own Cameron Highlanders (Foyers, Inverness-shire)
51st H. Div. P.O.W. Pool *(L.G. 11.10.45)*

Stewart, John, T/Warrant Officer Cl. II (T/Sgt.-Maj.)
7882538, 1st Fife & Forfar Yeomanry, T A
Between the 19th and 29th May 1940, this W.O. gave an outstanding example of leadership and endurance under fire. On all occasions when his troop was subjected to bombing and machine gun fire, he preserved complete calm and was a source of inspiration to all the men in his troop, which he used to the fullest advantage, obtaining accurate detail of enemy positions, etc., by his tactical skill. On the afternoon of 29th May at Vwyfeg, South of Bergues, considering that it was too dangerous to send a runner, he personally crossed some open ground on foot, under heavy M.G. fire, to tell one of his crews to withdraw, returning to his own Carrier, with total disregard for his own safety.
Recommended for M.M. *(L.G. 3.9.40)*

Stewart, Robert Reekie, Private
799700, 2nd Black Watch (Dunfermline) (Immediate)
On 21st November 1941 in the attack of the Bn. on Tiger from the Tobruk perimeter, Pte. Stewart, Coy. runner of the Light Coy., displayed the most conspicuous and continuous gallantry and devotion to duty.

At the intermediate objective of Jill he joined a section in the vicinity of Coy. HQ in a bayonet assault of an enemy M.G. post. When the sec. comdr. was killed on the wire, and the remainder were all casualties he succeeded in bombing the surviving enemy into silence and completed the destruction of the post with his bayonet.

Later, he accompanied his C.S.M. then in command of the Coy. to draw in a section on the extreme left and committed with an enemy wired post. Pte. Stewart joined in a bayonet assault on this and two other similar posts.

He then rejoined his Coy. HQ and continued his normal duties with the few remnants of the Coy. to the final objective.
Recommended for M.M.   *(L.G. 24.2.42)*

Stitt, Herbert Dixon, Corporal
B.70118, 3 Cdn. Armd. Rec. Regt. (Governor,
General's Horse Guards) (Immediate)
On the night of 16/17th April 1945, the Irish Regt. of Canada with, in support, 'C' Sqn., 3 Cdn. Armd. Rec. Regt. (G.G.H.G.) were holding a defensive position based on the village of Otterloo.

At midnight the enemy launched a strong counter-attack which came as a surprise and succeeded in penetrating the forward Coy. positions. By 0230 hrs. the enemy had infiltrated throughout the village, occupied numerous houses, and were digging in on both sides of the main road which was the Divisional Centre Line. The situation within the village was fast becoming critical.

Cpl. Stitt was ordered to patrol up and down the main road from his position with 'B' Coy. to the centre of the village, a distance of 500 yards and to clear the enemy who by this time commanded the road.

As his tank moved out on to the road it was immediately engaged by Spandau and Bazooka fire. One Bazooka bomb scored a direct hit on the turret rink and completely destroyed the traversing mechanism. Although the enemy were only ten yards away, Cpl. Stitt immediately climbed out of his turret and traversed the gun on the enemy by pulling it around by hand.

During the ensuing three hours of darkness, Cpl. Stitt continued to attack the enemy up and down the road, closing with them to point blank range. Throughout this period, he calmly remained on the outside of his tank, constantly exposed to enemy fire, pulling the tank guns on to the enemy by hand and engaging them with grenades and pistol.

By his aggressive action and courage well beyond the bounds of duty, Cpl. Stitt successfully cleared the main street of Otterloo, killing and wounding countless German infantry. His action was undoubtedly instrumental in restoring the situation within the village and keeping the Centre Line open.

Cpl. Stitt's courage, devotion to duty and aggressive spirit in the presence of the enemy have always been an example and an inspiration to all.   *(L.G. 22.9.45)*

Stockdale, William Richard, Troop Sergt. Major
6910706, RA, No. 4 Commando
Operation Jubilee, Dieppe Area 19th August 1942

Sgt Mjr Stockdale took command of the troop after all his Officers had been killed or had become casualties. Sgt Stockdale, while leading a bayonet charge, had part of his foot blown away by an enemy stick-bomb. Although in very great pain, Sgt Stockdale continued to engage the enemy. He set a splendid example, and was an inspiration to his men.   *(L.G. 2.10.42)*

Stocks, Ivor Henry James, Private
5495986, Hampshire Regt. (Rushden, N'hants)
M.E. 1942. P.O.W. Pool.   *(L.G. 14.2.46)*

Stocks, John William, T/Warrant Officer Cl. I (Sgt.-Maj.)
1072129, 21st Anti-Tank Regt., Royal Artillery
During the advance to East of the river Dyle and during the withdrawal to the river Senne, he commanded a Troop of 'BB' Anti-Tank Battery R.A. working with the Divisional Cavalry Regt. Throughout these operations he displayed skill, initiative and coolness in commanding his Troop. Largely due to his skilful handling his Troop avoided having any casualties to men or equipment.
                    (L.G. 27.8.40)

Stoddart, Robert Ray, Corporal
NX 68711, 2/1 Aust. Inf. Bn. (Immediate)
On 11th November 1942 at Gorari Ck. 'C' Coy. attacked a very strongly held enemy position NE of the Bridge. 13 Platoon of which Cpl. Stoddart is a member led the attack and Cpl. Stoddart's section was detailed to ascertain the position of the enemy's right flank where the platoon attacked and succeeded in surprising the Jap, killing 18 of them and taking the objective. Later when the Jap counter-attacked and by sheer weight of numbers forced the platoon to withdraw Cpl. Stoddart was wounded in 3 places, the head, shoulder and foot but despite his wounds and the fact that his T.S.M.G. had jammed he continued to fight on with a rifle. During this phase of the battle he killed 3 Japs and was the last member of his section to withdraw, after which he reported to his Platoon Comd. Later he was evacuated on a stretcher. During the action most of the 15 in the platoon were killed or wounded.

Cpl. Stoddart bold leadership and doggedness served as a shining example to his men and it is recommended that for his gallantry he be awarded the D.C.M.
                    (L.G. 30.3.43)

Stoker, Kenneth William, Warrant Officer Cl. II
24980, Royal Australian Infantry Corps
WO Kenneth William Stoker enlisted in the Australian Regular Army in 1951 and served in Korea with 1st Battalion, the Royal Australian Regiment. In 1954 he joined 3rd Battalion, The Royal Australian Regiment and between 1957 and 1965 he served with the Air Support Unit as a parachute jump instructor and with 1st Battalion, Royal New South Wales Regiment as an instructor. In October 1965 he was posted to the Australian Army Training Team, Vietnam.

On 8th December 1965 WO Stoker was a military advisor with the 1st Battalion of the 5th Vietnamese Regiment, engaged on offensive operations in Thang Binh District of Quang Tin Province, Republic of Vietnam.

At about 1500 hours on that day, the 1st Battalion was halted by heavy enemy fire and forced to adopt a hasty defensive position. This position was then attacked by a Viet Cong force estimated at two battalions, whose morale was high, having already over run another battalion of 5th Regiment on the right flank of 1st Battalion. The attack continued through the night. All Battalion Officers and the majority of its Non-Commissioned Officers were killed. The defences held and the attack was repulsed. Throughout this attack WO Stoker organised and reorganised defensive fire positions, directed mortar fire and personally incited the defenders to repel the enemy. He continually exposed himself to hostile fire with no regard to his personal safety.

In darkness at 0630 hours on the 9th December the Viet Cong again attacked under cover of heavy bombardment. It was evident that the superior strength of the enemy would over run the position and the decision to break out to the rear was taken. WO Stoker was wounded by shrapnel during this attack but disregarding this, he took charge of the situation, organised and directed an orderly withdrawal and by his example, encouragement and professional ability, prevented a probable rout. He regrouped the remaining Vietnamese troops into fighting squads and directed their movement to a point some 3,000 metres to the rear. Approximately 100 only men remained but with these, he organised a new defensive perimeter. This was attacked at 1200 hours and the defenders commenced to break. WO Stoker rallied them again and his coolness under fire, personal influence and control was such as to impel them to stand and fight effectively so that eventually the position was held and the attack repulsed with heavy casualties to the enemy.

In the series of attacks on the 8th and 9th December enemy casualties were estimated at 720 whilst 1st Battalion suffered some 500 casualties.

By his coolness and exemplary conduct under enemy fire, in the face of three consecutive enemy attacks in some twenty-four hours, WO Stoker prevented the defeat of the Vietnamese Unit to which he was advisor, was instrumental in saving the lives of friendly soldiers including United States Army Advisors and finally brought about the defeat of a numerically superior enemy force. The determination, professional competence and personal bravery which he displayed throughout the 8th and 9th December was outstanding and in the highest traditions of the Australian Military Forces. *[From L.G.]*
(L.G. 20.12.66)

Stone, Richard Coleman, Sergeant (temp.)
178093C [178093V on AFW 3121], Imperial Light
Horse/Kimberley Regt. (Periodic)
At C. Saligastro MR 771269, Italy on 13th January 1945 T/Sjt. Stone, R.C., No 178093V was being subjected, with his platoon to a very determined enemy counter-attack in superior numbers. The Western area of defence was being forced back and Sjt. Stone from his Eastern sector noted the absence of the Platoon Officer.

He at once made his way across to the West—found that the Platoon Officer had been wounded and was lying some 30 yards from where the Germans were now spraying the area with Spandau, Rifle fire and grenades. Assuming command, he ordered his men not to yield any further ground then went forward under the enemy fire, lifted and carried his Officer back and at once led his men forward against the enemy, killing and capturing 12 and restored the position completely. Sjt. Stone's courage, leadership and quick initiative was outstanding and saved the platoon from being forced off their area and certainly saved his Officer.

On 21st April 1945 at Caldarada De Reno MR 8356, Sjt. Stone's platoon was directed in an attack on an enemy strong point in the village. Under extremely heavy M.G. and Mortar fire, the platoon suffered casualties and the Platoon Officer was seriously wounded. The advance was held up – Sjt. Stone at once assumed command and, going forward himself under very heavy fire engaged with grenades and destroyed the first Spandau nest then, rallying his men, led them forward, destroyed the strong point of 4 M.G.s and 2 Light Mortars, cleared the area and occupied the centre of the village.

In 30 minutes he successfully repelled 3 counter-attacks and during the whole action took 40 PWs and killed 14 Germans.

On 29th April 1945 near Carturo Nuova MR 255688 Sjt. Stone brilliantly led his platoon against a strongly held enemy post of three houses. Using a Bren gun himself he accounted for 5 enemy L.M.G.s then, waving his platoon forward successfully neutralised the area taking some 50 P/Ws.

Sjt. Stone's magnificent courage, determination and fine leadership is always an example and inspiration to his men – his devotion to duty and total disregard for personal safety is always of the very highest order and on four occasions he has commanded and led his platoon with complete success on to and beyond his objective—his work has been consistently magnificent and of immense value. As the last remaining member of his

original platoon he is admired by all the men of his Coy.
and his courage never fails.   (*L.G. 13.12.45*)

Stott, John, Warrant Officer Cl. II (C.S.M.)
2921936, 1st Queen's Own Cameron Highlanders
On the early morning of 27th May when a combined
attack took place near La Bassee between French tanks
and his Coy., C.S.M. Stott led both parties to the canal
bank, guiding the tanks by hitting their sides. Though
wounded he continued in action until all enemy had
withdrawn to the southern bank of the canal. He set a
splendid example to his men.   (*L.G. 22.10.40*)

Strong, W., Corporal
343062, LancashireFusiliers
B.E.F.   (*L.G. 11.7.40*)

Stubbs, Samuel Basil Alexander, Lance Corporal
NX 200338, 2/2 Aust. Inf. Bn. (Immediate)
On 16th March 1945 a company attack was launched
against a strongly held enemy position which had halted
the advance to but just West of Ulban villages. The left
forward platoon was held up astride the coastal track
fifteen yards in front of the position which consisted of
four bunkers and a number of covered fox-holes.

L/Cpl. Stubbs, from the right section worked his way
forward and directed the fire of the section into the slits
of the two forward bunkers. Then, covered by the fire of
his section he rushed the bunkers throwing grenades into
each and killing four enemy. This done, he advanced
without hesitation to the third and fourth bunkers firing
into their slits and calling to his section to advance. He
killed three more Japanese with his Owen gun and finally
moved forward on to the track and covered the
consolidation of the platoon on the objective. His action
enabled the thrust which culminated in the capture of
the But Aerodrome and Jetty to be continued. His
outstanding gallantry undoubtedly saved the lives of
many of his comrades.   (*L.G. 3.7.45*)

Summers, Alfred, Gunner
1606075, 171 Light A/A Bty., 57 Lt. A.A. Regt. R.A.,
Royal Artillery (Long Eaton, Derby) (Immediate)
This man was an ammunition number and as such
engaged in feeding with ammunition the A/A guns during
the operations against the Martuba aerodromes on 21st
March 1942. One of the rounds mis-fired and although
it was extremely dangerous to do so, he told the number
one not to wait for the prescribed safety period as no
time must be lost in continuing to engage the enemy.
The gun was unloaded and although the fuse was still
burning, he carried the shell away to safety where it later
exploded. Later he was twice wounded but refused to
received any treatment and carried on with his work
supplying the guns with ammunition.   (*L.G. 12.5.42*)

Sunwar, Dambarbahadur, Sergeant
21141356, 10th Princess Mary's Own Gurkha Rifles
For Malaya   (*L.G. 27.4.51*)

Surkitt, Maurice, Warrant Officer Cl. II (C.S.M.)
2609513, 5th Northamptonshire Regt. (Shepton
Mallet, Somerset)
This W.O. took part in an engagement with the Germans
on the night of 24/25th December in the mountains North
West of Medjez-el-Bab in the direction of Tebourba.

During a period of 11/2 hours when the Germans
attempted to storm the position several times, C.S.M.
Surkitt moved freely about the locality under heavy small
arms and grenade fire, organising the distribution of
ammunition and encouraging the men of his Coy. He
removed several wounded to sheltered positions.

When it became necessary to leave the area, C.S.M.
Surkitt effected the evacuation of two wounded men on
mules. He then returned to a portion of the position on
which the enemy had got a footing. Only when he was
satisfied that no more wounded remained did he
withdraw. At all times during the engagement, C.S.M.
Surkitt showed complete disregard for is own safety.

I strongly recommend that this W.O. be awarded the
D.C.M. for his several acts of gallantry and his intense
devotion to duty.
Recommended for M.M.   (*L.G. 23.9.43*)

Sutherland, Alexander Davidson, Sergeant
311323, Royal Australian Infantry Corps
For Vietnam   (*L.G. 10.12.68*)

Sutton, A. F., Warrant Officer Cl. I (R.S.M.)
6190605, Essex Regt.
Gold Medal of the Order of Nassau (Dutch) L.G.
17.10.46   (*L.G. 11.7.40*)

Swain, Thomas, Corporal
7043839, 1st Royal Irish Fusiliers (Birmingham)
On the Kef El Tiour position on the night 24/25th April,
1943, Cpl. Swain took part with his Coy. in an attack on
an enemy strong point, Pt. 622. Throughout the attack
Cpl. Swain was always in the lead urging on his men.
He was the first to reach the objective and with another
man destroyed two enemy M.G. posts.

On the 26th April 1943, Cpl. Swain again took part
in a daylight attack on Pt. 622. Throughout the attack
Cpl. Swain was up with the Assault Gp. and displayed
great gallantry and resolution in pushing forward in the
face of M.G. fire and sniping. When the Gp. were held
up within 100 yds. of the objective, he voluntarily crept
forward with his Platoon Comd. and in spite of accurate
sniping, which killed four men directly behind him,
reached the rocks concealing an M.G. nest, climbed on
top in the face of stick grenades and took prisoner the
enemy gun crew. Cpl. Swain has shown the highest
qualities of leadership and courage throughout the
campaign.   (*L.G. 8.7.43*)

Swan, James Paxton, Lance Sergeant
7928964, 22nd Dragoons (Glasgow) (Immediate)
On 3rd December 1944 L/Sgt. Swan was troop sergeant of a troop of flail tanks which was ordered to make a lane through minefields on either side of the anti-tank ditch surrounding Blerick.

On the way to the forming up point for the assault the Troop Leader's tank was blown up on a mine and L/Sgt. Swan thus became responsible for the handling of the troop throughout the assault.

As the assault began his troop came under very heavy enemy fire, and, on reaching the outer wire defences, was met by exceptionally concentrated small arms fire from Infantry in slit trenches. Here L/Sgt. Swan's tank was completely immobilised by an electrical fault. Having no wireless, he hand signalled his tanks up, giving them covering fire by using his manual controls. One of his tanks was hit from close range and burned out; a second bogged in a slit trench. The third reached the ditch to await the arrival of an assault bridge.

Owing to the delay in its arrival L/Sgt. Swan expended all his ammunition. He therefore called for a reinforcement tank, and, under fire which was by this time increasing in accuracy and intensity, transferred to this second vehicle. By this time the assault bridge was in position, and he led his remaining flail through the deep minefield on the other side of the ditch.

After making a penetration of the minefield of a hundred yards, his tank was blown up and immobilised by a mine. L/Sgt. Swan, however, continued with the utmost determination to shoot his remaining tank in, and he was able to report a safe lane completed.

Whilst waiting for tank-borne infantry to arrive, L/Sgt. Swan once more expended all his ammunition. He was then ordered to evacuate his tank and, still under heavy fire, returned through the minefield with his crew, all of whom he brought back safely.

Having seen to the evacuation of his wounded men L/Sgt. Swan collected an A.R.V. and effected the recovery of the tank which had been bogged in a slit trench. This recovery was done during the assault and under heavy enemy shell fire.

Throughout the entire action L/Sgt. Swan showed magnificent determination and leadership, refusing to be turned from his objective by the difficulties and the enemy opposition with which he was faced. He displayed outstanding courage and devotion to duty and that this penetration of very formidable enemy defences was made good was due to this N.C.O.'s resolution and fearless energy. *(L.G. 5.4.45)*

Swan, William John, Sergeant
6012679, 5th Bn. The Essex Regt. (Saffron Walden) (Immediate)
On 22nd December 1943 Sgt. Swan was commanding the leading platoon of the Coy. ordered to assault the right half of the village of Villa Grande. The attack was held up and his Coy. could not be committed until late in the day.

On reaching the village Sgt. Swan found very stiff opposition and was unable to reach his objective. Nothing daunted, he proceeded to harass the enemy all night and by midday had succeeded in clearing twelve houses. At this stage a further company was sent forward only to meet an enemy counter-attack which succeeded in cutting off Sgt. Swan and his platoon from the rest of the Bn. On the morning of 24th this N.C.O. broke out of his position and rejoined the mainforce inflicting such casualties on the enemy by so doing that the houses lost could be re-occupied.

The next day a further assault was made on the centre of the village in the face of intense grenade and mortar fire from the enemy. Sgt. Swan insisted on leading this assault in person—with complete disregard for his personal safety swept on to his objective through the houses, killing and capturing any enemy still resisting. On arrival he organised the position for defence and, although still under heavy fire and surrounded on three sides was able to consolidate his gains during the night.

When he was wounded on 26th December, Sgt. Swan had been leading his platoon for 5 days of continuous action, always in the closest contact with the enemy and usually under heavy fire.

The determination and powers of leadership displayed by this N.C.O. were an inspiration to all who saw him, whilst his handling of that platoon was in no small measure responsible for the success of the final assault. *(L.G. 6.4.44)*

Swann, Joseph Edgar, Sergeant (A/Colour Sergeant)
6913155, 2nd Rifle Brigade (Cricklewood) (Immediate)
Sgt. Swann was troop sgt. of a troop of 6 pdr. anti-tank guns during an action on the Snipe position 866295 on 26 and 27th October 1942. As troop sgt. he should have gone back when the portees were withdrawn during the first night, but he was at the time firing a gun, and the portee withdrew without him. In this night action he personally accounted for 2 lorries and 1 88mm gun which was firing into the position at 300 yards range. During the day he acted as No. 1 on a gun, at the same time giving all possible help to his troop. Whenever tanks appeared he engaged them as soon as the range was suitable, even though his flank was exposed to M.G. fire from other tanks which were in dead ground and could not be engaged by any gun in the position. In the afternoon a shell landed behind the gun killing the loader and wounding the No. 4. He carried on firing with the No. 3 until the latter was also wounded. He then crawled across to another gun in the troop which was out of action and fetched its crew and ammunition to man his own gun. In the evening attack at 1700 hrs. 8 Mk IIIs advanced head-on towards his troop position; he saw that the gun to his right, belonging to another troop, was not being fired as the crew were all wounded. He crawled across

to it under shell and M.G. fire, loaded and laid it, and hit the turret of the nearest tank at 150 yards, halting it and putting it out of action. He then took on the second tank at 200 yards and set it on fire. This gallant action under intense fire, when there were only 20 rounds of ammunition left in the whole position and sixty German tanks were attacking South-eastwards down the valley turned the enemy and saved the day.   *(L.G. 14.1.43)*

Swanson, Leslie Ronald, Sergeant
NX 8748, 2/4 Inf. Bn., Australian Military Forces
During the campaign in Crete the C.O. 2/4 Bn. disposed 11 Platoon 'B' Coy. in an outpost position wholly separated from the remainder of the Bn. except for visual signal communication. The platoon was under command of Lieut. Kesteven with Sgt. Swanson as Platoon Sgt.

At dawn on 26th May 1941 reconnaissance by the Platoon Comd. revealed a large body of enemy approaching from the West. Further bodies of enemy were observed approaching from other quarters and after firing upon the enemy and holding them up sufficiently long to enable the despatch of a message to Bn. the Platoon Comd. decided to return to Bn. in accordance with instructions.

The route he selected would have passed through the F.D.L.s of a neighbouring Bn. and instructing Sgt. Swanson to lead the way he, Lieut. Kesteven, brought up the rear, as he thought nearest the enemy. Sgt. Swanson had not proceeded far when he became aware of another body of approx. 50 enemy lying in a vineyard and they opened fire upon the platoon. Realising that this was the only way out which offered any chance of returning to the Bn., Sgt. Swanson with great presence of mind shouted to Lieut. Kesteven and then calling to the men led a bayonet charge against the enemy. The enemy continued to fire but under the threat of the oncoming platoon with Sgt. Swanson at least 20 yds. in front, broke and fled. One of the enemy was killed with the bayonet and at least 30 others were shot as they emerged from cover. The prompt action of Swanson undoubtedly enabled the platoon and its Commander to return to Bn. HQ and they were able to furnish valuable information regarding the enemy's movements the purpose of which the platoon had originally been placed in position.
Recommended for M.M.   *(L.G. 4.11.41)*

Swart, Crispin, Sergeant
90225, 2nd Anti-Tank Regt., S.A. Artillery (Periodic)
Period October 1941 to February 1942.

This Sgt., who, since December 1941, has been acting as Troop Comd., has, by his coolness in action, keenness and cheerfulness, set an example which has been an inspiration to his men. Particular mention must be made of the gallant and successful covering action on 19th December 1941 N.W. of Sharean (Area 518360) when by his handling of his troop he disabled two enemy tanks and enabled a platoon of 2 R.D.L.I. under Lieut.

Anderson, to withdraw successfully and the S.A. Armd. Cars to evacuate wounded.

On 28th January 1942 this N.C.O. showed brilliant handling in an action with enemy tanks North of Msus, when his troop destroyed two heavy German tanks and disabled another.   *(L.G. 9.9.42)*

Sweeney, Christopher Percy Mackenzie, Corporal (A/ Sgt.)
32060, 1st Bn. Transvaal Scottish (Immediate)
For gallant leadership in action.

On the morning of 16th march 1942, Sgt. Sweeney, who was acting Platoon Comd., was in a F.O.P. West of Wadi El Frech in Cyrenaica, together with another N.C.O. While observing enemy movements further West of their position, they were surprised by a party of Germans, who called upon them to surrender. Sgt. Sweeney, however, decided to fight it out rather than surrender. They opened fire on the enemy from a range of about 60 x, one of the enemy fell wounded and the remainder dropped to the ground. In the ensuing exchange of shots, Sgt. Sweeney was wounded by two Tommy gun bullets in the left arm, but in spite of these wounds continued firing his Tommy gun, and only gave the order to withdraw when an A/Tk. gun opened fire from 80 X to 100 X range. Sgt. Sweeney then contacted the balance of his patrol and took them all back to Wadi Belfarais without further casualties.

During the whole action Sgt. Sweeney displayed great courage, devotion to duty and presence of mind.
                                                (L.G. 12.5.42)

Sweet, Henry John, Sergeant
2657931, 2nd Bn. Coldstream Guards
During the period 30th May/1st June on the Yser Canal North of Hondschoote, Sgt. Sweet showed initiative and resource on taking command of a platoon. He held an exposed position on the canal bank which was constantly subjected to mortar and shell fire. The litter of abandoned vehicles on the enemy bank gave cover to their snipers and machine gunners. By his handling of his platoon Sgt. Sweet minimised his own and inflicted heavy casualties on the enemy. He showed a cheerfulness under shell fire and disregard for his own personal safety which was a fine example to all ranks.

Finally he conducted the withdrawal of his platoon without casualties and in good order.   *(L.G. 27.8.40)*

Swinburn, Arthur, Warrant Officer Cl. II
4855159, Leicestershire Regt. (attd. S.S.T., No. 50 Commando) (Nottingham)
In recognition of gallant and distinguished services in the field.
M.E. P.O.W. Pool 1942.
M.I.D. 15.12.42.   *(L.G. 13.9.45)*

Sye, Henry, Lance Sergeant
7020431, 2nd Bn. London Irish Rifles, (Belfast) (since died of wounds) (Immediate)
Fontanelice 032255 Italy 1/25,000 Sheet 99 IV/NW.
On 21st October 1944 on the occasion of 'H' Coy's night attack on Hill 387 N of Monte Pieve the a/n N.C.O. was at the outset Platoon Sgt. Early in the attack his platoon which was leading the Coy. came under very intensive small arms fire and heavy shelling. Considerable casualties were caused and the Platoon Comd. was killed. L/Sgt. Sye immediately rallied the few remaining men of his platoon and continued to press up the steep slopes towards the objective. All the time he was facing heavy M.G. fire and grenades at short range, but despite this he pressed on with total disregard for his personal safety.

By crawling forward he attacked single handed one M.G. post and successfully killed or wounded all of its occupants.

Not content with this feat, he tried twice more to reach another enemy M.G. but was severely wounded in the attempt.

Throughout this attack, as on many previous occasions L/Sgt. Sye behaved with great personal courage and displayed the highest quality of leadership.
(L.G. 12.4.45)

Symons, Frank Thomas Verdun, Sergeant
7374502, R.A.M.C. (Torquay) (Immediate)
In the action in the vicinity of Montecorvino Airfield on 10th September a group of casualties were isolated ahead of a Bn. R.A.P. Repeated attempts to collect these casualties by sending forward a motor ambulance car and a carrier had failed and both vehicles were knocked out by direct hits from an enemy 88mm gun. This N.C.O. led his section forward under intense shell and machine gun fire using a ditch and disregarding the danger of enemy mines. He succeeded in collecting by hand carriage one Officer and eight wounded men. The task necessitated two journeys on foot. His courage and devotion to duty undoubtedly saved the lives of the wounded personnel.
(L.G. 27.1.44)

T

Tacon, Stanley James, Sergeant
*5825023, 4th Bn. The Queen's Own Royal West Kent
Regt. (Stratford-on-Avon)*
At Kohima in the D.I.S. area on 8/9th April 1944 Sgt.
Tacon was in command of a platoon in the forward area
which was subjected to continual attacks in strength by
night and day. By skilfully directing and controlling the
fire of his platoon he succeeded in beating off all attacks
with heavy losses to the enemy, at least 15 falling to his
own rifle; and later was severely wounded when
attempting to recover one of his forward section comds.
who had been wounded knowing full well that the area
was swept by M.M.G. fire.

His courage, devotion to duty and complete disregard
for his personal safety was an inspiration to his men and
of a very high order.

Recommended for an immediate award of the
Distinguished Conduct Medal.   *(L.G. 27.7.44)*

Talmey, Albert William, Corporal
*6397782, 1st Bn. The Royal Sussex Regt. (16, Henry
St., Brighton)*
During the attack on Sidi Omar Nuovo on 22nd
November 1941, Cpl. Talmey, although suffering from
several wounds continued to fight and lead his men
forward, Finally when unable through weakness to go
further forward himself, he gave covering fire with a Bren
gun and so enable two men to get forward and capture
an enemy post.

The courage and devotion to duty shown by this
N.C.O. were beyond all praise.   *(L.G. 23.1.42)*

Tamang, Makarpai, Corporal
21142129, 10th Princess Mary's Own Gurkha Rifles
For Malaya   *(L.G. 4.11.52)*

Tanidrala, Waisake, Sergeant
6170, Fiji Military Forces
No citation   *(L.G. 7.12.44)*

Tanui, Kiberen Arap, W.O. Platoon Commander
N15457, King's African Rifles
For Malaya   *(L.G. 7.10.52)*

Tate, Bertie, Sergeant
*NX.28467, 2/15 Field Regt., R.A., Australian Military
Forces*
During the action at Muar on 21st January 1942, Sgt.
Tate together with Lieut. Ross of the same unit displayed
great coolness and devotion to duty in engaging, under
most difficult conditions, enemy tanks which threatened
the position. As the result of this action two enemy tanks
were put out of action and possibly others. Throughout

the day's fighting Sgt. Tate displayed great devotion to
duty.   *(L.G. 10.1.46)*

Taute, Matthys, Flying Officer
*63776, 258 Squadron (R.A.F. Regt.), Far East
Command.*
On 14th February 1942 this officer, with about 20 men
of his Defence Unit, attacked and drove back a force of
about 150 Japanese parachute troops on the road leading
West from Palembang Aerodrome. As a result a battery
of No. 6 Heavy A.A. Regt. were shielded from attack,
and eventually extricated from their battery site almost
without loss. This officer showed great personal courage
and leadership, and was responsible with an airman for
the bringing up under fire and the operation of a Lewis
machine gun in an exposed position, thus causing the
Japanese attack on the site to be broken off. In subsequent
phases of the campaign Flying Officer Taute maintained
the high standard of leadership shown on this occasion.
Recommended for M.C.   *(1.10.46)*

Taylor, Alexander John, Lance Corporal
QX 2687, 18 Aust. Inf. Bde.
On the night of 3/4th May 1941, at Tobruk, during an
attack on enemy M.G. positions, L/Cpl. Taylor was
detailed to contact the Pl on his left. On three occasions
he crossed ground swept by enemy M.G. fire, located an
enemy M.G. post, advanced and wiped out the six men
in the post with his Tommy Gun. During the same night
he helped his Sec. destroy an A/T gun Post, and remained
behind alone to give the section covering fire during their
withdrawal after completing this task.

Again on completion of the Pl. task he remained
behind with his Pl. Comdr. and gave covering fire for
the Pl. withdrawal. During this action L/Cpl. Taylor was
wounded, but gallantly stuck to his job to the last. This
most distinguished conduct and display of courage was
a great inspiration to all members of his Pl.
    (L.G. 19.8.41)

Taylor, Douglas Roy, Sergeant
VX 5449, 2/7 Aust. Inf. Bn. (Immediate)
On 5th December 1942 in the vicinity of Cape Endaidere,
Papua, Sjt. Taylor was in command of a Bren carrier
which was ordered into an attack to support the advance
of U.S. Infantry.

Soon after he crossed the start line Sjt. Taylor's carrier
was engaged by M.G. fire from well concealed enemy
strong posts at a range of approx. 30 yards. He
immediately ordered the storming of these posts which
he engaged with M.G. fire and grenades.

At this stage the enemy scored a direct hit on the
carrier with a mortar bomb, killing one of the crew and

seriously wounding a second. The carrier was then moved to the rear of the enemy strong post and with complete disregard for personal safety, Sjt. Taylor continued to hurl grenades into the post until it was silenced. He then leapt from the carrier and engaged and killed with the bayonet an enemy soldier who had been hurling grenades at the carrier from behind cover.

He returned to the carrier and proceeded towards the beach to engage a second enemy M.F. post from the rear. This he did with M.G. fire and grenades. To complete the silencing of this post he ordered the carrier to move to the front of the post. The carrier was partly disabled and the driver was forced to make a wide detour which brought them under the close fire of a third enemy M.G. post which previously had remained silent. He immediately stormed this post and got the front of this carrier jammed in some coconut logs in front of this strong post.

The carrier stopped and could not proceed further. Sjt. Taylor stood up and immediately received a burst of M.G. fire which shattered one arm. Notwithstanding his injury he crawled forward to the opening in the enemy strong post and under cover of S.A. fire from the driver of the carrier (Pte. Cameron) he continued to hurl grenades inside the post until the enemy M.G. crew had been killed or disabled and the post completely silenced. He then lost consciousness. The driver of the carrier was wounded in the head but continued to fire his Bren gun until all his ammunition had been expended when he returned to the U.S. lines. Later Sjt. Taylor regained consciousness and made his way back to the U.S. lines.

Throughout the action he set an inspiring example to the men of his platoon which he commanded when Lieut. Fergusson, the Pl. Comd., was killed soon after the action commenced.   *(L.G. 22.4.43)*

Taylor, George Christopher, Sergeant
*320184, The Royal Dragoons, Royal Armoured Corps
(Pimlico, London)*
On 9th June 1941 at Khiam Sjt. Taylor was in command of the leading car of a Recce patrol which obtained valuable information. During the patrol the car had to carry out a withdrawal in reverse gear under heavy Machine Gun fire, A/T Gun fire and shell fire. During this withdrawal the R.E. Officer in the car was killed and another member of the crew was severely wounded. Sjt. Taylor showed exceptional bravery and powers of leadership in extricating his car from a very dangerous position.

Again at Qastal on 24th June 1941 he was in charge of the leading car of a patrol which came under very heavy A/T Gun fire and shell fire. His Troop Leader's car was overturned. He at once dismounted under heavy fire and, with the help of another man managed to get his Tp. Ldrs. car back on to its wheels again and thus enabled the patrol to complete its task.

Throughout all these operations Sjt. Taylor showed bravery and resource of the highest order.

Recommended for M.M.   (L.G. 30.12.41)

Taylor, George Frederick, Sergeant
*1061333, 107 S. Notts 'H' Regt. Royal Horse Artillery
(Manor Park, E. 12)*
Action 107 R.H.A. near Bir Tamar on 27 May 1942.

On the morning of May 27th 520 Bty. 107 R.H.A. was attacked by a very large enemy tank concentration. The first wave of tanks was stopped by the fire of the guns and turned to a flank. When the 2nd wave approached the guns, those on the flank closed in from the rear, machine gunning the detachments. During this action W/Sgt. Taylor fought his gun with great courage and determination in the face of heavy enemy fire until all the detachment were either killed or wounded. His personal coolness in action was an inspiration to his detachment. He was responsible for destroying 3 enemy tanks.   *(L.G. 24.9.42)*

Taylor, John, Lance Sergeant
14443359, 1st Bn. The Leicestershire Regt. (London, W.2) (Immediate)
At about 0830 hrs, 18th January 1945 when 'C' Coy. 1 Leicesters., had been attacked by the enemy at Zetten, 17 Platoon 'D' Coy., 1 Leicesters were ordered to Zetten to reinforce 'C' Coy. and came under their Comd. L/Sgt. Taylor commanded a section in 17 Platoon.

Moving up to Zetten, 17 Platoon came under heavy Spandau fire. L/Sgt. Taylor immediately ordered his section to return the fire and silenced it.

On arrival at Zetten, the platoon was ordered to clear a street and get to a platoon of 'C' Coy. which had been overrun. Co-operating with tanks the platoon cleared four or five houses of enemy who offered stiff opposition. L/Sgt. Taylor's section did most of this work and L/Sgt. Taylor led it with great bravery and dash.

17 Platoon reached the platoon of 'C' Coy. that had been cut off, but found it was pinned down by fire from a house opposite. A platoon attack was laid on and L/Sgt. Taylor's section was ordered to be house clearing section. L/Sgt. Taylor again led his section with complete disregard to his own personal safety against Spandau and rifle fire, took the house and occupied it.

At approx. 2000 hrs. the enemy put in an attack mainly against L/Sgt. Taylor's house. This was beaten off.

The enemy resumed the attack at approx. 2130 hrs. concentrating on L/Sgt. Taylor's house again. The house was subjected to Bazooka fire until it was practically demolished and caught fire. L/Sgt. Taylor inspired his section to fight back and inflicted considerable casualties. It was not until the fire was completely out of hand that L/Sgt. Taylor ordered his section to withdraw to platoon HQ. He was immediately ordered to occupy a house nearby which was considered vital to the defence. Three times he tried to get there, but his section met with such heavy fire that they had to withdraw. He was then ordered to take up positions in the house of platoon HQ.

At about 2330 hrs the enemy again attacked against the house where the platoon HQ and two sections (one of which was L/Sgt. Taylor's) were. The enemy Spandau and Bazooka fire was extremely heavy and the thatched roof of platoon HQ was set alight. L/Sgt. Taylor took the Piat himself and from a very exposed position, under very heavy fire, scored direct hits on the Bazooka and Spandau positions and silenced them. L/Sgt. Taylor's wonderful bravery on this occasion was mainly responsible for beating this attack off and giving time for the fire in the roof of the platoon HQ to be checked.

Throughout the night 18/19th January and until the platoon was relieved at about 1900 hrs on the 19th January L/Sgt. Taylor continued to lead his section with outstanding bravery and ability and inflicted very heavy casualties on the enemy.

In this action L/Sgt. Taylor showed personal bravery of a quite outstanding order. His determination and fighting spirit were an example to the whole platoon who on this day fought a most magnificent action. Both when his section was isolated and when he was fighting later with the rest of the platoon, his leadership and doggedness were superb, and an example of which the Regt. will be justly proud.   *(L.G. 3.5.45)*

Taylor, Samuel, C.S.M.
2754072, 4th Bn. The Black Watch, T.A
On 13th May 1940, the behaviour of C.Q.M.S. Taylor was magnificent. At all times during the height of the battle he was calm, encouraging the men, and showing a remarkable example of bravery. At one stage he was firing a Bren gun when it was hit by a stream of bullets down the flash eliminator. He was temporarily stunned but quickly changed the barrel and continued firing with complete calm and accuracy. His example had a far reaching effect on the men who were fighting, in the same post, a battle against very great odds.
          (L.G. 5.7.40 & 22.10.40)

Taylor, William Sutherland, Sergeant
2563362, 1st Argyll & Sutherland Highlanders
    (Edinburgh) (Immediate)
During the fighting East of Marradi.

On 7th October 1944, 'A' Coy. attacked and captured the feature, Pt. 744. Sgt. Taylor was in command of No. 8 Platoon which he led with great dash and skill on the objective, despite the confusion caused by our own smoke and heavy enemy mortar and Spandau fire. Just short of the objective Sgt. Taylor's platoon came under direct fire from an enemy M.G. post at very close range. Though by this time, wounded, Sgt. Taylor attacked the post single-handed with grenades and succeeded in knocking it out, killing one German, wounding a second and capturing a third. He then personally directed fire on to the fleeing enemy and rapidly reorganized his platoon (reduced to 14 strong) which was then sent forward to clear up a spur to which elements of the enemy had fled. The platoon succeeded in doing this but then

came under fire from Spandaus on both flanks. Sgt. Taylor was pinned down there for some hours but though unable to break out or attack either Spandau, he gallantly returned fire and kept the enemy at bay till his ammunition was exhausted. Sgt. Taylor then showing complete disregard for enemy fire moved about the remnants of his platoon instructing them to hold their positions at all costs, and tending the wounded. Sgt. Taylor's platoon held on. 'B' Coy. then attacked Pt. 685 in the late afternoon and this enabled Sgt. Taylor to bring in the remainder of his platoon (now reduced to 9 strong) to Pt. 744. He did not complain of the wound in his leg, and was indefatigable and invaluable in his efforts to assist in the organisation of the defence of Pt. 744 against counter-attack. The next morning after having his wound dressed he was most reluctant to leave the Coy. and had to be ordered to go back with a S.B. for evacuation. Throughout the whole operation Sgt. Taylor displayed outstanding leadership, coolness and determination to close with the enemy, and the capture of Pt. 744 was to a great extent due to his gallant and inspiring behaviour.
          (L.G. 12.4.45)

Teale, Charles Leslie, Sergeant
3445729, 1st Bn. The East Lancashire Regt.
    (Stretford) (Immediate)
On 4th January 1945 during the Bn. attack on Bois Du Grand Pouhon (MR 92/3583), Sgt. Teale's Platoon was held up by a well concealed and dominating enemy position in the woods, containing two Spandaus.

Owing to the difficulty of the development in the thick wood (all movement in the undergrowth caused snow to fall off the branches above and drew fire from the enemy) the platoon was detailed to work its way back and round the left flank of the enemy position.

Sgt. Teale then carried out a lone stalk of the position. The enemy continued to fire bursts into every bush and piece of cover in the vicinity, including those through which Sgt. Teale was moving, but undaunted by this, he calmly edged his way forward, inch by inch, to within a few yards of the position. Then without waiting for the rest of his platoon, he threw in his grenades and charged the position single-handed with his Sten gun. The enemy were completely surprised and quickly overwhelmed. One German was wounded and the remaining ten were taken prisoner by this one N.C.O.

Sgt. Teale's calm bravery and complete disregard of personal danger were of the highest order. He is an inspiration to all who serve under him. *(L.G. 12.4.45)*

Teale, John William, Sergeant
6850982, 2nd Bn. King's Royal Rifle Corps (N.
    Cheam) (Periodic)
Sgt. Teale has consistently shown the highest qualities of courage and leadership throughout the Campaign in Northern Europe, and indeed also in Africa and Italy. His section of carriers has often operated independently, and it is then that his initiative has been given full play.

On 28th October 1944 at Reijen (E.0536), Sgt. Teale was a member of a patrol of 1 Officer and 4 O.R.s. The enemy from short range hit the officer and a Corporal. Sgt. Teale carried back the officer returned and took back the Corporal. The Rifleman who was with him was wounded, so Sgt. Teale returned a third time and brought this Rifleman back. All this under heavy accurate fire.

On 9th April 1945 at Neuenkirchen (WO725), in an independent role Sgt. Teale's section found itself isolated and surrounded by the enemy. He directed the fire of his section with such effect that the enemy were driven back in confusion. It was a joy to hear his section firing all their weapons. After replenishing with ammunition, his section continued to play a gallant part in the attack, and in the evening lead the advance into the village driving the enemy before him by the weight of his well-directed fire.

The offensive spirit of this N.C.O. and his determined handling of his section, was on this occasion largely instrumental in the success of the attack. Often during the last year has Sgt. Teale shown a similar spirit in action with equally happy results. His example has inspired his company with the highest offensive spirit.

(L.G. 24.1.46)

Teare, Edward Herbert, Lance Corporal
3783471, 6th Bn. The Royal Inniskilling Fusiliers (Liverpool)
On 7th April 1943, during the bn. attack on Di Mahdi L/Cpl. Teare was a Bren gunner in a forward platoon, which was held up by a German machine gun. L/Cpl. Teare went forward alone with his LMG and some grenades and silenced the machine gun, taking the survivors prisoner, and occupying the position himself.

Throughout the day he displayed great personal initiative and his individual efforts were largely responsible for the gaining of the Coy. objectives.

On 27th April 1943 during the bn. attack on Kef Es Senrach L/Cpl. Teare was ordered to move to the left flank of the Coy. to fire at a German MG Post which was holding up the forward pls. He succeeded in silencing this post with his Bren gun from an exposed position. Suddenly he was rushed at from a concealed position by 4 Germans led by an officer. With great coolness L/Cpl. Teare opened fire, killing the officer and an N.C.O. after which the remainder gave themselves up. The handling of his Bren Group continued to be of the greatest assistance to his Coy. throughout the battle.

(L.G. 8.7.43)

Tekavesi, Sekonaia, Private
23892827, King's Own Royal Border Regt.
For Oman   *(L.G. 9.4.74)*

Telfer, James Alexander, Sergeant
3189201, 6th Bn. King's Own Scottish Borderers (Hawick)
During the assault on Goch on 18/19th February 1945, Sjt. Telfor was Platoon Comd. of the leading platoon of 6 K.O.S.B. On the night of 18th February he was given the task of advancing across open ground in front of an anti-tank ditch, crossing the ditch and establishing a firm base in the area of some houses on the far side.

On approaching the anti-tank ditch his platoon came under heavy M.M.G. fire, but Sjt. Telfor, fully alive to the importance of his task, pressed onwards. Thus he immediately came to close quarters with the enemy who now fired on his platoon with Bazookas and M.M.G.s and threw grenades. With great courage and determination, Sjt. Telfor then fought a hand-to-hand battle up the anti-tank ditch, killing many Germans, until he reached a bridge. Here he found that he was up against a prepared defensive position and that the bridge was defended by approx. one platoon of enemy with two 88 mm guns, three M.M.G.s and a number of Bazookas in support. Although casualties had by now considerably reduced the strength of his platoon Sjt. Telfor immediately put in an attack on the bridge. The enemy reacted fiercely but this N.C.O. with great courage and by his fine personal example, led his platoon forward and captured intact not only the bridge but two 88 mm guns and considerable enemy equipment.

Sjt. Telfor now reorganised his platoon while still under heavy fire from the houses on the far side of the ditch and mounted a successful attack on his final objective, clearing the houses and establishing the necessary firm base on the far side of the ditch. He then held this position throughout the night in face of strong enemy counter-attacks in which Bazookas were used against the houses.

During the entire period Sjt. Telfor's determined courage and leadership were a source of inspiration to his men and the subsequent capture of Goch can be directly attributed to this N.C.O.'s determination to capture his objectives in the early stages of the battle.

(L.G. 19.4.45)

Teneti, Wiwi, T/Corporal
39603, 28 N.Z. (Maori) Bn. (Immediate)
Cpl. Teneti commanded one of the section of the platoon that bore the brunt of the attack on Point 209 on 26th March 1943. Under heavy mortar and M.G. fire he succeeded in leading his men up the steep face of the hill and the boldness of his attack caused the enemy to evacuate strong dug-in positions that he held on the hill crest. At the same time the advance of the rest of his platoon on the right was held up by two enemy L.M.G. posts. Displaying great initiative and courage he took over the section Bren gun and firing from the shoulder in full view of the enemy succeeded in keeping their heads down. Then he ordered his men to rush the positions with hand grenades which they did so

effectively that the positions were wiped out. Enemy resistance collapsed and his platoon were thus able to consolidate on their objective. During the hours of darkness the enemy launched several counter-attacks in an all-out effort to recapture this high ground. Cpl. Teneti stood his ground and fought back till his whole section had become casualties, then he joined the remainder of his platoon and fought back tenaciously until he himself was finally wounded and it was only under severe persuasion that he agreed to be evacuated.

This soldier displayed courage and leadership of the highest quality. (*L.G. 17.6.43*)

Terry, Jack, Sergeant
880535, Royal Artillery, No. 11 Commando & SAS
(Bulwell, Notts.)
At Sidi Rafa

After capsizing in his boat during the landing from the submarine and after an exacting march over 18 miles of mountainous country in drenching rain Sgt Terry, in company with two officers, forced an entrance to the German HQ at Sidi Rafa. He covered the two officers while they investigated the ground floor and prevented enemy interference by firing his tommy gun at guards who attempted to descend from the first floor. He afterwards entered a room and; though fired at from the dark interior, he emptied two magazines into it. When the commander of his detachment was killed he conducted his party successfully back to the beach.

On retirement from the beach, after ordering his party to disperse and take to the hills in compliance with instructions, Sgt Terry remained behind under heavy fire and waited for his Commanding Officer, who had hurt his knee. He remained in his company behind the enemy lines for 41 days until they were able to rejoin our own advancing troops. (*L.G. 24.2.42*)

Tevendale, Lewis Ligertwood, Warrant Officer Cl. I (R.S.M.)
2873628, Gordon Highlanders, S.S. Bde. (Layforce)
(Stonehaven, Kincardineshire)
Litani River (Syria) 9—10 June 1941

R.S.M. Tevendale showed great initiative and daring when he assumed command of a detachment after all 3 of its officers had been killed. On being unable to contact the detachment on his right he led his party forward under heavy fire and succeeded in dispersing several enemy detachments. He remained in position covering the enemy's L of C to their forward positions and, by cutting field telephone lines and capturing or killing runners he prevented information being passed in either direction.

The detachment inflicted severe casualties on the enemy retiring to their secondary positions throughout the day but they were eventually surrounded and captured during the evening but were able to escape on the following morning during the advance of the Australian Brigade.
Recommended for M.M. (*L.G. 21.10.41*)

Thackray, Frederick, Lance Sergeant
4346494, 5th Bn. The East Yorkshire Regt. (Leeds 10)
(Immediate)

On 23rd March 1943, two companies of the East Yorkshire Regt. were holding the locality in the Mareth line known as Ksiba Ouest. During the afternoon of 23rd March the enemy attacked the locality with a party of infantry supported by about 10 tanks. The tanks approached to within about 400 yds. of the locality and then subjected the garrison to a very heavy and continuous bombardment with 88mm and A/Tk. guns and machine guns. Under cover of this bombardment three of the enemy infantry managed to effect an entry into the Southern end of the locality which was held by 'B' Coy. 5th East Yorks. and penetrated 50 yds. inside the locality. They then occupied a slit trench and opened fire on 'B' Coy. with machine gun fire—they also used grenades and were effectively covered by fire from their tanks. L/Sgt. Thackray who was commanding No. 11 Pl climbed out of his Pl locality and accompanied only by 4341644 Pte. Smith G. he charged the enemy and drove them completely out of the locality, wounded two of the enemy and captured one machine gun, a machine gun pistol and a quantity of grenades. There is no doubt that the resource and courage shown by L/Sgt. Thackray on this occasion prevented the enemy consolidating and strengthening his position in the locality and prevented our fwd. positions being cut off. Throughout the whole of the action the area was under heavy machine gun fire from the enemy tanks. (*L.G. 17.6.43*)

Thapa, Bhaktabahadur, Colour Sergeant
21135027, 1/6th Gurkha Rifles, Brigade of Gurkhas
For Malaya (*L.G. 21.3.50*)

Thapa, Bhaktabahadur, D.C.M., Colour Sergeant
Bar
21135027, 6th Gurkha Rifles
For Malaya (*L.G. 31.8.51*)

Thapa, Bhimlal, Rfn
21132255, Brigade of Gurkhas
For Malaya (*L.G. 25.7.50*)

Thapa, Pahalsing, Corporal
21134008, 6th Gurkha Rifles
For Malaya (*L.G. 30.3.52*)

Thapa, Pimbahadur, Lance Corporal
21135192, 6th Gurkha Rifles
For Malaya (*L.G. 21.7.53*)

Thapa, Tekgahadur, Sergeant
21145269, 6th Gurkha Rifles
No citation. (*L.G. 31.5.55*)

Thayer, Herbert Hedley, Private
112231, S.A. Irish, Union Defence Force
Whilst Prisoner of War.

Escaped from P.W camp after Italian Armistice and went into hiding in the mountains for some months. In February 1944 he managed to get hold of some arms and ammunition by disarming Fascists at Pacarara and started a Partisan Band which eventually in June 1944 totalled 120 men. Shot up German convoys, captured vehicles, food and clothing, shot Fascist spies and demolished bridges. Also sent 14 Allied ex-P/W through to Allied Lines. Was wounded three times. Eventually joined British Mission on 18th March 1945. Arrived at Naples 25th March 1945.

His keen sense of duty enabled him to make a most valuable contribution to the Allied cause and there is no doubt that, in spite of his rank, he was able to harass the enemy considerably. *(L.G. 5.12.46)*

Theodoulou, Iakovas (Jakovos on AFW 3121), Private
1104, Cyprus Regt., 4th Pioneer Corps
Pte. Theodoulou's company was stationed at Larissa, repairing the road to Tyrnavo, when the Germans advanced. They were moved down to Lamia by lorry, where they entrained for Piraeus. Their train was attacked by German aircraft and they dispersed and marched to Piraeus in small groups. They spent two days at Kokkinia Bridge camp in Piraeus, and were then moved by truck to Nauplia, for embarkation. They stayed two days at Nauplia but no ships came in to take them away, and they were ordered to proceed by truck to Calamata. They reached Asphrohoma, a small village near Calamata, where they waited for embarkation, going into Calamata for that purpose every night. Some British and Australian troops succeeded in embarking, but no Cypriots got away.

On the 28th or 29th April, at about 7 or 8 p.m. German tanks and motorised infantry entered Calamata and attacked the British forces there with machine guns, while Italian submarines shelled them from the sea. Our troops resisted, but one hour later surrendered. The Germans began rounding up our troops and concentrating them outside Calamata near the railway line, for transport to Athens.

Pte. Theodoulou escaped at about midnight to the hills with three friends. The next morning they walked in the direction of Sparta, and reached the village of Tripi near Sparta two days later, where they obtained civilian clothes. From Sparta they walked on in the direction of Athens.

At Tripoli his three companions remained behind with sore feet, and Pte. Theodoulou proceeded alone. On the way he made friends with two Greek soldiers from Kimolos an island of the Cyclades, with whom he reached Corinth, wearing a Greek Army cap, and passing as a Greek soldier. He was held up at the Canal for two days, and then allowed to cross over a pontoon bridge built near the sea shore by the Germans.

After crossing the canal he was put on the train with his two friends and other Greek troops, and taken to Piraeus where he lived seven or eight days with relatives of his two Greek friends.

On the 12th May, Pte. Theodoulou left Pireaus by motor caique with his two friends for Kimolos Island, after obtaining the requisite permits from the German military authorities on which he was described as a native of Kimolos.

On the 16th January, Pte. Theodoulou met the Greek captain and crew of the German auxiliary motor schooner 'Aghios Igannis,' which had arrived at Kimolos Island on its way to Bardia, with A.A. ammunition and explosives, who informed him of their plan to steal the schooner and escape to Alexandria. Pte. Theodoulou was against this plan as he said the Germans would advise their authorities on Crete and recapture them before they could reach safety, and suggested that they should put to sea, throw their two German guards over-board and then steer for Alexandria. This plan was agreed upon, but two members of the crew were afraid of the voyage and were replaced by two seamen from Kimolos.

Before sailing on the 17th January, they got 5 okes of wine and 2 okes of fish and had a big feast together with the two German guards. Pte. Theodoulou says he put cigarette ash into the Germans' wine to increase its potency. They sailed at about midnight, and the German guards were already too dazed to notice that two members of the crew had been changed. About 20/25 miles out they attacked their guards, threw them overboard, and continued their way southward towards Alexandria. When they were passing Cape Sidero, Crete, the German observation posts fired flares at them, and they changed course and slowed down their engine to avoid detection. The next day a strong wind blew them off their course and they finally ran ashore on the Palestine Coast South of Gaza, on the 22nd January at about 15 hours, where they were taken in charge by our authorities.

This private not only showed courage in his undaunted efforts to escape, but it was obviously due to his leadership and daring that the schooner 'Aghios Dannis' reached British territory. He also brought back useful information.
Recommended for M.M. *(L.G. 26.3.42)*

Thom, John Gordon, Warrant Officer Cl. II
2883476, 1st Bn. The London Scottish, Gordon Highlanders (Huntly, Aberdeenshire) (Immediate)
C.S.M. Thom was C.S.M. of 'C' Coy., 1 Lond. Scot., at Il Palazzo 862832, on the morning of 9th September 1944. The Coy. had for two days been heavily shelled, mortared and counter-attacked and on 9th September, after an enemy attack had been repulsed, a large calibre enemy gun was directed at the house occupied by Coy. HQ. Several direct hits knocked the house down and several of the Coy. were buried in the debris. Under continued enemy fire, he rallied the uninjured and set

them to digging their comrades out—at least three men's lives were saved thereby.

His Coy. Comd. was killed when the house was first hit and, in the absence of any other officer, this WO assumed control and personally reorganised the posn. He then conducted a vigorous defence, fearlessly exposing himself and personally leading a sally which drove the enemy back, and held off repeated enemy assaults until ordered to move within the perimeter of the adjacent Coy.

Continuously throughout the three days that the Coy.held the Il Palazzo feature C.S.M. Thom had shown great devotion to duty getting the Coy. organised when in danger of being broken up by the almost continuous shelling. His gallantry was an example to all and helped in no small way in keeping the Coy. together and holding the position.   *(L.G. 8.3.45)*

Thomas, Harry William, Sergeant
VX.3961, Australian Military Forces
No Citation   *(L.G. 30.12.41)*

Thomas, Hugh, Sergeant
4198746, 7th Bn. The Royal Welch Fusiliers
(Llangristulus) (Periodic)
This N.C.O. until wounded on 28th March 1945 after the Rhine crossing has served with his company throughout the NW Europe campaign. On all occasions he has displayed the utmost devotion to duty, while his personal bravery and his refusal to allow any circumstances to interfere with the conduct of operations has always been an inspiration to all who have served with him.

At the village of Fresney in Normandy, this N.C.O. then a L/Cpl., after his company had been pinned down by shell and machine gun fire, led his section through an orchard and although nearly every member of his section became a casualty, he drove out about 15 to 20 of the enemy in panic by firing a Sten gun, in the open from the hip, and enabled his company to secure a footing in the village.

At Valhuon during the move through France, Sjt. Thomas was a member of the leading platoon of a company ordered to carry out an outflanking move to the left of a village. The leading platoon became pinned in the open by an enemy M.G. which opened fire at some 40 yds. range, and inflicted 6 killed and 4 wounded in the platoon. Although lying in the open Sjt. Thomas engaged the post with rifle fire and encouraged the remainder of the platoon to do likewise. As a result the enemy post was silenced and the platoon enabled to move on to its objective. Shortly afterwards the enemy were seen to be withdrawing in considerable haste from the remainder of the village.

During the fighting in the Ardennes the enemy launched a counter-attack on the Bn. The enemy shelling severely wounded the company commander, and there were no officers left. Sjt. Thomas and one other Sjt. took command of the company, and although amn. was short, held the company to its ground, when a withdrawal was ordered, this was conducted in an orderly manner. For his part in this operation, the other Sjt. received the D.C.M.

During the fighting in the Reichswald Forest Sjt. Thomas became A/C.S.M. of his company. During the initial attack on the village of Asper by his company, the two leading platoons became pinned by heavy M.G. and Bazooka fire. Sjt. Thomas took comd. of a group of 2″ mortars. He crawled out under heavy fire some 200 yds. and engaged the enemy with H.E. and smoke so effectively that he enabled both pls to move from the positions in which they had been pinned.

During the subsequent night attack on the same village Sjt. Thomas was again a tower or strength and walked around encouraging each of the pls in turn.

His influence in enabling his company to secure its objective in the confused fighting cannot be over-emphasised.   *(L.G. 24.1.46)*

Thomas, Robert Reginald, Corporal (A/Sgt.)
QX 11632, 2/9 Aust. Inf. Bn. (Immediate)
During action on 18/22nd December 1942 Cape Endaidere Cpl. Thomas showed good leadership and great personal courage. He was always in front of his men and never failed to be first to the objective. His example was not only one to his section but to his platoon and Coy. One particular incident is cited here:— During the action on 18th December his Section came under fire from an enemy M.G. post. Cpl. Thomas charged the post and although slightly wounded in the face by a grenade pressed home his attack killing four of the enemy and capturing the rest.   *(L.G. 22.4.43)*

Thommason, Lorne George, Sergeant
D.77454, HQ 1st Cdn. Army Defence Coy. (RMR). att
Regina Rifle Regt. (Immediate)
On the 6th October 1944 in the area of Moerhuizen, Belgium, the 1st Cdn. Army HQ Defence Coy. (RMR) attached to the 1st Bn. The Regina Rifle Regt. was one of the two assault companies for forming the bridgehead across the Leopold Canal.

Sgt. Thomson was in command of his section crossing the Canal in the leading wave in the face of intense machine gun fire. His platoon was then ordered to move up the Canal bank. His was the leading section. Despite heavy machine gun fire and accurate sniping he moved his section to a forward position where they were pinned down by fire.

Later the section came under command of another company which was holding a pill box. As the Coy. had suffered heavy casualties including most of their officers and N.C.O.'s, Sgt. Thomson took over the task of defending the pill box. For the next 48 hours the enemy attacked again and again. There was much close fighting with grenades but the enemy failed to capture this position.

Throughout this entire battle Sgt. Thomson commanded his section, and later the pill box with coolness and efficiency and complete disregard for his own safety.

By his example, he steadied his men under his command, inspiring confidence by his calmness and devotion to duty and with his small force beat off one counter-attack after another during some of the fiercest fighting that took place in this sector.

Recommended for M.M.   *(L.G. 10.2.45)*

Thompson, Clifford Henry, Sergeant
7911409, 1st Northamptonshire Yeomanry (Kippax, Leeds) (Immediate)
On October 31st 1944 Sgt. Thompson was the Comd. of the leading tank of a coln. consisting of a troop and a platoon of 7 B.W. in Kangaroos, which was ordered to advance from Raamsdonk to Laan. During the advance an enemy SP gun was encountered on the road at very short range, and destroyed by Sgt. Thompson's gunner. In passing the destroyed SP the road gave way and Sgt. Thompson's tank fell four feet into a ditch; as the tank became ditched another enemy SP gun appeared from a side turning immediately in advance of Sgt. Thompson's veh: although the tank was falling at an angle, which subsequently overcame the powered traverse, Sgt. Thompson very quickly put his gunner on to the target and destroyed the SP gun with the first shot. The Tp. Ldr. then came up past the destroyed SP but owing to the bad visibility and the soft condition of the road became ditched himself. Throughout the whole action the area was heavily shelled and swept by fire from Spandaus, and the Tp. Ldr. who dismounted from his tank was killed by Spandau fire; whereupon Sgt. Thompson took charge of the operation from his ditched tank and gave the Sqn. Ldr. a very clear picture of the situation over the wireless. This enabled the C.O. of 7 B.W. to appreciate the situation and successfully send the remainder of the Bn. round an alternative route to Laan. Meanwhile Sgt. Thompson made contact with the platoon Comd. and informed him of the new plan to send the rest of the Bn. to Laan by the alternative route, and that they were to hold on until dark. He ordered the Tp. Cpl. forward to protect the coln. from the front, and continuously kept his Sqn. Ldr. informed of the situation and controlled the tp. over the wireless, and directed the actions of the dehorsed crews who remained with their tanks and fought with Sten guns and grenades. Finally, when ordered to withdraw he collected his crew and mounted on the back of the Tp. Cpl.'s tank; they attempted to advance to join the rest of the Bn. who had by this time successfully reached Laan, but ran into further enemy fire and Sgt. Thompson decided to return by the way he had come; this necessitated the negotiation in the dark of the obstacles made by the destroyed enemy vehs. and ditched tanks. On the way, the tank was fired at by a Bazooka which knocked Sgt. Thompson out, and wounded him. I consider that the coolness and initiative of Sgt. Thompson, and his skilful and inspiring leadership

of the troop after his tp. ldr. had been killed resulted in considerable damage to the enemy (the tp. accounted for three SP guns, three half tracked vehs. mounting 20 cm guns, and a number of Infantry) with correspondingly few casualties among his own troop.

I recommend this N.C.O. for an immediate award of the D.C.M.   *(L.G. 1.3.45)*

Thompson, Frederick, Sergeant (A/W.O.II (C.S.M.))
4455800, 9th Bn. The Durham Light Infantry (Newcastle-on-Tyne) (since killed in action) (Immediate)
C.S.M. Thompson, 'C' Coy. 9 D.L.I. crossed the River Simeto during the daylight attack on the Primosole Bridge on July 17th with Coy. HQ immediately behind the leading platoons. As soon as they set foot on the far bank they were attacked by Germans on all sides. During the hand-to-hand fighting the Coy. Cmdr. disappeared and both Pl. Cmdrs. became casualties. C.S.M. Thompson took charge. He organised the Pls. so that they fought off all efforts of the enemy to overrun his Coy. Finally, realising that they could not hold their ground, he skilfully arranged their withdrawal back across the river so that they suffered the minimum casualties. During the night attack on July 18/19th on the same position C.S.M. Thompson took charge of a portion of his Coy. who became very split up owing to well-hidden enemy strong-points in the vineyards. When dawn came his small party were taking cover with most of Bn. HQ in a ditch only 100 yds. from an enemy strong-point in No Mans Land where they were being shot up badly by both sides. C.S.M. Thompson volunteered to crawl 200 yds. back to get a smoke screen put down. So successful was the smoke screen that all the force got back without further loss. C.S.M. Thompson has at all times shown most distinguished and brave conduct in the field. Always cool, calm and full of zeal, he is an inspiration to the Bn. in battle.
M.I.D. 13.1.44   *(L.G. 21.10.43)*

Thompson, John Francis, Sergeant
1023358, 4th Royal Northumberland Fusiliers, T.A
On 21st May near Amas Sgt. Thompson showed especial gallantry and leadership in successfully organising the withdrawal of his scout car platoon after his platoon Comd. had been killed and his platoon had been attacked by tanks. In subsequent actions he carried out successful patrol and recce duties.   *(L.G. 11.7.40)*

Thompson, Keith Philbrock, Sergeant
K 53228, Seaf. of C., Canadian Infantry Corps (Immediate)
Ref. Map Italy 1/25,000 Sheet 100–1 SW San Giorgio Di Cesena.

During the night 21/22nd October 1944, The Seaforth Highlanders of Canada launched an attack across the Savio River. Bridgehead objectives were taken in the face of stiff opposition. K–53228 Sgt. Thompson was in charge of a Piat group working with 'C' Coy., which was right forward company.

As the Coy. was moving towards positions of consolidation at MR 57881110 it was suddenly counter-attacked by a force consisting of three Mk V Panther tanks, two self-propelled guns and about thirty infantry. Owing to the swollen condition and the steep and slippery banks of the river it had not yet been possible to construct a bridge and our troops were operating without the support of anti-tank guns or tanks. The Coys. position was very precarious and the success of the whole bridgehead operation was therefore threatened.

Sgt. Thompson, disregarding the heavy fire from the enemy tanks and guns, immediately went forward to organize his Piat group to break up the enemy attack. After siting the Piats to cover the approaches, he personally laid and camouflaged a string of mines across the road on which the main enemy armour was operating and took over the Piat position covering it. The leading self-propelled gun ran over these mines and a track was blown off, with the result that the road was completely blocked. An oncoming tank was thus placed in a very vulnerable position and was quickly dealt with by fire from the covering Piats.

As the action developed, Sgt. Thompson, with complete disregard for his own safety, moved across open ground swept by enemy fire, from one Piat position to another, encouraging his men, re-siting the weapons to counter the enemy's moves, and controlling the defence. In the course of this action, one Mk V Panther tank was destroyed, one knocked out and captured and one Volkswagon, one full track self-propelled gun and one half track 75 mm self-propelled gun were destroyed.

Largely through Sgt. Thompson's coolness and tenacity and his ability to coordinate the defensive effort under conditions of grave danger and also to the aggressive spirit to take counter measures which he inspired in his men by his example in knocking out the first vehicle, the counter-attack was broken up. This N.C.O.'s initiative and courage throughout the operation were highly commendable, and were beyond doubt mainly responsible for the preservation of the bridgehead in face of a determined and strongly supported counter-attack.
Recommended for M.M.   *(L.G. 17.2.45)*

Thompson, Leslie, Sergeant
907601, 4th Surrey Regt., Royal Artillery (Gateshead)
On 10th November 1942 whilst firing a forward post the enemy shell fire was of such intensity that he was delayed in four attempts but he persevered and in spite of continuous enemy action completed the work success-fully.

In face of extreme danger and difficulties he was always cheerful, effective and maintained his sections in action.

Whilst carrying out an extremely dangerous reconnaissance he was severely injured on a minefield and his eyes damaged by sandblast to such an extent that he is now totally blind.

At El Alamein the courage, resource and skill of this N.C.O. in the reconnaissance and survey of forward and exposed posts under heavy enemy shell and machine gun fire was a great inspiration to his section who had great confidence in him and respect for his personal courage and ability.   *(L.G. 18.5.43)*

Thompson, Robert Henry, Private (A/Cpl.)
WX 4274, 2/16 Aust. Inf. Bn. (since died)
During the dawn attack on Japanese positions on Gona beach on 1st December 1942, A/Cpl. Thompson showed great courage and bravery under heavy machine gun fire. During the night raiding party on 6/7th December 1942, A/Cpl. Thompson led his section across open ground to within grenade throwing distance of strongly held enemy positions and whilst attacking these posts with grenades he was wounded.

In spite of his wounds and without further supplies of grenades he led his section and endeavoured to storm the Japanese position. A/Cpl. Thompson was again wounded and four of his section were also hit and although it was some time before these four men could be evacuated he waited until they were safely out of the way before he withdrew.

His coolness and bravery were also displayed when he moved out into the open on the night of 1st December 1942 and under heavy fire carried out Cpl. Nicholls who had been badly wounded. Knowing that Lieut. Hill had been wounded also he again moved out and on two further occasions carried out this officer and a Pte. Watts.

By outstanding bravery and leadership during the close of the action and the bitter fighting experienced on the beach, his conduct was exemplary and it is recommended that he be granted the Immediate award of the Distinguished Conduct Medal.   *(L.G. 22.4.43)*

Thompson, Samuel, M.M., Corporal
*5724115, 1st Dorsetshire Regt. (Birmingham) (since
        died of wounds)*
During the assault in the Le Hamel area on 6th June 1944, Cpl. Thompson's section led the advance of the Coy. from the beaches to Asnelles and then on towards Buhot. His leadership in the face of heavy and accurate MG fire was an inspiration to all, he had no thought of danger and was the first into each successive enemy position. When an attack was made by the enemy on the flank of the Coy. whilst it was supporting an attack on Puits D'Herod, Cpl. Thompson immediately moved his section to deal with it and killed, wounded or captured all of them. Throughout the whole action this N.C.O. showed the most courageous and determined leadership without any thought for his own safety.
Recommended for M.M.; M.M. 4.11.43 (L.G. 31.8.44)

Thompson, Thomas Innes, Lance Sergeant
1501076, 4th Bn. Royal Welch Fusiliers (Airdrie)
(Immediate)
On 22nd September 1944 the Bn. was engaged in
attacking the village of Wintelre, which was later proved
to have been held by at least 300 enemy. For two hours
no news could be obtained from an attacking Coy. and
before another attack could be ordered it was essential
to find out whether this Coy. had in fact entered the
village and its general situation. Cpl. Thompson was IC
Carrier Sec. which was ordered to enter the village
regardless of enemy fire and obtain this information. His
section came under heavy MG and Bazooka fire on
reaching the outskirts of the village but continued right
through the village and one mile beyond, all the while
under continuous fire, with the enemy at the same time
attempting to throw grenades into the carriers. Cpl.
Thompson succeeded in locating the position of the
remnants of one platoon of 'B' Coy. which had entered
the village and informed them that another attack was to
be launched shortly after by the Bn. On his return journey
when one Carrier was hit and blown off the road into a
ditch, Cpl. Thompson remained covering the crew as
they removed themselves and their weapons to his
Carrier. Whilst proceeding through the village this Sec.
engaged many parties of the enemy both in the street
and in houses with LMG and Piat fire, inflicting casualties
on them. The success of the whole action was entirely
due to the fine leadership and complete disregard of
danger displayed by Cpl. Thompson and the information
obtained by him greatly assisted the Bn. in their
successful capture of the village a short time later.
(L.G. 1.3.45)

Thompson, Thomas William, Corporal
24114640, Royal Green Jackets
For Northen Ireland   *(L.G. 22.5.72)*

Thompson, Walter Louvain, Corporal of Horse
294997, Life Guards (Immediate)
On 5th September 1944 C. of H. Thompson's Tp. was
ordered to seize and hold a Br. over the R. Dyle at
Louvain. The Tp. encountered heavy fire from houses
and side streets. His Tp. Ldr. ordered C. of H. Thompson
to cross a small Br. to the left of the main Br. in order to
cover a rd. junc. of three roads. C. of H. Thompson found
a hole in the middle of the small Br; under heavy fire he
dismounted from his Armd. Car and pulled a door and
some planks over the hole which enabled his car to cross.
He then held the rd. junc. against the S.S. who made
many attempts to destroy him. Much of the time his
gunner was firing to the front whilst C. of H. Thompson
was firing with his revolver to flank and rear.
  C. of H. Thompson by his coolness and courage was
largely instrumental in enabling his Tp. Ldr. to hold the
Br.
M.B.E. 31.12.60   *(L.G. 1.3.45)*

Thomson, Albert, Warrant Officer Cl. II (C.S.M.)
2210727, 1st Bn. The Gordon Highlanders (Aberdeen)
(Immediate)
This W.O. was C.S.M. of 'C' Coy. which, in order to
reach its objective, had to pass through a heavy barrage
on the 24th October 1942 at the battle of Alamein, and
as a result lost 70% casualties. His fine example of
coolness under these exceptional circumstances and his
shouts of encouragement to his company were an
inspiration to all. Again, while on the objective, he never
ceased to spur on the few that were able to reach it. In
the task of consolidation the manner in which he kept
up his company's morale was marked and also essential,
as the remnants of the company, which consisted of only
24 men of all ranks, was now being heavily shelled. Later,
when the company was running short of ammunition and
three attempts to contact Bn. HQ had failed, Sjt.-Major
Thomson volunteered to his Coy. Comdr. to reach Bn.
HQ and succeeded in spite of the enemy's heavy and
accurate small arms fire as he crossed a thousand yards
of open ground. On arrival he gave a valuable and
detailed report to the Comd. Ofr. and then personally
guided up two carriers which evacuated the wounded
under the Red Cross.
Recommended for M.M.   *(L.G. 18.3.43)*

Thomson, John, Lance Sergeant
3190591, King's Own Scottish Borderers (attd. S.S.T.,
No. 9 Commando) (Southwock, Dumfries)
(Immediate)
Ref Map—Italy 1/25,000 Sheet 158 IV SE
  During the operation carried out by this unit in wadis
in square 8230 on 19th March 1944, this NCO
commanded two bren LMGs. which were sited well
forward of this troop main position. At one stage his
post was attacked by a party of ten Boche, who attacked
from a dominating position and under cover of strong
support from LMGs and rifle grenades. L/Cpl Thomson
was wounded in this attack, and one of his LM Gunners
killed, but he took over this bren himself and his small
force of four men succeeded in driving off the Boche
attack, killing two and wounding several more.
  Later in the day, although still wounded, he and his
other LMG covered the movement of his troop by
holding off a strong Boche counter-attack, which, had it
been successful, would have turned the flank of the whole
unit position.
  Throughout the entire action, Thomson was unable
to move from his position owing to accurate enemy
sniping which inflicted heavy casualties on the rest of
his troop and after he was wounded he refused to allow
attempts to be made to evacuate him owing to the danger
to the stretcher-bearers. In spite of his wound and
although being under continuous rifle, LMG and grenade
fire, he maintained his two LMGs in position in a most
determined manner, and it was entirely due to his
complete control of the situation while giving covering
fire to his troop that it was able to take up new positions,

which in turn covered the successful withdrawal of the whole force.

Throughout the action this NCO displayed a remarkably high standard of leadership, and his personal courage, determination and disregard for his wound set a magnificent example to all ranks.   *(L.G. 20.7.44)*

Thomson, Richard Heywood, Sergeant
5599, 39 (N.Z.) M.T. Coy., New Zealand Military Forces

This N.C.O. was in charge of troop carrying transport which conveyed 'B' Coy. Raj Rif. in the advance to attack Tu[...] East on 9th December 1940 when an enemy counter-attack suddenly developed on the flank. He showed the greatest disregard for danger and calmly moved his M.T. through a hail of M.G. bullets until ordered to stop for the troops to [...]. After this, he attached himself to a Bren gun section which attacked and forced to surrender an enemy det. of Light Machine Gunners. His example was an inspiration for the section throughout the operations.

M.I.D. 6.6.46   *(L.G. 25.4.41)*

Thomson, Robert Hair, Warrant Officer Cl. II
2694494, 1st Bn. Scots Guards (Kilmarnock) (Periodic)

For outstanding gallantry and devotion to duty throughout the Italian campaign.

C.S.M. Thomson has been C.S.M. of Left Flank (Coy.) since August 1944 having previously served as a Platoon Sergeant in the company.

During the final phase of the campaign from 1st April 1945 his company carried out five major operations in all of which he played a most distinguished part. At Porto Baribaldi and subsequently at the Fosso Marina his company provided the carrying parties and rowers in river crossing operations. Under extremely heavy shelling and small arms fire he organised these parties and by his complete disregard of danger and personal supervision was largely responsible for the completion of the operations in question. Later at the Canale Bianca on the approaches to the River Po, his company was heavily counter-attacked from both flanks by night and his Company Comdr. and the majority of Coy. HQ were taken prisoner. Knowing the intention of the Coy. Comdr. he succeeded in withdrawing the company with minimum casualties, and reorganised them behind the next canal. During this action, setting a superb example of self-confidence and leadership, he had an especially steadying influence on the company and was entirely responsible for the maintenance of control at a time when communications no longer existed.

In Jan–Feb 1944 on the R. Garigliano as Platoon Sergeant he assumed command of his platoon when the platoon commander was wounded and remained in command for about three weeks. During this time he carried out a number of difficult patrols most successfully. Subsequent he was in action on the R. Sangro and

throughout the advance from Rome to Florence, during most of which time he again commanded a platoon with great distinction. Having been appointed C.S.M., he took part in the company's attack on Monte Catarelto in October 1944 where his superb disregard of danger and fine fighting spirit were largely instrumental in driving off the bitter counter-attacks by troops of 16 S.S. Division.

This W.O. is now the only remaining man in the company who came overseas with it, and has never missed one single day's duty either in or out of the line. He has been an inspiration to his men in every action in which he has fought and through his fearless courage, acknowledged by all, has had a most marked effect on everyone who has fought with him.

M.I.D. 29.11.45 & 7.1.49, M.B.E. 31.12.61
(L.G. 13.12.45)

Thomson, William, Private (A/Cpl.)
3194543, 6th King's Own Scottish Borderers (Galashiels) (Immediate)

During the assault crossing of the Escaut Canal and the formation of the bridgehead North of Gheel on 17th September 1944, this N.C.O. was attached to one of the forward Coys. in the capacity of a Sniper. He was sited on the roof of a house occupied by the foremost section of the forward platoon. During the afternoon of 17th September, from his advantageous but exposed position he successfully accounted for a number of the enemy by his accurate sniping, in spite of heavy machine gun and mortar fire to which he was exposed. In the evening the position was attacked by a determined enemy force in some numbers, preceded by an intense arty concentration and heavy mortar fire. Throughout the attack L/Cpl. Thomson remained at his post and continued to snipe at the advancing enemy whenever a target offered itself. By his accurate shooting he inflicted many casualties and caused considerable confusion in the enemy ranks. Eventually, owing to the weight of the enemy attack, the position became untenable and the house in which this N.C.O. was situated was overran. Immediately prior to the enemy entering the house, the forward section which was occupying it was ordered to withdraw a short distance and did so. L/Cpl. Thomson however refused to leave his post and remained with one other sniper on the roof of the house throughout the entire night. The enemy occupied and surrounded the house and throughout the night made several determined efforts to dislodge the two snipers from the roof, but on all occasions failed to do so. During this period of close fighting L/Cpl. Thomson continued to cause casualties to the enemy from his position on the roof.

The following morning the house was still in enemy hands but a counter-attack from another Coy. eventually retook it and liberated the two snipers. The defence of the house was reorganised and L/Cpl. Thomson remained at his sniper's post on the roof for a further two days until his unit was relieved.

Throughout the whole engagement L/Cpl. Thomson displayed great coolness, courage and resolution.

His determination to hold his post at all costs though completely isolated enabled the counter-attack the next day to succeed. The recapture of this position was vital to the restoration of the unfavourable situation which at one time threatened the security of the entire bridgehead. *Recommended for M.M. M.I.D. 22.3.45* *(L.G. 1.3.45)*

Thorn, Charlton, Sergeant
VX14574, 2/5 Aust. Inf. Bn. (Immediate)
On the morning of 23rd February 1945, Sjt. Thorn's company was attacked for 4 hours by a determined enemy force of approx. 120. During the attack he volunteered to lead a fighting patrol to distract the enemy. With great determination and leadership he led his patrol from a flank into the midst of the attacking enemy inflicting heavy casualties and destroying L.M.G.s.

Held up by heavy fire, he moved his patrol around behind the enemy position from where he attacked the rear. He fiercely pressed home his attack despite heavy enemy fire and forced the enemy to break contact and withdraw hastily. This restored the L. of C. to his company.

Sjt. Thorn's outstanding personal gallantry, his complete disregard for his own personal safety and his cool and determined leadership were the deciding factors in the success of this operation. *(L.G. 21.6.45)*

Thornely, John Brandreth Cresswell, Sergeant
4535917, 2nd Bn. The West Yorkshire Regt. (Helsby, Warrington) (Immediate)
Operations at Cheren 15/29th March 1941.

This N.C.O. commanded a platoon which was sent forward to exploit and reconnoitre in front of the Fort on Mount Dologorodoc, immediately after it had been taken, on the morning of 16.3.41. The platoon had to cross open ground and came under severe fire. With seven casualties and though continuously subject to this fire he maintained the platoon in its position until ordered to withdraw. The withdrawal was carried out successfully under fire despite the presence of seven wounded. Sgt. Thornely personally carried one wounded man back across open country under enemy fire.

He set a fine example of coolness and efficiency during the rest of the operations, especially under shell-fire and in the repulse of counter-attacks.
M.B.E. 29.6.44 *(L.G. 18.7.41)*

Thornton, H. A., Sergeant
2026277, 213 Field Coy. Royal Engineers
On the 5th June 1940 he was in charge of a demolition party at Eu, faced with a strong approaching enemy force who were attempting to rush the position. With great coolness and presence of mind Sgt. Thornton cut down the length of safety fuse to a few inches and fired the charge at great personal danger to himself.

By this means the enemy, supported by motorised units, were unable to advance into the town and a serious situation was thereby relieved. *(L.G. 18.10.40)*

Thornton, Henry Albert, Sergeant
5951003, 1st Oxfordshire & Buckinghamshire Light Infantry (Wallasey) (Immediate)
On the night of 16th February 1945, 'B' Coy. 43rd Lt. Infty. were ordered to capture a group of farmhouses at 901476, to the East of the Reichswald and known to be held by the enemy. The objectives were quickly gained after a short sharp fight. While the company was reorganising on the objective, however, a party of Germans with three Spandaus established themselves about fifty to sixty yards from the objective, and opening fire caused casualties.

Sjt. Thornton—the platoon sjt. of No. 11 Platoon—seeing that this development was hampering the reorganisation of the Coy., immediately and alone, charged the enemy position firing his sub-machine gun and throwing hand grenades. He killed four Germans and captured two; the remainder fled leaving the three Spandaus on the field.

Sjt. Thornton by his prompt and courageous action prevented what might well have been a dangerous infiltration and certainly stopped many casualties being caused to his company; his conduct in this successful action resulting in the capture of over thirty prisoners, was throughout an inspiration to his men, and he behaved according to the high traditions of the N.C.O.'s of the Regt. *(L.G. 10.5.45)*

Threlfall, James, Conductor
3850338, Indian Army Corps of Clerks, 10 Ind. Inf. Bde.,
(Periodic)
On 5th June 1942 Conductor Threlfall was taken prisoner when Bde. HQ position was attacked by a strong force of tanks and lorried inf. After remaining for three days in enemy hands, he succeeded in escaping from Temimi by replacing the sanitary orderly who was employed in cleaning latrines some distance away from the P/W Cage, and taking cover in nearby marshes when the coast was clear. This was after several unsuccessful attempts to escape. Shortly after making his escape Condr. Threlfall found an Italian tunic. This he put to good use on several occasions; once when obliged to cross an enemy camp within speaking distance of groups of German soldiers and a second time when challenged by a German sentry, he replied in Italian. Condr. Threlfall finally reached the sea opposite the Gazala position and decided to swim across the bay which was at this point about three miles wide. He started to swim, taking his direction from a star but losing direction found he was going out to the open sea. He finally reached the S. African lines after some nine hours continuous swimming. He was taken to the G.O.C. 1 S.A. Div. to whom he gave full details of the German positions across the bay. This information

proved most valuable as the positions had been a source of trouble for some days and had been responsible for the loss of several patrols. Condr. Threlfall's escape is a splendid example of initiative, resource, courage and powers of endurance. His successful escape has demonstrated what can be done by a determined man who is imbued with the will to be free, and has always kept himself in magnificent physical condition. His achievement has been a fine example of devotion to duty to all ranks of this Bde.
Recommended for M.M. M.B.E. 31.5.55
(*L.G. 18.2.43*)

Thrussel, Kenneth, Sergeant
5381660, Oxfordshire & Buckinghamshire Light Infantry (Aylesbury)
145 Inf. Bde. P.O.W. Pool   (*L.G. 25.10.45*)

Tifineni, Kennedy, W.O., Platoon Commander
DN 24368, Northern Rhodesia Regt.
No citation.   (*L.G. 30.10.56*)

Tiller, William Leslie, Sergeant
VX 4026, 2/5th Aust. Inf. Bn. (since killed in action)
(Immediate)
For inspiring courage and resolute leadership: Sgt. Tiller was acting platoon commander of 7 Platoon during 'A' Coy. attack on Mt. Tambu on 16th July 1943. He led his platoon up a steep, heavily defended razorback spur under extremely heavy fire. Time and time again when his platoon was pinned down he urged them forward, showing a complete disregard of personal safety, and overran the enemy stronghold. His courage and initiative were an inspiration to his men.

When a Bren gunner was killed, Sgt. Tiller went seventy yards forward, alone, and wiped out the enemy gun crew with rifle fire. During heavy counter attacks at night, Sgt. Tiller moved from post to post encouraging his men and attending to wounded under mortar and small arms fire.

From before dawn until 1630 hrs on 19th July the enemy again attacked Tiller's positions in strength. The attack was almost continuous and at a most critical stage when ammunition was short, Tiller rose from his position and advanced towards the enemy throwing grenades and inflicted such casualties that the enemy was forced to withdraw.

His courage and extreme steadiness during the whole operations was a major factor in the capture and consolidation of the essential ground on the Mt. Tambu feature.
M.I.D. 30.12.41   (*L.G. 4.11.43*)

Tilley, Russell Frederick, Sergeant
552600, 2 Wing, Glider Pilot Regt., Army Air Corps
During the operations near Arnhem this N.C.O. was attached to the K.O.S.B. and distinguished himself throughout by his personal gallantry, initiative and

unflagging cheerfulness under the most trying conditions. On 20th September, when the M.O. and part of his staff were captured, Sgt. Tilley attached himself to the R.A.P. where he did sterling work in attending to the comfort and moral well-being of the wounded, many of whom he himself brought in under fire. When the R.A.P. was hit and set on fire he saved several lives by his coolness in organising the evacuation of the wounded. Later, when the medical staff had been reinforced and when casualties had decimated for HQ, he voluntarily assumed the duties of R.S.M. In this capacity he maintained the supply of ammunition, making numerous hazardous journeys to forward positions to do so. When rations ran out he organised a central kitchen from which he produced, out of the products of the country, a hot meal for every man daily. In addition to these activities, he volunteered whenever there was dangerous work to be done, and was constantly on anti-sniper patrols in and about the Bn. area.

On one of these, on 23rd September, he discovered an enemy post, on which he immediately organised and led an attack as a result of which six enemy were captured and many killed. This N.C.O.'s enthusiasm, complete disregard for personal safety and confident bearing had the most marked effect on all ranks of the Bn. and his conduct throughout the battle was in accordance with the highest traditions of the British Army.
(*L.G. 9.11.44*)

Tilling, Archibald, Lance Sergeant
6397485, 7th Royal Sussex Regt.
Prior to Capture.
On the 19th May the 7/R Sussex were travelled by train to Abbeville, when they were bombed just outside Amiens, and were ordered to take up defensive positions. They remained here during the night.
Capture.
On the morning of the 20th May, the Germans increased their attack and Tilling was hit in the thigh. In spite of this he continued for some time to fire on a machine gun post, and eventually managed to crawl to the temporary field dressing station, where stretcher bearers were attending to the wounded. About an hour later the station was surrounded by German tanks and a German officer demanded their surrender. As all ammunition was exhausted, those of the wounded that could walk out did so. All stragglers were rounded up by armoured vehicles and collected at the dressing station.

The Germans were heavily armed and adopted a menacing attitude throughout the interrogation on Unit, Bde., Div. and strength of Army. Questions were also put on the armament of the R.A.F.

About 40 P/W were put into tanks or armoured vehicles and 4 wounded (of which Tilling was one) were left under armed guard at the field dressing station. During this time there was no medical attention, food or water.

Escape.

That night Tilling discussed escaping with another P/W, but the latter decided against it. Tilling, who was determined to escape, eluded the guard, crawled down the road in a ditch and eventually found an abandoned bicycle, on which he freewheeled for about 2 miles into the next village. On reaching the village he fainted and was picked up by two villagers, who put him in a hand cart at first and then into a car and drove him to Beauvais to the French hospital.

On the 23rd May Tilling was taken from Beavais to Paris by a French ambulance and admitted to the Bichet hospital. On the same day, he was evacuated to a French Military hospital Franco-Hussulman—at Bobigny (Seine) and remained at this hospital until the 13th June. During this period he was operated upon and the bullet in his thigh extracted.

On the 13th June he was evacuated to Clermont Ferrand in an ambulance train and put into a large school which was being used as a hospital. During the time he spent there, he was disguised as a French soldier and was moved from hospital to hospital in order not to come under suspicion.

From here he was sent to a convalescent home at Gravanche about 5 kms. from Clermont Ferrand. At Gravanche there was a large aerodrome. From here he was sent back to Clermont Ferrand to another hospital— Hospital St. Hilaire—where he tried to persuade the M.O. in charge to discharge him but was not successful.

On the 9th August, with the help of an Irish nurse, he managed to persuade the M.O. to discharge him and was given a railway warrant to Marseilles. When he reached Marseilles he went to the American Consul and was passed on to the Annexe which was the unofficial British Consulate, after a period he was interned in Fort St. Jean.

During his internment, a scheme was in progress, whereby British soldiers should become Poles, be given Polish passports and obtain visas for Portugal and Spain. The plan however fell through.

In the Fort he contacted C.S.M. Moir and with him, they approached a man, giving him 1,000 frs. for a passage to Oran. When the time came for them to board the ship, the captain asked them for a further sum of money, which they were unable to give, so they had to come off the French troop carrier. However, they managed to get back 500 frs. of the 1,000 they had paid originally.

After this, they returned to the Poles again, who by then had another scheme and had managed to obtain a boat—S.S. 'Storm'—but after waiting about ten days on board ship, they heard that the scheme had fallen through, as the Poles were unable to obtain permission for the boat to leave the harbour.

Tilling then decided to try and get to Spain, so took the train to Perpignan and walked over the mountains near Le Perthus. In Spain he travelled at night by side roads and passed through Figueras and on to Gerona.

Just outside Gerona, he was arrested by the Guardia Civil and asked for papers, when he produced the British Emergency Certificate given to him by the American Consul at Marseilles. He was then taken to the Police Station and from there put into prison. He was then removed to Figueras where he remained for ten days.

His next prison was Castillo in Figueras where he remained for a week. From Castillo he was transferred to the concentration camp at Cevera for ten days and then sent on to Miranda Del Ebro, where he remained until he was released and sent to Gibraltar via Madrid.

Conditions of Spanish Concentration Camps.

At Figueras, internees slept on the floor and had one blanket between two. Food consisted of potatoes and soya beans with gravy. On Sundays instead of beans they were given cabbage.

At Castillo, the food was better. Here one of the internees escaped so the 80 internees were put into a small room about 15ft square and were not allowed downstairs, except at meal times, as the guards refused to bring food up to them.

At Cevera they slept on palliasses, were given blankets, and the food was more varied.

At Miranda Del Ebro many of the internees suffered from stomach trouble on account of the amount of potato which formed their diet.

On account of bad sanitation, no proper facilities for washing and bathing, they became very lousy.

At some camps, there was a great deal of bullying and at one time an Englishman, a mercantile marine, was very roughly-handled. *(L.G. 7.3.41)*

Tindall, Philip Joseph, Corporal
14339326, 18th London Regt. (1st Bn. London Irish Rifles) (Scarborough) (Immediate)
On 26th December 1944, at Bisaura near Faenza, Cpl. Tindall displayed a devotion to duty and aggressive courage beyond praise. His platoon had made a successful night attack on a group of houses and was immediately counter-attacked by a stronger enemy force, which infiltrated right among the farm buildings, firing at the house on 3 sides with MGs and endeavouring to knock it down with a 'Bazooka.' In this situation Cpl. Tindall showed a spirit which inspired his whole Platoon. During 3 hours of continual fighting, during which his Pl Comd. was killed, he handled his section with such energy, dashing from post to post, encouraging his men and directing their fire, that the enemy was continually beaten off: he himself used grenades and TMC to great effect, killing two enemy: twice with no thought for danger he dashed out of the house himself and cleared the enemy from the outbuildings. *(L.G. 21.6.45)*

Tirrell, Thomas Joseph, Warrant Officer Cl. II (B.S.M.)
4743421, 2 R.H.A., Royal Artillery
Did outstanding work as G.P.O. of 'L' Troop throughout the three weeks. Showed great courage in the Mont Des Cats, May 29th. Continuing to control the fire of a gun

under heavy and accurate fire. After all the detachment had been wounded, went on to the f[...] himself and continued to fire.

M.C. 18.2.43, Bar to M.C. 25.2.43, 2nd Bar to M.C. 12.4.45, M.I.D. 10.5.45   *(L.G. 27.8.40)*

Todhunter, Tom, Sergeant
3591528, Loyal Regt. (Whitehaven)

Sjt. Todhunter has served with this Bn. in action throughout the North African and Italian campaigns. During the Anzio beachhead campaign he served with great gallantry and distinction as a sec. comd. During the break-out to Rome and the capture of Florence he again distinguished himself as a platoon Sjt.

The following is an example of the many acts of gallantry in which he took part:—

On 25th August 1944 Sjt. Todhunter was platoon serjeant of a platoon sent out on a long distance patrol with the task of reaching the summit of Monte Ceceri. This feature is 400 metres high and is the dominating point of the Fiesole Ridge which overlooks Florence from the NE. It was of the utmost importance to find out whether the enemy still held this ridge. The patrol reached its objective and finding an enemy Spandau post, assaulted and wiped out the entire section, and gained a footing on one end of the ridge.

Sjt. Todhunter was in the van of the assault, killing several of the enemy with Tommy gun and grenades.

The enemy however were found to be in considerable strength and the patrol was ordered to withdraw.

The patrol reached the foot of the ridge successfully but was then caught by very heavy mortar fire and suffered 19 casualties.

Sjt. Todhunter was severely wounded in the abdomen, but although in very great pain, he assisted the platoon commander to render first aid to the other wounded.

He cheered and encouraged the men and despite his severe and painful wound personally helped to carry several men to shelter.

Not until all had been attended to would he allow his own wounds to be dressed.

His superb courage and devotion to duty were an inspiration to all.

Sjt. Todhunter recovered from his wounds, rejoined the Bn. in the autumn in the mountains of the Gothic Line and fought on with the same high courage, showing inspiring leadership and devotion to duty, until the Bn. was withdrawn from the theatre in January 1945.

(L.G. 13.12.45)

Tolley, Barry, Warrant Officer Cl. II (temp.)
53714, Royal Australian Infantry Corps

No citation.   *(L.G. 19.9.69)*

Tomany, James Eugene, Sergeant
3243004, 2nd Bn. The Cameronians

This N.C.O. commanded a section of Carriers throughout the period 11th to 31st May 1940.

On several occasions he displayed exceptional courage and powers of leadership.

In particular at Houthem on the 27th May 1940 he twice found the enemy working round his flanks. By his quick appreciation of the situation he undoubtedly saved many men of the Bn. from becoming casualties and he is known to have inflicted at least 50 casualties on the enemy.

His coolness and disregard of danger were a fine example to all who came in contact with him.

(L.G. 27.8.40)

Tomlinson, James Robert, Lance Corporal
4268833, 6th Bn. Argyll & Sutherland Highlanders
Webb, A. J., L/Cpl
2734077, 2nd Bn. Welsh Guards.
Tomlinson, J. R.
Account of escape.

I was alone on motor cycle patrol, making my way back to the quayside when I was captured at Boulogne on 3rd June. I was marched to Cambrai and worked for some weeks unloading food and ammunition.

I and others were captured in a farmhouse on 27th May at Bethine and then marched to Cambrai where we worked for some weeks unloading food and ammunition.

We were then put on the train with other P/W in closed cattle trucks, spent 2 days at Trier, Luxembourg, and were then sent to Thorn, Fort 13. The hospital is in the German Barracks nearby. From there we went to the working camp at Winduga, arriving on 21st July. We were not searched or interrogated. The Camp Leader was T.S.M. Briggs, appointed by seniority. (Camp conditions etc., are described in Briggs' report).

We were told that German troops were in England, and that the war would be over in September. The morale of the P/W was very good. The guards were not bribable. There was unrest among the older German soldiers who were fed up with the war, their wives complaining of shortage of food. But the young soldiers were full of confidence. We were made to work. We both escaped together on the night of 2nd August. The sentries had had no pay for a long time and were then suddenly given pay and all got drunk. We hid in the cookhouse where Webb was working, and about 12 o'clock got through the window and dodged the patrols, and got through the barbed wire into another unfinished compound where there was only wire in places.

We were in battle-dress uniform and had no food. We got down to the river and took a rowing boat and crossed to the other side. We walked all night intending to make South. At dawn we took a chance and went to a Polish house. Some Polish workmen in the camp had told us that the Poles would help us.

We were welcomed and given hot food and a complete change of clothing. The following night we set out intending to make for Rumania. After 3 days we decided to travel by day as we lost our way at night. We passed German troops but they never bothered about us.

The Poles had told us that we must raise our hats (this is important) and say 'Heil Hitler.'

After 12 days we were told that the Germans had occupied Rumania, and we decided to go East to Russia. We always got help from the Poles. Sometimes we met Poles who had been in America; otherwise we said 'Engelshe Soldat' and though at first doubtful they would become convinced that we were English. We eventually called at the house of a rich Polish captain, near Sochnezew, whose wife and sister spoke fluent English. They wanted us to stay there for the rest of the war. They would not give names. German officers used to visit the house. He sent us by train to Warsaw. There were no difficulties. Passports are not required in the Protectorate area. We followed the Polish family's servant and led us through Warsaw to the Radzeimedz road, where we left her. Very little damage had been done to the city.

The Captain had given Webb a new 'plus four' suit, and he played the part of a gentleman farmer and Tomlinson that of an agricultural worker, carrying the pack of food. The reason for this pretence was that it was harvest day. We had also been given money.

Outside Wyszkow we crossed the Bug by ferry. The ferryman was suspicious and we had to pay him well. There were plenty of German soldiers about.

We crossed the border into Russia on 22nd August, 3 kms. South of Ostrow. There were no German but plenty of Russian sentries with dogs, and we were taken by about 15 of them. Webb was kicked and beaten because he could not understand something they said. They made us lie down while they searched us, and everything was taken from us.

We were then taken, handcuffed, by 4 guards by train to Bailystow. We were asked every conceivable question on personal and military subjects—on the latter we were dumb. We were here for 14 days. Food and conditions were abominable. We were 120 in a small room—Poles, Germans, Russians and Jews. Four times we were searched, and had to strip naked in view of everyone—women included.

We were then sent to Moscow where we were put in the Luvianko Prison. We were in separate cells and did not see another at all. Webb went on food strike for 5 days in an attempt to see the Ambassador. They constantly asked us 3 questions (i) Who sent us?, (ii) Where did he send us to?, and, (iii) What for?

Eventually we were taken to another prison in Moscow where we met again, and also met Doyle, Massey and Corkney, and 3 Englishmen who had volunteered to fight for the Finns in September 1940. They had been in a Russian prison ever since. We left them there. Their names are Harold Watkins (a Dental Mechanic) and Frank Baxter (an ex Naval man). We were there until the Germans invaded Russia, when we were put on a train to go to Siberia. The train was halted and the British taken off. We were then sent to a hotel outside Moscow where we stayed for 12 days before being handed over to our Embassy on 8th July 1941.

(L.G. 4.11.41)

Toole, John Lawrence, Sergeant
2656974, 3rd Bn. Coldstream Guards
Matruh Fortress.

On 9th December 1940 Sgt. Toole was leading a section of the Carrier Platoon in the advance on Maktilla Camp. In order to obtain information he took his section across the main Barrani road to an O.P. quite close to and under heavy fire of all arms from the camp. He returned safely with the information required.

On 10th December when a patrol he was on ran into a very strong enemy position 7 Km. S.E. of Barrani and was ordered to withdraw Sgt. Toole's Carrier had a petrol stoppage. He succeeded in remedying this although under heavy fire from three sides. On 11th December in the main attack on the Camps East of Barrani the Carriers were pushed forward ahead of the Tanks and arrived on the 2nd objective alone where they tried to hold the enemy. When one Carrier was seen going back to report the enemy opened very heavy fire at close range. Sgt. Toole effected a most difficult withdrawal with the loss of only one man. His task was rendered more difficult by the fact that none of his L.M.G.s would fire owing to the sandstorm. The sense of duty, leadership and courage shown by this N.C.O. throughout the entire operation was of a very high order. *(L.G. 25.4.41)*

Tootle, James Gordon, Sergeant
D81688, Royal Canadian Armoured Corps
C.F., N.W.E. *(L.G. 24.1.46)*

Towler, Harold, Private
3655683, 1/4 Bn. Hampshire Regt. (Pendlebury, Swinton)
On 16th September 1943 Pte. Towler was a Coy. Sniper attached to a forward platoon of his Coy. which had been ordered to attack an important and dominating feature in the Salerno bridgehead. The Coy. came under heavy enemy M.M.G. fire and their advance was held up. Pte. Towler went forward alone and with complete disregard for his own safety he calmly and methodically put out of action three of the enemy M.G. posts thus enabling his Coy. to resume their advance.

At 0130 hrs., 17th September Pte. Towler was one of six men attached to another Coy. which attacked another enemy position. The Coy. came under heavy machine gun fire and though wounded himself Pte. Towler went forward and neutralised the enemy posts with hand grenades, causing great confusion and enabling the Coy. to secure the objective. Throughout this day and night action his personal courage and disregard of personal injury was an example to all ranks. *(L.G. 13.1.44)*

Townsend, George Eugene Atherton, Private
6213268, Devonshire Regt. (A/Sjt., 11th Bn. The
Durham L.I. on AFW 3121) (London, N.W.9)
(Immediate)
At Rauray, MR 8865, on 28th June 1944, Pte.
Townsend's platoon came under heavy machine gun fire
whilst attacking the village.

The platoon commander, platoon serjeant and two
section commanders became casualties—Pte. Townsend
took control of the platoon and led onto the objective.
Later certain enemy tried to infiltrate. Pte. Townsend
organised a quick local counter-attack and drove them
back. Throughout this period and later when on the
defensive, this man showed a fine example of leadership
and complete disregard of personal danger.
Recommended for M.M. M.C. 12.4.45 (L.G. 19.10.44)

Townsend, John Franklin, Corporal (A/Sgt.)
L.13235, 8 Cdn. Recce Regt. (14 C.H.) (Immediate)
During a night attack on the 8/9th August 1944, Cpl.
Townsend's troop came under very heavy mortar fire.
The officer and sergeant both were seriously wounded
and Cpl. Townsend took over command. He rallied his
troop and they fought their way right into the enemy
position. He himself cleared three enemy slit trenches
with hand grenades. He then located a friendly tank
which he lead into position in pitch darkness and directed
its fire against an 88mm gun which was firing on the
troop. It was knocked out and Cpl. Townsend took 11
prisoners in the gun position.

Throughout the night and until the end of the action
he remained in command. His initiative and resourcefulness inspired his comrades with absolute confidence
and won their immediate support. His spirited leadership,
courage and determination were an inspiration and an
example to all ranks of the Regiment. *(L.G. 20.1.45)*

Townsend, Melvill Keith, Corporal (now Sergeant)
23722726, Royal Signals
Oman   *(L.G. 20.7.76)*

Tracy, Arthur Herbert, Sergeant
817177, Royal Signals
Calais 1940 (from P.O.W. Pool)   *(L.G. 29.11.45)*

Traynor, George Bisset, Sergeant
2755915 (2755911 on AFW 3121), 6th Black Watch,
T.A
This N.C.O. was the senior N.C.O. of the Carrier Platoon.
During the action of May 2nd, he showed outstanding
gallantry whilst under fire, on one occasion leaving his
Carrier to engage an enemy Tank with his anti-tank rifle,
so successfully that it blew up at the second shot. In the
subsequent actions during the retreat to Dunkirk, this
N.C.O. continued to show great coolness and bravery
when at any time in the presence of the enemy and his
example to the men under his command (the officer i/c

Carrier Platoon having been wounded) was most
inspiring.
Recommended for M.M.   *(L.G. 22.10.40)*

Treeby, Alexander Stuart, Sergeant
2614627, 3rd Grenadier Guards (London, S.W.1)
(since killed in action) (Immediate)
On the night of 18/19th February Sgt. Treeby was in
command of No. 6 Platoon on Pt. 711 when the Germans
launched a Coy. attack, on his position. His platoon bore
the brunt of the attack for a considerable period. During
this time Sgt. Treeby was a continual source of inspiration
to his platoon, encouraging them and cheering them on
all the time, besides killing four Germans himself. His
whole platoon speak in glowing terms of his leadership
and example.

It was subsequently discovered that 40 Germans lay
dead in front of his platoon position.

For outstanding leadership and personal devotion to
duty I recommend that he be given an immediate award
of the D.C.M.   *(L.G. 29.6.44)*

Trevis, William Frederick, Bombardier (A/Sgt.)
1126866, 179 Field Regt. Royal Artillery (Hoddesdon,
Herts.)
On 9th July 1944 this N.C.O. was acting as O.P.A. to
Major Mapp who was commanding the battery in direct
support of the infantry at Chateau de Fontaigne.

Major Mapp was killed in the morning and both O.P.s
were deployed and pinned to the ground.

Bdr. Trevis at Bn. HQ then took command and
assumed the Major's responsibilities, co-ordinated the
work of the O.P.s and brought down fire wherever
required by the Bn.

The officer who crawled up from the gun area to
relieve him was wounded and it was not until 2000 hrs
that another officer could be made available.

Bdr. Trevis therefore commanded the battery for a
period of 12 hours for the greater part of which he was
under enemy mortar and shell fire. During this period it
was entirely due to his efforts that the artillery support
for the Bn. did not fail; and the information he passed
continuously to the Regt. was of immediate value to the
Divisional Artillery and to 214 Inf. Bde.

He did a job which would have been a credit to any
Battery Commander.   *(L.G. 21.12.44)*

Trewby, Norman, Sergeant
9217, 23 N.Z. Bn.
On 11th December 1941 when his Company attacked
very strong enemy positions on a ridge East of the Gazala
defences and after his officers had been wounded Sgt.
Trewby who was acting C.S.M. immediately took control
of two platoons of the Company. In face of very heavy
artillery, mortar and machine gun fire he reorganised
these platoons, allotted fresh positions and was
personally responsible for the beating off of a strong
enemy counter-attack.

His personal courage and coolness in face of danger was an inspiration to the men under his command. His actions were largely responsible for the defeat and destruction of a force overwhelmingly superior in numbers and proved to be the beginning of complete enemy withdrawal in that sector. *(L.G. 24.2.42)*

Trollip, Neville Oliver, Private
592092V, Royal Durban Light Inf. (Immediate)
For outstanding initiative, devotion to duty and personal courage of the highest order.

On the morning 25th April 1945, when R.D.L.I. had established a firm bridgehead with two rifle Coys. over the river Po, at MR 885053, acting on instructions to patrol forward, both Coys. sent out fighting patrols. One of these under Sgt. C. C. Buckley was briefed to proceed to Ca Zaghi MR 901065. The terrain was a very flat plain, fairly close country, with winding roads flanked on each side by drainage canals of approximately 3 feet wide and 5 feet deep. After advancing 200 yards across the open towards one of these roads, the patrol was fired on by the enemy. They were using MGs and automatic rifles from positions sited in one of these canals, and the patrol leader was instantly killed. The remainder of the patrol headed and urged on by Pte. Trollip, dashed for the canal where Pte. Trollip personally killed two enemy armed with a Spandau M.G. There was a bend in the canal and led by Pte. Trollip the patrol then began to advance along in single file. At the bend they were fired on at very close range and Pte. Trollip with aggressive determination stalked forward and positioned himself so as to enable him to kill three enemy with his rifle. At this stage the patrol was being fired on from the opposite side of the road as well. Two of our infantry, disengaged themselves from the rear of the patrol and attempted to work around to the right flank. Under cover of this diversion, without hesitation and with total disregard of his own personal safety Pte. Trollip leapt out of the ditch across the road and into the enemy trench bayonetting two, and causing the remainder to abandon their position and run away. Pte. Trollip immediately engaged them with his rifle killing a further two Germans and shouting to the retreating four to surrender.

Throughout the action he displayed a degree of leadership and devotion to duty far in excess of his rank. By his total disregard for his own personal safety, his brilliant initiative, his dogged determination and aggressiveness and by his fearless courage, Pte. Trollip personally accounted for nine enemy killed and four taken prisoner. *(L.G. 23.8.45)*

Troster, Albert George, M.M., Colour Sergeant (A/W.O.II (C.S.M.))
6093335, 2/6th Bn. The Queen's Royal Regt. (Dagenham) (Immediate)
On the morning of 23rd February 1944, 'C' Coy 2/6 Queen's was heavily attacked on their left flank. The Coy. Comd. was wounded and there was no other officer

in the Coy. at the time. C.S.M. Troster immediately took command. He led two hand to hand grenade attacks against the Germans and after about 1/4 hour of confused fighting, had got complete control of the situation. The Germans were finally beaten off with casualties. Throughout this action C.S.M. Troster showed the highest qualities of leadership and his personal courage, initiative and tremendous energy and drive turned an awkward situation into one solely to our advantage. His persistent cheerfulness under arduous and trying conditions were an inspiration to all ranks.
Recommended for M.M. M.M. 20.12.40
(L.G. 15.6.44)

Troughton, John William, Sergeant
3852230, 32 L.A.A. Regt. Royal Artillery (Preston) (Immediate)
This N.C.O. is detachment commander of a Bofors gun overlooking the Grand Harbour. On 24th March 1942 during heavy raids on shipping many bombs fell around his gun, two passing a few feet overhead and hitting Lascaris barracks.

While he was engaging an enemy plane, Sgt. Troughton was knocked out by blast, striking his head against the predictor stand.

After attending the Medical Post near the gun, (where he was told to go to bed), Sgt. Troughton immediately resumed command of his gun and remained at his post for 24 hours, until ordered to leave.

Sgt. Troughton has been in command of this gun detachment during the last three months while the Grand Harbour has been the target for attacks of increasing violence. None of his men had been in action before and by his personal example, leadership and devotion to duty, Sgt. Troughton has welded them into a first class detachment. *(L.G. 13.8.42)*

Tukaki, Ngakete, Lance Corporal (tem. Corporal)
65332, New Zealand Military Forces
No citation. *(L.G. 28.1.43)*

Tulloch, James, Sergeant (A/W.O.II (B.S.M.))
1095068, 19 Medium Battery Royal Artillery (Quetta)
On 25th March 1944 the regiment under my command was ordered to proceed to the Sinzweya 'box' at the East of the Ngakyedauk Pass on account of enemy infiltration to the rear of the position.

The Regiments' move involved passing along a road where the features on each side were strongly held by the enemy. The roads which had been mined, was swept by small arms fire and was subjected to heavy mortaring and shell fire. One tractor with a 5.5 medium gun on tow of 18 Medium Battery R.A. received a direct hit from a mortar bomb and was so severely damaged as to be incapable of continuing, while the gun detachment sustained three casualties.

B.S.M. Tulloch who was travelling on a vehicle in rear immediately took control of the situation and under heavy fire and sustained mortaring directed the unlimbering of the gun from the damaged tractor and organised its removal by another vehicle which was already loaded with ammunition. He personally assisted and arranged for the wounded to be removed and for the remaining members of the gun team to be transported.

The ammunition lorry, with the gun on tow, became the last tractor in the Regimental convoy. Whilst passing down a straight stretch of road enfiladed by enemy automatic fire, the gun ran over a filled in slit trench and was bogged.

B.S.M. Tulloch thereupon organised the further recovery of the gun with the assistance of a nearby tank whilst still under small arms fire. This was successfully accomplished and the gun finally brought into action in its new position.

Throughout, B.S.M. Tulloch showed complete disregard of his personal safety which was an inspiration to those whom he was directing. It was entirely due to his prompt action, sustained courage under fire and complete disregard of danger that the gun and its connected equipment was brought into action in the new position, together with the ammunition lorry.

(L.G. 22.6.44)

Tulloch, Thomas William, Sergeant
35163, 25 N.Z. Bn. (Immediate)
Cassino 15th March 1944.

Sjt. Tulloch was a Platoon Sjt. in 25 N.Z. Bn. during the attack on Cassino on 15th March 1944. During the early part of the attack his Platoon Comd. was wounded and Sjt. Tulloch himself wounded by grenade splinters. He immediately took command of this platoon and personally contacted a nearby tank and organised tank fire support which enabled him and his platoon to overcome the nearest enemy strong point. By this time his total strength was reduced to 12 men and he was beyond the limit of further tank assistance. He reorganised his platoon and with platoon weapons alone assaulted the next enemy strong point about 75 yards away.

He and his platoon were driven back and he was again wounded. He then led the remnants of his platoon round the flank of the strong point where he established them in a strong position. The strong point consisted of a group of strongly fortified houses at the base of Pt. 193. Sjt. Tulloch kept his men aggressively employed against this strong point and by his tactics partially neutralised it. He stayed with his men until ordered by his Coy. Comd. to report to the R.A.P. from which he was evacuated.

Despite the severe casualties suffered by his platoon Sjt. Tulloch, by his aggressive tactics and personal example, so led and encouraged his men as to keep them in the highest spirits.   *(L.G. 3.8.44)*

Turnbull, Allan Frederick, Warrant Officer Cl. II (C.S.M.)
D82922, Canadian Infantry Corps
C.F., N.W.E.   *(L.G. 24.1.46)*

Turner, Geoffrey Trenchard, Sergeant
*1479126, 65th Lt. A.A. Regt. Royal Artillery
   (Liverpool, 18) (Immediate)*
At 1800 hours on 22nd April 1942, this N.C.O. was on leave in Valetta when a heavy raid developed. Learning that bombs had fallen near a Light A.A. gun position causing casualties to a number of the men, he collected three Gunners who were with him and disregarding his own personal safety led his party to the gun position where he found the gun still in action, but most of the detachment wounded. Sgt. Turner ordered the detachment commander, who was wounded, to hand over to him and immediately manned the gun with his men and was able to engage further waves of bombers and remained with the gun in action until relieved two hours later.

Sgt. Turner has at all times shown a very high standard of leadership and great personal courage whilst in command of his own gun detachment which is situated in the defences of an aerodrome.
Recommended for M.M.   *(L.G. 14.7.42)*

Turner, George Penman, Sergeant (A/W.O.II (C.S.M.)
*2750855, 1st Bn. The Black Watch (Etrol, Perthshire)
   (Immediate)*
During the attack on the El Wishka Ridge on night 23/ 24th October 1942, Sjt. Turner displayed a complete disregard for his own safety and led his section twice through very heavy M.G. fire at short range into enemy posts, capturing them on each occasion. By his courage and bravery he set a magnificent example to his men. Nothing could stop him. Later, when his Coy. was reorganizing on its objective, this N.C.O. was sent with a patrol to gain touch with the flanking unit. During the journey, all but one man of his patrol became casualties, but Sjt. Turner completed his task. On the way back to rejoin his Coy. he suddenly came under fire from an enemy headquarters post. He immediately charged this post with the bayonet, accompanied by the only survivor of his patrol, and killed all the occupants.

The N.C.O.'s aggressive spirit and personal bravery on this night and in subsequent operations had a wonderful effect on his platoon, which had never once failed to carry out a task allocated to it, however dangerous or arduous.   *(L.G. 4.5.43)*

Turner, Peter Donaldson, Warrant Officer Cl. II (B.S.M.)
778247, 51st Fld. Regt. Royal Artillery (Whitehaven, Cumberland) (Periodic)
B.S.M. Turner was acting as B.S.M. of 'D' Troop at Gubi on 7th December 1941. When his Troop was coming into action B.S.M. Turner saw a Troop of 88

mm guns coming into action. He immediately took charge and went to one gun and, directing the shoot himself from the gun, he succeeded in knocking out one of the enemy guns and forced the others to withdraw. Later in the day his Troop was under prolonged and continuous heavy shell fire from which it suffered 12 casualties.

B.S.M. Turner, although he had to work in the open under heavy shell fire went to and dressed each casualty as it occurred and personally saw to its evacuation. Throughout the campaign B.S.M. Turner has shown the utmost coolness and determination in action. By his determination and his complete disregard for personal safety he has set an extremely high standard for his Troop to follow. *(L.G. 9.9.42)*

Tuttle, Norman Eugene, Corporal (actg.)
A.50218, Highland Light Inf. of Canada
On the 1st November 1944 A–50218 Cpl. Tuttle was acting as commander of 12 platoon, 'B' Coy., Highland Light In. of Canada. As a result of casualties the platoon was at that time 23 men strong.

The battle of the Lower Scheldt Estuary was nearing its close and the enemy had been forced into a pocket in the area of Heyst, Knock-Sur-Mer and 'Little Tobruk,' the German fortress along the Scheldt East of Knock-Sur-Mer. Ninth Cdn. Inf. Brig. was ordered to clear this pocket.

The H.L.I. of C. was given the task of cleaning up the East end of Knock-Sur-Mer and the 'Little Tobruk' fortress area which would allow the remainder of the Brigade to advance West to take out the balance of the enemy pocket.

'B' Coy. was given the task of attacking 'Little Tobruk,' the rapid capture of which was essential to the success of the battalion battle and the subsequent completion of the brigade task.

'Little Tobruk' was a self-contained fortress. It consisted of mutually supporting concrete and earth work positions situated on the high sand dunes just inland from the sea, and supplemented by normal infantry dug-in positions. The perimeter of the fortress was protected, from the landward side, by a belt of heavy concertina wiring 30 feet in depth and 100 yards of flat open ground, heavily mined.

'B' Coy. advance was held up when 12 platoon, in the lead, came under intense enemy machine gun fire from the fortress. The only approach was across the minefield and the wire, directly through the enemy fire.

A–50218 Cpl. Tuttle, seized the initiative. He sited the Brens of his platoon to provide covering fire and, with only this support and smoke from the 2 inch mortar, he crawled forward through the enemy fire. Using his bayonet to prod for mines he picked a path through the minefield to the barbed wire. The enemy machine guns continued firing through the smoke, the bullets landing throughout the wired area around Cpl. Tuttle.

Completely ignoring the enemy fire Cpl. Tuttle worked for twenty minutes cutting his way through the wire. He then called to his platoon to follow him through the gap. His men inspired by his act rushed through behind him and charged the enemy position. Cpl. Tuttle, in the lead, threw two 36 grenades into the first pill boxes, killing 5 Germans and wounding 12. He then led his platoon through the maze of wire, entrenchments, earthworks and pill boxes to force the surrender of a Lieut. Col., seven other officers and approx. 250 other ranks. The outstanding skill with which he commanded the platoon during this action contributed materially to the ultimate success of the battalion and the brigade operation.

Cpl. Tuttle's complete disregard for his own safety and courageous leadership were an inspiration to his comrades and will remain for all time an outstanding example of the high tradition of valour of the Cdn. Army.
Statement of A.37397 Pte. Berrington.
I was the platoon runner of No. 12 Platoon, 'B' Coy., The Highland Light Inf. of Canada, on 1st November 1944. 'D' Coy. and 'B' Coy. were the two leading companies in the attack against the German strong point we knew as 'Little Tobruk.' We came under extremely heavy fire from pill box positions on high ground. The situation seemed hopeless because the pill box positions were surrounded by thick belts of heavy concertina wire. Our officer and Sgt. had been knocked out and Cpl. Tuttle was in charge of the platoon. He asked us to give him covering fire. He crawled out through the anti-personnel minefields to the wire. He worked for twenty minutes cutting the wire and the bullets were flying all around him. Then he shouted 'Are you with me men,' and we followed him through the gap and charged the first pill box, killing or injuring the Germans who held it. Then we went on through the maze of slit trenches and concrete implacements.
Statement by Major J. C. King.
On the 1st November 1944, during an attack on 'Little Tobruk,' a German fortress East of Knock-Sur-Mer, Cpl. Tuttle was acting as Platoon Commander of No. 12 Platoon in my Coy.
No. 12 Platoon was leading and were forced to ground under heavy enemy fire. Cpl. Tuttle took the situation into his own hands. He placed his Bren guns in position and ordered smoke from the 2″ Mortar. Cpl. Tuttle under cover of this fire then crawled forward to the minefield. He reached his way through the enemy mines using the 'prodding' method, until he came to the thirty feet of barbed wire. All this time he was under enemy machine gun fire, the bullets could be seen landing all about him. For twenty five minutes under this intense fire he cut his way through the barbed wire before the task was finished.

His Platoon, inspired by this act, charged through the gap behind him. Cpl. Tuttle threw grenades into the first pill box killing five Germans and wounding twelve.

Pushing ahead he and his Platoon then forced the surrender of an Oberst Lieut., seven other officers and two hundred and fifty German soldiers.

Statement by B.142303 Pte. Dick

On 1st November 1944, Cpl. Tuttle, N.E. was acting as our Platoon Commander. We were attacking over the dykes and polders towards a series of enemy strong points. When our artillery stopped firing we came under heavy fire from the enemy strongpoints. Our platoon was forward and we were forced to lie in the ditch along the dyke because it was impossible to go any further in the face of such heavy machine gun fire. Cpl. Tuttle ordered the Bren gunners to give him covering fire and told the 2≤ Mortar men to smoke out the enemy position. Cpl. Tuttle then crawled out through the anti personnel minefield to the thick belt of barbed wire which surrounded the German position. He worked for a long time with lead flying around him. Then I heard him shout, 'Are you with me men.' We all rushed out through the gap he made until we reached the dead ground about 15 yards from the first pill box. Cpl. Tuttle then crawled forward and threw a couple No. 36 grenades in through a slit into the German pill box. He threw another one into a second slit and then we went in to clear out the place. I saw five Germans lying there dead and about twelve others were wounded. We then went forward through the network of trenches and concrete pill boxes.

Without Cpl. Tuttle leading the way we would never have been able to take the enemy strong points without a lot of additional support.

Statement by D.139128 Pte. Michailiuk,.

I was a rifleman in No. 2 section, 12 Platoon, 'B' Coy., The Highland Light Inf. of Canada, on 1st November 1944 when our company was one of the leading companies in the attack against a German position, which we were told was known as 'Little Toburk.' We bumped up against very heavy enemy fire from some pill boxes, which were on high ground. It seemed as though we could not advance because the pill boxes were surrounded with many belts of heavy concertina wire and mines. Our Platoon Officer and Platoon Sgt. had been casualties a couple of days previous, and Cpl. Tuttle, N.E. took over the platoon. He gave orders to give him covering fire. He then crawled out through the minefield, prodding the ground with a bayonet as he went, until he reached the wire. He then started to cut a path through the wire and worked at least twenty minutes in doing so. All the time he was cutting the wire and worked at least twenty minutes in doing so.

All the time he was cutting the wire, the bullets were hitting all around him. Then he shouted, 'Are you with me men' and we followed him through the gap he had cut, to charge the first enemy position. Cpl. Tuttle, still in the lead, threw two grenades into the first pill box, killing some and wounding quite a few more. We were then able to clean out the remainder of the dug outs and concrete emplacements, and in doing so killed and wounded many Germans, and captured a Lt. Col., 7 other officers and about two hundred and fifty other ranks.

Recommended for V.C.   *(L.G. 24.3.45)*

Tutton, Percy, Sergeant
5493022, 59 Fd. Coy. Royal Engineers
For gallantry and fine leadership throughout the operations in Belgium.

At the counter-attack at Warneton, although wounded in the wrist he continued to inspire his section by his fearless conduct. When finally relieved by infantry he did not withdraw from the battlefield until he had rallied and sent back all his section. On the beach at La Panne, although he and his section had been working in the forward area all night, he kept them working all the following day and night on the piers by his own personal powers of leadership and drive. Due to his coolness and organising ability his section arrived on the beach at La Panne complete with all its transport and equipment.

Recommended for M.M. M.I.D. 29.11.45(L.G. 20.6.40)

Twyman, William Henry, Warrant Officer Cl. II (C.S.M.)
3850823, Loyal Regt. (attd. 2 Gold Coast Regt.)
(Walthamstow, London)
This British Warrant Officer was Company Sergeant-Major of 'C' Coy. during the engagement at Bulo Brillo on 13th February, 1941. In the early stages, the Coy. Commander, 2nd-in-command and one of the Platoon Commanders were killed. Pending the arrival of a Platoon Commander to take over, C.S.M.Twyman continued to direct and control the advance of the Company with scarcely any pause. During the advance he personally subdued with grenades an enemy M.G. post which was holding up the advance of the neighbouring Coy. He also effectively controlled the fire of the mortar detachment allotted to his Coy. Throughout the engagement, C.S.M.Twyman's coolness and resource were an inspiration to the men about him and to the young officer who assumed command of the Coy. after the deaths of the Coy. Commander and 2nd-in-command.

(L.G. 21.10.41)

U

Udin, Ahmad bin, Private
8537, 6th Battalion, Malay Regt.
For Malaya   *(L.G. 10.5.57)*

Underwood, Robert, Sergeant
5880350, 2 Northamptonshire Regt. (Loughton, Essex)
During the whole of the period May 1st to June 6th this
NCO was acting CSM of C Coy. Throughout this period
he showed outstanding gallantry and devotion to duty.
It is not possible to record all his actions but the following
is given as typical.

In the early afternoon of 2 May the Coy was in a
position at Anzio known as the Fortress. The forward
platoon was counter-attacked. The enemy attacked in
considerable force and the whole area of the forwrd
company was subjected to very heavy mortar fire. The
counter-attack was checked but the forward platoon were
in danger of giving ground through running short of SAA
and grenades. This NCO immediately volunteered to lead
a party to the platoon. He collected two other men and
proceeded along the very narrow steep-sided valley.
Several times, as it was broad daylight, the party were
subjected to aimed and accurate automatic fire from the
enemy. Just short of Pl HQ Sjt. Underwood was blown
off his feet and was wounded in the leg. Despite this he
picked up his load of 1000 rounds of SAA and 20
detonated 36 grenades, and struggled to the Pl HQ. The
ammunition arrived in time and the Pl were able to hold
their ground.

Later the same afternoon, after his wounds had been
dressed, he led forward the nightly maintenance party.

with great devotion to duty and utter disregard for
his own safety, and outstanding leadership, this NCO
took his party with ammunition across ground which was
not normally crossed except in darkness. But for his
action this important feature would almost certainly have
been lost.   *(L.G. 19.4.45)*

Upton, Daniel Earl, Warrant Officer Cl. II (C.S.M.)
*G.18024, Carleton and York Regiment, Canadian
    Infantry Corps (Immediate)*
Reference Map Italy 1/100,000 Sheet 160 Cassino

At 0600 hours on 23 May 1944 the Carleton and York
Regiment supported by the 51 Royal Tank Regiment,
less one squadron, commenced the attack on the main
defences of the Adolf Hitler line, about two thousand
yards northeast of Pontecorvo (MR 736–186). 'A'
Company was on the right and 'B' Company was on the
left.

At about 0645 hours 'A' Company came under heavy
shell and mortar fire and the company commander was
killed. So intense was the fire that the company became
dispersed and company headquarters lost contact with
the forward platoons. G18024 Company Serjeant Major
Daniel Earl Upton realizing the seriousness of the
situation rallied his company headquarters and the
reserve platoon and led them forward under intense
shelling. Soon he contacted 'B' Company moving up on
'A' Company's left flank and the situation was partially
restored. On reaching the objective Company Serjeant
Major Upton placed what elements he had of his
company on the right flank of the battalion objective,
knowing this to have been his company commander's
intention.

This Warrant Officer's decisive action and determined
leadership ensured the protetion of the vulnerable right
flank at a time when the situation was very critical. His
devotion to duty and complete disregard for his own
safety were an inspiration to the men of his company.
M.B.E. 1.2.45   *(L.G. 30.9.44)*

Usher, Sidney Lewis, Warrant Officer Cl. III (Pl.S.M.)
3590396, 1st Border Regt. [2590496 on AFW 3121]
For exemplary courage and devotion to duty.

On two consecutive occasions near Tournai on 21st
& 22nd May 1940 this PSM was in charge of an isolated
rear-guard position when the post on his right and left
were destroyed by the enemy. Under heavy artillery and
mortar fire, he, by his example of cool determintion
inspired his platoon to maintain the position until ordered
to withdraw according to plan.   *(L.G. 11.7.40)*

V

Valentine, Arthur Frank, Warrant Officer Cl. III (Pl.S.M.)
6192888, Middlesex Regt., T.A
For conspicuous bravery and leadership in the Field.

At Nieuport on 30 May 40 PSM Valentine was holding a large frontage on the Canal with his platoon. During the day of 29 May his position was heavily mortared and he was ordered to move to another position on 30 May. This move was only made possible through the skilfull handling, coupled with the great confidence the men had in this W.O. On the afternoon of 30 May he was ordered to salvage the four guns of another platoon in a very exposed area. This proved unsuccessful owing to heavy mortar and shell bombardment. In the evening he asked whether he might make a second attempt to get the guns and was this time entirely successful even though he had to make several journeys to obtain all the ammunition in addition to the guns and equipment. His steadiness throughout the operations and his determination to carry through with any task he was given regardless of enemy action won the admiration of his platoon and did much to steady men when under severe fire.
Recommended for M.M. *(L.G. 3.9.40)*

Vallance, Royston Ivor, Sergeant
7953534, 2nd Fife & Forfar Yeo., Royal Armoured Corps (Hadleigh) (Periodic)
This NCO has commanded a tank in every battle from Normandy to the Baltic. His troop has seen more action than any other and for two separate periods of a fortnight he has commanded his troop in battle. In Germany, every time that his troop has been ordered to lead the advance or attack the enemy, he has either voluntarily become, without any orders, or volunteered to become the point tank.

His troop was doing a standing patrol on the bank of the Elbe, North of Winsen, when they were attacked by a bazooka patrol of 20 SS at first light in close country. Sjt. Vallance, as point tank, allowed the enemy to infiltrate past him, reporting their movements. He then moved under fire at close range into such a position that his guns covered all the enemy's line of withdrawal. None of the patrol got back with any information.

On another occasion, his and another tank were guarding an important road junction on the centre line. They were without infantry support and as darkness fell, a car full of enemy armed with bazookas and supported by further enemy infantry in the woods, approached his position. Realising that to misfire his tank gun would disclose his very vulnerable position, Sjt. Vallance went forward alone with a Bren gun. He brewed up the car at 10 yards range, killing all the occupants, and by firing

into the woods by the light of the burning car, he dispersed the remainder of the enemy, killing three of them.

In all engagements with the enemy, he has shewn similar initiative, determination and personal courage. He has always manœuvred his tank and his troop with such cunning, that although subject to heavy anti-tank and bazooka fire on innumerable occasions, he himself has never been knocked out and his troop has suffered fewest casualties of the Squadron.
M.B.E. 13.6.70 *(L.G. 24.1.46)*

Van Der Werff, George Bernard, Warrant Officer Cl. I
S/34968, R.A.S.C. (W. Croydon)
No citation. *(L.G. 20.6.46)*

Van Hende, Marcel Octave, Lance Sergeant
A.102717, The Hastings and Prince Edward Regt., Canadian Infantry Corps (Immediate)
Ref. Map Italy 1/50,000 Sheet 101 MR 837951 S. Fortunato Ridge.

On the 20th Sep. 1944 during the battle for the S. Fortunato Ridge, A–102717 Corporal (Lance Sergeant) Marcel Octave Van Hende took over command of 17 Platoon, 'D' Company, The Hastings and Prince Edward Regt., when his platoon commander was wounded. This platoon was ordered to clear the enemy positions at MR 837951 that were threatening the advance of the company. Heavy enemy M.G. fire originated from these positions, the ground was open and the enemy commanded all approaches.

From the outset L/Sgt. Van Hende and his men came under deadly mortar and M.G. fire. Quickly appreciating that for a platoon to advance across that terrain was suicide, L/Sgt. Van Hende halted his men and placed them in a position where they could harass the enemy with small arms fire. Then he, with two of his men, moved forward. Placing his two men in a position to cover him, he repeatedly dodged alone from cover to cover in the face of intense fire. One by one he cleared five M.G. posts, killing many of the enemy and taking thirty prisoners. The ground taken, he signalled his platoon forward and consolidated his position.

His great leadership and sterling courage in performing feats over and above the dictates of duty were an inspiration to all ranks and greatly assisted the advance of his company to their final objective, the commanding heights—near MR 836950. This N.C.O.'s conduct and gallant actions are deserving of this award.
(L.G. 20.1.45)

Van Niekerk, Gert Willem, Sergeant (temp.)
P/6191, 1 F.A. Regt, S.A.A., South African Forces
   (Immediate)
For conspicuous bravery on the 13th July 42.

His Battery was in action at El Alamein; preceding an attack on their position the Battery was heavily shelled and bombed, as the result of which he was temporarily blinded by a shell burst close to his gun, and one of his men was buried in a dug-out which collapsed. Hearing cries for help, he, although suffering extreme pain and although the position was under heavy shell fire, dug the man out with his bare hands refusing to be evacuated until the other man had been attended to.

                           (L.G. 24.9.42)

Vaughan, Ernest Edmunds,M.B., Assistant Surgeon
Indian Medical Department, att. 25 Fd Regt RA
On 17 Jun 41, during operations at Halfaya Pass

Asst. Surg Vaughan reached the Troop position whilst it was being heavily shelled by Medium Artillery, and tended the wounded. By this time enemy A.F.Vs had reached the lip of the Escarpment and the position was under continuous fire from open sights. Two men were hit on either side of this W.O. and this did not deter him from continuing his duty. I consider that Asst. Surg Vaughan showed great devotion to duty under exceptional circumstances.   *(L.G. 21.10.41)*

Verner, William Robert, Warrant Officer Cl. I (R.S.M.)
188227, South African Forces
M.E. (Repat. P.O.W.)   *(L.G. 3.2.44)*

Vernon, Sidney Morton, Sergeant
2039598, Royal Engineers (Newcastle-on-Tyne)
Middle East   *(L.G. 1.6.43)*

Vickers, Harry Cedric, Lance Sergeant (Actg. Sergeant)
324359, 2nd Spacial Air Service Regt., Army Air Corps (Kelsall)
During the course of operations in France, Sjt. Vickers was a troop sergeant in a squadron of jeeps fitted with machine guns operating against withdrawing enemy convoys behind the German front. Throughout the operation which began at Orleans and ended in the Vosges, lasting 5 weeks, Sjt. Vickers distinguished himself by a grim determination to inflict casualties on the enemy. His jeep alone accounted for some twenty enemy vehicles and his ceaseless courage was an inspiration to his whole troop.

On 30 August when his squadron attacked the German garrison in Chatillon-sur-Seine, Vickers and his jeep were to guard the rear on an important cross-roads while the rest of the squadron were heavily engaged in the town, a large enemy column of 30 trucks and 400 reinforcements arrived at these cross-roads. Sjt. Vickers held his fire until the enemy had closed to about twenty yards, and then set fire to the five leading vehicles with accurate shooting from his twin Vickers guns. The enemy attacked and enfiladed his position with heavy cross-fire, but Sjt. Vickers held the cross-roads until the whole squadron had extricated itself from the fierce fighting in the town. When his gunner was killed, he himself took the guns and standing in a completely exposed position, he inflicted heavy casualties on the enemy until the end of the action. On another occasion, his squadron was attacked by 4 armoured cars and 600 infantry, when receiving supplies by parachute behind the lines. Sjt. Vickers' prompt action in knocking out the German Headquarters' truck and killing their Commanding Officer, so disorganised the enemy attack that the squadron was able to escape the net, taking the enemy by surprise from the rear. In all these operations, his dauntless courage and tenacity was outstanding.

                           (L.G. 19.3.45)

Vincent, George Athol, Private
4464672, 1st Bn The West Yorkshire Regt.
   (Gateshead) (Periodic)
During the period May 9th—June 3rd Pte. Vincent performed the dangerous duties of Coy Stretcher Bearer in a manner which has filled all ranks with admiration. On occasions too numerous to specify he has crawled out under fire dragging a stretcher behind him to attend to the wounded; to administer morphia to the badly wounded and dying; or to satisfy himself that a man was past all help. On almost every one of these missions he has risked his life to get to the wounded man. On one occasion he crawled to within 20x of a Japanese post to get an Officer who was lying badly wounded. Assisted by other men he dragged this officer to safety on a stretcher. On another occasion he crawled up to a leading section which had been pinned down by fire and grenades and there gave morphia to a dying man. It was on one of these heroic missions of his that Pte. Vincent was ultimately seriously wounded. He was wounded in four places by a mortar bomb—the same bomb killing the wounded man whom he had been attending—but Pte. Vincent crawled back to his own lines and would not suffer any of his comrades to venture towards him in spite of his slow progress, until he was out of enemy fire. Subsequently his attitude while being attended by the Doctor was a model of calm fortitude and an example to all the wounded and others in the vicinity.

Although it must be expected that a stretcher bearer carrying out his duties is bound to run considerable risk, the actions of Pte. Vincent throughout the campaign were far over and above the normal requirements of his task. His devotion to duty coupled with the determination to carry that duty out, no matter at what cost has been a splendid example of *[line missing]* eagerness to do his job under the heaviest enemy fire without the possibility of returning it was an inspiration *[remainder missing]*.

                           (L.G. 28.6.45)

Vivier, John Douglas Haig, Corporal
53796V, 3 Recce Bn. S.A.T.C., South African Forces
On 4 Dec 41, ten days after his capture at Sidi Rezegh, Vivier and another NCO crawled under the wire surrounding Benghazi Camp. They made their way to Mechili but were recaptured by an Italian patrol.

Because he was a P/W at Chiavari (Camp 52) at the time of the Italian Armistice, Vivier came into German hands. However, when employed on a ration fatigue on 9 Sep 43, he and another P/W eluded the guards. After staying in the hills for six weeks they moved south-east to Sesta, where they were advised to wait for the Allies. At the end of Dec, when attempting to reach the fighting area, Vivier was again taken prisoner.

Although he had been badly treated by his captors, he and six other escaped from Florence gaol on 16 Jan 44, after removing a bar from one of the cell windows and climbing over a high wall using a blanket rope. For a month they stayed near Camerino, and then joined a partisan group at Copogna. One of the band betrayed the location of their H.Q. and Vivier was amongst those captured on 11 Mar 44.

Although their first plans to escape were frustrated by a disloyal Italian, Vivier and an officer arranged a mass break-out. This officer speaks highly of Vivier's resourcefulness, courage and behaviour whilst in gaol and during the escape. On 29 Apr 44, after an air raid alarm, the guards were attacked with sandbags fashioned from some of the prisoners' clothing and the P/W made good their escape.

Separated from his companions by an encounter with Germans, Vivier proceeded alone to Tuscany, where he joined a small rebel band, later becoming the leader. At the beginning of June, moving to Monte San Savino, he formed another group, whose work included the distribution of food, and harassing the German retreat.

On 4 Jul 44 a South African unit was encountered. Vivier's leadership and courage throughout his partian activities have been praised by another escaper who served with him.   *(L.G. 1.3.45)*

Voss, Alfred John, Corporal
H 29835, 18 NZ Bn. (Immediate)
During the morning of 15 July 42 in the attack on El Reweisat Ridge, Cpl. Voss attacked and destroyed an enemy medium machine gun post and its crew with hand grenades. Later in the morning when our troops encountered enemy tanks, Cpl. Voss with hand grenades being thrown at him by the crew, attacked a tank with a pick to damage the track, but was driven back by heavy fire from two other tanks in the vicinity. He then moved out and brought in two wounded men under heavy fire from mortars and tank machine guns.

During the whole of the attack Cpl. Voss showed indifference to personal safety and led his men with determination and vigour.

During the night attack of 22 July 42, Cpl. Voss' platoon attacked what at first appeared to be a machine gun post. On nearing the objective six enemy tanks were encountered supported by infantry. As the line of withdrawal was cut off by tank m.g. fire the attack was continued. Cpl. Voss led his section against two tanks and with the use of anti-tank grenades forced them to retire damaged. He also destroyed several of the enemy with hand grenades and forced the remainder to retire. When the order to retire was given Cpl. Voss rallied his section and brought them out intact.
M.C. 3.8.44, M.B.E. 28.4.59   *(L.G. 24.9.42)*

Vuniwawa, Eliki, Sergeant
4418, Fiji Infantry Regt.
For Malaya   *(L.G. 30.10.53)*

W

Wadai, Ibrahim, Sergeant
NA/32204, Nigeria Regt., Royal West African Frontier Forces
No citation.   *(L.G. 19.4.45)*

Wade, John, Corporal (A/Sgt.)
5048025, 2nd North Staffordshire Regt.
On 21 May 1940 following a counter-attack carried out by 'A' Coy 2 N. Staffs on the R. Escaut it was discovered that Capt. C. Birch had been wounded and left on ground which remained in enemy possession. Cpl. Wade who had taken part in counter-attack, volunteered to bring Capt. Birch and a wounded Guardsman of the Grenadier. During this operation which was carried out in broad daylight under heavy M.G. and small arms fire, Cpl. Wade acted with great courage, determination and with complete disregard for his personal safety.
(L.G. 22.10.40)

Wade, Leonard, A/Corporal
19034149, King's Shropshire Light Infantry
For Korea   *(L.G. 30.11.51)*

Wadge, Eric James, Lance Corporal
7358474, R.A.M.C., No. 3 Commando (Devonport)
L/Cpl Wadge is medical orderly in No. 3 Commando. At Amfreville on 12th June 1944 although wounded by shellfire he refused to have his wounds attended to until he had dressed and evacuated five of his wounded comrades. Throughout the campaign in Holland and Germany his conduct has been consistently excellent. At Linne in January 1945 he re-entered the town after a fighting patrol had withdrawn and with the assistance of a comrade managed to evacuate one of four wounded men left behind. At Leese after the crossing of the River Weser he walked out with the medical officer over completely open ground on two separate occasions and helped carry back a wounded officer and OR, during this time being under continual rifle fire from enemy troops some four hundred yards away. After the crossing of the River Aller and whilst the the initial fighting was still in progress he voluntarily went out through woods infested by the enemy to attempt an evacuation of two wounded men of his troop. Subsequently on hearing at 0200 hrs 13th April that a wounded Sgt of the Commando was in an enemy regimental aid post in a village some three miles away, he immediately went out, through the enemy lines to look for the Sgt, but was unsuccessful. He returned at first light, despite the fact that SS troops were holding the village, found the wounded Sgt, carried him back through the German lines, and saw him evacuated. By this action L/Cpl Wadge was largely instrumental in saving the amputation of one of the Sgt's legs. Again on

the crossing of the River Elbe L/Cpl Wadge distinguished himself by walking out, under fire from the cliffs above, and across ground which was being mortared and shelled, and successfully brought to cover, and then evacuated two wounded men from his troop who had been hit on disembarking from their Buffalo, and who were lying in the open.

L/Cpl Wadge's bearing, devotion to duty and complete disregard for his personal safety have been an inspiration to all throughout the entire campaign.
Recommended for periodic M.M.   *(L.G. 24.1.46)*

Wagner, Charlie Arthur, Sergeant
NX.29683, 2/8 Bn, Australian Military Forces
On 27th January 1942, and at a time when two companies were cut off from the rest of the Battalion, all communications severed, the runners unable to get through to Battalion Headquarters, this NCO worked his way through enemy positions under fire, obtained most valuable information as to the dispositions of both our own and the enemy forces, and returned under fire again. This action enabled the Battalion Commander successfully to engage the enemy with artillery fire and to attack with his riflemen. He later returned again to the same forward companies under fire with further orders. His coolness, courage and devotion to duty were most marked and his services most valuable at a difficult time in the operations which resulted in success.
M.I.D. 14.2.46   *(L.G. 10.1.46)*

Waisake, Tanichala, Serjeant
Fiji L.F.
S.W. Pacific   *(L.G. 7.12.44)*

Wait, Ronald Frank, Sergeant
4130391, Cheshire Regt., SBS (2 Cdo Bde) (Chester) (Immediate)
The action took place between the hrs 2300 and 0100 on the night 8/9 Apr in region (ref map Sheet 77 III SE, Commacchio 1:25,000) MR 569678. 'M' Sqn SNS were based on the island Casne Di Caldirolo Mr 5164 in Lake Commacchio. Orders were received on the 8 Apr to create the impression a maj attack was coming in this area and to take prisoners in the region SE of the town of Commacchio 5668. The main German def line at that time was along the North bank of the Canalone Canal (569672). Two patrols 'E' and 'Y' were detailed for this task. They successfully landed at MR 572673 approx 2300 hrs and formed up for the adv along the rd towards Commacchio town. Sjt. Waite who is a patrol sjt of 'E' patrol volunteered to go ahead of the patrols as fwd scout. He was 10 yds ahead of the patrols and they had travelled 500 yds when he was challenged by a sentry. He stood

still whilst an Italian-speaking member of the patrol replied. This man kept talking to divert the attention of the sentry. The other crept fwd with Sjt. Waite in the forefront. A spandau opened fire when they were approx 10 yds from the posn. Waite was hit in the leg and the leg broken. The others raced past to aslt the 1st posn. Owing to the wd Waite could not adv with the others. Neither could he fire as his own men intervened between him and the enemy. However, above the noise of firing and exploding gren he heard someone calling for help. Recognising the voice as belonging to one of the force and locating it as coming from a slit trench approx 10 yds away he in complete disregard of danger to himself from MG fire sweeping the rd side crawled towards the trench to discover the man in hand to hand combat with a German. The German had his man by the throat but Waite despite a 'game' leg managed to seize him and pull him off sufficiently to shoot him through the chest and kill him. By this deed which showed great determination and tenacity of purpose to destroy the enemy when and wherever posible, Sjt. Waite despite his own incapacity and whilst in great pain undoubtedly saved the life of one of his comrades. By this time the force had adv about 50 yds but not without cas so Waite decided to take 2 wd men back to the boats and await the withdrawal. During this 500 yd journey under continuous and accurate MG fire one of the wounded was killed and Waite continued the journey encouraging all the time the other man who had by now been hit again. By travelling half submerged in water they avoided further injury and were eventually joined by 3 other men who were withdrawing with the main body. One man went ahead to hold up the boats while the other 2 assisted Waite and his wounded companion. However they found the boats had already gone and only a one man rubber dinghy was left on the far bank of the canal. 2 men one of whom was drowned in the effort made unsuccessful attempts to swim across to it, but rather than relinquish this one chance of escape Waite himself despite weakness from loss of blood and with his undressed wd tried and by swimming on his back reached the dinghy and paddled it across with his hands. By ferry system he got the other three across the canal and then with himself and the other wounded hanging over the gunwales trailing their legs in the water and the two unwounded pushing, wading and swimming, the party after about an hr reached a spit of land about 700 yds from the lake shore; As dawn was nearly breaking Waite sent the 2 unwounded on to try and reach base and arrange a pickup that night 9 Apr and he and the other man lay all through the day without movement to betray their presence in intense heat plagued with flies and mosquitoes without any cover and still with wds undressed. They were picked up after dark. The leadership and determination displayed and the encouragement given to his men by Sjt. Waite throughout the whole time of his being wounded until his rescue cannot be too highly praised. He was able even though

wounded by sheer guts to save one man from death and 3 others from capture.   (*L.G. 23.8.45*)

Wakefield, Douglas, Private
4543537, 2nd Bn. The West Yorkshire Regt. (Leeds 7)
(Immediate)
For outstanding gallantry and magnificent fighting spirit during operations on the Tiddim Road.

On 31 July 44 Pte. Wakefield's section came under close and accurate enemy fire. Without orders and in full view of the enemy he carried out a wounded comrade. He then returned and taking command of the remainder of his section, he organised the evacuation of the remaining casualties, himself carrying out another seriously wounded man.

Later in the same day, his Pl again came under heavy fire from machine gun, rifles and grenades. The height of the grass and undergrowth precluded the use of any firing position except that of standing. Pte. Wakefield stood in full view of the enemy, keeping up a vigorous fire with his Bren gun at an enemy machine gun and a sniper. Entirely disregarding the enemy fire, which was largely directed at him, he persisted in shooting until he had killed both the machine gunner and the sniper. This action had the effect of causing the remainder of the enemy pl to break off the engagement and to retire.

His action, besides being extraordinarily gallant, contributed most materially to the eventual success of the operation.   (*L.G. 16.11.44*)

Waldron, Jack Godfrey, Corporal
6539356, King's Royal Rifle Corps (Queen Victoria's Rifles) (Northampton)
Calais 1940 (from P.O.W. Pool)   (*L.G. 20.9.45*)

Walker, Albert Baldwin, Lance Sergeant
2118582, 79 Assault Squadron Royal Engineers
This NCO commanded a tank which landed at H hr on the beaches on 6 Jun 44. During the assault he was wounded in the head and body but continued to fight his tank and finally took over the troop when his troop leader and troop officer were killed. During this time he showed great courage and endurance and his devotion to duty was a great inspiration to his troop. Later in the day he joined the Squadron in the attack on Ouistreham Lock Gates and that night remained on duty supervision three bren gun posts. The following morning he assisted a troop leader in clearing the streets of snipers and pockets of the enemy. This NCO gave an outstanding performance of leadership and bravery under most trying conditions.
                                                (*L.G. 31.8.44*)

Walker, Alexander Laird, Sergeant
7264530, 167 Field Ambulance, R.A.M.C. (Dartford)
(Immediate)
During the attack on the M Camino feature on 2–3 Dec Sjt. Walker was NCO i/c of bearer section of 167 Fd Amb in support of 9 RF. Soon after the attack had started

the RM of 9 RF was killed and Sjt. Walker immediately took charge of the RAP. In the meantime the RAP of 8 RF had been held back treating casualties from the initial attack. Sjt. Walker on his own initiative moved the RAP of 9 RF forward to a position from which it was able to treat the casualties of both Bns. Under intense shell and mortar fire for a period of many hours he worked continuously with the greatest cheerfulness and tenacity, utterly regardless of his personal safety. Even when seriously wounded he continued to direct the stretcher bearers, refusing to be evacuated until the RAP was clear of casualties. His initiative and courage during this period without doubt saved the lives of many of the wounded and was a magnificent example to all around him.
M.M. 23.8.45 (L.G. 4.5.44)

Walker, Alfred, Warrant Officer Cl. II (C.S.M.)
3707751, King's Own Royal Regt., Habforce Div.
(India)
At approximately 0800 hours on 22nd May, 1941 at Fallujah, C.S.M. Walker took over command of his coy as all the coy officers had become casualties. He had taken over, as coy H.Q. a house which commanded the entrance into Fallujah village from the Baghdad Road. His H.Q. was attacked several times by strong forces of the enemy, all of which were repulsed; and, though under continuous and heavy sniping fire, this W.O., by his extreme devotion to duty and good sense undoubtedly commanded his coy to such effect for nearly nine hours (until relieved) that, despite casualties which were heavy, not one inch of ground was lost and the important entrance to the village remained in our hands.
(L.G. 21.10.41)

Waller, Joseph, Private
4388769, 4th Green Howards
Roberts, W. J., Pte.
4457717, D.L.I.
Bainbridge, Cpl.
843466, 8/D.L.I.
I was captured on 22 May 40, South of Arras. I was searched and my paybook taken from me.
I was captured on 21 May 40, 8 kms South of Arras, cut off by German tanks.
I was captured on 21 May 40, 8 kms South of Arras, with the same party as Roberts.
We were all taken to Cambrai and thence by train, arriving at Thorn on 9 Jun 40, where we were put in Fort 11. We were not interrogated and personal property was not taken away.
From Thorn we were sent to Konitz on 15 Jul, a working camp. Waller had one letter, the rest none. There was one Red Cross parcel between 20 men, containing food but no cigarettes, although 'cigarettes' was written on the parcel. Letters were censored.
At Fort 17 there was an RSM called Davidson who was very friendly with the Germans. He made N.C.Os salute an English private because he could speak German.

We were punished if we stole raw materials, he reported us to the Germans and we got 7 days in the cells with no blankets.
At Thorn there was also a P/W who acted as interpreter. He spoke German perfectly and used to go out with the Commandant and could go in and out of the camp without being stopped. Once a German General and a high Air Force officer came and questioned a Welsh P/W about the chances of landing paratroops in Wales. The Welshman said that the only way to get there is to swim. They said he ought to be ashamed of wearing English uniform.
The Camp Leader at Konitz was Sjt. Nursery appointed by seniority.
We escaped on the night of 21 Sep by forcing a window. With us were also ptes. A. Hodgson and R. Hodgson (Green Howards) and Pawson (D.L.I.). We then forced the barbed wire with an axe. The sentries were partly drunk, it being Saturday night. They were mostly elderly men.
We travelled South by night for seven days to Tuchei and were nearly caught in a haystack. A German spotted us in a wood and called the Police, who surrounded us, but we got away. We then split into two parties of 3, and have not heard of the other 3 since then.
We got civilian clothes and a compass from an American Pole at S[...], who also got us a boat to cross the Vistula. We journeyed through Wabreszno to Rypin, where we came in contact with an organisation with Headquarters at Biezun. We lived at different houses and the Poles gave us food, clothing and collected 200 Marks for us. We subsequently had to get off on our own and ran into the organisation again later on. We went through Mlawa and Makow and crossed the frontier near Ostrow on 24 Feb 41 at night.
We were captured by about 20 Russian guards, with dogs and night flares, when we were 200 yards across the frontier. They thought we were Poles and treated us very badly. We were in prison at Lomza for a month, five weeks at Minsk and were then taken to the internment camp where we met the rest of the party and our subsequent story is the same as theirs, being released on 8 Jul. (L.G. 4.11.41)

Walmsley, Frank, Lance Corporal
2617752, 3rd Grenadier Guards (Stockport)
On February 5th 1943 at about 1330 hrs the bn together with 1st Bn Para Regt were ordered to withdraw from their position on Diebel Mansour. The withdrawal was carried out in daylight under heavy artillery, mortar and M.G. fire. The evacuation of casualties, which were considerable, was the most difficult problem. L/Cpl. Walmsley at once volunteered to take out his Carrier to bring in stretcher cases. Though under heavy fire and across open country he went out again and again to bring in the wounded with no regard for his own safety. His courage and initiative was an example to the other Carriers who all did excellent work. L/Cpl. Walmsley

not only helped in the collecting of our own wounded but also those of the 1st Bn Para Regt, and it was largely due to his coolness and devotion to duty that so large a number were successfully evacuated. When the last one was brought in, he again went out to satisfy himself that no one was left. His behaviour throughout won the greatest admiration of all who saw him. I recommend that L/Cpl. Walmsley be given the immediate award of the DCM.

This Non-Commissioned Officer was the driver of a Bren Carrier and did fine work in evacuating many wounded from the Ravine Post, the 'woggery' and the plain during the days of the Mansour engagement. On the last day of the battle, Corporal Walmsley drove his Carrier forward time after time and even when it seemed impossible, because of the heavy shell and mortar fire, for him to get through, he continued his work unpertured.

(L.G. 4.5.43)

Walsh, Stanley Richard, Warrant Officer Cl. II
Q.X.835, 2/15 Aust Inf Bn. Australian Military Forces
(Periodic)
Throughout the present campaign until he was evacuated sick in the middle of September Warrant Officer Walsh has evinced courage and coolness of a high order.

While 2/15 Australian Infantry Battalion was occupying the coastal sub-sector Walsh displayed resourcefulness and bravery on several deep patrols. In particular he accompanied Captain Angus on reconnaissance patrols into enemy territory in the early part of August, as a result of which a fighting patrol under the same officer was able to locate and destroy almost the whole of an enemy working party 25 strong.

During this fighting patrol Warrant Officer Walsh, who was second-in-command, was cut off behind the enemy forward posts, but was cool enough to avoid betraying his position until the enemy defensive fire had stopped, when he made his way back to our lines.

Again during an attack made by 2/15 Australian Infantry Battalion on enemy positions at West Point 23 near Tel el Eisa on 1 September 1942 Warrant Officer Walsh displayed outstanding resolution and devotion to duty. When his company reached its objective Walsh was sent to inform battalion headquarters of his company's location. After making the journey to and from battalion headquarters under extremely heavy shell fire, Warrant Officer Walsh saw a runner from another company who had been hit by a shell splinter about 50 yards from the post Walsh was occupying. Walsh went out to the man under heavy fire, brought him in, and dressed his wounds.

Later when the battalion was ordered to withdraw Walsh picked up the wounded man and carried him throughout the withdrawal, which took place under enemy fire. During this 500 yard carry the wounded man was hit a second time, and Walsh halted, dressed his second wound, and continued to carry him to safety.

The physical endurance, courage, and tenacity of this Warrant officer on this occasion were an inspiration to all troops who saw him, as was his steadiness under fire throughout the engagement on 1 September 1942.

(L.G. 18.2.43)

Walsh, Thomas James, Sergeant
68108, 35th Battalion, New Zealand Military Forces
This NCO performed outstanding work as a patrol leader right through the operations carried out by the 35th Bn. in the northern portion of Vella Lavella during the period 28th September to 2nd October '43. Repeatedly and at great personal risk, he pushed forward and gained information of the utmost value. His uncanny bush sense, combined with his absolute disregard for his own safety, enabled him to pin-point enemy machine-gun positions on at least three occasions. The result was that the artillery were able to concentrate on these positions and thereby enable the infantry to get forward without heavy casualties. This NCO set an example of leadership of the highest order.

(L.G. 9.12.43)

Walters, Richard Robert, Private
WX21015, 2/28 Aust Inf Bn.
For Distinguished conduct is action in the field
Ref Map Labuan South 1:25,000 North Borneo
WX21015 Pte. Richard Robert Walters was a member of the right forward platoon of D Coy 2/28 Aust Inf Bn which stormed across a canal following the landing on Labuan on 10 Jun 45. The canal and surrounding terrain were dominated by enemy who occupied the thickly wooded, rising ground, further inland. The platoon came under enfilade fire as it penetrated to the rising ground; which caused it to recoil slightly. If suffered casualties; and, Walters went to the left forward platoon for the purpose of obtaining their support. Eventually, he guided the leading section of the latter platoon to a position from which it could launch a flank attack on the enemy positions; but, as the section commenced its attack, the section leader and three others became casualties. Walters then collected as much ammunition for his sub machine gun as he could and attacked single handed. He captured the post, killed five enemy and put the remainder to flight. He then pursued the enemy in the direction of the next post. When his sub machine gun ammunition was exhausted, he plunged onward, flinging grenades, until he fell wounded in the leg. Thereupon, he shouted directions to the platoon which enabled them to locate the enemy and continue the attack. Eventually the enemy was overcome. Around the post which Walters captured, eighteen enemy dead were found, most of which were accredited to Walters. Had he not undertaken his daring close combat tactics the enemy posts would have been difficult to locate and would have caused greater loss to both forward platoons. As a result of Walters' bravery and initiative, the Coy was able to capture vital ground, overlooking the beach head, which

the enemy intended to defend stubbornly.

(L.G. 20.9.45)

Wara, Napolioni, Sergeant (temp.)
17222, Fiji Infantry Regt. (since killed in action)
For Malaya   *(L.G. 29.6.54)*

Warcup, James Albert, B.E.M., Sergeant (A/W.O.II
(C.S.M.))
*4391561, 12 Para. Bn., Army Air Corps (Langtoft,
Yorkshire)*
Sjt., now A/CSM, Warcup landed on D Day with his
Battalion by parachute. His cool courage and leadership
at Bas de Ranville on 6 June 44 and Breville on 12 June
44 were an inspiration to all. Wherever the fight was
hottest Sjt. Warcup was always to be found. After his
company had suffered severe casualties at Breville, and
it had lost all its officers, by great personal gallantry and
leadership he led the remnants into the village onto the
objective. On 19 Aug 44 at Putot en Auge as A/CSM the
leading platoon of his company was pinned by fire in
the graveyard of the Church by a machine gun firing at
25 yards range. Without hesitation A/CSM Warcup went
forward and led an attack by the leading section on this
gun. When about five yards away from the machine gun
he was dangerously wounded in the neck by a bullet.
Despite the loss of blood he went on until the MG post
was destroyed. It was only later that he could be
persuaded to go back to be attended to. Throughout the
period 6 Jun 44 to 19 Aug 44 CSM Warcup showed
complete contempt for enemy fire and complete contempt
for his own safety on numerous occasions. His gallantry
combined with magnificent leadership has been an
inspiration to the Battalion and he has contributed more
than any other man in the Battalion to its many successes
in battle during this period.
B.E.M. 7.7.44, M.I.D. 22.3.45   *(L.G. 19.3.45)*

Ward, Kenneth Robert, Private
WX 22431, 31/51 Aust Inf Bn.
8/9 Jun 45: Map ref 264722 Chabai Sheet (Bougainville
Island) 1:25000 dyeline print
    For courageous action and devotion to duty during
the Porton operation 8/9 Jun 45.
    Shortly after the initial landing at Porton Pte. Ward
was a member of 7 Pl which occupied the left flank of
the perimeter, Pte. Ward occupying the most forward
pit of the Pl sector. During the day 3 Japs with an LMG
crawled forward to within 10 yards of Ward's pit and
commenced firing into the perimeter. Ward promptly
threw a grenade, and, despite the intensity of the enemy
automatic and small arms fire in the area, jumped out of
his pit and rushed forward shooting the 3 Japs with his
rifle and knocked out the LMG; Four other Japs promptly
attacked him from a flank. He shot one, then taking cover,
killed the other 3 by rifle fire. Pte. Stewart who was on
listening watch in front of the pit occupied by Ward was
wounded. Ward immediately crawled forward again

under small arms and mortar fire and dragged Stewart
back to his pit and obtained medical attention for him.
    During the evacuation on 9 Jun, under a smoke screen
from the artillery a canister from our artillery landed in
some boxes tied on top of the engine of a stranded Alca
caught on a reef 40 yards from the shore. Pte. Ward was
in this Alca and although an intense amount of enemy
small arms fire was directed at the barge, Ward
immediately exposed himself to it and attempted to pick
up the canister with his bare hands. This was unsuccessful
and his hands were burnt. He then cut loose the burning
boxes with his bayonet and kicked them overboard. This
prompt action prevented the fire from spreading which,
if it had gained a hold, would have forced the personel
into the water helpless in the face of enemy fire.
    At 1930 hrs when another Alca came in under enemy
fire in an attempt to take troops off the barge Pte. Ward
volunteered to stay on the barge to help guard the
wounded personnel and was one of the last to leave the
craft.
    During the whole of the operation the conduct of this
Pte was outstanding. He was absolutely fearless in the
execution of his duty his courage and determination with
a total disregard for enemy fire, and his own personal
safety, won the admiration and respect of all.

(L.G. 24.8.45)

Wareing, Philip Thomas, Sergeant (now Pilot Officer)
748091, Royal Air Force Volunteer Reserve
This NCO was forced to abandon his aircraft by
parachute over Calais on 25th August 1940 and was
immediately captured by the Germans and sent to
Brussels. He was finally moved to a prison camp at
Schubin in Germany. He escaped from here and made
his way to Danzig where he hid in the hold of a Swedish
Steamer. He finally reached this country from Sweden
on 5th January 1943.   *(L.G. 14.12.43)*

Warren, Frank William, Warrant Officer Cl. III
(T.S.M.)
1422095, 2nd A.A. Bty., Royal Artillery
T.S.M. Warren showed conspicuous ability, leadership
and coolness under fire. His Section was attacked from
the air on several occasions and was also shelled out of
various positions. He always was a tower of strength,
and by his quiet, determined manner, a pattern to his
Section.   *(L.G. 20.12.40)*

Warren, L. G., Warrant Officer Cl. III (Pl.S.M.)
5947258, Bedfordshire & Hertfordshire Regt.
B.E.F.   *(L.G. 11.7.40)*

Waterston, David Rutherford Gordon, Sergeant
916446, 115 Field Regt, Royal Artillery, T.A
This NCO was in charge of a gun throughout the action
against tanks in Merville on 28 May 1940. He displayed
the greatest courage and devotion to duty. His calmness
and determination was a fine example to his sub-section,

which, in spite of heavy machine gun and shell fire from the tanks and an 18-pdr British Battery that had been captured, put out of a action five enemy tanks.

(L.G. 20.8.40)

Watson, George William, Lance Corporal
4753675, 9th Bn The York & Lancaster Regt. (Gilford, Co. Down) (Immediate)
Arakan
On the night of 11/12 Jan 45 at Yongon on the Kaladan River, L/Cpl. Watson was a member of an improvised party of boatmen detached to defend the left flank of a beachhead which was being fiercely attacked by Japanese. Shortly after midnight, the Sjt. in charge of the party was missing. L/Cpl. Watson found himself the senior NCO in the party. His party was hard pressed and he and 3 others were wounded. He reported the other 3 casualties, but not himself and continued to lead the resistance. Eventually the attack was beaten off although L/Cpl. Watson's party suffered further casualties. He then organised the collection, dressing of all wounded men in his area, and rejoined his party. There he remained till dawn revealed no further danger, when he reported himself a casualty and was evacuated.

His complete disregard for his own safety and his determination to hold his position were responsible for the fact that the flank of the bridgehead held firm despite determined attack.   *(L.G. 22.3.45)*

Watson, J., Warrant Officer Cl. III (Pl.S.M.)
6137239, East Surrey Regt.
B.E.F.
M.I.D. 15.3.45   *(L.G. 11.7.40)*

Watson, James Edward, Sergeant
318820, 12th Royal Lancers
He showed the finest leadership and courage during all the actions in which his troop took part between 10–25 May. He was always in the leading car of his troop which inflicted severe casualties on the enemy and obtained much invaluable & accurate information. On 25 May when his car was finally destroyed by enemy fire, although wounded, he got back with another wounded member of his crew whom he assisted, reported to his troop leader that his car was lost and pointed out the positions of the two enemy A/T Guns which had fired at his car, thereby, through his [...] and forethought ensuring the prevention of further casualties.
M.I.D. 23.5.46, M.B.E. 1.1.55(L.G. 5.7.40 & 22.10.40)

Watts, Harry Lindsay, Sergeant
NX 2057, 2/4 Bn. Australian Military Forces
During the Battle of Tobruck, on morning of 21 Jan 41, Sjt. Watts with Pte. Broinowski, attacked and caused to surrender, whilst under fire, a Machine Gun Post molesting 'B' Coys right flank. Throughout the whole of the Libyan campaign Sjt. Watts has done valuable work on patrols, obtaining accurate information. He has

always been one of the first to volunteer for any dangerous task.   *(L.G. 8.7.41)*

Weatherby, John Frederick, Sergeant
7357051, R.A.M.C. (permanently attd. 2nd Bn The Parachute Regt.) (Fallowfield)
From the 17th to the 20th of September 1944. The RAP was established in a building near the main Bridge at Arnhem in Holland. Over 150 casualties were collected and were treated and nursed in this building. As further evacuation was impossible Sjt. Weatherby, though greatly handicapped by lack of assistance and absence of facilities, organised the cellars, crowded with wounded, into orderly and efficient Sick Wards. Many lives and limbs were undoubtedly saved by his unceasing labours and devotion to duty under the most difficult conditions imaginable, during these four days.

On the 20th of September, a day of fierce fighting in which any movement provoked intense fire from the enemy, Sjt. Weatherby organised and led a large stretcher party to collect casualties from a company holding the main bridge. It was largely due to his great personal courage and cool management of the party under fire that all the casualties were recovered for the loss of three stretcher bearers, two of whom were killed.

This NCO, by his gallantry and conspicuous devotion to duty led a very fine example to the medical orderlies of the Unit who during a battle in which they could expect no quarter from the enemy, never hesitated to risk their lives on behalf of the wounded.   *(L.G. 20.9.45)*

Webb, Arthur Jess, Lance Corporal
2734077, 2nd Bn. Welsh Guards
See L/Cpl. J. R. Tomlinson

Webb, George Harry, Corporal (A/W.O.II (C.S.M.))
4342188, 2nd Bn. The East Yorkshire Regt.
(Manchester) (Immediate)
During an attack on ring contour 290 south of L'Aubesniere on the evening of 15 Aug this W.O. was CSM of one of the leading Coys. His Coy Comd was killed and the only other officer badly wounded. By his initiative and determination he rallied the remainder of the Coy, which had become very scattered and in spite of incessant mortar and arty fire, lead them on to the objective. He then reorganised the remainder of the Coy and was successful in exploiting to the final objective and in holding it. Isolated from the rest of the Bn he commanded the Coy until he was joined by one of the Coy's officers early in the morning. This WO displayed the very highest powers of gallantry, determination and leadership at a time when the impetus of the assault had been checked, and the whole success of the attack by his Coy was largely due to his example.
M.M. 21.12.44   *(L.G. 21.12.44)*

Webber, John James, Sergeant
2093392, Royal Engineers (attd. 44 Fd Park Coy
(Madras) I.E., Indian Army) (Cardiff) (Immediate)
On the evening 12th June 1942, Sjt. J. J. Webber, RE, in charge of two D.I. type crews comprising 9 I.O.R.'s was attached to 'F' Coy Scots Guards (1st Armd Div) located north of Rigel Ridge. His task was to dig vehicle and gun pits as required by that unit.

Although the area in which he was operating was intermittently shelled, he continued with his task. Later in the day, 13th June, owing to increased enemy shelling, he became separated from the Scots Guards, who had moved south on to Rigel Ridge, but although left on his own, he carried on until enemy shelling from enemy guns and tanks, from the south and west, made it impossible for him to continue.

He then decided to recover and load his bulldozer and equipment, and to withdraw them to a safer area. Whilst doing this under heavy fire, three of his I.O.R.'s were wounded, two of them severely. Sjt. Webber attended the wounded and evacuated them in one of the 10 ton lorries to H.Q. 1st Armd Div some 6 miles away. He then found that the first type of the other 10 tonner was punctured, which prevented the whole being moved any further.

He changed the tyre, and after joining up with his other 10 tonner, returned to his unit near Bvo-Bvo, via Aeroma—Tobruk and Salum.

His courage and coolness under fire was a great inspiration to his men and by his efforts, he collected and withdrew, under shell fire, his very valuable equipment, and brought it and his party ([...] wounded) safely back to his unit.

This act merits the immediate award of the D.C.M.
(L.G. 24.9.42)

Wedlick, Victor Warwick, Sergeant
VX.39136, 2/29 Bn, Australian Military Forces
On 18 Jan 1942 at Bakri Sjt. Wedlick was ordered to engage with his carrier an enemy machine gun post. Although wounded and forced to withdraw he returned three times to the attack under heavy fire and finally compelled the enemy Machine Gun party to withdraw. On 19 Jan Sjt. Wedlick again showed conspicuous gallantry in driving his carrier close in to an enemy machine gun post in an attempt to cover the passage of transport of his unit, with the result that two vehicles containing wounded were successfully withdrawn. On the 20 Jan this NCO made severl attempts to break through an enemy road block under heavy fire by attacking the block with his carrier at close quarters. *(L.G. 10.1.46)*

Weir, Robert, Trooper
556411, 8th King's Royal Irish Hussars. R.A.C.
(Stainforth, Yorks)
On 17 Nov 42 at Slonta—Cyrenaica, Tpr. Weir was driving the Sqn Leader's tank of 'A' Sqn 8 Hussars with the Sqn leader in front. The Sqn moved to attack a party of Germans mining the main raod. Guns opened fire from the Fort and the rd on the Sqn of only four tanks. The Sqn Leader, whose guns jammed, ordered his driver, Tpr. Weir, to run down an anti-tank gun on the rd. Negotiating a steep embankment a track broke and the tank, now immobile, was repeatedly hit by the anti-tank gun from 20 yds range. Ordered to 'bale out', Tpr. Weir opened the driver's flaps and saw a German a few yards away about to machine-gun the remainder of the crew. Unarmed he rushed the German, knocked him down and disarmed him. Although in the ensuing struggle the German escaped, the anti-tank gun was captured. By his devotion to duty, coolness and quick thinking under fire, Tpr. Weir saved the lives of the remainder of his crew, and by his personal bravery was instrumental in capturing an anti-tank gun. *(L.G. 25.2.43)*

Weir, Walter Thomas, Corporal
1176, Divisional Cavalry Regt., New Zealand Military Forces
For conspicuous gallantry.

At Galatos on the 22nd May 1941 the Div. Cav. detachment was defending the village occupying a defensive line along the western boundary of the village. A determined attack was made on that date by the enemy and the right flank was thrown back exposing the village. This was caused by the enemy gaining high ground on our right flank and enfilading our positions. Cpl. Weir covered the withdrawal with a captured enemy Maxim machine gun which he had acquainted himself with. This was done at great personal risk. In addition to covering the troops withdrawing, his action gave our troops time to organise and subsequently launch a counter attack which resulted in recapturing our original positions. Cpl. Weir later instructed others in the use of Maxim guns which were invaluable. During the whole Crete campaign his devotion to duty, example, and initiative were outstanding and an inspiration to others. *(L.G. 4.11.41)*

Welburn, Wilfred, Corporal (Acting Sergeant)
816620, 60 A.Fd Regt. Royal Artillery
For outstanding bravery, initiative and power of command at Houthem on 26th and 27th May 1940 while in charge of an 18-pr gun in an Anti-tank role. During this period he commanded and successfully directed the fire of his gun on numerous mortar, machine gun and infantry gun targets with conspicuous cool-headedness, decision and skill, enabling the infantry to re-occupy positions and evacuate their wounded. This work was carried out over open sights at ranges of between 800 and 300 yards under shell fire and direct rifle and machine gun fire and necessitated several changes of position in full view of the enemy. Sjt. Welburn displayed conspicuous powers of leadership and was a source of inspiration to his detachment. His conduct was beyond all praise. Sjt. Welburn's gun definitely destroyed at least one infantry gun two trench mortars and three machine guns.

On the 27th May, 1940, Sjt. Welburn was in Command of a Gun Detachment and one isolated field gun located in an Infantry Bn. area for the purpose of anti-tank defence.

The Infantry Bn. was holding a defensive position on the Ypres—Comines Canal near Wytchaete. During the morning some Germans with a macine gun took up positions in a house which was to close to your own front line to be shelled by our Artillery in the normal manner Sjt. Welburn on his own initiative, suggested that he should take his gun close up to the front line and fire at the house at point blank range. This he did, manhandling the gun to within 600 yds. of the house under heavy small arms fire. He then opened fire and quickly demolished the house. Many Germans must have been killed or wounded and their fire was completely silenced. He then withdrew his gun team and gun, and later rejoined his Battery. He showed a fine example of initiative, courage and resourcefullness in dealing with a situation by novel methods.
M.I.D. 20.12.40   *(L.G. 20.12.40)*

Welden, Harold, Lance Sergeant
352958, 1/7 Bn The Middlesex Regt. (Ashton-under-Lyne) (Immediate)
On the 13th July 1943, Sjt. Weldon commanded No. 1 Sectioin 13 Pl 'D' Coy 1/7 Mx in support of the 5 Seaforths in the battle for Francofonte.

On the afternoon of the 13th the leading inf were ambushed by paratroops. Showing great resolution and determination Sjt. Weldon got his section into action, opened fire and halted the enemy advance by causing them considerable casualties. Throughout this engagement he came in for very heavy M.G. and mortar fire. It was due to the speed in which he got his guns into action that the inf were able to take up positions and deal with this threat.

At 0400 hrs on the 14th July the section was in action about 70 yds in the rear of the leading inf. Sjt. Weldon's section had suffered severe casualties and only three men were left to man the guns; he himself acted as No. 1 to one of the guns. At 0500 hrs the enemy opened intense Spandau fire and caused the inf in front to withdraw, leaving the two Vickers guns in front; Sjt. Weldon held this position with only two guns for over three hours, inflicted very heavy casualties on the enemy and prevented them from making any further advance. The gun which Sjt. Weldon was firing soon became a target for the enemy and was damaged in several places. He repaired the gun and continued to fire.

During this engagement Sjt. Weldon was wounded by a burst of Spandau fire at very short range. He remained with his section and kept his guns in action until the situation had been restored when he allowed himself to be evacuated.

Throughout the two day's fighting Sjt. Weldon showed leadership and personal courage of a very high order. His complete disregard for his own personal safety

and his devotion to duty were an inspiring example both to his own section and to the inf coy which he was supporting during the battle.   *(L.G. 21.10.43)*

Wells, Leonard Joseph, Sergeant
2564758, 2nd Corps Tps, Royal Signals, T A
This NCO was responsible for the maintenance of important circuits forward from Brussels under continual shellfire and bombing. He repaired the lines personally, working all night to do so on occasion, and set a fine example to the men under his command. At a later stage he took a detachment into what was believed to be a tank-infested area and put through some important circuits successfully.   *(L.G. 22.10.40)*

Wells, William Alexander, Sergeant
NX 5174, 2/4 Aust Inf Bn. (Immediate)
For outstanding leadership and conspicuous bravery.

During the recent operations in the Wewak—Mt. Tazaki area Sjt. Wells has continuously commanded a rifle platoon and he has consistently displayed an outstandingly high degree of leadership and personal bravery far above the average. On patrol and in the attack he has always shown complete disregard for his own safety and his example has been an inspiration to his platoon.

In the attack on Mt. Tazaki on 26 Jun 1945, when the forward coy was held up by strong enemy positions, Wells took his platoon on an out-flanking movement to the left, and it was ultimately due to the success of this movement and the vigorous way in which Wells carried out his task, that the position was captured. The movement of the platoon was opposed by exposing himself and drawing their fire that Wells was able to locate positions and effectively silence them. On two occasions Wells deliberately drew the fire of enemy machine guns onto himself so that his platoon could move forward and carry out their task and there is no doubt that had it not been for the outstanding bravery he displayed on these occasions, the position would not have been taken without heavy losses to our own troops. During the attack Wells personally killed many of the enemy and several times narrowly escaped being killed himself. His great bravery and leadership was of a standard rarely seen in one of his rank and appointment.   *(L.G. 24.8.45)*

Welsh, Albert James, C.S.M.. (temp.)
Ex.1217, No. 42 RM Commando, Royal Marines (Immediate)
Arakan 1945
At Hill 170 near Kangaw on 31st January 1945, TSM Welsh's Troop were called up to reinforce No 1 Commando at a critical period when the enemy seemed likely to gain a footing o the crest of the hill. They were ordered to put in a counter-attack, which they did with great dash, the Troop Commander, the Platoon Commander of the leading platoon, and all but one of

the forward section on the left soon being killed. TSM Welsh took charge and reorganised the troops, his remaining Platoon Commander by then also having been hit. Himself occupying a forward trench he repeatedly drove off counter-attacks with grenades and tommy gun fire until he was twice wounded. It was only after he had pulled out a number of casualties that he went back to the regimental aid post refusing a stretcher. His aggressive fighting spirit, complete disregard for his personal safety and inspiring leadership did much to hold together the remnants of his troop. *(L.G. 15.5.45)*

Welsh, David Caldwell, Sergeant
19863, 26 NZ Bn. (Immediate)
This Sjt. displayed magnificent courage, coolness and unquestionable qualities of leadership up till the time he was wounded. On the morning of 16 Mar when his platoon had been ordered forward at dawn from Cassino Square to assist in mopping up in the direction of Highway 6, it came under heavy mortar and small arms fire directed from houses immediately in front. The platoon was pinned down by concealed snipers after they had advanced 150 yds. As soon as his men had got into position, Sjt. Welsh ran the gauntlet of snipers and Spandau fire over extremely difficult ground to get stretcher bearers to evacuate his casalties and was instrumental in getting them safely out. Later in the day when his Coy had been ordered to move forward to consolidate on the rly station he crossed the bullet-swept Square with the first platoon. A third of his platoon became casualties, and realising the desperate situation of the whole Coy and with complete disregard for his own safety, stood fully exposed, calling and encouraging the men over 300 yds of open ground and rushing them behind the shelter of covering tanks and buildings. Between the Church and the railway his Pl Comd and two forward sections became trapped under a building by snipers. Showing coolness and initiative he organised a quick flanking movement under harassing small arms fire and succeeded in extracting the two sections who were in a critical position and having casualties.

During the consolidation period he moved about among his platoon encouraging and cheering them until he too became a casualty. The success of the Company's operation was to a great measure due to the gallantry of this NCO. *(L.G. 3.8.44)*

Wenborn, Alfred, Bombardier (Lance Sergeant)
863999, 1st Regt. Royal Horse Artillery (Lee, London)
For similarly conspicuous gallantry in this campaign, as he showed in France. He has consistently shown the greatest resolution and devotion to duty and has set an exceedingly high example of personal courage to his comrades. He was especially conspicuous in the Capuzzo Tank action, when O.P. wireless operator, under heavy fire from enemy tanks and medium guns L/Sjt. Wenborn successfully passed fire orders with complete coolness enabling most effective artillery support to be given at a

critical time. He was equally conspicuous when under fire a Tobruk. *(L.G. 8.7.41)*

Wessels, Bernard Johannes, Corporal
SAP.197013, 2 S.A.P., Union Defence Force
(Immediate)
On 28.5.1942 Cpl. Wessels was a member of a composite company occupying a strong point at 'Commonwealth' (.209). The position was only partially prepared and the mine fields had not yet been completed. An enemy column, which had broken through in the south, at first by-passed the position, evidently making for the sea. Cpl. Wessels was in charge of a section of Infantry, which manned a .75 captured enemy gun. He and his section were quite untrained in the use of the gun and had had only one or two lectures on the subject.

The enemy column attacked their position from a northerly direction. Cpl. Wessels' gun had been dug-in in order to repulse an attack from the South. With his men he moved the gun under heavy fire, to a position—partly exposed—where he could bring it into action against the attacking enemy. He brought it into action and although wounded continued firing it, with good effect, until the gun was put out of action by a direct hit.

Some of his crew were put out of action early on but he kept the gun going with a reduced crew. He subsequently extricated himself and some of his men when the position was overrun by the enemy.

By his personal devotion to duty and bravery he accounted for some of the enemy tanks and enabled several of his comrades to get away so that the number of our men taken prisoner was exceptionally few.
(L.G. 19.12.46)

West, Herbert William, Corporal (actg.)
7932221, 12 Royal Tank Regt. (Wandsworth)
Ref Map Italy 1/50,000 sheet 76 I Copparo.
On the afternoon of the 24th Apr 45 Cpl. West led an attack with a single tank with some infantry on to a strongly held position north of 326957 which had held up the advance during the night of the 23rd and the morning of the 24th. As a result of his heavy and accurate shelling combined with machine gunning of the position the enemy were driven out and suffered casualties whilst [...]ping. He was then ordered to take his tank round the back of the strong-point on his own to clear the enemy machine guns to allow our infantry to continue.

In doing this his tank received a direct hit on the left track. Cpl. West attempted to reverse with no success and a second shot smashed the right idler. It was not until he realized the tank was completely immobilized and that he could not bring his guns to bear on the target, that he gave orders to evacuate the tank.

It was known that three enemy tanks were in position 250 yards away and he had no other tanks to support him during the action.

Still not wishing to give up the fight, Cpl. West immediately armed his crew with TSMGs and rifles from wounded or dead infantry, organised them into an inf sec and placed himself at the disposal of the inf who were then only at pl strength. Cpl. West and his crew remained and fought with the inf for four hours, and in so doing greatly assisted in beating off an enemy counter-attack against the vital bridge behind our small fwd party. It was not until a relief Coy and more tks could be got fwd that Cpl. West withdrew his men to his own Sqn HQ.

The capture and subsequent exploitation of the position was largely due to Cpl. West's initiative, outstanding leadership and determination to defeat the enemy with all means available.

I recommend he be awarded the D.C.M. (Immediate).

(L.G. 18.10.45)

West, Walter, C.Q.M.S.
4535094, 2nd Bn., The West Yorkshire Regt.
(Sheffield) (Immediate)
In the Arakan, East of the Ngakydauk Pass, on the 5th Feb 1944, a large Japanese force attacked the 9 Indian Infantry Brigade 'B' Echelon area and succeeded in cutting our lines of communication. CQMS West kept our positions supplied with ammunition, the route to which was under continual and heavy fire. This job finished, he then worked his way through the jungle, and took up a position behind two Jap LMG posts and dispersed them, thus opening the road again.

On the morning of the 7th Feb a Jap force broke into our positions, this force was completely smashed but several of the enemy dispersed into the jungle. CQMS West, again working alone, killed five of the enemy. Throughout the battle, this NCO, under constant shelling and mortar fire, brought rations and ammunition to our defence box. His conduct throughout was exemplary.

(L.G. 22.6.44)

Weston, Jack Keith, Corporal
SX.7808, 2/48 Aust Inf Bn.Australian Military Forces
(Periodic)
Corporal Weston has shown skill, daring and determin-ation in patrolling. He has led or accompanied twenty three patrols or raids between 11th April 1941, the date when his unit arrived in Tobruk, and 31st July 1941. His outstanding ability in movement by night has enabled him to perform especially meritorious service on reconnaissance patrols, going long distances outside our own lines and obtaining valuable information concerning the enemy. As a member of fighting patrols at night he has shown great enthusiasm and courage; and patrols led by him have inflicted many casualties on the enemy. The zest and bravery with which he has undertaken these duties have been a great encouragement to all men who have worked with him.
M.M. 24.9.42   *(L.G. 30.12.41)*

Weston, Joseph Edmund, Sergeant
2615873, Grenadier Guards (attd. 1/4 King's African
Rifles) (Welwyn Garden City, Herts)
For outstanding gallantry on March 31st at Soroppa when his company was held up by a Machine Gun post, he led a section to the attack with skill and promptitude; in spite of heavy enemy fire he took the position.

Having captured the latter another L.M.G. post opened at a range of some 150 yards, against which he immediately advanced with success. Throughout the action he displayed an admirable courage and an inspiring example to the men of his platoon.

(L.G. 21.10.41)

Westwater, Alexander, Bombardier
876932, 26 F.R.A. Royal Artillery, 1 S.A.S. (since
killed)
Captured at Tmimi on 23 Nov 41. Sent via Benghazi, Taranto, Bari, Udine, Servigliano and Imperia to Camp 53 (Macerata). While at Bari he escaped through the wire but after three days liberty he was recaptured and taken back to camp where he was 'beaten up' and kept without food for three days as a punishment. His second escape was by tunnelling at Servigliano; he was recaptured after 18 days and given 35 days solitary confinement. A third attempt was made in Feb 43 from Macerata, when he escaped wearing Italian uniform with faked insignia. He was recaptured the next day and given 30 days solitary confinement.

After the Armistice, Westwater escaped from Camp 53 on 13 Sep but was recaptured on the Gran Sasso and taken to Aquila. From here a fifth escape was made, but he was retaken at Castropignano by the Germans and sent to Sulmona. The next day he slipped through the wire, thus making his sixth escape, and his in a tree while the enemy peppered the surrounding woods with M.G. fire. He lay up until nightfall then made his way to our lines, finally meeting Allied troops at Trigno on 27 Oct 43.

Other successful escapers from camps where Westwater was imprisoned have reported that he was conspicuous for his high morale and continued determination to escape. He set a fine example to all ranks.   *(L.G. 29.6.44)*

Wheeler, Frank Robert, Sapper
1539676, 22 Mech. Equip. Pln. Royal Engineers
(Enfield) (Immediate)
On 20 Sep '44 during the advance of 5 Ind Inf Bde on the road Faetano—San Marino Sapper F. R. Wheeler of 22 Mech. Equip Pln RE was attached with his D4 angle-dozer to 'A' Pln 4 Fd Coy I.E. This sapper was filling in a blow which was in full view of the enemy from two sides, from Monte San Marino ahead and from the foothills on the left, where the enemy were firmly established. For 2 hours this sapper operated his dozer in full view with support tanks sitting on the hill at his side a few hundred yards away. The blow was almost

repaired when the enemy switched his SP guns from the tanks to the dozer & straddled the dozer with 3 shells. The pln took shelter but the dozer operator carried on until a further 2 shells fell dangerously close, when with apparent unconcern he parked his dozer under the shelter of a tree & himself took shelter. A further few shells followed but as the enemy had achieved his objective of stopping the work, further shells did not follow. The dozer driver was then told that he would not be ordered to work his dozer as further movement would receive shells & that the pln could work on the road and run to shelter if further shelling occurred. It was pointed out to him that it was then 1330 hours and the road was vital to supply traffic and had been promised open to all vehicles at 1400 hours & if he could work the dozer for another 15 minutes the road would be open. The operator immediately volunteered to carry on and after a short period had almost completed his task when the SP guns fired a salvo and scored a direct hit on the road. The next few minutes were full of bursting shells on the road & on both sides of the road. Through the dust caused by the shells came the operator and machine, still carrying on. With a final turn he back-paddled the dozer and smoothed out the bumps. The road was open at 1345 hrs. During both periods of shelling a total of *M.I.D. 24.8.44* (*L.G. 8.3.45*)

Wheeler, Frederick Walter, Lance Sergeant
328377, Nottinghamshire Yeomanry R.A.C. (Cardiff)
(*Immediate*)
On April 19th 1945 'B' Sqn were supporting the 1st Bn K.O.S.B. who were operating in an area SW of Bremen. L/Sjt. Wheeler commanded a tank in a troop supporting a company from the 1st Bn KOSB to capture an enemy strong point holding an important cross roads at MR 661982 NW of Huchting. The attack started at dark, but immediately the infantry crossed the open ground they were held up by intense enemy machine gun and mortar fire and were compelled to take cover.

L/Sjt. Wheeler immediately detailed the other 2 tanks in his troop to watch his left flank where an enemy SP gun has knocked out a tank in the Sqn—then using the maximum skill, he dashed across the open ground, right into the centre of the enemy position. When his tank came to a halt, he found himself surrounded by enemy, who were so close that he was not able to depress his gun to fire. Displaying the greatest coolness and complete disregrd for his own personal safety he stood on the outside of his tank behind his turret firing his pistol and throwing hand grenades, which his operator passed to him from the inside of the turret at the enemy who were endeavouring to engage his tank with bazookas.

The enemy, who were so surprised at his sudden appearance, and so overwhelmed by this offensive action, which had cost them heavy casualties, soon began to surrender. L/Sjt. Wheeler immediately summoned his other two tanks and the infantry, on whose appearance the whole of the enemy force surrendered and 200 PW

were taken. It was entirely through this outstanding example of coolness and courage and complete disregard for his own safety on the part of L/Sjt. Wheeler that this important cross road was captured together with so many prisoners without a single casualty to our supporting infantry.

Whilst standing on the outside of his tank he was repeatedly engaged by the enemy with rifles and spandau, and although the turret of his tank was continually hit, he himself was completely unmoved and fortunately unharmed. This action was an example of courage of the highest order, which was rewarded with such satisfactory and far reaching results. (*L.G. 23.8.45*)

Wheelwright, Harold, Signalman
2579803, 46 Div Signals, Royal Signals, T.A
On May 22, 1940, during the afternoon, having delivered despatches to 25th Inf Bde at Don. Returning he found an enemy unexploded bomb lying on the road near Rly junction towards Wavrin. With great coolness and disregard for personal danger he carried the bomb some distance off the road and placed it in a waterlogged ditch. He then proceeded to Armentieres to deliver further despatches to 3 Co[...] at the Rly bridge entering Armentieres he was subject to very heavy bombing but with his nose and ears bleeding from concussion of the explosions he delivered his despatches.

This Sgmn was at all times very cool and quite untiring in his efforts to deliver despatches to formations which were continually moving and a fine example to the other Sgmn in the detachment. He was frequently under M.G. fire from enemy aircraft when on roads delivering despatches. (*L.G. 22.10.40*)

Whelan, Timothy Patrick, Warrant Officer Cl. II
23654283, Royal Regt. of Fusiliers
For Northern Ireland (*L.G. 19.3.74*)

Whelch, Henry John, Corporal
596013, 22 NZ Bn. (Immediate)
On the night 18–19 Apr 45, Cpl. Whelch was acting as pl sjt of the res pl during the attack West of Villa Fontana across the River Gaiana. About midnight, just after an intermediate obstacle had been negociated, the pl was attacked by a strong force of German paratroopers. Because of a hy ground fog and the dust caused by the barrage, visibility had been reduced to zero. In the sharp fighting which developed immediately upon contact, Cpl. Whelch's pl not only lost comn with Coy HQ but it also became separated for a period of eight hours from its pl comd. To the difficulties of the situation, Cpl. Whelch responded with qualities of great personal courage and cool and sound judgment. Rallying the pl, he led it in determined assaults upon the enemy with such skill and dash that more than 20 enemy were killed and the remainder put to disorderly flight. Cpl. Whelch himself was foremost in the fighting and under his leadership his men fought outstandingly well.

Once more, Cpl. Whelch rallied his men and on his own initiative continued to the final objective. Close to the rly line, more enemy troops were encountered. They were engaged immediately and driven off after suffering cas. Before first light, Cpl. Whelch had led his men to the final objective and by first light the pl was firmly consolidated.

Throughout the attack, Cpl. Whelch's leadership was a factor of the greatest importance in the excellent work performed by the pl. On each occasion when the circumstances became critical, he reacted with a calm indifference to his personal safety and a bold determin-ation to push on the attack to the best advantage.

(L.G. 18.10.45)

Whitaker, Joseph William, Warrant Officer Cl. III (T.S.M.)
764415, 155 Lt.A.A. Bty. Royal Artillery, attd. 4th R.R.
This Warrant Officer commanded the Tp of 155 Lt.A.A. Bty which accompanied 4 Raj.Rif. column with attack on Tumar East on 9th Dec. 1940. When the column was counter attacked in the flanks by Inf [...] A.F.Vs he showed the utmost initiative resource and courage in face of heavy M.G. fire in immediately bringing his section into action. When this advancing infantry observed his sights he brought fire to bear on enemy infantry who were holding up the advance on the left front. Later he brought his L.M.G. into action. His prompt action undoubtedly helped to speed up the complete surrender of the enemy and saved many casualties.

(L.G. 25.4.41)

Whitbread, Thomas William Donald, Sergeant (actg.)
6102411, 1st Bn The Buffs (Royal East Kent Reg)
(London, N.5) (Immediate)
On 13th April 1945, 1st Battalion The Buffs was part of a force landed on the south western beaches of Lake Comacchio, with the object of securing two vital bridges. Sjt. Whitbread was in command of a platoon of 'A' Company which had been ordered to seize and hold the south bridge, which was more than a thousand yards inland.

On the original plan, Sjt. Whitbread's Platoon was to have been in reserve, but during the approach march the L.V.T. containing one of the assaulting platoons broke down and orders had to be quickly changed before beaching. In spite of this, Sjt. Whitbread quickly organized his Platoon on the beach and lead the attack with such force, initiative and spirited determintion that the bridge was captured before the enemy could demolish it.

On the way to the objective, the Platoon passed through a previously unlocated mine field and suffered casualties, but such was this NCO's leadership that no delay or unnecessary confusion was caused. He was joined by the second platoon of 'A' Company at the bridge, and over 30 enemy prisoners were taken. Except for wireless communications with Company HQ this

bridge party was out off from all assistance until it was relieved during the night 14th/15th April by Coldstream Guards working up from the South East.

The bridge was continually attacked but on every occasion the Platoons repulsed the enemy and inflicted heavy casualties. The Officer in Command of the second platoon at the bridge was killed on the early moring of 14th April; Sjt. Whitbread now assuming command of the entire bridge force.

This NCO showed inspiring leadership and cool determination throughout the operation, and his holding of this bridge was a major factor in the success of future operations.

(L.G. 19.7.45)

White, Alan George, Warrant Officer Cl. II (temp.)
16071, Royal Australian Infantry
No citation.

(L.G. 8.9.70)

White, Benjamin, Private (A/Cpl.)
VX 45139, Allied Intelligence Bureau, Australian
Military Forces (Immediate)
Cpl. White, as a member of Lt. Mason's Allied Intelligence Bureau patrol since 29 Nov 44 has been continuously engaged on dangerous and arduous patrols inside enemy territory on Bougainville. In Dec 44 Lt. Mason's party was near Kieta and a force of natives under Sjt. Warner, of Lt. Mason's party was besieging 25 armed Japs in a village nine miles south of Lt. Mason's position. The Japanese had been sent from Buin to try to eliminate the AI[...] party, but was met and defeated by Sjt. Warner's party.

Early in Jan 45 word was received that 100 armed Japs from Buin were on the way to relieve the garrison being besieged by Sjt. Warner. Cpl. White was instructed to intercept the Japanese relief party, and enlisting the aid of more than 200 natives he moved to Kekemona, approximately eight miles south of Sjt. Warner's position. His natives ambushed the relief party in a gorge. With a few captured rifles, their native weapons, and heavy stones rolled down on the enemy, they caused the relief party to panic and flee into the jungle, where they were pursued and almost annihilated. Eighty-five Japs were killed on the day of the ambush, and five later. The only native casualty was one wounded.

The relief party's rations, ammunition and stores and a large quantity of hand grenades were captured, and some sent to Sjt. Warner's party. The remainder of the weapons were distributed among Cpl. White's natives, who were then put to work to build a trail block at Kekemona.

On 10 Feb 45 a second large well armed Jap relief party reached the trail block and attacked Cpl. White's party with the support of a mobile 20 mm AA automatic cannon. The attack was beaten off, and the Japs held up for three weeks, until the natives' ammunition and grenades were exhausted. In that period 42 Japs were killed. The remaining 30 reached and relieved the garrison besieged by Sjt. Warner, but on their way back to Buin were again ambushed by the combined parties of Cpl. White and Sjt. Warner at Kekemona on 4 Mar 45, when 15 Japs were killed. The remainder sought refuge in a native village where they were surrounded, and on 25 Mar were still under siege.

Accompanied only by native scouts, Cpl. White has obtained valuable information on other patrols. On one occasion he travelled alone through enemy territory to Torokina and returned with urgently needed wireless parts with which communication with Lt. Mason's party was re-established. He has proved himself a splendid and intrepid jungle fighter and has personally killed 5 Japanese in combat.

He has been a constant volunteer for the most dangerous and arduous operations. He is still in enemy territory. In 1943 and early 1944 he carried out similar patrols in support of US Forces then in Bougainville.

(L.G. 3.7.45)

White, Cecil Frederick, C.Q.M.S.
4031837, 42nd Divisional Signals, Royal Signals
18th May 1940

F. of S. (C.Q.M.S.) White C. F. displayed great coolness and resource when an enemy bomb fell close to the workshop section. He put out the fire caused by the bomb and saved the workshop vehicles by evacuating them, showing no regard for his personal safety. One man was killed and two wounded on this occasion.

(L.G. 11.7.40)

White, Ernest George, Corporal
6341647, Queen's Own Royal West Kent Regt., No. 3 Commando (Gillingham)
Throughout the operations at Vaagsö in South Norway on 27th December 1941, Cpl White displayed leadership of a very high order coupled with a remarkable spirit. When his Troop Commander had been shot, the other officers in his troop put out of action and the Troop Sgt.-Major delayed, Cpl White took command of the remnants of the troop. He carried out a series of assaults and proceeded in destroying a hotel which was manned as a strong point and continued in charge until the end of the operation. He personally accounted for some fourteen of the enemy. His gallantry and leadership were of a high order, and had a direct bearing on the allotted tasks being carried out, within the time limit which had been laid down. *(L.G. 3.4.42)*

White, Evelyn Sydney, Sapper
1861570, Royal Engineers
Rfn. Hosington and Spr. White were taken prisoners at Calais in May 1940 and were taken to the P/W Camp Stalag XXI B at Schubin, in German occupied Poland. Later they were transferred, in a working party, to a camp at Wlocawsk.

Conditions at both these camps were deplorable; P/W were half starved and were obliged to eat roots found in the fields. As a result 75% were down with dysentery.

Preferential treatment was however given to P/W from Eire.

The working camp was enclosed by barbed wire and patrolled by sentries, but Rfn. Hosington and Spr. White nevertheless succeeded in slipping out during the night. Towards daybreak they hid in a haystack, where they were later found by two Poles. The latter informed friends, who provided food, cigarettes, money and civilian clothes and conveyed them to Crosnice. There they were put in touch with an underground Polish organisation, which thenceforth took charge of them.

From Krosnice they were passed on to Kutnow, whence, under the care of a Polish officer, they were taken to Dobzelia. Here they had to cross the very closely watched frontier between Reichspolen and Occupied Poland. A guide then took them by train to Warsaw, travelling on the Berlin—Warsaw express in the same second class compartment as a number of German officers.

Three months were spent in Warsaw, where they were sheltered in no less than fourteen different houses, British and Eire residents being particularly helpful.

From Warsaw they travelled by train viz Cracow to Samok and thence by wagon via Ramonov to Barakov in Slovakia. They then went by car to the Hungarian frontier and, after a successful crossing, made their way to Budapest.

As well as passing on extremely valuable information for the use of possible future escapers, Rfn. Hosington and Spr. White brought back many items of Intelligence. These concerned, for example, German operations in Calais, conditions in Berlin and Warsaw (a street map of the city was obtained and marked to show military objectives) and, with many illustrative details, conditions in Poland generally. *(L.G. 15.7.41)*

White, Fred Henderson, Lance Sergeant
5391063, 6th Bn Oxfordshire & Buckinghamshire Light Infantry (Windsor) (Immediate)
Ref Map:—Burma Hind 601 Sheets 85E/13/2 & 85E/13/3.

After forcing the crossing of the Me Chaung on 3 Mar 45, the Bn continued to advance towards Tamandu on 4 Mar 45. On the speed and success of this advance depended the whole Brigade's Operation.

No. 5391063 L/Sjt. F. M. White was in command of the leading platoon of the advance guard company. The platoon came under accurate M.M.G. and Rifle fire from a flank, L/Sjt. White's orders were to push on at all costs. He therefore immediately went forward to the leading section and led them in a charge on the enemy. An M.M.G. was captured intact and of the seven Japanese killed in the charge, L/Sjt. White personally accounted for two. By his bold leadership and quick appreciation of the situation he enabled the Coy to push on and seize its objective in the given time.

The ultimate effect of the action of L/Sjt. White's platoon in quickly overcoming the enemy opposition was to prevent the enemy disengaging, and thus to enable the rest of the Bn. to move forward and consolidate on a line vital to the further advance of the Brigade Group.

L/Sjt. White has now commanded a platoon in action for the last four months and has displayed outstanding leadership and resource. In my opinion he is thoroughly deserving of the Immediate Award for which he is recommended.   *(L.G. 21.6.45)*

White, Frederick Henry, M.M., Lance Sergeant
3535141, Loyals, Special Raiding Sqdn., S.S. Bde.
  (Urmston, Manchester)
L/Sjt. White was in charge of a subsection during a German counter attack in the Termoli area on the morning of 6 Oct 43 when he came under heavy shelling and mortar fire. The intensity of fire increased to such an extent that his section was forced to give ground, but fearing infiltration by German Infantry, he himself went back to hold his original position where he kept an L.M.G. in action for two hours despite the weight of the enemies fire.

He refused to fall back on the main line till the threat to that Section eased. Later, when his Officer was killed and several of his men wounded, he took over command of a section and led it with daring and initiative.

Throughout, he showed high powers of leadership and great courage and his example pulled the section through a very difficult time.
M.M. 14.10.43   *(L.G. 27.1.44)*

White, James Joseph, Sergeant
5249567, 7th Bn The Worcestershire Regt. (Kidder-
  minster) (Immediate)
At Maram on 19 June 1944, Sjt. White commanded a platoon during the battle for this important feature. During the attack his platoon came under heavy enemy fire from small arms and grenades and he himself was badly wounded. In spite of his wounds and at great personal danger due to continuing loss of blood, he continued to direct the fire of his platoon and successfully carried out a difficult manoeuvre of his men ordered by his Company Commander, standing in the face of enemy fire to direct the movement of his men to safety. His personal example and courage in this instance largely contributed to the eventual success of the day and to the rout of the Japanese forces in this area.

When unable to carry on any longer, he refused a stretcher and said he was too heavy to be carried down a steep hill in view of the enemy. He managed to get himself down the hill to the road where before collapsing through exhaustion and loss of blood, he related the situation on the hill to his Commanding Officer.
                                        (L.G. 5.10.44)

White, Percy, Warrant Officer Cl. II
2887, Royal Australian Infantry Corps
For Vietnam   *(L.G. 10.12.68)*

White, Raymond Ernest, Staff-Sergeant
952832, Glider Pilot Regt, Army Air Corps (Kettering)
Danville, June 6th 1944
In the early moring of Tuesday after landing and taking up a defensive position, S/Sjt. White was the only member of a 6 pr A/T gun crew. He manned his gun single handed and amid heavy mortar and shell fire, he stayed with his gun and fought it entirely himself. He destroyed a self propelled enemy gun with his first shot and continued to engage enemy tanks. Through this man's courage and determination and complete disregard for his own safety, he was responsible for delaying the advance of the enemy around.   *(L.G. 31.8.44)*

White, William George, Sergeant (actg.)
6031433, 2nd Royal Berkshire Regt. (Swansea) (since
  killed in action) (Immediate)
On 10 Mar 45 at Mandalay Sjt. White commanded a Pl of D Coy 2 R Berks, during the operations for the capture of the remaining portion of Mandalay Hill. In the first phase of this operation Sjt. White's Pl was in reserve, from where it was ordered to attack the right flank of a strong enemy posn which had held the main Coy attack. This Pl attack succeeded due to the outstanding leadership of Sjt. White, & the skilful handling of his men, & enabled the Coy to capture the whole of its objective, resulting in the killing of 27 of the enemy & the capture of 7 M.M.Gs. In the subsequent exploitation the Coy was faced with the task of destroying enemy in a tunnel which guarded the approach to the remainder of Mandalay Hill. Again Sjt. White showed initiative & with complete disregard for his personal safety managed to get petrol into the tunnel & set it afire & burn the enemy out at the same time positioning his men to fire grenades into the tunnel entrances. These efforts silenced the enemy & 11 were killed and 2 L.M.Gs captured.

In the second and final phase of this operation—the attack on the Pavilion area—Sjt. White's Pl was leading in the attack, again he skilfully manoeuvred his Pl in the face of well directed small arms fire. This attack succeeded, resulting in the routing of the enemy and the complete capture of the Mandalay feature. During the whole of this operation Sjt. White's example of leadership, initiative & complete disregard for personal safety was outstanding. It gave great inspiration & confidence to his men & thereby materially assisted in his Coy capturing its objectives.   *(L.G. 2.8.45)*

Whiteside, Robert Baden, Sergeant
M16475, The Loyal Edmonton Regt.. Canadian
  Infantry Corps (Immediate)
At first light on 23 October 1943, The Loyal Edmonton Regiment was attacking the town of Colle D'Anchise. 'A' Company, in which Sergeant Whiteside was Platoon Sergeant, had secured its objective. 'D' Company, however, moving forward to their objective which was a feature north west of the town, came under heavy fire from an enemy strong point with two machine guns

located between 'A' and 'D' Companies on the western edge of the town. Sergeant Whiteside obtained permission to attempt to knock out this machine gun position.

Dodging from building to building within the town and being continually sniped at by the enemy, Sergeant Whiteside worked his way forward 120 yards to a locality from which he could engage the enemy by rifle fire from 50 yards range. From this point of advantage he prevented the enemy from using the machine guns against the advancing Company. After the action it was found he had accounted for 11 enemy, killed and wounded. He also captured a German Non-Commissioned Officer and removed to safety from under very heavy fire one of our own wounded. Sergeant Whiteside's meritorious deed enabled 'D' Company to work forward at greater speed at a crucial time in the battle and secure their objective.

(*L.G. 16.3.44*)

Whitfield, Nigel, Sergeant
23945040, Royal Anglian Regt.
For Northen Ireland   (*L.G. 24.7.73*)

Whiting, Frederick William, Corporal
5623972, 15 (S) Reconnaissance Regt.,
  Reconnaissance Corps (Bristol) (Immediate)
This NCO was the Commander of the leading car which on 28 August was moving towards Fretteville after having crossed the R. Seine. On reaching the outskirts of this village, he was subjected to very heavy, accurate and short range machine-gun and mortar fire, but he returned the fire to such good effect that he silenced much of the machine-gun fire, thus allowing his patrol to withdraw and continue their mission to a flank. During his manoeuvre he killed at least 6 Germans attacking his car with his own Bren. On his patrol to the left flank he again ran into heavy opposition and his car was blown up and disabled, landing up in a small quarry, where for 45 minutes under accurate machine-gun fire he supervised the recovery of his car. His car was repeatedly hit by machine gun fire but he was determined that this operation, once started, should be successfully completed. The whole time he was exposing himself to accurate enemy fire. Although the steering of the car was damaged, the turret jammed, and his gun mounting useless, he continued to patrol and fought for the remainder of the day, causing very severe casualties to the enemy.

A less resourceful and determined Commander would easily have accepted the situation as hopeless when he was blown off the road and would have tried to evacuate the crew. He was given permission by his Troop Commander to leave the car and evacuate his crew as the enemy fire was so accurate and it appeared to be impossible that this vehicle could carry on. His car was, in fact, so shot to pieces by the enemy that on return it had to be written off as a complete loss.

Cpl. Whiting's determination, courage and devotion to duty were largely responsible for the unmolested passage of our leading infantry into Le Thuits as he dominated with his patrol the enemy in this area to such an extent that they were unwilling to open up on the infantry who were passing.

His actions throughout this day were an inspiring example; his leadership, coolness and complete disregard for his personal safety, and the information that he obtained and reported to his Squadron Commander was of the highest standard.   (*L.G. 1.3.45*)

Whittet, Charles Goodman, W.O.II (C.S.M.)
947747, 1st Bn The Royal Scots (Dunedin, N.Z.)
On 27th May 1940 at Le Paradis near Merville this Warrant Officer was commanding 'D' Company 1st Bn The Royal Scots. At about 0900 hrs. his position was heavily attacked by elements of the S.S. Division 'Totenkopf' supported by A.F.Vs, mortars and artillery. Very soon after the attack started the farmhouse, which C.S.M. Whittet's company was occupying, was set on fire and three trucks containing the battalion's reserve of S.A.A. and mortar ammunition, which were beside the farm, also caught fire.

C.S.M. Whittet successfully withdrew the remainder of his company, through the blazing farm and exploding ammunition, to some outhouses in rear of the farm occupied by HQ Company, which then became the rear of the battalion position. C.S.M. Whittet was ordered to occupy this position with his own company and stragglers from other companies of his own battalion and from other units. Although there were very few N.C.Os to assist him, C.S.M. Whittet occupied his position and set a very high example of courage and devotion to duty by remaining completely in the open, without any cover whatsoever, under aimed small arms fire from a range of some hundred and fifty yards, until the position was occupied. Later C.S.M. Whittet went out further into the open to bring back a wounded man.

For the remainder of the day, with a force finally reduced to about 10 effective men with one Gren Gun and very limited ammunition, C.S.M. Whittet maintained his position, himself directing the fire of his men from a most exposed position. It was largely due to C.S.M. Whittet's personal gallantry and leadership that his command was able to maintain its position in face of greatly superior numbers.

Throughout the day C.S.M. Whittet personally rendered first aid to some twenty wounded men, there being no medical assistance available and supervised their evacuation under continuous fire to a place of comparative safety.   (*L.G. 29.11.45*)

Whitton, Stanley Arthur Raymond, Corporal
NX 41284, 42 Aust Inf Bn. (Immediate)
On 19 July 1945 Corporal Whitton led a security patrol of three men operating south of the Bujin Road near the Mivo River. Whilst acting as leading scout the patrol

was fired on by a party of enemy who wounded Corporal Whitton in the wrist. Corporal Whitton continued to advance killing one and wounding three enemy who fled, Corporal Whitton remained on duty.

On 21 July Corporal Whitton led a security patrol of four men. When 600 yards from the Company position the patrol was fired on by ten enemy armed with two Light Machine Guns. The leading scout had entered a clearing and was forced to ground by heavy fire. With complete disregard for his personal safety Corporal Whitton advanced alone across the clearing and attacked the enemy. He silenced the first Light Machine gun with his Owen gun and was then wounded in the arm and the foregrip of his Owen was shot away. He continued to attack the second Light Machine Gun with grenades and silenced it killing three enemy and wounding three others. As a result of his gallant action the leading scout was able to move to cover. Corporal Whitton then returned with his patrol to his company and despite his wounds led a fighting patrol back to clear the enemy position.

At all times when in contact with the enemy Corporal Whitton has displayed outstanding personal courage, aggressive leadership and determination.   *(L.G. 12.10.45)*

Wichtacz, Harry, Private
B.37767, Royal Hamilton Light Infantry (Wentworth Regt.)
B/37767 Pte. Wichtacz, H. 12 Pl 'B' Coy R.H.L.I. landed on White Beach at Dieppe on 19 Aug 42. From first beaching the platoon came under heavy fire from a pillbox directly in front, which had practically wiped out No. 11 Pl and which swept a long stretch of beach, making it almost impossible to close on the objective, the Casino. Under cover of a quick smoke screen, Pte. Wichtacz went over a low sheltering wall and around to the back of the pillbox. He placed a Bangalore torpedo inside which destroyed the pillbox and its crew of fourteen Germans, thus clearing the way for the seizure of the main objective, the Casino.

In returning to join his platoon, he was hit by enemy M.G. fire, which later necessitated the amputation of his leg.

Pte. Wichtacz displayed the greatest courage and gallantry, and his intrepid action unquestionably saved the lives of many of his comrades.   *(L.G. 22.12.42)*

Wickman, Mervyn, Warrant Officer Cl. II
64698, 24 NZ Bn.
This soldier has been a member of B Coy since he joined 24 NZ Bn as a 7th reinforcement in Jan 42. Since that time he has taken part in many campaigns and battles rising from the ranks to WOII and finally being selected for UK Octu (4th Intake). CSM Wickman has at all times shown great devotion to duty. His coolness and courage in the face of the enemy has been a sterling example to all ranks. The following is a list of campaigns in which he has taken part: Alamein (campaign); Kaponga Box;

Mitiyria (battle); Wadi Matratin (battle); Tunisian campaign; El Hamma (battle—wounded); Italian Campaign; Sangro battle; Orsogna attack; Cassino battle (in town from 14–24 Mar 44). During the recent fighting WOII Wickman showed outstanding coolness and courage; his cheerful demeanour and tireless work at all times was a great help to both officers and men.
     (L.G. 21.12.44)

Wightman, George Cairns, Sergeant
6913204, 2nd Bn The Rifle Brigade (Maidstone)
On 8 May when approaching enemy defences at Halfaya Pass, sudden and very heavy fire was opened on this NCO's carrier pl from about 500 yds by 2 Field guns 4 or 5 A/Tk guns and numerous heavy and light M.G.s. The leading carrier was immediately hit, the officer [...]c pl was seriously wounded (he subsequently died) and the driver killed. Sjt. Wightman went forward in his carrier under this very heavy fire to tow the damaged carrier and occupants to safety. He made two attempts, each time leaving his vehicle under heavy close-range fire to adjust the tow ropes, but another direct hit made the carrier impossible to tow. He therefore removed the wounded officer and put him in his carrier. He then removed the weapons from the damaged carrier and rendered the wireless set unserviceable before abandoning the vehicle, and drove his carrier to safety. This was all carried out under heavy close range fire of all calibres of weapons. His action under heavy fire in full view of the enemy showed the greatest coolness gallantry and unselfish devotion to duty and to his platoon commander.   *(L.G. 19.8.41)*

Wilcox, Geoffrey, Sergeant
2613675, 2 Armd Grenadier Guards (Windsor)
     (Immediate)
This Tp Sjt was acting as Tp Leader during the whole of the battle for La Jouberie Wood. Throughout the whole of the day of 11 Aug 44, his tp were engaged in a very fierce fighting. Under the most difficult circumstance, he maintained complete control of his tp. Although he was under constant shellfire and very heavy small arms fire, he frequently exposed himself, regardless of all danger, and stood up on the back of his tk or walked forward to a nearby bank in order to observe better the movements of the enemy in the very thick country which lay immediately on his flank. By so doing, he manoeuvred his tp. time and again, into different posns to ward off the repeated efforts of the enemy to infiltrate amongst the tks of the remainder of his Sqn. His magnificent leadership and conduct throughout the whole day were of the highest order.   *(L.G. 21.12.44)*

Wilde, George, Warrant Officer Cl. II (C.S.M.) (A/ W.O.I (R.S.M.))
4027583, 1st King's Shropshire Light Infantry (Birmingham)

For conspicuous gallantry and devotion to duty in the Anzio Beach-head between 30 Jan and 11 Feb 44. This Warrant Officer's coolness and personal example throughout two recent actions has been an inspiration to all ranks.

On 3 Feb 44, in the Silos area, despite a part of the ammunition dump being on fire, this Warrant Officer continued to load ammunition and to supervise its carriage forward to the Rifle Companies. On 8 Feb 44, during the action at Buonriposo Ridge, when Bn HQ received a direct hit from enemy artillery, RSM Wilde quietly took command of relief parties and organised the move of Bn HQ to a safe area. RSM Wilde's cool determination has had a fine effect on all ranks with whom he came in touch and has resulted in forward Companies never having to look back for ammunition or stores.

M.B.E. 19.4.45   *(L.G. 15.6.44)*

Wildman, Edgar Owen, Sergeant (A/W.O.II (C.S.M.)
2987111, 7th Bn The Argyll & Sutherland Highlanders (Baildon, Yorks) (Immediate)

During the night attack on 10 Aug 1944 on a strongly defended enemy posn in woods, S.E. of St. Sylvain, Sjt. Wildman's platoon came under heavy machine gun fire and the platoon sustained a number of casualties which included the Pl. Officer. Sjt. Wildman immediately took command of the pl. and carried on to his objective although under a heavy cross fire the whole time. All through the night he was in constant and independent action against enemy posts and was unable to gain touch with his company Headquarters. He was not able to rejoin until 0930 hrs the following morning. Although he had only ten men of his pl. left, he took the whole of his pl. objective and captured 17 prisoners. It was undoubtedly due to his courage, leadership and determination that his pl. made this successful advance and captured a very important objective.   *(L.G. 21.12.44)*

Wilkes, Peter Duff, Warrant Officer Cl. II (temp.)
2411081, Royal Australian Infantry Corps
No citation.   *(L.G. 19.9.69)*

Wilkinson, Dennis, Warrant Officer Cl. II (C.S.M.)
4688371, 1/4 Bn. King's Own Yorkshire Light Infantry (Mansfield) (Immediate)

When temporarily under comd of Hallamshire Bn. CSM Wilkinson was an inspiring example to all ranks of 'D' Coy during the action at Barbee Ferme on 16 Jul 44. At 0645 hrs he organised four 2″ Mortars into a Battery to support the Coy forward to the objective. Although the Mortar Teams were heavily mortared in their position CSM Wilkinson kept them firing whilst support was required. He then brought forward the two remaining Mortars (the other two having been knocked out) to the objective through heavy Mortar and considerable S.A. fire. He immediately organised coy HQs and got the mortars and brens into fire posns.

The Coy was then isolated as one 18 Set had been mortared and knocked out and the other one was unable to get forward. CSM Wilkinson then returned across the fire swept ground to give the picture to the C.O. at Bn HQ (Hallams). He successfully did this and was able to inform the C.O. what was happening. It was then decided that another Coy should be sent to re-inforce 'D' Coy. CSM Wilkinson was detailed to lead them forward and show the Coy the way to their objective. Extremely heavy mortar fire was encountered but the CSM kept going arriving back at Barbee FM with one officer and two sections, the remainder being held up. From there until 'D' Coy's withdrawal this W.O. had a tremendous steadying effect on the men. His coolness, personal courage and presence of mind were an example to all. Finally he remained on the objective until all the others had withdrawn covering his Coy Comd out of the wood with his rifle.   *(L.G. 19.10.44)*

Wilkinson, Jack, Lance Corporal
2570986, 46 Div Sigs., Royal Signals (Seacroft, Yorks.)

For conspicuous gallantry and devotion to duty on 9th March 1943 at Tamara.

At approx. 0900 hours Lt. V. J. Sanger (RCOS) ordered L/Cpl. Wilkinson to execute the following tasks. (a) report to 457 Light Bty, R.A. with instructions about A. F. Gear of a W/T Set No. 21. (b) To repair the line from 457 Light Bty R.A. position to this Headquarters.

L/Cpl. Wilkinson on reaching the road and railway bridge near Tamara Station decided to leave his m/c in the woods and travel forward on foot. He set off under cover of the bushes and on approaching 457 Light Bty R.A. position saw a man with his back facing in the direction in which he was travelling, firing on members of the First Para Bn in that area, this man, a German Paratroop, he shot. A few minutes later he came within firing distance of another enemy—this one he shot through the lungs. These events happened whilst intense shell fire was being brought down on the whole area. Continuing on his way, still under shellfire, he delivered the message and A.F. gear to the Bty in question. L/Cpl. Wilkinson stayed on the position until wireless communications had been satisfactorily established to this H.Q. and then returned down the telephone wire, which he endeavoured to repair, but this was found impossible owing to the continuous shelling.

On his return journey to this H.Q. he saw a further enemy soldier firing in a kneeling position. This soldier he fired at and wounded in the thigh and then closed with the enemy who attempted to slash at him with a bayonet. L/Cpl. Wilkinson fired a second time and killed this Boshe, receiving himself only slight scratches on the left wrist. A few hundred yards further on he came across 3 German soldiers dressed in field-grey uniform, whom he captured and handed over to members of the 1st Para Bn as prisoners of war. On reaching Tamara railway bridge again he joined up with some more Paratroops who were fighting on the surrounding hills, during which time he shot another German soldier and finally returned to this H.Q.   *(L.G. 15.6.43)*

Wilkinson, Robert, Bombardier
*324626, 102/Northumberland Hussars, attd. Royal
   Artillery (Gateshead)*
Both in Greece and Crete Bdr. Wilkinson showed himself a brave, cool and dependable leader. He was a fine example to others at all times, as for instance on 20 May 1941 on the Akzotiri Peninsula, Suda Bay, Crete, when in charge of a bren gun section of four men at B.H.Q. Two German gliders landed on either side of B.H.Q. and Bdr. Wilkinson was ordered to deal with one of the gliders whilst his Battery Commander dealt with the other. Approaching the glider under cover, he set it on fire with a hand grenade, and whilst the German machine gunner's attention was thus distracted, he shot the gunner and knocked out the gun. The remainder of the glider crew took up a strong and heavily armed position, but Bdr. Wilkinson put up such a show of strength and determination that eventually the whole glider crew were either killed or taken prisoner. The prisoners included a German Hauptmann who was in charge of thirteen gliders and whose capture was of extreme importance.
                                            (L.G. 29.11.45)

Willans, Laurence Robert, Lance Corporal
WX 1488, Australian Military Forces
M.E. 1941, POW Pool   *(L.G. 15.11.45)*

Williams, Emrys Desmond, Staff Sergeant
24090754, Royal Welch Fusiliers
No citation.   *(L.G. 19.9.78)*

Williams, John, Warrant Officer Cl. II
22290559, Parachute Regt.
In the early morning of the 27th April 1965, Company Sergeant Major Williams was in his company base defended only by the Company Headquarters, a mortar section and one weak platoon of young soldiers, when they came under heavy attack by a force of Indonesian infantry more than 150 strong who were powerfully supported by rocket launchers, mortars, rifle grenades and machine guns from the surrounding hills.
The position was vulnerable and overlooked, the enemy fire intense and accurate, and there were several casualties. Company Sergeant Major Williams immediately took charge of the defence, controlled the defensive fire and steadied the young soldiers who were defending the base. He then moved round the position with complete disregard for his own safety, attending to the wounded, reorganising sections to meet each attack and, at one stage, took over a two inch mortar from the

wounded mortarman and fired illuminating bombs to light up the battlefield.
The enemy assault was rapid and determined, penetrated the inner wire and carried a mortar pit. A quickly organised section counter-attack had several casualties and was pinned down by enemy fire. Company Sergeant Major Williams then ran across the open ground under heavy fire to man a machine gun position from which he could fire into the mortar pit—and it was under cover of his fire that the enemy were ejected.
A second attack then developed directly against Company Sergeant Major Williams' position and he found himself under heavy fire from automatic weapons and rocket launchers at point blank range. He, himself, was hit by splinters and blinded in one eye, the radio set by his side was hit and the weapon he was using received direct hits on two occasions. He nevertheless continued to engage the enemy and was instrumental in breaking up the attack that had been pressed with fanatical determination. He killed one enemy soldier, who had a rocket launcher, within a few feet of his post.
He then reorganised the position, reported to his company commander and immediately took out a patrol to attack two more enemy parties which had again approached the perimeter. On his return, he was ordered to lie down and receive medical attention for his eye.
Throughout the whole action, Company Sergeant Major Williams showed outstanding bravery and devotion to duty, continually moving from one post to another under heavy fire—reorganising the defence, directing fire, carrying ammunition, attending the wounded, inspiring the men and setting a magnificent example to all ranks. The successful defence of the position against great odds was largely due to his courage, his example and leadership and to his own direct intervention in the battle at every crisis and at every point of maximum danger. *[From L.G.]*   *(L.G. 14.12.65)*

Williams, Kenneth Stanley, Gunner
*887308, 116 LAA Regt. Royal Artillery (Bexhill-on-
   Sea) (Immediate)*
On 27 Oct 44 during the attack on the outskirts of s'Hertogenbosch a tp of LAA SP guns was placed in sp of one of the leading bns. Gnr Williams was the dvr of the Tp commanders jeep. During this day the tp were given the task of supporting the carrier pl and throughout Gnr Williams drove the jeep about in the fwd area of the leading inf. On 28 Oct the tp was ordered to deploy in the Western half of s'Hertogenbosch and a recce party went fwd into the area in which it was known that there were many enemy snipers and which was under constant and heavy enemy fire. Gnr Williams drove about in the area totally ignoring this fire and showing utter disregard for his own safety. Several enemy prisoners were taken; these Gnr Williams took back to the Inf Coy HQ, through streets which were under fire, returning later to his tp comd. The tp had now deployed but were pinned to the ground, and one of the men became a cas. Gnr Williams

helped to load him on the jeep and drove back to the RAP under covering fire from a Bren mounted in the back of the jeep. Later in the day a further recce was made of the area, Gnr Williams accompanying his Tp Comd, throughout, who especially reported his complete coolness in the most dangerous circumstances. On the 29 Oct the inf located a spandau post near the canal, and Gnr Williams drove his jeep with the Tp Comd aboard, with great dash, followed by an SP gun into a fwd posn. Then with the SP covering the attack Gnr Williams drove the jeep with three others inside along the Canal bank and gook nine prisoners. The canal bank was in full view of the enemy and was under heavy fire. The Tp Comd and three others then took up posn and Gnr Williams kept them supplied with amn making several journeys and running the gauntlet along the canal bank fearlessly and without hesitation. This he continued to do throughout the day, and when the party were pinned down by enemy fire he and another came up and gave them covering fire. On the 30 Oct his Tp Comd and TSM were wounded, Gnr Williams took the latter back to the RAP and on the way back was hit in the hand, but successfully reached the scene of the fighting bringing with him a ladder with which to cross the canal to rescue his offr. In spite of his wounds he gave great assistance in carrying back his Tp Comd whilst being sniped and once again went back to the RAP over a route which was under enemy fire. His courage and complete devotion to duty throughout these four days of action were of the very highest order and there is no doubt that by his actions he contributed in no small measure to the success of the operation of his tp which enabled the leading tps to press on continuously. His gallant behavior is still the talk of his fellow men. *(L.G. 1.3.45)*

Williams, Thomas Garton, Sergeant
3129046, Royal Scots Fusiliers
No. 3129046 Sjt. T. Williams is recommended for the D.C.M., in recognition for his services during May 27th and 28th on the Ypres—Comines Canal.

This Sergeant was under my personal observation on many occasions under heavy enemy fire and was always noted to keep cool and use his brains. At about 9am on the morning of May 28th I took this NCO in a carrier from Bde H.Q. to try and establish contact with my Bn H.Q., we were unable to get nearer than the St. Eloi X rds on account of an enemy A/T weapon. At this point we found troops in the ditch unable to move as S.A. fire was coming from three sides. I ordered Sjt. Williams to drive the carrier to a covered position and dismount the Bren gun and engage the enemy on one front, he carried out my orders with perfect coolness and courage—on engaging the enemy with Bren gun fire the enemy fire from the fear ceased and the troops in the ditch managed to retire.

It is for this action in conjunction with continuous reports of coolness and courage that I recomment this NCO for the D.C.M.

M.I.D. 27.4.51 *(L.G. 27.8.40)*

Williams, Thomas, Sergeant
5332172, Royal Berkshire Regt.
This NCO was commanding the Carrier Pl. on the 15 May. On the 26 May having been ordered to secure by night the rd to Haverskerque. His pl came into contact with enemy A.F.B.s Several of his carriers were destroyed by the enemy in spite of this he still secured the road. His actions were always exemplary and he used his carriers vigourously throughout the operations.
(L.G. 22.10.40)

Williamson, Frank, M.M., Corporal
3241840, Army Air Corps (Bellshill, Lanark)
M.E. 1942, P.O.W. Pool.
M.M. 3.8.44 *(L.G. 11.4.46)*

Wilson, Alfred, Sapper
5885174, GSI(B), 8th Army Pool of Interpreters,
Royal Engineers (New York, U.S.A.) (since killed in action)
No: 5885174 Spr. Wilson was att 3/1 Punjab from 31 June to 12 Aug 44 as an official interpreter. On 1 Aug 44 he accompanied a reconnaissance patrol to Civitella, 738029 and when the patrol came under MG fire, he continued to advise the patrol comd regarding enemy posns.

Again on 5 Aug, Spr. Wilson accompanied a fighting patrol to Montone which became heavily engaged in a fierce fight with strong enemy posn. Spr. Wilson displayed great bravery and by his efforts and complete disregard for personal safety evacuated one wounded Ior several hundred yds down a steep hill in full view and under heavy fire. On this occasion, the infm Spr. Wilson was able to obtain from civilians in the neighbourhood was of extreme value and afforded considerable assistance to the patrol comd.

Between 20 and 24 Aug in the area Pt. 618, 6227, Spr. Wilson, frequently on his own initiative proceeded deep into enemy territory, to obtain valuable infm from civilian sources. Infm which he brought back, on one occasion enabled him to lead a patrol to within 200 yds of an enemy posn resulting in its capture and casualties on the enemy.

On 12 Aug, Spr. Wilson was att to Lovat Scouts, still in his capacity as interpreter. Whilst accompanying a patrol on 14 Aug in the Ponte Ale Piera area 3746, Spr. Wilson detached himself from the patrol and went ahead unaccompanied and approached a house occupied by the enemy, and succeeded in capturing single handed, 4 armed enemy soldiers. He continued to perform his duties in this manner until curtailed by OC Lovats, and it was with reluctance that Spr. Wilson permitted himself to be accompanied by an escort while performing his duties as interpreter and obtainer of infm from civilian sources behind the enemy lines.

Throughout his attachment to this fmn his conduct has been exemplary and the infm obtained of extreme value to our patrols and utmost importance to operations in this area.   *(L.G. 8.2.45)*

Wilson, Daniel, Sergeant
6968074, 7th Bn The Rifle Brigade (London, S.E.23)
(Immediate)
This NCO commanded a porteed 6 Pdr in the 7RB action between DJ Zemlet El Bieda and Dj Hadoudi north of El Hamma on 31 Mar 43. He gave magnificent support with H.E. from a forward and exposed position and personally directed the fire without a thought of his personal safety in spite of being continuously for three hours under very heavy artillery, mortar and S.A.A. fire. After all his H.E. had been expended he organised the unwounded Rfn. of his gun and a neighbouring gun into a defensive position and continued to fight his position with Brens and Rifles. When ordered to withdraw, Sjt. Wilson kept the advancing enemy infantry at bay until the remaining equipment had been withdrawn, finally pulling out himself when the enemy were only 150 yds away. Throughout the action—under continuous and heavy enemy fire Sjt. Wilson showed great courage and determination, which inspired all those under him to fight to the last.   *(L.G. 1.6.43)*

Wilson, Francis Wilfred, Private
NX 53925, 2/20th Bn. Australian Military Forces
During the action at Mersing in January 1942, No. 5 Section 11 Platoon, just prior to first light were ordered to re-occupy its section post north of Mersing River. The Section sucessfully crossed the river and approached within about 100 yards of its post, when heavy enemy mortar, automatic and rifle fire was brought to bear on it. One man was killed and two wounded. The Section Leader was wounded and Pte. Wilson, who had a bullet wound in the arm and a shrapnel wound in the back, took command of the Section and successfully drove the enemy out of the section post, killing most of them. The Section was then running short of ammunition, so Pte. Wilson ordered it to withdraw to the river, where he learned that the Section Leader, whom he thought was killed, was only badly wounded, so he and another volunteer moved forward again and endeavoured to bring him out. On the move forward the other man was badly wounded by mortar fire, but was able to return unaided. Pte. Wilson, though wounded himself, continued alone and was able to bring his Section Leader out under covering fire from our own troops. The Section then withdrew across the river, bringing out all the wounded.
                    (L.G. 10.1.46)

Wilson, Robert John, Sergeant
17108, 23 NZ Bn.
In the preliminary attack for the Orsogna Road Bridgehead on 7th Dec when his Pl Commander was wounded Sjt. Wilson immediately assumed command

of his Platoon which he controlled with outstanding skill. On the night of Dec 11th his Company advanced to a new position and had not completed their consolidation when they were unexpectedly counter attacked. In the absence of his Coy Commander Sjt. Wilson immediately and on his own initiative re-organised the defence to meet the attack. He inspired the men to move forward and meet the enemy standing up, controlling his fire until the enemy was at close quarters thus gaining a surprise which caused the enemy to withdraw with casaulties. Showing a sound military appreciation he anticipated a further more determined attack and in spite of heavy MG and small arms fire moved with complete disregard for personal safety amongst his men ensuring firm control and steadiness so that two further attacks were repulsed before artillery assistance was obtained to break up the enemy force. His conduct and bearing in action was at all times an inspiration to his company. *(L.G. 6.4.44)*

Wilson, Stanley Arthur, Colour Sergeant (A/W.O.II (C.S.M.))
16th Bn The Durham Light Inf. (Sutton) (Immediate)
On the morning of 13th September, 1943, the enemy got into position on the side of the hospital North of Salerno. As it was occupied by civilians the hospital building and grounds had been respected by us, but now it became apparant that the Germans were using it. 'A' Company, 16th Bn The Durham Light Infantry, to which Company Sergeant Major Wilson belongs were ordered to attack and drive the enemy off the position they had occupied. The time was about 1000 hours. 'A' Company supported by mortar fire (3") and smoke went up the hill into the attack. As the majority of the Company swung right handed to get round the enemy's flank they came under intense machine gun fire. The Company Commander and Second-in-Command were both wounded. The only other Officer was further over moving round the left flank. The Company Commander ordered the Company back and to move over to the left to join the other platoon who were using a more covered line of approach. Company Sergeant Major Wilson who has always shown real powers of leadership, courage and determination, came into his own at once. He directed the Company (less a platoon) over to the left. At that moment the enemy started to shell the area having registered it the day before. Company Sergeant Major Wilson continued to direct operations. He sent the men off to join the left platoon. He organized the evacuation of the wounded. Company Sergeant Major Wilson stayed forward for two hours and then slipped back. He satisfied himself that all wounded had been evcuated. The infomation he brought back greatly assisted the 2/4th Bn the King's Own Yorkshire Light Infantry to attack later that night. The way in which Company Sergeant Major Wilson controlled two thirds of the Company was splendid. His personal courage was an example to all ranks. I most strongly recommend this Warrant Officer

for the immediate award of a Distinguished Conduct Medal. *(L.G. 13.1.44)*

Windsor, Ernest Archibald, Gunner
968534, Royal Artillery (Stratford-on-Avon)
During the severe attacks by the enemy on the El Adem garrison on June 11th the name of Gnr. Windsor was recommended to 30 Corps H.Q. by W/T message for the Immediate Award of the D.C.M. on account of the conspicuously gallant, and meritorious service he had shown in the defence of the position. *(L.G. 13.8.42)*

Winstanley, John, Sergeant (temp.)
SR 598299V, First City / Cape Town
 HighlandersSouth African Forces (Immediate)
For great courage and devotion to duty
On the thirteenth of October 1944 the Battalion was engaged in the final attack [...]chi culminated in the capture of the Stanco feature in the mountains North of Camugnano. Starting at 04.45 hours the leading company was given the task of reaching it's objective, Point 602, before dawn. In this Company Sergeant Wintanley's platoon led the assault and soon encountered strong opposition, a number being killed and wounded including his platoon Commander. Appreciating the urgency of his task however Sergeant Winstanley rushed the enemy positions killing several, taking six prisoners and putting the rest to flight. These prisoners were interrogated and gave the valuable information that the division on this sector had been changed.

When dawn broke he had reached Point 602 and held on throughout the day in spite of persistent shelling and mortaring. Point 602 was the key to the defence of the whole sector and by holding on he enabled the company to consolidate and break up all attempts by the enemy to form up a counter attack. Although wounded himself he refused to leave the platoon and held his post until the battalion had reorganised on the ground they had won.

Throughout the battle Sergeant Winstanley displayed the greatest courage and skill in the control of his platoon and by his devotion to duty ensured the success of the action. *(L.G. 8.3.45)*

Winter, William Arthur, Warrant Officer Cl. I (actg.)
7263180, 5 Br Fd Amb. R.A.M.C. (St. Albans)
 (Immediate)
Burma 16 Feb—15 May 1945
During the complicated medical arrangements necessary to cover 2 Div's operation for the crossing of the Irrawaddy commencing on 24 Feb, RSM Winter's detailed organisation was beyond praise. For 72 hrs he toured the forward A.D.S's often under intense shell fire, giving assistance where necessary and ensuring that the evacuation of casualties worked efficiently. He crossed the river under machine gun fire and there under extreme difficulties organised collection of casualties within the Bridgehead. The embarkation point was at that time only 300 yards from the enemy, and was swept by machine gun fire. RSM Winter showed complete disregard for his own safety.

The smoothness of evacuation under the most difficult circumstances and the consequent excellent condition in which the patients reached hospital were undoubtedly due to the coolness and resourcefulness of RSM Winter and by his work many lives were undoubtedly saved.

During the whole period under review covering the crossing of the Chindwin up to and including, the crossing of the Irrawaddy, RSM Winter has shown outstanding initiative and leadership and coolness in the face of the enemy. *(L.G. 17.1.46)*

Winthrop, Colin Joseph, Gunner
26103, 6 NZ Fd. Regt.
On 10th Dec 1941, the 6 NZ Regt was heavily attacked by tanks and infantry. Gnr. Winthrop as driver of tractor B.4 stood throughout the action beside his tractor ready to bring his gun out of action. The gun was eventually disabled by a burst of hostile gunfire. At the same time Gnr. Winthrop was wounded through both arms and both legs. Despite this he crawled into his tractor drove it up to where the gun was collected a load of personnel and drove them quickly to the rear. After driving for about two miles he collapsed and had to be lifted out of his tractor. *(L.G. 20.1.42)*

Wisiki, Bauleni, WS/Cpl. (Immediate)
DN 9327, 22 (NY) K.A.R.
On 27th Oct. 44 No. DN 9327 Cpl. Wisiki Bauleni was the leading sec comd of 13 Pl of C Coy, during C Coys attack on Brown Hill, Burma. Within 100 yards of the start line, Cpl. Wisiki was wounded by a grenade, for the first time. Undeterred, Cpl. Wisiki continued to lead his sec forward, being wounded twice more before finally reaching his objective. In spite of weakness and loss of blood from three wounds, Cpl. Wisiki refused to be evacuated and continued to direct the fire of his sec on to a Japanese counter attack which was then launched. This attack was beaten off, but during the course of it Cpl. Wisiki was wounded for the fourth time, and then only, when unconscious, was he evacuated.

Wolsey, John, Sergeant
5102418, 1/7 Royal Warwickshire Regt.
When his Platoon position was being heavily shelled he saw one section post receive a direct hit, which killed the Section Commander. Without Orders he immediately ran forward and took command of the section and by his example raised the moral of the men who were rather shaken. In spite of being severely wounded himself and in considerable pain, a little later he refused to allow anyone to run the risk of carrying him in and remained there until dark. *(L.G. 22.10.40)*

Wongsue, Jack, Leading Aircraftman
83783, 'A' Special Unit, Royal Australian Air Force
(Periodic)
From 3 Mar 45 to 15 Aug 45 this NCO displayed leadership, gallantry and cold-blooded courage of the highest order. On 3 Mar 45 Sjt. Wonsue was a member of a small party of 4 officers and 3 NCO's who entered British North Borneo well knowing:— (a) That there was a large price on the head of the leader of the party as a result of his previous mission into the area (enemy posters were found bearing his portrait and offering a reward of $15000 for him dead or alive). (b) That having left the submarine there was no chance of withdrawal (c) That the coast was strongly held by the enemy and continuously patrolled by land and sea.

The landing was made by rubber boat and canoe midway between two strong enemy posts at Tegahanf and Pura Pura 3 miles apart. Owing to the hostility of the natives, 250 miles were travelled by canoe at night before finding a friendly contact enabling the party to move inland. The cold-blooded courage required to make a landing of the type above described is worthy of the highest commendation.

Whilst in the interior, this NCO did magnificent work in gathering intelligence, organising native guerillas and harassing the enemy, capturing considerable quantities of Japanese equipment and killing numbers of the enemy.

In addition, in 21 May 45, this NCO was extracted by Catalina with his party leader and when further infomation was required on behalf of 9 Aust Div he volunterred to enter Borneo again. On 29 May 45 with his party leader and another NCO and one native, Sjt. Wonsue was inserted by Catalina into the strongly held Beaufort area near Brunei Bay.

After a reconnaissance of the situation on 31 May 45, the party leader discovered that the railway stationmaster at Bongowan was a Chinese named Ah Lee known to him in pre-war days. In a particularly daring operation, covered at close range by the party leader and the other NCO, Sjt. Wonsue entered Bongowan railway station staffed and guarded by Japanese and in broad daylight extracted Ah Lee from the station for the party leader to interrogate. During the next 8 days, this NCO checked the information passed by Ah Lee and at great personal risk watched hundreds of Japanese move down the railway line. The information thus received and passed on was of the highest importance to 9 Aust Div. From 29 May 45 to 7 Jun 45, this small party operated in the heart of the most strongly held area in British North Borneo, necessarily on the alert 24 hours of the day.

On 7 Jun 45, this NCO with the party, was extracted by Catalina and a few weeks later returned to the interior of Borneo where his work continued to be of great value and earned the highest praise of his commander.
(L.G. 24.5.46)

Wood, Allen Campbell, Warrant Officer Cl. I (R.S.M.)
30485, 28 Maori Bn.
At Platanias on 21st May this Warrant Officer did excellent work in leading a party of men from Bn Headquarters in cleaning up parachutists who had landed in the Bn and Div Engineer areas. He personally accounted for many of the enemy, who had already come into action.

On the 22nd May, during the attack on Maleme he personally led several small bodies of our men in bayonet rushes against enemy posts and M.Gs. Later, when the attack had stopped, he and a soldier stalked and accounted for at least two enemy machine gunners and two snipers. During these operations he received a bullet wound on side of chest, but would not be evacuated. This Warrant Officer is apparently fearless and throughout operations in Greece and Crete has set the highest possible example to all ranks. *(L.G. 30.12.41)*

Wood, Harold John, Warrant Officer Cl. III (Pl.S.M.)
2611848, 3rd Bn. Grenadier Guards
For courage, [...] & leadership (recomendation DCM).

On 28 May 40 this W.O. handled the mortar pl with the greatest ability. He showed complete disregard for personal danger, when bringing his mortars into action on repeated occasions under heavy fire. His behaviour throughout the battle was an example to all.
(L.G. 27.8.40)

Wood, James Deans, Warrant Officer Cl. II (actg.)
P 21422, Princess Patricia's Canadian Light Infantry
(Immediate)
Reference Map Italy 1/25,000 Sheets 100 I SW S Giorgio Di Cesena and 100 II NW Cesena

On 20 October 1944, the Princess Patricia's Canadian Light Infantry was ordered to secure a bridgehead over the River Savio. 'A' Company's task was to establish a bridgehead in the area C Medri (MR 588102) to C Saladini (MR 599099). P21422 Serjeant (A/WOII) (Acting Company Serjeant Major) James Deans Wood was Company Serjeant Major of this company.

It had not been possible to make a thorough reconnaissance to the proposed crossing place or of the approaches to the river previous to the attack owing to their exposed position. The attack was launched at 1710 hours under extremely heavy fire from enemy machine guns, mortars and artillery and over ground that was found to be mined. The crossing was accordingly found to be an extremely dangerous undertaking owing to this enemy oppostion and to the swollen nature of the river. Completely disregarding these dangers, Serjeant Major Wood who arrived at the river with the leading elements, remained there under fire during the whole crossing and personally assisted seventeen non-swimmers across to the other bank.

A reconnaissance of the objective, in which he took part, revealed that it was very strongly held by machine guns from well concealed positions. While the Company moved to surround the position Serjeant Major Wood worked his way forward to within 85 yards of the position and then, dashing across the open stretch of ground he threw hand grenades into one of the machine gun posts killing two of the enemy and forcing three into the open where they were taken prisoners.

On the afternoon of 21 October 1944 while he was escorting a wounded officer to the river crossing at Tay (MR 595107) an enemy sniper opened fire at close range from a dug-in position. Serjeant Major Wood immediately attacked this position with hand grenades, killing one German and capturing two others.

Throughout the whole operation, covering two days, this Warrant Officer showed great courage and a complete disregard for his own personal safety. He personally killed three enemy in dug outs and captured five; at all times his actions, which were far beyond the normal call of his duty, were an inspiration to all ranks in his company and a contributing factor to the success of the operation. *(L.G. 17.2.45)*

Wood, Joseph William, Sergeant
2614780, Grenadier Guards
No citation. *(L.G. 22.10.40)*

Wood, Robert, Sergeant (actg.)
2616015, Grenadier Guards (now Army Physical Training Corps) (Ferry Hill)
No citation. *(L.G. 24.1.46)*

Woodcock, Clifford Arthur, Warrant Officer Cl. II
4744382, 1st Bn. York & Lancaster Regt. (Parkgate) (Immediate)
On 1 May 45, after the leading platoons of 'C' Coy had advanced through the village of Grosser Pampau, Coy HQ under CSM Woodcock advanced into the village. A party of enemy, under an officer, which had been left behind opened fire on them. CSM Woodcock immediately took command and returned the fire. A section of the reserve platoon which was in the vicinity was taken by him and added to his force. By skilful use of Coy HQ as a fire unit he outflanked the enemy with the section and forced what remained of the enemy to surrender. The German officer and six ORs were killed and about 20 others were captured. It was due to the great initiative and personal disregard for danger shown by this W.O. that this action was successful. *(L.G. 2.8.45)*

Woodgate, Reginald, Sergeant
142582, 15th A.A. Bty., Royal Artillery
Sjt. Woodgate displayed great gallantry in maintaining the service of guns during 1st–2nd June at Dunkirk dockyard whilst under heavy shell fire and low-flying bombing attacks of the enemy. He put up a very effective fire which dispersed severl low-flying attacks on the Mole and undoubtedly saved it from severe damage.
(L.G. 20.12.40)

Woodhouse, William George, Lance Sergeant
3914270, 6th Bn The South Wales Borderers (Birmingham) (Immediate)
Mayu Range, Arakan 26th March, 1944
During an attack on Maungdaw—Butidaung road positions on 26th March 1944 this NCO was in command a section which was wiped out by Japanese grenades. Sjt. Woodhouse continued the assault on the enemy positions alone, grenading the positions and killing a number of the enemy with his grenades and C.M.T. He captured the enemy position and cleared the bunker showing unsurpassed gallantry and complete disregard for himself. *(L.G. 22.6.44)*

Woods, Jack, Sergeant (temp.)
213636, Royal Australian Infantry Corps
For Vietnam *(L.G. 10.12.68)*

Woods, John, Sergeant
2614778, attd 143 Inf Bde, 1st Div, 1st Corps, 3rd Bn Gren. Gds.
For courage and leadership (recommandation DCM)
On 28 May 40 this NCO was commanding this Coy, as all his officers and WOs had become casualties. He organised the defence of his position with great skill and fought the Coy in the most gallant way against repeated attacks throughout the day. His leadership and personal gallantry were outstanding. *(L.G. 22.10.40)*

Woods, William Arthur, Private
QX 8178, 2/15 Aust Inf Bn. (Immediate)
On 13 Oct 1943 during the period of fierce and continuous fighting over difficult mountainous jungle country that followed the opposed landing north of Finschhafen by the 20th Australian Infantry Brigade Group, Private Woods showed most conspicuous leadership, resolution, and personal bravery. When his company attacked strong and well-sited enemy positions, concealed in a thick undergrowth of tangled cane west of the village of Kimawa, Woods was commanding his section, the section Corporal having been wounded in an earlier engagement. As the attack went in Woods' section came suddenly under heavy machine gun fire from a strong enemy post thirty yards away. Woods at once led an assault on the post and pressed it home although two of his men were killed and four wounded, leaving him with only one man to support him when he reached the enemy post, which they reduced with grenades. He then turned and engaged a flanking post which had already caused casualties to another section of his platoon and overcame its fire so effectively that the rest of the platoon were able to close with the two remaining enemy posts and destroy them. Private Woods' soldierly and methodical coolness under fire is illustrated by the fact that during the action he used twelve grenades against the enemy though he carried only two into the attack, and an Owen sub-machine gun though he began the attack with a rifle. The sub-machine

gun and several magazines for it and the extra grenades he obtained from our men who became casualties during the progress of the attack. His courageous conduct opened the way to the defeat of three heavily defended enemy positions and was one of the decisive factors in enabling our troops to clear the area of the enemy who withdrew in confusion leaving behind them thirty-nine of their dead and a number of weapons. *(L.G. 23.3.44)*

Woodward, Harold Henry, Craftsman
7622725, R.E.M.E., 3 Bn. R.T.R. (Leigh-on-Sea,
    Essex)
In 1941 April, Woodward was captured in Greece and later taken to a Prisoner of War Camp at Woltzburg in Austria. From this camp he was transferred to various small working camps which enabled him to gain information about the surrounding countryside and also gave him the opportunity of learning the language. On September 15 at a small camp near Vienna, Woodward and a friend arranged to escape. At 9 p.m. they attacked the two guards at the gate with bars unscrewed from some windows and struck out in a S.E. direction. As a result of previous unsuccessful attempts to escape it was decided not to travel by night, but masquerade as German Officers on leave in civilian clothes travelling openly by day. Whenever it looked as though they were to be spoken to, they said 'Heil Hitler' thus creating an impression of Gestapo in plain clothes.

As no help was forthcoming from the civil population of Austria they had to exist on what they could steal from the land such as turnips and grapes. On crossing the Border into Yugo-slavia they stopped at a house to ask for food and finding the Ustache in occupation, Woodward and his friend used great presence of mind in following up their story of German Officers on leave and convinced their hosts that their papers had been stolen. They spent the night in this house and left on their travels the following morning furnished with a considerable amount of information about location of units etc.

They were finally picked up by the Partisans and returned to the British after a very difficult spell trying to convince the Partisans that they were escaped British Prisoners of War and not German spies. Apart from making an outstanding escape and showing great initiative, Woodward was able to pass on valuable information which will help future escapees. He has also volunteered to go back into enemy occupied territory and help his companions escape in the same way. This is an excellent example of courage and initiative and I thoroughly recommend that this soldier be awarded the D.C.M. for his great achievement. *(L.G. 24.8.44)*

Worrall, Stanley, Private
32164, Transvaal Scottish
For acts of individual bravery in action.

At one stage of the attack on the main enemy positions on the night of the 23/24 Oct 42, at El Alamein, Pte.

Worrall's platoon was pinned down by heavy fire from a machine-gun post. There were no support weapons available to silence the post, and attempts to reach it with grenades had been unsuccessful. By this time, the general advance of the company had slowed up. Showing great initiative and presence of mind, Pte. Worrall fixed his bayonet and charged the post, killing the gunner at his gun and taking the remaining members of the post prisoner.

Pte. Worrall's presence of mind and initiative saved his platoon from heavy casualties, and enabled the advance to be continued. His display of courage was an inspiration to all.   *(L.G. 31.12.42)*

Worsdale, Ormonde, Gunner
1897, 4 NZ Fd Regt. (Immediate)
During the action of the 4 NZ Bde at Ruweisat Ridge on the morning of July 15th 1942, the armoured Arty OP in which Gnr. Worsdale was wireless operator, was set on fire by a hit from enemy tanks at close range. This soldier showed conspicuous gallantry and devotion to duty by climbing back into the burning vehicle soon afterward in order to man his wireless set and pass essential fire orders. He succeeded in getting through two complete sets of fire orders before being compelled to make his final exit under enemy fire from the now fiercely burning vehicle.

Again, during the operation of the 9 Armd Bde, which his Regt was supporting, the action in front of El Miteiriya [...]ge on the morning of 25 October, the officer commanding the light tank used as an Arty OP was wounded. Gnr. Worsdale, after assisting under fire in the removal of the unconscious officer, took immediate command of the tank and effected its safe conduct through the fighting of the heavier tanks, and its subsequent withdrwal through the heavily shelled gap of the minefield.

Throughout these operations this soldier has exhibited initiative, coolness and courage of an exemplary order and has been an example to all in contact with him.
                                          (L.G. 28.1.43)

Worsley, Austin Reginald, Warrant Officer Cl. II
6342368, 1 Queen's Own Royal West Kent Regt.
    (London, S.E.25) (Immediate)
Ref Map:— Italy 100/11 NW Cesena 1/25,000

On 24 Oct, 1944 'C' Coy was ordered to advance under cover of a barrage some 1000 yds on to an area round rd junc 568066. Just after the advance had commenced the Coy Comd and two signallers became casualties from shellfire. CSM Worsley immediately took over command of the Coy as the only two other officers were already deployed forward with their pls. He quickly re-organised his Coy HQ and 18 Set, and continued to command the Coy, shouting orders and encouragement to his men. Before long CSM Worsley was himself wounded in the back but despite this he continued to lead the Coy and to send back valuable information to

Bn HQ on his 18 Set. Despite the attempts of the Coy Stretcher Bearers CSM Worsley refused evacuation until word could be got to one of the Pl Comds to inform him of the loss of the Coy Comd. CSM Worsley himself supervised the consolidation and was eventually evacuated when his relief arrived.

Throughout this operation CSM Worsley displayed great powers of leadership, initiative and personal courage. His quick action and devotion to duty undoubtedly prevented any loss of efficiency in the Coy which might have arisen temporarily by the sudden loss of the Coy Comd and signallers, and his own personal courage was an inspiration to all around him.

(L.G. 26.4.45)

Wraight, Ernest Clarence, Private
745994, 14 Field Ambulance, R.A.M.C. (Smeeth, Kent)
While a prisoner at Halfaya, Pte. Wraight was unfaltering in his attentions to our wounded and sick. He never had any water available to wash wounds and had no clean bandages but he succeeded in saving the lives of everyone of them. He habitually climbed under shell and bomb fire, the face of the escarpment to the German caves (which were mainly at the top where the British prisoners were at the bottom) to beg for medicines, iodine and food for the wounded. The Germans were short of all these things. Not ony were our wounded suffering from their injuries but they were without pure drinking water (in some cases for eight weeks), they had only one third of a small tinof bully apiece a day, one eighth of a pint of liquid daily in the form of a salt-tasting soup or occasionally ersatz coffee (also very salt) and they were consequently half-starved and weakened with thirst. One night when the ration party, under a German guard, went out to get rations they were bombed by the R.A.F. and a New Zealander was killed and a German sentry wounded. Wraight heard the German crying in the night, went out, found him badly wounded and amputated his shattered arm with a pen-knife, applying a turniquet thereafter. The Germans were able to end to collect this man next day. The German Commander sent Wraight a packet of cigarettes and his thanks for his heroism, presence of mind and conscientious discharge of his duty as a medical orderly. Wraight was seven weeks a prisoner. He continued his work until too weak himself to carry on.
Report by Pilot Officer H. Earl, 201 Group Royal Air Force, on Pte. Ernest Wraight, RAMC
During my stay in the prison camp from January 2nd to 17th no medical officer attended to my wounds, apart from an initial dressing by an Italian doctor, and due to this man's frequent visits to the German medical officer which entailed a climb up the face of the escarpment of about 1 mile, he obtained sufficient supplies of iodine, dressings, quinine etc. to keep his patient in the best possible health. Had he not done this, and given all his attentions to the wounded, the consequences must have been serious, and it was noted that after the treatment he rendered to the German Guard, who was injured by the bomb, he was usually successful in adding to his stock of supplies. He attended cheerfully to all prisoners at any time of the day or night, and frequently shared his meagre liquid ration with others, and I felt we were fortunate in having an R.A.M.C. orderly in the camp.

(L.G. 9.9.42)

Wright, Frederick William, Sergeant
27215, 2 T.S., Union Defence Force (Periodic)
For devotion to duty while in command of the Mortar Section of the 2nd Battalion Transvaal Scottish in the Acroma Keep during the period 25th April to 19th June, 1942. His Section performed excellent work, on one occasion knocking out a German Mark II Tank by a lucky hit on its turret with a mortar bomb. Sjt. Wright was a leader of high degree and his efficiency and courage inspired his section to give of their best. He was a splendid soldier at all times, and it was mainly due to his splendid example that the 'Keep' held out against repeeated tank attacks by the enemy.
M.I.D. 5.12.46   *(L.G. 19.12.46)*

Wright, John, Warrant Officer Cl. II (actg.)
3317002, 10th Bn. Highland Light Infantry (Glasgow)
On 24 Mar 45 the bn carried out an assault crossing of the R. Rhine in the early morning. 'A' Coy was the left hand forward company and had the task of clearing about 500 yards of a bund which ran parallel to the river and about 50 yards from the water's edge. The company was unavoidably landed too far South and was confronted with the task of clearing up a portion of the bund which had been allotted to the right hand forward company. Heavy opposition from enemy spandaus and a 20 mm gun was encountered and the company sustained many caualties, one of whom was the Company Comd. While endeavouring to assault the 20 mm gun position, the only remaining officer in the company was killed. CSM Wright immediately took command of the company. Although the platoons were considerably reduced in strength, he was able to clear several MG positions from the bund and advanced up the main axis from the bund. During this advance, he came under heavy fire from a 20 mm gun at short range as a result of which one platoon was pinned to the ground. CSM Wright gathered the remnants of the remaining two platoons and successfully assaulted the enemy posn which was pinning down the third platoon. He t[...] consolidated and held the ground g[...]ed under enemy machine gun, shell and mortar fire, until he was reinforced by another company.

Throughout the entire action CSM Wright showed admirable initiative and bravery. The speed and readiness with which he accepted and carried out the responsibilities not only saved his company from suffering further casualties but also enabled the initial bridgehead to be taken and enlarged.   *(L.G. 12.7.45)*

Wright, Peter, CSM
2657545, 3rd Coldstream Gds. (Immediate)
On 25 Sep 43 3rd Bn Coldstream Guards attacked the Pagliarolli feature, a steep wooded hill near Salerno. Before they reached the crest the right hand company was held up by heavy spandau and mortar fire and all the officers had become casualties. CSM Wright, seeing that his company was held up, went forward to see what could be done. Finding that there were no officers left he immediately took charge and crawled forward by himself to see what the opposition was. He shortly returned, collected a section; informed them that three spandau posts were holding them up and put them into a position where they could give covering fire. Single handed he then attacked each post in turn with hand grenade and bayonet and silenced each one. He then led the company on to the crest but realised that the enemy fire made this position untenable. He therefore led them a short way down the hill again and up on to the objective from a different direction. Entirely regardless of enemy fire, which was very heavy, he then re-organised what was left of the company and placed them in position to consolidate the objective. Soon afterwards the enemy launched a counter attack which was successfully beaten off. Later, with complete disregard of heavy enemy shellfire on the area of company headquarters and the reverse slopes of the hill and of machine gun fire from the commanding slopes on the left flank of the position, he brought up extra ammunition and distriuted it to the company. It is due to this Warrant Officer's superb disregard of the enemy's fire, his magnificent leadership and his outstanding heroism throughout the action that his battalion succeeded in capturing and maintaining their hold on this very important objective.

I was watching this attack from the hill in rear. I saw the right hand company held up under heavy mortar fire. I then saw it move up to the crest, later withdrew and go up to the crest further to the left. All through this period the company was under heavy and accurate mortar fire and there was the sound of many spandaus firing. The results of the latter I was of course unable to see.
Subsequently cancelled and replaced by award of V.C., L.G. 7.9.44   *[L.G. 27.1.44]*

Wyeth, Reginald, C.Q.M.S. (A/W.O.II (C.S.M.))
5490220, 2 Royal Warwickshire Regt.
For gallantry in action at Hollain 20/21 May and Wormhoudt 28 May 40.

Driven by shell fire in the late afternoon of 20 May from his position in the open in rear of Company H.Q., C.Q.M.S. Wyeth set up his cookhouse in a cellar. Here, although the house was shelled, and in spite of an intense bombardment which went on continuously till after 1800 hrs on 21 May, he organised and distributed to the three platoons, three meals during the 24 hours. In his behaviour he displayed a great deal of common sense, coolness when under fire, and an organising ability of a high order. It was entirely due to his personal efforts

and no one else's that the Company was fed; and from the point of view of rations, kept in good heart.

After the Battle at Wormhoudt on 28 May he was placed in command of the rear group of the Company H.Q. party which had to cut their way out through the German lines after dark. During the course of this 'sortie' the whole party came under enemy automatic fire and got separated.

C.Q.M.S. Wyeth led his small party away to a flank towards a copse. Here he called over the names of the party, some of whom he found missing. With what he had left he wormed through the copse, and one of his party butt-striking a German on the way. [...] bold, skilfull leadership he led his small party through the southern end of the town; breaking into a house to get into the fields beyond. Here they encountered a German sentry who appeared to be asleep outside some H.Q. Giving him a wide berth, C.Q.M.S. Wyeth struck off in a North Easterly direction. He had nothing to guide him except the Pole Star and had not the slightest knowledge of the whereabouts of the Battalion or the Brigade. He merely worked on the instructions of his Company Commander that the latter intended to break through to the South of Wormhoudt and then march N.E. in the hope of finding the Battalion. On the morning 29th May, C.Q.M.S. Wyeth and his party found Bn H.Q. where he narrated his adventures calmly and in a manner as though nothing untoward had occurred.

In the course of these two actions C.Q.M.S. Wyeth has shown gallantry when under fire and that he possesses skill and courage in adversity together with grit and determintion.   *(L.G. 3.9.40)*

Wylie, James, Guardsman
2719527, 1st Bn. Irish Guards (Immediate)
On May 25th a company of the Irish Guards were occupying the front line in Pothus Wood. [...] platoon occupied the left front and a section was in the platoon centre. This section post was on the forward slope of the hill and further down than any other section. The duty of the section was to bring heavy fire on the enemy in the early stages of the attack and then to withdraw to an alternative position, already prepared, higher up the hill. Having fulfilled its first task, and by now being under heavy fire, the Platoon Commander ordered the section to withdraw to the second position. When the section had done this, it was discovered that a gun had been left behind. The Pl Commander then ordered the No. 1 to fetch the gun; he went off to do so but returned shortly afterwards saying the machine gun fire was too heavy for him to get through. The Pl Commander said the gun must be got back and Gdsmn. J. Wylie proceeded to the vacated position, fetched the gun, returned and fetched the tripod, then returned a third time and brought back the picks and shovels. All this was achieved under very heavy fire. the bravery and coolness this guardsman showed had a great effect on the morale of the section,

who had been under consistently severe fire, and shortly resumed their original forward post.
M.I.D. 23.9.43   *(L.G. 6.8.40)*

Wynn, Norman Samuel, Sergeant (actg.)
5621682, 1/4th Bn. Hampshire Regt. (Frinton)
    (Immediate)
For devotion to duty and Most Conspicuous bravery
Map Ref 250187 Brisighella, Italy 1/25,000 Sheet 99.I.SW.
On night 3/4 Dec 44 Sjt. Wynn was comd the leading Pl in the Bn attack across the R. Lamone and in a heavy mist attacked and captured an enemy strongpoint killing two and taking two prisoners. On night 4/5 Dec his Pl attacked again and drove the enemy from their posns at Casa Valle by attacking them from the rear after a fatiguing night move over mountainous country, killing and wounding five enemy. On night 5/6 Dec he led his Pl against strong enemy opposition on Pt 261 (map ref 235213 Castel Bolognese, Italy 1/25,000 Sheet 99.I.NW) and adjoining houses which he successfully captured.

He took 4 MG posts, killed 3 enemy and captured 11 prisoners. His Pl then held the ground against a counter attack inflicting heavy losses on the enemy. In all these actions Sjt. Wynn acted with utmost ability and skill and his capability and leadership were of the highest order. His courage and steadfastness in face of the enemy were a constant source of inspiration to his men.
(L.G. 10.5.45)

Wynn, Reginald, Sergeant
6088800, 5 Queen's Royal Regt.
27 May. A sec comd of the Carrier Pl, was given orders to take his carriers forward to Becque 3848 to deny to the enemy tanks access to Strazeele. In spite of the fact that there were three German tanks operating in that area, he concealed his carriers and by dismounted action, forced the enemy to withdraw to Borre. His really aggressive leadership was instrumental in saving the Bn many casualties, and he fought an unsupported battle for nearly three hours.   *(L.G. 11.7.40)*

Y

Yacalevu, Ropate, Private
4472, Fiji Military Forces
No citation.   *(L.G. 7.12.44)*

Yarrow, John, Lance Sergeant
4386530, 7th Green Howards (Spennymoor, Co.
*   Durham) (Immediate)*
Place—Mareth Line, Northern Sector
During the night 20/21st March 1943, L/Sjt. Yarrow was second-in-command of a fighting Patrol which was sent ahead of his Company in an attack on a strongly held enemy position, in order to cover a party of sappers who were to clear a path through the enemy minefield. On reaching the minefield, the R.E. mine detector failed to work and L/Sjt. Yarrow knowing the company was following up quickly, immediately went forward detecting the mine. Very heavy enemy defensive fire was coming down in the area all the time L/Sjt. Yarrow was at work, but with remarkable coolness he completed his task.

A heavy smoke screen later caused part of the patrol to become separated from the rest and L/Sjt. Yarrow immediately took over this handful of men, rushed and captured an enemy mortar post and then, with grenades, drove out a troublesome German M.M.G. section. He then led his men on to the final objective and rejoined his company, where he continued to be an inspiration to his men.

Throughout the whole action, L/Sjt. Yarrow, by his complete disregard for his own safety, inspired everyone with his own courage and devotion to duty.
                                               (L.G. 1.6.43)

Yarrow, William Herbert Thorborn, Lance Sergeant
QX4973, 2/13 Aust Fd Coy. R.A.E.
Distinguihed conduct in action during attack on enemy position West of El Alamein, 1 Sep 42.

L/Sjt. Yarrow was commander of a party RAE attached to a forward inf coy. Encountering minefields he commanded his party in making and marking a gap 50 yds wide by 160 yds deep through them under heavy M.G. and shell fire—so heavy that the entire first minelifting party on a nearby gap became casualties in the first ten minutes (before the completion of their task). L/Sjt. Yarrow was also hit on one hand; he carried on, completed his own gap, and later seeing that a neighbouring gap (Gap C) was incomplete through sapper casualties he completed it under very heavy enemy fire including A.Tk. gun fire. He was hit in the leg at this stage but remained on the gap until 30 minutes later he was able to contact a L/Cpl. and arrange for him to take over the position. He was then carried back to our own lines by two prisoners. L/Sjt. Yarrow remained very cool during the whole operation and took pains to advise the tanks and the infantry of the initial failure to complete Cap C, and later to report to them that the gap had been completed. He showed great personal courage, steadiness and qualities of leadership under very heavy enemy fire and would not leave the minefield gap although twice wounded, until the work was completed and it was possible to hand over to another NCO.
                                               (L.G. 5.11.42)

Yates, Samuel, Lance Corporal
24393, 24 Bn., New Zealand Military Forces
On 18 Apr 41, South of Ellason, when commanding a forward section in contact with the enemy he was in receipt of orders to withdraw. The enemy then advanced with 48 AFVs. He delayed his withdrawal until his Coy HQ had been advised of the changed situation and he had received confirmation of the order to withdraw.

On 24 Apr 41, during the enemy attack at Thermopylae, his section was surrounded by small parties of enemy who had dismounted from tanks. During the tank attack he kept his men under cover and afterwards led a party which successfully 'mopped up' the dismounted enemy tank crews.

From 27 to 30 Apr 41, in the vicinity of Kalamata beach he displayed courage and initiative in leading his section. In spite of unsuccessful attempts to escape he continued the attempts and by his leadership and tenacity succeeded in saving the majority of his section.
M.I.D. 30.12.41   *(L.G. 29.9.42)*

Yauwiga, Warrant Officer Cl. I
R416, Australian Military Forces
Recommended by Gov. Gen. Australia   *(L.G. 6.3.47)*

Yeates, Albert Edward, Lance Sergeant
D.15060, 16th Cdn Field Company, Corps of Royal
*   Canadian Engineers (Immediate)*
At Nieuwvliet on the 28 Oct 44, Lance Sergeant Albert Edward Yeates was in charge of a section detailed to clear the road of mines behind the advancing infantry. His instructions were to clear the road south from the coast towards Nieuwvliet. Approaching a cross-road and small village, he and his section came under MG fire from a hitherto unknown pillbox about 50 yds ahead. Ordering one sub-section to give him covering fire, Lance Sergeant Albert Edward Yeates at the head of the remaining sub-section and firing the Bren Gun from the hip charged forward onto the enemy position which was cleared and three prisoners were taken. Noticing that fire was still coming from a large pillbox in the centre of the village Lance Sergeant Albert Edward Yeates collected his sub-section and again led them forward to clear and

capture the position, this time taking nine prisoners. He then reorganised this section and held the position under intense concentration of mortar and shell fire until the arrival of a Coy of the 1 C Scot R made possible the capture of the remainder of the village.

The high courage and exceptional qualities of leadership shown by this NCO under the most exacting circumstances were an inspiration to his men and made possible the capture of these two vital pillboxes.

(L.G. 10.2.45)

Yeowell, Stanley William, Rifleman
6845500, 2 Bn. King's Royal Rifle Corps

I was captured at Calais on 26 May 40 with what remained of my Bn. We had left Dover only four days previously. After capture we were marched through France, Belgium and Holland into Germany, our journey lasting about three weeks. In Germany, we were sent first to Stalag VIIB (Lamsdorf), arriving about 26 Jun. After about three weeks in the camp I was sent to Laband (Upper Silesia), near the former Polish border. There the P/W were employed on the construction of factories. We lived in camp about a kilometre from the factories. Food and clothing were scarce.

I escaped alone from the camp at Laband on 21 Nov 40. Rfm. Beechinor, R., of my Bn, and I had planned to escape together, but he did not accompany me. There were civilian Polish workers employed alongside us, and I asked one of them if he could get me a map and a compass. He said he could help me to escape and pass me on to friends. I decided to trust him, and he planned my escape for me. He brought me a pair of overalls and a civilian hat, as well as a forged workman's pass. (The pass had been forged on a bread ration card, the paper of which was similar to that of workmen's passes in the camp). The card with which I was provided had someone else's photograph on it and was handed over to me in a wallet.

I escaped when going to work on the morning shift. I walked into the camp in the ordinary way about 0600 hrs and went to a hut, where I put on the overalls and hat. As the guard who had brought us to the camp was in another hut signing papers, I had no difficulty in mingling with the Polish night shift workers who were leaving the camp. The guards at the gate did not examine my pass carefully, and I got out. Following my Polish friend, I met another Pole who took me to a small place five or six kilometres away. There I was sheltered for the night and given clothing. Next morning (22 Nov) a son of the house took me to another house in Gleiwitz. From there another Pole took me by bicycle to Katowice (Kattowitz). I stayed in Katowice five days or more, and then travelled by train with still another Pole to a town about halfway between Katowice and Krakow—probably Chrzanow.

I stayed with a Polish family there for about five months. I had to remain indoors most of the time, though I was able to have occasional walks in the evening. An English-speaking Pole told me that it was very hard to get anyone out of the district. I had, however, no difficulty with the Germans. Once a German came round checking the number of rooms in the block of flats where I was living, but I was moved out while he was there.

I left Chrzanow about the end of Mar 41. A railway driver acted as my guide. We walked two or three kilometres to a small station, where we got a train for Krakow. There the railwayman took me out of the station through a goods yard to a house, where I remained for five or six days. I was then taken on a train journey, which lasted all night and half the next day, to Sanok, on the river San. As the river was too high and fast for me to cross I waited in Sanok for about a month. By 8 or 9 May the river had fallen sufficiently for me to ford it. My Polish host showed me where to cross—on the outskirts of the town. The road alongside the river was patrolled by German guards in pairs. We watched the guards out of sight at about 1735 hrs, and I began wading across. The river was abut 100 yards from edge to edge, but was shallow except for about 10 yards in the middle where it was breast-high and where I had difficulty in keeping my foot on the rocks and pools.

The river was the boundary between the German and Russian parts of Poland. On the Russian side I was arrested by four soldiers. They searched me and fired a rifle as a signal. Two officers came from a village about 500 yards down the river. The officers took me to the village. They gave me tea and lit a fire so that I could dry my clothes. Two or three hours later they sent me by lorry to a town a few miles away (I do not know the name of the town, but it was probably about 22 miles East of Sanok). Here I was put in prison.

In the prison I was asked questions in Polish, of which I knew a few words. The interrogators and I also made drawings and conversed by signs, and they seemed to understand that I was an escaped British P/W. I also handed over a piece of paper on which my Polish host had written in Polish that I was a British soldier escaped from Germany and had asked that I should be put in touch with the British Embassy. There were two periods to the interrogation—from 2100 hrs to 0100 hrs on the night of my arrival, and practically the whole of the next day till about 2300 hrs with breaks for dinner and tea. The Russians were quite friendly at the interview. They did not accuse me of being a German. I spoke English several times, but apparently they could not find anyone who could speak the language. During the time I was in this prison (about six days) I was in a cell by myself. The Russians made the cell comfortable by giving me a mattress and lighting a fire. The food was not too bad.

After about six days I was put with about ten other prisoners, mostly Polish and sent to Sambor, which was also in Russian-occupied Poland. For the five weeks I was there my treatment was pretty good. The food was quite good and there was as much of it as I wanted. We had 20 minutes exercise each day in the prison yard, and a bath every ten days. At first I was, for about a week and a half, in the same cell as the party with whom I had travelled. After that I was in a cell with 20 or 25 other prisoners—Ukranians, Poles and Jews. The cell was roomy enough for everyone to sleep and was comparatively clean.

I was twice interrogated in Sambor prison. The first interrogation was conducted, probably in Russian and Polish, by a soldier and two civilians. I could not understand them, and when I said so in Polish, I was sent back to my cell. During the interview I asked them in English for an interpreter, but they said they did not understand. I also asked as best as I could for the British Consulate. The interrogation lasted one and half to two hours. At the second interrogation there was a young lady who spoke Polish, but I understood very little of what she said. They then turned my face to the wall, and someone spoke to me from the doorway in English, asking my name, rank and regiment, and when I escaped from Germany. It was a man's voice, and the accent sounded like a Cockney's, though he might have been a Russian. When I asked for the Embassy the man had gone. I was then sent back to my cell.

From Sambor I was sent by train to Kiev. On the way there was a break of two days in the journey at Lvov. In Kiev I was put in prison in a cell with three others. The cell was clean and we had beds with sheets and blankets. The food was quite good. I was interviewed twice. The first occasion was on the afternoon after arrival. When the interrogator found I could not speak Polish he sent me back to my cell. About 2100 hrs on the same day I was taken back to the office. A young woman who spoke fairly good English asked my name, what I was, where I had come from, and how I had travelled through Poland. I told her I would like to get in touch with the Embassy and my people. She said that would be possible in two or three weeks, when everything was settled. The treatment in Kiev was good. I was even lent an English book—Fielding's 'Tom Jones.'

On 22 Jun 41, the day of the outbreak of the war between Germany and Russia, I was moved to the Butirka Prison in Moscow. Treatment was good. At first there was plenty of food; later it was rationed, but was still sufficient. I was in a big cell, in which there were sometimes as many as 40 others, although there were generally only between 20 and 30. The cell was clean and we slept on mattresses on platforms round the walls. The Russians paid no attetion when I asked to be put in touch with the Embassy, merely saying, 'Wait' and 'It won't be long.' I also kept asking for the prison governor and writing to him, but I never saw him.

When Moscow was evacuated in Oct 41 I was sent to Saratov by train. The prison in Saratov was the worst I was in while in Russia. The food was bad at first, because (I was told) of the large number of evacuees in the district, but improved later. Letters were allowed once in three weeks, and I wrote continually to the Embassy and to the prison governor. The Embassy did not receive any of the letters I wrote. About 23 May 42 I was at last interviewed in Saratov prison by a Russian major and a young lady interpreter. They told me my case was being taken up in Moscow and that everything would soon be all right. I was now living on my own in a comfortable cell. The treatment was the same as before, with sometimes a little extra food.

Nothing happened till the end of Sep, when without any explanation, I was put on a river boat, with two NCO's as escort, and sent to Kuibyshev. There I was put in a prison where conditions were like those Saratov. On the evening of my arrival I was sent for. I was taken to two men in civilian clothes. One told me in English that everything had been settled and that next day I would be going to the Embassy. Two days later (26 Sep) one of the men took me to the Embassy in a car. He put me out on the opposite side of the road and pointed the Embassy out to me. The Embassy officials were expecting me.

I left Kuibyshev on 4 Oct and travelled via Moscow to Archangel, where I embarked for the U.K.

(L.G. 7.1.43)

Yerwa, Dogo, Sergeant
NA 27209, Gold Coast Regt., Royal West African Frontier Forces (Immediate)

On 12 Dec 44 at Khabaw village, Burma (ref map 84 H/1052562) Sjt. Dogo Yerwa was in command of a recce patrol of one section which was heavily attacked by a stronger Jap force with LMGs and grenade dischargers. His patrol had three casualties, but he handled it so well that the enemy were repulsed and the wounded removed to cover from where they were later brought in.

On the night 15/16 Dec 44 at Tinma West (ref map 84 C/160458) Sjt. Dogo Yerwas was commanding the forward pl of A Coy astride a ridge at 049587. At 1915 hrs his posn was attacked by at least a company of enemy with considerable artillery support. The attack was pressed home with the utmost determination for seven hours without respite. The full force of the attack fell on Sjt. Dogo Yerwa's platoon the ridge being too narrow to allow reserves to do anything but supply amn. Early in the action he was wounded by grenade splinters, but refused to leave his platoon. Throughout the seven hours' fighting he went from section to section, directing and controlling their fire, and himself firing rifle grenades from the hip. His task was the more difficult as two section commanders and 14 men were wounded. Only when severely wounded himself at the end of the action was he evacuated. 16 enemy bodies were later found in and about his platoon position. It was mainly due to Sjt. Dogo Yerwa's magnificent leadership and personal gallantry that his platoon held their position and repulsed the enemy with heavy loss. (L.G. 22.3.45)

Yool, Robert, Corporal
312445, 2nd Royal Gloucestershire Hussars (Cheadle, Cheshire) (Immediate)

On 27.5.42 Cpl. Yool commanded a tank at Bir El Harmat. During a very heavy engagement with German tanks and guns his tank was hit and set on fire. Every effort was made to extinguish the flames without avail and he ordered the crew to bale out and try to reach our lines. When about 20 yards from the tank he observed that his 75mm. Gunner was not with him, and, accompanied by his [...]7 mm. Gunner returned to his tank evacuated the wounded 75 mm. Gunner and carried him safely back to our lines although under very heavy fire the whole time. Cpl. Yool thus showed great courage and coolness in saving his comrade's life.

On 5.6.42 Cpl. Yool commanded a tank during an abortive attack on the enemy at Bir El Aslagh. Only about 800 yards from the forward enemy positions his tank developed engine trouble and he could not continue withdrawal. He managed to get the tank into a vehicle pit and reported on the [...]ir to his Sqn. Leader who offered to return and try and pick up the crew. Cpl. Yool insisted that he would first try to repair the tank. Although under heavy fire he eventually succeeded and brought it back to our lines. Throughout the engagement he showed great coolness under fire and a strong sense of duty.

(L.G. 15.10.42)

York, Percy Sydney, Sergeant
5498630, 5th Bn The Hampshire Regt. (Totton)
For outstanding bravery and devotion to duty.

Ref maps:— Italy 1/100,000 Sheet 171 & 172.

On October 15th 1943 ater the crossing of the R Bolturno the Bn pushed forward to occupy some ground two miles ahead of its position (9673). The leading coys became heavily involved and German infiltration and sniping were causing heavy casualties. The Commanding Officer together with Sjt. York and three stretcher bearers moved forward by jeep to collect wounded. They were under constant fire. On arrival Sjt. York attended to twenty wounded. He loaded one jeep full of wounded and sent it off, looking after the remaining wounded. Orders were given that two more jeeps would come forward. In the meantime the Commanding Officer and Sjt. York were wounded, Sjt. York in the jaw and face. Sjt. York although in great pain loaded the two jeeps on their arrival and succeeded in getting all the wounded to the RAP nearly two miles back in spite of sniping at 7 yds range and enemy on the side of the road. The jeeps having to drive at over 40 mph to avoid accurate aimed arms fire. It was due to this NCOs magnificent behaviour under intense mortar and small arms fire, that the Commanding Officer and twenty men were able to arrive at the RAP.

During the Ornito—Cerasola operations 5–10 February 44 Sjt. York carried out the duties of RAP Sjt. in a roofless hut on the reverse slope of Mt. Ornito. This area was under continuous shell fire from medium guns for five days and nights and on the morning and afternoon of 10 Feb shells fell within 5 yards of the hut. Sjt. York assisted the R.M.O. to evacuate 180 casualties during this period working in pouring rain under most difficult and dangerous conditions.

His cheerfullness, courage and energetic medical assistance were of the highest order and greatly helped to keep the morale of the wounded so remarkably high.

Previously during the North African Campaign he took part in the actions at Sidi N'sir, Hunts Gap, Pichon and Bou Arada and displayed the highest devotion to duty and resourcefulness. His name is a by-word in the Battalion. *(L.G. 21.12.44)*

Young, H. W. A., Serjeant
U.F.
No citation.
M.I.D. 30.12.41 *(L.G. 16.4.42)*

Young, Joseph, Lance Corporal
4919942, 1st Bn The South Staffordshire Regt.
(Coventry)
At Henu on the 21st, 22nd March 44 the enemy launched a heavy attack on to the position held by the Company. In this attack they succeeded in penetrating the defence area and occupied a portion of Bare Hill feature. The Platoon in which this NCO was a Section Commander was ordered to counterattack. His Section was ordered to move forward on the left flank of the counterattack. This he carried out. During all of these preliminary moves, his Section was under constant fire from enemy LMGs and Mortars. However, he continued his advance in a most determined and courageous manner. In this movement he was wounded by shrapnel in the eye causing partial blindness. He still commanded and directed his Section into the attack. As his Section reached the assaulting stage he ordered charge, he himself leading. He threw grenades into enemy positions and bayoneted three more Japanese. His Section inflicted several casualties in this assault and it was due partially to the splendid example set by this NCO to his men that accounted for the success. In the final action he was again wounded by a bullet in the hand, but he still encouraged his Section, continued the assault and succeeded driving the enemy out of a wired trench which they had occupied. He remained in position commanding his Section until the area was clear. By this time he could not see and was only partly conscious. He was later evacuated. Throughout the whole action this NCO showed great courage and determination and was a most inspiring leader to his men.
Dated Henu 28th March 44. *(L.G. 4.1.45)*

Young, Keith Wellington, Sergeant
QX 2111, 2/13 Fd. Coy., Australian Military Forces
Tobruch—Period April/October 1941

For the six months up to October Sjt. Young as Section Sergeant of No. 2 Sec. 2/13 Fd. Coy. RAE has rendered extremely meritorious service. He has been employed continuously in the Western Sector of Tobruch Fortress, during which time he has worked day and night in the forward areas of the Salient. A lot of this work has consisted of supervising disarming and removing

German mines and 'booby traps' in 'No Man's Land' so that patrols might move with comparative safety. The whole area was constantly under extremely heavy mortar and machine gun fire and most of the forward work had to be carried out on moonless nights, which meant that the difficulty of locating 'booby traps' was extremely great, and it is difficult to exaggerate the personal risk entailed. The sergeant, by his cool actions and intimate knowledge of the ground, has been of great service in keeping up the morale, not only of his own men, but of the infantry in the line. Confirmation of this can be readily obtained from the C.O.'s of 2/9 Bn., 2/13 Bn., 2/15 Bn., 2/32 Bn and 2/43 Bn.

During the attack on the night 2/3 Aug. on Post R7, Sjt. Young did excellent work, and displayed great initiative during the action, and when all officers of the assaulting Coy. of the 2/43 Bn. were wounded, he, on the order of Capt. McCarten took command and withdrew what was left of the assaulting Coy. to our own lines.   *(L.G. 16.4.42)*

Young, William Grant, Sergeant
2692927, Scots Guards attd 2 Coldstream Gds (Witton Gilbert, Co. Durham) (Immediate)
This NCO was Platoon Sjt to No. 8 Platoon when the battle for Point 501 (Monte Lignano) was joined on 15th July 1944. When the leading Platoon was pinned down by heavy fire from entrenched German machine guns, he quickly organised his Platoon into a fire position crawling about in the open along the crest of a small hillock and assisting in the siting of the Bren Gun positions. This covering fire enabled the leading Platoon to extricate itself into dead ground and the remainder of the company to form up for the assault. When the C.S.M. was killed he became Acting C.S.M. and later when a Platoon Comd casualty occurred he took over command of a Platoon. During this time he showed strong powers of leadership and initiative and was an example to all. When heavy shelling was in progress Sjt. Young volunteered to crawl over the [...] to direct o[...] own gunfire. A piece of shrapnel from a 88mm shell tore the gascape on his back to shreds. Later when mortar bombs and shells were falling in our area, Sjt. Young crawled about the company encouraging the men, displaying great courage, cheerfulness & complete disregard for his own peronal safety throughout the battle.

(L.G. 7.12.44)

Youngman, Eric Walter, Sergeant
7911156, 1st Derbyshire Yeomanry (Swansea)
Owing to casualties, Sjt. Youngman has been acting alternatively as Troop Leader and Troop Sergeant in his Troop. On more than one occasion he has shown complete coolness when under fire and has continued to carry out his task to the very best advantage. At Tebourba, in November, he led a party which successfully recovered his Troop Humber Armoured Car under heavy fire and in close proximity to 12 enemy tanks. In Sidi Bou Zid area in February, he obtained most valuable information of 50 German tanks under conditions which necessitated him remaining under enemy fire in order to continue observing the enemy. On all occasions this NCO has shown organizing abilities and powers of leadership. By his complete disregard to enemy fire and his will to obtain information in the face of stiff enemy resistance, he has on all occasions shown great devotion to duty.

(L.G. 23.9.43)

Z

Zakare, Busanga, Lance Corporal
12572, 24 (GC) Inf Div, 12 (African) Corps, 2 G.C.R.
For conspicuous gallantry in action.

At Uadara on 5 May during an attack this NCO displayed great gallantry advancing on the enemy firing his Bren Gun from the hip without regard for his own safety. Later his platoon was heavily counter attacked in front and flank and forced to withdraw. L/Cpl. Zakare continued to maintain his gun in action alone thus enabling the platoon to withdraw with only slight casualties. L/Cpl. Zakare was consequently cut off. He spent the night in the enemy lines rejoining his unit the following morning with his Bren Gun while the enemy were sheltering from a British air attack. He brought back useful information with him.
Backdated to 30.9.41   *(L.G. 21.7.42)*

Zefaniya, Mayanja, C.S.M.
U/283, 21 E.A. Bde, 12 (African) Div, E.A. Forces Corps, 1/4 K.A.R.
For conspicuous gallantry on March 31st at Soroppa, he was throughout the action prominently in the fore-front of the fight regardless of his personal safety, and was active in forcing the enemy from several L.M.G. and rifle positions. He set a brave example to the men of his company and on several occasions used a Bren Gun with deadly effect.
Backdated to 30.9.41   *(L.G. 21.7.42)*

Printed in the United Kingdom
by Lightning Source UK Ltd.
125283UK00001B/53/A